Historical Dictionary
of the
French Second Empire,
1852-1870

Historical Dictionaries of French History

This five-volume series covers French history from the Revolution through the Third Republic. It provides comprehensive coverage of each era, including not only political and military history but also social, economic, and art history.

Historical Dictionary of the French Revolution, 1789-1799
Samuel F. Scott and Barry Rothaus, editors

Historical Dictionary of Napoleonic France, 1799-1815
Owen Connelly, editor

Historical Dictionary of France from the 1815 Restoration to the Second Empire
Edgar Leon Newman, editor

Historical Dictionary of the French Second Empire, 1852-1870
William E. Echard, editor

Historical Dictionary of the Third French Republic, 1870-1940
Patrick H. Hutton, editor-in-chief

Historical Dictionary of the French Second Empire, 1852-1870

Edited by
WILLIAM E. ECHARD

Greenwood Press
Westport, Connecticut

To Lynn M. Case

Library of Congress Cataloging in Publication Data

Main entry under title:

Historical dictionary of the French Second Empire.

Includes bibliographies and index.
1. France—History—Second Empire, 1852-1870—
Dictionaries.   I. Echard, William E., 1931-
DC276.H57   1985   944.07'03'21   84-8958
ISBN 0-313-21136-1 (lib. bdg.)

Library of Congress Catalog Card Number: 84-8958
ISBN: 0-313-21136-1

First published in 1985

Greenwood Press
A division of Congressional Information Service, Inc.
88 Post Road West
Westport, Connecticut 06881

Printed in the United States of America

10 9 8 7 6 5 4 3 2 1

Contents

Contributors

Julian Archer, Drake University, Iowa
Eric A. Arnold, Jr., University of Denver
Nancy Nichols Barker, University of Texas at Austin
Leland C. Barrows, University of Constantine, Algeria
James A. Bising, County College of Morris, New Jersey
James R. Bloomfield, Thiel College, Pennsylvania
Marvin L. Brown, Jr., North Carolina State University at Raleigh (emeritus)
Robert F. Brown, Sonoma State University, California
Stuart L. Campbell, Alfred University, New York
Robert B. Carlisle, Saint Lawrence University, New York
Lynn M. Case, University of Pennsylvania (emeritus)
Joel S. Cleland, Lander College, South Carolina
Jeffrey Cooper, Ph.D., Cornell University, New York
Raymond L. Cummings, Villanova University, Pennsylvania
William E. Duvall, Willamette University, Oregon
Christopher English, Memorial University of Newfoundland
Martin Fichman, Glendon College of York University, Toronto
Willard Allen Fletcher, University of Delaware
Charles E. Freedeman, State University of New York at Binghamton
Beverley Giblon, York University, Toronto
Patrick J. Harrigan, University of Waterloo, Ontario, Canada
Robert L. Hoffman, State University of New York at Albany
Natalie Isser, The Pennsylvania State University at Ogontz
Leo A. Loubère, State University of New York at Buffalo
Paul E. Michelson, Huntington College, Indiana
Barrie M. Ratcliffe, Université Laval, Quebec
Ann Pottinger Saab, University of North Carolina at Greensboro
Ivan Scott, University of Toledo, Ohio
Winyss A. Shepard, Ph.D., University of Pennsylvania
George J. Sheridan, Jr., University of Oregon
Mark W. Sholofsky, Villanova University, Pennsylvania
Dolorès A. Signori, University of Toronto

Dorothy E. Speirs, Research Associate, Research Program on Zola and
   Naturalism, University of Toronto
Warren F. Spencer, University of Georgia
David R. Stevenson, Kearney State College, Nebraska
Lee Shai Weissbach, University of Louisville, Kentucky

Preface

Not many years ago a historical dictionary of the French Second Empire could have been assembled only with the greatest difficulty, if at all. Information now available was still relatively inaccessible, and objectivity remained less the rule than the exception. The Second Empire and Napoleon III had not been well served by historians. There are, of course, experiences befalling a people that require fixing blame. That France, after its terrible year of military defeat and civil war (1870–1871), should have chosen Napoleon III as the symbol of all that had gone wrong did not surprise him and should not surprise us. But the biases of republican historians over more than two generations are less easy to justify. It is hoped that the articles composing this dictionary are indeed both accurate and objective. But it may also be that, taken in their entirety, they reveal more forcefully than is customary the importance of an era vital to French history and the qualities of the man central to its development.

Napoleon III made many enemies during his eighteen-year reign: the republicans, whose projects he frustrated until the last scene of the drama; the monarchists, who regarded him as a usurper; the radicals, who rejected his well-meaning projects because they did not go far enough or fast enough; the Catholics, who could not forgive him for his role in despoiling the pope; the notables, who resented his ideas and his ascendancy; even the avant-garde artists and many intellectuals, who blamed the regime for what they did not like in bourgeois taste and sensibility. After 1870 these opponents would make of their triumph an occasion for sustained vituperation of the former emperor, portraying him as inept, a self-indulgent sensualist, an adventurer without aim or scruple, a tool in the hands of unprincipled and meritless men. He was, we are now beginning to see, none of these things, and those who served him or supported him were often of greater worth than many who made it their chief objective to bring him down. What Napoleon III truly was we shall probably never know, but when—as in a work of this nature—we consider the facts alone, it becomes clear that he was certainly a masterly politician, able to rule France for more than eighteen years, to command its support until the end, and to exert an influence so pervasive on his era that it may without exaggeration be considered the Age of Napoleon III.

The richness and importance of that era, as well as the influence on it of the French emperor, are revealed in the articles that follow. Concerning foreign policy, that importance and influence cannot be doubted. French foreign policy *was* the policy of Napoleon III, and to a great extent it shaped such major events as the unification of Italy and of Germany, the establishment of a Rumanian state, the checking for a generation of Russian expansion, the ending of papal temporal power (and acquisition by the Italian kingdom of the former Papal States), the annexation of Nice and Savoy by France, the creation of a new French colonial empire (Indochina, Senegal), the organization of the Lebanon, the building of the Suez Canal, and the introduction into European diplomacy of the principle of nationalities. Even in the foreign policy failures of Napoleon III can be seen auguries of what was to come. His concept of an Arab kingdom of Algeria, his championship of the Poles, and his advocacy of European concert may be viewed in that light. Finally, the catastrophe of 1870 was to engender a century of turbulence, crisis, and war, not only for France but also for the rest of Europe and indeed for the world.

Historians would agree as well that the economic development of France between 1850 and 1870, which marks the emergence of a modern French economy, owed much to Napoleon III. There were fortuitous circumstances, of course (the boom years, especially until 1857; the major world discoveries of gold and silver), but for the first time economic leadership came from above and was both sustained and effective. The motives behind that leadership remain open to debate, although certainly the Saint-Simonian aspiration to raise the living standard of the masses was important. The results are undeniable. Credit was revolutionized; the national railroad network was built, and a tunnel was constructed under the Alps (Mont Cenis); the great French steamship companies were launched; an era of European free trade was inaugurated; merchandising was transformed through the invention of the modern department store; Paris was rebuilt; a major iron and steel industry was created; deregulation was promoted; and the laws governing business organization were revised for the century that would follow. Speculators and self-serving men abounded, but for every Mirès, there was a Fould, Rouher, Magne, Rothschild, Talabot, Béhic, Chevalier, or Arlès-Dufour. Napoleon III struck the balance between the free traders and the protectionists, the advocates of "productive deficits" (Persigny, the Pereires) and the champions of fiscal conservatism, the doers like Georges Haussmann, and those who rebelled at "unproductive" use of capital. He struck the balance, provided much of the impetus, and left a mark that was to be the first that his detractors could no longer deny.

Concerning politics, the rancor has been slower to disappear. Many Napoleonic ideas still have a nuance that is either quaint or suspect: the plebiscite, management of elections, the whole apparatus of democratic Caesarism. And yet the system had held remarkably well; universal manhood suffrage was established once and for all, and public opinion became the abiding concern of government. Perhaps it is even true that the coup d'état of December 1851 and the constitution of 1852 saved France from social chaos and civil war and that the establishment of the Second Empire reflected the wishes of the great majority of Frenchmen. What is certain is that the transformation of the authoritarian regime into the Liberal Empire between 1860 and 1870 is an event almost unparalleled in modern history and that France appeared to possess on the eve of the catastrophic war with Prussia institutions and a sense of direction that it would not regain for almost another century of experiment, crisis, and conflict.

Napoleon III undoubtedly would have wished for at least an equal success in regard to the social question. This "Saint-Simon on horseback" began his career by publishing a socialist tract (*L'extinction du paupérisme*), and certainly he was at least half sincere in proclaiming himself a socialist. He was the first French ruler to recognize the existence of a social question, and his was the first government to attempt a remedy for the ills that flowed from industrialization. Bonapartism, as Napoleon III defined it, not only rose above parties but based itself squarely on a sense of reponsibility for the well-being of the most numerous class. That, in effect, was one of the problems, since the emperor could never choose between the paternalism of men like Frédéric Le Play and the implications of trade unionism, encouraged for the first time in France by laws and actions of the Second Empire. Moreover, while sympathetic to the workers (Proudhon briefly supported him), Napoleon III could not ignore the wishes of the propertied classes on whom he also depended. Thus the lost initiatives (for example, the attempt to abolish *livrets d'ouvrier*) and the snail's pace of improvement that ensured that while the emperor had always an element of support among the workers and even among the moderate republicans, he could not prevent either the defection of the urban masses from the Empire or the reemergence of a revolutionary movement after 1864. Working-class gains during the Second Empire were nevertheless real. The standard of living rose, if barely perceptibly; workers' housing was built; the dignity of labor was enshrined in the great international expositions; strikers often received sympathetic understanding from the government; even the First International enjoyed, initially, a degree of government support; education, under the auspices of Victor Duruy and others, became more popular, practical, and effective; and from 1864 the labor movement was progressively unshackled. And yet the Second Empire ended in revolutionary violence and bitter, blood-stained strikes (as at La Ricamarie). It was one more disappointment for the "modern emperor" whose fate it seemed to be to release the genii of the future without always being able to ensure their control.

The future was an obsession with Napoleon III. The man who, in prison, had written treatises on electrical currents, beet sugar, and a canal across the isthmus of Central America and who always retained an intense interest in science and technology must have been delighted at the French innovations of the era: Dupuy de Lôme's ironclad frigates, Saint-Claire Deville's commercial production of aluminum, Lenoir's prototype automobile, Marinoni's rotary perfecting press, the Michaux and Lallement's development of the bicycle, Pierre Martin's open hearth process, Beau de Rochas' cycle engine (the first to use commercial gas), Duclos du Haroun's experiments with color photography, Nadar's aerial photography and photographs taken by artificial light, Bernard's discovery of the cause of diabetes and definition of the science of physiology, Pasteur's development of pasteurization, Tournaire's and Fourneyron's turbines, Ruolz's electroplating process, Planté's storage battery, Sommeiller's compressed air drill, Magnin's embroidery machine, Bergès' practical utilization of hydroelectric power, Tellier's refrigeration experiments, Foucault's pendulum, Mège-Mouriès' invention of margarine, Leclanché's dry cell battery, Marey's sphygmograph, Amécourt's "helicopter," and Bourdon's steam hammer. The Second Empire saw as well the development of chemical perfumes and dyes, of the structural use of iron and steel, of electric arc lighting, of photogravure, of meteorology (the first daily international weather bulletins), of anthropology (Paul Broca), and of psychiatry (French psychiatrists discovered the link between mania and melancholy, redefined hysteria, contributed greatly to the establishment of modern neurology, and applied psychiatry to history). Nor was the French emperor a spectator only but an important participant. His aid to and encouragement of French science and technology are only partially illustrated by his well-known association with Saint-Claire Deville, Le Play, and Pasteur and by his energetic sponsorship of the great Paris international expositions of 1855 and 1867.

Circumstances also placed Napoleon III at the center of turbulent and important developments in areas as diverse as the press and religion. Stern supervision of the political press (relaxed only at the end of the Empire) prevented neither flourishing opposition newspapers nor the emergence of modern journalism at the hands of Girardin (*La presse*), Nefftzer (*Le temps*), Villemessant (*Le Figaro*), Millaud (*Le petit journal*), and others. Newspapers became truly big business during the Second Empire and, for the first time, popular in every sense of the word, spurred by Marinoni's presses and the innovations of imaginative journalists. The emperor found himself once again at the point of balance, torn between his desire for the French to assume greater self-responsibility and his determination to maintain order. It was much the same in religious matters. Not himself overly preoccupied with questions of faith, Napoleon III cultivated the support of the church in politics but desired its modernization. In the era of Lourdes and Solesmes, the First Vatican Council, the *Syllabus of Errors*, and the dogma of papal infallibility, he defended Gallicanism, sympathized with liberal Catholicism (a sympathy briefly reciprocated by Montalembert), and proposed to Pope Pius IX the abandonment of his temporal power. Small wonder that for the Second Empire no solution could be found to the Roman Question or, indeed, to the constant tempests (Mortara affair, prosecution of Flaubert and of Baudelaire, the controversy concerning Abbé Gaume, the dismissal of Renan from his chair at the Collège de France) that regularly exercised or embarrassed the government.

As for the regime's supposed philistinism in matters of literature, art, and music, that would indeed have been a major accomplishment for an era of so great ferment and achievement. In the twenty years between 1850 and 1870, the theater attained a pinnacle of spectacle, of acting (Rachel), and of writing (Dumas fils, Meilhac, Halévy, Banville, Feydeau, Labiche, Sardou, Scribe, Sand, Vigny); Romantic opera reached its apogee; concert life assumed its modern aspect; and the operetta was invented. During the Second Empire, as well, literature passed from romanticism (Lamartine, Nerval, Sand) to realism (Flaubert, Champfleury, Duranty, the Goncourts) to naturalism (Zola), and even to science-fiction (Jules Verne), while in poetry the Parnassian movement was launched (Leconte de Lisle, Gautier, Coppée), and Baudelaire blazed his meteoric path. In art, while Delacroix and Ingres continued the glories of the romantic and neoclassical schools, the contest was joined between the technical perfection of the academy (Gérôme, Cabanel, Bouguereau, Couture) and the modern imagination of the rebels, who contemptuously termed their rivals *pompiers*, and who set the future course of art whether realist (Courbet, Bonheur, Corot, Daumier, Rousseau, Millet), impressionist (Pissarro, Renoir, Monet), or simply modern (Manet, Degas, Carpeaux).

The imperial couple had no artistic pretensions, but their patronage was nevertheless real and of major importance to many composers, writers, and artists who largely populated the *séries* of Compiègne. Intimates of the court (or supporters of the regime) included Vigny, Mérimée, Carpeaux, Viollet-le-Duc, and Sainte-Beuve. Moreover, the rapport that Napoleon III and Eugénie could not supply was provided by the salons of their Bonaparte cousins, Prince Napoleon and Princess Mathilde, or by figures closely associated with the imperial circle— Mérimée, Mocquard, Morny, Ollivier. The Salon des Refusés of 1863 and attempts to reform the Institute and the Académie des Beaux-Arts attest to an even more direct involvement by the emperor in an artistic and cultural ferment ultimately resolved in favor of a generation of painters, sculptors, and writers who believed, rightly or wrongly, that the Empire had been their enemy.

Architects, on the other hand, could have had no illusions concerning their debt to Napoleon III. The rebuilding of Paris provided opportunities that come rarely, and there seemed no lack of talent to profit from the occasion. Garnier's Opéra, Alphand's parks, Viollet-le-Duc's medieval restorations, Labrouste's libraries, Davioud's theaters, and, until very recently, Baltard's Halles Centrales still stand as monuments to the era when Paris gained its reputation as the modern Babylon, consolidated (under Charles Worth) its position as the fashion center of the world, and assumed the physical aspect that it was to retain for more than a century.

So many topics, then, to contend for a limited space! Roughly 350 entries, in alphabetical order, make up this dictionary, the first of its kind to be compiled in any language. The topics have been chosen not only for their significance but also because together they offer a comprehensive account of the Second Empire. Some articles are broader in coverage than their titles imply, as cross-references throughout the dictionary indicate. Entries generally will be consulted individually, but the reader who chooses to follow the suggestions under ''Related

Entries'' may begin at any point and traverse virtually the entire panorama of Second Empire history.

Articles have been written by specialists with the purpose of serving the needs of both students and scholars. The former will find here a concise introduction to each topic and a summary of the historical debate. The latter will value the many details that may have escaped memory or are difficult to find. Dates, for example, are given for all persons cited who are not themselves the subject of an entry. For readers who wish to know more about any topic, bibliographical suggestions are appended to most articles. A list of abbreviations used for frequently cited journals will be found at the front of the dictionary. Although the bibliographies are intended to point to further study rather than to indicate the author's indebtedness, it is understood that this dictionary, like all other similar works, has depended on certain standard compilations, among the most useful of which are: Eugène Hatin, *Bibliographie historique et critique de la presse périodique française* (Paris, 1866); *La grande encyclopédie: Inventaire raisonné des sciences, des lettres, et des arts*, ed. Marcellin Berthelot et al., 31 vols. (Paris, 1886–1902); *Grand dictionnaire universel du XIXe siècle*, ed. Pierre Larousse, 17 vols. (Paris, 1866–1890); E. Benezit, *Dictionnaire des peintres, sculpteurs, dessinateurs et graveurs*, new ed., 10 vols. (Paris, 1976); *Dictionnaire de biographie française* (in progress under the direction of Jean Charles Roman d'Amat); *Dictionary of Scientific Biography*, ed. Charles Coulston Gillispie, 15 vols. (New York, 1970–1976); *Dictionnaire des sculpteurs de l'école française*, ed. Stanislas Lami, 8 vols. (Paris, 1898); *Dictionnaire biographique du mouvement ouvrier français*, 2d part, *1864–1871*; ed. Jean Maitron and M. Egrot, 6 vols. (Paris, 1967–1971); *Dictionnaire des parlementaires français, 1789–1889*, ed. Adolphe Robert, Edgar Bourloton, and Gaston Cougny, 5 vols. (Paris, 1889–1891); L. G. Vapereau, *Dictionnaire universel des contemporains* (Paris, 1858, 1861, 1865, 1870, 1880, 1891–1893); Fayard's *Dictionnaire des lettres françaises: XIXe siècle*, 2 vols. (Paris, 1971); A. F. Frangulis, ed., *Dictionnaire diplomatique*, 5 vols. (Paris, 1954); *New Grove Dictionary of Music and Musicians*, 6th ed., ed. Stanley Sadie, 20 vols. (New York, 1980); Jacques Hillairet, ed., *Dictionnaire historique des rues de Paris*, 2 vols. and supplement (Paris, 1963–1972); and Russell Sturgis, ed., *A Dictionary of Architecture and Building*, 3 vols., (London, 1902). A more extensive *Bibliography of the History of the French Second Empire* is projected by Greenwood Press.

The comprehensive chronology that concludes this dictionary offers a view of events as a whole. Although every effort has been made to ensure accuracy, no such compilation can, by its nature, be free of errors and ambiguities, for which apology is offered in advance. Unsigned entries are the editor's, and his, too, the responsibility for any errors, whether in the entries written by himself or in those which he has edited to meet the exigencies of this work.

William E. Echard

Abbreviations of Journals in References

Act. h.	*Actualité de l'histoire*
AHR	*American Historical Review*
AMN	*Les amis de Napoléon III*
Annales	*Annales: économies, sociétés, civilisations*
ASMP	*Séances et [or Revue des] travaux de l'Académie des Sciences Morales et Politiques*
BM	*Burlington Magazine*
BSHM	*Bulletin de la Société d'Histoire Moderne [et Contemporaine]*
CA	*Connaissance des arts*
CAM	*Les cahiers de l'art mineur*
CHJ	*[Cambridge] Historical Journal*
CJH	*Canadian Journal of History*
CN	*Cahiers naturalistes*
Con.	*The connoisseur*
Corr.	*Le correspondant*
EcHR	*Economic History Review*
EcS	*Economies et sociétés: Cahiers de l'Institut de Sciences Economiques Appliquées*
EHR	*English Historical Review*
ES	*Etudes sociales*
FHS	*French Historical Studies*
GBA	*Gazette des beaux-arts*
HJ	See *CHJ*
HZ	*Historische Zeitschrift*
IH	*Information historique*
IHA	*L'information d'histoire de l'art*
JAA	*Journal de l'amateur d'art*
JEEH	*Journal of European Economic History*
JEH	*Journal of Economic History*
JES	*Journal of European Studies*
JHI	*Journal of the History of Ideas*
JMH	*Journal of Modern History*

JTH	*Journal of Transportation History*
MH	*Miroir de l'histoire*
MHF	*Monuments historiques de la France*
MS	*Le mouvement social*
NA	*Nuova antologia di lettere, scienze ed arti*
NALSA	See *NA*
PAPS	*Proceedings of the American Philosophical Society*
POQ	*Public Opinion Quarterly*
PWSFH	*Proceedings of the Western Society for French History*
RA	*Revue administrative*
RDM	*Revue des deux mondes and Nouvelle revue des deux mondes*
RE	*Revue économique*
REN	*Revue des études napoléoniennes*
RFHO	*Revue française d'histoire d'outre-mer*
RFSP	*Revue française de science politique*
R. gén	*Revue générale*
RH	*Revue historique*
RHD	*Revue d'histoire diplomatique*
RHE	*Revue d'histoire ecclésiastique*
RHEF	*Revue d'histoire de l'Eglise de France*
RHES	*Revue d'histoire économique et sociale*
RHLF	*Revue d'histoire littéraire de la France*
RHMC	*Revue d'histoire moderne [et contemporaine]*
RHS	*Revue d'histoire de la sidérurgie*
RHSA	*Revue d'histoire des sciences et de leurs applications*
RIN	*Revue de l'Institut Napoléonien*
R. 1848	*Révolution de 1848*
RM	*Revue de musicologie*
RPP	*Revue politique et parlementaire*
RSR	*Rassegna storica del Risorgimento*
RST	*Rassegna storica toscana*
SN	*Souvenir napoléonien*
SP	*Storia e politica*
SR	*Sociological Review*

The Dictionary

A

ABOUT, EDMOND (1828–1885), novelist, playwright, and journalist; born at Dieuze (Meurthe), 14 February 1828. About's father was a grocer of modest means who died when About was six. His ambitious and energetic mother was determined to provide her son with every available opportunity. She took him to Paris where his intellectual precocity earned him a scholarship to the Lycée Charlemagne and, subsequently, entrance to the prestigious Ecole Normale Supérieure (1848). Graduating in 1850 with the highest honors, About studied at the Ecole Française d'Athènes (1851–1853) and traveled extensively in Greece. But he decided against teaching and began his literary career with two travel narratives, one of which, *La Grèce contemporaine* (1855), attracted the attention of the writer Jules Barbey d'Aurevilly. Soon he had commissions to write for various Paris newspapers and reviews. With *Tolla* (1855), he began a long series of highly successful novels, fairly superficial in character but immensely popular (he was considered by some enthusiasts to be the heir of Voltaire).

About directed his literary efforts not only toward the novel but also toward the theater. Here, however, his efforts met with less success. His first play, *Guillery*, opened at the Théâtre Français on 2 February 1856 and ran for only two performances. Two later plays were banned by the censorship, and two one-act presentations enjoyed some success (1860, 1861). But *Gaëtana*, when presented at the Odéon 2 January 1862 (and subsequently in the provinces), was booed from the stage by a cabal of liberals and Catholics whom About's political writings had offended. In Paris the production had only four performances.

It is probable that About's lack of success in the theater was due at least in part to his political convictions and connections. Following his initial literary successes, he had been introduced to the most important literary salons and had become acquainted with the intellectual liberal faction of the imperial court, the emperor's cousins Princess Mathilde and Prince Napoleon, Achille Fould (one of the Empire's chief political figures), and their friends. About was firmly committed to the principle of nationalities (freedom and, if desired, unity for oppressed peoples) and to religious and press freedoms. He was a fervent anti-clerical and an enemy of ultramontanism (papal sovereignty). Through his new friends, who combined some of these aims and prejudices with a devotion to the regime, he was seduced into writing for the government.

Napoleon III, eager to enlist French support for an Italian confederation free of Austrian control and a reduction of papal temporal power used About's talents. The journalist wrote a series of articles for the official newspaper, *Le moniteur universel*, prior to the war with Austria in 1859 (Italian War). In May 1859, following a visit to Italy and to Rome, he published at Brussels an antipapal book, *La question romaine*, which, although based on earlier articles inspired by the emperor himself, was, for reasons of political expediency, officially banned from France. In the spring of 1860, About was again commissioned to write for Napoleon III. Two pamphlets, *La nouvelle carte de l'Europe* and *La Prusse en 1860*, both edited by the emperor, had enormous sales since rumors of their semiofficial character accompanied their publication. A few years later, About was offered a position as personal counsellor to Napoleon III, his function being to deliver regular, confidential reports to the sovereign on shifts in public opinion. He tried to interest L. A. Prévost-Paradol in sharing the task with him but was unsuccessful. Finally, About accepted the post. However, it was short-lived. After a few reports, the scheme fell through.

About was a prolific journalist, from his debut at *Le Figaro* in 1854 ("Lettres d'un bon jeune homme," signed Valentin de Quévilly) to *Le soir* in the last months of the Empire. He collaborated with or contributed to *Le constitutionnel*, *Le moniteur universel*, *L'opinion nationale* (1859–1860, a new series of "Lettres d'un bon jeune homme à sa cousine Madeleine," this time signed with his own name), *La nouvelle revue de Paris* (chronicles later published as *Causeries*), and *Le Gaulois* (where in 1868 he was a principal editor and the cause of its being banned from sale on the public way). The subjects that enlisted his concern were literature, the arts, politics, economics (in 1864 he published a book on political economy, *Le progrès*), foreign policy, and religion. His main targets were Catholic dogma and the temporal power of the pope. His chief adversaries were Louis Veuillot, Mgr. Félix Dupanloup, and Cardinal Antonelli (Pope Pius IX's secretary of state). In 1870 About gave his whole-hearted support to the Liberal Empire. For his services he was named to the Legion of Honor 15 August 1858 and became an officer in 1867. But he was soundly defeated for election to the Académie Française in May 1870.

The outbreak of war with Prussia in July 1870 found About at his family home in Lorraine. He became a war correspondent, and his cogent descriptions were read in *Le soir*. About accepted the Third Republic after the defeat of 1870 and the policies of Adolphe Thiers. In 1884 he was finally elected to the Académie but died at Paris 16 January 1885 before he could take his seat. Among his major novels written during the Second Empire, and mostly published by Hachette, are: *Tolla* (1855), *Les mariages de Paris* (1856), *Le roi des montagnes* (1857), *L'homme à l'oreille cassée* (1862; which imagines the favorable impressions of a colonel of the First Empire returned to France during the reign of

Napoleon III), *Le nez d'un notaire* (1862), *Madelon* (1863), *Le Turco* (1866), and *Les mariages de province* (1868).

E. About, *Théâtre impossible* (Paris, 1862), *Voyages à travers l'Exposition des Beaux-arts de 1855* (Paris, 1855), *Nos artistes au salon 1857* (Paris, 1858), *Salon de 1864* (Paris, 1864), *Salon de 1866* (Paris, 1867), and *Alsace* (Paris, 1873); M. Thiébaut, *Edmond About*, 7th ed. (Paris, 1936).

Natalie Isser
Dorothy E. Speirs

Related entries: BAUDRY; FOULD; GALLICANISM; HACHETTE; NA-TIONALITIES; PUBLIC OPINION; ROMAN QUESTION; THEATER.

ACADEMIE FRANCAISE, senior of the five academies constituting the French Institute; notable during the first half of the Second Empire less for the endless compilation of its dictionary and the annual distribution of its prizes than for its opposition to the regime. Three of forty members (Victor Hugo, Adolphe Thiers, and Charles de Rémusat [1797–1875]) were exiled at the coup d'état of December 1851. In January, however, the academy prudently rejected a proposal that it express sympathy for the exiles. The academy's opposition to Napoleon III was expressed more cautiously. Of twenty-three Immortals elected between 1850 and 1870, no more than a quarter can be considered to have been chosen for literary merit; a large majority were elected primarily to embarrass the emperor and to keep the academy a stronghold of opposition—primarily liberal, under the aegis of François Guizot (1787–1874), the "grand elector." Abel Villemain (1790–1870), perpetual secretary from 1834, was also an Orleanist. No government candidate was ever chosen, although Prosper Mérimée, elected in 1844, Charles Augustin Sainte-Beuve, elected also in 1844, and Désiré Nisard (1806–1888), elected in 1850, were bonapartists, and Octave Feuillet, elected in 1862, was a familiar of the Tuileries (Empress Eugénie attended his reception). The chief official candidate, Raymond Troplong, lost his bid twice, in 1856 and in 1866. Even Napoleon III was rejected in 1863, the academy preferring Jules Dufaure (1798–1881). And, of course, the empress' efforts on behalf of George Sand proved unavailing. Despite censorship by the academy's *commission de lecture*, notably of speeches by Samuel Silvestre de Sacy (1801–1879) in 1855 and Victor, duc de Broglie (1785–1870) in 1856, receptions of new members were almost invariably political statements, especially before November 1860. More than once the emperor graciously granted requests by newly received members to be excused from the customary courtesy call at the Tuileries. Tension was at its greatest in 1869 when Napoleon III responded to the triple election of Franz Nompère, comte de Champagny (1804–1882), the Comte d'Haussonville (1809–1884), and Auguste Barbier (1805–1882), all critics of the regime, by declining to receive the successful candidates. Although the Académie des Sciences Morales et Politiques (permanent secretary, François Mignet [1796–1884], also a liberal) elected Edouard Drouyn de Lhuys in 1861, it was not until the elections to the Académie Française of Jules Janin and, in particular, of Emile Ollivier in the spring of 1870 (a choice championed by Charles de Montalembert) that the senior academy relaxed its opposition to the now liberal Empire, while remaining divided in regard to other issues: romantics versus classicists, materialists versus idealists, Catholics versus freethinkers (the latter symbolized by opposition of the liberal Catholics to the unsuccessful candidacy of Emile Littré). Throughout the Second Empire, the organization of the academy, and, indeed, of the institute, remained basically unchanged. The academy, through its *bureau*, protested the decrees of 14 April 1855 (the "academic coup d'état") by which a new section of ten members, initially named by the government, was added to the thirty-member Académie des Sciences Morales et Politiques and the government acquired power to organize the public meetings and influence distribution of prizes. Napoleon III backed down in effect, and in two years nothing remained but the ten new members redistributed among the original sections (formalized by decree of 9 May 1866). The decrees of 14 April also set the date for the annual joint public session of the institute's five academies at 15 August (the fête nationale under the Empire), but this was changed in 1872.

Membership of the Academy 1851–1870 by Seats (*fauteuils*)

1. Comte de Saint-Aulaire, incumbent in 1851; succeeded by Victor, duc de Broglie in 1855, who was succeeded by Prosper Duvergier de Hauranne in 1870 (the last election under the Empire).
2. François Mignet (1836–1884).
3. Charles Brifaut, incumbent in 1851; succeeded by Jules Sandeau in 1858.
4. Eugène Scribe, incumbent in 1851; succeeded by Octave Feuillet in 1862.
5. Comte Louis Molé, incumbent in 1851; succeeded by Frédéric, comte de Falloux in 1856.
6. J.A.F.P. Ancelot, incumbent in 1851; succeeded by Ernest Legouvé in 1854.
7. François Guizot (1836–1874).
8. P.M.F.L. Baour-Lormian, incumbent in 1851; succeeded by François Ponsard in 1855, who was succeeded by Joseph Autran in 1868.
9. Victor Hugo (1841–1885).
10. Charles Augustin Sainte-Beuve, incumbent in 1851; succeeded by Jules Janin in 1870.
11. Jean Jacques Ampère, incumbent in 1851; succeeded by Lucien Anatole Prévost-Paradol in 1865.
12. Baron Guillaume Prosper Barante, incumbent in 1851; succeeded by Alphonse Gratry in 1867.
13. Sanson de Pongerville, incumbent in 1851; succeeded by Xavier Marmier in 1870.
14. Alexis de Tocqueville, incumbent in 1851; succeeded by Père Lacordaire in 1860, who was succeeded by Albert de Broglie in 1862.
15. Philippe, comte de Ségur (1830–1873).
16. Adolphe Thiers (1833–1877).
17. Prosper Mérimée (1844–1870).
18. Désiré Nisard (1850–1888).

19. Narcisse Achille, comte de Salvandy, incumbent in 1851; succeeded by Emile Augier in 1857.
20. Pierre Lebrun (1828–1873).
21. Charles Lacretelle, incumbent in 1851; succeeded by Jean Baptiste Biot in 1856, who was succeeded by Louis, comte de Carné-Marcein in 1863 (Carnet defeated Emile Littré who was supported by Thiers and opposed by Dupanloup).
22. Louis Vitet (1845–1873).
23. Saint-Marc Girardin (1844–1873).
24. Pierre Flourens, incumbent in 1851; succeeded by Claude Bernard in 1868.
25. Etienne Denis, duc de Pasquier, incumbent in 1851; succeeded by Jules Dufaure in 1863.
26. Paul, duc de Noailles (1849–1885).
27. Alphonse de Lamartine, incumbent in 1851; succeeded by Emile Ollivier in 1870.
28. Alexis de Guignard, comte de Saint-Priest, incumbent in 1851; succeeded by Antoine Berryer in 1852 (elected 1852, received 1855), who was succeeded by Franz Nompère, comte de Champagny in 1869.
29. Victor Cousin, incumbent in 1851; succeeded by Jules Favre in 1867.
30. Pierre François Tissot, incumbent in 1851; succeeded by Félix Dupanloup in 1854 (the first election under the Empire).
31. Abel Villemain (1821–1870; perpetual secretary from 1834).
32. Antoine Jay, incumbent in 1851; succeeded by Samuel Silvestre de Sacy in 1854.
33. Alfred de Vigny, incumbent in 1851; succeeded by Camille Doucet in 1855.
34. L.E.M. Dupaty, incumbent in 1851; succeeded by Alfred de Musset in 1852, who was succeeded by Victor de Laprade in 1858.
35. Henri Patin (1842–1876).
36. Charles de Montalembert (1852–1870; chosen in the first election following the coup d'état).
37. A.D.F.J. Simonis-Empis, incumbent in 1851; succeeded by Auguste Barbier in 1869.
38. Jean Pons Guillaume Viennet, incumbent in 1851; succeeded by comte Joseph d'Haussonville in 1869.
39. Charles de Rémusat (1847–1875).
40. André Dupin, incumbent in 1851; succeeded by Alfred Cuvillier-Fleury in 1866.

E. Charavay, *C. Baudelaire et Alfred de Vigny, candidats à l'Académie* (Paris, 1879); H. Moulin, *Jules Favre et son fauteuil académique* (Paris, 1881); *Recueil des discours, rapports et pièces diverses lus dans les séances publiques et particulière de l'Académie Française, 1850–1859* (Paris, 1856–1860, in two parts), and *1860–1869* (Paris, 1866–1872, in two parts); R. W. Reichert, "Anti-bonapartist Elections to the Académie Française, 1852–1870," *JMH* (March 1963).

Related entries: BAUDELAIRE; BONAPARTISM; FAVRE; *HISTOIRE DE JULES CESAR*; LITTRE; ORLEANISM; ORLEANS, BISHOP OF; SAND.

ADDRESS, RIGHT OF, the key concession granted by Napoleon III in 1860 to critics of the authoritarian Empire. The reform of 24 November 1860 attempted compromise between the authoritarian regime that had prevailed since December 1851 and demands for a return to parliamentary government. In order to increase the role of parliament, the emperor henceforth presented each year an annual report on the state of the Empire (the speech from the throne), in reply to which the Corps Législatif and the Senate could prepare, debate, amend, and vote an address, analyzing the throne speech paragraph by paragraph. During this exercise, three ministers without portfolio would clarify government policy and reply to questions—hence a limited right of interpellation. The address was prepared at the beginning of each legislative session. Customary procedures were followed, except that amendments could not be rejected by the commission preparing the draft or by the Conseil d'Etat. The exercise required an average of one to two months. Liberals protested that as a control on governmental action, the address was ineffectual, despite the newly granted right of publicity of debate, and a waste of parliamentary time, since it was always after the fact. On occasion, however, amendments were used to convey to the government, even when unsuccessful, the sentiments of the legislators—for example, the Senate amendment guaranteeing the temporal power of the pope, which on 7 May 1861 received sixty-one votes, and the amendment calling for further reform, which received sixty-three votes in the Corps Législatif on 19 March 1866. In June 1863 the three ministers without portfolio were replaced by the minister of state as sole representative of the government. The death of Auguste de Morny in March 1865 deferred the possibility of replacing the address with full right of interpellation. Demands for reform continued, however, and on 19 January 1867 a decree suppressed the address in favor of the right of interpellation.

Related entries: AUTHORITARIAN EMPIRE; CONSTITUTION; CORPS LEGISLATIF; LIBERALISM; MINISTER OF STATE; REFORM; ROMAN QUESTION; SENATE.

ALGERIA, for the Second Empire, as for subsequent French governments, a major colonial opportunity and problem (although Algeria was never officially classed as a French colony). The Second Empire completed and consolidated the conquest begun in 1830 by expanding French rule into the Sahara as far south as Laghouat and Ouargla and by imposing it on the mountainous Kabylie region between Algiers and Constantine. Having completed these two tasks by 1857, the permanent French garrison in Algeria, known as the Army of Africa, spent the rest of the Empire suppressing isolated revolts in various parts of Algeria and ruling the conquered Algerians, particularly those in military territory, where the army was supreme, and increasingly involving itself in administrative, educational, and developmental tasks, which presaged the later *rôle colonial de l'armée* of General Louis Lyautey (1854–1934).

In other respects, the Second Empire made vacillating attempts to reach a fair settlement between the conflicting claims of the European settlers, or *colons*, and the native Algerians. The latter, who during the period 1850 through 1870 numbered about 2 million, were a medley of mostly tribal Arab-Berber peoples, as well as a Jewish minority concentrated in the towns. Moved by a combination of motives (humanitarian, economic, Saint-Simonian) and, after 1860, by the emperor's personal concern, France of the Second Empire made attempts to stimulate economic, social, political, and educational development in Algeria in ways that would benefit not only the small but influential European population (181,000 in 1857) but the native Algerians as well. It seems ironic, therefore, that Napoleon III's first reaction to Algeria was negative: "[It is] a cannonball strapped to the feet of France," he said, "as much a drain on her strength as Ireland [on that of] England and Poland [on that of] Russia." Yet to some extent Louis Napoleon owed the inception and the success of his coup d'état of 2 December 1851 to the buccaneering spirit, the opportunism, and the ambition of many of the officers of the Army of Africa who had come, by the 1840s, to view the conquest of Algeria as a means for obtaining rapid promotions. Both Victor Fialin Persigny and Auguste de Morny had served in Algeria. In particular, General Leroy de Saint-Arnaud, who as minister of war in December 1851 directed the coup, had earned the promotion that qualified him for the post by leading a raid into the eastern Kabylie.

From the French point of view, the accession of Louis Napoleon to the presidency of France and then to the imperial dignity represented, for the *colons*, a loss of political power and an end to the institutional assimilation to France, which had been gained as a result of the revolution of February 1848, and a return to military rule and the *régime d'exception*. The constitution of January 1852 and legislation that followed ended the experiment in parliamentary representation for the *colons*, the *rattachement* of certain services in Algeria to their respective ministries in France, and the relative independence of the three Algerian prefects from control by the governor-general and the commanding generals of the three provinces. These measures in themselves contributed to maintaining an anti-bonapartist, radical sentiment among the settlers, which was augmented by the dissidents whom French governments began exiling to Algeria after June 1848. But on Algerian soil, democratic radicalism would ring hollow, for most of the so-called radicals invariably developed racist and bigoted feelings toward the native Algerians. The attitude of the settlers toward the Army of Africa was contradictory in the extreme. While cursing the *régime du sabre*, demanding an end to military rule of any kind and the creation of the full gamut of French civilian and parliamentary institutions in Algeria for *colons* only, these same *colons* continued to depend on the Army of Africa for their security, if not their lives, and to expect the army to be their willing partners in efforts to wrest more and more land from the native Algerians. This attitude would be increasingly opposed, particularly by those officers assigned to the *bureaux arabes*, the apparatus of native administration.

During the first seven years of the Second Empire, the settlers were fortunate in that they had in General Jacques Louis Randon a soldier-administrator as governor-general who was sympathetic to their wishes. Because Randon was occupied with the conquest of the Kabylie and the northern Sahara until 1857, he continued to view the native Algerians as so many opponents of France to be crushed at all costs. Later, from 1859 to 1867, when Randon served as minister of war, he began to have second thoughts about the proper roles of the native Algerians and the European settlers in a French Algeria. Even as governor he had come to prefer colonization by large land companies, the objects of which were to produce industrial cash crops like tobacco or cotton, over the proliferation of small freehold farmers (*petits colons*). The later governor-generals, Marshal Amable Pélissier (1860–1864), for instance, and Marshal Marie Edme Patrice de MacMahon (1864–1870), tilted toward the *colons* even while criticizing their excessive appetite for land.

But whether the *colons* were major landowners or small farmers, the limited quantity of land available in Algeria suitable for European settlement could only be taken, by fair means or foul, from the native Algerians. The problem for French jurists and the irresistible temptation for the *colons* was that Islamic Algerian conceptions of land tenure differed so greatly from those provided for in the Code Napoléon that the differences seemed to justify the French seizure of certain Algerian lands despite the objections of the native Algerians. That so much arable Algerian land was either collectively owned (*arch* land) or held inalienably in a sort of Muslim mortmain (*habbous* land), that so many of the rural Algerians were tribal and more or less nomadic, that the Algerian peasants worked their lands in ways that to the French seemed woefully inefficient and wasteful—all of these factors conspired to give the *colons* the conviction that the Algerians owned or controlled far more land than they would need if they practiced "more efficient," more intensive husbandry on smaller holdings.

From the start of the conquest of Algeria, the French authorities had pledged to respect the religious freedom and the property rights of the Muslims. But the fact of armed Algerian resistance to the French invasion gave the French authorities a justification for confiscating the property of their defeated opponents. Then, major land ordinances of 1844 and 1846 sponsored by Marshal T. R. Bugeaud, governor-general from 1844 to 1847, permitted the sequestration in certain cases of lands not properly registered with the French authorities and ended the inalienability of *habbous* land. Although a further land law of 1851 reaffirmed the inviolability of both *melk* and *arch* lands, the *colons* increasingly subverted the law.

The coming of peace simply meant that in the absence of military confiscations, the French authorities would have to find another way of satisfying the land hunger of the *colons*. The formula that evolved was called *cantonnement*, the idea of a certain Dr. Worms who, as early as 1844, had reasoned that by having defeated the *dey* of Algiers, the French government had acquired ultimate title to all land in Algeria. What Worms had chosen to overlook is that conquest did not permit the expropriation of those persons who paid a small supplementary land tax, the *kharadj*, by which the landowner acknowledged the overlordship of the *dey* and then of France. Thus, acting through administrative means, the French civil authorities used the *cantonnement* formula in civil territory and even to some extent in military territory to force Muslim individuals and whole tribes to hand their "surplus" land over to European *colons* who, it was said, would work them more efficiently and intensively than had been the case with the Algerian owners. Some officials salved their consciences by further arguing that because through *cantonnement* Algerian and European farmers would end up living and working in close proximity, the presence of Europeans would be a force tending toward civilizing and assimilating Algerians. The practical result of *cantonnement*, however, was that most Algerian tribes lost large quantities of their arable lands, 50 to 75 percent in some cases, with little to show in exchange. Pauperization ensued for many Algerian farmers who, because of lack of capital and of skills, could not adapt to the new farming methods required on reduced holdings. More often than not, they were left with the worst lands, and even these they might lose through debt foreclosure. Still, *cantonnement* continued unrestrained as an administrative procedure until 1861. At this point an attempt on the part of Mercier-Lacombe, the director of civil affairs under Governor-General Pélissier, to have it codified and made the object of a decree led to its undoing. The commission he created to propose the outlines of such a decree attracted so much negative publicity in France that *cantonnement* was roundly condemned. In fact, the emperor's personal opposition to *cantonnement* would contribute greatly to his developing interest in the Algerian Muslims.

Meanwhile, however, between 1858 and 1860, Algeria was the object of an experiment, not only in assimilation but in integrated colonial administration. In June 1858, Napoleon III created the Ministry of Algeria and the Colonies to take responsibility for the colonies proper (removed from jurisdiction of the ministry of the navy) and of Algeria (taken from the ministry of war). He gave the portfolio of the new ministry to his cousin Prince Jérôme Napoleon, who held it for ten months. In Algeria, Prince Napoleon abolished the governor-generalship and strengthened the prefects, giving them independence from the military authorities. Most services were attached to their respective ministries. Civil territory was expanded at the expense of military territory, and land transactions were completely freed in both. Although Prince Napoleon was more interested in freeing the *colons* from military rule than in helping the native Algerians resist *colon* pressure, he was at least moved by the desire to assimilate the Algerians completely. He attempted some liberal measures affecting the native Algerians. He ended collective punishment and attempted to reduce the arbitrary authority that both the *bureaux arabes* and certain native chiefs had exercised over the Algerian masses. Given Prince Napoleon's genuine liberalism and the regrets he later expressed for having been duped by *colon* spokesmen, one can only speculate as to what the outcome might have been had he held on to his ministry for a longer period. But he resigned in March 1859, for reasons not connected with Algeria. His successor, Prosper de Chasseloup-Laubat, cancelled most of his reforms.

By 1864 Algeria had passed once again almost completely under the control of the military, headed by the all-powerful governor-general. But this time the emperor intended military domination to serve in Algeria as the vehicle for protecting, emancipating, and educating the native Algerians. The fighting qualities that Algerian troops had demonstrated in the Crimea had awakened Napoleon III's interest in Algeria. When in September 1860 he and the empress paid a surprise visit to Algiers, he came away disgusted with the rapaciousness of the *colons* and determined to take measures to protect the interests of the native Algerians. But he was forced to move carefully because of the close links between *colon* interests on one hand and the gathering forces of liberalism in France on the other.

Influenced by Ismaïl Urbain, journalist and government interpreter, and by Colonel Lapasset, former commandant of the subdivision of Philippeville, the emperor denounced the evils of *cantonnement* in an article appearing in the 22 January 1863 issue of the *Moniteur universel*. Then, obviously influenced by a reading of Urbain's *L'Algérie française: Indigènes et immigrants*, he wrote his famous open letter of 6 February 1863 to Marshal Pélissier in which he called for an end to *cantonnement* and in general an end to the exploitation of the native Algerians. He proclaimed a close collaboration between the French authorities and the Muslims and a functional division between native Algerians and *colons*. The former would retain their lands on which they would engage in cereal farming and stock raising, traditional activities that they did best. The Europeans would confine themselves to irrigated agriculture and industry, which required capital investment on a large scale, both to be financed by investment from France. The letter ended with the often quoted declaration: ''Algeria is not strictly speaking a colony, but an Arab kingdom....I am as much emperor of the Arabs as emperor of the French.'' In short order came the *sénatus-consulte* of 22 April 1863, by which the French government completely renounced the Worms doctrine on which *cantonnement* in practice had been based. Once again the government stressed the inviolability of Algerian landholdings, both *melk* and *arch*, under Islamic law and practice. The *sénatus-consulte* also provided for the restitution to certain tribes of lands that the French authorities had confiscated. But since even in this pro-native period the French authorities still hoped to turn the Algerians into European-style farmers, a procedure was established by which tribal land could be individualized and distributed in individual holdings to each member of the tribe or *douar*. The massive surveying of land that this required would continue until 1873. Unfortunately, the good intentions of the measure were subverted by the great difficulties inherent in individualizing tribal land and by the settler establishment, which in some cases was able to continue effecting a form of *cantonnement* through its control over local administration.

This period of liberal military domination culminated in the visit of Napoleon III to Algeria between 3 May and 7 June 1865, during which the emperor was lionized by the native Algerians, this despite the subtle efforts of Governor-General MacMahon to discourage contacts between him and the Muslims. Moved by the obvious rapacity of the *colons*, the friendliness of the Algerians, the influence of Urbain, who served as his interpreter, and what seemed to him to be the doubtful attitude of the senior military administration, the emperor came away strengthened in his pro-Muslim Algerian sympathies. Back at Paris, and influenced by reports written by Colonel Lapasset and General Auguste Ducrot (1817–1882), Napoleon III wrote a second open letter dated 20 June 1865, addressed to Marshal MacMahon. He reiterated his earlier views and stressed that Algeria was "at once an Arab kingdom, a European colony, and a French [military] camp," all aspects of which should be made to coexist in harmony. He called on French officials in Algeria to show respect for their Algerian counterparts (*la politique des égards*). There followed a second *sénatus-consulte*, that of 14 July 1865, which granted the status of French subjects and full civil rights to the Muslim populations while facilitating the naturalization and the grant of political rights to those who wished to take full French citizenship. There were few takers, for the Muslims believed that by taking French citizenship they would be renouncing their religion. Also, the mostly civilian officials whose job it was to register naturalizations did everything possible to discourage them. A final liberalization in 1866 reformed the election criteria for the municipal councils of Algeria, permitting a greater level of Muslim representation and participation than in the past.

The reforms of the Arab Kingdom period lasted only a short time and gave only short-lived results. There had been several minor revolts in Algeria in 1864 and 1865, even before the emperor's visit. These would contribute to the opposition of the *colons* to the reforms in question. In 1866–1867 came a severe economic crisis and several natural calamities, including severe heat and drought, which followed an abnormally cold winter, then locust plagues and a cholera epidemic. The *colons* and their spokesmen put the blame for the famine that ensued on the primitive agricultural methods of the native Algerians, which, they argued, only *cantonnement*, assimilation, and an end to military rule would cure, views adopted by the influential agricultural investigative commission of 1868. The commission, headed by Count Léopold Le Hon, became a powerful lobby in favor of the *colons*. The greatest setback, however, to the Arab Kingdom and its pro-Muslim program of military liberalism was the success of the liberal movement in France. Its leaders, Jules Favre and Emile Ollivier, among others, gained strength by giving support to the *colons* in their opposition to the *régime du sabre*. Parliamentary liberalization in France enabled the settlers in Algeria to make a major political comeback. The paradox was that most of the *colons* voted "no" in the plebiscite of 8 May 1870, while hoping to benefit from the reforms it would entail. In short, the native Algerians were sacrificed, despite the better sentiments of the emperor, to the expediencies of French domestic politics. With the fall of the Second Empire, a decree of October 1870 would confirm the political ascendancy of the *colons*, which they would not begin to lose until 1959. The Warnier Law of 1873 would grant them full access to all land in Algeria.

Economic development in Algeria during the Second Empire came as an offshoot of the economic boom in France. Colonization by small farmers dropped off after 1851, even though the seven-year period 1851 through 1858 saw the founding of sixty-eight new villages. But these were settled by only 15,000 new *colons* in comparison to the 40,000 who had come during the Second Republic (1848–1851). Although the total European population of Algeria rose from 131,000 in 1851 to 181,000 in 1857 and to 215,000 in 1868, the majority of the new arrivals settled in the towns. At the start of the Second Empire, the French government, influenced by certain business interests, expressed a preference for settlement in Algeria by large land companies rather than by individuals. As General Eugène Daumas observed, it cost 4,000 francs to settle a French family in Algeria, but if such a family had 4,000 francs, it would prefer to remain in France. Thus the government and the authorities were willing to grant concessions to powerful land companies like the Société Genèvoise and Demonchy's Tipassa Domaine. Although these companies were able to obtain large grants of land, sometimes through *cantonnement*, and even official subsidies, they actually settled very few European *colons* on their properties, which they worked with hired Muslim labor or left fallow until they could sell them at speculative prices.

During the Second Empire, as in the past, the French authorities continued to try to produce exotic cash crops such as cotton, sugar, and indigo in Algeria. These attempts failed. Cotton, however, seemed to offer promise while the Union blockade of the Confederacy from 1861 to 1865 during the U.S. Civil War caused a surge in the world market price of cotton, but the promise faded with the victory of the North. On the other hand, tobacco cultivation flourished after it was introduced on a large scale in 1858. Viticulture also began during the Second Empire, although it would produce little more than table grapes until the end of the nineteenth century. Sheep and cattle raising, major economic activities of the native Algerians, were improved, as well as the growing and processing of olives. Still, the basic economic problem remained that Algeria produced best those same agricultural products that France also produced. Nevertheless, French tariff laws of 1851 and 1867 permitted the free importation of Algerian products into France. The second law, indeed, permitted the importation of foreign products into Algeria on better terms than their importation into metropolitan France. The year 1851 also saw the founding of the Bank of Algeria, the quasi-official bank for the issuing of bank notes and the deposit of government funds.

During the Second Empire, northern Algeria was systematically prospected. Workable deposits of lead and copper were discovered. The iron deposits of Mocta-el-Hadid near Bône were granted to Paulin Talabot's interests. As a result of the military campaigns in northern Algeria, the basic road infrastructure was completed linking all the principal cities to one another and to the Tunisian and Moroccan frontiers. In response to the pressure of the *colons* and the support of Marshal Randon, the Corps Législatif approved an Algerian railway bill that provided for an integrated Algerian network to connect the principal cities. The first section, linking Algiers to Blida, opened in 1862 and was followed in 1870 by the Philippeville-Constantine section. Since the operating body, the Algerian Railway Company, was undercapitalized, the PLM Railway of France obtained control of it and thus held a monopoly of Algerian railways until 1875.

In short, the Second Empire represented for Algeria a period of consolidation of French rule and of experimentation, both as to political forms and economic development, this despite a degree of pushing and pulling between the military authorities and the local settlers and both vis-à-vis the native Algerians. A remarkable feature of the period was the genuine sympathy for the Algerian population expressed by Napoleon III. Unfortunately, the effects of his good intentions were weakened by distance, the ill will of the settlers and their allies in the colonial administration, and then diluted by the advent of the Liberal Empire, and finally cut short by the fall of the Empire. The Arab Kingdom thus passed into Algerian history as another one of the *occasions manquées* of French Algeria.

C. Ageron, *L'Algérie algérienne de Napoléon III à de Gaulle* (Paris, 1980), "La politique Kabyle sous le Second Empire," *RFHO* (September 1967), and "La vie politique en Algérie sous le Second Empire," *IH* (1969 and 1970); L. C. Barrows, "L'influence des conquêtes algériennes et coloniales sur l'armée française (1830–1919): Une mise au point préliminaire," *Le mois en Afrique: Etudes politiques, économiques, et sociologique africaines* (December 1981–January 1982), and (January–February 1982); W. D. Gray, "French Algerian Policy During the Second Empire," *PWSFH* 3 (1975); C. A. Julien, *Histoire de l'Algérie contemporaine*, vol. 1: *La conquête et les débuts de la colonisation, 1827–1871*, 2d ed. (Paris, 1979); I. Loiseau, "Napoléon III et l'Algérie," *RDM* (15 March 1968); P. Rain, "Le premier ministère de l'Algérie, 1858–1859," *RDM*, 15 July 1956; A. Rey-Goldzeiguer, "Les plébiscites en Algérie sous le Second Empire," *RH* (January–March 1963), "Les problèmes algériens du Second Empire vus par les historiens français," *RHMC* (January–March 1974), and *Le Royaume Arabe* (Algiers, 1977); A. Sainte-Marie, *L'application du sénatus-consulte du 22 avril 1863 dans le province d'Alger, 1863–1870* (Paris, 1973); G. Spillmann, *Napoléon III et le Royaume Arabe d'Algérie* (Paris, 1975), and "Qu'est-ce que le Royaume Arabe d'Algérie?" *AMN* 45 (May 1974); X. Yacono, "Quelques remarques sur la politique indigène du Prince Napoléon en Algérie, 24 juin 1858–7 mars 1859," *Revue de l'Occident musulman et de la Méditerranée*, special number (1970).

Leland C. Barrows

Related entries: CHASSELOUP-LAUBAT; FAIDHERBE; INDOCHINA; MACMAHON; PELISSIER; PRINCE NAPOLEON; RANDON; REFORM; SAINT-ARNAUD; SENEGAL.

ALLIANCE POLICY, Napoleon III's real or presumed search for permanent allies with whose aid he could achieve the objectives of his foreign policy. Since those objectives included revision of the Treaties of 1815 and promotion of nationalities, conservative Austria offered little attraction. Clearly Napoleon III's first choice was Britain. The Crimean War (1854–1856) did, in fact, result in an Anglo-French alliance, and its aftermath seemed to offer the opportunity of including Russia, whose desire to escape the Black Sea neutralization clauses of the Treaty of Paris of 1856 had made it a revisionist power. Anglo-Russian antagonism combined, however, with growing British distrust of France to frustrate such a combination, despite the successful embassy to Russia in 1856–

1857 of Napoleon III's half-brother, Auguste de Morny, and the signature in December 1858 of a Franco-Russian alliance treaty. The Italian War of 1859 and subsequent French annexation of Nice and Savoy ended the Anglo-French entente, which had been made less attractive by Britain's refusal to enter commitments or even to discuss potential problems in advance and by its lack of enthusiasm for conference diplomacy. The possibility of substituting Prussia for Britain may have encouraged Napoleon III in his indecision during the Danish War of 1864 and in his consequent dalliance with Otto von Bismarck. The events connected with the Polish question, in particular the crisis of 1863, not only deepened the rift between France and Britain but also ended the Franco-Russian entente and initiated a flirtation with Austria. This could come to nothing, however, as long as Venetia remained Austrian and French foreign policy revisionist.

The Austro-Prussian War of 1866 created a new situation. Venetia became Italian, and the decisive Prussian victory at Sadowa posed a long-range threat to French security. Bismarck's refusal to enter into a useful arrangement with France, the Luxembourg crisis of 1867, and other factors combined to ensure that in the latter years of his reign, Napoleon III would increasingly seek allies not for change, as before 1866, but for defense of the status quo and thus of French security. He sought a triple alliance, of France, Austria, and Italy. This effort failed, partly because of Austrian uncertainty, partly because of the continued French presence at Rome, partly, perhaps, because of Napoleon III's abiding distaste for Hapsburg policies. In 1869 the emperor apparently returned to his first alliance preference, courting Britain through a proposal of disarmament (1870) and Russia through the mission of General Emile Félix, comte de Fleury to St. Petersburg. Nevertheless, the outbreak of the Franco-Prussian War found France still without a dependable ally.

Related entries: BIARRITZ; BOLGRAD; COBDEN-CHEVALIER TREATY; CONGRESS OF PARIS; CONGRESS POLICY; DANISH WAR; LATIN MONETARY UNION; POLISH QUESTION; REVISION; ROMAN QUESTION; TRIPLE ALLIANCE; VENETIA; WALEWSKI.

ALPHAND, ADOLPHE (1817–1891), assistant to Baron Georges Haussmann in the transformation of Paris; chiefly responsible for parks and landscaping; born 26 October 1817 at Grenoble. In 1851 Alphand was an engineer of roads and bridges at Bordeaux, where he constructed the harbor basin and prepared the setting of Louis Napoleon's triumphant reception in October 1852. As a protégé of Haussmann, the young engineer found his prospects magnificently improved with the coup d'état of December 1851. Brought to Paris in November 1854, he replaced the horticulturist Varé on 5 December 1854 as engineer in charge of the transformation of the Bois de Boulogne. By 1857 he had become the chief engineer of the park service (in 1867 his title was director of streets and parks, to which was added responsibility for municipal lighting). Haussmann called him his "right arm," and it is difficult to judge the accomplishments of the engineer apart from those of the prefect. Certainly Alphand, an engineer of artistic bent, creator of the city's nurseries and greenhouses (1855–1859), put flowers in fashion and, as designer of all the new parks, many squares, and the landscaping of the major streets, played a key role in creating the new Paris. He was the principal organizer of the international exhibition of 1867. In 1869 he was appointed inspector general of roads and bridges.

Alphand created the parks of the Bois de Boulogne, Bois de Vincennes, Buttes-Chaumont, Montsouris, and Monceau, as well as the smaller gardens of Trocadéro, Ranelagh, and the Squares St. Jacques and Louis XVI. He landscaped the avenue des Champs-Elysées, the avenue de l'Observatoire (1867), and many of the new streets and squares, notably the avenues de l'Impératrice, de l'Empereur, de l'Opéra, and de la République, and the boulevards Saint-Germain, du Prince Eugène, and Richard Lenoir. Following the overthrow of the Empire on 4 September 1870, he was, to some extent, Haussmann's successor in the early years of the Third Republic. Alphand died 6 December 1891 at Paris.

A. Alphand, *Les promenades de Paris: Histoire, description des embellissements, dépenses de création et d'entretien des Bois de Boulogne et de Vincennes, Champs-Elysées, parcs, squares, boulevards, places plantées* (Paris, 1867–1873); P. Strauss, ''M. Alphand et les travaux de Paris,'' *Revue bleue* 48 (1891).

Related entries: BOIS DE BOULOGNE; PARIS, REBUILDING OF.

ALUMINUM. In 1854 Henri Sainte-Claire Deville (1818–1881), professor of chemistry at the Ecole Normale Supérieure, perfected a process of reducing aluminum salts with sodium to produce marble-sized lumps of the pure metal. Deville's preliminary studies on the potential large-scale production of sodium, aluminum chloride, and aluminum were subsidized in part by a grant from the Académie des Sciences. When these studies showed sufficient commercial promise, Jean Baptiste Dumas in 1855 brought the matter to the attention of Napoleon III, who was intrigued with the possible military use of aluminum for strong yet lightweight equipment for his troops. Given an imperial grant for the cost of pilot-plant operations at Javel, Deville was quickly able to produce large ingots of the metal, which were displayed at the Paris international exposition of 1855 where they impressed visitors by their extreme lightness and resistance to tarnishing and corrosion.

Initially, aluminum remained a costly substance and was regarded as a precious and decorative metal. The first manufactured aluminum article appears to have been a baby's rattle for the prince imperial (made in 1856), and aluminum table service was used for the visit of the king of Siam to the French court. The pilot operations at Javel were followed by technical installations at Rouen and Nanterre where Deville and his colleagues launched the aluminum industry by so decreasing the cost of production that by the decade's close, aluminum could be used commercially, as in the manufacture of household utensils and marine instruments. Deville's process remained the basis for large-scale production in France—and later in Britain and the United States—until the discovery of the direct electrolytic production of aluminum simultaneously in 1886 by Charles Martin Hall of the United States and Paul Héroult of France. This process so radically reduced costs as to render commercially obsolete all chemical methods of aluminum production.

R. E. Oesper and Pierre Lemay, "Henri Sainte-Claire Deville, 1818–1881," *Chymia* 3 (1950); T. G. Pearson, "The Aluminum Industry," *Chemistry and Industry*, no. 46 (17 November 1951).

Martin Fichman

AMNESTY, during the Second Empire a political act that the emperor was empowered to exercise under the *sénatus-consulte* of 25 December 1852. In January 1853 there were some 6000 political *condamnés*, whether in prison (at Belle-Isle until 1857, then at Mont-Saint-Michel or Corte Fortress in the center of Corsica), *transporté* (to Guyana [Cayenne] or Algeria), *assigné à résidence* in France (i.e., required to report to the local authorities twice a month), *surveillés* (requiring permission to leave their communes), or exiled (in Belgium, Switzerland, Britain, Holland, Jersey, and Sardinia [Savoy], where they referred to themselves as *proscrits*). Motivated both by his habitual generosity and by his shrewd political sense, Louis Napoleon issued his first amnesty decree 8 August 1852 while still prince president (although technically he could not under the constitution of January 1852 extend *amnestie* but only *grâce*). Proclaimed in connection with the *fête nationale* on 15 August, the presidential decree applied notably to Adolphe Thiers and other former deputies exiled 10 January 1852 in the aftermath of the coup d'état. A wider amnesty was decreed 9 December 1852 on the occasion of the reestablishment of the Empire. It applied to all political exiles and detainees of the period 1848 through 1852 who would promise publicly not to engage in politics. Many eventually did so. On 1 February 1853, on the occasion of his marriage, Louis Napoleon amnestied 4,312 political prisoners. Three years later, partly as a bid to separate the republican leaders from their followers, partly in order to celebrate the birth of his son, the prince imperial, Napoleon III disregarded the advice of a number of his ministers (Jules Baroche, Adolphe Billault, J. P. Abbatucci, Eugène Rouher) and offered amnesty (16 March 1856) to all political *condamnés* (in France, Algeria, and Cayenne) and exiles who would give their word of honor "to submit loyally to the government which the nation has chosen." Most of those who had not accepted the 1852 amnesty now made their peace with the government and returned to France. Of those who did not (some 1000), all but a few (about 400, including Victor Hugo and Edgar Quinet, for example) accepted the general amnesty proclaimed without condition on 15 August 1859, in celebration of victory in the Italian War (this embraced as well those who had been victims of the repression following Felice Orsini's attempt on Napoleon III's life in January 1958). A final amnesty was granted political offenders 15 August 1869, in commemoration of the centenary of the birth of Napoleon I and in conjunction with the *sénatus-consulte* establishing the Liberal Empire.

Related entries: COUP D'ETAT; *FETE NATIONALE*; VICTOR HUGO; OATH; REPUBLICANISM.

ANGLO-FRENCH COMMERCIAL TREATY. See COBDEN-CHEVALIER TREATY.

ARLES-DUFOUR, FRANCOIS BARTHELEMY (1797–1872), industrialist; born at Cette (Sète). Arlès-Dufour is one of those notables of the July Monarchy and Second Empire who deserve more attention than they have received. Son of an officer of the Army of Italy, a product of the Lycée d'Orléans, briefly a defender of Paris in 1815, he worked in Germany for the textile firm of Dufour Frères at Leipzig, married the daughter of a partner, and founded a branch of the firm at Lyons. Later (1856) he would, with his father-in-law, help to found the Société Générale de Crédit de Leipzig. Anti-clerical and socialist in Lyons, the most conservative and Catholic of French cities, he there carved out a position of leadership in the business and political community, which under the Second Empire he extended to all of France, Britain, and Germany. He was *maire-adjoint* of Lyons, a member of the chamber of commerce, a founder of the Banque de Lyon, and an organizer of the Magasin Général des Soies de Lyon, of the Ecole de la Martinière, and of the Ecole Professionelle du Rhône. Arlès worked with Frédéric Le Play, Michel Chevalier, and Emile Pereire as an organizer and secretary general of the Paris international exposition of 1855 (he had been a member of the jury for that of 1851 at London). A longtime friend of Richard Cobden (1804–1865), he was consulted in the negotiations leading to the Anglo-French commercial treaty of 1860. In 1847 Arlès had organized an international Society for the Study of a Canal at Suez. He was of assistance to the eventually successful De Lesseps Company, although his group did not take part in the project. As a silk merchant, Arlès advocated the transformation of silk manufacture from the workshop to the factory. In October 1861 he launched the idea of sending a delegation of French workers to the London international exposition of 1862, and in 1867 he was one of the founders of the Ligue de la Paix. Not the least of Arlès' accomplishments was the energizing of the Lyonnais business community in the formation of the railways that would become the PLM network (he had formed a committee to work to this end as early as 1843).

The organizing principle of Arlès-Dufour's multifarious activities was derived from his lifelong friendship with Prosper Enfantin (1796–1864) and his association (from 1820) with the Saint-Simonian movement of which Enfantin became leader. Declaring to nobody's surprise at Enfantin's funeral "Je suis Saint-Simonien," Arlès manifested his devotion to the doctrine by his support of technical education, industrial expansion, the "organization of work," international trade and communications and international peace, and by his efforts to transform Lyons into a "French Birmingham." Throughout his life, he contributed to the support of needy Saint-Simonians and advanced the careers of artists with Saint-Simonian connections such as the painter Rosa Bonheur and the composer Félicien David (1810–1876). As a businessman he worked effectively within the network of former Saint-Simonians: the Pereires, Paulin Talabot,

Chevalier, who played a central role in the political and economic life of the Second Empire. Arlès was often at the Tuileries and a familiar of the emperor and empress. At his death, faithful to Saint-Simonian doctrine on the necessity of the transformation of the institution of property, Arlès-Dufour willed three-quarters of his estate to public purposes. The great disappointment of his life was the Franco-Prussian War, the great pride his conviction of having contributed to the making of the Suez Canal. He died at Golfe-Juan, 22 February 1872.

R. Carlisle, "The Saint-Simonians and the Foundation of the Paris-Lyon Railroad," (Ph.D. thesis, Cornell University, 1957).

Robert B. Carlisle

Related entries: BANKING; INTERNATIONAL EXPOSITIONS; RAIL-ROADS; SAINT-SIMONIANISM; SUEZ CANAL; TALABOT.

ARMY REFORM, the largely unsuccessful efforts of Napoleon III to modernize France's military organization. The structure of the French army during the Second Empire was determined by the Soult law of 1832. In theory, the 150,000 men who reached the age of twenty each year were to be called up for seven years of active service, thus ensuring a standing army of about 1 million. In practice, the Corps Législatif annually determined the number who were to be conscripted (the *contingent*). During the Second Empire, the *contingent* averaged 100,000, but when those who were dispensed (for example, for reasons of health or profession) and those who were exempted (for example, as sole support of a widowed mother) are subtracted, the number actually conscripted was closer to 80,000. All eligible young men drew lots (reviewed by *conseils de révision*). Those who drew a "*mauvais numéro*" and were not subsequently dispensed or exempted presumably would be inducted, but in practice only about half of them were; the others were maintained provisionally at home. Moreover, the holder of a *mauvais numéro* could, if he had the money (between 800 and 1,200 francs) hire a replacement to serve in his stead from one of the contractors who undertook this task for a fee. Since conscripts might be given indefinite leave at the end of three years, the French peacetime standing army (*effectifs*) tended to be small (320,000 in 1853, 420,000 in 1863, 389,000 in 1866, 370,000 in 1870) and professional. Perhaps only a quarter of the army were true conscripts. Another quarter were replacements. And the bulk (some 160,000 in the late 1860s) were enlistees or reenlistees who had made the army their life and who grew old in its ranks.

Few changes were made in this system before 1866. A law of 26 April 1855 provided that those who drew a *mauvais numéro* would, rather than themselves hire a replacement, pay a sum of money to the army (*caisse de dotation*). This money would be used to encourage enlistments and reenlistments and to pay pensions to soldiers and to noncommissioned officers. Insurance companies soon gave middle-class families the opportunity to ensure the redemption of their sons from military service. As a result of the personal efforts of Napoleon III, the rifled cannon was introduced in 1858 and the Chassepot rifle in 1866, and the main arsenal was moved from the east to the center of France at Bourges, where it remains today. The need for more fundamental reform was pointed up by the Italian War of 1859. The lack of trained troops was undoubtedly a factor in Napoleon III's decision to make peace with Austria at Villafranca. Even before the peace treaty had been signed, the emperor instructed his minister of war, Marshal Jacques Louis Randon, to prepare a reform plan, which was discussed at the end of October 1859. Nothing was achieved, however, except to provide a modicum of training for that part of the *contingent* that was not called up (as little as five months in three years). Then, in July 1866, Prussia's unexpectedly decisive victory over Austria at Sadowa produced a new sense of urgency. Because of its military system (all Prussian males served three years in the active army, four in the reserve, and a total of twelve in the *Landwehr*) Prussia, with a population of 23 million, had mobilized 750,000 men, while France in the days following Sadowa could have put only 80,000 men on the line, and no more than 250,000 within a month. Since 1843, Napoleon III (an artillery officer in his youth) had urged that the French system be brought closer to that of Prussia. Now he was determined to achieve effective reform. On 20 August 1866 he instructed General Henri Pierre Jean Abdon Castelnau (1814–1890) to draft a memorandum envisaging the establishment of universal military training (*service obligatoire*).

The reform efforts that began in the summer of 1866 were destined to be long and, in the end, largely fruitless. Marshals Randon and Jean Baptiste Vaillant, together with most of their colleagues, had no confidence in an army drawn from reserves. Interventions persuaded Napoleon III in September 1866 to satisfy himself for the time being with a vague call (La Valette Circular, 16 September) for military reform. That same month, however, a meeting of military leaders at Saint Cloud recognized the need for an army of a million men. On 31 October 1866 *Le moniteur* announced the creation of a commission to study the question. Its members (twenty-two) included the marshals, a number of generals, Prince Napoleon, and three ministers—Eugène Rouher, Achille Fould, and Adolphe Vuitry. Under the chairmanship of the emperor, the commission met through November and December 1866 at Saint Cloud and Compiègne, but it proved unable to choose from among six projects embracing three alternatives: universal military service (favored by Napoleon III), modification of the 1832 law (preferred by most of the military men), and maintenance of the existing system with the addition of a Garde Nationale Mobile. The proposal published in *Le moniteur* on 12 December 1866 came, therefore, not from the commission but from the emperor's cabinet and the Conseil d'Etat. It was subsequently modified by the new minister of war, Marshal Adolphe Niel (appointed 20 January 1867), whose project would be known as the "Niel law." The proposed system (after Niel's changes) would require that those drawing *mauvais numéros* should serve five years in the active army and three years in the reserves. Those drawing *bons numéros* would serve four years in the reserve army and then another five years in the Garde Nationale Mobile, a trained force that in time of war could take over garrison duty, maintain order, and handle other such chores. *Exemptés* and *dispensés* would also serve in the Garde Mobile, as would those who took advantage of the *caisse de dotation* to purchase exoneration from the active army. Thus every able-bodied French male would be required to undergo some military service, and France would have an offensive army of 800,000 and a defensive army of 1 million men.

From the moment that Niel's project was unveiled, opposition mounted from almost every quarter. The republicans, embracing the theory of the *levée en masse*, called for abolition of the regular army. Citizen levies, they argued, would suffice for defense, and the example given to Germany would inspire liberal elements there to take control, so that the German threat would disappear. Liberals fretted that parliament would no longer set the annual *contingent* and that 800,000 men could be called up by ministerial order (the first *ban* of reserves) or imperial decree (the second *ban*). They feared a strengthening of authoritarianism. The bourgeoisie, in addition to resisting higher taxes, did not want to lose the possibility of buying replacements for their sons, and the peasants wanted to keep the possibility of drawing *bons numéros*, which would allow their sons to remain on the land. The military insisted on the superiority of a small professional army over one composed largely of reserves. Especially influential were Generals Nicolas Changarnier (1793–1877) and Louis Jules Trochu (1815–1896). The latter published in March 1867 a book, *L'armée française en 1867*, which soon went through twenty editions and which proposed changes in tactics and organization rather than an increase in numbers. In sum, French opinion rejected any additional military burden, and Napoleon III, who would have gone to the country in the summer of 1867 in elections conducted on the issue, was dissuaded by Rouher, whose eyes were always on the constituencies. Most newspapers— even those like Emile Girardin's, which would cry the loudest for war in 1870— rejected the proposed reform. Only those areas bordering Germany (Flanders, Lorraine, and Alsace) were favorable.

The Conseil d'Etat reflected this popular mood in drafting the proposed law (February 1867). Only a very few *conseillers*, including Pierre Ernest Pinard, supported Napoleon III's efforts to establish universal military service. Consequently, the project, which on 7 March 1867 went to the Corps Législatif, was already much changed from Niel's proposals. In particular, the reserve army would not be trained, nor would it be called up except in case of war. The Corps Législatif met on 14 February 1867. "L'influence d'une nation," the emperor warned in his opening address, "dépend du nombre d'hommes qu'elle peut mettre en ligne." But the eighteen-member commission to which the bill was sent was composed almost entirely of opponents. By May 1867 the commission had virtually substituted a new project for the one that had come from the Conseil d'Etat. The legislative session ended 24 July 1867. Since the commission and the Conseil d'Etat could not agree, Napoleon III bowed to political necessity. When the Corps Législatif met again on 18 November 1867, he presented a drastically altered proposal for its consideration. The revised Niel law would allow the legislature to retain its right to determine the size of each year's *contingent*, and while suppressing exoneration and the *caisse de dotation*, it would return to the pre-1855 system of replacement. The holder of a *mauvais numéro* could hire a replacement (in 1868 the cost would be 1,700 francs, or about equal to two years of a school teacher's salary). Moreover, the reserve army could be called up only in time of war and class by class, the oldest first. As for the Garde Mobile, it would consist of all who drew *bons numéros* (five years' service), as well as *exemptés*, *dispensés*, and those who had hired replacements. But the training period could not be longer than fifteen days per year, and the men must be able to return to their homes each night. Thus the institution that was to introduce equality of service into French military organization was rendered largely ineffective from the outset.

Debate began in the Corps Législatif on 19 December 1867 and ended two days later. Adolphe Thiers, who considered himself a military expert, favored a small professional army. He intervened only briefly (and from his chair) to argue that greater numbers were not necessary. Jules Favre called for French disarmament. Jules Simon, the leading republican orator in the debate, demanded a citizens' militia like that of Switzerland, electing its own officers and organized solely for defense. Emile Ollivier, who had made the dropping of the Niel proposals a condition for his entering the government at the end of 1866, shared these sentiments. Niel proved a surprisingly effective and eloquent orator. "Vous voulez donc faire de la France une caserne," Favre cried. "Et vous," the marshal replied, "prenez garde d'en faire une cimetière." The law passed the Corps Législatif on 14 January 1868 by 199 votes to 65 and the Senate on 30 January 125 votes to 1 (that of Michel Chevalier). It was promulgated in early February, the government requesting a loan of 462 million francs to put the new system into effect.

Although Niel had shown great optimism both during and after the debate and Frenchmen were assured that the new law restored the military balance in Europe and prepared France for all eventualities (assurances that were widely accepted), little had changed. The standing army would remain a professional rather than a conscript force, subject to severe initiative-stifling discipline (soldiers could not marry without authorization until one year after entering the reserves, at age twenty-six). Moreover, it would not even increase appreciably in size (to 500,000 men) unless the Corps Législatif were to vote each year the full *contingent* of 100,000, an unlikely prospect. The reserve army of some 300,000 men would exist only on paper. And the Garde Mobile, totaling about 450,000, would be virtually untrained. Niel made strenuous efforts to reform the army's general staff and to organize the Garde Mobile in March and April 1868, despite riots at Bordeaux and elsewhere. His intention was to pour the Garde Mobile into line regiments in the event of war. However, Niel's optimism had contributed greatly to the false sense of security that now lulled France, and he died on 13 August 1869 during lithotrity for a bladder stone. Randon, his successor as minister of war, proved a willing ally of a Corps Législatif eager to spend as little as possible on the new army. (In the elections of May 1869, almost every candidate called for a reduction of the military burden.) In reality, the basic French military deficiencies remained: the lack of a trained reserve and of a true general staff. The first meant that in a war against Germany, France would be in a situation of grave numerical inferiority; the second, that there was no effective counterweight to the anti-intellectualism which, coupled with advancement of higher officers for reasons other than ability, and with an experience in the field (Algeria, Mexico, China, Indochina, Italy, Syria), which was far removed from the realities of continental warfare, ill prepared the French command for conducting a modern war. The French army had made possible the coup d'état of December 1851 and thereafter was guarantor of order and of the regime. It was rewarded with pomp and privilege. But the imposing facade masked a reality that was to be revealed fully only in the disasters of 1870.

Y. Barjaud, "La Garde Nationale Mobile (1868–1872)," *Bulletin de la Société de Borda*, no. 4 (1970); J. Casevitz, *Une loi manquée: La loi Niel (1866–1868): L'armée française à la veille de la Guerre de 1870* (Paris, 1959); R. D. Challener, *The French Theory of the Nation in Arms, 1866–1939* (New York, 1955); F. Engerand, "Le projet Niel et l'opinion," *Correspondant* 150, 25 March 1913; Etat-major de l'Armée de Terre (Service Historique), *Guide bibliographique sommaire d'histoire militaire et coloniale française* (Paris, 1969); A. F. Kovacs, "French Military Institutions before the Franco-Prussian War," *AHR* (January 1946); L. D. Oliver, "Reorganization of the French Army, 1866–1870" (Ph.D. diss., University of California, 1941); G. Wright, "Public Opinion and Conscription in France, 1866–1870," *JMH* 14 (March 1942).

Related entries: CHASSEPOT; FRANCO-PRUSSIAN WAR; NIEL; PUBLIC OPINION; RANDON; REPUBLICANISM; ROUHER; SADOWA; THIERS.

ASSASSINATION ATTEMPTS. See NAPOLEON III: ASSASSINATION ATTEMPTS.

ASSOCIATION, RIGHT OF. See COALITIONS LAW.

AUGIER, EMILE (1820–1889), dramatist; one of the most celebrated writers of social comedy during the Second Empire; born 17 September 1820 in Valence (Drôme). Little disposed toward the practice of law, Augier presented his first drama, *La ciguë*, 13 May 1844 at the Théâtre de l'Odéon. Its relative success encouraged him to pursue a career as a dramatist. Two years after his appointment as librarian to the Duc d'Aumale (1822–1897) in 1846, Augier made his first sally into republican politics, editing with fellow dramatist François Ponsard (1814–1867), journalist Taxile Delord (1815–1877), critic Gustave Planche (1808–1857), and historian Théophile Lavallée (1804–1866) *Le spectateur républicain* (29 July–7 September 1848). In 1852 he was elected *conseiller général* for the Drôme. Not an active participant at meetings, he resigned the post in 1855. The fruits of his involvement in politics took the form of a brochure, *La question électorale*, in which he proposed reform of the electoral system. Although conceived during this period, the pamphlet was not published until 1864, by which time Augier had become indifferent toward pure politics. He was elected to the Académie Française in 1857.

Augier is best remembered for approximately thirty comedies that premiered during the Second Empire. His first efforts, composed in verse, included two successful comedies, *L'aventurière* (Théâtre Français, 1848) and *Gabrielle* (Théâtre Français, 1849), for which he received the Prix Montyon; *Le joueur de flûte* (Théâtre Français, 1850); *Diane* (Théâtre Français, 1852; an unsuccessful play written for the actress Rachel); and *Philibèrte* (Gymnase, 1853). In collaboration with Jules Sandeau (1811–1883), Augier wrote a vaudeville, *La chasse au roman* (Variétés, 1851), and two comedies in prose, *La pierre de touche* (Théâtre Français, 1853) and *Le gendre de M. Poirier* (Gymnase, 1854). Throughout the 1850s he continued to write comedies of manners in prose: *La ceinture dorée* (Gymnase, 1855), *Le mariage d'Olympe* (Vaudeville, 1855), *La jeunesse* (in verse, Odéon 1858), and, in collaboration with Edouard Foussier (1824–1882), *Les lionnes pauvres* (Vaudeville, 1858) and *Un beau mariage* (Gymnase, 1859). In the following decade, he treated social problems in his comedies: *Les effrontés* (Théâtre Français, 1861), *Le fils de giboyer* (Théâtre Français, 1862), *Maître Guérin* (Théâtre Français, 1864), *La contagion* (Odéon, 1866), and *Lions et renards* (Théâtre Français, 1869). *Les effrontés* satirized the speculation mania of the time; *Le fils de giboyer* attacked the contemporary efforts to mix religion and politics, aroused intense indignation, and was Augier's greatest success. These solid, well-constructed plays concerned with bourgeois life and values won the respect even of such later demanding critics as Jules Lemaitre (1853–1914).

In addition to drama, Augier composed the libretto for Charles Gounod's opera *Sapho* (Opéra, 1851) and published a collection of poems, *Les pariétaires* (1855), some of which were set to music by Gounod. Although disinterested in politics, Augier was a frequent guest at the receptions of Auguste de Morny, the Palais Pompéien of Prince Napoleon (which was inaugurated by a production of Augier's *Le joueur de flûte*, starring Edmond Got [1822–1901], Madeleine Brohan [1833–1900], and Isidore Samson [1793–1871], attended by Napoleon III and Eugénie), and the salon of Princess Mathilde. He was named knight of the Legion of Honor in 1850, officer in 1858, and commander in 1868. He died at Croissy, 26 October 1889.

H. Parigot, *Emile Augier* (Paris, 1890); P. Morillot, *Emile Augier* (Grenoble, 1901).

Dolorès A. Signori

Related entries: THEATER.

AUSTRO-FRENCH WAR. See ITALIAN WAR.

AUTHORITARIAN EMPIRE, the period of personal rule following the coup d'état. From 2 December 1851 until the opening of the first legislative session 29 March 1852, Louis Napoleon governed France by decree, assisted by an appointive Commission Consultative, whose functions were never defined but which substituted for the Conseil d'Etat. Thereafter the constitution of 14 January 1852 placed overwhelming authority in the hands of the prince president and, after 21 November 1852, those of the Emperor Napoleon III. This was the period of the authoritarian Empire (formally proclaimed 2 December 1852). A change of mood, first noticeable about 1858, was catalyzed by the events of 1859–1860 arising from Napoleon III's Italian policy. The years 1860 through 1869, commonly referred to as the Liberal Empire, therefore may be seen as transitional to the establishment of a parliamentary regime. However, as the structure of the constitution was not altered until 8 September 1869 by the *sénatus-consulte*, this latter date may be taken as the formal end of the authoritarian Empire. An alternative dividing point, stressing noninstitutional factors, would be the crowning of the edifice between January 1867 and the spring of 1868, culmination of a period of reform that began with the decree of 24 November 1860. It might then be argued that the Liberal Empire began with the reform decree of January 1867 and that the parliamentary Empire was ushered in with Emile Ollivier's government of 2 January 1870 and confirmed by the *sénatus-consulte* of 21 May 1870.

Related entries: BONAPARTISM; *LES CINQ*; CONSEIL D'ETAT; CONSTI-TUTION; COUP D'ETAT; *IDEES NAPOLEONIENNES*; LIBERAL EMPIRE; MORNY; PRINCE NAPOLEON; OLLIVIER; PERSIGNY; PLEBISCITE; PRESS REGIME; PUBLIC OPINION; REFORM; ROUHER; SECOND EM-PIRE; UNIVERSAL MANHOOD SUFFRAGE.

B

BAKERIES, DEREGULATION OF, an important aspect of the free trade policy of the Second Empire. Because of the ever-present possibility of poor harvests, shortages of grain, and skyrocketing bread prices, there had developed in France from 1789 a body of regulations controlling every aspect of the bakeries industry and notably requiring state authorization in order to follow the trade and to open or to close a bakery. Reform had been discussed during the July Monarchy, but no changes had resulted. At the beginning of the Second Empire, a disastrous harvest (1853) led to a tightening of regulations (decree of 1 November 1854) and to the establishment by Georges Haussmann, prefect of the Seine, of a *caisse de boulangerie* for Paris and region (decrees of 27 December 1853 and of 7 January 1854), designed to keep bread prices stable through a system of taxation and of subsidies. The food crisis continued, although somewhat abated, until 1856 and led to the suspension (1853 and 1859) of the *échelle mobile* (a sliding scale of tariffs on imported agricultural products), which was subsequently abolished and replaced by a law of 15 June 1861 setting a single low duty. This led, in turn, to the ending of the tax on bread, the application of which had, in large part, necessitated the regulation of the industry.

These events added to the growing pressure for liberation of the bakeries. Already, by decree of 24 February 1858, regulation of the butcheries had been ended, and the Second Empire would also see the deregulation of taxi driving. As a result of measures proposed by the municipal commission of Paris, the Conseil d'Etat conducted an inquiry from June to July 1859 into the bakeries industry, during which Jules Baroche, minister presiding the Conseil d'Etat, and Frédéric Le Play argued for deregulation. Another bad harvest in 1861 interrupted the momentum of reform, but in 1862 Eugène Rouher, minister of agriculture, commerce, and public works from 3 February 1855 to 23 June 1863, entered the lists. Together he and Baroche persuaded a reluctant Napoleon III, who presided the two sessions of the conseil that discussed the issue. By decree of 22 June 1863, effective 1 September, all regulation of the bakeries ended (except for rules relating to public health). Henceforth, the price of bread would be determined by market forces, although the Paris *caisse de boulangerie* continued to function in modified form and was active one final time as a consequence of the poor harvest of 1867–1868. The timing of the deregulation was excellent since development of the railroads had largely ended the periodic shortages and wide price fluctuations that originally had justified control of the industry.

Egrot, "La boulangerie parisienne sous le Second Empire," *Act. h.*, (January 1956); T. Horii, "La caisse de la boulangerie du département de la Seine sous le Second Empire" (Paris thèse 3e cycle, Lettres, 1970).

Related entries: COBDEN-CHEVALIER TREATY; ECONOMIC CRISES; ROUHER.

BALLET. See MEYERBEER.

BANKING. During the Second Empire, the banking system saw important developments. New institutions were established to mobilize credit, the use of bank notes became more widespread, and there was a marked increase in bank deposits. Traditional historiography contrasts the dynamism of the new investment and deposit banks with the supposed conservatism of the Bank of France and the *haute banque* (the banking elite in the capital) and concludes that a banking revolution took place during the Second Empire and that this was an important factor promoting economic growth. Such views have been shown to be mistaken. In general terms, we know that banking structures are both growth induced and growth inducing and that growth and the banking sector are interdependent. The expansion of credit facilities in the 1850s and 1860s was, then, the result of prosperity and of the transport revolution, as well as of the favorable policies of the government. Recent studies also have shown that the Parisian *haute banque* was far from conservative and had long participated in loan flotations and insurance, railway, and metallurgical company flotations and, from the 1820s onward, had even supported innovations, such as attempts to set up joint-stock investment banks. Besides, the developments that took place during the Second Empire were far from complete in 1870. The acceptance of the bank note, the opening of bank branches in the provinces, the utilization of bank accounts, and the availability of banking services for different sectors of the economy and society were all incomplete and continued to trail far behind Britain's example.

The changes, then, were complex, were not an independent variable, and have to be understood in the context of the long-term evolution of the banking system. This is not to say, however, that there were not significant developments between 1852 and 1870. During that period, money in circulation doubled, the result of the influx of gold and the increase in bank notes. This increase was relatively modest but stood in marked contrast to the long period of stagnation down to mid-century. There was also an increase in the bank facilities available to institutions, companies, and individuals. And new banks were established to mobilize savings and invest them productively and thus promote growth.

There were two ways in which these changes were achieved. One was through the existing banking institutions, which continued to adapt to changing circumstances and to respond to new profit opportunities. Thus the Bank of France, the sole note-issuing bank and regulator of the system, was more dynamic than contemporary detractors were willing to allow. A law of June 1857 doubled its capital and extended its monopoly of note issue for thirty years beyond 1867 but required in turn that it establish a branch in each department and issue notes in smaller denomination. The bank began to grant loans to owners of railway shares (to help in placing railroad stocks and bonds), to open more branches (in 1848 there had been thirteen provincial branches; by 1870 there were seventy-four), and to increase note issue (in 1864 it offered a 50 franc note). Similarly, the *haute banque* continued to invest in heavy industry and railways and greatly extended its investments abroad, as evidenced in the struggle between rival groups of French bankers to secure railway concessions in central and southern Europe. Members of the financial elite not only invested in the new banks that were set up but dominated their boards of directors. There continued, however, to be a struggle over interest rates between those who favored cheap and plentiful credit (Victor Fialin Persigny, Auguste de Morny, Armand Béhic, and Emile and Isaac Pereire) and those who defended traditional methods (Eugène Rouher, Achille Fould, Jules Baroche, and James de Rothschild). Napoleon III, whose sympathies were probably with the former group, nevertheless played the role of a balance.

The second means by which credit facilities were extended was the establishment of new institutions. In 1852 two banks were founded that were to be imitated throughout Europe. One was the Crédit Foncier, a mortgage bank that invested in urban renewal. The other was the Crédit Mobilier, an investment bank that aimed to mobilize savings that otherwise would not have gone into financing industrial development. The Crédit Mobilier participated in company—and especially railway—formation in France and elsewhere in Europe, as well as in urban development at Paris and Marseilles and government loan flotations. It was imitated by such institutions as the Banque de Darmstadt (April 1853), and Jules Mirès' Caisse Générale des Chemins de Fer (July 1853), and the Rothschilds' Réunion Financière (January 1856). Equally important, the period from 1859 to 1864 saw the formation of mixed banks, those with both deposit and investment functions. These banks aimed to attract deposits, by publicity, by lowering the minimum sum required to open an account, by adopting the English practice of payment by check (legalized in France only in 1865), and by establishing branch offices. They also aimed to promote industry and underwrite issues of corporate and public securities. In 1859 the Crédit Industriel et Commercial, capitalized at 60 million francs, was established, principally by Eugène Schneider and Paulin Talabot, backed by the Rothschilds. The Réunion Financière, with its newspaper *La semaine financière*, had striven for three years to achieve this end; Talabot succeeded, despite the opposition of Rouher, who was worried by Morny's involvement. Four years later Henri Germain (1824–1905) founded the Crédit Lyonnais, with a capital of 20 million francs. This was destined to become France's largest bank. In 1864, Rothschild and allied

financiers (again the Réunion Finançière) set up the Société Générale pour Favoriser le Développement de l'Industrie et du Commerce en France (a union of
the Comptoir d'Escompte de Paris, the Crédit Colonial, and the Crédit Industriel
et Commercial), with an initial capital of 60 million. On the board of the Société
Générale sat such powerful figures as Schneider, Talabot, J. François Bartholony
(1796–1881), and Pierre Ernest Pinard. In the same period were founded the
Banque Impériale Ottomane (1863) and the Banque des Pays Bas (1864; in 1869
it merged with the newly created Banque de Paris). By the end of the Second
Empire, these banks were beginning to set up branches.

The old and new banking institutions both reacted to and contributed to the
economic growth of the period. The investment opportunities available to them
were limited by a number of factors, including the internal financing practiced
by most industrial firms. But they made important contributions to public works
and urban renewal, contributed to making Paris the financial center of the Continent, and helped to channel perhaps a third of French capital into foreign
investments, making 1852 through 1856 the greatest period of French capital
exports (which by 1870 had increased from 2 billion to 15 billion francs). From
1867, with the exception of the Franco-Prussian War and its immediate aftermath,
income from existing foreign investments equaled or exceeded new capital exports. Still, as peasants hoarded gold, and as specie accumulated in the vaults
of the Bank of France (about 1 billion francs by 1869), it is estimated that despite
an average annual investment in France of some 1.5 billion francs from 1852
to 1865, billions of francs remained uninvested and unproductive.

J. Bouvier, *Le Crédit Lyonnais de 1863 à 1882: Les années de formation d'une banque
de dépôts*, 2 vols. (Paris, 1961); F. Braudel and E. Labrousse, eds., *Histoire économique
et sociale de la France au XIXe siècle*, vol. 3: *L'avènement de l'ère industrielle* (2 vols.;
Paris, 1977); P. Cousteix, "Les financiers sous le Second Empire," *1848: Revue des
révolutions contemporaines* 43 (July 1950); P. Dauzet, "Conflit de banquiers sous le
Second Empire," *Monde française* (March 1948); P. Demarquette, "La Banque de France
sous le Second Empire," *SN* (1979); B. Gille, *La banque en France au XIXe siècle*
(Paris, 1970); H. G. Martin, "La Société Générale, 1864–1964," *RHES*, no. 3 (1965);
C. Michalet, *Les placements des épargnants français de 1815 à nos jours* (Paris, 1968);
Alain Plessis, *La Banque de France sous le Second Empire* (Paris, 1982).

Barrie M. Ratcliffe

Related entries: ARLES-DUFOUR; CREDIT MOBILIER; ECONOMIC
CRISES; FOULD; GOVERNMENT FINANCE; HAUSSMANN; LATIN MON-
ETARY UNION; MIRES; PEREIRE; RAILROADS; ROTHSCHILD; SAINT-
SIMONIANISM; *SOCIETES PAR ACTIONS;* TALABOT.

BANVILLE, THEODORE DE (1823–1891), poet, dramatist, and central figure
of the Parnassian school; born 14 March 1823 at Moulins to a noble but liberal
family. An ardent admirer of Victor Hugo, Banville has been called the last of
the romantic poets and the first of the Parnassians. His early readings in the
literature of classical antiquity, in the French poets of the fifteenth and sixteenth
centuries, fostered a desire to resuscitate verse forms of preclassical France.

With a group of young writers, notably Charles Baudelaire, whom Banville met at nineteen, and Henri Murger (1822–1861), he shared a hatred of the bourgeois and the philistine, and it was to the plaudits of his friends that he published two collections of poetry, *Les cariatides* (1842) and *Les stalactites* (1846). To support himself, Banville contributed theater reviews and verse to various ephemeral publications, *Le corsaire*, *Revue fantaisiste*, and *Paris*, the last a literary journal to which the Goncourt brothers also contributed. The short stories that appeared in *Paris* were published in volume form in 1853 under the title *Les pauvres saltimbanques*. A third collection of verse, *Les odelettes*, appeared three years later. Critic and poet Théophile Gautier acclaimed him.

With *Les odes funambulesques* (1857), Banville acquired a reputation as a verbal acrobat, his readers failing to take seriously his exposé of their foibles and frivolity. Tubercular since the early 1850s, the poet spent several months and a great deal of money in private sanatoriums. Falling at a time when he was only beginning to make a name for himself, these periods of convalescence were financially burdensome. The Ministry of Fine Arts came to his assistance, and the poet, no doubt out of gratitude, realized the impossibility of maintaining an overtly hostile attitude toward the society of his day, as did, for example, his close friend Félix Nadar. A much expanded second edition of the *Odes* appeared in 1859. This time the critical *esprit* of the volume as a whole went unnoticed in the sheer volume of material.

Banville was also productive in the genre of drama. *La mer de Nice, Lettres à un ami*, and *Nice française*, a *scène lyrique*, won for him the cross of the Legion of Honor in 1860. The *Fourberies de Nérine*, performed at the villa of Princess Mathilde in 1864 with Napoleon III and Eugénie in attendance, elicited compliments from the emperor, and two years later Banville was invited to attend a performance of his play *Gringoire* at the royal chateau at Compiègne.

The appearance of the *Revue fantaisiste*, founded by the poet Catulle Mendès (1841–1909) in 1859, drew the attention of younger poets of the day, François Coppée, Albert Glatigny (1839–1873), as well as Baudelaire and Banville. The Parnassian circle, as it came to be known, published its first anthology of verse, *Le Parnasse contemporain*, in 1866. The same year Banville married Marie Elisabeth Rochegrosse, a widow with one son, and the literary circle, which until then had met regularly on Thursday at Banville's, now gathered at the home of the couple in the rue de Buci. In 1867 Banville published one of his best-known collections, *Les exilés*. A more profound collection than some of his efforts—Banville reflects on the disappearance of art from human concerns—it refutes the charge that his verse was mere poetical buffoonery.

For three years (1866–1869), Banville composed principally for the theater—*Gringoire* was his most successful endeavor in the genre—and from 1869 through 1878 took charge of the theater bulletin in *Le national*. Among other works Banville published during the Second Empire were the following: *Esquisses parisiennes* (1859), *Occidentales* (1868), *Sang de la coupe* (1857), *Améthystes*, *nouvelles odelettes amoureuses* (1862), *Nouvelles odes funambulesques* (1869), and *Rimes dorées* (1869). He died at Paris, 12–13 March 1891.

M. Fuchs, *Théodore de Banville* (Paris, 1912); T. de Banville, *Petites études: L'âme de Paris: Nouveaux souvenirs* (Paris, 1890).

Dolorès A. Signori

Related entries: GAUTIER; LECONTE DE LISLE; THEATER.

BARBEY D'AUREVILLY, JULES (1808–1889), novelist, critic, and journalist; born 2 November 1808, at Saint-Sauveur-le-Vicomte. Grandson of a royal secretary who had been appointed to the parlement of Clermont-Ferrand in 1756, Barbey d'Aurevilly began his literary career in Paris as a left-wing dandy, working chiefly in journalistic circles. In 1846 overindulgence in alcohol and opium led to a breakdown in his health. On recovery, he rejected his former ways, returning to Catholicism and to absolutism. He began the *Revue du monde catholique*, whose first issue appeared in April 1847 and whose outlook was uncompromisingly ultramontanist. Further, he undertook works of religious propaganda, attempting to found a Catholic Society, and he even made political overtures to a workers' club but was rejected because of his strict Catholic stand. With this change in his life began the production of his greatest polemical works, in which he spoke out against Luther and Descartes and the principles for which they stood in favor of absolutism and theocracy. As the strength of the legitimists waned and democratic elements came to the fore, Barbey rallied to the bonapartist cause, staunchly supporting Louis Napoleon. As a journalist and literary critic, he continued to support the Second Empire and to attack the new liberalism. From 1851 he wrote literary articles for the semiofficial newspaper, *Le pays*. With Adolphe Granier de Cassagnac and others, he helped in April 1858 to found and edit *Le reveil*. He wrote also for *Le Gaulois*, *La situation*, *Le constitutionnel*, *Le veilleuse*, *Le Figaro*, and *Le nain jaune*. In all of his articles, Barbey spoke out fiercely against Emile Augier, Victor Hugo, Charles Augustin Sainte-Beuve, the Académie Française, Emile Zola, and the poets of the new Parnassian movement for their liberal and democratic tendencies, while at the same time praising Balzac and Charles Baudelaire.

During the period of the Second Empire, Barbey began to produce his great novels, all of them characterized by an odd mixture of satanism and Catholicism, essentially romantic in tone. He had published *Le Chevalier Des Touches* (1864) and *Un prêtre marié* (1865) when the Franco-Prussian War broke out. He joined the National Guard but was exiled by the Commune to Cotentin. At this point in his life, Barbey was accepted as one of the leading lights in Paris literary circles. He continued his newspaper work. *Les diaboliques* (1874) and *Une histoire sans nom* (1882), two of his best-known works, also belong to this postwar period. Among other novels written during the Second Empire are *Une vieille maîtresse* (1851) and *L'ensorcelée* (1855). In criticism, he published *Les oeuvres et les hommes* (Paris, 1860–1895). Barbey died at Paris, 23 April 1889.

J. Barbey d'Aurevilly, *Oeuvres complètes*, 17 vols. in 7 (Geneva, 1926–1927; reprint 1979); C. Buet, *J. Barbey d'Aurevilly: Impressions et souvenirs* (Paris, 1891); P. Colla, *L'univers tragique de Barbey d'Aurevilly* (Paris, 1965); G. C. Gille, *Barbey d'Aurevilly, critique littéraire* (Geneva, 1962).

Dorothy E. Speirs

Related entries: BONAPARTISM; PRESS REGIME.

BARBIZON SCHOOL. See DAUBIGNY.

BAROCHE, JULES (1802–1870), lawyer, early supporter of Louis Napoleon, a key political figure of the Second Empire, and distinguished minister of justice (1863–1869); born 18 November 1802 at La Rochelle. Early orphaned (his father was a shopkeeper), Baroche became a lawyer in 1823. Seven years later, his financial independence was ensured by an advantageous marriage. Elected to the Chamber of Deputies in 1847, he became a member of the dynastic opposition, played a modest role in the banquet campaign, and rallied sincerely to the Republic following the Revolution of 1848. Baroche was elected to the Constituent Assembly but soon took alarm at the threat from the Left. Concerned above all with the preservation of social order, he rallied on 22 December 1848 to Louis Napoleon following the latter's election to the presidency and was appointed procureur général and, later, minister of the interior. Baroche, who had disapproved of Louis Napoleon's attempt to restore universal manhood suffrage, was not a party to the coup d'état of 2 December 1851; however, he applauded it and accepted the vice-presidency of the Consultative Commission, which foreshadowed the Napoleonic Conseil d'Etat and which he chaired in the absence of the prince president. With Pierre Magne and Achille Fould, Baroche shaped the principal organic decree-laws of the regime. It was he who officially informed Louis Napoleon on 31 December 1851 of the results of the plebiscite sanctioning the new regime, and he was a member of the commission that established the electoral system of 2 February 1852.

Named vice-president of the Conseil d'Etat 25 January 1852 (president from 30 December), Baroche headed that body, with cabinet rank, until 23 June 1863, serving as chief spokesman for the government. Other honors accumulated. He was awarded the grand cross of the Legion of Honor 3 April 1855 and in 1860 became a member of the Conseil Privé and of the Regency Council, as well as one of the three ministers without portfolio responsible for representing the government before the Corps Législatif and the Senate. He was very briefly interim foreign minister between Alexandre Walewski and Edouard Thouvenel. On 20 October 1864 he was named to the Senate. In legal and economic matters, Baroche's views were liberal. He played a major role in preparing the 1860 free trade treaty with Britain (the Cobden-Chevalier Treaty) and with Eugène Rouher was instrumental in bringing about in 1863 deregulation of the bakeries. As president of the Conseil d'Etat and as minister of justice and cults (23 June 1863–12 July 1869), Baroche worked untiringly for reform of the legal system.

He secured such changes as the abolition of the *mort civile* (deprivation of the rights of citizenship) and of imprisonment for debt (*contrainte par corps*), establishment of the *casier judiciaire* (maintenance of criminal records; the system had been inaugurated in 1850), and reform of punishments and of the bankruptcy law. He championed copyright and patent laws and drew up the great legislation of 1862 governing public accountability. In matters concerning the church, Baroche was staunchly Gallican, opposing the "party of the pope," especially in those troubled years following 1859. On 16 October 1867 he was one of the three ministers who opposed the new Roman expedition that culminated at Mentana.

In matters of politics, however, Baroche remained consistently conservative. Fearful of revolution and socialism, he defended the authoritarian Empire to the end, viewing a strong executive and a controlled press as necessary for the preservation of social order and of good government. His was the policy of the strong hand. In 1856 he argued against Napoleon III's proposal of a generous amnesty. Imbued with bourgeois virtues, Baroche was an enemy of extravagance, whether in the form of foreign adventures (he opposed the Crimean War and the Italian War of 1859), Baron Georges Haussmann's projects for rebuilding Paris, or the financial methods of Isaac and Emile Pereire. Although keenly disappointed when succeeded as president of the Conseil d'Etat in June 1863 by Rouher, he remained an intimate friend and close political colleague of the new minister of state, and, his political influence having ended with the reform decree of 19 January 1867, he resigned his cabinet functions at the same time as Rouher on 12 July 1869.

Despite the savagery of Victor Hugo's attacks (motivated largely by personal considerations), Baroche must be judged an excellent public servant. Intelligent, tactful, an extremely effective orator, indefatigable in his activity, he was, besides, a man of great integrity who remained true to his principles and loyal to the emperor, whom he liked and admired. Although still a senator and a member of the Conseil Privé, his last years were clouded not only by the decline of the Empire but by the involvement of his son, Ernest, in the Jules Mirès scandal. Baroche blamed the war of 1870, in which Ernest was to die heroically, on Emile Ollivier and Antoine, duc de Gramont. On 4 September, he opposed the adjournment without resistance of the Senate by Rouher and made his way to Jersey, where he died less than two months later on 29 October 1870.

Mme. J. Baroche, *Second Empire: Notes et souvenirs, 1855–1870* (Paris, 1921); J. Maurain, *Un bourgeois français au XIXe siècle: Baroche, ministre de Napoléon III d'après ses papiers inédits* (Paris, 1936); O. de Vallée, *Paris journal*, 30 October 1875.

Related entries: CODBEN-CHEVALIER TREATY; CONSEIL D'ETAT; FOULD; GALLICANISM; MAGNE; ROUHER.

BARYE, ANTOINE LOUIS (1796–1875), animal sculptor and painter; born at Paris, 24 September 1796. Barye entered the Ecole des Beaux-Arts in 1818, having studied engraving, sculpture, and then painting with the romanticist Baron

Antoine Gros (1771–1835). He was unsuccessful in his attempts to win the Prix de Rome for sculpture but began to work for a goldsmith sculpting animals. He studied animals at first hand, as did Eugène Delacroix, at the zoo in the Jardin des Plantes, which received many animals during the Second Empire, such as Bengal tigers, Asian and African elephants, and hippopotamuses, a gift for Napoleon III from Egypt. In the 1830s, he sculpted a number of hunting scenes and animal combats for the duc d'Orléans, most of which depicted romantic themes. *Lion Crushing a Serpent* (1832, Brooklyn Museum), in which a savage beast was depicted looming victorious over its victim, is representative of Barye's work at this time. He exhibited in the Salon for the first time in 1827, but after a rejection in 1837 he did not submit again until 1850. During the 1840s he was associated with members of the Barbizon group, especially Théodore Rousseau. From 1848 to 1850, he was put in charge of plaster casts at the Louvre. In 1850, he exhibited *Theseus Fighting the Centaur Biénor* (1850, Metropolitan Museum of Art, New York), a work recalling the Parthenon frieze, in which a Greek hero is shown as he is about to commit the final act, the killing of a monstrous hybrid whom he now holds in his power. Barye presents the action at its most dramatic moment, just prior to the climax. His earlier works of the 1830s seem more restrained when compared to the later ones, which are more aggressively charged with movement and emotion, such as *Jaguar Devouring a Hare* (1850, Louvre, Paris). Typical of the romantic temperament is the idea of overpowering strength, violence, combat that leads to victory or death, of the struggle for dominance whether between man and animal, animal and animal, or man and the elements.

Barye was commissioned in 1855 to do a frieze for the Pavillon d'Horloge and, as part of the construction of the new Louvre, to decorate the Pavillon Denon and the Pavillon Richelieu with four stone groups of *War*, *Peace*, *Strength*, and *Order*. In 1857 in order to mass produce small bronzes for middle-class buyers, he once again established his own foundry, after earlier attempts from about 1839 had ended in failure. As an animalier, he was well received during the Second Empire, both by officials and critics who could accept the exotic subject matter and the ferocity and beauty of animals more readily than they could the exuberant activity and realism of Jean Baptiste Carpeaux's sculpted nudes. Barye received a commission for an equestrian portrait of Napoleon I. The theme he chose was *Napoleon I in Roman Garb*. The monument, which was to stand in Ajaccio, Corsica, was completed in 1865. Barye was appointed professor of zoological drawing at the Musée d'Histoire Naturelle, a post he held from 1854 to 1874. He was made an officer of the Legion of Honor in 1855 and won gold medals at the Paris international expositions of 1855 and 1867 for a group of small bronzes, which he showed in the industrial section. The latter fact was significant, for Barye, who became president in 1863 of the Commission Consultative de l'Union Centrale des Arts Appliqués à l'Industrie, was one of the few successful practitioners of the merger of art and industry much touted in the era. He died at Paris, 25 June 1875.

G. F. Benge, "Barye," in Jeanne L. Wasserman, ed., *Metamorphoses in Nineteenth-Century Sculpture* (Cambridge, Mass., 1975); S. Pivar, *The Barye Bronzes* (Woodbridge, Suffolk, 1974); C. O. Zieseniss, *Les aquarelles de Barye: Etude critique et catalogue raisonné* (Paris, 1954).

Beverley Giblon

Related entries: DELACROIX; INTERNATIONAL EXPOSITIONS.

BAUDELAIRE, CHARLES (1821–1867), poet and art critic; born at Paris, 9 April 1821. At the time of Baudelaire's birth, his father was sixty-two and his mother twenty-eight. The death of his father in 1826 and his mother's remarriage eighteen months later left a deep impression on the sensitive boy. Moreover, Baudelaire's stepfather, Jacques Aupick (1789–1857), who was destined to become a general, head of the Ecole Polytechnique, and ambassador to Spain and to the Ottoman Empire, was unable to deter his charge from becoming a writer, persuade him to obtain a conventional education, or separate him from his bohemian friends, despite sending the young man on a long voyage to Mauritius and the Ile Bourbon in 1841–1842. From 1842, a rift steadily widened between Baudelaire and his family, including his half-brother Claude Alphonse, and the mother to whom he had once been so close.

During the early 1840s Baudelaire, who from 1842 had the income from a fortune of 75,000 francs, lived the life of a spendthrift and a dandy. His fellow *noctambules* included Théodore de Banville, Jules Champfleury, Félix Nadar, Gérard de Nerval, Alfred de Musset (1810–1857), Henri Murger (1822–1861), and Charles Asselineau (1820–1874). Asselineau in 1869 would write the first biography of his friend. In 1844, however, Baudelaire's fortune was put in trust, and he had to live thereafter on a meager allowance, which ended the extravagant life-style that had centered around his Ile Saint Louis apartment. This existence of debts and poverty would continue through the rest of his life. These events also led to a gradual break in relations with his mother (1844–1847).

Turning to journalism, Baudelaire wrote a series of essays for *Le corsaire-Satan* and then entered a brief period of republican enthusiasm, during which he contributed to *Le salut public* (1848) and to *La république du peuple* (1851). He had met Gustave Courbet in 1847, and the two had become friends (the artist depicted Baudelaire in his painting, *L'atelier du peintre*). Through his association with *La république du peuple*, Baudelaire also made the acquaintance of Pierre Joseph Proudhon. But these years marked a decisive turning point in Baudelaire's attitudes. After the coup d'état of December 1851, he divorced himself from politics, abandoned political journalism, and turned away from realism and from the idea of material progress.

Baudelaire had not neglected literary contacts, with Balzac, Charles Augustin Sainte-Beuve, and, from 1849, Théophile Gautier. Moreover, in 1845–1846, he began his career as an art critic, reviewing the Salons of those years, and defending the talents of Honoré Daumier, Jean Baptiste Corot, and, especially, Eugène Delacroix, who became his friend and of whom he was the staunchest supporter. (Baudelaire is one of the figures included in Henri Fantin-Latour's 1864 painting, *Homage to Delacroix*.) Astute in recognizing talents that, like his own, were unappreciated, Baudelaire was particularly drawn, from 1846, to the works of Edgar Allen Poe (1809–1849). The attraction is understandable. In spite of obvious differences both men were fundamentally romantics in revolt against romanticism. Similar themes haunted them. Both were preoccupied by the idea of death; both rebelled against the limits of reality, experimenting with various types of evasion (eroticism, alcohol, drugs) in order to transcend their corporeal limitations. Baudelaire's study on Poe, *Edgar A. Poe, sa vie, et ses ouvrages*, appeared in 1852, and he devoted himself for fifteen years thereafter to translations (published first in *Le pays*) of the American's works. In 1854–1855 Baudelaire translated thirty-five of Poe's stories. There are those who still find his five large volumes of translations equal, and occasionally superior, to the originals.

Baudelaire's own poetry came painfully. It sometimes required years for him to complete a poem. He seems to have written only some thirty between 1837 and 1845 and to have published one (in 1845). In 1848 he published *Les limbes*. But from 1841 to 1842, he was at work on the compositions that would ultimately appear in his first book of poetry, *Les fleurs du mal*. Three women would figure prominently in this poetry: the mulatto actress Jeanne Duval or Lemer, with whom the poet lived on occasion from 1842 to 1861; Marie Daubrun; and, perhaps the most important, Apollonie Sabatier (born 1820). Mlle. Sabatier, who was the mistress of a Belgian banker, maintained a Sunday evening salon attended by such luminaries as Gautier (who called her "La Présidente"), Gustave Flaubert, Hector Berlioz, Ernest Meissonier, and, from 1851, Baudelaire, who in December 1852 sent La Présidente a letter including his poem, "A celle qui est trop gaie." He would pursue her with a highly idealized profession of love for the next five years. In 1855 Baudelaire published eighteen poems in *La revue des deux mondes* under the title *Les fleurs du mal*. Apparently he had chosen verses that were most likely to shock. As a result, the staid Orleanist journal would not again publish any of his poems. In its final form, the collection was composed of one hundred poems. The five sections dealt with several main ideas—time, death, ennui, love, and evasion—each intricately linked to the others. Although public reaction to Baudelaire's poetry had been lukewarm, to say the least, Auguste Poulet-Malassis, an editor and a friend of the poet, agreed to publish the book, which was dedicated to Gautier. *Les fleurs du mal* appeared in late June 1857, only to be impounded on 16 July at the printer's in Alençon. A few days before, Gustave Bourdin, who had already attacked the *Revue des deux mondes* offerings of 1855, had loudly condemned the "monstrosities" set out in the book, characterizing them as "unpardonable for an author over thirty years old." Baudelaire and his editor were now charged with offending both public and religious morals, and it was widely rumored that *Figaro*'s attack had been launched at the instigation of Adolphe Billault, then minister of the interior, although some other ministers, like Achille Fould, who later interceded on behalf of Edmond Duranty, and even the empress were said to have been opposed.

On 17 July Baudelaire, represented by Gustave Louis A. V. Chaix d'Est-Ange (1800–1876), appeared in court. The prosecutor, Pierre Ernest Pinard, who only a few months before had unsuccessfully presented the government's case against G. Flaubert for immorality in his *Madame Bovary*, underlined the "obscene" passages in certain of the poems and suggested that *Les fleurs du mal* could serve only to excite unhealthy curiosity and to corrupt French youth. Unlike Flaubert, Baudelaire was not acquitted. With his bohemian and republican reputation, he had little chance. Oddly, the charge of religious immorality was dropped (it could be argued, of course, that in his poetry Baudelaire, a lapsed Catholic, was seeking God in the nature of evil itself) but that of offending public morals was upheld. However, the 300 franc fine imposed on the poet on 20 August was reduced to 50 francs thanks to the intervention of the empress, to whom Baudelaire had appealed. Poulet-Malassis was fined 200 francs and ordered to delete six poems judged to contain "obscene or immoral passages or expressions." It was at this time that Mlle. Sabatier offered herself to the profoundly depressed Baudelaire and was repulsed.

Despite *Les fleurs du mal* and the publication of *Nouvelles histoires extraordinaires* and of Baudelaire's first group of prose poems, *Poèmes nocturnes*, it seems likely that had the poet died at the end of 1857, his reputation would not yet have been securely established. The next few years confirmed not only his poetic genius (a second edition of *Les fleurs du mal* was published in 1861, containing eighteen new poems) but also the brilliance of his art criticism. Baudelaire's innate romanticism led him to reject both realism and photography as an art form. He turned early from "art for art's sake." Withholding moral judgments, he reacted intuitively to each work of art. Above all, he sought an artist who would respond to what he had termed in his review of the 1845 Salon the "heroism of modern life." Such an artist he hailed in his friend, Edouard Manet, with whom he frequently dined and whom he accompanied on sketching expeditions to the Tuileries Gardens (Baudelaire appears as one of the figures in Manet's *Concert aux Tuileries*, a painting of the sort for which he had called since 1845). Having written a review of the 1855 Salon for *Le pays* and *Le portefeuille*, Baudelaire agreed to report on the Salon of 1859 for *La revue française*. The resulting articles secured his reputation as an art critic. His perception proved as remarkable in music, which he considered the most perfect of the arts. Baudelaire's article on *Tannhäuser* in the *Revue européenne* (1861) placed him in a small group of critics who represented Richard Wagner's admirers in France.

These years were marked, however, by continuing disappointments. Baudelaire's final break in 1861 with Jeanne Duval left him completely alone. Always plagued by debts, his health had now begun to disintegrate as the result of syphilis (perhaps contracted as early as 1842 although Nadar was to claim in 1911 that the poet had been impotent all his life) and the misuse of drugs and of alcohol. Baudelaire's conception of art was closely linked to his interest in hallucinogens. He had early formed a "Club des Hashischiens" with his friend Gautier, and in 1851 had published his first treatise on the subject, *Du vin et du hashish, comparés comme moyens de multiplication de l'individu*. In 1858 he published the first installment of *Les paradis artificiels* (1860) in the *Revue contemporaine*, once again investigating the means by which man can transcend space and time, thereby entering into a unity of all sense impressions. Frustrated at the lack of recognition accorded him, Baudelaire even campaigned, against the advice of Alfred de Vigny, for a seat in the Académie Française (1862). Sainte-Beuve, to whom the poet had been devoted and who had caused a scandal in the literary world in 1857 by his failure to defend *Les fleurs du mal*, treated this candidacy—unsuccessful of course—as a joke and Baudelaire as an eccentric.

Baudelaire wrote his last serious poems in 1863. At the end of that year, he published in *Le Figaro* (on 26 November) the first installment of his praise of Constantin Guys as "the painter of modern life." The last years were futile and tragic. In order to settle his debts, Baudelaire was obliged to sell the rights to his five volumes of Poe translations. In 1864 he was invited to Brussels to give a lecture series, which was so poorly attended that it had to be cancelled. Embittered, Baudelaire nevertheless remained in Belgium where Poulet-Malassis, ruined by financial reverses, had also taken refuge. Together they published in 1866 *Les épaves de Charles Baudelaire*, a collection containing the six poems condemned in 1857, together with sixteen new ones. Several copies were seized by French customs, and Poulet-Malassis was eventually convicted in absentia at Lille for smuggling (May 1868) and the confiscated copies destroyed. Baudelaire did not live to see these final indignities. In March 1866 while visiting the Church of Saint Loup with Félicien Rops (1833–1898) and Poulet-Malassis, he collapsed. Transported to a clinic in Paris, he lingered, speechless and partially paralyzed, for eighteen months until he died in the arms of his mother, 31 August 1867. Banville gave the oration at his grave.

Although far from being universally celebrated by his contemporaries, Baudelaire's genius was recognized by some—Victor Hugo, de Vigny, Jules Barbey d'Aurevilly, and Paul Verlaine (1844–1896), the last of whom he much influenced. Successive generations have hailed him as the source of the symbolist movement, even of all modern poetry, and the creator of modern art criticism. Certainly such artists of the succeeding generation as Paul Cézanne (1839–1906) and Auguste Rodin (1840–1917) admired Baudelaire and were influenced by him. Among his other major works published during the Second Empire may be listed: *Théophile Gautier* (1859) and *Richard Wagner et «Tannhäuser» à Paris* (1861).

M. Albert-Fernet, "Baudelaire à la *Revue des deux mondes*," *RDM* (January 1979); L. B. Hyslop and F. E. Hyslop, *Baudelaire, a Self-Portrait* (New York, 1957); L. B. Hyslop, *Baudelaire, Man of His Time* (New Haven, 1980); H. Peyre, ed., *Baudelaire: A Collection of Critical Essays* (New York, 1962); C. Pichois, *Baudelaire à Paris* (Paris, 1967), and ed., *La correspondance de Baudelaire*, 2 vols. (Paris, 1973); E. Starkie, *Baudelaire* (London, 1957).

Dorothy E. Speirs

Related entries: GUYS; MANET; NADAR.

BAUDIN, VICTOR (1811–1851), physician and politician; martyr of the coup d'état of December 1851; born at Nantua (Ain), 23 October 1811. Baudin, whose father, Pierre Camille (d. 1853), had served as a physician in Napoleon I's armies, studied medicine at Lyons and at the Val-de-Grâce (Paris). After graduating as a military surgeon, he served in Algeria from 1837 to 1839. Returning to Paris, he soon established himself as a "doctor of the poor" whose patients included Jules Michelet (1798–1874), Edgar Quinet (1803–1875), Louis Michel de Bourges (1797–1853), and Félicité de Lamennais (1782–1854). A republican and a Saint-Simonian, Baudin entered politics after the Revolution of 1848 and gradually gave up the practice of medicine. He declined an offer of the Ministry of Education from General Louis Eugène Cavaignac (1802–1857), whom he had known in Algeria, but was elected deputy from the Ain to the Legislative Assembly in May 1849, sitting on the extreme left and vigorously opposing Louis Napoleon's party and the policies of the government until the coup d'état of December 1851.

At 8 A.M. on 3 December, Baudin was one of some twenty deputies and journalists who met at a socialist café in the Faubourg Saint Antoine to plot resistance. Despite a marked lack of enthusiasm on the part of the workers of the *quartier*, a party of about one hundred was assembled, which hastily erected a barricade on the rue du Faubourg Saint Antoine (No. 151) at the intersection of the rue de Cotte and the rue Sainte Marguerite (now rue Trousseau). The flimsy structure, defended by mostly unarmed men, was intended chiefly to rally resistants, but the prevailing attitude was reflected in the taunt of a bystander that no one wanted to die so that deputies could continue to collect their daily stipend of 25 francs. "You'll see," Baudin is supposed to have replied, "How a man dies for twenty-five francs." Shortly afterward, troops appeared from the direction of the place de la Bastille. Most of the defenders fled. Seven deputies, including Victor Schoelcher (1804–1893), went forward to talk with the soldiers. There was a scuffle; a shot was fired from the barricade; the troops replied; and Baudin, as well as an unidentified youth, fell mortally wounded. On 5 December the martyred deputy was buried in Montmartre Cemetery, where he would lie forgotten for sixteen years.

Baudin's reentry into history was the result of a number of factors: the political decline of the Empire; the rise of an intransigent opposition on the left; the publication in July 1868 by Eugène Ténot (1839–1890), an editor at *Le siècle*, of *Paris en décembre 1851* (in which he described Baudin's death); and the establishment that same month of the radical newspaper *Le réveil* by Charles Delescluze (1809–1871). On 29 October 1868 *Le réveil* issued a vague invitation to a manifestation at Baudin's grave on All Souls' Day, 2 November. Some twenty persons made their way to the Montmartre Cemetery on that day, found the grave with considerable difficulty, recruited a slightly larger group meeting at the tomb of Godefroy Cavaignac (1801–1845), and applauded a speech extremely hostile to the Empire by Charles Quentin, a *Le réveil* editor. The next day *L'avenir national* and *Le réveil* announced a public subscription to build a monument to Baudin. Other newspapers joined or showed sympathy for the campaign: *La tribune*, the *Revue politique*, the *Journal de Paris*, *Le temps*. The great legitimist orator, Antoine Berryer, then on his deathbed, subscribed, as did a number of Orleanists. And yet the subscription aroused little enthusiasm. Some (for example, Auguste Nefftzer at *Le temps*) proposed that the emperor himself should contribute to the fund; others, like Eugène Rouher and Jules Baroche, preferred to adopt an attitude of indifference. But Napoleon III, sensitive to attacks in the press, decided to prosecute and instructed his inexperienced minister of the interior, Pierre Ernest Pinard, to do so under the law of general security, a dead letter since the aftermath of Felice Orsini's attempt on the emperor's life in 1858.

The trial opened before the sixth correctional chamber on 13 November 1868. In the dock were Quentin and Delescluze of *Le réveil*, Alphonse Peyrat (1812–1891) of *L'avenir national*, Théodore Duret (1838–1927) of *La tribune*, and Paul Challemel-Lacour (1827–1896) of the *Revue politique*. The last was defended by Clément Laurier (1832–1878); Peyrat and Duret were represented by Adolphe Crémieux (1796–1880) and Emmanuel Arago (1812–1896). But it was the lawyer who had been reluctantly accepted by Delescluze, the young Léon Gambetta, who created a sensation and made his reputation by turning the defense into an eloquent assault on the Empire and its origins. For the first time since the brief allusion by Ernest Picard in the Corps Législatif in January 1864, the coup d'état was publicly castigated as a crime. The defendants were found guilty that evening and on 28 November were again condemned, along with Adrien Hébrard (1834–1914) of *Le temps* and Jean Jacques Weiss (1827–1891) of the *Journal de Paris*. Delescluze was sentenced to six months' imprisonment, a fine of 2,000 francs, and loss of his civic rights.

The affair had proved a disaster for the regime. The behavior of the judge, Vivien, in a tribunal that traditionally tried political crimes, had signaled that the courts could no longer be regarded as docile (Vivien had permitted great latitude to the defense lawyers and did not prevent their speeches from being published). An implacable new enemy of the regime had emerged in the person of Gambetta. And Baudin, powerless in life, had become a potent symbol of opposition. On 3 December Pinard compounded the error by so overreacting to a further demonstration at the martyr's grave that he was compelled to resign in disgrace. Under the Third Republic, a statue of Baudin by Aimé Millet (1819–1891) would be erected in the cemetery and there, on 2 December 1888, would be held a great anti-Boulanger demonstration. More recently, modern Paris has commemorated the martyr of the coup d'état by naming a street in his honor.

A. Billiemaz "Le Docteur Baudin, député de l'Ain, martyr du point d'honneur," *Cahiers de marottes et violons d'Ingres*, n.s. no. 26 (1953); M. Dessal, *Un révolutionnaire Jacobin: Charles Delescluze, 1809–1871* (Paris, 1952); V. Schoelcher, *Histoire des crimes du Deux Décembre*, 2 vols. (Paris, 1852).

Related entries: COUP D'ETAT; GAMBETTA; REPUBLICANISM.

BAUDRY, PAUL (1828–1886), academic painter; born at La Roche-sur-Yon (Vendée), 7 November 1828. Baudry entered the Ecole des Beaux-Arts in Paris in 1845, having spent some time in Michel Martin Drolling's atelier, and won the Prix de Rome after four attempts in 1850, along with William Adolphe Bouguereau. He studied in Italy from 1851, where he met and became a close friend of the architect Charles Garnier. After his return to France, his work was exhibited in the Salon of 1857. *Saint John the Baptist* (Amiens Museum), shown in that Salon, was purchased by Napoleon III. With the purchase of two other works by the state, Baudry won immediate acclaim. His work was admired by Théophile Gautier, and Baudry's friend Edmond About wrote glowingly in his reviews. The artist received several commissions to paint decorative panels (usually depicting mythological scenes) for the mansions of wealthy individuals, including the magnificent Paris hotel of the Second Empire's most celebrated courtesan, La Païva. Further success came in the Salon of 1861 when he won a first-class medal and again in the Salon of 1863 when *The Wave and the Pearl* (Prado, Madrid) was exhibited and then purchased by the emperor. This work, like similar paintings of nudes by William Bouguereau, whose *Birth of Venus* was exhibited in the same Salon, exploits Baudry's ability to draw, aiming at classical purity. But for Baudry and other academic painters, there seems to have been no desire to invest the work with any personal expression. This results in an image that is, to our eyes, contrived in composition and often arid and mechanical in execution.

Baudry learned that he was to receive a commission to paint the foyer of Garnier's new Paris Opéra. He decided to return to Rome to study once more the masterpieces of decoration of Michelangelo in the Sistine Chapel, which he proceeded to copy. He later went to London in order to copy Raphael's cartoons. From 1865 onward, the Opéra decorations were his major preoccupation, almost to the exclusion of anything else. He stopped sending works to the Salon and painted only the occasional portrait. His *Portrait of Charles Garnier* (1868, Musée National du Château, Versailles) indicates the precise linearity and clear definition of forms that were the foundation for all his finished works. Baudry worked on the Opéra decorations until 1874, with a break in 1870 when he joined a French infantry unit during the war with Prussia. When later the public and art critics were able to recognize the new values brought to art by the more avant-garde artists, painters such as Baudry, Bouguereau, Alexandre Cabanel and Jean Léon Gérôme, who were the giants of their own age, receiving many awards and the patronage of the imperial family, were relegated to the ranks of *pompiers* and their works to an oblivion from which they have begun to emerge only in our own day. Baudry died at Paris, 17 January 1886.

A. Boime, *The Academy and French Painting in the Nineteenth Century* (New York, 1971), and *Art pompier: Anti-Impressionism: Nineteenth-Century Salon Painting* (Hempstead, N.Y., 1974); Shepherd Gallery, *Ingres and Delacroix through Degas and Puvis de Chavannes: The Figure in French Art, 1800–1870* (New York, 1975).

Beverley Giblon

Related entries: BOUGUEREAU; CABANEL; GEROME.

BAZAINE, FRANCOIS ACHILLE (1811–1888), marshal of France; one of the most controversial military commanders of the Second Empire, especially noted for his role in the ephemeral Mexican Empire of Maximilian and, more important, for his conduct during the Franco-Prussian War; born at Versailles, 13 February 1811. In 1830, having failed the entrance examinations for the Ecole Polytechnique, Bazaine enlisted voluntarily as a soldier in the Thirty-seventh Infantry Regiment. His advancement was extremely rapid, and his meritorious record reflects the major military involvements of the French army between 1830 and 1870. Promoted to lieutenant in 1835, Bazaine served in Spain, Algeria, the Crimea, Italy, and Mexico, where he was promoted to marshal of France on 5 September 1864. Bazaine is an example of the Napoleonic ideal of the simple soldier who found a marshal's baton in his knapsack.

Bazaine was commander in chief of the 38,000-member French Expeditionary Corps of Mexico from 16 July 1863 to 3 May 1867, most of the period of its existence. He replaced General Forey (1804–1872). Under Bazaine's command, the French troops, with the support of their Mexican allies, seized control of Mexico from the liberal forces of the legal government of Benito Juarez. In effect, Bazaine had conquered an area four times the size of France. Soon after the arrival of Maximilian at the end of May 1864, Bazaine found himself in the difficult position of trying to reconcile the increasingly divergent interests of Maximilian and Napoleon III. Bazaine, who married the seventeen-year-old daughter of an ambitious Mexican family, tried to destroy the continuing resistance to the new regime. As that resistance grew more bitter, he counseled Maximilian to approve a decree, which was later promulgated, calling for the summary judgment and execution of armed dissidents. Early in 1866, Napoleon III revised his unpopular Mexican policy and ordered Bazaine to prepare the withdrawal of the French troops. Before leaving Mexico, Bazaine tried to organize as solidly as possible the Mexican forces of Maximilian. His success was minimal. When the French left Mexico in March 1867, Maximilian's empire was near collapse.

Returned to France, Bazaine was given important military commands, including that of commander in chief of the Imperial Guard (October 1869). At the outbreak of the Franco-Prussian War, he was appointed to lead the III Corps of the Army of the Rhine under the command of Napoleon III. Following the defeat of Marshal Marie Edme Patrice de MacMahon in Alsace, Bazaine was appointed commander in chief of the Army of the Rhine on 12 August 1870. Trying to withdraw westward from Metz, he fought at Borny on 14 August, Mars-la-Tour on 16 August, and Gravelotte and St. Privat on 18 August. In these battles, Bazaine's army inflicted heavy casualties on the Prussian forces but also suffered them in return. Bazaine made the capital decision to retire under the protection of the guns of Metz in order to replenish supplies and care for the wounded. His army was quickly invested, and the siege of Metz began. Marshal MacMahon, in command of a new army, decided to attempt the relief of Metz. His ill-prepared force suffered disastrous defeat at Sedan, and Napoleon

III was taken prisoner. When the news of Sedan reached Paris, the Second Empire was overthrown and the Government of National Defense established on 4 September 1870. Bazaine's army, still besieged at Metz, represented the most powerful organized force left to France. Accordingly, great hopes were placed in the "glorious Bazaine," as he was called.

In fact, Bazaine did nothing to justify those hopes. His conduct during the rest of the siege has remained the subject of continuing dispute. From the moment he learned (on 10 September) of the defeat at Sedan and the fall of the Second Empire, Bazaine's chief concern seems to have been the safeguard of the Army of the Rhine. He and his chief lieutenants were unsympathetic to the leaders of the Government of National Defense and initially decided to await developments beyond Metz. Bazaine apparently hoped that the war would end before his food supplies were exhausted. Later he allowed himself to become involved in intrigues aimed at ending the war or at least at neutralizing his army. To explore such possibilities, Bazaine sent, on different occasions, Generals Charles Bourbaki (1816–1897) and Napoléon Boyer (1820–1888) to consult with the Empress Eugénie, who had taken refuge at Chislehurst in England. Bazaine hoped the empress would make a declaration with which he could associate himself and the army. His main motivation seems to have been neither personal ambition nor the restoration of the Empire but rather the maintenance of his army as a bulwark against social and political instability in France. At all times, Otto von Bismarck was fully aware of and even encouraged these tortuous negotiations. At the end of October, he terminated them. By then, Bazaine's food supplies were exhausted. Deciding that a final sortie was hopeless, he surrendered his army of over 170,000 men and the city of Metz on 27 October 1870. When he heard of the surrender, Léon Gambetta, minister of the interior in the Government of National Defense, denounced Bazaine as a traitor. In 1873, the marshal was court-martialed for his conduct at Metz. He was found guilty of having capitulated his army and the city of Metz, of having prematurely treated with the enemy, and of having failed to fulfill obligations imposed by duty and honor. Gambetta called the conviction of Bazaine "the first revenge of the rights and honor of France." Although condemned to death and military degradation, his sentence was commuted to life imprisonment by Marshal MacMahon, who had become president of the Republic. Bazaine escaped from prison in 1874. He lived out his life in discredited exile in Spain and died at Madrid, 20 September 1888.

M. Baumont, *L'échiquier de Metz: Empire ou république?* (Paris, 1971), and *Bazaine: Les secrets d'un maréchal (1811–1888)* (Paris, 1978); F. Bazaine, *L'Armée du Rhin, depuis le 12 Août jusqu'au 29 Octobre 1870* (Paris, 1872); K. Hammond, "Bazaine—Too Much, Too Late," *Army Quarterly Defense Journal*, no. 3 (1980); I. Loiseau, "Bazaine et le 4 Septembre," *RDM*, 1 January 1967; Gens. E. Ruby and J. Regnault, *Bazaine: coupable ou victime?* (Paris, 1960); and the service spécial du *Moniteur universel*: "Procès Bazaine, seul compte rendu in extenso des séances du 1er conseil de guerre de la 1er Division Militaire séant à Versailles" (Paris, 1873–1874).

Robert F. Brown

Related entries: FRANCO-PRUSSIAN WAR; MACMAHON; MEXICAN EXPEDITION.

BEHIC, ARMAND (1809–1891), industrialist, politician, and minister (1863–1867); born at Paris, 15 January 1809. After studying law, Béhic entered government service in 1826, becoming an *inspecteur des finances* in 1832 and *inspecteur général* in 1845. In the latter capacity he visited Corsica and the Antilles before moving to the post of *directeur du contrôle*, which had been created for him at the Ministry of Marine, where he reorganized the administrative services. In August 1846, he was elected to the Chamber of Deputies but resigned his seat at the revolution (February 1848) and became director of the Vierzon Ironworks. Named to the Conseil d'Etat by the Legislative Assembly in 1849, Béhic quit that post following the coup d'état of December 1851, returning to Vierzon and then, in 1853, becoming inspector general of the shipping company Messageries Impériales, with special responsibility for mail routes. The company, which after 1870 would be known as the Messageries Maritimes, enjoyed a great expansion under Béhic's skillful leadership, exercised first as director and then as president of the administrative council. It was Béhic who organized the transport of French troops to the east during the Crimean War. In 1856 he added to his company the Société des Forges et Chantiers de la Méditerranée. He also organized a maritime service to Indochina and created near Toulon the naval construction yards of La Seyne. Béhic was, as well, director of the Compagnie des Docks de Marseille and presided the commission charged with organizing a banking system for the colonies.

Although a member of the Conseil Général of the Bouches-du-Rhône and commander of the Legion of Honor (from 3 October 1860), Béhic was long suspected of Orleanist sympathies and consequently held at arm's length by the regime. But his close ties with the James de Rothschild-Paulin Talabot interests did not prevent him from sympathizing with the Saint-Simonian ideas of many who were close to the emperor. The decision of Napoleon III to liberalize his government following the elections of 1863 opened an opportunity for the widely admired Béhic, who on 23 June became minister of agriculture, commerce, and public works, replacing Eugène Rouher, who became minister presiding over the Conseil d'Etat. An able and energetic minister, Béhic was soon enlisted among the economic activists (Victor Fialin Persigny, Auguste de Morny, Isaac and Emile Pereire) against the "party of resistance" (Achille Fould, Jules Baroche, Rouher, and Rothschild). Napoleon III probably sympathized with the former but found it necessary to balance the two groups.

Béhic conducted important inquiries into agriculture (by decree of 30 March 1866), the railroads, and the Bank of France. He secured on 23 June 1866 a sanitary regulation against cholera and on 18 July 1866 the suppression of commercial brokers (*courtiers en marchandises*). He also played an important role in the establishment of the Latin Monetary Union of 23 December 1865, the revision of the maritime provisions of the commercial code, and the passage of a succession of laws that established for almost one hundred years the rules governing corporations in France. Béhic hoped to implement the economic program that Napoleon III had sketched in January 1860, and he strongly supported the proposal for a great loan (*emprunt de la paix*) of 500 million to 1 billion francs to finance public works. The project was blocked, however, by Fould, the finance minister, aided by a conservative coalition alarmed at the size of the floating debt and the funneling of so much capital into unproductive enterprises.

The political reforms of January 1867 and the consequent remaking of the cabinet marked the end of Béhic's ministry. Three days later he was named senator and grand cross of the Legion of Honor (20 January 1867). In November he was made a member of the Conseil de Perfectionnement de l'Enseignement Secondaire Spécial. Until the end of the Second Empire, he busied himself primarily with the Messageries Impériales and with his other business interests. After the fall of the Empire, he remained a bonapartist, serving briefly as vice-president of their society and as senator (1876–1879). Béhic died at Paris in March 1891.

Related entries: FOULD; GOVERNMENT FINANCE; LATIN MONETARY UNION; MESSAGERIES IMPERIALES.

BELGIAN QUESTION. See BELGIAN RAILROADS AFFAIR.

BELGIAN RAILROADS AFFAIR, an 1869 Franco-Belgian dispute that owed its importance to the mounting hostility between France and Prussia. As a new state, in existence only since the 1830s, seriously divided by language and cultural differences, and with a large French-speaking population, Belgium had seemed to many a likely target for expansion by its powerful neighbor, especially after the coup d'état of December 1851, which brought Louis Napoleon to power at Paris. Tensions were particularly high throughout 1852, fed by differences concerning tariffs, literary copyright, and political refugees from France living in Belgium. Books and newspapers from Belgian presses made their way into France, adding to the difficulties. In March 1852 Napoleon III seemed especially menacing in his complaints concerning the Belgian press. But King Leopold I, uncle of Queen Victoria, presided over a policy of moderation and conciliation, which gradually smoothed over the problems. In Belgium a firm hand was taken toward the refugees, who were soon reduced in number from several thousand to about four hundred, the others finding a more congenial reception on Jersey or Guernsey, or in Britain, especially in London. In return for this and for a January 1852 law against literary counterfeiting, a 22 August 1852 copyright convention, and a December 1852 press law making it illegal for Belgian newspapers to attack foreign heads of government, France at last agreed (9 December 1852) to a temporary economic treaty and, on 27 February 1854, to a formal commercial pact replacing that which had expired in August 1852. On 28 March 1856 Brussels bowed to French demands for a tougher extradition law and, at the beginning of 1858, responded to Felice Orsini's attempt on Napoleon III's life by clamping down even harder on the press and on the French refugees (by 1870 only 34 would remain in the country). Fears continued, and rumors of impending annexation by France broke out at intervals, as in June 1860. Napoleon III was restrained, however, not only by the limitations imposed by his own *politique des nationalités* but also by Europe's suspicion of him and especially by his determination not to break with Britain, a result that certainly would have followed any French move against Belgium. Prussia's victory over Austria at Sadowa in July 1866 introduced another complication, the need for territorial compensation for France in order to offset the dramatic increase in Prussian power. Nevertheless, the alliance proposed by France to Prussia in August 1866, which would have bound the latter to assist in an Anglo-French war arising out of the Belgian question, cannot be considered proof of a meditated French design on Belgium, however unwise such a proposal may have been. Still, it seems reasonable to believe that Napoleon III desired close ties with Belgium, perhaps even the customs union that had been bruited since the reign of Louis Philippe and had been suggested again in March 1852.

So matters stood when, on 8 December 1868, the French Compagnie des Chemins de Fer de l'Est, encouraged by a financial guarantee from the French government, signed an accord with two Belgian railroad companies (the Grand Luxembourg and the Liégeois Limbourgeois). The French company hoped to establish an integrated Franco-Dutch-Luxembourg-Belgian network. The Belgian companies, which were in financial difficulty, sold to the Compagnie de l'Est their lines radiating from Arlon in the southern tip of Belgium to Luxembourg, Liège, Languyon, and Brussels. In so acting, the owners of the Belgian lines (one of them a former minister) had ignored warnings from Brussels and the fact that by a law of February 1867 the sale would be invalid without government authorization. The ceded lines were of great economic and strategic importance; under French management they could be used during a crisis to compromise Belgian neutrality. Moreover, compliance at Brussels undoubtedly would have led to a protest from Berlin. Unsurprisingly, then, the Belgian government interposed its veto, obtaining from parliament on 13 February 1869 a law specifically annulling the cessions. More difficult to understand is the irritability of the French reaction, which created, from mid-February until the end of April, a crisis during which Napoleon III even contemplated the possibility of war (note to the French minister of war, 19 April 1869). It is true that the Belgian government's action was regarded at Paris as unnecessarily provocative, but the most likely explanation is that the dispute was viewed by the French government in terms of Franco-Prussian rivalry; Bismarck's hand was seen; the newly freed Parisian press reacted violently; and Napoleon III, sensitive to French opinion on the eve of elections to the Corps Législatif, was determined not to accept a new humiliation. Calmer second thoughts prevailed, however, encouraged perhaps by the strong British reaction (mobilization of the Channel fleet and representations to the French ambassador at London on 22 April). On 23 April Napoleon III received H.J.W. Frère-Orban, Belgian premier since January, with assurances that although he much desired a Franco-Belgian customs union, nothing would be done to compromise the independence, autonomy, and neutrality of Belgium. By 27 April the French emperor had, in effect, abandoned the projected purchase. A mixed commission was constituted, and the dispute, treated henceforth as a business matter, was quietly resolved by the organization on 9 July 1869 of an international railroad service. At the outbreak of the Franco-Prussian War in July 1870, France readily agreed not to violate Belgian neutrality.

Baron Beyens, "Napoléon III et la Belgique," *R. gén.* 109 (1923), and *Le Second Empire vu par un diplomat belge*, 2 vols. (Paris, 1924–1926); M. Blanchard, "D'une version de l'affaire des chemins de fer belges," *RH* (April–June 1940); G. Craig, "Great Britain and the Belgian Railways Dispute of 1869," *AHR* 50 (July 1945); R. Grenu, *La question belge dans la politique européenne de 1866 à 1870* (Paris, 1931); P. Hymans, *La Belgique et le Second Empire* (Paris, 1910), and *Frère-Orban, la Belgique, et le Second Empire* (Brussels, 1905); H. Lademacher, *Die belgische Neutralität als Problem der europäischen Politik, 1830–1914* (Bonn, 1971); K. Rheindorf, "Der belgische-französische Eisenbahnkonflikt und die grossen Mächte 1868/1869," *Deutsche Rundschau* 195 (May 1923); D. H. Thomas, "English Investors and the Franco-Belgian Railway Crisis of 1869," *Historian* 26 (February 1964), and "The European Press on the Belgian Railway Affair of 1869," in Nancy N. Barker and Marvin L. Brown, Jr., eds., *Diplomacy in an Age of Nationalism* (The Hague, 1971); E. Wanty, "Quand Napoléon III convoitait la Belgique," *R. gen.* (April 1968).

Related entries: LA VALETTE; LUXEMBOURG CRISIS; NATIONALITIES; RAILROADS; REPUBLICANISM; REVISION.

BENEDETTI, COMTE VINCENT (1817–1900), a professional diplomat who played a key role in Franco-Prussian relations between 1866 and 1870; born at Bastia, Corsica, 29 April 1817. The son of a judge on the court of criminal jurisdiction in Bastia, Benedetti entered the diplomatic corps after completing his legal studies at the University of Aix and served initially at Cairo, Palermo, and Constantinople. From 1855 to 1861 he was head of the *Direction Politique* at the Quai d'Orsay and served as secretary to the Congress of Paris of 1856. A member of the Italian faction in Second Empire politics, Benedetti had been sent on a special mission in 1860 to complete the Treaty of Turin by which Sardinia ceded Nice and Savoy to France. In August 1861 he became the first French minister to the new Kingdom of Italy. When, in anticipation of the elections in 1863, Napoleon III deemed it essential to bid for clerical support, the anti-papal Italian faction members Edouard Thouvenel, Benedetti, and Charles Jean, marquis de Lavalette, were dismissed (October 1862). In October 1864, however, Benedetti was named ambassador to the Prussian court. Diplomats viewed the appointment as a means to provide flexibility for French diplomacy regarding Prussia and Austria. Because of known antipathy toward Austria, Benedetti could hope to establish an effective relationship with the Prussian president of council, Otto von Bismarck. Between 1865 and 1866 Benedetti watched Bismarck's German policy with sympathy and actively promoted the conclusion of the Prusso-Italian alliance in 1866, hoping that the destruction of the status quo in Germany would bring France the long-coveted Rhine frontier. However, the swiftness and finality of the Prussian victory at Sadowa shattered that illusion, and Benedetti found himself engaged in long and unproductive territorial compensation negotiations with Bismarck in 1866–1867, relative to the Rhineland, Luxembourg, and Belgium. After 1867 (Luxembourg crisis, failure of a French bid for Prussian support in the Roman Question), he came to favor a rapprochement with Austria, mainly to check Bismarck's unification policy south of the Main River. During the Hohenzollern candidacy crisis in 1870, Benedetti was given the thankless task of conveying to William I escalating French demands to accept the blame for the crisis and to pledge that the candidacy would not be posed ever again. As in 1866, so in 1870 Benedetti's desire to be an effective negotiator caused him to commit serious errors of conduct (in 1866 he had ill-advisedly left in Bismarck's hands the draft of a proposed Franco-Prussian treaty anticipating future French annexation of Belgium), which Bismarck was able to exploit effectively. Except for these failures, which did not have a decisive impact on events, Benedetti had shown himself to be an able representative of French interests in both Italy and Prussia. He died at Paris, 28 March 1900.

V. Benedetti, *Ma mission en Prusse*, 2d ed. (Paris, 1871), and *Essais diplomatiques* (Paris, 1895), trans. as *Studies in Diplomacy* (New York, 1896); W. A. Fletcher, *The Mission of Vincent Benedetti to Berlin, 1864–1870* (The Hague, 1965).

Willard Allen Fletcher

Related entries: HOHENZOLLERN CANDIDACY; SADOWA.

BERNARD, CLAUDE (1813–1878), one of the nineteenth century's outstanding biologists and a prominent spokesman for science during the Second Empire; born 12 July 1813, at St.-Julien (near Villefranche, Beaujolais). The son of a wine-growing peasant, Bernard was educated by the village priest and later by the Jesuits. As student of, and then assistant to, François Magendie (1783–1855) at the Collège de France, Bernard established himself as a leading experimental physiologist during the years prior to the creation of the Second Empire. He was one of a group of younger scientists who founded the Société de Biologie in 1848 (as an institution more hospitable than the older academies to biologists of unestablished reputation) and was elected one of its two first vice-presidents. In 1849 he was named knight of the Legion of Honor, primarily because of his studies on the digestive functions of the pancreas.

Bernard's early scientific achievements are all the more noteworthy because of the grossly inadequate support for laboratory and research facilities for French scientists at mid-century. Typically, when the imperial government created a chair of general physiology for Bernard at the Faculty of Sciences at Paris (Sorbonne) in 1854, it failed to provide him with either a laboratory or an assistant. When, a year later, Bernard succeeded Magendie as professor of medicine at the Collège de France, he could describe the ill-equipped and unhealthy laboratory there as one of the "tombs of scientists." Such conditions were not to be remedied until the closing years of the Empire. Bernard was elected to the Académie des Sciences in 1854 (after two unsuccessful attempts) and to the Académie de Médecine in 1861.

Apart from strictly scientific activities, Bernard had philosophical and literary interests and was a gifted writer. His close colleagues at the Collège de France included Ernest Renan and Marcellin Berthelot, and, from 1862 on, he attended the bimonthly dinners at the Café Magny of the literary group led by Charles Augustin Sainte-Beuve. Bernard's famous exposition of the experimental method in biology may be credited with exerting some influence on literary developments, particularly the naturalism of Emile Zola, although Bernard himself remained within the Roman Catholic faith and did not approve of the conclusions drawn by positivists and naturalists from his work.

Invited to Compiègne in 1864, Bernard—after a private audience with Napoleon III—was finally able to secure for himself improved laboratory facilities and funds for an assistant, Paul Bert (1833–1886), who would succeed him at the Sorbonne in 1869. He still championed the cause of French scientists and, on the occasion of the Paris international exposition of 1867, took his campaign to the public in the famous *Report on the Progress and Achievements of General Physiology in France*, which deplored the obstacles facing the development of physiology owing to lack of government patronage and the hostility of established naturalists and anatomists.

Bernard had now become a major statesman of science. In 1868, along with Louis Pasteur, Henri Milne-Edwards (1800–1885), and Henri Sainte-Claire-Deville (1818–1881), he was invited by the emperor to confer with members of the imperial administration (including Eugène Rouher, Marshal Jean Baptiste Vaillant, and Victor Duruy) on the conditions of research laboratories in France. The scientists' arguments were persuasive, and major new laboratories were created for Bernard (at the Muséum d'Histoire Naturelle) and Pasteur (at the Ecole Normale). The conference also resulted in the establishment, under Victor Duruy's influence, of the Ecole Pratique des Hautes Etudes (31 July 1868). The final years of Bernard's life saw numerous honors, including the presidency of the Société de Biologie (1867), nomination to the post of commander of the Legion of Honor (1867) and to the Senate (1869), and election to the Académie Française (1868, reception 27 May 1869).

Bernard's scientific achievements constitute the founding of modern experimental physiology. They include experiments on the digestive action of saliva, gastric juice, and bile; studies on the digestive functions of the pancreas; discovery of the glycogenic function of the liver; studies on carbohydrate metabolism in muscle; experiments on the spinal and vagus nerves and the innervation of the vocal cords; discovery of the vasomotor nerves (demonstration of the existence of nerve centers independent of the cerebral-spinal core); research on animal heat production and its regulation; and studies of the effects of toxic and medicinal substances (notably curare). Bernard also made fundamental contributions to the philosophy of science and the psychology and logic of scientific research. His *Introduction à l'étude de la médecine expérimentale* (1865) is still considered a classic in the philosophy of biology. Finally, Bernard's research threw light on the causes of diabetes, and his concept of the *milieu intérieure* clarified fundamental ideas of regulatory mechanisms that maintain a constant and controlled internal environment (the blood system), which mediates between the cellular processes of an organism and the external environment. Bernard died at Paris, 10 February 1878.

C. Bernard, *Philosophie*, unedited manuscript (Paris, 1937), and *La science expéri-mentale* (Paris, 1878); R. Debre, "Ernest Renan et Claude Bernard," *RDM*, no. 1 (January 1977), and "La vie de Claude Bernard," *RDM*, no. 5 (May 1978); J.M.D. Olmsted and E. Harris Olmsted, *Claude Bernard and the Experimental Method in Medicine* (New York, 1952); Y. Ors, "Claude Bernard: Son rôle dans l'évolution de la médecine scien-tifique," *Clio medica* 13 (June 1978); J. Schiller, *Claude Bernard et les problèmes scientifiques de son temps* (Paris, 1967); J. Théodoridès, "Claude Bernard et les para-sites," *Histoire et nature* 14 (1979); R. Virtanen, *Claude Bernard and His Place in the History of Ideas* (Lincoln, Neb., 1960); E. Wolff, "L'oeuvre de Claude Bernard," *RDM*, no. 4 (April 1978).

Martin Fichman

Related entries: BERTHELOT; CHARCOT; PASTEUR; POSITIVISM; RENAN.

BERRYER, ANTOINE (1790–1868), lawyer, orator, politician; born 4 January 1790 at Paris. An ardent Catholic and a loyal legitimist, Berryer combined support of the Bourbons with attachment to a host of democratic principles and a will-ingness to provide victims of misfortune, such as Marshal Michel Ney, with legal defense, whether he agreed with their political views or not. Elected to the Chamber of Deputies in January 1830, he was the only legitimist to continue to serve after the July Revolution, retaining his seat as a deputy (in a position of almost permanent opposition) under Louis Philippe and in the Constituent and Legislative Assemblies of the Second Republic. During this time, he contributed the extraordinary oratorical talents that have earned him the reputation of one of the greatest of nineteenth-century orators to a defense of liberty of the press, of universal manhood suffrage, of the right of workers to unite in associations, of Catholic religious orders, and of many other causes, all the while preserving his reputation as one of the most able lawyers in France. He won Louis Na-poleon's gratitude by agreeing to participate in his defense after the abortive coup at Boulogne in 1840, but he did not favor his campaign for the presidency in 1848, worked to reconcile Bourbon and Orleanist factions in case circum-stances might permit a restoration, joined other deputies to vote the prince president's deposition at the time of the coup d'état in December 1851, and then retired to private life in protest against the regime. When he was elected to the Académie Française in February 1852, he declined to take his seat until 1855 and then requested that he be excused from paying the traditional call on the emperor at the Tuileries.

Though out of public office, Berryer remained in the public eye, for he handled many celebrated cases, including the defense of Charles de Montalembert in 1858 (prosecuted by the government for an article he had published in the *Correspondant*), of Bishop Félix Dupanloup in 1860 (prosecuted for a letter published in the *Constitutionnel*), and of the Paris typesetters arrested for striking in March and November 1862 (they were convicted but pardoned by Napoleon III). Berryer declined to seek election in 1852 to a Corps Législatif where his voice would have been muffled. In 1857 he failed to persuade the comte de Chambord to abandon the policy of abstention by legitimists from politics. Nevertheless, in the elections of 1863, he and Comte Frédéric Falloux (1811–1886) took the required oath and became candidates. Berryer was elected from Marseilles, under the Union Libérale label, thanks largely to republican votes, the only legitimist to win a seat. Henceforth he took a prominent part in legislative debates, often as a penetrating critic of imperial policy, especially financial. In 1867 he accused Baron Georges Haussmann of irregularities in financing the rebuilding of Paris. Illness forced his retirement in 1868, the year of his death. In 1863 the French bar, and in 1864 that of England, had honored him with ceremonies testifying to his outstanding service to the legal profession. He died 29 November 1868 at Augerville (Loiret) after subscribing, as his last political act, to a monument to Victor Baudin, the deputy martyred in December 1851.

A. Berryer, *Oeuvres, discours parlementaires*, 5 vols. (Paris, 1872–1874), and *Oeuvres, plaidoyers* (Paris, 1875–1878); P. Jacomet, *Berryer au pretoire* (Paris, 1938); C. de Lacombe, *Vie de Berryer*, 3 vols. (Paris, 1895); M. Pierchon, *Pierre Antoine Berryer, 1790–1868* (Montpellier, 1977).

Raymond L. Cummings

Related entries: CHAMBORD; CORPS LEGISLATIF; LEGITIMISM.

BERTHELOT, MARCELLIN (1827–1907), chemist, public administrator, and senator; born at Paris, 25 October 1827. One of France's most brilliant chemists and an able public administrator, Berthelot was active during both the Second Empire and the Third Republic. In 1851 he secured a post as demonstrator to the chemist Antoine Balard (1802–1876) at the Collège de France, a position he held until he was appointed professor of organic chemistry at the Ecole de Pharmacie in 1859. Berthelot was awarded the *prix Jecker* by the Académie des Sciences in 1861 for his important research on the laboratory synthesis of organic chemicals. Under pressure from Balard and other prominent chemists from the Collège de France and the Académie des Sciences, Victor Duruy, then minister of education, created a chair of organic chemistry at the Collège de France in 1865, a post that enabled Berthelot to pursue his studies on organic synthesis, physical chemistry, and thermochemistry.

Berthelot's scientific achievements were wide ranging. He was one of the major figures in the development of organic chemistry and played a fundamental role in establishing the concept that the production and reactions of organic chemicals follow the same laws as those that govern inorganic chemistry. Berthelot effectively attacked the idea that the chemistry of living things is different from that of inanimate matter and discredited the theory of vital forces. Berthelot's researches on the synthesis of organic compounds (including acetylene, benzene, glycerin, and numerous esters, alcohols, and sugars), on thermochemistry, on vegetable chemistry, and on the laws governing the mechanism of chemical reactions were instrumental in raising nineteenth-century chemistry from the level of a descriptive to a theoretically mature science. Stimulated by a visit to Egypt in 1869 for the inauguration of the Suez Canal, Berthelot also made significant contributions to the history of alchemy and chemistry.

Berthelot was elected to the Académie de Médecine in 1863, the Académie des Sciences in 1873 (of which he would become permanent secretary in 1889), and numerous other French and foreign scientific societies. He was made knight of the Legion of Honor in 1861 and officer in 1867 and would become commander in 1879 and grand officer in 1886. He received the Grand Cross in 1900. Berthelot played an important role in the reorganization of French education in the latter half of the century. He assisted in the foundation of the Ecole Practique des Hautes Etudes and was minister of education from 1886 to 1887. An ardent republican and anti-clerical, he fought for the greater inclusion of scientific subjects in the curriculum and for the increased secularization of education.

During the siege of Paris in the Franco-Prussian War, Berthelot distinguished himself as president of the Comité Scientifique pour la Défense de Paris (from 2 September 1870) and directed the manufacture of explosives. Because of his services rendered, Berthelot received a large vote in the Paris general election of February 1871, although he had not declared himself a candidate. He first took a seat in the Senate in 1871 and would be elected a permanent senator in 1881. Berthelot subscribed to a positivist philosophy—although his views were largely independent of the Comtists—and devoted much of his career to the elucidation of science's social and cultural functions. He was later chief editor of the *Grande encyclopédie* (1885–1901) and throughout his life was a strong influence on Ernest Renan, his close friend since 1842. In the last years of his life, Berthelot published books extolling the moral value of science and progress. He died at Paris, 18 March 1907.

A. Horeau, "Marcellin Berthelot," *RDM*, no. 7 (1980), no. 8, no. 9; L. Velluz, *Vie de Berthelot* (Paris, 1964); R. Virtanen, *Marcellin Berthelot: A Study of a Scientist's Public Role* (Lincoln, Neb., 1965).

Martin Fichman

Related entries: BERNARD; DUMAS; PASTEUR.

BIARRITZ, the tiny sardine fishing village just inside the French border with Spain, which became, thanks to the Empress Eugénie, a fashionable seaside resort during the Second Empire. Eugénie and her sister, Paca, first visited Biarritz in August 1847 (it had been "discovered" by Carlist exiles from Spain in 1838 when the population was about a thousand). Eugénie loved the wildness of the Basque coast where the Atlantic merged with the sandy pine forests of the Landes. She persuaded her new husband to holiday there for the first time from 21 July 1854. From October 1854 Napoleon III supervised the construction at Biarritz of a large but informal palace, built in the Renaissance style to his specifications by Auguste Déodat Couvrechef (1827–1857), as a holiday home for the imperial family. Constructed on a slope leading down to the Grande

Plage and the sea, the Villa Eugénie, with its attendant structures (including a private chapel), commanded a splendid view. Nearby was a model farm owned by the emperor. Until 1857 the imperial family holidayed each summer at Biarritz, where Eugénie, leading an almost private life in the informal surroundings she preferred, could invite friends and acquaintances, including those too unconventional to fit the guest lists of Fontainebleau, Compiègne, Saint-Cloud, or the Tuileries.

After 1857 Napoleon III's annual summer visit to the military camp at Châlons meant that the holiday took place in the autumn, usually from the beginning of September to early October. Biarritz, sometimes called "Eugénieville," grew rapidly during the Empire, reaching a population of nine thousand by the late century and becoming one of the most fashionable of French Atlantic resorts. The emperor and empress last saw the Villa Eugénie in October 1868. After the fall of the Empire, it became a casino and burned down in 1903 (the Hôtel du Palais now occupies the site). The Chapelle Notre-Dame de Bon Secours, rebuilt in the Roman style in 1855 as the Chapelle Sainte Eugénie, still stands. It was on the beach at Biarritz in October 1865 that Bismarck and Napoleon III had their famous conversation concerning the latter's plans for Germany.

M. F. Chauvirey and E. Goyhénèche, *Biarritz* (Capbreton, 1972); "Inauguration du monument à l'Impératrice Eugénie à Biarritz [et discours]," *SN* 18 (1954); J. Laborde, "Biarritz, de la domination anglaise au Second Empire," *Société des Sciences, Lettres et Art de Bayonne*, n.s., no. 108 (1965); J. Laborde, "L'Impératrice Eugénie à Bayonne et à Biarritz," *Société des Sciences, Lettres et Arts de Bayonne*, n.s., no. 74 (1955).

Related entries: BIARRITZ INTERVIEW; COMPIEGNE.

BIARRITZ, INTERVIEW OF, conversations between Napoleon III and the Prussian president of council, Count Otto von Bismarck (1815–1898), in October, 1865, which are considered to have made possible the Austro-Prussian War of 1866. Bismarck had decided on war with Austria to secure Prussian domination of Germany, but French neutrality was essential. Moreover, the Prussian general staff insisted on the participation of Italy in order to impose a two-front war on Austria. In early October 1865, Bismarck, who had been minister to France briefly (May–September 1862), was a guest at the Villa Eugénie at Biarritz. There the French emperor confirmed his opinion that Bismarck was too conservative to play a great European role, while the Prussian found in Napoleon III "a great unrecognized incapacity." More important were the soundings the two men made of each other's intentions. At Paris, en route to Biarritz, Bismarck had had on 2 October interviews with the minister of state, Eugène Rouher, as well as with the foreign minister, Edouard Drouyn de Lhuys. Of his conversations with the emperor between 4 and 11 October, we have only Bismarck's account to King William I, subsequently published by Heinrich von Sybel. Before leaving France, the Prussian met with Napoleon III on one further occasion, at Saint-Cloud, 3 November.

It would appear that neither Bismarck nor Napoleon III wished to enter into commitments. Bismarck's chief purpose was to assure himself that France would not ally with Austria in the event of war between the two great German powers. This he accomplished. Napoleon III wished above all to know that Prussia had not guaranteed Austrian possession of Venetia. He too was satisfied. Possibly Bismarck was able to foresee that Napoleon III's overwhelming desire to complete the work of 1859 by obtaining Venetia for Italy would open the way to a Prussian-Italian alliance, which, in fact, it did. Napoleon III may have intended either to use the threat of war to extort Venetia from Austria, or, in the event of a protracted conflict, to intervene and impose his preferred solution to the German and Italian questions on the exhausted combattants. Speculation aside, however, the essential fact remains that the French emperor could, with a word, have prevented war between Austria and Prussia. Neither at Biarritz nor subsequently did he speak that word. The Biarritz conversations appear, in retrospect, to be the first step on the slope leading to Sedan and the fall of the Second Empire.

P. Bernstein, ''Les entrevues de Biarritz et de Saint-Cloud (octobre–novembre 1865),'' *RHD*, no. 4 (1964), and ''Napoleon III and Bismarck: The Biarritz-Paris Talks of 1865,'' in N. Barker and M. Brown, eds., *Diplomacy in an Age of Nationalism* (The Hague, 1971); E. A. Pottinger, *Napoleon III and the German Crisis, 1865–1866* (Cambridge, Mass., 1966).

Related entries: ALLIANCE POLICY; DROUYN DE LHUYS; LUXEMBOURG CRISIS; NATIONALITIES; VENETIA.

BICYCLE. While forms of foot-operated vehicles appeared in the eighteenth century and a steerable two-wheeled bicycle was certainly in use by 1818, the first pedal-operated bicycle was built in Scotland in 1839. It was in France, however, that the first commercially significant production was undertaken by a Paris coachmaker, Pierre Michaux (1813–1883), and his son Ernest (1849–1889). Their prototype design of 1861 featured cranks attached to pedals by which the front wheel was driven (there is some question whether the idea was Pierre's, Ernest's, or that of a mechanic with the firm, Pierre Lallement). The Michaux *vélocipède* was put into regular series production in 1862. That first year, 142 machines were manufactured and sold. By 1865 annual production was more than 400. The Michaux *vélocipède* shown at the Paris international exposition of 1867 was modern in appearance, although its two wheels, of almost similar size, were made of wood and shod with iron. A second Paris factory, employing 300 workmen, was opened in 1868. The Michaux family continued in business until 1869, the year in which solid rubber was used for the first time to rim the wheels, and a Parisian, Magee, built a bicycle completely of iron and steel. In 1869 the Michaux firm was sold to the Olivier family for 200,000 francs and its name changed to Compagnie Parisienne Ancienne Maison Michaux.

During the 1860s, the *vélocipède* acquired prominence in French sporting life. Princess Mathilde presented to the prince imperial his first bicycle on the occasion of his thirteenth birthday in 1869 (it is now in the Museo Napoleonico at Rome).

Public demonstrations of the improved design of the machines and of the increased skill of riders functioned also as important social events. The first bicycle race was held at Saint-Cloud on 31 May 1868 and the first such race on French roads (Paris-Rouen) on 7 November 1869. The latter was won by a naturalized Frenchman of English origin, who covered the 126 kilometers in 10 hours and 40 minutes. That race had been organized by the first bicycle journal, *Le vélocipède*. It was also in 1869 that Le Véloce Club de Paris was formed, and a permanent cycle track was constructed on the Vesinet race course near Paris.

In addition to the Compagnie Parisienne, other important manufacturers appeared, and by 1870 France had established itself as the world's leading manufacturer of bicycles. The Franco-Prussian War cut short production, however, and leadership passed to other countries, notably Britain. Ironically, it was a subcontracting order for four hundred Michaux-type machines, placed from Paris in 1869, that led ultimately to making the English city of Coventry the center of the world's cycle industry.

The bicycle would not become truly popular and socially acceptable until the development of pneumatic tires in the 1890s had softened its bone-crushing ride, and even then the problem would remain that to increase the distance covered by each turn of the pedals, the front wheel would have grown disproportionately large, thus making the machine extremely unstable.

F. Alderson, *Bicycling: A History* (New York, 1972); C. F. Caunter, *The History and Development of Cycles* (London, 1955); J. Richardson, *La vie parisienne* (London: 1971).

Martin Fichman

BILLAULT, ADOLPHE (1805–1863), a key political figure of the Second Empire, first president of the Corps Législatif, senator, minister of the interior, minister without portfolio, and minister of state; born 12 November 1805 at Vannes. Without fortune (his father was a customs collector), Billault studied law at Rennes, became a lawyer at Nantes in 1830, and by dint of ability, ambition, and great self-confidence not only created a successful law practice but married a wealthy young woman of the Nantaise liberal bourgeoisie. Elected deputy in 1837, he aligned with Adolphe Thiers against François Guizot, voting sometimes with the Left although more often with the Right. In the Constituent Assembly, following the Revolution of 1848, Billault revealed his interest in economic and social reform in a speech for which conservatives never forgave him. He envisaged, in fact, a cradle-to-grave system of *providence sociale*.

Although Billault (who had not been elected to the Legislative Assembly) was not involved in the coup d'état of December 1851, he rallied to Louis Napoleon and did so early in the Second Republic. Like the prince president, Billault was a Saint-Simonian, eager for economic and social progress, solicitous of the welfare of the workers (at Nantes he had organized apprentice schools, and later, as minister of the interior, he would interest himself greatly in charitable institutions). He was devoted to French glory and grandeur. And although he embraced the principles of 1789, parliamentary government did not seem to him the best way of achieving these ends. Indeed, Billault was—as were so many of his fellow bourgeoisie at mid-century—a devotee of authoritarian government by a strong executive in the interest of order. His value as a minister was increased by a willingness to support and to advocate even those ideas he opposed. Thus, during the Second Empire, Billault defended the rebuilding of Paris (although he was an enemy of Baron Georges Haussmann) and Napoleon III's free trade policy, although he was himself a protectionist.

Elected as an official candidate to the Corps Législatif in 1852, Billault was named its first president, presiding with a firm but light hand. He was appointed minister of the interior 19 June 1854 and, in handling the press, showed a similar approach, issuing only fifty-seven *avertissements* from March 1854 to February 1858. The attempt on Napoleon III's life by Felice Orsini in January 1858 was an embarrassment to the minister. Although he prepared and submitted to the Corps Législatif the *loi de sûreté générale*, he was on 8 February replaced at the ministry by General Charles Espinasse (1815–1859). Recalled as minister of the interior 1 November 1859, Billault continued to show the concern for authority and order that had led him to oppose the generous amnesty of March 1856 and to propose a moratorium on construction of new factories at Paris. Although a critic of the reform decree of 24 November 1860, Billault agreed to become one of three ministers without portfolio who under the new system would defend government programs before the chambers. His special responsibility was foreign affairs and religious matters (*cultes*). In regard to the latter, he evidenced a Gallicanism that vigorously asserted the authority of the state against the church. Following the elections of 1863, Billault was one of those who worked successfully to end the political career of Victor Fialin Persigny. On 23 June 1863 he accepted the position of minister of state, becoming sole official spokesman for the government. His eloquence, high-mindedness, and éclat might have made a difference in the political struggle that lay ahead, but on 13 October 1863 Billault died unexpectedly at his château of Grésilières, near Nantes.

For Napoleon III, the sudden death of Billault was a great loss. The two men had understood each other and worked well together. The generous emperor rewarded this service well. Billault was named senator 4 December 1854, made commander of the Legion of Honor, and, when he became a minister without portfolio, given a house worth 700,000 francs. He was accorded a state funeral. Although some aspects of Billault's character remain ambiguous (for example, the Sandon affair), there seems little doubt that he was an able, conscientious, honest, and extremely hard-working minister, representative in that sense of the best traditions of his class.

A. Billault, *Oeuvres*, 2 vols. (Paris, 1865); N. Blayau, *Billault, ministre de Napoléon III, d'après ses papiers personnels, 1805–1863* (Paris, 1969, 1975).
Related entries: BAROCHE; FOULD; MAGNE; MINISTER OF STATE; ROUHER.

BOIS DE BOULOGNE, one of the earliest and most impressive results of the rebuilding of Paris by Napoleon III; a center of brilliant social life during the

Second Empire. Inspired by his London experiences and especially by the example of Hyde Park, Louis Napoleon in July 1852 ceded the state forest that is now the Bois de Boulogne (beyond the city's fortifications on the west and then in a wild state) to the city of Paris on condition that the city spend 2 million francs in four years to transform the terrain into a park. The Bois was entirely the prince president's idea, and he interested himself personally in the smallest details. Work began in the spring of 1853, even before the appointment of Georges Haussmann as prefect of the Seine. Varé, originally charged by Louis Napoleon with the task, proved unequal to the engineering problems and was replaced by Adolphe Alphand, a young protégé of Haussmann (December 1854). Landscaping was supervised thereafter by Alphand's chief gardener Jean Barillet, called Barillet-Deschamps (1824–1875). Louis Napoleon was forced, reluctantly, to accept two artificial lakes rather than a single serpentine modeled on that of Hyde Park. The two lakes, the roadway around them, and the adjoining lawns were completed in 1854. The Bois had assumed its present aspect by 1858 at a net cost to the city of some 3.5 million francs.

The Bois de Boulogne was approached by the avenue des Champs-Elysées (which, under Alphand's ministrations, was decked with masses of rare flowers, assuming its present-day aspect) and the avenue de l'Impératrice (now avenue Foch), built between 1854 and 1856, an incredible 460 feet wide. Access from the south was by the avenue de l'Empereur, opened in 1858 and extended in 1860 (now the avenues du Président Wilson, Georges Mandel, and Henri Martin). Water from the artesian well at Passy (drilled from 1855 to 1866) fed the smaller upper lake, dropped into the cement-lined lower lake over a cascade of artificial rocks, and then flowed westward via a brook to the spectacular Longchamp cascade (operated only briefly, once each day) complete with the then obligatory grottoes. Restaurants (the Pré-Catalan), chalets, islands, docks, an excursion barque, bridges, streams, ponds, footpaths, some forty-three miles of curving carriage roads and bridle paths, signposts, shelter houses, benches, and almost 500,000 newly planted trees and shrubs completed the promenade. In the north the Société d'Acclimatation (founded 1854) opened to the public in October 1860 a Jardin Zoologique d'Acclimatation for breeding and acclimatizing animal and vegetable species recently introduced into France. In the west, on the Plain of Longchamp (added to the Bois by a law of April 1855), the architect Gabriel Davioud (1823–1881) created the Longchamp racetrack (authorized 1854) on land leased to the Jockey Club in 1856. The track, inaugurated April 1857, soon established a passion for horse racing in France.

The Bois quickly became an essential part of the social life of Paris. Used by all classes on Sundays and holidays (between the late 1850s and 1867, Alphand laid out a popular park in the Bois de Vincennes, again in the English mode, much nearer the more crowded part of Paris), it was thronged every fine afternoon by the bourgeoisie and the rich, thousands of carriages making the tour of the lakes, a scene colorfully described by Emile Zola in *La curée*.

E. Gourdon, *Le Bois de Boulogne* (Paris, 1861); T. Vacquer, *Le Bois de Boulogne architectural* (Paris, 1860).

Related entries: ALPHAND; PARIS, REBUILDING OF.

BOLGRAD, a town in Bessarabia, center of a diplomatic dispute in 1856. The Congress of Paris had authorized Russia to retain Bolgrad (while giving up much of Bessarabia to Moldavia), on the ground that the town was the *chef-lieu* of a Bulgarian colony. The boundary commission soon discovered, however, that the congress maps had been faulty and that the Bolgrad claimed by Russia had direct access to the Danube via Lake Yalpuck and its tributaries. At this point Britain and Austria objected, since the intention of the peace treaty was to remove the Russians from contact with that strategic river. The issue was symptomatic of mutual suspicions concerning the carrying out of the Treaty of Paris. The British navy was still in the Black Sea, the Austrian army in the Danubian Principalities, and the Russians remained in possession of Serpents Island, some 90 miles off the mouth of the Danube. Napoleon III, hoping to conciliate Russia while retaining an alliance with Britain, proposed transaction, but London refused. British marines seized Serpents Island (it was turned over to Turkey), and Lord Palmerston blustered concerning Bolgrad. The Russian foreign minister, Alexandre Gorchakov (1798–1883), probably hoped to drive a wedge between Britain and France. While requesting that the Congress of Paris be reconvened, St. Petersburg offered through the French ambassador, Auguste de Morny, who was also Napoleon III's half-brother, to accept any compensation for Bolgrad proposed by the French emperor if he in turn would enter into an alliance with Russia to constrain Britain to carry out the peace treaty. Unwilling to risk the alliance with Britain, Napoleon III declined. He pressed relentlessly, however, for a conference to resolve the Bolgrad dispute and arranged (4 November) that Sardinia should vote against Russia, thus enabling France to support the Russian claim without alienating London, since Turkey and Austria would also join Britain in opposition, making a majority. Moreover, by skillful diplomacy Napoleon III contrived that compensation for Russia should be agreed on in advance and that the conference should meet to ratify the solution without a vote. Thus the conference, which met at Paris from 31 December 1856 to 6 January 1857 under the presidency of France's foreign minister, Alexandre Walewski, resolved a dispute that might have had serious consequences. The new rapprochement between France and Russia, the growing strains on the Anglo-French alliance, the rather unsatisfactory conclusion of the Crimean War, and the penchant of Napoleon III for conference diplomacy were all reflected in the Bolgrad dispute.

W. E. Mosse, *The Rise and Fall of the Crimean System, 1855–1871* (New York, 1963); E. Schüle, *Russland und Frankreich von Ausgang des Krimkrieges bis zum italienischen Krieg, 1856–1859* (Berlin, 1935); H. Temperley, "The Treaty of Paris and Its Execution," *JMH* 4 (1932).

Related entries: ALLIANCE POLICY; CONGRESS OF PARIS; CONGRESS POLICY; CRIMEAN WAR.

BONAPARTE, JEROME. See PRINCE NAPOLEON.

BONAPARTE, LOUIS NAPOLEON. See LOUIS NAPOLEON.

BONAPARTE, MATHILDE. See MATHILDE.

BONAPARTISM, a species of political theory and practice best understood in the context of the divisions and conflicts of post-Revolutionary France. Above all, bonapartism espoused an authoritarian democracy to bridge the gap between the tradition of absolutist monarchy and the democratic tradition of the Revolution. Or, as one pamphleteer put it, a bonapartist rejected both monarchy and republic, entrusting to a Bonaparte the duty of defending him against both, although it should be noted that some forms of republicanism (utopian, fraternal, aiming to abolish class) had much in common with bonapartism and that until the 1830s they were closely allied. Louis Napoleon began his political career, of course, as a republican. Bonapartism recognized the democratic right of the people to determine the form of their government (a right denied by the monarchist) and favored the retention of power in a hereditary dynasty as a guarantee of stability (an idea the republican rejected). Possible abuse of power by the emperor would be held in check not by the caprices of political parties or the parochial interests of parliamentary deputies but by the sovereign will of the people, expressed through periodic plebiscites. Bonapartism meant representative government, the Bonaparte representing the will and aspirations of the people, with no mediator. Further, it meant overcoming the unwillingness or inability of both legitimist and Orleanist governments to take up the social question and to promote social and economic reform while at the same time avoiding the tendency of the Republic to open the door to chaos and violent disorder. Finally, bonapartism meant glory for France in Europe and the rest of the world.

On St. Helena, Napoleon I had portrayed himself as consolidator of the Revolution and as savior of France. His Caesarian democracy, standing above party or geographical factionalism, offered neither monarchical inflexibility and irresponsibility nor revolutionary anarchy. Rather, it provided order on which liberty, not license, would be established and the ideals of 1789 would be preserved. His nephew found the image credible and convincing, and in 1839 he developed the Napoleonic ideas in clear and coherent form in his book, *Des idées napoléoniennes*. He too was confident that the victory of the Empire had been the establishment of civil order but that its ultimate goal was liberty: "The name of liberty was not, it is true, placed at the head of every law . . ., but every law of the Empire prepared for its peaceful and certain reign. . . . It is necessary to reconstruct a civil order. . . before liberty is possible." Louis Napoleon's well-known response to the plebiscitary results in 1852 reflected exactly the same understanding of the political mission to which his name was attached.

The Napoleonic tradition was capable of yielding both an authoritarian and a liberal bonapartism. When Louis Napoleon was elected president of the Second

Republic, it was far more expedient to emphasize order and authority; fear of the "reds" and of new terror and fresh memories of the June Days explain this. But there was remarkable consistency between the theory and practice of bonapartism for the prince president, and he made it clear that peace, prosperity, the principles of 1789, and, above all, liberty were the ultimate objects of the hard-fisted regime he established following the coup d'état of December 1851. What is more, he desired that his Empire be democratic and representative, in contrast to the previous governments of his century. Periodic plebiscites having proved to be a weak means for the people to communicate their views and opinions to their government, by 1857 the Empire was in danger of being merely a dictatorship, democracy in danger of being an illusion. Therefore, with order and prosperity achieved and the regime enjoying widespread support (although not all the opposition was a loyal opposition, as the bonapartists wished), the emperor took the initiative on 24 November 1860 to promulgate what Pierre de La Gorce called "the first, the most important of the successive evolutions which transformed the authoritarian Empire to the liberal Empire." In the subsequent ten years, a series of reforms affecting budget processes, labor laws, and press and public assembly laws were proposed by Napoleon III and passed by the Corps Législatif. Then, following the elections of 1869, the emperor issued a decree expanding legislative powers, and a new majority emerged, composed largely of members converted from the old majority of official candidates, led by Emile Ollivier. Finally a liberal ministry under Ollivier took office in early 1870 and produced a new constitution. The Liberal Empire, a virtual parliamentary monarchy, had arisen from the reforms of the 1860s.

The Liberal Empire was not Orleanism reinstated, as some historians have argued. The emperor was still a democratic representative and was to rule as well as reign. Nor had Napoleon III merely buckled under the pressure of opposition. The opposition of the Right was of decreasing significance and that of the Left he recognized as irreconcilable. As Theodore Zeldin (1958) noted, "The theory that Napoleon was merely yielding in his weakness before the attacks of the opposition was invented by that opposition to flatter its own importance." The emperor was fulfilling his long-standing desire to reconcile order, democracy, and liberty. Liberty had crowned the edifice of order as the theory of bonapartism had promised. In fact, however, the Empire had succeeded neither in reconciling nor in co-opting its opponents of the Left and Right. It may not be unreasonable to suggest that the war with Prussia in the summer of 1870 denied Napoleon III sufficient time to accomplish his bonapartist bridge building. Nonetheless, failure in the war effort rather fully discredited the emperor's liberal bonapartism, and the conservatives and authoritarians were left to bear the bonapartist standard under the early Third Republic. The necessary conclusion is that despite the promises of bonapartist theory and despite Napoleon III's commitment to a consistency of theory and practice, bonapartism in practice in the nineteenth century was unable to build an effective and durable bridge over the conflicts of post-Revolutionary French political life. This was perhaps not surprising since Napoleon III was not the only interpreter of bonapartism during the Second Empire. To understand fully the meaning (or meanings) of that doctrine, attention must also be paid to the romantic bonapartism of Victor Fialin Persigny, the left-wing bonapartism of Prince Napoleon, the parliamentary bonapartism of Ollivier, Eugène Schneider, and (perhaps) Auguste de Morny and Alexandre Walewski, and the conservative bonapartism of Achille Fould, Jules Baroche, Pierre Magne, Adolphe Billault, Raymond Troplong, Adolphe Granier de Cassagnac, Jérôme David, and Eugène Rouher.

S. L. Campbell, *The Second Empire Revisited* (New Brunswick, N.J., 1979); H.A.L. Fisher, *Bonapartism* (New York, 1914); L. Gall, "Bismarck und der Bonapartismus," *HZ* 223 (1976); K. Hammer and P. Hartmann, eds., *Le bonapartisme: Phénomène historique et mythe politique* (Munich, 1975); J. Rothney, *Bonapartism after Sedan* (Ithaca, N.Y., 1969); T. Zeldin, *The Political System of Napoleon III* (London, 1958), and "Bonapartism," in T. Zeldin, *France, 1848–1945: Politics and Anger* (Oxford, 1979).

William E. Duvall

Related entries: CONSTITUTION; COUP D'ETAT; CROWNING THE EDIFICE; DAVID; GRANIER DE CASSAGNAC; *DES IDEES NAPOLEONIENNES*; LABOR REFORM; LOUIS NAPOLEON; NATIONALITIES; PERSIGNY; PLEBISCITE; PUBLIC OPINION; ROUHER; SECOND EMPIRE; TROPLONG; UNIVERSAL MANHOOD SUFFRAGE.

BONHEUR, ROSA (1822–1899), painter of animals and rustic scenes, sculptor; born at Bordeaux, 22 March 1822. Rosa Bonheur's father, Raymond, a painter and Saint-Simonian socialist, encouraged his daughter's independent attitude. She refused to become a seamstress and she, as well as her sister and two brothers, became a painter. Bonheur's overriding interest in animals (she kept several domestic as well as exotic animals, including a lion, as pets in the chateau she bought at Le By near Fontainebleau) provided her with ample subject matter for her paintings, which recall the seventeenth-century works of Paulus Potter and Albert Cuyp. Her earliest studies were sketches of animals in the Bois de Boulogne, but she also pursued her interests to horse fairs, cattle markets, and even to slaughterhouses. After a try at sculpture, she devoted herself to painting, exhibiting in the Salons in the 1840s. She won a first-class medal in 1848 and *Plowing in Nivernais* (1848, Fontainebleau), whose subject matter recalls a passage in George Sand's *La mare au Diable*, was purchased by the government. Bonheur's independent behavior (she cut her hair short, smoked and wore male attire, and subscribed to Saint-Simonianism) necessitated her obtaining a waiver from the police to permit her to appear in such a manner in public.

The work proclaimed as her masterpiece, *Horse Fair* (Metropolitan Museum of Art, New York), shown in the Salon of 1853, was of major proportions in both scale and acclaim. It recalled some of the form and the romantic content of Théodore Géricault. The dimensions of the canvas, 8 by 16 1/2 feet, permitted Bonheur to emphasize her close observations of life-size horses with objective, precise detail. This effort toward greater realism is counterpoised against the more dramatic and expressive content. The horses are depicted as straining against tightly held reins, a confrontation between man and animal in the romantic vein. The work is vigorously painted, with an emphasis on the horizontality of the composition, recalling a Greek frieze but a highly energized version thereof. When her native city of Bordeaux failed to purchase it, she sold it to the London dealer Gambart, much to the regret of Napoleon III and the Empress Eugénie, whose offer to purchase came too late. The work had successful showings in England and was especially admired by Queen Victoria, who had it brought to Buckingham Palace. Bonheur visited England and the Scottish Highlands in 1856 and saw the work of Sir Edwin Landseer, the English animal painter.

Although she no longer exhibited in France at the Salons after 1855, she received widespread renown and awards from Belgium, Spain, Portugal, and Mexico. Empress Eugénie, who as regent in 1865 secured for her the Legion of Honor, came to the studio at Le By to present the award. Bonheur exhibited at the Paris international exposition of 1867 as she had done in 1855. She was made an officer of the Legion of Honor in 1894, the first woman to achieve this status. She died at Le By in 1899.

D. Ashton and D. B. Hare, *Rosa Bonheur: A Life and a Legend* (New York, 1981).

Beverley Giblon

BOUDIN, EUGENE (1824–1898), pre-Impressionist seascape painter; born at Honfleur, 12 July 1824, the son of a sea captain. Boudin spent some of his early years on a ship but later owned a stationery and framing shop in Le Havre where he sold artists' supplies. In the shop window, he exhibited works by such artists as Constant Troyon (1810–1865), Thomas Couture, and Jean François Millet. These came to Normandy to paint and in turn encouraged Boudin to paint also. He was awarded a three-year scholarship to study in Paris in 1851. On his return to Le Havre, he worked as a marine painter with a special interest in the sky and light. He encouraged Claude Monet, whom he met in 1858 when Monet exhibited some of his caricatures in Boudin's former shop, to study nature and paint out of doors, *en plein air*, without any preconceptions as to how one ought to paint landscapes. This was a decisive factor in the development of Monet's painting and for Impressionism. Boudin's own work demonstrates the freshness and directness he was able to achieve through close contact with the sea and the sky, painted at first-hand. Camille Corot called Boudin the "King of the Skies." Boudin traveled to several centers along the coast painting the harbors, fishermen, and beach scenes. He introduced Gustave Courbet to the Saint-Siméon farm at Honfleur, with its view of the Seine estuary where Corot and the Barbizon painters Narcisse Diaz de la Peña and Charles François Daubigny also came to paint. Charles Baudelaire visited Boudin's studio and praised his pastel sketches in his review of the 1859 Salon. Boudin's quick and free brushwork produced a sketchy effect, which brought into question whether the works were merely sketches (and thus preparatory works) or finished works of art. His paintings such as *On the Beach at Trouville* (1863, Metropolitan Museum of Art, New York) are generally small in format, concentrating on the changes of light, its brightness in this case, as it affects the environment. The small figures, mainly fashionable middle-class vacationers, serve as accents of color, animating the seaside scenes at Deauville and Trouville, his favorite sites, and providing a social commentary on the Second Empire. Boudin was influenced by Monet but exhibited only at the first Impressionist exhibition in 1874, preferring to show his work in the Salon. He died at Deauville, 8 August 1898.

C. C. Cunningham, *Jongkind and the Pre-Impressionists: Painters of the Ecole Saint-Siméon* (Williamstown, Mass., 1977); G. Jean-Aubry, *Eugène Boudin, la vie et l'oeuvre d'après les lettres et les documents inédits*, 2d ed. (Neuchâtel, 1977; trans. into English 1969); G. de Knyff, *Eugène Boudin raconté par lui-même: sa vie, son atelier, son oeuvre* (Paris, 1976); Santa Barbara Art Museum, *Louis Eugène Boudin: Precursor of Impressionism* (Santa Barbara, 1976–1977); R. Schmit, *Eugène Boudin, 1824–1898* (Paris, 1973), and "Eugène Boudin, le roi des ciels," *L'oeil*, no. 290 (1979).

Beverley Giblon

Related entries: DEAUVILLE; MONET.

BOUGUEREAU, WILLIAM ADOLPHE (1825–1905), academic painter; born at La Rochelle, 30 November 1825. After studying at the Ecole des Beaux-Arts in Bordeaux and then at Paris, Bouguereau had his paintings accepted in the Salon of 1849. He (and Paul Baudry) won the Prix de Rome in 1850, which allowed him to go to Italy. He returned to Paris in 1854, after having studied the remains of antiquity in Italy and the Renaissance masters, in particular Raphael and Giotto. Bouguereau was well received on his return, winning several awards, including a first-class medal in the Salon of 1857, and obtaining many commissions for portraits and church decorations. Bouguereau concentrated his efforts on painting women as erotic beings displaying faultless flesh, often in the guise of mythological nymphs or Venuses, such as *Zénobie trouvée sur les bords de l'Araxe* (1850, Ecole des Beaux-Arts, Paris). His paintings were avidly sought by aristocrats and the upper middle class who could recognize technical skill in imitating reality and who welcomed anecdote and sentimental subject matter. Based on a firm foundation of drawing, craftsmanship, and high finish, which at times becomes mechanical, works such as the allegory *Spring* (1858, Harry Glass Collection, New York), commissioned by the banker Emile Pereire, readily illustrate what Bouguereau was striving for—the ideal, the noble, the sublime. Characteristic of his more literal pursuits is *All Souls' Day* (1859, Musée des Beaux Arts, Bordeaux), a work in which pathos is pushed to the extremes of tolerance and where the naturalistic intent is most ably fulfilled with meticulous precision. Bouguereau was awarded the Legion of Honor in 1859 and received commissions to decorate churches, private homes, and a newly constructed theater at Bordeaux in 1865.

Much of Bouguereau's career was devoted to decorative mural painting, including those in the newly constructed Paris churches of Sainte Clotilde and Saint Augustin and the Pereire mansions where he shared the work with Alexandre Cabanel. He was appointed professor at the Ecole des Beaux-Arts in 1875 and, as an important member of the jury determining which works were to be admitted, continued to exert influence through the Salons, where his work served the more conservative critics as examples of ideal painting whose virtues ought to be emulated by the Impressionists. Bouguereau's best-known subjects were painted during the Third Republic. He died at La Rochelle, 19 August 1905.

R. Isaacson, ''The Evolution of Bouguereau's Grand Manner,'' *Minneapolis Institute of Arts Bulletin* 62 (1975), and *William Bouguereau* (New York, 1974); M. Schiff, ed., *William Bouguereau* (Montreal, 1984).

Beverley Giblon

Related entries: BAUDRY; CABANEL.

BUDGET. See FOULD.

BUFFET, LOUIS (1818–1898), politician and minister, leader of the Tiers Parti; born at Mirecourt (Vosges) 26 October 1818 to a bourgeois, bonapartist family. Buffet's father, who had campaigned in Spain and Russia as a soldier of the Imperial Guard, was mayor of Mirecourt and conseiller général of the Vosges (1843–1852), but the son did not inherit an enthusiasm for bonapartism. By 1848, Buffet, a lawyer at Nancy, had committed himself to politics. Elected to the Constituent Assembly, he sat slightly to the left and preferred General Louis Eugène Cavaignac (1802–1857) to Louis Napoleon in the presidential election of December 1848 (Second Republic). Following the election, however, Buffet rallied to the new president and was appointed minister of agriculture and commerce in place of Jacques Bixio (1808–1865), the sole republican member of the cabinet, on the latter's dismissal in December 1848. Elected to the Legislative Assembly, Buffet now sat to the right of center. His departure from the cabinet at the end of 1849 signaled his growing discontent with Louis Napoleon's move toward personal power. But Buffet, who had come to like and to admire the president and was in sympathy with his defense of order, returned in April 1851 to the Ministry of Agriculture, only to resign once again (14 October 1851) when the prince president espoused the cause of universal manhood suffrage against the restrictive electoral law of May 1850, which Buffet had helped to frame. Arrested at the coup d'état (2 December 1851) but soon released, the ex-minister returned to Mirecourt, where he was elected to the conseil général of the Vosges.

Although Buffet contested the election of 1857 in the Vosges (unsuccessfully), it was Napoleon III's reform decree of 24 November 1860 that permitted his return to national politics by opening the prospect of a parliamentary regime. Loyal to the dynasty but devoted to bourgeois parliamentary government (he believed that only men of independent income should be deputies), Buffet, after his election to the Corps Législatif in 1863, quickly emerged as the most notable and influential member of a group of like-minded men, eventually known as the Tiers Parti. Inspired as well by Adolphe Thiers, Buffet helped to draft the proposed amendment to the address of March 1866 calling for a complete parliamentary regime, which received 63 votes. Napoleon III, although he had named Buffet to the Legion of Honor in 1851, found repugnant his former minister's parliamentarianism, protectionism, lack of social policy, fiscal conservatism, and resistance to a vigorous foreign policy (Buffet was a proponent of good relations with Austria and in 1868 voted against the government's military reform bill). Nevertheless, political evolution favored the Tiers Parti. Buffet was reelected almost unanimously in 1869. During that year's legislative session, he signed the "interpellation of 116" demanding responsible government.

When Emile Ollivier formed on 2 January 1870 the first government of the parliamentary Empire, he was constrained, despite the advice of Eugène Rouher and his own preferences, to appoint Buffet minister of finance, since the Tiers Parti leader whose *centre-gauche* faction was indispensable to Ollivier would not collaborate with any men of the authoritarian Empire. Together with Comte Napoléon Daru, Buffet imposed protectionist measures on the new government and pressed for a relaxation of the emperor's power to appoint mayors. Buffet could not, however, accept the plebiscite of May 1870, although he had reluctantly agreed to enshrine the plebiscitary power in the new constitution, finding it incompatible with a parliamentary regime. He resigned as finance minister 8 April. Following Napoleon III's disastrous defeat at Sedan, Buffet and several other deputies tried to persuade the empress to surrender her powers of regent to the Corps Législatif. Nevertheless, Buffet protested the events of 4 September by which the regime fell victim to a popular uprising at Paris. He retired once again to Mirecourt, from which, as an Orleanist, he would enjoy a second political career during the Third Republic. He died at Paris 7 July 1898.

Duc de Broglie, "Louis Buffet," *Corr.* (May and June 1899); J. Buffet, *Essai d'une synthèse de la vie de Louis Joseph Buffet, homme d'état, 1818–1898* (Nancy, 1975); Baron de Courcel, "Notice sur la vie et les travaux de M. Buffet," *ASMP* 157 (January 1902).

Related entries: CORPS LEGISLATIF; DARU; LIBERAL EMPIRE; LIBERALISM; ORLEANISM; REFORM; THIERS; TIERS PARTI.

C

CABANEL, ALEXANDRE (1823–1889), academic painter; born at Montpellier, 28 September 1823. Cabanel entered the Ecole des Beaux-Arts in 1840, having won a government award, exhibited in the Salon of 1844, and won the Prix de Rome, allowing him to go to Italy to continue his studies in 1845. His return to Paris was greeted with commissions, including twelve panels representing the months of the year for the Room of the Caryatids in the Hôtel de Ville (executed 1852–1853; destroyed in the Commune of 1871). He won a first-class medal at the Paris international exposition of 1855 for another work commissioned for the St. Louis chapel in the Château de Vincennes, *Apotheosis of St. Louis*. The remainder of the decade was spent completing further commissions for ceiling decorations for wealthy individuals (for example, *The Five Senses*, 1858, for the banker Emile Pereire), and painting portraits. *Nymph Abducted by a Faun* (1860, Musée des Beaux-Arts, Lille) was shown in the Salon of 1861 and purchased by Napoleon III. It is carefully and painstakingly drawn in the classical manner yet presents as well sensuous overtones that verge on the erotic and result in insipid prettiness. This is even more evident in his *Birth of Venus* (1863; Louvre, Paris), which refers to Boucher's sensuous nudes of the eighteenth century and attempts to combine this with the classical tradition. It was the sensation of the Salon of 1863 and was purchased, again, by Napoleon III, who also had his portrait painted by Cabanel in 1865. The critic Jules Castagnary (1830–1888) denigrated it, along with, although to a lesser extent, similar nudes by the academic painters Paul Baudry and Eugène Amaury-Duval (1808–1885), for its poor color. Other critics, however, admired Venus's agreeable curves. While Cabanel aspired to serious subject matter and classically perfect form, the results he achieved were most often weak, the nudes banal, and the concept pretentious. Following his success in the Salon of 1863, he was promoted in the Legion of Honor (1864), and elected to the Académie des Beaux-Arts (1863) in the place of Horace Vernet (1789–1863). In 1863–1864 both Cabanel and Jean Léon Gérôme were made professors at the reformed Ecole des Beaux-Arts and their *ateliers* were assimilated into the school. Cabanel's influence as a habitual member of the jury of the Salons, like that of other conservative artists such as Gérôme and William Bouguereau, prevented the more avant-garde artists such as the Impressionists from being accepted. He died at Paris, 23 January 1889, having become a veritable institution in the French art world.

A. Boime, *The Academy and French Painting in the Nineteenth Century* (New York, 1971), and *Art Pompier: Anti-Impressionism: Nineteenth-Century Salon Painting* (Hempstead, N.Y., 1974); J. Nougaret, "Alexandre Cabanel, sa vie, son oeuvre: Essai de catalogue" (University of Montpellier thesis, 1962); R. Rosenblum and H. W. Janson, *19th-Century Art* (New York, 1984).

Beverley Giblon

Related entries: BAUDRY; BOUGUEREAU; GEROME; VAILLANT; VIOLLET-LE-DUC.

CABINET. See MINISTRY.

CAFES AND RESTAURANTS. See DUGLERE.

CANDIDATURE OUVRIERE, worker candidacy for election to the Corps Législatif in the general elections of May–June 1863 and in the Paris by-election of March 1864. In 1863 J. J. Blanc, printer and page setter for *L'opinion nationale*, and Jean Baptiste Coutant, also a printer, ran as worker candidates in the first and sixth electoral districts, the former against Léonor Havin, a candidate of the opposition. Henri Tolain, engraver on bronze, was briefly a candidate but withdrew before the election. Chabaud, most prominent of the Palais Royal workers, was proposed as a candidate but refused to run. This first workers' candidacy was a failure, attracting only 332 voters for Blanc and 11 for Coutant. The by-election of 1864 was more eventful but hardly more successful. In this election, Tolain stood as the only workers' candidate against Louis Antoine Garnier-Pagès (1803–1878), republican veteran of 1848, and against a partisan of the Empire. Although accused of dividing the opposition and thus serving the interests of the regime, Tolain affirmed his adherence to republican doctrine and therefore his anti-imperial stance. He received only 424 votes. This second workers' candidacy occasioned the drafting of the *Manifesto of the Sixty (Manifeste des Soixante)*, for which the *candidature ouvrière* has been celebrated as much as for the electoral event itself.

The idea of workers' candidacies was first proposed in meetings of republican electoral committees in Paris in preparation for the 1863 election. Workers had demanded a more active voice in the selection of opposition candidates, as well as more emphasis on social issues in the program of the opposition. In response to these demands, certain bourgeois republicans, notably a disciple of Pierre Joseph Proudhon and some veterans of June 1849, invited workers from the faubourgs du Temple et Saint Antoine to participate in electoral deliberations. Amid these discussions the candidacies of J. J. Blanc and Tolain were proposed and accepted; Tolain later withdrew, however, and Coutant joined the contest. A number of republicans gave their enthusiastic support, among them Gustave Tridon (1841–1871), a disciple of Auguste Blanqui, Léon Gambetta, Adrien

Hébrard (1834–1914), and especially the young journalist Henri Lefort, who served as intermediary between the worker candidates and the electoral groups of the bourgeois opposition.

Although historians disagree as to the position taken by *Le temps*, many other opposition newspapers, such as *Le siècle,* attacked the candidacies, claiming that they were divisive and fostered a politics of class. After the elections, Tolain responded to these charges in *Quelques vérités sur les élections de Paris*. He specified a program of practical reforms, most notably freedom for workers to organize unions and other associations, as the goal of workers' candidacies and affirmed the necessity of workers' representation by members of their own class to realize such reforms. Tolain made no secret of the socialist lineage and orientation of this program but emphasized the concrete, practical nature of the reforms, differentiating them from the more utopian socialist proposals of the Second Republic. Tolain's brochure, it has been argued, effectively linked the workers' candidacies with the socialist movement, now revived in a more pragmatic form.

These notions were developed further in the *Manifesto of the Sixty*, published in the 17 February 1864 issue of *L'opinion nationale*. Drawn up at the home of Henri Lefort, whom historians have credited with a major role in drafting this document (though perhaps less important than that of Tolain), the manifesto proclaimed social emancipation for workers as a necessary complement to their political emancipation (achieved through universal suffrage) for realizing true equality according to the principles of 1789. Because workers alone were sufficiently knowledgeable and interested in social questions, selection of candidates from their own class to represent these interests in the legislature was imperative. While favoring the same political program as the democratic bourgeoisie and the liberal opposition, the signers of the manifesto expressed their determination to achieve social equality on their own—notably through labor chambers composed exclusively of workers. This document has been classed, along with the *Manifesto of Equals* and the *Communist Manifesto*, as affirming clearly and sharply the split between bourgeois and proletarians. Among contemporaries it generated intense debate about the position of workers in French government and society. Proudhon was inspired by the manifesto to write his last work, *De la capacité politique des classes ouvrières*, where he proposed a *mutuellist* organization of economy and society, based on reciprocal contracts, as the best means for social emancipation through the workers' own efforts. The more typical bourgeois response however—including that of the bourgeois opposition—was denial of the existence of classes since 1789 and therefore rejection of a specifically working-class representation. Even some workers opposed the propositions of the manifesto. A group of workers inspired, perhaps, by Emile Ollivier replied with a counter *Manifesto of the Eighty*, published in the 28 February 1864 issue of *Le siècle*.

Tolain's candidacy in the March 1864 by-election, announced slightly more than two weeks after the appearance of the manifesto, thus encountered widespread resistance among both republicans and members of his own class. Tolain received support from some well-known democrats, including Emmanuel Arago (1812–1896), Jean Macé (1815–1894), Charles Delescluze (1809–1871), Noël Parfait (1813–1896), and Léon Laurant-Pichat (1823–1886). The last three signed a public letter testifying to Tolain's loyalty to republican principles. But the candidate still faced accusations by some of being in league with the Palais Royal. Others assailed him as a class candidate, inciting revolution, and perhaps circumstances did impel him in that direction despite his personal moderation and conciliatory intentions. The entry of Chabaud into the race heightened speculation on both accounts. The suspicion that this latter candidacy was designed only to discredit Tolain's seems justified in the light of Chabaud's withdrawal from the contest on the day of the election. Tolain's defeat thus came as no surprise. Tolain himself attributed it to "the force of reaction armed with all the privileges," especially the privilege of the right to meet. Historians, however, have pointed to other causes of failure—to the "fear of the red specter," to the unconscionable machinations of certain opposition leaders, especially Adolphe Guéroult (1810–1872), editor of *L'opinion nationale,* who may have initiated Chabaud's candidacy and then used it to editorialize against that of Tolain or, more commonly, to the strangeness and lack of appeal that the idea of class representation had for both workers and leaders of the bourgeois opposition. The event has been regarded, nevertheless, as a significant step in the development of an autonomous workers' movement after 1860.

E. Dolléans, *Histoire du mouvement ouvrier, 1830–1871* (Paris, 1948); I. Tchernoff, "Les candidatures ouvrières sous le Second Empire," *La revue socialiste*, 43 (January–June 1906); A. Thomas, *Le Second Empire, 1852–1870*, vol. 10 of J. Jaurès, ed., *Histoire socialiste, 1789–1900* (Paris, 1907); A. Zévaès, "Les candidatures ouvrières et révolutionnaires sous le Second Empire," *R. 1848* 29 (March 1932–February 1933).

George J. Sheridan, Jr.

Related entries: ELECTIONS; LABOR REFORM; PALAIS ROYAL GROUP; TOLAIN.

CANROBERT, FRANCOIS (1809–1895), marshal of France, commander of French forces in the Crimean War; born François Certain, 27 June 1809, at St. Céré (Lot). The Certains were a royalist Breton family by origin. Canrobert (it was the name he had adopted by the 1850s) entered St. Cyr in 1825, graduating 1828 as a sublieutenant of the line. In Algeria from 1835 to 1839, he distinguished himself by his energy, dash, and bravery. Promoted to captain, decorated, and named to the Legion of Honor, he returned to France in 1839, where he was charged with organizing a Foreign Legion battalion from the remnants of Carlist bands who had survived the Spanish civil war. By the end of a second period in Algeria (1841–1850), Canrobert, then general of brigade (13 January 1850) and a commander of the Legion of Honor, had became one of those young, ambitious officers of the African army cultivated by Louis Napoleon, president of the French Republic. Recalled to France, although he had voted for General

Louis Eugène Cavaignac (1802–1857) in the election to the presidency, Canrobert
soon attached himself to Louis Napoleon, whose aide-de-camp he became. Not
involved in the planning of the coup d'état of December 1851 and apparently
troubled by it, Canrobert nevertheless obeyed orders to help crush resistance at
Paris. It was his brigade, although not at his command, that fired on a crowd
of innocent bystanders (massacre of the boulevards) on 4 December. In March
1852 Canrobert was sent, together with General Charles Espinasse (1815–1859),
and Alexandre Quentin Bauchart (1809–1887), to review the sentences imposed
on those who had resisted the coup d'état in the provinces. Assigned responsibility
for the central area (Massif Central), he pardoned only 779 of 4,655, probably
contrary to Louis Napoleon's wishes for a greater leniency.

At the beginning of the Crimean War, Canrobert, who had been named general
of division on 14 January 1853, received command (March 1854) of the First
Division of the Armée d'Orient, subsequently decimated by cholera along the
Danube. In the Crimea, Canrobert, serving under Marshal Leroy de Saint-Arnaud, conducted himself gallantly at the Battle of the Alma, where he was slightly
wounded. Dying of cholera, Saint-Arnaud, obeying Napoleon III's secret instructions, confided command to Canrobert on 26 September 1854. Although he
undertook the investment of Sebastopol with customary energy and was popular
with his soldiers, Canrobert lacked the power of decision necessary for high
command. Quarreling with the British commander, Lord Raglan, he voluntarily
resigned and was succeeded by General Aimable Pélissier on 16 May 1855.
Canrobert returned to the First Division and, two months later, to France. In
November 1855 he was sent to Scandinavia to negotiate a treaty of alliance with
Sweden (signed 21 November 1855). Following the war, he was named marshal
of France (18 March 1856), at the same time as Generals Pierre Bosquet (1810–
1861) and César Alexandre Randon.

Canrobert was one of five marshals who, following the attempt on Napoleon
III's life in January 1858 by Felice Orsini, was named to execute martial law
throughout France (his command was at Nancy). During the 1859 war against
Austria in Italy, he exercised subordinate command with great bravery, leading
III Corps at the battles of Magenta and Solférino. A quarrel with General Adolphe
Niel resulted from his role in the latter action. Following the war, Canrobert
was named on the death of Marshal Victor Castellane (1788–1862) commander
of the Fourth Army Corps at Lyons (September 1862). Although genuinely
devoted to the emperor, he declined Napoleon III's invitation to take the place
of Auguste de Morny in the Conseil Privé, pleading that he was only a soldier
and wanted nothing more. The emperor, perhaps suspicious, granted the marshal
his wish and for the rest of the Empire, although a senator by virtue of his rank,
and a member of the Conseil Général of the Lot, Canrobert pursued a purely
military career. His services, however, were generously rewarded; he received
a salary that on occasion reached 160,000 francs (100,000 as commander of an
army corps, 30,000 as a marshal, and 30,000 as a senator). On the death of

Marshal Bernard Pierre Magnan (1791–1865), he was named commander of the army at Paris.

During the Franco-Prussian War, Canrobert confirmed his reputation as a brave and able subordinate. Unable to make a useful force of the undisciplined Paris Garde Mobile gathered at Châlons, he took command of VI Corps and, after the Battle of Forbach, placed himself under Marshal Achille Bazaine, although senior to him. Declining Empress Eugénie's invitation of 10 August 1870 that he become commander of Paris, Canrobert rejoined Bazaine and fought gallantly at Gravelotte and St. Privat (18 August). Besieged at Metz, he opposed (26 August) the attempt to break out but argued later (7 October) that the army should make such an attempt whatever the cost if not given honors of war. After the fall of the Empire, Canrobert attached himself to the Thiers government but, at his own request, attended the funeral of Napoleon III in England (January 1873). His career as a Bonapartist deputy during the Third Republic was without great importance. Canrobert died at Paris, 28 January 1895, the last surviving marshal of the Second Empire.

G. Bapst, *Le Maréchal Canrobert: Souvenirs d'un siècle*, 6 vols. (Paris, 1898–1913); Count L. Grandin, *Le dernier maréchal de France: Canrobert*, 8th ed. (Paris, 1904). *Related entries:* CRIMEAN WAR; FRANCO-PRUSSIAN WAR; ITALIAN WAR; MACMAHON.

CARPEAUX, JEAN BAPTISTE (1827–1875), sculptor of portraits and works for public buildings, painter and engraver; born at Valenciennes (Nord), 11 May 1827. Although Carpeaux's father, a stonemason, wanted him to study architecture and agreed to his entering the Petit Ecole, Carpeaux soon became aware of his greater interest in sculpture. It was at the Petit Ecole, where he was a fellow student of Charles Garnier, that he learned the basic skills of ornamental decoration and sculpture. In 1844 he began to study at the Ecole des Beaux-Arts, later with François Rude, the major sculptor of the romantic period, and then with Francisque Duret (1804–1865) in order to be better prepared to compete for the Prix de Rome. With persistent effort, despite grinding poverty, he finally won the Grand Prix in 1854 with the neoclassical *Hector Imploring the Gods in Favour of His Son Astyanax* (Ecole des Beaux-Arts). He arrived in Rome at the beginning of 1856 and spent most of his time there (1856–1862) observing the life of the city, the antiquity, and the work of Michelangelo. His second *envoi*, a work sent back to Paris as part of the fulfillment of his obligation, was *Fisherboy with a Shell*, exhibited in 1858. There is a springiness in the pose of this young boy and a lively expression that presages the animated works that followed. It won public recognition but also the disapproval of the academy. The next major work achieved in Rome was *Ugolino* (Louvre, Paris) whose tragic theme was inspired by a passage in Dante's *Inferno*, Canto XXXIII. Reminiscent of the *Laocöon* and of Michelangelo, the dynamic forms of the original plaster, the expressive content, and the multifigured composition were a considerable achievement. Yet when it arrived in Paris in 1862 and was shown in the Salon of 1863, it met with unfavorable reactions from such critics as Théophile Thoré (1807–1869), although it gained Carpeaux a first prize and the attention of the press.

By 1863, Carpeaux had been introduced into the salon of the Princess Mathilde, cousin of Louis Napoleon, where important artists and writers such as Charles Augustin Saint-Beuve and Théophile Gautier gathered. Entry into this milieu brought with it commissions, including a bust of the *Princess Mathilde* (Petit Palais, Paris). It indicates Carpeaux's ability to capture not only a likeness but the dynamic quality of life that makes his portrait busts so vital. The liveliness of the modeled surface and sensitivity to the personality of the model is evident as well in *Marquis de La Valette*, (1863, Petit Palais), with its bittersweet smile and stately dignity. It is apparent also in the bust of *Eugénie Fiocre* (1869, Petit Palais), a dancer at the Opéra, whose youthful freshness is caught by Carpeaux in the animated forms and sensitive modeling.

Carpeaux received an important commission for pediment and cornice ornaments for the Pavillon de Flore of the new Louvre, and Baron Georges Haussmann requested a group for the new Church of La Trinité in 1863. Carpeaux's *Triumph of Flora* (1863–1866) for the Pavillon de Flore was criticized when it was unveiled because of the Rubensian voluptuousness of the female goddess. The sculptor had, in fact, quarreled violently with the architect, Hector Lefuel (1810–1881), and Napoleon III, following public opinion, had decided for Carpeaux, who from this point entered into intimacy with the court. (He had earlier, in 1853, managed to gain the attention of the emperor with a bas-relief titled *The Emperor Receiving Abd-el-Kader at Saint-Cloud* and had been commissioned to assist in decorating the Pavillon de Rohan.) He became virtually a court artist, recording its personages in sculpture and in paintings, the latter having recourse to a remarkably modern style in order to capture the color and activity of the imperial milieu. Commercial versions of Carpeaux's bust of the prince imperial and the enormously popular *The Prince Imperial and His Dog Nero* became the basis of the sculptor's personal fortune. In 1865 Carpeaux was asked by his friend, Garnier, to provide one of four reliefs for the facade of the new Opéra. The theme of the dance was completed in a large relief by Carpeaux in 1869. When it was unveiled to the public, *La Danse*, consisting of a group of female dancers surrounding a male figure or genie with a tambourine, caused a great scandal. Accusations that the work was morally offensive were accompanied by violent actions—a bottle of ink was thrown at the work by an outraged observer. The figures show Carpeaux's considerable understanding of the human body in motion (Carpeaux, like Edgar Degas somewhat later, studied the dancers at the Opéra), and the grouping of the figures a sure knowledge of structure and balance; however, the bacchanalian feeling of abandonment to sensuality is projected with enormous spirit and energy and is made all the more striking because the figures are so fresh and real. The critic Charles Blanc (1813–1882) complained that if you were to touch their skin, your finger would leave an imprint. The contrast with the three other reliefs by academic sculptors in the classical tradition is quite evident. Carpeaux's method was not to repeat the classical past but to observe nature closely and then create a work that maintained that living quality. Although he was supported by Garnier, it was decided that the group be replaced by another commissioned work, which would show greater respect for decency. The Franco-Prussian War, however, put an end to any such action.

The project Carpeaux was commissioned to do in 1867, the Fontaine de l'Observatoire, was completed and unveiled when he returned to Paris in 1874 after an interval spent in London during the war. The work was shared with the architect Gabriel Davioud and the sculptor Emmanuel Frémiet (1824–1910), but it is Carpeaux's sculpture that became famous. This sculpture represents the four continents with female figures of different races who uphold an armillary sphere surrounding a globe. Although not as successful as *La danse*, it nevertheless conveys a sense of movement on a monumental scale. During his stay in England, he sculpted a bust of *Charles Gounod* (1871, Fitzwilliam Museum, Cambridge), giving it a sense of pulsating life with the mouth open as if about to speak. Carpeaux also sculpted a head of *Jean-Léon Gérôme* in which the deeply modeled forms imply the painter's sense of determination. He visited Napoleon III in exile at Chislehurst and undertook a sculptured portrait of the deposed emperor, who died just a few days after its completion. In 1875, shortly before his death, Carpeaux was made an officer of the Legion of Honor, to which he had been named in 1866. Auguste Rodin (1840–1917), whose teacher Carpeaux was at the Petit Ecole in 1854, was considerably influenced in his early work by Carpeaux's concern for direct observation and lively modeling. Carpeaux died at Courbevoie, 11 or 12 October 1875, tormented until the end by a persecution complex derived from his painful early years of poverty.

V. Beyer et al., *Sur les traces de Jean Baptiste Carpeaux* (Paris, 1975); P. Fusco and H. W. Janson, *The Romantics to Rodin: French Nineteenth-Century Sculpture from North American Collections* (Los Angeles, 1980); R. Mirolli, *Nineteenth-Century French Sculpture: Monuments for the Middle-Class* (Louisville, 1971).

Beverley Giblon

Related entries: OPERA; RUDE.

CARVALHO, LEON (1825–1897), opera impresario; born Léon Carvaille at Port Louis, Ile Maurice, 18 January 1825. After studying briefly at the Paris Conservatoire, Carvalho sang supporting baritone roles at the Opéra Comique (1851–1855) and in 1853 married his more successful colleague, the soprano Marie Miolan (1827–1895; pupil of the celebrated tenor Gilbert Duprez [1806–1896], and winner of a *premier prix de chant* at the Conservatoire). Quarreling with the management of the Opéra Comique, Carvalho broke his contract and at the beginning of 1856 used his position as a principal creditor of the Théâtre Lyrique to become its director in place of Emile Perrin (1814–1885).

The Théâtre Lyrique had opened 27 September 1851 as the Opéra National, under the direction of Edmond Seveste. Its purpose, initially at the site of the former Théâtre Historique (Boulevard du Temple), was to rival the Opéra, the

Opéra Comique, and the Théâtre des Italiens as a producer of music drama at Paris. Seveste died in February 1852, and, under the direction of his brother Jules (died 30 June 1854), the theater asumed the name Théâtre Lyrique, which it kept until its demise in 1870. The Opéra Comique was its most immediate rival. Located at the Salle Favart during the Second Empire (except fot the 1853 season), directed by Perrin from 1848 to 1857 and again from 1862 to 1876, the Opéra Comique was distinguished from the Opéra primarily by its retention of spoken dialogue (the Théâtre Lyrique did not insist on the latter but sometimes used it). From 1825 through 1870, however, the opera of the Salle Favart languished under the domination of Eugène Scribe and Daniel François Auber (1782–1871; director of the Paris Conservatoire, 1842–1871, and chapel master at the Tuileries). The Théâtre Lyrique, on the other hand, was to enjoy its greatest élan under Carvalho's direction.

In particular, Carvalho's theater became a mecca for promising younger composers, whom he treated with a courtesy uncommon for the day. The first production under his direction (1 March 1856) was *La Fanchonette* of Louis Clapisson (1808–1866). Marie Carvalho enjoyed a great success, which she repeated on 19 September in *Les dragons de Villars* of Aimé Maillart (1817–1871) and on 27 December in *La Reine Topaze* of Victor Massé (1822–1884, chorus master at the Opéra from 1860 to 1876). In the following years Carvalho revived Weber's *Oberon* (1857), Mozart's *Marriage of Figaro* (also 1857; sung by Marie Carvalho and Delphine Ugalde [1829–1910]), and Gluck's *Orféo et Euridice*, the latter (19 November 1859) in a version prepared by Hector Berlioz (1803–1869) and sung by Pauline Viardot and Marie Constance Sass (1834–1907). On 3 October 1857 the Théâtre Lyrique produced *Maître Griffard*, the first opera of Léo Délibes (1836–1891). But it was in 1858 that Léon Carvalho began his most famous collaboration, staging on 15 January 1858 *Le médecin malgré lui* of Charles Gounod; on 19 March 1859 Gounod's *Faust* (with spoken dialogue, Marie Carvalho creating the role of Marguerite and enjoying perhaps her greatest success); and on 18 February 1860 the same composer's *Philémon et Baucis*. Mme. Carvalho thus arrived at the peak of her celebrity, having compensated magisterially for a rather light soprano voice through charm, style, and perfection of phrasing.

Worn out and in debt, Léon Carvalho withdrew on 1 April 1860 as director of the Théâtre Lyrique, leaving the theater in the charge of his secretary, Charles Réty. Marie Carvalho, who had sung every season at Covent Garden, now toured Germany, Belgium, and the French provinces. She and her husband returned, however, to the Théâtre Lyrique in 1862, on its move to Gabriel Davioud's new building on the place du Châtelet. The new theater (since 1968 the Théâtre de la Ville) was inaugurated 30 October 1862 with a performance of Gounod's *Hymne à la musique*, sung by an ensemble including Mme. Carvalho, Viardot, and the famous baritone Jean Baptiste Faure (1830–1914). In this second period of his directorship (1862–1868), Carvalho continued to reveal the character that had won him both fame and notoriety. While composers complained, with justification, of the Carvalhos' tendency to alter and to prune scores, none could deny Léon Carvalho's intelligence and skill as a producer, his charm and amiability, and, above all, his boldness. There were many examples of the last. Carvalho commissioned *Les pêcheurs de perles* of George Bizet (1838–1875) on the strength of a state subsidy not due until the following year (the opera premiered 30 September 1863 and, despite Berlioz's praise in the *Journal des débats,* was a comparative failure), and he offered to Berlioz, France's greatest living composer, a stage often denied him. Berlioz had completed *Les Troyens* in April 1858, words and music, but had been unable to arrange its production despite appeals to the emperor and empress, Prince Napoleon, the Opéra, and the minister of fine arts. Carvalho required the work to be cut in half (it would have taken five hours to stage it in its entirety) and presented the last three of its five acts as *Les Troyens à Carthage* on 4 November 1863. Even so, and despite praise by Jean Baptiste Camille Corot, Giacomo Meyerbeer, and Bizet, the work enjoyed no great popular success, although the income enabled Berlioz to quit his job as music critic for the *Journal des débats.* During the 1860s Carvalho staged other notable premières: Verdi's *Rigoletto* (24 December 1863; it had received its Italian première in 1851), Gounod's *Mireille* (19 March 1864; Marie Carvalho created the role of Mireille), the Paris version of Verdi's *Macbeth* (21 April 1865), Gounod's *Roméo et Juliette* (27 April 1867; with Marie Carvalho as Juliette), and Bizet's *La jolie fille de Perthe* (26 December 1867; a failure).

Financial problems continued. By 1868 the Théâtre Lyrique was bankrupt, although Marie Carvalho had not drawn her salary for four years. Léon Carvalho's attempt to combine the Théâtre Lyrique and the Théâtre des Italiens under one direction failed, and in 1868 he resigned the former into the hands of Jules Pasdeloup. From 1872 to 1874, Carvalho directed the Vaudeville theater before becoming, in January 1874, chief producer at the Opéra. Marie Carvalho, who sang at the Opéra from 1869 to 1872 and at the Opéra Comique from 1872 to 1874, returned to the Opéra in 1875 at a salary of 60,000 francs, before following her husband once again to the Opéra Comique in 1877. She retired in 1885 and died at Puys (Seine-Inférieure) 10 July 1895. One of Léon Carvalho's last services to the composers of the Second Empire was to present Jacques Offenbach's *Les contes d'Hoffmann* at the Opéra Comique in February 1881. He died at Paris, 29 December 1897.

E. Accoyer-Spoll, *Mme Carvalho* (Paris, 1885); M. Cooper, *Opéra comique* (London, 1949); G. Cucuel, *Les créateurs de l'opéra comique français* (Paris, 1914); *RDM*, no. 40 (1933); A. Soubies and C. Malherbe, *Histoire de l'Opéra Comique: La seconde Salle Favart (1840–1887)* (Paris, 1892–1893); A. Soubies, *Soixante-neuf ans à l'Opéra Comique en deux pages, 1825–1894* (Paris, 1894); T. J. Walsh, *Second Empire Opera: The Théâtre Lyrique, Paris, 1851–1870* (London, 1981).

Related entries: CONCERT LIFE; DAVIOUD; DELIBES; GOUNOD; MEYERBEER; OFFENBACH; PASDELOUP; SCRIBE; THOMAS; VIARDOT.

CATHOLICISM. See GALLICANISM.

CAVAILLE-COLL, ARISTIDE (1811–1899), organ builder, called the "creator of the French romantic organ"; born at Montpellier, 4 February 1811, where the family, whose surname of Hyacinthe had been changed by Aristide's father, Dominique (1771–1862), had built organs and pianos since the mid-eighteenth century. Encouraged by Gioacchino Rossini (1792–1868), Aristide came to Paris in the fall of 1833 to compete for a contract to build an organ for the abbey church of Saint Denis.

The revival of French organ music had already begun, with the appointment of François Boëly (1785–1858) to the Paris Conservatoire. The achievements of the Cavaillé-Coll family, combined with the playing and teaching of the Belgian organist Nicolas Jacques Lemmens (1823–1881) and of his teacher, the German Adolphe Friedrich Hesse (1809-1863), were to play a decisive role in the great élan that was to characterize organ music at Paris during the Second Empire. Aristide won the Saint Denis contract, and the organ was built (completed 1841) by a family consortium according to his designs. Later the family moved its business to Paris. Aristide Cavaillé-Coll designed and built (or rebuilt) organs for the Paris churches of Saint Jean-Saint François (1844), La Madeleine (1846–1848), Saint Vincent de Paul (1850), Saint Sulpice (completed 1862–1863; with 6,500 pipes the Saint Sulpice organ was the largest in Europe), Saint François Xavier, La Trinité, Saint Augustin (1868), and Sainte Clotilde (1859; the last three were churches built as part of Baron Georges Haussmann's embellishment of the "new Paris"). In addition, Cavaillé-Coll rebuilt the organs of Notre Dame (1863–1858). After the fall of the Second Empire, he built (in 1878) the organ of the Salle des Fêtes of the newly constructed Palais du Trocadéro.

The greatest French organ virtuosi and composers of the day were inspired by these instruments. And Paris of the Second Empire boasted many talented organists. In 1853 the government had extended support to the Ecole de Musique Religieuse et Classique of Louis Niedermeyer (1802–1861) in an attempt to reinvigorate church music. A number of key organ appointments also contributed to that end: Antoine Batiste (1820–1876) and Bazille to Saint Eustache (late 1850s and early 1860s), where the great organ, built in 1854, was one of the most beautiful in Paris; Louis Lefébure-Wély (1817–1869) to Saint Roch (1831–1847), La Madeleine (1847–1857), and Saint Sulpice (1863–1869); Charles Chauvet (1837–1871) to Saint Merri (1866–1869) and La Trinité (from 1869); Eugène Gigout (1844–1925), a student of Camille Saint-Saëns and a professor at the Ecole Niedermeyer, to Saint Augustin (1863–1925); François Benoist (1794–1878), professor at the Conservatoire, to Saint Germain l'Auxerrois (from 1837); Charles M. Widor (1845–1937) to Saint Sulpice (from 1870 to 1937); and Léo Delibes (1836–1891) to Saint Pierre de Chaillot (1853–1862) and Saint Jean-Saint François (1862–1871). Especially important were the appointments of Camille Saint-Saëns to La Madeleine, 7 December 1857 (replacing Lefébure-Wély), and of César Franck (1822–1890) to Sainte Clotilde in 1859.

Saint-Saëns, who had been a pupil of Boëly and Benoist and who had a strong religious sense, had been organist briefly at Saint Séverin (1853) and at Saint

Merri (1853–1857) before coming to La Madeleine, where he remained until 1876 (from 1861 to 1865 he was also professor of piano at the Ecole Niedermeyer). The position of organist at La Madeleine was much sought after, for it commanded prestige and a good salary. César Franck, born at Liège, Belgium, the son of a banker, had been brought by his father to the Paris Conservatoire in 1837 where he proved a brilliant pupil. Later, straitened financial circumstances imposed on him an austere routine. He composed music from 5 A.M. to 7 A.M., as well as in the evenings and on holidays, but most of his time was devoted to lessons and to his duties as organist, first at Saint Jean-Saint François and then, from 1858, at Sainte Clotilde, where, with Lefébure-Wély's help, he inaugurated Cavaillé-Coll's newly installed organ on 19 December 1859. A great organist and an incomparable improviser, Franck became the center each Sunday of a circle of pupils and such friends and admirers as Franz Liszt (1811–1886). His saint-like modesty belied the fact that after 1870 he would help to engender a rebirth of French music. During the Second Empire, he wrote little (although his *Six pièces* for organ, based on his after-service improvisations and written between 1860 and 1862, profoundly influenced French organ music, and in 1869 he began his masterwork, *Les béatitudes*). The Second Empire public knew Franck only as a painfully shy Belgian organ virtuoso (he would become a naturalized Frenchman in 1873).

Aristide Cavaillé-Coll during his lifetime built almost five hundred organs in France, Spain, and South America, although many have since been altered. The family exhibited at all the international expositions, winning first-class medals. Aristide, who was named knight of the Legion of Honor in 1849 and officer in 1878, died at Paris on 13 October 1899, leaving three sons to continue the family's activities in Europe, the Americas, and Australia.

C. and E. Cavaillé-Coll, *Aristide Cavaillé-Coll: Ses origines, sa vie, ses oeuvres* (Paris, 1929); L. Davies, *César Franck and His Circle* (London, 1970); C. Noizette de Crausat, "Aristide Cavaillé-Coll (1811–1899)," *Acta organologica* 10 (1976); F. N. Speller, "Aristide Cavaillé-Coll: Organ Builder" (Ph.D. diss., University of Colorado, 1968); M. Vanmackelberg, "L'esthétique d'Aristide Cavaillé-Coll," *L'orgue*, no. 127 (1968). *Related entry:* SAINT-SAENS.

CENSORSHIP. See PRESS REGIME.

CENTRAL MARKET. See LES HALLES CENTRALES.

CHAMBERY, the ancient capital of the Duchy of Savoy, significant for nineteenth-century history because it served as the diplomatic stage for Italian unification. At Plombières in July 1858, Napoleon III had promised the Sardinian prime minister, Count Camillo Benso di Cavour, that he would support the Italian cause in a war against Austria. Sardinia would receive at least the provinces of Venetia and Lombardy, and France would be rewarded for its services by the annexation of the duchies of Nice and Savoy. However, at Villafranca in July 1859, the French emperor made peace with Emperor Francis Joseph of Austria before he had wrested Venetia from him. Napoleon III therefore did not lay claim to Nice and Savoy. By the Villafranca terms (and by the peace treaty of Zurich, signed 10 November 1859), the French emperor was required to encourage the populations of the Italian states that had overthrown their rulers (notably the Romagna, Parma, Modena, and Tuscany) to return to the prewar status quo. He did so. But since force was not to be used and since Sardinian agents were active and Sardinian troops present, the sentiment for annexation to Sardinia grew steadily.

During the summer of 1859, constituent assemblies were elected with instructions to vote for annexation. On 9 September 1859, in an interview with Count Francesco Arese at Saint-Sauveur in the Pyrenees, Napoleon III agreed that Sardinia could have Parma as well as Lombardy. His hope was to reserve other decisions for a European congress. However, Britain consented in November to the annexation of central Italy by Sardinia, and the publication at Paris in December 1859 of a semiofficial pamphlet, *Le Pape et le congrès*, which called on Pius IX to surrender the Romagna (and, indeed, all of his provinces), marked the indefinite adjournment of the congress. In January 1860 Cavour, who had resigned at the time of Villafranca, once again became prime minister, and Edouard Thouvenel replaced Alexandre Walewski as French foreign minister. Thouvenel was determined that France should allow the people of central Italy to join Sardinia in return for the annexation of Nice and Savoy by France. The bargain was struck in March and April 1860. Pope Pius IX deeply resented the loss of the Romagna and Napoleon III's acquiescence in Cavour's actions (letter of Napoleon III to Pius IX, 31 December 1859; Pius IX's allocution of 1 January 1860), but worse was to follow. Giuseppe Garibaldi, a Niçoise, had planned a filibuster to undo the French annexation of Nice and Savoy, but his attention was diverted (with the connivance of Cavour) to Sicily where a rebellion against Neapolitan rule had failed in early April. On 5 May 1860 Garibaldi sailed from Genoa with some twelve hundred to fourteen hundred men, the Red Shirts. Within several weeks, he had gained control of the island and stood poised to cross over to the mainland. Although without sympathy for the Neapolitan Bourbons, Napoleon III still cherished his schemes for an Italian confederation. In June 1860 he suggested mediation of the crisis in southern Italy with a view toward preserving the Neapolitan state. In July he proposed that Britain and France together should prevent Garibaldi from crossing the Straits of Messina. London refused; France declined to act alone; and on 18 August 1860 Garibaldi landed in southern Italy. The outcome had now become inevitable, despite the resistance of the young Neapolitan king, Francis II, who had announced reforms and, on Napoleon III's suggestion, entered into negotiations with Sardinia. As Garibaldi advanced northward, apprehension grew that his ultimate destination might be Rome, Nice, or Venetia.

In late August, Napoleon III and Eugénie paid an official visit to Savoy on their way to Algeria. Meanwhile Cavour, fearing a confrontation between the

French garrison at Rome and the advancing Garibaldians, had devised a solution. He would prepare an ultimatum for Rome, demanding that the papal volunteers (led by a Frenchman, General Louis Lamoricière [1806–1865]) be disbanded. If the ultimatum were rejected, Sardinia would send troops into the provinces remaining to the pope (Umbria and the Marches). With its army on papal territory, Sardinia could interject a force between Rome and Garibaldi. At the same time, such an action would throttle the revolution in southern Italy that threatened to revive the republican enthusiasms of 1848 and would open the way to further annexations of papal territory. But French consent was needed. Cavour therefore sent two emissaries to Chambéry, General Enrico Cialdini and Luigi Farini, president of the Italian National Society. Cavour's plan was submitted to Napoleon III on 28 August 1860 and received his approval. "Do it," he is reported to have said, "but do it quickly." He then departed (1 September) for Algeria, thus becoming almost inaccessible to his ministers. On 7 September Cavour sent his ultimatum to Rome; on 10 September he launched an invasion of the Papal States; on 18 September Lamoricière was defeated at Castelfidardo; on 26 October 1860 Garibaldi met King Victor Emmanuel II of Sardinia and made his submission. Thus Cavour, with the complicity of Napoleon III, converted Garibaldi's filibuster into a military conquest by Sardinia of Naples, Umbria, and the Marches (confirmed by plebiscites in early November 1860).

Although Napoleon III had permitted this final unification of Italy, it seems reasonable to believe that he regretted the absorption of Naples by Sardinia (French ships protected Gaeta, to which Francis II fled on 7 September, from mid-October 1860 until the end of January 1861, and it was on a French ship that the king left Gaeta for papal territory on 14 February 1861). Moreover, the French emperor seems to have felt that he had been misled at Chambéry by Cavour who (Napoleon III believed) had agreed not to invade the Papal States without the pretext of an insurrection and to go subsequently to a European congress. In mid-September 1860, France broke diplomatic relations with Sardinia, and it was not until June 1861, following the death of Cavour, that Paris recognized the Kingdom of Italy, which had been proclaimed in March 1861.

G. del Bono, *Cavour e Napoleone III: Le annessioni dell'Italia centrale al regno di Sardegna, 1859–1860* (Turin, 1941); F. Boyer, "L'affrontement des escadres françaises et piémontaises à Gaëte, Octobre 1860," in *Studi in memoria di N. Cortese* (1976); "La marine française et Garibaldi [mai-août 1860]," *Archivio storico messinese* 9–10, series 3 (1957–1959), and "La politique de Napoléon III et l'escadre française à Gaëte, novembre 1860–janvier 1861," *RSR* 59, no. 2 (April–June 1972); L. M. Case, "Thouvenel et la rupture des relations diplomatiques franco-sardes en 1860," *RHMC* 7 (April–June 1960); R. L. Cummings, "The French Effort to Block Garibaldi at the Straits, 1860," *Historian* 31 (February 1969); C. Pouthas, "La médiation de Napoléon III entre le roi de Naples, les Siciliens, et le gouvernement piémontais, mai–août 1860," *RSR* 39 (October–December 1952); C. Vidal, *La reconnaissance du Royaume d'Italie par Napoléon III, juin–juillet, 1861* (Paris, 1954).

Ivan Scott

Related entries: ITALIAN CONFEDERATION; NATIONALITIES; ROMAN QUESTION; VILLAFRANCA.

CHAMBORD, HENRI CHARLES FERDINAND MARIE DIEUDONNE D'ARTOIS, DUC DE BORDEAUX, COMTE DE (1820–1883), legitimist pretender to the French throne; born 29 September 1820 in Paris. The most dramatic point in the life of the comte de Chambord, grandson of Charles X, posthumous son of the duc de Berry, was in 1873 when he dashed monarchist hopes by refusing to accept the tricolor as a condition to ascending the throne. He was, however, a considerable factor in shaping French political life in the days of the Second Empire. During the chaos of 1848–1849, the legitimists were not in a position to take advantage of the basic strength of the Bourbon pretender, but by 1851 fusionist activity (efforts to secure an agreement between Bourbons and Orleanists) no doubt was a factor in causing Louis Napoleon to stage his coup d'état when he did. From 1851 to 1857 various overtures were made by the princes of Orleans to effect a fusion (Chambord detested the word, preferring *union*, which implied subordination of the younger branch). Particularly the duc de Nemours, who had legitimist leanings, pushed these negotiations far. Chambord himself showed signs of conciliatory attitudes toward the usurping family of 1830, but he would never compromise on the principle of hereditary monarchy, of which he regarded himself the symbol, and therefore would not grant the Orleanists the guarantees they demanded or accept the tricolor. By 1857 the cause of fusion was ruptured, but had there been a reconciliation, Napoleon III's reign would have been threatened.

During the Second Republic, a group of monarchist parliamentarians called themselves the Bureau du roi, but by the early 1850s another group of royalists, more truly representing the cause of legitimacy, carried on in Paris the business of the pretender, who divided his time between Frohsdorf in Austria (near Wiener Neustadt) and, in winter, Venice (Goritzia after 1866). Despite the efforts of "attachés," who shuttled between Paris and the court in exile, the distance between the legitimate king and his people widened. Chambord had obstacles to overcome, including a limp resulting from a fall from a horse in 1844, but the wife he had taken in 1846, Marie-Thérèse of Modena, tended to reinforce his ideological and actual distance from Paris. Had he married the Grand Duchess Olga of Russia, he might have had a powerful ally. Chambord not only lacked such reinforcement, he did not even have an heir, a circumstance that goes far in explaining why the Orleanists were willing to accept subordination in the 1870s.

While in exile in Austria in the 1860s, Chambord, often called Henri V, formulated a large part of his legitimist program. Basing everything on traditional and hereditary monarchy, he offered decentralization as his key to political freedom. His letter on decentralization (14 November 1862) was his principal statement against the administrative centralization of the Revolution and Napoleon. His letter on workers (20 April 1865), although couched in traditional terms, actually reflected Christian socialist ideas and the thinking of Frédéric Le Play. He advocated the revival of corporatism, which had been disrupted by revolutionary individualism. His letter on agriculture (12 March 1866) was innovative. His court was high-minded, but the death of the skillful duc de Lévis in 1863 may have been the loss that accounts for some of the failure of the legitimist cause.

In the 1850s Napoleon III appeared to be the champion of the pope, thus undermining much of Chambord's appeal, but by 1859 he was actively building Italy at the expense of the pontiff. By 1870 the fall of Rome, as well as the fall of France, made Chambord again the hope of the Catholics as well as the legitimists. The comte de Chambord died at Frohsdorf, 24 August 1883.

M. L. Brown, Jr., *The Comte de Chambord* (Durham, N.C., 1967); A. Jossinet, *Henri V, duc de Bordeaux, comte de Chambord* (Paris, 1983).

Marvin L. Brown, Jr.

Related entry: LEGITIMISM.

CHAMPFLEURY (pseudonym of JULES HUSSON [1821 1889]), novelist and art critic; founder of the realist school of literature in France; born at Laon, 10 September 1821. On arriving at Paris, Champfleury shared lodgings with Henri Murger (1822–1861) and lived a bohemian life not particularly suited to his practical and ambitious nature and that he described more accurately than in Murger's *Scènes de la vie de bohème* (1847–1849). Taking the name Fleury and then Champfleury, he moved in the Café Momus circle of Murger, Félix Nadar, Théodore de Banville, Charles Baudelaire (with whom he briefly edited *Le salut public* in 1848), and Gérard de Nerval. At the editorial offices of *Le corsaire-satan*, he met a number of left-wing intellectuals and artists, including Pierre Joseph Proudhon and Gustave Courbet. Champfleury began his literary caeer as an art critic, and it was in this context that he first used the term *realism*. He was one of Gustave Courbet's few defenders and praised his painting, *The Burial at Ornans*, as a landmark of a new movement. His first articles appeared in *Le corsaire-satan* and in *L'artiste*. After a brief period at Hippolyte de Villemessant's *L'événement*, Champfleury contributed a great many articles, once again on art, to *Le messager de l'Assemblée*. It was here that he published the first draft of his study on the Le Nain brothers, seventeenth-century painters of his native Laon, which appeared in 1852. The coup d'état of December 1851 and its subsequent effects on the press decided the left-wing journalist to turn his attention to the novel.

Champfleury's realist theories carried over into his novels. *Chien caillou* (1847) had already attracted some attention and had been praised even by Victor Hugo. But it was with *Les aventures de Mademoiselle Mariette* (1853), a narrative based on his early life and on his friendship with Murger and Banville, that Champfleury's name and the philosophy he expounded came into prominence. *Mademoiselle Mariette* and the novels produced over the next few years were far from being outstanding literary creations. Champfleury suffered from two major handicaps. Because of his lack of formal education, the language of his novels is often banal and even incorrect. Further, his precarious financial situation forced him to produce novels at a much quicker rate than he might otherwise have done. Nonetheless, his stories, based on provincial life and often on characters he had known in his youth, enjoyed wide popularity. He wrote for a class that was relatively new to literature—the lower middle class—and his stories, simple in plot and theme and characterized by humor and a sometimes facile sentimentality, were understood and appreciated by this relatively uncultured public.

In the 1850s Champfleury became the recognized leader of the realist movement, with his novels appearing in serialized form in several newspapers, among them *La presse,* the *Revue de Paris,* the *Journal pour tous,* and *L'opinion nationale.* Furthermore, the restrictions placed on political journalism during the Second Empire inevitably led to greater emphasis in the press on quarrels between schools of literary and artistic thought. The controversy between the realists and their detractors (who viewed realist writings as dull and vulgar) reached its height in 1855–1856. Champfleury in 1855 joined the *cénacle* centered around Courbet, which met on Thursdays at the Brasserie Andler. He wrote the catalog for the realist artist's private showing of his paintings in that year (*Le Réalisme—G. Courbet*) and published his first manifesto on realism in the 2 September 1855 issue of *L'artiste* in the form of a letter to George Sand on Courbet. The next year, which was marked by the publication of the serialized version of Flaubert's *Madame Bovary,* saw the publication of the first issue of the journal *Le réalisme.* Although it was in fact Edmond Duranty who founded the periodical and who, under various pseudonyms, wrote many of the articles, the ideas expressed in it were Champfleury's to a large extent. The first issue was devoted to theoretical considerations. Subsequent numbers (six in all) were chiefly composed of panegyrics to "approved" writers (such as Nicolas Restif de la Bretonne, H. Stendhal, H. Balzac, and, of course, Champfleury), alternating with attacks on those who espoused other theories of literature, especially Victor Hugo and the romantics. Finally, in 1857, Champfleury himself collected his own articles, added a preface, and published them under the title of *Le réalisme.*

Champfleury and his followers insisted that realism as a theory represented no more than the codification of precepts currently being followed by predominant novelists of the day. They rejected the historical novel (as popularized by Alexandre Dumas and Hugo) because of the degree of imagination involved in its creation. For them, serious literature was characterized by a minimum of invention and a maximum of scrupulously recorded observation. Further, they took exception to the romantic writers' focusing on exceptional individuals in extraordinary circumstances. Realism, for them, was concerned with observation of the actions and interactions of ordinary people in day-to-day life. This depiction had a socially useful function insofar as it served to make readers more aware of their environment and signaled the need for reform. To these ends, Champfleury advocated the use of the simplest language possible in order to reach a wide sector of the reading public. Because realism depended not only on aesthetic but also, to some extent, on political affiliations, Champfleury, with his vaguely republican leanings, had his share of difficulties with censorship during the Second Empire. His publisher, Louis Hachette, was forced to destroy the remaining copies of the 1856 edition of *Mademoiselle Mariette*; in 1857, *La succession de Camus* was banned in France and had to be published in Belgium.

As the 1860s progressed, Champfleury's production of novels virtually ceased, the one notable exception being *Le violon de faïence* (1862), which Charles Augustin Sainte-Beuve praised in his *Nouveaux lundis*. After 1860, Champfleury turned his attention back to art, producing works on the history of caricature, popular imagery, ceramics, and porcelain. To the other unpopular causes he had espoused (the paintings of Courbet, the novels of Flaubert, the poetry of Baudelaire), he added the music of Richard Wagner (1813–1883). In 1872, he was named curator of the museum at Sèvres, a post he retained until his death at Sèvres, 6 December 1889.

Other Champfleury novels written during the Second Empire include: *Les bourgeois de Molinchart* (1854), *Les souffrances du Professeur Delteil* (1857), *Grandeur et décadence d'une serinette* (1857), *Les amoureux de Sainte-Périne* (1858), and *La mascarade de la vie parisienne* (1859). As an art critic and historian, Champfleury produced: *Les peintres de Laon et de Saint-Quentin* (1855), *De la littérature populaire en France* (1861), *Grandes figures d'hier et d'aujourd'hui* (1861), *Nouvelles recherches sur la vie et l'oeuvre des frères Le Nain* (1862), *Histoire de la caricature antique* (1865), *Histoire des faïences patriotiques sous la Révolution* (1867), *Les chats* (1869), *Histoire de l'imagerie populaire* (1869), and *Histoire de la caricature au Moyen Age* (1870).

G. and J. Lacambre, *Champfleury: Le Realisme* (Paris, 1973).

Dorothy E. Speirs

Related entries: COURBET; DURANTY; FLAUBERT; GONCOURT; ZOLA.

CHARCOT, JEAN MARTIN (1825–1893), neurologist and psychiatrist; born 29 November 1825 at Paris. Charcot belonged to the Parisian petite bourgeoisie (his father was a manufacturer of coaches). Awarded the M.D. degree in 1853, he entered bonapartist circles with his appointment as Achille Fould's family physician but after 1870 would be adopted by the republicans as a consequence of his links with Léon Gambetta. Charcot was made physician to the Salpêtrière Hospital in 1862, where he shortly afterward created a major neurology department. Although his main scientific interest lay in pathological anatomy, of which he was appointed professor in the Faculty of Medicine in 1872, Salpêtrière's numerous mental patients afforded Charcot the opportunity to observe and classify a wide variety of nervous disorders. He established clinical neurology as an autonomous discipline and assumed the newly created Chair of Clinical Diseases of the Nervous System in 1882.

Charcot, a brilliant teacher, succeeded in establishing the Salpêtrière as one of Europe's preeminent centers of postgraduate neurological education and research. His pioneering, if controversial, researches and lectures on hysteria (which he defined as nervous rather than physical in origin), neuroses, and hypnosis influenced the later psychological theories of Sigmund Freud (who studied at the Salpêtrière from 1885 to 1886) and Pierre Janet (1859–1947).

Charcot's most significant theoretical and clinical achievements include differentiating multiple sclerosis from Parkinson's disease (1868) with which it had been confused; studies on cerebral localization; description of the neurogenic arthropathies now known as Charcot's joints; studies on gout and chronic rheumatism; description of amyotrophic lateral sclerosis (also called Charcot's disease); and (with his pupil Charles Jacques Bouchard [1837–1915]) studies on the secondary degeneration of the spinal cord and on the pathogenesis of cerebral hemorrhages. Thus he stands as one of the founders of modern neurology.

Charcot became a member of the Société de Biologie in 1851 and was elected vice-president in 1860; he was elected to the Academy of Medicine in 1872 and to the Academy of Sciences in 1883. In his psychiatric interests, he may be seen as the best known of those mid-century figures who made the Second Empire almost as revolutionary in psychiatry as in economic development and finance: J. P. Falret (1794–1870), J. G. F. Baillarger (1809–1890), C. Lasègue (1816–1883), P. Briquet (1796–1881), L. F. Calmeil (1798–1895), A. J. F. Brière de Boismont (1797–1881), and Ulysse Trélat (1829–1890). Charcot died near Vézelay, 16 August 1893.

J. M. Charcot, *Oeuvres complètes*, 13 vols. (Paris, 1880–1893); G. Guillain, *J. M. Charcot: Sa vie, son oeuvre* (Paris, 1955); A. R. G. Owen, *Hysteria, Hypnosis, and Healing: The Work of J. M. Charcot* (London, 1971); T. Zeldin, *France, 1848–1945: Anxiety and Hypocrisy* (New York, 1981).

Martin Fichman

Related entry: BERNARD.

CHASSELOUP-LAUBAT, PROSPER, MARQUIS DE (1805–1873), one of the ablest ministers of the Second Empire, noted especially for his role as minister of marine and colonies; born 29 March 1805, Alexandria (Italy). Chasseloup-Laubat was the third son of Napoleon I's general, François Chasseloup-Laubat (died 1833). Napoleon I and Josephine were his godparents. He succeeded to the title on the death of his elder brother, Justin Prudent (1802–1863), a general much honored under the Second Empire.

A graduate of the Lycée Louis Le Grand, Chasseloup-Laubat enjoyed an active administrative career under the July Monarchy. He was a member of the Conseil d'Etat, president of the conseil général of the Charente-Inférieure, deputy, and railroad company president. From the Revolution of 1848, his political allegiance altered from Center-Left to conservative. As a member of the Legislative Assembly from May 1849, he rallied to Louis Napoleon, serving as minister of marine from 10 April to 26 October 1851. At the coup d'état, Chasseloup-Laubat was appointed, as was his brother, to the Consultative Commission (a temporary Conseil d'Etat) and played a major role in shaping the new legislative lower house, the Corps Législatif, to which he was elected in 1852 and 1857 as an official candidate. He succeeded Prince Napoleon as minister of Algeria and the colonies on 24 March 1859, visited Algeria in April, and sponsored a number of reforms in its administration.

With his appointment as minister of marine and colonies on 24 November 1860, Chasseloup-Laubat began his most important role in the Second Empire. His ministry (1860–1867) coincided with the transition from sail to steam, wood to iron and steel, and paddle wheel to screw-propeller. He presided over these crucial developments with a skillful hand, championing Stanislas Dupuy de Lôme's pioneering efforts in the development of ironclad vessels, and streamlining naval administration. Chasseloup-Laubat was also influential in the development of the French colonial empire. He seconded General Louis Faidherbe's efforts in Senegal, played an important role in the development of the Antilles, Réunion, and Nouvelle Calédonie, and persuaded a reluctant Napoleon III (no great enthusiast for collecting colonies) to annex Cochinchina. Named to the Senate in 1862 and awarded the grand cross of the Legion of Honor in 1866, Chasseloup-Laubat was not renamed to the cabinet in the aftermath of the 19 January 1867 reform decree.

Although a sincere friend of the emperor, Chasseloup-Laubat was always a moderate within the bonapartist ranks. From 1852 to 1857, he had been one of those calling for greater control over the budget by the Corps Législatif (the *budgétaires*) and was a regular contributor to the *Revue des deux mondes*. A man of uncompromising integrity (he sold all his stock when he entered government and, later, as president of the Conseil d'Etat refused to draw his salary), Chasseloup-Laubat was an early advocate of liberalization of the regime. Within the Council of Ministers, only he and Comte Alexandre Walewski supported the reform decree of November 1860. It was to the former minister of marine that Napoleon III turned as the parliamentary Empire emerged in 1869. Called to preside over the Conseil d'Etat on 17 July 1869, Chasseloup-Laubat directed the revision of the constitution that followed the elections of that year. He gave a liberal interpretation to the thought of the emperor, including among the new prerogatives of the Corps Législatif that of initiating legislation. Unacceptable to some opponents of the Empire, although Emile Ollivier would have had him in the government of 2 January 1870, Chasseloup-Laubat in December 1869 retired to the Senate and to his various nonpolitical duties including that of president of the Société de Géographie de Paris (from 1864). He died at Versailles, 29 March 1873.

A. Duchêne, *Un ministre trop oublié, Chasseloup-Laubat* (Paris, 1932); F. Lombard, *Un grand ministre de Napoléon III, Chasseloup-Laubat* (Poitiers, 1970).

Related entries: DUPUY DE LOME; LIBERAL EMPIRE; REFORM.

CHASSEPOT, the first modern military rifle, standard infantry issue of the French army from 1866 to 1874. Prussia had adopted in 1848 the first true breech-loader (the Dreyse). This weapon, which was later rifled, made use of a self-contained cartridge fired by a long needle; hence its usual designation, "needle gun." Antoine Alphonse Chassepot (born Mützig, 4 March 1833; died Gagny, 1905), son of an arms controller and himself destined for the same career, began in 1857 a series of inventions improving on the Dreyse. The new rifle was perfected between 1863 and 1866. The chassepot was a breech-loading, bolt-action rifle that expelled its 11 millimeter projectile by means of a percussion cap exploded by a firing pin at the rate of seven to eight shots per minute. It had several advantages over the Dreyse: a gas-tight chamber (achieved by using a rubber ring seal), a barrel drilled from a single steel bar, and a range of sixteen hundred yards, compared with the Dreyse's six hundred. Its smaller-caliber ammunition was also lighter to carry. Thought was given to its adoption from 1863, when field trials began, but objections were raised, especially by Marshal Jacques Louis Randon: it was untried; it would use too much ammunition; it recoiled too violently; and, because of the small caliber, it fouled easily. When, however, the Prussian needle gun contributed dramatically to the defeat of Austria at Sadowa on 4 July 1866, Napoleon III intervened. The chassepot was patented 27 August 1866 and adopted by the state three days later. By April 1867 ten thousand had been issued. It was used by the French force that defeated Garibaldi's troops at Mentana in November 1867 and became the cause of a diplomatic incident when a telegram in which the French commander praised the efficiency of the new weapon was published in the *Moniteur*. Chassepot was rewarded for his inventions by being named to the Legion of Honor and receiving 30,000 francs. Still an arms controller, he sold his patents to the firm of Cahen and Lyon, himself becoming a partner. The transaction led to a quarrel with the army, and he resigned from the central arms control depot 1 March 1867. The chassepot was not enough to turn the tide of war in 1870–1871. Modified for use with new metallic percussion cartridges, it became the Gras rifle in 1874.

P. Chassepot, "Antoine-Alphonse Chassepot, l'inventeur et l'homme," *Armes et uniformes de l'histoire*, no. 14 (1973).

Related entries: FRANCO-PRUSSIAN WAR; MENTANA.

CHASSERIAU, THEODORE (1819–1856), painter and engraver of biblical, mythological, and Oriental scenes and murals. Born at Santa Barbara de Samana (Santo Domingo), 20 September 1819, where his father was stationed as a French diplomat, Chassériau and his family moved back to France when he was two years old. He drew at an early age and began to study with Dominique Ingres in 1830. His first work, accepted in the Salon of 1836 when he was only seventeen years old, was a diptych with a religious theme. He went to Italy in 1840 to join Ingres, who had been there since 1834, but since Chassériau had already come into contact with artists such as Eugène Delacroix who expressed a romantic sensibility, he felt he could no longer gain from his association with Ingres. Chassériau received several commissions to do large wall decorations when he returned to Paris, such as the frescoes at the Church of St. Séverin in 1841, and, in 1844, those of the stairway at the Palais de la Cour des Comptes, Quai d'Orsay, whose theme was an allegory of war and peace. It was these latter frescoes that inspired Pierre Puvis de Chavannes, but unfortunately they were destroyed by fire during the Commune in 1871 except for a few fragments now in the Louvre. A trip to North Africa in 1846 provided Chassériau with subject matter and motifs in the form of drawings and sketches, which were to occupy him for the remainder of his short life. Representative of these interests are *Jewesses on a Balcony* (1849) and *Arab Horsemen after Battle* (1850, both Louvre, Paris). The subject and treatment recall the works of Delacroix but lack his expressive power.

In 1852 Chassériau received a commission to decorate the apse of the Church of Saint Philippe du Roule and in 1855 the walls of the baptismal chapel of the Church of Saint Roch. His smaller easel paintings, portraits, and mythological scenes show his attempt to combine the classical training dependent on line derived from Ingres with the more expressive color and forms of Delacroix. A painting that demonstrates Chassériau's endeavor to reconcile these two streams is *Tepidarium, the Hall Where the Women of Pompeii Came to Rest and Dry Themselves on Emerging from the Bath* (1853, Louvre), shown in the Salon of 1853, and purchased that year by the state. Inspired by the recent uncovering of such a room in Pompeii, Chassériau painted a scene based in part on factual knowledge of an archeological discovery, combining the drawing skills and classicist nude female figures derived from Ingres with the exoticism and sensuality of Delacroix. Chassériau was named to the Legion of Honor in 1849 and was awarded a second-class medal at the Paris international exposition of 1855. His friend Théophile Gautier praised his work in his writings, as did Edmond About, and he was admired by Gustave Moreau. He died at Paris, 8 October 1856.

L. Bénédite, *Théodore Chassériau: Sa vie et son oeuvre*, 2 vols. (Paris, 1932); M. Sandoz, *Théodore Chassériau: Catalogue raisonné des peintures et des estampes* (Paris, 1974); M. Sérullaz and R. Bacou, *Théodore Chassériau, 1819–1856, dessins* (Paris, 1957).

Beverley Giblon

CHEVALIER, MICHEL (1806–1879), economist, expert on public works, senator, *conseiller d'état*, and influential figure during the Second Empire. Chevalier was one of the chief architects of the 1860 Anglo-French treaty of commerce. Born the son of a minor civil servant at Limoges, 13 January 1806, he early proved to be an outstanding student at the Ecole Polytechnique and the Ecole des Mines, from which he graduated in 1829. He first achieved notoriety when, abandoning his engineering career, he joined the Saint-Simonian sect, edited its journal *Le globe* (1830–1832), and was tried, found guilty, and imprisoned along with the leader of the sect, Prosper Enfantin (1796–1864). On his release from Sainte Pélagie Prison (Adolphe Thiers had intervened on his behalf), he carefully rebuilt his career, cultivated friends in high places, and was sent by Thiers to North America to study communications there. He stayed two years, touring the United States, Canada, Mexico, and Cuba, and his first major work, *Lettres sur l'Amérique du Nord* (1836), resulted. This book was remarkable for the flair for observation and writing its author demonstrated and the message in favor of economic development it contained. Two years later he published another influential study, *Des intérêts matériels en France* (1838), in which he proposed a public works program for France that was to cost nearly 1,200 million francs. It was this work that led to Chevalier's appointment in 1840 to the chair of political economy at the Collège de France, a chair he held, except for a brief period in 1848, until his death in 1879. When he took up his chair he was thirty-four years old.

A supporter of François Guizot (1787–1874) during the July Monarchy, Chevalier, who attacked the socialists in 1848 (the cause of his suspension from the Collège de France), rallied to Louis Napoleon Bonaparte after the coup d'état of December 1851 (his brother Auguste [1809–1868] had been since 1848 secretary of the prince president's cabinet) and was in 1852 named to the Conseil d'Etat. Although he maintained his intellectual and political independence (in 1858 he was one of those who, in the Conseil d'Etat, opposed the general security law), Chevalier was to play a significant role as an economist and as a policy adviser to Napoleon III.

As an economist, Chevalier made up in enthusiasm and clarity of exposition for his lack of depth and originality. His optimistic brand of modified classical economics provided an intellectual underpinning for the transport revolution, new credit institutions, and economic policies of the Second Empire. Borrowing from J. B. Say (1767–1832), Frédéric Bastiat (1801–1850), and Saint-Simonianism, he praised industry as the motor of human progress, advocated public works built by an alliance of private enterprise and government, defended bimetallism (the French monetary policy), and combatted socialism, workers' trade unions, and strikes. An early advocate of the need to endow France with a modern transport system—(he published his first proposal in 1832, *Système de la Méditerranée*, when he was a Saint-Simonian)—he continued to press for improvements and for government encouragement, such as the guarantee of interest on railway capital. As an economist, his contribution was practical rather than theoretical. He thus provided a justification for the attitudes and strategies of French business and for the economic policies of the Second Empire. His writings won him election in 1851 to the Académie des Sciences Morales et Politiques.

Long interested in industrial exhibitions, Chevalier was also a leading figure in the expositions of the period. He chaired one of the committees for the 1855 Paris exposition (for which he was rewarded with promotion to commander of the Legion of Honor, 1855), headed the French delegation to the London exposition of 1862, and presided over the international jury for the 1867 Paris exposition, working closely with his friend Frédéric Le Play. His most important practical contribution, however, was the role he played in persuading the emperor to sign the 1860 Anglo-French commercial treaty, commonly known as the Cobden-Chevalier treaty. A pacifist and lifelong proponent of a United States of Europe (he was president of the Ligue Internationale de la Paix in June 1869), Chevalier was formally converted to free trade only in 1846. In that year and under the influence of Britain's new tariff policy and Bastiat's writings, he joined the French tariff reform association and as a result was defeated in his bid to remain in the Chamber of Deputies. After Bastiat's death in 1850, it was Chevalier who became the leading reform advocate, frequently in the pages of the *Revue des deux mondes*. His best-known attack on protection, *Examen du système commercial connu sous le nom de système protecteur*, was published in 1852. In it he proposed changes similar to those that the government itself was to propose in 1856 and to bring about from 1860. Chevalier was probably the author of an anonymous memorandum, drawn up in the summer of 1859, that Napoleon III saw and used to sound out opinion among ministers that autumn. He was certainly the principal French negotiator of the commercial treaty with Britain that was signed in January 1860 (the chief British negotiator, Richard Cobden [1804–1865], had been his close friend since 1846). In March 1860 he was rewarded with a seat in the Senate, where he would prove a vigorous defender of the Mexican expedition. In January 1861 he was promoted to grand officer of the Legion.

In 1870 Chevalier, who had opposed Napoleon III's rearmament plans, was the only senator to vote against the war with Prussia. After the fall of the Empire, he played no further political role, although he continued to write and even founded a study group for a Channel tunnel. In his career, he had achieved fame and fortune, but his achievement was flawed, and he never fulfilled the promise of his early years, despite a remarkable capacity for work. For many of his contemporaries, he was an arriviste who shed friends and principles to further his career, just as he abandoned Prosper Enfantin in 1833 and Emile and Isaac Pereire, his friends of forty years, when their Crédit Mobilier fell in 1867. For many of his fellow Saint-Simonians, he was an apostate who gave up all the radical elements in the sect's doctrine—concern for the working class, abolition of inheritance, women's emancipation—for conservative economics. As an economist he made no real theoretical contribution, and as a politician he never quite achieved the positions for which his ambition and talent seemed to destine him. Chevalier died at Lodève (Hérault), 28 November 1879.

A. L. Dunham, "Chevalier's Plan of 1859: The Basis of the New Commercial Policy of Napoleon III," *AHR* 30 (1934); J. B. Duroselle, "Michel Chevalier et la Guerre de 1870–1871," in *Mélanges offerts à Ch. H. Pouthas* (1973), and "Michel Chevalier et le libre-échange avant 1860," *BSHM* (1956); E. James, "Note sur les propositions de Michel Chevalier en matière monétaire," *EcS* 5 (1971); J. Walch, *Michel Chevalier, économiste Saint-Simonien, 1806–1879* (Paris, 1975).

Barrie M. Ratcliffe

Related entries: COBDEN-CHEVALIER TREATY; INTERNATIONAL EXPOSITIONS; LE PLAY; SAINT-SIMONIANISM.

CHEVREAU, HENRI (1823–1903), prefect and minister; born at Belleville (Seine), 27 April 1823. At first Chevreau was drawn to literature and in 1844 published, with Léon Laurent-Pichat (1823–1886), a volume of verse. But having rallied in 1848 to the cause of Louis Napoleon, as had his father, Jean Henri Chevreau (1794–1854; member of the Corps Législatif, 1852–1854), he was named prefect of the Ardèche, 10 January 1849. Following the coup d'état of

December 1851, he was appointed *conseiller d'état en service extraordinaire hors section* as well as *secrétaire général et chef du personnel* of the Ministry of the Interior, Agriculture, and Commerce. In the latter capacity he defended the budget in 1853 before the Corps Législatif but, having quarreled with his minister, Victor Fialin Persigny, he was sent as prefect-first-class to Nantes (Loire-Inférieure), where he remained until transferred 12 September 1864 to Lyons as prefect of the Rhône, replacing Claude Marius Vaïsse (1799–1864), who had served at that post since 1854 and had initiated a great series of public works at Lyons similar to those of Georges Haussmann at Paris.

Chevreau was one of the ablest and most vigorous of the Second Empire's prefects. At Lyons he continued his predecessor's public works projects and supported the efforts of Victor Duruy, minister of public instruction, on behalf of education for girls, organizing a program of free professional instruction. Chevreau had a reputation for making excellent speeches, although he never published them. His services to the regime were amply rewarded: knight of the Legion of Honor, 1850; officer, 1852; commander, August 1855; grand officer, August 1861; and senator, 15 March 1865. However, he had also a reputation for being worldly and a lover of pleasure and was vetoed by Eugène Rouher in 1867 as a candidate for minister of the interior.

Although a loyal bonapartist, Chevreau survived the transition to the Liberal Empire. On 5 January 1870 he was named to replace Haussmann as prefect of the Seine. His first major act was to request (March) a loan of 250 million francs. The Conseil d'Etat proposed to increase the amount so that he might complete necessary projects as well as retiring Haussmann's debts, but war intervened. When Ollivier's government fell on 9 August following French defeats in the war with Prussia, Chevreau became minister of the interior in the comte de Palikao's government, while remaining prefect of the Seine. On 14 August he was responsible for suppressing an uprising at La Villette by a small group of Blanquistes. Chevreau undertook to organize the National Guard at Paris and the Garde Mobile and *francs-tireurs* throughout the country (to that purpose he dispatched ten *conseillers d'état*).

On the afternoon of 4 September, Chevreau and his brother Léon (1827–1910), then a high functionary in the Ministry of the Interior, were among the handful who stood at Eugénie's side during the last hours of the regime and who persuaded her to flee the Tuileries into exile. Although Léon Gambetta asked him to remain at Paris, Chevreau refused to abandon the emperor and empress. From Brussels he rejoined Eugénie in England. Returning to France in 1871, he remained a bonapartist and in 1885 was elected deputy from the Ardèche, although the election was subsequently invalidated. Chevreau died at Yerres, 26 May 1903. His brother Léon also had a distinguished career as prefect of the Ardèche (1853), Sarthe, and Oise (1860–1870) and was named commander of the Legion of Honor in 1868.

Related entries: HAUSSMANN; JANVIER DE LA MOTTE; PREFECTS.

CHINA EXPEDITIONS, armed diplomatic expeditions to China dispatched in
1857–1858 and in 1860 by the British and French governments. While national
prestige, the defense of Roman Catholic missions, and hopes for increased trade
were publicly proposed as French aims, these were in reality subordinated to a
desire for close cooperation with Britain. The principle of joint diplomatic intervention, based on a clause of the French Treaty of Whampoa (24 October
1844), which permitted the reopening of negotiations after twelve years, had
been decided before the *Arrow* affair of 8 October 1856 in which a British ship
was attacked at Canton. The judicial execution of the Lazarist missionary, Auguste Chapdelaine, in the interior of Kiangsi Province on 29 February 1856
provided the occasion to act. Almost identical instructions were issued to the
plenipotentiaries, Baron Jean Baptiste Gros (1793–1870) and James Bruce, eighth
earl of Elgin, supreme diplomatic and military commanders of the respective
missions. Each was to seek diplomatic access to Peking, the opening of new
ports to trade, and security for French missionaries. Stressing the need for *une
parfaite entente* between the two powers, Comte Alexandre Walewski, then
French foreign minister, abandoned long-standing hopes of annexing the island
of Chusan at the mouth of the Yangtze as a French Hong Kong. The expedition
of 1857–1858 was a largely British enterprise (fifty-five hundred men, of whom
about eight hundred were troops), supplemented by some French marines and
seamen. Unable to win either satisfaction from Viceroy Yeh in Canton or a
common front with the United States and Russia, the allies captured Canton
(December 1857) and the Taku Forts at the mouth of the Peiho River in the
north (20 May 1858), to sail unopposed upstream to Tientsin. The treaty of
Tientsin (27 June 1858) granted France an indemnity of 2 million taels (15
million francs), occasional diplomatic access to Peking, extraterritorial jurisdiction over French citizens, trade with six new ports, missionary access to the
interior when carrying passports endorsed by both French and Chinese officials,
and most-favored-nation status. In six secret articles, French grievances over the
Chapdelaine affair were resolved.

Two weeks after Gros returned to France, allied plenipotentiaries, Alphonse
de Bourboulon, French minister in China (1851–1863), and Frederick Bruce,
Lord Elgin's brother, were defeated at Taku (25 June 1859) when trying to force
their way upstream to exchange the ratified treaties of 1858. When the news
was received in Paris on 13 July, Napoleon III instructed his ministers to work
closely with London in preparing a new expedition. Three times the French
government changed the command structure of its mission to make it accord
with Britain's. First, it transferred the diplomatic functions of General Charles
Guillaume Cousin-Montauban (1796–1878), appointed to lead the expedition in
November 1859, to Bourboulon. Then it named (May 1860) Admiral Joseph
Charner (1797–1869), equal in rank to Montauban, to command French naval
forces. Finally, in response to Britain's decision to appoint Lord Elgin, Gros
superseded all three to become once again supreme commander. Napoleon III
held that only Gros had the ability, tact, and prestige to ensure "an entente with

the English Government...and...simultaneously, the defense of our interest.'' Because of the good relations between Gros and Elgin in 1858, London welcomed Gros' appointment and acceded to Paris' wish for ''a perfect identity'' in their titles, powers, and instructions. Gros was to act within the entente to win a Chinese apology for Taku, the exchange of the treaties of 1858 in Peking, and an indemnity. Like Elgin, he was permitted ''wide discretionary powers of appreciation and action.'' His secret instructions called for an indemnity of 60 million francs, safeguards for the practice of Christianity (including the recovery of former Christian churches and cession of land for a church in Canton), and China's reacceptance of the secret clauses of 1858. No mention was made of French hopes for Chusan. This time the expeditionary force consisted of about seven thousand French and thirteen thousand British. Garrisoning Canton, Chusan, Shanghai, and Chefu, the allies moved north via Pehtang and Taku to Tientsin (26 August 1860). Abortive negotiations, interspersed with military skirmishes like Montauban's success at the Bridge of Palikao (21 September), led the allies to Peking (15 October) as Emperor Hsien-feng fled to Mongolia. On 22 October, against Gros' advice, Elgin ordered the destruction of the Imperial Summer Palace, which had already been sacked by allied troops. The act was in revenge for the murder of a number of European prisoners by the Chinese. Whether it also served to speed the pace of negotiations is still debated. The second Sino-French treaty of Tientsin (25 October 1860) provided for China's disavowal of the activities of its officials at Taku in 1859, the exchange of the ratified treaties in Peking in 1861, an indemnity of 8 million taels (60 million francs), the opening of Tientsin as a treaty port, the recovery of former missionary properties, negotiations to regulate the flow of Chinese emigrant laborers, and diplomatic residence in the capital. When Bourboulon established his embassy in Peking in March 1861, the last of the French expeditionary force was being withdrawn from China. Its total losses in the fighting had been a dozen men. Thereafter relations were smooth. French troops assisted China's imperial forces in suppressing the Taiping Rebellion by 1865. On 21 June 1870, however, a crowd attacked the French compound in Tientsin, killing eighteen French citizens and destroying the cathedral, orphanage, and consulate. A Chinese apology, an indemnity, and the execution of the rioters brought an amicable settlement at a time when France was in a position to do no more than protest. Napoleon III amply rewarded General Cousin-Montauban for his victories. The general was named grand cross of the Legion of Honor, given the title comte de Palikao, and appointed to the Senate. To the emperor's chagrin, however, the Corps Législatif refused (February 1862) to approve a hereditary annual pension of 50,000 francs for Palikao, who had to content himself with a gift from Napoleon III of 600,000 francs taken from the indemnity paid by China.

H. Cordier, *L'expédition de Chine de 1857–1858* (Paris, 1905), and *L'expédition de Chine de 1860* (Paris, 1906); A. Dansette, ''Il y a cent ans: Quand les Français et les Anglais occupaient la Chine,'' *Historia*, no. 166 (1960); C. English, ''Napoleon III's

Intervention in China, 1856–1861: A Study of Policy, Press, and Public Opinion'' (Ph.D. diss., University of Toronto, 1972); D. Hurd, *The "Arrow" War* (London, 1967); Comte de Palikao, ed., *Souvenirs sur l'expédition de Chine de 1860* (Paris, 1932); Jen Yu-wen, *The Taiping Revolutionary Movement* (New Haven, 1974).

Christopher English

Related entries: ALGERIA; ALLIANCE POLICY; INDOCHINA; MEXICAN EXPEDITION; SYRIAN EXPEDITION.

CHISLEHURST, the town in England (Kent), fifteen miles from central London where Napoleon III lived in exile for the last years of his life. After his surrender at Sedan, the emperor was taken to Germany via Belgium, reaching the chateau of Wilhelmshöhe in Kassel, capital of Hesse-Kassel, on the evening of 5 September 1870. That same day, the Empress Eugénie left Paris. She arrived in England on 8 September and was reunited with the prince imperial who had reached Dover two days earlier from Belgium. On 24 September, the former empress and her son took up residence at Camden Place, a twenty-room house on the edge of Chislehurst Common. The house had been leased to Eugénie by an Englishman who had known Louis Napoleon thirty years before.

For six and a half months, Napoleon III lived comfortably at Wilhelmshöhe as a prisoner of war, surrounded by a large retinue and receiving many visitors, including Eugénie for four days in early November. Neither he nor Eugénie would negotiate with Otto von Bismarck. Napoleon III was released in March 1871, following the conclusion of a preliminary peace treaty between France and Prussia. Having decided shortly after his arrival at Wilhelmshöhe to live in exile in Britain, he reached Dover in the early morning of 20 March 1871, where he was met by Eugénie and the prince imperial and given a warm welcome by the British.

At Chislehurst Napoleon III was visited by many distinguished acquaintances, including Queen Victoria and her son, the prince of Wales. The prince imperial was enrolled in the military school at Woolwich. The imperial family made visits to Cowes (the Isle of Wight), Torquay, Sheerness (to see the *Great Eastern*), Bath, Windsor, and Brighton. Among the friends and courtiers at Camden Place (which accommodated some forty gentlemen and ladies and twenty servants) were Dr. F.A.H. Conneau, Dr. François Rémy Lucien Corvisart (1824–1882), Prince Joachim Murat (1843–1901), and the prince imperial's former tutor, Augustin Filon (b. 1841). A number of French delegations also visited Chislehurst. Napoleon III fully intended to return to France, confident that the chaos there would cause the people to rally to him. His plan was to enter the country through Belgium, gather a few loyal regiments, and march on Versailles. He therefore agreed to a risky operation for his bladder stone but died in its course on 9 January 1873.

Eugénie remained at Camden Place for another eight years following the death of her husband before leaving it on 23 March 1881. Resettled at Farnborough in Hampshire, she built an abbey and a mausoleum to hold the bodies of her son, killed in the Zulu Wars in 1879, and of Napoleon III. These were moved to the mausoleum in January 1888, and there, too, Eugénie was buried on her death in 1920. Today the monks (now Benedictine) continue to offer their prayers for the souls of the former imperial family.

General H. Castelnau, "Sédan et Wilhelmshöhe" journal du Général Castelnau, aide-de-camp de Napoléon III; ed. Louis Sonolet), *La revue de Paris* 36 (1, 15 October, 1 November, 1929); P. Guériot, *La captivité de Napoléon III en Allemagne (Septembre 1870–Mars 1871)* (Paris, 1926); J. Kühn, "Après Sedan: Bismarck et Napoléon III," *REN* 33 (1924); Comte de La Chapelle, ed., *Posthumous Works and Unpublished Autographs of Napoleon III in Exile* (London, 1873); J. Ridley, *Napoleon III and Eugénie* (New York, 1979); H. Welschinger, "La captivité de Napoléon III à Wilhelmshöhe (5 September 1870–Mars 1871)," *RDM*, 56 (March–April 1910).

Related entries: EUGENIE; NAPOLEON III: HEALTH; PRINCE IMPERIAL.

CHURCH. *See* GALLICANISM.

LES CINQ, the first republican opposition members of the Corps Législatif. In the elections of 1857, two generations of republicans were unable to present a common front. Younger men, advanced by the journalist Léonor Havin, opposed at Paris the veterans of 1848. Of the former, Emile Ollivier and Alfred Darimon were elected and took the oath and their seats. Three men of 1848, Hippolyte Carnot (1801–1888), General Louis Eugène Cavaignac (1802–1857), and Michel Goudchaux (1797–1862), were also successful. Carnot and Goudchaux refused the oath and were not seated. Cavaignac died a month before the new chamber met. By-elections the following year to replace the three returned two more republican candidates, Ernest Picard and Jules Favre, who were willing to take the oath as the price of political effectiveness, as had been Jacques Louis Hénon (1802–1872), elected at Lyons in the previous year—thus the five (*les Cinq*), all (except Hénon) representing Paris. Seated on the left rear benches, ignored by the majority, the Five were from 1857 to 1863 the major opposition to the authoritarian Empire, making up in oratorical and debating skills what they lacked in numbers. Favre and Ollivier were generally regarded as leaders of the small group. None were extremists. They opposed the law of general security in 1858, the press regime, and the management of elections. Following Napoleon III's first major reform of his regime in November 1860, the Five used amendments to the address in order to criticize the authoritarian system, demanding repeal of the law of general security, suppression of the system of official candidates, a free press, jury trial, the right of reunion, increased powers for local government (such as a municipal council for Paris), decentralization, and full guarantees of individual liberty. They were persistent critics as well of the government's finances and, especially, of Baron Georges Haussmann and his plans for Paris. They attacked monopolies, government aid to railroads, the occupation of Rome by French forces, and the Mexican intervention but were divided concerning Napoleon III's 1859 Italian intervention. In the spring of 1861, Ollivier began his movement toward the regime by accepting the reform decree of 24 November 1860. Darimon would follow him after 1863. This rift in the republican ranks combined with the elections of 1863 in which the Five, all reelected, were joined by twelve additional republican deputies, to end a political era and to initiate the transition to the Liberal Empire.

A. Darimon, *Histoire d'un parti: Les Cinq sous l'Empire, 1857–1860* (Paris, 1885), and *L'opposition libérale sous l'Empire, 1861–1863* (Paris, 1886).

Related entries: CORPS LEGISLATIF; DARIMON; ELECTIONS; FAVRE; OATH; OLLIVIER; PICARD; REFORM; REPUBLICANISM.

CLARETIE, JULES (1840–1913), novelist, playwright, and journalist; born 3 December 1840 in Limoges. After studying at the Lycée Bonaparte in Paris, Claretie began a career in business but soon realized that literature was his real vocation. At the age of twenty-two he became a journalist, writing during the 1860s for such newspapers as *La France* (as "Olivier de Jalin"), *Diogène, Le Figaro* (as "Candide"), and *L'illustration*, while at the same time publishing his first short stories and novels. In 1867 he succeeded Francisque Sarcey (1828–1899) as drama critic for *L'opinion nationale.* By the mid-1860s, Claretie had established his reputation as a novelist with such works as *Un assassin* (1866) and *Mademoiselle Bertin* (1868). During the last years of the Second Empire, his liberal leanings (he was a republican and a Freemason) led him into some difficulty. He was gagged by government censors in February 1865 and April 1868 and in 1868 was prosecuted and convicted for having resurrected in *Le Figaro* a forgotten execution associated with the coup d'état of 1851. In early 1868 he helped to found an opposition newspaper, *Le Corsaire.* And at the beginning of 1870, he testified as a friend of Victor Noir in the trial of Pierre Bonaparte for murder. During the Franco-Prussian War, Claretie worked as a press correspondent for *L'opinion nationale* and *Le rappel.* The following year, he served as a captain in the National Guard during the siege of Paris.

After the war, Claretie became even more popular with the general public. His many novels, depicting for the most part Parisian life in a dramatic and colorful style, were widely serialized. He drew on these novels as the basis for a series of plays, which also enjoyed considerable success. Furthermore, Claretie wrote as an historian. He not only recounted his experience during the Franco-Prussian War but also wrote on the French Revolution. Having been named to the committee whose task it was to make an inventory of the documents of the imperial family, Claretie drew on this information and in 1871 published *L'Empire, les Bonapartes, et la cour.* Finally, Claretie's interest in literary and artistic life produced several biographies—of Petrus Borel, for example—and studies such as *La vie moderne au théâtre* (1869, 1875), and *Peintres et sculpteurs* (1882), whose charm was less in the historical perspective they provided than in the lively, anecdotal information they contained. Claretie continued to contribute regularly to the Paris press, including the *Revue française, L'artiste, La presse, L'opinion nationale,* and *Le temps.* Among other major novels written by Claretie during the Second Empire are the following: *Une drôlesse* (1863), *Les victimes de Paris* (1864), and *Mademoiselle Cachemire* (1867). For the theater, he wrote *La famille des gueux* (1869) and *Raymond Lindey* (1870). His historical works include *Le champ de bataille de Sedan* (1871), *Paris assiégé* (1871), *La France envahie* (1871), and *Petrus Borel le Lycanthrope* (1865). Claretie died at Paris, 23 December 1913.

G. Grappe, *Jules Claretie* (Paris, 1906).

Dorothy E. Speirs

Related entries: PRESS REGIME; THEATER.

CLOTHING. See CRINOLINE.

COALITIONS LAW (1864), one of the first major reforms of the Second Empire in the interest of workers, revising articles 414, 415, and 416 of the Penal Code of 1810 and thus recognizing the right to strike. Voted 25 May 1864 by the Corps Législatif, this law removed the act (material fact) of workers' coalition from the category of criminal offenses but identified certain acts associated with coalitions as punishable crimes. These were (1) the use of "violence, coercion (*voies de fait*), threats or fraudulent maneuvers" in the attempt "to bring about or maintain a concerted work stoppage, for the purpose of forcing an increase or reduction of wages, or for interfering with (*porter atteinte à*) the free exercise of industry or work" (new article 414) and (2) the use of "fines, prohibitions, prescriptions, or bans pronounced according to a concerted plan" as an "aid" to "interfering with the free exercise of industry or labor" (new article 416). The law also imposed more stringent penalties for these acts when accomplished in association with strikes than when performed in other contexts regulated by the common law (articles 305, 308, and 209ff of the Penal Code). The 1864 law recognized neither the right of assembly nor the right of association; thus trade unions were not legalized along with strikes.

The Second Empire had, in fact, continued the legislation of Napoleon I, of the July Monarchy (law of 1834), and of the Second Republic (law of 27 November 1849) concerning association, meeting, and coalition. Organizations and meetings of more than twenty persons were illegal unless authorized by the government. Political and economic organizations and meetings were never authorized (except in the case of electoral meetings during election campaigns), and such groups as were allowed to form for charitable or similar purposes were closely supervised. The courts, moreover, interpreted the 1849 law as prohibiting the mere fact of coalition, regardless of intent. This interpretation fell more heavily on workers than on employers because of the relative ease of identifying workers' coalitions. Consequently there were demands, in the name of equality, for revision of the offending law and provisions of the Penal Code. Freedom to strike was also increasingly regarded as an ideological corollary of the liberalization of trade after 1860, especially by liberal economists, journalists, and politicians. Without such freedom, argued the liberals, the government had to be prepared to intervene in the labor market to protect workers from the more competitive economic environment created by the 1860 Cobden-Chevalier commercial treaty with Britain. The emperor's personal intervention in a printers' strike of July 1862 to grant clemency (November) to nine workers convicted of coalition under the 1849 law implicitly recognized the validity of this argument. This intervention also highlighted the anomaly of the existing law in a regime priding itself on legal equality. Demands by worker delegates to the 1862 London Exposition were reinforced in February 1863 by an unsuccessful attempt of Alfred Darimon to secure abolition of articles 414 through 416 of the Penal Code. Napoleon III requested a study. Its result and the growth of the opposition in the 1863 elections finally persuaded him to remove existing anomalies by legalizing strikes. In thus satisfying one of the workers' oldest and most popular demands (it was repeated in the *Manifeste des Soixante* of sixty Seine department workers during by-elections of February 1864), he also sought to rally them to the Empire, to replace some of the lost support among conservatives alienated by imperial policy in Italy and among industrialists discontented with the commercial treaty of 1860. In this sense, most historians have interpreted the coalitions law of 1864 as the first of a series of liberal measures designed to head off the opposition by anticipating its demands and to establish a workers' constituency favorable to the regime. The emperor might also have hoped to divide the republicans on the issue—as did happen. His personal role is clear, beginning with his call for reform in opening the legislative session in November 1863. The Conseil d'Etat's project (deposed in February 1864) having been judged too vague, Auguste de Morny, president of the Corps Législatif and half-brother of the emperor, obtained the appointment of Emile Ollivier to the commission (and as *rapporteur*) and helped him to draft the proposed legislation. Despite opposition from Left and Right, the coalitions law was approved by a vote of 121 to 31. Theodore Zeldin (1963) has credited this largely to Ollivier, noting that Napoleon III wavered as opposition mounted.

The law had a mixed reception. Critics on the Left attacked it for imposing special prohibitions and penalties for strike-related activities and for seeming to legalize only spontaneous strikes, since, in the absence of unions, the right to strike was likely to prove either meaningless or a trap. As well, the law heavily reflected Ollivier's moralizing (he preferred to eliminate strikes altogether and had even argued for compulsory arbitration), and the protection of "freedom to work" would mean, in practical terms, protection of "blacklegs." Besides, the republicans were unwilling to accept any reform emanating from the Empire. Opponents on the Right predicted disruption of industry, commerce, and social peace as a result of strikes that the law now made legal. The first group of critics demanded the right of coalition pure and simple, leaving to common law the proscription of aggravating acts. They argued that the vague language of the revised penal articles, especially "fraudulent maneuvers," effectively empowered the courts to decide arbitrarily the legality of individual strikes. In 1865 the prosecution of striking velvet weavers of Saint-Etienne under a penal article prohibiting permanent associations showed how fragile the new freedom was. Not surprisingly, reaction of workers to the coalitions law was cool. They continued to demand the right of meeting, without which, they argued, the right to strike was empty. In fact, however, the right to meet and even to form de facto unions was implicit in the 1864 law. Although the government continued vigilant against illegal political organizations (prosecution in 1864 of *les Treize*, accused of having coalesced during the elections of 1863), a circular of the minister of the interior (February 1866), and a letter of the minister of commerce (21 March 1866) prescribed for the prefects a broad tolerance of workers' organizations and meetings. The workers had long used their mutual aid societies (*sociétés de secours mutuels*) as substitutes for unions. After 1864 there was a growth of *chambres syndicales*, which flourished in the atmosphere of government tolerance that became official policy with the approval on 31 March 1868 by the emperor of a report by commerce minister J.L.V.A. de Forcade La Roquette recommending that the *chambres syndicales* be tolerated in the same way as were the patronal organizations.

Although historians have generally accepted as valid the criticisms of the coalitions law of 1864 offered by the Left and have been inclined to judge the law a failure in rallying the workers to the regime, some have stressed its significance as the first major break with the legal regime in effect since the Le Chapelier Law of 1791, which regarded strikes and unions as incompatible with economic liberty. In this sense, the 1864 law was a first step toward the legalization of union activity finally achieved in France in 1884. And there is an obvious relationship between the coalitions law of 1864 and the liberalization in 1868 of controls on public meetings. That law, voted 209 to 22 and promulgated 6 June 1868 as part of the reform program announced by Napoleon III in January 1867, distinguished for the first time between association (which remained subject to government authorization) and meetings. It permitted the latter, if not political or religious (the nature of political meetings was not specified, although the definition was understood to exclude economic matters), subject to certain conditions, which applied as well to electoral meetings during political campaigns for the period prior to five days before the balloting. A declaration signed by seven residents of the commune had to be submitted three days before the meeting certifying place, time, and subject to be discussed. The meeting was required to be indoors and presided over by a specified bureau. Finally, a government agent, in attendance, would have the power to suspend proceedings at once if the meeting strayed from the agreed topic or if public order were threatened. In fact, the authorities could always suspend operation of the law in the name of public order. Primarily for this latter reason, the Left rejected the law on public meetings, although it would be the first to profit from its provisions.

G. Bourgin, "La législation ouvrière du Second Empire," *REN* (July–December 1913); P. L. Fournier, *Le Second Empire et la législation ouvrière* (Paris, 1911); E. Levasseur,

Histoire des classes ouvrières et de l'industrie en France de 1789 à 1870, 2 vols., 2d ed. (Paris, 1904); E. M. Saint-Léon, *Histoire des corporations de métiers*, 3d ed. (Paris, 1922); T. Zeldin, *Emile Ollivier and the Liberal Empire of Napoleon III* (Oxford, 1963).

George J. Sheridan, Jr.

Related entries: COMITE DES FORGES; LABOR REFORM; LA RICA-MARIE; OLLIVIER.

COBDEN-CHEVALIER TREATY, a tariff agreement signed in January 1860 whereby Britain and France lowered or eliminated duties on each other's goods and France abolished prohibitions. The treaty was the first of a series of similar bilateral commercial agreements between European states and was thus a major catalyst of the European low-tariff era of the 1860s and 1870s. The treaty raises two difficult questions. One concerns the reasons for its signing when most French industrialists and politicians were against it and when there was no organized reform campaign (the pressure group set up under Frédéric Bastiat [1801–1850] in 1846 had collapsed in 1850 and had not been revived). The other concerns the economic consequences of its signing. The answers to these questions were controversial at the time and remain so for historians.

A proper understanding of the 1860 agreement can be gained only if the treaty is put in the secular context of tariff policy and foreign trade. Although some attempts had been made to eliminate excesses and inconsistencies in the system, French tariffs after 1815 remained highly protective and, for some manufactured and semimanufactured goods in which Britain excelled, prohibitive. Their purpose was twofold: to afford protection for French industrialists (textile and metallurgical concerns in particular) and to provide revenue for the state through duties on colonial and raw material imports. The effectivenss of the French tariff is reflected in the import list. Manufactured goods made up only 8.5 percent of imports in the late 1820s, a proportion that had fallen to 4 percent by the late 1850s. Raw materials and semimanufactures, on the other hand, constituted 64 percent of imports in the early 1830s and 71 percent two decades later. However, French tariffs and the similar tariffs adopted by most of France's trading partners did not stifle trade. France's commerce increased markedly in the first two-thirds of the nineteenth century. From 1845 to 1854 exports averaged 1,049 million francs a year; from 1855 to 1864 they averaged 2,148 million; and they reached 3,188 million a year in the 1865–1874 period. As a proportion of gross national product, foreign trade was the equivalent of 13 percent in 1830, 19 percent in 1850, 29 percent in 1860, and 41 percent by the end of the Second Empire. During the Second Empire, France had a surplus on its commercial balance that averaged 277 million francs between 1848 and 1866. Only in the last three years of the regime was there a deficit, a harbinger of the changed situation of the following decades, and even then the total balance of payments was positive.

The Second Empire thus inherited a tariff system that was protectionist and yet a foreign trade that was growing more rapidly than the economy itself. It was to facilitate expansion (especially of the railroad network), and thus to increase the standard of living of the lower classes, that the government undertook from 1853 a reduction of tariffs. In December 1853 duties on iron, steel, and coal were decreased by an average 20 percent (those on cotton textiles were maintained, following an inquiry); and other piecemeal reductions were effected during the Crimean War, although the idea of seeking an elimination of all prohibitions was put aside in 1854. In June 1856, following a successful war and an impressive French showing at the Paris international exposition of 1855, the government tried to go further when it proposed the abolition of all prohibitions, as well as a series of tariff reductions. So vociferous, however, was the outcry these proposals provoked among industrialists, and so threatening was the economic climate as the crisis of 1857 approached, that not only did the government desist, it even promised not to initiate any major reforms before July 1861 and then only after undertaking an official inquiry. Although the inquiry was not carried out and although the *Moniteur* article of October 1856 announcing the government's decision stated that the regime of prohibitions would not be allowed to continue beyond January 1861, when Napoleon III signed the 1860 agreement, he was able to do so only because the *sénatus-consulte* of 25 December 1852 gave the executive the right to sign commercial treaties without having to submit them for parliamentary ratification. The treaty and the other agreements that followed effected a major breach in the protectionist system. Customs duties as a proportion of the value of imports had fallen from 17.2 percent in 1847–1849 to 11 percent in 1855–1859. By 1865–1869 they would be only 4 percent.

A treaty that was negotiated in such secrecy that neither the Corps Législatif nor the Council of Ministers was informed and that was signed by an emperor who left historians few written documents has proved difficult to explain. Scholars have stressed the role of various individuals who, they claim, persuaded Napoleon III to conclude the treaty: Richard Cobden (1804–1865), president of the British Board of Trade, champion of free trade, and close friend from 1846 of Michel Chevalier; Chevalier, who sent a memo to Napoleon III in October 1859 and was received by the emperor, together with Cobden; Emile Pereire, who also wrote a memo; Eugène Rouher, then minister of agriculture, commerce, and public works and a free trader since 1851; and Victor Fialin Persigny. They have also emphasized that motives for signing the agreement were complex and involved political and economic considerations. France thus sought to improve relations with Britain that had deteriorated with the 1859 Italian War and were in danger of being further jeopardized when France annexed Nice and Savoy. Napoleon III also sought to stimulate an economy that was still suffering the effects of the 1857 commercial crisis, to halt the increase in prices, and to encourage a return of the prosperity of the 1852–1856 boom. As was made clear in his famous letter of 5 January 1860 to Achille Fould (published in the *Moniteur* of 15 January), lower tariffs was one of the incentives he chose.

The decision made, negotiations proceeded at Paris in strictest secrecy during the fall of 1859. On the French side, only Rouher, Chevalier, and, later, Jules

Baroche (interim foreign minister in January 1860) were involved. The cabinet was not informed until 21 December 1859, at which time all ministers but Rouher were hostile. The British negotiators were Cobden and Britain's ambassador at Paris, Lord Cowley (1804–1884). On 12 January 1860, the first intimation of the talks appeared in the *Morning Post* (London) and was reproduced three days later by the protectionist *Moniteur industriel*. Negotiations were accelerated. On 22 January 1860 the treaty was signed (published 23 January). By its terms, France substituted for all prohibitions a maximum ad valorem duty of 30 percent, to be reduced to 25 percent. Existing duties were reduced—on coal by 50 percent, on most metals by two-thirds. An inquiry would determine which items should have special protection and at what rate, while mixed commissions would convert ad valorem duties to fixed ones for most cloth and metals. All French products would be admitted free to Britain, except for wines and spirits, on which duties were reduced. The treaty was for ten years, and included a most-favored-nation clause by which France and Britain would benefit automatically from any favorable terms negotiated by either with a third party. Finally, a French law of 1 August 1860 created a credit of 40 million francs to provide twenty-year, 5 percent loans to industries harmed by the new rates. Nevertheless, many in France continued to oppose the treaty, which they regarded as a betrayal. Opposition was unanimous only in the textile industry, however, and others (silk, wine) gave enthusiastic support. Moreover, while many protectionists remained intransigent (notable spokesmen included Adolphe Thiers and Auguste Pouyer-Quertier [1820–1891]), others like Eugène Schneider and Paulin Talabot came to accept and even to approve the emperor's initiative.

Debate has long raged on the treaty's impact on the economy and trade. Protectionists at the time attributed deleterious effects, while economic liberals insisted the new policy benefited France. The classical study of the treaty that A. L. Dunham published in 1930 reiterated liberal claims. But more recent historiography has tended to play down the effects by insisting that previous tariff policy had not been as ill adapted to the needs of the economy as reformers and many historians had claimed and that patterns of foreign trade are determined by a complex of factors, of which government policy is but one. As for French exports, they continued to expand, increasing in volume by 30 percent in 1857–1860 and by 36 percent in 1861–1864. Two provisos have to be made, however. One is that the greatest expansion occurred in nonmanufactured goods. The other is that the rate of growth fell markedly after 1865, and between 1875 and 1895 exports would rise by a mere 0.5 percent a year. As far as imports were concerned, there was an increase of nearly 30 percent in 1861 alone, but this was due in large part to a massive influx of grain made necessary by a poor French harvest. The momentum, however, was not maintained. Nor was the much-feared invasion of British goods realized. Imports from Britain nearly doubled between 1855–1859 and 1866–1870, but the total remained extremely small as a proportion of British exports and in relation to Britain's importance as a market for French exports.

The consequences, then, were by no means as important as proponents and opponents of the treaty claimed, and the new commercial policy did not radically alter patterns of trade—as the statistics of long-term trends indicate—or of economic change. It is not possible, however, to be more specific than this about the impact of the new tariff. Not only were other factors involved, but the treaty's inception coincided with a series of conjunctural and long-term changes: the cotton famine that cut off U.S. raw cotton and closed France's second most important market; the pebrine epidemic that struck the Lyons silk industry from the 1850s and the phylloxera that hit the French vineyards, especially after 1875; and the slowing down of the rate of French economic growth from the 1860s. Certainly the treaty initiated an era of free trade; France negotiated a series of commercial treaties similar to that of January 1860 with most other European states: Turkey, 29 April 1861; Belgium, 1 May 1861 and 12 May 1863; Prussia and the Zollverein, 2 August 1862; Italy, 17 January 1863; Switzerland, 30 June 1864; Sweden-Norway, 14 February 1865; Mecklenburg-Schwerin, 9 June 1865; Spain, 18 June 1865; Netherlands, 7 July 1865; Portugal, 11 July 1866; Austria, 11 December 1866; and the Roman States, 29 July 1867.

P. Bairoch, *Commerce extérieur et développement économique de l'Europe au XIXe siècle* (Paris, 1976), and "Commerce extérieur et développement économique: Quelques enseignements de l'expérience libre-échangeiste de la France au XIXe siècle," *RE* (January 1970); J. Coussy, "La politique commerciale du Second Empire et la continuité de l'évolution structurelle française," *EcS* (1961); A. L. Dunham, *The Anglo-French Treaty of Commerce of 1860 and the Progress of the Industrial Revolution in France* (Ann Arbor, 1930), and "Michel Chevalier et le traité de 1860," *RH* 171 (1933); A. A. Iliasu, "The Cobden-Chevalier Commercial Treaty of 1860," *CHJ* 14 (March 1971); C. P. Kindleberger, "The Rise of Free Trade in Western Europe, 1820–1875," *JEH* 35 (March 1975); B. M. Ratcliffe, "The Tariff Reform Campaign in France, 1831–1836," *JEEH* 7 (1978), and "Napoleon III and the Anglo-French Commercial Treaty of 1860: A Reconsideration," in B. M. Ratcliffe, ed., *Great Britain and Her World, 1750–1914* (Manchester, 1975); M. S. Smith, *Tariff Reform in France, 1860–1900: The Politics of Economic Interest* (Ithaca, N.Y., 1980); G. Wright, "Origins of Napoleon III's Free Trade Policy," *EcHR* (1938–1939).

Barrie M. Ratcliffe

Related entries: ARLES-DUFOUR; BAKERIES, DEREGULATION OF; CHEVALIER; COMITE DES FORGES; COTTON FAMINE; ECONOMIC CRISES; GOVERNMENT FINANCE; INTERNATIONAL EXPOSITIONS; NICE AND SAVOY; OIDIUM-PHYLLOXERA; PEREIRE; RAILROADS; ROUHER; SCHNEIDER; TALABOT.

COCHINCHINA. See INDOCHINA.

COMITE DES FORGES, one of France's earliest and most successful employers' federations. The Comité des Forges was set up in February 1864 by ironmasters, representing the largest and most modern metallurgical concerns in the country. This was not the first time that French ironmasters had come together to concert action, but whereas previous agreements and pressure groups had remained shadowy and proved transitory, the Comité des Forges was open and, if not officially sanctioned, tolerated by the government. While previous pressure groups representing metallurgical interests had generally restricted themselves to combatting any lowering of protective tariffs, the Comité des Forges had wider and more forward-looking aims. It was to gather and disseminate commercial and technical intelligence, as well as to act as a pressure group in the capital. In its membership and its activity, the Comité des Forges represents the coming of age of a modern and competitive French metallurgical sector anxious to continue to innovate and compete with British and Belgian producers on foreign markets. The prestige and power that successful ironmasters had achieved by the time of the Second Empire is evidenced in the career of the organization's first president, Eugène Schneider. Schneider was not only the successful director of Le Creusot, one of the largest metallurgical concerns, but also mayor of Le Creusot, regent of the Bank of France, deputy, vice-president, and (from 1867) president of the Corps Législatif.

The founding of the Comité des Forges, then, has to be understood in the context of a dual revolution: metallurgy was undergoing both a technical and a structural transformation. These changes had proceeded only slowly in the first half of the century but had accelerated under the stimulus of orders from the expanding railway network from the 1840s onwards. A new peak was reached between 1850 and 1857 when production of rails increased seven-fold and represented between a quarter and a half of total iron production. At the same time, the market was widening, with new uses for iron products, such as iron-hulled ships, and framework for buildings. The Second Empire witnessed the triumph of technically advanced and large-scale metallurgical concerns over the small-scale, charcoal-based ironworks that had dominated previously. Already in 1837 coke-produced cast iron had surpassed that made with charcoal. In 1852 pig iron produced by coke exceeded that produced by charcoal. By the end of the Empire, 93 percent of pig iron was produced by coke. Steel production was also transformed as the Bessemer process was adopted from 1862 and the Siemens-Martin from 1864. By the early 1860s, then, metallurgy employed 100,000 workers, and its annual production was estimated to be worth nearly 500 million francs.

The industry came to be dominated by a dozen large concerns. While the ten largest firms had controlled 14 percent of the market in 1854, they controlled 55 percent in 1869. The largest metallurgical concern, de Wendel, alone was responsible for 11 percent of total output. The triumph of these large, integrated concerns had been facilitated by a market that favored mass production—iron rails for railways, for example. It had been achieved by horizontal and vertical integration and large-scale inputs of capital. Thus firms in the same region came together, as did the small foundries in Franche-Comté in 1855, and firms at different stages in the production process, like the Fourchambault ironworks that joined with the Commentry coal concern in 1853 (by the end of the following year the firm's capital stood at no less than 24 million francs). It was leaders of these large concerns who came together to found the Comité des Forges in 1864.

Cooperation among ironmasters in a region or among producers of common products was far from unique to the Second Empire. During the Restoration and July Monarchy, there are instances of agreements to keep down wages or share raw materials. There are also numerous instances of joint efforts to maintain or increase tariff protection. At first these were limited to the drawing up of petitions, but forgemasters in the 1840s set up a more permanent committee to defend existing tariff legislation and cooperated with other protectionist organizations like the Association pour la Défense du Travail National. During the Second Empire, then, there was no novelty in the ad hoc agreements to share rail orders, like that in 1854 for the Paris-Caen railway, or the defense groups like the committee called the Comité des Maîtres de Forges that seems to have been established in 1850 with Léon Talabot of the Denain-Anzin concern as chairman. Even before 1864, indeed, the name Comité des Forges appears in correspondence to the government on the Anglo-French commercial treaty of 1860.

There were, though, particular reasons why the largest metallurgical concerns should have created the Comité des Forges in 1864. The principal of these was that the industry faced permanent problems that had been lost sight of in the euphoria of the 1851–1856 boom but became visible in the more difficult years from 1857. The economic crisis of 1857 brought a fall in demand for rails and hit metallurgy particularly hard. Pessimism among ironmasters lingered on into the early 1860s as ralway orders failed to return to earlier levels. There also was concern about high transportation charges and the high price of borrowing, both of which raised production costs. The expense of financing new plants was especially worrisome in the early 1860s when new processes in steel production were being perfected. Ironmasters were anxious to cooperate to improve their competitiveness against British and Belgian producers on international markets. However, since they had come to dominate the home market, major producers were less worried about the Anglo-French treaty of commerce that was signed in 1860. Finally, although declining profit margins were not universal among the major producers, some large concerns faced difficulties, and one of the most famous of all, Decazeville, failed in 1865. Thus the early 1860s were a turning point for French metallurgy in many ways. New challenges and mounting pressures led to the establishment of the Comité des Forges.

The organization was set up by leading figures in the industry. Apart from Schneider, its president, there were Jules Hochet of Fourchambault, who became vice-president, Charles de Wendel (1809–1870), and Benoist d'Azy (1796–1880), and all the leading firms were represented. The Comité des Forges had four objectives: to provide members with information on new techniques, to represent the industry in relations with the government, to act as a source of intelligence on prices and markets abroad, and to disseminate information on the domestic market and to work to establish uniform prices for iron products. Such aims could be met only if the ironmasters were willing to cooperate and the government to close its eyes to what was, after all, an illegal organization. The Comité des Forges represented new and powerful interests, and the government tacitly accepted its existence. Legal from 1887, it was destined to play an important but not always visible role in the French economy.

B. Gille, *Recherches sur la formation de la grande entreprise capitaliste (1815–1848)* (Paris, 1959), and *La sidérurgie française au XIXe siècle* (Geneva, 1968); M. Lévy-Leboyer, ed., *Le patronat de la seconde industrialisation* (Paris, 1979); R. R. Locke, *Les fonderies et forges d'Alais à l'époque des premiers chemins de fer: La création d'une entreprise moderne* (Paris, 1978); R. Priouret, *Origines du patronat français* (Paris, 1963); P. Rousseau, "Pour Napoléon III [Bessemer] invente l'acier," *Historia* 339 (February 1975); J. Vial, *L'industrialisation de la sidérurgie française, 1814–1864* (Paris, 1967).

Barrie M. Ratcliffe

Related entries: COBDEN-CHEVALIER TREATY; COALITIONS LAW; ECONOMIC CRISES; SCHNEIDER; *SOCIETES PAR ACTIONS*; TALABOT.

COMPAGNIE GENERALE TRANSATLANTIQUE (also known as the Transat and the French Line), the shipping company established by the Pereire brothers (Emile and Isaac) and their Crédit Mobilier group 25 February 1855. Its early years, when it was called the Compagnie Générale Maritime, were marked by daring and by failure, and it was only when the Pereires secured the North Atlantic postal concession in October 1860 that the company was renamed and reorganized (21 April 1861) and achieved a measure of success. Along with the Messageries Impériales, the Transat was to become France's leading shipping line.

Earlier attempts to set up a steamship company had failed, and at the mid-century France had no rival to the Cunard or the Hamburg-Amerika on the North Atlantic. Indeed, France's merchant marine remained small—under 700,000 tons and only 3 percent of this made up of steam vessels. Part of the explanation for the failure of French shipping is to be found in the structure of French trade, which was geographically concentrated within Europe and thus favored coastal shipping and export by the land frontier. French ports received twice as much freight as they exported, an imbalance that limited shipping profits and favored foreign carriers. Part of the explanation is also to be found in the poor dock facilities and the absence of government funding. This situation was remedied during the Second Empire. Technical innovations—iron hulls, screw propellers, compound engines—solved the problems of safety and fuel efficiency that had hindered the success of earlier steamships. The growth of intercontinental trade and the unprecedented increase in emigrant traffic also stimulated shipping enterprise. Greatest encouragement was given by the state. From the 1840s European governments increasingly subsidized steamship companies. In France these subsidies stood at only 5 million francs in 1859 but had risen to 26 million a year by 1869. At the same time, French government funding of port modernization rose to 18 million francs a year between 1859 and 1867.

Despite these favorable circumstances and the alliance of Parisian capital and

Norman shipping interests, the early years of the Compagnie Générale Maritime were difficult. The Pereires, who had no experience in the shipping business, were too ambitious in their aims, and the company's activities were too diverse. At the time the company was founded, wheat supplies were cut off by the Crimean War, and food prices, for a number of reasons, were high in France. The Pereires therefore calculated that their new line would profit from buying and transporting American wheat and other foodstuffs. Such plans were to prove premature, and, in any case, the return to peace in 1856 and the commercial crisis of the following year undermined their projects. Lack of confidence in the company helps explain why the government awarded the North Atlantic postal concession to a rival group in 1858. It was only the collapse of the latter company that enabled the Pereires successfully to tender again in 1860. In October of that year, the government gave them an annual subsidy of 9.5 million francs and a twenty-year interest-free loan of 18.6 million. In return, the Pereires agreed to build a fleet of steamships and to maintain regular services to Mexico, the Caribbean, and the United States. The new company ordered some of its new steam vessels in Britain, whose shipbuilding industry enjoyed a considerable lead over others, and built some at its own shipyards, at Saint-Nazaire. On 14 April 1862, it inaugurated the Mexico route from Saint-Nazaire and on 15 June 1864 opened its New York run (two ships each month). Thanks to the subsidy and loan from the French state, Napoleon III's Mexican expedition, and the growth of traffic, the Transat was able to establish itself in the 1860s as a viable competitor to established North Atlantic shipping lines. By 1865, the voyage from Le Havre to New York required an average of ten days.

The prestige and success the company enjoyed were bought at a price, and in the last years of the Empire the Transat faced mounting financial difficulties. Competition on the North Atlantic was more severe than, for example, on the routes served by the Messageries Impériales, and the U.S. Civil War disrupted commercial relations. Moreover, the Transat made a serious mistake when it ordered paddle steamers rather than the new screw propellers, for the screw beat out the paddle wheel in the 1860s. When the new company was established in 1861, the Pereires had exaggerated the value of the Compagnie Générale Maritime, and the Transat had to bear this burden in the 1860s. In 1868, therefore, the Pereires were forced off the board of directors, and the government stepped in to aid the company. When it granted the Transat the Valparaiso-Panama concession, the government also gave a large subsidy and, for the first time to a shipping line, offered a guarantee of interest on its shares. In the early years of the Third Republic, the Transat faced further problems; the Pacific route was operated at a loss, sailing ships and German steamship lines offered stiffer competition, and several company ships suffered spectacular shipwrecks. To combat these problems, Isaac Pereire and his sons were invited back on the company's board of directors. Eugène Pereire proved to be a successful chairman of the Transat from 1877 until 1904.

M. Barbance, *Histoire de la Compagnie Générale Transatlantique: Un siècle d'exploitation maritime* (Paris, 1955); P. Guiral and M. Barak, "La navigation française dans
l'Atlantique de 1814 à 1914," *Annuario de estudios americanos* 25 (1968); M. Mollat,
ed., *Les origines de la navigation à vapeur* (Paris, 1970); J. Trogoff, "La 'Transat' à
cent ans," *Historia* (April 1955).

Barrie M. Ratcliffe
Related entries: CREDIT MOBILIER; DUPUY DE LOME; GOVERNMENT
FINANCE; MESSAGERIES IMPERIALES; PEREIRE; RAILROADS.

COMPIEGNE, a favorite imperial residence of Napoleon III. Each year, beginning in 1856, the court moved to Compiègne during late October or early
November, remaining there for a month to six weeks. To the palace, which
Napoleon I (who made it a *maison impériale*) had had restored by Charles Percier
and P.F.L. Fontane, were invited during the season a total of four or five groups
(in 1861, six) of about seventy to eighty guests each, chosen by the empress
from various classes and professions, including artists—the famous *séries de
Compiègne*. (It was at Compiègne in December 1852 that Louis Napoleon probably formed his resolution to marry Eugénie de Montijo, one of the 101 guests
in attendance that Christmas season.) Despite republican suspicion of orgies and
English consternation at the lack of *convenances*, the relatively informal four-
day house parties at the woefully overcrowded chateau were rather staid affairs,
even if the guests were kept busy with dinners (the food was plentiful but not
very good), theater, representations of proverbs and of *tableaux vivants*, balls
(especially that of 15 November, Eugénie's feast day), excursions to nearby
Pierrefonds, the medieval castle then being restored by Eugène Viollet-le-Duc,
and to the Roman ruins of Champlieu, walks in the surrounding forest, and,
especially, the great stag hunt on the last day of each *série*, for which Napoleon
III had revived the elaborate ritual and uniforms of the Bourbon royal hunt.
Frequently the emperor took the opportunity of these contacts with businessmen,
politicians, and diplomats to pursue matters of state, especially since the *saison
de Compiègne* traditionally marked the beginning of preparations for the new
political year and Compiègne was only a two-hour train ride from Paris. On
occasion he entertained other rulers, of whom a favorite was William I of Prussia.
A Museum of the Second Empire was opened at Compiègne in 1953, including
the Musée de l'Impératrice which had earlier been assembled privately at
Pierrefonds.

J. M. Moulin, "La cour à Compiègne sous le Second Empire," *Journée d'étude,
Compiègne 1978, SN* 41 (1978), and "The Furnishing of the Palace of Compiègne during
the Second Empire," *Connoisseur* 199 (1978); C. Sykes, "The Emperor Entertains:
Napoleon III at Compiègne," *History Today* 3 (January 1953). There is a vivid account
of a *série* at Compiègne in Emile Zola, *Son Excellence Eugène Rougon* (Paris, 1876).
Related entries: BIARRITZ; DORE; VIOLLET-LE-DUC.

CONCERT LIFE. During the Second Empire and particularly in the 1860s,
concert activity in France increased dramatically. The French musical capital

was clearly Paris, which maintained this position by attracting the provinces' most talented musicians. But Parisian musical life was less than adventurous, and many foreign works received their French premieres at provincial festivals.

Parisian concerts took place throughout the social season—that is, from November through May. The height of concert activity lasted from February through April. Many groups and individuals gave series, most commonly presenting four to six programs at biweekly intervals. A contemporary source reported about seven hundred Parisian concerts in 1869, not counting café and outdoor summer concerts or programs in salons. In late summer, musicians followed their audience to resorts. Provincial festivals also occurred during the summer.

Parisian concert halls, of which there was a perpetual shortage, had seating capacities ranging from about four hundred to approximately five thousand, although few held more than two thousand. Among the small halls were several maintained by piano manufacturers (for example, Pleyel), which provided the pianos, thereby gaining publicity for their products. Numerous private salons offered musical entertainment; at some salons, the programs resembled full-length concerts.

Programs consisting of works for a single medium—that is, works exclusively for string quartet, for orchestra, or for a solo pianist—were slowly becoming fashionable but remained in the minority. More prevalent were programs that juxtaposed orchestral music, choral works, and opera arias, or piano pieces, instrumental and vocal solos, and chamber works for various ensembles.

The most popular composers of orchestral and chamber works were five Germanic composers, all deceased: Beethoven (whose music was performed more than twice as often as anyone else's), Mendelssohn, Mozart, Haydn, and Weber (the last known mainly for orchestral works). Trailing these musicians at some distance were Schumann and Adolphe Blanc (b. 1828), a contemporary Frenchman then known for chamber works and long since forgotten. Other significant native composers, such as Hector Berlioz (1803–1869), Camille Saint-Saëns, Georges Onslow (1784–1852), and Louise Farrenc (1804–1875), were played occasionally. The standard vocal repertory emphasized works by many of the same composers—especially Mendelssohn, Haydn, Mozart, and Beethoven— but encompassed a broader chronological span, including excerpts from operas of J. P. Lully, J. P. Rameau, C. W. Gluck, and Handel (whose oratorios were also sampled) and various works of J. S. Bach, as well as contemporary *romances* and *mélodies*, lieder of Schubert and eventually Schumann, and selections from popular nineteenth-century operas, among them works of Gioacchino Rossini (1792–1868), G. Spontini, V. Bellini, Giacomo Meyerbeer, and Giuseppi Verdi (1813–1901). Choral and operatic works of L. Cherubini and Charles Gounod were also essayed at concerts.

A large portion of the solo instrumental repertory involved works of contemporary virtuosos, such as the pianists Anton Rubinstein (1829–1894), Henry Litolff (1818–1891), and Emile Prudent (1817–1863) and the violinists Henri

Vieuxtemps (Belgian; 1820–1881) and Delphin Alard (1815–1888). Slightly earlier piano pieces of Beethoven, Hummel, and Chopin were also played often.

Many of the orchestras, chamber ensembles, and choruses that presented series were labeled (or can be regarded as) societies. The most famous orchestral societies included the Société des Concerts du Conservatoire (from 1828), a Société Sainte Cécile (founded about 1849–1850 by François Seghers), and two groups organized by the conductor Jules Pasdeloup, the Société des Jeunes Artistes (1852–1853) and the Concerts Populaires (1861). The Société des Concerts du Conservatoire, whose orchestra and chorus consisted of roughly 160 faculty, graduates, and students of that institution, was the aristocrat of French concert societies. Admired throughout Europe for its high performance standards and supported not only by the state but also by dedicated subscribers, it nonetheless drew criticism, especially from composers, for its old-fashioned and unchanging repertory. Its conductors during the Second Empire were Narcisse Girard (1797–1860) from January 1849 to 1860, Théophile Tilmant (1799–1878) from January 1861 to 1863, and Georges François Hainl (1807–1873) from January 1864. The latter was chosen over Berlioz and Edouard Ernest Deldevez (1817–1879). The Société des Concerts gave less than a dozen concerts each year, primarily between January and April, in the concert hall of the Conservatoire, rebuilt in 1866 and still in use. The Société Sainte Cécile, an orchestra and chorus of about 130, also had conservative programs but devoted one concert a year to contemporary works. (The Société Sainte Cécile, which performed until 1856, was resurrected by Théodore Weckerlin [1821–1910] without an orchestra in the mid-1860s.) The sixty-two instrumentalists and forty choristers of the Société des Jeunes Artistes (first performance 7 December 1856) were students and graduates of the Conservatoire. They too played the standard repertory, but also essayed music of contemporaries, among them Schumann, Gounod, L. T. Gouvy, and Wagner. The Jeunes Artistes performed at the small Salle Herz and despite receiving financial aid from the Conservatoire accumulated a large deficit. Consequently, in 1861 Pasdeloup decided to replace this society with a more traditional series in a larger hall. He enlarged the orchestra to over one hundred members, engaged a number of celebrated guest soloists, and moved to the Cirque Napoléon, which seated about five thousand. Billing his presentations as the Concerts Populaires, he succeeded in filling the hall by charging low admission fees. Pasdeloup's achievement in attracting a substantial audience to programs of art music perhaps outweighs his musical contribution. Programs of the Concerts Populaires were almost exclusively orchestral and were largely conservative, although Pasdeloup did lead performances of Schumann, Lachner, Wagner, Meyerbeer, Berlioz, and Gounod.

Provincial towns had *sociétés philharmoniques*, ostensibly similar to Parisian institutions. But many of the provincial orchestras were small and incapable of playing symphonic literature. Programs were therefore designed around guest artists who performed solos, while the orchestras presented overtures and dance music. Concerts Populaires that appeared in several cities in the 1860s attempted more ambitious programs of symphonies (or movements thereof) and overtures.

Before the late 1840s, chamber music had been associated mainly with salons. The best known of the series that brought it to Parisian concert halls in the following decades were the Société de Musique de Chambre (from about 1847), the Société des Derniers Quatuors de Beethoven (from about 1851), the Quatuor Armingaud-Jacquard, which began as the Société de Musique de Chambre Armingaud (1856–1867), and the *séances* of the violinist Charles Lamoureux (1834–1899; from 1860). The Société de Musique de Chambre, organized by the violinist Alard and cellist Auguste Franchomme (1808–1884) and also known as the Société Alard-Franchomme, was regarded as a miniature counterpart of the Société des Concerts du Conservatoire, for its members, the best string players and pianists, presented polished renditions of classical sonatas, trios, quartets, and quintets. The Société des Derniers Quatuors de Beethoven was established by the violinist Jean Pierre Maurin (1822–1894) and cellist Alexandre Chevillard (1811–1877). Through carefully prepared performances (at the Salle Pleyel) and persistent programming, the société promoted Beethoven's difficult late quartets, works previously little played in Paris and still controversial. Slowly the group's repertory widened, and from 1855 the quartet was joined by a pianist, who played both chamber music and solo works. The société's success may have inspired the formation of the Quatuor Armingaud-Jacquard (after the violinist Jules Armingaud [1820–1900] and cellist Léon Jacquard [1826–1886], which at first devoted its attention to Mendelssohn's works and was known briefly as the Société des Quatuors de Mendelssohn. Lamoureux's *séances* adopted the name Séances Populaires de Musique de Chambre in 1863 and thereafter emulated the successful Concerts Populaires by performing a relatively traditional repertory and charging a low admission fee that attracted a sizable audience. The participants, a string quartet and pianist, occasionally sampled works of contemporaries such as Brahms and Blanc. The double bass player Achille Gouffé (1804–1874) and the cellist Charles Lebouc (1822–1893) each sponsored long-lasting series of chamber music *séances* that were especially significant for musicians. Both actively promoted recent compositions. As concert series multiplied, new series tried to establish a distinctive identity by specializing. Some concentrated on single genres (the Société des Trios Anciens et Modernes, the Société des Quintettes Anciens et Modernes, a Société des Quintettes Harmoniques); some on recent works (the Société Nationale des Beaux-Arts, the Grands Concerts des Compositeurs Vivants); some on both (the Société des Quatuors Français); and some on individual composers (the Société Schumann, for example).

Concert performances of choral music were heard mainly at programs of orchestral-choral societies. The most famous Parisian choral organization was the Orphéon, founded as a children's group in 1833. When Gounod became its conductor in 1852, there were two thousand *orphéonistes*, among them men, women, and children, and after 1860 (when Pasdeloup and François Bazin [1816–1878] were codirectors) there were separate Orphéons for the Left and Right banks. *Orphéons* were also established in the provinces. At the Première Réunion Générale des Orphéonistes de France in Paris in 1859, six thousand performers from two hundred four societies presented sacred works, secular choruses, and opera excerpts. Similar festivals occurred in the 1860s. Other Parisian choruses included L'Union Chorale (about 1848 to 1858, for mixed voices), the Société des Concerts de Chant Classique (from 1860; performed early religious works and oratorios), the Société Chorale d'Amateurs de Guillot de Sainbris (from 1865), the Société Bourgault-Ducoudray (from 1868; an amateur group that sang Renaissance and Baroque works), and the Société des Oratorios (also from 1868; led by Pasdeloup). In the provinces, choral works were presented at regional festivals in which musicians from several towns joined forces to perform oratorios, orchestral works, and music for military band. The most significant festivals were those of the Association Musicale de l'Ouest (established in 1835). The choral movement reached its peak during the Second Empire, with 147,000 members (by 1868) in 3,243 societies.

Many series and most single concerts were organized by individuals—vocalists, pianists, other instrumentalists, composers, and teachers. Often the single events were considered benefit concerts, of which the beneficiary was the organizer. There were also benefit concerts for charitable causes, particularly for the assistance of needy musicians and other artists. These usually involved large forces, which in turn drew large audiences.

Concerts of light music enjoyed great success at Parisian cafés and hotels and, in summer, at various outdoor locations, especially on or near the Champs Elysées (nightly) and at the Pré Catelan in the Bois de Boulogne (on Sunday afternoons). In 1865 Thérésa, the reigning *café-concert* star, was able to command a salary of 5,000 to 6,000 francs a month. Orchestras, military bands (including the Guides and Garde of Paris), choruses, and vocal and instrumental soloists presented diverse combinations of dance music, overtures, virtuosic solos, opera excerpts, choral works, and occasionally symphonies or movements thereof. Such concerts proliferated in the 1860s as crowds enjoyed the opportunity to listen, dance, eat, and drink in fashionable surroundings. *Concerts de famille* offered an atmosphere reputedly more refined than that of events frequented by beer drinkers.

Both the success of café and outdoor concerts and the dramatic increase in other concert activity demonstrate the phenomenon that best characterizes the musical scene in the Second Empire (and especially in the 1860s): the popularization of musical entertainment. The change from a patronized to a commercial concert world had taken place by mid-century, and musicians and entrepreneurs had already discovered that if admission fees were low (no more than a franc), a sizable segment of the population would pay to hear light music. After 1850 musical interests of the audience and the ability of concert organizers to meet these interests continued to develop. Undoubtedly for the growing crowds who attended outdoor or café concerts, music was a pleasant diversion at an event that was essentially social (although even at these concerts some art music was performed). But as the establishment of chamber music series in public concert halls and, even more convincingly, the overwhelming success of the Concerts Populaires demonstrated, appreciation of the best orchestral and chamber music was growing rapidly. The participation of a vast new audience for music previously associated with the elite provided a refreshing change for musicians and prepared the way for the widely acknowledged resurgence of French music after the Franco-Prussian War.

E. Bernard, "Jules Pasdeloup et les Concerts Populaires," *RM* 57 (1971); J. Cooper, *The Rise of Instrumental Music and Concert Series in Paris, 1828–1871* (Ann Arbor, 1983); J. Fulcher, "The Orphéon Societies: 'Music for the Workers' in Second Empire France," *International Review of the Aesthetics and Sociology of Music* (1979); C. Marcel-Robillard, "Une étoile sous le Second Empire: Thérésa (1837–1913)," *Vieux papier* 28 (1978); W. Weber, "Artisans in Concert Life of Mid-Nineteenth-Century London and Paris," *Journal of Contemporary History* 13 (April 1978); and "How Concerts Went Classical in the Nineteenth Century," *PWSFH* 5 (1978).

Jeffrey Cooper

Related entries: CAVAILLE-COLL; GOUNOD; HALEVY; MEILHAC; MEYERBEER; OFFENBACH; PASDELOUP; SAINT-SAENS; SCHNEIDER, H.; SCRIBE; *TANNHAUSER* PREMIERE; THOMAS; VIARDOT.

CONFEDERATION, ITALIAN. See ITALIAN CONFEDERATION.

CONGRESS OF PARIS, the peace congress following the Crimean War; the most important European assemblage between the Congress of Vienna of 1815 and the Congress of Berlin of 1878. The fall of Sebastopol on 10 September 1855 achieved perhaps the only goal that could justify for French opinion a continuation of the war. Britain having refused in November to envisage a revolutionary war (for the liberation of Poland) and Austria having at last agreed (in December) to impose the Allied war aims (the Four Points) on Russia by an ultimatum, Napoleon III firmly drew a reluctant Britain to the conference table. On 15 January Russia yielded to Austria's ultimatum. The Congress of Paris met on 25 February 1856 under the presidency of the French foreign minister, comte Alexandre Walewski. In addition to their ambassadors at Paris, Britain was represented by Lord Clarendon, Russia by Count Orlov, Austria by Count Buol, and Turkey by Ali Pasha. Prussia was excluded, on British insistence, for having refused to abandon neutrality during the war. The peace treaty was quickly sketched in absolute secrecy; only in regard to the new Bessarabian frontier was there significant debate. Austria and Britain were successful in removing Russia from the Danube, but Napoleon III intervened to secure important modifications in Russia's favor, including retention of the town of Bolgrad. Prussia, as a signatory of the Straits Convention of 1841, was admitted to the congress on 18 March.

The Treaty of Paris (30 March 1856) neutralized the Black Sea, reaffirmed the Straits Convention, guaranteed freedom of navigation of the Danube (it was to be organized by a European commission), and demilitarized the Aaland Islands. Turkey, which had independently promised to ameliorate the condition of its Christian subjects, was admitted to the European concert, its territorial integrity guaranteed, and provision made for collective mediation of disputes involving the sultan and a signatory or signatories of the treaty. The Ionian Isles, Serbia, and the Danubian Principalities were placed under the protection of the signatory powers. Concerning the last, it was decided to consult the peoples of the Principalities as to their wishes in regard to national self-determination. A future conference would bring about definitive reorganization. But the Principalities would be autonomous and with an independent, national administration. Nothing was done for Poland, the czar having intimated that he would act positively. At the twenty-second session of the congress, held on 8 April, a free-ranging discussion embraced the condition of Italy (especially the Papal States and the Kingdom of the Two Sicilies), questions of maritime law, and abuses by the Belgian press.

In addition to the Treaty of Paris, the congress, on the initiative of France, adopted the Declaration of Paris, formalizing in a humanitarian and civilizing sense certain rules of naval warfare, notably the abolition of privateering, protection of enemy goods (other than contraband) by a neutral flag, protection of neutral goods (if not contraband) even under an enemy flag, and abolition of paper blockade. There was, however, no adequate definition of contraband. Within two years, over forty additional countries (but not the United States) adhered to the declaration. The Congress of Paris also adopted, on the motion of Lord Clarendon, a resolution urging mediation between signatories of the Treaty of Paris before resort to war.

Napoleon III's was a dominant influence at the congress. Although scrupulously avoiding a break with Britain, he resisted a number of additional British demands on Russia while successfully wooing his former enemy. The birth of the prince imperial on 16 March contributed to make the Congress of Paris, whose final session was held on 16 April, the apogee of the reign.

W. Baumgart, *Der Friede von Paris, 1856* (Munich, 1972; trans. A. P. Saab, 1981, as *The Peace of Paris, 1856*); F. de Bernardy, "Le Congrès de Paris," *RDM* (15 March 1956); W. E. Mosse, "How Russia Made Peace, 1855–1856," *CHJ* (1955); F. Piggott, *The Declaration of Paris, 1856* (London, 1919); W. F. Spencer, "The Mason Memorandum and the Diplomatic Origins of the Declaration of Paris," in N. Barker and M. Brown, eds., *Diplomacy in an Age of Nationalism* (Hague, 1971); H. Temperley, "The Treaty of Paris and Its Execution," *JMH* 4 (1932); F. Valsecchi, "Cavour al Congresso di Parigi," *Risorgimento*, no. 2 (1956).

Related entries: ALLIANCE POLICY; CONGRESS POLICY; CRIMEAN WAR.

CONGRESS POLICY, an important aspect of the foreign policy of Napoleon III. In his writings of the period before 1852, the French emperor appears as a sincere European, a subscriber to the myth of St. Helena, convinced that the prudent statesman should take the lead of the ideas of the day and that these ideas could be realized only within the context of a European community and concert. During the early years of power, Napoleon III showed a tenacious predilection for conference diplomacy, which can be traced in a long series of congresses or conferences held or proposed: the Vienna conferences of 1853–1855; the Congress of Paris of 1856; the conferences on Bolgrad (1856), Neufchâtel (1857), and the Danubian Principalities (1858 and 1859); the proposed congresses to prevent a Franco-Austrian war in 1859 and to organize Italy (in 1859 and 1860); the two conferences on Syrian intervention (1860–1861); and the proposed congress on Poland (spring of 1863). Out of the Polish crisis of 1863 came the dramatic proposal by Napoleon III on 4 November of a general European congress that would confront the major European problems before they could lead to war. The proposal was vetoed by the British government, which distrusted France and had, besides, an aversion to taking positions in advance of crises. Yet Napoleon III's sincere disappointment at the failure of the congress to meet would seem to indicate that here had been revealed if not the goal at least the method of his foreign policy: to bring about, through alliances if possible, a general congress that would revise the Treaties of 1815 and solve Europe's problems without conflict. In this way, France would exercise its natural moral hegemony (and perhaps gain some frontier rectifications), the European peoples would be liberated and consolidated, the Ottoman Empire would pay the cost (would, in fact, cease to exist), and Europe's disputes henceforth would be solved by discussion and arrangement rather than by war. This congress idea persisted in French policy from 1863 through 1867, manifesting itself in conferences on Schleswig-Holstein (1864) and the Danubian Principalities (1866), the congress proposal to avert war between Prussia and Austria (May 1866), the conference on Luxembourg (1867), and the proposed congress on Rome of that same year.

With the rise of Prussia, however, and the decline of the authoritarian Empire at home, Napoleon III, while retaining his commitment to the European concert, seems increasingly to have seen it in conservative terms. The role of the congress policy in his mind ceased to be revision and became that of preserving the status quo. A general European congress could, for example, put the Treaty of Prague, which had ended the Austro-Prussian War, under European sanction and thus prevent the clash between France and Prussia that must inevitably follow any further Prussian expansion. In January 1869 a European conference met at London to prevent war between Greece and Turkey over Crete. The French government expressed the hope that the success of this effort might serve as a precedent. But the crisis of July 1870, which culminated in war between France and Prussia, could not be averted by a sense of European community that was at least a century ahead of its time. The congress idea foundered in the short run on various difficulties; in the long run it was probably doomed to failure by the physical decline of Napoleon III and the relative decline of France. Both of these factors played important roles in what may be regarded as the crisis of the French emperor's congress policy, his failure to impose a European congress, by force if necessary, after the decisive Prussian victory over Austria at Sadowa in July 1866.

W. E. Echard, *Napoleon III and the Concert of Europe* (Baton Rouge: Louisiana State University Press, 1983).

Related entries: ALLIANCE POLICY; BOLGRAD; CONGRESS OF PARIS; CRETAN REVOLT; ITALIAN WAR; LUXEMBOURG CRISIS; NATION-ALITIES; REVISION; ROMAN QUESTION; RUMANIAN UNITY; SYRIAN EXPEDITION; VENETIA.

CONNEAU, HENRI (1803–1877), chief physician and long-time friend of Louis Napoleon; born 4 June 1803 at Milan. Conneau's father was a French functionary in Milan; his mother was Italian. While studying medicine at Florence in 1820, he served for nine months as secretary to Louis Napoleon's father, Louis Bonaparte. Physician at Rome in 1831, he formed, during the insurrection of that year in the Papal States, a friendship with Louis Napoleon and became physician to Hortense, the prince's mother. As personal physician of Louis Napoleon, he accompanied him into exile in England, participated with him in the unsuccessful Boulogne adventure of 1840, shared his prison cell at Ham, refusing amnesty in 1844 and remaining on as a companion after the termination of his own five-year prison sentence in October 1845. On 25 May 1846 Conneau assisted Louis Napoleon to escape from prison and as a consequence was himself jailed for three months, after which he rejoined the prince in London where Louis Napoleon bought him a medical practice. Conneau encouraged the coup d'état of December 1851, although he was not a party to it.

On reestablishment of the Empire, Conneau became chief physician of the imperial household, in charge of charity. He was a member of the Corps Législatif, 1852–1867; senator, 1867–1870; conseiller général in Corsica and vice-president of the conseil; and member of the Academy of Medicine for his work in meteorology and on electricity and his inventions of precision instruments. He was named grand officer of the Legion of Honor in 1867. Conneau was one of five doctors who examined Napoleon III on 1 July 1870 and decided that an immediate operation was not necessary. He remained loyal to the deposed emperor after 1870, attending him at Chislehurst until the end. Napoleon III made use of his friend, an ardent champion of Italian unity, in his secret Italian diplomacy, most notably in March 1858 when a visit by the physician to Turin arranged the fateful interview of Napoleon III and of the Sardinian prime minister, Count Benso di Cavour, at Plombières four months later, and in August 1860 when he talked with the Italian emissaries before their interview with the emperor at Chambéry. Conneau died at La Porta, Corsica, 14 August 1877.

M. de Baillehache, *Grands bonapartistes* (Paris, 1899); M. de Fontbrune, "Le docteur Conneau," *MH*, no. 130 (1960).

Related entries: CHAMBERY; CHISLEHURST; LOUIS NAPOLEON; PLOMBIERES.

CONSEIL D'ETAT, the chief administrative body of the Second Empire and, in the form it assumed between 1852 and 1870, a major innovation of the constitution of 14 January 1852. The Conseil d'Etat linked the executive and legislative functions of the government while screening one from the other. The Conseil d'Etat of the Second Empire was installed in its palace of the Quai d'Orsay 1 April 1852. It was abolished by decree of the provisional government 15 September 1870.

Modeled on its predecessor of 1800–1814, Napoleon III's Conseil d'Etat headed the administrative apparatus, drafted regulations, gave advice, settled disputes (a function restored to it by the Second Empire), regulated and supervised incorporated enterprises (*sociétés anonymes*), decided issues of competence and jurisdiction between the administrative and judicial authorities, received petitions, and judged the acts of functionaries when requested by the emperor. As a political body, the Conseil d'Etat provided liaison between the executive and legislative functions, advised the emperor concerning projects of law, drafted all proposed legislation (including budgets) and defended the proposals before the Corps Législatif and the Senate, and approved or rejected all amendments after discussing them with delegates from the Corps Législatif. The conseil might also be asked to examine projects of *sénatus-consultes*. *Conseillers* were occasionally sent *en mission* by the emperor to the departments. The Conseil d'Etat lacked the power of initiative; it could only advise, even in administrative matters. During the Second Empire, however, its advice was never rejected.

The organization of the Conseil d'Etat was determined primarily by the constitution of 14 January 1852, the organic decree of 25 January 1852, and the decrees of 30 January, 22 March, and 31 December 1852. *Conseillers d'état* were named and dismissed by the emperor. They received an annual salary of 25,000 francs. There were a maximum of 165: 40 to 50 *conseillers d'état en service ordinaire*, 15 *conseillers d'état en service ordinaire hors section*, 20 *conseillers d'état en service extraordinaire*, 40 *maîtres de requêtes*, and 40 *auditeurs*. The last two categories, each divided into two classes, also served, at need, the *service extraordinaire*. The *auditeurs*, chosen in effect by examination from lists that until March 1870 were established by the emperor, were apprentices in high administration, a revival of the system of Napoleon I that did not prove notably successful during the Second Empire. The size and classification of the *auditorat* varied. In 1852 there were twenty first class and twenty second class; in 1853, twenty and sixty; in 1860, forty and forty; and in 1869, thirty-two and sixteen.

Conseillers in ordinary service and *maîtres de requêtes* could not be senators or deputies or functionaries but could be military or naval officers on inactive service. Meetings were secret. The emperor presided the Conseil d'Etat by right (until the constitutional changes of 1870) but designated a president to preside in his absence. Jules Baroche held this post from 30 December 1852 until 23 June 1863 and often exercised a high hand. From June 1863 the title was *ministre président le conseil d'état* and was held successively by Eugène Rouher (23 June

1863), Gustave Rouland (18 October 1863), Adolphe Vuitry (28 September 1864), Prosper Chasseloup-Laubat (17 July 1869), M.L.P.F. Esquirou de Parieu (1815–1893; 2 January 1870), and Julien Henri Busson-Billaut (1823–1888; 9 August 1870). The emperor also appointed a vice-president (increased to three from 18 October 1863 to January 1867). The president had ministerial rank from 1853. He received an annual salary of 80,000 francs, increased to 100,000 in 1854, as well as expenses and lodgings. There was also a *secrétaire-général*, named by the emperor from among the *maîtres de requêtes*. The ministers were full members of the Conseil d'Etat, as were, with the emperor's permission, adult male French princes. The conseil was divided into six sections, each presided by a president named by the emperor:

1. Legislation, justice, and foreign affairs.
2. Contentions (*contentieux*).
3. Interior, public instruction, and cults.
4. Public works, agriculture, and commerce.
5. War and marine.
6. Finances.

Contentions (*affaires contentieuses*) were dealt with by a special assembly composed of the *section du contentieux* and ten other *conseillers*, chosen two from each of the other five sections by the emperor and renewed by one-half every year. The president of the Conseil d'Etat, presiding the assembly, had *voix prépondérante*. *Affaires contentieuses* were introduced by report in public session, but deliberations were in secret. Projects of law were sent to the Conseil d'Etat by the emperor either directly or through the minister of state, who was kept fully informed of proceedings. Projects were referred to the sections within whose competence they fell. The drafted legislation was returned to the emperor, who forwarded it by decree to the Corps Législatif or to the Senate, naming, on advice of the president of the Conseil d'Etat, the three *conseillers* who would serve as "government orators" before the chambers during consideration of the proposal. Proposed amendments were sent directly to the general assembly of the Conseil d'Etat for examination. They could be rejected or incorporated into the project. The Conseil d'Etat in general assembly decided measures by simple majority, through a show of hands.

The Second Empire left only nine of forty former *conseillers d'état en service ordinaire* in place. Subsequent appointees were men of weight, mostly from the legal profession and the middle bourgeoisie, holding good university degrees, although there were complaints that too often the Conseil d'Etat was regarded as an Invalides for failed bureaucrats. More than half had had experience under other regimes, often as ministers, deputies, or *conseillers*. Perhaps one in ten was bonapartist. No *conseiller* was ever dismissed. The average age increased during the Empire from fifty to fifty-eight.

Even critics recognized the usefulness of the institution, the competence of the *conseillers*, and the burden of work borne. From January 1852 to December

1865, the Conseil d'Etat dealt, for example, with 30 projects of *sénatus-con-sultes*, 3,491 projects of law (932 of general interest), 1,924 proposed amend-ments (842 were wholly adopted, 468 partially accepted, and 602 rejected), 235,000 administrative affairs, 14,927 *affaires contentieuses,* and 230,957 pe-titions. Only in regard to the decrees confiscating Orleans property in 1852 did Napoleon III interfere with a decision of the Conseil d'Etat, arguing then that the *conseillers* were not magistrates but *des hommes politiques*. More often he listened patiently to criticism and more than once abandoned plans in the face of opposition. The conseil appears, in fact, to have regarded him as a utopian, to be carefully watched. There were other grounds for disagreement as well. The Conseil d'Etat only narrowly and reluctantly approved the general security law proposed after the attempt on Napoleon III's life by Felice Orsini in 1858. Opposition increased as the influence of Orleanists and other liberals within the conseil grew, although party spirit remained subdued. The emperor rarely pre-sided the Conseil d'Etat and often sought advice elsewhere. Indeed, the Conseil d'Etat failed in its essential political purpose. Prefects balked at cooperating with *conseillers-en-mission*; ministers managed to establish effective if unconstitu-tional contacts with the deputies; the Corps Législatif gradually reasserted its rights vis-à-vis the Conseil d'Etat, and some *conseillers* welcomed this devel-opment. Formal changes brought about by the evolution toward the Liberal Empire recognized a situation already largely accomplished in fact. Even before its suspension following 4 September 1870, the "Napoleonic" Conseil d'Etat had ceased to exist, having lost successively its monopoly in representing the government before the chambers (from 24 November 1860 the president of the Conseil d'Etat had to share the task with two other ministers; from 23 June 1863, he became simply an assistant, together with three vice-presidents, to the minister of state; on 19 January 1867 interpellation was reintroduced), its control of amendments (24 November 1860, 3 February 1861, 18 July 1866, 8 September 1869, and 20 April 1870), and its regulatory power over the *sociétés anonymes* (1863, 1865, 1867). In its administrative role, however, the Conseil d'Etat of the Second Empire did important and sometimes innovative work.

V. Wright, *Le conseil d'état sous le Second Empire* (Paris, 1972).

Related entries: CHASSELOUP-LAUBAT; CONSTITUTION; CORPS LEG-ISLATIF; MINISTER OF STATE; MINISTRY; REFORM; ROUHER; ROU-LAND; SENATE; VUITRY.

CONSEIL PRIVE, an appointive council whose functions were to advise the emperor on great occasions and to become a council of regency if required—that is, to take over the day-to-day tasks of government in case of the absence or incapacity of the emperor. The *sénatus-consulte* of 17 July 1856, which had established plans for a regency following the attempt on Napoleon III's life by Pianori (28 April 1855) and the emperor's projected trip to the Crimea during the Crimean War (February–March 1855), provided that the empress should preside the government or, in default of that, a French prince, unless otherwise decreed by the emperor. A regency council was envisaged that would consist of French princes designated by the emperor (or, if he failed to so designate, the two closest to the throne) and other persons also appointed by him or, failing that, five persons named by the Senate. Throughout 1857, Napoleon III considered creating a conseil privé that would become, if required, the contemplated regency council. His original preference was for the membership to include not only individuals named by him (Marshal Aimable Pélissier, Victor Fialin Persigny) but also the archbishop of Paris, the minister of state, and the presidents of the Senate, Corps Législatif, and Conseil d'Etat.

Felice Orsini's assassination attempt on 14 January 1858 made the organization of a regency council imperative. Napoleon III agreed reluctantly to the demand of his uncle, Prince Jérôme, former king of Westphalia, that he be permitted to preside over meetings of the Council of Ministers in the absence of the emperor or the regent and that Jérôme's son, Prince Napoleon, be named minister of Algeria. But fearing that in the event of the latter's becoming regent, he could control the council of regency by naming his friends to preside the great organs of state, Napoleon III decided that appointments to the Conseil Privé would be of persons rather than by office. The decree of 1 February 1858 so provided, whereupon Jérôme and his son declined to be members. At its first meeting (12 March 1858) the Conseil Privé included Raymond Troplong, Auguste de Morny, Pélissier, Achille Fould, and Jules Baroche. However, by the *sénatus-consulte* of 17 July 1856 and in the absence of other arrangements, the Conseil Privé, on becoming the Council of Regency, would include Prince Napoleon and his father. The prince did in fact become a member of the Conseil Privé and was its vice-president in January 1865, at a time when its members included Alexandre Walewski and Pierre Magne. Throughout the latter part of the Empire, the Conseil Privé met on occasion, often together with the Council of Ministers, to advise the emperor concerning exceptional questions.

Related entries: CONSEIL D'ETAT; EUGENIE; NAPOLEON III: ASSASSINATION ATTEMPTS; ORSINI; PRINCE IMPERIAL; PRINCE NAPOLEON; SECOND EMPIRE.

CONSTITUTION OF 14 JANUARY 1852, the organic law constituting the Second Empire. The coup d'état of 2 December 1851 effectively ended the Second Republic, although some of its forms were retained for another year. The coup suspended the constitution of 4 November 1848 and called the nation to a plebiscite (21–22 December 1851) that invested Louis Napoleon with constituent powers to prepare a new constitution based on the principles of 1789, universal manhood suffrage, and the supremacy of the executive. These Louis Napoleon had drawn from his meditation on the Napoleonic legend, his reflections on recent history, and his experience as president of the Second Republic from 10 December 1848.

The new constitution was deliberately brief (fifty-eight articles) and lacking in detail. It had been discussed for several weeks by a commission named by

Louis Napoleon (Joseph, comte de Flahaut [1785–1870], Victor Fialin Persigny, Eugène Rouher, Raymond Troplong, and Jacques André Mesnard [1792–1858]) and then, at his insistence, quickly drafted by Rouher, perhaps in a single night, and signed on 14 January. It had no preamble. An accompanying proclamation related the new regime to its Napoleonic precedents. The constitution was held to have been ratified in advance by the plebiscite. It became effective with the convocation of the newly elected legislature on 29 March 1852. Article 1 guaranteed the principles of 1789, which were held to form the "bases of French public law." The constitution created a regime still ostensibly republican but in which the supremacy of the executive ("le president de la République gouverne au moyen des ministres, du Conseil d'Etat, du Sénat et du Corps législatif") was ensured in three ways: by accretions to the executive power, by restraints on other government organs and a denial of parliamentary government, and by repudiation of the principle of separation of powers. The president of the republic was responsible only to the people. In addition to the usual executive powers, he could name his successor at the end of a ten-year term, appeal directly to the nation through plebiscites, dissolve the lower chamber (the Corps Législatif) and appoint the members of the other two (the Conseil d'Etat and the Senate). He appointed and dismissed the ministers, who were responsible only to him. He concluded and ratified treaties. He alone could initiate projects of law, and all acts were promulgated at his pleasure. He declared martial law, named all mayors, and controlled the Haute Cour de Justice, established to judge without appeal all acts against the president or the state. Moreover, he participated in the constituent power since he could propose constitutional changes through the Senate (*sénatus-consultes*) or by plebiscite.

These specific accretions to executive power were enhanced by restraints on other government organs and by an explicit denial of parliamentary forms. All deputies, senators, and other officials were required to take an oath to the person of the prince president, as well as to the constitution. The Senate, while designated repository (together with the people) of constituent powers and charged with supervising and completing the constitution, was deprived of legislative functions and restricted to secret sessions whose timing and length depended on the president. The Senate could not choose its own officers or design its own rules. The Corps Législatif was elected every six years by universal manhood suffrage. All laws required its approval, but great care was taken to deny this elective body a parliamentary character and to restrict its essential activity to a simple vote for or against the projects of law prepared, on initiative of the president, by the Conseil d'Etat. The Conseil d'Etat, in turn, was appointed by the president and had no power of initiative. The Corps Législatif could debate but could not publicize its debates; it could not freely amend; it could not interpellate. The ministry depended entirely on the president; moreover, cabinet solidarity was explicitly repudiated.

It was the stated philosophy of the constitution of 1852 that there was but one government, having legislative, executive, and judicial functions—hence no separation of powers. In practice, this meant a government consisting of the chief of state on the one hand, and on the other of his instruments. Of those instruments none was more important than the Conseil d'Etat; because ministers could not appear in the Senate or the Corps Législatif, it was the *conseillers* who played the vital role of intermediary, drafting legislation, shepherding it through the chambers, and approving or rejecting proposed amendments.

The constitution was completed between 2 December 1851 and the end of the dictatorship on 29 March 1852 by a series of decrees that not only filled in its sparse framework but also served methodically to isolate the individual, depriving him of freedom of action and of the possibility of combination and cooperation, whether physically or in the realm of opinion and ideas. A decree of 31 December 1851 consigned press offenses to correctional tribunals (criminal court). There followed, in early 1852, decrees of 11 January: reorganizing the National Guard; 22 January: organizing the ministry; 24 January: reestablishing titles of nobility; 25 January: organizing the Conseil d'Etat; 30 January: setting procedures of the Conseil d'Etat; 2 February: organizing the electoral regime so that every advantage would be given to official candidates; 12 February: establishing costumes for public and court officials; 17 February: organizing the regime of the press (a combination of judicial and administrative control, which, in the case of the periodical press, amounted to an effective censorship and control); 17 February: designating the *fête napoléonienne*, 15 August, as the sole national holiday; 1 March: setting retirement age for judges; 8 March: establishing the oath required of all officials; 9 March: reorganizing public instruction so that the government could expel any member of the University and name members to the Conseil Supérieur to which those expelled would no longer have the right of appeal; 16 March: reorganizing the Legion of Honor; 22 March: organizing the Senate and the Corps Législatif and defining the relations among the organs of government; 25 March: reorganizing the prefectoral system in order to increase greatly the authority and responsibilities of the prefects; 25 March: proscribing unauthorized public meetings or political organizations when either involved twenty persons or more. In addition, a decree of 31 December 1852 reestablished censorship of the theater, and a *sénatus-consulte* of 12 July 1852 organized the Haute Cour de Justice.

Few changes were necessary, therefore, to convert the regime of 1852 into an imperial one. The *sénatus-consulte* of 7 November 1852, ratified by plebiscite of 21–22 November, reestablished the imperial dignity, designated Louis Napoleon as its possessor with the title of Napoleon III, set the succession in his male line, dealt with the consequences of a lack of male heirs (a decree of 18 December 1852 set collateral rights of succession in the family of Prince Napoleon), called for a plebiscite on the reestablishment of the Empire, and concluded: "The constitution of 14 January 1852 is maintained in all dispositions which are not in contradiction with the present *sénatus-consulte*." A *sénatus-consulte* of 25 December 1852 defined *prince français* and *prince imperial* and stipulated the changes necessary to make the constitution compatible with an imperial regime. Substantial additions were made to the prerogatives and powers of the head of state. He could preside the Senate, alter tariffs through treaties (which did not require legislative ratification), initiate public works projects without legislative authorization, amend the organic decree of 22 March 1852 organizing the relations of the major government bodies, distribute by decree within ministries the global amounts voted for each ministry by the Corps Lég-islatif, transfer by decree money from one section to another of a ministerial budget (*virement*), and open extraordinary credits subject to later approval by the Corps Législatif. In addition, the annual report by the head of state to the chambers was abolished, and it was stipulated that the *procès-verbal* of the Corps Législatif would state simply the operations and votes of that body. Finally, an organic decree of 31 December 1852 made the necessary modifications to the decree of 22 March. Essentially the imperial constitution created a government that has been called one of democratic caesarism. To rule, Napoleon III required the explicit support of the French people, but, given such support, he could rule with few trammels.

From 1852 until 1869, the imperial constitution was preserved in its essentials but not without change. Whether by the will of the emperor or by force of circumstances or a combination, the constitution and the regime were modified through a series of decrees, laws, and *sénatus-consultes*: 21 June 1853: abolishing the Ministry of Police; 17 July 1856 (*sénatus-consulte*): setting the conditions for a regency; 29 May 1857 (*sénatus-consulte*): adding six more deputies to the Corps Législatif; 1 February 1858: establishing the Conseil Privé; 17 February 1858 (*sénatus-consulte*): requiring candidates for election to the Corps Législatif to take the oath; 27 February 1858: promulgating the *loi de sûreté générale*; 10 October 1859: increasing the powers of the prefect of the Seine; 24 November 1860: reestablishing the annual speech from the throne and permitting an address to the throne by the chambers in reply; granting to the chambers a limited right of interpellation during preparation of the address, appointing two ministers without portfolio to join with the minister presiding the Conseil d'Etat in pre-senting projects of law to the chambers (*conseillers d'état* could still be delegated to this task), and permitting publication of debates of the Senate and Corps Législatif; 2 February 1861 (*sénatus-consulte*): organizing publicity of debate of the two chambers, *Le moniteur* to publish both a *compte rendu analytique* and a *compte rendu in extenso*; other papers could reproduce either but only *in extenso* for any topic); 3 February 1861: permitting preliminary discussion of projects of law in secret session by the Corps Législatif (before referral to the *bureaux* and a *commission*) and in the presence of government commissioners authorized to take part in the discussion; granting permission to the Corps Législatif to elect six secretaries each session and to discuss but not vote any amendment supported by at least five deputies, even if previously rejected by the *commission* or the Conseil d'Etat; 13 April 1861: effecting a degree of administrative decentrali-zation; 15 November 1861: renouncing extraordinary credits opened by decree; 31 December 1861 (*sénatus-consulte*): revising budgetary procedures (proposals for each ministry to be presented to the Corps Législatif by sections, chapter, and articles, and voted by sections; supplementary or extraordinary credits to be opened only by law); 31 May 1862: establishing modern principles of public accountability (budget); 23 May 1863 (law): reducing the role of the Conseil d'Etat in regulating limited liability companies; 23 June 1863 (*sénatus-consulte*): making the minister of state sole representative of the government before the chambers (assisted by the minister presiding the Conseil d'Etat); 6 January 1864: ending censorship and control of the theaters; 25 May 1864 (law): granting limited right of coalition to workers; 18 July 1866 (*sénatus-consulte*): reserving debate on constitutional revision to the senate; requiring amendments rejected by the Conseil d'Etat or the *commissions* of the Corps Législatif to be referred to the Corps Législatif and, if taken into consideration, to be reexamined by the *commissions* and the Conseil d'Etat; permitting the Corps Législatif to determine the length of its sessions; 19 January 1867: suppressing the address and permitting the chambers to interpellate the government (if supported by two Senate and four Corps Législatif *bureaux*); 5 February 1867: restoring the tribune in the Corps Législatif; 14 March 1867 (*sénatus-consulte*): empowering the Senate to request that the Corps Législatif reconsider a project in its subsequent session; 29 July 1867 (law and *sénatus-consulte*): withdrawing control of limited liability companies from the Conseil d'Etat.

Until the end of 1869, despite these numerous modifications, the imperial constitution and regime of 1852 remained structurally intact, although the laws of 25 May 1864 and of 6 June 1868 on associations and meetings and that of 11 May 1868 on the press had compromised the deliberate isolation of the individual in face of the state. In the last two years of the Empire, however, events precipitated toward liberalization, culminating in an almost complete reworking of the constitution. The Ministry of State was abolished 17 July 1869, following the elections of that year. The *sénatus-consulte* of 6 September 1869 added to the powers and prerogatives of the Corps Législatif the right to initiate legislation (shared with the emperor and Senate), to elect its own *bureau*, to adopt amendments even against the advice of a *commission* or of the Conseil d'Etat, to vote the budget by chapters (rather than sections), to make its own rules, and to control tariffs (which could no longer be changed by treaty without Corps Législatif consent). The Senate's meetings were made public, and it was given the right of self-regulation. The Senate also obtained a suspensive veto and control over changes in the decree regulating relations among the public powers (such changes would henceforth require a *sénatus-consulte*). Ministers could be members of both chambers, and interpellation was freed of restraints. Wording and context of the *sénatus-consulte* of 6 September did not, however, make clear whether ministers were to be responsible to the chambers as well as to the emperor.

Finally, a new constitution, defined by the *sénatus-consulte* of 20 April 1870, approved by the plebiscite of 8 May, and promulgated on 21 May, replaced the revised constitution of 14 January 1852. It reaffirmed the principles of 1789, the imperial dignity, the oath to the emperor's person, and the right of the emperor to appeal directly to the people through plebiscites. But it stated, "L'empereur gouverne avec le concours des ministres, du Sénat, du Corps législatif et du Conseil d'Etat." Henceforth the legislative function, including the right of initiative, was to be exercised collectively by the emperor, the Senate (which became a full legislative body), and the Corps Législatif. The Corps Législatif could receive petitions and must be the first chamber to act on tax legislation. The ministers were made responsible to the emperor and to the chambers. The emperor continued to name senators (but no more than twenty per year) and the chief officers of the Senate, but he no longer presided that body by right. The Senate lost its constituent powers ("la Constitution ne peut être modifiée que par le Peuple sur la proposition de l'empereur"). The Conseil d'État, no longer presided by the emperor, continued to draft projects of law and to argue them before the chambers, but its loss of control over amendments was confirmed. Moreover, article 33 of the constitution of 1852, by which the emperor could exercise emergency powers in cooperation with the Senate, was suppressed. Thus in two decades the constitution had evolved from the charter of a dictatorship to that of a parliamentary democracy.

H. Berton, *L'évolution constitutionnelle du Second Empire* (Paris, 1902); P. A. Cucheval-Clarigny, *Histoire de la constitution de 1852* (Paris, 1869); L. Girard, "Histoire et constitution, 1851–1855," *BSHM* no. 2 (1963); M. Prélot, "La signification constitutionnelle du Second Empire," *RFSP* (January–March 1953); T. Zeldin, *The Political System of Napoleon III* (New York, 1958).

Related entries: AUTHORITARIAN EMPIRE; COALITIONS LAW; CONSEIL D'ETAT; CORPS LEGISLATIF; CROWNING THE EDIFICE; DECENTRALIZATION; GOVERNMENT FINANCE; LIBERAL EMPIRE; MINISTRY; MINISTER OF STATE; OATH; PLEBISCITE; PREFECTS; PRESS REGIME; REFORM; SECOND EMPIRE; SENATE; UNIVERSAL MANHOOD SUFFRAGE; TROPLONG.

LE CONSTITUTIONNEL, largest and most important of the daily Paris semiofficial newspapers during the Second Empire (the others were *La patrie* and *Le pays*). Founded in 1815, *Le constitutionnel* had supported the regime during the July Monarchy. Its owner from 1844, Louis Véron, known as Docteur Véron (1798–1867), was a Parisian dilettante, a physician, journalist, director of the Opéra, politician, businessman, and boulevardier, who was persuaded by Achille Fould to support Louis Napoleon after 1848. Auguste de Morny, Louis Napoleon's half-brother, was also an important stockholder in the paper. Although Véron applauded the coup d'état of 2 December 1851, he did not prove pliant enough for Victor Fialin Persigny, the minister of the interior (1852–1855). After serving two *avertissements* on *Le constitutionnel*, Persigny encouraged *Le pays* as a competitor. Véron, sensitive to the political currents, sold his newspaper in 1852 for the huge sum of 1.9 million francs to the financier Jules Mirès, whose Société des Journaux Associés already controlled *Le pays* and the *Journal des chemins de fer* (founded 1842). It was a profitable transaction for Véron and also for Morny, whose shares in *Le constitutionnel* Véron repurchased. When Mirès' financial empire collapsed in 1861, Morny took the opportunity to replace him as the dominant voice in the Société.

All of the semiofficial newspapers exchanged the same personnel, and all sustained constant supervision of their affairs. *Le constitutionnel* and *Le pays* often had a single director. Nevertheless, the papers differed in content and style. *Le constitutionnel* was the more respected. It enjoyed special privileges, including important official releases and articles that were written in the Tuileries. Its *secrétaire de la rédaction*, Joseph Xavier Saintine or "Boniface" (1798–1865), was understood to sign articles written by Napoleon III. *Avertissements* were issued, but usually either to create the fiction of independence or to deflate unsuccessful trial balloons. Pierre Grandguillot (1829–1891) succeeded Amédée Renée (1808–1859) as director on the latter's death. From 1863 through 1865, he directed both *Le constitutionnel* and *Le pays* as Renée had also done from 1857 to 1859. He was succeeded by Gibiat. August Chevalier (1809–1868), brother of the noted economist, was political director from November 1862. Among the editors-in-chief were Philippe Cucheval-Clarigny (1822–1895), Antoine Grenier (1833–1881), Paulin Limayrac (1817–1868), and Robert Mitchell (1839–1916). Limayrac, who became chief editor in 1861, also wrote the literary review. In 1868 he was named prefect of the Lot. His immediate successor, Henri Joseph Baudrillart (1821–1892), was followed by Mitchell in April 1869. Charles Augustin Sainte-Beuve wrote his celebrated column, "Causeries du lundi," for *Le constitutionnel* until he was enticed to *Le moniteur universel*. Other collaborators included Amédée de Césèna (1810–1889), Adolphe Granier de Cassagnac, Nestor Roqueplan (1804–1870), Auguste Vitu (1823–1891), Louis Enault (1824–1900), Henri Alexis Cauvain (1815–1858), Ernest Dréolle (1829–1887), and Jules Barbey d'Aurevilly. *Le constitutionnel* was one of ten Paris newspapers prosecuted in January 1868 for violating the law concerning the reporting of parliamentary debate.

Despite frequent changes of editors and collaborators, continual government subventions, lowered subscription rates, and the constant insertion of special official and judicial notices, *Le constitutionnel*, although maintaining the largest circulation of the government press, saw its sales decline throughout the Second Empire. Circulation was 25,450 in April 1853, 22,000 in 1855, 24,502 in July 1857, 26,530 in July 1858, 19,448 in August 1861, 12,000 in 1866, 8,900 in October 1868, and only 7,600 in March 1869.

Dr. M. E. Binet, *Un médecin pas ordinaire, le Docteur Véron* (Paris, 1945); M. Mouchot, "Le constitutionnel" (Ecole des Chartes thesis, 1968).

Natalie Isser

Related entries: MIRES; *LE MONITEUR UNIVERSEL*; *LA PATRIE*; *LE PAYS*; PRESS REGIME; PUBLIC OPINION.

COPPEE, FRANCOIS (1842–1908), poet and dramatist, one of the central figures of the Parnassian school; born 12 January 1842 at Paris. For several years employed by the Ministry of War, Coppée left this position in 1869 for a post at the Senate library. Three years later, he was appointed archivist at the Comédie-Française on the recommendation of his patroness, Princess Mathilde. He retained that post until his election to the Académie Française in 1884. Encouraged and stimulated by his association with Catulle Mendès (1841–1909), coeditor with Louis Xavier de Ricard (1843–1911) of *Le Parnasse contemporain*, Coppée published several poems in this first anthology of Parnassian verse in 1866. In the same year, he published his first volume of poetry, *Le reliquaire*, which established his reputation as an elegiac poet and *chanteur* of the common people. His poems were admired by both Sully Prudhomme (1839–1907) and Charles Augustin Sainte-Beuve. His popularity increased with the appearance of his poetry in several newspapers of the day: *Nain jaune, Revue nationale, Revue libérale*, and *L'artiste*. Other collections followed: *Intimités* (1868) and *Poèmes modernes* (1869), for which the Académie Française awarded him the Prix Lambert. To the second anthology of Parnassian poetry (1869), Coppée contributed *Promenades* and *Intérieurs*. Thirty years later, he was to remember with awe his weekly visits to the salon of the Parnassian master, Charles Leconte de Lisle.

Even better known as a dramatist than as a poet, Coppée made his début at the Odéon on 14 January 1869 with the verse play *Le passant*, a comedy immensely successful for both himself and for Sarah Bernhardt (1844–1923), who played the role of the minstrel boy, Zanetto. A few days later *Le passant* was performed at Princess Mathilde's house on the rue de Courcelles, again on 29 April, with Napoleon III present, and yet again at the Tuileries after a dinner for the visiting queen of the Netherlands. The play and the actors were warmly praised by Théophile Gautier. Sarah Bernhardt's career (she had signed a contract at the Odéon in 1865) was ensured. In March 1870 the emperor and empress attended at Princess Mathilde's another of Coppée's plays, *Deux douleurs*. Coppée subsequently published several lyrical dramas, novellas, and short stories. He died at Paris, 17 May 1908.

H. Schoen, *François Coppée* (Paris, 1909); F. Coppée, *Mon franc parler*, 4 vols. (Paris, 1894–1896).

Dolorès A. Signori

Related entries: BANVILLE; GAUTIER; LECONTE DE LISLE; THEATER.

COPYRIGHT and TRADEMARK, protections established in France largely through decrees, legislation, and treaties of the Second Empire. A law of 5 July 1844 codified the extensive French legislation concerning patents (*brevets d'invention*), but at mid-century literary and artistic property was still inadequately protected. A law of 23 June 1857 established the right of trademark in France (*marque de fabrique et de commerce*) for fifteen years, with the possibility of renewal for an equal period. At the same time, as a result of the efforts of such men as Louis Hachette and comte Alexandre Walewski (who as minister of state and of fine arts from 1860 to 1863 established the Commission de la Propriété

Littéraire et Artistique and named its first members), two decrees (17 February and 28 March 1852) and two laws (8 April 1854 and 14 July 1866) regulated for France the right of literary and artistic property, enjoyable during the lifetime of the author/artist and for fifty years following death. The French legislation foresaw the establishment of reciprocal arrangements among states, but this required a series of international treaties, whose negotiation consumed a great deal of the time and energy of Second Empire diplomats: with Portugal, 12 April 1851 and 11 July 1866; Britain, 3 November 1851; Brunswick, 8 August 1852; Belgium, 22 August 1852, 1 May 1861, and 7 January 1869; Hesse-Hamburg, 2 October 1852; Reuss (Elder Line), 24 February 1853; Nassau, 2 March 1853, and 5 July 1865; Reuss (Cadet Line), 30 March 1853; Hesse-Cassel, 7 May 1853; Saxe-Weimar-Eisenach, 17 May 1853; Oldenburg, 1 July 1853; Spain, 15 November 1853; Schwarzburg-Sondershausen, 7 December 1853; Schwarzburg-Rudolstadt, 16 December 1853; Waldeck and Pyrmont, 4 February 1854; Baden, 3 April 1854, 2 July 1857, and 12 May 1865; Netherlands, 29 March 1855 and 27 April 1860; Saxony, 19 May 1856; Luxembourg, 4 June 1856, and 16 December 1865; Switzerland, 30 October 1858 and 30 June 1864; Russia, 6 April 1861; Italy, 29 June 1862; Prussia-Zollverein, 2 August 1862; Free City of Frankfurt, 18 April 1865; Wurtemberg, 24 April 1865; Saxony, 26 May 1865; Mecklenburg-Schwerin, 9 June 1865; Hesse-Darmstadt, 14 June 1865; Hanover, 19 July 1865; Austria, 11 December 1866; Papal States, 14 July 1867. Although the United States on 16 April 1869 signed a trademark convention with France, the U.S. government refused to enter into an agreement concerning the reciprocal protection of literary and artistic property.
Related entries: HACHETTE; WALEWSKI.

COROT, JEAN BAPTISTE CAMILLE (1796–1875), landscape and figure painter; born at Paris, 16 July 1796. Corot's family provided him with a modest income, which allowed him a certain degree of independence to become an artist once they were convinced he would not be successful in the textile business. He was already twenty-six years old. His early training with Jean Victor Bertin (1775–1842) and Achille Etna Michallon (1796–1822) was followed by trips to Italy, first from 1825 to 1828, in 1834, and again in 1843. It was there that he was impressed by the Italian light, and the influence of Claude Lorrain becomes evident in his paintings. After experiencing swings in popular and critical acceptance of his work, he was awarded a first-class medal in the Salon of 1848 and was appointed to the jury in 1849. Although not a member of the Barbizon school, Corot was associated with its participants, sketching motifs from the Forest of Fontainebleau. His early interest in the intensity of light, which characterizes his early works such as *The Bridge at Narni* (National Gallery of Canada, Ottawa), shown in the Salon of 1827, is transformed in the works of the 1850s, corresponding to the more diffused light and damp atmosphere of the region near Paris. Typical of this period is *Ville d'Avray* (c. 1855; private collection, New York; another in Des Moines Art Center), which depicts a motif found near his parents' property and painted frequently by Corot. Corot was not a colorist (he used very few colors, in fact) but rather painted in terms of *valeurs*, achieving a harmony based on about twenty values of one color. The feeling is one of intimacy, the hazy atmosphere adding to the gentleness and tranquility of mood. The diffused light is depicted as though seen through a veil. The silvery effect resulting from Corot's manipulation of values contributes a poetic lyricism to an otherwise carefully observed scene.

At the same time that he painted motifs from nature, Corot sometimes composed works where nymphs frolic among the feathery trees such as in *Morning: Dance of the Nymphs* (1850, Louvre, Paris) exhibited in the Salon of 1850–1851. This more poetic approach to nature becomes pronounced during the 1860s when Corot, painting his *Souvenir* series, called on memory. One such remembrance, *Recollection of Mortefontaine* (1864, Louvre), shown in the Salon of 1864, was purchased by Napoleon III and hung at Fontainebleau where the court gathered in the summer. Painted in a wooded region north of Paris where Antoine Watteau had been inspired a century and a half before, Corot's work is executed with brushwork unique to him and influential for the Impressionists who followed. Each dab of paint is set on the canvas in such a way that it is detached from the object depicted rather than following the volume or the surface of the object. The detached brushwork results in flat dabs of paint, which contribute to the feathery quality of the trees and figures and produce a soft vibration. The gradual transitions of his *valeurs*, the elimination of contours, the diffuse silvery haze, and the effects of memory add to the elegiac mood.

Corot's late figure paintings, primarily of single females in his studio or in an indefinable outdoor setting, done in the 1860s, extend his mastery of brushwork and tonal values to this new motif. These are not portraits of individuals or particular women but rather women in unassuming poses who seem to be daydreaming. The subject matter is somewhat ambiguous, even enigmatic. Activity is not emphasized, books are held but not read, musical instruments lean against the sitter, silent. Works such as *The Studio* (1865–1968, Louvre) and *Interrupted Reading* (1865–1870, Art Institute, Chicago) in which the figures appear to be monumental nevertheless convey a meditative, pensive mood. With few exceptions, these paintings were not exhibited by Corot but remained in his studio during his lifetime.

A gentle and modest man throughout his life, Corot was generous to his colleagues, especially to Honoré Daumier when the latter was old and blind, giving him a house in Valmondois where he spent his last years. Corot received a second-class medal at the Paris international exposition of 1867 and was promoted to officer of the Legion of Honor. In the 1870s he was influenced by the Impressionists and began to paint some works *en plein air*. He died at Ville d'Avray, 22 February 1875.

D. Baud-Bovey, *Corot* (Geneva, 1957); M. Hours, *Corot* (New York, n.d.); J. Ley-marie, *Corot* (Geneva, 1966); G. Monnier, M. Servot, and H. Toussaint, *Hommage à Corot: Peintures et dessins des collections françaises* (Paris, 1975).

Beverley Giblon

Related entries: COURBET; MILLET; ROUSSEAU.

CORPS LEGISLATIF, the elected body that, under the constitution of 14 January 1852, shared the legislative function of the government with the emperor, the Senate, and the Conseil d'Etat. Laws could not be made or taxes levied without its consent. The Corps Législatif first convened at the Palais Bourbon 30 March 1852; it met for the last time on 4 September 1870.

The organization of the Corps Législatif reflected, as did its name, an intended apolitical character and subservience to the executive power. The experience of the Legislative Assembly (1849–1851) was not to be repeated under the Empire. The president of the Corps Législatif, whose special role was indicated by his annual salary of 100,000 francs and his lodgings in the Palais Bourbon, was named by imperial decree from among the deputies at the beginning of each session, as were the vice-presidents and *questeurs* who assisted him. The Corps Législatif could not draw up its own by-laws, convene, adjourn, or dissolve itself, or extend its single, short annual session, but waited in these matters on the will of the emperor. It could not initiate legislation or receive petitions. Projects of law came to it by intermediation of the minister of state from the Conseil d'Etat, whose consent to amendments was also required.

A project of law, in the form of an imperial decree, went first to each of seven *bureaux* into which the Corps Législatif was divided by lot at the beginning of the session. After discussion, each *bureau* chose by secret ballot one member of a seven-member *commission* (fourteen for a major project, increased to nine and eighteen in February 1861 when the number of *bureaux* was increased by two), which, following secret discussion in collaboration with government commissioners and the Conseil d'Etat, reported the project through a *rapporteur* to a public sitting of the Corps Législatif. Until the report was deposed, amendments could be proposed, through the president, to the *commission*. If accepted, they would be referred by the president to the Conseil d'Etat and if there approved would be incorporated into the project of law. Once debate by the full legislative body had begun, no further amendments were possible.

Sittings were public except when in *comité secret* at the request of five deputies. Debates could be published only in the form of *procès-verbaux* prepared under supervision of the president at the close of each sitting. Although honest, the *procès* were in the third person, deliberately colorless, and much abbreviated. Deputies could publish their speeches, with consent of the Corps Législatif, but this consent was rarely granted in the early years of the Empire, except to members of the majority. Voting was open, required the presence of at least one-half of the deputies, and was by absolute majority, first on the project section by section as presented by the president and then on the project as a whole.

Votes could not be justified or qualified, the function of the Corps Législatif at that point being simply to accept or to reject en bloc. The tribune had been abolished, its place taken by a bench reserved for the *conseillers d'état*. Deputies spoke from their places after being recognized by the president. Expressions of approval or disapproval of the speaker's words were forbidden. It was not possible to question (interpellate) the ministers, who never appeared in the chamber and could not be deputies. Instead, for each debate the emperor named three *conseillers d'état*, usually including the president of the Conseil d'Etat, to defend the project as *commissaires du gouvernement*, having the right to speak when they wished. The principle of ministerial responsibility to the legislative body was firmly repudiated. Although the budget required Corps Législatif approval, it could be accepted or rejected only by ministry, en bloc, with no changes permitted once debate had begun. A project of law passed by the Corps Législatif went to the Senate, to be examined for constitutionality, and then to the emperor, who promulgated it as law if he so chose. From 25 December 1852, the emperor could, however, act by decree concerning public works projects and could, without consulting the Corps Législatif, alter tariffs through treaties.

Thus deprived of most parliamentary trappings (initiative, petition, address, interpellation, amendment, publicity of debate, self-regulation, and responsibility), the Corps Législatif was expected to serve a useful but unthreatening legislative role made more efficient by the precautions taken against political maneuvering. All depended, however, on the results produced by a carefully contrived electoral system. Deputies were elected (one for each 30,000 to 35,000 voters) to six-year terms by direct universal male suffrage; 265 were elected in 1852, 267 in 1857, 283 in 1863, and 292 in 1869. From 25 December 1852, deputies were paid 2,500 francs for each month of session, later (1866) 12,500 francs for a regular session, augmented by 2,500 francs for each month that the Corps Législatif sat in extraordinary session (in 1852, 1855, 1869, and 1870). Deputies could not be ministers, councillors of state, prefects or subprefects, magistrates, or on active military service. Regular sessions averaged four and one-half months during the Second Empire, although originally intended not to exceed three.

Until 1869 an overwhelming majority of the deputies elected were pledged to support the emperor. All were required to take an oath of loyalty. For the most part, these were able, public-spirited men who came from the same social groups that had provided the deputies of previous regimes. In 1852 19 percent were landed proprietors, 26 percent had been government functionaries, 8 percent were military men, 20 percent were lawyers or from other professions, and 24 percent were businessmen. There was a tendency for the last to replace intellectuals. Incumbents were usually returned. Only a small minority of deputies were bonapartists in the full sense. The others, although rallied to the Empire in the name of order and loyal to the emperor, were independents or sympathetic to other parties. In 1852, for example, half of the elected deputies were Orleanists, some thirty were legitimists, and only a third were bonapartists. Moreover, the number of declared opponents of the regime grew with each election, In 1852, seven were elected, but two republicans refused the oath, one rallied to the regime, and three legitimists resigned following the proclamation of the Empire. Thus only Charles de Montalembert, who had been elected as an official candidate but had quickly broken with the regime, represented the opposition. In 1857–1858 that opposition grew to nine or ten, including five republicans (*les Cinq*), and in 1863 to some thirty-two to thirty-five, including eighteen to twenty republicans. Although it would yield to an imperative expression of the emperor's will, the Corps Législatif would never prove to be a mere rubber stamp.

The first session of the Corps Législatif convened on 29 March 1852 in the Salle des Maréchaux of the Tuileries and adjourned on 28 June, almost three weeks later than planned. In his opening address, Louis Napoleon called on the deputies to help him save the Republic and described the state of society as having been once more set on a broad base after tottering like a pyramid placed on its apex. Adolphe Billault was named president on 22 March, a nomination that would be renewed for the sessions of 1853 and 1854. Montalembert soon broke with the government and joined a few other independent spirits in protesting the Orleans confiscation decrees and, particularly, the budget process. In a speech of 22 June, which the Corps Législatif voted to permit him to print and to distribute, he warned against the long-term consequences of a lack of parliamentary control. In three months, fifty-six laws of local interest and twenty-five of general interest were voted, including provision for the recasting of copper money, the rehabilitation of convicts, modification of the criminal code (concerning crimes committed abroad), continuation of the state's tobacco monopoly, and cession of the Bois de Boulogne to the city of Paris. An extraordinary session (25 November–3 December 1852) was required in order to validate the plebiscite that restored the Empire. And on 22 January 1853 Napoleon III met with the *conseillers d'état* and with representatives of the Senate and Corps Législatif to announce his coming marriage.

The 1853 session of the Corps Législatif lasted from 14 February to 28 May (prolonged to allow the budget to be voted). The legislators feted the new empress at a great ball at the Palais Bourbon. Montalembert continued his opposition, rejecting the proposed budget because it sanctioned the *sénatus-consulte* of 25 December 1852, as well as the Orleans decrees. The *budgétaires* (including Prosper de Chasseloup-Laubat, Charles Louvet [1806–1882], François Jules Devinck [1802–1878], and Alfred Leroux [1815–1880]) also protested aspects of the budget. In the face of opposition, the government withdrew four projects of law, including restoration of the death penalty for political crimes. Still, the legislature functioned much as its creators had hoped. In forty-two sessions and without real debate, it passed 145 laws of local interest and 55 of general interest, including provision for reorganizing the general staff of the navy, reforming the penal code, purchase of canals by the state, establishment of a retirement fund for functionaries (at age sixty after thirty years of service; the legislation would endure until after World War II), and reorganization of the *conseils de prud'hommes*.

Circumstances surrounding the 1854 session (2 March–1 June) were less favorable. Crop failures had led to high prices and considerable suffering, and the Crimean War was imminent. Napoleon III announced the creation of a *caisse de la boulangerie de Paris* and in his war message offered assurance that the era of conquests had passed, never to return. A war loan of 250 million francs was voted (it would be oversubscribed more than two times), the army contingent from the class of 1853 was set at 100,000, and the budget was discussed and voted in two days. The government, attempting to prosecute Montalembert for his polemics, won the right to do so, after two days of stiff debate, but there were fifty-one negative votes, twenty-six abstentions, and the *commission* had been opposed, so the government relented. The session passed laws reorganizing public instruction (*bifurcation*), the University, and higher education. It also abolished *mort civile* (deprivation of civil and political rights), renewed the law requiring workers to carry *livrets d'ouvriers*, and provided for the regulation of land drainage.

By decree of 12 November 1854, Auguste de Morny replaced Billault as president of the Corps Législatif. He would be renamed to the post each year until his death in March 1865 and would function with such skill that both government and chamber would come to regard him as its champion. The war and military matters preoccupied the 1855 session (26 December 1854–14 April 1855). A second war loan (of 500 million francs) was unanimously authorized, and the contingent was increased to 140,000. After a debate during which Montalembert spoke impressively in opposition, a new system of conscription was adopted, substituting *exonération* for *remplacement* (204–46). The budget was presented early (22 February) at the legislators' request. A new tax on dogs was voted, and the government agreed that decrees authorizing extraordinary expenses would be issued only when the Corps Législatif was not in session and would be submitted for sanction at the following session. Other laws dealt with the organization of municipal government, Paris public works, industrial property, and reform of the criminal code. An extraordinary session (2 July–13 July 1855) unanimously approved a third war loan (750 million francs) and later voted 72 million francs in new taxes, including a *décime* on the indirect tax, and surtaxes on alcohol and rail transport. A Turkish loan of 125 million francs was guaranteed.

The 1856 session met under happier auspices on 3 March 1856 (adjourned 2 July 1856). The Crimean War was over, a great peace congress had just opened at Paris, and Empress Eugénie was about to give birth to an imperial heir. Nevertheless, the session was agitated. Montalembert pressed his attacks (against the fever of speculation, against the decision of the *cour de cassation* to permit government distribution of electoral ballots); protectionists and free traders clashed; and deputies criticized the growing debt (of about 900 million francs) and called for stricter, more conventional budget procedures. A Paris tax on horses and carriages passed, but there were 55 negative votes, and the Senate refused to concur. Moreover, there was criticism of Napoleon III's project (approved) of pensioning wives and children of deceased functionaries. The session approved a tax on transfer of *valeurs mobilières*, increased pensions to widows of servicemen killed in action, reformed old age retirement legislations (*caisse de retraites pour la vieillesse*), and passed a major law regulating *sociétés en commandite*.

By contrast, the 1857 session, which convened on 16 February, was calm. On 28 May the first Corps Législatif of the Second Empire was dissolved in preparation for the elections of 21–22 June. In the interval, besides voting the 1858 budget (there was a small surplus), the session extended the privileges of the Bank of France for thirty years, voted an annual income for Marshal Aimable Pélissier, conqueror of Sebastopol, revised the code of military justice and the *code rural*, voted a trademark law (*marque de fabrique*), and revised the regulations governing *sociétés anonymes* in order to permit foreign companies to operate in France.

The Corps Législatif elected in 1857 contained an increased number of opponents of the Empire. Montalembert had been defeated, but three republicans and some six opponents of other persuasion were returned. Two more republicans, Jules Favre and Ernest Picard, were elected in by-elections of 27 April and 10 May 1858—hence, *les Cinq*. At the meeting of 28 November 1858, convened to organize the new legislature, Morny refused to allow Emile Ollivier to discuss the elections. On 18 January 1858, four days after the attempt on his life by Felice Orsini, Napoleon III opened the 1858 session with a firm speech, announcing that henceforth candidates as well as elected deputies would be required to take the oath. Orsini's *attentat* dominated the session. On 1 February a *loi de sûreté générale* was presented by Achille Fould, with Morny serving as *rapporteur*. Despite the opposition of Ollivier, Jules de Jacquot, marquis d'Andelarre (1803–1885), Pierre Legrand (1804–1859), and August Bonamour, marquis de Talhouët-Toy (1819–1884), and efforts of the *commission* to limit its duration and effect, the law was voted 227 to 24 on 19 February. Once again debate on the budget was vigorous. The *rapporteur*, Devinck, called for reform of the budget procedure; Adrien Charles Calley de Saint-Paul (1808–1873) demanded that the budget be voted by section rather than ministry; and forty-five deputies voted against a proposed 60 million francs subsidy for Paris public works. Before adjourning 8 May 1858, the Corps Législatif also voted laws dealing with the code of maritime justice, sale and guarantee of merchandise by stores, agricultural loans for drainage, and patents (*brevets d'invention*).

The 1859 session (7 February–27 May 1859) met in the shadow of the impending war with Austria. Although in his opening speech Napoleon III offered assurances of peace, Jules Baroche requested authorization for a 500 million franc loan and a contingent (for the class of 1858) of 140,000. Despite criticism of the government's Italian policy by Ollivier and Favre (who spoke for the first time at the end of April) and demands by Catholic deputies for guarantees for the pope, the contingent was authorized unanimously and the loan by 247 votes.

On the outbreak of war, the Corps Législatif voted (3 May) to raise a contingent of 140,000 from the class of 1859. In the budget debate the *commission* requested fifty-two amendments (for a reduction of 4.4 million francs) and were granted thirty-nine by the Conseil d'Etat. The budget was voted 260 to 5. The session also passed laws reforming the administration of *délits forestiers*, providing for the annexation of its suburbs by the city of Paris and (by a vote of 221 to 11, against the vigorous opposition of *les Cinq*) guaranteeing the interest from investment by the railroads in construction of local lines.

During the 1860 session (1 March–20 July 1860) deputies showed a disquieting independence and spirit of parliamentarianism. After the emperor, in his opening address, had signaled the coming annexation of Nice and Savoy, the Corps Législatif managed (11–13 April) to achieve a de facto interpellation concerning both Italy (during discussion of a proposal to reduce the contingent) and the new treaty of commerce with Britain (during discussion of a law on cottons). On the treaty issue, even the right wing showed resentment of the government's infringement on the "rights" of the legislature. Baroche's speeches in behalf of the government won a great success, however; Morny, who had informed *les Cinq* of his wish for a liberal evolution of the regime, directed the debate with a firm if gentle hand; and despite the opposition of the republicans and Raymond Larrabure's (1799–1875) criticism of the "permanent deficit," the 1861 budget was accepted with only five negative votes. The session (which was extended twice) also passed laws creating the departments of Savoie, Haute-Savoie, and Alpes-Maritimes, regulating manufacture and sale of military weapons, purchasing canals by the state, and providing state aid for the modernization of industries threatened by competition as a result of the commercial treaty with Britain.

The government had obviously drawn its conclusions from the performance of the Corps Législatif, however. The reform decree of 24 November 1860 reinstated the annual speech from the throne as a formal parliamentary ritual and empowered the Corps Législatif and the Senate at the beginning of each session to debate, amend (on the initiative of at least five deputies), and vote an address in reply. For the occasion the emperor would allow two ministers without portfolio together with the minister presiding the Conseil d'Etat to appear as government commissioners or orators and to give explanations. Thus was granted a limited right of interpellation. The three commissioners would, throughout the session, explain and defend government projects unless they delegated this task to *conseillers d'état*. Early 1861 saw further changes. An organic decree of 3 February increased the number of Corps Législatif *bureaux* from seven to nine, permitted the election of six secretaries for the session, and provided for an initial consideration of projects of law *en comité secret*, with the government commissioners present and taking part in the debate, before referral to *bureaux* and *commission*. This decree also provided that an amendment could be discussed by the Corps Législatif at the request of five deputies, even if it had been rejected by a *commission* or by the Conseil d'Etat, although it could not be adopted without their approval. A *sénatus-consulte* of 2 February required, as promised by the decree of 24 November 1860, that a detailed account of the day's debates (*compte rendu*), as well as a summary (*compte rendu analytique*), be prepared for publication in the *Moniteur* and in other newspapers, but, in the latter case, only *in extenso* for any topic and without comment.

The 1861 session (4 February–27 June 1861) was opened with great pomp by Napoleon III, the empress in attendance. In his speech from the throne, the emperor promised that in future he would present a department-by-department survey of the state of the Empire, accompanied by documents (the *Livres jaunes*). Despite Morny's cautionary advice, the debate on the address was long and stormy. Emile Keller (1828–1909) and Charles Ignace Plichon (1814–1888) expressed, on behalf of the despoiled pope, their hatred of Italy. Keller, in particular, electrified the chamber on 13 March with his pro-papal attack on the government (''Etes-vous révolutionnaire? Etes-vous conservateur?''). A clerical faction quickly formed that would gather ninety-one votes for an amendment deleting from the address a phrase critical of papal policy. Meanwhile *les Cinq* proposed collectively an amendment to the address calling for full liberty, and demanded election of the Lyons and Paris municipal councils, vote of the budget by article, and representation of the colonies (especially Algeria) in the Corps Législatif. On the other hand, Ollivier, frightened by the threat of reaction implicit in the reception given Keller's speech, had on 14 March, after a sleepless night, spoken in support of Napoleon III if he continued in the spirit of the 1860 reforms. Only after a discussion requiring eleven sessions was the address voted (on 22 March by 213 to 13). Discussion of the 1862 budget gave rise to further acrimony. Extraordinary and supplementary credits had put the previous budget into deficit by more than 300 million francs, and the proposed budget was for almost 2 billion francs. The *commission* managed to obtain only miniscule reduction, but Pierre Magne promised reform, agreeing to a discussion and vote by chapters, and the budget was passed 242 to 5, together with a disguised loan of up to 132 million francs to pay for the state's part of railroad construction. The government proposed and obtained by unanimous vote certain changes in press legislation—the end of the practice of suppressing a newspaper after two *délits* or *contraventions* and of suspension after two *avertissements* (which henceforth would expire in two years). The opposition was not satisfied, but Billault stood firm: ''Le décret de novembre a dit son dernier mot.'' The session also abolished the sliding scale and established free trade in grains, reformed tariff legislation for the colonies and the system of military pensions, and authorized construction of a new Opéra and acquisition of the Campana collection for the Louvre Museum.

Following adjournment of the Corps Législatif, Napoleon III appointed Achille Fould minister of finance (November 1861) and agreed to further financial reform, culminating in the *sénatus-consulte* of 31 December 1861, which provided for a vote on the budget by chapters (sections within each ministry) and required the passage of a law for opening supplementary or extraordinary credits after the budget had been voted.

In his speech from the throne opening the 1862 session (27 January–27 June 1862), Napoleon III admitted the financial difficulties and offered assurances concerning the French intervention in Mexico. In reality, despite Fould's efforts (including the conversion of the *rentes* of 41/2 percent and 4 percent to 3 percent, the Mexican expedition was largely to frustrate efforts to ameliorate government finances. *Les Cinq* attacked the conversion and posed a new series of amendments, calling for freedom of press, elections, and meetings, direct nomination of mayors by the people, evacuation of Rome, reduction of government expenses (such as the civil list), and ending of the Mexican intervention. After thirteen days of debate, the address was voted 244 to 9. But the legislature remained prickly. Almost unanimously it blocked the emperor's efforts to secure a pension for the comte de Palikao as reward for his services in China. The deputies also complained about the 193 million francs addition to the 1862 budget (mostly for Mexico) and the size of the budget for 1863 (which contained a surtax on sugar and coffee and continued the Crimean War *décime de guerre* on registration while imposing a new tax on horses and carriages). Moreover, Favre once again warned against what he saw to be the government's intentions in Mexico.

The 1863 session (12 January–7 May 1863) was dominated by the pending elections. Alfred Darimon called for granting to both employers and workers the right to organize. The 1864 budget was balanced by a variety of expedients. Before dissolution on 7 May, the Corps Législatif made further changes in the penal code and in the regulations governing *sociétés anonymes* (principle of limited responsibility; government authorization required only for larger enterprises), abolished the *droit de tonnage* for Algeria, and confirmed the state's tobacco monopoly.

As a result of the elections of 1863, opposition to the Empire in the Corps Législatif grew to more than thirty deputies, including eighteen to twenty republicans. Again, the government drew its conclusions. It was provided by decree of 23 June 1863 that the minister of state would be the emperor's sole representative to the Corps Législatif, assisted by the president of the Conseil d'Etat, who also held ministerial rank, and three vice-presidents. The premature death of Billault meant that Eugène Rouher would undertake this important role of government orator in the session of 1864. There he would face not only Ollivier and Favre but also, as a result of the elections, the redoubtable Adolphe Thiers and Pierre Antoine Berryer. Before the new Corps Législatif convened, Napoleon III remade his government in a more liberal mold.

The 1864 session (5 November 1863–28 May 1864) inevitably involved an electoral postmortem. During the debate on the address, *les Cinq* called for freedom of elections, while Rouher hinted at a more liberal orientation ("Sans doute le résultat des élections signale des pensées libérales, et pourquoi pas? Ces pensées sont celles du gouvernement!") Thiers, Favre, and Berryer spoke against the Mexican intervention, and Thiers, in a resounding address of 11

January 1864, called for reestablishment of the "five necessary liberties." Ernest Picard made the first public criticism (January 1864) of the coup d'état. On 29 January the address was adopted, and the legislature tackled a heavy work load. The budget presented its usual difficulties, since expenditures had grown from 1.5 billion francs in 1852 to almost 2 1/3 billion for 1864. The total debt was 972 million francs (Thiers spoke, attacking official prodigality), and the Corps Législatif reacted with misgivings to a request for supplementary credits and a loan totaling 300 million francs. However, Adolphe Vuitry skillfully defended the government's views. The great achievement of the session was the passage on 25 May by vote of 222 to 36 of a coalitions law suppressing article 414 of the penal code and permitting temporary coalitions for the purpose of a strike. The project's author and *rapporteur*, Ollivier, officially separated on this occasion from his former colleagues, the republicans. The session also modified the statutes of the old age retirement fund and made provision for reforestation and sodding of mountainous terrain.

The 1865 session (15 February–8 July 1865) witnessed the official acceptance by Ollivier of the regime. He voted for the address, explaining that he wished to forge an alliance of liberty, democracy, and authority. Despite opposition from the Left, the Corps Législatif authorized a Mexican loan but balked at the government's request for a loan of 250 million francs for Paris and 270 million francs for other public works (including a new post office building) and for alienation of the state forests. The government withdrew its requests. The session was marked as well by the effort of clerical deputies to secure guarantees for the pope's temporal power, culminating in a minority vote of 84 favoring changes to this effect in the address. Morny died on 10 March 1865. His chair was taken, for the rest of the session, by Eugène Schneider. Before adjourning, the Corps Législatif voted laws on special secondary education, syndical associations, and local railroads and for the first time gave legal recognition to the bank check in France.

Before the Corps Législatif convened again, Napoleon III, on 1 September 1865, named Alexandre Walewski as its president, a choice that did not please the legislature. In his speech from the throne opening the 1866 session (22 January–30 June 1866), the emperor cautioned against too much haste in reform while calling for debate on the constitutional question and the system of government. He also announced the coming end of the Mexican intervention. In March the Tiers Parti emerged (it had been bruited since the previous session). Forty-two deputies who wished to put particular emphasis on economic reform and civil liberties signed an amendment to the address pledging support to the dynasty but calling for further development of the reform initiative of 1860. The reforms envisaged were the right of interpellation, fuller power of amendment, access of ministers to the chambers, liberalization of the press laws, and more freedom of reunion during elections. Despite a three-hour speech in opposition by Rouher, the amendment received 63 votes. Acrimony also resulted from events in Germany. To Rouher's declaration of French neutrality in the coming

Austro-Prussian War, Thiers replied on 3 May with a scathing speech opposing German unification. The government, however, refused to debate the issue. The 1867 budget provided for a surplus and the beginning of an effort to retire the debt. In addition, the Corps Législatif passed laws broadening the powers of the *conseils généraux* and establishing the duration of literary copyright at fifty years.

At the end of the 1866 session, a *sénatus-consulte* (18 July 1866) introduced further changes into the organization of the Corps Législatif. Henceforth it could determine the length of its sittings; the pay of deputies was increased; and the right to consider all proposed amendments was further strengthened, although the Conseil d'Etat retained, after reconsideration, its veto. On 19 January 1867 Napoleon III moved at last to "crown the edifice," at least so far as the Corps Législatif was concerned. The address was suppressed and the right of inter-pellation introduced. (The tribune was reestablished, at Walewski's urging, by decree of 5 February 1867). On each debate topic, pertinent ministers would appear before the Corps Législatif, together with the minister of state, to respond to questions and to defend the government's proposals. Such interpellation, requested in writing by at least five deputies, required the consent of at least four *bureaux*. A subsequent *sénatus-consulte* (14 March 1867) gave a suspensive veto to the Senate, meaning that it could return a measure passed by the Corps Législatif for reconsideration in the following session.

The 1867 session (14 February–24 July 1867) was particularly tumultuous. In his opening speech, Napoleon III called for the additional reforms stipulated in his 19 January letter, particularly of the press and of reunion. He also warned of the necessity for military reform. There followed interpellations on the seizure by postal authorities of a letter of Chambord on the projected reforms, and on foreign policy. During the latter, Thiers and Rouher clashed violently (Thiers: "Il n'y a plus une faute à commettre"; Rouher: "Il n'a été commis aucune faute"). Rouher, incensed at Walewski's ineptitude to control the chamber, viciously attacked him during the debate of 18 March and on 29 March obtained his resignation as president but then had to accept the appointment of Schneider in Walewski's place (2 April). These events seemed to the public to mark a defeat for liberalism, although the government deposed during the session proj-ected laws on the press and on public meeting, as well as a project for reform of the army. Three demands for interpellation on the Luxembourg crisis were defeated in April and May. Discussion of the budget (there was a new deficit as a result of armaments related to Luxembourg and the proposed army reform) provided opportunity for further attacks on the government. Thiers once again condemned the Mexican intervention (just ended), and Ollivier, who had been blocked by Rouher as *rapporteur* for the proposed press law, termed the minister of state on 12 July *vice-empereur sans responsabilité* and called for suppression of the Ministry of State and establishment of responsible government. The 1867 session nevertheless passed a number of important laws, increasing the powers of the municipal councils, providing a pension for Alphonse de Lamartine, establishing the modern system of *sociétés anonymes*, organizing primary education, and abolishing imprisonment for debt (*contrainte par corps*).

New crises preceded the next meeting of the Corps Législatif, particularly a growing economic recession and threats to the pope's safety at Rome (Mentana). Moreover, the 1868 session (18 November 1867–28 July 1868) was critical in the fate of political reform, which Napoleon III promised, in his speech from the throne, to continue. First, however, came another heated debate on the Roman Question, which culminated in a clash between Thiers and Rouher and the latter's assertion (5 December) that Italy would never be permitted to seize Rome. Military reform was discussed in the last two months of 1867. Earlier, after vigorous debate, the Corps Législatif had returned a veritable counterproposal, much emasculated, to the Conseil d'Etat. Dissuaded by Rouher from calling an election on the issue, Napoleon III on 18 November 1867 withdrew Marshal Adolphe Niel's project and substituted a proposal restricted to changes in the 1832 law. This came before the chamber on 19 December, *commission* and Conseil d'Etat having failed to agree. It was voted (199 to 65) on 14 January 1868, shortly after the legislature reconvened following the Christmas break. Discussion of the press law required twenty-four sessions and witnessed two abrupt changes of mind by the emperor. It was passed on 9 March 1868 only because of the insistence of the government, which seven irreconcilable bonapartists defied (on 31 January 1868 Adolphe Granier de Cassagnac had made a great speech against the proposed law). The same hesitations and passionate debate characterized the law on public meeting, which was voted 209 to 22 on 25 March. The session ended with a discussion of finances, highlighted by Thiers' analysis, and passage of a law establishing equality of oath of worker and employer in a court of law.

The 1869 session (18 January–26 April 1869), again presided by Schneider, was held under the shadow of the impending elections. Four interpellations were proposed and rejected: on the application of the law on public meetings and on the internal situation (moved by the Left), on the riots on Réunion, and on the direction taken by internal politics. The last, moved by Louis Buffet on behalf of the Tiers Parti, was only narrowly rejected. The attack on Baron Georges Haussmann's administration of Paris culminated in February. By abandoning the prefect, Rouher was able to obtain authorization for a contract between the city of Paris and the Crédit Foncier, but it proved necessary to agree that henceforth extraordinary Paris budgets would be approved by law. In addition a large loan was approved to begin retiring the city's debt. There were other interpellations (on electoral corruption, on alienation of Luxembourg Garden lands). Before dissolution on 26 April, the session also voted an indemnity for holders of Mexican bonds and adopted, at Napoleon III's insistence (and almost without discussion), a law granting pensions to survivors of the Grande Armée (1869 was the centenary of the birth of Napoleon I).

Failure of the Corps Législatif to pass promptly and decisively the reform laws promised in January 1867 undoubtedly contributed to the results of the elections of May 1869. Of 292 deputies returned, 74 (including some 30 republicans) were opponents of the regime; about 80 were "pure bonapartists" or "Arcadiens"; the remaining 138 retained varying degrees of independence but without a common program. Thus there was no longer a majority of any sort.

The extraordinary session of 1869 was held in two sittings (28 June–13 July and 29 November–27 December 1869). In his opening speech, Napoleon III affirmed his commitment to reform. That day Schneider resigned as president to protest Jérôme David's having been named grand officer of the Legion of Honor but withdrew his resignation at the emperor's request. The purpose of the session was to validate the elections and certify the powers of the newly elected deputies, and Rouher asked that all substantive discussion be deferred until the ordinary session, when the government would propose further reforms. Two requests for interpellation were repulsed by the *bureaux*, but 116 deputies had signed that of the Tiers Parti on responsible government. On 12 July Rouher sketched the reforms to come and announced his resignation. The emperor, reluctantly and on advice of Schneider, had decided to accept the resignation of his minister of state, together with that of the rest of the cabinet. Also on Schneider's advice the Corps Législatif was prorogued (13 July), although fifty elections remained to be validated. On 3 October an imperial decree set 29 November as the date for reconvening the chamber, and this date was maintained despite much agitation (particularly on the Left) for an earlier sitting. In by-elections of 21–22 November, four more republicans were elected from Paris, including Henri Rochefort.

On 6 September 1869, a *sénatus-consulte* established the promised reforms. These granted to the Corps Législatif full right of initiative (shared with the emperor), interpellation, amendment, and self-organization. Henceforth ministers could be deputies, and the Corps Législatif could elect its own officers and determine its own rules. In addition the lower house could vote the budget item by item and control tariff legislation, even in treaties. Historians disagree as to whether ministerial responsibility was effectively established by this *sénatus-consulte*. The extraordinary session reconvened at the Louvre on 29 November. Napoleon III opened the session with a firm speech ("L'ordre, j'en réponds...aidez-moi à sauver la liberté"). Just days before, the Tiers Parti had been opened to all, and, with the emperor's blessings, its ranks had swelled to 163. The demand for an interpellation on responsible government was dropped (although the Left, via Favre, deposed four requests for interpellations, as well as a projected law giving the lower house constituent powers). When at the end of November the Corps Législatif for the first time elected its own officers, it chose Schneider (272 to 151) as president and two conservatives, David and Talhouët, as well as comte Napoléon Daru, as vice-presidents. The republican deputies declared their independence of the Paris radicals. J.L.V.A. de Forcade la Roquette made a masterly speech on behalf of the government, and the Corps Législatif returned to the task of certifying election results (that of Isaac Pereire was invalidated).

The regular 1870 session (27 December 1869–21 July 1870) followed immediately on the conclusion of the extraordinary one and witnessed the formation (2 January 1870) by Emile Ollivier of a government representing a majority of the Corps Législatif. The situation remained confused and uncertain, however. The Tiers Parti had split into a left and right wing, the latter led by Ollivier. A vociferous debate erupted on the free trade issue, with Thiers speaking for the protectionists. On 10 January Léon Gambetta refused conciliation, and the republicans multiplied their demands; the murder of Victor Noir by Pierre Bonaparte created a new crisis. The government responded by prosecuting Rochefort (approved 222 to 34 by the Corps Législatif), establishing four special commissions (on decentralization, the government of Paris, higher education, and the commercial treaties), and abandoning official candidacy (following a tumultuous interpellation, which culminated on 26 February in a vote of confidence). In March the Corps Législatif debated Algeria. The *sénatus-consulte* of 20 April 1870, confirmed by a plebiscite of 8 May—(brilliantly interpellated in the Corps Législatif by Jules Grévy (1807–1891)—at last substituted for the constitution of 1852 a new one, which clearly vested sovereignty in the people, deprived the Senate of constituent powers, and made the ministers responsible to both chambers as well as to the emperor, while the Senate became a full legislative body, autonomous and coequal with the Corps Législatif, which obtained the right to receive petitions. Thus in ten years a remarkable political transformation had been accomplished, one of the most remarkable in modern history. But the experiment was soon to be frustrated by events.

Prorogued until after the plebiscite, the Corps Législatif met again on 12 May 1870. On 23 May the plebiscite was sanctioned in a solemn Louvre ceremony at which Schneider and Napoleon III spoke, the latter calling for an end to the constitutional debate. Picard organized a *gauche ouvert* (May), while Gambetta continued his evolution toward respectability. On 26 June a law was deposed aiming at effective regulation of hours and conditions in mines and factories. On 30 June the Corps Législatif approved reduction of the contingent from 100,000 to 90,000, Ollivier having offered assurances concerning the state of affairs in Europe. On 2 July the chamber voted 173 to 31 against permitting the return of the Orleans princes. The next day, word reached Paris of the Hohenzollern candidacy. On 6 July the foreign minister, Antoine, duc de Gramont, assured the Corps Législatif in strong terms that French honor would be maintained. Despite the militancy of the Right and a widespread sentiment among the deputies for guarantees, Gramont returned to the chamber on 13 July to announce the resolution of the crisis. The Ems telegram incident (evening of 14 July) aroused, however, an irresistible war sentiment in the Corps Législatif, which on 16 July voted war credits and other measures with only ten negative votes, after shouting down Thiers' pleas for delay and for further documentation (supported by a few voices on the Left), and listening to Ollivier's assurance that he accepted the war with a *coeur léger*. On 17 July the last constructive law was voted, allowing *conseils généraux* to choose their own officers (another project of law was deposed, to establish voluntary pension programs for workers from age sixty). On 19 July France declared war, and on 21 July, after authorizing a 500 million francs war loan and very rapidly voting the 1871 budget, the Corps Législatif adjourned.

The military reverses of early August spurred the reconvening of the Corps Législatif on 9 August. Despite Ollivier's defiance, the government was ignominiously overthrown that evening, only the ministers opposing Clément Duvernois' (1836–1879) contemptuous motion of dismissal ("La Chambre, décidée à soutenir un cabinet capable d'organiser la défense nationale, passe à l'ordre du jour"). The following day a right-wing government under the comte de Palikao was confirmed, and on 22 August six deputies, including Daru, were named to the Committee of National Defense. The denouement quickly followed. On the evening of 4 September, some two hundred deputies, assembled in the dining room of the Palais Bourbon, heeded Thiers' advice to adjourn without recrimination at the behest of the new republican government. The following day, the last Corps Législatif of the Second Empire was dissolved.

Grande encyclopédie, vol. 12; J. F. Kahn, ed., *Ainsi parlait la France: Les heures chaudes de l'Assemblée Nationale entre 1848 et 1938: Discours et débats* (Paris, 1978); T. Zeldin, *The political system of Napoleon III* (N.Y., 1958).

Related entries: ADDRESS; ARMY REFORM; BILLAULT; *LES CINQ*; CONSTITUTION; ELECTIONS; GOVERNMENT FINANCE; HOHENZOLLERN CANDIDACY; LIBERAL EMPIRE; MINISTER OF STATE; MORNY; OLLIVIER; REFORM; ROUHER; SCHNEIDER; SENATE; THIERS; TIERS PARTI; WALEWSKI.

LE CORRESPONDANT, a moderate Catholic Paris journal, founded 1843, published fortnightly. In October 1855 *Le correspondant* came under the control of a group of liberal Catholics led by Charles de Montalembert and including Albert de Broglie, Louis Buffet, Augustin Cochin (1823–1872), and Joseph Foisset (1800–1873; a Dijon magistrate). The newspaper became the channel through which Montalembert and others (such as comte Frédéric de Falloux, 1811–1886) could voice liberal Catholic opinion, urge a restoration of freedom in France, moderate a growing anti-clericalism, and attenuate the influence of Louis Veuillot and the conservative Catholic newspaper *L'Univers*. François Lenormant (1837–1883), a professor of archaeology at the Sorbonne, was director of the paper; Père Henri Lacordaire and Mgr. Félix Dupanloup were its patrons. Franz Nompère, comte de Champagny (1804–1882) was a principal editor during the Second Empire.

The reviving of *Le correspondant* heralded a rebirth of Second Empire journalism, and the newspaper's writers soon clashed with government censors. It was an 1861 article in *Le correspondant* that brought about the dismissal of Victor Laprade from his position at the University of Lyons. Earlier, in October 1858, Montalembert had used the Sepoy rebellion in India as an occasion not only to defend the British East Indian Company (at a time when most other

French newspapers were attacking it) but also to praise the principles and practices of the British parliamentary system. For this article, he and the manager of *Le correspondant*, Douniol, were prosecuted and, despite the efforts on their behalf of the renowned lawyer Antoine Berryer, found guilty in November of "inciting hate and scorn of the government." The next month, however, their appeals having failed, the two men were pardoned by the emperor. The case proved important for the reputation of the newspaper. The sympathy it aroused among intellectuals (although the Académie Française declined to assist Montalembert), and foreign personalities, and the intervention of the archbishop of Paris gave *Le correspondant* added prestige and importance. During the Italian War of 1859 and the subsequent development of the Roman Question, Montalembert's paper joined in defending papal interests, but sometimes with a heavy heart, for liberal Catholicism represented only a minority opinion within the French church and increasingly clashed with the intransigence and conservatism of Pope Pius IX. The general tone and erudite quality of *Le correspondant* limited the size of its circulation, which was 3,290 in August 1861, 5,000 in October 1868, and 4,500 in March 1869.

A. Flavia, "*Le correspondant,* French liberal Catholic journal, 1843–1855" (Ph.D. diss., Catholic University of America, 1959).

Natalie Isser

Related entries: GALLICANISM; MONTALEMBERT; PRESS REGIME; SO-CIAL CATHOLICISM.

COTTON FAMINE, a period when the French cotton industry confronted a series of difficulties that resulted in part from blockade of Confederate ports during the U.S. Civil War, which cut off most of France's supply of raw cotton. Textiles, and the cotton industry in particular, were a major driving force in French industrialization. In the 1850s, the process of technical change in cotton was accelerating as the self-acting mule and the power loom were increasingly adopted, first in Alsace, then in the north and in Normandy. Between 1830 and 1861, the number of cotton spindles increased by 80 percent and production by 200 percent. By 1861, the French had the second largest cotton industry in Europe, with 5.5 million spindles, compared with Britain's 31 million and Germany's 2.2 million.

Since the United States furnished 90 percent of France's raw cotton needs, the closing of U.S. Southern ports by the end of 1861 had serious repercussions. This is evidenced in statistics of French imports of U.S. cotton. From 624,600 bales in 1861, imports fell to 271,570 in 1862, 381,539 in 1863, and 460,880 in 1864. With the ending of hostilities in April 1865, supplies again returned to European markets, and in 1866 France imported a record 689,890 bales of U.S. cotton, although by 1867 the United States supplied only 38 percent of France's imports of raw cotton. Drastically reduced supplies had the effect of raising prices—by September 1862 prices had tripled—but the same situation encouraged speculation, which led to marked price fluctuations. The difficulties of the 1861–

1865 crisis should not be attributed exclusively to the Civil War. The immediate impact of the war was lessened by the existence of large stocks of raw cotton in France, the result of the bumper American crops of 1859–1860. The long-term impact was mitigated to some extent by increasing supplies from other sources, such as Egypt and India. Three other elements constituted the so-called cotton famine. One was the mechanization of industry and the concomitant transport revolution, which meant increased pressure and competition for smaller and less efficient producers. Another was the Anglo-French commercial treaty of 1860, which came into effect for textiles in October 1861. Although the flood of British piece goods never materialized, fears of British competition, particularly in Normandy and the north, added to the malaise. Finally, the wheat harvest of 1861 was poor, and this raised food prices and depressed the market for cheap cottons.

The impact of this series of problems is difficult to assess because we lack adequate statistics on bankruptcies, closures, unemployment, and short-time working and because the impact varied over time, among areas, sectors, and firms. The worst moment of the crisis was October 1862 to April 1863. Thereafter, alternative supplies of raw cotton provided some respite, and the wheat harvests of 1862 and 1863 were good. The worst-affected area was Normandy, the largest of France's three cotton manufacturing regions. Here, industry was the least mechanized and specialized in coarse cloths in which raw materials formed a large proportion of production costs. Perhaps two-thirds of Norman textile workers were unemployed, and a national subscription was organized to offer some relief. Alsace was less affected because its innovative manufacturers had better credit possibilities, produced finer cloths, already drew part of their raw materials from Egypt and Brazil, and always carried large stocks. In the north, the third area, other local textile industries (wool, linen) were to profit from cotton's difficulties and thus take up the slack. The firms most affected by the cotton famine were the smaller, inefficient enterprises, which did not have the credit possibilities larger firms had. The workers who fared the worst were the rural handloom weavers, in Normandy especially, who were the first to be laid off and whose suffering was more discrete but probably greater than that of the urban workers. The crisis, together with technical progress during the Second Empire as a whole, accelerated the movement toward concentration and hastened the decline of rural hand weaving.

A. L. Dunham, *The Anglo-French Treaty of Commerce of 1860 and the Progress of the Industrial Revolution in France* (Ann Arbor, 1930); C. Fohlen, *L'industrie textile au temps du Second Empire* (Paris, 1956); W. O. Henderson, "The Cotton Famine on the Continent, 1861–1865," *EcHR* 4 (1932–1934).

Barrie M. Ratcliffe

Related entries: COBDEN-CHEVALIER TREATY; ECONOMIC CRISES; MEDIATION PROPOSALS (U.S. CIVIL WAR).

COUNCIL OF STATE. See CONSEIL D'ETAT.

COUP D'ETAT, the seizure of power by Louis Napoleon, 2–10 December 1851. On Tuesday morning, 2 December 1851, Parisians woke to find the city covered with placards announcing that Louis Napoleon Bonaparte, president of the Second French Republic, had dissolved the Legislative Assembly and proclaimed martial law. Universal manhood suffrage was restored, and the French people were summoned to a plebiscite that would decide if the prince president should govern France for ten years under a constitution based on the Consulate of Napoleon I. At some point during the year, most probably following his failure on 19 July to achieve an amendment to the constitution that would have allowed him to seek reelection in 1852, Louis Napoleon had reluctantly yielded to arguments favoring a coup d'état. The sentiment of the country in favor of amending the constitution had been frustrated by the Left and by the requirement of a three-fourths majority; anarchy and perhaps civil war seemed a possibility for 1852, when France would have to elect almost simultaneously a president and a legislature. The conspirators were few: Auguste de Morny, who was to be minister of the interior; C. E. de Maupas (1818–1888), Paris prefect of police; Victor Fialin Persigny; General Leroy de Saint-Arnaud, minister of war and commander of the Paris garrison; Joseph, comte de Flahaut (1785–1870); and General E. F. Fleury (1815–1884). An attempt by Louis Napoleon to restore universal manhood suffrage was defeated by the Assembly at the beginning of November. Several times scheduled and adjourned, the coup was finally carried out on the anniversary of Austerlitz, greatest of Napoleon I's military victories. Some eighty arrests were made in the course of the night of 1–2 December, including Adolphe Thiers, General Nicolas Changarnier (1793–1877), and General Louis Lamoricière (1806–1865), and at dawn the troops were in control of Paris. The population of the city did not respond to the scattered calls for resistance; the attempted meeting of a number of deputies was dispersed with many arrests; and the high court was dissolved. On the morning of 3 December, some barricades rose but were quickly cleared by the soldiers. In the fighting, perhaps fifteen were killed, including a republican, Victor Baudin, much later to be hailed as a martyr. That evening the troops were withdrawn to barracks. During 4 December, new resistance was organized in Paris. The return of the army early in the afternoon resulted in a clash on the boulevards in which many were killed or wounded, including a number of innocent bystanders ("massacre of the boulevards"). By evening it was over; the few barricades to appear the next day were easily cleared. In the meantime, centers of resistance had developed in the provinces (3 December), particularly in the center and south. Some towns were taken by republican forces (5–6 December), but by 10 December the army was in control throughout France. Under a stringent deportation decree (8 December), mixed commissions administered rude punishment: over seventy republican deputies were exiled; eventually twenty thousand were sentenced, half of them deported to Algeria. The total of those killed between 2 and 10 December was probably fewer than four hundred.

The coup d'état had succeeded; the "Men of December" were in power; and a period of dictatorship had begun that would last until the end of March, to be succeeded first by an authoritarian republic and then by the Second Empire. The plebiscite of 20–21 December 1851 indicated that an overwhelming majority of Frenchmen were willing to approve what had occurred. And yet the cost of the coup d'état, moral and in terms of lives lost, was more than Louis Napoleon had intended, possibly because both he and Morny had overestimated the resistance. The republicans would never forgive the violence committed against the constitution of 1848, which Louis Napoleon, as president, had sworn to uphold, and historians would long refuse to extend to 2 December the nuanced judgment accorded other such events, often with less justification. As for Napoleon III, the coup d'état was for him, by his own admission, a ball and chain from which he could never escape.

M. Agulhon, "La résistance au coup d'état en province," *RHMC* 21 (1974); F. de Bernardy, "L'Angleterre et le 2 décembre," *RDM*, 1 December 1951; A. Dansette, "Le deux décembre," *Revue de Paris* (December 1960); P. Dominique, *Le deux décembre* (Paris, 1966); H. Guillemin, *Le coup d'état du 2 décembre* (Paris, 1951); J. B. Halsted, ed., *December 2, 1851: Contemporary Writings on the Coup d'Etat of Louis Napoleon* (Garden City, N.Y., 1972); T. W. Margadant, *French Peasants in Revolt: The Insurrection of 1851* (Princeton, 1979); J. M. Merriman, *The Agony of the Republic: The Repression of the Left in Revolutionary France, 1848–1851* (New Haven, 1978); E. Ténot, *Paris en décembre 1851: Etude historique sur le coup d'état* (Paris, 1868) and *La province en décembre 1851* (Paris, 1865); L. Willette, *Le coup d'état du décembre 1851: La résistance républicaine au coup d'état* (Paris, 1982).

Related entries: AUTHORITARIAN EMPIRE; BAUDIN; CONSTITUTION; LOUIS NAPOLEON; MAUPAS; MORNY; PERSIGNY; PLEBISCITE; PRINCE PRESIDENT; REPUBLICANISM; SAINT-ARNAUD; SECOND EMPIRE; UNIVERSAL MANHOOD SUFFRAGE.

COURBET, GUSTAVE (1819–1877), realist painter; born in Ornans in Franche-Comté on 10 June 1819 of middle-class farmers who owned their property. Courbet arrived in Paris in 1839. He was largely self-taught and achieved his skill primarily by copying works in the Louvre. Of the twenty-four works he submitted to the Salons from 1841 to 1847, only three were accepted. Many of his works during this decade were self-portraits, which he considered autobiographical. They are rather romantic in character.

Because there was no jury to reject his works in the 1848 Salon, seven of Courbet's paintings were exhibited. He won the gold medal at the 1849 Salon for *After Dinner at Ornans* (1849; Musée des Beaux-Arts, Lille), which the government purchased. He had already received recognition from the critic Jules Champfleury, who was to continue to publish his admiration for Courbet's work. In the following year, of the works Courbet exhibited, two in particular warrant discussion: *The Stonebreakers* (formerly Dresden, destroyed), and *Burial at Ornans* (Louvre). The Salon opened late in December 1850 because of the uncertainty of the political situation and continued into the new year. These two works were considered an affront to the viewers. Their enormous scale meant that the figures were life-size and thus doubly offensive since they and the subject matter were thought to be vulgar, coarse, impious, and totally inappropriate. Both works represent the life of the here and now, unembellished, in a manner that attempts to record as objectively and accurately as possible that which the artist saw and experienced. There are conflicting opinions as to whether the paintings have significant political and social content as criticism of the government (Courbet is somewhat confusing about this in his own writings), but some of his ideas correspond to those of his friend, Pierre Joseph Proudhon. What is clear is the innovation of the theme and the formal elements. In the hierarchy of acceptable subject matter in the nineteenth century, works dealing with historical events in the distant past were most important. Courbet had the temerity to paint commonplace events that he himself had witnessed—a man and a boy working by the side of the road, a group of provincial townspeople gathered together for the funeral of one of their members—on a scale that rivaled the *grandes machines* of the Salon, with their elevated subjects and noble themes. Compositionally, *Burial* appears to be rather unorthodox. The space does not recede in the traditional manner clearly and logically into depth. The figures are displaced horizontally across the canvas, with little indication of a focal point or a sense of continuity. It is an additive composition with no preconceived notion of unifying elements. Each individual in the town posed separately for a portrait, which Courbet later combined, giving the work a matter-of-fact actuality rather than an idealized quality. Public and critical response was negative. The people were considered ignoble and ugly, the event too insignificant.

Courbet called himself a realist, "a sincere friend of the truth," who drew his inspiration from ordinary people. Unwilling to have his work defined or judged by any official government body, he refused the invitation of comte Alfred Nieuwerkerke (1811–1892; at the time director of fine arts) to contribute a commissioned work to the international exposition of 1855 at Paris. Instead he set up his own rival exhibition in a "Pavilion of Realism" he had constructed nearby, showing forty of his paintings. One of the major works of that exhibition, *The Painter's Studio, a Real Allegory Summing up Seven Years of My Artistic Life* (1855; Louvre), with its paradoxical title and ambiguous content, remains a much debated subject for interpretation. Once more Courbet demonstrated his desire to paint only what he himself visually and sensually experienced—the artistic milieu of his time, including Charles Baudelaire on one side, and various types of people of different classes on the other: a nude model, a child and a cat in the center, with Courbet painting in their midst. Furthermore, his emphasis on the immediacy of the moment—he has limited the time period to the past seven years of his own life—is a clear demonstration against themes dealing with the distant historical and personally unrelated past to be seen in abundance in the paintings in the official Salon.

Supported verbally by a few critics and financially by a well-to-do patron from Montpellier, Alfred Bruyas (1821–1877), Courbet continued to explore new themes, such as in *Young Women on the Banks of the Seine* (1857, Petit Palais, Paris), to produce animal and hunting scenes, such as *Stags Fighting in a Wood* (1861, Louvre), and landscape paintings, *The Wave* (1869, National Gallery of Victoria, Melbourne). Courbet enjoyed hunting and spent time in Frankfurt indulging in this sport, as well as painting the German landscape. He was fortunate also to find several admirers there to provide financial support. Courbet's landscape paintings such as *Le puits noir* (1865, Louvre) demonstrate his ability to capture the appearance of nature, not seeking its transcendent or sublime character but its tactile qualities, applying the pigment heavily in a thick impasto with both brush and palette knife, mixing the colors on the canvas. The sensuous qualities of nature, the heaviness or hardness of rocks, their physical and material properties, were especially well interpreted and rendered by Courbet. The accuracy and reality of the object depicted as a principle of Courbet's painting is demonstrated in a journalist's record. He writes of seeing a reddish ox, serving as a live model, tethered in the studio of the school that Courbet set up for a short time in 1862. Courbet refused the role of teacher in the usual academic sense, consistent with his philosophy, demanding of those who sought his advice that they experience life themselves in direct contact with it.

In the 1860s Courbet painted several works devoted to female nudes, such as *Woman with a Parrot* (1866, Metropolitan Museum of Art, New York) and *The Sleepers* (1866, Petit Palais), where the sensuous appeal and not the ideal, as was the case with Alexandre Cabanel's and Paul Baudry's academic nudes, was the overriding intent. Recalling Venuses, Psyches, and nymphs of the past, Courbet's works, however, expressed not allegory or mythology but the direct and frank presence of sensuous, ample, tactile flesh of naked women.

Courbet continued to exhibit at the Salon in Paris, at another one-man exhibit he installed on the Place d'Alma in 1867 during the international exposition of that year, in smaller centers in France, and in major cities in Belgium and Germany. Having maintained and demonstrated both a sympathy with the leftist opposition to the Second Empire and a long-standing dislike for Napoleon III (Courbet believed he was struck from the list of recipients of the Legion of Honor in 1861 because of Napoleon), Courbet refused to accept the Legion of Honor award when it was offered in 1870. Elected chairman of the art commission set up for the protection of works of art in Paris during the Commune, Courbet recommended the dismantling of the Vendôme Column as it was of no artistic value and was a reminder of war and conquest. Having been a member of the Commune, he was later convicted and sentenced to prison for his role in the destruction of the Column, a sentence he protested vehemently. He was ordered to pay for the cost of reconstructing the Column in 1873, whereupon he fled to Switzerland, remaining there in exile until his death at Latour de Peilz, 31 December 1877.

Arts Council of Great Britain, *Gustave Courbet, 1819–1877* (London, 1978); P. ten-Doesschate Chu, ed., *Courbet in Perspective* (New York, 1977); R. Fernier, *Gustave Courbet: Catalogue raisonné de l'oeuvre* (2 vols.; Paris, 1978–79); P. Lafille, "Une confession-plaidoyer de Gustave Courbet sur son rôle depuis 1848, sous l'Empire, la République et la Commune [written in prison, June-Sept. 1871]," *Les amis de Gustave Courbet*, no. 53 (1975); J. Lindsay, *Gustave Courbet: His Life and Art* (New York, 1973); C. R. Mainzer, "Gustave Courbet, Franc-Comtois: The Early Personal History Paintings, 1848–1850" (Ph.D. diss., Ohio State University, 1982); B. Nicolson, *Courbet: "The Studio of the Painter"* (New York, 1973).

Beverley Giblon

Related entries: CHAMPFLEURY; DAUMIER; INTERNATIONAL EXPOSITIONS; MILLET; POSITIVISM; PROUDHON; SALON DES REFUSES.

COUTURE, THOMAS (1815–1879), painter and teacher of painting; born at Senlis (Oise), 21 December 1815. Son of a shoemaker, Couture received his early training in the Ecole des Arts et Métiers (1829), the studio of Antoine Jean Gros (1830), the Ecole des Beaux-Arts, Paris (1831), and, for a short time, with Paul Delaroche (1838). His work was accepted for exhibition in the Salons from 1840 to 1844. With the exhibition of his huge *Romans of the Decadence* (1847, Louvre, Paris) in the Salon of 1847, Couture received overwhelming acclaim. The work was seen as an expression of profound morality presented in a manner recalling the highest tradition of history painting. The precise drawing, range of classical poses, complexity of detail, and accumulation of narrative incident reflect the academic historicism of the period, and it was thus welcomed as a revival of the best of the old masters. The painting was purchased by the government after the reestablishment of the Empire and then shown again in the Paris international exposition of 1855. Following on this major success, Couture obtained commissions from the government of the Second Republic for *Enrollment of the Volunteers*, in 1848, and from that of the Second Empire for several works, including *Baptismal Ceremony of the Prince Imperial*, in 1856. Neither commission was fulfilled by a finished work, but the preparatory works for each continued to be produced throughout the last decades of Couture's life. These consisted of quantities of drawings, studies, and oil sketches that show a much greater liveliness of expression and interest in color than Couture's finished works demonstrate. In order to accommodate the new demands of the Second Empire, Couture was obliged to alter the form and conception of the *Enrollment*, deemphasizing the concept of "La Liberté." The long period of preparation and the many steps involved in the process, necessary for the painting of history, are characteristic of the traditional approach to the creation of a work of art, a rule of painting that the Impressionists so vigorously opposed.

With an attitude typical of the more conservative stream of painters at this time, Couture, although he did renounce the academy and establish his own school, aimed to combine history, allegory, and reality and to reconcile classicist and romanticist principles of painting. Unable to sustain some of the freedom of brushwork and animation of the figures of the oil sketches in the final works, Couture resorted to compromises, which resulted in works that have been tamed to the point of the prosaic. Uninspired are his murals for the Chapel of the Holy

Virgin in the Church of Saint Eustache, Paris, commissioned in 1851, finished in 1856, his last completed major work. The murals are indicative of a revival of religious subject matter at the same time that realists such as Gustave Courbet were refusing to paint angels never having seen any. Couture was made a knight of the Legion of Honor in 1848 and was sought out as a teacher. Some of his pupils—for example, Henri Fantin-Latour, Pierre Puvis de Chavannes, Edouard Manet (his student for six years), and several American artists—were influenced by his teaching. Couture wrote two treatises on painting, *Méthode et entretiens d'atelier* (Paris, 1867), and *Paysage—Entretiens d'atelier* (Paris, 1869), which were required reading for the period. Despite his many commissions (including murals for the Pavillon Denon in the new Louvre, Couture ended by quarreling with the regime, feeling himself unappreciated. He retired to Villiers in 1868. In 1870, German troops appropriated his villa for a year, destroying or removing many of his works. He died at Villiers-le-Bel (Seine-et-Oise), 30 March 1879.

A. Boime, *"Enrollment of the Volunteers": Thomas Couture and the Painting of History* (Springfield, Mass., 1980), *The Academy and French Painting in the Nineteenth Century* (New York, 1971), and *Thomas Couture and the Eclectic Vision* (New Haven, 1980).

Beverley Giblon

Related entries: FANTIN-LATOUR; MEISSONIER; PUVIS DE CHAVANNES.

CREDIT MOBILIER, a joint stock investment bank established 20 November 1852 by Emile and Isaac Pereire, who directed it until October 1867 when the bank's financial difficulties were publicly revealed and they were forced to resign. The Crédit Mobilier profited from and contributed to the prosperity and growing capital exports of the Second Empire period in general and the 1850s in particular. The originality of the institution and its contribution to economic growth have been affirmed by some, questioned by others. For some it was the application of Saint-Simonian banking theories; for others, like Antoine Berryer, who called it "the greatest gaming house in Europe," it was typical of the speculation and lack of business probity among Second Empire elites. The truth lies somewhere in between these extremes.

In aims and structure, the Société Générale du Crédit Mobilier was a three-fold innovation. First, while the merchant banks that made up the *haute banque* were family firms or limited partnerships, the new bank was a joint stock undertaking with a larger capital base than any of the others, with the exception of the Parisian Rothschilds. The Pereires, indeed, hoped to expand greatly even these resources through the issue of short- and long-term debentures. They were never to be allowed to do so. Second, the primary purpose of the bank was investment banking (deposit accounts, which it also accepted, were a secondary activity). This was not the case with the merchant banks, for which industrial investment was a recent and ancillary function. The Pereires aimed, above all, to channel funds into railways and associated industries in France and abroad. Third, the new institution sought its clients not just in a small group of the wealthy, as did the merchant banks, but in wider groups whose savings would not otherwise have gone into public works and industry. Indicative of this aim was the low share denomination the Crédit Mobilier issued at its inception in 1852. Its capital of 60 million francs was divided into 120,000 shares of only 500 francs each. The Pereires' originality, however, should not be overstated. Their bank was a synthesis of earlier projects and institutions: Jacques Laffitte's proposals of the 1820s and his Caisse set up in 1837; the Caisse des Actions Réunies that Jules Mirès had established in 1851; and the Belgian Société Générale, which from 1830 had invested heavily in industry and transport. Nor should it be supposed that the Crédit Mobilier was formed in the teeth of opposition from the *haute banque*. In fact its founding owed much to the financial support of leading merchant banks and especially to the backing of Benoît Fould (1792–1858), brother of Achille (Fould was the Crédit Mobilier's first president, until that position was assumed by Isaac Pereire). It also owed much to Napoleon III, who saw its establishment (like that of the Crédit Foncier, set up a few months earlier) as a means of promoting economic recovery. Thus the emperor disregarded James de Rothschild's memo of 15 November 1852 cautioning against the Pereires' project and, encouraged by Victor Fialin Persigny (who wanted to break the Orleanist stranglehold on finance), established the Crédit Mobilier by decree.

In France the Crédit Mobilier made particularly significant contributions to two sectors, railways and urban development. It contributed to the establishment and strengthening of the Midi (1852), Eastern (1854), and Western (1858) railroad networks. At Paris it set up in 1854 the Compagnie des Hôtels et des Immeubles de la Rue de Rivoli, which became in 1858 the Société Immobilière de Paris, the largest private company involved in the rebuilding of the capital. In 1858 the Crédit Mobilier formed the Compagnie Générale des Omnibus de Paris and the next year fused six competing companies into the Société Parisienne d'Eclairage et de Chauffage par le Gaz. Much has been made of the struggles for railway concessions and through-routes in France and abroad between the Crédit Mobilier group and rival groups, especially that dominated by James de Rothschild. Rather than being conflicts of personality or principle, however, these struggles were to secure or to break monopolies, to make profits at a time when the major networks were still being formed and rounded out. In these struggles, the Pereires scored victories and, more often, suffered defeats. By 1857 the high tide of competition had passed. In the early 1860s, the Crédit Mobilier transferred the focus of its efforts to the acquisition of insurance companies and to construction at Marseilles by the Société Immobilière.

The Crédit Mobilier also channeled French capital and enterprise abroad, chiefly to Southern and Central Europe. It did this in two principal ways. First, it stimulated the creation of banks of a similar kind either by directly promoting them or by serving as an example. In Northwest Europe the Crédit Mobilier was a model, for example, for the Darmstädter Bank, set up in 1853, which was to be the first of the German great banks. In Southern Europe, by contrast, it founded similar banks. The most successful of these were in Spain and Italy. The Sociedad General de Credito Mobiliario Español, capitalized at 60 million francs, was set up in 1863 and made important contributions in industrial promotion and government loan flotation. The Società di Credito Mobiliare was created in 1863 and until its demise in the 1890s was the second most important bank in Italy after the Banca Nazionale. The second way in which the Crédit Mobilier promoted capital exports was through building railways. If it had failures in this field (for example, the Great Russian Railway Company established in 1857), it also had successes, such as the Austrian State Railways concession it purchased in 1855, the Franz Josef Orientbahn, which it took over in 1856, and the North of Spain, which it started to build in 1857.

Whatever its contributions (and these must include an estimated 4 billion francs placed at home and abroad, the founding of two important insurance companies, the reorganization of the salt industry, and the spurring of competitors), the Crédit Mobilier lost its original élan by the late summer of 1856 and fell into serious difficulties in 1866–1867, difficulties that eventually led to the Pereires' resignation. Although the institution survived into the Third Republic, it ceased to be a major force in French finance. The explanation of this failure remains as controversial today as it was for contemporaries. Three related causes can be invoked. One is that the bank's capital base was not as wide as the Pereires wished to make it and not wide enough for the promotions in which they involved it. Refused permission to issue debentures in order to bring capitalization to the originally contemplated 600 million francs (in 1853, September 1855, and 1866, although in the last year capitalization was doubled, to 120 million), the Pereires tried a number of other expedients, including using the Bank of Savoy, after the annexation of that region in 1860, in order to issue bank notes throughout France. None of them succeeded. Another cause is that the type of investment favored immobilized ever greater amounts of capital. If the Crédit Mobilier could sell its shares in French and foreign railways and in the banking institutions it set up abroad in order to gain liquidity, the same was not true of its real estate investments in Paris and, especially, Marseilles, which absorbed ever more funds in the 1860s and yet failed to yield expected returns. Thus by 1866 the Crédit Mobilier had advanced 52 million francs to the Société Immobilière, and in the following year the figure had risen to 70 million. A final explanation of the Pereires' discomfiture in 1867 is more controversial: their financial methods. Their empire was built on confidence, on expectations of continued growth and success, and this led them to put inadequate funds in reserve (only 4.38 percent of profits between 1853 and 1865) and to prefer instead to distribute large dividends. These weaknesses that the Pereires had cleverly managed to hide from shareholders were finally revealed. In March 1867 Napoleon III ordered a solution to be found, but the enemies of the Pereires were implacable, and in October 1867 the brothers and their friends were forced to resign as the price of a rescue operation by the Bank of France. The losses suffered at that time were roughly the equivalent of the dividends which the Crédit Mobilier had distributed from 1853.

R. E. Cameron, "The Crédit Mobilier and the Economic Development of Europe," *Journal of Political Economy*, 61 (1953), and *France and the Economic Development of Europe, 1800–1914* (Princeton, 1961); B. Gille, "La fondation du Crédit Mobilier et les idées financières des frères Pereire," *Bulletin du Centre de Recherches sur l'Histoire des Entreprises* 3 (1954); B. M. Ratcliffe, "Some Ideas on Public Finance in the 1830s: The Example of Emile and Isaac Pereire," *Revue internationale d'histoire de la banque* 6 (1975).

Barrie M. Ratcliffe

Related entries: BANKING; COMPAGNIE GENERALE TRANSATLAN-TIQUE; ECONOMIC CRISES; GOVERNMENT FINANCE; MIRES; PARIS, REBUILDING OF; PEREIRE; RAILROADS; ROTHSCHILD; SAINT-SIMON-IANISM; *SOCIETES PAR ACTIONS*; TALABOT.

CRETAN REVOLT (1866–1869), the last flare-up of the Eastern question during the Second Empire. France had helped Greece win independence from Turkey (September 1829) and had become by the Treaty of London of 1832 one of the three guarantor powers of the new kingdom, sharing that role with Britain and Russia. As prince president of the Second Republic from December 1848, Louis Napoleon had taken a firm stand in regard to Lord Palmerston's attempt (18 January–21 June 1850) to extort from Greece by a naval blockade of Athens a huge financial compensation for a British subject, Don Pacifico. It was in part through the good offices of France that the affair was finally resolved, but not before the French ambassador had been recalled from London. The ambitions of King Otto of Greece to create a great Greek kingdom from parts of the Ottoman Empire stirred sympathy in Napoleon III after 1852, not only because of his support for the principle of nationalities but also because of his antipathy toward the Turks. Although as an ally of Turkey during the Crimean War Napoleon III had agreed to an Anglo-French occupation of Greece in order to prevent Athens from carrying out an anti-Turkish policy, he still talked in 1857 of creating a large Greek kingdom, of which Crete (then a Turkish province called Candia) would be part.

There had been revolts in Crete against Turkish rule in 1841, 1852, and 1863. When the most serious uprising began in August 1866, the situation of France and of Napoleon III had much changed from that of the 1850s and of the early 1860s. The emperor's health was in sharp decline, and Prussia's astounding victory over Austria at Sadowa in July 1866 had altered the European balance of power and called French security itself into question. The subsequent phases of French policy concerning the Cretan revolt mirror the broader evolution of Napoleon III's foreign policy in the final years of the Second Empire. From September 1866 until the spring of 1867, the French emperor seems to have flirted with the idea of gaining Russian support against Prussia, or perhaps of creating a Franco-Prussian-Russian-Austrian grouping, by supporting the dismemberment of Turkey in the name of reform. Thus in December 1866, he proved amenable to Russia's suggestion that Crete be separated from the Ottoman Empire (the Cretans had declared their annexation to Greece and were being supplied by Greek ships) and opposed the idea of a general congress of the signatories of the Treaty of Paris of 1856. But neither a Russian alliance against Prussia nor a Franco-Prussian understanding proved feasible, and the spring of 1867 witnessed a steady reorientation of French policy from one of revision to one of defending, or at least of supervising, the status quo. At the beginning of April 1867, the French foreign minister, Lionel, marquis de Moustier (1817–1869), dropped his resistance to Russia's proposal of "a collective démarche at Constantinople with a view of ending the bloodshed" and at the same time began backing away from the idea of a Turkish cession of Crete. By October 1867 Paris was content to end negotiations, disengage the responsibility of the powers, and leave the sultan and his rebellious subjects to settle matters among themselves. The revolt subsided briefly as 1867 came to an end.

In February 1868, hostilities recommenced on Crete. On 2 December 1868, the Porte unexpectedly broke off diplomatic relations with Greece and nine days later sent a ultimatum to Athens threatening to expel all Greeks from the Ottoman Empire (rejected by Greece 15 December). Paris at once accepted the suggestion made by Prussia of a conference. In fact, Charles Jean, marquis de La Valette, then foreign minister (Moustier had suffered a heart attack in December) not only pressed hard for the conference but eagerly supported the idea that it should meet in connection with the wish expressed at the Congress of Paris of 1856 that states, before resorting to war, should have recourse to the mediation of a third party (Clarendon mediation proposal). Paris was obviously more interested in the fact of the conference than in the question of Crete. He was, La Valette told the British ambassador, "entirely in favour of referring all international disputes to the decision of the general voice of Europe." To secure the conference, France was willing to agree in advance that the Greeks would be prevented from helping the rebels and that no proposal of cession should be made. Invitations were sent on 2 January 1869. The conference of the great powers that had signed the Treaty of Paris of 1856 plus Italy and Turkey met at Paris from 9 to 20 January and concluded its business in seven meetings. After some delay, the Greek government fell in line, and within a few months the insurrection had been crushed.

The Cretan crisis was particularly significant for what it did not become and for what it revealed of French policy. Had war in the East erupted among the great powers, France might well have escaped the isolation that was to prove fatal to it in 1870. But clearly Napoleon III had abandoned his earlier policies of revision and of an active concert of Europe, dedicated to bringing about change before conflict could occur. His aim had become the preservation of the status quo, and his hope was that such European actions as the conference on Crete could serve to prevent changes that, from being opportunities for France, had now become dangers.

D. Bosch, *Frankreichs Griechen landpolitik, 1857–1867: Im Spiegel der französischen Gesandtschafts Berichte*, 2 vols. (Augsburg, 1971); W. E. Echard, "Conference Diplomacy in the German Policy of Napoleon III, 1868–1869," *FHS* 4 (Spring 1966); V. J. Puryear, *France and the Levant from the Bourbon Restoration to the Peace of Kutiah* (Berkeley, Calif.: University of California Press, 1941).

Related entries: ALLIANCE POLICY; CONGRESS POLICY; NATIONALITIES; TRIPLE ALLIANCE.

CRIMEAN WAR (1854–1856), fought between Russian forces and the allied armies of Great Britain, France, the Ottoman Empire, and Sardinia. The Prussians were neutral; the Austrians were also neutral but became heavily involved in diplomatic efforts to end the war.

The war grew out of problems in the Near East and in Europe. For the British, the strategic and commercial prizes attainable in the Near East were paramount. The French, on the other hand, were attracted to the area because their interests there were relatively unimportant and so they had little to lose. Unlike the British, Napoleon III and most of his associates did not believe that the Ottoman Empire could be maintained except as a short-term barrier to Russian ambitions. The eastern Mediterranean, accordingly, was an ideal area for resolving European problems, for jousting with diplomatic rivals, pledging new alliances, and playing with the principle of nationalities. In response to Russian intervention in Hungary in 1849 and rumored Russian intrigues throughout the Balkans and in the hope of gaining favor with clerical circles in France, Napoleon III from 1849 to 1850 championed the rights of the Latin (Roman Catholic) pilgrims at the Holy Places in Palestine against the Greek Orthodox. His success led the Russians to riposte in 1853 with the Menshikov mission. Hoping for British support against the Russians, Napoleon III sent his fleet to Salamis in March 1853. When the British refused to join the demonstration, he feared that the Russians might back down and all the powers combine against France. Saved by Russian demands for a *sened* (treaty) recognizing the czar's right to protect the Greek Orthodox subjects of the Porte, Napoleon III furthered his goal of cooperation with the British when the joint fleets moved up to Besika Bay in June. But as the situation deteriorated during the summer, with Russian occupation of Moldavia and Walachia, the French took a leading part in attempts to resolve the crisis between Russia and the Ottoman Empire through the Vienna Note. When this démarche failed and the Ottomans declared war on Russia (4 October 1853), the French agreed to move the Anglo-French fleet to the Bosporus, but as late as November, Napoleon III had raised no additional troops and resisted British efforts to draw his navy into a forward position in the Black Sea. Russian destruction of a Turkish fleet at Sinope on 30 November 1853 was a humiliation to the French bystanders at Constantinople and impelled Napoleon III to send his fleet into the Black Sea. In a last, probably sincere gesture toward peace on 29 January 1854, he wrote directly to Czar Nicholas I proposing an accommodation. Nicholas's haughty reply led to the French treaty of alliance with Britain and the Ottoman

Empire on 12 March 1854 and the declaration of war on 27–28 March. Although Napoleon III's policy seemed contradictory, the diplomatic machine had functioned effectively to further his aims. A diplomatic solution was his first choice, but war, with the chance of gilding the new bonapartist regime with military glory, was always preferable to loss of face. Napoleon III had used the crisis to end France's pariah status. He had achieved a long-sought alliance with Britain and had isolated Russia, although, despite the French emperor's skillful use of threats against Austria in Italy, a four-power military alliance (France, Britain, Austria, and Prussia) did not result.

The French military command was less than impressive during the war. Napoleon III had considerable difficulty in securing army commanders who were both able and loyal. The forces sent to Gallipoli and then to Varna in April 1854 were commanded by Marshal Leroy de Saint-Arnaud, the hero of the December 1851 coup d'état. They had contracted cholera in France before embarkation and were ravaged in the unhealthy climate of Bulgaria. Unexpectedly effective Turkish resistance and the presence of the allied forces helped prevent a rapid Russian march on Constantinople, but it was Austrian occupation of Moldavia and Walachia (August 1854) that separated the belligerents in the Balkans and led to adoption of the plan Napoleon III had always favored, an attack on Sebastopol, the chief Russian port in the Crimean peninsula. After a successful landing at Eupatoria, the French and British forces foiled Russian attempts to dislodge them at the Battle of the Alma (20 September 1854), but on Saint-Arnaud's insistence missed the opportunity for pursuit, although it is true the allied forces were in need of rest and regrouping. Another mistake was the failure to march immediately on Sebastopol. The Russians were given time to build up the city's defenses under the supervision of General E. I. Totleben (1818–1884) but were unable to end the siege by the battles of Balaclava (25 October) and Inkermann (5 November), which instead perpetuated the stalemate. Severe winter conditions during 1854–1855 were especially hard on the British. The French benefited from better-organized supply systems, sanitary facilities, and medical care but suffered from leadership problems. After Saint-Arnaud's death (September 1854), General François Canrobert proved an indecisive replacement, while Napoleon III's attempts to direct operations from Paris by telegraph confused matters and relations with the allies remained tense.

Meanwhile, efforts to end the war by diplomacy continued. The program for a negotiated settlement laid down in the Four Points (summer 1854) was made the basis for Austrian mediation by a treaty of 2 December 1854 among France, Britain, Austria, and Prussia and was discussed extensively with the Russians during the Vienna Conference (spring 1855) but was frustrated primarily by British distrust of Austria. The breakdown of negotiations did not lead to a declaration of war by the German powers on Russia as hoped. Although Sardinia entered the war in January 1855 and sent a contingent of some fifteen thousand to the Crimea, France continued to bear the brunt of the fighting. In September 1855 the allies launched a major assault on Sebastopol. The bold and even

insubordinate leadership of the new French commander, General Aimable Pélissier, paid off with the capture of the key outworks at the Malakoff (MacMahon:
"j'y suis...j'y reste"). The British were not able to take the Redan, however.
Nonetheless the Russians, themselves decimated by disease and facing problems
of resupply even greater than those of the allies, decided to surrender the city
(9–10 September) and eventually agreed to an armistice (January 1856), following the delivery of an Austrian ultimatum at the end of December 1855. There
was no imperative reason why defeat at Sebastopol should have brought peace.
That it did so is partially owing to the intense activities of Napoleon III who
brought pressure to bear on the Russians through the Austrian government and
through private channels (including his half-brother, Auguste de Morny), as well
as on the British government. His motives included the impending collapse of
French medical services in the East and growing problems at home where the
war, never popular, had contributed to food shortages and mounting inflation.

The Peace of Paris ended the war on 30 March 1856. It was the work of the
Congress of Paris, which met during February and March under the presidency
of the French foreign minister, Alexandre Walewski. Although many scholars
have considered the Crimean War a brilliant success for Napoleon III's policy,
others have seen it as an empty victory. At issue is the question of what Napoleon
III really wanted. If he intended to make the war the occasion for a redrawing
of the map of Europe in accordance with the principle of nationalities as expounded in his *Des idées napoléoniennes*, then the results were meager. The
equivocal decision to put Moldavia and Walachia (later Rumania) under protection of the powers and the hollow encouragement to Sardinia represented the
major successes for the nationalities principle. On the other hand, Napoleon III
had effectuated a diplomatic revolution. He had ended for the next fifteen years
a system of European diplomacy in which Austria, Russia, and Prussia had
frustrated France and Britain, unable to overcome their own mutual hostility.
And he had brought the Ottoman Empire into the concert of Europe. But he did
not succeed in forging firm new alliances for France nor was he able to seize
control of the European nationalist movements he encouraged, although Russia's
desire to revise the Treaty of Paris would open opportunities—in Italy, for
example. Napoleon III's army had been the most effective fighting force in the
Crimea; but the French, unlike the other powers, did not learn from the war,
and the army did not prove to be the instrument Napoleon III needed in later
European conflicts. The conflict had been costly, taking the lives of about 24,000
British out of 96,000 sent, 63,000 French (out of 400,000 sent), about 150,000
Turks, and 250,000 to 500,000 Russians. Most of the deaths were due to ex-
posure, starvation, disease, and inadequately treated wounds.

L. M. Case, *Edouard Thouvenel et la diplomatie du Second Empire* (Paris, 1976); J.
S. Curtiss, *Russia's Crimean War* (Chapel Hill, N.C., 1979); Guillemin, "Guerre de
Crimée: Les opérations navales dans le Pacifique," *Revue historique des armées* 4 (1977),

and *La Guerre de Crimée* (Paris, 1981); L. Monnier, *Etude sur les origines de la Guerre de Crimée* (Geneva, 1977); A. P. Saab, *The Origins of the Crimean Alliance* (Charlottesville, Va., 1977); P. W. Schroeder, *Austria, Great Britain, and the Crimean War* (Ithaca, N.Y., 1972).

Ann Pottinger Saab

Related entries: ALLIANCE POLICY; ARMY REFORM; BOLGRAD; CONGRESS OF PARIS; CONGRESS POLICY; GUYS; HOLY PLACES; NATIONALITIES; PELISSIER; REVISION; RUMANIAN UNITY; SAINT-ARNAUD; WALEWSKI.

CRINOLINE, the characteristic style in feminine dress during the Second Empire. By 1850, as skirts became fuller, it proved necessary to support them with petticoats made of a stiff material such as horsehair interwoven with linen, hence ''crin'' (hair) and ''linum'' (thread) or ''crinoline.'' Other methods of stiffening were also used, including the gumming or varnishing of silk and cotton. The voluminous skirts, called ''crinolines'' by extension of the word, had been accepted by 1853. As they grew steadily larger (the waist tightly laced to accentuate the flare of the skirt), even six stiffened petticoats could no longer support the weight. Hoops of steel or of whalebone were introduced, and in 1856 the cage crinoline appeared. Made of steel ribs, light in weight, and inexpensive, the cage not only permitted the skirt to swing freely from the waist but guaranteed that the new fashion would be accessible to all classes. By 1859–1860 the crinoline had expanded to its maximum dimensions. In the 1860s its shape gradually changed to an oval, then the front and sides flattened and fullness was concentrated at the back, creating a bustle or *tournure*. Under the influence of the couturier Charles Worth, the crinoline shortened from 1867, becoming in 1868 the demi-crinoline. Thus, despite ridicule and even anti-crinoline movements (the ''bloomer girls'' in Britain and the United States), the fashion endured throughout the Second Empire.

Certainly the crinoline posed problems of transportation (the landau proved especially adaptable in this respect), safety (the flaring skirt was particularly susceptible to fire), and accommodation. The theater at Compiègne, which had comfortably held eight hundred in Louis Philippe's day, now was crowded with five hundred. The crinoline, with its garish colors and over-ornamentation (especially in lace), has been considered symbolic of the poor taste, ostentation, materialism, and wastefulness of the era. But there was more to it than that. The new fashion reflected the new technology: aniline dyes, developed in the 1860s; widespread use of the sewing machine; merchandising techniques introduced by the *grands magasins*; mass production of steel products; in general, a great and growing industrialization and ingenuity (a Frenchman, Delirac, invented a *crinoline magique*, which could be made smaller or wider). Moreover, the fashion stimulated a number of industries, in particular textiles. Even a modest taffeta dress required 17 yards of material; by 1865 a more elaborate garment might use 37 yards, not including trimming. The congruence was perfect: the crinoline, born with the Empire, did not survive its passing.

P. L. Giafferri, *L'histoire du costume féminin français: Les modes du Second Empire, 1852–1870* (Paris, 1922); P. Perrot, *Les dessus et les dessous de la bourgeoisie: Une histoire du vêtement du XIXe siècle* (Paris, 1981); A. Troux, "Sur l'élégance de l'habillement à la fin du Second Empire," *Information historique* 39 (September 1977) and 40 (March 1978); N. Waugh, *Corsets and Crinolines* (London, 1970); J. P. Worth, *A Century of Fashion* (Boston, 1928).

Related entries: WORTH.

CROWNING THE EDIFICE, the promise of Napoleon III, often evoked, to restore political liberties in France when conditions were favorable. In February 1853 Napoleon III told the French people: "To those who might regret that larger concessions had not been made to liberty, I would answer: liberty has never helped to found a lasting political edifice; it crowns the edifice when time has consolidated it." For the liberals, this statement and similar ones constituted a promise that liberty would gradually be restored. Consequently, the first reform decree of November 1860 merely whetted appetites for more. Speaking for the bonapartists of the Left, Prince Napoleon at Ajaccio in May 1865 called for "progress toward liberty through dictatorship." The enduring historical judgment made of Napoleon III and of key figures associated with him (such as Emile Ollivier) will depend greatly on how historians decide concerning the sincerity of the emperor's 1853 promise. Judgment in recent years has tended to give greater weight to Napoleon III's liberal intentions than has been accorded by past generations. But a question remains whether certain concessions (freedom of the press, ministerial responsibility) would ever have been granted had the emperor felt strong enough to withhold them.

Related entries: AUTHORITARIAN EMPIRE; BONAPARTISM; CONSTITUTION; REFORM.

D

DANISH WAR, the 1864 conflict between Denmark and the two German great powers that set the stage for the decisive clash between Austria and Prussia two years later. The root cause was the long-simmering rivalry between German and Danish nationalisms over the duchies of Schleswig and Holstein, historically attached to the Danish crown. Traditionally, France was a guarantor of Denmark's territorial integrity, but it was a Danish initiative that, at the end of 1863, challenged the status quo (sanctioned by the great powers at London in 1852) by seeking to apply one constitution to all possessions of the Danish crown, including Schleswig and Holstein. The Prussian president of council, Otto von Bismarck, chose to champion the 1852 Treaty of London and to this end entered into an alliance with Austria. Napoleon III opted for neutrality, for many reasons: the weakness of Denmark's case when measured by the principle of nationalities (only northern Schleswig was ethnically Danish); Bismarck's skillful tack of defending a treaty that all the great powers had signed; the French emperor's disappointment at British failure the preceding year to act vigorously in defense of Poland against Russian violations of the 1815 treaties and to support the French proposal (November 1863) for a general European congress; and, perhaps, the sheer difficulty of acting alone against the combined strength of Prussia and Austria. British actions (or, rather, inaction) soon confirmed that no material help for Denmark could be expected from that quarter.

The war began 1 February 1864 with Prussia's invasion of Schleswig, France having rejected the previous month London's proposal for a conference. The key Danish position of Düppel (Schleswig) fell to Prussian assault 18 April, and the Danes were constrained to attend a conference that, this time with French support, met at London 25 April. Although Napoleon III proposed a division of the duchies along national lines, the Danes remained obdurate, and the conference ended with Prussia and Austria demanding cession (28 May). The war recommenced 26 June. Defeated, Denmark was compelled to accept an armistice and, on 1 August, peace preliminaries, by which it surrendered Schleswig-Holstein to the victorious allies. The Treaty of Vienna of 30 October 1864 ended the Danish War. By consigning the conquered duchies to an Austro-Prussian condominium, this treaty may be said to have initiated events that would lead to the Austro-Prussian War of 1866. French liberal opinion at the time, and historians since, have argued that by failing to check Bismarck in this first of his ventures, Napoleon III lost his opportunity to halt the swing in Europe's balance of power. There was, however, nothing in French actions of 1864 inconsistent with Napeoleon III's earlier predilections and policies. Moreover, the failure of the conference of London well illustrated the intractability of the problem. Nor could Napoleon III have known, from information available to him in 1864, the scope of Bismarck's plans or the peril they posed for French. Under such circumstances, it is probably unreasonable to have expected him, by siding with Denmark, to repudiate both a solemn treaty and the principle of nationalities. The decisive events in the German question still lay ahead.

K. Döhler, *Napoléon III et la question danoise* (Halle, 1913); E. Driault, "La diplomatie française pendant la Guerre de Danemark," *RH* 107 (May–June 1911); P. Muret, "La politique française dans l'affaire des duchés et les premiers essais d'intervention européenne jusqu'à l'invasion du Sleswig (25 décembre 1863–16 janvier 1864)," *RHMC* 16 (1911); L. D. Steefel, *The Schleswig-Holstein Question* (Cambridge, Mass., 1932). *Related entries:* CONGRESS POLICY; DROUYN DE LHUYS; NATIONALITIES; POLISH QUESTION.

DANUBIAN PRINCIPALITIES. See RUMANIAN UNITY.

DARIMON, ALFRED (1819–1902), republican journalist and politician who, together with Emile Ollivier, rallied to the Empire as it became more liberal; born at Lille, 17 December 1819. Before 1852 Darimon had pursued an interest in archaeology, declared his republicanism, and attached himself to Pierre Joseph Proudhon as his secretary and disciple. Economics editor of the *Presse* in 1854, Darimon was nominated in 1857, along with Ollivier, by the journalists Auguste Nefftzer and Léonor Havin to contest Paris seats sought also by the "republicans of 1848," Jules Bastide (1800–1879) and Louis Antoine Garnier-Pagès (1803–1878). Darimon was narrowly elected in the second round, took the required oath and his seat, and became part of the small group of opposition deputies known as *les Cinq*, although his relations with Prince Napoleon caused the others to treat him with a certain amount of reserve.

Darimon made economic and financial matters his specialty, attacking government aid to railroads, monopolies, and scandals on the Bourse. He was an advocate of cooperatives for the workers and in February 1863 issued a call for legalization of labor unions, which became the first step toward the coalitions law of 1864. Although a committee of 1848 republicans attempted to eliminate Darimon and Ollivier as candidates in the elections of 1863 (for insufficient vigor in attacking the Empire), both were nominated through the efforts of several journalists, notably Emile Girardin. Darimon was reelected by a large majority and subsequently followed his friend Ollivier in a gradual movement toward support for a liberal Empire, encouraged by the attentions of Auguste de Morny, president of the Corps Législatif, through whose efforts he became in 1865 *rapporteur* of the important law establishing the bank check in France. He received the decoration of the Legion of Honor in August 1865, served as secretary of the Corps Législatif from 1865 to 1867, attended receptions of the empress in court dress, and cultivated contacts with members of the government. Disowned by the republicans after voting for the address in 1865, Darimon became a principal founder of the Tiers Parti and a propagandist for Napoleon III among the workers. He did not seek reelection in 1869 but retired to private life. Named consul at Rotterdam by Ollivier's government in 1870, he did not take up the post before the overthrow of the Empire on 4 September.

A. Darimon, *Histoire de douze ans: Notes et souvenirs, 1857–1869* (Paris, 1883); *A travers une révolution, 1847–1855* (Paris, 1884), *Histoire d'un parti: Les Cinq sous l'Empire, 1857–1860* (Paris, 1885), *L'opposition libérale sous l'Empire, 1861–1863* (Paris, 1886), *Histoire d'un parti: Le Tiers Parti sous l'Empire, 1863–1866* (Paris, 1887), *Histoire d'un parti: Les Irréconciliables sous l'Empire* (Paris, 1888), and *Le ministère du 2 janvier* (Paris, 1889).

Related entries: LES CINQ; OLLIVIER; REPUBLICANISM.

DARU, COMTE NAPOLEON (1807–1890), politician; foreign minister in 1870; born at Paris, 11 June 1807, son of Comte Pierre Daru, historian, and a soldier and minister of Napoleon I. Napoleon and Josephine were Daru's godparents. He studied at the Lycée Louis-le-Grand and the Ecole Polytechnique, served as a captain of artillery in Algeria, and resigned his commission in 1847 to follow the political career opened to him by his succession to Louis Philippe's chamber of peers in January 1833. Although Daru supported the July Monarchy, showing particular interest in railroads and other public works, he rallied to the Republic after the Revolution of 1848 and was elected to the Constituent Assembly from the Manche, where he held important properties, and, in May 1849, to the Legislative Assembly, of which he was vice-president in 1850–1851. His policies were conservative. He voted for the Falloux law and for the expedition to Rome and was one of the *Burgraves* who prepared the legislation of 31 May 1850 restricting universal manhood suffrage. However, Daru rejected the coup d'état of December 1851. It was in his home on the rue de Lille that protesting deputies first met before going on to the meeting at the *mairie* of the tenth arrondissement where Louis Napoleon was formally "deposed." There Daru was arrested. Detained several days at Vincennes, he retired to private life, subsequently rejecting several advances from the emperor, a boyhood friend.

The reforms of 1867 at last opened the way for Daru's return to politics. His close friend, Louis Buffet, had been elected to the Corps Législatif in 1863; in June 1869 Daru, too, was narrowly elected as an opposition candidate. In the short session of July, he became a leader of the Tiers Parti and one of the promoters of the interpellation, signed by 116 deputies, that precipitated the establishment of the Liberal Empire. In December he was elected one of the vice-presidents of the Corps Législatif. A liberal Catholic, a friend of Charles de Montalembert, and united with legitimism by the marriage of his daughter to Benoist d'Azy, Daru was nevertheless ready to serve the Empire on condition that it become a parliamentary regime. He therefore agreed to enter the cabinet formed on 2 January 1870 by Emile Ollivier. Before accepting the post of foreign minister, however, he required that Napoleon III state his conviction that he, Daru, was not an Orleanist. As representatives of the Center-Left faction, Daru and Buffet successfully insisted on a total revision of the constitution of 1852. They could not, however, in the face of opposition from Ollivier and Napoleon III, achieve their plan to have mayors named from lists drawn up by the municipal councils. They accepted, in the *sénatus-consulte* of August–September 1869, the ambiguity concerning ministerial responsibility as well as the retention in principle of the emperor's plebiscitary power. By an interesting aberration, however, Daru went further and urged that a plebiscite be held on the reforms carried out since 1860. Undoubtedly he hoped to secure an additional guarantee for the Liberal Empire, but he could not deny the force of Buffet's argument that such a plebiscite was incompatible with a parliamentary regime. Buffet resigned 8 April 1870, and Daru, after failing to persuade Napoleon III not to use his plebiscitary power without the consent of the chambers, followed the next day.

Although foreign minister for only three months, Daru played a not-insignificant role in the last days of the Empire. Despite his limitations as an orator, he was chosen to reply on 22 February 1870 to Jules Favre's interpellation on the government's internal policies. Daru's term at the foreign office coincided with the meeting of Pope Pius IX's Vatican Council, toward which the foreign minister wisely maintained a position of strict neutrality. His chief initiative, however, was the proposal in January 1870 of a mutual arms reduction by France and Prussia. The thought of arms limitation was not new. In January 1849 Louis Napoleon had suggested to the British ambassador that France and Britain reduce their naval forces, and although the ambassador demurred, Louis Napoleon subsequently reduced his military budget and, in fact, returned again to the subject during the Crimean War. France was among the first of the great powers to accept general disarmament as the basis for a conference proposed to meet in April 1859 to avert war in Italy. In November 1863 Napoleon III listed, as one of the priorities of the general European congress he had just proposed, the reduction of "exaggerated armaments." It would appear that by the end of 1868, the emperor had become wary of the pitfalls involved in such negotiations, but he nevertheless agreed to allow Daru to make one further effort, provided that the proposal not be made directly by Paris to Prussia. The foreign minister, who undoubtedly hoped to improve relations with Britain, asked Lord Clarendon, British foreign secretary, to suggest at Berlin a mutual Franco-Prussian arms reduction (24 January 1870). This effort had failed by the beginning of February, and a second approach that same month was equally fruitless. Nevertheless, Daru, whose sincerity seems undeniable, proposed a unilateral reduction of the French contingent from one hundred thousand to ninety thousand men. This measure (applying only to the reserve) was approved by the Corps Législatif 30

June, two months after Daru's resignation, which had led to the fateful appointment of his successor, the duc de Gramont.

Daru voted for war with Prussia in July 1870. He accompanied Buffet and Charles Kolb-Bernard (1798–1888) to the meeting with Empress Eugénie of 12:30 P.M., 4 September, at which they urged her to stand aside in favor of a commission named by the Corps Législatif. Daru had been named on 2 August a member of the *comité de défense*. After Quatre September he retired to the department of the Manche, where he had long been a member and president of the conseil général, to help organize its defense. He was elected to the National Assembly in February 1871 and to the Senate of the Third Republic in 1876 but failed to win reelection three years later. Daru had been an officer of the Legion of Honor since April 1840 and a *membre libre* from April 1860 of the Académie des Sciences Morales et Politiques. His brother, Vicomte Paul Daru (1810–1877), a financier and industrialist, remained in private life throughout the Second Empire. Daru died at Paris, 20 February 1890.

L. Buffet, *Le Comte Daru* (Paris, 1893); J. L. Herkless, "Lord Clarendon's Attempt at Franco-Prussian Disarmament, January to March 1870," *HJ* 15 (September 1972); A. Pingaud, "Napoléon III et le désarmement," *Revue de Paris* 3 (1899), and "Un projet de désarmement de Napoléon III de 1863,' *ASMP* 21 (November 1931).

Related entries: BUFFET; LIBERAL EMPIRE; QUATRE SEPTEMBRE; TIERS PARTI.

DARWINISM IN FRANCE, the reception accorded the theory of evolution by natural selection (first announced jointly by Charles Darwin and Alfred Russel Wallace in 1858) in the decade following the publication of *Origin of Species* (1859). The initial French response to Darwinism was generally negative or noncommittal and must be interpreted within the political and philosophical framework of the Second Empire, as well as within the framework of French biology. Evolutionary theories were not new to France. Jean Baptiste de Lamarck (1774–1829), to cite the most influential figure, had put forward speculations that established a native school of transformist doctrines by the start of the nineteenth century. In the 1820s and 1830s, however, the eminent paleontologist Georges Cuvier (1769–1832) argued on the basis of an apparently overwhelming body of evidence against the possibility of the mutability of species and effectively discredited evolutionary speculation within the French scientific community. Cuvier's influence was still strong in 1859 and posed a major obstacle to the spread of Darwinian ideas. Ironically, some of those biologists who maintained a more open attitude toward evolution tended to equate, or confuse, Darwin's theory with Lamarck's and to underestimate, therefore, the significance or originality of the principle of natural selection as the mechanism of the origin of new species from preexisting ones.

The empiricist bias of French science at mid-century further militated against an early acceptance of Darwinism. While few denied the impressiveness of the data marshaled in *Origin*, French critics repeatedly deplored what they perceived to be the excessively hypothetical character of natural selection and the doctrine of species transformation itself. The author of *Origin* could, therefore, be praised for the accuracy and brilliance of his observations while at the same time denounced for unwarranted and unsupported theoretical statements. Many argued that Darwin's work failed to satisfy the rigorous canons of experimental proof associated (in particular) with the methodological guidelines of Claude Bernard and that, although evidence of the mutability of species might be forthcoming in the future, Darwin's evolutionary hypotheses were without foundation in the present state of biological knowledge. Significantly, when Darwin was finally elected as a corresponding member of the Académie des Sciences (in the Botanical Section) in 1878, it was not for his evolutionary theories but, more probably, to honor his strictly empirical studies. Positivism contributed also to the initial opposition to Darwinism. Committed to the belief that true science is limited to observation, experiments, and to those general laws that can be legitimately inferred from the data, the disciples of Auguste Comte (1798–1857), including both the orthodox group and the Littréists, greeted the theory of natural selection with extreme skepticism as a hypothesis lacking experimental evidence. Emile Littré, moreover, contended that Darwin had contributed nothing novel to Lamarckianism.

The scientific and philosophical forces arrayed against Darwinism were strengthened by potent political and religious ones. Despite its official empiricism, French science—particularly biology—was embedded in the political and religious controversies of the Second Empire. Evolutionary theory had obvious, if ultimately ambiguous, implications for theology and social thought, and Darwin's work appeared at a time when church and state were particularly vigilant against presumed threats to orthodoxy. Although republicanism, atheism, and materialism had no necessary connection with Darwinism, it is clear that such doctrines could be (and were) read into the argument of *Origin*. Darwin himself, at least publicly, had been reticent with respect to religious or social implications of evolutionary biology, as well as with respect to the sensitive question of the origin of life, but the French translation of the *Origin of Species* rendered vigorous reactions to Darwinism inevitable. The translation, which appeared in 1862, was the work of the anti-Catholic, republican, and materialist writer Clémence Royer (1830–1902). Her lengthy introduction was a strident polemic, which cited Darwin's theory as a "rational revelation of progress" wholly opposed to centuries of Catholic error and oppression. She also asserted that the earliest forms of life must have arisen from nonliving substances in a purely naturalistic manner and thereby embroiled Darwinism in the debate on spontaneous generation then taking place in France. Thus, Louis Pasteur's celebrated (albeit inconclusive) refutation of that doctrine provided a major additional scientific argument for the opponents of Darwinism. Finally, Royer's emphasis that *Origin*'s argument had significant moral and social implications ensured that Darwinism would be associated with radical ideas in the Empire. Darwin himself had been surprised by the nature of her introduction and felt that it injured the *Origin*'s reception in France. Darwin's most influential critics included Catholic biologists such as Pierre Flourens (1794–1867; permanent secretary of the Académie des Sciences), who interpreted Darwinism as theologically suspect because of its presumed materialism. Their formal objections to Darwin were advanced, however, on (then) legitimate biological grounds. The Catholic church, therefore, whose doctrines, including providential design, were threatened by the theory of natural selection, found itself in the enviable position (in the 1860s at least) of having members of the French biological establishment spearheading the attack against Darwinism.

If, aside from the support of a few minor figures, the initial response among biologists to the theories of Darwin and Wallace was generally either overtly hostile, as typified by Flourens' *Examen du livre de M. Darwin sur l'origines des espèces* (1864), or judicious but critical, as typified by the series of articles published in 1868–1869 by the naturalist and anthropologist Armand de Quatrefages de Bréau (1810–1892) in the *Revue des deux mondes*, the situation in other disciplines was more favorable. Anthropology, a recently professionalized and hence possibly less tradition-bound science in the Second Empire, employed evolutionary explanations in studying human prehistory, racial characteristics, and cultural institutions, including religion, language, and law. By the late 1860s, the discussions of the Société d'Anthropologie de Paris, founded in 1859 by Paul Broca (1824–1880), concentrated on transformism and made positive references to Darwin (Royer was a member). It must be emphasized, however, that it was not strict Darwinism that was endorsed (that is, the mechanism of natural selection) but rather a general evolutionary framework. Analogies drawn from evolutionary biology also began to appear in fields such as history, sociology and philosophy. Ernest Renan's writings, for example, bear an evolutionist imprint, and in a well-known letter to the chemist Marcelin Berthelot (1863), he referred positively to Darwin's ideas and their broader philosophical significance. Here again, however, it is not a question of an endorsement of Darwinism but of Renan's and certain other French intellectuals' appropriation of the language of science, particularly a broad (and vague) evolutionary paradigm, to articulate alternatives to received ideas on man and nature. Under the Empire, Darwinism, both as science and as cultural metaphor, could make little headway. And when, during the first years of the Third Republic, evolution gained increasing acceptance in France, it was not of the Darwinist guise.

E. Arquiola, "Darwinism in the Société d'Anthropologie de Paris," *Clio medica* 14 (May 1980); D. Biucan, "L'accueil de Darwin à l'Académie des Sciences," *Revue de synthèse* 103 (January 1982); L. L. Clark, "Social Darwinism and French Intellectuals, 1860–1915" (Ph.D. diss., University of North Carolina, 1968), and "Social Darwinism in France, 1860–1915: Some Reactions from Political Quarters," *PWSFH* (1977); Y. Conry, *L'introduction du Darwinisme en France au XIXe siècle* (Paris, 1974); J. Farley, "The Initial Reactions of French Biologists to Darwin's *Origin of Species*," *Journal of the History of Biology* 7 (1974); H. W. Paul, *The Edge of Contingency: French Catholic Reaction to Scientific Change from Darwin to Duhem* (Gainesville: University Presses of Florida, 1979); J. Roger, "Darwin in France," *Annals of Science* 33 (1976); R. E.

Stebbens, "French Reactions to Darwin, 1859–1882" (Ph.D. diss., University of Minnesota, 1965), and in T. F. Glick, ed., *The Comparative Reception of Darwinism* (Austin, Texas, 1974).

Martin Fichman

Related entries: BERNARD; GALLICANISM; LITTRE; PASTEUR; POSITIVISM; RENAN; REPUBLICANISM; SAINTE-BEUVE.

DAUBIGNY, CHARLES FRANCOIS (1817–1878), Barbizon landscape painter; born at Paris, 15 January 1817. Daubigny was initiated into painting by his father, Edme, a landscape painter. As a young student, he worked for François Granet (1775–1849) in the Louvre restoring paintings. He traveled to Italy in 1836 and later studied with Paul Delaroche (1797–1856) in Paris in order to be able to compete for the coveted Prix de Rome (he failed to get it). Some of his works were exhibited in the Salon beginning in 1838. He frequented the Barbizon area from 1843 onward, eventually befriending Jean Baptiste Camille Corot and traveling with him to Switzerland in 1852. Daubigny spent the 1850s traveling throughout France and continued to exhibit in the Salon, receiving a first-class medal in 1853. *Les bords de la Seine* was purchased by the state in 1852 and *The Pond of Gylieu* (Cincinnati Art Museum) privately by Napoleon III in 1853. The emperor also purchased (in 1857) *The Great Valley of Optevoz*.

Daubigny was especially attracted to rivers, streams, and ponds. He spent his time traveling up and down the Marne, the Oise, and the Seine in a boat, the *Botin*, which he converted to a studio in 1857. In his floating studio, he could be close to the nature he loved, the water and the sky, and paint more directly from the motif, *en plein air*. During this decade, works such as *The Pond with Herons* (1857; Louvre, Paris) achieve a flowing, moving quality due to the lightness of touch and the point of view (the artist locates the viewer of the scene in the water as he himself was). Charles Baudelaire complained that Daubigny's works were too sketchy, others that they were unfinished. The motifs, seen from the river and accessible only by water, seem to have been come on by accident. They are not composed in the tradition of Nicolas Poussin but rather seem to be taken from nature just as it appeared to Daubigny. The small formats also contribute to the feeling of quiet intimacy with an unknown aspect of nature. Having visited Auvers-sur-Oise beginning in 1854, Daubigny established himself there in 1860. At Auvers he was visited by Corot, Honoré Daumier, and others. Named to the Legion of Honor in 1857, he received a number of government commissions, including one to paint the park at Saint Cloud, a favorite imperial summer residence near Paris. He continued to find new vantage points to paint during the 1860s, showing in the Salon and attracting buyers. He went to London for the first time in 1865, where he met James McNeil Whistler (1834–1903), and again in 1866. He was elected to the jury of the Salon in 1866 and used his influence to have a work by Camille Pissarro, a future Impressionist, exhibited. He also advocated works by Pierre Auguste Renoir and Paul Cézanne, which were not accepted. Elected to the jury again in 1868, he once more promoted the younger artists' works, among whom were Pissarro, Claude Monet, Frédéric Bazille (1841–1870), Edgar Degas, Renoir, Alfred Sisley (1839–1899), and Berthe Morisot (1841–1895), all but Bazille (who died in the Franco-Prussian War of 1870) future members of the Impressionist group. Daubigny later resigned from the jury in 1870 because of their refusal to admit Monet to the Salon. He sought refuge in London during the war, this time encouraging the French dealer Paul Durand-Ruel (1831–1922), who had opened a gallery in London, to purchase works by Monet and Pissarro, who had also gone to London. Daubigny's devotion to painting *en plein air* was his important contribution to Impressionist painting of the 1870s. His son, Karl Pierre (1846–1886), was a talented painter in his own right, who first exhibited in the Salon of 1863. Daubigny died at Paris, 19 February 1878.

J. Bouret, *The Barbizon School* (Greenwich, Conn., 1973); M. Fidell-Beaufort and J. Bailly-Herzberg, *Daubigny* (Paris, 1975); R. L. Herbert, *Barbizon Revisited: A New Appraisal of the Art of Corot, Daubigny, Diaz, Dupré, Jacque, Millet, Rousseau, Troyon* (New York, 1963).

Beverley Giblon

Related entries: COROT; DIAZ DE LA PENA; MILLET; ROUSSEAU.

DAUMIER, HONORE (1808–1879), lithographer, sculptor, painter; born at Marseilles, 26 February 1808. While Daumier was referred to by Honoré de Balzac as having something of Michelangelo about him, it was as a lithographer and caricaturist that he won public acknowledgment. The Michelangelo aspect of his work was its monumental quality. Daumier achieved renown and notoriety in the 1830s when he began creating biting political cartoons for *La caricature* and *Le charivari*, mocking King Louis Philippe and the legislators. For his pains he was sentenced to prison. His deep sympathy for the poor and oppressed is strikingly summarized in *Rue Transonain le 15 avril 1834*, a lithograph depicting an incident in the attempted insurrection at Paris of that year, which stands as a memorial to the senseless slaughter of helpless members of society. The monumentality of the image, despite the medium used and its small format, is achieved by the dramatic foreshortening of the figure of the dead man. With simple means, Daumier created a masterpiece of expressive power and penetration.

Born to an artisan father, Daumier had moved at an early age with his family to Paris, where he began to develop his extraordinary draftsmanship. His first major commission was a series of some forty-five small portrait busts of political figures, which he made in 1832 in an unorthodox medium, unbaked clay. These caricatures were manipulated with unusual tools, such as a comb, and then painted, thus demonstrating an attitude to creativity in keeping with the individuality and independence of spirit of the artist. His major sculpture, *Ratapoil* (1850, Louvre), is a trenchant statement against the exploiters of society represented by a single male figure. It is a deeply felt response to the current political atmosphere in which the demise of the Second Republic was momentarily expected. As a republican, Daumier found ample targets for his penetrating satire.

When his political caricatures were suppressed by the government of the Second Empire, he pursued another interest, the negative characteristics of human nature in general, its hypocrisy, falsity, and vulgarity, for which he found an abundance of inspirations. He produced about four thousand lithographs in all, some dealing with theatrical subject matter, others aiming their scathing satire at the professions, in particular, the law, but also at social mores and customs, not without a measure of humor. Meanwhile, he continued to earn his meager livelihood by producing cartoons at a prolific rate for *Le charivari*, except for a period of four years from 1860 to 1864, when he was dropped from the staff as the result of government pressure.

The Third-Class Carriage (1856; National Gallery of Canada, Ottawa) is a painting that indicates Daumier's concern with a new feature of modern, urban society—its railways, crowded conditions, its chance mingling of classes and types, treated with understanding and compassion. His observation and depiction of ordinary people in commonplace activities bring Daumier's work close to the realism of Gustave Courbet. Daumier's paintings, done for his own pleasure beginning in 1848 and seen by only a few friends until *The Washerwoman* was shown at the Salon of 1862, were his abiding interest. He devoted more time to painting during the 1850s and 1860s when his political caricatures were suppressed. As an academically untrained artist, he could be innovative and experiment with boldness and daring. He carried over into his painting his graphic skills but also his intuitive sense of what was permissible and necessary. His lack of inhibition and his unorthodox methods allowed him to paint quickly, often in series, setting up twenty canvases in a row, and to exaggerate form and line for their dramatic and expressive qualities in such works as *Don Quixote and Sancho Panza* (1865, Courtauld Institute, London). Daumier portrayed Don Quixote as a modern hero, fighting for truth despite all obstacles and lack of success, much as Daumier himself experienced life. Daumier also depicted the ordinary man in his everyday life with admirable qualities of honesty and dignity in the face of hardship and misery, elevating him as well to the level of the heroic. Daumier's message proclaimed the universality of heroism in modern life. This can be seen in *The Heavy Burden* (c. 1860, Glasgow Art Gallery), which depicts a theme the artist explored repeatedly in painting and in sculpture.

Toward the end of the 1860s, Daumier began to lose his sight and, never financially secure, became even more destitute. He had been given only one government commission—for a drawing in 1863. He was supported by friends, especially Jean Baptiste Camille Corot, who bought a house for him in Valmondois where he spent his remaining years, from 1865. Others among his republican artist friends were François Bonvin (1817–1887), Jean François Millet, Edouard Manet, Gustave Courbet, Jules Dalou (1838–1902), and Auguste Préault. He firmly declined the medal of the Legion of Honor, which was offered to him in 1869, for he was a firm enemy of all forms of authority. Daumier died at Valmondois, 10 February 1879, in debt, and was buried in a pauper's grave.

Today he is hailed by some as the first modern painter and the founding father of realism.

J. Adhémar, *Honoré Daumier* (Paris, 1954); Musée Cantini, Marseilles, *Daumier et ses amis républicains* (Marseilles, 1979); O. W. Larkin, *Daumier, Man of His Time* (New York, 1966); R. Passeron, *Daumier* (New York, 1981); R. Rey, *Honoré Daumier* (New York, 1965); J. Wasserman, *Daumier Sculpture: A Critical and Comparative Study* (Cambridge, Mass., 1969).

Beverley Giblon

Related entries: CHAMPFLEURY; COURBET; MILLET; REPUBLICANISM.

DAVID, BARON JEROME (1823–1882), deputy, vice-president of the Corps Législatif, and minister; born at Rome, the grandson of the painter Jacques-Louis David (1748–1825). Jérôme Bonaparte (1784–1860), youngest brother of Napoleon I and former king of Westphalia, was Jérôme David's godfather (and rumored to be his father) and as such directed the boy toward a naval career, which he abandoned in favor of training at Saint Cyr. He left that academy in 1844 as a sublieutenant to join the infantry, serving under Generals Louis Eugéne Cavaignac (1802–1857), Louis de Ladmirault (1808–1898), and Jacques Louis Randon in the conquest of Algeria. David remained in Algeria in the military administration of the territory until the coup d'état of December 1851, when he was recalled by his godfather to be aide-de-camp (with the rank of captain) to King Jérôme's son, Prince Napoleon. He accompanied Prince Napoleon in battle in the Crimean War, seeing combat at the Alma and Sebastopol. In 1853 David had married into a wealthy Girondin family and subsequently became mayor of Langon and a member of the Conseil Général of the Gironde. When in 1857 he resigned from the military, he stood as an independent for election to the Corps Législatif. He was defeated in this first attempt but gained a legislative seat in the by-elections of 1859 in the Gironde, this time as an official candidate.

In the Corps Législatif, David took a special interest in Algerian affairs. He was also a committed free trader, supporting Napoleon III's tariff treaty with Britain in 1860, and was a vigorous supporter of the temporal power of the pope and of the expedition to Mexico. Above all, David distinguished himself as an avid proponent of conservative bonapartism and as an opponent of the movement toward a liberal Empire. When the emperor in 1867 announced his legislative reforms and promised reform of the laws regulating the press and the right of reunion, David apparently believed the Empire was on the verge of collapse. He took the initiative, with his equally conservative and energetic colleague, Adolphe Granier de Cassagnac, to form an extraparliamentary opposition to the reforms in the Club of the Rue de l'Arcade. At first merely a gathering place for deputies of all parties, the Club of the Rue de l'Arcade, under David as president, quickly became the domain of the Right, of those who were more bonapartist than the emperor himself, of a loyal opposition intending to pressure the throne and ministry into withdrawing the reform proposals. Despite David's opposition to official policies, Napoleon III named him vice-president of the

Corps Législatif (David's friend, Eugéne Rouher, had hoped that the leader of the Arcadians would succeed Alexandre Walewski as president of the Corps Législatif, but the emperor had instead designated Eugène Schneider). When the laws on the press and reunion were voted, David (with Cassagnac) abstained. During the spring of 1869, in his zeal to oppose further reform, to maintain a conservative majority in the Corps Législatif, and to prepare for the coming elections, David, although he spoke poorly and therefore had spoken seldom, engaged the ministers in debate. He interpellated the government on how it intended to check electoral corruption, hoping the ministers would respond by reaffirming clearly and unmistakably their support for the practice of official candidature. The move backfired. A torrent of speeches from the Left attacked official candidature as the most extreme example of electoral corruption. David, in a panic, withdrew his interpellation, but the Left immediately replaced it by one of their own.

David stood for reelection in 1869 but in a new district of the Gironde, having given his seat to Ernest Dréolle (1829–1887), a journalist who had supported the conservative bonapartist opposition. Both were elected without difficulty. Following the elections, Napoleon III reappointed David vice-president of the Corps Législatif and raised him to grand officer of the Legion of Honor, moves that did little to clarify the emperor's intentions for the political future of his government. Momentarily, David and the conservatives rejoiced in the confidence that their star once more was rising. In November 1869, the Corps Législatif, for the first time electing its own officers, chose Schneider as president and David as vice-president. But the emperor continued his course toward liberalization, and when he charged Emile Ollivier with the formation of a ministry, David's opposition to the Liberal Empire became unqualified and unceasing. In the summer of 1870, David was most insistent (he interpellated the government 13 July) that France secure a guarantee for the future from Prussia regarding the withdrawal of Leopold's candidacy for the Spanish throne. He voted for war with Prussia, was shrill in his efforts to blame Ollivier for the early defeats, and on Ollivier's overthrow took the portfolio of public works in the short-lived right-wing government of the comte de Palikao (1796–1878). It was David who carried word of the disaster at Sedan to the Empress Eugénie, of whom he had long been a confidant. After 4 September, David went with other conservative bonapartists to London, where he lapsed into a period of despair. He resumed his political life in 1876, however, when he was elected to the Chamber of Deputies and sat among the bonapartist *Appel au Peuple*. He did not stand for election in 1881. David died at Langon (Gironde), 27 January 1882.

J. David, *Actualités et souvenirs politiques* (Paris, 1874); R. Dufourg, "Un homme politique Girondin au siècle dernier, Jérôme David," *Revue historique de Bordeaux et du département de la Gironde* 6 (April–June 1957); A. Sapaly, "Le Baron Jérôme David, maire de Langon (1860–1861)," *Les cahiers du Bazadais* (1978).

William E. Duvall

Related entries: BONAPARTISM; GRANIER DE CASSAGNAC; LIBERAL EMPIRE; PRINCE NAPOLEON; REFORM; ROUHER; SCHNEIDER.

DAVIOUD, GABRIEL (1823–1881), architect, one of those chiefly responsible for the transformation of Paris during the Second Empire; born at Paris, 30 October 1823. Davioud studied under Adolphe Marie François Jaÿ (1789–1871) and Léon Vaudoyer (1803–1872) and at the Ecole des Beaux-Arts and the Ecole Spéciale de Dessin. After a brilliant student career, he executed his first major commission (the Théâtre d'Etampes, 1850–1851) and joined the host of architects recruited for Baron Georges Haussmann's rebuilding of Paris. In 1855 Davioud was named *sous-inspecteur*, under Victor Baltard (1805–1874), of construction of the new central market, the Halles Centrales, and a little later was promoted to chief architect *des promenades et plantations de Paris*. The scope of his duties is indicated by the fact that in 1860–1862 he directed major works involving the square des Arts et Métiers, the Canal Saint Martin, and Parc Monceau, the Jardin d'Acclimatation, and the place du Châtelet.

Davioud's contributions to the embellishment of Paris were numerous. He built the Nouvelle Panorama of the Champs Elysées (1859–1860) and helped to shape two new parks, designing (1860–1862) the four entrance grills of the Parc Monceau and (1866–1867) the decorations of the Parc des Buttes Chaumont. To the Bois de Boulogne he contributed a number of pavilions (including those of Armenonville and the Pré-Catelan), kiosks, chalets, and restaurants and designed the guard dwellings of the gates. On the periphery of the Bois, he created the Jardin d'Acclimatation (1854–1860), and, with Antoine Nicolas Bailly (1810–1892), the grandstands of the Longchamp race course (1857). Davioud also created the squares Montholon, des Batignolles (1862), and Monge (1859) and changed the aspect of a number of other Paris squares. In 1860–1862 he created the two basins and the Crimean War column of the square des Arts et Métiers and in 1865 moved and restored Jean Goujon's fountain in the square des Innocents. He also created the boulevards de Grenelle and de Charonne (1864) and constructed the basins of the place Pigalle (1862). In addition he undertook private commissions, building a number of houses (hôtels) on the boulevard Sébastopol and the place Saint Michel, as well as the Magasins Réunis (1866) on the place du Château d'Eau (now place de la République).

The place du Châtelet most impressively bears Davioud's stamp. While building (1858–1860) the monumental fountain of the place Saint Michel, which faces the Châtelet, he moved the Fontaine du Palmier (also known as the Fontaine de la Victoire) of the place du Châtelet (1858) and built for it an impressive sphinx-decorated stepped pedestal (restored 1900). From 1860 to 1862 he built in the square two immense theaters, the eighteen hundred seat Théâtre Impérial or Cirque Impérial (now the Théâtre du Châtelet) and the sixteen hundred seat Théâtre Lyrique (now the Théâtre de la Ville). Work began on the Théâtre Impérial 1 May 1860. The theater was inaugurated 19 August 1862, two months before the Théâtre Lyrique (30 October). Davioud was named to the Legion of Honor that same year.

Davioud's career continued after the fall of the Empire. In 1872 he was named inspector general of the buildings of the city of Paris. Between 1874 and 1878 he built the fountain of the place du Château d'Eau (now on the Place Daumesnil), the two fountains of the place du Théâtre Français, and the basins of the Fontaine de l'Observatoire. His final major undertaking, with Jules Désiré Bourdais (b. 1835), was the Palais du Trocadéro, built for the exposition of 1878 and replaced in 1935–1937 by the Palais de Chaillot. Davioud died 6 April 1881 at Paris, where, fifteen years later, a street was named in his memory.

C. Daly and G. Davioud, *Les théâtres de la Place du Châtelet* (Paris, n.d.); D. Destors, "Notice sur la vie et les oeuvres de M. Davioud," *Revue générale de l'architecture et des travaux publics* 38 (1881).

Related entries: ALPHAND; PARIS, REBUILDING OF.

DEAUVILLE, Norman (Calvados) seaside village between Caen and Le Havre, which became an exclusive holiday resort during the Second Empire. Trouville, across the Touques River, was already at the beginning of the Empire a popular bathing center but too crowded and democratic in its clientele for Auguste de Morny (Napoleon III's half-brother) and Morny's preferred physician, the Irish-born, Paris-educated Joseph Oliffe. In 1859 Oliffe and a financier friend, Pierre Donon, undertook to build at Deauville (the nearest sandy beach to Paris) a resort that would lure the capital's *beau monde* from its usual summer haven of Baden-Baden. They purchased the site from the commune for 800,000 francs and enlisted Morny, whose contacts were invaluable. Morny hoped not only to establish a major race course at Deauville but also to make of the town a rival railroad center to Paris. He took a personal interest in the work, which advanced rapidly after 1860 under the direction of architect D. F. Breney (conveniently elected mayor in 1861): a bridge over the Touques, a harbor and jetties, a yacht basin, a granite quay bordered by a boardwalk, and a wide terrace along which stood a number of impressive buildings facing the sea. In the center of the terrace rose the casino, backed by a large English garden. Morny's villa ("Sergevna"), Oliffe's ("Victoria Lodge"), and Donon's ("Villa Elisabeth"), built side by side and, together with the casino, since demolished, were soon joined by a number of similar creations, including Prince Demidov's Palais Italien, as well as by hotels for the somewhat less affluent. The *Grande rue* led to Morny's racetrack whose inauguration 15 August 1864 launched the first Deauville season. Also that year the railroad was completed, and control of the venture transferred to a limited liability company. Although Morny's larger railroad schemes failed, and Napoleon III could never be persuaded to visit the resort, Deauville succeeded, leading the way to similar Calvados developments (Paris-Plage, Cabourg) and becoming in a short time the favored resort of the wealthy and influential. It was from Deauville 7 September 1870 that Empress Eugénie sailed to exile in England following the overthrow of the Empire. A statue of Morny by Henri Iselin (1824–1905), erected in the Place Morny in 1867, was torn down that same month.

R. Deliencourt, "Le Duc de Morny et le nouveau Deauville," *Le pays d'Auge* 12, (1961); R. Deliencourt and J. Chennebenoist, *Deauville: Son histoire* (Grenoble, 1952); R. Kain, "Deauville/Trouville: The Evolution of These Northern Counterparts to Cannes and St-Tropez," *Con*. 204 (June 1980).
Related entries: BIARRITZ; MORNY; RAILROADS.

DECENTRALIZATION, the objective of various political movements during the Second Empire that opposed the highly centralized administrative system created by Napoleon I. Napoleon had not, of course, invented French centralization, nor was its appeal limited to the Right. Jacobin republicans were also among its supporters. In his proclamation of 14 January 1852, Louis Napoleon made clear his intention to apply the centralist ideas of the Consulate to French local government, and this was done in a series of decrees and laws, notably the law of 7 July 1852 concerning local councils. While both the department councils (*conseils généraux*) and those of most communes (*conseils municipaux*) were elected, the central government named their officers. A special law of 5 May 1855 organized the governments of Paris, the Seine communes, and Lyons. In all three cases, the councils were named every five years by the emperor, who also appointed the president of each. The Paris municipal council (or "commission") consisted of thirty-six members, increased to sixty when in 1860 the number of Paris arrondissements was expanded from twelve to twenty. Each arrondissement was administered by an appointed mayor and two appointed *adjoints*. The Commission Départementale de la Seine consisted of forty-four members (later increased to sixty-eight) who were named by the central government (only eight represented non-Parisian communes). All mayors throughout France were named by Paris. The decree of 25 March 1852, which organized the prefectoral powers, must be seen in this context. The aim was not to decentralize but to make the action of the centralized government more effective by decentralizing purely administrative functions. Thus the powers of the prefects were increased vis-à-vis the *conseils généraux* (over whose actions they obtained a veto), and the prefects were granted increased powers of appointment and of action without reference to Paris.

Theorists like Raymond Troplong and C. B. Dupont-White (1807–1878) could argue that this centralization was not antithetical to democracy but, rather, was the best instrument for liberating the masses from feudalism and aristocracy. The fact that Orleanists, with their elitism, and legitimists, with their memories of 1830, advocated decentralization (letter of the comte de Chambord, 14 November 1862) gave encouragement to this point of view, so that a predilection for centralization was one of the many attitudes held in common by bonapartists and republicans. On the other hand, among the paradoxes of Napoleon III was his belief in laissez-faire and his desire to encourage Frenchmen to escape from their "let the government do it" attitude. Decentralization was not, therefore, a program he inflexibly opposed.

The agitation for decentralization that began shortly after the Crimean War was very much a partisan movement, however. Legitimists (Claude Marie Raudot [1801–1879]) joined with Orleanists like Charles de Rémusat (1797–1875), Lucien Anatole Prévost-Paradol, and Victor, duc de Broglie (1785–1870) and with republicans like Jules Simon (1814–1896), Jules Ferry (1832–1893), and Ernest Desmarest (1815–c. 1893) in attacking the centralization of the Empire, although their ultimate objectives were quite different. The Left wanted a moderate (Girondin) republic; the Right wanted monarchy and aristocracy, with rule by the provinces and conversion of the *conseils généraux* into estates generals. The common cry was to free the provinces from the domination of Paris and to liberate local initiative from prefectoral control. Certainly decentralization was a very live topic during the latter half of the Second Empire; books and pamphlets flowed from the presses. The campaign reached a crescendo in 1865. In September 1865 the congress at Berne of the Société Internationale Pour le Progrès de Sciences Sociales brought together Orleanists and moderate republicans and led to the Nancy movement, which culminated in the publication of a program by several Lorrain notables.

The Nancy movement was too blatantly partisan to have much political importance. It was rejected, for example, by the main body of republicans. On the other hand, the accelerating transformation (from 1866) of the authoritarian regime into the Liberal Empire bore fruit in a number of important decentralization laws. As early as 1863, Napoleon III had reopened the issue of decentralization, which a commission of 1849 had confronted without results. The law of 18 July 1866 greatly extended the powers of the *conseils généraux* in local matters, in fact reduced the prefect to the role of agent, while that of 24 July 1867 did the same service for the *conseils municipaux*. The latter, however, still required the approval of the mayors (in cases of dispute, the prefect would arbitrate, except for Paris and Lyons where Napoleon III performed that role). At the beginning of the Liberal Empire the Corps Législatif undertook a great debate on decentralization in which Lucien Prévost-Paradol distinguished himself, arguing that the movement could become both an instrument of social peace and a school of practical politics. In February 1870 a commission was appointed to consider the matter, chaired by Odilon Barrot (1791–1873) with Edouard Drouyn de Lhuys as vice-president. Also at the beginning of February 1870 at Lyons appeared the journal *La décentralisation* and at Paris a weekly, *Revue de la décentralisation*. A law of 17 July 1870 ended the government's power of nominating the officers of the *conseils généraux*. It seems probable that except for the outbreak of the Franco-Prussian War, the process would have continued and that one of the most difficult problems, the appointment of mayors by Paris, would have been resolved in a decentralist sense, but the opposition of Napoleon III and of Emile Ollivier to the proposal that mayors be named from lists drawn up by the municipal councils meant that the issue remained unresolved at the end of the Second Empire.

G. Calamarte, ed., *Décentralisation et déconcentration en France depuis 1789* (Paris, c. 1965); J. Droz, "Le problème de la décentralisation sous le Second Empire," in

Festgabe für Max Braubach (Münster, 1964); R. Riemenschneider, "Décentralisation et régionalisme au milieu du xixe siècle," *Romantisme*, 12, no. 35 (1982); O. Voilliard, "Author du programme de Nancy, 1865," in *Régions et régionalisme en France: Colloque Strasbourg 1974* (Paris, 1977); V. Wright, "Administration et politique sous le Second Empire," *ASMP* 126 (1973).

Related entries: LIBERALISM; ORLEANISM; PREFECTS; PREVOST-PARADOL.

DEGAS, EDGAR (1834–1917), Impressionist painter and sculptor; born at Paris, 19 July 1834. Having given up the study of law, Degas began to study art with a student of Dominique Ingres beginning in 1853. His studies at the Ecole des Beaux-Arts from 1855 to 1856 were followed by a trip to Italy, where he met Gustave Moreau. After returning to Paris in 1859, he painted works with biblical (*The Daughter of Jephthah*, c. 1861–1864, Smith College Museum of Art, Northampton, Massachusetts) or classical (*The Young Spartans*, 1860, National Gallery, London) themes. During this time, his paintings were based on many works of the Renaissance he had copied and absorbed while in Italy, but he was also familiar with more contemporary works by Eugène Delacroix. He was introduced to Ingres by his (Degas') close friends and patrons of Ingres, the Valpinçons. Ingres' advice to Degas to draw constantly served him admirably throughout his career. The early years were also devoted to several self-portraits, as well as portraits of family members who resided in Italy. *The Bellelli Family* (1860, Louvre, Paris) is a group portrait that includes Degas' uncle, the Baron Gennaro Bellelli, his wife, and their two daughters. Classically ordered and tightly yet unusually composed for a family portrait in a shallow space, treated with a subdued range of colors, the painting shows a sophistication of drawing, knowledge of structure, and also a personal expression based on his psychological insight into the family relationships. The portrait of *Edmondo and Thérèse Morbilli* (1867, Museum of Fine Arts, Boston) continues to show this concern for accurate likeness and psychological penetration, built on a firm linear foundation.

In 1865, Degas made his debut at the Salon with *Misfortunes of the City of Orléans* (1865, Louvre), one of his last paintings with a historical theme. By this time he had discovered another interest that would thereafter occupy him: race horses and jockeys. He was first attracted to the depiction of horses in motion by Géricault's paintings of the 1820s, which he could see in the Luxembourg Museum. He was also stimulated by English racing prints and was familiar with the military scenes painted by Ernest Meissonier. One of his first paintings on this theme, *At the Races* (1862, Fogg Art Museum, Harvard University), is indicative of this new direction. The horses are closely observed for their actual movements, not their heroic or idealized forms. The work is executed with a looseness of brushwork, an openness of form, and a casualness of composition, moving toward the abrupt cropping of his later works, that give it the lively freshness of a sketch. Degas was to carry his exploration of movement even further in the 1870s both with horses and jockeys but especially with ballet dancers, for which he is most renowned.

Degas' fascination with the theater and opera began during this period as well. Attracted by the effects of interior light, as his fellow Impressionists were to be by outdoor light, he frequently attended performances and noted the changes brought about by the light on the performers, the members of the orchestra, and the audience. *Mlle Fiocre in the Ballet "La Source"* (1866–1868, Brooklyn Museum) is based on a performance at the Opéra with Mlle. Eugénie Fiocre in the leading role (Jean Baptiste Carpeaux sculpted a bust of her in 1869). The scene Degas painted is the one in which she dips her feet into a pool of water (actually part of the set, as is a real horse), looking at her reflection in it. As with all of Degas' works, distinguishing him from other Impressionists, this painting was based on carefully drawn preparatory studies and was painted in his studio. Closer still to Degas' more modern approach and future explorations is *The Orchestra of the Paris Opera* (1868–1869, Louvre). In this painting, unconventional in composition, with the ballet dancers chopped off at the top and the musicians cut off along the sides, Degas depicts his friend Désiré Dihau playing a bassoon. He and several of his friends in the orchestra are compressed into a shallow space and are seen from above. On the other hand, the ballet dancers' skirts are seen from below, thus distorting the space, denying traditional rules of perspective and giving the work a greater sense of dynamic movement. The artificial illumination, carefully observed and emphasized with flickering highlights and sharp contrasts, also contributes to the sense of instability and thus to the actuality of a moment about to change.

Degas' *Collector of Prints* (1866, Metropolitan Museum of Art, New York) and *Portrait of James Tissot* (1867, Metropolitan Museum), which can be compared with Edouard Manet's *Portrait of Zola* (1868; Louvre), present another aspect of his conception that proved to be of major importance for Impressionist art in the 1870s. The framed collection of memorabilia on the upper right of the *Collector* contains Japanese silk fabrics, and a framed Japanese print decorates the wall above Tissot's head. Degas' admiration of Japanese woodblock prints was not just another facet of exoticism but resulted in his adapting the stylistic characteristics in his own work. The new mode of spatial composition, based on asymmetry and flat areas of color, in part attributable to an acceptance of Japanese principles of art and an integration of those principles into Western art, finds its beginnings here with Degas and his fellow Impressionists. Japanese prints were a topic of interest and discussion in the Café Guerbois where the Batignolles group of pre-Impressionists, which included Degas from 1861, met.

The major part of Degas' oeuvre was yet to be created during the next five decades. After the Franco-Prussian War (1870–1871), in which both he and Manet served as artillery officers, he experimented with various media, created outstanding pastels, and developed new subject matter in his works devoted to ballet dancers or women seen at their most private moments, washing themselves or combing their hair. He produced remarkable monoprints as well as some exceptional sculptures of horses and dancers, which were done primarily for his own personal satisfaction. He died at Paris, 26 September 1917.

J. Boggs, *Portraits by Degas* (Berkeley, 1962); J. P. Crespelle, *Degas et son monde* (Paris, 1972); I. Dunlop, *Degas* (New York, 1979); C. W. Millard, *The Sculpture of Edgar Degas* (Princeton, N.J., 1976); T. Reff, *Degas: The Artist's Mind* (New York, 1976); J. Rewald, *The History of Impressionism*, 4th ed. (New York, 1973); D. C. Rich, *Degas* (New York, 1966).

Beverley Giblon

Related entries: PISSARRO; RENOIR; SALON DES REFUSES.

DELACROIX, EUGENE (1798–1863), leading painter of the romantic movement; born at Charenton-Saint-Maurice, 26 April 1798. By the time Napoleon III was proclaimed emperor, Delacroix was already long established as the major painter of romanticism. Critics like Charles Baudelaire who admired his work recognized and welcomed the profound expression of feeling in his choice of themes, but especially his means of expression—the bold and free brushwork and the vibrant color. The traditional critics, of a more classicist frame of mind, like Gustave Planche (1808–1857), objected to the sketchy quality as being more appropriate to a preparatory work, not a finished painting worthy of exhibition in the official Salon. Although there was a long-standing controversy between Dominique Ingres and Delacroix on the question of whether painting was based on line or on color, both achieved considerable honors during their long and productive lives. Delacroix was honored with a retrospective exhibition of his works at the Paris international exposition of 1855, as was Ingres. Delacroix also returned in his late period to subjects he had dealt with earlier, often producing new variants on a previously treated theme. Some of his most important works were created during this later period of his life, including some major wall decorations.

The commission for a section of the enormous uncompleted ceiling decoration of the Galerie d'Apollon in the Louvre was received by Delacroix in 1850. The painting, *Apollo Destroying the Pythean Serpent*, was completed in 1851. The flying figures are posed in a baroque manner to emphasize the illusion of infinite depth and to express violent movement. The sensation of turbulence is made more striking by means of the broad areas of intense reds, blues, and purples. The contrast with other ceiling decorations by the seventeenth-century academic painter Charles LeBrun becomes even more apparent in the vigorous execution and the dynamism of the composition. In 1851, Delacroix received a commission to paint the ceiling for the Salon de la Paix in the Hôtel de Ville. The allegory, *The Triumph of Peace*, was completed by the artist in 1854; it was destroyed by fire during the Commune in 1871. The next major commission, for the Chapel of the Holy Angels in the Church of Saint Sulpice, was the culminating masterpiece of Delacroix's career. The two paintings, *Jacob Wrestling with the Angel* and *Heliodorus Driven from the Temple*, were preceded by the development of ideas in sketches and drawings early in the decade. The actual paintings were begun in 1856 and completed in 1861. The violent theme of *Heliodorus* is emphasized by the complexity of swirling movements and an extensive range of figural poses, made more evident and dramatic by contrast with the solid architectural setting. This is augmented by the expressive effects of the yellows, oranges, and blues. *Jacob*, on the opposite wall, is treated in a less violent manner yet displays a similar feeling of heightened passion, with the two struggling figures set against majestic oak trees. The intensity of color, here using reds, greens, and violets, seems to illuminate the chapel itself. Delacroix's thorough understanding of the effects of color, especially that of complementaries, and the resultant brightness of some passages, the quantity of color in the shadows as well as in the light areas, makes his intent to convey a passionate spiritual message explicit.

At the same time that Delacroix was working on these major state commissions, he was also working on smaller-format paintings. Taking up the theme of an earlier work of 1836–1838, with his great powers of invention, imagination, and memory, he transformed it, in *The Fanatics of Tangier* (1857, Art Gallery of Ontario, Toronto), into a new composition by means of simplification of details without diminishing the feverish expression of the frenzied fanatics. The explosiveness of the content is amplified with the spontaneous brushwork, the thick impasto, and the heightened color contrasts of red and green. Other Oriental themes, having their basis in Delacroix's first trip to Morocco in 1832 when he filled several notebooks with drawings and watercolor sketches, are returned to during this period with renewed vigor, as in *Arabian Horses Fighting in a Stable* (1860, Louvre, Paris). Here the wildness and strength of the animals is equaled by the impassioned means. It is typical of Delacroix's romantic spirit in content, in the exotic theme, and the struggle of ferocious animals. It is executed with both broad sweeps and short, agitated jabs of his brush, along with large areas of unmodulated colors. The haze of memory has allowed Delacroix to obscure some of the detail and to combine several incidents where he viewed horses fighting in various places and times, thus creating a more emotionally charged effect.

A literary source of inspiration, Scott's *Ivanhoe*, was explored twice in Delacroix's later period in *The Abduction of Rebecca* (1846, Metropolitan Museum of Art, New York; 1858, Louvre). Delacroix often looked to Shakespeare, Goethe, Scott, and Byron for stimulus and subject matter. In this instance, it is a scene in which Rebecca is taken from Front-de-Boeuf's burning castle by the Templar Bois-Guilbert. We see in these two versions how Delacroix is stimulated by the narrative but does not follow it precisely. He contributes with his own imaginative invention, and with the second version it is the knight himself who struggles with her. Delacroix effectively renders the excitement of the moment in a composition based on diagonals, with his characteristic free brushwork and abundance of color. The sketchiness and impulsiveness of the brushwork and the brilliance of the colors excite the viewer's senses and provoke a feeling of active participation.

Delacroix had a cultivated intellect, a deep understanding and knowledge of music, and wrote essays and a remarkable *Journal*, which be began in 1822, contributing to it with only a few interruptions until his death in 1863. Much of the *Journal* was, in fact, compiled during the Second Empire. In it he recorded some of the most profound thinking on the theories of art, illuminating his own work as well as providing insights into the artistic world around him. In 1857 he planned to write a dictionary of the fine arts, which he did not complete. Delacroix was a superb painter whose skills with brush and color proved enormously influential for Théodore Chassériau, Henri Fantin-Latour, Gustave Moreau, Pierre Auguste Renoir, and Vincent Van Gogh. The controversy surrounding him in his youth never completely disappeared. Although awarded many major commissions by the government during the Second Empire, he was not elected to the Académie des Beaux-Arts until 1857. After *The Abduction of Rebecca* and others of his paintings shown in the Salon of 1859 met with considerable criticism (such as from Maxime Du Camp, 1822–1894), Delacroix withdrew from any further exhibits. In his final years, he devoted himself to his work, husbanding his declining strength, discouraging approaches by all but a few close friends. He died at Paris, 13 August 1863.

R. Hugghe, *Delacroix* (New York, 1963); W. Pach, ed. and trans., *The Journal of Eugène Delacroix* (New York, 1972); F. Anderson Trapp, *The Attainment of Delacroix* (Baltimore, 1971).

Beverley Giblon

Related entries: CHASSERIAU; FANTIN-LATOUR; INGRES.

DELIBES, LEO (1836–1891), composer; known chiefly during the Second Empire as an organist and a composer of operettas; born at Saint-Germain-du-Val, 21 February 1836. Delibes' father was in the postal service; his mother was an able musician, daughter of an opera singer, and sister of the organist Antoine Batiste (1820–1876). An only child, the boy learned music from his mother and uncle and, after the death of his father, moved with the family to Paris in 1847. Although money was in short supply, Delibes was enrolled at the Conservatoire where he studied organ with François Benoist (1794–1878), piano with Félix Le Couppey (1811–1887), harmony with François Bazin (1816–1878), and composition with Adolphe Adam (1803–1856), whose portégé he became.

It was on Adam's recommendation that Delibes at seventeen (in 1853) was appointed organist at Saint Pierre de Chaillot (in 1862, he moved to Saint Jean-Saint François, where he would remain as organist until 1871). Also in 1853 Adam secured Delibes' appointment as accompanist at the Théâtre Lyrique, and it was in the musical theater that the young composer would find his true vocation. Having a good voice, he had been a chorister at La Madeleine as a boy and had sung in the chorus at the Opéra premiere of Giacomo Meyerbeer's *Le prophète* in 1849. He became chorus master at the Théâtre Lyrique, where he worked on the production of Charles Gounod's *Faust* (the arrangement of the vocal score was his), *Les pêcheurs de perles* of Georges Bizet (1838–1875), and *Les Troyens à Carthage* of Hector Berlioz (1803–1869). In 1864 Delibes became accompanist at the Opéra and (1864–1872) second chorus master under Victor Massé (1822–1884).

On 9 February 1856 Florimond Hervé (1825–1892) produced at his Folies Nouvelles the first of sixteen operettas that Delibes was to compose (two in collaboration) during the Second Empire, *Deux sous de charbon*. There followed *Deux vieilles gardes* (Bouffes Parisiens, 8 August 1856; enormously successful for its wit, melody, and lightness of touch), *Six demoiselles à marier* (Bouffes Parisiens, 1856), *Maître Griffard* (Théâtre Lyrique, 3 October 1857), *La fille du golfe* (1859), *L'omelette à la Follembuche* (Bouffes Parisiens, 8 June 1859), *M. de Bonne-Etoile* (Bouffes Parisiens, 4 February 1860), *Les musiciens de l'orchestre* (Bouffes Parisiens, 25 January 1861), *Les eaux d'Ems* (1861), *Le jardinier et son seigneur* (Théâtre Lyrique, 1 May 1863), *La tradition* (Bouffes Parisiens, 5 January 1864), *Le serpent à plumes* (Bouffes Parisiens, 16 December 1864), *Grande nouvelle* (1864), *Le boeuf Apis* (Bouffes Parisiens, 25 April 1865), *L'Ecossais de Chatou* (Bouffes Parisiens, 16 January 1869), and *La cour du Roi Pétaud* (Variétés, 24 April 1869; Delibes' last operetta).

Delibes' operettas were produced mostly at the Bouffes Parisiens, the theater of his close friend Jacques Offenbach. Delibes admired Meyerbeer, Bizet (although they were never close friends), and Richard Wagner. During the Second Empire he also wrote a number of now-neglected choral works, including a cantata, *Alger*, written at the request of the Opéra's director, Emile Perrin (1814–1885), and performed at the Opéra 15 August 1865 on the occasion of the *fête de l'empereur*. On 12 November 1866 the Opéra performed another work commissioned by Perrin, the ballet *La source*, composed by Delibes and the Russian composer Louis Mincus (1827–c. 1897), and choreographed by Arthur Saint-Léon (c. 1815–1870) (the book was by Charles Nuitter [1828–1899]). The great success of Delibes' part encouraged him to compose the work for which he is today best remembered, the ballet *Coppélia ou la fille aux yeux d'émail*, first performed at the Opéra on 25 May 1870.

In 1871 Delibes gave up his duties at the Opéra and as an organist, married, and devoted himself to composition. Ahead lay two major works, the ballet *Sylvia* (1876) and the opera *Lakmé* (Opéra Comique, 14 April 1883). Delibes died at Paris, 16 January 1891.

M. V. Boston, "An Essay on the Life and Works of Leo Delibes" (Ph.D. diss., University of Iowa, 1981); A. Coquis, *Léo Delibes: Sa vie et son oeuvre* (Paris, 1957); H. de Curzon, *Léo Delibes* (Paris, 1926).

Related entries: CAVAILLE-COLL; CARVALHO; GOUNOD; OFFENBACH.

DEMOCRATIC CAESARISM. See UNIVERSAL MANHOOD SUFFRAGE.

DEPARTMENT STORE. SEE *GRANDS MAGASINS*.

DEPRESSIONS. See ECONOMIC CRISES.

DEREGULATION. See BAKERIES.

DIAZ DE LA PENA, NARCISSE (1807–1876), Barbizon landscape painter; born at Bordeaux, 20 August 1807, the son of Spanish refugees. Diaz's childhood was marred by the early death of his parents and the loss of a leg following a snake bite. His first career as a printer was followed by that of porcelain painter. His early works, shown in the Salon beginning in 1831, were primarily of figures of bathers, nymphs, Oriental women, themes from his imagination recalling the fetes of Watteau, and reflecting the influence of Correggio, Titian, Prud'hon, and Eugène Delacroix.

Diaz met Théodore Rousseau, was introduced to the Barbizon area and to painting from nature at the end of the 1830s, and learned a great deal from the association. During the 1840s he concentrated on landscape painting, the figures growing smaller in scale and providing animation to the scene through touches of color. *Autumn—The Woodland Pond* (1867, Metropolitan Museum of Art, New York) and *Forest Scene* (1867, City Art Museum, St. Louis), a sunlit clearing in the forest, illustrate the liveliness of his brush, the accents of color, and the luminosity characteristic of his painting in the 1850s and especially in the 1860s. Diaz was considered to be the colorist of the Barbizon group and was admired for his handling of the textures of nature by means of a thick impasto yet without the heaviness and solidity of form typical of Rousseau. The surfaces were enlivened in Diaz' paintings with flecks of gold or white paint, which served both to soften the effect and to create a feeling of vibrancy. After meeting Diaz, Pierre Auguste Renoir claimed to have lightened his palette considerably, and Adolphe Monticelli's association with Diaz brought about a decided increase in the variety and quantity of color he employed and a more spontaneous and loose brushwork. Diaz was made an officer of the Legion of Honor in 1851, much to the disappointment of Rousseau, who felt he had been overlooked. Diaz, for his part, took advantage of every opportunity to promote the work of Rousseau and the other Barbizon masters. Diaz' work was admired by the future Impressionists. He died at Menton, 18 November 1876. His son Eugène (1837–1901) had already won recognition as a composer of operas.

J. Bouret, *The Barbizon School* (Greenwich, Conn., 1973); R. L. Herbert, *Barbizon Revisited* (San Francisco, 1962); C. Bourgeois, "Le peintre Narcisse Diaz," *IHA* 13 (1968).

Beverley Giblon

Related entries: COROT; DAUBIGNY; MILLET; ROUSSEAU.

DINING. See DUGLERE.

DISARMAMENT. See DARU.

DORE, GUSTAVE (1832–1883), illustrator, engraver, painter, and sculptor; born at Strasbourg, in the shadow of the cathedral, 6 January 1832. Doré's father was a civil engineer; his grandfather had been an officer of the First Empire, dead at Waterloo. The family moved to Bourg-en-Bresse in 1842, and there Doré attended school, revealing a precocious talent for drawing (he published his first lithographs in 1843). He visited Paris with his father in 1847 and contrived to stay on. When the elder Doré died two years later, Doré settled at Paris with his mother in a large house she had inherited in the rue Saint Dominique. He would never marry.

Doré's earliest patron at Paris was Charles Philipon (1806–1862). A three-year contract at Philipon's newly launched *Journal pour rire* (renamed in 1857 the *Journal amusant*) enabled the sixteen-year-old to complete his education at the Lycée Charlemagne. At the *Journal* he worked and collaborated with Charles Bertall (1820–1881) and Félix Nadar, who became his friend. By 1848 he had painted his first picture, compiled his first albums, and sent his first drawings to the Salon. Since there was little money, Doré worked hard, at the *Journal*, as a collaborator with other journals (*L'illustration, Journal pour tous, Tour du monde, Monde illustré*), and, from 1852, with Paul Lacroix (1806–1884), also known as the Bibliophile Jacob. Blessed with great manual dexterity and a photographic memory and stimulated by his habit of heavy smoking, Doré worked incessantly sixteen to eighteen hours at a time, and with great productivity (by 1864 he had completed fifty thousand designs). He divided his time between illustration, which earned him his living, and to which he devoted his mornings in the splendid rue Saint Dominique studio, and painting (in a second studio). It was his activities as an illustrator, however, that won him celebrity, fortune, and enduring fame.

In 1854 J. Bry Aîné published an edition of Rabelais' works illustrated with 104 Doré wood blocks. That same year appeared Doré's *Histoire dramatique, pittoresque, et caricaturale de la Sainte Russie* (500 illustrations). But it was the illustrations for Balzac's *Les contes drolatiques* (Dutacq, 425 illustrations) that made Doré's reputation, opening the way to world fame and great wealth. From 1855 to 1860 he illustrated only one book (Pierre Dupont's *La légende du Juif errant*; Librairie du Magasin Pittoresque; 12 illustrations) while producing a number of lithographs on such topics as the Crimean and Italian wars. But in 1862 Doré announced his intention to illustrate all the literary masterpieces, and, in fact, since 1861 the production of his atelier had been "industrialized." Doré, who had begun as a lithographer, drawing directly on the stone, now provided the sketches and turned them over to engravers like his lifelong friend Héliodore Joseph Pisan (b. 1822), to execute on wood blocks under his supervision. The blocks could then be duplicated indefinitely through the new electrolytic process. By the end of his life, Doré would have thus illustrated some two hundred books. Most notable during the Second Empire were Dante's *Inferno* (Hachette, 1861; 76 illustrations; perhaps the artist's finest achievement), Perrault's *Contes* (Hetzel, 1861; 40 illustrations), Chateaubriand's *Atala* (Hachette, 1862), Cervantes' *Don Quichotte* (Hachette, 1863; 370 illustrations), *La Sainte Bible* (Alfred Mame [Tours], 1865; 241 illustrations; earlier [1859–1863] Doré had helped illustrate

Cassell's *Illustrated Family Bible*), Milton's *Paradise Lost* (Cassell, 1866), La Fontaine's *Fables* (Hachette, 1868), Dante's *Il Purgatorio* (Hachette, 1868; 60 illustrations); and Tennyson's *Les idylles du roi* (Hachette, four volumes, 1867–1869; each with 9 illustrations). In 1876 Doré would illustrate Coleridge's *The Rime of the Ancient Mariner* and in 1883 Poe's *The Raven*. He died before being able to undertake his great ambition of illustrating Shakespeare.

By the 1860s, Doré was the world's foremost illustrator. His success derived from his energy and also from his imagination (to which he often gave free rein without much concern for the text), verve, and dramatic sense. It was as a painter, however, that he yearned to be recognized. From 1851 he sent his often huge and elaborate canvases to the Salon, but his French contemporaries persisted in seeing them as drawings translated into color without the benefit of a classical training, for Doré, as an artist, was essentially self-taught. Only in England, where he made a long visit in 1868, were his paintings popular. A huge Doré Gallery, built by a group of bankers at 35 New Bond Street, would remain in business until 1914 (it is currently the salesroom of Sotheby). Doré's last major work of illustration was for Blanchard Jerrold's *London: A Pilgrimage* (1872; 180 illustrations). Here he displayed a realism that contrasted with his habitual and rather brooding romantic bent (as in the sinister "Rue de la Vieille Lanterne").

Although Doré traveled widely in Switzerland, Spain, the Black Forest, and Britain, he preferred to use photographs and the treasures of the Louvre as sources for his illustrations. And despite his travels, long hours of work, and interest in sports, he still found time for bohemian activities and a wide circle of friends. He loved the theater and could be found in the notorious company of Cora Pearl (Emma Crouch) and Alice Ozy (who had been Théodore Chassériau's model). In 1868 Doré designed the costumes for the first spectacularly successful operetta of his friend Jacques Offenbach, *Orphée aux enfers*. His Sunday evenings in the impressive rue Saint Dominique house brought together such friends and intimates as Offenbach, Felix Nadar, Théophile Gautier (who early recognized Doré's genius, and who traveled with him in Spain), the publisher Jules Hetzel (1814–1886), Edmond About, the art critic Balloz, Gioacchino Rossini (1792–1868), Adeline Patti (1843–1919), and Christine Nilsson (1843–1921), as well as Marietta Alboni (1826–1894), Alexandre Dumas (father and son), Franz Liszt (1811–1886), Pauline Viardot, and Charles Gounod. Doré earned a fortune (the *Sainte Bible*, at 200 francs a copy, sold out its first run in less than a year) and spent it lavishly.

Although republicans were among Doré's friends, he was himself uninterested in politics. He found the society of the Second Empire agreeable, and it in turn welcomed his gay, sociable, childlike surface nature. On 15 August 1861 he was named knight of the Legion of Honor. By 1864 he had sufficiently overcome his legitimist sympathies to be a guest of the emperor at Compiègne where he created a series of *tableaux vivants* based on the biblical scenes he was then preparing for Mame's edition of the Bible. Doré's cooperation with the regime extended to assisting in the preparation of imperial balls. In 1869 he was invited to accompany the empress' party on her trip to the Suez Canal.

In 1870 Doré turned to sculpture and to etching. Thus he called all the resources of art to the service of his imagination. But for him as for the Empire, the happy days were past. Although still outwardly cheerful and childlike, he yielded more and more to melancholia as his artistic pretentions continued to be rejected in France. In 1878 he developed heart disease. Doré died suddenly at Paris, 23 January 1883. Perhaps he would have taken some consolation from the judgment that in his influence on such artists as Vincent Van Gogh (1853–1890), Odilon Redon (1840–1916), and the surrealists he appears neither romantic nor realist so much as modernist before his time.

J. Adhémar, ed., *Catalogue de l'exposition Gustave Doré, organisée à la Bibliothèque Nationale, Paris, 18 juillet-ler septembre 1974* (Paris, 1974); P. Dessau, "Gustave Doré," *CAM*, no. 21 (1979); L. Dézé and J. Valmy-Baysse, *Gustave Doré: Bibliographie et catalogue complet de l'oeuvre* (Paris, 1930); K. Farner, *Gustave Doré, der industrialisierte Romantiker* (Munich, 1975); N. Gosling, *Gustave Doré* (Newton Abbot, [1973]); J. Richardson, *Gustave Doré* (London, 1980).

DROUYN DE LHUYS, EDOUARD (1805–1881), diplomat and statesman; twice minister of foreign affairs during the Second Empire (28 July 1852–8 May 1855 and 15 October 1862–1 September 1866); born at Paris, 19 November 1805, into an ancient Soissonais family, nobility of the robe since 1611. Drouyn de Lhuys' inheritances combined with those of his wife made him reputedly one of the wealthiest men in France. Educated at the Collège de Louis-le-Grand (1818–1823) and the Paris law faculty, he entered the foreign service in 1831, serving as unpaid secretary at Madrid (1831–1833) and Brussels (1833–1835), paid chargé at Madrid (1835–1840), and director of commercial affairs at the Ministry of Foreign Affairs (1840–1844). Elected as a government supporter to the Chamber of Deputies in 1842, he opposed the policies of François Guizot (1787–1874). Dismissed from the Foreign Ministry, Drouyn de Lhuys allied with Odilon Barrot (1791–1873), becoming a reformist active in the "banquet campaign." During the 1848 Revolution, he served as a National Guardsman and won reelection to the Constituent Assembly (April 1848) where he chaired the Committee on Foreign Affairs. President Louis Napoleon appointed him minister for foreign affairs (December 1848–June 1849) in the Barrot cabinet. He conducted the diplomacy of recognition of the Second Republic and dealt with questions related to the Austro-Sardinian war and the occupation of Rome by French forces. As ambassador to Great Britain (July–December 1849 and February 1850–January 1851), he negotiated the Don Pacifico affair. He was briefly foreign minister (9–24 January 1851) during the Changarnier affair.

After the December 1851 coup d'état, Drouyn de Lhuys was a member of the Consultative Commission (precursor of the imperial Conseil d'Etat), and accepted appointment 28 January 1852 as vice-president of the Senate, a post he held until January 1856. On 28 July 1852 he became foreign minister for the third time, handling negotiations for recognition of the Second Empire and issues surrounding the Crimean War. Miffed over Czar Nicholas' refusal to address Napoleon III as "brother," he developed an antagonism against Russia that reinforced his preference for strong ties with Austria. He negotiated the neutral rights question with England, formulated the Four Points and Black Sea neutralization policies, and negotiated the Tripartite Treaty of 2 December 1854 (Britain, France, and Austria). As chief French delegate at the Conference of Vienna (1855), he accepted a compromise concerning postwar status of the Black Sea in order to ensure Austrian entry into the war and to cement Austrian ties with the allies. When Napoleon III rejected the compromise, Drouyn de Lhuys wrathfully resigned (8 May 1855). Nevertheless the Treaty of Paris (1856) was based on the Four Points, neutralization of the Black Sea, and closer ties with Austria.

Drouyn de Lhuys opposed Napoleon III's intervention in Italy (1858–1859) as destructive of Franco-Austrian ties. He therefore refused appointment as foreign minister in 1859. Edouard Thouvenel succeeded comte Alexandre Walewski, but when Thouvenel's Italian policy became a political burden, the emperor turned once again to Drouyn de Lhuys (15 October 1862) who tried to use political leverage to force dismissal of other pro-Italian diplomats. He had to accept a compromise that authorized him to replace diplomatic representatives in Constantinople, Rome, Turin, and London. During this last ministry, Drouyn de Lhuys dealt with the Polish crisis of 1863 and the Danish War and negotiated the 1864 September Convention. During the U.S. Civil War, he handled the mediation proposals and recognition questions. He opposed the Mexican expedition but cleverly combined it with Civil War issues to create with U.S. Secretary of State William H. Seward a mutual neutrality in the two conflicts. German events led to Drouyn de Lhuys' final departure from the foreign ministry. He warned that the Gastein agreement (1865) between Prussia and Austria over Schleswig-Holstein was a Prussian victory detrimental to French security. He resented Napoleon III's personal diplomacy with Bismarck at Biarritz (1865) and vainly sought to learn its substance from Bismarck. After the Prussian victory at Sadowa, Drouyn de Lhuys, backed by Marshal C. A. Randon and Empress Eugénie, advocated mobilization on the Rhine and forceful mediation. Marquis de La Valette and Prince Napoleon opposed him. When the emperor finally decided on peaceful mediation, Drouyn de Lhuys initiated demands for territorial compensation from Prussia, but realizing the futility of this policy he resigned effective 1 September 1866.

As a senator (he was reappointed 5 May 1865) and member of the Conseil Privé (1866–1870), Drouyn de Lhuys continued to advise on foreign policy matters, opposing the attempt to acquire Luxembourg (1867) and even rejecting the usefulness of an Austrian alliance (1867–1869) in view of Prussian dominance in Germany. Instead he advocated military preparedness (1867–1870) for a Prussian war he considered to be inevitable. Drouyn de Lhuys' diplomacy was based on his conviction that France derived its security from being the largest European state composed of a single nation. He sought to preserve that status by concentrating French power in Europe; thus he opposed the Asian and Mexican expeditions. He saw Austria (Austria-Hungary after 1867) as a bulwark against German national unity and pan-slavism, and Italian unity as a step toward Austro-Hungarian disintegration. Nonetheless he accepted change, demanding only creation of protective "conglomerations," which he perceived to have been Napoleon I's policy. This inevitably clashed with Napoleon III's policy of nationalities and contributed to the indecisive French response to Sadowa. Although Drouyn de Lhuys' support in foreign affairs came chiefly from bonapartist conservatives (Eugénie, whose marriage to the emperor he had opposed, Walewski, Randon, Pierre Magne) and the opposition to him from the liberals (Prince Napoleon, Eugène Rouher, La Valette), he is difficult to classify. He supported domestic social and political reform to prevent, as he put it in 1835, "the war between *les prolétaires et les propriétaires.*" He saw the Second Empire as the "best of all possible Governments for France," and yet he considered his life's services to have been not "to parties, but to France."

Drouyn de Lhuys' private services to France centered on agriculture, although he also was president of the boards of the Société d'Acclimatation and (1855–1862) the Compagnie des Chemins de Fer de l'Est. By combining the resources of the Société des Agriculteurs de France, which he founded in 1867 and presided over until the end of the Empire, and the agricultural penal colony for young offenders at Mettray, whose board he presided from 1861, he established the first French experimental center to adapt steam-driven machinery to agriculture. He used the international membership of the Société des Agriculteurs to provide seed and machinery to farmers in areas devastated by the Franco-Prussian War, thus avoiding hardship and famine. He most cherished the Colonie de Mettray, endowing it generously and retaining the presidency until his death.

Drouyn de Lhuys was showered with honors during his lifetime. He was recipient of the grand cross of the Legion of Honor and was elected 16 November 1861 to the Académie des Sciences Morales et Politiques. He was decorated by the sovereigns of Portugal, Spain, Sardinia, Turkey, and Austria. He died at Paris, 1 March 1881, and was buried, as he had requested, in the cemetery of the Colonie de Mettray.

B. d'Harcourt, *Les quatre ministères de M. Drouyn de Lhuys* (Paris, 1882); P. L. E. Pradier-Fodéré, *M. Drouyn de Lhuys* (Paris, 1881), and *Documents pour l'histoire contemporaine* (Paris, 1871); W. F. Spencer, "Edouard Drouyn de Lhuys and the Foreign Policy of the Second Empire" (Ph.D diss., University of Pennsylvania, 1955), and "The Making of a Notable Revolutionary: Edouard Drouyn de Lhuys, 1844–1848," *PWSFH* (1983).

Warren F. Spencer

Related entries: CRIMEAN WAR; DANISH WAR; MEDIATION PROPOSALS; MEXICAN EXPEDITION; POLISH QUESTION; RECOGNITION QUESTION; ROMAN QUESTION; SADOWA; SEPTEMBER CONVENTION; THOUVENEL.

DUGLERE, ADOLPHE (1804–1884), perhaps the most distinguished chef of the Second Empire. During that era a number of new ingredients were added to the already celebrated Paris culinary scene. In 1853 a low-price self-service restaurant opened at the Barrière Rochechouart (Le Petit Ramponneau); on 9 July 1865 the first butcher shop for the sale of horse flesh was inaugurated; brasseries began to compete with the cafés; catering by famous restaurants to private homes came into vogue, as did dining en masse at popular restaurants (the main dining room of the Grand Hôtel could seat six hundred); Baron Léon Brisse (1813–1876) published in *La liberté* and *Le petit journal* what was perhaps the first cooking column to appear in a daily newspaper; and, after much resistance, cooking on gas stoves was accepted, even by the most discriminating. For the general public, new standards of economical dining were set by a Paris butcher, Louis Duval (1811–1870), who in the 1850s began his chain of Bouillons Duval (the first was on the rue de la Monnaie; by 1870 there would be a dozen). In Duval's establishments, diners at clean, marble tables, attended by neat and efficient waitresses, could choose from a printed, fixed-price menu. A complete meal—with wine—cost less than 2 francs, or one-third the price of a typical meal at the Grand Hôtel.

For more affluent diners, fashionable restaurants were numerous. During the Second Empire, they became even more opulent and expensive as the center of fine eating shifted from the area around the Palais Royal to the boulevards. Among the best known of these restaurants were Bignon's at nos. 2,4, boulevard des Italiens (Gioacchimo Rossini [1792–1868] lived upstairs, and regular patrons included Thackeray and Jacques Offenbach); Aux Trois Frères Provençaux at no. 88, Galerie Beaujolais, in the Palais Royal (became Goyard's in 1867; there the banker Raphaël Bischoffsheim [1823–1906] gave banquets); Véfour's at nos. 106–112, Galerie de Valois, in the Palais Royal (gambling salons overhead; owned by Guibert in 1867); Durand's at the Madeleine (there chef Joseph Voiron devised sauce Mornay); Ledoyen's on the Champs Elysées (frequented by the journalist Hippolyte de Villemessant); the Grand Hôtel at no. 12, boulevard des Capucines; Foyot's at no. 33, rue de Touron (purchased in 1848 by one of Louis Philippe's cooks, Diguet, and in 1864 by Lesserteur; had a heavily political clientele); Voisin's at the angle of the rues Cambon and Saint Honoré; Maire's at the corner of the boulevard de Strasbourg and the boulevard Saint Denis (there lobster thermidor was invented); and two English restaurants established in 1860—Peter's at no. 24, passage des Princes, off the boulevard des Italiens (where the owner, Pierre Fraisse, may have named "lobster à l'américaine") and Hill's on the boulevard des Capucines.

Five Second Empire restaurants deserve special attention. Magny's at no. 3, rue Contrescarpe Dauphine (now no. 9, rue Mazet) was, from November 1862 until the end of 1869, the site of the famous *dîners Magny*, attended by Charles Augustin Sainte-Beuve, among others. When those literary diners left Magny's, they found a new home at Brébant's, no. 32, boulevard Poissonière, which was also the locale for the *dîners des spartiates*, grouping such figures as Jules and

Edmond Goncourt, Paul, comte de Saint-Victor (1827–1881), Charles Dalloz (1829–1887), Francis Magnard (1837–1894), Jules Claretie, Agénor Bardoux (1829–1897), and Prince Georges Galitzin (1825–1872). At Brébant's were held as well the *dîners des Rigobert*, where painters like Edouard Detaille (1848–1912) and Alphonse de Neuville (1836–1885) paid for their dinners with drawings and sketches, and the *dîners Bixio*, grouping financiers, industrialists, and writers like Prosper Mérimée, Charles Augustin Sainte-Beuve, Jules Claretie, Victorien Sardou, Alexandre Dumas fils, and Ernest Legouvé (1807–1903). At Verdier Frères (better known as the Maison Dorée or the Maison d'Or), no. 20, boulevard des Italiens, near the rue Taitbout, Ernest Verdier and his chef, Casimir, offered both public and private rooms (some sixteen, of various sizes). Nestor Roqueplan (1804–1870) dined there every night, for Verdier's *soupers* were famous. The Café Riche, founded in 1785, was enlarged and given new kitchens in 1865, becoming a virtual palace. Located at no. 16, boulevard des Italiens, and run from 1865 by the elder Bignon brother, its restaurant (there was also a café from which, as was the custom of the day, respectable women were excluded) attained its greatest fame in the last years of the Second Empire. There gathered writers, musicians, lawyers, journalists, and painters, including Edouard Manet, Jacques Offenbach, Edmond About, the Goncourt brothers, and Charles Baudelaire. It was in a private room of the Café Riche that Maxime and Renée in Emile Zola's *La curée* initiated their incestuous relationship. But *le temple de la gastronomie* during the Second Empire was undoubtedly the Café Anglais at no. 13, boulevard des Italiens, near the Opéra Comique and directly across from the Café Riche. After the closing in 1856 of the Café de Paris, the Café Anglais became the ultra-chic Paris restaurant, noted for its great wine cellar, its labyrinth of twenty-two private rooms (including "The Marivaux" or "Le Cabinet des Femmes du Monde," and, in particular, "Le Grand Seize"), and a chef whom Rossini termed the "Mozart of French cooking," Adolphe Dugléré.

For a long time, Dugléré had directed the kitchens of the Rothschild family. Leaving that employment in 1848 and failing in his efforts to establish his own restaurant, he spent a short time at Aux Trois Frères Provençaux before coming to the Café Anglais in 1866. There he would remain until his death, except for a short period (about 1880) at the Café de la Paix. Restaurants could prove very profitable during the Second Empire, and the owner of the Café Anglais, who himself lived the life of a country gentleman, paid his celebrated chef 25,000 francs per year. Inventor of sole dugléré and potage germiny, Dugléré also collaborated with Alexandre Dumas père, a noted gourmet, in writing *Livre de cuisine*. The undoubted apex of his career was the dinner he prepared on 7 June 1867 in Le Grand Seize for Alexander II of Russia, his son (the future Alexander III), King William I of Prussia, and Otto von Bismarck (hence the "Dinner of the Three Emperors"). Its memorabilia can still be seen at the Tour d'Argent Restaurant and well illustrate the *service à la française* of the day, when first a great variety of moderate portions of *potages, relevés,* and *entrées,* and then of *rôtis* and *entremets*, and finally of desserts were served with elaborate ostentation ensuring that the food (if in a large group, one were lucky enough to get anything other than hors d'oeuvres) would be eaten cold. As an ardent collector of art, Dugléré befriended and gave financial assistance to Jean François Millet, Narcisse Diaz de la Peña, and Thomas Couture. He left to his wife and daughter a small but valuable collection of paintings. When he died at Paris, 5 April 1884, Adolphe Dugléré was hailed as "une des gloires de la gastronomie française."

H. d'Alméras, *La vie parisienne sous le Second Empire* (Paris, 1933); J. P. Aron, *Le mangeur du 19e siècle* (Paris, 1973); "Eating and Drinking," in T. Zelden, *France, 1848–1945: Taste and Corruption* (New York, 1980); F. Fosca, *Histoire des cafés de Paris* (Paris, 1934); R. Mandrou, *Introduction à la France moderne, 1500–1940* (Paris, 1961); J. Richardson, *La vie parisienne* (London, 1971); L. Sonolet, *La vie parisienne sous le Second Empire* (Paris, 1929); *Le vocabulaire des moeurs de la "Vie parisienne" sous le Second Empire* (Louvain, 1976).

DUMAS, ALEXANDRE, FILS (1824–1895), major dramatist and popular novelist; born at Paris, 27 July 1824, the illegitimate son of Alexandre Dumas père (1802–1870) and a serving girl. By the beginning of the Second Empire, Dumas had made his debut as a poet and author of prose fiction. A collection of his poetry, *Péchés de jeunesse,* an unsuccessful venture published privately at the expense of his father, appeared in 1847. There followed a series of novels that focused on contemporary society, in particular on the *demi-monde: Diane de Lys* (3 vols., 1851), *Le Régent Mustel* (2 vols., 1852), *Contes et nouvelles* (1853), *Un cas de rupture* (1854), *La dame aux perles* (4 vols., 1853), and *Sophie Printemps* (1857). Written principally to ensure an income and to pay off debts, they were a source of embarrassment to him in subsequent years, and he later withdrew many from publication. During the same period, Dumas published in serial form in the *Gazette de France* a set of historical novels under the general title *Les quatre restaurations.*

The sensational success of *La dame aux camélias,* based on his 1848 novel of the same name and presented at the Théâtre du Vaudeville in February 1852, launched Dumas' career as a dramatist. Initially rejected by the censorship board then under the direction of Léon Faucher (1804–1854), the play was finally licensed when Auguste de Morny, a personal friend of the author, intervened (Morny was Napoleon III's half-brother). Due to the absence of set principles regarding censorship, Morny was able to argue that no influential segment of society was offended by revealing, as the play did, that young men frequented the houses of courtesans. The subsequent popularity of the play is attested to by the fact that it provided the plot for Giuseppi Verdi's opera *La Traviata* (Teatro La Fenice-Venice, 1853). Moreover, *La dame aux camélias* initiated a lively debate concerning the shady world of not-quite-respectable women and their male attendants. The Second Empire was a golden age for the courtesan in perhaps every area except respectability. Dumas was blamed for regarding this world too indulgently. A rival playwright, Théodore Barrière (1823–1877), indignantly presented the counterview in his popular play, *Les filles de marbre,* but after 116 performances, it was succeeded by a rerun of *La dame aux camélias*. Perhaps it was Barrière's play that persuaded Dumas to write *Le demi-monde*, first performed in 1855. Thus was coined what became the accepted word for the twilight world that lived in the shadow of respectability. The next year *La bourse*, a play by François Ponsard (1814–1867), won the congratulations of Napoleon III for its attack on the speculation mania of the day. In 1857 Dumas produced *La question d'argent*, which launched the aphorism "Les affaires, c'est l'argent des autres." Other successful Dumas plays at the Gymnase included *Diane de Lys*, 1853 (Napoleon III intervened with the censor to ensure its production), *Le fils naturel*, 1858, and *Un père prodigue*, 1859.

In the mid-1860s Dumas began to develop his ideas on social ethics more vigorously. Proposing a *théâtre utile* in opposition to the Parnassian credo of art for art's sake, he put forth his views on such questions as prostitution, abortion, infanticide, the birthrate, illegitimacy, adultery, love, marriage, and divorce. Conservative, he nevertheless preached social reform, greater freedom from conventions, and, especially, a higher status for women. Although his plays *L'ami des femmes* (1864) and *Les idées de Mme. Aubray* (Gymnase, 1867) and his novel *L'affaire Clémenceau, mémoire de l'accusé* (1866) reflect these opinions, he also had recourse to other forms, such as prefaces to his plays, pamphlets, and brochures, especially after 1870.

Dumas was perhaps the most successful and famous playwright of the Second Empire. Rated higher than his father by contemporaries, he was a friend of Princess Mathilde, a frequenter of her salon, and moved in high social circles (as early as 1846, he had met Eugénie de Montijo, the future empress, and had fallen in love with her). He would be elected to the Académie Française in 1874. He amassed a sizable fortune, becoming a noted collector of paintings and objets d'art. But Dumas was also a close friend of the nonconformist Félix Nadar and, with his father, a member of Nadar's Société des Aéronautes. Dumas fils died at Marly-le-Roi, 27 November 1895.

N. C. Arvin, *Alexandre Dumas fils* (Paris, 1939); F. A. Taylor, *The Theatre of Dumas fils* (Oxford, 1937).

Dolorès A. Signori

Related entry: THEATER.

DUMAS, JEAN BAPTISTE (1800–1884), chemist, scientific administrator, senator, and educational reformer; born 14 July 1800 at Alais (now Alès). One of the most influential French chemists and teachers of the nineteenth century, Dumas' scientific contributions—largely completed before the establishment of the Second Empire—include systems for the classification of organic compounds and of the elements, a new method for measuring the vapor densities and (indirectly) the relative molecular weights of different substances in the gaseous state, precise determination of the atomic weights of many elements (including that of carbon, in 1840—a crucial step in the development of organic chemistry), and the theory of substitutions (which successfully explained the mechanism of substitution reactions in organic chemistry). Dumas also did important research in applied chemistry, including studies on dyes, the treatment of iron ores, the properties of commercial glasses, and pharmaceutics. He was elected to the Académie des Sciences in 1832 and during the following decade was appointed to professorial posts at the Faculty of Science (Paris), the Ecole de Médecine (Paris), the Sorbonne, the Collège de France, and the Ecole Polytechnique. He became one of France's more notable and powerful beneficiaries of the system of multiple professorships (the *cumul*). Dumas also cofounded (1829) the Ecole Centrale des Arts et Manufactures.

After 1847, Dumas devoted less attention to chemical theorization and research and turned increasingly to public life, particularly in his advocacy of industrial progress. A moderate conservative, he became directly involved in politics after the Revolution of 1848 and was elected to the Legislative Assembly from Valencienne following the overthrow of Louis Philippe. Dumas served as minister of agriculture and commerce from October 1850 to January 1851 and, after the coup d'état of December 1851, was one of the first men to be named a senator by Napoleon III. Dumas had no strongly defined political affiliation and served different regimes equally well. He refrained from overt political discussion as senator but played a leading role in scientific, commercial, industrial, and—particularly—educational debates. As dean of the Faculty of Science (Paris), Dumas had submitted a report in 1847 to the minister of education proposing major actions to improve scientific education at all levels in France. When Napoleon III's first minister of education, Hippolyte Fortoul, chose Dumas as his chief aide, the 1847 proposals became the basis for the educational reforms of 1852, and Dumas emerged as the most powerful scientific figure within the University, a position he continued to hold under successive ministers during the Empire. Dumas was a major architect of *bifurcation*, which established science as a viable alternative to classics in secondary education. Although Victor Duruy officially abolished *bifurcation* in 1865, the presence of science in the curriculum could no longer revert to its pre-1852 status of relative obscurity, and Dumas' reforming efforts therefore may have been a more direct influence than Saint-Simonianism or positivism in the Second Empire's attempt to use the power of the state to promote scientific and industrial progress. Finally, Dumas—along with his former pupil Louis Pasteur—was mainly responsible for those improvements achieved in public funding for scientific research laboratories during the Second Empire.

As member, vice-president (1855), and president (1859) of the Paris municipal commission, Dumas was a major agent in Baron Georges Haussmann's modernization of the capital (supervising the installation of modern drainage systems, water supply, and electrical systems). He enjoyed many public honors, including promotion to commander of the Legion of Honor (1845), grand officer (1855), and grand cross (1863). Dumas became perpetual secretary of the Académie des Sciences in 1868, following the death of Pierre Flourens (1794–1867), and was awarded the prestigious Faraday medal of the Chemical Society (London) in 1869, the first French scientist to be thus distinguished. He died at Cannes, 11 April 1884.

Martin Fichman

Related entries: BERTHELOT; DURUY; FORTOUL; PARIS, REBUILDING OF; PASTEUR.

DUPANLOUP, FELIX (1802–1878), bishop, educator, orator, polemicist, politician; born 3 January 1802 at Saint-Félix (Haute-Savoie). Dupanloup's mother was a peasant girl; the identity of the father remains unknown. Ordained as a priest on 18 December 1825, he moved in the fashionable circles of Paris, becoming confessor and teacher of high nobles. Because of his exceptional talent as catechist and teacher, he was entrusted with the religious instruction of the Bourbon heir to the throne (the duc de Bordeaux) and of the younger Orleanist princes. He won attention as a successful director of the famous Paris seminary St. Nicolas du Chardonnet in the late 1830s and still wider acclaim for his role in bringing about Talleyrand's deathbed reconciliation with the church in 1838. Named professor of sacred scripture at the Sorbonne in 1841, he was suspended for his attacks on Voltaire, a bête noire for Dupanloup throughout his life. Disciplined for excessive zeal by his clerical superiors, he lost his diocesan offices and was appointed an assistant at Notre-Dame. During the 1840s, Dupanloup increasingly identified with the small, liberal Catholic faction. On 16 April 1849 he was named bishop of Orleans. From this episcopacy, his fervor and talents soon made him, with the possible exception of Cardinal Pie, the best known and most influential of French bishops during the Second Empire.

In the 1850s and 1860s, Dupanloup was preponderant in the realm of Catholic education. Active in the lobby for liberty of education, he was appointed to the commission that prepared the Falloux law of March 1850. He acted as leader of the Catholics on the commission, fashioning many of the law's provisions and consistently arguing that neither church nor state could monopolize schooling. Shortly afterward he defended traditions of Catholic classical humanism against Gaumism; twenty years later, he would again shield classical studies, that time against secular forces led by Jules Simon (1814–1896). These efforts were a factor in his election to the academy in 1854. Dupanloup was one of the few bishops actively to promote diocesan Catholic schools. His three-volume *De l'éducation* (1849), in the tradition of Jesuit humanism, became a bible for French Catholic teachers. He shared with Abbé Joseph Gaume a conviction that society was in mortal danger and that education was at once disease and cure, but his prognosis was more hopeful and his prescription more moderate. Not in curriculum but in tone, atmosphere, and direction did schooling need reform. His major contribution was an emphasis on the distinctions between *éducation* and *instruction*. *Instruction* was but one part of true *éducation*, which encompassed as well religion, discipline, and physical exercise, whose whole was greater than the sum of its parts and whose object was the whole man whereas

instruction attended only the mind. *Education* concerned itself with mental powers, man's spirit, and ends; *instruction* confined itself to knowledge, the mind
and means. *Education* made men, *instruction* savants. Like most other French
intellectuals of his time, including Victor Duruy, Dupanloup believed that students had predestined occupational roles (Duruy alluded to "natural destiny,"
Dupanloup to "Providence") for which there was an appropriate education:
primary for the popular classes, vocational for the intermediate, literary for the
upper. Consequently, Dupanloup never questioned the structure of French schooling, only its moral direction. An elitist who acknowledged individual mobility,
Dupanloup wrote mainly about secondary and higher education. Although he
shared Catholics' emphasis on parental authority as prior to and superior to the
authority of the state, concerns about increasing secularism in society and the
malleability of children (a position between that of Puritans' sinfulness and
Rousseauian purity) led him to recommend a greater emphasis on boarding
schools—a recommendation that presaged and may have influenced a significant
shift from day to boarding among Catholic high schools in the 1860s and 1870s.

During the 1850s, Dupanloup was a liberal and positive force on church-state
relations; 1863 marked a turning point, however, with the question of public
education for women. Thereafter Dupanloup more often was polemical against
the state and the University than he was conciliatory. Despite what unsympathetic
historians have claimed, Dupanloup did not consistently oppose education for
women or regard them as inferior. Earlier, in *Femmes savantes et femmes stu-
dieuses*, he had, against the prevailing opinion of his age, argued for women's
higher education. Duruy's proposal produced Dupanloup's virulent opposition
because he perceived it to be part of a conspiracy to diminish the church's
educational role (an exaggerated but not fallacious assumption) and because he
had determined that the single means left to rechristianize France was through
Catholic education of women, who had been a key force in his battle to rechristianize his diocese. The disappointment and even fear that Dupanloup felt fueled
an innate intemperance that grew worse with age. As in other disputes in his
last fifteen years, his polemics grew worse as he became embroiled in controversy. He insisted that women were more prone to a vanity that *instruction*
without *éducation* would encourage and were incapable of advanced learning—
judgments inconsistent with ideas he had held in his youth. Although he had
consistently worked for liberty of both secondary and higher education of men
(spearheading a crusade for the latter between 1867 and 1875), he demanded a
clerical monopoly of women's schooling.

In his own diocese, Dupanloup established a modern administrative machinery,
encouraged libraries, sodalities, and retreats, built schools and churches, and
demanded good conduct from his priests. His self-stated goal was to rechristianize
a diocese in which only one man in forty was making the Easter Duty. During
his episcopate, the physical and financial state of the diocese improved, as did
priestly conduct; vocations rose along with religious practice, while "superstitious beliefs" declined. Orleans was rare in witnessing its low point of religious

practice in 1849 and an increase in the third quarter of the nineteenth century. Nevertheless, religious practice peaked during the 1860s at only one woman in three and one man in fifteen and was beginning to decline before Dupanloup's death. After his death, the administrative machinery functioned less well too. His success was an ephemeral one, lasting his lifetime. His larger hope for reconciliation of the church with the modern world must be deemed a failure— an inevitable one. Increasing formalism within the church and aggressiveness may have discouraged informal religious practice and increased anti-clericalism in an environment within which the church had not many footholds and no stronghold.

A legitimist and a defender of the existing social order (he opposed the first stirrings of social Catholicism in *L'avenir*, although he consorted with that group in the search for liberty of education), Dupanloup preferred the France of the seventeenth century but nevertheless searched for an accommodation with a secular order he disliked. He has been harshly treated by conservative Catholics and anti-clerical republicans alike, for he searched for ways to reconcile mutually irreconcilable groups. Louis Veuillot's judgment that he failed in everything he did was too harsh; he was a greater success than was Veuillot. But his successes were short-term. In pursuit of his professed goal of reconciling the church of Pius IX with modern society, he was, indeed, as Duruy proclaimed him, "a valiant soldier of a lost cause." As he grew older and realized that his goals were unreachable, he became more obstructionist, recalcitrant, and obstreperous. He died 11 October 1878 at Lacombe (Savoy).

L. Branchereau, *Journal intime de Mgr. Dupanloup* (Paris, 1902); A. M. Carré, "Qui fut Mgr. Dupanloup?" *RDM* (December 1978); F. Dupanloup, *De l'éducation,* 3 vols. (1849) and *De la haute éducation intellectualle*, 3 vols. (1850–1866); F. Lagrange, *Vie de Mgr. Dupanloup, évêque d'Orléans*, 3 vols. (Paris, 1883–1884); C. Marcilhacy, *Le diocèse d'Orléans sous l'épiscopat de Mgr. Dupanloup, 1849–1878* (Paris, 1962).

Patrick J. Harrigan

Related entries: ACADEMIE FRANCAISE; *CORRESPONDANT*; DURUY; FALLOUX LAW; GALLICANISM; GAUME; LITTRE; ORLEANS, BISHOP OF; PIE; PIUS IX; POSITIVISM; ROMAN QUESTION; SOCIAL CATHOLICISM; *SYLLABUS OF ERRORS*; L'UNIVERS; VATICAN COUNCIL; VEUILLOT.

DUPUY DE LOME, STANISLAS (1816–1885), naval architect and marine engineer; pioneer in the construction of ironclad warships; born 15 October 1816 at Ploemeur, near Lorient, a port and naval station in northwest France. After passing through the Ecole Navale and the Ecole Polytechnique, Dupuy de Lôme entered the naval construction corps in 1835. His superiors selected him in 1842 to go to the shipyards of England to study British techniques of building iron ships. Metallurgical advances in Great Britain had enabled the English to introduce the first iron merchant vessels and unarmored iron warships. Dupuy de Lôme's *Mémoire sur la construction des bâtiments en fer*, published by order of the minister of the marine in 1844, came to be recognized as a classic. Several iron despatch boats and liners immediately began to be constructed in accord with his ideas, which long set the standard for iron shipbuilding in French shipyards, but he recognized that the project that he submitted in 1845 for an armored iron-hulled warship would have to be deferred until circumstances inclined his superiors to be more receptive to the idea. Tests in England and France demonstrating the vulnerability of iron ships to the improved shot and shell of modern ordnance convinced English and French naval authorities that iron warships were less practical than wooden ones. Dupuy de Lôme succeeded, however, in winning approval for a proposal that, by boldly reducing sails to a strictly auxiliary role and providing for an engine of great horsepower, permitted him to build the first high-speed, screw-propelled, steam-driven battleship of the line. This was the *Napoléon*, launched in 1850 and faster than any ship in the British squadron during the Crimean War. Its success on 22 September 1853 in not only defying the currents and head winds of the Dardanelles but towing the French flagship of 112 guns through the straits behind it, amazed the British, who soon found themselves forced to follow suit as the French began to launch a series of similar vessels.

The naval lessons acquired in the Crimean War turned men's minds to iron as well as steam, for armored floating batteries in the Battle of Kinburn had sustained less damage than wooden ships had suffered in their engagements, as for instance, before Sebastopol in October 1854. Profiting from this experience and from a long series of tests of different types of armor, in which Napoleon III took a personal interest, Dupuy de Lôme was able to press for a project similar to the one he had first advanced in 1845. He urged that ironclads be substituted for wooden ships in the program for a large steam fleet advanced by the Commission Supérieure Centrale in August 1855. His appointment on 1 January 1857 (the same day on which subsidies were granted to the three major French transatlantic maritime services) to the key position of *directeur de matériel* gave him, at age forty, an opportunity to inaugurate a new era in naval construction. He designed the *Gloire*, the world's first high-seas ironclad, which was launched in 1859. In the midst of a fleet of wooden battleships, it would resemble, in his words, a lion amid a flock of sheep. Screwed to the sides of its wooden hull were 10 to 12 centimeters of iron armor. Although the *Gloire* possessed many features of the speedy *Napoléon*, its increased weight and lower height posed fresh technical problems with which Dupuy de Lôme had had to wrestle. Its successful trials in August and September 1860 marked the beginning of the end of wooden capital ships. Shortly before the trials, the French had already launched a sister ship, the *Normandie*, destined to become the first armored naval vessel to cross the Atlantic. They would complete construction of another sister ship, the *Invincible*, early in 1861. These vessels were quickly followed in June 1861 by two more ironclads built in accord with Dupuy de Lôme's plans, the *Magenta* and the *Solférino*. Dupuy de Lôme fostered experimentation, advised against adopting his designs as the sole norm, and encouraged the members of the construction corps to present new ideas. He had favored the construction of the iron-hulled ironclad frigate, the *Couronne*, built at the same time as the *Normandie* and *Invincible* but in accord with another engineer's plans. Most French ironclads of the period would have been ironhulled (Dupuy de Lôme's original preference) had it not been for the limitations of the French iron industry. In 1860 the government gave orders to build ten more ironclads, nine of them woodenhulled (the French navy in 1860 consisted of 51 ships of the line plus 398 other vessels, including those on order). This impressive creation during the Second Empire of the first French ironclad fleet would have been impossible without the active participation of the emperor himself, who saw the need for change, picked a man of extraordinary talent to direct the process, and provided the funds necessary to carry it out. He thus helped to revolutionize the navies of the world. For this he paid a price. The English, already alarmed at French innovations with respect to steam, reacted with suspicion and fear to the French navy's rapid thrust to technological superiority with the ironclad warship. The British ironclad fleet built in response gave greater prominence to sails and overall was less homogeneous than the French. French naval competition was an important factor in subverting healthy relations between the two countries during and even beyond the Second Empire.

Dupuy de Lôme became a grand officer of the Legion of Honor in 1863 and a member of the Academy of Sciences in 1866. After the construction of the ironclad fleet, he left public service to devote sixteen years to the Cie des Messageries Maritimes and the Société des Forges et Chantiers de la Méditerranée, in whose employ he contributed significantly to the improvement of the French merchant marine. Elected to the Corps Législatif in 1869, he advised the imperial government during the Franco-Prussian War, and then counseled the Government of National Defense when the Empire fell. The acceptance by the latter of his proposal for a dirigible led to the construction of an airship whose successful trials in 1872 contributed to the development of lighter-than-air travel. He had already helped improve turret designs for warships and later in life played a role in persuading the Third Republic to adopt plans for a submarine. He replaced General Nicholas Changarnier (1793–1877) as a life senator in 1877. Dupuy de Lôme died at Paris, 1 February 1885.

L. Basch, "*La Gloire*, the First Ironclad, 1859," *Mariner's Mirror* (August 1972); J. P. Baxter, *The Introduction of the Ironclad Warship* (Cambridge, Mass., 1933); M. Martin, "La renaissance de la marine militaire française sous Napoléon III," *SN*, 42 (1979); F. W. Wallin, "The French Navy during the Second Empire: A Study of the Effects of Technological Development on French Governmental Policy" (Ph.D. diss., University of California at Berkeley, 1954), and "French Naval Conversion and the Second Empire's Intervention in Industry," in F. J. Cox et al., eds., *Studies in Honor of Franklin Charles Palm* (New York, 1956).

Raymond L. Cummings

Related entries: CHASSELOUP-LAUBAT; COMPAGNIE GENERALE TRANSATLANTIQUE; MESSAGERIES IMPERIALES.

DURANTY, EDMOND (1833–1880), novelist, art critic, and theoretician of the realist school in literature; born 5 June 1833, at Paris. Duranty began his career in government administration in 1853, obtaining a post through the good offices of his father, Louis Edmond Antoine, an auditor attached to the Conseil d'Etat. He gave up his position a few years later to devote himself to literature. Having met Jules Champfleury, the father of the realist movement, at one of the literary evenings of Louise Colet (1808–1876), poet, and friend of Gustave Flaubert, he was profoundly impressed and became Champfleury's disciple. He joined the staff of *Le Figaro* on 13 November 1856 and two days later published the first issue of the journal *Le réalisme* in collaboration with J. Assézat and Doctor Thulié (who was later to become president of the Paris municipal council). The ideas expounded in the review were largely those of Champfleury, although he never in fact contributed to the periodical. Under various pseudonyms, Duranty wrote most of the articles, with Thulié offering a series of theoretical essays. In their theoretical manifestos, the collaborators of *Le réalisme* underlined above all the social and practical functions of a literature based on observation rather than imagination. From this vantage point, they launched their attacks, aimed chiefly at the writers of the romantic school. To them, Victor Hugo was a "monster," Alfred de Vigny a "hermaphrodite." Poetry, especially that of the Parnassian school, was totally rejected, Théodore de Banville characterized as a "drum filled with little pebbles." The admiration that the editors expressed for Champfleury and for the other realist writers was unbounded. The periodical was short-lived; disputes between Duranty and Assézat, coupled with a dwindling number of new ideas, hastened the demise of *Le réalisme*, after six issues, in May 1857.

Duranty next turned his attention to the novel, publishing his only successful work, *Le malheur d'Henriette Gérard*, in *Le pays* (1858). His next work, *La fille dédaignée,* appeared shortly after in *Courrier de Paris* but had very little appeal. Although they were a powerful and sometimes dramatic representation of provincial bourgeois life, Duranty's novels were, for the most part, narrow in their horizons and lacking in the creative touch that made Balzac's novels so popular.

In 1859, Duranty was hired to review the Paris art Salon by the *Courrier de Paris*. As an art critic, he was to contribute greatly to the public's recognition of Edouard Manet and of other artists of his generation. Duranty also obtained a concession, through the intervention of Achille Fould, a cabinet minister, to direct a marionette theater in the Tuileries gardens in Paris. The sketches he wrote for his theater (which closed with the advent of war in 1870) were published under the title *Théâtre des marionnettes* and are filled with the same sort of cynical realism that characterizes his novels.

Duranty continued to write novels, producing *La canne de Mme. Desrieux* in 1861 and *La cause du beau Guillaume* a year later, neither of which brought him recognition or revenue. In 1864, Duranty joined the *Progrès de Lyon* as that newspaper's literary critic. Two years later, he traveled to London to study contemporary trends in English art. On his return, he pursued his career as an art critic, contributing to *L'étendard*, the *Revue littéraire*, and Jules Vallès' *La rue*. His reviews of the 1869 Salon led to an estrangement between Duranty and Henri Fantin-Latour and Manet. And a heated debate with Manet early in 1870 led to a duel. Honor was satisfied on 23 February 1870, and the two settled their differences shortly after.

In spite of his lack of success as a novelist, Duranty persisted in his vocation, publishing, with only moderate success, *Les combats de François Duquesnoy* in *L'événement illustré* (1868). Hampered by his lackluster style and his lack of imagination, Duranty had no true authority as a novelist. As an art critic, he was more successful. Perceptive, severe, and ironical, he was little loved by his contemporaries, but interest in him and his work has nevertheless continued. He died at Paris, 9 April 1880.

M. Crouzet, *Un méconnu du Réalisme: Duranty* (Paris, 1964; R. Dumesnil, *Le Réalisme et le naturalisme* (Paris, 1955); M. Parturier et A. Luppé, *La naissance de Duranty* (Paris, 1947).

Dorothy E. Speirs

Related entries: CHAMPFLEURY; COURBET; FLAUBERT; GONCOURT; ZOLA.

DURUY, VICTOR (1811–1894), historian and politician; minister of education 23 June 1863 to 17 July 1869; born at Paris 10 September 1811. Of modest birth, Duruy was the son of an anti-clerical, republican craftsman at the Gobelin factory in Paris. As an apprentice, Duruy obtained a scholarship at the Collège Sainte-Barbe and later graduated from the Ecole Normale Supérieure. In his early years, he was tutor for two of Louis-Philippe's sons, secretary to Jules Michelet (1798–1874), and teacher of history at the Lycées Henri IV and Saint Louis. He wrote about fifty history texts that became the standard for a generation of *lycéens*. They expounded themes of progress, deism, secular morality, and, occasionally, caesarism. From his histories developed a personal friendship with Napoleon III (whom he assisted in the writing of his *Histoire de Jules César*) and his surprising appointment as minister. Although Duruy's career had been of some distinction (inspector of the Académie de Paris, *maître de conférences* at the Ecole Normale, *inspecteur général* of secondary education, professor at the Ecole Polytechnique), his appointment was all the more surprising because he had not been an ardent bonapartist, had voted for General Louis Eugène Cavaignac (1802–1857) and against Louis Napoleon for president of the Second Republic on 10 December 1848, had opposed, although silently, the coup d'état of December 1851 and had voted "no" in the plebiscites of 1851 and 1852. The emperor, however, had come to value what he considered to be Duruy's democratic sentiment and generous instincts, his faith in ideas, idealistic patriotism, and philosophical love of humanity.

Not a creative intellect, Duruy shared dominant assumptions of the age— dedication to French glory, the omnipotence and omniscience of the state, *culture générale* (although he did not restrict that notion to the classics), education as a tool of progress, and fear of the untutored masses. Uninterested in constitutional forms, he could support a government based on universal manhood suffrage that maintained order and developed public instruction. More confident than his predecessors that education, including that of the working class, was the key to progress, he encouraged expansion and improvement of elementary instruction, developed a program of special education—which he claimed was one of his great innovations—established public high schools for girls, and attempted to strengthen the public sector of education at the expense of the church.

Although he required fewer reports from his inspectors than did his predecessors, Duruy began by seeking out statistics, and his massive inquiries remain among the best historical sources from the nineteenth century. A report of 1863 which claimed an illiteracy rate of about 30 percent and 500,000 to 750,000 children without schooling turned the ministry's attention from secondary to primary education, which would prepare the masses for the exercise of universal suffrage, raise their moral level, and act as a vehicle for the downward transmission of elite culture. To the same goal, Duruy supported public libraries and, after hesitation in 1866, the Ligue de l'Enseignement of Jean Macé (1815–1894). He gave libraries to primary schools and stressed practical subjects. He proposed free and compulsory education fifteen years before it became law. Failing to achieve fundamental reform through the emasculated law of 10 April 1867, he succeeded by administrative fiat in expanding the budget for schooling and improving the lot of *instituteurs*. Duruy upgraded teachers' colleges, required communes of 500 people (rather than 800) to provide a girls' school, and removed the quota on the number of free places in schools although he did not encourage the day-care centers recommended by the Pillet report. He also encouraged adult classes, which by 1869 involved 800,000 auditors, including 100,000 women, and did all that he could to enlarge the exercise of *gratuité*, a principle he had advocated in a circular of February 1864.

Like republicans who followed him and some of whose philosophies he anticipated, Duruy mainly encouraged completion of trends in primary schooling established and largely achieved before his ministry. The report of 1863 had, for example, exaggerated local resistance to and the failings of primary education; 97 percent of the communes, obeying the provisions of the Guizot Law of 1833, then had a school and many of the children deemed "without schooling" were absent only in that particular year. Enrollment in primary schools had risen by 965,218 students (29 percent) in the thirteen years prior to Duruy's ministry. It grew by 7 percent during his six years of office. Both schooling and literacy were growing rapidly in France before Duruy's time. By 1870 illiteracy had fallen to 29 percent and enrollment was 100 percent of the school-age cohort (irregular attendance meant that some children had to enroll for more than seven years to complete studies).

In secondary education Duruy implemented two major reforms—he did away with the vestiges of *bifurcation* and established *enseignement spécial*. Neither was so original as often supposed. His first step (29 July 1863) was symbolic, restoring philosophy's name and honor in the final year of *division supérieure*, and ending Hippolyte Fortoul's despised "logic." By the end of the year he had terminated the bifurcated *baccalauréat*; the last particle of *bifurcation* was swept away in 1864. Duruy's opposition to *bifurcation* reflected both the opposition by teachers (opposition decreasing according to Duruy's own inquiry in 1864) and his own philosophy that opposed specialization and supported the old division between theoretical and applied sciences.

Introduction of *enseignement spécial* (i.e., without Greek or Latin) resulted in part from an admiration of Germany's technical education, but French special education was neither technical nor equal to other segments of secondary studies. A second-rate program which did not give access to the *grandes écoles* but which charged the same fees as did *enseignement classique*, special education was not radically different in goals or content from the preexisting *cours de français*. Designated for and attracting the lower-middle classes, it seems to have widened the social base of secondary education only slightly while restricting radical social mobility by funnelling the lower-middle classes into a program that provided limited mobility. Its effects were consistent with Duruy's faith in both mass education and elitist culture. Enrollment within the program grew rapidly but few completed it. A school at Cluny for training teachers offered great promise but soon closed. Like Napoleon III and Gustave Rouland, Duruy saw vocational education both as a way of furthering material prosperity and reducing social strains; nevertheless, he regarded it as inferior to a *culture générale*. Duruy differed from contemporaries not in a denigration of *culture générale* but in his incorporation of modern elements into a classics-based notion. He introduced modern (nineteenth century) as well as economic and intellectual history as part of the regular curriculum, despite charges of introducing propaganda—a charge that had some substance, for Duruy believed that history guided understanding of contemporary civilization. A proposal to reduce exercises in the classics to leave time for modern subjects achieved limited success, but the study of modern languages, music, design, and gymnastics was made obligatory.

Noting that universities were barren of students, Duruy attempted first to attract students by stressing methodology and offering scholarships. In 1867 he even supported a Catholic campaign for the right to open Catholic universities, although he insisted on the jurisdiction of the state over degrees. As in other areas, Duruy's most original ideas came to fruition after his regime. His major achievement in higher education was the establishment in 1863 of the now famous Ecole (Pratique) des Hautes Etudes. Also created during his tenure was the Ecole Nationale d'Agronomie. Duruy worked toward creation of law faculties in the provinces and establishment of new chairs (including one, at Paris, for political economy) and of laboratories. He also made it possible for professors to defend themselves before dismissal.

In 1868 the first *lycée* for girls opened its doors. Intended as schools for upper-class women to prepare them "for the roles nature has assigned them" and to transfer the education of women "from the church to the state," girls' public high schools have had much wider social implications than their founder foresaw when he launched the idea in October 1867. In memoirs, Duruy claims to have founded girls' secondary education, but the church long had conducted schools. The impetus for the reform derived more from a desire to check clerical influence than to advance the place or thoughtfulness of women and the result was an acrimonious debate. Because girls' education did not include classical studies, it did not prepare for the *baccalauréat*; appropriately, the first woman to pass the *baccalauréat* was a teacher who had studied independently, passing it before the introduction of public high schools and over the objection of the previous ministry. Women's education burgeoned only after the Camille Sée law a decade later.

Like other ministers of the Second Empire, Duruy had to concern himself with competition from the church. Neither religious nor expressly anticlerical, Duruy did believe that the state should dominate education and that the church should have little role in the University. In both 1866 (for primary schooling) and in 1867 (for universities) Duruy was willing to permit more liberty for Catholic schools to expand schooling provided the state retained jurisdiction over private schools. By the end of his regime, church and state had responded to social demand for education, the prime stimulus for growth in the first half of the century. In the future, they would compete for the same clientele. Duruy attempted to ensure that the state would be victorious. These efforts, together with his deficiencies as a politician (he was not a good speaker and was above all an enthusiast), increased his isolation and made him a growing liability to the emperor who had never given him instructions but had simply allowed him to act. Following the elections of 1869, Duruy was sacrificed to his opponents in the church, liberals as well as conservatives. In retirement he completed his monumental *Histoire des Romains*. He died at Paris, 15 November 1894.

Duruy has been acclaimed as France's greatest education minister. Such a judgment derives too much from the inadequacies of other ministers and the favorable judgment of socially conservative, republican *universitaires* who laid the historical foundation. (Ernest Lavisse was a collaborator and secretary of the minister.) Accomplished reforms owed much to his predecessors. The reforms he himself claimed—inauguration of special education, abolishment of *bifurcation*, establishment of women's education—appear respectively as unoriginal, retrograde, or disingenuously motivated. Only in his failures, which were many, was he ahead of his time. Like the uncle of his mentor Napoleon III, Duruy was most successful as a synthesizer of the best ideas of those who preceded him.

R. Anderson, *Education in France, 1848–1870* (New York, 1975); V. Duruy, *L'administration de l'instruction publique de 1863 à 1869* (Paris, 1878), and *Notes et souvenirs*, 2 vols. (Paris, 1901); S. Horvath, *Victor Duruy and French Education: Liberal Reform in the Second Empire* (Baton Rouge, La., 1984), and "Victor Duruy and the Controversy over Secondary Education for Girls," FHS 9 (Spring 1975); A. Dansette, "Un grand ministre," *Revue de Paris*, no. 12 (1967); R. Grew and P. J. Harrigan, with J. Whitney,

"La scolarisation en France, 1829–1906," *Annales*, no. 1 (1984); P. Harrigan, *Mobility, Elites, and Education in French Society of the Second Empire* (Waterloo, Ontario, Canada, 1980); J. Rohr, *Victor Duruy, ministre de Napoleon III: Essai sur la politique de l'instruction publique au temps de l'Empire Libéral* (Paris, 1967); M. Schwab, *Victor Duruy et les premiers pas de l'enseignement laïque* (Paris, 1963); G. Weisz, *The Emergence of Modern Universities in France, 1863–1914* (Princeton, N.J., 1983); W. H. Wilkins, "The Debate over Secondary Education for Women in Nineteenth-Century France," *North Dakota Quarterly* 49 (Winter, 1981).

Patrick J. Harrigan

Related entries: DUPANLOUP; FALLOUX LAW; FORTOUL; GALLICAN-ISM; GAUME; *HISTOIRE DE JULES CESAR*; PASTEUR; ROULAND.

E

ECONOMIC CRISES UNDER THE SECOND EMPIRE. Economic crises— in the mid-nineteenth century they were termed *commercial crises*—have proved to be imponderable but regular occurrences in industrial societies. The Second Empire witnessed two, those of 1857 and 1866–1867, and emerged out of another, the economic and political crisis of 1846–1851. Not surprisingly, contemporaries were struck by the serious consequences and by the unpredictability of business fluctuations. Clément Juglar (1819–1905), who pioneered the study of trade cycles, was trained as a physician and turned to economics only after living through the mid-century crisis and that of 1857. His first major work dates from 1862. Another contemporary, Karl Marx, carefully charted the progress of the 1857 crisis in the belief that it would bring about the demise of capitalism. Although it did not do so, he went on to develop his theory that the economic system would be subject to ever-deepening economic crises.

Neither of the economic crises that afflicted the major European economies and that of the United States in the 1850s and 1860s was as serious in France as elsewhere, and both were short-lived. Of the two, that of 1857 has greater symbolic importance. The economic crisis of that year brought to an end the great boom of the early years of the Empire. The increase in gold supply—an increase of one-third in gold in circulation between 1848 and 1856—had helped make possible the lowering of interest rates and had lubricated the wheels of international exchange. In France a combination of factors, including the return of political stability, railway building, and continuing technical innovation in textiles, had led to high economic growth rates. The crisis of 1857 marks a watershed that separates the relatively rapid growth achieved in previous decades from the deceleration and even stagnation of the later decades of the nineteenth century. By the late 1850s France was the leading industrial power of continental Europe. Thereafter, it lost its lead. The 1866–1867 crisis also had significance, for it was one element in the decline of the authoritarian Empire and the catalyst of the collapse of the Crédit Mobilier in October 1867.

There are no universally accepted explanations for either of these crises. Economists, like Juglar and, in the 1920s, N. D. Kondratieff, have classified business fluctuations according to the length of the cycle, but they have not been able to offer the tools that would enable historians to explain periodic crises. Three difficulties in particular limit our understanding of the 1857 and 1866–1867 crises. One is that although some scholars stress the importance of such monetary factors as money supply and rates of interest in the generation of crises, others emphasize underconsumption, overproduction, or stock market slumps. Another is that like the crisis of 1846–1851, crises during the Second Empire were mixed, that is, they were both agricultural and industrial in origin. They shared features with the pre-Revolutionary crises that had been determined by poor harvests and raised food prices and reduced income available for other consumer goods like textiles. This kind of crisis, so admirably analyzed by the French historian Ernest Labrousse, would persist in France to 1870. Thereafter, agricultural prices would tend to move down in times of economic crisis rather than up, as had been the case before. Crises also reflected the growing importance of industry in the French economy, and industry had its own boom-and-slump sequence. The crises of 1857 and 1866–1867 were mixed; that is, they consisted of two kinds of crises that were linked and yet had a certain independence. There is a third difficulty. Business fluctuations at this time, as later, are internationally transmitted, and France is but one epicenter among others. Thus the first sign of crisis in 1857 occurred in July in the United States when the collapse of the Ohio Life Insurance and Trust Company was the signal for tumbling share prices and bank failures.

The 1857 crisis in France, then, had more than one trigger. Wheat prices had been high in the 1850s, but the harvest of 1856 was particularly poor. The cost of the Crimean War was borne with greater difficulty in France than in Britain, and, because of growing specie exports to the Near and Far East, the Bank of France's specie reserves fell by nearly 40 percent between June and November 1857. This led the bank to raise its discount rate to 10 percent. However, a crisis in confidence was the most obvious trigger, a crisis that was the sequel to the exaggerated optimism and speculation engendered by rising prices, the railway boom, and prosperity of the 1852–1857 period. Railways had attracted massive investments, but returns on new lines proved to be not as high as expected and the Pereires' Grand Central scheme failed. Railway share values fell, and as a result railway construction declined by 5 percent in 1858. The metallurgical industry was affected because railway orders were reduced. The textile industry was also hit, and raw cotton consumption was 13 percent lower in 1857 than it had been in 1856. Banks that had invested in railways and public works were also touched by the crisis, none more than the most spectacular of the banking creations of the early years of the Empire, the Crédit Mobilier. It issued a dividend of 23 percent in 1856 but of only 5 percent in 1857, and by the end of that year its shares that had stood at just under 2,000 francs in March 1856 had declined to 700. Although the number of bankruptcies increased by 10 percent in 1858, there were already signs of recovery. Besides, the new agreements the government signed with railway companies, agreements that became the 1859 railway law, guaranteed interest on new lines and helped bolster confidence in railway shares.

The second crisis, that of 1866–1867, came after some difficult years in the early 1860s and especially the so-called cotton famine. Like its predecessor, this was a mixed crisis. It coincided with, and was influenced by, high agricultural prices, which reduced textile sales. The cotton industry was also affected by overproduction resulting from the ending of the U.S. Civil War and bumper cotton crops. The crisis was also international. Its onset was signaled by the failure of one of the most important London banks, Overend and Gurney, in May 1866. The same month saw a marked fall in share values on the Paris Bourse. Again, disappointing returns on railway, and above all foreign railway, stocks affected confidence. Although the crisis in France was not as deep as in Britain, it had one important victim. The overextended Crédit Mobilier, its funds locked in investments that failed to yield early returns, was in difficulty in the first half of 1866 when its shares dropped by half. The general crisis and the refusal of the Bank of France to bail out the Pereires led to their resignation in October 1867 and to the effective end of the Crédit Mobilier as a major force in French finance.

J. Bouvier, "Les crises économiques: Problématique des crises économiques du XIXe siècle et analyses historiques: Le cas de la France," in J. Le Goff and P. Nora, eds., *Faire de l'histoire*, vol. 2 (Paris, 1974); M. Flamant and J. Singer-Kérel, *Crises et récessions* (Paris, 1968); C. P. Kindleberger, *Manias, Panics, and Crashes: A History of Financial Crises* (New York, 1978); H. Rosenberg, *Die Weltwirtschaftskrisis von 1857–1859*, 2d ed. (Berlin, 1974); J. A. Schumpeter, *Business Cycles: A Theoretical, Historical and Statistical Analysis of the Capitalist Process* (New York, 1939); G. W. Van Vlack, *The Panic of 1857: An Analytical Study* (New York, 1967).

Barrie M. Ratcliffe

Related entries: BANKING; COBDEN-CHEVALIER TREATY; COTTON FAMINE; GOVERNMENT FINANCE.

ELECTIONS, during the Second Empire regarded as periodic plebiscites on the regime. Elected bodies included the councils of the departments (*conseils généraux*), of the arrondissements, and of the towns (*conseils municipaux*). Most important was the lower house of the legislature, the Corps Législatif, which was elected every six years. All elections were by universal manhood suffrage, regulated by the decree-law of 2 February 1852, which had been formulated by a commission consisting of Jules Baroche, Victor Fialin Persigny, Eugène Rouher, and Louis Napoleon. Members of the Corps Législatif were chosen in single-member constituencies (*circonscriptions*) drawn to allow one deputy for every 35,000 people (or fragment over 25,000). Elections were held in two rounds (*tours*) separated by two weeks (the additional *tour* was an innovation of the Second Empire). If in the first balloting no candidate had a majority of the votes cast or if the winner did not receive support from at least 25 percent of the total registered electorate, a plurality would decide at the second *tour*. Voting was secret (the ballot was handed folded to the poll chairman, who deposited it in the ballot box) and extended over two days (Sunday and Monday), during which time the mayor of each commune was entrusted with the ballot box (*urne*). The government, which had determined the constituency boundaries, drawn up the electoral lists, and set the election dates, also prescribed the electoral period, which was kept as short as possible since it was only then that public meetings or any form of party activity were permitted. The government also chose the candidates to be recommended to the voters. This concept of official candidature had existed since 1815, but the Second Empire married it to the new idea of universal manhood suffrage. In 1852 the official candidates were nominated primarily by the prefects. Thereafter they were generally approved by the Council of Ministers on the recommendation of the minister of the interior, who took his orders from the emperor and was greatly influenced by the prefects. Napoleon III did not choose the candidates except in two or three cases. Nor were all official candidates bonapartists. Men of all parties were adopted, on condition that they accept the regime and pledge to support it or, at least, to constitute a loyal opposition. Once the official candidates had been designated, it was the function of the mayors and prefects, all of whom were appointed by the government, to "make the elections," using all means of patronage, persuasion, and pressure at their disposal. Even during the electoral periods, associations of more than twenty persons were forbidden, and newspapers were kept under close surveillance. Only official candidates could use white paper for their posters, which were hung by the official *afficheurs* and watched over by the local police. To be an official candidate was, therefore, to avoid the greater part of campaign costs, which by 1869 could be as high as 20,000 francs. Ballots (*bulletins*) of the official candidates were also white and were sent directly to each voter, along with the voter registration card (*carte d'électeur*). By a decision of the *cour de cassation* of 1856, ballots were held to be subject to the *colportage* laws and hence to government control. A voter who did not wish to cast the white ballot might have to request another at the polling place. Thus the full weight of government was dedicated to ensuring a good result for the elections, and that result could even be known, at least theoretically, fairly well in advance. This system was justified by invoking the political inexperience of the people, the deleterious effect of parties, and, somewhat later, the principle of noncontradiction; the people, having supported the emperor in the plebiscites, should be consistent and send him deputies ready to assist him in his work. All successful candidates were required to take an oath to Napoleon III before they could be seated in the bodies to which they were elected. From February 1858, candidates had to take such an oath before they could run.

The first elections to the Corps Législatif following the coup d'état of December 1851 were held on 29 February and 1 March 1852 while martial law was still in effect. Persigny, then minister of the interior (from 22 January 1852), made a major effort to secure a sweeping government victory and was largely successful. Zealous local authorities often deprived opposition candidates of opportunity to be heard, but it seems likely that under any circumstances the government would have won an enormous majority. Of 9.8 million registered voters, 6.2 million cast ballots. Official candidates, mostly chosen by the prefects and accepted by Persigny even when, as in some instances, they were moderate legitimists, obtained almost 5.2 million votes, the opposition only several hundred thousand. Of 265 elected candidates, no more than 7 could be considered opponents of the regime, and only 3 of those—Robert Constant Bouhier de l'Ecluse (1799–1870); Marie Henri Louis, marquis Durfurt de Civrac (1812–1884); and Paul Audren de Kerdrel (1815–1889), all from Brittany and the Vendée—had defeated an official candidate. Of three republicans—Hippolyte Carnot (1801–1888), Jacques Hénon (1802–1872), and Pierre Legrand (1804–1859)—all but Legrand (Lille) refused the oath and were not seated. Legrand rallied to the regime. After the proclamation of the Empire, Bouhier de l'Ecluse, Durfurt de Civrac, Kerdrel, and another legitimist deputy resigned and were replaced by official candidates. And so, the 1852–1857 Corps Législatif contained only one declared opponent, Charles de Montalembert, who had been elected an official candidate. And yet it remained true that official candidates received support from only 53 percent of the electorate; 37 percent of the registered voters abstained (55 percent at Marseilles, 75 percent at Saint-Etienne). There had been 250 opposition candidates, including some 35 legitimist leaders, despite the comte de Chambord's sudden injunction (issued against the advice of the comte de Falloux [1811–1886]) to his supporters to abstain. Moreover, abstentions, as well as the opposition vote, were concentrated in the towns and cities. At Paris 133,513 voted for official candidates, but 89,732 voted for opponents of the regime, and 91,772 abstained. Perhaps most significant, the official candidates were by no means all bonapartists. In fact, no more than one-third could be so labeled. Orleanists, legitimists, and others had been accepted in return for their promise of support. Only the leaders of the old parties had been systematically excluded, and as a result some seventeen of the former followers of François Guizot (1787–1874) were elected. Sixty-nine official deputies showed some independence: two Catholics (including Montalembert), eighteen conservatives, seventeen Orleanists, and thirty-two legitimists. Nor were the bonapartists necessarily supporters of an indefinitely prolonged authoritarian regime. Bonapartists of both Left and Right had from the beginning reservations concerning the emperor's virtually unrestrained powers.

The next elections were held eight months before the expiration of the Corps Législatif's mandate. The question was whether the regime, aided by almost six years of remarkable prosperity and by the victory of France and its allies in the Crimean War (1854–1856), could further consolidate itself. But the economic surge had reached its zenith and had already begun to recede, while the Crimean War had been followed by a period of uncertainty and of malaise in international relations. The minister of the interior, Adolphe Billault, undertook to support almost all sitting deputies (a notable exception was Montalembert); in fact, the government withdrew its support from only nine former official candidates and did not oppose several moderate independents. However, official candidacy was maintained in full force, and the republican newspaper *Le siècle* was warned for attacking the practice. All means of government management were once again used, and, as in 1852, some prefects and other local officials went to extreme lengths, so that public meetings and electoral committees were often forbidden, and there was, as a result, practically no real campaign. Although divided on the issue, many republicans decided against abstention and against rejecting the oath should they be elected. At Paris there was a quarrel concerning the republican list. Auguste Nefftzer and Léonor Havin managed to have Louis Garnier-Pagès (1803–1878) and Jules Bastide (1800–1879) replaced by Emile Ollivier and Alfred Darimon. The Orleanists stood aside, but some legitimists presented themselves. Voting in the first round took place on 21 and 22 June 1857 (28 June in Corsica). On 28 June the government announced the arrest of a group of conspirators against the emperor's life (an offense dating to April). Once again the results could be interpreted as a resounding victory for the government. Almost 65 percent of those eligible voted. Government candidates received 5,470,000 votes, or nearly 85 percent of those cast, the opposition candidates only 665,000. In the Doubs, Montalembert was roundly beaten by Napoleon III's chamberlain, Charles Adrien Gustave, marquis de Conegliano (b. 1820). In fact, the government conquered the west, formerly a legitimist stronghold. Of the 267 elected candidates, no more than 14 (and perhaps as few as 9 or 10) could be considered in opposition to or independent of the regime. As in 1852, however, there was another way of interpreting the results. Opposition had not disappeared; it had grown; and it had changed in nature from legitimist to republican. After the by-elections of April 1858, in which the government regained one *circonscription* but lost two (to Jules Favre and Ernest Picard), the death of General Louis Eugène Cavaignac (1802–1857), and the refusal of Michel Goudchaux (1797–1862) and of Hippolyte Carnot (1801–1888) to take the oath (all three had been elected at Paris in the first *tour*), five republicans (*les Cinq*) were seated in the Corps Législatif: Ollivier, Alfred Darimon (both elected at Paris in the second *tour*), Jules Favre, Ernest Picard, and Jacques Louis Hénon (1802–1872), the last elected at Lyons. Another republican, Louis Jean Ambroise Gustave Curé (1799–1876), was elected at Bordeaux but rallied to the Empire. At Paris the largely republican opposition had obtained 96,000 votes to the government's 110,000, winning five of the ten *circonscriptions*. Republicans also won a majority of votes at Toulouse but no seat and were strong at Marseilles, Lille, Saint-Etienne, and Angers. Moreover, in 1857 as in 1852 there were many abstentions, and these, like the opposition vote, were concentrated in the cities. In fact, some ministers took alarm. Achille Fould talked of abolishing universal manhood suffrage. Others advocated stern measures against the intractable urban workers. Displeased by the election results at Paris, the emperor recalled that he had always wanted to ban the building of new factories there. It could be argued that both the short-lived repression after the attempt on Napoleon III's life by Felice Orsini in 1858 and the more important first steps toward the Liberal Empire which followed, had their roots in the 1857 elections.

Six years later, new elections were held in the midst of greatly changed circumstances. The first steps had been taken toward liberalization of the regime, while events connected with the Italian War of 1859 had alienated from the government some of its staunchest supporters in the church and among the bourgeoisie. The crisis of 1852 was now more than ten years past, and the elections of 1863 could be construed as a plebiscite on the general direction indicated for France by the emperor in his reform decree of November 1860 and, especially, on the proposition that the decree constituted the crowning of the edifice so long promised. The economic crisis resulting from civil war in the United States was a further complication, as was the uprising that had begun in Poland in January. Under these circumstances, the government resolved to maintain the electoral regime unchanged, rejecting the argument of Auguste de Morny, president of the Corps Législatif, that all deputies should be endorsed for reelection. Instead, Persigny, once again minister of the interior, found opponents for those who had shown themselves too independent in the preceding legislature (forty-eight sitting deputies were denied official candidacy). Persigny hoped that out of the elections would emerge a homogeneous bonapartist party. Every device was used to ensure victory. The electoral map was redrawn, gerrymandering fourteen departments (4 January 1863) in order to underrepresent Paris. Electoral lists were published at the last moment, leaving only ten days for corrections. The campaign period was kept to a minimum length (10–31 May), the association's laws were rigorously enforced against meetings and organizations of more than twenty persons, and *avertissements* were multiplied against the press. Functionaries were enlisted in the cause and opposition printers and distributors harassed. Moreover, grants for railroads and other projects were liberally dispensed. Persigny, fulminating against the revival of the parties ("coalitions of hostility, bitterness, and spite against the great causes of the Empire"), designated the formidable Adolphe Thiers, who had at last decided to reenter the political arena, public enemy number one.

But in the campaign of 1863, the government had to contend not only with electoral machinery that was beginning to break down but also with an opposition much more vigorous than in the past. In particular, the republicans, strengthened by the return, under successive amnesties, of many of their exiles and by the arrival on the scene of a new generation, mounted an effective campaign. Despite the efforts of the men of 1848, most republicans agreed to take the oath, if only for tactical reasons. The republican list at Paris was largely the work of a committee composed of the five republican deputies plus Léonor Havin of *Le siècle* and Adolphe Guéroult (1810–1872) of *L'opinion nationale*. It was perhaps Auguste Nefftzer and *Le temps* who persuaded Thiers, recently attacked by Persigny in *Le moniteur*, to run as a republican. Thiers agreed to be an enemy of the Empire, but only within the law. In the end, the republican candidates at Paris consisted of *les Cinq* (despite the opposition of the old-line republicans),

Jules Simon (1814–1896), Eugène Pelletan (1813–1884), Havin (opposed by Ferdinand, comte de Lasteyrie du Saillant [1810–1879]), Guéroult, and Thiers. Jules Ferry (1832–1893) and Léon Gambetta contested seats in the provinces. Although the legitimists once more abstained on instructions from the comte de Chambord, some, like Antoine Berryer (at Marseilles) and the comte de Falloux, did put themselves forward. Of the ninety-one Catholic deputies who had approved the proposed amendment to the address of 1861, seven did not stand, twenty-four were opposed by the government, and twenty-four were unopposed, although not all were considered official candidates. Those who regarded themselves as Catholic above all—Emile Keller (1828–1909), comte Anatole Lemercier (b. 1820), Ignace Plichon (1814–1888), Maurice Adolphe Charles, vicomte de Flavigny (1799–1873), and C.L.H. Kolb-Bernard (1798–1888)—ran as independents, although they were forbidden to use that designation, but only Keller was an implacable enemy of the regime. The Orleanists put forward a number of candidates: Charles de Rémusat (1797–1875) in the Haute-Garonne, Saint-Marc Girardin (1801–1873), Lucien Anatole Prévost-Paradol, Jules, marquis de Lasteyrie (1810–1883, grandson of Lafayette), Jean Jacques Weiss (1827–1891) (these last three at Paris), Auguste Casimir-Périer (1811–1878) at Grenoble, Victor, duc de Broglie (1785–1870), Jules Dufaure (1798–1881), Odilon Barrot (1791–1873), and the Duc Decazes (1819–1886) at Libourne. In addition, they supported Thiers and Berryer. Those Orleanists and legitimists who could accept the Empire if it were to become liberal advocated a Union Libérale, to embrace the entire moderate opposition from republicans through legitimists. But while Le temps and Le siècle called for a united front and a few moderates rallied to the idea (Bastide, Carnot, Simon, Montalembert, Berryer, Falloux, Thiers), the time had not yet arrived for such a coalition. The Roman Question, if nothing else, was an insuperable barrier. Besides, the church hierarchy was itself divided. While Bishop Félix Dupanloup supported the Catholics in a pamphlet signed by six bishops, ten others supported official candidates. The opposition did cooperate at some point but failed notoriously to do so at many others. Nevertheless, 300 opposition candidates contested 283 seats, and the contest this time was a real one.

The first round of the elections was held on 31 May and 1 June 1863 (7 June in Corsica). Of 9,938,000 electors, 7,262,000 voted. Of those voting, 73 percent (5,308,000) cast their ballots for official candidates and 27 percent (1,954,000) for the opposition. About 23 percent (2,291,000) of the registered voters abstained. The last were mostly workers, especially in the Seine department. Obviously, many of those who had abstained in 1852 and 1857 now voted for opposition candidates. Most significant was the result in the big cities. At Paris, where in August 1861 opposition newspapers had outsold those of the government by 166,000 to 53,000, all ten opposition candidates were elected—nine republicans (Ollivier, Darimon, Favre, Picard, Simon, Carnot, Guéroult, Garnier-Pagès, Pelletan) and Thiers, against whom Persigny had personally led the campaign. These candidates won 63 percent of the Paris vote (150,000 to 84,000 for the official candidates), and four were elected on the first ballot. Of the other large towns and cities, only Strasbourg, Orleans, Angers, Rouen, Rennes, and Amiens voted for the government. On the other hand, the peasants once again proved their loyalty to the regime. In the end, only 32 to 35 of the 283 newly elected deputies could be considered in opposition to or independent of the regime, and only 18 to 20 of those were republicans. The "Catholic party" had almost completely failed, as had the Orleanists, who obtained a majority only at Nantes, Bordeaux, and Le Havre. Fourteen of the twenty former deputies blacklisted by Persigny because of their attitude toward the Roman Question were defeated. In fact, no more than 24 deputies in all, and perhaps as few as 15 (6 opposition, 9 official deputies), could be considered to belong to the "Catholic party," and none of those were pure clericals. Thiers, although victorious at Paris, was defeated in three other constituencies. Of legitimist candidates only Berryer was elected (at Marseilles). Among the opposition, the true victors were the republicans.

The elections of 1863 could be interpreted in several ways. The government had won a massive majority, routed the clericals, legitimists, and Orleanists, frustrated the grand coalition, gained votes over 1857 in a third of the departments, and continued its conquest of the West from the legitimists. With better planning and more attention to detail, the already small number of opposition deputies might have been reduced by half. And yet there was cause for discontent. The electoral machinery had functioned poorly; many abstainers of 1857 had voted against the government, and many workers had continued to abstain; eloquent and powerful opposition voices had appeared for the first time in the Corps Législatif (Thiers, Berryer, Simon, Louis Buffet, Alexandre Marie [1795–1870], and Victor Ambroise Lanjuinais [1802–1869]), or had reappeared (Ollivier, Picard, Favre, Darimon); the cities had been lost and, as a consequence, an exaggerated impression created of opposition successes. Moreover, many government candidates were too independent to be counted on, at least for continued support of an authoritarian Empire. All of this Napoleon III understood. Persigny, blamed for poor management as well as excessive zeal, was relieved of his ministry and retired from active politics. And the emperor, perhaps recognizing the need to disengage from the new Corps Législatif a great center party of support, ignored the cries from the Right that political change introduced in 1860 had been to blame for the election results. He embarked from 1863 on a policy of reform and of liberalization.

The final elections of the Second Empire, in 1869, were held under circumstances that had greatly changed from those of six years before. Since 1863, foreign policy reverses had seriously undermined Napoleon III's prestige. No means had been found to reanimate the economic boom that had reinforced the regime during the 1850s. Moreover, the political and social reforms of 1867–1868 had been so mishandled as gravely to compromise their effectiveness, and yet they had opened new arenas to the opposition. In fact, the reappearance of a revolutionary party from 1864 had even caused the government to turn back toward its alienated clerical supporters. The new republican party, led by men like Léon Gambetta, pledged intransigent opposition to the regime. It was clear that the elections must lead to change or to revolution. Rouher conducted the government's electoral campaign and, against the objections of the interior minister, Pierre Ernest Pinard, once more designated official candidates, all of whom were from the *parti autoritaire et conservateur*. The electoral districts were gerrymandered; special enemies designated; in a word, all of the old methods were brought into play. Moreover, on the eve of the elections, Napoleon III secured a generous military pensions law and talked of abolishing the *livrets* that workers had to carry. But the system no longer worked. Candidates, once nominated, were left largely to their own devices, as the government failed to control its chief electoral instruments—the mayors. No government candidates contested Paris' nine seats or those of Lyons. Some twenty-seven opposition candidates were unopposed, for the government did not combat independents. On the other hand, no opposition coalition proved possible. Although a Union Libérale was again proposed, legitimists and Catholics on the one hand and democrats on the other made no attempt to agree, so that the grouping embraced only monarchists. Despite the fact that all republicans rejected the regime, the left wing (*démocratie radicale*) ran candidates against fellow republicans. At Belleville, Gambetta flaunted his *mandat impératif* against Carnot, pledging "irreconcilable opposition" to the regime and strict loyalty to the "contract" that bound him to his constituents. The campaign (3–22 May 1869) was violent, especially at Paris, punctuated by meetings (newly legal under the 1868 law on public reunions) and demonstrations. Voting took place on 23 and 24 May. At Paris the Left won almost 80,000 votes, the entire opposition 234,000 to the government's 77,000. Radicals like Désiré Bancel (1822–1871) and Gambetta were elected in the first round against Ollivier and Carnot respectively. So, too, were more moderate republicans (Picard, who alone was unopposed by the radicals, Simon and Pelletan). There were disturbances at Saint-Etienne, Lille, Toulouse, and Strasbourg. In the second round of voting on 7 June, fifty-eight *ballottages* were decided (a record number), including four at Paris. Except at Paris, where François Raspail (1794–1878) and Henri Rochefort persisted without success against their more moderate republican adversaries, Garnier-Pagès and Favre, the opposition agreed on common candidates. In the final count, government candidates received almost 4.5 million votes (or more than 5 million if all candidates not actually opposed to the regime are included). All nongovernment candidates together received somewhat fewer than 3.4 million votes—a shift of about 1 million votes from government to opposition candidates since 1863. In the cities the opposition proved overwhelmingly successful, but in the provinces, republican successes were rare. Even at Paris the rioting (7–11 June) that followed the second round of voting was easily contained, and on 11 June Napoleon III and Eugénie were cheered as they rode through the boulevards.

At Paris eight republicans and Thiers were elected: in the first *tour* Bancel, Gambetta, Picard, Simon, and Pelletan; in the second Favre, Garnier-Pagès,

Ferry, and Thiers. Bancel, Gambetta, Picard, and Simon accepting other seats, in the by-elections of 21 and 22 November 1869, Adolphe Crémieux (1796–1880), Alexandre Glais-Bizoin (1800–1877), Emmanuel Arago (1812–1896), and Henri Rochefort were returned for Paris—another republican (but not a radical) sweep. Ollivier, defeated at Paris, was elected in the Var against Clément Laurier (1832–1878), with the unofficial support of Napoleon III. Except for Thiers who triumphed over Edmond, comte d'Alton-Shée (1810–1874) at Paris, the old Orleanist and legitimist leaders of the Union Libérale (Albert de Broglie, [1821–1901], Falloux, Prévost-Paradol, and Rémusat) were decisively beaten, as were all of Prince Napoleon's left-wing bonapartist candidates. Of 292 deputies, 186 had been official candidates, but at least 130 of those had taken positions opposed to some of the government's policies. The irreconcilable republicans and their allies held about twenty-five seats (there were perhaps thirty republicans of all persuasions). Other opponents of the regime numbered some forty-nine, making seventy-four deputies who wished to bring the Second Empire to an end. Of those not opposed to the regime, about eighty were pure bonapartists (or "Arcadiens"). The others were government liberals (ninety-eight) or opposition liberals (forty). The new element was this decisive mass of liberal bonapartists. No majority existed as a result of the elections, but the division of the republicans into moderate and radical wings and the existence of a large group of middle opinion (a third party between the irreconcilable Right and Left) pointed to a possible restructuring of the regime and to the emergence of a Liberal Empire.

No final assessment has yet been made of the electoral history of the Second Empire. For eighteen years, universal manhood suffrage had been so managed, without significant corruption, as to secure massive majorities for an authoritarian regime. That in itself was a remarkable achievement. But it could also be argued that the electoral battles of those years contributed to the emergence of a republican party capable—as it had not been in 1848—of winning power and of exercising it. Moreover, it may well be that the electoral history of the Second Empire constituted for France a necessary apprenticeship in democracy, during which the political power of the notables was decisively shaken and the political education of the peasants irreversibly begun.

M. Boivin, *Elections et plébiscites, 1848–1914* (Rouen, 1971); L. Girard et al., *Les élections de 1869* (Paris, 1960); A. Lefèvre-Pontalis, *Les lois et les moeurs électorales en France et en Angleterre* (Paris, 1864); L. Puech, *Essai sur la candidature officielle en France depuis 1851* (Paris, 1922); G. D. Weil, *Les élections législatives depuis 1789* (Paris, 1895); T. Zeldin, *The Political System of Napoleon III* (New York, 1958).

Related entries: AMNESTY; BONAPARTISM; *CANDIDATURE OUVRIERE*; *LES CINQ*; COALITIONS LAW; CORPS LEGISLATIF; DECENTRALIZATION; GAMBETTA; LEGITIMISM; LIBERAL EMPIRE; OATH; ORLEANISM; PERSIGNY; PLEBISCITE; PUBLIC OPINION; PREFECTS; PRESS REGIME; REFORM; REPUBLICANISM; ROUHER; THIERS; TIERS PARTI; UNIVERSAL MANHOOD SUFFRAGE.

EMPRESS. See EUGENIE.

ERCKMANN-CHATRIAN, collaborators on plays and novels that enjoyed a great vogue, especially toward the end of the Second Empire. Emile Erckmann was born 20 May 1822 at Phalsbourg (Lorraine), near the German border, and died on 14 March 1899 at Lunéville. In 1847, he made the acquaintance of Alexandre Chatrian, who was born 18 December 1826 in Soldatenthal (Grand-Soldat) and who died on 3 September 1890 at Villemomble. Their collaborative efforts, which were to last for some forty years, began with a play, *Georges ou le chasseur des ruines*, which ran at the Théâtre de la Gaieté and later at the Ambigu in Paris. For the next few years, the partnership continued, with Erckmann writing in Phalsbourg and Chatrian living in Paris, attempting to find publishers for their novels, plays, and essays. By 1856, the works of Erckmann-Chatrian, as they were now known, were widely accepted in the Paris press. By the early 1860s, a whole series of highly successful novels had assured them of a comfortable income. Sixteen months after *Les romans nationaux* was published in 1865, over a million copies had been sold.

Because of their highly readable character, the novels reached not only the bourgeoisie but also members of the working class. They mirror the simple life of the people whom both writers had known in their youth—farmers in the Rhine valley, whose concern was less with French or German nationalism than with a spirit of mutual tolerance and friendship. When the Franco-Prussian War broke out in 1870 and Prussian soldiers threatened Phalsbourg, Erckmann joined Chatrian in Paris, where their literary successes continued unabated through the early years of the Third Republic. *Le rappel*, *Le siècle*, *Le globe*, and *Le temps*, among other newspapers, published their stories and novels, while their plays were well attended at the Opéra Comique, the Ambigu, and the Théâtre du Châtelet. This profitable relationship lasted until 1887, when a financial and political dispute caused the dissolution of the partnership. Among Erckmann-Chatrian's major works published during the Second Empire are *L'illustre docteur Mathéus* (1859), *Contes de la montagne* (1860), *Contes fantastiques* (1860), *Maître Daniel Rock* (1861), *Le fou Yégof* (1862), *Contes des bords du Rhin* (1862), *Madame Thérèse* (1863), *L'ami Fritz* (1864), *Confidences d'un joueur de clarinette* (1865), *Histoire d'un conscrit de 1813* (1864), *Histoire d'un homme du peuple* (1865), *Waterloo* (1865), *La maison forestière* (1866), *Contes populaires* (1866), *La guerre* (1866), *Le blocus* (1867), *Histoire d'un paysan* (1869), *Le Juif polonais* (1869), and *Histoire d'un sous-maître* (1871).

Bulletin de la Société Erckmann-Chatrian (Nancy, 1914–1932); *Europe*, no. 549–550 (1975); L. Schoumacker, *Erckmann-Chatrian: Etude biographique et critique d'après des documents inédits* (Paris, 1933).

Dorothy E. Speirs

Related entry: PONSON DU TERRAIL.

EUGENIE (1826–1920), empress of the French (1853–1870); Spanish-born wife of Napoleon III. Eugénie Marie de Montijo de Guzman, countess of Teba, was born 5 May 1826 at Granada. She was the daughter of the count of Montijo, a Spanish grandee, and of Maria Manuela Fitzpatrick, of Scottish descent. Noted for her beauty and her leadership in the world of fashion, she lent to the imperial regime glamor and individuality, which had been lacking in the French monarchy after the Bourbon restoration. She took a serious interest in affairs of state, served three times as regent (1859, 1865, and 1870), and drew down on herself much criticism for her influence on imperial policy, especially in foreign affairs.

She first attracted the attention of Louis Napoleon, then prince president of the Second Republic, when she visited Paris in the company of her mother. After unsuccessful attempts to find a bride in one of the royal families of Europe, the prince, by now emperor of the French, married Eugénie on 30 January 1853 in a ceremony at Notre Dame in Paris. On 16 March 1856, she gave birth to their only child, Eugène Louis Jean Joseph, known as the prince imperial.

Although the empress never clearly thought out or articulated her political credo, she tended to be conservative, with an instinctive attachment to legitimate monarchy. She resisted liberalization of the Empire in the 1860s and as regent in 1870 dismissed the cabinet headed by Emile Ollivier. In religion, she was a devout Roman Catholic although never the narrow bigot her enemies made her out to be.

Her serious interest in foreign affairs began late in the 1850s when the emperor decided to ally with Piedmont-Sardinia against Austria. Although at first attracted to the cause of Italian unity, she soon came to see it as a threat to the Hapsburg monarchy and to the temporal power of the pope. By the end of the Italian War, she was strongly opposed to the *Italianissimes* in the French court and was firmly austrophile. In the 1860s she cooperated with Prince Richard von Metternich, Austrian ambassador, in trying to curb the emperor's support of Sardinian-Italian aggrandizement and to effect a rapprochement with Austria. Her influence in foreign affairs reached its zenith in the years 1861 through 1863. She worked successfully for the dismissal of Edouard Thouvenel in 1862, for a French intervention in Mexico to create a throne for an Austrian archduke, and in 1863 for the emperor's proposal to Austria of an alliance to remake the map of Europe. When Austria rejected the French offer the same year, the empress and the other austrophiles in the French court lost much of their ability to influence imperial policy.

In the last years of the Empire, the empress watched the success of Prussian policy under Otto von Bismarck with growing alarm. In 1866, after the Prussian victory over Austria at Sadowa, she advocated, in vain, a French military demonstration on the Rhine and active resistance to the Prussian terms of peace. But by this time, the disasters of French policy in Mexico, for which she bore much responsibility, had discredited her views. In 1870 she was among those who, mistakenly believing in the preparedness of the French army, advised the emperor to declare war on Prussia. Her Spanish connections in Madrid had enabled her to penetrate to some extent Bismarck's role in the Hohenzollern candidacy for the Spanish crown, which she had strongly resented. However, having no entrée into the Ollivier cabinet then in office, she probably had little influence on the decision to go to war.

After the emperor's defeat at Sedan and during the subsequent uprising in Paris, she fled the capital and made her way to England, where she was joined by her husband and son at Camden Place, Chislehurst. She became a close friend of Queen Victoria. After the prince imperial was killed in the Zulu War in 1879, she went to Africa to bring back his body to be buried beside his father in England. During the remainder of her long life, she lived at Farnborough Hill, Hampshire, and in a villa she built at Cap Martin on the Riviera. She traveled extensively, retained her interest in public affairs, and corresponded with, visited, and entertained royalty across Europe. Eugénie died 11 July 1920 at Madrid.

N. N. Barker, *Distaff Diplomacy: The Empress Eugénie and the Foreign Policy of the Second Empire* (Austin and London, 1967); S. Desternes and H. Chandet, *L'Impératrice Eugénie intime* (Paris, 1964); D. Duff, *Eugénie and Napoleon III* (London, 1978); H. Kurtz, *The Empress Eugénie, 1826–1920* (London, 1964); J. Ridley, *Napoleon III and Eugénie* (New York, 1979).

Nancy Nichols Barker

Related entries: BIARRITZ; CHISLEHURST; COMPIEGNE; MERIMEE; PRINCE NAPOLEON; PRINCE IMPERIAL; QUATRE SEPTEMBRE; ROMAN QUESTION; WINTERHALTER; WORTH.

EXPOSITIONS. See INTERNATIONAL EXPOSITIONS.

EXTINCTION DU PAUPERISME, a pamphlet written by Louis Napoleon Bonaparte during his imprisonment at Ham and published in May 1844. Louis Napoleon's purpose was to relate bonapartism to the growing social awareness of the 1840s. In *Extinction du paupérisme,* he criticized France's economic system for improperly distributing the benefits of the community's productive capacity. As a result, he argued, economic injustice spawned needless working-class poverty and threatened society's foundation. Louis Napoleon's solution was to loan government funds to workers' associations to establish agricultural colonies for the urban and rural poor on France's 9 million hectares of uncultivated wastelands. Military-like in organization, the colonies were to provide healthy surroundings, increase the productive wealth of the poor, support higher wages (since workers would not leave their pleasant havens except for adequate pay), and shelter the working class against the threat of unemployment. The plan also emphasized the principle of association, and leaders of the colonies, although answerable to the minister of the interior, were to be chosen by the workers through a complicated series of elections.

Extinction du paupérisme sketched a program typical of the advanced thought of the period with its utopian schemes to foster class harmony. Clearly Louis Napoleon's ideas on poverty were not original. Although their exact source remains unknown, scholars have determined that while imprisoned at Ham, Louis Napoleon immersed himself in the progressive literature of the period, made numerous contacts with the leftist opposition, and even hosted Louis Blanc (1811–1882). Whatever the source of its inspiration, *Extinction*, which enjoyed a large circulation, certainly established Louis Napoleon's reputation as a political figure concerned with the social question. George Sand, to whom he had sent a copy of the pamphlet, replied approvingly, as did Pierre Béranger (1780–1857), and an address signed largely by workingmen thanked the prince for his interest in their behalf. Although republicans and socialists remained suspicious, *Extinction du paupérisme* undoubtedly contributed to Louis Napoleon's election as president of the Second Republic in December 1848. Some scholars have attributed the Second Empire's reputed Saint-Simonianism to the concerns first expressed in the pamphlet. Undoubtedly those concerns were sincere, and, within the context of the first part of the nineteenth century, Louis Napoleon's socialism was genuine. "How could you expect the Empire to function smoothly?" he would later ask: "The Empress is a legitimist; my half-brother, Morny, is an Orleanist; my cousin Jérôme, is a republican, and I am a socialist. Among us, only Persigny is a bonapartist, and he is crazy."

H. N. Boon, *Rêve et réalité dans l'oeuvre de Napoléon III* (The Hague, 1936); M. Emerit, "Les sources des idées sociales et coloniales de Napoléon III," *Revue d'Alger* 3 (1945); A. Dansette, "La formation intellectuelle, morale, et politique de Louis Napoléon Bonaparte," *ASMP* 119 (1960); Louis Napoleon, *Extinction du paupérisme*, in *The Political and Historical Works of Louis Napoleon Bonaparte* (New York, 1972; reprint of an 1852 collection published in London).

Stuart L. Campbell

Related entries: BONAPARTISM; *HISTOIRE DE JULES CESAR*; *DES IDEES NAPOLEONIENNES*; LABOR REFORM; LE PLAY; LOUIS NAPOLEON; SAINT SIMONIANISM.

F

FABRE, HENRI (1823–1915), entomologist and scientific popularizer who made major discoveries in the biology and behavior of insects, particularly in the area of instincts; born 22 September 1823 at Saint-Léons, Aveyron. Although possessed of only a modest income (he taught at various lycées), Fabre was able to publish a series of important scientific memoirs from 1855. His abilities were recognized early. He was awarded the Prix Montyon (for experimental physiology) by the Institut de France in 1856, and Charles Darwin utilized his observations on the instinctual behavior of certain species of wasps in preparing *Origin of Species*, although Fabre himself was not an evolutionist. From 1855 to 1879, Fabre continued to produce a series of important scientific papers and in 1879 would begin publication of the ten-volume *Souvenirs entomologiques* (1879–1907), an influential and popular work. In 1866, he developed a process of extracting alizarin, the active chemical component of the natural (vegetable) red dyestuff madder. For this method, which permitted much quicker and less expensive dyeing than the traditional French procedure, Fabre was named to the Legion of Honor and was received by Napoleon III. Fabre's (and France's) hopes for significant financial gain were soon dashed, however, when a few years later processes for synthesizing alizarin from coal tars were developed by W. H. Perkin in England and by the Badische firm in Germany. The commercial success of synthetic alizarin rendered Fabre's method irrelevant, caused the ruin of the French madder agricultural industry, and signaled the replacement of natural colorants by artificial dyes. In the remaining years of his life, Fabre turned to the writing of textbooks and other works of scientific popularization. He was elected a corresponding member of the Académie des Sciences on 11 July 1887 and died at Sérignan (Vaucluse) 11 October 1915.

H. Cuny, *Jean-Henri Fabre et les problèmes de l'instinct* (Paris, 1967); A. Fabre, *The Life of Jean Henri Fabre, the Entomologist*, trans. B. Miall (New York, 1921); M. Gauthier, "Vie et oeuvre de Jean-Henri Fabre, poète de la flore et de la faune des collines provençales," *Marseille*, no. 114 (1978); J. Rostand, "Jean-Henri Fabre," in *Hommes de vérité*, ser. 2 (Paris, 1948).

Martin Fichman

Related entry: DARWINISM IN FRANCE.

FAIDHERBE, LOUIS (1818–1889), French general in the army engineers, best known for his role as governor of Senegal, 1854–1861 and 1863–1865, and as commanding general of the Army of the North during the Franco-Prussian War; born at Lille, 3 June 1818. Of modest origins, the son of a hosier who had been a sergeant-major in the French army, Faidherbe in 1838 won a half scholarship to the Ecole Polytechnique. Here, although the record he compiled was not impressive, he was able to earn admission to the engineers.

Both to increase his chance of promotion and to earn a higher salary, Faidherbe sought assignments in Algeria and then in the colonies, beginning with Guadeloupe. He served in Algeria from May 1844 to June 1846 and from December 1849 to June 1852. On the latter occasion, he participated in the Kabylie expedition, which provided justification for promoting its commander, General Leroy de Saint-Arnaud, and then naming him to head the Ministry of War. Letters that Faidherbe wrote at the time to his mother indicate both his correct understanding of why the expedition had been undertaken and his very poor opinion of Saint-Arnaud's generalship.

In between Algerian assignments, Faidherbe served in Guadeloupe from March 1848 to August 1849. An unsubstantiated myth later grew up about Faidherbe that he was recalled from Guadeloupe through the efforts of the planters because he had become too enthusiastic in his efforts to organize the newly freed slaves politically in favor of the candidacy of Victor Schoelcher (1804–1893) as deputy from Guadeloupe. The truth is that Faidherbe left Guadeloupe as the result of a routine reduction in staff and would have returned in 1852 had he not instead been able to obtain an assignment to Senegal. All that one can say for sure about his attitude toward slavery is that he only expressed strong views against it in his latest writings, particularly in *Le Sénégal: La France dans l'Afrique Occidentale* (1889), which he dedicated to Victor Schoelcher. As governor of Senegal, he was particularly tolerant of traditional African slavery—as were most other European colonial figures of the time.

When Captain Faidherbe landed at Saint-Louis-du-Sénégal in November 1852 to head the local engineer detachment, he was already prepared intellectually from his prior experience in Algeria and in Guadeloupe for what would follow. He threw himself into his work with gusto; he traveled throughout the French sphere in Senegal and even went with Captain Auguste Baudin (1800–1877), commander of the French West African Squadron, to visit the two *comptoirs* on the Ivory Coast, Assinie and Grand Bassam, and then the one at Gabon, the three at the time attached administratively to Senegal. He quickly took to heart the plan of 1854 to establish French economic dominance along the Senegal River. In 1854, Faidherbe published his first scholarly article, ''Les Berbères et les arabes des bords du Sénégal,'' in *Bulletin de la Société de Géographie de Paris* and played a crucial role in the military expedition that from March to May of that year undertook the rebuilding of the French fort at Podor in Fouta-Toro and defeated a Toucouleur army at Dialmath. The relatively high number of casualties resulting from this action added to the already growing disenchantment with Captain Auguste Protet (1808–1862), governor of Senegal since 1850, and led to Faidherbe's promotion to major and his nomination to the governorship in November 1854 to replace Protet.

In the next four years, Faidherbe would realize the plan of 1854, despite very limited means at his disposal and the strong resistance of his African foes. Indeed, one foe, the Toucouleur state builder El-Hadj Omar Tall, who began campaigning in the upper Senegal in the summer of 1854, had been completely unanticipated by the creators of the plan. By 1859, Faidherbe's forces had expelled Omar and his armies from the Senegal Valley west of Balfoulabé, but at the same time the French authorities had agreed to coexist with the empire Omar built to the east. Adapting the system of lightning raids (*razzias*) as they occurred in Algeria to the exigencies of a river system, Faidherbe used his small fleet of steam gunboats to pacify the Senegal River. By 1858, he had forced the gum producers to agree to trade on French terms, to end the system of customs payments they had required of French traders in the past, and to content themselves with a yearly duty, paid by the French authorities, which was based on the value of trade. From the other riparian polities, Faidherbe obtained the recognition of French sovereignty on the Senegal River and an end to all African-imposed restrictions on French navigation.

Having finished with the Senegal Valley, albeit at a high material and human cost to the native Africans, Faidherbe turned next to the Woloff and Serrer societies, which extended down the coast from Saint-Louis south past Cape Verde to the Gambia River. He attempted to pacify the major Woloff kingdom, Cayor, which lay between Saint-Louis and Cape Verde, without conquering it, thus to link Saint-Louis with Cape Verde by road and by telegraph and to encourage the peasantry to produce groundnuts for sale to French wholesalers without interference by the ruler or his warriors, the *tyeddos*. Since a land route could not be as distinct from the polity through which it passed as a water route and because Cayor as a whole resisted even these minimal encroachments, Faidherbe's attempts at applying a riparian strategy to a land axis failed. Forced to fight numerous campaigns in Cayor and to appoint a puppet ruler who proved ineffective, he was never able to achieve a satisfactory relationship with this polity, which he finally annexed completely to the colony just before he left Senegal for good in 1865. Elsewhere, south of Cayor, Faidherbe's subordinates, particularly fellow *polytechnicien* Pinet-Laprade, commandant of Gorée after 1858, had better luck.

That Faidherbe was far more interested in intimidating the various Senegambian polities within French reach than he was in annexing them to the French-ruled enclaves in the area is attested both by what he said about what he was trying to do and what others, particularly his friends in the business community, said about him while he was actually in Senegal. As with Faidherbe's feelings about slavery, the distinction between what he and others said at the time and what was said later is important because later, after he had left Senegal, Faidherbe became an avid partisan of French expansion into the far interior of West Africa.

Also, the fact that his limited political and economic objectives required far more military operations than the French had ever attempted before in Senegambia gave rise to a myth that he had effected the total conquest of Senegal just as Marshal Bugeaud was said to have effected the total conquest of Algeria. Of course, Faidherbe did introduce many of the administrative structures and much of the terminology of French Algeria into Senegal, but without giving them much substance, a fact that his successor from December 1861 to May 1863, Captain Jean Bernard Jauréguiberry (1815–1887), soon discovered. In May 1863 Jauréguiberry was recalled. His replacement was Faidherbe, himself transferred from command of the subdivision of Sidi-Bel-Abbès in Algeria, and promoted to brigadier general as an added inducement to return to Saint-Louis. Faidherbe restored the status quo by intimidating the most restive of the hinterland polities and by annexing Cayor before making his final departure from Senegal. The situation would once again deteriorate, however.

Faidherbe earned a reputation as a builder and innovator for projects that he undertook within the confines of the small French enclaves. He is credited with having ordered the paving of the principal streets of Saint-Louis, the construction of the two bridges (one short and the other long) that connected Saint-Louis Island to the mainland, the refurbishing of official buildings and the construction of new ones, and much more. He presided over the opening of the government printing press and then sponsored two official periodicals, the *Moniteur du Sénégal* and the *Annuaire du Sénégal*. Faidherbe himself and his talented subordinates published articles of major anthropological, sociological, and historical value in both organs. Despite Faidherbe's reputation as a builder, however, he took little interest in the largest Senegalese development project of the era, the construction of major port facilities at Dakar. The guiding spirits behind this project were, on one hand, Pinet-Laprade in his role as commandant of Gorée, and on the other hand, the French government, for reasons unrelated to the development of Senegal. In 1863 Faidherbe, who retained an emotional, almost irrational attachment to Saint-Louis, wrote that it would always be the largest city in the colony even if, one day, Dakar should become the capital, as Jauréguiberry had suggested. As late as 1889, Faidherbe would still claim that Saint-Louis was a viable seaport, despite the bar at the river's mouth.

On leaving Senegal in May 1865, Faidherbe insisted on taking a long period of sick leave in Algeria, which he devoted not only to recovering his health but to scholarship. In 1867 he was able to prolong his stay in Algeria by having himself named subdivisional commandant of Bône, in which position he periodically served as interim divisional commandant of Constantine Province. During this last period of Faidherbe's Algerian-colonial career, he seems to have been popular with all segments of the population: the *colons*, the native Algerians, and the French military. He won praise for his role as president of the court-martial that in April 1869 took place as a result of the *Affaire de l'Oued-Mahouine*. This affair, like the *Affaire Doineau* of 1856, had had the effect of putting the French military regime in Algeria on trial. Two years later, Claude

François Colas (b. 1829), later a radical deputy from Constantine, attempted to have Faidherbe appointed divisional commandant of Constantine with the argument that by his very presence he would cause the province, then wracked by the Kabylie rebellion, to "return to order." Still Faidherbe's position in Algeria was never as influential as it had been in Senegal, something he resented greatly.

At the start of the Franco-Prussian War, the minister of war ordered Faidherbe to remain in Bône. Later, in November 1870, the Government of National Defense named him commander in chief of the Army of the North with responsibility for the defense of the three northern departments of France. At the head of seventeen thousand poorly trained regulars and several thousand *gardes mobiles*, Faidherbe fought several successful battles, or rather holding actions, against Prussian troops, which together contributed to salvaging some glory for France in an otherwise disastrous war. Although Faidherbe never actually retired from the army, he would hold no more active commands. His health was shattered; by 1875, rheumatism had confined him to a wheelchair. But he remained active both in public affairs and in scholarship, serving briefly in the National Assembly as deputy from Lille and after 1879 in the Senate. In 1880 Freycinet would appoint him grand chancellor of the Legion of Honor.

Faidherbe's scholarly writings were eclectic, touching on African history, linguistics, and anthropology. His longest work, *Le Sénégal: La France dans l'Afrique Occidentale*, was both a skilled apologia for his role as governor of Senegal and good public relations in favor of the French conquest of the western Sudan, which had got underway after 1879. Indeed, as a senator Faidherbe would give this effort his blessing. The young proconsuls who brought about the conquest of French West Africa and who kept in touch with Faidherbe until his death would give rise, with Faidherbe's tacit consent, to the myth that he had been the founder of French West Africa while serving as governor of Senegal during the Second Empire. Faidherbe died at Paris, 28 September 1889, and was given a hero's funeral.

L. C. Barrows, "Louis Léon César Faidherbe," in L. H. Gann and P. Duignan, eds., *African Proconsuls: European Governors in Africa* (New York, 1979); A. Demaison, *Faidherbe* (Paris, 1932).

Leland G. Barrows

Related entries: ALGERIA; SENEGAL.

FALLOUX LAW, education law of 15 March 1850 named for Frédéric, comte de Falloux (1811–1886), a liberal Catholic, who became minister of education on 20 December 1848 and who appointed the extraparliamentary commission that drafted the law. The law is noteworthy for having given the church more influence in schooling, according it a role in secondary education like that the Guizot law had entrusted to it in primary instruction, allotting the clergy a larger place on educational councils at the expense of lay teachers and encouraging growth among private elementary schools. Although the Falloux law was important, it was not a sudden turning point. It followed a long Catholic campaign, generaled by Charles de Montalembert, for "liberty of education," a principle promised by the Carnot project and incorporated in the republican constitution (1848). Fears issuing from the Revolution of 1848 ensured reduced autonomy for the University, and Louis Napoleon seems to have promised liberty of education in return for Catholic support in the presidential elections of December 1848.

The Falloux commission, an extraparliamentary one because leftists controlled the chambers in 1848–1849, included Montalembert and Mgr. Félix Dupanloup from the Catholic camp but also Adolphe Thiers, Victor Cousin (1792–1867), Saint-Marc Girardin (1801–1873), and the director of the Ecole Normale, Paul François Dubois (1793–1874)—six representatives of the church (but only one cleric), nine from the University, and nine supposed neutrals, who actually tended to favor some form of liberty of education. Hardly anyone demanded monopoly either for the church or the state. It was a commission of moderates, for Falloux had deliberately excluded vocal anti-clericals and Catholic extremists like Louis Veuillot and his episcopal allies. Surviving verbatim records of the commission's debates reveal that although the law became renowned for its provisions concerning secondary schools, the dangers of elementary instruction preoccupied commission members. Therein has lain much of the historical controversy. The historiography has wrongly found in conservative arguments for restricting mass primary education the reasons for the adoption of liberty of education at the secondary level. The two issues were distinct. Thiers, so concerned about socialist tendencies among lay primary school teachers that he offered a monopoly of primary schooling to the church only to find that Montalembert, Dupanloup, and the Christian Brothers wanted no part of it, insisted on state supervision of secondary schools and was abashed that the final bill did not exclude the Jesuits from teaching.

Despite concern about elementary schools, the law made adjustments, not transformations, in the system. Both teachers and their training schools (écoles normales) suffered more regulation; enseignement primaire supérieure disappeared—a backward step that explains in part the popularity of special secondary programs during the Second Empire—but the curriculum was expanded, a girls' school was required of communes of eight hundred or more (exemption for poor communes meant enforcement would be lax, however), and teachers enjoyed a guaranteed if modest minimum wage. In the area of secondary education, the celebrated article 17 permitted anyone who was twenty-five years of age or older and had a baccalauréat or five years of teaching in a recognized secondary school to establish a secondary school. The law further permitted any town to transfer its public collège to the clergy; so many did that the number of collèges communaux declined by 25 percent in the next decade, when other secondary schools were enjoying substantial growth. The silences of the law were important too; it did not forbid schools run by the unauthorized religious congregations, the most notable of which was the Society of Jesus. Administratively, the law reduced the power of the *universitaires*. The new highest council for education consisted of seven clergymen (four Catholic), three representatives from private education, nine government officials, and eight lay teachers. The new legislation also granted government officials the right to inspect all schools and the state alone the right to grant the *baccalauréat*. Church and state each won rights from the teaching establishment.

As a result of the Falloux law, enrollment in Catholic secondary schools multiplied. By 1854 21,195 students attended ecclesiastical schools (about 20,000 in Catholic ones); by 1867 the number was 36,924 and another 20,000 to 25,000 were enrolled in minor seminaries, most without any intention of following a priestly vocation. Private lay schools, taking advantage of the law, prospered too; their enrollment in 1854 was, in fact, twice that of Catholic schools, but such schools usually offered only a few years of secondary studies and, unable to compete against the twin powers of the church and state, they atrophied. Catholic schools, however, enjoyed a sustained growth rate of 75 percent versus 34 percent for the whole secondary system between 1854 and 1867. For a time church and state responded to social demand for more education with more schools. By the end of the Second Empire and the early years of the Third Republic, however, cooperation gave way to conflict as they competed for the same social groups. Anti-clericalism and worries about competition from Catholic schools would lead to the abrogation of most of the libertarian provisions of the Falloux law between 1880 and 1886. Granted a foothold, however, Catholic secondary education survived anti-clerical legislation during the Third Republic and remains an important part of French secondary studies today. In primary education, the church did substantially increase its share of elementary schooling (from 21 to 34 percent by 1863), but total enrollment grew by 1 million students between 1850 and 1863. Girls' schooling particularly expanded during those years. The law had little effect on growth, nor did it direct students to the church. But the church took advantage of the law's provisions to expand its role and probably was better equipped to respond to social demand for schooling then than was the state with its much smaller army of teachers.

The Falloux law was certainly not a victory for reactionaries; Louis Veuillot, *L'Univers* and Abbé Joseph Gaume vigorously opposed it. A compromise, it permitted the church to operate schools while the state supervised them. The church conceded the state's right to supervise education; the state conceded the church's institutional right to conduct schools. The Falloux law represented the center of French politics, a center too often missed in historians' captivation by the disputes of Catholic and anti-clerical extremists. The growth of Catholic schooling during the Second Empire reflected the law's response to the age.

G. Chessenau, *La Commission extraparlementaire de 1849: Texte intégral inédit des procès-verbaux* (Paris, 1937); H. Michel, *La Loi Falloux* (Paris, 1926); J. Huckaby, "Roman Catholic Reaction to the Falloux Law," *FHS* 4 (Fall 1965); P. Harrigan, "The Social and Political Implications of Catholic Secondary Education during the Second

Empire," *Societas* 5 (Winter 1976); A. May, "The Falloux Law, the Catholic Press, and the Bishops: Crisis of Authority in the French Church," *FHS* 8 (Spring 1973).

Patrick J. Harrigan

Related entries: DUPANLOUP; DURUY; FORTOUL; GAUME; LOUIS NA-POLEON; MONTALEMBERT; ROULAND; THIERS; VEUILLOT.

FANTIN-LATOUR, HENRI (1836–1904), portrait and still-life painter and lithographer, born at Grenoble, 14 January 1836, to a Russian mother and French father who was also a portrait painter. Fantin grew up in Paris after his family moved there in 1841. He was taught drawing at an early age by his father, and he began to do copies in the Louvre in 1853. He could not gain full entry to the Ecole des Beaux-Arts but continued to learn from the old masters in the Louvre during the 1850s, making copies also to earn a living. It was in the Louvre that he met Berthe Morisot (1841–1895) and James McNeil Whistler (1834–1903). In 1861 Fantin visited England, where his work was admired. On returning to Paris he studied with Gustave Courbet in his school of realism. He joined the newly formed Société des Aquafortistes in 1862, and it was in printmaking that he allowed himself to experiment. A portrait of Fantin's sister was accepted for the Salon of 1863, another painting was exhibited in the Salon des Refusés of 1863, and he began work on *Homage à Delacroix* (1864, Louvre, Paris) inspired by Eugène Delacroix's death. This group portrait (a genre often repeated by Fantin), which includes among others Edouard Manet, Whistler, Alphonse Legros (1837–1911), Charles Baudelaire, and J. Champfleury, as well as Fantin arranged around a portrait of Delacroix, was shown in the 1864 Salon. In this horizontal composition, recalling seventeenth-century Dutch group portraits, each figure is presented with Fantin's careful observations accurately rendered. Restraint of form and color almost to the point of austerity is characteristic of most of Fantin's group portraits. The *Homage* was to be one of a series of five paintings whose purpose was to proclaim the new spirit of art, music, and literature. A devotee of the music of Richard Wagner, Fantin painted *Tannhäuser on the Venusberg* (1864, Los Angeles County Musuem) as a tribute to Wagner. The work was also accepted in the Salon of 1864. It is full of poetic charm and grace that recalls the rococo, but the artist has combined with it his knowledge of the Venetian masters.

The still lifes and flower pieces to which Fantin devoted much time from this point on were well received by the public, especially in England, and provided him with a modest income. Recalling the influence of Courbet, these paintings such as *Fruit and Flowers* (1865, Museum of Fine Arts, Boston) are more vibrant in brushwork, color, and texture than are Fantin's portraits or mythological scenes. Fantin joined the Batignolle group at the Café Guerbois, meeting Manet whose portrait (Art Institute of Chicago) he painted in 1867. The group portrait *L'atelier des Batignolles* (1870, Louvre) shows Manet seated at an easel surrounded by admirers, including Claude Monet, Pierre Auguste Renoir, and Emile Zola. While it brings to mind Courbet's *Atelier* painted fifteen years earlier, it lacks the complexity of subject matter and the skillful treatment. It does not sustain the interest as does Courbet's more ambitious work and seems to be concerned more with illustration and documentation than making a statement about the reality of life. Although associated with those artists who would later become known as Impressionists, Fantin refused to show his work in the first Impressionist exhibit in 1874, as was the case also with Manet. He did not agree with the Impressionist process of painting *alla prima* or the manner of creation *en plein air*. His devotion to the old masters left little room for innovation or experimentation in painting but found its release in his graphic work. A rather modest man, he spent his later years as somewhat of a recluse, painting in much the same manner as in his early years. He died at Buré (Orne), 25 August 1904.

C. Chetham, *Henri Fantin-Latour* (Northampton, Mass., 1966); D. Druick and M. Hoog, *Fantin-Latour: A Retrospective* (Ottawa, 1983); E. Lucie-Smith, *Henri Fantin-Latour* (New York, 1977); M. Verrier, *Fantin-Latour* (Paris, 1978).

Beverley Giblon

Related entries: COURBET; MANET; *TANNHAUSER* PREMIERE.

FASHIONS. See CRINOLINE.

FAVRE, JULES (1809–1880), lawyer and republican politician, leading spokesman of the irreconcilable opposition to Napoleon III; born at Lyons, 21 March 1809, of a bourgeois family. Favre studied law at Paris, where he briefly flirted with utopian socialism. He became a republican when he defended several of the leaders of the 1834 Lyons uprising in a highly publicized trial. During the Second Republic, Favre briefly held minor posts in the ministries of the interior and foreign affairs. As a deputy in the assemblies, he defended the Republic against the wave of reaction that intensified from 1850. Already an opponent of Louis Napoleon, especially regarding the Roman expedition of 1849, whose purpose he accused the government of betraying, Favre attempted, with Victor Hugo, to organize resistance to the coup d'état of December 1851 and was forced briefly into hiding but was not arrested, perhaps because of the intercession of his friend Adolphe Billault. Contentious by nature, Favre would quarrel as much during the following years with his republican colleagues as with the monarchists and bonapartists whom he opposed politically.

During the early years of the Empire, when normal channels of dissent were closed, Favre made effective use of the courts to criticize the regime, assailing in particular its heavy-handed prosecution of political opponents, the corruption of military government in Algeria (as a deputy Favre would persistently advocate a civil administration for Algeria), and the manipulation of elections. He became, with Antoine Berryer, perhaps the most esteemed member of the Paris bar. As defender of Felice Orsini in February 1858, Favre made no attempt to save his client but focused instead on the frustrated nationalism that had led to the unsuccessful attempt on Napoleon III's life. This highly publicized plea helped the emperor (who lent Favre tacit support by allowing him to read at the trial a letter of Orsini's) to prepare the ground for his 1859 alliance with Sardinia against Austria.

The Orsini trial pushed Favre into political prominence and led to his election to the Corps Législatif in a Paris by-election of April 1858. Taking the required oath, he joined Emile Ollivier and three other republicans in the group known as *les Cinq*. A masterly orator, excelled only by Berryer and rivaled only by Ollivier and Adolphe Thiers, Favre found little opportunity for effective opposition until the gradual liberalization of the Empire after 1860. Even as he drifted apart from Ollivier, however, he reconciled his differences with the republicans of 1848 and was one of seventeen republicans elected to the Corps Législatif in 1863 and the leader of that group. (Returned from both Paris and Lyons, Favre chose the latter, allowing fellow republican Louis Antoine Garnier-Pagès [1803–1878] to claim the Paris seat.)

Favre's forte as a deputy was foreign affairs. He condemned French military support of the Papal States (and occupation of Rome) and especially criticized French intervention in Mexico. On the other hand, he sympathized with Napoleon III's attempt to drive Austria out of Italy. Favre's position on German affairs was somewhat erratic. He first warned of Prussian militarism but later defended German nationalism and opposed increased French armaments, arguing that if France gave the example of disarmament, liberalism would triumph in Germany. In domestic affairs, Favre spoke eloquently for more secure civil liberties, freedom of the press, judicial and legal reform, and administrative decentralization. With Thiers he was probably the orator most listened to in the chamber. Throughout 1864 Favre defended the *Treize* (accused of illegal association during the elections of 1863) and quarreled with Ollivier as the latter moved toward reconciliation with the Empire. The two men broke over the coalitions law of 1864, but the real issues were Favre's implacable opposition to the imperial regime and Ollivier's willingness to accept the emperor's policy of gradual liberalization. Favre worked closely with Thiers and liberal monarchists who, on occasion, formed a loose coalition with the moderate republicans called the Union Libérale. Favre's key position was signaled by his election to the Académie Française in May 1867 in place of Victor Cousin. Younger, more radical republicans found their older colleague's moderation distasteful. His alliance with the Orleanists, his profession of spiritual faith at the time of his reception at the Académie (April 1868), his bourgeois suspicion of the workers, and, perhaps, his personal (although not political) sympathy for Napoleon III, whom he saw for the last time in 1868, aroused hostility on the extreme Left. In the elections of 1869, the radicals nearly unseated Favre, although he contested fifteen constituencies. At Paris he defeated the demagogic journalist Henri Rochefort only on the second ballot.

In the closing years of the Second Empire, increasing liberalization made no difference to Favre's implacable opposition. With Ernest Picard, Jacques Louis Hénon (1802–1872), and Jules Ferry (1832–1893) he founded (1868) an opposition newspaper, *L'électeur libre*. He proposed a law that would have granted constituent power to the Corps Législatif, and he was one of Eugène Rouher's most indefatigable opponents. This intransigence helped to restore some of Favre's credibility with the younger republicans, who had even suspected the government of favoring his candidacy over that of Rochefort. On the other hand, in November 1869 Favre led in the repudiation by the moderate republican deputies of the *mandat impératif* by which the radicals had pledged to carry out the wishes of their constituents.

Favre joined Thiers in trying to prevent a declaration of war against Prussia in July 1870, and it was he who, in the last meeting of the Corps Législatif, on 4 September, moved the "déchéance de Louis Napoléon Bonaparte et de sa famille" and who, with Léon Gambetta, led the crowds to the Hôtel de Ville and, in order to avert a "Red Republic," proclaimed a provisional government of which he became vice-president and minister of foreign affairs. Favre was inept in negotiating an armistice with Otto von Bismarck several months later, resigning as foreign minister in February 1871. He would serve as deputy and later senator under the Third Republic. Favre died at Versailles, 28 January 1880.

J. S. Cleland, "Jules Favre and the Republican Opposition to Napoleon III" (Ph.D. diss., University of South Carolina, 1974); Mme. Vve. Jules Favre, née Velten, ed., *Discours parlementaires, 1848–1879*, 4 vols. (Paris, 1881), *Plaidoyers politiques et judiciaires*, 2 vols. (Paris, 1882), and *Plaidoyers et discours du bâtonnat*, 2 vols. (Paris, 1893); Paul Maritain, ed., *Mélanges politiques, judiciares et littéraires* (Paris, 1882); H. Moulin, *Jules Favre et son fauteuil académique* (Paris, 1881); M. Reclus, *Jules Favre, 1809–1880: Essai biographique, historique, et moral* (Paris, 1912).

Joel S. Cleland

Related entries: ARMY REFORM; *LES CINQ*; GAMBETTA; LIBERAL EMPIRE; OLLIVIER; ORSINI; QUATRE SEPTEMBRE; REPUBLICANISM; ROUHER; THIERS.

FETE NATIONALE, the national holiday of France during the Second Empire. Not 14 July, with its associations of revolution and republicanism, but 15 August, the birthday of Napoleon I (*la fête de l'Empereur* or *fête napoléonienne*), was the national French holiday from 17 February 1852 through 1870. The *Marseillaise* was prohibited until the last weeks of the Empire, its place taken by *Partant pour la Syrie*, the unofficial anthem of the day, a tune written (or inspired) by Hortense de Beauharnais, mother of Louis Napoleon. The occasion, marked by charitable donations, solemn masses, and the issuing of an honors list, was celebrated with great pomp, particularly at Paris, where there were decorations, illuminations, entertainments in the public squares, galas at the opera, fireworks, and military reviews. The *fête de l'Empereur* was first celebrated 15 August 1852 in the midst of a violent storm. That day flags were distributed to the reorganized National Guard, and a number of those proscribed following the coup d'état were amnestied, notably Adolphe Thiers. On 15 August 1853 there was, for the first time, a free matinee at the Théâtre Français (*Phèdre* and *Le* *médecin malgré lui*). On 15 August 1855 the money normally devoted to the fête was used to aid families of soldiers dead in the Crimean War. On 15 August 1857 the new Louvre was inaugurated with great ceremony. On 15 August 1859 the march through Paris of the victorious Army of Italy was accompanied by a general amnesty and cancellation of *avertissements* in effect against newspapers. On 15 August 1867 the facade of the new Opéra was unveiled. Two years later, on 15 August 1869, special pomp marked the celebration on the occasion of the centenary of the birth of Napoleon I: political offenders were amnestied, pensions were granted or increased to survivors of the Grand Army, and the troops were reviewed by the prince imperial, the emperor being ill. The final fête nationale of the Empire was darkened by accumulating defeats in the war with Prussia.

R. Boutard, "La célébration de la fête de l'Empereur sous le Second Empire," *Mémoires de la Société des Sciences Naturelles et Archéologiques de la Creuse* 31 (1953); E. Drumont, *Les fêtes nationales à Paris* (Paris, 1878); R. Sanson, *Les 14 juillet: 1789– 1975: Fête et conscience nationale* (Paris, 1976).

Related entries: AMNESTY; BONAPARTISM; SECOND EMPIRE.

FEUILLET, OCTAVE (1821–1890), novelist and dramatist, one of the most successful writers of the Second Empire; born 11 August 1821 at Saint-Lô (Normandy). Abandoning his legal studies, much to his father's displeasure, Feuillet began his literary career in the 1840s. With Paul Bocage (1822–1884), he collaborated on a novel parodying the style in vogue and a children's story, both of which were published in *Le national*, and on three plays for the Théâtre de l'Odéon and the Comédie Française. Attracted by his worldly manners, modesty, and gentleness, François Buloz (1803–1877) solicited his collaboration for the *Revue des deux mondes* in 1848. Here he published novelettes and several plays, some of which were not staged until much later: *La crise*, *Le pour et le contre*, *La fée*. In 1850 his first collection of stories, *Bellah*, appeared in the *Revue* and six years later three short stories, *La petite comtesse*, *Le parc*, and *Onesta*. In 1850 a reconciliation with his father brought Feuillet back to his birthplace, where he remained for some time, eventually settling his family in Palliers near Saint-Lô.

Two plays in the style of Marivaux, *Péril en la demeure* and *Dalila*, which premiered 19 April 1855 and 29 May 1857, respectively, established Feuillet's reputation as a playwright. His first novel, *Le roman d'un jeune homme* (1858), was an instant success, selling forty thousand copies in the first year of publication. The dramatized version of the novel, which premiered at the Théâtre du Vaudeville the same year, fared equally as well, its popularity being ascribed in part to a digestible mixture of familiar elegance and gentle didacticism, in part to its exaltation of *les bons sentiments*.

Feuillet was a welcome guest at court, the Tuileries, Compiègne, and Fontainebleau, where the Feuillet family often staged salon comedies for the empress and her circle of intimates. He also frequented the receptions of Auguste de Morny and the salon of Princess Mathilde. In 1862 he was elected to the Académie Française where he occupied the chair of Eugène Scribe. Empress Eugénie attended his reception. Six years later the emperor appointed him librarian of the chateau at Fontainebleau. Feuillet was particularly valued, perhaps, because he was one of the relatively few intellectuals friendly to the regime. At the outbreak of the Franco-Prussian War, Feuillet settled his family in Jersey and then joined the National Guard in his home town of Saint-Lô. After the overthrow of the Empire on 4 September, he resigned his post as librarian. Among other comedies of Feuillet that premiered during the Second Empire are: *Le pour et le contre* (Gymnase, 1853), *La Crise* (Gymnase, 1854), *La fée* (Vaudeville, 1856), *Le village* (Théâtre Français, 1856), *Le cheveu blanc* (Gymnase, 1860), *Montjoye* (Gymnase, 1863), and *Le cas de conscience* (Théâtre Français, 1867). Esteemed even more as a novelist, Feuillet strengthened the tradition of the *roman mondain*. During the Second Empire he published, in addition to *Le roman d'un jeune homme*, *L'histoire de Sibylle* (1863) and *Monsieur de Camors* (1867). Feuillet died at Paris, 28 December 1890.

L. Deriès, *Un historien et une histoire du grand monde, Octave Feuillet* (Saint-Lô, 1901); Madame O. Feuillet, *Quelques années de ma vie* (Paris, 1894), and *Souvenirs et correspondances* (Paris, 1896).

Dolorès A. Signori

Related entries: COMPIEGNE; PRINCESS MATHILDE; THEATER.

FEYDEAU, ERNEST (1821–1873), novelist and dramatist, one of the most widely read authors of the day; born at Paris, 16 March 1821. Employed by the stock exchange as a broker, Feydeau pursued his interest in ancient civilizations privately. The fruits of his studies took the form of articles on Egyptian archaeology in *Le moniteur*, *La presse*, and *L'artiste* and a two-volume work, *Histoire des usages funèbres et des sépultures des peuples anciens* (1856–1858). In 1858, capitalizing on the greater freedom that writers had won since the publication of Gustave Flaubert's *Madame Bovary*, Feydeau published his first novel, *Fanny*. A sensational best-seller, hailed as a triumph of realism, it went through over thirty editions and launched Feydeau's literary career. Over the next ten years, he published several novels, four of which were first serialized in newspapers and *revues* of the day: *Daniel* (4 vols., 1859), *Catherine d'Overmeire* (2 vols., 1860), *La Comtesse de Châlis* (1867), and *Les aventures du Baron de Féreste* (1868). Although he was accused of corrupting public taste and morals, Feydeau's novels were extremely popular with contemporary readers. In *Sylvie* (1859), a *roman à clef*, the heroine was inspired by Mme. Apollonie Sabatier, *"présidente"* of a famous Bohemian salon, and the hero by Charles Baudelaire, whom Feydeau heartily disliked.

In 1865 Feydeau presented two comedies at the Théâtre du Vaudeville: *Monsieur de Saint-Bertrand* and *Louise Reynolds*. The same year he founded a daily newspaper *L'époque*, which was short-lived, ceasing publication within a year. From 15 January 1869 to 15 February 1870, he was director of *Revue internationale de l'art et de la curiosité*. Among other novels of Feydeau published during the Second Empire are: *Un début à l'Opéra* (1863, a saga in three parts); *Monsieur de Saint-Bertrand*; *Le mari de la danseuse* (1862–1863); *Le secret du bonheur* (2 vols., 1864); *Les amours tragiques*; and *Le roman d'une jeune mariée* (1868). He was also the author of travel books: *Alger* (1862) and *L'Allemagne en 1871* (1871). His son, Georges (1862–1921), was a talented writer of the Third Republic whose comedies and vaudevilles, successful abroad as well as in France, are still revived today. Feydeau died at Paris, 29 October 1873.

E. Feydeau, *Mémoires d'un coulissier* (Paris, 1873).

Dolorès A. Signori

Related entry: THEATER.

LE FIGARO, the newspaper of Hippolyte de Villemessant that began, for France, what its established rivals, the great political journals, scornfully dubbed the *petite presse*. Founded, directed, and edited by Villemessant, a flamboyant but capable journalist and businessman, *Le Figaro* first appeared 2 April 1854 as a weekly literary review, with special emphasis on the theater (on 28 December 1856, Villemessant began to publish a daily theater review with a bulletin on activities at the Bourse, *Figaro-Programme*). In 1856 *Le Figaro* became a biweekly and in November 1866 a daily literary journal. In May 1867 it was transformed into a political newspaper, specializing in satire and clever irony. Literary or political, Villemessant's paper was constantly involved in lawsuits and its editors in duels (twelve in fewer than ten years). Villemessant had weak political commitments. For a time he claimed to be Orleanist; then, always the opportunist, he seemed to favor the imperial cause. Most felt that his sympathies were legitimist. Because of his seemingly wavering political opinions, he remained a source of controversy.

But *Le Figaro* prospered. Its circulation of 1,500 in 1855 and 3,000 in 1860–1861 had become 55,000 by the end of 1866, declined to 39,400 in March 1869, and once again reached 56,000 in February 1870. Among the many journalists who contributed to or collaborated with *Le Figaro* were Nestor Roqueplan (1804–1870), Louis Enault (1824–1900), Emile Blavet (1838–1924), Léo Lespès (1815–1875), Paschal Grousset (1845–1909, scientific editor), Henri de Pène (1830–1888; signed his articles "Nemo"), Auguste Villemot (1811–1870; briefly chief editor when Villemessant gave up management of the paper for several months following Henri de Pène's notorious duel with two military officers), Louis Ulbach (1822–1889; contributed as "Ferragus"), Amédée de Césèna (1810–1889; one of the anonymous editors in 1869), Jules Claretie (1840–1913; signed his articles "Candide"), Jean Jouvin (1810–1886; Villemessant's son-in-law; wrote the musical criticism as "Benedict"), and Charles Monselet (1825–1888). Villemessant had the ability to exploit the talents of a succession of writers, many of whom he would later attack. Even more important was his knack of discovering new talent. Writers who worked for *Le Figaro* soon gained recognition and wealth. Among noted writers who contributed to the newspaper were Jules Barbey d'Aurevilly, Henri Murger (1822–1861), Léon Gozlan (1803–1866),

Aurélien Scholl (1833–1902; titled his column "Les coulisses"), Théodore de Banville (1823–1891), Emile Zola, Edmond Duranty, and Edmond About.

Whatever his own political persuasions, Villemessant was remarkably broad-minded. Jules Vallès (1832–1885), the anarchist, made his name at *Le Figaro*, initially as a writer on the Bourse. Henri Rochefort wrote for both the weekly and the daily *Le Figaro*, was paid the huge salary of 30,000 francs, and when his vitriol brought government wrath to bear on the paper (its sale was banned on the public way), Villemessant helped him to establish the notorious *La lanterne*, which Rochefort hoped to make "a republican *Figaro*." And after the suppression of Louis Veuillot's clerical newspaper *L'Univers*, Villemessant would have been willing to give the noted conservative Catholic a voice in the columns of his newspaper.

Le Figaro sometimes judged hastily and harshly. A criticism of Charles Baudelaire's *Les fleurs du mal* (5 July 1857) initiated the prosecution of that work for offenses to morality. But it was in the pages of *Le Figaro* that Baudelaire at the end of 1863 revealed the genius of the painter Constantin Guys and defended "modern art." In a word, Villemessant's paper was more than froth generated by a frivolous era. It emphasized original wit and created an aura of Parisian style by combining gossip, fashion, news, theater criticism, and society affairs. Moreover, it created a new press genre, one that invented the literary, dramatic, and gossip *chronicles*, that sought to attract readers through sensation, novelty, and anecdote, and that soon added to its ranks, in frank imitation of *Le Figaro*, such journals as *Le monde illustré* (1857) and *La vie parisienne* (1863).

J. de Lacretelle, *Face à l'événement: "Le Figaro," 1826–1866* (Paris, 1966).

Natalie Isser

Related entries: MARINONI; PRESS REGIME; VILLEMESSANT.

FINANCES. See GOVERNMENT FINANCES.

FINANCIAL REFORM. See FOULD.

FIRST INTERNATIONAL (1864–1872), a working-class organization seeking the emancipation of labor. Organized in September 1864 by British and French working-class leaders, the International Working Men's Association, better known later as the First International, was the first attempt to organize labor on local, national, and international levels simultaneously. Its creation came about from the contacts established by workers attending the London International Exposition of 1862, though the concept of an international association of workingmen had surfaced on a number of occasions in the preceding twenty years. The International was coordinated by an administrative committee, the General Council, based in London, and its ideological orientation was hammered out in annual conferences and congresses, usually held in September (London, 1865; Geneva, 1866; Lausanne, 1867; Brussels, 1868; Basel, 1869; London, 1871; The Hague,

1872). The essential strength of the International, however, lay with its branches in each European country. A branch was established at Paris in January 1865, just four months after the International was created, and within three years there were several dozen in the provinces located in cities such as Lyons, Marseilles, Bordeaux, Rouen, and Vienne. At Paris the first headquarters was situated at no. 44, rue des Gravilliers. Prominent in the establishment of the International in France were Henri Tolain, Ernest Fribourg, and Charles Limousin (1840–1909). Moderate republicans like Henri Martin (1810–1883), Ferdinand Buisson (1841–1932), and Jules Simon (1814–1896) belonged, but the organization in France showed a prejudice against those who were not manual workers (by the end of 1866 it had perhaps twelve thousand members).

Initially the International had no ideological cast, being scarcely more than a forum for the exchange of views. But the French delegates at the Geneva congress sought to commit the International to the emancipation of labor through Pierre Joseph Proudhon's mutualism, a cooperative association of artisan producers where individuals made reciprocal promises but were not bound by any organizational rules. Although the congress went on record as favoring producers' cooperatives, it did not adopt the limitations sought by the French. Throughout its existence, the International stood by the cooperative as the agency for obliterating capitalist production. Within France the branches worked tirelessly to create or assist cooperatives, and when labor unions appeared at the end of the 1860s they received their whole-hearted support, for they were seen as elements that could evolve naturally into producers' cooperatives. The French branch, which wanted to reform the existing order, not destroy it, was even hostile to strikes at first. Cooperation and mutualism were goals of which the imperial government could approve, and initially the International was tolerated in France and even encouraged. At the same time, the International endorsed collectivization of agricultural property, which most of the French members accepted because they saw it as extending the cooperative idea to agriculture. Moreover, the organization grew increasingly activist after 1866. In February 1867 it supported a successful strike of bronze workers. In October and November 1867 it organized political demonstrations in Paris, and on the last day of that year the government undertook prosecution of its leaders.

The International was three times suppressed in France: in March 1868, June 1868, and June–July 1870. Following the first repressions, many of the Proudhonists quit the organization and left it in the hands of a younger generation of activists: Benoît Malon (1841–1893) and Eugène Varlin in Paris, Albert Richard (1846–1918) in Lyons, André Bastelica (1845–1884) in Marseilles, and Emile Aubry (1829–1900) in Rouen. The strikes of 1868–1870 brought many recruits to the International in France, but by 1870 it probably had no more than 20,000 to 40,000 members, despite the government's estimate of up to 250,000. The arrests and trials of 1870 effectively destroyed the organization of the French branch. When war between France and Prussia threatened in 1870 and even after it broke out, French leaders of the International made frequent declarations of solidarity with workingmen in Germany and condemned the war as a dynastic struggle. Once the Third Republic had been proclaimed and Prussia sought to annex French territory, the testimonials of solidarity ceased, and the leaders rallied to national defense. Taking advantage of the turmoil within France and relying on the support he had cultivated within the International's Lyons branch, the Russian anarchist Mikhail Bakunin (1814–1876) came to Lyons and carried out an ill-starred attempt to overthrow the state through a seizure of the city hall that lasted scarcely one day. In the provinces the International was effectively dead, however, although in Paris activity would continue through May 1871. The years 1870–1871 saw the creation of approximately sixty-five branches in Paris and the adherence of some seventy-five trade unions to the International, but this apparent growth was largely ephemeral. Immediate political and military questions occupied the members, and in a real test of strength, the National Assembly election of 8 February 1871, only five (only two of whom were workers) of the forty-three candidates proposed by the International were elected. In private it was admitted that the International in Paris was in disarray. A thorough reorganization was underway, but when the Paris Commune was created, it again absorbed all the energies of the International's leadership, and the suppression of the Commune in May effectively ended the last arena of the International's existence in France.

J. Archer, "The Cooperative Ideal in the Socialist Thought of the First International in France," *PWSFH* (1979); J. Braunthal, *History of the International, 1864–1914* (New York, 1967); J. Freymond, *La Première Internationale*, 2 vols. (Geneva, 1962); J. Guillaume, *L'Internationale: Documents et souvenirs, 1864–1878*, 4 vols. (Paris, 1905–1910); U. Marzocchi, "La Première Internationale et son développement," *Rue*, no. 23 (1977); M. Moissonnier, *La Première Internationale et la Commune à Lyon, 1865–1871* (Paris, 1972); *Mouvement social* (April–June 1965).

Julian Archer

Related entries: INTERNATIONAL EXPOSITIONS; LABOR REFORM; PROUDHON; REPUBLICANISM; TOLAIN; VARLIN.

THE FIVE. See *LES CINQ*.

FLAUBERT, GUSTAVE (1821–1880), one of the most prominent novelists of the Second Empire; born 13 January 1821 at Rouen, son of a surgeon. In the mid-1840s Flaubert established himself with his widowed mother in the family estate at Croisset, having abandoned his unsuccessful legal studies in favor of a literary career. From the period immediately following the Revolution of 1848 dates his preliminary work on *La tentation de Saint-Antoine*, Inspired by a Breughel painting, *The Temptation of Saint-Antony*, which he had seen in Genoa in 1845 and conceived as a fresco about man's folly, the work was not published until after the collapse of the Second Empire.

Poor health prompted Flaubert to undertake an extensive voyage to the Near East with his friend Maxime Du Camp. Resettled in Croisset in 1851, Flaubert, whose dedication to his art imposed on him a hermit-like existence, began work on *Madame Bovary*, referring to his labor on the novel as a "terrible *pensum*." Four years passed before he submitted the completed manuscript for publication in serial form to Du Camp (1822–1894), then an editor of the *Revue de Paris*, an opposition newspaper with a reputation for a socialist viewpoint. The serialization of the novel in six installments beginning in October 1856 provoked a court case against Flaubert. The charge of outraging public and religious morality was regarded by both the author and the editor of the *Revue* as a politically motivated attack against the *Revue* for its liberal tendencies. Flaubert was reprimanded "for the unbridled, unrestrained fashion in which the passions [were] depicted" but not censored. The case if anything stimulated interest in the novel; an edition of fifteen thousand copies appeared later in 1857. A study of the human capacity for self-illusion—today referred to as *bovarysme*—*Madame Bovary* became a classic among the realist novels of the nineteenth century.

In 1862 the publisher Michel Lévy agreed to print Flaubert's second novel, *Salammbô*. Based on an episode drawn from the history of Carthage, revealing the romantic side of Flaubert's talent, the novel is remarkable as a great poetic work that aspired to epic grandeur. Its appearance provoked mixed reactions among contemporary writers and critics. Charles Augustin Sainte-Beuve, Flaubert's friend, who had recognized the value of *Madame Bovary* while criticizing its "vulgarity," was highly critical of the new work; George Sand and Victor Hugo were enthusiastic. Despite the mixed response, the novel sold well and drew attention to Flaubert. The year 1863 was one of great social activity for Flaubert. He frequented the salon of Princess Mathilde and attended the suppers at the Restaurant Magny where he met Ivan Turgenev (1818–1883). The emperor and empress invited him to the country chateau at Compiègne, and in 1866 Flaubert was named a knight of the Legion of Honor, but he never took a position for or against the Empire.

In the late 1860s Flaubert began a readaptation of a novel he had begun some twenty years earlier. His most ambitious effort to portray bourgeois society of the 1840s, *L'éducation sentimentale*, was submitted to Lévy in 1869. In return Flaubert received 32,000 francs. Unprepared for the novel's initial failure with the press and public, Flaubert suffered one of the greatest disappointments of his life. Ten years passed before critics reversed their decision and hailed it a masterpiece. During the siege and the Commune, Flaubert continued to work on the manuscript of *La tentation de Saint-Antoine*.

The *Correspondence* of Flaubert has been regarded by some readers as his greatest masterpiece. Comprising five volumes of the sixteen-volume edition of Flaubert's *Complete Works*, the correspondence spans practically his entire life. Among his most frequent correspondents were his mother; Madame Louise Colet (1808–1876), with whom he was involved in a tempestuous liaison for many years; his faithful friend, the poet Louis Bouilhet (1822–1869); and George Sand, with whom he carried on lively discussions about literature, art, and politics. In this correspondence, Flaubert reveals himself as a profound cynic and misanthrope, contemptuous of all forms of government (and, indeed, of France), and with no hope or illusions for France or mankind. Flaubert died at Croisset, 8 May 1880.

Maître J. Bariller, "Le procès de Madame Bovary (1857)," *Les amis de Flaubert*, no. 52 (1978); B. F. Bart, *Madame Bovary and the Critics* (New York, 1966); G. Flaubert, *Oeuvres complètes, XII–XVI: Correspondance, 1831–1880* (Paris, 1974–1975); D. Lacapra, *"Madame Bovary" on Trial* (Ithaca, 1982); J. F. Lemaire, "Gustave Flaubert, médecin passif," *RDM*, (September 1981); J. P. Sartre, *L'idiot de la famille: Gustave Flaubert, 1821–1857* (Paris, 1971); E. Starkie, *Flaubert: The Making of a Master* (London, 1967), and *Flaubert: The Master, 1856–1880* (London, 1971); F. Steegmuller, ed. and trans., *The Letters of Gustave Flaubert*, 2 vols. (Cambridge, Mass., 1981–1982); C. Tricotel, *Comme deux troubadours: Histoire de l'amitié Flaubert-Sand* (Paris, 1978).

Dolorès A. Signori

Related entries: CHAMPFLEURY; DURANTY; GONCOURT; SAND.

FORCADE LA ROQUETTE, JEAN LOUIS VICTOR ADOLPHE DE (1820–1874), functionary, politician, minister, deputy, and senator; born 8 April 1820, at Paris, son of a Parisian *juge de paix* (1811–1846). Forcade La Roquette was a half-brother of Leroy de Saint-Arnaud. After earning his law degree at Paris, he began a career that remained undistinguished until his acceptance of the coup d'état of December 1851. He was then named to the Conseil d'Etat as *maître des requêtes* on its reorganization in January 1852. His administrative career culminated in 1857–1859 with appointment first as director of forests and then (1859) as director of customs and of indirect taxation. In connection with the latter post, he was also named *conseiller d'état en service extraordinaire et hors section*. It is possible that Forcade La Roquette's Orleanist contacts precluded his political promotion until the beginning of reform in November 1860. On 26 November 1860 he was named finance minister, but his tenure was brief (only until 14 November 1861, when he was replaced by Achille Fould) and relatively uneventful (*émission trentenaire*, June 1861). Named to the Senate 14 November 1861, Forcade la Roquette was sent on several missions, notably to Algeria in March 1863 to study commercial questions. On 18 October 1863 he was named a vice-president of the Conseil d'Etat (1863–1867).

It was with the further reforms of January 1867 that the most brilliant phase of Forcade La Roquette's career opened. On 20 January 1867, he was recalled to the cabinet as minister of agriculture, commerce, and public works. In this position he manifested his enthusiasm for free trade and was said to have been the promoter of the Le Havre International Maritime Exposition of 1868. Moreover, he proved a willing instrument of a policy of labor reform. As a result of a report of Forcade La Roquette, approved by the emperor on 31 March 1868, administrative tolerance of trade unions (*chambres syndicales*) assumed an official character. In July 1868 two voluntary insurance funds were established. And a law of 18 August 1868, suppressing article 1781 of the Civil Code, established equality of oath for workers and patrons during legal actions. On 17

December 1868, Forcade La Roquette replaced Pierre Ernest Pinard as minister of the interior, a particularly delicate and difficult post at the time. The recently enacted laws on the press and on public meetings had to be administered while preparations went ahead for elections in the spring of 1869. The new minister, by now a zealous partisan of the regime, did not distinguish himself for liberalism in these few months, either in regard to the press or to the government's electoral preparations. On 8 March 1869 he skillfully defended before the Corps Législatif the system of elections, which until then had worked so well for the regime. And yet it was Forcade La Roquette who in effect abandoned the government's utilization of the mayors as electoral instruments.

Forcade La Roquette resigned with the rest of the cabinet, including his friend Eugène Rouher, on 13 July 1869 but was reappointed minister of the interior on 17 July. Although he opposed Prince Napoleon's call in September for a "democratic Empire," the minister became increasingly the champion of liberalization, which he brilliantly defended in the Corps Législatif on 7 December 1869. He was, however, too closely identified with the authoritarian Empire to be a principal in the new government, and he resigned on 27 December, with the rest of the ministers, to make room for the ministry of Emile Ollivier. Subsequently resigning his Senate seat, Forcade La Roquette won election to the Corps Législatif in a Lot-et-Garonne by-election on 10 January 1870. A member of the Commission d'Enquête Commerciale, which was to conduct a massive inquiry into the tariff question, he helped in February to turn back the protectionist assault on the government's free-trade policy. Although sitting on the right of the chamber, with Pinard and Jérôme David, he gave general support to the Liberal Empire.

Following the disasters of 1870–1871 and a six-month exile in Spain, Forcade La Roquette failed in his attempt to reenter politics. He died suddenly, at Paris, 15 August 1874. Forcade La Roquette has been cited by enemies of the Second Empire as an example of mediocrity advanced in reward for servility. In reality, he was an able, honest, and energetic public servant who certainly made no monetary gain from his years of office. He was a member of the Conseil Général of the Gironde from 1852 to 1867 and seven times its president. Named to the Legion of Honor in 1855, he was promoted to officer on 2 August 1858, commander on 2 August 1861, and grand officer on 2 April 1864.
Related entries: COBDEN-CHEVALIER TREATY; LABOR REFORM; REFORM.

FORTOUL, HIPPOLYTE (1811–1856), educator and politician, minister of education and religion, 1851–1856; born at Paris, 8 April 1811, the son of a mayor. In his youth a republican with Saint-Simonian connections, later a supporter of Louis Napoleon, Fortoul had a variety of distinct careers. In the 1820s he was an art and literary critic, then a popular lecturer at the University of Toulouse and professor of modern languages at Aix. He turned to politics during the Second Republic, being elected to the Legislative Assembly in 1849 and appointed minister of the navy in 1850. Louis Napoleon appointed him minister of education (public instruction) 3 December 1851.

The conservatism of Fortoul's tenure as minister of education reflected general fears in French society about education after the Revolution of 1848. He himself attributed the revolution to "misguided instruction" while asserting that right instruction would put France back on the proper track (report to the prince president, 2 December 1851). Purges of teachers—about 125, including Victor Cousin (1792–1867), Emile Deschanel (1819–1904), Jules Michelet (1798–1874), Edgar Quinet (1803–1875), and a future minister of education, Jules Simon (1814–1896), suffered some sanction—, pressures on them to demonstrate "proper" religious and political attitudes (they were required to submit course plans in advance), a dress code that required black coats and forbade beards and mustaches, and the hated loyalty oath (which actually predated his ministry by a year although most teachers signed it during his tenure) followed from an ambivalence about whether the rewards or dangers of mass education were greater, whether order should be put above culture. Unlike most other ministers, Fortoul was not committed to unbridled expansion of schooling; the budget for education was reduced by 2.5 million francs in 1853 and was lower in 1859 than it had been in 1852; particularly did the budget for mass primary schooling suffer, although enrollment was growing in secondary schools at an annual rate of 2 percent, a rate that would never in future be exceeded. He reduced the number of scholarships in secondary schools and made parental service to the state rather than need or aptitude the criterion for selection. The apocryphal comment ascribed to him, "Right now all lycéens throughout France are explicating the same passage from Virgil," is apt. A desire to monitor teaching throughout France marked his ministry and determined the reorganization of the University in 1852, whose basic structure was preserved into the twentieth century and components of which survived the student revolts of the late 1960s. First, he reconstituted the Imperial Council for Education, subordinating it to Paris and reducing clerical representation rather than have it "reflect the social forces of the nation" as stipulated by the Falloux law. On 14 June, 1854, sixteen academies were reinstituted, with their prefects given authority over all schooling, both public and private, in their regions. Anomalously, the proposed Fortoul bill would actually have divided public and private education into two separate sectors and been closer to twentieth-century practices than to the unitary model that resulted from the 1854 legislation. A decree of 25 April 1855 (the "academic coup d'état") attempted a reorganization of the Institute in the interest of greater government control but was largely unsuccessful.

During Fortoul's ministry, Catholic schools, especially secondary ones, grew even at the expense of public ones. This growth was due in part to a conservative reaction to the Revolution of 1848, in part to the removal by the Falloux law of former restrictions on Catholic schooling, in part to the ability of decentralized private schools to respond to local needs. Some forty public high schools closed as a result of competition from Catholic schools in his first three years. Enrollment in Catholic secondary schools rose from 21,195 to 30,744 between 1854 and 1861, their growth rate being 45 percent, while growth in the public sector was only 25 percent. In secondary education, Fortoul's ministry was on the defensive. Out of this competition, however, resulted a major innovation in curriculum known as *bifurcation*.

The decree of 10 April 1852 made two major changes in the traditional curriculum amid a general reemphasis on modern subjects: the applied sciences, modern languages, modern history, and gymnastics. It elevated science to the level of the classics and deemphasized philosophy, renaming the final year Logic rather than Philosophy. Although the last was the most immediately contentious, the *bifurcation* of the final four years of secondary studies into two separate, equal streams (science and classics) after four years of a common base had deeper pedagogical repercussions. *Bifurcation*, which owed much to the 1849 report of Jean Baptiste Dumas (1800–1884), differed from Victor Duruy's program and that of Narcisse Salvandy (1795–1856) for an inferior special education by making science equal to letters. Dumas' report attracted Fortoul because of the latter's conviction that science was the source of wealth and political supremacy among nations and that it was less politically dangerous than were the humanities. Fortoul also envisioned the scientific section as a section that Catholic schools (traditionally weak in science) would be unable to rival soon. Within *bifurcation*, common teaching remained for some subjects—history, geography, French literature, modern languages, logic, and some Latin—but each division was to prepare for different careers: science for the *grandes écoles* and medicine, letters for law, universities, and government service, each with its own *baccalauréat*. Classicists and teachers attacked the reform as utilitarian; Catholics claimed that it would foster materialism and would prevent the education of the whole man; doctors disliked it for they thought their status would decline if they lacked a classical education. Fortoul himself claimed that it was the only way to save classical studies in an age of science and that it would permit different aptitudes to realize themselves. Everybody opposed it except students and parents, who flocked to science. In the lycées enrollment in the scientific section soon surpassed enrollment in letters; more *baccalauréats* were given in science than in letters by 1854–1855.

Most historians have treated Fortoul too harshly. Even his sympathetic biographers, Raphael and Gontard, describe him as a "failure" in all of his careers because of his "lack of patience," although they do credit him with saving the University from the Catholic offensive and note the lasting features of his 1854 administrative reforms. *Bifurcation*, in fact, was a major reform that might have saved the French system from the pedagogical stultification and restricted social access that marked it during the Third Republic. His bad press has resulted from his authoritarianism within the University, his restrictions on the church, and the unattractiveness of his personality. His policies in secondary education were probably the most innovative of any minister in the next hundred years. He died at Paris, 7 July 1856.

N. Hulin, "A propos de l'enseignement scientifique: Une réforme de l'enseignement secondaire sous le Second Empire: La 'bifurcation' (1852–1864)," *RHSA* 35 (July 1982); G. Massa-Gille, ed., *Journal d'Hippolyte Fortoul*, vol. 1: *ler janvier-30 juin 1855* (Geneva, 1979); P. Raphael and M. Gontard, *Un ministre de l'instruction publique sous l'Empire autoritaire* (Paris, 1975).

Patrick J. Harrigan

Related entries: DUMAS, J. B.; DUPANLOUP; DURUY; FALLOUX LAW; GAUME; ROULAND.

FOUCAULT, LEON (1819–1868), physicist; born 19 September 1819, at Paris. One of the outstanding experimental physicists of the nineteenth century, Foucault made fundamental contributions to both science and technology. His best-known achievements are the experimental demonstration of the earth's rotation (using a pendulum attached to the dome of the Panthéon) in 1851 and the precise determination of the speed of light (1850, 1862). In collaboration with Hippolyte Fizeau (1819–1896), Foucault executed major researches in optics, providing powerful evidence for the wave theory of light, and in astronomical photography, including the first daguerreotype of the sun in 1845. In 1852 he invented the gyroscope, a device of practical importance and one that also stimulated the development of theoretical physics. Foucault's technological contributions include: a regulator for the arc lamp (1843, 1849), which made it possible for electricity to replace gas in the supply of silvering glass to produce mirrors for reflecting telescopes (1857); accurate methods for constructing and correcting mirrors and lenses (1858); and sophisticated mechanical regulators used in both machines for keeping a telescope pointed continuously at a given celestial object and in steam engines. He exhibited a 31.5 inch reflecting telescope at the London international exposition of 1862. Foucault was also an effective scientific popularizer, writing excellent articles in the *Journal des débats* from 1845. He was named knight of the Legion of Honor in 1851 (for the pendulum experiment) and then made officer in 1862. In 1855 Napoléon III created a place for him as physicist at the Paris Observatory, a post that enabled Foucault to pursue his work on lenses and mirrors. He received the Copley Medal of the Royal Society (London) in 1855 and became a member of the Bureau des Longitudes in 1862 and a foreign member of the Royal Society in 1864. After one unsuccessful attempt (1857), Foucault was elected to the Académie des Sciences in 1865. He died at Paris, 11 February 1868.

Martin Fichman

FOULD, ACHILLE (1800–1867), minister of state from 1852 to 1860, senator, and twice minister of finance (1849–1852, 1861–1867). Fould was the second son of a wealthy Jewish merchant banker, Beer Léon Fould (died 1855), who founded the family bank. He was born at Paris, 17 November 1800, studied at the Lycée Charlemagne, completed his education by travels in southern France, Italy, and the East, and became an amateur of art before settling down to run the family banking house with his brother Benoît (1792–1858), one of the founders of the Crédit Mobilier in 1852.

Elected to the Chamber of Deputies in 1842 from Tarbès (Hautes-Pyrénées), where the family had large properties and where he would long sit on the conseil général, Fould supported François Guizot (1787–1874) and was reelected in 1846 but at the Revolution of 1848 offered his financial expertise to the Republic while refusing the post of finance minister. He was elected to the Constituent Assembly from Paris in the by-elections of July 1848, obtaining (as an Orleanist candidate) a third fewer votes than Louis Napoleon, who was returned in the same poll. Disillusioned with the course of the Republic, Fould rallied to Louis Napoleon at the end of the year. Before the coup d'état of December 1851, he was finance minister from 1 November 1849 to 24 January 1851 and from 10 April to 27 October 1851. Fould approved the coup d'état, although he was not an accomplice, and on 3 December 1851 accepted the finance ministry but resigned 22 January 1852 in protest against the Orleans confiscation decrees. Nevertheless, he was named to the Senate on the first list of appointments, 26 January. Fould was the first Jew to be named senator, although it should be noted that, while never formally renouncing Judaism, he married a Protestant, raised his children as Christians, and would be buried according to Protestant rites.

On 29 July 1852 Fould became minister of state, a post to which was added in December that of minister of the imperial household (*maison de l'empereur*). Already Louis Napoleon's personal banker, Fould was thus assured a unique influence and role (it was he, for example, who delivered the letter in which Napoleon III formally requested the hand of Eugénie de Montijo in marriage). His prominence brought into the field a coalition of enemies, including Victor Fialin Persigny (who in 1854 complained that the emperor was in Fould's hands), Empress Eugénie (who, although the minister of state was one of the few to favor her marriage, resented his having "procured" Virginia de Castiglione [1837?–1899] for her husband in 1857), Alexandre Walewski, Auguste de Morny, and Georges Haussmann.

While of the greatest importance, Fould's role during these years is difficult to assess. He presided over the Paris international exposition of 1855, the administrative reorganization of the Opéra (bringing it directly under the jurisdiction of the Ministry of State), and the completion of the new Louvre and was elected to the Académie des Beaux-Arts in November 1857. He favored the amnesty of March 1856, which his friend Eugène Rouher and others opposed, but after the elections of 1857 talked of abolishing universal manhood suffrage. In tariff matters, he was a strong protectionist and in church affairs a Gallican, hated by the ultramontanes as a Jew and for favoring withdrawal of French troops from Rome (in 1858 Napoleon III sent him to Lourdes to make sure the grotto, closed by the prefect and the minister of education, was reopened to the public as the emperor had ordered). With the political reforms of November 1860, Fould's enemies secured his resignation (23 November) and the diminution of the Ministry of State but not his fall from favor. Napoleon III, who had made Fould grand cross of the Legion of Honor on 8 March 1856 and who would have made him a duke had the honor not been declined, immediately named him to the Conseil Privé.

Fould's subsequent career under the Second Empire can best be understood against the background of the regime's financial history. Under the constitution of January 1852 and the *sénatus-consulte* of 25 December 1852, the budget was voted by the Corps Législatif en bloc by ministry. These global amounts were then distributed within each ministry by imperial decree rendered in Conseil d'Etat or, if the occasion later presented itself, the funds could be redistributed (*virement*) in the same way. Moreover, if a need for additional money arose after the Corps Législatif had adjourned, supplementary or extraordinary credits could be opened by imperial decree rendered in Conseil d'Etat, subject to approval in the next legislative session. Partial reform of the system in 1855 did not change its essentials, and by 1858 additional credits of more than 2 billion francs had been opened, to the alarm of the other European powers (who suspected hidden military projects) and of conservative and prudent bankers.

Fould had first come to public notice in 1848 when he published two controversial pamphlets on the finances of the Second Republic, *Opinion de M. Fould sur la situation financière* and *Observations sur la situation financière*. Indeed, his first major achievement had been to balance the 1851 budget. In the following years, he remained a proponent of a conservative fiscal policy, clashing in particular with Pierre Magne, finance minister from 3 February 1855 to 26 October 1860. Although Fould had declined the finance ministry in November 1860, he prepared after his resignation as minister of state a memo critical of the government's financial practices and calling for reduction of the debt and for controlling it, which he sent in November 1861 to the emperor. Napoleon III read the memo to his cabinet on 12 November. J.L.V.A. de Forcade La Roquette, Alexandre Walewski, and Victor Fialin Persigny were opposed to the proposed changes; Jules Baroche and Rouher favored them. On 15 November the *Moniteur* published Fould's memo, an announcement of his appointment as minister of finance, and an explanation from the emperor promising financial reforms to be embodied in a *sénatus-consulte*. That of 31 December 1861 provided that henceforth the budget would be voted by sections within ministries (*virement* by decree was retained) and that a law would be required for the opening of extraordinary credits (by 1869 the Corps Législatif would have won the right to discuss the budget by chapters and articles and to vote it by chapters).

In office Fould sought to balance the budget by reducing the cost of the national debt, successfully converting 4 percent into 3 percent bonds, and by introducing a number of administrative reforms, the best known of which was the new (and long-lasting) system of public accounting he introduced in May 1862. However, the Mexican expedition made it impossible to eliminate the deficits. Extraordinary credits of 200 million francs were voted in 1860 and 350 million in 1861. Moreover, the decree of 31 May 1862 permitted the minister of finance to open credits and then to present a *budget rectificatif* to the Corps Législatif. There would be such a budget every year from 1863. In March 1863 both Magne and Fould resigned as the result of a quarrel. Fould returned to his ministry, but Magne was named to the Conseil Privé. In June 1863 Fould joined with Morny and Billault in securing the dismissal of Persigny. That year, as well, two of the finance minister's sons, Edouard Mathurin (1834–1881) and Adolphe Ernest (1824–1875), were elected to the Corps Législatif as official candidates (a third son, Gustave Eugène [1836–1884], was elected deputy in 1869). In January 1864 a new state loan of 300 million francs was necessitated by Mexican expenditures, and the budget of 1868 (the last prepared by Fould) would require yet another loan. In November 1865 the finance minister persuaded Napoleon III to suppress the post of *payeur du trésor* in the departments, assigning their tasks to the *receveurs généraux*. Fould was not renamed to the cabinet that resigned in January 1867 following the emperor's letter promising further political reforms. The Finance Ministry was assumed by Rouher. On 5 October 1867 the ex-minister died unexpectedly at Laloubère in the Hautes-Pyrénées. He was buried at Paris with great pomp.

Fould's role, except as minister of finance, remains ill defined and obscure, for, unlike other leading political figures of the Second Empire, he has not been the subject of a biography. His role as finance minister remains controversial. Some historians, and Louis Girard (*La politique des travaux publics du Second Empire*) in particular, have been critical, blaming Fould's financial orthodoxy and his part in limiting Napoleon III's financial prerogatives and thus depriving the emperor of his ability to stimulate the economy. However, we should be wary of attributing too much to Fould. There are grounds for believing that both the importance of government spending in the 1850s and the freedom of maneuver that the minister of finance enjoyed in the 1860s have been exaggerated. Besides, the slowdown in the growth of government expenditures (in monetary terms) in the 1860s reflected not only Fould's prudent policies but also a falling off in inflation and in economic growth.

S. L. Campbell, *The Second Empire Revisited: A Study in French Historiography* (New Brunswick, N.J., 1978); A. Fould, *Journaux et discours* (Paris, 1867); L. Girard, *La politique des travaux publics du Second Empire* (Paris, 1952).

Barrie M. Ratcliffe
William E. Echard

Related entries: BANKING; BILLAULT; BAROCHE; GOVERNMENT FINANCE; MAGNE; MEXICAN EXPEDITION; MINISTER OF STATE; MORNY; PERSIGNY; PRINCE NAPOLEON; ROTHSCHILD; ROUHER.

FOUR SEPTEMBER. See QUATRE SEPTEMBRE.

LA FRANCE, newspaper launched by Arthur de La Guéronnière on 8 August 1862. La Guéronnière, a faithful supporter of Napoleon III who had often written articles and brochures at the emperor's request, received a government subsidy to establish the newspaper, assisted as director by Henri de Pène (1830–1888), an uncompromising enemy of republicanism. But *La France*, edited by L. de Saint-Poncy, was a bonapartist newspaper of liberal persuasion, its program sketched in La Guéronnière's 1862 brochure, *De la politique intérieure et extérieure de la France*. The British press had welcomed its appearance as a turning point in Second Empire political development. The new paper was therefore not immune from government criticism (*avertissements*). Moreover, La Guéronnière had become so identified in the public mind with Napoleon III's thought that he could not express his own opinions without embarrassment to the government. He therefore sold his interest in *La France*, which, with Charles Genty as director, continued to give support to the emerging Liberal Empire. Among collaborators and contributors to the paper were Jules Claretie, Charles Aubertin (1825–1908), Paul L. E. Pradier-Fodéré (b. 1827), Paul, comte de Saint-Victor (1827–1881), Louis de Viel-Castel (1800–1887), Joseph Cohen (1817–1899), and the philosopher Elme Marie Caro (1826–1887). *La France* had a circulation by 1866 of eighty-nine hundred, which it maintained until the end of the Empire.

Related entries: BONAPARTISM; LA GUERONNIERE; PRESS REGIME.

FRANCO-AUSTRIAN WAR. See ITALIAN WAR.

FRANCO-PRUSSIAN WAR (19 July 1870–10 May 1871), the conflict that saw the humiliation and overthrow of the French Second Empire, the final unification of Germany, and a major readjustment in the balance of power on the Continent. Although the war sprang immediately from a diplomatic incident (the Hohenzollern candidacy), its real cause lay in an amalgam of Otto von Bismarck's ambitions for Germany, the yearning of the imperialist party in France for a reestablishment of the authority of the emperor, French miscalculations concerning France's diplomatic position and military will, and the volatility of French public opinion.

Napoleon III well understood the implications of Prussia's victory over Austria at Sadowa in July 1866, but he was unable to overcome resistance to effective French military reform. All that he could accomplish was the introduction of the excellent chassepot breech-loading rifle and the *mitrailleuse* (a machine gun that was France's equivalent of the U.S. Gatling gun). The French standing army remained at its pre-1866 strength of under 400,000 men, and France continued to lack an effective system of mobilization, a true general staff, and trained reserves. By contrast, Prussia, with a system of territorial reserves, lavished money and attention on its army. Helmuth von Moltke, the brilliant chief of staff, and Albrecht von Roon, the minister of war, were denied nothing by Bismarck to prepare for the final confrontation with France, a confrontation made necessary by French resistance to incorporation of the south German states into a united Germany under Prussian control. Moreover, if France were to appear the aggressor, Bismarck would be able to take the field with a unified German army under Prussian command. Nevertheless, urged on by public opinion, the French Corps Législatif voted war credits on 16 July and shouted down the few voices (Adolphe Thiers, Léon Gambetta) that urged restraint and second thoughts. Emile Ollivier's government declined to communicate the diplomatic documents; and the foreign minister, Antoine, duc de Gramont, hinted at an alliance with Italy and Austria-Hungary that did not in fact exist. Moreover, the minister of war, Marshal Edmond Leboeuf (1809–1888), exuded confidence. French hopes and the calculations of Europe's military experts held that the Napoleonic professionalism of the French army would prove irresistible. Granted that the total German forces would exceed 1 million men, the belief was that since most of these would be conscripts, while the French army was based on long-term voluntary enlistment, the latter would be more quickly mobilized and deployed and would prove more efficient in battle. On 19 July, France declared war on Prussia, asserting that its quarrel was not with Germany but with Bismarck's policies. Bismarck, however, was able to bring not only the North German Confederation but also the four south German states into a coalition against the French.

Unrealistic French joy and overconfidence at the declaration of war soon vanished, although because of censorship (voted by the Corps Législatif on 16 July) the French people would not know the true course of events until early September. French mobilization was chaotic. Troops raised at Lyons found that their chassepot rifles were at Dunkirk on the channel coast; deployment of colonial regiments to the frontier was hamstrung by the necessity of going through Paris; French units, in expectation of a war to be fought on German soil, were issued maps of Germany but not of France; the French military command proved unwilling to take initiatives at the local level; and complacency in the memory of victories over Russia and Austria in the 1850s led the French to make much less effective use than did the Germans of such relatively new technical developments as the railroad and the telegraph. On 21 July the Corps Législatif adjourned; on 23 July Empress Eugénie was appointed regent; on 28 July, Napoleon III, in agony from a flare-up of his bladder stone, left without fanfare for the front from his private railroad station at Saint-Cloud and the next day assumed command at Metz of the French forces. Those forces consisted of, from right to left (south to north): I Corps, Marie Edme Patrice de MacMahon (Strasbourg); V Corps, Charles de Failly (Saargemunde and Bitche); II Corps, Charles Auguste Frossard (St. Avold); IV Corps, Louis de Ladmirault (Thionville); III Corps, Achille Bazaine (Metz); and, in support, the Imperial Guard, Charles Bourbaki (Nancy); VI Corps, François Canrobert (Châlons); and VII Corps, Félix Douay (Belfort). The eight corps of this Army of the Rhine were commanded by Napoleon III, seconded by Edmond Le Boeuf. The ten corps of the main Prusso-North German force, grouped in three armies, were deployed along a line Wittlich-Neunkirchen-Landau, while one Prussian corps and the Saxon Corps covered Mainz and were in a central position to aid either wing of the main field force. When the south German states entered the war on Prussia's side (20 July), their troops were divided among these three armies. By the end of July, when active operations were about to begin, France had put 230,000 to 250,000 men into position; Prussia and its German allies disposed of nearly 500,000. Further, the French had few reliable reserves (apart from the relatively worthless Garde Mobile and National Guard), while Prussia and its allies still had substantial reserve strength on which to draw (perhaps another 500,000). The Prussian order of battle was, from right to left (north to south): Second Army (Prince Frederick Charles), First Army (Karl Frederik von Steinmetz), Third Army (Crown Prince Frederick William of Prussia). Of total French effectives at the beginning of the war (370,000), 66,000 were out of France.

Not only were the French outnumbered, but their mobilization soon degenerated into chaos. Part of the reason was the last-minute decision (July) not to group the French troops into three field armies. Because of this change, which did not allow for a strategic reserve, the coordinated movement of men and material broke down almost completely, dangerously delaying the beginning of the French offensive. The French delay in starting the offensive, combined with the entrance of the south German states, reduced the already slim possibility that Austria and/or Italy would enter the war on France's side. Nevertheless, by herculean effort and in the face of increasing chaos in the rear areas, II Corps, under Frossard (1807–1875), began to advance on Saarbrücken on 1 August. The Prussian screening force, part of Steinmetz's First Army, fell back in the direction of the main force behind Saarbrücken. Had Frossard and the two French corps (I and III) on his flanks advanced more vigorously and with greater coordination, they could have put Steinmetz, who had not yet completed his deployment, in an awkward position. The French advance, however, was tentative and poorly coordinated, and Steinmetz was able to dispose his forces without French interference, although Saarbrücken was occupied by the French on 2 August. This would not be the last time that French complacency or passivity would vitiate initial success.

While the French were beginning, however tentatively, their move to Saarbrücken in the center of the front, the Prussian Third Army, commanded by Crown Prince Frederick William, had begun its advance in the south. On 4 August it fell on a small detachment (4,000) of MacMahon's corps at Wissembourg, guarding the Pigeonnier Pass through the Vosges Mountains. After determined resistance in this first battle of the war, the French retreated. The defeat caused confusion and consternation both within MacMahon's staff and the War Ministry at Paris. The northern corps were ordered to concentrate at Cadenbronn, which necessitated Frossard's retreat from Saarbrücken. Frossard then took up a strong position at Spichern. When the Prussian First Army entered Saarbrücken (5 August), they found that the retreating French had failed to blow up the bridges over the Saar River, which meant that their continued advance was not delayed as it should have been. Frossard's troops were soon engaged by the advancing Prussians, while units of the Prussian Second Army, commanded by the Prussian Prince Frederick Charles, began a rapid march to the sound of the guns, a Napoleonic response typical of the Prusso-German commanders that was not emulated by the French. In spite of a steady trickle of German troops arriving before his position, Frossard was confident of holding and requested that nearby French units be sent to reinforce his position. The neighboring French corps commanders did not reinforce him, however, nor did Bazaine take overall direction of the fight, and Frossard, hard-pressed, began an orderly retreat. By default, then, Steinmetz's First Army had won a victory, with the aid of units of the Second Army (Prince Frederick Charles had assumed overall command). On the evening of 5 August, however, neither Steinmetz nor Frederick Charles fully appreciated the importance of their victory. On the following day while Frossard was once again defeated (at Forbach), units of the Prussian Third Army began to probe the lines of MacMahon's corps. At first, the French held their position, but in the early afternoon, their right gave way under the Prussian assault. By the end of the afternoon, the French at Wörth (Froeschwiller) had been defeated and were retiring to Reichshofen. Because of the ineffectiveness of the pursuing Prussian cavalry, the French were able to get away completely via Lunéville. Units of the French forces that had fought at Wörth were later to fight at Sedan. The events of 6 August were particularly bitter for the French because on that day Paris had celebrated rumors of a great victory. When word of Wörth was received in the capital on 7 August, a state of siege was proclaimed at Paris; as events were to show, Ollivier's government was doomed.

The combination of the French defeats at Wissembourg, Spichern, and Wörth was serious. The Prusso-German armies had driven a wedge between the northern and southern corps of the French Army of the Rhine, so that their operation in support of one another would henceforth be difficult, it not impossible (on 9 August Bazaine was formally charged with conducting French operations in Lorraine). Moltke could now direct his armies with near impunity in such a way as to defeat the French forces piecemeal. Moreover, with the complete failure of the French offensive, the hopes for Austrian and Italian intervention were ended. The French were now (14–18 August) forced back into the confines of the fortress of Metz, as much by Bazaine's hesitancy and indecision as by the tactical ability of Frederick Charles, commander of the attacking Prussian First and Second Armies. In spite of the increasingly obvious deficiencies of Bazaine's administrative and command abilities, on 12 August he was named to the supreme command, replacing the emperor whose health no longer permitted him to discharge his responsibilities. On 9 August Ollivier's government had been overthrown by the Corps Législatif, convened to vote additional credits and levies. Ollivier's successor was the comte de Palikao (1796–1878). On 10 August, the siege of Strasbourg began.

In a sense, the fate of Bazaine as well as that of the Rhine Army was settled on 14 August when, after hard fighting, the French, who enjoyed local superiority, were defeated at Colombey-Borny. After the battle, Bazaine's troops began their retirement on to the forts at Metz. Strangely, at this time Bazaine had not yet made up his mind whether to retreat to the Meuse River (and, possibly beyond), thereby keeping his still formidable army in the field, or to stand a siege within Metz. Initially, Frederick Charles seems to have been convinced that Bazaine would not bottle himself up in the fortress but would seek instead to retain some mobility and unite with the other French forces. Consequently, Frederick Charles pursued the French retreat from Colombey-Borny without taking proper precautions. Thus, General Gustav von Alvensleben, one of Frederick Charles' corps commanders, blundered into the main body of Bazaine's army at Vionville (or Mars-la-Tour) in the early morning of 16 August. All day the Prussian III, IX, and X Corps, as each arrived on the field, entered the battle. Of the five French corps under Bazaine's command, however, only about half were actually committed to the battle. Had Bazaine engaged all his troops, as he should have done, the day might well have ended with a much-needed French victory. By contrast, Frederick Charles acted decisively and promptly and rushed Prussian reinforcements to the battlefield throughout the night of 16–17 August. As a result, the bitter fighting at Vionville ended in a stalemate, which effectively prevented Bazaine from retreating toward Verdun. On 18 August the reinforced Prussians, with additional troops arriving on the field for most of the day, again began to probe Bazaine's position. Frederick Charles (now enjoying the numerical superiority that Bazaine had had over the previous three days) sought to find the French flank and get around it. In early afternoon Bazaine's position at Gravelotte (Rezonville) was broken, and in the early evening the French were also driven from Saint-Privat-la-Montagne. The consequence of Gravelotte and Saint-Privat was that Bazaine's freedom to decide his own course was lost. His army was forced back into Metz, there to withstand a siege. Any remaining chance of a French victory was lost.

Complete disaster might yet have been avoided, however. On 15 August the French navy (nine ironclads) had begun a blockade of Germany's Baltic coast; on 19 August the last of France's Rome garrison left the port of Civita Vecchia en route to the front. *Francs tireurs* had taken the field, much to the disgust of the Germans. And on 16 August Napoleon III, accompanied by the prince imperial, had reached Châlons-sur-Marne from Verdun. At Châlons (near Reims, about 100 miles east of Paris) the Second Empire had maintained, since 1857, a great military camp. From the moment of the initial defeats, the emperor's military instinct had counseled a withdrawal to Châlons and, indeed, to Paris. Now some 100,000 men with 419 cannons, remnants of the southern army corps, were gathering at the camp to be hastily reorganized into the Army of Châlons. Although exhausted and demoralized, they constituted the only remaining French force, for there were virtually no reserves that could be called up. On the morning of 17 August, a council of war (Napoleon III, Prince Napoleon, MacMahon, and General Louis Jules Trochu [1815–1896]) decided, with the emperor saying little, that Napoleon III would return to Paris where Trochu, head of a military Comité de Défence, would be governor and that the Army of Châlons would fall back on the city where its strength could be boosted to 250,000 men, supplemented by the Garde Mobile and the National Guard. This prospect had already been debated in the capital. Ollivier (before his overthrow), Maurice

Richard (1832–1888), and Joachim Pietri, the prefect of police, had favored it and had persuaded the empress on the morning of 9 August to agree. She was, however, reluctant, fearing the political consequences for the dynasty, and the Council of Ministers that afternoon followed instead the advice of Victor Fialin Persigny (a romantic bonapartist to the end), Eugène Rouher, and Palikao. Frightened of revolution, the government advised Napoleon III by telegram in the afternoon of 17 August that it could not accept responsibility for his return. The emperor undoubtedly shared these misgivings. He postponed the projected return to Paris and dispatched Prince Napoleon to Florence. Trochu, having arrived at Paris at midnight, failed to sway the government, which now ordered MacMahon to march to the relief of Metz (on 19 August, the same day that the telegraph line to Metz was cut). Two days later, Rouher, at Reims, to which MacMahon had marched the army from Châlons, was converted to the necessity of Napoleon III's return to Paris, but he too failed to shake the government's resolve. On 22 August, MacMahon was once again instructed to march toward Metz, but the marshal, having that same day received word that Bazaine would attempt to break out to the north, had already decided that he must attempt a relief operation. The next day began the maneuver that was to culminate in the disaster of Sedan, the surrender of Napoleon III and of the last French army (2 September), and the overthrow of the Second Empire by a revolution at Paris (4 September). Thereafter the war was the concern of the emerging Third Republic, but despite the efforts of such men as Léon Gambetta, the cause proved hopeless. On 19 September the siege of Paris began; on 27 October Bazaine surrendered Metz and his army of almost 180,000 (including Marshals Le Boeuf and Canrobert, the Imperial Guard, and some 400 artillery pieces). The new French armies, raised by the provisional government, lacked professionalism, discipline, and adequate training, although they displayed temporary enthusiasm, patriotism, and ingenuity. With the capitulation of Paris on 28 January 1871 and the final defeat of the Army of the Loire (4 December 1870), France had no choice but to sign Bismarck's harsh peace terms on 10 May 1871 (Treaty of Frankfurt).

The French defeat is best explained by a complex of factors. First, although Napoleon III was a man of undeniably noble intentions and military expertise, his poor health, on the one hand, and the strident and unrealistic stance of much of the growing liberal opposition, on the other, together had prevented effective diplomatic and military preparations before war broke out. The French declaration of war, provoked by French popular hysteria, must therefore be considered an irresponsible act.

Second, on the military level, France (and the emperor knew it) was far behind Prussia in terms of military doctrine and preparation. Although the rank and file repeatedly displayed great courage and endurance, the French army was behind the times regarding such matters as organization, mobilization, and planning. There was no French general staff worthy of the name to plan and oversee. The fact that, beyond the standing army, there were no trained reserves was perhaps the most important factor in explaining the French defeat, although it was at least equaled by the passivity, hesitancy, and indecision repeatedly shown by senior French officers. The rank and file of the army surely deserved better civil and military leadership than it was given. The Prussian generals not only commanded a much larger force, with ample reserves, but time and again they outperformed their French counterparts in maneuvering large bodies of men so that the German forces almost always enjoyed numerical superiority at the point of conflict. In terms of arms, the French chassepot rifle eclipsed the Prussian needle gun. But Prussian artillery (steel, rifled, breech-loading) proved infinitely superior to the French (bronze, rifled, muzzle loading). As to the *mitrailleuse*, it was developed in such secrecy that its murderous effectiveness at close range was not appreciated until too late, and those trained to use it were few. Moreover, Prussian artillery proved deadly in eliminating the weapon when it became a danger. The French navy had a clear mastery, but a navy is of little use in a short land war, such as the Franco-Prussian. France of the Second Empire was not prepared for modern war in which the totality of a nation's resources are focused; Prussia, under Bismarck, Moltke, and Roon, was so prepared. Thus the Second Empire ended after twenty years, not because of a political but rather because of a military failure, although it might be argued that political considerations partially underlay the failure to carry out effective military reform, the decision to go to war, and the equally fateful decision to direct MacMahon's army toward Metz rather than Paris and to bar Napoleon III's return to the capital.

T. J. Adriance, "The Mobilization and Concentration of the French Army in 1870" (Ph.D. diss., Columbia University, 1968); G. Bourgin, *La Guerre de 1870–1871 et la Commune* (Paris, 1971); M. Crosland, "Science and the Franco-Prussian War," *Social Studies of Science* 6 (1976); W. German, "Les généraux français de 1870," *Revue de la défense nationale* (August–September 1970); W. V. Groote and U. V. Gersdorft, eds., *Entscheidung 1870: Der Deutsche-Französische Krieg* (Stuttgart, 1970); M. Howard, *The Franco-Prussian War: The German Invasion of France, 1870–1871* (New York, 1961); A. Leclerc and A. Jacques, *Prodomes de "l'Année Terrible": Victoires manquées, Rezonville, Saint-Privat, août 1870* (Paris, 1972); J. Madaule, "1870: La Guerre Franco-Allemande," *Historia* (May 1968); Colonel Rocolle, "Anatomie d'une mobilisation," *Revue historique des armées* 2 (1979); G. Roux, *La Guerre de 1870* (Paris, 1966).

Eric A. Arnold, Jr.

Related entries: ARMY REFORM; BAZAINE; CHASSEPOT; GAMBETTA; HOHENZOLLERN CANDIDACY; LIBERAL EMPIRE; MACMAHON; NAPOLEON III: HEALTH; OLLIVIER; PUBLIC OPINION; QUATRE SEPTEMBRE; SADOWA; SEDAN; THIERS.

FRENCH ACADEMY. See ACADEMIE FRANCAISE.

G

GALLICANISM, the doctrine that denies sovereignty to the pope within the church and insists that secular matters be reserved to secular authorities. In regard to the question of papal sovereignty, the Second Empire maintained at first a position of neutrality. The struggle was, in fact, unequal. Although the Gallicans within the French church had important centers (the two faculties of theology, the Ecole des Carmes, the seminary of St. Sulpice), they were a tiny minority within a hierarchy that accepted the theocratic ideas of Pius IX. The Vatican Council of 1869–1870 and, in particular, the proclamation of the doctrine of papal infallibility (1870) marked the complete victory of the proponents of papal sovereignty (ultramontanists). This outcome was not particularly welcome to the regime, whose initial indifference perhaps played a role in the triumph of ultramontanism.

The question of relations between church and state was a more complex matter. Napoleon III was influenced in his attitude by two legacies, the Principles of 1789, which he had inherited via his uncle from the Revolution, and the Concordat (treaty) of 1801, which Napoleon I had negotiated with Pope Pius VII and to which he had attached in 1802, without papal approval, certain Organic Articles further restricting the pope's authority within the French church. The Principles of 1789 and the Concordat of 1801 required a clear division between secular and spiritual concerns and rejected all aspects of clericalism (church intervention in such secular areas as government and education). But the Concordat of 1801 firmly subordinated the church to the state and placed the state as an intermediary between Rome and the church hierarchy in France—thus what might well be termed *Napoleonic Gallicanism*. Throughout the Second Empire, for example, it was customary for Napoleon III to name bishops and then to inform the pope. On the other hand, Napoleon III, while not a religious man, clearly saw the value of the church as a bulwark of order and as a political instrument, particularly in rallying legitimist populations to the regime. As Louis Napoleon he had cultivated church support during the Second Republic and rewarded Catholics for that support with the Falloux law, by which responsibility for education was shared between church and state. Significantly, however, intransigent Catholics had wanted not a share but a monopoly. The church, for its part, saw in Louis Napoleon the savior of society, and its hierarchy supported the coup d'état of December 1851 and the proclamation of the Empire in December 1852. This marriage of convenience was both durable, in that the regime and the church remained mutually dependent, and fragile, in that Napoleon III regarded the church as simply a means of government and resisted its substantive demands. Cardinals became members, by right, of the imperial Senate; the pay of the hierarchy was increased; and money was lavished on the church, whose public prominence greatly increased. Most church leaders responded by heaping extravagant praise on Napoleon III and his regime, although a small group of legitimists and of liberals kept their distance. From the beginning, however, the administrators of the Empire stubbornly maintained the principles of Napoleonic Gallicanism. The University retained control of education, and Hippolyte Fortoul was succeeded as minister of education by Gustave Rouland, a Gallican, and Rouland in 1863 by Victor Duruy, a determined foe of clericalism. Jules Baroche as minister without portfolio and, from 1863 to 1869, minister of justice and of cults was an uncompromising Gallican in the Napoleonic tradition. The regime staunchly resisted efforts by Catholics to extend church control of education, to have the Organic Articles abolished (although they were not used) or the Civil Code altered in order to subordinate civil to religious marriage. In his foreign policy, Napoleon III often seemed to seek when possible to please the church, as in the dispute over the Holy Places (1849–1853), the Crimean War (which some saw as a new crusade), the Syrian, China, Japanese, Mexican, and Indochina expeditions, and in the expressions of French sympathy for Poles and Rumanians. The first two foreign ministers of the Empire, Edouard Drouyn de Lhuys and Alexandre Walewski, were perhaps influenced by their religious convictions. But the touchstone of church-state relations in the area of foreign policy proved to be the Roman Question, and while Napoleon III maintained a French garrison at Rome from 1849, he refused after 1858 to abandon his advocacy of Italian independence or to be dissuaded from a course that resulted in the progressive loss to the pope of all his territories save Rome.

The French emperor was unwilling to break completely with the Catholic party. He restrained the virulent anti-clericalism of his cousin, Prince Napoleon and in 1862 sacrificed perhaps the ablest of his foreign ministers, Edouard Thouvenel, to Catholic opinion. But his ideal for the papacy (reform and acceptance of the loss of temporal power) was anathema to Pius IX and to intransigents of the nature of Louis Veuillot and of Bishop Louis Pie. They were, however, generals without troops. In the confrontation between church and state of 1860–1861, the government easily won. Veuillot's newspaper, L'Univers, was suppressed, Pie constrained to urge moderation on his clergy, and the Society of St. Vincent de Paul was in effect disbanded by Victor Fialin Persigny, then minister of the interior. There is serious doubt, at any rate, if the church, in its fear of anarchy and of atheistic socialism, had any desire to carry its quarrel with the Empire beyond a certain point.

The issue of Gallicanism versus ultramontanism was complicated by the clash between liberal and conservative Catholics. Liberal Catholicism, in its most extreme form, called for the separation of church and state, for a "free church in a free state," and for an acceptance by Catholics of responsibility for social reform and for adapting the church to the modern world. Devoted to parliamentary government, liberal Catholics would not, despite the temporary aberration of Charles de Montalembert, accept the authoritarian Empire. So far as church-state relations were concerned, they rejected completely the principles of Napoleonic Gallicanism. Concerning the government of the church, however, their sympathies were Gallican, since they preferred the sovereignty of a council to that of the pope. They were a small if vociferous minority within the French church, including, notably, Montalembert, Père Henri Lacordaire, Georges Darboy (1813–1871), Père Alphonse Gratry (1805–1872), Armand de Melun (1807–1877), Frédéric de Falloux (1811–1886), Augustin Cochin (1823–1872), Charles de Coux (1787–1864), Frédéric Le Play, Père Hyacinthe, François Tircuy de Corcelle (1802–1892), and Henri Maret (1805–1884). Their journal, the *Correspondant*, clashed noisily with Veuillot's *L'Univers*, but the contest was unequal. Would-be mediators between the two camps (such as Bishop Félix Dupanloup) found themselves in an impossible position as the tides that had overwhelmed Gallicanism as an ideal of church government gathered against the liberal Catholics. Pius IX's *Syllabus of Errors* (1864) and the difficulties encountered by social Catholicism during the Second Empire signaled the victory of the conservatives, who were also, invariably, ultramontanes.

The double victory within the church of ultramontanism and of conservative Catholicism over Gallicanism and liberal Catholicism made even more difficult the relations between church and state in the closing years of the Second Empire. As political embarrassments accumulated, Napoleon III remained capable of making semiturns toward the church (refusal to withdraw from Rome, 1867; dismissal of Duruy, 1869). But the movement of the Empire toward political liberalization and Napoleon III's personal commitment to social and economic liberalism as well as to Napoleonic Gallicanism in church-state relations meant that the alliance between the church and the regime remained troubled and equivocal until the end.

A. Debidour, *Histoire des rapports de l'Eglise et de l'état en France de 1789 à 1870* (Geneva, 1977; reprint of 1898 ed.); J. K. Huckaby, "Liberal Catholicism in France, 1843–1870" (Ph.D. diss., Ohio State University, 1957); J. Maurain, *La politique ecclésiastique du Second Empire de 1852 à 1869* (Paris, 1930); J. R. Palanque, *Catholiques libéraux et Gallicans en France face au Concile du Vatican, 1867–1870* (Aix-en-Provence, 1962); G. Riou, *Le Père Hyacinthe et le libéralisme d'avant le Concile* (Paris, 1910); G. Weill, *Histoire du Catholicisme libéral en France, 1828–1908* (Paris, 1909). *Related entries: CORRESPONDANT;* DARWINISM IN FRANCE; DUPANLOUP; FALLOUX LAW; GAUME; HYACINTHE; INFALLIBILITY, DOCTRINE OF; ITALIAN WAR; LACORDAIRE; LEGITIMISM; LOURDES; MARET; MONTALEMBERT; PIE; PIUS IX; ROMAN QUESTION; ROULAND; SOCIAL CATHOLICISM; SOLESME; *SYLLABUS OF ERRORS; L'UNIVERS;* VATICAN COUNCIL; VEUILLOT.

GAMBETTA, LEON (1838–1882), a major figure in the revival of republicanism during the last years of the Second Empire; born in Cahors, son of a grocer of Genoese origin. Gambetta went to Paris to study law in 1857 and in 1861 was admitted to the bar. Attracted by the cliques of younger republicans that met in the cafés of the Left Bank (Procope, Voltaire) and inspired by Pierre Joseph Proudhon and by the opposition of the small group of republican deputies in the Corps Législatif known as *les Cinq*, he decided to stay in Paris and become involved in political life. A bohemian, very unprepossessing appearance and a penchant for radical speeches masked Gambetta's essentially moderate and pragmatic nature. His ability as an orator (he had the power to move his audiences deeply) and his personal charm and charisma made him a valuable addition to the struggling republican opponents of the Second Empire. Neither revolutionary nor anti-religious (despite his anti-clericalism), Gambetta denied the existence of classes in France and sought the creation of a single class, which would include the *nouvelles couches* of small proprietors, industrialists, and shopkeepers through such instruments as a citizens' army and universal education in common schools.

Gambetta first won notice as a defense lawyer in 1862 in the trial of a number of workers charged with plotting to assassinate Napoleon III (Greppo affair). In the 1863 elections, he campaigned vigorously for the opposition. He gained notable attention, however, only in 1868 as defense attorney for Charles Delescluze (1809–1871), one of three republican journalists prosecuted for collecting subscriptions to erect a monument to Victor Baudin, a republican martyr of 1851. In his plea for Delescluze, Gambetta denounced the coup d'état and the imperial regime, the first such public denunciation since that of Ernest Picard's in the Corps Législatif in January 1864. The resulting publicity propelled him into the legislative elections of 1869 when he stood as a candidate at Marseilles and in the Belleville working-class district of Paris. Gambetta's Belleville campaign manifesto, cast into the form of a contract (*mandat impératif*) with his constituents, called for the repression of standing armies, disestablishment of the church, freedom of the press, of assembly, and of association, and free elementary education. The manifesto was probably fashioned more for appeal to the Belleville voters than by Gambetta's personal ideological commitments, but it later came to be viewed as an important statement of radical republican objectives. Gambetta won election in both constituencies on the first ballot but chose to represent Marseilles.

The elections, which sent forty republican deputies to the Corps Législatif, convinced Gambetta that a final republican victory through electoral success was inevitable. Buoyed by such optimism, he became one of the chief architects of the *gauche fermée*, a party adhering to strict republican principles and distinguishing itself from other opponents of the Empire who were simply liberal. On the other hand, he continued to advocate a strong, if decentralized, state, and in October 1869 he led the republicans in breaking with the socialists. In notable speeches of 10 January and 5 May 1870, Gambetta reaffirmed his intransigent opposition to the Empire, denouncing the liberal constitution proposed by Napoleon III and Emile Ollivier. The overwhelming popular endorsement that the constitution received in the subsequent plebiscite, despite Gambetta's best efforts, confounded his hope for a republic in the immediate future. During the remaining months of the Empire, however, he remained irreconcilable to the liberal regime, which he interpellated on the issue of sending troops to Le Creusot during the strikes of 1870.

In the crisis of July provoked by publication of the Ems dispatch, Gambetta joined with Adolphe Thiers in counseling against haste in declaring war on Prussia but then broke with more pacifist colleagues such as Jules Favre to vote for war credits requested by the government. He also called for revival of the popular-based National Guard. After the emperor's capitulation at Sedan on 2 September, Gambetta favored a quick but orderly transition of power to a new government sanctioned by the Corps Législatif. On 4 September, when crowds of Parisians broke up the deliberations of the Corps Législatif, Gambetta urged the demonstrators not to interfere and tried unsuccessfully to assuage them by reading a motion of *déchéance*, but fearing that more revolutionary elements, such as Delescluze or Henri Rochefort, might gain control of the crowds, he ended by joining Favre in leading the demonstrators on a march to the Hôtel de Ville. There he joined the other republican deputies from Paris in proclaiming a Government of National Defense.

Gambetta assumed the post of minister of the interior in the new government. With Paris soon besieged by German armies, he left the city, in a dramatic escape by balloon, and took charge of the war effort in the provinces. His energetic conduct of the war did not save the capital, however, or prevent defeat for France. In fact, his policy of war to the knife and the virtual dictatorial control he briefly assumed led to a period of eclipse of his career. By 1873, however, Gambetta would reemerge as a major political force, although his key role in shaping the Third Republic was to be cut short by his premature death at Ville d'Avray (Seine-et-Oise), 31 December 1882.

Bertol and Plantié, eds., *Léon Gambetta, souvenirs, 1838–1882* (Paris, 1883); J. Chastenet, *Gambetta* (Paris, 1969), and "Gambetta méconnu," *Historia*, no. 375 (February 1978); J. Dautry, "Gambetta contre l'Empire et l'ordre moral," *Cahiers internationaux* (June 1959); J. Gaillard, "Gambetta et le radicalisme entre l'élection de Belleville et celle de Marseille en 1869," *RH* 519 (July–September 1976); P. B. Gheusi, *Gambetta: Life and Letters* (London, 1910); D. Halévy and E. Pillias, eds., *Lettres de Gambetta* (Paris, 1938); J. Reinach, ed., *Discours et plaidoyers politiques de Gambetta*, 11 vols. (Paris, 1881–1885); G. Wormser, *Gambetta dans les tempêtes* (Paris, 1964).

Joel S. Cleland

Related entries: BAUDIN; QUATRE SEPTEMBRE; REPUBLICANISM.

GARNIER, CHARLES (1825–1898), architect of the Paris Opéra; born 6 November 1825 at Paris. Son of a Parisian blacksmith and carriage-maker, Garnier might have entered his father's profession had it not been for poor health.

Encouraged by his mother, he began the study of design and entered the Ecole des Beaux-Arts at the age of seventeen. He studied under Hippolyte Lebas (1782–1867) and, to gain funds, worked as a draftsman for Eugène Viollet-le-Duc and other architects. In 1848 he won the academy's Grand Prix de Rome in architecture, which enabled him to spend four years at the Villa Medicis and to travel in Greece (1852) and Turkey, where he met Théophile Gautier, thereafter his champion, and studied, in particular, the architectural polychromy of the Temple of Jupiter at Aegina.

Returning to Paris in 1854, Garnier became *sous-inspecteur* of the restoration work at the Tour Saint Jacques and designed an apartment building on the new boulevard de Sébastopol. The Paris of Baron Georges Haussmann provided great opportunities for architects. Garnier soon became architect of the City of Paris for the fifth and sixth arrondissements (Left Bank; Luxembourg Gardens, Jardin des Plantes) and in 1855–1856 and 1859–1860 was auditor of the Conseil Général des Bâtiments Civils. Nevertheless, he was still virtually unknown when the competition for a design for the projected new Opéra opened 29 December 1860. Although barely surviving the initial round, Garnier's design was chosen in the final competition. An irascible man of great pride, Garnier undertook to create a distinctly Second Empire synthesis, a "style Napoleon III." Begun in 1861, the Opéra was not completed until 1875. This single work, although appreciated by few at the time, linked the name of Garnier forever with the transformation of Paris and with the architectural achievement of the Second Empire (today the Opéra is known, appropriately, as the Palais Garnier). Garnier died at Paris, 3 August 1898.

Catalog of the exhibition "Charles Garnier et l'Opéra" (Paris, 1961); L. Garnier, "Charles Garnier par Mme. Garnier," *L'architecture* 38 (1925); J. Gaudet, *Charles Garnier: Notice historique* (Paris, 1899); G. Larroumet, *Notice historique sur la vie et les oeuvres de M. Charles Garnier* (Paris, 1904).

Related entries: OPERA; PARIS, REBUILDING OF.

GAUME, JOSEPH, ABBE (1802–1879), priest and polemicist, vicar general of the diocese of Nevers and director of its minor seminary, and apostolic prelate (1854). Gaume received brief notoriety in the three years following the Falloux law with the publication of *Le ver rongeur* (1851), *La question des classiques* (1852), and *Lettres à Mgr. Dupanloup* (1853). In them he insisted that social ills since the fifteenth century were due to paganism in European society and that the church could make no compromise with decadent, contemporary society. The source of social illness was to be found in the educational direction of European society during the four centuries since the Renaissance, particularly in the teaching of what he referred to as pagan classics (those written by non-Christian authors). Gaume went on to insist that all subjects had to be regarded as "servants of the spiritual order." The proper understanding of geometry, then, became not the theorems of geometry but rather that those theorems were the expressions of divine law; the object of history was the understanding of the working of God's Providence on earth.

The denunciation of pagan classics was not new. Gaume's *Du Catholicisme dans l'éducation* was published in 1835; a few years earlier a disciple of Félicité de Lamennais (1782–1854) had spoken against paganism in French schooling at the Collège de Juilly. What was new in the 1850s was that church leaders paid attention to such extremism. Initial support indicated the extent to which denunciation of secularism had become part of standard Catholic rhetoric. Liberal Catholics' toleration for Gaume's simplifications dissolved quickly as they realized the implications for Christian humanism and for the church's role in modern society. Reactionaries, however, found in his attack an expression of their own alienation from modern society and of their dissatisfaction with the Falloux law. *L'Univers*, and the *Revue de l'enseignement chrétien*, which had opposed the Falloux bill, became the leading proponents of Gaumism. The elimination of secular literature was but a part of their goal, which was nothing less than the construction of a society dominated by the Catholic church or, failing that, creation of a wall isolating church and modern society, behind which Catholics would withdraw. The close temporal relationship between the wide reception of Gaume's ideas from 1851 to 1853 and the passage of the Falloux law was not coincidental. Gaumist ideology represented the dissatisfaction of those Catholics who, while advocating freedom of education, had hoped for the establishment of clerical supremacy.

Recognizing that at stake was the propriety of Christian humanism and the future direction of Catholic education, Catholic liberals—notably Mgr. Félix Dupanloup, Mgr. J.B.F.A.T. Landriot (1816–1874), and Jesuits like Charles Daniel (1818–1892)—mounted a counterattack. They insisted that study of all creation was proper, that religion and knowledge were compatible, that the development of the mind was essential to the development of Christians. Because Gaumists were never more than a small minority within the church, the controversy ended quickly, raging from 1851 to 1855, raising its head again briefly in 1858 and again in 1871, but never capturing the imagination or energy of many Catholics after 1854. Mgr. Dupanloup condemned *L'Univers* on 6 June 1852. Other bishops, including Gaume's superior, soon joined Dupanloup; they rejected the philosophy formally in 1856. A year earlier *Revue de l'enseignement chrétien* had terminated publication with a subscription list of fewer than one hundred.

The defeat of Gaumism marked the defeat of reactionary elements within the church concerning the conduct of schools. Disunity within the church, however, also precluded pedagogical innovations from Catholics during the next decade. In a peculiar about-face, Catholics in the 1870s would become the great defenders of classical studies against secular efforts at change.

P. J. Harrigan, "French Catholics and Classical Education after the Falloux Law," *FHS* 8 (Fall 1973).

Patrick J. Harrigan

Related entries: DUPANLOUP; GALLICANISM; *L'UNIVERS*; VEUILLOT.

GAUTIER, THEOPHILE (1811–1872), journalist and poet, a major precursor of the Parnassian school; born at Tarbès (Pyrénées), 31 August 1811, son of a tax official. By the beginning of the Second Empire, Gautier had written a collection of poems (1830), a novel (*Mademoiselle de Maupin*, 1835), and the librettos of two ballets (*Giselle*, 1841, and *Péri*, 1843). As well, he was at the time drawing considerable attention as the powerfully influential chief drama critic of *La presse* (1836–1855) who assiduously turned out "verbal photographs" of premieres of plays and ballets in Paris. In 1855 he moved to *Le moniteur universel*, publishing the first of fifty-two articles on the Paris international exposition of that year, and in 1869 to the *Journal officiel*. From December 1856 Gautier was also director of the influential *L'artiste*. In fact, throughout his entire career until his appointment as private librarian and reader to his friend and patroness Princess Mathilde in the winter of 1868, Gautier was never free from the demands of journalism, a fact he often bitterly lamented both privately to his friends and publicly in his reviews. His *Voyages en Espagne* (new ed., 1845) and *Voyages en Russie* (1867) record travels abroad that were undertaken largely to escape from the burdensome task of turning out copy. And yet it has been estimated that while Gautier in twenty years earned 20,000 francs from his books and plays, he earned 100,000 francs from his journalism, which, during the Second Empire, was a well-paid profession.

Having elevated journalistic criticism to the level of literature, Gautier longed to be recognized as a poet. His early poetry had been in a decidedly romantic vein, but by mid-century he had moved down another path. In 1852 his most famous collection of poems, *Emaux et camées*, appeared. Initially a slim volume of eighteen poems, subsequently expanded in later editions, it expressed Gautier's conception of the relationship of poetry to the plastic arts (he had studied painting as a young man). In the second edition (1858) Gautier published the poem "L'art," one of the best-known statements of the credo "'art for art's sake," which was to contribute greatly to the emergence of the Parnassian school centered on Charles Leconte de Lisle. Gautier's view was that art should be cultivated for its own sake and that its only purpose was the achievement of beauty: the perfect expression of the unity of form and content. Of necessity, this philosophy would restrict the appreciation of art to a small, elite circle.

The respect attached to Gautier's opinion as an art critic is testified to by the fact that in 1863 he was a member both of the Conseil Supérieur d'Enseignement pour les Beaux-Arts and of the Salon jury and president of the Société Nationale des Beaux-Arts. That same year he presided, with fine arts superintendent comte Emilien Nieuwerkeke (1811–1892) and Prosper Mérimee, over the disastrous installation of Eugène Viollet-le-Duc as professor of the history of art at the Ecole des Beaux-Arts. Still a romantic at heart, Gautier, despite his best efforts, could not accept realism in painting. Although he recognized, for example, the great gifts of Gustave Courbet, he rejected him because Courbet appeared to have abandoned the search for beauty.

Gautier was one of the relatively few intellectuals who were friendly to the

Second Empire (his social contacts included Prince Napoleon and Nieuwerkeke as well as Princess Mathilde), and it was probably for that reason, although he was in reality little interested in politics, that he was defeated by Auguste Barbier (1805–1882) for election to the Académie Française in 1869. Nevertheless, Gautier counted among his personal friends some of the most important literary figures of the age: Victor Hugo, Honoré de Balzac (1799–1855), Charles Augustin Sainte-Beuve, Gustave Flaubert, the Goncourt brothers, Théodore de Banville, and Gérard de Nerval (a fellow student at the Lycée Charlemagne). Gautier had traveled with Charles Garnier, future architect of the Paris Opéra, in Greece in 1852 and became his close friend and a champion of his work. He was a friend of Gustave Doré and, from earliest days, of the bohemian photographer Félix Nadar, who photographed him on more than one occasion. Gautier and his fellow poet Charles Baudelaire met in 1849. They formed a close attachment, experimented together with drugs, and it was to Gautier ("the impeccable poet, the perfect magician of French literature, my most dear and most venerated master and friend") that Baudelaire dedicated in 1857 his *Les fleurs du mal*. Gautier, in turn, published a preface to the first posthumous edition of the collection, which established Baudelaire's reputation as the father-founder of French decadent literature. Gautier was a regular at the *dîners Magny*, which from the end of November 1862 grouped on alternate Mondays such luminaries as Sainte-Beuve, the Goncourts, Paul Gavarni (1804–1866), Ernest Renan, Hippolyte Taine, Marcellin Berthelot, and George Sand (on occasion).

Among other works published by Gautier during the Second Empire are: *Portraits contemporains* (Paris, n.d.), *Le roman de la momie* (1858), *L'histoire de l'art dramatique en France depuis vingt-cinq ans* (6 vols., 1858–1859), *Le Capitaine Fracasse*, and *Poésies nouvelles* (1863). In June 1870 Gautier returned to Paris from Geneva for the funeral of Jules de Goncourt and remained there throughout the siege of the city by the Germans (Franco-Prussian War). The *Tableaux de siège* (1871) records his experience as a poet and Frenchman from within the capital. The siege and the defeat of France broke his health and spirit; he died at Neuilly, 23 October 1872.

E. Feydeau, *Théophile Gautier: Souvenirs intimes* (Paris, 1874); J. G. Lowin, "Théophile Gautier et ses Juives," *Revue des études juives* 131 (July–December 1972); J. Richardson, *Théophile Gautier, His Life and Times* (London, 1958), and "Théophile Gautier: Social Historian," *History Today* (April 1972).

Dolorès A. Signori

Related entries: BAUDELAIRE; LECONTE DE LISLE; MATHILDE; NADAR.

GEROME, JEAN LEON (1824–1904), academic painter of history and genre; born at Vesoul, 11 May 1824, son of a prosperous goldsmith. Gérôme began his training with the painter of French history Paul Delaroche (1797–1856). He went with Delaroche to Rome in 1844. Wishing to compete for the Prix de Rome, Gérôme returned to Paris in 1846 and entered the studio of Charles Gleyre (1808–1874), later the teacher of Pierre Auguste Renoir and Claude Monet. He did not win the coveted award but acquired from Gleyre an interest in Oriental subject matter that would often be the basis of his paintings.

The Cock Fight (1847, Louvre, Paris), Gérôme's first work accepted in the Salon (of 1847, where it competed with Thomas Couture's *Romans of the Decadence*), elicited praise from Théophile Gautier for its clarity of form and color. Gérôme and some fellow artists set up a studio that they shared and came to be known as Les Pompéistes or Les Néo-Grecs. They wanted to revive the classical tradition but also to purify it. The large figures set in a frieze-like composition in *The Cock Fight* reflect these ideas. In the early 1850s Gérôme received several government commissions for wall decorations in churches and also some private commissions such as the design for a Sèvres urn, which was shown in the Paris international exposition of 1855. His Salon entry in 1855 was *The Age of Augustus* (Amiens), which won a second-class medal and was purchased by the state. He was also made a knight of the Legion of Honor (in 1867 he was promoted to the rank of officer). His interest in depicting history as literally and accurately as possible left little room for the imagination. His traditional training was so strongly embedded that what becomes most evident in his anecdotal scenes is his technical competence and the lack of any sense of vitality.

Gérôme's trips to Egypt beginning in 1856 contributed to his explorations of exotic themes of remote places and foreign cultures. While similar in subject matter to the paintings of Eugène Delacroix, there is a considerable difference. Delacroix's horses, lions, and figures as in *Horses Fighting in a Stable* (1860, Louvre), also based on sketches he did on his trip to North Africa, are full of energy and turbulent motion and often express violent conflict; Gérôme's animals and figures as seen in *The Last Prayer* (1863–1883, Walters Art Gallery, Baltimore) or in *Slave Market* (1867, Sterling and Francine Clark Institute, Williamstown) seem to record factual data with cold observation and a polished finish. This can be seen as well in *Napoleon in Egypt* (1863, Art Museum, Princeton) where the effort to reproduce actuality in a deliberate manner results in a bloodless portrait.

In 1858 Gérôme received a commission to paint Pompeian decorations for the Palais Pompeien of Prince Napoleon (no longer extant). In 1861 he was commissioned to commemorate the visit of a Siamese embassy to Napoleon III and the Empress Eugénie in the Salon d'Hercule at the chateau of Fontainebleau. The occasion was the signing of a treaty opening Siam to Western trade. Gérôme's careful attention to detail is manifested with painstaking diligence (he had attended the reception and included his self-portrait on the left) in this large, horizontally composed work entitled *Reception of the Siamese Ambassadors by Napoleon III and the Empress Eugénie at Fontainebleau, June 27, 1861* (Versailles) completed in 1864. The scene is crowded with small figures, including miniature portraits of some eighty Second Empire dignitaries, set in the far distance in order to accommodate all of them. Preparatory work included precise drawings for which attendants at the ceremony later posed. Photographs taken by Gérôme's friend, Félix Nadar, were also used by Gérôme as an aid to greater verisimilitude. His *Duel after the Ball* (1857–1859, Walters Art Gallery), another version of which was shown in the Paris international exposition of 1867, is typical of the artist's anecdotal conception presented in a modest format. The duel in a clearing in the Bois de Boulogne is given a picturesque quality and sentimentalized (the victim is dressed as a Pierrot, the surgeon as a Venetian doge, the victor an American Indian), thus adding a touch of exoticism. The clarity and detail of the figures is so evident, the finish so polished, that the work seems to concentrate on an accumulation of separate incidents of form, line, color, as well as narrative, distracting the viewer from experiencing as a whole the feeling appropriate to such a dramatic event.

Gérôme was lionized during the Second Empire. In 1863 he was appointed professor at the reorganized Ecole des Beaux-Arts (Edouard Vuillard and Thomas Eakins, the great American realist, would eventually count among his pupils) and in that same year was elected to the Académie des Beaux-Arts, after four rejections. A frequent guest at Compiègne and the salon of Princess Mathilde, he was also able to indulge his taste for travel and exotic safaris, sometimes in the company of the Rothschilds. In 1867 he won the Grand Medal of Honor of the Paris international exposition. But he outlived his fame and in his latter years was bitterly attacked by advocates of Impressionism who blamed him for suppressing avant-garde art during his day. He numbered Claude Monet and Edgar Degas among his friends, however, and was not as devoid of sympathy for innovation and for experimentation as he has been depicted. Gérôme died at Paris, 10 January 1904.

G. Ackerman, "Gérôme: The Academic Realist," *Art News Annual* 33 (1967), and "Gérôme: Reassessing a Scorned Painter," *Art News* 72 (January 1973); A. Boime, *The Academy and French Painting in the Nineteenth Century* (New York, 1971); E. Strahan, ed., *Gérôme: A Collection of Works*, 2 vols. (New York, 1881–1883).

Beverley Giblon

Related entries: BAUDRY; BOUGUEREAU; CABANEL; COUTURE; MEISSONIER.

GIRARDIN, EMILE DE (1806–1881), the most influential journalist of the Second Empire, regarded as the founder of the modern mass press in France; born at Paris, 22 June 1806, the illegitimate son of an aristocratic general, comte Alexandre de Girardin. The fact of illegitimacy deeply influenced Girardin's entire life. Neglected by his parents and raised by strangers, he was determined to achieve fame, power, and fortune and to redeem his cloudy origins. To this end, he turned to journalism, founding his first newspaper, *Le voleur*, in 1828. A digest of other papers, *Le voleur* was soon making a fine profit, its circulation boosted by vigorous advertising. In June 1831 Girardin (then Eugène Delamothe) married the writer Delphine Gay (1804–1855) and in 1837 formally adopted his rightful name (ten years later General de Girardin publicly claimed paternity). Selling his interests in a number of other newspapers, Girardin in July 1836 founded *La presse*, a daily political paper. Before the Revolution of 1848, he had established himself as a major innovator in French journalism. He had set the subscription price of *La presse* at 40 francs, half that of other newspapers. The loss was recovered through increased advertising and a greatly increased circulation. Thus Girardin anticipated the sort of thinking that was to emerge in merchandising (the *grands magasins*) and in government finance during the Second Empire. He actively sought readers, expanding the content of his newspaper to include serials, sports, and other special features. He also published novels in serial form, paying 130,000 francs for George Sand's *Histoire de ma vie*. And like Napoleon III's half-brother, Auguste de Morny, he dabbled without great success in writing for the stage.

In politics, Girardin had diffidently opposed Louis Philippe's governments during the July Monarchy (1830–1848) but without becoming associated with any party or faction. He professed indifference to the form of government—so long as it took his advice! Following the Revolution of 1848, he supported the provisional government, then quarreled with General Louis Eugène Cavaignac (1802–1857) and was briefly imprisoned. Angered, Girardin turned to Prince Louis Napoleon. He was the first to propose in print (October 1848) that the prince present himself as candidate for president. As one of Louis Napoleon's few influential supporters and an important factor in his election (December 1848), Girardin was offered several government posts but declined because his ideas for remodeling the government were not accepted. *La presse* entered once again into opposition, taking a stand only slightly to the right of the republican *Le siècle*. Consequently Girardin was exiled in January 1852 following the coup d'état of December, but his friendship with Prince Napoleon enabled him to return to France, and he quickly made his peace with the regime, devoting his harshest attacks not to the government but to the church. He remained a liberal, however, and *La presse* was considered part of the left-wing opposition. His wife having died of cancer in June 1855, Girardin married in October 1856 an aristocratic German woman and, in December, irritated by the restrictions placed upon newspapers, sold his interest in *La presse* to the banker, Moïse Millaud. Girardin retained his ties with the regime, however (he was a friend of both Prince Napoleon and Princess Mathilde), and on 1 December 1862 unexpectedly returned to *La presse* as editor in chief, only to relinquish control once again, four years later, under circumstances similar to those of 1856. He subsequently busied himself with his investments and with publishing many political pamphlets.

In June 1866 Girardin returned to journalism by purchasing a recently established political daily, *La liberté*, which he immediately priced below cost at 10 centimes per copy. Within its columns, Girardin supported those who advocated a liberal Empire. *Avertissements* and fines followed (notably on 6 March 1867), and in April 1867 public sale of the paper was temporarily forbidden. But the next year Girardin saw the establishment of a degree of press freedom that Napoleon III had assured him (at Compiègne in 1863) would never be. And in 1870 his friend, Emile Ollivier, whom the journalist had helped to retain as a candidate to the Corps Législatif in 1863, became the first chief minister of a parliamentary regime. Girardin's volatility and independence prevented his appointment to the cabinet, and he continued his criticisms. The rise of Prussia had alarmed him and inspired angry articles in *La liberté* condemning Otto von Bismarck's policies. In the end, although he had earlier resisted plans for army reform and even flirted with the idea of disarmament and although he had sold *La liberté* to his nephew in June 1870, Girardin helped to orchestrate the demand for war with Prussia in July 1870. Appointed a senator that month, he was prevented from taking his seat by the war and the fall of the Empire. After 4 September he was reconciled to the Republic. He assumed control of *Le petit journal* in 1872 and of *La France* in 1874. His newspapers continued to prosper (he left an estate of 8 million francs) until his death at Paris, 27 April 1881.

H. Malo, *La gloire du Vicomte de Launay: Delphine Gay de Girardin* (Paris, 1925); J. Morienval, *Les créateurs de la grande presse en France: Emile de Girardin, H. de Villemessant, Moïse Millaud* (Paris, 1934); M. Reclus, *Emile de Girardin, le créateur de la presse moderne* (Paris, 1934); J. Richardson, "Emile de Girardin, 1806–1881: The Popular Press in France," *History Today* 26 (December 1976); G. Thuillier, "Les idées politiques d'Emile de Girardin," *RA*, no. 68 (1959).

Natalie Isser

Related entries: LIBERTE; MILLAUD; NEFFTZER; *PRESSE*; PRESS REGIME; VILLEMESSANT.

GOBINEAU, JOSEPH ARTHUR (1816–1882), sociologist and diplomat, author of *Essai sur l'inégalité des races humaines* (1854), which propounded the thesis of racial superiority and thus laid the intellectual foundation for racist ideologies for the next hundred years. Gobineau was also the promoter of a philosophy of conservatism that was enriched and to some degree shaped by his association (1843–1859) with Alexis de Tocqueville (1805–1859). Born near Paris (Ville d'Avray) 14 July 1816 to a bourgeois family long associated with Bordeaux, Gobineau aspired to the world of the nobility. The family had appropriated the particle *de* in their name. Louis de Gobineau père had been persecuted by Napoleon I's regime for his loyalty to the Bourbons, and Joseph Arthur called himself comte when an uncle with that title died in 1855. However, the Gobineau family was not rewarded by the Restoration governments, and the fortunes of the elder Gobineau collapsed altogether with the destruction of his marriage in the 1830s.

Young Gobineau, armed with an elementary education provided by a German tutor, entered college at Bienne and later at Redon with the intention of becoming an orientalist, but he was compelled in 1835 to seek his fortune in the real world of Paris. After stints of clerical work with a gas company and the postal service, Gobineau became a journalist and plunged into the social and political life of the legitimist salons. Reacting to the misfortunes of his father, Gobineau was politically conservative and yet contemptuous of political conservatives. His situation was similar to that of de Tocqueville. The European revolutions of 1848 consolidated the conservative emphasis of Gobineau's thought, and the rise of Louis Napoleon Bonaparte—and especially de Tocqueville's momentary acceptance of him—lured Gobineau into a diplomatic career in Persia, Germany, Greece, Brazil, and Sweden (1848–1877). In addition to his *chef d'oeuvre* (which he nursed through a number of editions), Gobineau reiterated his racial theories and conservative outlook in a novel, *Les Pléiades* (1874), an extended essay, *La Renaissance* (1877), dozens of articles, and an enormous correspondence highlighted by the exchange with de Tocqueville. His diplomatic service was honorable, but he was forced into early retirement at sixty-one (1877).

Gobineau believed that the race called Aryan, Teutonic, or Germanic (basis of the French nobility) was superior to all others, but he also believed that it was being adulterated by miscegenation, which at first had positive effects but then led to domination of the traits of the inferior race. Unlike later racial theorists, Gobineau was paralyzed morally and politically by his insights and conclusions. In *Essai sur l'inégalité*, to whose premises he constantly returned, Gobineau argued that miscegenation was debilitating to the Aryan (or any other superior) race but was unpreventable. In contrast to his intellectual descendants who registered moral outrage at racial mixing and worked for legislation to prevent it, Gobineau remained bleakly aloof from and indeed scoffed at moralists and politicians who responded pragmatically to his formulation of the problem. Two reasons have been advanced to explain Gobineau's passive pessimism. From the sociological standpoint, he identified himself with a French aristocracy that was, in his view, deservedly without prospects; for although he had deserted them to make a living, he retained with bitterness their world view. Moreover, Gobineau was a scientific determinist who had derived his racial theories from a body of thought concerning genetics and inheritance which was itself most deterministic. He died in voluntary exile at Turin, 13 October 1882.

J. Barzun, *Race: A Study in Modern Superstition*, Rev. ed. (New York, 1965); M. D. Biddiss, ed., *Gobineau: Selected Political Writings* (London, 1970), and *Father of Racist Ideology: The Social and Political Thought of Count Gobineau* (New York, 1970); J. Buenzod, *La formation de la pensée de Gobineau* (Paris, 1967); J. Gaulmier, "A propos de Gobineau, légende et vérité," *ASMP*, no. 2 (1971), and "Poison dans les veines: Note sur le thème du sang chez Gobineau," *Romantisme* 11, no. 31 (1981); J. F. de Raymond, "Le dossier personnel d'Arthur de Gobineau," *RHD*, 93 (April–December 1981).

David R. Stevenson

Related entries: BERNARD; POSITIVISM; RENAN; TAINE.

GONCOURT, EDMOND DE (1822–1896) **and JULES DE** (1830–1870), novelists whose works were appreciated mainly by contemporary professional writers. Edmond was born at Nancy, 26 May 1822; Jules at Paris, 17 December 1830. On the deaths of their rich and aristocratic parents in 1834 and 1848, the Goncourt brothers were able to live in reasonable comfort on income derived from inherited wealth (the family had moved to Paris from Nancy in the 1820s). An interest in drawing and painting encouraged them to undertake a hiking tour through Burgundy and Provence and on to Algeria. The fruits of their observations were recorded in their first literary work, a long description of Algiers, which appeared in 1852 in *L'éclair*, a weekly review devoted to literature and the arts founded by their cousin, the comte de Villedeuil (1831–1906). Offered posts as editors with the publication, the brothers began their career as journalists. To *L'éclair*, *Paris*, and *L'artiste* they contributed reviews of current dramas, literature, and vignettes of Parisian life.

The offices of these papers provided the brothers with a circle of colleagues. They became devoted to the lithographer Sulpice Guillaume Chevalier, known as Paul Gavarni (1804–1866), and were instrumental in securing his collaboration on *L'éclair* and *Paris*. Grief-stricken at the news of his death in 1866, the brothers wrote *Gavarni, l'homme et l'oeuvre* (1873), a biographical tribute to their close friend. At the Café Riche, the refuge of writers scorned by more bohemian circles, they met other journalists and aspiring writers: the novelist Mario Uchard (1824–1893) and the literary critic for *La Presse*, Charles Edmond Chojecki, known as Charles-Edmond (1822–1899). From the 1850s as well date their first contacts with Gustave Flaubert, Théodore de Banville, and Théophile Gautier.

In December 1852 the Goncourts became involved in a court case that aroused their hostility toward the regime. Proceedings were brought against them for publishing an article on Parisian life in which they had quoted mildly erotic verse by a Renaissance poet. Charged with offending public morality, they were acquitted in February 1853. The incident, which embittered them toward the regime and its repressive measures against the press, hastened their departure from the world of journalism. They took little interest in politics, however (few writers of the day did), and had nothing but contempt for politicians. Still, they resented the indifference of the court to them and to their writings, although Edmond was decorated in August 1867.

The brothers now turned to a more serious study of French history and in particular of the history of French art. They were passionate collectors of art and tapestries, and the drawings of the eighteenth century held a particular fascination for them. From the 1850s date several publications that attest to their researches: *Histoire de la société française pendant la Révolution* (1854); *Histoire de la société française pendant la Directoire* (1855); *Portraits intimes du XVIIIe siècle* (2 vols., 1857–1858); *Histoire de Marie-Antoinette* (1858); *Les maîtresses de Louis XV* (2 vols., 1860). From 1859 to 1870 they published privately and at their own expense studies on painters of the preceding century: Saint-Aubin, Watteau, Prud'hon, Boucher, Greuze, Chardin, Fragonard, Debucourt, La Tour, and vignettists Gravelot, Cochin-Eisen, and Moreau. These monographs appeared later (1875) in a collection under the general title *L'art du dix-huitième siècle*, recognized as an important work.

In the 1860s the Goncourts became interested in Oriental art and participated in the general enthusiasm for collecting *japonaiseries*. No doubt their collection was the subject of conversation at the salon of Princess Mathilde, which the brothers unfailingly frequented from 1862 to the end of the Empire, together with Flaubert, Gautier, Hippolyte Taine, Charles Augustin Sainte-Beuve, and many other literary figures. From the same year date the *dîners Magny*, a bi-monthly gathering of writers, critics, and artists. Records of both the gatherings at the home of Princess Mathilde in the rue de Courcelles and of the suppers at the Restaurant Magny were kept by the Goncourt brothers in their *Journal*. Begun 2 December 1851 by Edmond and Jules, the *Journal* was kept until the death of Edmond in 1896. A collection in twenty-two volumes of anecdotes, portraits of contemporaries (often acid), literary conversations, and confidences, its value as a commentary on the society of the *boulevard*, the realist-naturalist writers, and artists of the Second Empire and first years of the Third Republic is still acknowledged today.

As dramatists, the Goncourt brothers were unsuccessful. Two vaudevilles intended for presentation at the Palais Royal in 1850 were refused, as was a third play, *La nuit de Saint Sylvestre*, destined for the Comédie Française. The première of *Henriette Maréchal* at the Comédie in December 1865 drew violent protest from students who were convinced that Princess Mathilde had been instrumental in having the play presented. Curiously enough, it was opposition to the play from within the imperial circle that finally decided its fate (with-drawal). *La patrie en danger*, completed in 1867 after a holiday in Rome, was not produced until after the death of Jules.

As novelists, the Goncourt brothers chose to be realists and to depict all facets of modern life. Aiming for both documentary accuracy and art, they analyzed physiological and psychological crises that manifested themselves in mysticism, degradation, and erotic obsessions. Their first novel appeared the day after the coup d'état and was therefore a failure. But others followed. *Charles Demailly* (the title by which it is remembered today) appeared in 1860 and was greeted with less than enthusiasm, critical hostility being due in part to its focus on venal journalism and on the bohemian literary world. *Soeur Philomène* (1861) had a charity hospital for its setting; *Renée Mauperin* (1864) was a novel of manners, the first to concern itself with the *jeune fille moderne*; *Germinie Lacerteux* (1864) was based on the life of a depraved family servant, Rose; *Manette Salomon* (1867) was also a novel of manners; and *Madame Gervaisais* (1869), the brothers' last joint work of fiction, was a study of religious mania, inspired by the example of an aunt. A desire to be modern led the Goncourts to create an *écriture artiste*, a style and a language appropriate to the examination and presentation of the spiritual states of their protagonists. The death of the more vivacious and extrovert Jules at Paris, 20 June 1870, probably of syphilis, was a terrible blow to his melancholy and protective older brother. Nevertheless, Edmond continued for twenty-six years to write their journal, and he published on his own another twelve novels.

In addition to their chronicle of literary life, the Goncourt brothers are re-membered today as the founders of the Académie des Goncourt. Created in 1896 in accordance with Edmond's testament, the Académie is composed of ten prom-inent literary figures whose task is to award annually a prize of 5,000 francs to a promising young writer. Among those so honored have been André Malraux for *La condition humaine* (1933), Simone de Beauvoir for *Les mandarins* (1954), and Antonine Maillet for *Pélagie la charrette* (1980). Edmond de Goncourt died at Champrosay (Seine-et-Oise), 16 July 1896.

E. and J. de Goncourt, *Journal: Mémoires de la vie littéraire*, 8 vols. (Paris, 1956–1957; abridged translation by L. Galantière, New York, 1937); R. B. Grant, *The Goncourt Brothers* (New York, 1972); R. Ricatte, *La création romanesque chez les Goncourt, 1851–1870* (Paris, 1953); J. Richardson, "The Goncourt Brothers," *History Today* 25 (August 1975).

Dolorès A. Signori

Related entries: CHAMPFLEURY; DURANTY; FLAUBERT; THEATER; ZOLA.

GOUNOD, CHARLES (1818–1893), composer, recognized today as perhaps the most important figure in French music during the Second Empire; born at Paris, 17 June 1818. His father, who died in 1823, was a talented painter, professor of drawing at the Ecole Polytechnique. Gounod obtained his early musical education from his mother, a distinguished pianist. After graduating from the Lycée Saint Louis and receiving private instruction from Anton Reicha (1770–1836), he entered the Paris Conservatoire in 1836. There he studied composition with Jean François Lesueur (1760–1837), counterpoint with Fromental Halévy (1799–1862), and piano with Pierre Zimmerman (1785–1853), whose daughter, Anna, he would marry in 1847. Having won the Grand Prix de Rome in 1839, Gounod spent from December 1839 until 1843 at the Villa Medici in that city. The celebrated painter Dominique Ingres, who then directed the Villa and was himself a talented musician, had known Gounod's father and was so taken with the young composer's sketches that he offered to arrange an art scholarship for him. The three years at Rome were pivotal in Gounod's artistic development. There he fell under the influence of Palestrina's church music, spending a great deal of time at the seminary, and was much moved by the Paris sermons of Père Lacordaire, whose reputation had reached Italy. At Rome, as well, he met two remarkable women, the singer Pauline Viardot and the pianist Fanny Hensel (1805–1847), eldest sister of Félix Mendelssohn (1809–1847). Hensel introduced Gounod to Bach, Beethoven and Mendelssohn. On his way back to Paris, the young composer visited Vienna and Germany, meeting Schumann and, at Leipzig, Mendelssohn, who offered encouragement. Gounod returned to France with a broad knowledge of the musical trends of his day.

Gounod had a strong religious sense, and the years between 1843 and 1849 saw him drawn toward church, as opposed to secular, music. This tension between sacred and profane love was to dominate his musical life. Before leaving for Rome, he had had a Mass commissioned and performed (at Saint Eustache). While at Rome a second Mass was performed at a French church, S. Luigi dei Francesi (May 1841). Now, on his return to Paris, Gounod was attached for six months to the Eglise des Missions Etrangères (rue du Bac) as *maître de chapelle*.

Living at that time with his mother, he attended courses at Saint Sulpice Seminary as an external student (1846–1848), but his religious calling appears not to have been very strong, and the termination of his Saint Sulpice studies marked as well his entry into that area to which all serious French composers turned by preference at mid-century—opera.

After a brief visit to Britain in 1851, during which parts of his *Messe solennelle* were played with great success (he had also produced a symphony in 1850), Gounod was encouraged by Viardot, who opened the way for him, to compose an opera, *Sapho*, in the grand opera tradition then predominant in France. Produced at the Opéra, 16 April 1851, with Viardot singing the lead role, *Sapho* (libretto by Emile Augier but lacking the requisite ballet) was coldly received, despite the praise of Hector Berlioz, music critic for the *Journal des débats*. On the other hand *Sapho* did win Gounod appointment in 1852 as conductor of the Paris choral society, the Orphéon, and as director (1852–1860) of music education in the communal schools of the city of Paris (such education was then under Orphéon supervision). That same year the composer wrote incidental music for the production at the Théâtre Français of a play, *Ulysse*, by François Ponsard (1814–1867). Still under Viardot's influence, Gounod tried his hand once more at grand opera, with *La nonne sanglante* (libretto by Eugène Scribe and Germain Delavigne [1790–1868]; Opéra, 18 October 1854). It too was a failure. Now at the height of his powers, Gounod won his first great success with a masterpiece of church music, the *Messe solennelle de Sainte Cécile*, performed at Saint Eustache 22 November 1855. He would write no more Masses during the Second Empire. Gounod also composed during the period 1850–1858 three symphonies (two for the Société des Jeunes Artistes, 1855 and 1856), a cantata on the occasion of Queen Victoria's visit to France in the summer of 1855, and incidental music for Molière's *Le bourgeois gentilhomme* (1857). In August 1857 he was made a knight of the Legion of Honor.

In 1858 Gounod began his long association with the Théâtre Lyrique, then directed by Léon Carvalho, assisted by his wife, Marie Miolan, a celebrated soprano. Critics of today would argue that in the successful comic opéra *Le médecin malgré lui* (libretto by Jules Barbier [1822–1901] and Michel Carré [1819–1872]; Théâtre Lyrique, 15 January 1858), Gounod at last found his true musical self. However, the lure of Meyerbeerian grand opera would not be denied, and *Faust* (libretto by Barbier and Carré; Théâtre Lyrique, 19 March 1859) had the perhaps unfortunate effect of encouraging Gounod in that direction, for *Faust* was a great success, both for the composer and for Mme. Carvalho, who created the role of Marguerite. Although at first a greater sensation at London than at Paris (the original version contained spoken dialogue and lacked a ballet), *Faust* made Gounod's name with the large public. It had almost two hundred performances at the Théâtre Lyrique (in 1860 Gounod provided it with recitatives) before a reworked version, containing a full-length ballet, premiered at the Opéra on 3 March 1869. *Faust* was given its five hundredth performance in 1887.

Other successes followed: *Philémon et Baucis* (libretto by Barbier and Carré;

Théâtre Lyrique, 18 February 1860); *La colombe* (libretto by Barbier and Carré; Baden Baden, 3 August 1860, and Paris, Opéra Comique, 7 June 1866); *La reine de Saba* (libretto by Barbier and Carré, based on a story by Gérard de Nerval; Opéra, 28 February 1862; sung by Louis Guéymard [1822–1880] and his wife, Pauline Lauters-Guéymard [born 1834]); *Mireille* (libretto by Carré, based on Frédéric Mistral's poem; Théâtre Lyrique, 19 March 1864); and *Roméo et Juliette* (libretto by Barbier and Carré; Théâtre Lyrique, 27 April 1867). *Mireille* was a great success for the composer and for Mme. Carvalho, who sang the title role. And *Roméo et Juliette* (Mme. Carvalho created the role of Juliette) marked the culmination of Gounod's career, receiving about one hundred performances at Paris before touring Europe. In May 1866 Gounod was elected to the Académie des Beaux-Arts, in place of Louis Clapisson (1808–1866), and in August he was named officer of the Legion of Honor.

After 1867 Gounod turned increasingly to religious music, including an oratorio, *Sainte Geneviève*, with words by Abbé Charles Freppel (1827–1891). Gounod was at the seaside when war broke out between France and Prussia in July 1870. He wrote a patriotic cantata, *A la frontière*, which was performed at the Opéra on 8 August. On 13 September he fled with his family to London and did not return until June 1874. Gounod's operas are still performed, but his reputation today rests even more on the great influence he exerted on French composers of the succeeding generation. Cultivated, interested in all the arts, Gounod had friends ranging from Hector Berlioz (1803–1869), whose genius he early recognized, to Dominique Ingres. He helped to discover and to encourage a number of young composers, including Camille Saint-Saëns, Georges Bizet (1838–1875), Jules Massenet (1842–1912), Edouard Lalo (1823–1892), and Gabriel Fauré (1845–1924). Bizet's first opera, *Les pêcheurs de perles*, was closely modeled on Gounod's works. Worried at the younger man's despondency following the failure of *Les pêcheurs*, Gounod introduced him to the salon of Napoleon III's cousin, Princess Mathilde, where he could make useful acquaintances and exploit his great talent as a pianist.

Because Gounod at last superseded the Meyerbeerian mold that had dominated opera at Paris for thirty years, he is credited with having initiated the revival of French music following 1870. Ironically, he achieved this not through what he would himself have considered his serious music but through his gift for unpretentious lyrical melody, believable dramatic presentation, and delineation of character by musical means. Gounod died at Saint Cloud, 18 October 1893.

M. Cooper, "Charles Gounod and His Influence on French Music," *Music and Letters* 21 (1940); M. Curtiss, *Bizet and His World* (New York, 1958); N. Demuth, *Introduction to the Music of Gounod* (London, 1950); C. Gounod, *Mémoires d'un artiste* (Paris, 1896); J. Harding, *Gounod* (London, 1973).

Related entries: CARVALHO; CONCERT LIFE; MEYERBEER; PASDELOUP; *TANNHAUSER* PREMIERE; THOMAS; VIARDOT.

GOVERNMENT FINANCE. The government budget did not undergo major changes during the Second Empire. Although in monetary terms the budget increased by 43 percent between 1850–1854 and 1865–1869 (the 1852 budget was 1.5 billion francs; that of 1869 was 2.2 billion), this represented a slight decrease in government expenditure as a proportion of gross national product (7.8 percent for the Second Empire as opposed to 8.4 percent for the 1820–1849 period). This stability is doubly surprising. It is surprising, first, because the long-term trend was toward a massive increase in state spending, not only in absolute terms but as a proportion of national income (between 1815 and 1969 this proportion would triple), the most marked development being in productive spending. It is surprising, second, because the Second Empire was perhaps the first regime to emphasize not only the central importance of the economy but that of the state in the economy, as witnessed, for instance, in Napoleon's Bordeaux speech of October 1852 or his letter to Achille Fould published in the *Moniteur* in January 1860. Some of the emperor's closest advisers, and Victor Fialin Persigny in particular, also believed in the advantages of productive spending: government spending to increase the tax base and, consequently, revenues. The regime, indeed, maintained a high profile in the economy, subsidizing railways and shipping and granting loans to agriculture and industry.

Government revenue increased as a result of increased prosperity, economic growth, and inflation (the cost of living rose perhaps 30 percent between 1852 and 1870), but no changes were made in the taxation system that had been established under the Revolution and the Empire. What did change was the increase in budget deficits and the consequent recourse to loan flotations. There were six government loans before 1870: those of 1854 (250 million francs), 1855 (500 million and 750 million), 1859 (500 million), 1864 (300 million), and 1868 (450 million). As a result, the national debt doubled between 1853 and 1869 (from 5.560 billion francs to 11.603 billion), while under the July Monarchy it had increased by only 20 percent. The cost of servicing this debt also increased. It rose from an annual average of 218 million francs in the 1840s to 363 million in the 1860s, by which time it represented a fifth of all government expenditures, second after defense spending. Contemporary critics of government finance, including those members of the Corps Législatif called *budgétaires*, attacked both deficits and the cost of loans in a period of rising interest rates and called for orthodox methods and a return to balanced budgets. The increase in the burden of debt under the Second Empire should not be exaggerated, however. It was to increase even more dramatically in the later nineteenth century and would double in the 1870–1874 period alone.

As far as the nature of government spending was concerned, regime apologists liked to claim that productive spending had increased. This was not the case. Defense spending continued to be responsible for over a third of all expenditures, while spending on public works made up only 6 percent and subsidies to business 5 percent. During the 1840s, in contrast, public works expenditures had constituted a larger proportion of state spending (9 percent). Thus while the government had provided roughly a quarter of railway capital prior to 1852, it furnished only about a tenth under the Second Empire. The only exceptions to the trend were subsidies to the merchant marine that stood at 5 million in 1859 but had risen to 26 million in 1869 and the loans to agriculture in 1856 and to industry in 1860 (to help in adjustment to the new tariff system). Only 1 percent of the state budget went to education and just over 6 percent to the colonies, a situation that was to alter from 1881 on. Without the wars of the Second Empire, probably revenues would have balanced expenditures.

One cause of the immobility in government finances and slight decline in productive spending was the prosperity of the period, as compared, for example, to the decades from 1870 when war and less favorable economic conditions led to increased expenditures. Another was the mobilization of credit. The preference share (*obligation*) provided 80 percent of new railway capital under the Second Empire, and government funding became less necessary. Besides, the canal and road networks that had absorbed large government funds were nearly complete by midcentury. (In this connection, it might also be noted that Second Empire loans were for the first time placed directly by the government. Banks continued to receive subscriptions, in return for a commission, but no longer guaranteed the placement.) Above all, financial orthodoxy with regard to the taxation system and even spending was successfully defended by the powerful budget commission of the Corps Législatif. As a result, indirect encouragement to the economy, through political stability and liberal policies toward bank and company formation and fusions, was probably more significant in promoting growth than direct government intervention.

L. Fontvieille, *Evolution et croissance de l'état français, 1815–1969* (Paris, 1976); M. Marion, *Histoire finançière de la France depuis 1715*, vol. 5 (Paris, 1928); R. Schnerb, *Deux siècles de fiscalité française, XIXe–XXe siècle* (Paris, 1973).

Barrie M. Ratcliffe

Related entries: BANKING; COBDEN-CHEVALIER TREATY; COMPAGNIE GENERALE TRANSATLANTIQUE; CORPS LEGISLATIF; CREDIT MOBILIER; ECONOMIC CRISES; FOULD; LATIN MONETARY UNION; MAGNE; MESSAGERIES IMPERIALES; PARIS, REBUILDING OF; PEREIRE; RAILROADS; ROTHSCHILD; ROUHER.

GRAMONT, ANTOINE, DUC DE (1819–1880), diplomat, foreign minister at the time of the outbreak of war with Prussia in 1870; born at Paris, 14 August 1819, descendant of an aristocratic family. After studying at the Ecole Polytechnique (1837–1839), he married the daughter of a wealthy English merchant. Despite the legitimist traditions of his family, Gramont attached himself to the cause of Louis Napoleon and was rewarded by appointment as French representative to Cassel, then to Stuttgart (1852–1853), and, in April 1853, to Turin. As French minister to Sardinia, he negotiated the entry of that country into the Crimean War. Appointed ambassador to Rome in the latter half of 1857, Gramont opposed the efforts of the foreign minister, Edouard Thouvenel, to negotiate a treaty that would lead to the evacuation of French troops in Rome. In November 1861 he was named ambassador to Austria. The Vienna posting proved a congenial one for the conservative diplomat. Handsome, with exquisite manners, he was at home in Viennese society and soon became committed to an Austrian alliance. In this he had the sympathy of the Empress Eugénie. Gramont performed his duties skillfully and effectively. The apex of his career was, perhaps, the 1866 treaty by which Austria ceded Venetia to France (and thus to Italy) and for which he was awarded the grand cross of the Legion of Honor.

The Prussian victory over Austria in the war of 1866 opened a new phase of Gramont's career. Convinced that he was at least the equal of Prussian chancellor Otto von Bismarck, the ambassador from July 1866 favored decisive French action to counter the rise of Prussian power. He contributed over the next four years to the development of French hostility toward Prussia. The resignation of Comte Napoléon Daru led to the appointment of Gramont in mid-May 1870 as foreign minister by Emile Ollivier on advice of Prince Napoleon. Emperor Francis Joseph bestowed on the departing ambassador the grand cross (diamonds) of St. Stephen.

Gramont, the faithful servitor of Napoleon III, was about to contribute to the collapse of the Second Empire. From the moment (3 July) when the candidacy of Prince Leopold of Hohenzollern-Sigmaringen for the Spanish throne was known at Paris, the new foreign minister favored a strong stand that would signal Prussia as the instigator. With Napoleon III's consent, he wired Berlin demanding an explanation of the candidacy. On 6 July, with unanimous approval of the cabinet, he delivered a statement to the Corps Législatif clearly threatening war if the matter were not resolved to the satisfaction of France. Gramont claimed, and with much justification, that French public opinion would not have tolerated any less vigorous a response. On 12 July, Prince Leopold having withdrawn his name, Gramont and Napoleon III decided, without consulting the cabinet, to demand that King William of Prussia bind himself never again to permit such a candidacy. Although on 13 July Ollivier won the cabinet to a policy of peace, Gramont undoubtedly had French opinion on his side, and Bismarck's subsequent actions easily infuriated that opinion into a war fury. At three cabinet meetings on 14 July, Gramont urged intransigence and opposed the alternative of a European congress. At its third meeting, the Council of Ministers decided for war. From the beginning, Gramont had held out the hope of effective Austrian assistance. Probably he was himself deceived, but undoubtedly this confidence was a factor in the decision of the Corps Législatif on 15 July to vote war credits. The nefarious result of these decisions for France cannot be doubted, but Gramont's personal responsibility must depend to some extent on an objective assessment of the role played by French opinion. On 9 August the foreign minister was preparing for the evacuation from Rome of French troops desperately needed at home when the fall of Ollivier's government ended his career. Gramont died at Paris, 17 January 1880.

Antoine, duc de Gramont, *L'Allemagne nouvelle, 1863–1867* (Paris, 1878) and *La France et la Prusse avant la guerre* (Paris, 1872); C. de Grünwald, *Le duc de Gramont,*

gentilhomme et diplomate (Paris, 1950); G. C. Patterson, "The Viennese Mission of the Duc de Gramont, 1861–1870" (Ph.D. diss., University of Notre Dame, 1974).
Related entries: ALLIANCE POLICY; HOHENZOLLERN CANDIDACY; PUBLIC OPINION.

GRANDS MAGASINS, the first modern department stores, an economic innovation of the Second Empire. The *grand magasin* was unique not for its size alone or for being a department store but for the combination of these factors supplemented by many new and successful retail techniques. Newly rebuilt Paris provided the essential ingredients: a large and wealthy population, efficient mass transportation, bulk manufacture of items for retail, acceptance of innovation, and the innovators, of whom the first (and the only one of genius) was Aristide Boucicaut (1810–1877). Although Jules Parissot's (d. 1861) Belle Jardinière (founded 1824, premises moved in 1866) anticipated developments, Boucicaut's Bon Marché was the world's first great modern department store. Son of a shopkeeper of modest means, an itinerant peddler from 1828, in Paris in 1835 and employed thereafter at the Petit St. Thomas store where he acquired a reputation as a brilliant buyer and seller, Boucicaut retired in 1852 and with his savings entered into partnership with the owner of a tiny shop, Au Bon Marché, at the corner of the rue de Sèvres and the rue du Bac. Over the next eleven years, he multiplied the innovations characteristic of the *grand magasin*: entry without obligation, marking of prices (which previously had been adjusted to the proprietor's assessment of the customer's ability to pay), right of return and refund, sales commissions, offering of a great variety of merchandise (division into departments), seductive display, home delivery, liquidation of stock every three months through advertisement and sales, and the principle of minimal profit margin on a greatly increased volume of sales (450,000 francs in 1852, 5 million in 1860, 7 million in 1863, and 21 million in 1869).

On 31 January 1863 Boucicaut bought his partner's interest. In 1867 he inaugurated catalog sales for the benefit of the provinces, borrowing for the purpose, and issuing the first French mail order catalog. That same year he engaged the architect L. A. Boileau (1812–1896) to build a new store incorporating features already embodied in the Coin de Rue (1864) and the Magasins Réunis—a huge central hall flanked by several levels of galleries, the whole constructed entirely of iron and covered by a great skylight. The cornerstone was laid 9 September 1869, the year of a strike by Paris department store clerks, but the project was not completed (by Boileau's son) until after the Franco-Prussian War. Boucicaut also created an emergency fund for employees (*caisse de prévoyance*) supported exclusively by the company. He launched other social security measures and introduced profit sharing by employees according to rank.

Until 1870 Bon Marché remained the only truly *grand magasin*, but there were imitators and competitors. Hippolyte Alfred Chauchard (1821–1909) and two associates persuaded Emile Pereire in 1854 to allow them to establish a store on the ground floor of the new Hôtel du Louvre. A year later, assisted by

the Pereires' Compagnie Immobilière, they established a society with capital of
1.1 million francs. The Grands Magasins du Louvre opened 9 July 1855 during
the international exposition of that year. The new store, luxuriously appointed
with salons and a buffet, catered to a wealthier clientele than that of Bon Marché.
It soon added a trade in household items and prospered so well that it later took
over the premises, the hotel moving across the street. Of even more humble
origins, Xavier Ruel in 1856 made a pioneering use of market research. Manager
of a group of street peddlers, he determined that the corner of the rue de Rivoli
and of the rue des Archives would be a promising site, and there he established
a small shop, which he expanded by 1860 into the Grand Bazar de l'Hôtel de
Ville. Ruel, a Lyonnais, invented the *prix fixe* (1 to 10 sous), a formula destined
later to great success. Jules Jaluzot (1834–1916) had received his training at Bon
Marché. With his wife's money, he founded Au Printemps in 1865, on the
boulevard Haussmann at the intersection of the rue du Havre and the rue de
Provence (a new quarter, close to the Gare Saint-Lazare). It was an immediate
success. Ernest Cognacq (1839–1928), after years of poverty and failure, established a small shop in 1869 near the Pont Neuf, which he and his wife (Louise
Jay; also trained at Bon Marché) would laboriously build into La Samaritaine
without recourse to bankers. Of course, this followed the Empire. But it remains
true that of the great modern Parisian department stores, only the Galeries Lafayette was founded after 1870. It might also be noted that during the Second
Empire was established the first grocery store chain selling its own packaged
products, Félix Potin.

Small merchants in the vicinity of the new stores—the "houses of temptation"
as Emile Zola named them—were easily overwhelmed. But while the *grands
magasins* were imitated throughout the world (for example, by John Wanamaker
in Philadelphia, 1876), their economic importance should not be exaggerated in
a time when of some 944,000 Frenchmen and French women engaged in commerce, 700,000 were owners of their own business.

M. Dasquet, *Le Bon Marché* (Paris, 1955); B. Gille, "Recherches sur l'origine des
grands magasins," *Mémoires des Sociétés savantes de l'Ile de France* 7 (1956); R. Héron
de Villefosse, *Cent ans de jeunesse: Le Bon Marché* (Paris, 1952); F. Laudet, *La Samaritaine* (Paris, 1933); P. MacOrlan, *Le Printemps* (Paris, 1931); M. B. Miller, *The
Bon Marché: Bourgeois Culture and the Department Store, 1869–1920* (Princeton, N.J.,
1981); H. Pasdermadjian, *The Department Store: Its Origins, Evolution, and Economics*
(London, 1954); E. Zola, *Au Bonheur des Dames* (Paris, 1883).

Related entries: PARIS, REBUILDING OF; PEREIRE; ROUGON-
MACQUART.

GRANIER DE CASSAGNAC, ADOLPHE (1806–1880), deputy to the Corps
Législatif, one of the most important semiofficial journalists of the Second Empire, vocal representative of conservative and authoritarian bonapartism; born at
Avéron-Bergelle (Gers), 11 August 1806, into an old noble family of modest
means. Granier de Cassagnac attended school in Toulouse and became a jour-

nalist, a choice that upset his family. He also taught school and wrote poetry. His first political brochure, *Aux électeurs de France*, appeared in 1831, proclaiming his belief in democracy, a position he would later abandon. As was so often the case with young, ambitious provincials when they had gained maturity, Granier de Cassagnac headed for Paris. He left Toulouse in 1832 with a letter from a local lawyer introducing him to Charles de Rémusat (1797–1875), who in turn presented him to François Guizot (1787–1874). With the assistance of these two distinguished men, he found employment as a journalist for the Orleanist journals, *Revue de Paris* and *Journal des débats*. Primarily writing as a literary critic, he fancied himself the champion of romanticism, particularly that of Victor Hugo. But he also served Guizot as a spokesman for conservatism. Brash and arrogant (he was forced to leave the *Journal des débats* but was immediately hired by *La presse*), he nonetheless wrote with clarity and style and conducted himself with a charm that commanded respect in the literary and social circles of the July Monarchy. He was named to the Legion of Honor in 1838 for his literary excellence and his defense of the political order.

The young Granier de Cassagnac had been disturbed by the revolutionary days of 1830, and when the Revolution of 1848 began, he was horrified and immediately left Paris for the south. At Le Couloumé, the chateau he had purchased from the abbé de Montesquieu, he wrote the three-volume *Histoire des causes de la Révolution française*, a polemic designed to show that the Revolution of 1789 had been unnecessary and that its consequences were far from positive for France. Granier de Cassagnac, the historian, is clear confirmation of the idiom that in the nineteenth century a Frenchman's politics were derived from his view of the great Revolution. His retirement from public life was brief, for in the fall of 1848 he declared his support for the presidential candidacy of Louis Napoleon Bonaparte. He returned to Paris in 1850 as editor of *Le pouvoir* where, after what he described as virtually a religious conversion to loyal confidence in Louis Napoleon and after having been taken into the pay of the government, he styled himself the ranking defender of bonapartism. He supported the president's attempt to revise the constitution (1851), and when the Legislative Assembly blocked revision, he found the blindness of the politicians clear justification for the coup d'état of December 1851. His *Récit authentique des événements de Décembre 1851* was commissioned by the prince president as a defense of the coup d'état. Following these events, Granier de Cassagnac ran as an official candidate for deputy to the Corps Législatif and was elected with 75 percent of the vote. He remained a deputy until 1870. Throughout the period of the Empire, he was also mayor of Plaisance, member of the Conseil Général of the Gers, and a semiofficial journalist of the Empire, albeit a rather independent one. He wrote first for *Le constitutionnel*, where he helped to persuade the proprietor, Dr. Louis Véron (1798–1867), to support the new regime, but in 1857 established *Le reveil*. He contributed numerous articles to all the semiofficial papers and to the official *Le moniteur*, frequently under direct inspiration of the emperor or of his ministers. In 1859 he gained the editorship of *Le pays*, where he remained until 1861. From 1861 to 1866, with the exception of six months in 1863 during which he edited *La nation*, preparing for the elections of that year, he was retired from journalism. In 1866 he returned to *Le pays* and remained there as a vigorous conservative bonapartist until September 1870, assisted by his son Paul (1842–1904).

The stability and prosperity of the 1850s allowed Granier de Cassagnac to enjoy his timely conversion to bonapartism and to reflect on the failures of the regimes that had preceded the Empire. Each regime had collapsed, he believed, because it had invested authority in legislative bodies. When on 24 November 1860, his own emperor began to move in the same direction, Granier de Cassagnac initially offered loyal support but was quick to assure his readers that the fundamental bases of power established in 1852 would not be disrupted. During the next few years, in spite of his discomfort with Napoleon III's initiatives toward liberal reform, he supported the imperial foreign policy and defended the Empire by arguing that the demands for liberty of the press, electoral liberty, and expansion of parliamentary power were dangerous and unnecessary. As late as 1866, he relaxed in the confidence that a liberal Empire was not imminent.

The reform proposals of 1867 caught Granier de Cassagnac off guard, and he was forced into a dual combat, defending the Empire against attacks from the Left while also defending bonapartism against the Bonaparte in power who, he was convinced, was straying too far and too fast from his principles. With the assistance of Jérôme David, he made the debating club in the rue de l'Arcade a domain of the Right, an extraparliamentary pressure group (the "Arcadiens") designed to urge the emperor to withdraw his reforms. When the new laws on the press and public assembly were voted, Granier de Cassagnac abstained, after first making (31 January 1868) a great speech against the proposed reform of press laws. The speech helped to decide Napoleon III on a free vote, although later he again changed his mind and instructed Eugène Rouher to bring the conservative bonapartists into line. Granier de Cassagnac's columns in *Le pays* reflected discouragement, disillusionment, and a sense of isolation from the emperor. Unwittingly the journalist contributed to the notion that the Empire was weakening by brashly asking, "Where are we going?" and by accusing Napoleon III of not "daring to govern." Granier de Cassagnac's despair crystallized into hostility directed at Emile Ollivier's Liberal Empire, and he complained that the politics of 1869–1870 were Parisian, not French, and above all, not bonapartist, although he did defend the plebiscite of May 1870. The criticism of Ollivier reached a furious pitch in the summer of 1870 in the face of the threat from Bismarck's Prussia. *Le pays* branded the government a "ministry of shame" and cried out for war to ensure the future of the dynasty.

Following the defeat of France in the Franco-Prussian War, Granier de Cassagnac settled in Brussels, where he founded *Le drapeau* and from which he launched an appeal to the people of France to restore the Empire. He regained the editorship of *Le pays* in 1872, was elected deputy from the Gers in 1876 and again in 1877, sat with the *Appel au peuple* group in the chamber, and remained a vigorous and loyal defender of authoritarian bonapartism until his death at Le Couloumé, 31 January 1880. His son Paul continued to direct *Le pays*.

W. E. Duvall, "Bernard Adolphe Granier de Cassagnac and Right-Wing Bonapartism under the Second Empire" (Ph.D. diss., University of California, 1973); A. Granier de Cassagnac, *Souvenirs du Second Empire*, 3 vols. (Paris, 1879–1882); K. Offen, "The Political Career of Paul de Cassagnac" (Ph.D. diss., Stanford University, 1970).

William E. Duvall
Natalie Isser

Related entries: BONAPARTISM; DAVID; LIBERAL EMPIRE; *PAYS*; *PRESSE*; PRESS REGIME; PUBLIC OPINION; REFORM.

GUYS, CONSTANTIN (1802–1892), painter; born at Vlissingen (Flushing), Holland. His father was a high French naval official. Remarkably little is known of his life. He was, it would seem, with Lord Byron in Greece during that country's struggle for independence from Turkey (1823–1824). From about 1848, Guys was a correspondent for the *Illustrated London News*, for which he covered the events of 1848 in France and, later, the Crimean War (1853–1855). In 1851 he met Félix Nadar, the photographer, in London, and the two men became lifelong friends. After having traveled to the Orient, Guys settled in Paris about 1862, making frequent excursions thereafter to Britain, for he was a noted Anglophile and seems to have possessed some private means. He was much admired by Charles Baudelaire, who in November 1863 published in *Le Figaro* the first installment of *Peintre de la vie moderne*, in which he recognized Guys' modernity and praised the artist's ability to capture quickly the essence of a motif without belaboring it. Guys' subjects were often women, both aristocrats and courtesans, depicted in a lively manner in watercolor, as can be seen in *Woman in a Blue Crinoline on a Yellow Background* (1860, Petit Palais, Paris). In his choice of motifs and animated handling, he is a forerunner of Henri de Toulouse-Lautrec. Not only Nadar but also Edouard Manet collected Guys' drawings. But the artist's passion for anonymity was such (even Baudelaire in his celebrated work referred to him as "M-G") that it was not until the 1895 exhibition arranged by Nadar, one of his very few friends, that he was recognized as a minor master. Guys died at Paris in 1892, seven years after he had been invalided as a result of a traffic accident.

G. Geffroy, *Constantin Guys, l'historien du Second Empire* (Paris, 1920); C. Holme, ed., *The Painter of Victorian Life, including an Introduction and Translation of Baudelaire's "Painter of Modern Life" by P. G. Konody* (London, 1930); J. Richardson, "The Painter of Modern Times," *History Today*, 24 November 1974; K. W. Smith, *The Crimean War Drawings of Constantin Guys* (Cleveland, 1978).

Beverley Giblon

Related entries: BAUDELAIRE; MANET; MEISSONIER; NADAR; PILS.

H

HACHETTE, LOUIS (1800–1864), founder of the great Paris publishing house; born at Rethel (Ardennes), 5 May 1800. A graduate of the Ecole Normal Supérieure (1822), Hachette studied law but in 1826 founded a press to publish school textbooks. By 1850 Hachette's was already a large and thriving business, specializing in science and history as well as literature. The press published travel guides (for example, Joanne's) and, from 1860, a travel journal (*Tour du monde*), dictionaries (Vapereau's *Dictionnaire universel des contemporains*, Emile Littré's *Dictionnaire de la langue française* [1863–1873]), and works of classical literature. Although Hachette's published from 1852 the best of contemporary foreign literature in translation and although these books in their red covers constituted a new threat to the well-being of French writers, Louis Hachette was noted for the respect and dignity with which he treated his authors. As one who contributed greatly to the establishment of protection for literary and artistic property in France (decrees of 17 February and 28 March 1852), he invariably tried to persuade writers to hold on to their property. From 1836 he had been the proponent of an absolute right of ownership of literary property, as opposed to reciprocity.

In 1855, with Charles Lahure, Hachette established the *Journal pour tous* to serialize novels in illustrated form. In 1862 Emile Zola began his Paris career as a clerk and later director of advertising at Hachette's. Louis Hachette avoided politics, but he wrote a number of *rapports* and *mémoires* on questions of social organization and public assistance. Hachette's flourished under the leadership of its founder and of his relatives and collaborators, Louis Bréton (d. 1883) and Emile Templier (d. 1891), who carried on after Louis Hachette's death, together with his second son, Georges (1838–1892; involved in the business from 1863). In one important respect, Louis Hachette helped to shape the reading habits of France. His press, which received permission in 1850 from the post office to transport newspapers, obtained between 1852 and 1855 exclusive rights to sell books and newspapers from kiosks on railway station platforms and kept the monopoly, except for 1896 to 1905, until World War II. There were 442 stalls in 1874, although newspapers were more important than books by 1865. Hachette died at Paris, 31 July 1864.

J. Mistler, ''Un grand éditeur et ses auteurs,'' *RDM* 14 (1964), and *La librairie Hachette de 1826 à nos jours* (Paris, 1964 and 1979).
Related entries: COPYRIGHT AND PATENT; LAROUSSE.

HALEVY, LUDOVIC (1834–1908), librettist, dramatist, and novelist, sometimes under the pseudonyms Jules Servières or Paul D'Arcy; best known as coauthor with Henri Meilhac (1831–1897) of numerous successful vaudevilles (short comedies using popular songs) and comedies; born at Paris, 1 January 1834, to a family well known in musical and artistic circles. Halévy's uncle was Fromental Halévy (1799–1862), composer of the grand opera *La juive*; his father, Léon, was an author and dramatist. Halévy made his debut in the theater when only twenty-one. In 1855, on Fromental Halévy's recommendation, he was approached by Jacques Offenbach at the government ministry where he was employed. For the opening of his new theater, Les Bouffes Parisiens, Offenbach solicited a prologue from the young Halévy entitled, ''Entrez, messieurs, mesdames.'' That same year Halévy composed his first libretto for Offenbach, *Bata-clan*. Enthusiastically received by audiences, the play launched Halévy's career. He subsequently collaborated with Hector Crémieux (1828–1892) on Offenbach's *Orphée aux enfers* (1858) and in 1861 *La chanson de Fortunio* and *Le Pont des Soupirs*.

In 1860 Napoleon III's half-brother, Auguste de Morny, then president of the Corps Législatif, called on Halévy to assist him with a vaudeville he was writing, *M. Champfleury restera chez lui*. The two men got along well. The play, with which Offenbach and Crémieux also assisted, was produced in September 1861, and Morny obtained for Halévy an appointment (1860) as the secretary of the Corps Législatif responsible for drafting the *procès-verbaux* of its sessions. Their collaboration and friendship continued until Morny's death in 1865. Halévy's post and his friendships (including with Lucien Anatole Prévost-Paradol) made him an invaluable memorialist of the Second Empire.

It was also in 1860 that Halévy undertook his most important collaboration, with Meilhac, an old school friend, on librettos for Offenbach's operettas. Success followed success: *La belle Hélène* (Théâtre des Variétés, 1864); *Barbe Bleue* (Variétés, 1866); *La vie parisienne* (Palais Royal, 1866); *La Grande Duchesse de Gérolstein* (Variétés, 1867); *La Périchole* (Variétés, 1868); and *Les brigands* (Variétés, 1869). *Le chateau à Toto* (1868) and *La diva* (1869) were less successful. Offenbach-Halévy-Meilhac became the favorite entertainers of Parisian audiences during the 1860s. Halévy and Meilhac also collaborated in writing a variety of comedies: *Le Brésilien* (Palais Royal, 1863), *Les brébis de Panurge* (Vaudeville, 1862), *Fanny Lear* (Gymnase, 1868), and *Froufou* (Gymnase, 1869). After the Franco-Prussian War, which Halévy recorded in his *L'invasion, souvenirs, et récits* (1872), he and Meilhac turned increasingly to comedy. It was a play of theirs, *Le reveillon* (1872), that became the basis for Johann Strauss' operetta *Die Fledermaus* (1874). Halévy died at Paris, 7 May 1908.

L. Halévy, *Carnets*, ed. Daniel Halévy (Paris, 1935); H. A. Parys, *Histoire anecdotique de l'operette* (Brussels, 1945).

Dolorès A. Signori

Related entries: MEILHAC; MORNY; OFFENBACH; THEATER.

HALLES CENTRALES, the innovative Paris central market whose construction after nearly half a century of delay was one of the first and most important achievements of the rebuilding of Paris by Napoleon III and Georges Haussmann. The site had been chosen in 1811 by Napoleon I, near the historic market center. The plan of the architects Victor Baltard (1805–1874) and Félix Callet (1791–1854) was approved in 1847. Only on the insistence of Louis Napoleon, however, did work begin in the summer of 1851. While still president of the Second Republic, he posed the initial cornerstone (15 September 1851) and ordered an enlargement of the area (26 March 1852). As emperor, he found Baltard's first building, a massive stone structure ("le fort des Halles"), unacceptable and ordered an informal design competition in June 1853. Haussmann encouraged his former school friend Baltard to adopt the principle of a glass and iron umbrella favored by Napoleon III and foreshadowed in the designs of the eccentric architect Hector Horeau (1801–1872) and the engineer Eugène Flachat (1802–1873), both of whom would later claim paternity. The emperor accepted Baltard's design and decorated him without knowing that he had also built the rejected building.

Construction recommenced in May 1854. Six huge pavilions, each devoted to a distinct function, separated by three covered streets, were completed by 1857 when Napoleon III inaugurated the new market. Four more were built between 1858 and 1866 (the initial stone building was torn down and replaced in 1863). Consisting of 21 acres (half of it covered), with gas lights, an emergency reservoir of water, great basements, and underground passages linking the pavilions (a railroad was intended but never built), les Halles was quickly accepted by artists and public alike and became in some sense, as Emile Zola depicted it in his novel *Le ventre de Paris*, a symbol of the prosperity and materialism of the Second Empire. Notably successful, imitated throughout the world, the new market would serve Paris for a century with the addition, in 1936, of only two pavilions (completing the design as modified in 1857). The twelve pavilions were demolished in 1972 and the market moved to the outskirts of Paris at Rungis. But one of Baltard's structures has been preserved at Nogent-sur-Marne as an example of what had come to be recognized as a masterwork of nineteenth-century architecture.

V. Baltard and F. Callet, *Monographie des Halles Centrales de Paris construites sous le règne de Napoléon III* (Paris, 1863); F. Boudon, A. Chastel, H. Couzy, and F. Hamon, *Système de l'architecture urbaine: le quartier des Halles à Paris*, 2 vols. (Paris, 1917); A. Lecointre, *Un quartier de Paris sous le Second Empire: Les Halles dans "Le Ventre de Paris" de Zola* (Paris, 1971); R. Manal, "En marge du quartier des Halles: Aspects et finalités du remodelage du centre de Paris sous le Second Empire," *RA* 28 (1975). *Related entry:* PARIS, REBUILDING OF.

HAUSSMANN, GEORGES EUGENE, BARON (1809–1891), administrator, charged with the task of carrying out the gigantic construction projects proposed for Paris by Napoleon III; born at Paris, 27 March 1809, into a Protestant (Lutheran) family from Alsace, which had long been French. Haussmann was the grandson of a member of the Convention and son of an Orleanist journalist and officer in Napoleon I's armies, who had married the daughter of General Baron Dentzel. His godfather was Prince Eugène de Beauharnais—hence his middle name. Early appropriating the title "baron," Haussmann was educated at the Collège Henri IV and the Collège Bourbon before studying at the Paris Conservatoire de Musique and then taking a degree at the Paris faculty of law. He became an *avocat* and after 1830 entered government administration under Orleanist auspices, serving successively as secretary general of the Vienne prefecture (1831–1832) and as subprefect at Yssingeaux (Haute-Loire; 1832), Nérac (Lot-et-Garonne; 1832–1840), Saint-Girons (Ariège; 1840–1841), and Blaye (Gironde; 1841–1848). Before the Revolution of 1848, he had taken a wife at Bordeaux and had been named to the Legion of Honor (1837) and advanced to the rank of officer (1847).

Although in 1848 Haussmann consented to be called a republican, his ambition, bonapartist precedents, and authoritarian bias early propelled him toward Louis Napoleon, whose election as president of the Second Republic he vigorously supported while a member of the prefectural council of the Gironde. When Louis Napoleon won 78 percent of that department's votes, he met Haussmann for the first time and named him (24 January 1849) to the prefecture of the Var, a difficult department, close to the Italian border and threatened by republican agitation. Although he had sought an appointment to the Gironde, the new prefect undertook his commission wholeheartedly, gained a conservative majority in the elections to the Legislative Assembly, and earned the undying animosity of a young Var republican, Emile Ollivier, for the vigor with which he acted against the Left. Transferred to another challenging post, the Yonne, on 11 May 1850, Haussmann had his second meeting with Louis Napoleon when the prince president visited Auxerre that year. Also in the Yonne the prefect became a close friend of Louis Frémy (1807–1891), then a member of the Legislative Assembly and future general director of administration in the Ministry of the Interior (1853), and governor of the Crédit Foncier (1857). The Crédit Foncier, a mortgage bank established by decree in December 1852, was destined to play a significant role in Haussmann's work at Paris. On 26 November 1851 Haussmann at last gained his reward; he received the long-coveted appointment as prefect of the Gironde.

At Paris to thank Louis Napoleon for his appointment, Haussmann saw the president during his Elysée reception the night of 1 December and was told to leave for Bordeaux as early as possible the following morning, after taking instructions from the minister of the interior. Thus, unwittingly, Haussmann became the first caller on the new minister, Auguste de Morny, the morning of the coup d'état of 2 December 1851. At Bordeaux, as extraordinary commissioner of the Republic, Haussmann presided over an efficient transition of power, maintaining order without having to declare a state of siege. With equal competence he organized the reception for Louis Napoleon at Bordeaux in October 1852 during the president's provincial tour, which culminated in the decision to restore the Empire. Thus the stage was set for the decisive event of the young prefect's career.

By 1853 Napoleon III, having failed to win the conservative prefect of the Seine, Jean Jacques Berger (1790–1859), to his plans for rebuilding Paris, was looking for a replacement. Victor Fialin Persigny, minister of the interior, reduced the list of candidates to five, dined with each, and was won over by the sheer force of Haussmann's personality, a lion to place among the Parisian foxes. The emperor readily agreed, exclaiming, when he had reached Haussmann's name on the list, "useless to go farther; there's the man I need." Always drawn to "a benevolent and efficient autocracy," the prefect promised at his oath taking on 29 June 1853 "that he belonged to the emperor without reserve." It was a declaration in regard to which he never wavered. The two men would work together for more than sixteen years, growing in regard for each other, although their relations were not always smooth. Haussmann had free access to Napoleon III, often seeing him every day, and while his great contribution was to carry out the emperor's plans, he also made his own mark. Notably, sewage and water supply were largely the prefect's ideas.

Above all a force of nature, Haussmann was also a skilled administrator, rich in expedients, with an iron will, and a great capacity for work. He could manipulate men, outmaneuver and intimidate them, but also command their loyalty. And he was, despite the calumny of the day, personally incorruptible. Haussmann generally got along well with Persigny but had few friends in high places; his enemies included Pierre Marie Pietri, the prefect of police (with whom he clashed over jurisdiction), Jules Baroche (a conservative who opposed Haussmann's methods and his bid for ever greater power), Adolphe Billault, Achille Fould, and Emile Ollivier. Eugène Rouher was undoubtedly jealous of Haussmann's access to the emperor and tended to treat him as a simple agent. Although Haussmann attempted with some success to win over the conservative Paris municipal commission (appointed, as was the conseil général of the Seine, by the emperor), and its president, Claude Alphonse Delangle (1797–1869), a supporter of Berger, his plethora of enemies and opponents may have contributed to his continuing demands for greater authority (Napoleon III early legalized his title of baron so that he might not be at a social disadvantage, promoted him grand officer of the Legion, 11 June 1856, and named him to the Senate, 9 June 1857). Baroche in 1858 won a head-on clash over Haussmann's expropriation tactics and bid for increased powers, but with Delangle as minister of the interior following the initial reaction to the Orsini *attentat* (which Haussmann had witnessed), a decree of 10 October 1859 enlarged the authority of the prefect of the Seine. By the end of 1860 Haussmann had almost persuaded his master that he should be "minister of Paris." Even his threat to resign, however, could not overcome the combined resistance of Baroche and Rouher, and the prefect had to be content with greater authority vis-à-vis the minister of the interior and (decree of 22 December 1860) permission to sit in the Conseil d'Etat and even in the Council of Ministers when the latter body considered matters relating to the city of Paris. On 8 December 1862 he was named grand cross of the Legion of Honor.

In the end it was the problem of financing his projects that led to the downfall of the once all-powerful prefect. Haussmann in fact divided those projects into three *réseaux*, according to their financing. The first were those authorized before 1858 and built with financial aid from the state (as well as projects subsidiary to these whether subsidized or not); the second were those listed in the 18 March 1858 contract between the state and the city (to be financed jointly). The third *réseau* consisted of all other projects, to be carried out by the city without state subsidy. The money for rebuilding Paris was to come from Paris budget surpluses, government subsidies, state-authorized city loans, and profits from sale by the city of appropriated properties and materials salvaged from demolitions. Napoleon III forebade an increase in taxes and was only persuaded with difficulty by Haussmann to maintain taxes at their existing level. But budget surpluses were small (at the beginning only about 4 million francs per year on budgets of 50 million to 60 million). Loans under Haussmann totaled about 460 million francs before 1869 (60 million in 1855, 130 million in 1860, and 270 million in 1865). And government subsidies were never very large (53 million francs by 1857 and another 50 million under the 1858 contract).

The year 1858 was critical. The economic boom had broken in 1857; costs of expropriation were rising sharply; and in December the Conseil d'Etat allowed owners to keep condemned property until work actually began, thus depriving Haussmann of a good portion of profits from resale of expropriated properties and demolition salvage. Expedients had clearly become necessary. In 1858 the prefect established the Caisse des Travaux de Paris (charged with supervising and paying for all projects) and began the practice of taking bids from contractors for proposed construction (until 1858 the city had usually been its own contractor). A successful bidder undertook not only to carry out the agreed work but also to dispossess the property owners and tenants, pay indemnities, and dispose of condemned property outside the right-of-way. Moreover, he would not be paid until the work was completed, and payments would be extended over a period of as long as eight years. In effect, the city enjoyed the privilege of an enforced loan from the contractor, a fact recognized by the paying of interest on sums owed. In the early 1860s circumstances led to a final refinement of this system. In December 1861 the Crédit Foncier agreed to discount the city's promises to pay (*bons de délégation*) issued to a major contractor, which meant that the city owed not the contractor but the Crédit Foncier. In 1863, to save the builder from bankruptcy, the Caisse des Travaux agreed to designate the entire project assigned to him as completed although it was still in progress, thus enabling the contractor to discount the city's debt to him at once. By 1864 this practice had become routine. When the Caisse had received a deposit from a contractor, it designated his work as completed, and he then discounted his *bons de délégation* with the Crédit Foncier. In this way Haussmann bypassed the requirement for authorization from the Corps Législatif to borrow money and fully embraced a policy of deficit finance or "productive spending" (spending borrowed money to increase future revenues), which he shared with Persigny and would later claim for his own. By 1868 banks would hold 54 million francs worth of *bons de délégation* and the Crédit Foncier almost 400 million. (Haussmann would estimate the next year that his works at Paris had cost a total of 2.5 billion francs.)

From the beginning, and especially from about 1857, Haussmann had borne the brunt of criticism from a host of opponents, including vested interests, provincials appalled at the expenditures lavished on Paris, fiscal conservatives yearning for a balanced budget as well as for an end to unproductive expenditures, and those whose real target was the emperor himself. The prefect's financial expedients were therefore especially vulnerable, as Fould warned the emperor from 1865. A series of articles by economist Léon Say (1826–1896) in the *Journal des débats* of January-February 1865 and speeches by Ernest Picard in the Corps Législatif in April and June 1865 signaled the beginning of a new campaign by Haussmann's enemies. Against Picard and Antoine Berryer in April 1867, Rouher, on the floor of the Corps Législatif, defended the *bons de délégation* as a simple transfer of credit. But criticism of the practice by Eugène Forcade (1820–1869) in the *Revue des deux mondes* would be followed by a series of articles in *Le temps* (20 December 1867–11 May 1868), written by Jules Ferry (1832–1893), and subsequently published by him as *Les comptes fantastiques d'Haussmann* (May 1868). Rouher, who in January 1867 added to his duties those of minister of finance, had already insisted that Haussmann regularize his dealings with the Crédit Foncier. The resulting contract of 8 November 1867 called for the city to repay 398 million francs in semiannual installments over sixty years. On 2 December the Paris municipal commission approved this agreement (the Corps Législatif had rejected Picard's motion that the capital be given an elected council), and on 11 December Haussmann published his methods, admitting to no legality but urging that the Paris budget be debated and approved each year by the legislature.

In reality, the decisive test was at hand. The new contract required Corps Législatif approval. After delay of more than a year, during which the Cour des Comptes joined the chorus of criticism, debate began on 22 February 1869. As the government's majority collapsed, Napoleon III reluctantly abandoned his prefect. On 26 February Rouher admitted to irregularities and promised they would not be repeated. That, together with agreement that henceforth the extraordinary budget of Paris would be approved by a law, was the price required for Corps Législatif approval on 6 March 1869 of the November contract, modified to stipulate a payment of 465 million francs in forty annuities. But that was not all. Incensed at the near doubling of Crédit Foncier dividends from 1861 to 1868, the Corps Législatif also required that a loan of 250 million francs be floated to retire part of the city's debt. This was done in May. On 19 April 1869 the Caisse des Travaux had been dissolved by imperial decree.

An unrepentant Haussmann defended himself during the Senate debate of the Crédit Foncier contract (6 April 1869), and indeed the prefect continued to enjoy

his master's support. But it was a support weakened by the progressive liberalization of the regime, and Haussmann now had no resources other than those
of a Paris budget devoted largely to retiring the existing debt. The emergence
of a Liberal Empire dominated by Ollivier was the final blow. Summoned to
resign, the prefect refused and was *relevé de ses fonctions* by decree of 5 January
1870. His successor was Henri Chevreau. Declining the offer from a still loyal
Napoleon III of a large sum of money, Haussmann, who had arranged his own
impressive departure from the Hôtel de Ville, retired with full pension of 6,000
francs to his villa at Nice (March 1870). He left France briefly following 4
September but returned in 1871 and in September 1871 was named director of
the Crédit Mobilier. From 1877 to 1881 he would serve as a bonapartist deputy
in the Chamber of Deputies, having been elected at Ajaccio (against Prince
Napoleon) with the support of the government, the prince imperial, and the
church. Haussmann died at Paris, 11 January 1891, having published the first
two volumes of his memoirs the previous year (the third appeared posthumously
in 1893).

Haussmann, who styled himself an *artiste démolisseur*, had pretensions beyond
those of an administrator. Elected a free member of the Académie des Beaux-
Arts on 7 December 1867 (replacing Fould), member of the Conseil Impérial
de l'Instruction Publique, sponsor of the collection of Paris historical materials
at the Musée Carnavalet, member of the commission for organizing the Paris
exposition of 1867, he prided himself on the aesthetics of his transformation of
Paris, which others would dismiss as mania for the straight line. Haussmann
brutally destroyed much of medieval Paris (although he refused Fould's injunction to raze the Church of St. Germain l'Auxerrois), but he made the modern
city possible. No doubt controversy will remain linked to his name as inextricably
as that name is linked to the history and the fact of contemporary Paris.

B. Chapman and J. M. Chapman, *The Life and Times of Baron Haussmann: Paris in
the Second Empire* (London, 1957); J. Des Cars, *Haussmann, la gloire du Second Empire*
(Paris, 1978); J. Gaillard, "Un bourgeois conquérant: Le baron Haussmann," *Histoire*,
37 (1981); L. Girard, "Le financement des grands travaux du Second Empire," *RE*, no.
3 (May 1951); Baron G. Haussmann, *Mémoirs*, 3 vols. (Paris, 1890–1893); G. N.
Lameyre, *Haussmann, "préfet de Paris"* (Paris, 1958); H. Malet, *Le baron Haussmann
et la rénovation de Paris* (Paris, 1973); G. Massa-Gille, *Histoire des emprunts de la ville
de Paris, 1814–1875* (Paris, 1973); D. H. Pinkney, "Money and Politics in the Rebuilding
of Paris, 1860–1870," *JEH* (March 1957); H. Saalman, *Haussmann: Paris Transformed*
(New York, 1971); C. Schoull, "Haussmann, préfet de la Gironde," *Annales du Midi*
80 (April–May 1968); P. Touttain, *Haussmann: Artisan du Second Empire, créateur du
Paris moderne* (Paris, 1971).

Related entries: OLLIVIER; PARIS, REBUILDING OF; PERSIGNY; PRINCE
PRESIDENT; ROUHER; SECOND EMPIRE.

HAVIN, LEONOR (1799–1868), journalist and politician; director of *Le siècle*;
born at Paris, 2 April 1799. Trained in the law, Havin had an active political
career under the July Monarchy (1830–1848). In the Chamber of Deputies he
sat with the dynastic Left but rallied to the Republic after the Revolution of

1848. Disapproving of the coup d'état of 2 December 1851, Havin resigned his offices and entered into opposition. He had become director of the moderate republican newspaper *Le siècle* in 1851. Partly because of his moderation (some would call it opportunism), partly because of powerful friends at court such as Narcisse Vieillard (1791–1857), long associated with the Bonaparte family, and Napoleon III's half-brother, Auguste de Morny, Havin was permitted to continue publishing *Le siècle* after the coup. As an adroit and diplomatic politician, he had revealed qualities that were soon apparent in his management of *Le siècle*. He always remained the pragmatic and prudent bourgeois. In political opposition to the Empire, Havin was careful never to offend the government enough to warrant suspension or suppression, although he frequently received warnings (*avertissements*). Nevertheless, *Le siècle* made its director a powerful force in Parisian politics. It was Havin and his fellow journalist Auguste Nefftzer who imposed the successful republican candidacies of Emile Ollivier and Alfred Darimon in the elections of 1857 to the Corps Législatif. Havin himself, however, was defeated, as he had been in 1852. He was elected to the Corps Législatif in 1863 from both Paris and the Manche (he chose the latter) and sat as an independent with the Left, although he was distrusted because of his boasting during the campaign that Napoleon III's private secretary, Jean Mocquard, had written to say the emperor was pleased with his candidacy. Even as a deputy, Havin's opposition remained muted. He pleaded the cause of Poland, the continued liberalization of the educational system, freedom of the press, and was especially eloquent in requesting (unsuccessfully) removal of the stamp tax on newspapers. He died at Thorigny-sur-Vire (Manche), where he had long been a member of the Conseil Général, 12 November 1868, leaving a fortune of 14 million francs.

Natalie Isser

Related entries: LES CINQ; PRESS REGIME; *LE SIECLE*.

HISTOIRE DE JULES CESAR, written by Napoleon III and published 1865–1866. After he assumed power, Napoleon III continued to give occasional vent to his literary inclinations, mostly in the form of open letters, memoranda to his cabinet, speeches (especially the annual speech from the throne after 1860), and certain anonymous pamphlets. His later writings included an extensive study concerning Algeria (1865), the sketch of a novel illustrating the changes brought about in France under the Second Empire, a profile of Empress Eugénie (published in *Le dix décembre*, 15 December 1868), a pamphlet, *Les titres de la dynastie napoléonienne* (1868), and an 1872 pamphlet on the Franco-Prussian War. Most significant was the project he contemplated in 1860, began in 1861, and wrote largely after 1863—a biography of Julius Caesar. At first it was intended to be a short book, but the emperor, who in June 1861 had toured the excavations at Alesia, became increasingly absorbed in the work as his health declined. Although typical of the period's tendency to employ history for political purposes, *Jules César* was relatively serious scholarship by nineteenth-century standards. Napoleon III made use of a veritable research team, headed by the learned Alfred Maury (1817–1892), whom the emperor had chosen in 1860 as librarian of the Tuileries. Maury gathered the material and served as intermediary with scholars whose assistance was sought, like Ernest Renan and Theodor Mommsen (1817–1903). Napoleon III was also greatly assisted by C.E.L.G. Froehner (1834–1925), the German archaeologist whom he naturalized by decree, and Victor Duruy, minister of education from 1863, as well as by his lifelong friend, Mme. Hortense Lacroix Cornu (1812–1875), and Prosper Mérimée. Until his death in 1864, Jean Mocquard, the emperor's private secretary and *chef de cabinet*, corrected the dictated text, but much of the manuscript Napoleon III wrote himself. The preface was dated 20 March 1862 at the Tuileries and signed "Napoléon." At the end of that year, Duruy was requested to give an honest criticism of the first draft of the book. (He was appointed minister of education in June 1863.) The first volume, including a lengthy introduction to the history of Rome and ending with Caesar's appointment as proconsul of Gaul, was published in March 1865; the second, ending with the crossing of the Rubicon, appeared in December 1866. A projected third volume was never written. And there were some, including Victor Fialin Persigny, who regretted the energy poured by the ailing emperor into the initial two volumes.

Because the First and Second Empires rested on a Caesarist principle clearly understood by all, opponents of bonapartism had long criticized the Napoleonic regimes by castigating Julius Caesar. Napoleon III's response in the *Histoire de Jules César* was to return to themes originally found in *Des idées napoléoniennes*: that great men play a providential role in history and thereby contribute to human progress. Further, in an obvious attempt to justify the coup d'état of December 1851, Napoleon III argued that factionalism and disorder had necessitated Caesar's action against the contentious parties that troubled the Roman Republic and that it is foolish and useless to resist a great man when he appears on the scene. The historical parallel could be used by opponents of the regime as well, however. The emperor had asked that the newspapers be instructed to write honest reviews. Most were sycophantic, although the noted critic, Charles Augustin Sainte-Beuve, refused to review the book, but on 4 March 1865 there appeared in the leftist journal, *La rive gauche*, a scathing review by Louis Auguste Rogeard (b. 1820) entitled "Les propos de Labienus," a frank attack on Napoleon III's policies in the guise of a discussion of the politics of ancient Rome. After the second part was published (by another printer, *La rive gauche* having been suppressed) on 18 March and quickly sold out, Rogeard fled to Belgium.

Napoleon III apparently hoped that his scholarly contribution would gain him admission to the Académie Française. That august body, however, was controlled by leaders of the liberal opposition who perceived the historian's task as one of affirming the values of parliamentary government, not Caesarism. As a result the Immortals in 1863 preferred Jules Dufaure (1798–1881) and in 1865 Lucien Anatole Prévost-Paradol to the "crowned historian." Nevertheless, *Histoire de Jules César* has survived and can still be read with pleasure and even with admiration.

M. Kranzberg, "An Emperor Writes History: Napoleon III's *Histoire de Jules César*," in H. S. Hughes, ed., *Teachers of History: Essays in Honor of Laurence Bradford Packard* (Ithaca, N.Y., 1954); E. Loudon, *Etude sur les oeuvres de Napoléon III* (Paris, 1857); M. G. Molinari, *Napoléon III publiciste: Sa pensée cherchée dans ses écrits—analyse et appréciation de ses oeuvres* (Brussels, 1861); Napoleon III, *History of Julius Caesar* (New York, 1865–1866), and *Exposé de la situation de l'Empire présenté au sénat et au Corps Législatif* (10 v.; Paris, 1861–1869); Comte de La Chapelle, ed., *Posthumous works and unpublished autographs of Napoleon III in exile* (London, 1873); *Oeuvres de Napoléon III* (5 v.; Paris: Henri Plon, 1856–1869), and *La politique impériale exposée par les discours et proclamations de l'Empereur Napoléon III depuis le 10 décembre 1848 jusqu'en février 1868* (Paris, 1868).

Stuart L. Campbell

Related entries: BONAPARTISM; *DES IDEES NAPOLEONIENNES*; DURUY; *EXTINCTION DU PAUPERISME*; MOCQUARD.

HOHENZOLLERN CANDIDACY, the event that precipitated the Franco-Prussian War of 1870–1871. Prince Leopold of Hohenzollern-Sigmaringen, a Catholic nephew of the Prussian king, an officer in the Prussian army, and a brother of King Ferdinand of Rumania, acceded in the spring of 1870 to repeated effort by the Spanish government and posed his candidacy for the Spanish throne, vacant since the overthrow of Queen Isabella in September 1868. He seemed to meet all the requirements the Spanish government had deemed essential and was even distantly related to Napoleon III through the Murat and Beauharnais families. Initially the prince had been reluctant to become a candidate, even after royal advisers had urged him to do so following a Prussian crown council in March 1870. He had refused short of a royal command, an order King William refused to give. Favorable reports, however, by two Prussian emissaries to Spain, sent to assess the viability of such a candidacy and dynasty, as well as renewed Spanish efforts, produced a more positive attitude on the part of the prince. Although the Prussian king viewed a Hohenzollern candidacy with decided misgivings, his chancellor, Otto von Bismarck, took a new and active interest in the matter. Not surprisingly, therefore, the Spanish agent, Salazar y Mazareddo, was able on 19 June to obtain Leopold's agreement to pose his candidacy officially, subject to royal approbation. William agreed, reluctantly, and the stage seemed set for a speedy and secret election by the Cortes, Spain's lower house of the legislature, so as to minimize the likelihood of French interference. However, a decoding error in Salazar's message announcing his return to Madrid by 9 July (it should have read 1 July) led to a premature adjournment of the Cortes. Worse, the secrecy surrounding the negotiations and the decision by Leopold was compromised in the process. By 3 July the news of Leopold's candidacy was known at Paris, and on 6 July the French foreign minister, Antoine, duc de Gramont, announced to the Corps Législatif that France would not tolerate a Prussian prince on the Spanish throne. Gramont later claimed that French opinion had made so strong a statement necessary, but others have argued it was, rather, the attitude of the government that enflamed public opinion.

Following the declaration of 6 July, comte Vincent Benedetti, France's minister at Berlin, was ordered to Bad Ems to persuade the king, as monarch and as head of the Hohenzollern family, to advise Leopold to withdraw his candidacy. French resentment grew when the official demarche at Berlin and Bad Ems did not meet with success. William was reluctant to take the initiative in a matter that constituted a personal decision by Leopold and that supposedly did not concern the Prussian government. Although he was cordial in his attitude toward Benedetti, the king would only consent to communicate to the ambassador whatever decision Prince Leopold might choose to take. Obviously, William was unwilling to take the responsibility for a concession that might insult public opinion in Germany. In fact, it was Charles Anton, the father of the prince, who in the absence of Leopold (who was on holiday) made the decision to withdraw late in the evening of 11 July. The news was related to Benedetti by King William the next afternoon, and the ambassador telegraphed word of the happy dénouement to Paris, where confirmation had been received from other sources as well.

Late in the evening of 12 July, however, Benedetti received new and ominous instructions from Gramont—to the effect that he obtain a guarantee from the king that he would not again authorize the candidacy. Napoleon III, after conversations with Baron Jérôme David, Adolphe Granier de Cassagnac, and Gramont (but without consulting the chief minister, Emile Ollivier), had decided the evening of 12 July that public opinion demanded—as Gramont argued— guarantees for the future. Benedetti, greatly disturbed by the new development, approached the king next morning at the *Brunnenpromenade* at Ems and, after William had told him that he was still waiting for the official communication from Charles Anton, decided to use the occasion to acquaint the king briefly with the further request of the French government. William did not comment on the matter, and Benedetti fully expected to discuss the issue in an afternoon audience. In the meantime, Bismarck, who had returned from Varzin to Berlin and planned to proceed to Bad Ems, had grown impatient with the imprudence and conciliatory attitude of the king and his entourage at Ems. He advised William through an intermediary that no further negotiations on the Hohenzollern candidacy be carried on with Benedetti. Later in the day, on 13 July, Benedetti was informed by an aide-de-camp that the king had received official word of Leopold's withdrawal and that the king of Prussia had given his entire approbation to the prince's communication. Beyond that the king had nothing further to discuss with the ambassador, and Benedetti learned that the audience had been cancelled. To be sure, the original French demand had now been met, and nothing further could be obtained at Ems.

The focus of events had now shifted to Berlin where Bismarck, fearing a diplomatic defeat, edited King William's account to him of the events that had transpired at Bad Ems (Ems despatch) and published it during the evening of 13 July in a way calculated to ignite both French and German chauvinism and to precipitate a war that Prussia was confident of winning. The French government, goaded by public opinion, responded as Bismarck had anticipated. Last-minute thoughts of a congress were swept aside, and on 15 July the process was begun that culminated in France's declaration of war on 19 July.

N. N. Barker, "Napoleon III and the Hohenzollern Candidacy for the Spanish Throne," *Historian* (May 1967); G. Bonnin, ed., *Bismarck and the Hohenzollern Candidacy for the Spanish Throne: The Documents in the German Diplomatic Archives*, trans. I. M. Massey (London, 1957); W. A. Fletcher, *The Mission of Vincent Benedetti to Berlin, 1864–1870* (The Hague, 1965); S. W. Halperin, "The Origins of the Franco-Prussian War Revisited: Bismarck and the Hohenzollern Candidacy for the Spanish Throne," *JMH* 45 (March 1973); D. W. Houston, "Emile Ollivier and the Hohenzollern Candidacy," *FHS*, no. 2 (1965); L. Steefel, *Bismarck, the Hohenzollern Candidacy, and the Origins of the Franco-Prussian War of 1870* (Cambridge, Mass., 1962).

Willard Allen Fletcher
Related entries: ARMY REFORM; BENEDETTI; FRANCO-PRUSSIAN WAR; GRAMONT; OLLIVIER; PUBLIC OPINION; SADOWA.

HOLY PLACES, a group of Christian shrines in Palestine, most notably the Church of the Holy Sepulchre in Jerusalem and the Church and Grotto of the Nativity at Bethlehem. Under Ottoman control since 1516, the shrines were maintained and used by the local Christian sects (Roman Catholic, Greek Orthodox, and Armenian) under a complicated schedule of rights and duties. Since the Roman Catholic church in the Ottoman Empire did not have an indigenous local head until the revival of the pre-Ottoman Latin Patriarchate of Jerusalem in 1847, Roman Catholic privileges had come to be defended by the kings of France. The high point of French influence was the Capitulations of 1740, which gave extensive rights to the Roman Catholics at the shrines and provided for protection of Catholic pilgrims and French nationals by the French government. During the French Revolution, more laically minded rulers questioned this orientation of French policy. In 1790, a ministerial council determined that the sultan, not the king of France, should in principle protect French nationals in the Ottoman Empire. However, in the nineteenth century, the rebirth of clericalism and of conservative patriotism centered around the church led to renewed French commitment to the Holy Places. Similar developments in other European nations, particularly Russia, increased general popular interest in the Holy Land at a time when governmental rivalries in the area were intensifying.

On 28 May 1850, the French demanded a return to the status quo of 1740, based on the argument that the Capitulations, as a bilateral agreement between two sovereign states, could not be modified without French consent. Napoleon III undoubtedly wished to curry favor with clerical groups in France, but he also wanted to curtail Russian influence in the Balkans, which had expanded as a result of Russia's role as policeman in the 1848 Revolution, and he believed that he had found a way of doing so without provoking a war. The Ottomans met the French demands with a series of masterly delays. The question was investigated first by an international commission and then by a commission of Ottoman legal scholars. These deliberations turned on symbolic points, such as the restoration of the Latin silver star missing from Bethlehem and the possession of the keys to the church there, and ended, after a welter of conflicting notes and a show of force by the French, in a special Ottoman mission to the Holy Land under Afif Bey with instructions to settle outstanding issues in favor of the Roman Catholics. At this point (February 1853) the Russians, contrary to Napoleon III's calculations, sent a mission headed by Prince Alexander Menshikov to Constantinople with instructions to resolve the Holy Places question once and for all in Russia's favor. Although the Russian government had often spoken up for Greek Orthodox claims, the Orthodox church in the Ottoman Empire had always been headed by the powerful patriarch of Constantinople, who was technically superior to the Russian patriarch, and its status was regulated by domestic law. To counter the French argument that these arrangements were less binding on the sultan than the international treaties with the French on behalf of the Catholics, Menshikov was instructed to conclude a treaty converting vague Russian rights to protect coreligionists in the Ottoman Empire into an explicit legal agreement. Faced with this vast extension of foreign control over Ottoman subjects, the Porte felt obliged to resist. Although Napoleon III proved willing to accept a Russian victory in the original dispute concerning symbolic points, frantic attempts to resolve the broader problem by negotiation foundered on the contradiction between differing views of the nature and extent of Ottoman sovereignty over the corporate christian church groups or Millets and great power distrust and rivalry. The Crimean War (1854–1856) was the result.

E. Bapst, *Les origines de la Guerre de Crimée: La France et la Russie de 1848 à 1854* (Paris, 1912); J. R. Broadus, ''Church Conflict in Palestine: The Opening of the Holy Places Question during the Period Preceding the Crimean War,'' *CJH* 14 (December 1979); A. P. Saab, *The Origins of the Crimean Alliance* (Charlottesville, Va., 1977); H.W.V. Temperley, *England and the Near East* (London, [1936]).

Ann Pottinger Saab

Related entries: CRIMEAN WAR; LA VALETTE; PRINCE PRESIDENT.

HUGO, VICTOR (1802–1885), poet, playwright, and novelist; perhaps the best-known and most influential literary opponent of the Second Empire; born 26 February 1802, at Besançon, the son of a general in Napoleon's armies. By the time of the Revolution of 1848, Hugo was already a towering romantic poet and playwright, a member of the Académie Française, and, through the intercession of the duchesse d'Orléans, a peer of France (1845). His political views were changeable. Although he had praised Napoleon and then supported the July Monarchy, he sought election to the Constituent Assembly in 1848 as a moderate republican. Successful, he placed seventh on 4 June in a poll in which Louis Napoleon Bonaparte, who was also elected, ranked eighth. The two men were at first political allies. Louis Napoleon cultivated Hugo; the poet and his two sons (Charles, 1825–1871, and François Victor, 1828–1873) founded a newspaper, *L'événement*, to support the bonapartist pretender in his triumphant campaign for the presidency (December 1848). Hugo was elected to the Legislative Assembly in May 1849. But friction soon developed, leading to a final break in October 1849. There were many reasons: Hugo's republicanism (formally proclaimed in the spring of 1850); his rejection of authoritarian rule (reflected in opposition to the 31 May 1850 law limiting universal manhood suffrage); his objections, as an ardent anti-clerical, to the government's education policy (Falloux law), and to the destruction of the Roman Republic. But there were personal factors as well: Hugo's feeling that he had been deceived and, perhaps most important, Louis Napoleon's decision, in view of the stand taken by his advisers, not to bring the poet into his cabinet of 31 October 1849 or to accept him as an *éminence grise*. Instead Hugo was offered the embassy at Madrid, which he declined. Subsequently he opposed efforts to revise the constitution in order to permit Louis Napoleon to seek reelection. His July 1851 speech ("What! Because we had Napoleon the Great must we have Napoleon the Little?") in which he offered a long defense of socialism prompted Jules Baroche to contrast Hugo's earlier conservatism with his present extremism and earned that estimable minister of the Second Empire a share of the poet's hatred of the regime and of its servitors. At the coup d'état (December 1851), Hugo, as "president of the provisional government," drafted an appeal to the people, which was published on 3 December, outlawing Louis Napoleon. He tried vainly to stir the workers to resistance, escaped arrest, made his way to Belgium on 11 December under the name Firmin-Lanvin (followed by Juliette Drouet, his mistress since 1832), and was temporarily banished from France on 10 January along with sixty-five other deputies.

Hugo's exile of almost twenty years was largely self-imposed. He could have returned to France as early as April 1852 under certain conditions or without condition from August 1859. The first place of refuge for the poet, his wife, and his two sons was Brussels. In August 1852 the family moved to the Channel island of Jersey, anticipating the Faider law, which would have expelled them from Belgium. On Jersey the small group of some one hundred exiles became increasingly unpopular with the authorities as the Crimean War, which Hugo opposed, brought Britain and France together. In April 1855 the poet published a pamphlet, "England's Disgrace," opposing Napoleon III's projected visit to that country. When the *émigré* newspaper of Hugo's fellow Jersey exile, Charles de Ribeyrolles (1812–1861), was suppressed for publishing a similar appeal by Félix Pyat (1810–1889), and three *proscrits* were expelled from the island, Hugo signed a protest that resulted in his own expulsion toward the end of 1855. He took his family to the neighboring island of Guernsey and there, at Hauteville House, he would live and work until the end of the Second Empire, with occasional visits to Belgium and to Switzerland.

From the moment of his exile, Hugo had begun to write his scathing denunciations of Louis Napoleon, vowing that he would speak as the conscience of France. The morning after his arrival in Brussels, he began an account of the coup d'état, *Histoire d'un crime*, a violent, distorted polemic, completed in May 1852 but not published until 1877. Before leaving Brussels, Hugo completed *Napoléon le Petit* (1852), in which he gave full rein to his almost pathological hatred of the man who would soon be Napoleon III. Immediately on settling on Jersey in the winter of 1852–1853, the poet published *Les châtiments*, a collection of some one hundred poems expressing his deep sense of indignation at events in France (the book appeared at Brussels in two editions, one expurgated and sold openly, the other clandestine and without name of editor). Soon copies of these works were being smuggled into France in overcoat linings and even in hollowed-out busts of Napoleon III. It seems likely, however, that Hugo's attacks were too excessive to be effective, particularly at a time when the Empire was undeniably popular in France.

Hugo's literary career continued in exile. *Les contemplations*, a collection of poems (1856), enjoyed tremendous popularity in France, where the first edition sold out as soon as it appeared. Hugo's publisher, Hetzel, paid him 20,000 francs in royalties for the work, and letters of praise came to Guernsey from such notables as Jules Michelet, (1798–1874), Alexandre Dumas fils, and George Sand. Encouraged by this great success, Hetzel demanded more, and in 1859 Hugo produced another collection, the first books of *La légende des siècles* (completed 1883). The decade after 1859 was a period of immense activity for Hugo, marked by the publication of poems, essays, epics, and novels, the most remarkable of which was undoubtedly *Les misérables*. Since the 1840s Hugo had planned a great novel based on the trials and privations of the working people. On 3 April 1862 the first installment appeared. Albert Lacroix, a young Belgian, had agreed to Hugo's terms, paying 30,000 francs for twelve years' exclusive rights to the novel. The book was an immediate success. Despite the editor's precautions (*Les misérables* was published simultaneously, translated into eight languages, in Paris, Brussels, Leipzig, London, Milan, Madrid, Rotterdam, Naples, Budapest, Saint Petersburg, and Rio de Janeiro), twenty-one counterfeit editions were on the stands before the last of five installments had appeared in June. Some, like Alphonse Lamartine and Jules Barbey d'Aurevilly, praised the novel with reservations, but all admired its scope and powerful style. A banquet at Brussels celebrated Hugo's triumph. One guest, the photographer Félix Nadar, not only photographed the writer but also smuggled back into France thirty-eight copies of *Les châtiments* and *Napoléon le Petit*. Later Hugo would give enthusiastic support to Nadar's campaign for a heavier-than-air flying machine. The serialized publication of Hugo's next novel, *Les travailleurs de la mer* (1866), in *Le soleil* increased that paper's circulation—in spite of the fact that the novel had already been published—from 28,000 to 80,000 copies. Hugo's popularity continued to grow in France. The year 1867 was the international exposition at Paris, and so, risking disfavor in certain quarters, the Comédie Française revived *Hernani*, originally presented in 1830. It was the first Hugo play to be performed in France since the coup d'état and was enormously successful.

Throughout these years, however, and despite his literary triumphs, Hugo maintained his resolve not to return to France while the Empire existed. When Adèle, his wife of forty-six years, died in Brussels on 28 August 1868, the poet followed her coffin only to the French border. But the Empire was in decline. Six months earlier, students had rioted in the Latin Quarter to protest the banning of Hugo's play, *Ruy Blas*. And when Henri Rochefort, the radical journalist, fled to Brussels after ruthlessly pillorying Napoleon III in *La lanterne*, Hugo greeted him with open arms. The poet now encouraged his sons to take advantage of the liberalized press laws in order to establish a newspaper, *Le rappel*, at Paris in 1869. The staff included Auguste Vacquerie (1819–1895), Paul Meurice (1820–1905), and Edouard Lockroy (1838/40–1913). Hugo, Pyat, and Louis Blanc (1811–1882) were among the contributors. The paper immediately gained a circulation of fifty thousand copies. Although Hugo's play, *Lucrèce Borgia*, was presented at the Théâtre Porte Saint Martin in February 1870, the exile remained intransigently opposed to the Empire, even a Liberal Empire. His opposition to the plebiscite of May 1870, expressed in *Le rappel* and in a pamphlet, *Non*, earned him a summons before the courts (11 May).

With the outbreak of the Franco-Prussian War in July 1870, Hugo, a prominent member of the peace movement and an advocate since 1849 of a United States of Europe, found himself torn by conflicting emotions. He moved back to Brussels in order to follow events more closely. On 5 September 1870, the day after the overthrow of the Second Empire, he returned at last to Paris amid a tumultuous welcome from thousands who had come to meet his train. Among other major works written by Hugo during the Second Empire are: *Les chants du crépuscule* (1857), *William Shakespeare* (1864), *Littérature et philosophie mêlée* (1864), *Les chansons des rues et des bois* (1866), *La voix de Guernsey* (1867), and *L'homme qui rit* (1869). Hugo died at Paris, 22 May 1885.

P. Angrand, *Victor Hugo raconté par les papiers d'état* (Paris, 1961); J. P. Houston, *Victor Hugo* (New York, 1974); V. Hugo, *Choses vues* (Paris, 1887; English translation as *The Memoirs of Victor Hugo*); A. Maurois, *Olympio ou la vie de Victor Hugo* (Paris, 1954), and *Victor Hugo and His World* (London, 1966); J. Richardson, " 'French of the French': Victor Hugo and Politics," *History Today* 24 (January 1974), and *Victor Hugo* (New York, 1974); P. Souchon, *Victor Hugo: L'homme et l'oeuvre* (Paris, 1949); A. Strugnell, "Contribution à l'étude du républicanisme de Victor Hugo: Lettres inéditées et oubliées à Jean Claude Colfavru et autres, 1848–1860," *RHLF* 78 (1978).

Dorothy E. Speirs

Related entries: AMNESTY; BAROCHE; LOUIS NAPOLEON; PRINCE PRESIDENT; REPUBLICANISM.

HYACINTHE, PERE (CHARLES LOYSON) (1827–1912), renowned preacher, apostate priest; born 10 March 1827 at Orléans. Ordained as a Sulpician in 1851, Loyson taught philosophy in the seminary at Avignon and theology in that of Nancy until moving to Paris in 1856 as curate at the church of Saint-Sulpice. He joined the Dominicans in 1859, took Hyacinthe as his religious name, and then, five months later, in 1860, transferred to the Carmelite order. His talents as an orator began to attract attention in the early 1860s. Called to preach in a number of provincial dioceses, he finally went to Paris where his success as a preacher at the Madeleine led to his being hailed as a successor to Père Henri Lacordaire, whom he rivaled in eloquence. In 1864 Archbishop Georges Darboy (1813–1871) of Paris chose him to present the Advent sermons at Notre Dame. Here, like Père Lacordaire, he established a national reputation as a powerful orator. For five years, Darboy called on him to preach despite the fact that from the beginning intransigent Catholics and the superiors of his own order complained of his liberal views; some questioned his orthodoxy. Among his sermons on marriage and the family, two lengthy ones devoted to conjugal love aroused astonishment. In 1866 his name appeared on a list composed of Protestants, Catholics, and Jews who had founded a society to work on a new translation of the Bible. This evoked criticism, as did his assistance in organizing (1867) and his participation in an International League of Peace whose membership included Protestants and freethinkers.

By 1868 the criticism directed against Loyson, problems with his superiors, and his profound disapproval of any type of authoritarianism had shaken his belief in the institutional church. He left his order in September 1869, protesting in a public letter against "those doctrines and practices which are called Roman but which are not Christian." Charles de Montalembert and Mgr. Félix Dupanloup tried in vain to persuade him to change his mind. His refusal, which led to his excommunication in October 1869, prompted Montalembert to accuse him of having "betrayed our cause, the cause of liberty." Louis Veuillot, in fact, did use Loyson's defection to argue that being liberal was close to being schismatic. Subsequently Loyson denounced the decisions of Vatican Council I, especially the adoption of the doctrine of papal infallibility, adhered to the Old Catholics of Germany, married an American (1872), and, still protesting his orthodoxy, founded a "French Catholic Church" in Paris, which attracted few disciples. He died at Paris, 9 February 1912.

A. Houtin, *Le Père Hyacinthe dans l'Eglise romaine, 1827–1869* (Paris, 1920); A. Houtin and P. L. Couchoud, eds., *Du Sacerdoce au mariage, le Père Hyacinthe (1867–1870): Lettres et journaux intimes* (Paris, 1927); C. Loyson, *Discourses on Various Occasions by Father Hyacinthe* (New York, 1869); G. Riou, *Le Père Hyacinthe et le libéralisme d'avant le Concile* (Paris, 1910).

Raymond L. Cummings

Related entries: DUPANLOUP; GALLICANISM; LACORDAIRE; MARET; MONTALEMBERT; VEUILLOT.

I

DES IDEES NAPOLEONIENNES, a book written by Louis Napoleon Bonaparte at London in 1839, designed to gain public attention for the Napoleonic cause. In the years before power, Louis Napoleon often wielded his pen, revealing a not-inconsiderable literary ability and a penchant for effective propaganda. Among the more important of his works, in order of publication, are: *Rêveries politiques* (15 pages, 1832); *Considérations politiques et militaires sur la Suisse* (83 pages, 1833); *Manuel d'artillerie* (1834); *Des idées napoléoniennes* (155 pages, 1839); *L'idée napoléonienne* (11 pages, 1840); *Fragments historiques: 1688 et 1830* (106 pages, 1841); *Analyse de la question des sucres* (130 pages, 1842); *Extinction du paupérisme* (43 pages, 1844); *Quelques mots sur Joseph Napoléon Bonaparte* (45 pages, 1844); *Le canal de Nicaragua ou projet de jonction des Océans Atlantique et Pacifique au moyen d'un canal* (69 pages, 1846); and *Du passé et de l'avenir de l'artillerie* (first volume, 1847; never completed). In addition he wrote a number of articles and shorter pieces for such newspapers as *Commerce, Capitol, Progrès du Pas-de-Calais, Guetteur de Saint-Quentin, Journal du Loiret, Journal de Maine-et-Loire, Paix, Revue de l'Empire,* and *Almanach populaire de la France.* Of these earlier writings, *Des idées napoléoniennes* was certainly the most important and the most noted.

Completed in July 1839, *Des idées napoléoniennes* was published shortly afterward, not long before the unsuccessful Boulogne conspiracy. The book (which Louis Napoleon summarized early in 1840 in *L'idée napoléonienne*) was priced at only a half-franc and enjoyed a large sale. Not only were four French editions sold out within several months, but the work was also translated into English, German, Italian, Spanish, and even Russian and Portuguese. Written primarily for the less-educated classes, *Des idées napoléoniennes* was part of Louis Napoleon's efforts to return France to a bonapartist politics while establishing his credentials as the leading heir to the Napoleonic legacy. Its political argument indicated Louis Napoleon's familiarity with contemporary historical theorizing about the meaning of the Great Revolution. In his opinion, 1789 was part of a progressive history leading toward liberty. However, the Revolution was also to be seen as one of several transitional points in history that necessarily brought division, confusion, and struggle. During these periods, governments—

led by heroic figures such as Alexander, Caesar, Constantine, Charlemagne, and Napoleon—had fortunately assumed control, established order, and directed the reconstruction of society on the basis of new principles. Louis Napoleon further argued that in the case of the Revolution, struggle between supporters of the *ancien régime* and proponents of radical change had threatened to destroy the nation. The emperor, however, had possessed a special understanding of the community's needs, including those of the lower classes, thus enabling him to become a symbol and instrument of national consensus. Napoleon may have been forced temporarily to employ authoritarian methods, but his role was fundamentally democratic and laid the foundations for a system of political liberty. Finally, Louis Napoleon argued that his uncle's work had been interrupted, and thereby remained unfinished, because of war imposed by England, which had failed to understand the Emperor's intentions: a federated and peaceful Europe. For Louis Napoleon the meaning was obvious. In order to establish a national reconciliation transcending Left and Right and to regain a sense of purpose, Frenchmen should return to a politics of bonapartism.

L. N. Bonaparte, *Des idées napoléoniennes*, in *Napoleonic ideas*, ed. B. Gooch (New York, 1967); *Political and Historical Works of Louis Napoleon Bonaparte*, 2 vols. (New York, 1972; reprint of 1852 edition), *Oeuvres de Napoléon III*, 5 vols. (Paris, 1856–1869), and *Recueil historique des pensées, opinions, discours, proclamations, lettres et beaux traits de Napoléon III...précédé des maximes de Napoléon Ier* (Paris, 1857); M. G. Molinari, *Napoléon III publiciste: Sa pensée cherchée dans ses écrits-analyse et appréciation de ses oeuvres* (Brussels, 1861).

Stuart L. Campbell

Related entries: BONAPARTISM; *EXTINCTION DU PAUPERISME*; *HISTOIRE DE JULES CESAR*.

ILLNESS: NAPOLEON III. See NAPOLEON III: HEALTH.

INDOCHINA, the French colony whose origins trace to the Second Empire. The term *Indochina* was created by the Danish geographer Konrad Malte-Brun (1775–1826) to apply collectively to Burma, Thailand, the Tonkin, Annam, Cochinchina, Laos, and Cambodia. *L'union indochinoise*, established by France in 1885, included all but the first two of these countries. From 1802 until 1867, Annam, the Tonkin, and Cochinchina formed the Empire of Viet-Nam, whose capital was Hué. From 1858 to 1867 France gradually assumed control of Cochinchina, the southernmost Indochinese region.

The July Monarchy had granted a modest subsidy and free passage on naval vessels to members of the Société des Missions Etrangères. Several of these priests entered Viet-Nam to convert the inhabitants. Minh Mang, emperor of Viet-Nam from 1820 until 1841, viewed these Frenchmen as blasphemous intriguers undermining a divinely sanctioned social order that he embodied. In 1832, he began to persecute all Christians in his empire. His successor, Thieu Tri (1841–1847), continued the oppression, and the next emperor, Tu Duc (1848–

1883), intensified it, executing several French clerics. In 1843 and in 1845 elements of the French navy forced the Vietnamese government to release imprisoned missionaries. But when Louis Philippe's indifference led to withdrawal of this protection, persecution resumed. Napoleon III was more sensitive to the fate of French missionaries. In 1856 his government dispatched a diplomatic mission to Indochina to ask the Vietnamese government to allow religious freedom, grant trade concessions, and permit establishment of a French consulate. The Vietnamese rejected these proposals and refused the head of the mission, Charles de Montigny, an audience with Emperor Tu Duc.

In 1857, Admiral Charles Rigault de Genouilly (1807–1873), while in command of a squadron in Indochinese waters, notified his superiors in Paris that only a *coup de vigueur* could lead to meaningful negotiations with the Vietnamese. In September 1858 he arrived at Tourane (now Da Nang) with a Franco-Spanish expedition of three thousand soldiers and a number of warships. Mutual distrust between French and Vietnamese led to a battle that the French won easily. Heat and disease forced the French from Tourane in a few months. As they were leaving, monsoon winds blew them south to Saigon, the granary of Viet-Nam and a deep-water port. Saigon fell to the French on 17 February 1859 after a brief skirmish. By the spring of that year, however, war in China diverted many French troops from Saigon. The eight hundred who remained were in a precarious position until the arrival of reinforcements from China in February 1861 under the command of Vice-Admiral Joseph Charner (1797–1869). Charner had 158 ships (including 68 warships) and 10,000 men (including a small Spanish auxiliary corps of some 200). On 24 and 25 February he seized the fortifications of Ki-oa and relieved Saigon. In April My-thô fell. After Charner's return to France (29 November), Rear Admiral Bonnard continued the conquest, taking the citadel of Bien-Hoa 18 December 1861. Thus, using Saigon as a base, the French conquered most of eastern Cochinchina in 1861. Tu Duc also faced a rebellion encouraged by French missionaries in the Tonkin. Therefore, on 5 June 1862 his government signed a treaty acknowledging French sovereignty over the three eastern provinces of Cochinchina—Bien-Hoa, Gia-Dinh (Saigon), and My-thô—and over the island of Poulo Condore. The treaty also promised toleration of Christians. The western provinces—Vinh-Long, Soc-Trang, and Chau-Doc—remained in Tu Duc's empire. In 1863, France and Viet-Nam exchanged diplomatic missions, fueling rumors that Napoleon III wished to sell his part of Cochinchina to Tu Duc. Lobbying by partisans of the colony began in France and lasted until the French emperor, at first indifferent and even hostile, seemed to change his mind in 1864. Edouard Drouyn de Lhuys and Achille Fould opposed the French presence in Cochinchina, but Prosper de Chasseloup-Laubat, minister of marine and of the colonies from 1860 until 1867, ardently supported the colony there. A protectorate treaty was signed at Hué 15 July 1864, but Chasseloup-Laubat managed to prevent its ratification, determined to consolidate French control. He urged his admirals in Cochinchina to counter opposition in France by making the colony as financially self-supporting as possible. This goal was never reached during the Second Empire. Chasseloup-Laubat believed that a permanent French presence in Cochinchina depended on the Vietnamese acknowledging the material and moral superiority of French civilization. Additional expansion in Indochina, he warned his admirals, would compromise France's civilizing mission there. Rigault de Genouilly, who succeeded Chasseloup-Laubat in 1867, continued these warnings, adding that they represented the feelings of Napoleon III.

Admiral Pierre Paul Marie de La Grandière (1807–1876), governor of French Cochinchina from 1863 to 1868, disobeyed these instructions. In 1863, he sent into Cambodia Lieutenant de Vaisseau Ernest Doudart de Lagrée (1823–1868), who induced King Norodom to make that country a French protectorate by a treaty of 11 August 1863. In January 1867, La Grandière ordered a military expedition there to support Norodom. In June 1867 he personally led the invasion of those Cochinchinese provinces remaining to Viet-Nam (Vinh-Long, Chau-Doc, and Soc-Trang, in the extreme south of the country) and annexed them by proclamation. Napoleon III quickly accepted this fait accompli, as did Tu Duc in 1874. Coincidental similarity between Vietnamese *phus*, *huyens*, and *tongs* and French *départements*, *arrondissements*, and *cantons* led French naval officers to believe that they could master the political complexities of Cochinchina. A few junior officers therefore volunteered for positions in the administrative infrastructure of the country and, beginning in 1863, received the title *inspecteur des affaires indigènes*. They took charge of native functionaries, most of whom revered Tu Duc, their former emperor. Each step of the Vietnamese educational system had inculcated this reverence. In each *huyen*, a few gifted students from village schools read in Chinese the canonical books of Confucius. Those passing requisite examinations advanced to schools in provincial capitals. There they faced tests qualifying them for diplomas similar to the *baccalauréat*. A few continued to Hué for the Vietnamese equivalent of doctoral examinations. Successful candidates qualified for high governmental positions. The few Vietnamese who attended French schools during the Second Empire learned little and lost face with their compatriots. Attempts to convert the Vietnamese to Christianity were slightly more successful; however, less than 5 percent of the population were Catholics by 1870. The navy maintained the French presence in Cochinchina during the Second Empire and in the early years of the Third Republic. Naval personnel patrolled the rivers, organized militia, and manned outposts. They chased pirates and bandits and crushed revolts by Tu Duc's partisans, often executing suspected ringleaders. From 1866 to 1868 Francis Garnier (1839–1873) and Doudart de Lagrée extensively explored the Mékong River and Laos. It was not until 1879 that the navy relinquished control of Cochinchina to civilian authority.

J. A. Bising, "The Admirals' Government: A History of the Naval Colony that was French Cochinchina, 1862–1879" (Ph.D. thesis, New York University, 1972); J. F. Cady, *The Roots of French Imperialism in Southeast Asia*, 2d ed. (Ithaca, N.Y., 1967); J. Chastinet, "Quand les Français s'intallaient en Indochine," *Historia* (May 1978); M.

E. Osborne, *The French Presence in Cochinchina and Cambodia: Rule and Response, 1859–1905* (Ithaca, N.Y., 1969); G. Taboulet, "Les origines immédiates de l'intervention de la France en Indochine (1857–1858)," *Revue d'histoire des colonies*, (third and fourth quarter, 1954), and "Le voyage d'exploration du Mékong (1866–1868): Doudart de Lagrée et Francis Garnier," *RFHO* no. 1 (1970); R. S. Thomson, "The Diplomacy of Imperialism: France and Spain in Cochinchina, 1858–1863," *JMH* (September 1940); E. Vo Duc Hanh, *La place du Catholicisme dans les relations entre la France et le Vietnam de 1851 à 1870*, 2 vols. (Leiden, 1969).

James A. Bising

Related entries: ALGERIA; CHASSELOUP-LAUBAT; CHINA EXPEDITIONS; MESSAGERIES IMPERIALES; MEXICAN EXPEDITION; SENEGAL; SYRIAN EXPEDITION.

INFALLIBILITY, DOCTRINE OF, adopted by the Catholic church at the Vatican Council of 1870. On 18 July 1870 the council voted in favor of the doctrinal constitution *Pastor aeternus*, which defined the infallibility of the pope and his jurisdictional primacy. According to *Pastor aeternus*, the Roman pontiff, when speaking *ex cathedra*—that is, when defining a doctrine of faith and morals for the entire church in his official capacity as pastor, teacher, and successor to St. Peter—is free from error. Convinced that Christ had promised to be with the church until the end of time, Catholics had already demonstrated in 1854 that they were prepared to accept a definition that recognized infallibility as a characteristic of the papal office itself, for in that year they had readily assented to Pius IX's proclamation on 8 December of the dogma of the immaculate conception of Mary without a church council's having been convened. In France none of the doctors of theology had raised an objection. A lively debate over papal infallibility developed in 1869–1870, however, both before and after the convening of the council. Mgr. Henri Maret, a theologian of note, published his *Du concile générale et de la paix religieuse* (1869), which, while not denying infallibility, contended that it was inoperative without the consent of the episcopacy. Mgr. Louis Pie of Poitiers, the ultramontane (supremacy of Rome) leader of the French infallibilists, promptly denounced Maret's position, while Louis Veuillot employed his newspaper, *L'Univers*, to organize a petition requesting that the council proclaim the doctrine. When in 1870 the Oratorian Fr. Alphonse Gratry (1805–1872) ventured into history to uncover a heretical pope and papal use of false decretals, it called forth a telling response from the scholarly Benedictine abbot of Solesmes, Dom Guéranger (1805–1875). The few surviving proponents of French Gallicanism, such as Maret, Gratry, and Archbishop Georges Darboy (1813–1871) of Paris, along with liberal Catholics, such as Charles de Montalembert and Mgr. Félix Dupanloup, constituted the minority, which struggled in France against the infallibilists. For the most part, their quarrel was less with the doctrine itself than with practical considerations, which, they judged, rendered its proclamation inopportune. Between the infallibilist majority and the inopportunist minority, there stood a third group. Some sixteen French bishops hoped to reconcile the contending sides.

The wording of the statement on infallibility as it was finally proclaimed at the council reflected the desire of the ultramontane majority to vanquish doctrinal Gallicanism for good, for the definition explicitly excluded the juridical necessity of church consent. At the same time, it did not exclude the need for prior consultation to determine the universal *sensus ecclesiae*, as Pius IX had consulted the bishops and theologians before proclaiming the dogma of the immaculate conception. Those who fashioned the definition did not contemplate a pope's acting apart from the belief of the church or apart from an essential fidelity to the deposit of faith within the church. That a pope could err as a private person no one doubted, but, in addition, the definition imputed infallibility only to a pope's declarations on faith and morals as an official person, not to his judgments as a private theologian or to all of his public acts. Nor was infallibility made an exclusive prerogative of the pope; it pertained to the church and so, according to some theologians, could be exercised also by the entire episcopacy when jointly, formally, and definitively defining a matter of faith or morals.

Not only by formally recognizing papal infallibility but also by stipulating that it could be exercised independently of a council, the proclamation of 1870 routed Gallicanism, affirmed papal sovereignty within the church, endowed the pope with a prestige that made it more difficult for the clergy or laity to resist his spiritual instruction, and drew Catholics throughout the world into closer cohesion about him. It need be noted, however, that a plurality of interpretations of the doctrine had existed within the council and persisted after it came to an end. The extreme ultramontanes had failed to win as sweeping a victory in the phrasing of the definition as they had hoped. Undaunted, ultramontanes, such as Louis Veuillot, stretched the doctrine's applicability to cover as wide a range of papal pronouncements as they possibly could. Maximalist interpretations of this type gained wide currency, especially in Anglo-Saxon countries.

T. Caffrey, "Consensus and Infallibility: The Mind of Vatican I," *Downside Review* 88 (April 1970); G. G. Coulton, *Papal Infallibility* (London, 1932); A. Hasler, *Pius IX: Papstliche Unfehlbarkeit und 1. Vatikanum*, 2 vols. (Stuttgart, 1977); J. Hoffman, "Histoire et dogme: La définition de l'infaillibilité pontificale à Vatican I à propos de l'ouvrage de A. B. Hasler," *Revue des sciences philosophiques et théologiques* 62 (October 1978); G. Thils, *L'infaillibilité pontificale: sources, conditions, limites* (Gembloux, 1969).

Raymond L. Cummings

Related entries: DARU; DUPANLOUP; GALLICANISM; PIE; PIUS IX; ROMAN QUESTION; *SYLLABUS OF ERRORS*; VATICAN COUNCIL.

INGRES, DOMINIQUE (1780–1867), classicist painter of portraits, history, and nudes, born at Montauban (Tarn-et-Garonne), 29 August 1780. The last two of the almost six decades of Ingres' long career spanned the greater part of the Second Empire. During that time, while often taking up themes he had explored earlier or completing or reworking works begun earlier, he also added some completely new ideas to his extensive oeuvre.

From his early training in the Academy at Toulouse to his studies with Louis

David in 1797 and his several stays in Italy after winning the Prix de Rome in 1801 (1806–1820, Rome; 1820–1824, Florence; 1834–1841, Rome again), Ingres developed a solid and strong classical foundation, exemplified by his consummate draftsmanship. The precision of his line is not just a matter of fidelity to the contour of silhouette of an object. Certainly observation of nature is taken into account in his drawing. But this would merely serve to make him an accurate transcriber of physical reality like many academic painters, such as Alexandre Cabanel and William Bouguereau. Ingres' genius resides in his ability to achieve both truthfulness of representation and idealization, beauty, and perfection through his skillful manipulation of line and form. The two demands of verism and perfection are superbly met in the portraits, which Ingres painted throughout his life, from the exquisite *Madame Rivière* (1805, Louvre, Paris) to the arresting *Madame Moitessier* (1856, National Gallery, London). Although he professed disdain for portraiture, since it was not as important as history painting, which he would have preferred to devote time to (maintaining the traditional hierarchy of subject matter), it is in his portraits that Ingres excels, more so than in his representations of history. The portrait of Mme. Moitessier is a striking example of Ingres' continuing ability to produce an exceptional work in advanced age, without any loss of skill or control. Ingres had completed an earlier portrait of *Mme. Moitessier* (1851, National Gallery, Washington), rendering the varied textures of her black velvet and lace dress, the nacreous quality of the pearls, the metallic gleam of the gold, the fullness and softness of bare flesh, with astonishing fidelity. The later painting, in which she is portrayed seated with the full splendor of her flowered silk gown taking up almost one-third of the painting, was commissioned in 1844–1845, discontinued in 1851, and resumed in 1852. The formal arrangement shows Ingres' thorough knowledge of a Roman wall painting from Herculaneum, which he synthesizes with the imposing grandeur of Greek art in Mme. Moitessier's pose. The luxurious silks, laces, damasks, and the sensuous dimpled flesh provide a counterpoint for the glassy hardness of the mirror, which occupies the upper half of the painting. We see two versions of her head: one a three-quarter pose clearly defined, the other, reflected in the mirror, an idealized profile as though seen through a veil. A continuous curving line follows her fleshy right arm and fingers, the crown of her head, the soft oval of her face, along the extended bare shoulder and exaggeratedly attenuated left arm and hand. The elongated ellipse is echoed and reinforced by the decorative ribbons that fall from the bodice and shoulder of her dress. All is held in harmonious balance by the repeating verticals of the mirror frame, reflected several times over. Ingres' conception of beauty does not hold to traditional ideas. He dares to distort by suppressing or exaggerating what he observes in nature in order to achieve a pure, more timeless, more sublime effect.

Ingres' persistent effort to present nature in its most perfect form can be seen in another work, not of the same magnitude as the portraits but one that did become renowned and widely imitated (it was an inspiration for Théophile Gautier's "La Source"), *The Source* (1856, Louvre). In conception it shows similarities to the *Venus Anodyomene* (Musée Condé, Chantilly), begun in 1808 but not completed until 1848. Both works present a standing female nude whose pose is a transformation of the classical Venus Pudica. Once more, drawing is the basis for Ingres' treatment of fluid, sinuous curves and sensuous, breathing flesh, recalling Botticelli's *Birth of Venus* and Raphael's *Galatea*. The idyllic quality of the *Venus Anodyomene* is repeated in *The Source*, but the figure of the female alone without the addition of cupids conveys the feelings of timeless innocence, tempered with palpable sensuality. *The Source*, which also had been started much earlier, in the 1820s, is a late version of the type of nude Ingres had introduced in such masterpieces as the *Bather of Valpinçon* (1808), and the *Grande odalisque* (1814, both Louvre).

That his portraits and nudes were more successful than the history painting that he aspired to is demonstrated in a late work, *Joan of Arc at the Coronation of Charles VII* (1854, Louvre). This state commission to paint an episode in the life of Joan of Arc was treated by Ingres with his usual precise recording of detail, historically correct except for the introduction of his own features for her equerry at the rear; however, there is a feeling of disharmony, so atypical of Ingres, in the congestion of objects and in the choice of dissonant colors. The result is a painting that is overly sentimental, too precious and contrived, and somehow lacking in the forcefulness that makes Ingres' portraits so remarkable. His last work, *The Turkish Bath* (1859–1863, Louvre), which in a sense summarizes his oeuvre, is a tour de force. A reprise of the nudes who previously populated his series of bathers, odalisques, and goddesses, this masterly expression of his old age is still full of invention and surprise. His ability to compose in a tondo format so many figures, displaying a whole gamut of poses in a compressed space, and to maintain the sensuous atmosphere and mood of the exotic setting is unsurpassed.

In 1850 Ingres was named president of the Ecole des Beaux-Arts. In 1855, he was honored, as was Eugène Delacroix, with an extensive retrospective exhibition at the Paris international exposition. (Both men were members of the imperial commission that planned the exposition.) Ingres was given a room solely for his work and was made a grand officer of the Legion of Honor. His influence as a teacher in the Academy in Rome and then in the Ecole des Beaux-Arts in Paris was pervasive and sometimes stifling. This was most apparent with the academic painters such as Cabanel, Paul Baudry, Bouguereau, and Jean Léon Gérôme who took over the precision and accuracy of transcription but disguised it with a pseudoclassical veneer. Yet such an important artist as Edgar Degas owed a considerable debt to Ingres, which Degas often demonstrated in his insistence as well that drawing is the basis of all art.

M. Davies, "A Portrait of the Aged Ingres," *BM* 68 (June 1936); R. Rosenblum, *Ingres* (New York, 1967); G. Wildenstein, *Ingres* (London, 1954).

Beverley Giblon

Related entries: BAUDRY; BOUGUEREAU; CABANEL; COUTURE; DELACROIX; GEROME; MEISSONIER.

INTERNATIONAL EXPOSITIONS (1855, 1867), the first of the great world's fairs to be held at Paris. From 1798 to 1849 France sponsored eleven national expositions, and there had been a sentiment to make that of 1849 international in scope. The proposal having proved impracticable, however, it was the 1851 Crystal Palace Exhibition at London that inaugurated the series of world's fairs that continues to our day. The French exhibits at London were second in importance only to those of Britain. French participation was supervised by the eminent archaeologist Léon, comte de Laborde (1807–1869), whose report laid the basis for the two French *expositions universelles* that were to follow. Laborde called on his countrymen to emphasize the rapprochement of art and industry and proposed that a permanent Palais de l'Industrie be constructed. Realization of this latter proposal—an old idea—was decreed on 27 March 1852, shortly after the coup d'état of December 1851. Not until 8 March 1853 would another decree authorize transforming the French national exposition scheduled for the following year into the Paris Exposition Universelle, opening 1 May 1855. Architect Jean Viel (1796–1863) and engineer Alexandre Barrault (1812–1865) were charged with erecting the Palais de l'Industrie on a site now covered by the Rond Point of the Champs Elysées. Work began in earnest in February 1854.

In the meantime, other decrees set the contours of the 1855 exposition. It was to commemorate the forty years of peace since Waterloo, would incorporate the fine arts, and would be financed by the government and planned by an imperial commission under the general supervision of Prince Napoleon, cousin of the emperor. The commission, established in December 1853, was divided into two sections, one for agriculture and industry, the other (under Empress Eugénie's patronage) for fine arts. The first *commissaire générale*, General Arthur Jules Morin (1795–1880), director of the Conservatoire des Arts et Métiers, was replaced at the beginning of 1855 by the pioneer sociologist Frédéric Le Play, who devised a highly intellectualized (and rather impractical) plan for classifying the exhibits. Napoleon III involved himself directly in both the planning and the details of the exposition, while Prince Napoleon, despite his absence from Paris from April 1854 to February 1855, proved to be an able and energetic administrator. Among others who played major roles in the planning were François Barthélemy Arlès-Dufour, Michel Chevalier, and Emile Pereire. All were Saint-Simonians or were heavily influenced by that doctrine, with its emphasis on the transformation of society and, in particular, the amelioration of the lot of the masses through the development of science and industry under government sponsorship. It has even been suggested that the replacement of Morin by Le Play represented a Saint-Simonian coup d'état, although doubts concerning Morin's vigor probably played a part.

From the point of view of its physical planning, the 1855 exposition stands at an intermediate point. It was the first to incorporate thematic exhibits, but it lacked an adequate center, was on the wrong site, and gave a general impression of confusion and disorder. The exposition was concurrent with an agricultural fair (*comice agricole*) at Trappes, a horticultural show, and *essais nautiques* on the Seine. The fine arts exhibits were displayed in a separate Palais des Beaux-Arts built in the French Renaissance style by Hector Lefuel (1810–1881) on the avenue Montaigne. The Rotonde du Panorama (built 1838), between the Palais de l'Industrie and the Seine and linked to the former by a walkway, displayed the imperial jewels and examples of decorative art from the imperial residences. The Palais de l'Industrie itself proved only partially successful. Not quite as large as the Crystal Palace, it was one of the first buildings in France to be constructed largely of iron and became, as a result, the prototype of a number of significant Second Empire buildings. But the architect chose to cocoon his iron and glass structure (the roof was partially covered by 408 windows of roughened glass) within a stone facing. Nor had he solved the ventilation problem, which led to some discomfort in the hot summer of 1855, despite the use of muslin screens. The Palais de l'Industrie faced the Elysées Palace. Rectangular in shape, it consisted of a central nave 35 meters high, covered by an arched semicircular roof and paralleled by two smaller galleries. A transverse gallery at each end, outside the gables, completed the structure, which was 250 meters long and 108 meters wide. The sculptures of Elias Robert (1821–1874) could not relieve its essential ugliness. An inaugural exhibition in the spring of 1855 having shown that the Palais was indeed too small, a long gallery (4,000 feet) was built on the Quai de Billy, paralleling the Seine, to house the exhibits of machines. The Palais de l'Industrie would stand on the present site of the Grand and Petit Palais until demolished in 1897 to make way for the world's fair held at Paris in 1900.

The exposition of 1855 was opened by Napoleon III and Prince Napoleon on 15 May. It had been preceded by the Great Industrial Exhibition at Dublin in 1853 and the World's Fair of the Works of Industry of All Nations at New York City in 1853–1854. Twenty-four thousand exhibitors (eleven thousand were French) came from thirty-four countries. But there was no longer a forty-years' peace to commemorate, for the Crimean War had begun the previous spring. Nevertheless, Russia had been invited, and although it declined to participate, Russian traders were issued passes and Russian officers who were prisoners of war in France were allowed to attend on their word of honor. In all respects other than attendance, the Paris exposition was almost twice the size of its London predecessor. Its final deficit was equally impressive: 8.3 million francs (not including the cost of the Palais de l'Industrie), despite the fact that visitors to the fair's 34 acres had, for the first time, to pay an entrance fee of 1 franc, increased to 5 francs—and then reduced to 2—on Fridays and reduced to 20 centimes on Sundays. There were an estimated 5,162,330 entries as opposed to more than 6 million at London in 1851. The some 500,000 foreign and provincial visitors were thus introduced to a newly established Empire and to a Paris whose transformation at the hands of Napoleon III and his prefect, Baron Georges Haussmann, had just begun. In fact, the exposition inaugurated the era of middle-class railroad excursions to the capital, and the Pereire brothers had prepared for the influx by building in 1854 the splendid Hôtel du Louvre and sponsoring the Grands Magasins du Louvre, which opened on 9 July 1855. It was already a brilliant city. On 30 April Hector Berlioz (1803–1869) conducted his *Te Deum* in the Eglise Sainte Eustache. Adélaïde Ristori (1822–1906) appeared at the Théâtre Italien. Giuseppi Verdi (1813–1901) presented on 13 June at the Opéra *Les vêpres siciliennes*, written at Paris 1853–1855. And on 5 July Jacques Offenbach offered *Les deux aveugles* at his newly acquired tiny theater, the Bouffes Parisiens, achieving at last his first real success. In June the king of Portugal arrived. Two months later Queen Victoria, accompanied by Prince Albert, the prince of Wales, and the princess royal, became the first reigning monarch of Britain to visit France since Henry V and the Hundred Years War (she was returning the state visit made by Napoleon III and Eugénie to England in April). Britain held more exhibition space at the fair than any country other than France, and Anglophilia was at its height. During her visit (18–27 August), the queen attended the exposition. Napoleon III and Eugénie made numerous appearances. The empress even had her own private apartment in the Palais de l'Industrie where she entertained guests. The precipitous rise in the cost of living at Paris and an attempt on the emperor's life on 8 September (the day of the victorious French assault on Sebastopol) could not dampen the mood. That same month a Congrès International de Statistique, meeting at Paris, called for a uniform system of weights and measures and established an international commission to work toward that end. In the fall of 1855, Paris truly seemed en route to becoming the capital of Europe.

In retrospect three aspects of the Paris exposition of 1855 command attention: the emphasis given to the fine arts, the celebration of French industrialization, and the concern evinced for the social question. At London in 1851, painting had been excluded and sculpture represented only as related to manufacturing. In 1855, however, the Salon was replaced by a retrospective display of the works of artists throughout the world who had been living in January 1853. This exhibition, considered to be an integral part of the exposition, also opened on 15 May. Five thousand works of 2,054 artists from twenty-nine countries were chosen for exhibition by national juries. French artists predominated with 3,634 entries. Neither the decorative arts nor sculpture impresses from our perspective of a century and a quarter. There was certainly a mastery of technique but a paucity of imagination and originality. Eclecticism, imitation, and overornamentation flourished. Sculpture was dominated by François Rude, who died two weeks before the official closing at which he was awarded a medal of honor (the other two such medals for sculpture also went to Frenchmen, Francisque Duret, 1804–1865, and Augustin Dumont, 1801–1884). Painting and, in particular, the retrospective exhibitions of Dominique Ingres and Eugène Delacroix, were the glory of the arts section of the exposition. Both men were among the twelve members of the fine arts section of the planning commission, and both were awarded medals of honor. But their styles (classicism and romanticism, respectively) were opposed, and Ingres' triumph was by far the greater. He was promoted grand officer of the Legion of Honor and saluted as a "national glory."

Ironically, the true hero of painting in 1855 from the viewpoint of art history was the realist Gustave Courbet, who reacted to the rejection of two of his paintings, *Burial at Ornans* and *The Studio of the Painter* (eleven were accepted), by setting up his own exhibit of forty paintings in a pavilion opposite the Palais des Beaux-Arts under the name "Le Réalisme, G. Courbet." Admission cost 1 franc and the catalog, with a preface said to have been written by Jules Castagnary (1830–1888), 10 centimes. The show's success was limited, but the realist movement in painting was launched.

Some contemporaries, notably Ernest Renan, condemned the 1855 exposition for its materialism. Certainly industry played a great part. All day, until 5 P.M., the machines (there was even a calculating machine) worked in their long gallery, while agricultural machines were demonstrated at Trappes. Significantly, the exposition demonstrated how dramatically France had closed the industrial gap with Britain in less than five years and in doing so helped to prepare the way for Napoleon III's policy of economic liberalism, and notably for tariff reductions. A trademark law had been adopted in France two weeks before the opening of the exposition, at which for the first time exhibits (which, on Prince Napoleon's suggestion, the French government had admitted without tariff and transported without charge from the frontiers) were priced and sold. The great event of 1855 was the extension of the applications of science and of industry to the arts. The silver electroplating process of Henri Catherine, comte de Ruolz-Montchal (1808–1887), applied by Charles Christofle (1805–1863), now came into its own. Encouraging the new technique, Napoleon III ordered a 1,200-place service of ruolzware for 800,000 francs. The emperor was also responsible in part for the appearance of a new, exotic metal, aluminum, which Henri Sainte-Claire Deville (1818–1881) had just succeeded with government help in producing in laboratory quantities (it was at this time considered a semiprecious metal). The animal sculptor Antoine Louis Barye exhibited his *Jaguar Devouring a Hare*, not at the Palais des Beaux-Arts but at the Palais de l'Industrie. Democratization and industrialization of art and especially of interior decorating had become a fact. (There was a section reserved for industrial design.) And photography, too, had arrived. Adolphe Eugène Disderi (1819–1890?) photographed the exposition, and Charles Nègre won a first-class medal for a photogravure process.

But industry and science were expected to do more than produce novelties or advance the fine arts. For the first time, an international exposition assumed a social aspect. The influences to this end included the ideas of Napoleon III, of Prince Napoleon, and of Le Play, as well as the spirit of social Catholicism (such as of Augustin Cochin, [1823–1872]) and of Saint-Simonianism. The last, especially, permeated the 1855 exposition and was invoked by Prince Napoleon's call in his final report for progress toward "the industrial and commercial organization of the world." An English idea for an *exposition économique* featuring articles for the use of the working class was realized, at Napoleon III's insistence, and proved extremely popular when it opened in July. There were exhibits, too, of models of workers' housing and of new materials likely to be useful to the workers. Le Play exhibited thirty-five of his monographs. Prizes were offered to excellent workers and foremen, as well as to employers who had especially benefited their workers (candidates in both categories were disappointingly few), and workers' excursions were organized to the exposition, although they were not much patronized. In a word, the exposition had as an avowed aim to consecrate all forms of labor and was, like the publications of Louis Hachette and Pierre Larousse, an experiment in popular education.

The Paris exposition of 1855 was officially closed by the emperor on 15 November. Forty thousand attended the ceremony at which Berlioz conducted his cantata *L'impériale* with twelve hundred performers, Prince Napoleon bestowed ten thousand awards, and Napoleon III decorated forty artists, including thirteen foreigners, with the Legion of Honor. The exposition would be remembered as unique in possessing an intellectual importance. It marked the triumph of modern industry and its arrival in France and signaled the growing importance of colonialism and of the non-European world, particularly the United States. It had summarized many of the dominant ideas, realistic or naive, of the century: its belief in indefinite material and moral progress, its assumption that the development of industry and science would bring wisdom and happiness, its hope for the rapprochement of the classes and for European peace (Napoleon III made his closing address the occasion for a plea for an end to the Crimean conflict). The exposition represented as well the triumph of the imperial regime, confidence in its stability, and notice of its concern for the social question.

Between 1855 and 1867 there were international expositions at London (the London International Exhibition, 1862) and Dublin (the International Exhibition of Arts and Manufactures, 1865). The former covered 24 3/4 acres, lasted almost six months, and registered 6,211,103 entries, in spite of which it suffered a small financial loss. In the spring of 1863, six months after the closing of the London exposition, Napoleon III announced that Paris would host an international exposition in 1867. Once again Prince Napoleon was placed in overall charge (he would resign this commission in May 1865), but real responsibility was consigned to the *commissaire général*, Le Play, who, under Laborde, had organized the French participation at London in 1862. Also essential in the planning was Chevalier, chief *rapporteur* and president of the International Jury. Le Play imposed a far more rigorous order than had been apparent in 1855, and it was his plan of classification that determined the nature of the main exposition building, a vast structure of oval design whose galleries formed concentric rings (each longer and higher than the preceding) surrounding a central garden. These oval galleries represented themes, while transverse avenues divided the building into national sections. Thus visitors could, in theory, choose either to follow a theme through the various national exhibits by walking the length of a gallery, or national exhibits through the various themes, by following an avenue, although few countries could do justice to all themes, and the clutter of exhibits often created cul-de-sacs. Out of the interplay of various influences came the central theme of the exposition ("The history of labor and its fruits") as well as its secondary purposes: to symbolize the prosperity and material achievements of the Second Empire, to show off the new Paris, and to state the case for economic liberalism (as witnessed by Chevalier's six-hundred-page introduction to the *Rapport du jury international*).

The exposition occupied the entire site of the Champ de Mars (more than 110 acres), opposite the Butte de Chaillot, which had been leveled in preparation for the exposition. Only one annex was required, on the Ile de Billancourt, to house agricultural exhibits (there were also exhibits on the banks of the Seine of models illustrating the history of naval construction and of artillery). The great central building, elliptical in shape and unadorned, covered almost 40 acres. Its chief engineers, Gustave Eiffel (1832–1923) and Jean Krantz (1817–1899), for the first time properly computed the stresses and strains before construction. Seven concentric galleries were covered with a roof hung from external supports that masqueraded as flagpoles. The dimensions were vast for the time: 1,245 feet in width, 1,500 feet in length, a circumference of 1,600 yards, and a floor space of 6.75 million square feet (three times that of 1855). From the central garden, parallel galleries were devoted, successively, to the history of work, fine arts, materials and their application to the liberal arts, furniture, textiles, raw materials, and machinery. The outermost (machinery) gallery, built by Eiffel, was also the highest (85 feet) and most spacious (115 feet in width). Hydraulic elevators, designed by Léon Edoux (1827–1910), lifted visitors from ground floor to roof where there were walkways offering splendid views. But the true novelty was the extensive outer garden. The 1867 exposition was the first to have an outdoors, the first to have national pavilions (101 small structures built in a variety of styles by the exhibitors and scattered throughout the park), and the first to offer a carnival atmosphere. Every French wine district had its own exhibits and cellar (the classification of Bordeaux wines based on price, which is still in effect, had been drawn up for the 1855 exposition). Cafés and restaurants offering a variety of international cuisines encircled the main building and opened on to the outer gardens where visitors could stroll among mosques, slobodas, chalets, kiosks, sarcophagi, bamboo houses, porcelain pagodas, and bazaars (the Tunisian Bardo survives today in Parc Montsouris, where it serves as a meteorological observatory). The French pavilion, an exquisite palace in miniature, was used as a lounge for the imperial family and guests. Everywhere dominated the exotic and, in particular, the Oriental. It was through the 1867 exposition that Japanese art burst fully on Europe.

Although a major last-minute effort succeeded in opening the exposition on time on 1 April 1867, only four of the national pavilions (the British, Russian, Swedish, and Danish) were ready and poor weather throughout the month, as well, perhaps, as the threat of war between France and Prussia over Luxembourg, kept attendance disappointingly low. Then in May the sun came out, the Luxembourg crisis was resolved, and Paris became the mecca of Europe. More than 11 million entrances to the exposition grounds were recorded, and a handsome profit of 2.88 million francs rung up despite the cost of 20 million francs for mounting 52,000 exhibits (the word for the first time won currency), of which 12,000 were French.

Visitors who, ignoring the pleasures of the outer gardens and such attractions as the ascensions, twelve passengers at a time, in Félix Nadar's captive balloon, would cross the Pont d'Iéna, mount the flag-lined avenue d'Europe, and enter the main building through the Porte d'Honneur, might penetrate at once to the innermost gallery where the theme of the exposition was illustrated by a "History of Work" exhibit, the first attempt at an international thematic display. (It was Le Play's idea.) The French section, covering the period from the Stone Age to the eighteenth century, was easily the best. French exhibits of all sorts occupied nearly one-half of the total ground space of the main building, while those of Britain were second in extent. As in 1855 Napoleon III insisted that the social question be stressed throughout the exposition. There was a special section devoted to inexpensive and useful goods, and the emperor himself exhibited (in the outer gardens) government-built workers' housing for which he won the highest award. There were even low-price restaurants for workers. As in 1862 the French government encouraged and subsidized workers' delegations to the exposition (from 1866 to 1870 these delegations, meeting at the *mairie* of the eleventh arrondissement, would form a sort of workers' parliament, formulating demands for presentation to the government). However, Le Play's paternalism— he sponsored a system of awards for philanthropic employers—was generally rejected by those at whom it was aimed.

Next to the inner gallery, the exhibitions of fine art looked out on the central garden. Representing paintings and sculptures from fifteen countries executed between 1855 and 1867, it was the largest collection of contemporary art that had yet been assembled. Unfortunately, the process of selection (each country had its own selection committee and shipped and set up its own section) ensured the imposition of official taste and in fact a virtual regimentation of European art. In France the jury, which also served for the Salon of that year (the best works were later sent to the exposition), was two-thirds elected by former medal winners and members of the Académie des Beaux-Arts and of the Legion of Honor and one-third appointed by the exposition's commission. It was dominated by such academic artists as Alexandre Cabanel, Jean Léon Gérôme, and Thomas Couture. Predictably the avant-garde painters were rejected. Camille Pissaro and Paul Cézanne (1839–1906) were excluded. Edouard Manet's submissions were not even sent on to the jury, with the result that he decided to hold his own exhibition on the avenue de l'Alma just outside the exposition grounds (Courbet had a nearby *baraque* where he showed 135 of his canvases). Manet from 24 May exhibited fifty paintings, including *Luncheon on the Grass*, *Olympia*, *Child with Sword*, *Lola de Valence*, *The Street Singer*, and *The Fifer*. As well, he provided a catalog with an unsigned preface by Emile Zola, who would publish *Thérèse Raquin* in 1867. That year Manet would paint *The Execution of Maximilian* and *View of the Exposition*, perhaps inspired by the glimpses he had when collecting the 50 centimes required for admission to his exhibition. Within the exposition building, official art held sway. Four of eight medals of honor for painting went to Frenchmen—Ernest Meissonier, Cabanel (for his *Birth of Venus*), Gérôme, and Théodore Rousseau—and sculpture was dominated by Jean Joseph Perraud (1819–1876) and Eugène Guillaume (1822–1905). The latter displayed a series of busts of Napoleon I at various stages of his life. Only the sculptor Jean Baptiste Carpeaux, winner of a second-class medal (among his works displayed were *Fisherboy with Shell*, *Ugolino*, and *The Prince Imperial*), impresses in retrospect. In the decorative arts as well, lack of originality vied with superlative execution.

In the outer galleries novelties competed for attention. There was a major medical exhibit from the United States, including a complete Civil War field hospital, a patented American rocking chair, such new materials and processes as petroleum distillation, aluminum, and sulfuric acid, and even a "locomobile." Railroad and photographic exhibits were very important. Of the latter, France had 165, Britain 105, Austria 58, Germany 52, Italy 42, and the United States 17. There was even an official photographer of the exposition, Pierre Petit (1832–1909), who took over twelve thousand photographs. The Suez Canal Company had its own exhibit where Ferdinand de Lesseps presided. Louis Pasteur won a medal for his work on pasteurization, and the Michaux brothers of France displayed a bicycle that was strikingly modern in appearance. But the heart of the exposition was the machinery gallery. From the raised balcony down its center, visitors could observe machines for every purpose, including some powered by gas or by compressed air. This was the apotheosis of the Age of Steel—Pierre Martin was awarded a gold medal for his open-hearth process. Le Creusot had its own pavilion, featuring locomotives and a huge marine engine; the heart of Prussia's exhibit was a gigantic fifty-ton Krupp cannon made of steel (everyone else still used bronze) that could fire a thousand-pound shell.

Our understanding of the 1867 exposition has suffered from the tendency, in hindsight, to view it either as the last excess of an age about to be punished for its frivolity or the final flare of a *belle époque* just before its extinction. Certainly it was in 1867 that Paris earned its reputation as the modern Babylon. From newly inaugurated Seine excursion boats (the *bateaux mouches*) or vehicles of the two recently consolidated transportation companies of omnibuses and of *petites voitures*, visitors could view the city that Haussmann had built. They could dine well for 80 centimes or sinfully in the private rooms of notorious restaurants such as the Grand Seize of the Café Anglais where Adolphe Dugléré would prepare dinner for the czar and czarevitch of Russia and the king of Prussia (the so-called Banquet of the Three Emperors, at which Bismarck was also a guest). They could hear Giacomo Meyerbeer's *L'Africaine* or Verdi's *Don Carlos* (the latter written for the exposition year and first performed 11 March) at the Opéra or Charles Gounod's *Roméo et Juliette* at the Théâtre Lyrique. They could see Victor Hugo's revised *Hernani* at the Théâtre Français or plays by François Ponsard or Alexandre Dumas fils. They could listen to the renowned café-concert singer Thérésa (1837–1913) at the Alcazar or, if important enough, whirl at a

Tuileries ball whose orchestra was conducted by Johann Strauss, Jr. They could watch a horse race at Longchamp for a stake of 100,000 francs or view in the Bois de Boulogne great military reviews attended by kings and emperors. Above all, they could join *tout Paris* (and Europe) at the Variétés for a performance of Jacques Offenbach's *Grande Duchesse de Gérolstein*, starring Hortense Schneider. Offenbach's career, which had received its first major impetus during the exposition of 1855, reached its pinnacle during the festivities of 1867. And the visitor might well be himself a prince or a king, for few failed to visit Paris in the summer and fall of 1867. Royal guests included the brother of the tycoon of Japan, the king of Greece (both in late April), the king of Belgium (May), the czar of Russia, William I of Prussia, and the khedive of Egypt (all in June), the sultan of Turkey and the king of Portugal (July), the king of Sweden and the queen of Württemberg (August), and in October the emperor of Austria. Add the kings of Bavaria and Denmark and a host of princes and princesses, granddukes and duchesses (only Queen Victoria and the king of Italy failed to appear). All was symbolized by the review at Longchamp of some thirty-five thousand French troops, where Napoleon III rode with the czar of Russia on his right and King William of Prussia on his left.

There were ample auguries of disaster: the unsuccessful attempt on Czar Alexander II's life by a Pole, Berejowski, as the French emperor and the czar returned (6 June) in a carriage from the Longchamp review; famine and cholera in Algeria; the beginning of Giuseppi Garibaldi's menace to Rome; economic stagnation; and the arrival at the end of June of word of Emperor Maximilian of Mexico's execution, final fruit of the disastrous French intervention in that country. Returning from his visit to Salzburg in August, where he had gone to meet Francis Joseph, Napoleon III referred somberly, at Lille, to the *points noirs* that had appeared on the horizon. But the exposition existed in the present, not the future, and it was a present of considerable accomplishments and even of much cause for hope. Victory Duruy, the minister of education, sponsored for the occasion a mammoth publication of twenty-nine volumes of reports on the state of arts and letters in France, and there was great emphasis on internationalism, symbolized by Victor Hugo's rather extravagant evocation of *universalité*. The exposition was officially closed on 3 November, but the great ceremony for the distribution of prizes by Napoleon III had been held earlier, on 1 July in the Palais de l'Industrie, before twenty thousand invited guests. For that occasion Gioacchino Rossini (1792–1868), whose *Hymn to the Emperor* had opened the exposition, wrote another hymn, sung this time by a chorus of twelve basses. Several days before the official closing, Napoleon III in a speech to the Corps Législatif (31 October) characterized the exposition as having tightened "the ties of fraternity between nations" and having destroyed "forever a past of prejudices and errors." "The shackles of labor and of intelligence," he concluded, "the barriers between peoples as well as among classes, and international hatreds—these are what the Exposition has cast behind." The exposition buildings were demolished at once and the Champ de Mars returned to its former state. But the great world's fair of 1867 was destined to launch a hundred years of similar celebrations on a similar scale.

J. J. Bloch and M. Delort, *Quand Paris allait "à l'Expo"* (Paris, 1980); M. Carmona, "Les expositions universelles," *Historia*, 437 (April 1983); Comte Fleury and L. Sonolet, "Il y a cent ans: L'Exposition de 1867," *Historia* (July 1967), and "Il y a cent ans: Tous les souverains du monde à l'Exposition Universelle à Paris," *Historia* (August 1967); E. G. Holt, ed., *The Art of all Nations: 1850–1873: The Emerging Role of Exhibitions and Critics* (New York, 1981); R. Isay, *Panorama des expositions universelles* (Paris, 1937); F. Laisney, "L'architecture industrielle dans les expositions universelles," *MHF*, no. 3 (1977); M. Pointon, "From the Midst of Warfare and Its Incidents to the Peaceful Scenes of Home: The Exposition Universelle of 1855," *JES*, 11 (December 1981); M. Rebérioux, "Approches de l'histoire des expositions universelles à Paris, du Second Empire à 1900," *Bulletin du Centre d'Histoire Economique et Sociale de la Région Lyonnaise* 1 (1979); H. Rollet, "Le Play, l'art, et la mode en 1867," *ES* n.s., no. 105 (1977); F.A. Trapp, "Expo 1867 revisited," *Apollo* 89, no.84 (1969).

Related entries: CHEVALIER; COURBET; LE PLAY; MANET; NAPOLEON III: ASSASSINATION ATTEMPTS; PARIS, REBUILDING OF; PRINCE NAPOLEON; RAILROADS; SAINT-SIMONIANISM.

INTERNATIONAL WORKING MEN'S ASSOCIATION. See FIRST INTERNATIONAL.

ITALIAN CONFEDERATION, the favorite scheme of Napoleon III for the reorganization of Italy. In 1852 Italy remained, as Prince Klemens von Metternich had described it, "a geographical expression." The peninsula was divided into a number of sovereign states, of which the most important were Sardinia, Tuscany, Modena, Parma, Lucca, the Papal States, and Naples or the Two Sicilies. All of these states, with the exception of Sardinia, were under Austrian control or influence; the provinces of Lombardy and Venetia had been part of the Austrian Empire since 1815. For Napoleon III there seemed good reason, therefore, to desire the expulsion of Austria from the peninsula and the consolidation of the Italian states. Such an objective was compatible with the policy of nationalities and with French national interests, provided that the new Italy would not itself pose a threat to France. To avoid this and because, knowing Italy and the Italians well, he did not believe unity to be feasible, Napoleon III had long advocated not a unitary but a confederated state. Since at least 1848, he had pondered the details of such a confederation, which would have the additional advantage of allowing the pope to retain his temporal power and even to exercise a sort of honorary presidency. We may assume that Napoleon III would have advocated this solution had he succeeded in bringing the Italian question before a European conference in 1849, 1856, or 1859, as he attempted to do.

At Plombières in July 1858, the French emperor and Count Camillo Benso di Cavour, prime minister of Sardinia, plotted a war against Austria that would drive it from the peninsula and reorganize Italy into a confederation of four states: Sardinia (enlarged by at least the addition of Lombardy and Venetia), the

Papal States, a central state, and the Kingdom of the Two Sicilies. It is possible that had France been able to win a complete military victory over Austria in the war that began in May 1859, an Italian confederation somewhat resembling the one sketched at Plombières would have been established. But Napoleon III found it expedient to make peace at Villafranca in July 1859 before having driven the Austrians from Venetia. This military failure soon became a chief reason for the failure of the Italian confederation scheme. Although such a confederation, including Venetia, had been agreed to at Villafranca, Italian patriots soon realized that an Italian confederation containing Austrian Venetia might easily fall under the influence or control of Vienna. Thus the already powerful sentiment for annexation to Sardinia was reinforced. Even had the proposed congress on the Italian question met in early 1860, it is unlikely that the creation of a unitary state would have been averted.

Napoleon III nevertheless remained convinced that the Italian confederation envisaged at Villafranca was "the only possible remedy for the evils to which Italy had been so long subjected." No state would be forced to enter; if any irrevocably refused, the idea would fail. Each state would have votes according to population. The seat would be at Rome, and the pope would be honorary president, but the real head would be the Italian sovereign having the largest possessions, and he would be represented, as in the German Confederation, by a minister. The states composing the confederation would help each other in resisting aggression and in putting down internal discontent, but only federal troops could be employed and only by order of the confederation. Venetia would be a part of the confederation, but the Austrian emperor would rule there by a purely Italian administration and only with Italian troops, and the Venetian fortresses would be federal. So, at least, ran the ideas of the French emperor on the subject, and he was certainly among the last to admit their futility. Even after the proclamation of the Kingdom of Italy in March 1861, he continued to believe (at least as late as 1866) that out of disorder in the peninsula or a new war with Austria could come a return to three or four sovereign Italian states— and confederation. But however prescient Napoleon III's analysis of the troubles in store for an Italy too hastily unified, the possibility of an alternative had been lost at Villafranca and disappeared forever with Prussia's victory over Austria at Sadowa in July 1866.

A. Blumberg, "The Demise of Italian Federalism, 1859," *Historian* 18 (1955); L. Giangrasso, "La politica inglese e il piano di confederazione italiana dopo Villafranca," *Risorgimento*, 22, no. 3 (1970); M.J. McDonald, "Napoleon III and His Ideas of Italian Confederation, 1856–1860" (Ph.D. diss., University of Pennsylvania, 1969), and "The Vicariat Proposals: A Crisis in Napoleon III's Italian Confederative Designs," in N. Barker and M. Brown, Jr., eds., *Diplomacy in an Age of Nationalism* (The Hague, 1971); A. Pingaud, "Napoléon III et ses projets de confédération italienne," *RH* 155 (May– August 1927).

Related entries: ITALIAN WAR; NATIONALITIES; NICE-SAVOY; PLOM-BIERES; ROMAN QUESTION; VENETIA; VILLAFRANCA.

ITALIAN QUESTION (1860). See CHAMBERY.

ITALIAN WAR (1859), the war of France and Sardinia against Austria for the purpose of driving the latter from the Italian peninsula. At the beginning of the Second Empire, Austrian influence in Italy was predominant. Only one state, Sardinia, remained free of its direct or indirect control. When Count Camillo Benso di Cavour became prime minister of Sardinia in 1852, he was determined to weaken or to destroy the influence of Austria with the aid of a great European power. As a liberal, Cavour's choice would have been Britain; as a realist, he turned to France. Napoleon III, long sympathetic to Italy, antithetic to conservative Austria, devoted to the principle of nationalities, and eager to increase French prestige, needed little persuasion. Moreover, once Austria was gone from Italy, Napoleon III believed that he could manage Sardinia's territorial ambitions (for example, in regard to the Romagna, a papal province where Austrian troops had exercised martial law since 1848) and at the same time obtain an increased leverage for forcing reform measures on Pope Pius IX. The problem was timing. Although Sardinia at the end of January 1855 entered the Crimean War against Russia on the side of Britain and France and sent a contingent of ten thousand men in May to fight before Sebastopol, it did not prove possible to bring the Italian question before the peace congress at Paris, except for the single session of 8 April 1856 where Britain and France castigated Austria for its Italian policy. Napoleon III, however, had openly displayed his sympathy for Italy and his eagerness to help, and Cavour continued his efforts to modernize and liberalize the Sardinian state in order that it might emerge as the leader of the peninsula.

On 1 August 1857 the Italian National Society was founded on Cavour's initiative. Six months later the attempt on Napoleon III's life by Felice Orsini led to the fateful interview at Plombières of Cavour and the French emperor. There a pact was concluded calling for a war between Sardinia and Austria in which France would assist the former. After the war, there would be a reorganization of the Italian peninsula on a confederated basis. In return for French aid, King Victor Emmanuel II would permit the marriage of his daughter, Clotilde, to the emperor's cousin, Prince Napoleon. At the conclusion of the war, Sardinia would cede to France the Duchy of Savoy (the ancestral home of Victor Emmanuel's family, the ruling Carignano line) and also the county of Nice. On 26 January 1859 Napoleon III contracted a formal alliance with Sardinia (Treaty of Turin).

Cavour's task, which he undertook at once following Plombières, was to goad Austria into declaring war on Sardinia. Through the National Society he created disturbances on both Austrian and papal territory and sponsored anti-Austrian propaganda. He increased Sardinia's armaments and interfered in the quarrel between Austria and certain *émigrés* from the Austrian territories of Lombardy and Venetia. On 1 January 1859 Napoleon III expressed publicly to the Austrian ambassador, Count Joseph Alexander von Hübner (1811–1892), his unhappiness that relations with Austria had deteriorated. On 18 January Victor Emmanuel, in a speech the French emperor had edited, announced that he could not be insensible to the "cry of anguish" mounting from various parts of Italy. And on 30 January Prince Napoleon married Clotilde at Turin (the treaty of alliance that Prince Napoleon signed for France four days before his wedding was officially dated December 1858 to conceal the connection between the alliance and the marriage). Although Napoleon III's diplomatic efforts to secure the neutrality of the great powers were partially successful (treaty with Russia, 3 March 1859), he quickly grew alarmed at the state of European opinion and, in particular, at the attitude of the British government, which, in mid-February, sent the British ambassador at Paris, Lord Cowley (1804–1884), to Vienna on a mission of mediation. Always drawn toward conference diplomacy, the French emperor accepted a European congress proposed by Russia on 16 March and brought great pressure to bear on Cavour to participate. The Sardinian was in despair. But on 23 April Austria, weary of provocations and preferring to lose a province by war rather than by negotiation, sent a peremptory ultimatum to Turin and invaded Sardinia on 29 April. Napoleon III was thus able to begin the war with the support of French public opinion and without appearing to be the aggressor.

France declared war on Austria on 3 May 1859. Napoleon III arrived at Genoa by sea on 12 May to take personal command of his troops in Italy. The French army of some 100,000 was far from prepared for war and had no adequate campaign plan. Nevertheless, partly because of Austrian ineptitude, partly because Napoleon III showed a greater strategic skill than is usually credited to him, partly because of the fighting qualities of the French troops, and partly because of luck, the first major battle, at Magenta on 4 June 1859, was a success for the allies, whose force of about 55,000 suffered some 4,500 casualties, to more than 10,000 for the somewhat larger Austrian army. Following the battle, the French emperor reprimanded Victor Emmanuel for having failed to give proper support. On 8 June Napoleon III and Victor Emmanuel entered Milan. The Austrian emperor, Francis Joseph, took command of his army, grown to some 160,000. The Battle of Solferino on 24 June 1859 pitted some 120,000 Austrian troops (with 451 cannons) against an equal number of French and Sardinians (with 320 cannons, including very effective new French rifled artillery). The engagement was confused and indecisive and nearly a disaster for the French, part of whose cavalry panicked the following day. But the Austrians withdrew from the field. Napoleon III had once again played a creditable role. He was, however, undoubtedly aware of his own deficiencies and of those of his army, and he was much moved by the loss of life and the suffering he had witnessed during and immediately after the fifteen-hour battle, which (together with the Sardinian action at San Martino) cost more than 20,000 Austrian and 18,000 allied casualties (4,000 Sardinian out of a force of only 25,000). Out of the carnage would come by 1870 the International Red Cross. The unpursued Austrian forces had withdrawn from the field of Solferino into a virtually impregnable redoubt, the Quadrilateral (four fortresses on the Mincio River). For these and other reasons, Napoleon III suddenly made peace with Francis Joseph at Villafranca on 11 July 1859. The final peace treaty was signed at Zurich on 10 November 1859. Fatefully, the Italian War had reopened the Italian question without resolving it. As a result, more than ten years of complications lay ahead for France.

F. de Bernardy, ''Alexandre Walewski et la question italienne,'' *RHD*, 90 (July-December 1976); H. Contamine, *Souplesse napoléonienne et rigidité autrichienne en 1859* (Paris, 1959); P. Defrasne, ''La Prusse et la France face à face en 1859,'' *Revue militaire générale* (April 1973); J. E. Jordan, ''Matrimony and Machiavellianism: The Marriage of Prince Napoleon,'' *PAPS*, 20 August 1971; K. B. Rose, ''Napoleon III and the Austro-Sardinian War of 1859'' (Ph.D. diss., University of Texas, Austin, 1963); B. H. Sumner, ''The Secret Franco-Russian Treaty of 3 March 1859,'' *EHR* 48 (January 1933); V. L. Tapié, ''Le traité secret de 1859 entre la France et la Russie,'' *RHMC* 5 (1953); G. J. Thurston, ''The Italian War of 1859 and the Reorientation of Russian Foreign Policy,'' *CHJ* 20 (March 1977); R. Ugolini, *Cavour e Napoleone III nell'Italia centrale: Il sacrificio di Perugia* (Rome, 1973); F. Valsecchi, ''La mediazione britannica nella Guerra del 1859: La missione Cowley [da Parigi] a Vienna, 10 febbraio–10 marzo 1859,'' *Mitteilungen des österreichischen Staatsarchiv* 31 (1978), and ''La paix de Zurich,'' *RHMC* (April–June 1960).

Ivan Scott

Related entries: ARMY REFORM; CONGRESS POLICY; CRIMEAN WAR; FRANCO-PRUSSIAN WAR; ITALIAN CONFEDERATION; NATIONALITIES; NICE-SAVOY; PRINCE NAPOLEON; ORSINI; PLOMBIERES; PUBLIC OPINION; ROMAN QUESTION; VENETIA; VILLAFRANCA; WALEWSKI.

J

JANIN, JULES (1804–1874), journalist and literary critic; born 16 February 1804, at Saint-Etienne. The son of a lawyer, Janin was destined for a law career, but after completing his education at the Collège Louis le Grand, he entered journalism and began to write novels, the first of which (*L'âne mort et la femme guillotinée*, a parody of the romantic style) appeared in 1829. Janin rallied to Louis Philippe and to moderate Orleanism and was named to the Legion of Honor in 1836. That same year he became a political editor of the *Journal des débats* but moved almost at once to the post of drama critic, which he was to hold without interruption until September 1873. His column, which appeared every Monday, earned him the epithet "Prince of Critics," and, indeed, a word from Janin could make or break careers. It was he who in 1837–1838 discovered the great tragic actress Rachel—and who turned against her in 1855 to hymn the praises of her young Italian rival, Adelaide Ristori. Even an attack by Janin could have momentous consequences. Thus, his condemnation of Jacques Offenbach's *Orphée aux enfers* in the fall of 1858 drew curious Parisians to the operetta in such numbers that Offenbach's theater was saved and his reputation made.

Janin's fame rested on his personality and his wit. His judgments were arbitrary, based on no clearly defined principles, and often inconsistent. Enemies proclaimed, as well, that his reviews were not always disinterested. Although an opponent of the Second Empire and possessing Orleanist credentials, the celebrated critic did not find it easy to join the ranks of the Immortals at the Académie Française. In 1863 he was defeated by Jules Dufaure (1798–1881) and, more surprisingly, in April 1865 by a younger *Journal des débats* colleague, Lucien Anatole Prévost-Paradol. Despite public support for Janin's candidacy, it was only on 7 April 1870 that he was elected to the seat left vacant at the Académie by the death of his fellow critic Charles Augustin Sainte-Beuve. The Franco-Prussian War intervened, and by the time Janin took his seat (November 1871), he was already in full intellectual decline. He died at Passy, 20 June 1874.

Sainte-Beuve's reputation has completely eclipsed that of Janin in our day, but it seems probable that if Janin did not deserve the extravagant praise of his contemporaries, neither has he merited the complete neglect that followed. Certainly his critical writings, which may be found in his own collection, *Histoire de la littérature dramatique* (6 vols., Paris, 1858) and in M. A. de la Fizelière's *Oeuvres choisies* (12 vols., Paris, 1875–1878) and, especially, his letters, constitute a valuable source for historians of the Second Empire. Among the novels written by Janin during the Second Empire are: *Les gaîtés champêtres* (1851), *Les symphonies de l'hiver* (1858), *Les contes du chalet* (1859), *Barnave* (new ed., 1860), *La fin d'un monde et du neveu de Rameau* (1861), *Les petits bonheurs de la vie* (1861), *La semaine des trois jeudis* (1861), *Contes non estampillés* (1862), *Les contes bleues* (1863), *Les oiseaux bleus* (1864), *Le talisman* (1866), *Les amours du Chevalier de Fosseuse* (1867), *Circé* (1867), *L'interné* (1869), *Petits romans d'hier et d'aujourd'hui* (1869), and *Le crucifix d'argent* (1870). Janin also wrote during the same period: *Rachel et la tragédie* (1858), *La poésie et l'éloquence à Rome* (1863), *La Révolution française* (2 vols., 1862–1865), *Béranger et son temps* (2 vols., 1866), *L'amour des livres* (1866), *Lamartine* (1869), and *Le livre* (1870).

J. Bonnerot, "Sainte-Beuve et Jules Janin," *RDM*, no. 7 (1958); Mergier-Bourdeix, ed., *Jules Janin: 735 lettres à sa femme, 1842–1855*, 2 vols. (Paris, 1976); A. Piedagnel, *Jules Janin*, 3d ed. (Paris, 1884); H. Ryland, "Jules Janin, 'Prince of Critics,' " *Kentucky Foreign Language Quarterly* 6 (1959); J. L. Wilbrich, "Jules Janin et son temps d'après des lettres inédites" (Ph.D. diss., Northwestern University, 1966).

Related entries: JOURNAL DES DEBATS; SAINTE-BEUVE.

JANVIER DE LA MOTTE, EUGENE (1823–1884), politician and administrator, prefect of the Eure department (Normandy) from 1856 to 1869; born at Angers, 27 March 1823. Janvier de la Motte was the son of Comte Elie (1798–1869), whose Roman peerage title was granted to him by Pope Pius IX in March 1851. Elected to the Corps Législatif as an official candidate in 1852, Comte Elie remained a deputy until his death. His son, after studying law, was appointed subprefect at Dinan in 1847 and at Saint-Etienne in 1850. In 1853 he was named prefect of the Lozère and in 1856 of the Eure, where he remained for twelve years.

At the time of Janvier de la Motte's appointment, the Eure was an Orleanist fief, dominated by the Passy, Broglie, and Orleans families. The last owned extensive properties in the region, which they frequently visited. The new prefect, an ardent bonapartist of the democratic variety who believed that the emperor should draw his strength directly from the people, immediately undertook to win popular support for the regime. A ribald, gregarious, outspoken man, with great energy and tact and a superb memory for names, he organized the peasants as village firemen (*pompiers*), regaling them at lavish banquets with the assurance that "l'Empereur est le père des pompiers, de tous les pompiers." He traveled incessantly, from fair to fair and from market to market, freely distributing largesse and haranguing the large open-air meetings, which gave best scope to his political skills. In order, as he said, never to refuse anything, Janvier de la

Motte ran through the fortunes of two wives, and when diversion of budget funds (*virements*) no longer sufficed, he accumulated a deficit for his department of 700,000 francs in seven years (1860–1867). But the prefect achieved his purpose, winning an ascendancy so great that, as he claimed, "the people obeyed him blindly." In December 1861 he was promoted officer of the Legion of Honor, to which he had been named in 1852. Some were more critical, however. Although Janvier de la Motte took care to defer to such powerful figures as Raymond Troplong, president of the Conseil Général of the Eure, the mounting deficit combined with the advance of political reform to erode his position. A quarrel in 1868, during which the prefect slapped a *conseiller général* named Alaboisette, led to suspension, a trial, and a fine of 3,000 francs. Undaunted, Janvier de la Motte threatened to run for election to the Corps Législatif and was offered the prefecture of the Gard, which he accepted, exchanging it a few months later for that of the Morbihan. Only the advent of the Liberal Empire could finally end his administrative career. Dismissed on 1 February 1870, the ex-prefect returned to Paris, where he became one of the most enthusiastic advocates of the plebiscite of that year.

Following the overthrow of the Second Empire on 4 September 1870, Janvier de la Motte made his way to Switzerland, from which he was extradited in June 1871 at the demand of Adolphe Thiers to stand trial for misdemeanors in office. His conviction was mandatory, for he had become an almost legendary symbol of the imperial *préfet de poing*, and would, indeed, have served as model for a novel which Gustave Flaubert, toward the end of his life, had planned to write about the Second Empire's prefects. Irrepressible, Janvier de la Motte won election to the Chamber of Deputies from the Eure in 1876 and again in 1881. He died at Paris, 26 February 1884.

I. Cloulas, "Joséphine, impératrice; Janvier de la Motte, préfet d'Empire: Deux images du XIXe siècle ébrocien," *Nouvelles de l'Eure*, no. 35 (1969); J. P. Defrance, "Eugène Janvier de la Motte, préfet de l'Eure, 1856–1866," *Annales de Normandie*, 32 (March 1982).

Related entries: AUTHORITARIAN EMPIRE; BONAPARTISM; CHEVREAU; PREFECTS.

JEROME, PRINCE. See PRINCE NAPOLEON.

JOURNAL DES DEBATS, perhaps the most prestigious of the Orleanist daily newspapers. Founded by the two Bertin brothers during the July Monarchy, its preeminent position was eroded during the Second Empire. Yet the patronage and support of the Rothschilds, the paper's close ties with academic and diplomatic circles, and the collaboration of very brilliant writers (at least six Academicians were among its contributors) gave it an important aura, which was enhanced by high journalistic standards, excellent literary criticism, and philosophical discussions of great clarity. Among the contributors to the *Journal des débats* were Adolphe Franck (1809–1893), Hippolyte Rigault (1821–1858), Narcisse Salvandy (1795–1856), Jules Janin (the newspaper's long-time drama critic), Philarète Chasles (1799–1873), Clément Caraguel (1819–1882), Saint-Marc Girardin (1801–1873), Hippolyte Taine, Alfred Cuvillier-Fleury (1802–1887), Jean Louis Antoine Alloury (1805–1884), Edouard Laboulaye (1811–1883), John Lemoinne (1815–1892; a chief editor during the Second Empire), Lucien Anatole Prévost-Paradol, Ernest Renan, Emile Littré, Michel Chevalier, Ernest Bersot (1816–1880), Hector Berlioz (1803–1869; the paper's music critic), Etienne Jean Delécluze (1781–1863; art critic, followed in the post by his nephew Adolphe Etienne Viollet-le-Duc, brother of the architect), Emile Deschanel (1819–1904), Samuel de Sacy (1801–1879; an editor-in-chief who after December 1851 wrote only literary articles), and Jean Jacques Weiss (1827–1891). Weiss, who wrote the political chronicle from 1860, was typical of the many academics who during the Second Empire found more interesting careers in journalism. The two sons of Louis François Bertin (1766–1841) directed the *Journal des débats* during the Second Empire—Louis Marie Armand (1801–1854) until his death and then his older brother, Edouard François (1797–1871). Edouard was little interested in politics. The most important of the newspaper's chief editors during the Empire, Samuel de Sacy, was very cautious and careful to avoid government censure. (Later, like Prévost-Paradol, he became reconciled to the regime and even accepted appointment to the Senate in 1865.) The *Journal des débats* did not, however, deny its liberal beliefs and remained in opposition, as did its sister publication, the bimonthly *Revue des deux mondes*. Although circumspect in its allegations, the newspaper was not immune from censure (Saint-Marc Girardin earned an *avertissement* for his comments on the constitution of 1852, and Prévost-Paradol's pen more than once stung the government press office into action). Allusions to and reports of parliamentary governments in Belgium and Britain were generally indirect attempts to criticize imperial authority and to convey the newspaper's belief in parliamentary government and in religious and press freedoms. The circulation of the *Journal des débats* was 8,000 in 1855, 8,455 in July 1858, 12,842 in August 1861, 10,000 in 1866, and 8,750 in March 1869.

C. Ledré, *Le livre du centenaire du "Journal des débats"* (Paris, 1889); A. Pereire, *Le Journal des débats politiques et littéraire* (Paris, 1924).

Natalie Isser

Related entries: JANIN; LIBERALISM; ORLEANISM; PRESS REGIME; PREVOST-PARADOL; *REVUE DES DEUX MONDES*.

K

KONNIGSGRATZ. See SADOWA.

L

LABICHE, EUGENE (1815–1888), dramatist, master of the vaudeville form (short comedies using popular songs); born 5 May 1815 in Paris. Labiche's bonhomie and gaiety afforded him easy access to theatrical circles at an early age. Two one-act vaudevilles, *Major Cravachon* and *Deux papas très bien*, presented at the Théâtre du Palais Royal in 1844, met with relative success. A third, *Frisette* (1846), depicting the proletariat, also belongs to this period of apprenticeship.

In 1851 Labiche experienced his first major triumph with *Un chapeau de paille d'Italie* (Palais Royal). The following year he wrote six one-act plays for Paris theaters, among which was his famous satire of vanity and hypocrisy, *Le misanthrope et l'Auvergnat* (1852, Palais Royal). By the mid 1850s he was well on his way to becoming the "king of Vaudeville." In 1860 he wrote his first major comedy, *Le voyage de M. Perrichon*. A year later he was named to the Legion of Honor. In 1864 his comedy in three acts, *Moi*, was presented at the Théâtre Français, and in the same year *Le point de mire*, a comedy-vaudeville in four acts, was staged at the court theater at Compiègne in the presence of Napoleon III and Eugénie. *La cagnotte* (1864), performed at the Palais Royal, was a stunning success and impressed even critics who had previously scorned him as a mere manufacturer of plays.

Labiche composed over fifty plays in the course of his career, many in collaboration. Among those of which he was sole author are: *Un jeune homme pressé* (Palais Royal, 1848), *Un garçon de chez Véry* (Palais Royal, 1850), *Le petit voyage* (Vaudeville, 1868), and *29 degrés à l'ombre* (Palais Royal, 1873). Among those who collaborated with Labiche by supplying ideas and serving as critics or first readers were Alfred Delacour (1815–1883), Edmond Gondinet (1828–1888), Emile Augier, Ernest Legouvé (1807–1903), Marc Michel (1812–1868), and Edouard Martin (1828–1866). Labiche is best remembered for *Un chapeau de paille d'Italie*, *La cagnotte*, and *Le voyage de M. Perrichon* (written in collaboration with Edouard Martin. From a bourgeois family himself, he was most successful in his satire of the vanities, manners, and preoccupations of the bourgeoisie during the Second Empire, especially their preoccupation with money and with speculation (see, for example, his play *Les chemins de fer*, recently revived). He died at Paris, 22–23 January 1888.

P. Soupault, *Eugène Labiche* (Paris, 1945).

Dolorès A. Signori

Related entry: THEATER.

LABOR MOVEMENT. See LABOR REFORM.

LABOR REFORM, an important part of Napoleon III's political program, and, in the end, one of his tragic failures. At mid-century perhaps 28 to 29 percent of the French population belonged to the working class (about 60 percent in Paris). Although far from homogeneous, the French workers generally shared harsh working conditions (average eleven- to twelve-hour days with Sundays off), low wages, and poverty, especially in the big cities (over 1 million Parisians lived in want). Louis Napoleon had become interested in the problems of labor during the 1830s. On the basis of his extensive travels, particularly in Britain, and his wide reading, he had not only become familiar with the condition of the urban industrial working class but had also decided that the support of labor, and popular support generally, were crucial to the success of bonapartism. In *Des idées napoléoniennes* (1839), *L'extinction du paupérisme* (1844), and other writings, Louis Napoléon emphasized the link between bonapartism and social reform, and thus he was able to win the support even of some republicans and democrats. The bonapartists increased their propaganda among the working class in 1848, and Louis Napoleon benefited from some labor support in his election to the presidency of the Second Republic. Following the coup d'état of December 1851, even Pierre Joseph Proudhon briefly rallied to the regime. But although Louis Napoleon wanted to satisfy the interests of the lower classes, he also sought the support of the upper classes and therefore could not act against the almost unanimous wishes of the latter. By March 1852 Proudhon announced that the prince president had abandoned his "grand projects."

Despite Louis Napoleon's expressed interest in social reform, his government initially did not display any intention of initiating changes that would affect the conditions of labor but was content to pursue a policy that, while stressing imperial concern with the problems of the working class and trying to relieve unemployment and to control prices where possible, made it clear that the administration intended to prevent worker agitation, whether collective or individual. For political reasons, workers' organizations had been dissolved at the coup d'état, and under the Empire (reestablished in December 1852) both unions and strikes were illegal. Napoleon III put great faith in traditional charitable activity as a way of ameliorating the conditions of the working class. Personally generous, he preferred that charity be private but recognized that in some instances only government involvement could prove effective. And so the imperial government, and the royal family itself, engaged in many philanthropic activities. These activities included the provision of aid to expectant mothers and to orphaned apprentices (a decree of 3 February 1853 placed all maternal charity under the Empress Eugénie), the establishment of facilities for convalescent workers, the construction of low-rent housing, and the institution of adult education courses. The empress used 600,000 francs with which the city of Paris had proposed to buy her a diamond necklace to establish vocational schools for young women. And at the birth of the prince imperial, an orphanage was created in his name. At the same time, the government took steps to see that the working class would not threaten order and tranquillity, a major concern of the regime. For example, in June 1853 the administration restructured the *conseils de prud'hommes* (labor mediation committees) so that they would not become forums for the expression of worker demands (Napoleon III was to name their presidents and vice-presidents, and the workers could vote for their representatives only after three years' domicile), and in June 1854 a law was passed reinvigorating the requirement that every worker carry a *livret*, an identity card detailing his employment history.

The only major legislation regulating working conditions in French factories that was in effect at the beginning of the Empire was the child labor law of 1841. This law, which prohibited the employment of children under the age of eight, applied in mechanized shops and in shops with twenty or more workers. The law also limited children under twelve to an eight-hour workday and children between the ages of twelve and sixteen to a twelve-hour day. The incomplete implementation of the 1841 law troubled the imperial government, and throughout the 1850s the administration considered various schemes for its regular enforcement while rejecting the option of revising the factory law or extending its scope. The administration also issued numerous clarifications of the 1841 law and urged France's more industrialized departments to appoint salaried factory inspectors at the local level, but the law remained largely ineffective. During the first half of the Second Empire, then, the keywords were paternalism and order. To the examples already cited may be added the regulation of pawnshops (*monts de piété*), by decree of 24 March 1852, the establishment of an unemployment bureau in Paris (25 March 1852), the creation of retreats (*asiles*) for old, ill, and infirm workers from 1855 (at Vésinet and Vincennes, Rouen, and Mulhouse), and an effort to organize medical services for the workers in the cities and in some thirty-six departments.

In these years, the most serious government efforts were directed at encouraging mutual aid societies (*sociétés de secours mutuels*). At Louis Napoleon's request, Armand de Melun (1807–1877), a precursor of social Catholicism, drafted the decree of 26 March 1852, which allowed mutual aid societies to constitute themselves freely although the government named their presidents, and only those that were officially approved could receive financial aid from the state. Ten million francs from the sale of the Orleans estates confiscated in 1852 went to these societies. (Another 10 million francs from the same source were devoted to workers' housing projects, although these were only partially successful.) On the birth of the prince imperial, Napoleon III gave a personal gift of 500,000 francs to the societies' pension funds. From 1852 to 1869 the number of mutual aid societies increased from twenty-four hundred to six thousand, and the membership from 260,000 to 900,000. However, only the better-off workers belonged.

By the late 1850s those elements within the working class that rejected the notion that their poverty was inevitable and opposed the government's position on labor reform became more vocal in their demands as Proudhon's complicated mutualism (exchange of services) began to lose its appeal. Especially in the skilled trades, some workers were beginning to develop a proletarian class consciousness, and they laid the foundation for a new labor movement. These workers demanded the legalization of strikes, cooperatives, and unions, as well as abolition of the *livret* and revision of that section of the Civil Code that gave the testimony of an employer greater weight than that of a worker. Other factors were also at work: the end around 1856–1857 of the great era of economic expansion, the persistence of a large opposition vote in the elections of 1857, and in 1859 the ill-starred French intervention in Italy. The government responded to these changed circumstances with a much more vigorous social reform policy from 1860.

Social reform was always linked in Napoleon III's mind with economic reform, and it was also about 1860 that he launched his major effort to modernize the French economy. Tariff reform had as one of its major purposes, for example, the lowering of prices, and the great public works projects, although they displaced the workers from the center of Paris, also provided jobs. During these years, the government responded to worker demands in part by developing a more sophisticated public relations effort, which admitted some shortcomings in dealing with the problems of the working class and at the same time held out hope for improvements in the workers' life within the framework of existing institutions. The emperor's cousin, Prince Napoleon, took a special interest in working-class concerns, and he had some influence on government policy in the 1860s. He led the Palais Royal group, which from 1861 to 1862 conducted a vigorous pro-government propaganda among the workers. Prince Napoleon, who was president of the French section of the international exposition at London in 1862, joined with Armand Lévy (1827–1891) and Adolphe Guéroult (1810–1872) of *L'opinion national*, Henri Tolain, and Napoleon III himself in arranging for French workers to organize in February 1862, through their mutual aid societies, a delegation of some two hundred to the London exposition.

Whether because of Napoleon III's calculated plan to win working-class support or because of the emperor's genuine desire to liberalize his regime (political liberalization also began in 1860), the imperial government undertook a number of policy decisions that spoke directly to the demands of the increasingly articulate working class. From 1860 the government was especially lenient in its treatment of strikes, and in May 1864 a new coalitions law made strikes legal under certain circumstances. At about the same time the government began to provide legislative and financial support for producer cooperatives organized by workers. Doubtless Napoleon III was gratified by the failure in 1863–1864 of Tolain's efforts to establish workers' candidacies to the Corps Législatif. The international exposition at Paris in 1867 contained a section devoted to the history of labor, displays of cheap goods, and examples of workers' housing. In its aftermath, the government allowed the election of a sort of workers' parliament of 354 delegates, which held meetings from July 1867 to August 1869 in the Passage Raoul at Paris and in January 1869 presented to the minister of commerce a report calling in particular for worker education and legalization of trade unions.

Social reform in the last years of the Second Empire once again received high priority. In 1868 administrative tolerance was extended to *chambres syndicales*, a partial step toward the full acceptance of trade unions. In July 1868 two voluntary insurance funds were established, one for life insurance and one for accidents (the latter received some state assistance). And a law of 18 August 1868 suppressed article 1781 of the Civil Code, thus giving equal weight to the testimony of worker and employer. Also in 1868 the government prepared a bill to amend significantly the 1841 child labor law, and as a temporary expedient it charged by decree France's mining engineers with the task of inspecting factories and enforcing the existing factory legislation (a bill was deposed 26 June 1870 to control work hours in mines and create an inspection corps). The government's interest in child labor reform was stimulated not only by a continuing concern with the efficient enforcement of the law but also by worker demands that the welfare and education of working-class children be given greater attention and by the increasingly pervasive belief that every youngster deserved intensive nurturing and protection during childhood. Finally, in July 1870 a bill was deposed to establish voluntary pension programs.

The government continued, however, to measure out its concessions, for it feared that working-class protest and strike activity remained a threat to the peace and stability of France. Emile Ollivier dreaded revolution as much as he favored reform. It was in order to restrain worker agitation that the government took action against the Paris section of the First International in 1868 and 1870. Moreover, despite the new labor policy adopted by Napoleon III's government after 1860, a militant trade unionism became increasingly important among workers in the last years of the Empire. Although the emperor had some popularity among the workers, he never won their leaders, and much of the working class was decidedly republican by 1870. During the Second Empire real wages grew (reaching their peak in 1858–1865), but far from dramatically. Workers ate more meat but remained very poor. There were real reforms, but much remained to be done. The *livrets* that Napoleon III had favored suppressing in 1869 (despite a report to the contrary) would remain until 1890; unions would not be fully legalized until 1884 nor an inspection corps created for mines and factories until 1892. And there would be no pension scheme, even voluntary, until 1894, and that only for miners. Unemployment insurance would have to await the twentieth century. Napoleon III was undoubtedly sincere in his efforts on behalf of the workers, but the burden of the past was heavy, the difficulties great, and, in the end, the time too short.

G. E. Boilet, *La doctrine sociale de Napoléon III* (Paris, 1975); H. N. Boon, *Rêve et réalité dans l'oeuvre économique et sociale de Napoléon III* (The Hague, 1936); E. Bornecque-Winandy, *Napoléon III, "empereur social"* (Paris, 1980); G. Bourgin, "La législation ouvrière du Second Empire," *REN* 14 (1913); F. Chavrot, "Les sociétés de secours mutuel sous le Second Empire," *Cahiers d'histoire de l'Institut Maurice Thorez* 11 (1977); A. Dansette, "La politique sociale de Napoléon III," *RIN*, no. 86 (1963); E. Dolléans, *Histoire du mouvement ouvrier, 1830–1871*, vol. 1 (Paris, 1967); P. Douchy and P. Périer, "La doctrine sociale de Napoléon III et Le Play," *ES*, n.s. nos. 83–84 (1970); P. Fournier, *Le Second Empire et la Législation ouvrière* (Paris, 1911); D.L. Kulstein, *Napoleon III and the Working Class* (Sacramento, 1969); M. Leroy, *Histoire des idées sociales en France d'Auguste Comte à P.J. Proudhon* (Paris, 1954); P. Louis, "Le sort de l'ouvrier français sous le Second Empire," *RPP* (December 1946); B. Ménager, "Force et limites du bonapartisme populaire en milieu ouvrier sous le Second Empire," *RH*, 265 (April 1981); G.J. Sheridan, Jr., *The Social and Economic Foundations of Association among the Silk Weavers of Lyons, 1852–1870* (New York, 1981); K. Tacke, *Die Sozialpolitischen Vorstellungen Napoleons III* (Cologne, 1969).

Lee Shai Weissbach

Related entries: BONAPARTISM; COALITIONS LAW; COBDEN-CHEVALIER TREATY; ECONOMIC CRISES; *EXTINCTION DU PAUPERISME*; FIRST INTERNATIONAL; FORCADE LA ROQUETTE; LA RICAMARIE; LE PLAY; LIBERAL EMPIRE; LIBERALISM; *LIVRET D'OUVRIER*; ORLEANS DECREES; PALAIS ROYAL GROUP; PRINCE NAPOLEON; PROUDHON; REPUBLICANISM; SAINT-SIMONIANISM; SOCIAL CATHOLICISM; TOLAIN; VARLIN.

LABROUSTE, HENRI (1801–1875), architect, known especially for his construction of the Bibliothèque Sainte Geneviève and the reading room of the Bibliothèque Impériale (now the Bibliothèque Nationale); born at Paris, 11 May 1801. Labrouste's father was an important functionary in the Ministry of Finance; his elder brother, Théodore (1799–1885), was also an architect whose early career closely paralleled that of Henri. Both studied at the Collège Sainte Barbe and then in the *ateliers* of Léon Vaudoyer (1803–1872) and Hippolyte Lebas (1782–1867), as well as at the Ecole des Beaux-Arts. Both won the *grand prix d'architecture* (Henri in 1824) and studied at the Villa Médicis in Rome, producing works honored in the international exposition of 1855 (Henri's won a first prize). From the early 1830s, however, Henri Labrouste's reputation began to eclipse that of his brother. He returned from Rome in June 1830 a romantic rationalist and, at the request of dissident students, established an *atelier*, which he conducted from 1831 to 1856. Thus romanticism was introduced into official French architecture. Among Labrouste's students were Pierre Bossan (1814–1888) and Jean Baptiste Antoine Lassus (1807–1857).

Labrouste joined his brother, who had returned from Rome in 1833, in constructing several new buildings for the Collège Sainte Barbe (1840). He was also inspector, under Jacques Duban (1797–1870), for the construction of the new Palais des Beaux-Arts. In 1840, together with Louis Visconti (1791–1853), he prepared the decorations for the funeral of Napoleon I (*Retour des Cendres*). But his great opportunity came when in 1838 he was named architect of the proposed Bibliothèque Sainte Geneviève. The library, perhaps the architectural masterwork of the July Monarchy, was completed in 1850. For its construction, Labrouste for the first time made major use of structural ironwork, a technique that made possible the great markets, railroad stations, department stores, and other public buildings of the Second Empire. Attached by 1854 to both the Conseil des Monuments Historiques and the Conseil des Bâtiments Civils, Labrouste in 1855 became architect of the Bibliothèque Impériale. That library had clearly outgrown its premises, and in August 1858 a commission chaired by Prosper Mérimée recommended that it be rebuilt. Labrouste's plans were approved at the end of April 1859. Construction began on 1 June and continued beyond the architect's lifetime. But Labrouste was responsible for the facade on the rue de Richelieu, the pavilion on the corner of the rue des Petits Champs, and, especially, for the splendid glass and iron reading room (substantially completed in 1866).

Both Henri and Théodore Labrouste were amply recognized during the Second Empire. Théodore, a member of the jury of the Ecole des Beaux-Arts, was named to the Legion of Honor in 1855 and promoted to officer in August 1869. He was a member of the Conseil des Bâtiments Civils and, from 1845 to 1876, chief architect for hospitals and hospices in Paris. Henri was a member of the Ecole juries from 1848 to 1855. He was named to the Legion of Honor in 1841 and promoted to officer in January 1852. In 1857 he was made *inspecteur général des edifices diocésains* and in 1865 *inspecteur général du Conseil des Bâtiments Civils*. On 23 November 1867 he was elected to the Académie des Beaux-Arts in place of Jacques Ignace Hittorff (1792–1867).

Among Henri Labrouste's private commissions during the Second Empire may be noted the seminary at Rennes (1854–1874; he was architect for the diocese), the Hôtel Fould (1856–1858; rue de Berri), the Thouret Villa in Neuilly (1860), the administration building of the Paris-Lyons-Mediterranean Railroad (1862), and the Hôtel Villgruy (1865; place François Ier). Henri Labrouste died at Fontainebleau, 24 June 1875.

P. d'Espezel, "Henri Labrouste," *JAA* 7 (1953); *Exposition Henri Labrouste, architect, Brussels, Milan, Rome, Turin* (Paris, 1977); B. Foucart et al., "Henri Labrouste," *MHF* 6 (1975); N. Levine, "Architectural Reasoning in the Age of Positivism: The *Néo-Grec* Idea of Henri Labrouste's Bibliothèque Sainte Geneviève" (Ph.D. diss., Yale University, 1975) and [article on Labrouste], in A. Drexler et al., *The Architecture of the Ecole des Beaux-Arts* (New York, 1977), pp. 325–93; *Souvenirs d'Henri Labrouste, architecte, membre de l'Institut: Notes recueillies et classées par ses enfants* (Fontainebleau, 1928). *Related entry:* PARIS, REBUILDING OF.

LACORDAIRE, PERE HENRI (1802–1861), liberal Catholic and celebrated Dominican preacher; born 12 May 1802, Recey-sur-Ource (Côte d'Or, Burgundy). After a brief law career Lacordaire sought spiritual fulfillment in the priesthood. Impulsive and convinced that the church should be free of state tutelage, he accepted in 1830, only three years after his ordination, the invitation of Félicité de Lamenais (1782–1854) to help found a newspaper, *L'avenir*. Under the direction of Lamenais, he and Charles de Montalembert wrote most of its articles, arguing for separation of church and state and for freedom of press, association, and education. Although Lacordaire submitted to the papal censure that doomed the paper, he remained convinced that, to prosper, Catholicism had to associate itself with liberty.

In 1835 Lacordaire delivered a series of conferences (lecture-sermons) at Notre Dame that were so spectacularly successful that they attracted the literary, social, and political elite of Paris, brought him nationwide fame as a preacher (by some he is still considered the greatest preacher of the nineteenth century), and led to subsequent addresses at Notre Dame (seventy-five in all) stretching into 1851. He preached throughout the country, arousing a more favorable disposition to-ward the church among the educated classes, especially in Paris, but could not retard an erosion of faith among the urban workers and peasants, which became increasingly more serious during the Second Empire. A more enduring contri-bution that Lacordaire made to the church was his restoration of the Dominican order in France. He donned the white habit of the order in 1839, founded the first post-Revolutionary house at Nancy in 1843, and served as French provincial from 1850 to 1854 and from 1858 until the year of his death in 1861.

Following the Revolution of 1848 Lacordaire, the abbé Henri Maret, and Frédéric Ozanam (1813–1853) launched a newspaper, the *Ere nouvelle*, dedicated to democracy, the Republic, and social justice. With Lacordaire as editor-in-chief, the paper enjoyed a spectacular but brief success. Mob violence shook Lacordaire's faith in the Republic; he resigned his seat in the Constituent As-sembly (May 1848) and separated from the *Ere nouvelle* (August 1848). Never-theless he deplored the political reaction that led to Louis Napoleon's rise to power. Following the coup d'état of December 1851, he refused to speak again at Notre Dame and in February 1853 delivered in the church of Saint Roch a sermon considered highly offensive to the imperial government. Thereafter he preached in the provinces, founded a Third Order of Dominicans dedicated to teaching, and assumed direction of a school at Sorèze in southern France (Tarn).

Lacordaire's efforts in behalf of liberty within the church and without had not ended, however. Having predicted that *L'Univers* and its reactionary supporters would cause the next revolution to turn on the priests, he lent his cooperation to the *Correspondant*, revived in 1855, as a voice for those Catholics committed to the belief that political liberties were in no way incompatible with the Catholic faith. His attachment to freedom for all peoples drew him into rare agreement with the government and separation from most other Catholic leaders as he supported Napoleon III's Italian War, a stance publicized by the government immediately upon becoming aware of it. Subsequent developments in Italy that threatened the existence of the temporal power prompted him to write in late

February 1860 the pamphlet *De la liberté de l'Eglise et de l'Italie*, supportive of both an Italian confederation and of the temporal power. He deemed the latter necessary for papal independence but desired reform at Rome. On 2 February 1860, Lacordaire, sponsored by Victor Cousin (1792–1867), was elected to the seat in the French Academy made vacant by the death of Alexis de Tocqueville (1805–1859). His reception by François Guizot (1787–1874) 24 January 1861 was an occasion for great excitement at Paris in view of Pius IX's quarrel with Napoleon III's Italian policy, but the new academician's equivocal feelings on that subject led to a general disappointment with his speech. Montalembert and Frédéric, comte de Falloux (1811–1886), themselves members of the academy, viewed the election as testimony to the progress Lacordaire had made in winning acceptance for the religious habit in post-Revolutionary French society. Père Lacordaire died suddenly at Sorèze on 21 November 1861.

  J. Cabanis, *Lacordaire et quelques autres: Politique et religion* (Paris, 1982); B. Chocarne, *Le R.P.H.-D. Lacordaire*, 2 vols., 10th ed. (Paris, 1912); M. Escholier, *Lacordaire ou Dieu et la liberté* (Paris, 1959); H. Lacordaire, *Oeuvres*, 9 vols. (Paris, 1888–1914), and *Correspondance du r.p. Lacordaire et de Madame Swetchine*, 14th ed. (Paris, 1920); G. Michel, *Le coeur humain de Lacordaire* (Paris, 1962); L. C. Sheppard, *Lacordaire* (New York, 1964).

Raymond L. Cummings

Related entries: CORRESPONDANT; GALLICANISM; MONTALEMBERT.

LA GUERONNIERE, ARTHUR DE (1816–1875), journalist, politician, and noted pamphleteer; born at Dorat (Haut-Vienne), 6 April 1816, the second son of five children of an old aristocratic family. La Guéronnière's father, who had been an inspector general of hospitals during the Restoration, lost his position after the Revolution of 1830. He retired to his estate in Haute-Vienne, where his children were educated. At the age of twenty, La Guéronnière wrote for a legitimist paper, *L'avenir national*, founded by his older brother Alfred (1810–1884) at Limoges. An admirer of both René Chateaubriand (1768–1848) and Alphonse de Lamartine (1790–1869), the younger La Guéronnière espoused a belief in legitimacy sanctioned by popular sovereignty. He left his brother's newspaper and went to Clermont to plead his political beliefs. During the February Revolution of 1848, he moved to Paris, becoming a "republican" and Lamartine's aide. He also worked successively on *Le bien public* and *L'ère nouvelle*, both of which eventually failed. As a result of his journalistic efforts, however, he was hired by Emile de Girardin for *La presse*, which he left shortly (1850) for Lamartine's new journal, *Le pays*, becoming editor in chief under the poet-statesman's patronage.

  At the end of 1848, Louis Napoleon had been elected president of the Second Republic. La Guéronnière at first angrily opposed the prince president but was gradually converted into supporting him. A favorable sketch of Louis Napoleon in *Le pays* late in 1851 led to a break with Lamartine, whose political star was in eclipse. Although La Guéronnière in *Le pays* condemned the coup d'état of

December 1851, he soon openly declared his loyalty to the new regime, visiting the Tuileries and publishing the emperor's dictated articles, and his fortunes rose as the government amply rewarded him for his services. In the elections of 1852 he was sponsored as a candidate for the Corps Législatif and elected as a deputy from the Cantal. In September 1854 he was named to the Conseil d'Etat, where he sat until July 1861, having resigned his editorship of *Le pays*. Also in 1854 La Guéronnière succeeded Pierre Latour-Dumoulin (1823–1888) as director of publishing and press in the Ministry of the Interior. In that capacity he continued the government's policy of supervision, repression, and manipulation, made somewhat more palatable by his conciliatory character. In 1856 La Guéronnière published a book of flattering portraits of important personalities of Second Empire France and abroad: *Etudes et portraits politiques contemporains*. Two years later he was commissioned by Napoleon III to write semiofficial brochures, and this role as ghost writer for the emperor's foreign policy quickly became known and brought him much fame. Among his most important pamphlets were *L'Empereur Napoléon III et l'Angleterre* (1858), *L'Empereur Napoléon III et l'Italie* (February 1859), *Le Pape et le congrès* (December 1859), *La coalition* (April 1860), and *La France, Rome et l'Italie* (February 1861; perhaps written by Victor Fialin Persigny although signed by La Guéronnière). Named to the Legion of Honor in 1852, La Guéronnière was made a commander of the order 21 July 1858 and a grand officer 14 August 1866. He was further rewarded by appointment to the Senate (5 July 1861), and he sat on the Conseil Général of the Haute-Vienne.

Although La Guéronnière's career as a semiofficial pamphleteer ended with his elevation to the Senate, he remained outspoken on the issues of the day and made a number of notable speeches as a senator, particularly on the questions of Italy and of the development of liberty in France. In fact, La Guéronnière became a champion of liberalization of the Empire. In 1862 he received a government subsidy to found his own newspaper, *La France*, in which he continued to defend and praise government policy while adopting a liberal line. Unfortunately for La Guéronnière, however, he could no longer express his personal views without having them interpreted as those of Napoleon III. His brochure, *L'abandon de Rome* (1862), aroused controversy and proved embarrassing to the government. His usefulness having ended, he resigned from all his offices (except the Senate) and sold his interest in *La France*, but his poor financial condition and past services eventually necessitated a new appointment. La Guéronnière was named minister to Belgium in August 1868, in time to negotiate the matter of the Belgian railways affair (March–April 1869). His appointment as ambassador to Turkey (12 June 1870) was short-lived, for he resigned following 4 September 1870. Returning to France, La Guéronnière became director of *La presse* (1871) and founder of *Le salut*, which soon failed. He died at Paris 23 December 1875.

N. Isser, *The Second Empire and the Press* (The Hague, 1974); D. I. Kulstein, "Government Propaganda and the Press during the Second Empire," *Gazette*, no. 2 (1964);

Comte de La Guéronnière, *La Guéronnière, publiciste, 1810–1884* (Paris, 1937); A. Saitta, *Il problema italiano nei testi di una battaglia pubblicistical: Gli opuscoli del Visconte de La Guéronnière, vol. 3: Italia e Europa* (Rome, 1963).

Natalie Isser

Related entries: BONAPARTISM; *FRANCE*; *PAYS*; PRESS REGIME.

LAMARTINE, ALPHONSE DE (1790–1869), poet, historian, and politician; born 21 October 1790 at Mâcon. By the beginning of the Second Empire, Lamartine's remarkable career as a romantic poet and as a statesman was virtually at an end. For a brief period following the Revolution of 1848, he had been the first hero of universal manhood suffrage, the most popular man in France. But political incapacity had destroyed his popularity before the appearance of Louis Napoleon on the scene. Ironically, although Lamartine fought hard (and unscrupulously) to keep the bonapartist pretender out of France and opposed him thereafter, his program was not unlike that of Louis Napoleon. Lamartine used his remaining influence to ensure that the president of the new Republic would be popularly elected, but as a candidate in December 1848, he received only 17,910 votes to Louis Napoleon's 5,434,226. Elected deputy to the Legislative Assembly, Lamartine opposed revision of the constitution to permit a second term for Louis Napoleon. Following the coup d'état of December 1851 he retired to private life. With these events came a dramatic fall from power and a drastic change in Lamartine's life-style. Besieged by creditors, he was forced to live on a much more modest scale than in the past. Formerly much celebrated and even idolized, he was now largely ignored, except by critics who jeered at his misfortune. Worse, it became necessary for the poet to resort to hack writing in order to meet the demands of his creditors. From 1851 to 1853, Lamartine singlehandedly published *Les foyers du peuple*, a periodical composed largely of his old poems, political speeches, and travel anecdotes. In *Le civilisateur* (1852–1854), he attempted to educate the workingman through a series of biographies of great men (Homer, Milton, Caesar, Columbus, and others); however, the articles provided few insights, and were regarded in general as reiterative and uninteresting. The critics brought the same complaint against the histories that followed. Lamartine treated the Restoration (1852), the Near East (1853), the French Revolution, Russia, and Turkey (1855) in a style that occasionally recaptured the verve of his early *Histoire des Girondins* (1846) but for the most part lacked imagination and originality. Prosper Mérimée was a particularly acerbic critic, attacking Lamartine's history of Russia as being dull and poorly documented.

Lamartine's chief literary work during the last fourteen years of his life was his *Cours familier de littérature*, a series of twenty-eight volumes begun in 1856 and published in regular installments. The *entretiens* (conversations) were devoted to literary criticism, history, biography, philosophy, theology, and topics of general interest. Lamartine's few remaining friends praised his initial efforts, hailing him as a second La Harpe. His far more numerous enemies saw in the

Cours only more hack writing destined to pay off ever-mounting debts. By 1857, Lamartine was near bankruptcy and made a request to the government that a national subscription fund be opened in his name. The campaign was a humiliating failure. In 1862, the poet refused a pension that Napoleon III offered him, declaring himself unable to remain in the debt of a government in which he did not believe. Further reverses, however, forced him to accept the offer. In May 1867, the Corps Législatif voted him a life annuity of 25,000 francs as *une récompense nationale*. Dejected and suffering from ill health, he nonetheless continued to produce his *Cours familier* and to play a role in French literary life as he had done in 1859 by his encouragement of Frédéric Mistral. When Lamartine died at Paris, 28 February 1869, he was mourned by very few. The man whom George Sand had dubbed "the old, dethroned king" had been rejected by the new poets and by the realists for his excessive sentimentality. Historically, however, the importance of his role in the evolution of romantic poetry in the 1830s cannot be challenged. Less attention has been paid to the enormous body of prose he produced at the end of his life. Undoubtedly, it lacks the brilliance of his early work, yet some volumes, like the *Cours familier*, are, in spite of their uneven quality, a valuable record of Lamartine's views on his contemporaries and on literature in general. Among other major works written during the period of the Second Empire are *Nouveau voyage en Orient* (1853), *Les visions* (1853), *Nelson* (1853), *Histoire de la Turquie* (8 vols., 1855), *Histoire de la Russie* (2 vols., 1855), *Histoire des Constituantes* (4 vols., 1855), *Vie des grands hommes* (5 vols., 1855–1856), *Vie d'Alexandre le Grand* (2 vols., 1859), *Oeuvres complètes: Mémoires politiques* (1863), *La France parlementaire (1834–1863)* (6 vols., 1864–1865), *Shakespeare et son oeuvre* (1864), *Portraits et biographies* (1865), *Civilisateurs et conquérants* (1865), *Les hommes de la Révolution: Mirabeau, Danton, Vergniaud* (1865), and *Antoniella* (1867).

H. Guillemin, *Lamartine, l'homme et l'oeuvre* (Paris, 1940); M. Guyard, "Les idées politiques de Lamartine," *ASMP*, no. 2 (1966); C. K. Lombard, *Lamartine* (New York, 1973); J. Lucas-Dubreton, *Lamartine* (Paris, 1951); M. Toesca, *Lamartine ou l'amour de la vie* (Paris, 1969); H. R. Whitehouse, *The Life of Lamartine*, 2 vols. (Boston, 1918).

Dorothy E. Speirs

LA LANTERNE, weekly Paris journal created by Henri Rochefort in 1868. Rochefort, a writer for Hippolyte de Villemessant's *Le Figaro*, had so antagonized the government with his vitriolic attacks and scurrilous wit that it seemed politic for him to take advantage of the new press law of 11 May 1868 in order to establish his own paper. *La lanterne*, in a seventy-four-page format with red-orange cover (almost a brochure), first appeared 30 May 1868. It was immediately successful. The 15,000 initial copies sold out; 80,000 copies were sold the first day. Eventually, including reprints, 120,000 copies of the first issue were circulated, and the paper's maximum circulation reached 170,000 copies. The keys to its success were outrageous satire and barbed jokes poked at every public figure and event. *La lanterne*'s irreverent style, its absurd humor (Rochefort had been, after all, a prolific writer for vaudeville), even its bad puns captured the public interest at a moment of instability and tension when concern for the future was great. The paper cost 40 centimes (twice the price of other journals), and still it sold widely, even in the provinces, despite prohibition, after the first issue, of its sale on the public way. It was also partially financed by Villemessant and heavily advertised by him in *Le Figaro*, which helped stimulate sales. After three months, the eleventh issue was seized and Rochefort sentenced to prison and a fine for his extravagances. He fled to Brussels, where he continued to publish *La lanterne*, but police seized most copies sent into France. Nevertheless, the paper was read surreptitiously in France (where it was widely imitated) and enjoyed a large readership throughout Europe, even in its French text, although there were also translations in English, Spanish, Italian, and German. However, suppression and the passage of time reduced interest in the paper, and it eventually declined. In December 1869 Rochefort directed his energies to a new journal, *La Marseillaise*.

E. Vatre, "Henri Rochefort et sa *Lanterne*," *RDM* (January 1982); R. L. Williams, "Unkindly Light: Henri Rochefort's *Lanterne*," *FHS*, no. 3 (1960).

Natalie Isser

Related entries: PRESS REGIME; ROCHEFORT; VILLEMESSANT.

LAPRADE, VICTOR DE (1812–1883), poet and academic; born 13 January 1812 at Montbrison (Loire). Mostly elegiac in nature, the early poetry of Laprade reflected the inspiration of the romantic poets and especially of Alphonse de Lamartine. Published in the *Revue du Lyonnais* during the persecutions in Poland of the early 1830s, these early poems attested to Laprade's sympathy with socialism and his convictions regarding the necessity of reconstructing society. The publication of *Eleusis* (1841) in the *Revue des deux mondes* provoked interest in his work in Parisian circles. In Paris in 1843 to prepare his manuscript of *Odes et poèmes* for publication the same year, Laprade paid several visits to Félicité de Lamennais (1782–1854) and was a frequent guest at the home of George Sand. In spite of his admiration for both, however, he remained more of a sympathizer with than an apostle of socialist philosophy, and the Revolution of 1848 marked his final disillusionment. His pessimism is reflected in the *Poèmes évangéliques* (1852), published during his appointment to the chair of French literature at Lyons. Thereafter his legitimist sympathies were reflected in a correspondence with the comte de Chambord. Laprade's hostility toward the Second Empire is voiced in *Les symphonies* (1855) and *Les idylles héroïques* (1858), selections of which appeared first in a liberal Catholic paper, *Le correspondant*. Elected to the Académie Française in 1858, partly because of his opposition to Napoleon III, Laprade continued to satirize the society of the Second Empire. Deprived of his professorship by Gustave Rouland in 1861 for a poem (*Les muses d'état*) published in *Le correspondant*, Laprade found sympathy and encouragement among republicans and legitimists alike. During a visit to Paris in 1862, his observations of social life in the capital convinced him that the Empire had suppressed freedom of thought and had bred servility. The Empire, therefore, was in his opinion directly responsible for the ruin of morals and the general decline of France.

In the early 1860s, Laprade continued to submit satires to *Le correspondant*: *Un entretien avec Corneille* (1862), *L'âge d'or* (1862), *Un conseil de famille* (1862). The year 1865 saw the publication of a collection of poems, *La voix du silence*, which included new verse as well as several satirical works printed earlier in the *Revue du Lyonnais* and *Le correspondant*. Four years later Laprade published *Pernette* (1869), a tragic idyll inspired by Goethe's *Hermann und Dorothea*. From this same period date three comedies under the general title *Tribuns et courtisans*; their publication was postponed until 1875. By 1863 Laprade had almost completed work on his lengthy prose work, *Histoire du sentiment de la nature*. It appeared in three volumes: *Le sentiment de la nature avant le Christianisme* (1866), *Le sentiment de la nature chez les modernes* (1868), and *Prolégomènes* (1882). During the Franco-Prussian War, he composed patriotic poems, many of which became popular. In 1871 he was elected to the Assemblée Nationale, where he remained for two years. In addition to the works mentioned, the following also appeared during the Second Empire: a tragedy, *Harmodius* (1870); and three prose treatises: *Questions d'art et de morale* (1861), *L'éducation homicide* (1866), and *Le baccalauréat et les études classiques* (1869). In his works on French education, Laprade was extremely critical, arguing that the teachers had made the schools a combination of monastery, barrack, and prison. Laprade died at Lyons, 13 December 1883.

P. Séchaud, *Victor de Laprade: L'homme, son oeuvre poétique* (Paris, 1934).

Dolorès A. Signori

LA RICAMARIE, coal-mining town in the department of the Loire, between Saint-Etienne and Firminy, scene of the massacre of the Ricamarie on the night of 15–16 June 1869. This was the most dramatic incident in the coal miners' strike of that month in the Loire basin, involving fifteen thousand miners. The strike was among the first in a wave of walkouts throughout France in the summer and fall of 1869, described as unexpected by most contemporaries and historians, although agitation had been brewing for some time. The government's dispatch of troops to the Loire coal basin to protect the freedom to work created the situation leading to the massacre. Some strikers at the Quintin pits of La Ricamarie tried to block the loading of coal and were arrested by the commanding officer of the troops guarding the pit. The arrest provoked demonstrations by other strikers, some of whom tried to block the soldiers' path. Some soldiers panicked and fired on the crowd, killing thirteen and wounding nine. More arrests followed. On 24 June the strike committee called for an end to the walkout. The prefect of the Loire subsequently pressured the mining companies to grant concessions to their workers, and the emperor pardoned the sixty-two miners convicted of violating freedom of work a few days after their trial in August. The massacre of the Ricamarie nevertheless remained a symbol of government repression of labor to contemporaries and subsequently to labor militants of the region. La Ricamarie became something of a local shrine to the heroic miners engaged in the struggle between capital and labor.

Under the Second Empire (until 1864) as under previous regimes since the Revolution, workers' coalitions were illegal, and consequently strikes were in effect proscribed, since it was easy to find a coalition behind any stoppage of work. Nevertheless, strikes did occur, more frequently in bad economic times than in good, but with generally greater success when the economy was on the upturn. In the first half of the Empire, the demands were most often nonpolitical: shorter working days (the demand was for a ten-hour day, then common in Britain), higher wages, a relaxation of factory discipline, worker management or co-management of mutual aid funds. Statistics exist only for strikes that involved prosecutions, usually of the leaders, who were sometimes sentenced to several months in jail, or of workers involved in incidents. There were 86 such strikes in 1852, 109 in 1853, 68 in 1854, 168 in 1855, 73 in 1856, 56 in 1857, and 53 in 1858. (There had been at least 382 strikes during the July Monarchy.) From 1859 strikers were prosecuted much less often, and the judicial statistics therefore become unreliable as a gauge.

Throughout the Second Empire, the government's attitude toward strikes remained equivocal. It rarely intervened, except to maintain order, but on a few occasions it did take the workers' side, as during the strike of Paris typesetters (*typographes*) in 1862. In 1833 the typesetters had formed an Association Libre Typographique, which Napoleon III allowed to survive as a friendly society (*société de secours mutuel*), whose officers he named. When the printers resisted demands for a wage increase (the government had inaugurated a study in December 1861) and even hired women at lower wages, a strike began on 25 March 1862. Six strikers were arrested, and four of them were sent to jail for ten days and fined 16 francs. Continued intransigence by the printers led to a renewal of the strike in July; this time eleven workers were arrested. Although freed provisionally by the emperor and defended by Antoine Berryer, they were condemned in September, but when two of them went to Compiègne, Napoleon III received them and two days later (November) pardoned all eleven. Three years later (May 1865), during a strike of farriers at Paris, the empress, acting as regent during Napoleon III's visit to Algeria, intervened to prevent the army from supplying blacksmiths to the Paris transportation companies.

Although strikes did not become notably more numerous following the coalitions law of 1864, which legalized workers' coalitions under certain conditions, a variety of factors contributed to increasing violence in the last years of the Second Empire. Economic depression (particularly in the building, textile, and metallurgy industries) and a decline in real income of the workers certainly contributed, as did, no doubt, the erosion of the authoritarian Empire. Perhaps, too, the First International played a hand, although its role is by no means clear. Certainly when strikes broke out, the International sent representatives and was helpful in such areas as the organizing of strike funds.

Historians generally attribute the massacre of the Ricamarie to chance and have focused attention on the government's role in the strike. Some historians have seen the strike as a test of the government's official policy of neutrality in disputes between capital and labor and, more fundamentally, of the latitude of strike freedom under the 1864 coalitions law. The miners of the Loire basin, it has been argued, counted on the government's neutrality and on the liberality it had demonstrated in most other walkouts since 1864 in deciding to launch their own strike in 1869. Their recent dealings with the prefect of the Loire, who had promised a delegation of miners support for their demands in return for the miners' cooperation in the May 1869 legislative elections, strengthened this conviction. Not only did the prefect fail to carry out his part of the agreement, but he also was forced to intervene more actively in their strike than either he or the miners had anticipated. The minister of the interior's determination ''to isolate and hem in the strikers'' and the government's eventual decision to send troops to the site rudely deceived the miners' expectations of government neutrality. Historians have interpreted these decisions as a shift from a policy of conciliation to one of repression, demonstrating the limits of strike freedom in the late Second Empire. Explanations for this shift have included the political circumstances of the late Empire and the government's concern with work stoppage in a large industry of vital national importance. Perhaps, too, there was a suspicion of conspiracy. It should be recalled that on 26 June, the Carmaux miners, on the other side of the Massif Central, went on strike. In July the Loire silk workers, in August the Vienne carpenters, and in September the Elbeuf textile workers followed suit, as did, in October, the miners of Aubin (in the Aveyron, some 60 kilometers from Carmaux). And there were other strikes as well—in Normandy and in the Champagne. The Aubin strike had many features similar to the Loire walkout, including the despatch of troops and the fusillade of Gua of 8 October 1869 corresponding to the massacre of the Ricamarie (attacked by miners, the troops fired, killing fourteen and wounding some twenty). Historians have related these two strikes by the repressive nature of the government's response rather than by any workers' conspiracy inciting walkouts in two different areas.

The questions of political conspiracy and of the government's sympathies remain largely unanswered, however, for the evidence is unclear and occasionally contradictory. In regard to the Loire miners' strike, for example, the workers' demands were mostly related to material interest, including higher wages and shorter hours, rather than to general social reform. But one demand—the centralization of company accident funds throughout the mining region—involved power considerations, for it reflected the miners' determination to increase their control of these funds. Agitation for these matters had been the main activity of the miners' Caisse Fraternelle, organized in November 1866, and by 1869 involving five thousand miners (half the Loire total). Ostensibly for providing accident insurance and pensions to miners but eventually for social and political action as well, the Caisse, under the leadership of Michel Rondet (1841–1908), became involved in the 1869 walkout. Although the extent of spontaneity of the strike is disputed, the Caisse probably gave the signal to initiate it, financed it once begun, and was vitiated physically and morally by the course the strike assumed. As for the government's sympathies, minister of the interior J.L.V.A. de Forcade La Roquette instructed the prefects to maintain law and order but to be reserved otherwise. Rondet was sent to jail for seven months for having interfered with the right to work. On the other hand, the Carmaux strike ended in at least a half success for the miners, and at the end they cheered the emperor. As for the Elbeuf workers, three hundred of their total four hundred struck for a 15 percent wage increase. The bosses used every device, including strike-breakers, and although the workers succeeded in avoiding provocation and after a month's strike obtained an 8 percent raise, half of those on strike were not rehired.

In 1870 the wave of strikes continued, the focus shifting from mines to factories. Most notable were those at Le Creusot in January and March and in Alsace (Haut-Rhin), where fifteen thousand were on strike in July 1870. But in both instances the government was not only an opponent (troops were sent to protect property) but also the strikers' best source of support. This was particularly true in Alsace, where the bosses were opponents of the Empire (and Protestants) while the workers, mostly Catholic, had voted yes in the May 1870 plebiscite, and received no support from the republican deputies, who feared them. In the end the Alsace workers greeted the prefect with cries of "Vive l'Empereur!"

M. Chalendard, "Le puits Devillaine à La Ricamarie, est-il le puits de *Germinal*?" *Les amis du vieux Saint-Etienne*, no. 56 (1964); P. Guillaume, "Grèves et organisations ouvrières chez les mineurs de la Loire au milieu du 19e siècle," *MS*, no. 43 (April–June 1963); P. Léon, "Les grèves de 1867–1870 dans le département de l'Isère," *RHMC* (October–December 1954); Y. Lequin, *Les ouvriers de la région lyonnaise (1848–1914); Les intérêts de classe et la République* (Lyons, 1977); F. L'Huillier, "L'évolution des principales grèves à la fin du Second Empire," *BSHM* (June–July 1951), and *La lutte ouvrière à la fin du Second Empire* (Paris, 1957); A. Philippe, *Michel Rondet* (Paris, 1948); P. Ponsot, *Les grèves de 1870 et la Commune de 1871 au Creusot* (Paris, 1958).

George J. Sheridan, Jr.

Related entries: COALITIONS LAW; ECONOMIC CRISES; FIRST INTER-NATIONAL; LABOR REFORM; *LIVRET D'OUVRIER*; SCHNEIDER; TO-LAIN; VARLIN.

LAROUSSE, PIERRE (1817–1875), grammarian, publisher, and lexicographer; born at Toucy (Yonne), 23 October 1817, of a humble family (his father was a blacksmith). As a teacher at Toucy, Larousse formed the idea of publishing a series of school texts. After years of self-education at Paris (1840–1848) he again taught (1848–1851). In 1852 he founded his press in association with Augustin Boyer (1821–1896). Larousse published first a *Lexicologie des écoles*, which had considerable impact on the teaching of grammar. In 1858 he began publication of *L'école normale*, a monthly education newspaper, and in 1860, *L'émulation*, a monthly paper addressed directly to students. Thus as in the case of most of the other great publishing houses founded during the Second Empire (Fayard, 1855; Dunod, 1858; Delagrave, Gauthier-Villars, Lethielleux, 1864; Picard, Armand Colin, Tallandier, 1870) Larousse began by publishing materials for the schools. With the fortune accumulated from these enterprises, Pierre Larousse published the fifteen volumes of his *Grand dictionnaire universelle du XIXe siècle*, between 1865 and 1876, the ancestor of today's vast series of Larousse dictionaries and encyclopedias. An indefatigable worker, Larousse did not strive for objectivity. In fact, he used his *Dictionary* as a weapon. His treatment of contemporary figures and institutions reflects a deep hostility to the Second Empire and must be regarded as polemic. He died at Paris 3 January 1875.

A. Rétif, *Pierre Larousse et son oeuvre, 1817–1875* (Paris, 1974), "L'attitude religieuse de Pierre Larousse," *Mélanges de science religieuse* 33 (November 1976), and "Le *Dictionnaire* de Pierre Larousse et le progrès social," *MS*, no. 101 (1977). *Related entry:* HACHETTE.

LATIN MONETARY UNION, a monetary convention signed at Paris 23 December 1865 at the instigation of Napoleon III. By this treaty the original signatories (France, Belgium, Italy, and Switzerland) agreed to mint gold and silver coins of common size, weight, and fineness and for the public treasuries of each to accept these coins. Other states, such as Greece (1868), Spain (1871), and Austria, were to sign agreements with the Latin Union, and by 1880 eighteen countries would use the French franc as the basis of their currency system. The union would be formally dissolved only in 1927.

The signing of the Paris accord has to be understood in a dual context. The one is the unprecedented economic growth and increasing international, and above all European, trade in the 1850s and 1860s. Intra-European exchange prompted and was itself encouraged by a growing number of international agreements to lower tariffs, such as the Anglo-French commercial treaty of 1860, to eliminate tolls on major rivers like the Rhine and the Danube, or to link currencies (the Austro-German monetary union of 1857). The other is the disturbance to monetary systems caused by the increases in the supply of gold that resulted from the major gold discoveries in California and Australia at mid-century and, to a lesser extent, greater gold exports from Russia. The value of gold fell relative to that of silver, and this led to a withdrawal of silver coins from circulation and to renewed debates in the major European countries as to the most appropriate metallic standard: the gold, the silver, or the bimetallic. The catalyst of the December 1865 Paris conference was the dysfunction in commercial and financial transactions that resulted from a difference of thirty-five-thousandths in the fineness of Swiss coins compared with those of France and Italy.

The results of the Latin Union, however, were disappointing. Napoleon III saw the treaty as the first step toward an even wider international monetary union. But while a conference was held at Paris in 1867, no agreement could be reached in the face of the French insistence on maintaining bimetallism and British defense of the gold standard and reluctance to adopt a decimal currency. The bimetallism of the Latin Union would even prevent any links being established with the Scandinavian monetary union that was established between 1873 and 1875 and adopted the gold standard. Even the Latin Union had weaknesses. It was hardly propitious for cooperation that Napoleon III saw the union as a means of increasing French prestige and perhaps power. Cooperation was made the more difficult because the treaty did not set up any permanent secretariat to deal with problems as they arose. Worse, the Latin Union had been prompted by the decline in the value of gold relative to that of silver. In the years after the agreement, the process was reversed, and silver fell in value relative to gold. This development would force member states to suspend free coinage of silver in 1878.

R. J. Bartel, "International Monetary Unions: The Nineteenth-Century Experience," *JEEH* 3 (1977); Y. Bitar, *Les unions monétaires* (Louvain, 1953); H. P. Willis, *A History of the Latin Monetary Union* (Chicago, 1901).

Barrie M. Ratcliffe

Related entries: BANKING; COBDEN-CHEVALIER TREATY; GOVERNMENT FINANCE.

LA TOUR D'AUVERGNE LAURAGUAIS, HENRI GODEFROI, PRINCE DE (1823–1871), diplomat and minister; born at Paris, 21 October 1823. On the death of his father, Prince Melchior, in 1849, La Tour d'Auvergne became head of the last branch of the medieval comtes d'Auvergne. Under the July Monarchy, he had enjoyed a brilliant diplomatic career, becoming at eighteen the youngest French diplomat, as his brother, the archbishop of Bourges, was the youngest French prelate. La Tour d'Auvergne's diplomatic career had been especially oriented toward Rome, where he began as secretary of the embassy (chargé d'affaires in 1852) and where he played an active role during the crisis of 1849. By family tradition and by character, La Tour d'Auvergne was attached to the clerical party and to its views. His diplomatic ideas closely accorded with those of Edouard Drouyn de Lhuys, twice foreign minister under the Second Empire.

On 4 December 1854 La Tour d'Auvergne was named minister to the Grand Duchy of Saxe-Weimar and on 30 December 1855 to Tuscany. In August 1857 he was appointed minister to Turin. In that capacity he pressed the Sardinian prime minister, Count Camillo Benso di Cavour, to curb the radical press (December 1857) but was unsuccessful. La Tour d'Auvergne's tenure, which ended 7 December 1859, included the periods of crisis following Felice Orsini's attempt on Napoleon III's life in January 1858 and preceding the Italian War of 1859. It was also during his stay at Turin that the young diplomat fell under the spell of Cavour's cousin, the beautiful Countess Virginia Castiglioni (1837–1899), whom Cavour contrived to make the mistress of Napoleon III in 1857–1858. La

Tour d'Auvergne's correspondence with her spans the period 1859–1863. His next assignment was as minister to Berlin, where he arrived 17 February 1860. In August 1862, at Aspromonte, the Italian army halted an expedition by Giuseppi Garibaldi against Rome, but shortly afterward a circular issued by General Giacomo Durando so angered French Catholic opinion by its references to Rome as the future capital of Italy that, in addition to the replacement of Edouard Thouvenel as foreign minister by Edouard Drouyn de Lhuys, Charles Jean, marquis de La Valette, was recalled from Rome and La Tour d'Auvergne appointed ambassador in his place on 17 October 1862. But the new ambassador's tasks—to persuade Pope Pius IX to adopt reforms and to achieve a conciliation of Rome and Turin—were impossible ones, however persona grata he might be with the pope. In the autumn of 1863, La Tour d'Auvergne requested transfer on the grounds that his health could not stand the Roman climate. On 13 October 1863 he was appointed to replace Jean Baptiste, baron Gros (1793–1870), as ambassador at London. There he would remain until July 1869. On 10 August 1867 La Tour d'Auvergne was named grand cross of the Legion of Honor.

On 12 July 1869, accepting the consequences of the electoral results of May, Napoleon III promised further reforms and undertook to form a new ministry. Although La Tour d'Auvergne resisted appointment as foreign minister, arguing that he lacked the necessary parliamentary skills, he yielded to the emperor's insistence (17 July). The appointment was widely regarded as a concession to the clerical party at a time when Pius IX was preparing to convene a great church council at the Vatican. In regard to the council, La Tour d'Auvergne announced (circular of September 1869) that France would act unofficially to defend its national interests and to counsel moderation. As foreign minister, La Tour d'Auvergne's most pressing task was to consolidate an alliance with Austria that could become the cornerstone of a triple alliance of Austria, France, and Italy. In this he failed. The arrival of Emile Ollivier at power (ministry of 2 January 1870) marked the end of La Tour d'Auvergne's tenure. Although urged by Ollivier to retain his post, he declined for reasons of health and was replaced by Napoléon, comte Daru.

Daru's subsequent resignation and replacement by Antoine, duc de Gramont (15 May 1870), left vacant the post of ambassador to Austria that La Tour d'Auvergne accepted on 16 July. His stay at Vienna was brief. An alliance with Austria in the Franco-Prussian War, which began three days later, required French military victories. Instead, a series of defeats led to the overthrow of Ollivier's government on 9 August. On 12 August La Tour d'Auvergne accepted the post of foreign minister in the new government of the comte de Palikao. It was his belief that the pressure on Berlin from the conservative powers would have enabled the defeated imperial government to obtain better peace terms from the victorious Prussians than were later accorded to the republic that followed the overthrow of the Second Empire on 4 September 1870. Ill and discouraged, La Tour d'Auvergne survived the regime by less than a year. He died at the Château d'Angliers, near Loudun, 5 June 1871.

E. Lesueur, *Le Prince de La Tour d'Auvergne et le secret de l'impératrice: Contribution à l'histoire diplomatique du Second Empire* (Paris, 1930).
Related entries: ROMAN QUESTION; TRIPLE ALLIANCE; VATICAN COUNCIL.

LA VALETTE, CHARLES JEAN MARIE FELIX, MARQUIS DE (1806–1881), diplomat, minister, and senator; born at Senlis, 25 November 1806. Entering the diplomatic corps, La Valette served from 1837 to 1846 in a variety of posts in Sweden, Persia, Egypt, and Hesse Cassel. He was elected from Bergerac to the Chamber of Deputies in 1846 where he voted with the conservative majority, but after the Revolution of 1848 he retired to private life and rallied to the cause of Louis Napoleon Bonaparte. The reward for this political decision came with La Valette's appointment as ambassador to Turkey in January 1851. The young, relatively inexperienced, and ambitious diplomat probably pressed French claims in regard to the Holy Places more vigorously than Louis Napoleon had intended. Nor was he successful in the long run. Recalled in February 1853 to be replaced by Edmond de la Cour (1805–1873), La Valette was named to the Senate 23 June 1853. He returned to Constantinople, however, in May 1860 to replace Edouard Thouvenel, named minister of foreign affairs, arriving just in time to preside at Constantinople over the development of the Syrian crisis, which erupted in June. A year later (August 1861) Thouvenel named him ambassador to Rome.

It was a difficult time in Franco-papal relations, and La Valette soon earned himself the hatred of the pope's supporters in France by his advocacy of Italian unity and his opposition to the temporal power of the papacy. When Thouvenel fell in October 1862, La Valette, too, was recalled, to be replaced by Henri Godefroi, prince de La Tour d'Auvergne. This political eclipse was not very prolonged, however. Named grand cross of the Legion of Honor on 10 July 1861 (he had been grand officer since 15 April 1852), La Valette in March 1865 was appointed minister of the interior, succeeding Paul Boudet (1800–1877). Although some now saw him as having liberal credentials and although he did show tact in the execution of his functions, La Valette nevertheless suspended the newspaper *Le courrier du dimanche* on 2 August 1866 for publishing an article by Lucien Anatole Prévost-Paradol. The minister also dissolved the municipal councils of Toulouse, Arles, and Roubaix when disturbances followed the putting into effect of the 1864 coalitions law, and in March 1867 he repressed further disturbances at Roubaix. From 1 September to 2 October 1866, following the resignation of Drouyn de Lhuys, La Valette took on the additional responsibility of interim foreign minister until Drouyn de Lhuys' successor, Lionel, marquis de Moustier (1817–1869), could reach Paris from Constantinople. It was therefore La Valette who signed the circular of 16 September (La Valette Circular) in which Napoleon III accepted the changes brought about in Germany by Prussia's unexpectedly decisive victory over Austria at Sadowa. The circular, whose chief authors were probably Michel Chevalier and La Valette's friend,

Eugène Rouher, attempted to prove that the results of Prussia's victory were favorable to France but ended with a call for the reform and strengthening of the French army. All but this last conclusion was undoubtedly acceptable to La Valette, whose pacificism led him to oppose the new French intervention at Rome, which culminated in the Battle of Mentana, 3 November 1867. On 13 November, La Valette resigned and was named to the Conseil Privé, where he argued vigorously for continuing the liberalization signaled by Napoleon III's letter of 19 January 1867.

The illness and death of Moustier led to La Valette's appointment as foreign minister on 17 December 1868. In the next six months, he executed (and defended before the Corps Législatif) a pacifistic and conciliatory policy, presiding over the Belgian railroads affair and the complications resulting from the Cretan revolt against Turkey. The imperial message of 12 July 1869 announcing the imminence of the Liberal Empire necessitated La Valette's resignation. He was, however, named ambassador to Britain replacing La Tour d'Auvergne, who became foreign minister. La Valette supported the efforts of La Tour d'Auvergne's successor, Napoléon, comte Daru, to arrange a mutual arms reduction between France and Prussia, but his career effectively ended with Emile Ollivier's formation of a government on 2 January 1870. La Valette returned to the Senate where he witnessed the final tragic months of the Second Empire. (His son, Welles de La Valette, had been elected to the Corps Législatif from the Dordogne in 1863 and 1869.) La Valette died at Paris, 2 May 1881.

Related entries: BELGIAN RAILROADS AFFAIR; CRETAN REVOLT; DARU; HOLY PLACES; LA TOUR D'AUVERGNE; ROMAN QUESTION; SADOWA; TRIPLE ALLIANCE.

LAVISSE, ERNEST (1842–1922), historian and publicist; born at Nouvion-en-Thierache (Aisne), 17 January 1842. A liberal and democratic nationalist who made the transition from bonapartism to republicanism after 1870, Lavisse represents a line of continuity linking certain features of the Second Empire's educational policies with the school system of the Third Republic.

Lavisse graduated from the Ecole Normale Supérieure, which he attended from 1862 to 1865, and taught history in lycées at Nancy and Versailles before becoming the secretary of Victor Duruy in 1868 and, shortly after, tutor to the prince imperial. He was a strong supporter of Duruy's program for educational reform, believing that democratic politics required a system of universal education in which the teaching of history would shape a citizenry committed to national and patriotic values. Although frequenting both Léon Gambetta and Georges Clemenceau (1841–1929), Lavisse did not compromise himself and was still a strong supporter of the bonapartist cause after 1870. But he adroitly rallied to the Republic in 1878–1879 and soon rose to prominence in the republican educational establishment. Convinced that a superior program of education had contributed to the Prussian victory over France in 1870–1871, Lavisse spent the years 1873–1875 in Berlin, mastering the so-called scientific methods of German historical research (his first major work was a seven-volume history of Prussia, which he began to write in 1875). The author both of scholarly works and of a series of textbooks noteworthy for their nationalistic themes, Lavisse by 1883 was the director of historical studies at the Sorbonne and in 1903 director of the Ecole Normale. He died at Paris, 18 August 1922.

W. R. Keylor, *Academy and Community: The Foundation of the French Historical Profession* (Cambridge, England, 1975); D. F. Lach, "Ernest Lavisse," in S. W. Halperin, ed., *Essays in Modern European Historiography* (Chicago, 1970); E. Lavisse, *Souvenirs* (Paris, 1912); C. V. Langois, "Ernest Lavisse," *Revue de France* (1922).

Stuart L. Campbell

Related entries: DURUY; REPUBLICANISM.

LECONTE DE LISLE, CHARLES (1818–1894), the acknowledged master of the young Parnassian poets; born 22 October 1818 in Saint-Paul on the island of Réunion in the Indian Ocean to a former surgeon in the armies of Napoleon I. His mother was of the island. By the beginning of the Second Empire, Leconte de Lisle had two important experiences behind him, both of which were reflected in his literary production of the following years. The first was his contact with the teachings of the utopian socialist Charles Fourier (1772–1837); the Fourierist message was evident in the poems Leconte de Lisle published in the journal *La phalange* in the mid-1840s. The second was his activity in the republican clubs in 1848 (he had come to France to study law in 1837 and settled nine years later in Paris). Quickly disillusioned by the indifference of the public, the poet gave up politics, becoming fiercely apolitical. He never lost faith in the Republic, however, or in social progress.

The events of 1848 impoverished Leconte de Lisle's family and resulted in the loss of his private allowance. Thereafter he supported himself by journalism, translating, and private tuition in classical languages. In 1864 in order to devote more time to his translations of the masterpieces of Greek literature, he accepted a small pension from Napoleon III, the disclosure of which later at the time of the collapse of the Empire brought him considerable criticism. His first collection of poems, *Poèmes antiques*, appeared in 1852. It contained the poetry published in *La phalange* in which he retraced the Greek myths of the heroic age in addition to those poems composed after 1848 in which he presents the Greece of his dreams. A second collection, *Poésies barbares* (1862), testifies to the poet's familiarity with Greco-Roman civilizations, the mythologies of Egypt, India, and Scandinavia, and the sacred lore of Oriental antiquity.

Leconte de Lisle's stature as a poet, his high-minded character, and his lofty nature made him, despite his rigid self-discipline and a certain severity, the much revered leader of a group of younger poets who, like himself, had chosen to follow in the steps of Théophile Gautier and Charles Baudelaire in their pursuit of art for art's sake. In rebellion against romanticism, they attached great importance to intelligence, objectivity, exact descriptions, and, above all, to perfection of form and expression. Theirs was a sort of realism in poetry. About

1860 the *Revue fantaisiste* of Catulle Mendès (1841–1909) offered an outlet for the new movement. In 1866 Alphonse Lemerre (1838–1912) established a publishing house that between 3 March and June issued eighteen fascicles of poetry by thirty-seven poets under the title *Le Parnasse contemporain*. An attack by the critic Jules Barbey d'Aurevilly in *Le nain jaune* of November confirmed the christening of the movement as Parnassian. A second publication, scheduled for 1869, was delayed and did not appear until after the Franco-Prussian War. Although the Parnassian poets found a meeting place in Lemerre's offices in the passage Choiseul, their true mecca was the apartment of Leconte de Lisle, boulevard des Invalides. There assembled, among others, José Maria de Heredia (1842–1905; Leconte de Lisle's favorite disciple), Théophile Gautier, Théodore de Banville, Armand Sully-Prudhomme (1839–1907), François Coppée, Catulle Mendès, Auguste Villiers de l'Isle-Adam (1840–1889), Stéphane Mallarmé (1842–1898), and Paul Verlaine (1844–1896).

Among other works written or published by Leconte de Lisle during the Second Empire (in addition to translations of Theocritus, Homer, and Hesiod) are: *Poèmes et poésies* (1855), *Le chemin de la croix* (1856), *Poésies complètes* (1858), *Catéchisme populaire républicain* (1870), *Histoire populaire du christianisme* (1871), and *Histoire populaire de la Révolution française* (1871). Leconte de Lisle died at Louveciennes (near Paris), 17 July 1894.

R. T. Denommé, *Leconte de Lisle* (New York, 1973); P. Flottes, *Leconte de Lisle, l'homme et l'oeuvre* (Paris, 1954); P. Martino, *Parnasse et symbolisme* (Paris, 1925); M. Souriau, *Histoire du Parnasse* (Paris, 1929); A. Thérive, *Le Parnasse* (Paris, 1928).

Dolorès A. Signori

Related entries: BANVILLE; BAUDELAIRE; COPPEE; GAUTIER.

LE CREUSOT. See SCHNEIDER, E.

LEGION OF HONOR, French national order of merit, acknowledging outstanding public and military achievements; reorganized under the Second Empire by the decrees of 31 January and 16 March 1852. The Légion d'Honneur was created at the suggestion of Napoleon Bonaparte by consular decree on 19 May 1802 and inaugurated under the First Empire. In its initial form, the legion was composed of a large administrative council and sixteen cohorts, each composed of 7 grand officers, 20 commanders, 30 officers, and 350 legionnaires, all appointed for life. In 1814, Louis XVIII restructured the order, taking away from its members many of the political advantages they had enjoyed as a result of the 1802 legislation. Louis Philippe left the revised structure virtually untouched.

With the advent of the Second Empire, Napoleon III and his government made sweeping changes. Henceforth the Legion of Honor was to be awarded in recognition of extraordinary accomplishments in civilian or military life. The head of state was to be grand master of the legion, whose administration would be by a grand chancellor and by a council named by the head of state. The grand chancellor remained in direct contact with the emperor and, when necessary,

attended meetings of the ministerial council. The decree of 16 March replaced
Napoleon I's cohorts with five grades of membership, four of which were limited
in number. At the top of the hierarchy were the eighty grand crosses. These
were followed by 200 grand officers, 1,000 commanders, 4,000 officers, and
an unlimited number of knights (chevaliers). The prerequisite for admission to
the legion was twenty years of outstanding service to the nation. Cabinet ministers
took charge of the nomination of civilians in their respective areas, while the
grand chancellor was responsible for the nomination of other civil servants and
military personnel. Foreigners were also eligible. All admissions were made at
the rank of knight, and candidates were required to advance step by step through
the hierarchy. Unless granted dispensation for extraordinary merit, they would
spend a minimum of four years as knight, two as officer, three as commander,
and five as grand officer, although military campaigns (no more than one per
year) were counted double. Membership in the Legion of Honor brought with
it certain prerogatives: invitations to official functions, a financial stipend, state
funerals, eligibility of a legionnaire's children to attend special schools. On being
named to the legion, the members took the following oath: "I swear to be faithful
to my honor and to my country; I swear to devote myself to the good of the
state and to fulfill the duties of a brave and loyal knight of the Legion of Honor."
By decrees of 22 January and 21 March 1852, Napoleon III created a supplement
to the legion in the form of a Médaille Militaire whose stipend of 100 francs
per year for life was awarded to military personnel below officer rank. It was
also during the Second Empire that the Legion of Honor received its first woman
officer, the painter Rosa Bonheur.

    R. Laurant, "Histoire de la Légion d'Honneur," *Historia* (January 1969).

Dorothy E. Speirs

LEGISLATIVE BODY. See CORPS LEGISLATIF.

LEGITIMISM, the ideology associated with hereditary and traditional monarchy
as symbolized by the line of Charles X (reigned 1824–1830). Although legitimacy
was the basis of the restoration of the Bourbon monarchy in 1814, French
legitimist doctrines took special shape as the nineteenth century progressed.
Louis, vicomte de Bonald (1754–1840) and Joseph, comte De Maistre (1753–
1821), gave a theocratic basis; René, vicomte de Chateaubriand (1768–1848),
Pierre Royer–Collard (1763–1845), Antoine Berryer, Blanc de Saint-Bonnet,
and La Rochejacquelein made their own special contributions. The comte de
Chambord, however, became the rallying point for legitimists with the death of
Charles X in 1836 and particularly with the manifestations of fealty at Belgrave
Square in 1844. He declared that his person was nothing but his principle
everything, and for more than one-third of a century his correspondence and the
doings of the "Bureau du Roi," his twelve-man unofficial staff at Paris,
coordinated the legitimist movement, whose organization he closely controlled.
The theory of absolutism as developed by Bishop Jacques Bossuet (1627–1704)

fell into disuse in this period, and the emphasis on traditional and hereditary monarchy came into vogue. The natural bond of the legitimate monarch with the nation was stressed. Liberal constitutionalism had no place in the scheme, but representation of the nation and a role in making the laws did. The bond between church and state was stressed. As social Catholicism appeared, it became associated with legitimism, at least until the death of Chambord. The social theories of Frédéric Le Play influenced this association.

The failure of Orleanists and legitimists to effect a fusion contributed to the strength of Napoleon III, though even the empress had legitimist leanings, which caused her to ask Chambord after the death of Napoleon III in 1873 to adopt the prince imperial. The legitimists could have placed Chambord on the throne in the 1871–1873 era if only the uncompromising and childless prince had accepted the symbol of the Revolution and popular sovereignty, the tricolor. The spread of various modern characteristics in the 1870s suggests, however, that a legitimist restoration would have encountered troubles and at best would only have provided a means for an eventual Orleanist monarchy. Even during the Second Empire, most Frenchmen may well have regarded legitimism as an anachronism. Certainly it did not constitute a political threat to Napoleon III. The Empire made steady political gains in legitimist strongholds of the south and west and easily dealt with the propaganda of the legitimist newspapers (there was from 1848 a press agency under De Saint Chéron), the few direct plots, and the Chambord-inspired campaign for political abstention. Such monarchist-dominated organizations as the Society of Saint Vincent de Paul were ruthlessly controlled. Some legitimists were even co-opted by the Empire, preferring Napoleon III to the ''reds.'' Others, like Berryer and Frédéric, comte de Falloux (1811–1886), while remaining in opposition, rejected Chambord's injunction to abstain from politics and reached out to the right wing of the Orleanists. In fact, a great number of legitimists disregarded Chambord's injunction to resign their government or elective posts: in 1852 there were four hundred to five hundred legitimists among the twenty-five hundred members of the departmental *conseils généraux*. At least until many clergy became disaffected with Napoleon III's Italian policy after 1859, the legitimists lacked natural agents and could do little more than harass the regime in the salons and in the Académie Française.

Chambord's will provided on his death in 1883 that the Spanish Carlist pretender be his heir, but only a small part of French royalists gave their support to the ''Spanish whites.'' Most rallied to the Orleanist pretender, the comte de Paris (1838–1894). The Ralliement (the attempt by the church in the 1890s to promote a reconciliation with the Third Republic) deprived the legitimists of Albert de Mun (1841–1914) and many others. The theories of La Tour du Pin and Charles Maurras (1868–1952) further divided the legitimists, and the successful dissertation of Prince Sixte de Bourbon-Parme, by which he showed that the line of Louis XV was not the proper inheritance for France and that it was he himself who was the legitimate claimant, added the most interesting note. By World War I the legitimist movement was tiny, but subsequent study has stimulated interest in a first marriage of the duc de Berry (son of Charles X, assassinated 1820, father of the comte de Chambord) and in the various claims of descent from Louis XVII, the lost dauphin.

C. N. Desjoyaux, *La fusion monarchique, 1848–1873, d'après des sources inédites* (Paris, 1913); A. Gough, "Catholic legitimism and liberal bonapartism," in T. Zeldin, ed., *Conflicts in French Society* (London, 1970); S. Holmes, "Liberal Uses of Bourbon legitimism, *JHI*, 43 (April–June 1982); B. Jacquier, *Le légitimisme dauphinois, 1830–1870* (Grenoble, 1976); C. Muret, *French Royalist Doctrine since the Revolution* (New York, 1933); S. Rials, *Le légitimisme* (Paris, 1983).

Marvin L. Brown, Jr.

Related entries: BERRYER; CHAMBORD; ORLEANISM; ROMAN QUESTION; SAINT VINCENT DE PAUL, SOCIETY OF.

LE PLAY, FREDERIC (1806–1882), engineer, traveler, propagandist, *conseiller d'état*, senator, and social scientist; born near Honfleur, 11 April 1806. His father, a customs official, died six years later, and Le Play was sent to Paris to be raised by an uncle who was a conservative anti-Napoleonic royalist. At the Collège Sainte Barbe and then the Ecole Polytechnique (1825–1827), Le Play was a brilliant student. He received the highest marks ever given by the Ecole des Mines, entered the *corps des mines*, and by 1848 was *ingénieur en chef de première classe*. Known for his technical writings as early as 1830, he was appointed professor at the Ecole des Mines and became a *sous-directeur* there.

In 1830 Le Play was seriously injured in a laboratory explosion. During his long and painful convalescence, he resolved to spend half his time thereafter trying to discover the cause of social strife and instability and to concentrate on the most numerous segment of society, the workers (including agricultural workers). This resolve was strengthened by the engineer's distaste for the revolutionary movements of his day, which were to culminate in 1848. For the next fifteen years, Le Play spent six months of each year traveling over much of Europe (he made his last trip abroad in 1848) and meditating on his observations. Those observations consisted of close study, for periods varying from a week to a month, of some three hundred families representing a wide variety of economic activities (and eight languages). At the heart of the resulting monographs was a minute scrutiny of family budgets. Thus Le Play became a pioneer of the social survey method. In 1855 he published, under the title *Les ouvriers européens*, a number of his monographs, as well as an exposition of his method. Thereafter Le Play had little to do with engineering, although he would be named honorary inspector general in 1868.

It was inevitable that Le Play's contacts and interests would bring him to the attention of Napoleon III. The engineer was a close friend of Michel Chevalier (whose daughter his son married) and had grown up among Saint-Simonian influences. In 1853, during preparations for the Paris international exposition of 1855, he was named to the organizing commission (*sous-commission impérial*), of which he became vice-president and, on the withdrawal of General Arthur Morin (1795–1880), president. Le Play's reward was to be promoted commander of the Legion of Honor (15 December 1855) and named to the Conseil d'Etat, 29 December 1855. He was appointed *commissaire de l'Empire français* for the international exposition of 1862 at London and presided over the organization of that of 1867 at Paris, following which he was made a grand officer of the Legion of Honor (30 June 1867) and appointed to the Senate, 29 December 1867. In 1856 Le Play had founded the Société Internationale des Etudes Pratiques d'Economie Sociale, whose journal (*Les ouvriers des deux mondes*) published case studies. The sociologist-engineer became a close adviser of Napoleon III in matters concerning social reform, and the emperor encouraged him to publish in 1864 his *La réforme sociale en Europe déduite de l'observation des peuples européens*.

Although Le Play, like Chevalier, supported the Second Empire as the regime most likely to ensure economic and social progress for France, and although he like the Saint-Simonians, advocated a liberal laissez-faire position in economic matters, his thought was too individualistic to be claimed by any school or party. Le Play sought, above all, to discover by his laborious statistical studies the truths known to wise men in all cultures, truths that would make possible happiness and social peace. He departed from Saint-Simonianism because he sought a practical reform alternative rather than a utopian new world and because he had no faith in linear material progress or in technocracy and he preferred agriculture to industry. He broke with the liberals because he would not surrender the workers entirely to the mercies of laissez-faire economics, did not believe the form of government to be very important, and was an innate conservative who saw value in authoritarianism. And although Le Play has been hailed as a pioneer in France of social Catholicism and undoubtedly influenced such leaders of that movement as Augustin Cochin (1823–1872) and Armand de Melun (1807–1877), he was far from an orthodox Catholic. Moved more by the Old Testament than by Christianity, he was not even a practicing Catholic until the last years of his life.

In summary, Le Play concluded that the social goals he sought could be obtained only through a restoration of religious belief, an increase in the power of the father within the family, and legislation to make "seduction" of women more difficult. Thus he extolled the value of religion and wished for the collaboration of the clergy in social reform, but like his friend Charles de Montalembert and other liberal Catholics, he believed that this could be effective only if the church were separate from the state, divorced from politics, and tolerant. Concerning the family, Le Play inclined toward authoritarianism and paternalism. Reaffirming the doctrine of original sin, he hoped for an authority in the paterfamilias sufficient to instill in children an obedience toward necessary social precepts that was not natural. Perhaps his key thought was that this authority (and hence "stable" families, which alone could make possible a stable society) required restoring to the father the right to bequeath all of his property to the son of his choice. The resultant "stem family" (*famille souche*) would be superior both to the unstable family that resulted from the dispersion of increasingly impoverished individuals (who had inherited equally) and to the patriarchal family in which several generations lived together. Le Play's ideal society would be rural, composed of large, autonomous stem families under strong paternal authority. It would be a society in which great stress was placed on obedience, chastity (for which the male would have sole responsibility), patronage, and custom, a strange mingling of medieval and modern elements. These ideas, and the fact that it was Le Play's misfortune to have been captured by the conservatives, go a long way to explain why he has rarely been classed among the great sociologists. And there was perhaps an additional reason: his close association with Napoleon III and the Second Empire. Although Le Play ended his career at the Conseil d'Etat on 9 January 1868, he remained, in the Senate, a supporter of the regime until its overthrow in 1870. Emile Ollivier sought his advice concerning a *chambre de travail* that the Liberal Empire hoped to establish (it would have consisted one-third of workers, one-third of employers, and one-third of economists and publicists). The Franco-Prussian War prevented the realization of this and other projects, and the end of the Empire meant a return for Le Play to private life. He died at Paris, 5 April 1882.

M. Z. Brooke, *Le Play: Engineer and Social Scientist* (London, 1970); P. Douchy and P. Périer, "La doctrine sociale de Napoléon III et Le Play," *Etudes sociales*, n.s., nos. 83–84 (1970); P. Farmer, "The Social Theories of Frédéric Le Play," in *Essays in Honor of L. B. Packard* (1954); W. L. Goldfrank, "Reappraising Frédéric Le Play," in A. Overschall, ed., *The Establishment of Empirical Sociology* (New York, 1972); F. Le Play, *Les ouvriers européens: Etudes sur les travaux, la vie domestique, et la condition morale des populations ouvrières de l'Europe, précédées de la méthode d'observation*, 6 vols., 2d ed. (Paris, 1879), *La réforme sociale en Europe déduite de l'observation des peuples eruopéens*, 5th ed. (Paris, 1874), *L'organisation du travail selon la coutume des ateliers, et la loi du Décalogue* (Paris, 1870), *Les ouvriers et la réforme sociale* (Paris, 1871), and *L'organisation de la famille* (Paris, 1871); H. Rollet, "L'apport de Le Play au Catholicisme social," *Etudes sociales*, n.s., nos. 79–80 (1969); P. Secretan, "Le destin d'un grand sociologue, Frédéric Le Play (1806–1882)," *ES*, n.s., nos., 73–74 (1967), and "Le Play et son école," *RDM*, no. 17 (1956); D. Sureau, "La sociologie de Frédéric Le Play," *ES*, n.s., no. 108 (1979).

Related entries: CHEVALIER; INTERNATIONAL EXPOSITIONS; LABOR REFORM; SOCIAL CATHOLICISM.

LIBERAL CATHOLICISM. See GALLICANISM.

LIBERAL EMPIRE, the name given to the regime resulting from the elections of 1869. From 1852 until 1860 the authoritarian Empire had endured unchanged. During the next decade, Napoleon III had attempted to "crown the edifice" by granting reforms, which, nevertheless, left intact the constitution of 1852. The elections of May 1869 marked the failure of that policy and seemed to leave no choice between a new coup d'état and espousal of a parliamentary regime. The emperor hesitated, partly because of natural caution, partly because of ill health, but mostly because he saw no resolution to the problem of satisfying the demand for further reform without losing the power to maintain order. Thus in June he wrote to the president of the Corps Législatif, Eugène Schneider, of the need to conciliate ''a strong government with sincerely liberal institutions,'' while at the same time in another letter to the young bonapartist deputy Anne Ferdinand Armand, baron de Mackau (1832–1918), he stressed that governments do not yield to rioters.

On 28 June 1869 the newly elected Corps Législatif was called into extraordinary session to validate the elections. Eugène Rouher, as the government's spokesman, promised vaguely that the wishes of the country would be met. In fact, Napoleon III's advisers were divided. Victor Fialin Persigny, while regretting the demise of the authoritarian Empire, frankly accepted that the role of the ''men of December'' was over and that further reforms were necessary. Prince Napoleon proposed not only that new men should be brought in but that ministers should be made responsible to parliament, the Senate transformed into an elective body, Paris given an elected municipal council, and provision made for election of mayors throughout the country (the prince also suggested withdrawing French troops from Rome and adopting a pacifistic policy toward Germany). Others cautioned against too precipitate change. The emperor seems to have contemplated a continuation of the reform policy espoused since 1860, adding to the powers of the legislature and of the *conseils généraux*, and providing for press offenses to be tried by special juries rather than by judges. Ministerial responsibility, however, remained anathema to him.

But events were outstripping the government's desire for caution. In June began a series of violent strikes, destined to continue into 1870. And in the Corps Législatif the group of deputies known as the Tiers Parti framed an interpellation with ministerial responsibility in view that by 6 July had obtained 116 signatures. Adolphe Thiers and the republicans abstaining in order to give the movement a greater chance, even so loyal a bonapartist as Antoine Juste Léon Marie de Noailles, duc de Mouchy (b. 1841; married Anna Murat in 1865), whose chateau Napoleon III had recently visited, signed the demand for an interpellation. Annoyed, the emperor nevertheless yielded to advice, particularly from Schneider, that Rouher must at last go. The latter on 12 July, in announcing his resignation to the Corps Législatif, also read a message from Napoleon III enumerating reforms to be submitted to the Senate. The Rubicon had indeed been crossed. To guard against second thoughts, the Ministry of State was suppressed (17 July) and the Corps Législatif indefinitely prorogued (13 July), even before it had completed its verification of powers. Also on 13 July the Senate was convoked for 2 August.

Since Emile Ollivier was still unwilling to assume office (only he and one other member of the Tiers Parti were approached), the government of 17 July 1869 was a transitional one of conservative technicians. Although Prosper, marquis de Chasseloup-Laubat, as minister presiding the Conseil d'Etat, gave a liberal interpretation to the reforms promised by Napoleon III on 12 July (reforms permitting the legislature to elect its own officers and make its own rules, extending the right of amendment, making interpellation easier, increasing the Senate's role, enabling the budget to be voted by chapters, and allowing ministers to be deputies and senators), the impression remained that of a government taken by surprise and swept along against its will. Nor, until the emperor spoke out clearly, could the Tiers Parti hope to enlist enough bonapartist official candidates to constitute a majority.

On 2 August 1869 the Conseil d'Etat submitted a project of *sénatus-consulte* to the Senate. Rouher introduced the legislation; Prosper Duvergier de Hauranne (1798–1887) commented; Adrien Marie Devienne (1802–1883) was *rapporteur*. The public debate coincided with the launching of the centenary of Napoleon I's birth and a prolonged illness of Napoleon III, as well as with the granting of a general amnesty (15 August). Only a handful of senators (Prince Napoleon, Michel Chevalier, Louis Bernard Bonjean [1804–1871]) gave more than lip-service to the proposed reforms, as Prince Napoleon pointed out in his ultraliberal speech of 1 September. But since the emperor would have the reforms, they were approved on 6 September, in the midst of an apparent public indifference, with only ten senators in opposition. A liberalizing amendment by Bonjean having been rejected by the *commission*, the proposals of the Conseil d'Etat were accepted almost without change, adding to the reforms promised by the emperor: the granting of legislative initiative to the Corps Législatif and to the Senate, opening of Senate meetings to the public, transferring control of amendments from the Conseil d'Etat to the legislature, conferring on the Senate a suspensory (one-year) veto, and requiring legislative approval of tariff provisions in treaties. Thus the Corps Législatif became a parliamentary assembly with full powers of initiative, amendment, self-organization, and interpellation, and the transformation of the Senate into a second legislative body was all but completed. However, Napoleon III could not be said to have granted ministerial responsibility, and the Senate retained its constituent powers. The constitution of 1852 yet remained in effect.

Napoleon III was ill from 19 August until September. He would have preferred to delay the regular session of the Corps Législatif until 1870, but the republicans demanded convocation for 26 October, and the emperor on 3 October set the date for 29 November. In the interval the republican deputies broke with their more radical brethren, and the Paris by-elections of 21–22 November proved to be only a partial victory for the latter. Attempts to form a liberal ministry in advance of the session failed, but on 26 November the Tiers Parti, urged by Ollivier, opened its ranks to all deputies of goodwill, and, Napoleon III this time having indicated his sympathy for liberalization, forty-seven official candidates accepted the invitation. The Tiers Parti, grown to 163 and having abandoned its demand for interpellation, now constituted a majority in the Corps Législatif, which convened at the Louvre to hear the emperor's opening speech on 29 November. "L'ordre," he affirmed, "j'en réponds." But he continued, after the applause had subsided, "aidez-moi à sauver la liberté." Pessimistic, Napoleon III apparently expected an uprising, but he nevertheless continued negotiations with Ollivier, which had begun at the end of October. On 27 December the Corps Législatif, having elected Schneider president and Jérôme David vice-president and having completed the verification of powers, adjourned until 10 January. That same day Napoleon III wrote to Ollivier asking him to form a homogeneous cabinet that would faithfully represent the majority in the Corps Législatif. Although the emperor had not yielded on the issue of ministerial responsibility (he would name and convoke the ministers, and there would be no prime minister) and although he continued to insist on his right to dissolve the legislature and to appeal to the people by plebiscite, Ollivier this time accepted, for a variety of reasons, including his genuine affection for the emperor, his desire for office, his indifference to forms of government, and his fear of revolution.

Ollivier's task was greatly complicated by the division that had appeared within the Tiers Parti from the end of November. One group of 130 deputies, the *centre droit* or Right-Center (Ollivier, Alexis Emile Segris [1811–1880], the marquis de Talhouët-Toy [1819–1884], Henri Germain [1824–1905], J. P. E. N. Chevandier de Valdrôme [1810–1878], Charles Louvet [1806–1882]), accepted the liberalized Empire. Placing much emphasis on social reform, they might be called liberal bonapartists. A smaller, more socially conservative group of 33 deputies, the *centre gauche* or Left-Center (Charles Louis Henri Kolb-Bernard [1798–1888], Louis Buffet, Emile Keller [1828–1909], Jules de Jacquot, marquis d'Andelarre [1803–1885], Pierre Latour-Dumoulin [1823–1888], Ignace Plichon [1814–1888], Napoléon Daru), would accept the Empire only if it were to become parliamentary to the extent that the Corps Législatif could vote on changes in the constitution and that mayors would be chosen from lists prepared by the municipal councils. At issue, then, were the electoral law and the question of constituent powers. But both groups agreed on responsible government, freedom of press and elections, a measure of decentralization, liberty of higher education, and the need for an inquiry regarding the treaty of commerce with Britain. Moreover, both feared a reaction by the minority of authoritarian bonapartists and both needed the emperor as a bulwark against the intransigent Left. On 31 December Ollivier formed a ministry composed of the Right-Center and containing four former ministers of the authoritarian Empire. Then Pierre Magne, Ollivier's choice for finance minister, insisted that the Left-Center be included, and on 2 January 1870 this was accomplished with the acceptance of portfolios by Buffet and Daru, although the price was the elimination of the former ministers, including Magne. In the subsequent election of three Corps Législatif vice-presidents, the Right-Center obtained two.

The ministry of 2 January was still responsible to the emperor, who continued to preside the Council of Ministers (he would have given Ollivier the title of vice-president of council but the other ministers were opposed). When the ministers met two or three times each week at the Tuileries as *conseil des ministres*, the emperor presided. When they met as *conseil de cabinet* (usually at the chancellery on the Place Vendôme), Ollivier, as minister of justice, presided; the emperor and Marshal Vaillant stayed away. On 3 January twelve prefects were fired and five were assigned other functions. On 6 January the dismissal of Baron Georges Haussmann as prefect of the Seine was announced. Restrictions against foreign newspapers were lifted, Alexandre Ledru-Rollin (1807–1874) was pardoned, as were those condemned for activities during recent strikes at La Ricamarie and Aubin, and permission was given for leftist newspapers to be sold publicly. On 9 January several decrees in a protectionist vein were obtained by Buffet. The new government further strengthened its credit by firm action during the crisis precipitated by the murder on 10 January 1870 of the left-wing journalist Victor Noir by Pierre Bonaparte (prosecution and condemnation of Henri Rochefort). By the end of February, the government was formulating projects to rescind the general security law of 1859 and to reform the press law so that offenses would be tried by juries. In addition to the inquiry concerning the 1860 commercial treaty with Britain, three commissions were also at work: on the administrative organization of Paris, on decentralization and the method of choosing mayors (headed by Odilon Barrot [1791–1873], and on freedom of higher education (chaired by François Guizot [1787–1874]). Ollivier also planned a permanent *chambre du travail*, consisting equally of workers, employers, and economists. And in February the government abandoned official candidacy in elections (fifty-six authoritarian deputies voted against the government on the occasion).

The constitutional issue remained, however. Some further revision had been agreed, but how extensive should it be? On 4 March 1870 Napoleon III bluntly rejected Prince Napoleon's plea for a parliamentary regime. But the question of how mayors were to be chosen (no agreement between the government and the Left-Center proved possible) raised the further question of constituent powers, and the Corps Législatif inclined decisively to Daru's view that there should be a total revision of the 1852 constitution. Reluctantly, the emperor instructed Ollivier on 21 March to prepare a *sénatus-consulte* "fixant la constitution de l'Empire" in such a way that constituent power would devolve to the people and that the Senate would become a true legislative body coequal with the lower house. On 28 March the required project was submitted to the Senate, debated for only a few days, and voted unanimously on 20 April 1870. The new constitution recognized the constituent power as being in the people, not the Senate. It took away from the Conseil d'Etat and bestowed on the legislature the rights of initiating legislation and of supervising amendments. It gave the Corps Législatif the right to receive petitions, and it made the Senate autonomous and coequal with the lower house, except that only the latter could initiate tax legislation. And it suppressed article 33 of the constitution of 1852, which had given the emperor emergency powers in conjunction with the Senate. But ministers remained responsible to the emperor as well as to the legislature, and a new article 13 stated: "L'Empereur est responsable devant le peuple français auquel il a toujours le droit de faire appel.'' Equally, article 44 stipulated that only the people "sur la proposition de l'Empereur" could change the constitution by a plebiscite. Thus Napoleon III retained the plebiscitary power. In fact, article 46 provided for a plebiscite on the constitution of 1870 and the newly established Liberal Empire.

The government's overwhelming victory in the plebiscite of 8 May 1870 (7.35 million to 1.5 million) had a number of immediate consequences. The republicans were greatly discouraged, and while most remained committed to Léon Gambetta's 10 February 1870 pledge of intransigent opposition, others followed Ernest Picard in accepting the new constitution and thus the regime (*gauche ouverte*). Ollivier's government was shaken by the resignation of Buffet, Daru, and Talhouët in April in protest against the plebiscite, but just before the promulgation of the constitution on 21 May, it was reconstituted with two Center-Right deputies and Antoine, duc de Gramont (the latter as foreign minister). The new government now took a stronger stand against the Left, condemning certain newspapers, arresting and trying the leaders of the Paris section of the Workingmens' International, and it launched a flurry of some 128 projects of law.

The question is whether the Liberal Empire could have survived. Ollivier found himself in the unenviable position of governing without a majority in a chamber divided into a fragmented Left (*gauche radicale*, *gauche fermée*, *gauche ouverte*), a Left-Center, a Right-Center, and an unrepentant authoritarian Right. Attacks on him, especially from the extreme Right, doubtless helped to preserve his government, and the plebiscite results strengthened his hand, but the necessity of building a new majority on each issue combined with his mercurial and somewhat idealist nature to make it appear that the government lacked direction and principle. The commissions labored to produce nothing, or very little. And there were rumors that the emperor was himself contemplating a new coup d'état. And yet it seems contrary to common sense that such should have been the case, especially following the plebiscite. Quite probably Napoleon III was both unhappy with and loyal to the government that events had given him. Moreover, those who disliked or distrusted Ollivier but who regarded both the authoritarians and the Left with apprehension had nowhere else to turn than to the Liberal Empire, which, after all, combined electoral democracy, full personal liberties, and effective parliamentary control with retention by the emperor of powers sufficient to make him a pillar of order in the event of another revolutionary crisis. Many former opponents rallied to the regime, including Guizot, Charles de Rémusat (1797–1875), Victor, duc de Broglie (1785–1870), Charles de Montalembert, Jules Claretie, George Sand, Picard, Louis Veuillot, Lucien Anatole Prévost-Paradol, Frédéric Masson (1847–1923), and Jean Jacques Weiss (1827–1891). The symbol of this acceptance was the election of Ollivier to the Académie Française in place of Lamartine on 8 April 1870. Perhaps France might have found in the Liberal Empire the stability that was to elude it for almost another century. It was not political factors but military defeat that led to the fall of

Ollivier's government on 9 August 1870 and to the collapse of the Second Empire on 4 September.

P. C. Chesnelong, "Les cinq dernières années de l'Empire," *Corr.*, 318 (1932); A. Dalotel, A. Faure, and J. C. Freiermuth, *Aux origines de la Commune: Le mouvement des réunions publiques à Paris, 1868–1870* (Paris, 1980); S. Elwitt, *The Making of the Third Republic: Class and Politics in France, 1868–1884* (Baton Rouge, La., 1975); J. J. Weiss, *Combat constitutionnel, 1868–1886* (Paris, 1977; 4 microfiches); R. L. Williams, *The French Revolution of 1870–1871* (New York, 1969); T. Zeldin, *Emile Ollivier and the Liberal Empire of Napoleon III* (New York, 1963).

Related entries: AUTHORITARIAN EMPIRE; BONAPARTISM; BUFFET; CHASSELOUP-LAUBAT; CONSTITUTION; CORPS LEGISLATIF; CROWNING OF THE EDIFICE; DARU; DAVID; DECENTRALIZATION; ELECTIONS; LIBERALISM; VICTOR NOIR AFFAIR; OLLIVIER; PLEBISCITE; PRINCE NAPOLEON; QUATRE SEPTEMBRE; REFORM; REPUBLICANISM; ROUHER; SCHNEIDER, E.; SENATE; THIERS; TIERS PARTI.

LIBERALISM, a congeries of attitudes that constituted throughout the Second Empire a point of opposition to bonapartism. Characteristically, the nineteenth-century liberal advocated parliamentary (and minimal) government, laissez-faire economics, and individual liberty (defined as freedom from various political, legal, or religious constraints). Much of this viewpoint was outlined in Adolphe Thiers' brilliant Corps Législatif speech of 11 January 1864 on the "necessary liberties." Liberals lacked neither targets for attack in Second Empire France nor dreams for the future. They particularly rejected managed elections, executive and administrative dominance over parliament, and arbitrary restrictions on association, assembly, and the press. They opposed a budgetary process that, because it escaped parliamentary control, made possible such uses of public money as the rebuilding of Paris or the numerous military expeditions of the Second Empire, especially that to Mexico. Liberals sought to avoid extremes and believed that if the line could be held between radicalism and reaction, an inevitable evolution would lead to a middle-class society in which people would have all the happiness they deserved and as much prosperity as the economic laws would allow. Moreover, once all governments had become liberal, war would disappear and people would live in peace and harmony. Liberals rejected class struggle as the basis of history. Rather, they tended to ascribe its existence to the conspiracies and machinations of the radical Left.

A liberal could be monarchist, republican, or bonapartist, but in reality the leadership of French liberalism came largely from the ranks of the Orleanists, and its major newspapers and journals (the *Journal des débats*, the *Revue des deux mondes*) tended to be Orleanist in tone. As a political force, liberalism had two great weaknesses: it lacked a popular base and was divided on a number of issues. Liberals regarded universal manhood suffrage with resignation—and considerable distaste. Their theory of leadership was elitist and reduced in the end to a small coterie who found in their undeniable abilities and shared education, values, and goals a right to govern. Behind the insistence by many liberals on political decentralization lay the wish of these notables to regain the positions of local dominance they had lost or were in danger of losing. Above all, liberals lacked almost entirely a social and economic program. Beyond individual philanthropy and a certain amount of grudging paternalism, their chief concern was not with reform but with order. Similarly, liberals rejected an active foreign policy as they rejected a large standing army. Wars were expensive, and although certain ends might be desirable (such as the removal of Austrian influence from Italy and the unity of the peninsula), they should be left to the slow working of time. Moreover, liberals disagreed among themselves on many points, especially concerning the proper relationship of church and state, the merits of free trade, and the role of government in economic affairs. Liberals who supported the temporal power of the pope and a role for the church in education (all in the interest of order), as well as protective tariffs and government subventions to industry, were not uncommon.

These weaknesses explain in part the relative political ineffectiveness of liberalism during the Second Empire. Its leaders were defeated for election to the Corps Législatif much more often than they won. Its attempts to form a great electoral coalition, the Union Libérale, floundered time and again. Even the elections of 1869 marked a triumph for republicanism as such rather than for liberalism. Undoubtedly liberalism contributed to the slow dismantling of the authoritarian Empire between 1852 and 1870, but the advent of the Liberal Empire need not be read as a victory for liberalism. Bonapartism had always included a *bonapartisme de gauche*, and Napoleon III had promised from the beginning a "crowning of the edifice," by which lost liberties would be restored at the proper moment. The constitution of 1870 remained bonapartist in the retention by the emperor of the plebiscitary power and in the continued responsibility of the ministers to him. Nor did the new government incline to limit its ambitions and interventions in accord with the inhibitions of liberalism. It would be as justified, therefore, to argue that bonapartism by 1870 had preempted liberalism and captured a number of its leaders (Emile Ollivier, Alfred Darimon, Lucien Anatole Prévost-Paradol) as to insist on the enforced liberalization of the regime.

S. Gavronsky, *The French Liberal Opposition and the American Civil War* (New York, 1968); P. Guiral, "Der Liberalismus in Frankreich (1815–1870): Grundlagen, Erfolge, Schwächen," *Liberalismus* (1976); G. Palmade, "Le *Journal des économistes* et la pensée libérale sous le Second Empire," *BSHM*, no. 3 (1962); L. A. Prévost-Paradol, *La France nouvelle* (Paris, 1869; reprint 1980); D. Sherman, "The Meaning of Economic Liberalism in Mid-Nineteenth-Century France," *History of Political Economy* (Summer 1974).

Related entries: BAKERIES, DEREGULATION OF; BONAPARTISM; BUFFET; COBDEN-CHEVALIER TREATY; *CORRESPONDANT*; CROWNING THE EDIFICE; DARIMON; DECENTRALIZATION; *JOURNAL DES DEBATS*; LEGITIMISM; LIBERAL EMPIRE; MONTALEMBERT; OLLIVIER; ORLEANISM; PREVOST-PARADOL; REFORM; REPUBLICANISM; *RE-*

VUE DES DEUX MONDES; *TEMPS*; THIERS; TIERS PARTI; UNIVERSAL MANHOOD SUFFRAGE.

LA LIBERTE, newspaper of Emile de Girardin. In June 1866, after leaving *La presse* for the second and final time, Girardin bought the paper that Charles Muller had established in July of the previous year. Dropping the price far below cost to 10 centimes per copy and capitalizing on the excitement created in France by the Austro-Prussian War, which had just broken out, Girardin achieved for *La liberté* a circulation of forty thousand. The price soon had to be increased, but the new paper, boasting the first sports column ever carried by a French journal ("Le monde sportique"), settled down to a more than respectable circulation: 21,000 in 1867, 17,000 in March 1869, and 10,250 in February 1870. Girardin hired young, adventurous writers, including Jules Vallès (1832–1885), Clément Duvernois (1836–1879), Auguste Vermorel (1841–1871), Edouard Drumont (1844–1917), Wilfrid (1824–1914) and Ulrich de Fonvielle (1833–1911), Hector Pessard (1836–1895), Paul de Saint-Victor (1827–1881; drama critic from January 1868), Alfred Assolant (1827–1886), Emile Boutmy (1835–1906), and vicomte Henri de Bornier (1825–1901). Many had followed him from *La presse*.

   Although *La liberté* did not oppose the regime, it stood for a liberal parliamentary Empire and immediately printed a number of articles extremely critical of the government. One of these, signed by Girardin, caught the attention of the emperor himself, and on 6 March 1867 Girardin was sentenced to a fine of 5,000 francs. Unrepentant, he received a second fine. Yet the next year *La liberté* was one of those journals that opposed the subscription for a monument to Jean Baptiste Baudin, martyr of December 1851. Although Girardin sold his paper to a nephew by marriage, Détroyat, in June 1870 for 1 million francs, he returned to the fray in its columns to urge war with Prussia over the Hohenzollern candidacy (July).

   A. Sirven, *Journaux et journalistes: "La presse," "La liberté"* (Paris, 1866).
Related entries: GIRARDIN; PRESS REGIME.

LITTRE, EMILE (1801–1881), philologist, historian, journalist, and leading expositor of positivism and of republicanism during the Second Empire; born 1 February 1801 at Paris. Educated at the Lycée Louis le Grand, Littré became proficient in Latin, Greek, and Sanskrit, as well as German and Italian. Although he was trained as a physician, he never practiced medicine but turned instead to journalism. During the 1830s and 1840s, Littré was an active contributor to the republican newspaper, *Le national*, and to the Orleanist *Revue des deux mondes*, distinguishing himself as a popularizer and advocate of science. He also commenced his critical edition and translation of Hippocrates, which appeared in ten volumes from 1839 to 1861. The work established him as a leading philologist and medical historian and is still considered authoritative. During the 1850s and 1860s, he contributed frequently to the *Journal des débats* and the *Journal des savants*.

After reading in 1840 the *Cours de philosophie positive* of Auguste Comte (1798–1857), Littré published a series of articles in *Le national* (subsequently printed together in 1845 as *De la philosophie positive*) that distilled the essential arguments from Comte's own prolix work and made positivism well known in France. Littré became a leading figure in the Positivist Society organized by Comte in 1848, but, repelled by the latter's approval of the coup d'état of 1851 (Littré was an outspoken foe of bonapartism), he left the group in 1852. He emerged as the focus of a group of dissident positivists who, in opposition to the orthodox disciples of Comte (led by Pierre Laffitte [1823–1893] after Comte's death), rejected the increasingly theocratic and authoritarian aspects of Comte's later writings and activities. Littré's secular rendition of positivism, expressed lucidly in *Auguste Comte et la philosophie positive* (1863), exerted considerable influence on republican strategists, most notably on his friends Léon Gambetta and Jules Ferry (1832–1893), during the last years of the Empire and during the formative years of the Third Republic. In 1867 Littré founded (and edited), along with the Russian-born scientist Grégoire Wyrouboff (1843–1913), the journal *Revue de la philosophie positive*, which became a major agent for the diffusion of positivist ideas and propaganda. When he was first put forward in 1863 as a candidate for membership in the Académie Française, Littré's republicanism and his eminent status in freethinking and anti-clerical circles enabled Bishop Félix Dupanloup to prevent his election despite Adolphe Thiers' support. Littré's successful candidacy in 1871—his literary credentials, including the *Histoire de la langue française* (1862) and the monumental *Dictionnaire étymologique, historique et grammatical de la langue française* (7 volumes plus supplement, published by Louis Hachette, 1863–1878), were by then indisputable—provoked Dupanloup's celebrated resignation from the Académie.

Littré welcomed the fall of Napoleon III, whose regime (despite the plebiscite) he regarded as having its origin in perjury and as the cause of war and ruin for France. Elected to the National Assembly in 1871 as a deputy for the Seine, he sat among the moderate republicans. He was named senator for life in 1875. Throughout the 1870s, Littré was an active political commentator, and his articles in *La philosophie positive* provide a perceptive chronical of the establishment of the Third Republic. He died at Paris, 2 June 1881.

S. Aquarone, *The Life and Works of Emile Littré, 1801–1881* (Leyden, 1958); L. Guinet, "Emile Littré (1801–1881)," *Isis* 8 (1926); E. Littré, *Auguste Comte et la philosophie positive* (Paris, 1863), and *Conservation, révolution et positivisme* (1852); A. Rey, *Littré* (Paris, 1970).

Martin Fichman

Related entries: DARWINISM IN FRANCE; DUPANLOUP; POSITIVISM; REPUBLICANISM.

LIVRET D'OUVRIER, industrial worker's passbook, recording employment history, debts owed previous employers, and certification of completion of work obligations. Instituted by the Law of 22 Germinal Year XI and by the decree of

9 Frimaire Year XII, both of which expanded on regulations of 1749 and 1781 (Turgot), the *livret* guaranteed employers, in theory at least, the fulfillment of commitments by their workers. A worker could not be hired by a new employer without first obtaining from the present one the *congé d'acquit*, certifying completion of work. The *congé* could be denied for failure to pay sums owed the present employer, or the latter could inscribe these sums in the *livret* and claim up to a fifth of the worker's wage in his new job until the debt was repaid. Employers hiring workers without the *congé* were liable to damage suits by the former employer, and workers without *livrets* were subject to arrest and prosecution for vagabondage, at least until 1832. Moreover, the Napoleonic requirement that the mayor must also sign a departing worker's *livret*, naming the town to which he was going, made of the document a sort of internal passport. Reformers complained that the existing law on *livrets* exposed industrial workers (artisans and agricultural laborers as well as provincial domestic servants were exempt) to excessive dependence on their employers by tempting them to accumulate debts without limit. In Paris the *livret* served, in addition, as a means of exercising surveillance over workers. Workers from the provinces were required to have their *livrets* stamped by the prefecture of police when accepting employment in the city, and the same visa was required for all workers in the city, immigrant or native, at each change of job.

Legislation of the Second Republic and Second Empire eliminated some of the worst abuses associated with the existing law on *livrets*. The law of 14 May 1851 prevented employers from noting more than 30 francs in debts in their workers' *livrets*, regardless of total sums owed, and allowed retention of no more than one-tenth of the wage earned by the worker in the new job for repayment. The law of 22 June 1854, supplemented by the decree of 30 April 1855, gave workers the right to retain their *livrets* in their possession during their period of employment and entitled them to receive the *congé d'acquit* simply on demand, once they had fulfilled their work commitments. The law also reduced the penalty against workers' not carrying *livrets* and imposed the same penalty on employers hiring workers without *livret* or *congé*. Moreover, employers were prohibited from making any annotation, favorable or unfavorable, on *livrets* (a practice that many had taken on themselves) and were required to keep a register of entries and departures of their workers for inspection by the police. For the first time, women were included. This law of 22 June 1854 was the Second Empire's most significant contribution to the institution of the *livret*. The law of 26 March 1852 on mutual aid societies also affected usage of the *livret* by allowing diplomas issued by approved societies to serve in place of workers' passbooks.

The imperial government hailed the 1854 law as a benevolent measure in favor of workers and as an advance in legal equality between workers and employers. But most historians have interpreted it as motivated primarily by concern for more effective policing of urban workers. Retention of *livrets* by workers—the law's most significant innovation—enabled the government to impose the requirement of the *livret* on a larger number of urban workers, notably on those having two or more employers simultaneously. The exemption of agricultural workers has been cited as further evidence of the *livret*'s police function, since these workers were not regarded by the authorities as a threat to public order. As some historians have noted, the 1854 law effectively placed urban workers in the same position as persons subject to high police surveillance.

This interpretation of the *livret* as essentially a police measure prevailed among the workers themselves, especially in Paris. Resistance to the *livret* increased after 1860, and delegates of several trades to the international expositions of 1862 and 1867 demanded its abolition. A government inquiry on the *livret* in 1868 revealed widespread dissatisfaction among both workers and employers, many of whom simply ignored the law. The inquiry revealed a division of opinion, however, not only between workers and employers but also among workers, concerning the desired status of the *livret*. While most employers' associations favored its retention and most Parisian workers wanted it abolished, some workers, especially in the provinces, favored retention of the *livret* as a certification of basic competency in a trade. The surveillance aspects of existing law on *livrets*, however, encountered universal hostility among workers, who argued that these provisions accentuated resentment against the authorities. In March 1869 a draft law to abolish the *livret* was submitted just before the elections of that year, to the Conseil d'Etat, on the emperor's initiative (the Council of Ministers was divided), but failed to reach the Corps Législatif because of resistance by industrialists. The Liberal Empire proposed in 1870 to abolish the *livrets*, but events intervened. Not until 1890 was the obligatory *livret* removed from the law code, although by then it had fallen into disuse.

H. Bressolette, "Le livret d'ouvrier d'un scieur de long livradois," *Revue d'Auvergne* 90 (1976); A. Chatelain, "A propos d'une contrainte sociale au XIXe siècle: Le monde paysan et le livret d'ouvrier," *Etudes de la Société d'Histoire de la Révolution de 1848* 25 (1953); E. Levasseur, *Histoire des classes ouvrières et de l'industrie en France de 1789 à 1870*, 2d ed. (Paris, 1904); A. Plantier, "Le livret des ouvriers" (University of Paris thesis, 1900).

George J. Sheridan, Jr.

Related entry: LABOR REFORM.

LOUIS NAPOLEON (1808–1873), third son of Louis Bonaparte and Hortense de Beauharnais; emperor of France from December 1852 to September 1870. Louis Bonaparte, brother of Napoleon I, was king of Holland when Hortense, daughter of the emperor's wife, Josephine, gave birth at Paris 20 April 1808 to a son who on 4 November 1810 at Fontainebleau was christened Charles Louis Napoleon Bonaparte. Relations between Hortense and her husband (they had married 4 January 1802) had been strained for some years and were particularly so following the death of their eldest son, Charles Napoleon, on 5 May 1807. Rumors that Louis Napoleon was not, in fact, the child of the king of Holland were to persist throughout the Second Empire. The historical consensus is overwhelmingly for legitimacy, but the case cannot be proved.

A physically weak child, Louis Napoleon was nursed by a Mme. Bure, with whose son, his foster brother, he formed a lifelong friendship. Even as a child he showed evidence of the natural generosity and compassion for the poor that was to persist throughout his life. Influenced by his mother and by his elder brother (Napoleon Louis, born 11 October 1804), to both of whom he was closely attached, Louis Napoleon also appears to have early developed a sense of his destiny to rule France in the name of the ideas of his great uncle.

After the fall of the First Empire, Hortense separated from her husband and was forced to give up her eldest son in October 1815. She settled with Louis Napoleon in Switzerland, since a French law of 12 January 1816 banned all Bonapartes from France. Immensely rich, Hortense purchased the estate of Arenenberg in Thurgau (Switzerland), February 1817, as well as a house in Augsburg, and it was in these places that Louis Napoleon received his education, first under his tutor Philippe Le Bas (1794–1860), a Jacobin republican (from 1819 to September 1827), and in the Augsburg *Gymnasium* (from April 1821); and then (from June 1830) at the Swiss military college of Thun.

Beginning in 1823–1824 Hortense and her son spent six months of each year at Rome or en route. Italy was, in fact, the meeting place of the Bonapartes. It was there that Louis Napoleon and his brother became involved in the 1831 rebellion against papal authority (the two young men considered themselves republicans) and that Napoleon Louis died, probably of measles, on 17 March 1831. Louis Napoleon, who seems to have been not a member but a fellow-traveler of the revolutionary *carbonaro* society, was helped by his mother to escape to England via France in April and early May 1831. Louis Napoleon spoke English with reasonable fluency although with a heavy accent, and he thrived in the English Whig society of the day, but in August 1831 he returned with his mother to Arenenberg. There he began to write the political pamphlets that were to make his name known and in which he publicized the bonapartist cause as he would have it understood. *Rêveries politiques* appeared shortly after his return to Switzerland and *Considérations politiques et militaires sur la Suisse* in July 1833. In April 1832 he had become a naturalized Swiss citizen of the canton of Thurgau. He was, as well, a captain in the artillery and author of a well-received artillery manual. From November 1832 to May 1833, Louis Napoleon visited Britain with his friend Count Francesco Arese (c. 1806–1881). At Arenenberg (November 1835 and April to May 1836) he renewed relations with two younger cousins, Prince Napoleon Joseph and Princess Mathilde, the children of Napoleon I's brother Jérôme. He fell in love with the flirtatious Mathilde, and their marriage was envisaged.

But Louis Napoleon had already (in 1835) met the man who was to have a perhaps decisive influence on his life, Victor Fialin Persigny. The death of Napoleon I's son, the duke of Reichstadt, in July 1832 and the unwillingness of the emperor's surviving brothers to enter the political arena had made Louis

Napoleon the bonaparte pretender, a role in which Persigny, an ardent bonapartist, encouraged him. On 30 October 1836 an attempt to rally the garrison of Strasbourg against Louis Philippe's regime failed. Louis Napoleon was transported to America and there released (Norfolk 30 March 1837). He was condemned by all of the family except Hortense. The marriage with Mathilde was no longer to be considered. In June 1837, having heard that his mother was dying of cancer, Louis Napoleon returned to Europe, arriving at Arenenberg on 4 August. Hortense died 5 October, at the age of fifty-four.

The next year, to relieve Switzerland of the growing threats accompanying French demands for his expulsion, Louis Napoleon voluntarily entered into exile in England, where he arrived 25 October 1838, accompanied by Persigny. Here in the summer of 1839 he published his propaganda masterpiece, *Des idées napoléoniennes*, and from here on 6 August 1840 he led a forlorn expedition to Boulogne. The attempted insurrection was an ignominious failure, and Louis Napoleon, after a six-day trial before the Chamber of Peers (he was defended by Antoine Berryer), was convicted on 6 October and condemned to life imprisonment in the fortress of Ham in Picardy. There he and his few companions were guarded by some four hundred men. At Ham, Louis Napoleon's already prominent characteristics continued to manifest themselves: his sensual nature (he had two illegitimate children by his prison laundress), his uncertain health and lack of robustness (he contracted rheumatism), his intellectual ability (he studied chemistry, wrote articles on the sugar beet industry, unemployment, a Nicaraguan canal), and his fatalistic determination to rule France. Since the death of his brother, he had styled himself "Napoleon Louis Bonaparte" and so he signed his new major propaganda brochures, *Fragments historiques, 1688 et 1830* and *Extinction du paupérisme*. The death of Joseph Bonaparte in July 1844 made Louis Napoleon's father, King Louis, emperor by right in the eyes of the bonapartists, but the former king of Holland was dying. On 25 May 1846, the sentences of his co-conspirators having expired, Louis Napoleon made a dramatic escape from prison, aided by his personal physician and long-time friend, Dr. F.A.H. Conneau. Two days later he was once more in England. On 25 July 1846 his father died.

Helped financially by a rich English mistress, Elisabeth ("Henrietta") Howard, Louis Napoleon awaited his opportunity. It came with the revolution of February 1848 in Paris and with his fortuitous rejection by the politicians who asked him on 29 February to leave France, to which he had returned the day before, and persuaded him in June to decline the seat in the Constituent Assembly to which he had been elected. In London, Louis Napoleon remained untainted by the terrible events of 23–26 June in the French capital. Elected in the September by-elections at the top of the poll, Louis Napoleon rushed to Paris (24 September). He presented himself as a candidate for the presidency of the Second Republic and was elected 10 December by an overwhelming majority. Thus began the events that were to culminate in a protracted struggle between a popularly elected president and assembly, the coup d'état of December 1851, and, one year later, the proclamation of the Second Empire. But already, in signing the constitution of January 1852, the prince president (as he was known in society, although not officially) had signed himself not "Louis Napoleon Bonaparte" but simply "Louis Napoleon."

A. Castelot, "La conspiration de Boulogne," *Historia* 324 (November 1973); A. Chatelle, *La route des coups d'état: Strasbourg 1836–Boulogne 1840: Le Prince-Président, 10 décembre 1848* (Paris, 1982); A. Cobban, "Louis Napoleon Bonaparte in 1838," *EHR* (July 1968); A. Dansette, *Louis-Napoléon à la conquête du pouvoir* (Paris, 1961); M. de La Fuye and E. Babeau, *Louis-Napoléon Bonaparte avant l'Empire* (Paris, 1951); Louis Napoleon, *The Political and Historical Works of Louis Napoleon Bonaparte* (New York, 1972); J. Savant, *L'énigme de la naissance de Napoléon III*, 2 vols. (Paris, 1971); F. A. Simpson, *The Rise of Louis Napoleon, 1808–1848* (London, 1925); H. Thirria, *Napoléon III avant l'Empire*, 2 vols. (Paris, 1895–1896).

Related entries: BONAPARTISM; COUP D'ETAT; *EXTINCTION DU PAUPERISME*; *DES IDEES NAPOLEONIENNES*; MATHILDE; MOCQUARD; MORNY; NAPOLEON III: HEALTH; PERSIGNY; PIETRI; PRINCE NAPOLEON; PRINCE PRESIDENT.

LOUIS NAPOLEON: WRITINGS. See *DES IDEES NAPOLEONIENNES*.

LOURDES, a small village on the Gave de Pau River near the Pyrenees where on 11 February 1858 Bernadette Soubirous (1844–1879), the illiterate child of a poor miller, saw a vision of the Virgin Mary in a grotto on the riverside. Instructed by the apparition, the young girl later discovered a miraculous spring (25 February). By March more than twenty-thousand persons accompanied her on her visits to the grotto. None but Bernadette, however, saw the apparition. On 25 March the vision pronounced, in the Lourdes dialect, "I am the Immaculate Conception" (the dogma of the immaculate conception had been proclaimed by Pope Pius IX on 8 December 1854). After sixteen appearances, the apparition appeared for the last time on 16 July 1858. The church, skeptical, appointed a commission (28 July) and waited, while the civil authorities tried to dampen public enthusiasm (the spring and grotto were closed "for hygienic reasons" from June to October 1858 on orders of the minister of education and religion, Gustave Rouland, and of the prefect of the Hautes-Pyrénées), clerical and anticlerical newspapers waged a press war, and the popularity of the site steadily grew.

Louis Veuillot defended Bernadette in his clerical newspaper, *L'Univers*, and visited the grotto in defiance of the law, as did the prince imperial's governess, Mme. Bruat. The first miraculous cure was reported in 1858. At length (September 1858) the government yielded to public opinion. After an interview with the archbiship of Auch in September 1858 at Biarritz, the emperor rescinded Rouland's order and sent the minister of state, Achille Fould, to Lourdes to ensure that the grotto was reopened. The mayor of Lourdes was replaced, and the church officially confirmed the miracle, approving a public cult of Our Lady of Lourdes (1862). Construction began of a gothic church on a rock overlooking the grotto (completed in 1871 at a cost of 2 million francs). Bernadette entered the convent of the Sisters of Charity and Christian Instruction at Nevers in 1865. She was beatified in 1925 and canonized in 1933. The site of her visions had become by the end of the Second Empire one of the major shrines of Catholicism, today visited by millions each year.

R. P. Cros, *Histoire de Notre Dame de Lourdes d'après les documents et les témoins*, 3 vols. (Paris, 1925–1927); R. Laurentin, *Lourdes: Histoire authentique des apparitions de Lourdes*, 6 vols. (Paris, 1961–1968); T. A. Kselman, *Miracles and Prophecies in Nineteenth-Century France* (New Brunswick, N.J., 1983); G. MacGrath, "Lourdes, 1858–1862," *Précis analytique des travaux de l'Académie des Sciences et Belles Lettres et Arts de Rouen* (1971–1972).

Related entry: GALLICANISM.

LOUVRE. See TUILERIES-LOUVRE.

LUXEMBOURG CRISIS, episode in the Franco-Prussian territorial compensation negotiations following Prussia's defeat of Austria in 1866 and the creation of the North German Confederation in 1866–1867. French demands for compensation—to balance Prussia's territorial expansion in Germany—initially centered on the Rhine frontier and were presented to Otto von Bismarck on 5 August 1866. Revelations about the secret talks appeared in the press on 10 August and made clear that Prussia would reject any alienation of German territory. Accordingly, the imperial government shifted the focus of its demands to Luxembourg (a property of the Dutch king) and to Belgium. Inspired in part by suggestions from the North German chancellor, Bismarck, France's minister to Prussia, comte Vincent Benedetti, drafted a treaty project based on specific demands formulated by Eugène Rouher, Napoleon III's minister of state, on behalf of the imperial government. By public convention Prussia and France were to agree to the acquisition of the Luxembourg grand duchy by France, with suitable compensation for the Dutch king. In a secret convention, which Benedetti ill-advisedly left in Bismarck's hands, Prussia was to agree to an eventual absorption of Belgium into France and, if necessary, to lend military support to such an undertaking (against Britain). Bismarck's delaying tactics, explained in part by his preoccupation with the constitutional and territorial reorganization of north Germany, prolonged the quest for compensation into the spring of 1867. Eager *à mettre les fers au feu*, the imperial government pressed the issue at The Hague. But while Britain and Austria were disposed to endorse the French acquisition of Luxembourg, Bismarck could ill afford the risk of public wrath should Prussia accede to the French demand for the federal fortress and for an area many thought to be German. When a formal Dutch inquiry at Berlin and an interpellation in the North German Parliament forced the Prussian government to take a stand, Bismarck voiced an implied opposition to the sale of Luxembourg to France. Under the circumstances, Napoleon III could not hope any longer for

Prussian adherence to the proposed treaty and for Dutch acquiescence to the transfer of Luxembourg. Although until 5 April the threat of war seemed to hang over the situation, the French emperor proved willing to accept a peaceful resolution of the conflict, to see the fortress dismantled, the Prussian garrison withdrawn, and the grand duchy neutralized in perpetuity under a European guarantee. A conference at London, proposed by France and convoked by King William III of the Netherlands in his capacity as the grand duke of Luxembourg, was attended (7–11 May) by representatives of Britain, Russia, Austria, Prussia, France, and Luxembourg. In a treaty dated 11 May 1867, the signatories pledged themselves to respect the neutrality of the grand duchy. Furthermore, they agreed that the city of Luxembourg would cease to be a federal fortress, that its fortifications would be demolished, and that orders for the withdrawal of the Prussian garrison would be issued immediately following ratification of the treaty, which was placed under a collective European guarantee. With these decisions, French compensation hopes were effectively ended, and French diplomacy had suffered a serious setback. Moreover, Prussian behavior during and after the treaty negotiations further exacerbated French susceptibilities. War, however, had been averted, if only for the moment.

J. Dontenville, "L'affaire du Luxembourg en 1866–1867: Documents nouveaux," *Revue des études historiques* 93 *(1927),* and "La France, la Prusse, et l'Allemagne au lendemain de Sadowa," *Nouvelle revue* 51 (1921); M. R. D. Foot, "Great Britain and Luxemburg, 1867," *EHR* 67 (1952); E. Haag, "Was wollte Bismarck mit der Luxemburger Affäre, 1867?" *Hémecht,* no. 1 (1971); G. Pagès, "L'affaire du Luxembourg," *RHMC,* 1 (1926).

Willard Allen Fletcher

Related entries: ARMY REFORM; BENEDETTI; CONGRESS POLICY; NATIONALITIES; PUBLIC OPINION; SADOWA.

M

MACMAHON, MARIE EDME PATRICE MAURICE, COMTE DE (1808–1893), duc de Magenta, marshal of France, governor of Algeria, disastrously defeated at Sedan in the Franco-Prussian War; born at Sully (Saône-et-Loire), 13 July 1808, to a royalist family of Irish origin. MacMahon's father was a peer of France and a personal friend of Charles X. Destined for the priesthood, he studied briefly at the seminary of Autun, but soon left to begin a military career. He graduated fourth in his class from Saint Cyr (1827) and took part in the Algiers expedition of 1830, the siege of Antwerp (1832), and various Algerian campaigns. A captain in 1833, MacMahon was named to the Legion of Honor in 1837 for his part in the assault on Constantine. His energy and bravery through twenty years in Algeria brought him a rapid advancement: general of brigade, 12 June 1848; commander of the Legion of Honor, 1849; general of division, 6 July 1852; and grand officer of the Legion of Honor, 10 August 1853.

It was the Crimean War, however, that established MacMahon's reputation as France's outstanding soldier. Sent to the Crimea in August 1855 to command the First Division in the corps of General Pierre Bosquet (1810–1861), he found his forces at the most advanced angle of the siege lines. On 8 September he personally led the assault that took the Malakov Tower, Sebastopol's key defense. MacMahon then defended the position against repeated counterattacks ("J'y suis, j'y reste"), forcing the Russians to yield the city. For this exploit he was named grand cross of the Legion of Honor (22 September) and, somewhat later, senator (24 June 1856). More sympathetic to the monarchy than to the Empire, uninvolved in the coup d'état of December 1851, MacMahon was nevertheless willing to serve whatever regime existed. He was not entirely subservient, however. In February 1858, he was the only senator to vote against the sweeping general security law passed following the attempt on Napoleon III's life by Felice Orsini.

After a brilliant role in Marshal Jacques Louis Randon's campaign against insurrection in the Kabylia (Algeria) in 1857 (he commanded the Second Division), MacMahon was named military commander of the colony (31 August 1858), but soon he was recalled to participate in the Italian War of the following year as commander of the Second Corps of the Army of Italy. He led the first

French troops across the Ticino River on 2 June 1859 and arrived on the battlefield of Magenta in time to play an important part in the French victory and perhaps to save Napoleon III and his Guards from being taken prisoner by the Austrians (4 June). MacMahon was named marshal of France and duc de Magenta the following day. On 24 June he contributed to the victory of Solférino. Now firmly established in the service of the Empire, MacMahon represented the French emperor, with considerable pomp, at the coronation of King William I of Prussia (18 October 1861). A year later he succeeded Marshal François Canrobert as commander of the Third Corps at Nancy (14 October 1862).

On 1 September 1864 MacMahon was named to succeed Marshal Aimable Pélissier as governor of Algeria. The appointment brought to a total of 185,000 francs per year the stipends he drew from his various posts. But he was required to enact the policies related to Napoleon III's dream of converting the colony into an Arab Kingdom (*royaume arabe*). Against resistance from the *colons* and from the church, led by Charles Martial Lavigerie (1825–1892), archbishop of Algiers, MacMahon displayed a heavy hand, especially concerning the press. Famine and cholera (1867–1868) further complicated the situation, as did continued insurrection. The Liberal Empire at length abandoned the experiment and returned Algeria to full colonial status. MacMahon offered to resign in March and June 1870, but his resignation was not accepted.

The outbreak of war with Prussia in July 1870 brought MacMahon once more to the forefront. In command of the First Corps of the Army of the Rhine, he soon fell victim, as did the other French generals, to chaotic organization and inexperience in maneuvering great masses of troops, with the result that he was crushed by overwhelming numbers at Reichshoffen and Froeschwiller (6 August) and forced to fall back to Châlons with barely eighteen thousand men. Heavily reinforced and placed in command of the new army by Napoleon III who was too ill to continue in the field, MacMahon agreed with the emperor on the wisdom of falling back on Paris. He was dissuaded, however, by politically motivated orders from the capital and by receipt of word from Marshal Achille Bazaine, besieged at Metz, that he was about to attempt to break through the enemy's line. On 23 August MacMahon marched toward Metz; four days later, foreseeing the developing trap, he would have turned back but was urged on by the government of the comte de Palikao (1796–1878). On 1 September he was decisively defeated by a numerically superior force near Sedan. Seriously wounded, the marshal was forced to surrender command. With the capitulation of the city, he entered internment in Germany, returning to France in March 1871 to commence a distinguished career under the Third Republic. MacMahon died at Paris, 17 October 1893.

L. Laforge, *Histoire complète de MacMahon*, 3 vols. (Paris, 1898); J. Silvestre de Sacy, *Le Maréchal MacMahon, duc de Magenta (1808–1893)* (Paris, 1960).

Related entries: ALGERIA; BAZAINE; CANROBERT; CRIMEAN WAR; FRANCO-PRUSSIAN WAR; ITALIAN WAR; NIEL; PELISSIER; RANDON; SAINT-ARNAUD; SEDAN; VAILLANT.

MAGNE, PIERRE (1806–1879), politician and minister; with Eugène Rouher and Jules Baroche responsible for much of the work of government of the Second Empire; born at Périgueux 3 December 1806 of a poor and obscure family. Magne's father was an artisan. Under the patronage of General Thomas Bugeaud, he became a lawyer at Périgueux and was elected to the Chamber of Deputies in 1843 and 1846. Favorable to François Guizot (1787–1874), he functioned with high competence in several subcabinet posts. Lacking ideology, Magne found it possible to serve any government that would maintain order and advance the interests of France. He rallied to Louis Napoleon after the Revolution of 1848, served him following his election as president in December 1848, and approved the coup d'état of December 1851 although not taking part in it. On 3 December 1851 Magne was appointed minister of public works in the first cabinet following the coup d'état but resigned shortly after (22 January) as a protest against the decrees confiscating property of the Orleans family in France. His parting from the prince president was amicable, however. On 25 January he was named to the Conseil d'Etat and made president of a section. This tenure was also brief, for on 29 July 1852 Magne was once again named minister of public works, resigning the Corps Législatif seat that he had won overwhelmingly in a Dordogne by-election of 6 July (his son-in-law was later elected to that body). He was named senator 31 December 1852 and was elected to the Conseil Général of the Dordogne. On 3 February 1855 he exchanged the Ministry of Public Works for that of Finance, which he surrendered when named on 26 October 1860 one of two ministers without portfolio, with special responsibility for defending before the legislative bodies government policies regarding Algeria, public works, and finance. In disaccord with Achille Fould, Magne resigned 31 March 1863. He was appointed the next day to the Conseil Privé. He returned to the Finance Ministry 13 November 1867 and at the beginning of 1868 undertook a major loan of over 400 million francs required to finance reorganization of the French army. Although reappointed to the cabinet that followed Napoleon III's announcement of new political reforms in July 1869, Magne was unacceptable to Louis Buffet and to the liberal opposition, and he retired 27 December 1869, although Emile Ollivier would have preferred him to Buffet as finance minister in the cabinet of 2 January 1870. The outbreak of war with Prussia, which he regarded as folly, and the subsequent overthrow of Ollivier's government brought Magne back to the Finance Ministry on 10 August 1870. He presided over the successful launching of a 750 million franc war loan. But 4 September and the fall of the Empire soon followed.

Magne was an excellent example of the longevity of Napoleon III's ministers. He exemplified other of their characteristics as well: honesty (although he was well rewarded for his services, receiving as a gift a furnished house in Paris), competence, conscientiousness, industriousness, and devotion to the emperor. Rouher, a demanding critic, put him at the head of his list of ministerial possibilities in 1867. Magne was conservative in economics and politics. With Rouher and Jean Mocquard, he helped to block a projected expansion of the

Crédit Mobilier in 1855; with Fould he urged in 1858 the purchase by the state of four canals as a counterweight to the railroad companies; with Adolphe Billault he opposed in cabinet the 1860 commercial treaty with Britain, defending the protectionist position; with Alexandre Walewski and Marshal Jacques Louis Randon (the Empress Eugénie's "clan") he favored indefinite French occupation of Rome and in 1862 helped to bring about the dismissal of Foreign Minister Edouard Thouvenel. But while Magne throughout the 1860s joined Fould, Baroche, and Rouher in resisting Napoleon III's efforts to introduce political reforms and while he favored the church as a force for order, he did not lack flexibility. He sent his daughter to one of the new high schools for girls established by the minister of education, Victor Duruy, from the end of 1867 and from July 1869 made a conscientious effort to carry out the emperor's reform intentions. Magne recommended Ollivier to lead the first government of the "parliamentary Empire," although he soon concluded that the eloquent former republican was not up to the task. Above all, Magne was a faithful servitor. A regular house guest at Compiègne, he spoke frankly and without reserve to both Napoleon III and Eugénie, but he refused to abandon the former emperor after the fall of the Empire. Magne was elected to the National Assembly of the Third Republic. Monarchist in sympathy, he even served once more (1873–1874) as finance minister. He died at his Chateau de Montaigne (Dordogne) 17 February 1879.

J. Durieux, *Le ministre Pierre Magne, 1806–1879, d'après ses lettres et souvenirs*, 2 vols. (Paris, 1929); J. Saint-Martin, "A propos de Pierre Magne," *Bulletin de la Société Historique et Archéologique du Périgord* 88 (1961); J. Secret, "Victor Hugo et Pierre Magne," *Bulletin de la Société Historique et Archéologique du Périgord* 99 (1972).

Related entries: BAROCHE; BILLAULT; FOULD; GOVERNMENT FINANCE; OLLIVIER; REFORM; ROUHER.

MANET, EDOUARD (1832–1883), painter; born at Paris 23 January 1832, the son of a high official in the Ministry of Justice. Manet early expressed a desire to pursue a career as an artist despite his family's wishes that he study law. His attempts at becoming a naval officer were unsuccessful, thus allowing him the opportunity to undertake artistic studies (1850) in the studio of Thomas Couture. He also attended the Académie Suisse in the evenings, while on Sundays he painted and sketched in the Forest of Fontainebleau. During the 1850s, Manet copied works in the Louvre of the old masters such as Tintoretto, Rubens, and Velasquez and obtained permission from Eugène Delacroix to copy his *Dante and Virgil in Hell*, then in Luxembourg. His reflective and eclectic attitude to the art of the past during this early period was augmented by travels to Italy in 1853, again in 1856, as well as to Belgium, Holland, Germany, and Austria. Having left Couture's studio in 1856 to establish one of his own, Manet continued to seek his advice on occasion.

Manet's first major work, *The Absinthe Drinker* (Ny Carlsberg Glyptotek, Copenhagen), was refused by the jury of the Salon of 1859. *The Absinthe Drinker* presaged several concerns that would occupy Manet's attention to a greater degree in the 1860s. The subject matter, while recalling Dutch genre scenes of the seventeenth century, emerged from a more modern attitude to the contemporary social milieu. Avoiding the anecdotal and without moralistic content, the painting presents the motif with honesty and directness. It was during the 1860s that Manet achieved some success and recognition. Two of his works, for which he was awarded an honorable mention, were accepted and well received at the Salon of 1861. *The Spanish Singer* (1860, Metropolitan Museum, New York), exhibited in the 1861 Salon, is one of the first examples of Manet's interest in Spanish themes. More daring in composition and painterly skills is the work of the following year, *Mademoiselle Victorine in the Costume of an Espada* (1862, Metropolitan Museum of Art, New York). Spanish culture had achieved popularity during the reign of Empress Eugénie, and Manet was inspired by the Spanish dancers, singers, and bullfighters, who made a considerable impression on Parisian society. *Mademoiselle Victorine* demonstrates several of Manet's interests during this time, as well as the development of his facture. A major source typical for this period in Manet's oeuvre, and this painting in particular, is Goya's series of etchings, the *Tauromaquia*. The bullfighters and bulls in the middle distance of Manet's painting are a direct quotation. What is unique to Manet is the startling composition and the form. The motifs seem to be isolated fragments not linked by a clearly readable spatial position which indeed appears to be flattened. Victorine is placed in a position very close to viewers, confronting them with her direct gaze. Her form is silhouetted and also rather flattened. Manet works with contrasts of black and white, dark and light, avoiding tonal gradations and thus interior modeling. The brushwork is clearly evident in several areas and especially in the cape she holds, thus animating the cape and the painting as a whole. Having been rejected by the Salon of 1863, this painting was exhibited in the Salon des Refusés, established in 1863 to accommodate those works (in the hundreds) not accepted by the official Salon. *Luncheon on the Grass* (1863, Louvre, Paris), another of the works rejected by the official Salon and shown in the Salon des Refusés, was the first of several paintings by Manet considered scandalous by the public and some of the critics. With its two women, one clothed, one naked, and two fully dressed men, it provoked such abusive comments, on both moral and aesthetic grounds, as "shameless" and "slipshod." What was completely disregarded were its links with Raphael, Giorgione, and the tradition of female nudes in a landscape setting. The overt realism and frankness of the four participants and their somewhat ambiguous activity aroused indignation against what was considered blatant effrontery. The subject matter seemed neither mythological nor historical, nor was it ennobling.

Negative reaction did not deter Manet from further exploring contemporary subject matter ("one must be of one's time"). *Olympia* (1863, Louvre), surprisingly accepted in the Salon of 1865, demonstrates Manet's brilliant use of free and spontaneous brushwork, especially in the bedding and bouquet of flowers, and his daring composition and colorism. The contrasts of whites against rich browns and blacks create a heightened sense of immediacy and vibrancy.

Olympia, for which Victorine Meurend served as model, as she had done for the nude female in *Luncheon on the Grass*, was considered to be shocking, a representation of an unidealized, rather thin courtesan, brazenly staring at the viewer, who was suddenly made to feel too close to what should have been a private and discreet moment. This public flaunting of private affairs was met with moral indignation, despite Manet's truthfulness and the actuality of this aspect of modern Parisian life. So vociferous was the critical response that the work was rehung in an almost inaccessible location. That Manet was giving a modern interpretation to a long-standing tradition was generally ignored. Manet's sources of inspiration, specifically Titian's *Venus of Urbino*, but even more recently the *Odalisques* of Dominique Ingres and Eugène Delacroix, were disregarded by the writers of the period. Derogatory comments focused on the meaning and appropriateness of the cat, the black servant, and the provocative nakedness, baseness, and lack of nobility of Olympia herself. This reception can be contrasted with that given to Thomas Couture's *The Modern Courtisan*, whose subject matter was allegorized and thus met with no reproach. The title *Olympia*, as well as the poem by Zacharie Astruc (1837–1907), part of which Manet attached to the painting, rather than clarifying the subject matter contributed to the enigma and indeed was interpreted as a further affront. More recent authors, however, have recognized contemporary literary sources in *Olympia* and affinities to passages in Charles Baudelaire's *Les fleurs du mal*, published in 1857. Manet and Baudelaire were close companions, their friendship having begun in 1860, and there is little doubt that they discussed aesthetic matters and that Manet was familiar with Baudelaire's writings. The motifs of the cat, the Negress, and the description of female beauty in Baudelaire's poems can be linked with those in *Olympia*, not as illustrations for the poetry but as a parallel expression. Other references to an Olympia in the writings of the period appear, for example, in Alexandre Dumas fils' *La dame aux camélias*, published in 1848, where Olympe is Marguerite Gautier's rival, and also in Emile Augier's play *Le mariage d'O-lympe*, performed in 1855.

In 1866, although *The Fifer* (Louvre) was rejected by the Salon, Manet's work was admired for its originality and modernity and perceptively analyzed by Emile Zola. Writing for *L'événement*, Zola defended Manet's paintings, especially *Olympia* and *The Fifer*, to such a degree that he was forced to resign. Manet's *Portrait of Zola* (1868, Louvre) was not only a tribute to Zola (now become a close friend) for his public support but also demonstrated Manet's further stylistic developments, as well as clearly indicating a new source of inspiration. Critics who complained of the awkwardness of the perspective and the flatness of the figure failed to notice the clues to a more insightful interpretation. In the upper right corner, Manet combined a reproduction of his own *Olympia*, an engraving of Velasquez' *Triumph of Bacchus* (Manet visited Spain in 1865 and had more direct contact with the Spanish masters), and, audaciously, a Japanese woodblock print by Utagawa Kuniaki. The Japanese screen on the left reiterates the important stimulus that Japanese treatment of space and large flat areas of color were for Manet and later for the Impressionists.

In theme, *The Execution of Emperor Maximilian* (1867, Stadtische Kunsthalle, Mannheim) deals with a contemporary event, the recent death of Maximilian, brother of Francis Joseph of Austria, who had been proclaimed emperor of Mexico after the invasion of French troops sent by Napoleon III. While recalling Goya's masterpiece, *The Third of May, 1808*, Manet's modern work had the abruptness and impact of a particular moment, caught just as it was happening. Facts and details were based on newspaper accounts and photographs, another new stimulus for avant-garde artists of the period. The *Execution* did not meet with much success in Paris, where it was taken as a comment on the incompetence of the administration in foreign affairs (the soldiers were wearing French uniforms). It was eventually exhibited in New York in 1879 and in Boston in 1880 by the singer Emilie Ambre while on a concert tour. In the United States it found a more receptive audience.

Manet's frustration and disappointment with the Salon and with the fine arts section of the Paris Exposition Universelle of 1867 prompted him in that year to organize an exhibition of fifty of his works in a temporary structure on the place de l'Alma, much as Gustave Courbet had done in 1855. The exhibition brought further disappointment since it was ignored by most critics and became the target for three pages of caricatures in a journal. Despite the many setbacks and adverse criticism, Manet persisted and indeed was beginning to gain recognition from a small group of young artists—the Batignolles group, which included Claude Monet, Alfred Sisley (1839–1899), Pierre Auguste Renoir, Edgar Degas, Camille Pissarro, and Paul Cézanne (1839–1906) among others— who all met at the Café Guerbois toward the end of the decade. Both as a forerunner of and an influence on the Impressionists in the 1870s and as a recipient of some of their ideas, which he incorporated in his own works, Manet remained a central figure of the art scene of Paris during the latter half of the Second Empire. He died at Paris, 30 April 1883, of complications resulting from tertiary syphilis.

F. Cachin and C. Moffet, eds., *Manet, 1832–1883* (New York, 1983); K. Champa, ed., *Edouard Manet and the "Execution of Maximilian"* (Providence, R.I., 1981); P. Courthion, *Edouard Manet* (New York, 1962 and 1978); G. H. Hamilton, *Manet and His Critics* (New York, 1969); A. Coffin Hanson, *Manet and the Modern Tradition* (New Haven, 1977); H. Perruchet, *La vie de Manet* (Paris, 1959); T. Reff, *Manet: Olympia* (New York, 1976), and *Manet and the Modern World* (Chicago, 1983); R. Rosenblum and H. W. Janson, *19th-Century Art* (New York, 1984).

Beverley Giblon

Related entries: BAUDELAIRE; DEGAS; INTERNATIONAL EXPOSITIONS; MONET; PISSARRO; RENOIR; SALON DES REFUSES; ZOLA.

MARET, HENRI (1805–1884), bishop, theologian, educator; born at Meyrueis (Lozère), 20 April 1805. Ordained in 1830 after having studied at the seminaries of Issy, where he knew Père Lacordaire, and of Saint-Sulpice, Maret was an obscure vicar in Paris when his *Essai sur le panthéisme dans les sociétés modernes* (1839) revealed him as a cogent thinker ready to do battle in behalf of orthodoxy against the prevailing eclecticism of the University. His tone was neither abrasive nor intransigent. One of his major concerns was the growing estrangement between Catholicism and the intellectual currents of his day. His book secured for him a professorship of dogmatics at the Sorbonne (1841). Maret's talents, combined with his enthusiastic support for Louis Napoleon, led to his being appointed in 1853 dean of the Sorbonne's theological faculty. In this position, he worked to attract the most capable men to his staff, such as Louis Bautain (1796–1867) and Alphonse Gratry (1805–1872), and to promote an improvement in clerical education in France, a real need. Most of the clergy were unaware of the science of criticism or of advances in the natural sciences. The church's two faculties of theology, the one at the Sorbonne and the other at Toulouse, suffered from state control and papal distrust. Many bishops hesitated to send young priests to them, despite the mediocrity of seminary education, for fear they might be tainted by the Gallicanism associated with both faculties. One of Maret's achievements was his success in obtaining Vatican recognition of the Sorbonne faculty, which conferred on it an ecclesiastical status previously lacking.

Influenced in part by the Catholic socialist Philippe Buchez (1796–1865), Maret combined his sensitivity to the academic deficiencies of the French church with a social awareness equally rare among his clerical colleagues. He joined with Lacordaire and Frédéric Ozanam (1813–1853) in launching *L'ère nouvelle* in April 1848, a paper dedicated to democracy and social justice that floundered in 1849 before episcopal hostility and the general reaction against the revolutions of 1848. The staff of the Catholic *L'Univers* dubbed the *Ere nouvelle* the *Erreur nouvelle*. Both Maret and *L'Univers* welcomed the rise of Louis Napoleon, from whom they expected support for the religious elements in society, but Maret, unlike *L'Univers*, also viewed him as an authentic heir of the French Revolution.

Maret established close relations with Gustave Rouland, Napoleon's pro-Gallican minister of religion and public instruction. He functioned as a theological adviser to Rouland and to Napoleon III himself and was able to influence the regime's nomination of bishops. From the beginning Maret openly backed Napoleon's Italian policy. The antipathy of most liberal as well as conservative Catholic leaders to the Risorgimento prompted him to comment: "Liberals in France, absolutists in Italy." When the government nominated him to the see of Vannes (1860), Pius IX, who disliked both his Gallicanism and his liberalism, refused confirmation. A compromise in 1861 made Maret titular bishop of Sura. In the hope that it might lead to a church policy more compatible with modern ideas, Maret was one of the earliest advocates of the convocation of a general council but rejected the subsequent promulgation by the Vatican Council (1869–1870) of the doctrine of papal infallibility. In 1869 he published, thanks to government subsidies, his two-volume *Du concile générale et de la paix reli-*

gieuse, in which he argued in a respectful manner and with copious historical citation that the spiritual leadership of the Catholic church did not require absolutism; the governmental tradition of the church harbored aristocratic, even democratic, as well as monarchial elements, the latter requiring qualification by the former. Although it took the pope to summon the episcopate to make a solemn declaration, Maret insisted, infallibility could not be ascribed to pronouncements unless they rested on the consent, at least tacit, of the bishops. Infallibility did not pertain to the pope himself nor was it necessary for his authority. Maret attended Vatican Council I where he saw his Gallican principles repudiated. He submitted to the council's decision in a letter to Pius IX of October 1870. He died at Paris, 16 June 1884.

G. Bazin, *Vie de Mgr Maret, évêque de Sura, son temps et ses oeuvres*, 3 vols. (Paris, 1891); C. Bressolette, *L'Abbé Maret: le combat d'un théologien pour une démocratie chrétienne, 1830–1851* (Paris, 1977); "Maret and Gratry," in B. Reardon, *Liberalism and Tradition: Aspects of Catholic Thought in Nineteenth-Century France* (London, 1975); A. Riccardi, *Neo-galicanesimo e cattolicismo borghese: Henri Maret e il Concilio Vaticano I* (Bologna, 1976); R. Thysman, "Le Gallicanisme de Mgr. M. et l'influence de Bossuet," *RHE* 52 (1957).

Raymond L. Cummings

Related entries: DUPANLOUP; GALLICANISM; INFALLIBILITY, DOCTRINE OF; LACORDAIRE; SOCIAL CATHOLICISM; VATICAN COUNCIL.

MARINONI, HIPPOLYTE (1823–1904), developer for France of the modern rotary printing press, which, using rolls of paper, could print on both sides, cut, and fold; born at Givry-Courty (Seine-et-Marne), 8 September 1823, the son of a police sergeant. Marinoni began his career as apprentice in a small machine shop and proved so quick, clever, and full of inventive promise that he was quickly promoted by his master, Gaveau, to machinist and then foreman. Gaveau had built the first practical French cylinder machines for printing (used by *Le national* in 1831), and by 1848 the two men, working in concert, had constructed a four-feeder cylinder machine for Emile de Girardin's newspaper *La presse*, which could print ten thousand papers per hour (sixteen thousand uncut and unfolded). Gaveau's workshop grew into one of the larger French factories.

In 1854, Marinoni established his own factory for the manufacture of printing presses. Under the patronage of Girardin, champion of the new mass press, the engineer improved the machinery used in the various operations of printing the daily news. His goal was to provide the industry with new inventions that would both improve the quality and lower the price of newspapers. He invented a more efficient lithographic machine. In 1866–1867 he created a high-quality rotary press with six cylinders that could print twenty thousand papers per hour, and was employed by *La liberté*. In 1872 a web-fed rotary machine was used by *La liberté* to double that production. These improved presses were exploited to their fullest advantage on *Le petit journal*. Marinoni also created a polychrome press using six colors, which printed the *Supplément illustré du Petit journal*. In 1883, having assumed nine years earlier the post of director of *Le petit journal*, he invented an even more advanced model of the rotary press, which became the forerunner of the modern offset press. His inventions were adopted and adapted throughout the world, earning him the Legion of Honor (1875) and an immense fortune. He died in 1904.

Natalie Isser

Related entries: GIRARDIN; *PETIT JOURNAL.*

MARKET, CENTRAL. See LES HALLES.

MARTIN, PIERRE EMILE (1824–1915), inventor and industrialist; born at Bourges, 18 August 1824. Martin's father, Emile, scion of an iron-making family, operated a forge at Fourchambault (near Nevers) and then at Sireuil (near Angoulême in the Charente). The younger Martin, after studying at the Ecole des Mines, went to work for his father and directed the Forges de Sireuil from 1854 to 1883. Until the late 1850s, the only practical way of making steel was the method invented by Sir Henry Bessemer in 1854-1855. The Bessemer process burned the carbon from pig iron by blasting hot air through the molten metal (hence "blast furnace"). In use by 1858, the Bessemer process had a number of shortcomings, including the lack of control, relative impurity of the steel, and the long furnace time required.

In 1856 the German-born English engineer, Sir William Siemens, invented a different type of furnace, capable of attaining a very high temperature. By the 1860s both the Bessemer process and Siemens' open-hearth furnace were in use in France. Martin entered into relations with Siemens in 1862 and about 1863 was licensed to build an open-hearth furnace (at Sireuil, 1864). Siemens developed his own process, but so did Martin. The latter's method, worked out by 1865, involved the mixing together of scrap steel and pig iron. Products made in this way won a gold medal at the Paris international exposition of 1867. By 1870 some ten forges were using Martin's process; in the 1930s half the world's steel would be so made (and one-third as late as 1963). Martin's patents were challenged, however, and the subsequent litigation reduced him to near poverty. When he was eighty-three, the Comité des Forges of France instituted a fund for him to which all the world's major steel-making companies contributed. The remarkable growth of the French steel industry during the Second Empire owed much to Martin. By 1870 that industry was producing iron and steel in sufficient quantities and at low enough cost to make possible its widespread use in architecture, naval construction, and railroads. Martin died at Fourchambault, 23 May 1915.

G. Husson, "Un retour aux sources de l'industrie: L'oeuvre de Pierre Martin: De la forge de précurseur de Sireuil aux aciéries de 1963," *RHS* 4 (1963); Sireuil, Le Comité de la Fête du Centenaire, *L'invention du procédé Martin* (Sireuil, 1963); A. Thuillier, *Un grand chef d'industrie au XIXe siècle: Emile Martin* (Nevers, 1967).

Related entries: COMITE DES FORGES; SCHNEIDER, E.

MATHILDE, PRINCESS LAETITIA WILHELMINE (1820–1904), first cousin of Louis Napoleon Bonaparte and, when he had become emperor, a princess and art patron of the Second Empire; born at Trieste, 27 May 1820. Mathilde's father was Jérôme Bonaparte (then prince de Montfort), youngest brother of Napoleon I and former king of Westphalia. Her mother was Catherine of Württemberg, daughter of King Frederick of Württemberg. Her brother, Joseph Charles Paul, would be known under the Second Empire simply as Prince Napoleon. At Rome the new Bonaparte generation played together as children, but visits by Mathilde to Louis Napoleon and his mother, Hortense, at Arenenberg (Switzerland) in November 1835 and April–May 1836 led to romance and to the engagement of Mathilde and Louis Napoleon. The indecision of the latter's father, Louis Bonaparte, and difficulties concerning a dowry delayed the wedding. Louis Napoleon's unsuccessful insurrection attempt at Boulogne in October 1840 ended all consideration of the match. In fact, Mathilde failed even to write to her former fiancé during his exile in America (1837).

On 10 October 1841 the comtesse de Montfort, as she was then styled, married at Florence a dissolute and sadistic but very rich Russian, Anatole Demidov. She was perhaps persuaded to enter the marriage by her father's financial problems but did so willingly. It was a disastrous alliance, childless, and ended by separation in December 1845. As Demidov's wife, Mathilde was able to settle in France (1841) despite a law excluding the Bonapartes, and to live comfortably there after the separation on the allowance of 200,000 rubles, which the sympathetic czar had secured for her. She never again saw her husband. An ardent bonapartist from childhood, Mathilde worked for Louis Napoleon's political success before his election as president in December 1848, and it is possible that in 1850 he renewed his offer of marriage. By Mathilde's account, she declined. In fact, she had already entered into a liaison (which would last until 1870) with the sculptor Emilien de Nieuwerkerke (1811–1892), son of a Dutch officer. She did not wish to be an empress and perhaps sensed the incompatibility between herself and her cousin. However, from 1849 through 1852 she served as hostess at the Elysée and (after December 1851) at the Tuileries Palace. She was one of those who opposed the Orleans decrees. On the restoration of the Empire in December 1852, Mathilde received the title *Altesse* and an income of 200,000 francs per year (later increased to 500,000), with which she purchased a country house, Saint Gratien, an hour from Paris near Lake d'Enghien. She vigorously but unsuccessfully opposed the marriage in 1853 of Napoleon III and Eugénie de Montijo, whom she did not consider to be suitable for the throne and whom she subsequently disliked with intensity.

The role Mathilde chose for herself was artistic, not political. She had no influence over the emperor, and although they remained friends, she saw him only a few times each year. But at her Paris mansion (rue de Courcelles, now destroyed) and at Saint Gratien, she established one of the great salons of the nineteenth century, gathering together the artists, writers, actors, and actresses of the day, encouraging their works, and serving as a conduit for the distribution of honors and awards (Nieuwerkerke under her aegis became director of museums and eventually superintendent of fine arts). It was a valuable service for a regime that wanted to patronize the arts but whose emperor and empress had little knowledge or appreciation of them. Mathilde, although she did not enjoy music, was herself a talented painter, a pupil of Eugène Giraud (1806–1881). She exhibited watercolors in 1859, 1861, 1863, and 1865, winning a third-class medal in 1865. Among her close friends were Charles Gounod, Théophile Gautier (her "accredited poet" and librarian), Alexandre Dumas père and fils, the playwright François Ponsard (1814–1867), Jules and Edmond Goncourt, Gustave Flaubert, Louis de Viel-Castel (1800–1887), and Charles Augustin Sainte-Beuve. She saw Sainte-Beuve every week and consulted him on her private affairs. And yet she did not hesitate to break with him violently and finally when in the last year of his life he became literary critic for an opposition newspaper, *Le temps*. Mathilde was, in fact, always ready to sacrifice even the closest and longest friendship to the devotion to bonapartism that colored her life. When the Empire fell in September 1870, she made her way to Belgium, returning after the war (1872) to Paris and to Saint Gratien. She died at Paris, 2 January 1904.

A. Augustin-Thierry, *La Princesse Mathilde* (Paris, 1950); A. de Gaigneron, "Le salon de la Princesse Mathilde, rendez-vous du tout-Paris des arts sous le Second Empire," CA, no. 310 (December 1977); J. Kühn, *La Princesse Mathilde, 1820–1904, d'après des papiers de la famille royale de Wurtemberg et autres documents inédits*, trans. by J. G. Guidau (Paris, 1935); M. Castillon du Perron, *La Princesse Mathilde: Un règne féminin sous le Second Empire* (Paris, 1953); M. Querlin, *Le Princesse Mathilde* (Lausanne, 1966); J. Richardson, *Princess Mathilde* (London, 1969).

Related entries: BONAPARTISM; LOUIS NAPOLEON; PRINCE NAPOLEON; SAINTE-BEUVE; SECOND EMPIRE.

MAUPAS, CHARLEMAGNE EMILE DE (1818–1888), executant of the coup d'état of December 1851, minister of police, and senator; born at Bar-sur-Aube, 8 December 1818. Maupas' father, Memmie Rose Maupas (1799–1861), inherited a large fortune derived from the acquisition and sale of confiscated property during the Revolution. He attached himself to Louis Napoleon Bonaparte's cause following the coup d'état (and added "de" to his name), was elected as an official candidate to the Corps Législatif in 1852 and again in 1857, became a *conseiller général* of the Aube, was named knight of the Legion of Honor, and died in May 1861. Charlemagne Emile de Maupas studied law at Paris. He served as subprefect at Uzès (1845) and Beaune (1847) but was retired by the provisional government following the Revolution of 1848. He joined his fortunes to those of Louis Napoleon, who undoubtedly saw advantage to be gained from the young bureaucrat's ambition and lack of scruples. Following Louis Napoleon's election as president of the Second Republic in December 1848, Maupas was successively appointed subprefect at Boulogne-sur-Mer (1849), prefect of the Allier (1849), and prefect of the Haute-Garonne (1850). On 27 October 1851 he replaced Pierre Carlier (1799–1858) as Paris prefect of police.

Maupas was intimately involved in preparing and executing the coup d'état, during which he seems to have shown much less *sang froid* than the minister of the interior, Auguste de Morny, who distrusted and detested his colleague. But on 22 January 1852 Napoleon III named Maupas to head the newly created Ministry of Police, instructing him to "faire parvenir jusqu'au prince la vérité qu'on s'efforce trop souvent de tenir éloignée du pouvoir." His task, the new minister informed his agents, was to "know everything." Theoretically the Ministry of Police had at its disposal the National Guard, the Republican Guard of Paris, and the agents of police and the gendarmerie throughout France. But the minister of war, Leroy de Saint-Arnaud, resisted giving up control of the latter. Maupas' ambition (he established a network of commissars), his unscrupulousness (he openly admitted forging documents to secure condemnation of political enemies), his heavy hand (he issued ninety-one *avertissements* to the press between January 1852 and June 1853 and in 1853 arrested twenty-one persons, including several journalists, proposing to transport them without trial to Africa) brought into the field against him a coalition of enemies, including Victor Fialin Persigny, the minister of the interior, whose prefects resented loss of control of their police; Saint-Arnaud; Pierre Marie Pietri, the Paris prefect of police; Emile de Girardin, who courageously protested the arrests of journalists; and Eugène Rouher. It seems likely that Maupas delivered himself to his enemies when, attempting to bolster his position by staging a riot, he employed an *agent provocateur* whose testimony Rouher used to persuade Napoleon III to suppress the Ministry of Police (21 June 1853). That same day the former minister was named, in compensation, to the Senate. Maupas never again played an important political role. Sent as ambassador to Naples, he was replaced there in April 1854 (when the post became of some importance following the outbreak of the Crimean War) by Edmond de la Cour (1805–1873). At the end of September 1860, Maupas was named prefect of the Bouches-du-Rhône, a position he held until relieved at his own request in December 1866. On 28 December 1866 he was named grand cross of the Legion of Honor (knight, 1849; commander, 2 March 1852; grand officer, 14 August 1862).

In the Senate Maupas was noted as a defender of the authoritarian Empire and of the dynasty. Asked to be *rapporteur* of the proposed law on public meetings (coalitions law), he declined in order to be free to attack it, which he did vehemently at the end of May 1868. On 5 February 1869 he interpellated the government on the abuses he said had arisen from the relatively liberal 1868 law on the press. And yet, whether from a sense of inevitability or out of hatred of Rouher, Maupas in early 1869 announced his conversion to parliamentary government (ministerial responsibility) as a means of shielding the person of the emperor. The revolution of 4 September 1870 retired him to private life, from which he emerged in 1876 and 1877 to seek, unsuccessfully, election to the Senate before rallying to Boulangisme. Maupas died at Paris, 18 June 1888.

C. E. de Maupas, *Mémoires du Second Empire* (Paris, 1884–1885); H. C. Payne, *The Police State of Louis Napoleon Bonaparte, 1851–1860* (Seattle, 1966); V. Wright, "Les préfets de police sous le Second Empire," in J. Aubert et al., *L'état et sa police en France, 1789–1914* (Geneva, 1979).

Related entries: AUTHORITARIAN EMPIRE; COUP D'ETAT; PIETRI; PREFECTS.

MEDIATION PROPOSALS (U.S. Civil War), the two diplomatic efforts made by France to mediate the U.S. Civil War. The first (30 October 1862), addressed to Great Britain and Russia, proposed a joint recommendation to the belligerents to establish a six-month truce during which all military action on land and sea should cease and the Southern ports should be opened to commerce. Both governments declined the French overture. The second (9 January 1863) was a unilateral offer of French good offices to the United States to establish "conversations between the belligerent parties" without a truce. The offer was rejected by Washington. The first proposal implied that the three European powers could not accept rejection of their offer (most likely by the United States) and would react to such a rejection by some intervention in the war (probably diplomatic recognition of the Confederate States). The British cabinet had been considering such an action but had delayed a final decision following the Battle of Antietam (September 1862). It therefore declined the French overture as unfeasible "at the present moment." The Russian demurral was unconditional. Washington rejected the French unilateral effort as unwarranted interference in the domestic affairs of the United States.

To the French government, however, the "present moment" was not only appropriate but necessary. Both notes were written when the French economy was most adversely affected by the war. During the winter of 1862–1863, there was 50 percent unemployment in the textile industry (resulting from the high cost of cotton), high unemployment among workers in the luxury industries (gloves, silks, hats, perfumes, leather goods) because of the loss of the U.S. markets, and a serious decline of commercial activity in the ports (especially that of Bordeaux). Also the November 1862 elections in the United States manifested widespread opposition to the war, and the Copperhead peace movement was at its height. France's minister to Washington, Henri Mercier (b. 1816), reporting these conditions, advised that the time was right for some attempt to reestablish peace. French domestic needs and U.S. political conditions coalesced, therefore, to justify the French action. But the compelling factor was French domestic needs. Both notes contained references to the war's impact on the French economy. The government published the 30 October note on 13 November, prior to receiving the responses, and the 9 January note on 28 January, before it reached Washington. In both cases, extensive press and public debate was permitted. The object was to publicize the government's efforts to reestablish peace in order to relieve French suffering. The emperor referred to the mediation proposals when he successfully requested unemployment relief appropriations from the Corps Législatif in January 1863 (the legislators approved direct relief, a retraining and relocation program, and public works projects where unemployment was highest).

By the summer of 1863 cotton imports began to rise, unemployment eased, and the domestic crisis passed. As a result, the diplomatic failure of the mediatory overtures proved less important to Napoleon III than the fact that he had made the efforts. However, the mediation proposals created a residual coolness between France and the United States. French foreign minister Edouard Drouyn de Lhuys' explanation that France was motivated by humanitarian concerns and friendship for the Americans was not convincing. U.S. Secretary of State William H. Seward remained suspicious of Mercier and U.S. Minister to France William L. Dayton thereafter sharply questioned every French action related to the Civil War. Undoubtedly this cooling of relations also played a role in the disastrous failure of France's Mexican intervention (1861–1867).

D. B. Carroll, *Henri Mercier and the American Civil War* (Princeton, N.J., 1971); L. M. Case and W. F. Spencer, *The United States and France: Civil War Diplomacy* (Philadelphia, 1970); F. V. Husley, "Napoleon III and the Confederacy" (Ph.D. diss., Mississippi State, 1970); J. G. Larrégola, *Le gouvernement français, face à la Guerre de Sécession* (Paris, 1970); W. F. Spencer, *The Confederate Navy* (Tuscaloosa, Ala., 1983).

Warren F. Spencer

Related entries: COTTON FAMINE; DROUYN DE LHUYS; MEXICAN EXPEDITION; RECOGNITION QUESTION; THOUVENEL.

MEILHAC, HENRI (1831–1897), dramatist and librettist, chiefly remembered as coauthor with Ludovic Halévy of many successful vaudevilles (short comedies with popular songs), operettas, and comedies; born 21 February 1831 in Paris. As a caricaturist and humorist, Meilhac collaborated on the *Journal pour rire* from 1852 to 1855 and on *La vie parisienne*, initially under the pseudonyms Ivan Baskoff and Talin and later under his real name. Meilhac made his debut as a writer of comedies in the early 1850s with a one-act vaudeville, *Garde-toi, je me garde*, for Charles Contrat-Desfontaines, known as Dormeuil (1794–1882), the director of the Théâtre du Palais Royal. In the following years, he wrote two vaudevilles for the same theater, *La sarabande du cardinal* (1856) and *Satania* (1856), and a one-act play, *L'autographe* (1858), for the Théâtre du Gymnase. In 1859 *Un petit-fils de Mascarille*, a comedy in five acts, was presented at the Théâtre du Gymnase and in 1860 *Ce qui plaît aux hommes* at the Théâtre de l'Odéon. Throughout the 1860s Meilhac devoted himself exclusively to the theater, writing vaudevilles, comedies, and libretti, often in collaboration with such other authors as Philippe Gille (1831–1901) and Charles Truinet, known as Nuitter (1828–1899), with whom he wrote the libretto for Jacques Offenbach's 1869 operetta, *Vert-vert*.

The year 1860 marked the beginning, for Meilhac, of a lengthy collaboration with his school friend, Ludovic Halévy, already librettist for Offenbach. There-after the three men produced an astounding succession of operettas, appealing to the taste of the day but also satirizing, with *boulevardier* eye and wit, the social and political foibles of the Second Empire. Their first collaboration was on a vaudeville, *Le Brésilien* (Palais Royal, 1863). There followed: *La belle Hélène* (Variétés, 1864), *Barbe-Bleue* (Variétés, 1866), *La vie parisienne* (Palais Royal, 1866), *La Grande Duchesse de Gérolstein* (Variétés, 1867), *Le château à Toto* (1868), *La Périchole* (Variétés, 1868), *La diva* (1869), and *Les brigands* (Variétés, 1869). Meilhac and Halévy also coauthored several comedies: *Les brébis de Panurge* (Vaudeville, 1862) and *Fanny Lear* (Gymnase, 1868). *Frou-frou* (Gymnase, 1869), one of their most successful comedies, offers a picture of the frivolous, elegant, carefree society at the end of the Second Empire. Meilhac died at Paris, 6 July 1897.

H. A. Parys, *Histoire anecdotique de l'operette* (Brussels, 1945).

Dolorès A. Signori

Related entries: HALEVY; OFFENBACH; THEATER.

MEISSONIER, ERNEST (1815–1891), academic painter; born at Lyons, 21 February 1815. Meissonier's early works in the 1830s and 1840s were devoted to scenes of smokers, readers, and card players in the seventeenth-century Dutch tradition. He won a first-class medal in the Salon of 1843 and again in 1848 and in 1846 was made a knight of the Legion of Honor. Eugène Delacroix admired *The Barricade, Rue de la Mortellerie (June 1848)* (1849, Louvre, Paris), which he saw in the artist's studio. Meissonier achieved great popularity with his small-format works on unpretentious themes and as a book illustrator. He won the gold medal in the Paris international exposition of 1855 for *The Brawl* (H. M. the Queen of England), which was purchased by Napoleon III for 25,000 francs and presented to Prince Albert and Queen Victoria when they visited France that year. In 1859, Napoleon III invited Meissonier to record the events of the French military campaign in Italy against Austria, which he did in *Emperor Napoleon III at Solférino* (1864, Louvre).

From this point, military scenes became Meissonier's principal interest. He conceived of a series of five paintings devoted to important dates in the military career of Napoleon I. Meissonier followed academic precepts with careful, almost fanatic, attention to precise and accurate detail in such works as *1814* (1864, Louvre), which depicts Napoleon's withdrawal into France. Another work, *Friedland—1807* (Metropolitan Museum of Art, New York) was finished in 1875 after Meissonier had spent twelve years preparing for it with separate studies. He was especially interested in the depiction of horses and studied them at great length, even making wax models in order to achieve greater verisimilitude. The artist was a friend of Charles François Daubigny and thus became interested in *plein air* landscape painting and natural light. There was, however, a considerable difference between the studies he did of nature and the completed work, which conformed to academic standards. Typical for the period was the attitude that there is a distinct separation between the lively sketch based on direct observation and the final studio-produced painting, which suppressed lively and personal expression for a more ideal end. As usual under the Second Empire, this attitude was amply rewarded. The artist was elected to the Académie des Beaux-Arts in 1861 and awarded a medal of honor at the Paris international exposition of 1867. He died at Paris, 31 January 1891.

A. Boime. *The Academy and French Painting in the Nineteenth Century* (New York, 1971); P. Guilloux, "Meissonier, ou l'érudition dans l'art," *Uniformes*, no. 48 (1979); C. C. Hungerford, "The Art of Jean-Louis-Ernest Meissonier: A Study of the Critical Years, 1834–1855" (Ph.D. diss., University of California, Berkeley, 1977); J. Sloane, *French Painting between the Past and the Present: Artists, Critics, and Traditions from 1848 to 1870* (Princeton, 1951).

Beverley Giblon

Related entries: BAUDRY; BOUGUREAU; CABANEL; COUTURE; GUYS; PILS.

MENTANA, an Italian village on papal territory approximately 10 miles from Rome. There, on 3 November 1867, a French expeditionary force and the papal army routed a contingent of volunteers led by Giuseppe Garibaldi. Garibaldi, the liberator of southern Italy in the summer of 1860, had long chafed at the French occupation of Rome. In 1862 he made a first attempt to seize the city but was blocked by Italian troops, wounded, and taken prisoner at Aspromonte (29 August). In September 1864 Paris and Turin agreed on a French withdrawal from Rome (September Convention). As the last French troops left the Holy City in mid-December 1866, they were replaced by a volunteer force of French soldiers "on leave," the Legion of Antibes. The papal army, popularly called the Pontifical Zouaves, was reorganized and greatly enlarged under General Hermann Kanzler (1822–1888), papal minister of war.

Garibaldi had denounced the September Convention, by which Turin was pledged to resist attacks on Rome. The failure of the Romans to rise against the pope's government of the city and of its immediate hinterland (all that now remained of the temporal power of the papacy) made action seem imperative to Garibaldi. During the summer of 1867, he took advantage of the Italian national elections to assemble volunteers. Harassment of papal territory began. On 24 September the Italian government arrested Garibaldi on the Roman frontier and returned him to his island home of Caprera, from which he escaped in mid-October. Alarmed, the French Council of Ministers decided (16 October) on the principle of intervention, with only Victor Duruy, Jules Baroche, and marquis Charles Jean de La Valette arguing against. Three days later, the Italian prime minister, Urbano Rattazzi, resigned rather than act against the volunteers, and no one could be found to take his place. A second French council meeting on 24 October decided on the immediate dispatch of an expeditionary force to Civita Vecchia, the port of Rome. Several days later an insurrection failed at Rome, but Garibaldi defeated a contingent of the papal army at Monte Rotondo.

On 28–29 October 1867, the French expedition, commanded by General Charles de Failly (1810–1892), disembarked. These forces (approximately three thousand men) joined with some three thousand pontifical troops. By 1 November Garibaldi's volunteers had swelled in number to about twelve thousand. But it is thought that in the next forty-eight hours, approximately half of these deserted, leaving the opposing armies roughly equal in numbers. Poorly armed and equipped, possessing only five cannon of any real capacity, Garibaldi's volunteers were routed in a short skirmish on 3 November 1867. Their leader was arrested, briefly detained by the Italian government, and then returned once again to Caprera.

Napoleon III had apparently hoped that once Rome was secure, a European congress would meet to dispose of the Roman Question. Paris formally proposed such a congress on 9 November. But emotions ran high. On 10 November the French emperor allowed the official newspaper, the *Moniteur*, to print a report submitted by General Failly. According to that account of the battle, only a few of the papal and French forces had died at Mentana, while the Garibaldian volunteers had suffered large losses, and the newly developed French breech-loading rifle, the chassepot, had done wonders. Napoleon III's motive was to warn the Italians that they must not attempt to take Rome by force and to advertise the superiority of the French rifle at a time when Franco-Prussian relations were increasingly strained. Within France, the emperor found it necessary for political reasons to conciliate the Catholic party—thus the pronouncement by Eugène Rouher before the Corps Législatif on 5 December 1867 that Italy would never be allowed to take Rome. Rouher's speech effectively ended the possibility of a congress as Mentana had effectively ended the September Convention. French troops returned to Rome where they would remain until the Franco-Prussian War.

M. Brignoli, ''Mentana,'' *Risorgimento*, no. 3 (1967); R. Di Nolli, *Mentana* (Rome, 1966); H. R. Marraro, ''Unpublished American Documents on Garibaldi's March on Rome in 1867,'' *JMH* 16 (1944); E. Ollivier, ''L'empereur et le Pape après Mentana,'' *Corr.*, 25 June 1905.

Ivan Scott

Related entries: CHASSEPOT; ROMAN QUESTION; SEPTEMBER CONVENTION.

MERCHANT MARINE. See COMPAGNIE GENERALE TRANSATLANTIQUE.

MERIMEE, PROSPER (1803–1870), man of letters, archaeologist, and friend of the imperial family; born 28 September 1803 at Paris. A writer of great versatility, Mérimée composed plays, essays, short stories, and novels and translated many Russian classics. Although his work was neither epic nor pretentious, it constitutes a timeless and perceptive commentary on the human condition, examining man's plight in a variety of circumstances. Among his best-known works are *La Jacquerie* (1828), *La chronique du temps de Charles IX* (1829), *Colomba* (1840), *Arsène Guillot* (1844), *Carmen* (1845), *Le faux Démétrius* (1852), and *Les Cosaques d'autrefois* (1865). Appointed inspector general of historical monuments in 1834, Mérimée was responsible for saving from destruction and for renovating many outstanding buildings, among which are the basilica of Vézélay, the Palace of the Popes at Avignon, the Roman theaters at Orange and Arles, and the cathedrals of Laon and Strasbourg. He presided (1857–1858) over the commission that recommended reconstruction of the Bibliothèque Impériale (now the Bibliothèque Nationale). Through his acquaintance from the early 1830s with the countess of Montijo, mother of Eugénie, he obtained entrée into the court and became the trusted and valued private friend of the emperor and empress. He was made a senator in 1853.

Mérimée's letters, published after his death, provide a unique insight into the character and thought of the imperial couple and are a valuable tool for historians. Anti-clerical in his views, Mérimée deplored French support of the temporal power of the pope, and he especially regretted the clerical influence of the empress on foreign policy. Yet he remained a devoted supporter of the regime and its ruler. His grief at the emperor's defeat at Sedan and the subsequent revolution in Paris undoubtedly shortened his life. He died at Cannes, 23 September 1870.

J. Autin, *Prosper Mérimée: Ecrivan, archeologue, homme politique* (Paris, 1982); P. Léon, *Mérimée et son temps* (Paris, 1962); P. Mérimée, *Oeuvres complètes*, ed. P. Trahard and E. Champion (Paris, 1927), and *Correspondance générale, établie et annotée par Maurice Parturier avec la collaboration de Pierre Josserand et Jean Mallion*, 17 vols. (Paris, 1941–); A. Raitt, *Prosper Mérimée* (New York, 1970); P. Trahard, *La jeunesse de Prosper Mérimée, 1803–1834*, 2 vols. (Paris, 1925), *Prosper Mérimée de 1834 à 1853* (Paris, 1928), and *La vieillesse de Prosper Mérimée, 1854–1870* (Paris, 1930).

Nancy N. Barker

MESSAGERIES IMPERIALES, France's first major steamship line; one of the two major lines developed during the Second Empire, established at Marseilles in February 1851. In 1851, Achille Fould, then finance minister, awarded the line the concession of postal and passenger services to the western Mediterranean, which had previously been operated at a loss by the government. The driving force behind the new company was the old Messageries Nationales, a road transport firm that, faced with the prospect of competition from the rapidly expanding rail network, was seeking to diversify its activities. After failing with steamboats on the Rhône and Saône in the 1840s, the company joined with the Rostand shipping firm of Marseilles to tender for the Mediterranean services, which was granted to it 8 July 1851. Until 1852 the new company was known as the Messageries Maritimes.

The Messageries Impériales was doubly successful. First, it increased the number of routes it served. Beginning its first service to Italy in September 1851, it extended services to Malta, Alexandria, and Constantinople, to Greece, Algeria, and Tunisia (1854), and to the Black Sea in the 1850s and Senegal in

1857. In the following decade, moreover, the company expanded beyond the Mediterranean. In May 1860 it inaugurated services to South America (Brazil, La Plata) and in 1860–1861 secured the concession for postal services to Indochina and the Far East. Saigon became its principal base outside Europe and increased in importance as lines were opened to other Asian destinations (Réunion, Ile Maurice, and Oceania from 1864, Japan from 1865). Second, the company's fleet increased markedly. When services began, it consisted of sixteen small vessels, most of which had been acquired from the government. In 1852 alone, however, the company ordered thirteen screw-driven steamers in Britain. More important, it began to build its own ships, taking over and modernizing the shipyards at La Ciotat, near Marseilles. By 1866 the company owned forty-three steamships, most of them new vessels driven by screw propellers.

This remarkable early success of the Messageries Impériales needs explaining. After all, the French merchant marine at the mid-century was less modern and less successful than those of other major European nations. Attempts in the 1840s to establish a major French steamship company had failed, and only about a third of France's foreign trade was carried on French vessels. Part of the explanation of the Messagerie Impériale's success is to be found in favorable international conditions: an unprecedented increase in international exchange and a series of innovations that increased the efficiency and hence feasibility of steam-shipping. But there are three specific explanations of the company's success. One is the support of the state. The government aided municipalities in improving port facilities, especially in the last years of the Second Empire, and it also gave subsidies to shipping companies. Thus when the Messageries Impériales secured its original concession in 1851, it was granted an annual subsidy of 3 million francs. The South America concession brought an even larger annual subsidy of 4.7 million, and the Far East route entailed an annual subsidy based on the length of the routes served together with an interest-free loan of 12 million francs. Through its military campaigns and colonial expansion, the government also aided the company indirectly. Thus company ships carried troops and supplies during the Crimean and Italian wars, as well as the Syria and China expeditions, and the company benefited for nearly a century from French involvement in Indochina. The Crimean War, for instance, meant that an army of 200,000 men had to be transported and supplied in a war zone some 3,000 kilometers and nineteen sailing days from Marseilles, the nearest French port. The second explanation for the company's success is the dynamism of its principal base, Marseilles, whose facilities were improved and whose traffic increased with the prosperity of the Mediterranean and the growth of French Algeria and would increase even more rapidly after the opening of the Suez Canal in 1869. During the Second Empire, Marseilles became France's greatest port, center of Mediterranean traffic and gateway to Algeria. The third explanation is the dynamism of company management in general and of Armand Béhic (1809–1891) in particular. Béhic was responsible for the reorganization of the shipyards at

La Ciotat in the 1850s, and in 1867 he became chairman of the board, a post he held, with one break in 1865–1867, until his death.

Although after 1870 the company (which again became the Messageries Maritimes) was to face renewed competition from sailing ships and from other shipping lines, it would exploit the new facilities offered by the Suez Canal, continue to benefit from government subsidies and colonial expansion, and to expand its fleet and its services.

M. Barbance, *Vie commerciale de la route du Cap Horn au XIXe siècle: l'armement A.-D. Bordes et fils* (Paris, 1969); R. Carour, *Sur les routes de la mer avec les Messageries Maritimes* (Paris, 1968), and "La Compagnie des Messageries Maritimes: Son passé, son avenir," *RHES* 50 (1972); P. J. Charliat, *Trois siècles d'économie maritime française* (Paris, 1931); M. E. Fletcher, "The Suez Canal and World Shipping, 1869–1914," *JEH* (1958); P. Guiral, "Marseilles et la navigation à vapeur vers l'Amérique latine de 1840 à 1870," *RHES* 34 (1956).

Barrie M. Ratcliffe

Related entries: ALGERIA; BEHIC; COMPAGNIE GENERALE TRANSATLANTIQUE; GOVERNMENT FINANCE; INDOCHINA; RAILROADS; SENEGAL; SUEZ CANAL; TALABOT.

MEXICAN EXPEDITION, the abortive attempt of Napoleon III to place the Austrian Archduke Ferdinand Maximilian on a Mexican throne (1861–1867). This French military expedition to Mexico grew out of decades of friction between the two countries during which an ideology of intervention built up. The French colony in Mexico, the largest group of foreign nationals in Mexico except the Spanish, had long suffered from the chronic instability of the Mexican governments and their constant financial destitution. The commerce of French subjects had been interrupted, their property pillaged and destroyed, their houses of business subjected to heavy and capricious taxation, and at times their persons attacked and robbed. Previous French governments had been helpless to alleviate the situation. The Bourbon Charles X had been on the point of sending out an armed fleet when he lost his throne in 1830. His successor, Louis Philippe, had blockaded and bombarded Veracruz in 1838 in a futile expedition dubbed the "Pastry War." By the late 1850s the plight of the French in Mexico was even worse. During the civil war of that time, the *Guerra de la Reforma*, marauding armies plundered the country while the contending governments subjected the French to forced loans and confiscated their property.

Redress of grievances of French subjects in Mexico was merely the ostensible purpose of Napoleon III's intervention. His true aim was to end the political anarchy of the country and to release its productive energies by the establishment of a monarchy. Like most of his contemporaries, the French emperor was convinced that a monarchical form of government was a necessity for *les races latines*. The decades of chaos in republican Mexico since it had won its independence from Spain in 1821 seemed evidence of the truth of the monarchist thesis. Nor was this all. The emperor's *grande pensée du règne* (great idea of the reign) for Mexico called for the newly regenerated nation to form a barrier against further encroachments of the United States on its territory. And in accordance with Napoleon III's belief in the economic theories of Saint-Simon, it provided for the construction of a transoceanic canal across the Isthmus of Tehuantepec that was not only to make Mexico the hub of a great commercial empire but also was to bring to Europe the rich trade of the Orient. The emperor could also make good use of these plans for Mexico in his diplomacy in Europe, where he was attempting to persuade Austria to accept his designs for the continent. By offering a throne to Ferdinand Maximilian, younger brother of the Austrian emperor, he could provide compensation to Austria for its losses in Italy and perhaps encourage its cooperation.

Among immediate triggers of the intervention were the arguments of Napoleon's Spanish-born wife, Eugénie, a passionate partisan of the *grande pensée*, and of prominent Mexican monarchists in Mexico and in the European courts; the sordid financial schemes of the French minister in Mexico, Alphonse Dubois de Saligny, who was urging intervention in order to line his own pockets; and the outbreak of civil war in the United States in April 1861, an event that precluded U.S. opposition to French action.

The intervention began under the guise of a simple debt-collecting expedition of all three European maritime powers. On 31 October 1861 special ambassadors from England, France, and Spain signed a convention in London agreeing to deploy military forces to oblige Mexico to pay its outstanding debts and claims allegedly owed to the subjects of the signatory powers. Their troops, modest in number, arrived off Veracruz in December 1861 and January 1862. The accord between the powers quickly broke down when the monarchist aims of France, supported by the outrageously excessive claims presented by Dubois de Saligny, became apparent. The British and Spanish withdrew their forces and left the French to march alone into the interior. From this point Napoleon's Mexican policies encountered mounting difficulties. The mass of the Mexicans did not flock to welcome the French as their saviors, as the monarchists had confidently predicted. The French army experienced a humiliating defeat 5 May 1862 in an abortive attempt to assault Puebla. Not until June 1863 were the French, now strongly reinforced, able to enter the capital as conquerors. There they hastily nominated a provisional government, which immediately offered the Mexican crown to Ferdinand Maximilian.

In Paris the emperor was having serious misgivings about his *grande pensée* but could think of no feasible way of disengaging short of humiliation. He decided to go ahead, therefore, and try to transfer to the shoulders of the archduke the burden of the crown he had created. The convention he signed with Ferdinand Maximilian in April 1864 required Mexico to pay France an indemnity, to bear all expenses of the French occupation, and to concede to France the product of the silver mines of Sonora. Napoleon offered no more than a military occupation of three years and neither guaranteed the territorial integrity of the Mexican empire nor promised to defend it against the United States. Only the genuine eagerness of Ferdinand Maximilian and his Belgian wife, Charlotte, to mount a Mexican throne induced the idealistic young couple to accept the crown on the basis of these inadequate guarantees (Convention of Miramar, 10 April 1864) and depart.

Entering Mexico City 12 June 1864, the new Emperor Maximilian found his regime doomed from the start. Rejected by the republican supporters of Benito Juárez (1806–1872), whose army mounted persistent guerrilla warfare against French forces, Maximilian, by his liberal policies, alienated the clericals and conservatives who should have been the base of his support. Financially and militarily he was entirely dependent on France. The fall of his empire became inevitable when in December 1865 the United States, having emerged from the Civil War, demanded the withdrawal of French troops from Mexican territory. Napoleon III, faced with a challenge from Prussia on the Rhine, could but acquiesce and began withdrawing his troops in 1866. Empress Charlotte traveled to Europe in July 1866 in a desperate attempt to reengage the support of Napoleon III and of the pope. Failing completely, she began to lose her reason. She was conducted to a family estate near Brussels where she remained, never recovering her sanity, until her death in 1927. Meanwhile in Mexico, the position of Maximilian deteriorated rapidly as the French forces retired. On 15 May 1867, having transferred his headquarters to Querétaro, he was betrayed by one of his own men and captured by the army of Juárez. He was court-martialed, convicted, and, despite international appeals for mercy, was shot by a firing squad on 19 June.

In addition to the personal tragedies experienced by those involved, the Mexican intervention had far-reaching effects. In France, where it had been very unpopular with the public, it was a severe blow to the prestige and popularity of the emperor and especially of the empress. By tying down some forty thousand French troops, it had weakened French resistance to the growing strength of Prussia, especially in the Sadowa crisis of 1866. Military experts believe that the French army had still not recovered from its loss of materiel by the time of the outbreak of the Franco-Prussian War in 1870. For the United States it marked the coming of age of the Monroe Doctrine and the emergence of the United States as the defender of republican states in the Western Hemisphere. In Mexico, among other things, the intervention saw the beginning of a kind of cult around Juárez, who became a national hero, and of the consolidation of the Mexican republic as a national entity.

N. N. Barker, *The French Experience in Mexico, 1821–1861: A History of Constant Misunderstanding* (Chapel Hill, N.C., 1979); C. H. Bock, *Prelude to Tragedy: The Negotiation and Breakdown of the Tripartite Convention of London, October 31, 1861* (Philadelphia, 1966); L. M. Case, ed., *French Opinion on the United States and Mexico, 1860–1867: Extracts from the Reports of the Procureurs Généraux* (1936; reprint by Archon Books, 1969); J. A. Dabbs, "French Imperial Policy in Mexico," in W. D. Raat, ed., *Mexico from Independence to Revolution, 1810–1910* (Lincoln, Nebraska, 1982); A. J. Hanna and K. A. Hanna, *Napoleon III and Mexico: American Triumph over*

Monarchy (Chapel Hill, N.C., 1971); F. E. Lally, *French Opposition to the Mexican Policy of the Second Empire* (Baltimore, 1931); C. Schefer, *La grande pensée de Napoléon III: Les origines de l'expédition du Mexique, 1858-1862* (Paris, 1939).

Nancy N. Barker

Related entries: BAZAINE; CHINA EXPEDITIONS; EUGENIE; FOULD; GOVERNMENT FINANCE; INDOCHINA; LATIN MONETARY UNION; MEDIATION PROPOSALS; NATIONALITIES; SYRIAN EXPEDITION.

MEYERBEER, GIACOMO (1791–1864), composer, one of the major influences on the development of French *grand opéra* in the middle decades of the nineteenth century. At the beginning of the Second Empire theater music, and in particular opera, still dominated the French musical scene, and French opera, particularly the Opéra, still dominated Europe. From 1852 to 1870 the major musical theaters at Paris were the Théâtre des Italiens (or Théâtre Italiens), the Théâtre Lyrique, the Bouffes Parisiens, the Opéra Comique, and the Opéra, although there were a number of others. The Théâtre des Italiens, housed in the Salle Ventadour, rue Méhul, presented Italian opera (sung in Italian) every autumn and winter. Singers included Giulia Grisi (1811–1869), Fanny Persiani (1812–1867), Giovanni Mario (1810–1883), Luigi Lablache (1794–1858), and Antonio Tamburini (1800–1876). The director from 1850 to 1852 was Benjamin Lumley (1811–1875), who also managed Her Majesty's Theater, London. The Italiens was very much in fashion during the Second Empire. The success in those years of the Théâtre Lyrique and of the Bouffe Parisiens owed much to the relative decline of the Opéra Comique. The latter during the Second Empire was housed in the Salle Favart, except for the period June to July 1853 spent in the Salle Ventadour. By mid-century productions at the Opéra Comique had become increasingly "serious." Under the successive administrations of Emile Perrin (1814–1885), Nestor Roqueplan (1804–1870), Alfred Beaumont (?–1869), and Adolphe de Leuven (1800–1884), the repertoire was dominated by Daniel Auber (1782–1871), Ambroise Thomas, Fromental Halévy (1799–1862) and Meyerbeer. Thomas' *Mignon* was produced there in 1866 and the first opera of Jules Massenet (1842–1912), *La grand' tante*, in 1867. Works by Adolphe Adam (1803–1856) and Victor Massé (1822–1884) were frequently presented. Although the latter pioneered the operetta form that Jacques Offenbach would fully develop, the standard fare at the Opéra Comique was formally distinguished from that of the Opéra only by the fact that spoken dialogue was prohibited by the latter.

Indeed, by 1852 a French style of grand opera had developed with its center at the Opéra, housed during the Second Empire in the rue Le Peletier (1,954 seats; Charles Garnier's magnificent new building, with 2,156 seats, would not open until 1875). The conventions of this grand opera reflected the facts that music still served a primarily social function and that opera, to a great extent, was a conservative club for the elite. That elite wanted its operas sung in French; it wanted spectacle, drama, pomp, pageantry, great choral ensembles, rich orchestration, showy singing, special effects; and it insisted on a ballet, placed not so early in the work as to be missed by those arriving fashionably late. These conventions the directors of the Opéra faithfully enforced: Nestor Roqueplan from 1849 to 1854; Louis Crosnier (1792–1867), from 1854 to 1856; Adolphe Royer, from 1856 to 1862; and Emile Perrin, from 1862 to 1871. Conservatism was reinforced by the fact that the state managed the Opéra from June 1854 until 1866 and by the rule that conductors could not conduct their own works, which lent special authority to the Opéra's chief conductors: Narcisse Girard (1797–1860), from 1846 to 1860; Louis Dietsch (1808–1865), from 1860 to 1863; and Georges François Hainl (1807–1873), from 1863 to 1872. Composers who did not conform, even when of the caliber of Hector Berlioz (1803–1869) or Richard Wagner (1813–1883), were denied access to the stage of the Opéra or subjected to rough treatment. Others who, like Giuseppe Verdi (1813–1901), disliked the Opéra, its bureaucracy, its emphasis on spectacle, and its insistence on construction over inspiration, nevertheless allowed themselves on occasion to be shaped by it, for they recognized Paris to be the musical center of Europe. Thus Verdi, whose first worldwide success, *Rigoletto*, had been produced at Venice 11 March 1851, wrote *Les vêpres siciliennes* for the Opéra (13 June 1855) and, twelve years later, *Don Carlos* (11 March 1867). The latter, featuring a first-rate cast (Marie Sass [1834–1907] as Elisabeth de Valois; Jean Baptiste Faure [1830–1914] as Posa; Armand Castelmary [1834–1897] as the Grand Inquisitor, and Jean Morère [1836–1887] as Don Carlos), was not greatly successful, although it was performed forty-three times and was said to have offended Empress Eugénie with its anti-clericalism. It was Verdi's last Paris opera, for the Opéra belonged not to the great Italian's romantic genius but to the inspired eclecticism of Giacomo Meyerbeer.

Meyerbeer was born Jakob Liebmann Beer at Vogelsdorf (near Berlin), 5 September 1791. His father was a rich Jewish banker, and by adding the prefix *Meyer* to his name in honor of his maternal grandfather, Meyerbeer secured an additional inheritance. Throughout his life, he was a wealthy man. Beginning as a pianist (he was a child prodigy), Meyerbeer was drawn to the musical stage, composing his first opera in 1812. After an Italian phase (he Italianized his first name to Giacomo), he settled for several years at Paris from 1826, avidly studying French opera. Thereafter Meyerbeer, a truly international man, would often spend several months a year at Paris, which he had first visited in 1814, but he would never settle or buy a home there. His first production at the Opéra, *Robert le Diable* (1831), was a tremendous success, and Meyerbeer became a man to emulate. Fromental Halévy (1799–1862) was clearly influenced by him in composing his masterpiece, *La Juive* (Opéra, 1835), one of the most important works of French grand opera. *Robert le Diable* marked another landmark, the beginning of the collaboration with librettist Eugène Scribe, for whom the composer had the highest regard. From 1831 until his death, Meyerbeer would be the central figure in French grand opera, a success explained by his genius, culture, and great wealth and also by his willingness to give the public what it wanted, his skillful use of the press (he might be said to have pioneered modern press relations) and of publicity, and the lack of major rivals at the Opéra. Meyerbeer's contemporary, Gioacchino Rossini (1792–1868), lived at Paris but wrote no more operas after *Guillaume Tell* in 1829.

Meyerbeer composed slowly and often over many years. *Les Huguenots* (1836) was not as rapturously received as had been *Robert le Diable* five years earlier, but in many ways it was "the grandest of all French grand opera" and is the work of the composer that has longest survived in repertoire outside France. Like other composers of the day, Meyerbeer often wrote with particular singers in mind (star singers were lionized and paid huge salaries). *Le prophète* (April 1849) was written for Pauline Viardot, his favorite singer. Besides Viardot's Fidès, the cast included Jeanne Anais Castellan (born 1819) as Bertha, Gustave Roger (1815–1879) as John of Leyden, and Nicolas Levasseur (1791–1871) as Zacharie. Staged with electric lighting, *Le prophète* was a sensational success (once again Scribe was the librettist), receiving its one hundredth Opéra performance on 14 July 1851. Meyerbeer, who had been honored by the previous regime, was now named commander of the Legion of Honor.

After *Le prophète* Meyerbeer turned to opera comique. Although it was a form in which his librettist, Scribe, was more happy than he, *L'étoile du Nord* (Opéra Comique, 16 February 1854) was a brilliant success. The emperor and empress attended, and within a year the work had received one hundred performances. *Le pardon de Ploërmel* or *Dinorah* (Opéra Comique, 4 April 1859; libretto by Jules Barbier [1822–1901] and Michel Carré [1819–1872] also had a successful premiere, following which a wreath was thrown to the composer from the imperial box. Napoleon III had urged Meyerbeer to prepare a new grand opera for Paris and had hinted that the reward could be promotion to grand officer of the Legion. Since 1838 the composer had, in fact, been at work on *L'Africaine*, but it was not until 1863 that rehearsals began, and by then Meyerbeer was already in poor health. He became seriously ill on 23 April 1864 and died, at Paris, the night of 2 May. A great official funeral service was conducted at the Gare du Nord on 6 May before the composer's body was taken to Berlin for burial.

After a final revision of Scribe's libretto by the Belgian musicologist François Joseph Fétis (1784–1871), *L'Africaine* was staged at the Opéra on 28 April 1865. The cast included Marie Sass as Selika, Faure as Nelusko, and Castelmary as Don Diego. Emilio Naudin (1823–1890), the celebrated tenor, was paid 110,000 francs for singing the role of Vasco da Gama. The opera was on a grand scale (in its original version it was six hours in length), featuring spectacular scenery (a ship wrecked and sunk on stage), and an orchestra of one hundred players, some sixteen more than the Opéra's normal complement. *L'Africaine* was extremely popular, receiving sixty performances in its first four seasons, and is generally considered the composer's finest opera. But Meyerbeer paid for his overwhelming popularity in the nineteenth century with neglect in our own. Wagner and Wagnerism were partly responsible. Although Meyerbeer assisted Wagner at Paris in 1839, and, as *Generalmusikdirecktor* at Berlin from 1842 to

1849, secured production of his *Rienzi* and *Der fliegende Holländer*, the younger composer bitterly attacked Meyerbeer's music from the late 1840s and broke with him completely toward the end of 1850. And yet Meyerbeer's critics have never succeeded in removing him from the operatic pantheon, for despite his faults, eclecticism, and inconsistencies, he was a composer of genius. Moreover, his influence on his contemporaries was immense and can be discerned not only in such works as *Herculanum* (1859) of Félicien David (1810–1876) but also in Verdi's *Les vêpres siciliennes*, *Don Carlos*, *Aida* (1871), and *Otello* (1887), Fromental Halévy's *La Juive*, Charles Gounod's *Sapho* (1851), *La nonne sanglante* (1854), *Faust* (1859), and *La Reine de Saba* (1862), Ambroise Thomas' *Hamlet* (1868), and even Wagner's *Rienzi* (1842), the Paris version of *Tannhäuser* (1861), and *Die meistersinger von Nürnberg* (1868).

H. Becker, ed., *Giacomo Meyerbeer: Briefwechsel und Tagebücher* (Berlin, 1960–1975); W. L. Crosten, *French Grand Opera: An Art and a Business* (New York, 1948); L. Dauriac, *Meyerbeer*, rev. ed. (Paris, 1930); I. Guest, *The Ballet of the Second Empire, 1858–1870* (London, 1953), and *The Ballet of the Second Empire, 1847–1858* (London, 1955); O. Meslin, *L'Opéra de Paris* (Paris, 1975); J. L. Thomson, "Meyerbeer and His Contemporaries" (Ph.D. diss., Columbia University, 1972).

Related entries: CARVALHO; DELIBES; GOUNOD; OFFENBACH; OPERA; SAINT-SAENS; SCRIBE; *TANNHAUSER* PREMIERE; THOMAS; VIARDOT.

MILITARY. See ARMY REFORM.

MILLAUD, MOISE (known as POLYDOR MILLAUD) (1813–1871), journalist, banker, and speculator; born 27 August 1813 at Bordeaux to a poor Jewish merchant family. After only a primary education and an unsuccessful venture into journalism, Millaud went to Paris in 1836 to seek his fortune. There he founded several short-lived newspapers, including the first to be sold at theater doors (*Le gamin*, 1836), the first to deal exclusively with business affairs (*Le négociateur*, 1838), and a paper concerned only with crime and the courts (*L'audience*, 1839). The last, in which Léo Lespès (1815–1875) and Félix Nadar were collaborators, enjoyed success and notoriety until its demise in 1845. On 24 February 1848 Millaud founded *La liberté*, which sold 122,000 copies per issue for four months until it was suppressed after the June Days for its vigorous support of Prince Louis Napoleon Bonaparte.

Since his Bordeaux days, Millaud had been associated with another Jewish journalist and speculator from that city, Jules Mirès. In October 1848 the two men bought the *Journal des chemins de fer* for 1,000 francs payable in four months. Aided by the fluid financial situation, they quickly made their new acquisition into the first French stock market newspaper. It became a center of speculative finance and the foundation of their respective fortunes (subsidies were quietly paid to the paper for printing advertisements that masqueraded as independent financial assessments). Together, the two men established in 1849 the *Conseiller du peuple* to exploit the popularity of Alphonse de Lamartine

(1790–1869), and together, in 1851, they organized the Caisse des Actions Réunies, a business bank that in two years paid dividends of 90 percent to its shareholders. Mirès and Millaud each realized profits of 3 million francs, but in 1853 the latter withdrew, yielding his place to Félix Solar (1815–1871), yet another speculator and journalist from Bordeaux (Solar and Mirès in 1854 transformed the company into the Caisse Générale des Chemins de Fer, an emulator and rival of the Crédit Mobilier).

After separating from Mirès, Millaud proved less successful in his business ventures. A company he formed in 1854 to speculate in urban property failed for want of subscribers, although Millaud himself made a large profit. In 1856 he turned the journal *Le dock* into the *Journal des actionnaires* and with Léopold Amail, Louis Jourdan (1810–1881), Charles Duveyrier (1803–1866), and others formed the Caisse Générale des Actionnaires, a financial association with nominal capitalization of 25 million francs. It had, in addition to regular banking functions, the task of exploiting the new journal. Millaud thus returned to journalism as the chief instrument of his speculations, having acquired *La presse* from Emile de Girardin in December 1856 for 800,000 francs, thanks in part to the patronage of Prince Napoleon, another investor in the paper. But Millaud's affairs did not prosper. In financial trouble (1859), he sold his enterprises, including *La presse*, to Solar, who had also acquired the *Journal des chemins de fer* from Mirès.

Millaud's greatest success, however, still lay ahead. On 1 February 1863 he began to publish a newspaper, *Le petit journal*, which was destined to rebuild his fortune while revolutionizing French journalism by introducing the nonpolitical information press. Other papers followed—*Le journal illustrée*, *Le soleil*, *Le journal des voyageurs*, and others—in the management of which he was aided by his son Arthur (1836–1892) and his nephew Alphonse Millaud (born 1829). Millaud dabbled in the theater, winning some success in February 1859 with a three-act vaudeville staged at the Palais Royal theater, *Ma mère et mon ours* (written in collaboration with Louis François Niolaie, dit Clairville [1811-1897] under the pseudonym Frascati). The journalist in 1856 built a palatial hotel on the place Saint Georges (Adolphe Thiers' house was also on the place) where he delighted in staging lavish parties. But his renewed financial and commercial speculation once again led to difficulties, and the heavy investment required at *Le petit journal* was not offset by the profit. Millaud finally lost the greater part of his fortune. He sold his share of *Le petit journal* in 1869, and the following year his affairs were liquidated. Millaud died at Paris, 13 October 1871.

J. Morienval, *Les créateurs de la grande presse en France: Girardin, Villemessant, Millaud* (Paris, 1934).

Related entries: GIRARDIN; MIRES; NEFFTZER; PEREIRE; *PETIT JOURNAL*; VILLEMESSANT.

MILLET, JEAN FRANCOIS (1814–1875), figure and landscape painter; born at Gruchy (near Cherbourg), 4 October 1814, to a family of peasant farmers. Provincially trained in art in his youth, he later moved to Paris where he studied with the academic painter Paul Delaroche (1797–1856). He also frequented the Académie Suisse, an open studio where artists could meet, exchange ideas, and paint in a liberal atmosphere. Millet's early paintings were devoted to nudes and mythological scenes (he was well read in the classics). His *Oedipus* (1847, National Gallery of Canada, Ottawa) was exhibited in the Salon of 1847 and received some recognition from the critic Théophile Thoré (1807–1869). The following year, 1848, Millet began to paint subject matter that would occupy him for the remainder of his life: peasants performing their daily tasks. He did this not so much because he liked or even understood the peasants but because these scenes were what he knew best. It was in 1848 that Millet exhibited *The Winnower* (Louvre, Paris), and in 1850–1851 *The Sower* (Museum of Fine Arts, Boston), in the Salon where Gustave Courbet's *Stonebreakers* was also shown. The monumental and rustic figure in a landscape setting became his prime concern, especially after he had joined the already established group at Barbizon, the small village close to Paris where he was closely associated with Theodore Rousseau (his anonymous patron on occasion) and remained until his death.

During the 1850s Millet painted works for which he is best known, *The Gleaners* (1857, Louvre) and *The Angelus* (1859, Louvre), both representing the simple, unchanging rural life. These works are composed with a classical order and attention to form (the influence of Poussin and Michelangelo) and imbued with a spiritual essence arrived at through a generalization of motifs and a tranquil atmosphere. Millet enriched the content with a deep religious spirit, conveyed by peasants who embody eternal verities and faith in God's active presence in the world. Millet was not as interested in the trees of the nearby Forest of Fontainebleau as were the other Barbizon artists. He was more concerned with broad, panoramic stretches of plain, the setting where his bearers of moral values carried on their age-old and never-ending tasks (see *The Man with a Hoe*, 1863). Despite the toil and impoverished conditions, there is a biblical sense of peacefulness, dignity, and harmony, which could be appreciated and perhaps envied by the urban public and collectors. This attitude was well suited to Napoleon III's social policies, and although Millet was a republican (but not a militant one), and many found his view of peasant life too gloomy and too little concerned with the picturesque, he received a state commission in 1852 and Salon medals in 1853 (second class) and 1864 (first class). The latter finally alleviated the financial difficulties that had caused him to spend much of his early life in poverty (he had nine children by a Breton servant girl with whom he lived without his family's knowledge, marrying her only in 1875). In 1867 he was given a retrospective exhibition at the Paris international exposition. In 1868 he was named to the Legion of Honor. That same year an industrialist commissioned from Millet four pictures of the seasons, one of which, *Spring* (Louvre) was finished in 1873, two, *Haystacks, Autumn* (Metropolitan Museum of Art, New York) and *Buckwheat Thrashers* (Boston) in 1874, with one remaining in an unfinished state. The works reveal Millet's attempt to convey the reality of nature and man's relationship to it, tempered with intermixed feelings of melancholy, resigned acceptance, and yet a sense of well-being. It was Millet's sympathetic treatment of humanity that so attracted Vincent Van Gogh in the 1880s and cemented his friendship with Honoré Daumier. Millet died at Barbizon, 20 January 1875.

J. Ady and M. Cartwright, *Jean-François Millet* (New York, 1971); J. Bouret, *The Barbizon School* (Greenwich, Conn., 1973); R. L. Herbert, *Jean-François Millet* (London, 1976), and "Millet revisited," *BM* (April 1962); L. de Poittevin, *J. F. Millet, portraitiste* (Paris, 1971).

Beverley Giblon

Related entries: COROT; COURBET; DAUBIGNY; DAUMIER; DIAZ DE LA PENA; DUGLERE; INTERNATIONAL EXPOSITIONS; ROUSSEAU.

MINISTER OF STATE, the key figure, from 1852 to 1869, of the ministry of the Second Empire. Although there was no premier or president of council before 1870, the minister of state had precedence over all other ministers (formally by decree of 21 December 1860). He was meant to be the indispensable intermediary between the head of state and the major organs of government and a conduit for transactions involving other ministers. His responsibilities were defined in decrees of 22 January and 14 February 1852. He was responsible for the relations of the government with the Senate, Conseil d'Etat, and Corps Législatif and for communications between the head of state and his ministers. He countersigned decrees nominating ministers, senators, *conseillers d'état*, and presidents of the Senate and Corps Législatif, as well as those relating to articles 24, 28, 31, 46, and 54 of the constitution of 1852 or pertaining to matters not falling within the jurisdiction of any particular minister. He kept the records of the Council of Ministers, directed the official portion of the *Moniteur universel*, and supervised the administration of the national palaces and manufactures. These responsibilities were subsequently enlarged and defined by decrees of 14 December 1852, 11 February 1853, 23 June 1854, July 1856, and November 1859 to include supervision of the *maison de l'empereur* (civil list, *dotation de la couronne*, budget of the Legion of Honor, libraries of the national palaces); of fine arts and the Opéra, and of the imperial archives; of public (civil) buildings, nonsubsidized Parisian theaters, theaters of the provinces, and of the censorship of the theater (*la censure dramatique*) and of extraordinary pensions of Empire functionaries.

The reform decree of 24 November 1860 deprived the minister of state of his role as intermediary between the government and the chambers, delegating that task to three ministers without portfolio. The same decree separated from the ministry of state those functions relating to the *maison de l'empereur*, a significant diminution. However, by decree of 5 December 1860, the minister of state was assigned a major cultural role involving responsibility for every official aspect of the arts, letters, and science not directly related to public instruction or to the University—for example, the Institute, the imperial libraries, the Ecole des Chartes, the Academy of Medicine, the *Journal des savants*, administration of the Opéra, patronage of arts and letters, and encouragement of scientific research. In 1861 the Ministry of State, as supervisor of the Commission des Manuscrits Historiques, became responsible for publishing the letters of Napoleon I. The decision of Napoleon III in June 1863 to appoint the minister of state as his sole official spokesman before the Senate and Corps Législatif required that the ministry be shorn of all administrative functions, most of which were transferred to the *maison de l'empereur* or to the Ministry of Public Instruction. Five ministers occupied the hotel of the Ministry of State (in the Louvre, opening on the rue de Rivoli) from 1852 to 1869: François Xavier, comte de Casabianca (1796-1888) from 22 January to 30 July 1852; Achille Fould from 30 July 1852 until the changes of 24 November 1860; Alexandre Walewski from 23 November 1860 until the decree of 23 June 1863; Adolphe Billault from 23 June 1863 until his premature death in October 1863; and Eugène Rouher from 18 October 1863, under whom the ministry enjoyed its period of greatest influence. In shepherding legislation through the senate and the Corps Législatif Rouher was aided by three vice-presidents, Gustave Louis A. V. Chaix d'Est-Ange (1800-1876), J.L.V.A. de Forcade La Roquette, and Adolphe Vuitry. The Ministry of State was suppressed 17 July 1869.

A. Laporte, *Les ministres d'état sous le Second Empire et la IIIe République* (Paris, 1958; law thesis).

Related entries: BILLAULT; CONSEIL D'ETAT; CONSTITUTION; CORPS LEGISLATIF; FOULD; MINISTRY; *MONITEUR*; REFORM; ROUHER; WALEWSKI.

MINISTRE D'ETAT. See MINISTER OF STATE.

MINISTRY, under the Second Empire an experiment in government without, properly speaking, a cabinet. The ministry of the Second Empire was organized by decree, 22 January 1852. Its nature had been stipulated in article 13 of the constitution of 14 January 1852: "The ministers depend only on the head of state; they are each responsible only for their own acts; there is no solidarity at all among them." In that sense, until 1870 there would be no cabinet, only meetings of ministers, and, of course, no prime minister. By decree of December 1860, ministers had precedence by date of appointment, except for the minister of state, who had precedence over all of the others.

Ministers were appointed and dismissed by the emperor and were responsible only to him. They could be put in accusation by the Senate. They received an annual salary of 40,000 francs, could not be deputies, and could not appear before the Corps Législatif or the Senate, that function being a monopoly of the Conseil d'Etat. Ministers were, however, full members of the Conseil d'Etat. The Council of Ministers met twice each week, at 9 A.M., at the Tuileries, Napoleon presiding. From the time of her regency in 1859, Empress Eugénie occasionally attended. The agenda was set in advance and maintained. The emperor made his decisions following the council, usually after meeting with the pertinent minister but often without further consultation. The ministers of the Second Empire, drawn largely from the upper middle class, were able men, already successful, seldom intellectuals, but well educated, sober, for the most part public spirited and hard working. They were loyal to Napoleon III, but few were bonapartists. Many had been Orleanists and remained so to a degree. Although they divided into factions and on occasion opposed the emperor's policies, he was reluctant to dismiss his ministers and, moreover, found it hard to replace them, so that few key men were added after 1852. The average age, forty-eight in 1852, had become fifty-nine in 1867.

Until 1869 ministerial crises were virtually nonexistent, and most changes involved men rather than policies. Certain exceptions may be noted. The first government following the coup d'état was constituted 3 December 1851. In January the resignations of Auguste de Morny, Eugène Rouher, Achille Fould, and Pierre Magne as a result of the Orleans decrees necessitated a number of changes. All ministers resigned at Louis Napoleon's request. Retained were Leroy de Saint-Arnaud (War), Théodore Ducos (1801–1855; Marine), Louis Félix, marquis de Turgot (1796–1866; Foreign Affairs), and Hippolyte Fortoul (Public Instruction). Replaced were Rouher by J. P. Abbatucci (1791–1857; Justice), Morny by Victor Fialin Persigny (Interior), Fould by Jean Martial Bineau (1805–1855; Finance), and Magne by Noël Jacques Lefèbvre-Duruflé (1792–1877; Public Works). At the same time, the decree of 22 January 1852 organized what was to be the ministry of the Empire (proclaimed 2 December 1852). A Napoleonic Ministry of State was created under François Xavier, comte de Casabianca (1796–1888), and a Ministry of Police (*ministère de la police générale*) under C. E. de Maupas. The Ministry of Agriculture and Commerce was abolished and its functions added to those of the Ministry of the Interior. Magne returned to the cabinet 28 July 1852 (Public Works) and Fould 30 July as minister of state (from 14 December 1852 *ministère d'état et maison de l'empereur*).

From 1853 the president of the Conseil d'Etat held the status of minister. On 23 June 1853, the Ministry of Police was abolished, its functions transferred to the Ministry of the Interior, while those of the recently defunct Ministry of Agriculture and Commerce were now added to the Ministry of Public Works, which Rouher would later (3 February 1855) return to head. The resignation of Edouard Drouyn de Lhuys as foreign minister and his replacement by Alexandre Walewski on 7 May 1855 resulted from policy disagreements between the emperor and his foreign minister arising out of the Vienna conference of that year. The Orsini *attentat* led to the appointment of General Charles Espinasse (1815–1859) on 7 February 1858 as head of a *ministère de l'intérieure et sûreté générale*. The latter functions was suppressed 14 June 1858 and Espinasse replaced by Claude Alphonse Delangle (1797–1869). Prince Napoleon was appointed 24 June 1858 to head a new Ministry of Algeria and the Colonies, the latter function having been detached from the Ministry of Marine. He resigned and was replaced by Prosper, marquis de Chasseloup-Laubat, 24 March 1859, intending in that way to protest the slowness with which Napoleon III was approaching war with Austria for Italian independence. The outbreak of the Italian War led to a change of men, Delangle, E.L.H.H. Arrighi de Casanova, duc de Padoue (1814–1888), and Marshal Jacques Louis Randon entering the cabinet 5 May as ministers of justice, interior, and war, respectively. The resignation of Walewski as foreign minister and his replacement by Edouard Thouvenel 4 January 1860 signaled a change in the Italian policy of the Second Empire.

The reform decree of November 1860 was issued against the advice of a majority of ministers and was accompanied by significant ministerial changes. The Ministry of Algeria and the Colonies was abolished, colonies becoming once again a function of the Ministry of Marine (*ministère de la marine et colonies*), headed by Chasseloup-Laubat from 24 November. The functions of the *maison de l'empereur* were separated from the Ministry of State (24 November) and confided to Marshal Jean Baptiste Vaillant as *grand maréchal du palais* (4 December). He now held ministerial rank. Two ministers without portfolio were named (Adolphe Billault and Magne). Together with the president of the Conseil d'Etat (who also became minister without portfolio 3 December 1860), these ministers would represent the government before the chambers during discussion of the address. Persigny replaced Billault at Interior and J.L.V.A. Forcade La Roquette succeeded Magne at Finance (26 November). Thus a first step was taken toward reintroducing ministers into the Corps Législatif. In reality, however, ministers had from the beginning found ways of defending their interests and in particular had established effective if unconstitutional direct contacts with deputies and senators. The appointment of Fould as minister of finance 14 November 1861 was associated with important reforms in the budget process.

In October 1862 Napoleon's attempt to replace Thouvenel at the Foreign Ministry and Persigny at Interior as a concession to French Catholic opinion resulted in the proffered resignations of Fould, Rouher, and Jules Baroche and perhaps the first true cabinet crisis of the Empire. Thouvenel was dismissed, but the three others withdrew their resignations on condition that Persigny should remain (they had no love for Persigny but resented so great a concession to the Catholic party), and the emperor thus took a first reluctant step toward recognizing the principle of cabinet solidarity. The elections of 1863, with their gains for the opposition, occasioned further changes involving policy and structures as well as men. By decree (23 June 1863) the responsibility for cults was taken from the Ministry of Public Instruction and entrusted to the Ministry of Justice (*ministère de la justice et cultes*), headed by Baroche. Persigny was replaced at Interior and the appointments of Victor Duruy (Public Instruction) and Armand Béhic (Public Works) indicated that the regime had taken a liberal orientation. Most important, the Ministry of State was shorn of its administrative functions, its minister (Billault) becoming the sole representative of the government before the chambers, assisted by the president of the Conseil d'Etat, now titled *ministre présidant le conseil d'état*. Responsibility for fine arts devolved to the *maison de l'empereur*.

Napoleon III's decision to "crown the edifice" at the beginning of 1867 was opposed by his ministers and might well have led to major changes had efforts to bring Emile Ollivier into the government succeeded. However, Rouher's indispensability to the emperor ensured that the resignation of the cabinet at Napoleon's request (19 January) was followed only by a change of men, although the appointment of Marshal Adolphe Niel as minister of war signaled a commitment to army reform. The elections of 1869 ended the dominance of Rouher. Ollivier not yet being ready to enter the government, on 17 July 1869 the emperor named a new cabinet, essentially one of technicians pledged to constitutional reform. The Ministry of State was abolished; the Ministry of Agriculture and Commerce was reestablished. The *sénatus-consulte* of 6 September 1869 delineated a parliamentary ministry. Ministers henceforth could be deputies or senators and were fully subject to interpellation by the chambers. The issue of ministerial responsibility remained clouded. From 2 January to 9 August 1870, Ollivier as minister of justice was in fact but not in name prime minister (*président du conseil*): when ministers met in *conseil des ministres* the emperor presided; when in *conseil de cabinet* Ollivier chaired the meeting (as *chef du cabinet*) and Napoleon absented himself. The new constitution, ratified by plebiscite on 8 May 1870, resolved the issue of responsibility. Ministers were to be responsible to both the emperor and the two chambers. Reverses suffered in the Franco-Prussian War led on 9 August 1870 to the fall of Ollivier's government (which had already been twice altered, on 13 April and 15 May) and the creation of a government headed by General Charles Guillaume Cousin-Montauban, comte de Palikao (1796–1878). The Ministry of Fine Arts, created for the cabinet of 2 January 1870, was abolished and its functions transferred to the Ministry of Public Instruction (23 August). This last government of the Second Empire ceased functions on 4 September 1870.

The ministries (listed in alphabetical order) and ministers (listed in chronological order by date of appointment within ministries) of the Second Empire were:

Agriculture and Commerce (abolished and its functions added to the Ministry of Interior, 22 January 1852, and then to the Ministry of Public Works, 23 June 1853; reestablished 17 July 1869): Lefèbvre-Duruflé (3 December 1851), Alfred Leroux (1815–1880; 14 July 1869), Charles Louvet (1806–1882; 2 January 1870), Clément Duvernois (1836–1879; 9 August 1870).

Algeria and the Colonies (created June 1858, taking colonial responsibilities from the Ministry of Marine; abolished 24 November 1860, responsibility for colonies returning to the Ministry of Marine): Prince Napoleon (24 June 1858), Chasseloup-Laubat (24 March 1859).

Finance: Fould (3 December 1851), Bineau (22 January 1852), Magne (3 February 1855), Forcade La Roquette (26 November 1860), Fould (14 November 1861), Rouher (20 January 1867), Magne (13 November 1867), Louis Buffet (2 January 1870), Alexis Emile Segris (1811–1880; 14 April 1870), Magne (9 August 1870).

Fine Arts (created 2 January 1870; became Ministry of Letters, Science, and Fine Arts 15 May 1870; abolished and its functions added to Public Instruction 23 August 1870): Maurice Richard (1832–1888; 2 January 1870).

Foreign Affairs: Turgot (3 December 1851), Drouyn de Lhuys (28 July 1852), Walewski (7 May 1855), Thouvenel (4 January 1860), Drouyn de Lhuys (15 October 1862), Lionel François René, marquis de Moustier (1817–1869; 1 September 1866), Charles Jean, marquis de La Valette (17 December 1868), Henri Godefroi, prince de La Tour d'Auvergne (17 July 1869); Napoleon, comte Daru (2 January 1870), Antoine, duc de Gramont (15 May 1870), La Tour d'Auvergne (9 August 1870).

Interior (Ministry of Interior, Agriculture, and Commerce from 22 January 1852 to June 1853 when the latter two functions were transferred to the Ministry of Public Works and the functions of the Ministry of General Police were absorbed by the Ministry of the Interior; Ministry of the Interior and of General Security [*sûreté générale*] from 7 February until 14 June 1858): Morny (3 December 1851), Persigny (22 January 1852), Billault (23 June 1854), Espinasse (7 February 1858), Delangle (14 June 1858), Padoue (5 May 1859), Billault (1 November 1859), Persigny (23 November 1860), Paul Boudet (1800–1877; 23 June 1863), La Valette (28 March 1865), Pierre Ernest Pinard (13 November 1867), Forcade La Roquette (17 December 1868), J.P.E.N. Chevandrier de Valdrôme (1810–1878; 2 January 1870), Henri Chevreau (9 August 1870).

Justice (Ministry of Justice and Cults from 23 June 1863): Rouher (3 December 1851), Abbatucci (22 January 1852), Paul de Royer (1808–1877; 16 November 1857), Delangle (5 May 1859), Baroche (23 June 1863), J.B.M. Prosper Duvergier de Hauranne (1798–1887; 17 July 1869), Ollivier (2 January 1870), M.E.A.T. Grandperret (1818–1890; 9 August 1870).

Maison de l'Empereur (separated from the Ministry of State November 1860, combined with the functions of the grand marshal of the palace and given ministerial status; absorbed functions of Fine Arts 23 June 1863 to 2 January 1870): Vaillant (4 December 1860).

Marine and Colonies (see Ministry of Algeria and the Colonies): Ducos (3 December 1851), Vice-Admiral François Alphonse Hamelin (1796–1864; 19 April 1855), Chasseloup-Laubat (24 November 1860), Admiral Charles Rigault de Genouilly (20 January 1867).

Police (created 22 January 1852 as the Ministry of General Police; abolished 23 June 1853 and its functions transferred to the Ministry of the Interior): Maupas (22 January 1852).

Public Instruction (until 23 June 1863 Ministry of Public Instruction and Cults; Ministry of Public Instruction and Fine Arts from 23 August 1870): Hippolyte Fortoul (3 December 1851), Vaillant (acting minister from 1 July 1856), Gustave Rouland (13 August 1856), Duruy (23 June 1863), Louis Olivier Bourbeau (1811–1877; 17 July 1869), Segris (2 January 1870), Richard (acting minister from 14 April 1870), Jacques Philippe Mège (1817–1878; 15 May 1870), Jules Louis Joseph Brame (1808–1878; 9 August 1870).

Public Works (Ministry of Agriculture, Commerce and Public Works, 23 June 1853 to 17 July 1869, when a Ministry of Agriculture and Commerce was reestablished): Magne (3 December 1851), Lefèbvre-Duruflé (25 January 1852), Magne (28 July 1852), Rouher (3 February 1855), Béhic (23 June 1863), Forcade La Roquette (20 January 1867), Edouard Valery Gressier (1815–1892; 17 December 1868), Auguste Elisabeth Joseph Bonamour, marquis de Talhouët-Toy (1819–1884; 2 January 1870), Ignace Plichon (1814–1888; 15 May 1870), Jérôme, baron David (9 August 1870).

War: Saint-Arnaud (3 December 1851), Vaillant (11 March 1854), Randon (5 May 1859), Niel (20 January 1867), Marshal Edmond Leboeuf (1809–1888; 21 August 1869), Pierre Charles, vicomte Dejean (1807–1872; acting minister from 20 July 1870), Palikao (9 August 1870).

In addition Billault and Magne (both from 26 November 1860) and Baroche (from 3 December 1860) were ministers without portfolio. From 1853 the ministers presiding the Conseil d'Etat were also members of the Council of Ministers: Baroche (30 December 1852), Rouher (23 June 1863), Rouland (18 October 1863), Adolphe Vuitry (28 September 1864), Chasseloup-Laubat (17 July 1869), M. F. Esquirou de Parieu (1815–1893; 2 January 1870), Julien Henri Busson-Billault (1823–1888; 9 August 1870). The ministers of state (from 14 December 1852 until November 1860 Ministry of State and of the Imperial House [*maison de l'empereur*]) during the Second Empire were Casabianca (22 January 1852), Fould (29 July 1852), Walewski (23 November 1860), Billault (23 June 1863), and Rouher (18 October 1863).

P. Guiral, ''Les cabinets ministériels sous le Second Empire,'' in M. Antoine et al., *Origines et histoire des cabinets des ministres en France* (Geneva, 1975); V. Wright, ''Les directeurs [de ministère] et secrétaires généraux sous le Second Empire,'' in F. de Baecque et al., *Les directeurs de ministère en France (XIXe–XXe siècles)* (Geneva, 1976). *Related entries:* ALGERIA; BONAPARTISM; CONSEIL D'ETAT; CONSEIL PRIVE; CONSTITUTION; GOVERNMENT FINANCE; LIBERAL EMPIRE; MINISTER OF STATE; ORLEANS DECREES; REFORM.

MIRES, JULES (1809–1871), financier who enjoyed spectacular success in the 1850s, creating a newspaper empire, establishing an investment bank and promoting metallurgical concerns in the Midi, the reconstruction of Marseilles, and government loans and railways abroad. In his time Mirès was a controversial figure, and he remains so. For some, he was an adventurer and an unscrupulous speculator whose spectacular rise and fall between 1849 and 1861 seemed to symbolize the stock jobbing and corruption of journalists and financiers during the Second Empire. For others he was a genius who profited from the growth of investment opportunities and left his mark but who made too many powerful enemies in business and government circles.

Like Emile and Isaac Pereire and the newspaper tycoon Moïse (Polydore) Millaud, Mirès was a Jew from Bordeaux, where he was born 9 December 1809. His origins were modest (his father was a watchmaker), his formal education minimal, and his early career unremarkable even after he came to Paris in 1841. In 1848 he was still a simple *courtier d'affaires*. His rise dates only from 1849–1850. From then until his career was brought to an end with his trial for fraud in 1861, he engaged in two complementary activities, journalism and finance. It was the purchase of the *Journal des chemins de fer*, which he made with Millaud in 1849, that launched his career. The two men changed this technical journal into a financial paper, addressing itself above all to provincial investors. They also founded the *Conseiller du peuple*, for which Alphonse de Lamartine (1790–1869) wrote. Mirès subsequently bought the bonapartist papers *Le pays* (1850) and *Le constitutionnel* (1852). In 1851, again with Millaud, he set up the Caisse des Actions Réunies, an investment company capitalized at 5 million francs. In view of its success and that of the Pereires' Crédit Mobilier (established in 1852), Mirès reorganized his company in 1853 as the Caisse Générale des Chemins de Fer with a nominal capital of 50 million francs, which made it a powerful financial institution. He took control of the new company, in association with Félix Solar (1815–1871). These activities were linked, for Mirès used his newspapers to promote his investments, as did many major companies and banks during the Second Empire. Those investments included the Crédit Foncier of Nevers and that of Marseilles, as well as the Société Générale des Ports de Marseille, where, in partnership with Solar, Mirès competed with the Pereires from 1856.

Such was Mirès' success that he became a flamboyant millionaire and in 1860 was awarded the Legion of Honor by Napoleon III, who was then visiting Marseilles. He married his daughter to the Prince Alphonse de Polignac and negotiated the Turkish loan of 1860. However, in December of the same year one of Mirès' collaborators in the Caisse Générale des Chemins de Fer brought a suit against him, perhaps at the instigation of the Pereires or the Rothschild group, both of whom he had alienated. He was arrested 17 February 1861, thrown into Mazas Prison, held in strict secrecy for some time, brought to trial for fraud, and found guilty 11 July 1861. Mirès was sentenced (together with Solar, who was tried in absentia) to five years in prison and a fine of 3,000 francs. The sentence was confirmed on appeal in August but revoked at the end of December by the *cour de cassation*, which ordered a retrial (at Douai). On 21 April 1862 the original judgment was quashed and Mirès was released. The question is still open as to whether Mirès' business practices were any more reprehensible than those of others at the time. Nor should his dubious methods blind us to his contribution to French finance and to capital exports. He promoted the investment habit, was a leading advocate of the first government loan to be floated without the use of *haute banque* intermediaries, that of 1854, and his Caisse des Actions Réunies was a major catalyst in the foundation of the better-known Crédit Mobilier. Even his promotional activities left a permanent mark in two domains: in Marseilles where he obtained the gas-lighting concession in 1855, developed land around the new port at La Joliette and even proposed a major redevelopment scheme for the old city; and in railways in Spain (the

Pamplona-Saragossa, opened in 1855) and in the Papal States. He died at Marseilles, 6 June 1871.

L. Girard, "L'affaire Mirès," *BSHM* (1951), and *La politique des travaux publics du
Second Empire* (Paris, 1952); P. Gueyraud, *La chronique des Gueyraud* (Marseilles,
1976); M. Martin, "Presse, publicité et grandes affaires sous le Second Empire," *RH*
256 (1976); J. Mirès, *A mes juges, ma vie et mes affaires* (Paris, 1861).

Barrie M. Ratcliffe

Related entries: BANKING; CREDIT MOBILIER; GOVERNMENT FI-
NANCE; MILLAUD; PEREIRE.

MISTRAL, FREDERIC (1830–1914), Provençal poet, author of *Mirèio*; born
at Maillane (Bouches-du-Rhône), 8 September 1830, to a family of moderately
well-to-do landowners. Mistral's father was fifty-five, his mother barely twenty.
The boy was sent to Avignon for a classical education but clung obstinately to
his mother tongue, Provençal. At Avignon he formed a close friendship with
one of his instructors, the Provençal poet and orator, Joseph Roumanille (1818–
1891). After taking his law degree from the University of Aix-en-Provence in
1851, Mistral returned to Maillane and to the family homestead, determined to
write poetry in Provençal and to restore the language to literary dignity.

On 21 May 1854, at the Chateau de Fontségur, Mistral, Roumanille, Théodore
Aubanel (1829–1886), and four others formed a society to purify and proclaim
the Provençal language and literature, which came to be known (the reason is
not clear) as the Félibrige. The next year appeared the group's official journal,
Armana prouvençau (*Almanach provençal*). And on 2 February 1859, Mistral
published at Avignon his epic poem, *Mirèio*, a rustic idyll in twelve cantos, with
French translation on the opposite page. The work struck Paris as a literary
bombshell, revealing the existence of a genuine Provençal literature. The poet
Alphonse Lamartine (1790–1869) hailed the poem and its author, to whom he
was introduced. Mistral also formed a close friendship with Alphonse Daudet
(1840–1897) but spent little of his life in Paris, despite the fact that *Mirèio*
(translated into French as *Mireille* and into many other languages) sold ten
thousand copies a year, was crowned by the Académie Française and, with
Mistral's collaboration, was made into an opera in 1864 by Charles Gounod. In
1867 appeared Mistral's *Calendau*, reflecting the deep conservatism of the Félibrige, its resistance to centralization (before 1870 Mistral proclaimed himself
a republican and showed sympathy for Pierre Joseph Proudhon's federalist ideas),
and to the hectic changes accompanying economic and social developments under
the Second Empire. In 1869 Mistral greeted the formal alliance of Félibrige and
the Basques (Catalans) with his poem *Chant de la coupe*. He died at Maillane,
25 March 1914.

R. Aldington, *Introduction to Mistral* (London, 1956); L. Bayle, *Grandeur de Mistral:
Essai de critique littéraire* (Paris, 1964); J. Bornecque, ed., *Histoire d'une amitié: Correspondance inédite entre Alphonse Daudet et Frédéric Mistral, 1860–1897* (Paris, 1979);

J. P. Clébert, *Mistral ou l'empire du soleil: Première époque, 1830–1860* (Paris, 1983); J. Pélissier, *Frédéric Mistral au jour le jour* (Paris, 1968); G. Place, *Frédéric Mistral* (Paris, 1970); P. Rollet, ed., *Frédéric Mistral: Mémoires et récits; correspondance* (Paris, 1969).

MOCQUARD, JEAN FRANCOIS (1791–1864), writer, senator, private secretary and *chef du cabinet* of Napoleon III; born at Bordeaux, 11 November 1791. Mocquard studied law at Paris. After a brief diplomatic career (he was named secretary of legation at Wurtzburg in 1812), he completed his law studies, became a lawyer, and had some brilliant successes (1818–1826) defending liberal and bonapartist causes before illness forced him to leave the bar. He was subprefect from 1830 to 1839 but resigned in that latter year to devote himself to the service of Prince Louis Napoleon Bonaparte, whose newspaper, *Le commerce*, he directed. In fact, Mocquard had long known Queen Hortense (1783–1837), Louis Napoleon's mother, helped her with her business affairs, assisted her in writing her memoirs, and was even rumored to have been her lover. He spent time with Louis Napoleon at Arenenberg and London and visited him regularly in prison at Ham from 1840. After the Revolution of 1848, Mocquard headed Louis Napoleon's secretariat at the Hôtel du Rhin (Place Vendôme), was one of the most active members of the committee to elect him president in December 1848, helped to draft the election manifesto, and after the election was named *chef du cabinet* of the new president. Mocquard was one of the first to be involved in the conspiracy that culminated in the coup d'état of December 1851. During the first part of the Empire, he remained Napoleon III's private and confidential secretary and *chef du cabinet*. His brother, Constant Amédée, was the emperor's notary and was named to the Legion of Honor.

Courteous, kindly, the soul of tact and, above all, of discretion, Mocquard was involved in the most intimate affairs of his master and undoubtedly served him in many confidential missions. On the eve of Napoleon III's marriage to Eugénie, Mocquard negotiated the settlement with the emperor's discarded English mistress, Elizabeth (Henrietta) Howard. He corrected Napoleon III's letters and from 1860 performed the same service in regard to the manuscript of the *Histoire de Jules César*, attempting to make the imperial style less wordy while retaining its flowing and monumental quality.

Mocquard was, in fact, a writer who collaborated on a number of plays, notably with Victor Séjour (1817–1874): *Masque de poix* (1855), *Fausse adultère* (1856), *Fiancés d'Albano* (1858), *Tireuse de cartes* (1859), *Massacres de Syrie* (1860), and *Volontaires de 1814* (1862). One of his plays, denouncing the role of the church in the Mortara affair, was applauded at the Porte Saint Martin theater by both the emperor and the empress. In 1861 Mocquard published a novel, *Jessie*, in the *Revue contemporaine*. It was he, with his theatrical contacts, who introduced Napoleon III to the actress Marguerite Bellanger (Justine Marie Leboeuf), one of the last loves of the emperor. But Mocquard also played a role in less frivolous matters. He was an opponent of the financial methods of Isaac and Emile Pereire and, toward the end of his life, an ally of those who advised liberal, anti-clerical reform that would gain the support of elements on the left.

His health failing, Mocquard was named to the Senate 7 May 1863. He died at Paris 12 December 1864, discreet to the end, taking with him to the grave his incomparable knowledge of the Second Empire. He was succeeded as *chef du cabinet* by the emperor's secretary and friend, Etienne Conti (1812–1872).

MONET, CLAUDE (1840–1926), Impressionist painter; born at Paris, 14 November 1840. Monet moved at an early age to Le Havre. As a youth he showed a precocious aptitude in drawing, doing caricatures that were exhibited in the stationer's shop where he met Eugène Boudin. It was through Boudin that Monet was introduced not only to landscape painting but to the direct observation of nature and painting out of doors. Returning to Paris in 1859, against his parents' wishes, he studied at the Académie Suisse, meeting Camille Pissarro, and frequenting the Brasserie des Martyrs where Gustave Courbet and the other realists gathered. He served in the army in Algeria from 1860, returning to Paris late in 1862. The light and color of North Africa made a stong impression on him as it had on Eugène Delacroix in 1832. It was after his return that he met Johann Jongkind (1819–1891), the Dutch artist who painted landscapes in Normandy with a concern for the qualities of light. Monet enrolled in the open studio of the academic painter Charles Gleyre (1808–1874), where he met Frédéric Bazille (1841–1870), Alfred Sisley (1839–1899), and Pierre Auguste Renoir. In 1863, he and his fellow students spent time at the Forest of Fountainebleau, absorbing ideas from Charles François Daubigny, Théodore Rousseau, and other Barbizon painters. The year 1864 was spent primarily in Normandy at Ste. Adresse and Honfleur, where Monet painted with Bazille. Two of his works, seascapes, were finally accepted in the Salon of 1865 (like most other painters of his day, he had longed for this conventional sign of success) and received some favorable comment. A very large work, now extant in only two fragments (Louvre and Eknayan Collection, Paris) and an oil sketch (Pushkin Museum, Moscow), *Luncheon on the Grass*, was also begun in 1865. Monet followed some of Courbet's suggestions and altered the work. It was later claimed for nonpayment of a debt and left in a damp place where it deteriorated. The painting was Monet's response to Edouard Manet's earlier *Luncheon* (1863) and showed both Manet's influence and Monet's departures. The freedom of brushwork and the concern for outdoor light are the features that distinguish Monet's rendering. His entry in the Salon of 1866 was the large figure painting *Camille* (1866, Kunsthalle, Bremen), for which his future wife posed. Emile Zola praised it, recognizing its lively appearance, something that set it apart from the other rather dry works in the Salon. However, it was not indicative of Monet's future direction.

With *Women in the Garden* (1866–1867, Louvre) Monet returned to painting figures set in a landscape. The composition is unusual in the manner in which it was painted. The large canvas, painted completely out of doors, was suspended by a system of pulleys, which allowed Monet to lower it into a trench dug in the ground, thus permitting him to paint the upper portions. Camille posed once more for the four female figures. The striking quality of this work is the light, which illuminates the figures and leaves with such brightness that one senses the actuality of the sun's rays directly observed at a particular time. It was rejected by the jury for the Salon of 1867. The light seems even more intense, the colors more brilliant in *The Terrace at Sainte Adresse* (1867, Metropolitan Museum of Art, New York). In this painting, the sense of a particular moment that will change immediately, the integration of figure and environment owing to similar treatment, the juxtaposition of complementary colors, the interpenetrating forms, the high viewpoint, and the flattening of space are some of the characteristics that Monet would explore even further during the Impressionist period in the decades to follow and that would confound all but a few of the Second Empire's art critics.

Several paintings done in Normandy in 1867, such as *Route de la Ferme St Siméon, Honfleur* (Fogg Art Museum, Harvard University, Cambridge and Lewyt Collection, New York), depict snow scenes, bringing Monet closer to his later landscapes where figures, if present, are incidental. An important aspect of these works, which are based on Dutch landscapes but are transformed in effect and meaning, is that the viewer enters the painting by a wide pathway that very quickly narrows. It seems to move upward in space rather than backward, as is also the case in *Rue de La Bavolle, Honfleur* (1865, Museum of Fine Arts, Boston), thus making the entry more rapid and the space shallower. Monet could also find similar effects in Japanese woodblock prints, which he as well as other Impressionists admired and which he collected. Another painting of this pre-Impressionist period that points toward later developments during the full bloom of Impressionism is *La Grenouillère* (1869, Metropolitan Museum). Monet and Renoir painted this motif of a café and swimming area in the Seine near Bougival together, producing canvases with quite similar stylistic features. In Monet's painting, the brushwork is quick and spontaneous in some areas of the background and organized in horizontal broken dabs in the water. Seemingly uncomposed in the traditional meaning of the term, the canvas conveys the feeling of a scene come upon by accident, directly experienced, viewed as a fleeting, ephemeral event, and captured with a variety of brushwork and color that is the equivalent of the vivacity of the moment itself. The contemporaneity of the here-and-now that Honoré Daumier, Courbet, and Manet sought has here been brought to an even more precise experience, based on the immediacy of perception and rendering of changing conditions of light and atmosphere. Temporal values, so important and richly explored in Monet's later works, find their roots in this period. But these characteristics were unappreciated at the time, and 1867 marks the beginning of a long period of critical obscurity, poverty, and occasional misery for the artist.

Monet left for London during the Franco-Prussian War, discovering at first hand the paintings of Turner and Constable and making contact, through his friend Daubigny, with the dealer Paul Durand-Ruel (1831–1922). On his return to Paris in 1871, he proceeded to experiment even further with light, achieving luminosity through the juxtaposition of fragmented patches of complementary colors. His series of *Haystacks* and *Cathedrals* in the 1890s and still later his *Water Lilies* were an important new development with major repercussions in the art of the twentieth century. Monet died at Giverny (Eure), 6 December 1926.

K. S. Champa, *Studies in Early Impressionism* (New Haven, 1973); M. Hoog, "L'oeuvre peint de Claude Monet," *Etudes*, (October 1979); J. Isaacson, *Monet: "Le Déjeuner sur l'herbe"* (New York, 1972); J. Rewald, *The History of Impressionism* 4th ed. (New York, 1973); W. Seitz, *Monet* (New York, 1960); D. Wildenstein, *Claude Monet: Biographie et catalogue raisonné, Vol. 1: 1840–1881* (Lausanne, 1974).

Beverley Giblon

Related entries: BOUDIN; COURBET; DAUBIGNY; MANET; PISSARRO; RENOIR; ROUSSEAU.

MONETARY UNION. See LATIN MONETARY UNION.

LE MONITEUR UNIVERSEL, until 1869 the official daily Paris newspaper of the Second Empire. From 1789 the Librairie Panckoucke contracted with the government to carry an official section in its newspaper. Thus *Le moniteur universel* maintained, under its editor in chief Paul Dalloz (1829–1887, nephew of Panckoucke) and its director Ernest Panckoucke (1806–1886, grandson of the founder) a limited independence, although the official section was supervised by the minister of state and contained official notices, speeches, and news releases unavailable to other newspapers. (In 1860 a *Bulletin* was added, collecting and summarizing for the public communications from the various ministries.) The provincial press relied heavily on *Le moniteur*, frequently reprinting its articles and columns. The nonofficial section incorporated literature, criticism, serials, and miscellaneous news. The literary figures who wrote for *Le moniteur* included such well-known authors as Théophile Gautier (*Le moniteur*'s art critic), Champfleury (Jules Husson), Octave Feuillet, Arsène Houssaye (1815–1896), Prosper Mérimée, Alexandre Dumas fils, Henry Murger (1822–1861), and Charles Augustin Sainte-Beuve, who early came over (6 December 1852) from *Le constitutionnel* as an editor, bringing with him his column of literary criticsm, "Causeries du lundi." Among the collaborators of the paper were Philippe Cucheval-Clarigny (1822–1895), Edmond About, and Jules Levallois (1829–1903). Sainte-Beuve left *Le moniteur* in 1858 for an Ecole Normale appointment, but returned in 1867, before leaving finally (for *Le Temps*) in 1869.

Concerned with encouraging a wide circulation, the government at the beginning of the Empire lowered the subscription price of *Le moniteur* from 120 francs to 40. In 1863, however, Moïse Millaud published a nonpolitical newspaper, *Le petit journal*, at 5 centimes (1 sou) per copy. Its success was so great that

Dalloz imitated the formula by creating his own inexpensive version of *Le moniteur*, *Le moniteur du soir* (known popularly as the *Petit moniteur*). With a subscription price of only 20 francs (15 for teachers), or 6 centimes per copy, the new paper, edited in 1869 by Léo Lespès (1815–1875; known as Timothée Trimm) who had been lured from *Le petit journal* by a salary of 100,000 francs, fulfilled expectations. It quickly enjoyed a circulation some four times greater than that of *Le moniteur universel*, which was 25,000 in 1855, 16,402 in July 1858, 17,242 in August 1861, and 25,000 in 1866. However, the minister of state, Eugène Rouher, unhappy with the Panckoucke contract since it allowed government ministers to publish independently, took the opportunity of its expiry to create by decree of 16 November 1868 an entirely official newspaper, *The Journal officiel*, on 1 January 1869. The first director was Norbert Billiart. By March the evening edition, *Le petit journal officiel*, had a circulation of 160,000.

Natalie Isser

Related entries: *CONSTITUTIONNEL*; MARINONI; MINISTER OF STATE; *PATRIE*; *PAYS*; PRESS REGIME.

MONTALEMBERT, CHARLES, COMTE DE (1810–1870), liberal Catholic leader, politician, orator, publicist, and historian; born of an English mother and *émigré* father at London, 15 April 1810. Raised in England until 1819 and strongly influenced by his maternal grandfather, the author James Forbes, Montalembert throughout his life looked to the English system as the model to be followed by France. Although more conservative than Félicité de Lamennais (1782–1854) or Père Henri Lacordaire, he enthusiastically collaborated with them in 1830–1831 on the liberal Catholic daily, *L'avenir*, which he also helped to finance and whose banner, "God and Liberty," he henceforth took as his personal motto. When Gregory XVI condemned the principles propagated by *L'avenir*, he submitted, but he failed to dissuade his friend Lamennais from breaking with the church. Active in the July Monarchy's Chamber of Peers from 1837 to 1848 (he had succeeded to this title in 1831), he organized and led an impressive movement for liberty of education aimed at advancing the cause of religious instruction by breaking the state's monopoly over higher and secondary schools.

Although most Catholics rallied, with varying enthusiasm, to the Second Republic in February 1848, the Whigish Montalembert greeted the revolution with cool reserve. Shocked by the June Days of 1848, he and the majority of his coreligionists looked about for security for religion and property against the "socialist" threat. Montalembert queried presidential candidates General Louis Eugène Cavaignac (1802–1857) and Prince Louis Napoleon concerning their views on freedom of education and the restoration of Pius IX; Napoleon eventually gave the necessary assurances. The Catholic Committee still refrained from designating an official candidate, but Montalembert's energetic support for Louis Napoleon as the only man capable of strengthening a weak government and of ensuring order was a major asset for him during his campaign. After Louis Napoleon's election in December 1848, Montalembert sat on the commission that prepared the famous Falloux law (1850) providing for liberty of education, and he defended the measure against Catholic intransigents, such as Louis Veuillot, who attacked it as an inadequate compromise.

As a member of the Legislative Assembly, Montalembert fought for the constitutional revision desired by Louis Napoleon to permit his reelection, but on the day of the coup d'état of December 1851, he organized a protest of deputies against it. Disturbances in Paris and uprisings in the provinces, combined with an appeal made to him by a number of bishops, quickly caused him to veer about. He agreed to be a member of the Commission Consultative (a sort of preliminary Conseil d'Etat) and urged Catholics to vote yes in the approaching plebiscite, arguing that to do so was not to approve all that Louis Napoleon had done but constituted a choice of authority over revolutionary socialism. In February 1852 Montalembert was elected to the Corps Législatif as an official candidate. This stance represented a brief aberration, for the autocratic nature of the new regime, its Gallicanism, its disregard for parliamentary government and civil liberties, its seizure of Orleanist property in January 1852, led him to refuse appointment to the Senate and to publish a pamphlet in October 1852, *Catholic Interests in the Nineteenth Century*, entreating Catholics not to identify the church with despotism and, in fact, to demand the separation of church and state. In the first legislature of the Second Empire, Montalembert was the only declared opponent of the regime. In June 1852, during a session attended by Louis Napoleon, he warned of the consequences that would follow from a lack of control (his speech was printed for distribution). In 1853 he, alone of the deputies, refused to contribute to a ball offered in honor of Napoleon III and Eugénie by the Corps Législatif and in the same year was threatened with prosecution by the government for publishing a correspondence critical of the regime. The Corps Législatif voted 184 to 51 with 26 abstentions to permit prosecution, but the government then allowed the matter to drop. In the elections of 1857, Montalembert was one of only nine incumbents refused government approval. Moreover, the regime campaigned vigorously against him. As a result he was soundly defeated in the Doubs (Besançon), an experience repeated in 1863 when he ran unsuccessfully as a Union Libérale candidate but did not actively campaign. This opposition also cost Montalembert his position as the foremost Catholic political leader, for most of his coreligionists embraced the authoritarian Empire and preferred Veuillot's viewpoint. An ultramontane (favoring the supremacy of Rome), Montalembert watched with dismay the spread of a new ultramontanism that emphasized authority rather than liberty in both the church and the state. Despite his eclipse, his name still commanded attention. He was able to exert some influence among cultivated laymen through his writings in the *Correspondant*, which he and other liberal Catholics had revived in 1855, and through his membership in the Académie Française, to which he had been elected in 1850. In politics he was an Orleanist who supported unsuccessfully the cause of fusion of the two branches of the Bourbon family. A champion not of universal suffrage, which he opposed, but of English parliamentarianism, Montalembert was prosecuted in November 1858 for an article published in the *Correspondant* criticizing the French regime while praising England's ("Un débat sur l'Inde au parlement anglais"). Defended by Antoine Berryer, Montalembert was convicted and sentenced to six months in prison and a fine of 3,000 francs. Rejecting a pardon, he appealed, was again convicted, and was pardoned a second time by the emperor.

Unlike Catholics of the Veuillot variety, Montalembert and his liberal colleagues experienced no embarrassment when they began in 1860 to assail Napoleon III's Italian policy, for they were already in opposition to the regime. Montalembert's stinging critiques in his pamphlet *Pie IX et la France en 1849 et en 1859* and in the *Correspondant* called forth police proceedings against him by the state, congratulations from Rome, and a supportive formal visit from Adolphe Thiers. The favor he had found with Pius IX for this defense of papal temporal power was short-lived, however, for, invited to address the first international Catholic congress in August 1863 at Malines, Belgium, he proclaimed in eloquent but unguarded language his attachment to the liberties associated with the modern state. His two speeches represented his political testament and his last great attempt to reconcile the church with the principles of 1789. It was an attempt that gained nothing from the provocative title "The Free Church in the Free State," which he chose for his speeches on publishing them, a title that by evoking Cavour's favorite phrase could only be offensive to Rome. Montalembert was appalled at the *Syllabus of Errors* in 1864 by which the pope condemned many tenets of liberal Catholicism and bitter as he recognized that the Vatican Council, whose summoning he had applauded in 1869, was moving toward a proclamation of papal infallibility. In his view, such a doctrine, whether acceptable or not as a private belief, would, if pronounced, only reinforce the policies of the man he called the "Louis XIV of the papacy." Seriously ill from 1865, Montalembert approved the evolution of the regime toward a liberal and, eventually, a parliamentary Empire. Since 1858 he had favored Emile Ollivier to lead such a government and in the last months of his life proposed Ollivier for a seat in the Académie Française.

Significant for his leadership in behalf of freedom of education, for the support he won for Louis Napoleon during his rise to power, for his opposition to authoritarianism, and for his valiant but discouraging struggle to persuade the Catholic church to adjust to the political realities of a new age, Montalembert never appreciated the nature of the social problems that developed during his lifetime. His narrowly nineteenth-century-liberal and paternalistic approach led socialists to dub him the "Jeremiah of property." He died at Paris, 13 March 1870.

J. Finlay, *The Liberal Who Failed* (Washington, D.C., 1968); A. Latreille, "Les dernières années de Montalembert," *RHEF* (July–December 1958); R. Marlin, "La dernière tentative électorale de Montalembert aux élections législatives de 1863," RHMC (October-December 1970), "Montalembert et l'Europe," *RHEF* 56 (1970); C. de Montalembert, *Oeuvres* (9 vols.; Paris, 1860-1868), *Les moines d'occident* (Paris, 1860-1877; his main literary achievement), and *Catholicisme et liberté, correspondance inedit avec le Père Lacordaire, Mgr. de Mérode [Montalembert's brother in law], et A. de Falloux, 1852-1870* (Paris, 1970); A. Trannoy, *Montalembert, Dieu et liberté* (Paris, 1970).

Raymond L. Cummings

Related entries: CORRESPONDANT; DUPANLOUP; FALLOUX LAW; GALLICANISM; HYACINTHE; INFALLIBILITY, DOCTRINE OF; LACORDAIRE; LOUIS PIE; ROMAN QUESTION; SOCIAL CATHOLICISM; *SYLLABUS OF ERRORS*; VATICAN COUNCIL; VEUILLOT.

MONT CENIS TUNNEL, the first great Alpine tunnel to be completed. The Mont Cenis tunnel was the product of Franco-Italian cooperation and a major engineering achievement. It was built under the Col de Fréjus over which Napoleon I had constructed a military road in the first decade of the nineteenth century.

The tunnel and the railway link between Sardinia and Savoy of which it is part were the result of two favorable circumstances. On the one hand, Cavour promoted the economic development of Sardinia in the 1850s and was anxious to secure the help of foreign enterprise and capital. On the other, the 1850s saw a remarkable outflow of French capital that went, above all, to central and southern Europe and was directed principally into railway promotion and construction. In Italy, for instance, France provided half of the capital for railways down to 1880. The Victor Emmanuel Railway Company was established in 1853. This French-controlled company under the banker Charles Laffitte (b. 1803) was to build a line to link Sardinia with Savoy with extensions to Lyons in France and Geneva in Switzerland. The line, except for the section that was to be the Mont Cenis tunnel, was completed in 1858 and the following spring carried 200,000 French troops to the Italian campaign.

Laffitte's company lacked both the financial resources and the courage to build the tunnel, and in 1857 the Sardinian government agreed to do so. It calculated that construction would cost 40 million francs and proposed to sell the completed tunnel to the Victor Emmanuel Railway for half this sum. After Nice and Savoy were ceded to France, the new French frontier went over the proposed tunnel. The French government therefore agreed to assume part of the construction costs.

The main interest of the Mont Cenis tunnel lies in the technical difficulties posed by its construction and the techniques used to solve them. Studies made in the 1840s had concluded, in fact, that the tunnel was not feasible since no rock-drilling equipment that could accomplish the task existed. Blasting was still done by gunpowder rather than by the more powerful dynamite that later tunnel builders were able to use. A first solution to the technical problems was offered by Germain Sommeiller (1815–1871), working at the University of Turin. Sommeiller devised a rail-mounted drill carriage and, as chief engineer for the tunnel project, was to perfect a pneumatic drill that speeded up tunneling. He was also to solve ventilation problems by the use of forced air from water-powered fans and the problem of recruiting and retaining the large labor force needed by setting up elaborate camps equipped with schools, hospitals, and recreational facilities. It is indicative of the magnitude of the tunnelers' task that, despite these innovations, it still took fourteen years to complete the 14 kilometer horeshoe-shaped tunnel that ran from Modane on the French side to Bardonecchia on the Italian. Work was completed in December 1870, and the tunnel opened to traffic in September the following year. The Mont Cenis tunnel, the example it offered, and the machinery that was perfected to build it opened the way for other Alpine tunnels. In 1872 work began on the Saint-Gotthard and in 1898 on the Simplon.

M. Abrate, "A cento anni del traforo de Moncenisio," *Risorgimento* 24 (1972); R. E. Cameron, "French Finance and Italian Unity: the Cavourian Decade," *AHR* 62 (April 1957); B. Gille, "Les capitaux français au Piémont (1849-1859)," *Histoire des entreprises* 3 (1959); F. Kossuth, "The Mont Cenis Tunnel," *Engineering* 11–13 (1871–1872).

Barrie M. Ratcliffe

Related entry: RAILROADS.

MONTICELLI, ADOLPHE (1824–1886), painter of landscapes, still lifes, and imaginary fetes; born at Marseilles, 16 October 1824. Monticelli had a provincial upbringing and remained outside the center of art and culture until his arrival in Paris in 1846. He came to art only after he had not succeeded in either pharmacy or music, receiving his first formal lessons in drawing in 1841. During his first stay in Paris, he studied with Paul Delaroche (1797–1856) and was no doubt influenced by Eugène Delacroix's use of color. He returned to Marseilles, traveled through Provence, and painted portraits and landscapes of little note during the 1850s. Monticelli returned to Paris in 1856, and it was during this period that Narcisse Diaz' influence predominated. Monticelli spent considerable time painting with Diaz, becoming more actively interested in the subject matter of the rococo period and thus associating with the rococo revival and its renewal of interest in nymphs, fetes galantes, and fantasy. It should be noted that the Empress Eugénie was attempting to recreate aspects of the eighteenth century in her residences, reflecting her admiration of the *ancien régime*. Monticelli's paintings in the 1860s such as *Confidences* (1867) and *A Dream of Woods and Sunlight* (1869, both Corcoran Gallery, Washington) demonstrate the lessons learned from Diaz: small format, vibrant colors, thickly applied impasto, objects and figures dissolving in the background, and vigorous and expressive brushstrokes. The dense impasto became progressively more so in the 1870s and 1880s, the artist's facture becoming so arbitrary that it could be described as verging on the chaotic. Monticelli achieved notable success in Marseilles and was admired by Paul Cézanne (1839–1906) and Vincent Van Gogh (1853–1890). Monticelli died at Marseilles, 29 June 1886.

A. Sheon, *Monticelli: His Contemporaries, His Influence* (Pittsburgh, 1978).

Beverley Giblon

Related entry: DIAZ.

MONTIJO, EUGENIA. See EUGENIE.

MOREAU, GUSTAVE (1826–1898), painter of mythological and symbolic scenes; born at Paris, 6 April 1826. Moreau, who won a drawing prize at age thirteen, was interested in art at an early age. He began his serious studies at the Ecole des Beaux-Arts in 1846 with the neoclassicist painter François Picot (1786–1868) and received government commissions (with the help of his father, an architect for the city of Paris) to copy works in the Louvre as well as for works of his own composition. He participated in the Salon of 1852 for the first time with his *Pieta* (1851, location unknown). Subsequently his paintings were accepted every year up to and including 1855.

Moreau's subject matter was most often mythological, as in *Anthenians Delivered to the Minotaur in the Cretan Labyrinth* (1855, Musée de l'Ain, Bourg-en-Bresse), commissioned by the minister of state for 4,000 francs and shown at the international exhibition of 1855. His works at this time show the influence of Théodore Chassériau, his close friend, in subject matter, and of Eugène Delacroix in color and dynamic form, bringing his paintings closer to romanticism than his earlier academic training would have indicated or permitted.

In Italy from 1857 to 1859, Moreau studied the old masters as well as doing freely sketched watercolors directly from nature, developing some of his taste for richness of color. Moreau's return to the Salon in 1864 with *Oedipus and the Sphinx* (Metropolitan Museum of Art, New York), recalling Dominique Ingres' work done fifty-six years earlier, caused a sensation. It combined the linearism of his academic training and the strong colorism and content underlying the romantic spirit. It was the focus of a caricature by Honoré Daumier and others but was purchased by Prince Napoleon for 8,000 francs. Moreau intended it to convey a message, although one imbued with an enigmatic symbolism. An aura of mysticism, of the inscrutable, and a feeling of the visionary pervades. Moreau was striving for a more indirect form of expression, one that evokes or suggests rather than clearly states. He sought not what he could see or touch, as was the case with Gustave Courbet, but what he felt, his inner sentiment. A favorite theme, woman as evil, sensuous, seductive, treacherous, is seen repeatedly in his later works devoted to Delilah, Europa, or Leda. Typical of this romantic image of woman as a femme fatale is Salome in *Salome Dancing before Herod* (1876, Los Angeles County Museum) exhibited in the Salon of 1876. It is one of several versions that depict Salome in a congested atmosphere, suggestive of opulence in the profusion of incident, ornament, and architectural detail. The painting speaks of a bizarre kind of eclecticism. It projects the heat of the Orient, with the figures and objects reinforcing the dream-like mystical quality with their insubstantial forms.

Moreau had attained sufficient security by the time of the 1869 Salon that he was able, subsequently, to retire from public life and to devote himself to the development of his style. He would be made an officer in the Legion of Honor in 1883 and appointed as teacher at the Ecole des Beaux-Arts in 1892. In this latter capacity he would teach Henri Matisse and Georges Rouault and exert an important influence on Odilon Redon. Moreau represents a more conservative stream, which, however, through its suggestive, evocative character, full of complexity and abundant with ideas, linked the romanticism of the early part of the century with the symbolism of the end of the century, skirting the intervening innovations in style and subject matter of the Impressionists. He died at Paris, 18 April 1898.

P. Hahlbrock, *Gustave Moreau, oder das Ungehangen in der Natur* (Berlin, 1976); J. Kaplan, *Gustave Moreau* (Los Angeles, 1974); P. L. Mathieu, *Gustave Moreau* (Boston, 1976); R. Von Holten, *L'art fantastique de Gustave Moreau* (Paris, 1960), and *Gustave Moreau, Symbolist* (Stockholm, 1965).

Beverley Giblon

Related entries: CHASSERIAU; DELACROIX.

MORNY, AUGUSTE, DUC DE (1811–1865), half-brother of Napoleon III; one of the conspirators of the coup d'état (2 December 1851); *homme d'affaires*, politician, sportsman, social figure, amateur of the arts, and a key statesman of the Second Empire: minister of the interior (1851–1852), ambassador to Russia (1856–1857), president of the Corps Législatif (1854–1865). Morny was born at Paris, 22 October 1811, illegitimate son of Louis Napoleon's mother, Hortense, and Joseph, comte de Flahaut (1785–1870), himself the illegitimate offspring of Talleyrand and Adélaïde Filleul, the illegitimate daughter of Louis XV. Although officially the child of a Prussian officer named Demorny who was living at Versailles, the boy was raised by Flahaut's mother, Mme. de Souza, while his father's influence watched over him. After a period of military service in Algeria, during which he saved the life of his commanding officer, Morny returned to France (1838), appropriated the title "comte," styled himself de Morny, and began a business career that soon made him a leader of the French beet sugar industry (he owned a refinery near Clermont-Ferrand).

Elected to the Chamber of Deputies from Puy-de-Dôme in 1842 and reelected in 1846, Morny at first supported the regime, but as troubles mounted for the July Monarchy, he passed over to the moderately progressive side of the chamber, attempting to mediate between the government and its opponents. Morny attempted, too, to warn the regime of the need to respond to the social question ("Quelques réflexions sur la politique actuelle," *Revue des deux mondes*, 1 January 1848). After the Revolution of 1848, he retired temporarily from politics but was again chosen deputy in 1849. Following the election of Louis Napoleon as president in December 1848, he arranged an introduction to his half-brother through a mutual friend, Félix, comte Bacciochi. Louis Napoleon, who may not have known of Morny's existence during their mother's lifetime, soon came to value him as an adviser, and perhaps as a friend, but always with a certain amount of reserve and even distrust. Certainly Morny played an important role in urging a reluctant Louis Napoleon to carry out the coup d'état of 2 December 1851 and in helping, as minister of the interior, to ensure its success, but he did not in any way dominate the president, the coup, or its aftermath. In fact, opposed and checked by Victor Fialin Persigny (whom Morny considered crude and stupid), C. E. de Maupas, and Achille Fould, blocked in his wish to be appointed president of the Corps Législatif, and genuinely upset by the Orleans confiscation decrees, he resigned on 22 January 1852. Although elected that same year to the legislature from Clermont-Ferrand and awarded the grand cross of the Legion of Honor on 2 December 1852, he stood aloof from politics until his appointment on 14 November 1854 to succeed Adolphe Billault as president of the Corps Législatif.

Morny had found his political niche. He was in many ways the perfect head of an assembly which, while accepting the authoritarian Empire, had no intention of being only a rubber stamp. Suave, cool, gracious, tactful, but mockingly witty, disdainful of "speechifying," Morny controlled the Corps Législatif with a firm hand and yet managed to win its acceptance as defender of the legislative prerogative. He was reelected, virtually unanimously, to the chamber in 1857 and 1863. A staunch opponent of the Crimean War, member of the Paris circle of Princess Dorothea Lieven (1785–1857), Morny was the logical choice to execute Napoleon III's policy of conciliation of Russia after 1856. His Russian embassy (1856–1857) did not succeed either in converting Russia into a vast market for France or in persuading the French emperor to abandon the alliance with Britain in favor of one with the former enemy. While at St. Petersburg, however, Morny wooed and married (January 1857) Princess Sophia Troubetskoy, half his age, and much in favor with the czar, who provided her with a dowry of 500,000 francs. Returned to Paris, Morny unceremoniously discarded his mistress of some twenty years, Mme. Le Hon, wife of a former Belgian minister to France and mother of Morny's illegitimate daughter, Louise, who later married Prince Joseph Poniatowski. Mme. Le Hon resisted; Napoleon III and Eugène Rouher became involved and took the side of the lady, to whom Rouher, asked by the emperor to arbitrate, awarded a large indemnity (3.5 million francs) from the privy purse. The affair made enemies of Morny and his former protégé Rouher, whom (together with Pierre Magne) he had brought into Napoleon III's service. Thereafter, the two men would be almost always in opposition.

Returned in July 1857 to his Corps Législatif post, Morny soon became aware of the new mood in that body and, indeed, in the country. Whether from ambition, statesmanship, or, more likely, both, he advocated political reform. He had little support in the imperial entourage, however, and was not on good terms with the few who shared his ideas (Prince Napoleon, for example, and Alexandre Walewski). After the reform decree of 24 November 1860, Morny's advice seemed to have little effect on the emperor. He had opposed the Italian War (but favored the 1860 liberalization of tariffs with Britain, although formerly a protectionist), resisted the break with Russia over Poland in 1863, and advised a stand against Prussia during the Danish crisis of 1863–1864. Convinced by the 1863 elections (he had favored supporting all of the sitting deputies) that it was necessary to come to terms with democracy, Morny undertook to cultivate Emile Ollivier as savior of the Empire and introduced the eloquent republican orator to Napoleon III. In December 1863 Morny advanced a program for suppressing the address, expanding the right of amendment, granting a limited right of interpellation, and allowing ministers to appear before the Corps Législatif. His statesmanlike aim was to ensure survival of the Empire after Napoleon III by endowing it with solid institutions. Perhaps what he really sought, as he intimated to Ollivier in 1862, was to be himself a prime minister, responsible to the emperor but naming the ministers, who would be individually responsible to but not members of the Corps Législatif. The time, however, was not yet ripe, and it is even possible that except for his death in March 1865, Morny might have been dismissed as president of the Corps Législatif by a master who distrusted his independence and questioned his reading of French public opinion.

It has been suggested that Morny was the only true statesman in Napoleon III's entourage. Despite the reservations the emperor held in his regard, it is clear that the two men were bound in a mutual dependence and that Napoleon III valued his half-brother as an adviser. Morny almost alone of the imperial entourage had encouraged Louis Napoleon's 1853 marriage to Eugénie de Montijo. In 1862, the emperor chose the occasion of a visit by himself and the empress to the Auvergne to bestow on Morny the title of duke. From 1858 he had been a member of the Conseil Privé. It is also clear, however, that Morny's frenetic activities, some of them less than exemplary, complicate a final appraisal. In business and financial affairs, he was devoid of morality, and his iron was in every fire. "Morny is in it" was an almost legendary refrain of the day. His business interests were many: the Crédit Mobilier; a projected Anglo-French bank (1856–1857), which in 1859 became the Crédit Industriel et Commercial despite Rouher's opposition; a proposed Grand Central Railroad (from April 1853, in collaboration with the Péreires) whose failure by 1857 led to the reorganization of French rail lines (later Morny went over to the Rothschilds and involved himself in their projects outside France); a scheme to replace Lesseps' Suez Canal company with an Anglo-French group; and even newspapers (in 1861 Morny obtained control of *Le pays* and *Le constitutionnel*). He was also a developer and a speculator, important in the creation of the resort town of Deauville from 1859. His role in having the claims of the Swiss banker J. B. Becker included in France's 1860 reclamations against Mexico remains a subject of controversy but was probably of minor importance in motivating France's illfated intervention.

Morny's interests were myriad. Jockey Club member, enthusiastic sports amateur, he played a major part in the establishment of horse racing in France. He was largely responsible for the Longchamp (April 1857) and Deauville (August 1864) courses and prizes, although his own horses seldom won. He was an epicure and gourmet, an amateur of painting and of theater. His collection of paintings was magnificent, favoring Delacroix and the Barbizon school but including pre-Impressionists (the collection was sold on his death). Alphonse Daudet was Morny's private secretary from 1861 to 1865 and Ludovic Halévy his intimate (from 1860). His receptions included Emile Augier, Edmond About, Octave Feuillet, Arsène Houssaye (1815–1896), and Eugène Labiche. Morny was himself a talented writer of libretti for operettas, a number of which were staged and one of which, M. Choufleury restera chez lui le 24 janvier (1861; written in collaboration with Halévy and Jacques Offenbach), has survived. Morny assisted Offenbach in obtaining a theater (Bouffes-Parisiens) for his productions. He saved Le Figaro, literary newspaper of his friend Hippolyte de Villemessant, from censorship, obtained permission for Alexandre Dumas fils to stage his play La dame aux camélias, protected Daudet and Halévy as well as the great actress Rachel. And it was on Morny's advice that the acting career of Sarah Bernhardt (1844–1923), daughter of his mistress of the moment, was launched. Morny's activities undoubtedly undermined his health, a situation made worse by his reliance on medical quackery in the person of one ''Doctor'' Joliffe. He died at Paris, 10 March 1865, after a brief illness, leaving four children (two boys and two girls) and an estate of several million francs. In his last hours, he destroyed many personal papers. Doubtless his death was a great loss for the Empire, and it can be surmised that had he lived, he would have played a major role in the evolution to a liberal regime. Yet there can be no certainty of this. Napoleon III's reservations in his regard, Morny's dislike for the political game, and, above all, his lack of character might have proved insuperable obstacles. In the words of the British ambassador, Lord Cowley, ''He had it in him, if he had been honest, to be a very great man.''

T. Charles-Vallin, ''Le Duc de Morny dans l'historiographie du Second Empire,'' RHMC 21 (January–March 1974); A. Dansette, ''Napoléon III et le Duc de Morny,'' BSHM (1962–1963); C. Dufresne, Morny, l'homme du Second Empire (Paris, 1983); G. Grothe, Der Herzog von Morny (Berlin, 1966; French translation, 1967); M. Parturier, ''Morny, ambassadeur en Russie,'' Revue de Paris 76 (1969), and, Morny et son temps (Paris, 1969); R. Pflaum, The Life of the Duke of Morny (New York, 1968); Morny himself put little into writing. See his Une Ambassade en Russie (Paris, 1892) and the fragment of memoirs published by his grandson (''Le genèse du coup d'état'') in the RDM of November-December 1925.

Related entries: BAROCHE; BILLAULT; CORPS LEGISLATIF; COUP D'ETAT; DAUDET; DEAUVILLE; HALEVY; MAGNE; OLLIVIER; ORLEANISM; PERSIGNY; REFORM; ROUHER; THEATER; WALEWSKI.

MORTARA AFFAIR, a cause célèbre of the 1850s, involving Pius IX and the Catholic church. In the summer of 1858, Edgardo Mortara, a younger child of a Jewish family living in the city of Bologna in the Roman states, fell ill and was secretly baptized by a Catholic servant girl. Canon law counseled Catholics to baptize infidels or heretics if they were dying. Although the child recovered, the nursemaid revealed her action to her priest during confession. The church authorities, having been informed, removed the boy from the custody of his parents. According to canon law, once the child had been baptized, he must be educated as a Christian. Edgardo was installed in the House of Catechumens in Rome; all efforts by the parents to recover their child were ineffectual. Jewish communities throughout Europe strongly protested this action, invoking public opinion and political assistance. Both the Jewish and secular press of Europe joined in a militant and bitter protest against the kidnapping. The most acrimonious, the most agitated, and the most polemical debates occurred in France. The discussions in the press transcended the fate of the participants because the issues concerned relationships between church and state and family rights versus religious law. The problem of the Mortara child was also important in French foreign policy because French troops protected the pope's temporal power in Rome.

The most ardent champion of papal sovereignty within the church (ultramontanism) was the journalist Louis Veuillot. In his newspaper *L'Univers*, he vociferously proclaimed the supremacy of Rome and the moral validity of its actions in the Mortara case. Those who opposed the position taken by the church were either pagans or socialists or radicals, he charged. On the other hand, anticlericals felt the Vatican had behaved in an inhumane fashion, in clear violation of French principles. The issues were irreconcilable, and no compromise was possible. The French government protested vigorously to the papacy citing reasons of humanity, decency, and parental rights and also stressing the fact that the kidnapping would weaken the church's influence as an institution of order and lessen respect for the papacy. The pope remained obdurate. The arguments in the press grew more bitter and prolonged and included antisemitic rhetoric. The government, preparing for conflict in Italy, wished to reduce friction with the ultramontanes and suppressed all articles on the Mortara affair. The affair had created a passionate and politically divisive controversy in French life, which marked the beginnings of the destruction of the tenuous alliance between the clericals and Napoleon III, as many of the former transferred their support to the legitimists.

N. Isser, "The Mortara Affair and Louis Veuillot," *PWSFH* (1981); G. Volli, *Il caso Mortara nel primo centenaria* (Rome, 1960).

Natalie Isser

Related entries: GALLICANISM; PIUS IX; ROMAN QUESTION; VEUILLOT.

MUSIC. See CONCERT LIFE.

N

NADAR, FELIX (1820–1910), writer, caricaturist, photographer, and aeronautic pioneer; born Gaspard Félix Tournachon, 5 or 6 April 1820, at Paris. Nadar's father was a Lyons printer of royalist persuasion; his parents did not marry until after the birth of their second and last child, Adrien. From the first Nadar was radical and freethinking. In Lyons, to which his father returned in 1838 and where he died bankrupt, Nadar, who at Paris had attended the Collège de Versailles and the Collège Bourbon, studied medicine but soon turned to journalism. In the early 1840s, he returned to Paris where he wrote for various minor newspapers under the pseudonym, by which he now became known, of Nadar. He lived a bohemian life, scrounging for jobs, which included six months as secretary to Charles de Lesseps, Ferdinand's brother. The revolutionary years 1848–1849 were a time of adventure for the young Nadar, who was arrested in Prussia en route to Poland (March 1848) and later spent six weeks as a particularly ineffectual French government "secret agent." He then visited London for the first time (1849), spent August 1850 in debtors' prison at Clichy, and returned to London in 1851 for the world's fair. It was there that he met the artist Constantin Guys, initiating a lifelong friendship. In the later 1840s, Nadar was a journalist (he founded *La revue comique* in 1849), a playwright (he produced *Pierrot ministre* at the Funambules in 1847 and *Pierrot boursier* at the Folies Nouvelles in 1854), an author (*La robe de Déjanire*, 1845), and increasingly a self-taught caricaturist.

By 1854 Nadar had undertaken an ambitious project to produce four sheets illustrating some one thousand celebrities of his day in literature, drama, art, and music. The literature sheet of this "Panthéon" appeared with 270 portraits in March 1854. It made Nadar himself a celebrity, especially abroad, but failed financially, and the project was abandoned. Perhaps, however, it was while working on this enterprise that Nadar became interested in photography. The new invention was already well established at mid-century. By 1855 there were at least twenty-seven different (and difficult) photographic processes available and eight or nine photographic journals. Stereoscopy was an industry of some importance, and photography had been introduced to the general public at the Paris world's fair of 1855.

Nadar drifted into photography, first with his brother Adrien in a studio at 11 boulevard des Capucines and then, between December 1854 and January 1855, following a quarrel with Adrien, in a studio in his own house, 113 rue Saint Lazare. It was at this time that he married a Protestant woman named Ernestine Lefèvre; his only son, Paul, was born in 1856. In December 1857 Nadar finally won a long lawsuit against his brother for sole use of his pseudonym.

Nadar's studio flourished, but he continued to interest himself in other activities (publication of *Quand j'étais étudiant* in 1856 and of *Le miroir aux alouettes* in 1859; contributions to *Charivari* and *Journal pour rire*; and editorship of the *Journal amusant* in 1859). About 1860, however, he turned his energies almost entirely to photography. In that year he rented a large studio comprising the two top floors and the roof of 35 boulevard des Capucines, premises that had once been used by Gustave Le Gray (1820–1882), painter, photographer, and inventor, who in 1856 had photographed the empress at Saint-Cloud (eventually Eugénie would gather a photographic collection—destroyed in 1870–1871—that was rivaled in France only by that of Nadar himself) and in 1857 was asked by Napoleon III to record the military camp at Châlons. In his new quarters, the flamboyant, red-headed, red-mustached Nadar soon became perhaps the most famous photographer of France, rivaled only by Disderi and by Etienne Carjat (1828–1906).

Although Nadar concentrated almost entirely on portraits, his was not the society patronage accorded to Louis Auguste Bisson (b. 1814, a student of chemistry under Jean Baptiste Dumas and Antoine Becquerel [1788–1878]) and his younger brother Auguste Rosalie (b. 1826) who had also earlier occupied the 35 boulevard des Capucines address. Nadar, an incorrigible republican and nonconformist, who coined the pun "Le Second Tant Pire," and who steadfastly refused all official honors (his studio took, nevertheless, about 1865 a famous photo of the top-hatted, dreamy-eyed emperor), gathered about him a variegated group of friends, including Jacques Offenbach, Charles Baudelaire, Honoré Daumier, Henri Murger (1822–1861), Isaac and Emile Pereire, Théophile Gautier, Gérard de Nerval, and Théodore de Banville. With Nerval, Banville, Murger, Alfred de Musset (1810–1857), Jules Champfleury, Gustave Courbet, and other *noctambules*, Nadar frequented the smoky cafés of Paris, especially the Café Momus. His portraits were very often of friends or of friends of friends. They aimed at sincerity and a straight-forward encapsulation of the character of the subject, a difficult enough task under any circumstances but particularly so in the day when either the wet or dry collodion process (adopted by Nadar after 1861) required that the photographer work with at least one assistant and that the subject remain motionless for several minutes. Already great photography required the eye of an artist, as Nadar would recognize in his 1900 book, *Quand j'étais photographe*. In fact, despite the fulminating of Baudelaire against photography's artistic "pretensions," and the rejection by most artists of photography's aspirations to be considered an art form, art and photography were intertwined from the beginning. In 1857 for the first time a photographic exhibition was held side by side with the Salon, and in that same year took place the first sale of photographs at the Hôtel Drouot. Eugène Delacroix and the realist Jules Champfleury were members of photographic societies and the former, along with Théophile Gautier, was named to an 1857 commission to consider inclusion of photographs in the Salon (it was not done during the Second Empire). Thomas Couture probably used Le Gray's photographs for his painting of the baptism of the prince imperial (1856), as Jean Léon Gérôme would use Nadar's for *The Reception of the Siamese Ambassadors at Fontainebleau*. And Edouard Manet was greatly interested in the new invention (he used photographs, for example, in preparing his painting *Execution of the Emperor Maximilian*). Moreover, the Alsatian Adolphe Braun (1811–1877) began in 1862 the systematic photographing of works of art and within five years employed more than 100 at the task.

Although Nadar's forte was studio portraiture, his irrepressible energy, interest in science, and restless taste for adventure led him constantly into new undertakings. After winning an award for artificially lit photography in February 1861, he became the first to take photographs in the newly constructed sewers of Paris and in the Catacombs, using galvanic arc lights. Earlier Nadar, after four unsuccessful attempts, had succeeded (autumn of 1858) in taking aerial views of Paris from a balloon, including the Arc de Triomphe, the avenue de l'Impératrice, and the new quartier of l'Etoile. The next year Napoleon III offered the photographer 50,000 francs if he would make aerial surveys during the war in Italy against Austria, but Nadar, an ardent opponent of the Empire, declined. These events foreshadowed a new obsession for the mercurial Nadar. He had long been a champion of heavier-than-air flight. In July 1863 he organized the Society for the Encouragement of Aerial Locomotion by Means of Heavier-Than-Air Machines. Jules Verne, who was secretary, would later use his friend Nadar as model for Ardan, the hero of *De la terre à la lune* (1865), and was probably inspired by the photographer's example to write *Cinq semaines en ballon*. For the next few years, Nadar would spend money with reckless abandon in promoting his latest enthusiasm, at first through the journal *L'aéronaute* and then through construction of a great balloon, the largest ever built, named *Le Géant*, which ascended, with varying fortunes, from Paris' Champ de Mars 4 October and 18 October 1863 (on the second occasion Napoleon III inspected the balloon and its two-story passenger basket, large enough to hold eighty passengers and a small printing press), from Brussels 26 September 1864, and from Lyons 1865. Two hundred thousand had watched the first Paris ascent, and in Brussels Nadar enlisted the support of Victor Hugo, but *Le Géant* had been intended to win public support and money for the cause of heavier-than-air flight, and in the latter sense at least it had failed. A lawsuit between Nadar and the designers of *Le Géant*, Napoleon III's official balloonists Louis Godard (1829–1885) and his brother, Eugène (1827–1890), ended the enterprise. Nevertheless, Nadar, who organized a Société des Aéronautes in 1866, attracting such eminent members as Offenbach, George Sand, and Alexandre Dumas fils and père, remained all his life an enthusiast for heavier-than-air flight. In 1864 he wrote *Les mémoires du Géant* and in 1865 *Le droit au vol* (the two works were characteristically separated by *La grande symphonie des punaises*).

The affair of *Le Géant* had exhausted Nadar's finances. He found it necessary to return full time to his photography and to move his studio from the prestigious boulevard des Capucines address to the rue Saint Lazare and then, in 1872, to the rue d'Anjou, where two years later he was to play host to the first Impressionist exhibition. In this latter part of his photographic career Nadar accepted the consequences of a rapid technical development. About 1852–1853 Adolphe Eugène Disderi (1819–1890?), born at Genoa, had established a studio on the boulevard des Italiens. In 1854 he patented a process for making small-format photographic portraits (about 6x9 cms.), later to be called *cartes-de-visite*. For the first time portraits were available at moderate prices (12 for 20 francs, as compared with the earlier price of 50 to 100 francs for a single photo). Although Disderi after winning fortune and fame (Napoleon III had his portrait taken by him in May 1859 enroute with his army to Italy and awarded him a court appointment) would die at Nice in poverty and obscurity, others like Nadar were able to profit from the growing commercialization of photography. The Studio Nadar would continue in existence until World War II. Nadar himself would live long enough to see the beginning of that propeller-driven, heavier-than-air flight he had championed for so long. He died at Paris, 15 March 1910.

M. F. Braive, "Nadar, aéronaute," *Connaissance du monde*, no. 77 (1965); N. Gosling, *Nadar* (London, 1976); B. Hemmerdinger, "Nadar et Jules Verne," *Belfagor* 20, (1965); A. Jammes and E. P. Janis, *The Art of French Calotype with Critical Dictionary of Photographers, 1845–1870* (Princeton, N.J., 1982); A. V. Mozley, "Nadar, the Second Empire's 'King of Photographers,' " *Art News* 78 (1979); J. Prinet and A. Dilasser, *Nadar* (Paris, 1966); J. Richardson, "Nadar: A Portrait, 1820–1910," *History Today* (October 1974); H. Schwarz, "Daumier, Gill, and Nadar," *GBA* 49 (1957).

Related entries: DAUMIER; GAUTIER; GUYS; NEGRE; NERVAL; VERNE.

NAPOLEON, LOUIS. See LOUIS NAPOLEON.

NAPOLEON, PRINCE. See PRINCE NAPOLEON.

NAPOLEON III: ASSASSINATION ATTEMPTS. The nature of the Second Empire, especially during its authoritarian phase, encouraged opponents of the regime to achieve their purposes by trying to end the life of the emperor. From 1852 to 1870 there were many such attempts, although it is possible that a number of the conspiracies that were discovered existed more in the bureaucratic mind than in reality (during 1861–1862 thirteen of the twenty-eight *procureurs généraux* noted the existence of assassination plots). Certainly the police proved generally efficient and the emperor consistently courageous in those attempts that did occur.

On 29 June 1852 thirteen men and women were arrested at Paris while making weapons in a building on the Reine Blanche, although these may not have been intended for use in an assassination. On 23 September 1852, as Louis Napoleon was touring the provinces preceding proclamation of the Second Empire, police announced discovery of an ''infernal machine'' awaiting him at Marseilles. This announcement may, however, have been a propaganda stroke. On 7 June 1853 some three hundred were arrested at Paris in connection with a plot of three recently merged secret societies (the Société des Deux Cents, the Société des Ecoles, and the Cordon Sanitaire) to assassinate Napoleon III either at the Cirque de l'Hippodrome or while he attended an exposition of the Société d'Horticulture. One month later, on 5 July, a Belgian named de Meren was arrested with several others near the Opéra Comique (then housed in the Salle Favart) waiting with knives and pistols the arrival of the imperial carriage.

In 1854 there were a number of plots. Belgian police arrested a man named Magen for manufacturing a bomb intended to kill Napoleon III. In France eighty-five were arrested in connection with a similar conspiracy. And in September 1854 a secret society planted a bomb near Pérenchies on the railroad from Calais to Tournai (Belgium) which the emperor was to use. At the end of 1855 another infernal machine was discovered, built by a secret society, the Militante (recruited from Angoulême and Bordeaux). Earlier in that year, on 28 April, an Italian named Pianori fired two pistol shots at Napoleon III as he rode on horseback with an aide on the Champs Elysées (the emperor and empress had just returned from a state visit to England). Pianori, who had wanted to avenge the overthrow of the Roman Republic in 1849, was executed on 15 May, but the example (which received only a few lines in the *Moniteur*) did not deter a cobbler named Delmarre from awaiting the emperor's arrival for a performance by Adélaïde Ristori (1822–1906) at the Théâtre Italien (Salle Ventadour) on 10 September 1855 and firing at the first court carriage to appear. He was found insane and sent to the asylum at Bicêtre. In 1857 occurred the peculiar conspiracy of Tibaldi. On 28 June, the day of the second round of balloting in the general elections, the government announced that Tibaldi and fellow Italians Bartolotti and Grilli had been arrested a month earlier for an attack on Napoleon III. Rumors circulated that the emperor had been set upon in April during a late-night visit to his mistress, Countess Virginia di Castiglione (1837–1899), and had been saved only by the quick action of his coachman. It seems more likely, however, that Tibaldi, betrayed by a letter addressed to him by Mazzini that had fallen into police hands, was arrested at his lodgings before he could act. On 3 September he was condemned to life imprisonment, and Mazzini, as well as the exiled French radical, Alexandre Ledru-Rollin (1807–1874), who had also been implicated, although without evidence, were condemned in absentia.

Six months later, on 14 January 1858, came the fateful Orsini *attentat*. Small wonder that Napoleon III was at last persuaded to establish a Conseil Privé, capable of transformation into a Council of Regency (the prince imperial had been born only in 1856). In 1862 Léon Gambetta began his legal career defending a former *transporté*, Greppo, accused of organizing a plot that would have had eight hundred workers from the Cail factory scale Tuileries walls to seize the emperor. For lack of evidence, the accused were found guilty only of belonging to a secret society. On 6 June 1867 a Pole, Berezowski, fired his pistol at Czar Alexander II of Russia as he rode in a carriage side by side with Napoleon III at Paris following a great military review during the Paris international exposition of that year. Both rulers were unharmed.

The Second Empire ended as it had begun. In early May 1870, on the eve of the plebiscite that established the Liberal Empire, Emile Ollivier arrested a number of persons for involvement in a plot against the emperor (the Beaury complot).

A. Dansette, L'attentat d'Orsini (Paris, 1964).

Related entries: AUTHORITARIAN EMPIRE; CONSEIL PRIVE; ORSINI; PIETRI; SECOND EMPIRE.

NAPOLEON III: HEALTH. Louis Napoleon Bonaparte, future emperor of the French, was not blessed with robust health. Athletic as a young man, he had nevertheless a delicate constitution, and imprisonment for five years (from age thirty-eight) contributed to problems that were to persist for the rest of his life: hemorrhoids and a condition variously described as neuralgia or rheumatism (probably a muscular manifestation of the gout) that was, like the hemorrhoids, a result of too-rich diet and a sedentary life. Far more significant was the gradual development of a bladder stone, caused, as is gout, by an accumulation of uric acid. The condition may have made itself felt as early as 1853; in June 1855 Dr. Jobert de Lamballe (1802–1867), one of the Tuileries staff of physicians under Dr. F.A.H. Conneau, spoke of a "bladder spasm." From 1856 Napoleon III's physicians sent him each summer (excepting only three in twelve years) to take the waters at Plombières or (from 1861) Vichy. Mineralized and alkaline waters could only make his condition worse. By the end of 1863, symptoms, including difficulty in urinating, were apparent. The emperor's walk had changed, and he made occasional use of a cane.

Napoleon III was ill from January to March 1865. In August he endured a terrible attack of the stone while on his annual summer visit to the great military camp at Châlons. On that occasion Dr. Hippolyte Larrey (1808–1895), another of the Tuileries' medical staff, made the first formal diagnosis of a stone, but the emperor refused to be sounded by catheter and enjoined his doctors to secrecy. Fifteen days later came another attack and then no more until August 1866. Undoubtedly Napoleon III's sexual adventures combined with the burden of his responsibilities to worsen his illness. He was sexually obsessed to a great extent, and his propensity for sexual activity outside marriage was doubtless encouraged by the fact that Empress Eugénie, advised to have no more children after her difficult confinement with the prince imperial, was probably reluctant to have sexual relations with her husband after 1856. At any rate, he had already been unfaithful to her. In subsequent years there would be a succession of mistresses, most notably Virginia Castiglione (from January 1856), Marianne de Walewski, wife of his foreign minister (from the autumn of 1857), and the actress Marguerite Bellanger (from the summer of 1864).

In the late 1860s, Napoleon III's illness worsened. At the height of the German crisis of 1866, he endured a vitiating attack of the stone and at the end of July was sent by his doctors to Vichy where he approved the ill-fated French demand for compensation from Prussia. During 1867 his health improved, but there was a new bout of illness from May to June 1868 and an even more serious one beginning in August 1869, which persisted until the first week of November. On this occasion, the public took alarm. Although the emperor was attended daily by his doctors, including the noted urologist Philippe Ricord (1800–1890), the government insisted that only rheumatism was involved. On 1 July 1870 Napoleon III was examined by four specialists (in addition to his chief household physician and long-time friend, Conneau): Ricord, Auguste Nélaton (1807–1873), Germain Sée (1818–1896), and François Rémy Lucien Corvisart (1824–1882, nephew of Napoleon I's great physician). The stone was again diagnosed, but it was decided that an immediate operation was not essential. Shortly after began the international crisis that culminated in the Franco-Prussian War. The emperor took command in the desperate agony of a new flare-up of his illness. The problem continued after his exile in England, especially from the summer of 1872. There he consulted not only Conneau and Corvisart but the eminent British physicians Sir William Gull, Sir Henry Thompson (in July 1872), and Sir James Paget (in October 1872). Thompson was a leading practitioner of the procedure of crushing stones within the bladder and removing the debris, which had been developed by a French surgeon, Civiale, in 1822 and used successfully by Thompson on King Leopold I of Belgium in 1863. On Christmas Day 1872 the former emperor at last permitted a sounding under chloroform. Now for the first time Eugénie was informed of the nature of her husband's illness. Thompson undertook the crushing operation on 2 January 1873. It was repeated on 6 January and again on 7 January. The morning of 9 January, as a fourth operation was about to commence, Napoleon III died suddenly, perhaps as the result of a dose of chloral too strong for a constitution that was more severely undermined by kidney disease (caused by the stone) than his doctors could have realized. He would at any rate have had only a few more years to live.

Historians disagree as to the extent to which Napoleon III's policies, and indeed the results of his reign, were affected by his illness. The disease was certainly of a nature to undermine his energy and will while leaving his intelligence intact and could account for the increasing difficulty he had after 1862 in freeing himself from his hesitations. It could also have contributed to the bouts of indolence and lassitude that are perhaps symbolized by the writing of his *Histoire de Jules César* between 1860 and 1865. In better health, Napoleon III might well have acted other than he did in moments requiring great efforts of will, such as the aftermath of Prussia's victory at Sadowa (July 1866) or the days following the arrival at Paris of word of the Hohenzollern candidacy for the Spanish throne (July 1870). He might even (although that is more problematic) have managed in a different way the fatefully awkward transition between 1867 and 1870 from an authoritarian regime to the Liberal Empire.

A. Dansette, "La maladie de Napoléon III," *Revue de Paris* 70 (September 1963); G. C. N. Lecomte, *Napoléon III, sa maladie, son déclin* (Lyons, 1937); R. L. Williams, *The Mortal Napoleon III* (Princeton, 1972).

Related entries: CHISLEHURST; CONNEAU; LOUIS NAPOLEON; SADOWA.

NAPOLEON III: WRITINGS. See *HISTOIRE DE JULES CESAR*.

NAPOLEONIC IDEAS. See *DES IDEES NAPOLEONIENNES*.

NATIONALITIES, a key concept in the foreign policy of Napoleon III. As early as 1839, in his *Idées napoléoniennes*, Louis Napoleon attributed to Napoleon I the aim of creating a confederated Europe of satisfied nationalities. Seeing in this theory of nationalities one of the ideas of his time, he returned to it frequently as emperor. Historians have disagreed not only as to the importance of this idea in Second Empire foreign policy but also as to its exact meaning in the mind of Napoleon III. Clearly, as Emile Ollivier stressed, it was not based on language or ideas of race or geography but rather on the right of any people to constitute itself a nation and to dispose of itself as it might wish. At a minimum the *politique des nationalités* implied the right to cultural autonomy; at a maximum the right to independence. Its achievement would require an undoing of the treaties of 1815 and a revision of the map of Europe. The efforts made by Napoleon III to free Italy from Austrian control (1859–1866), to secure the autonomy and unity of Rumania (1856–1866), and to help Poland in 1863 are notable examples of the policy of nationalities in action, as is the failure to block Prussian ambitions in Germany before 1867. However, French intervention at Rome (1849–1870) and in Mexico (1862–1867), possible designs on Belgium and the Rhine, schemes for placing an Austrian prince on the Rumanian throne, preference for a separate Rhineland state after 1866, and veto of a union of northern and southern Germany (1866–1870) indicate that the theory was often sacrificed to French national interests.

G. I. Bratianu, *Napoléon III et le problème des nationalités* (Paris, 1934); P. Henry, *Napoléon III et les peuples, à propos d'un aspect de la politique extérieure du Second Empire* (Paris, 1943); H. Joly, "Les nationalités sous Napoléon III et aujourd'hui," *Revue hebdomadaire*, 9 January 1915; E. Ollivier, "Napoléon III, son dessein international," *RDM* 146 (1898); G. Weill, *L'Europe du XIXe siècle et l'idée de nationalité* (Paris, 1938).

Related entries: ALGERIA; CONGRESS POLICY; DANISH WAR; *DES IDEES NAPOLEONIENNES*; ITALIAN WAR; LUXEMBOURG CRISIS; MEXICAN EXPEDITION; NICE-SAVOY; OLLIVIER; *L'OPINION NATIONALE*; PLEBISCITE; POLISH QUESTION; PRINCE NAPOLEON; PUBLIC OPINION; REVISION; ROMAN QUESTION; RUMANIAN UNITY; THIERS.

NAVY. See DUPUY DE LOME.

NEFFTZER, AUGUSTE (1820–1876), journalist, founder of *Le temps*; one of the most important publicists of the Second Empire; born at Colmar (Haut-Rhin, Alsace), 3 February 1820. Nefftzer studied Protestant theology at Strasbourg and commenced his journalistic career in that city. At Paris in 1844 he began his long association with Emile de Girardin's *La presse*, first as *gérant* and then, in 1856, as political director. For *La presse*, Nefftzer wrote especially on foreign policy, philosophy, and religion, all in a liberal vein. He was responsible, as well, for the daily political bulletin. But he left the paper in November 1857 when it was purchased by Moïse Millaud, forced out by Prince Napoleon, who had originally sponsored his appointment but who had become convinced that the political director was "too Orleanist." The next year (31 January 1858) Nefftzer founded, with Charles Dollfus (1827–1913), *La revue germanique et française*, renamed in March 1865 *La revue moderne*. Collaborators included Ernest Renan, Emile Littré, Prosper Mérimée, Hippolyte Taine, Philarète Chasles (1799–1873), Alfred Maury (1817–1892), and Lefebvre de Laboulaye (1811–1883). In 1859 Nefftzer returned to *La presse* but left for the second and final time in January 1861.

Nefftzer received permission to publish his own newspaper, perhaps because, as a Protestant, he was an enemy of the pope and of the Catholic clergy, and Napoleon III at the time was engaged in a quarrel with the church hierarchy over his Italian and Roman policies. *Le temps* appeared on 25 April 1861. It was destined to become, under Nefftzer's leadership (he was both director and chief editor), one of the most respected newspapers of the Second Empire. In *Le temps* Nefftzer opposed the authoritarian Empire but fairly and with moderation. During the elections of 1863, he played a major role in securing Adolphe Thiers as an opposition candidate for election to the Corps Législatif from Paris. Nefftzer was one of the few representatives in French journalism of the neo-Hegelian viewpoint. With Dollfus he translated and published David Strauss' *Life of Jesus*. In 1872 Nefftzer gave over the direction of *Le temps* to his long-time collaborator, Adrien Hébrard (1834–1914), and retired to Switzerland. But he remained an active contributor to the paper until his death at Basel 20 August 1876.

R. Martin, *Le vrai visage de l'Alsace: La vie d'un grand journaliste, Auguste Nefftzer, fondateur de "La revue Germanique" et du "Temps"...d'après sa correspondance et des documents inédits*, 2 vols. (Besançon, 1953); G. Pariset, *"La revue germanique" de Dollfus et de Nefftzer, 1858–1868, d'après la correspondance des deux directeurs* (Paris, 1906).
Related entries: GIRARDIN; MILLAUD; *PRESSE*; PRESS REGIME; *TEMPS*; VILLEMESSANT.

NEGRE, CHARLES (1820–1880), photographer; born at Grasse, the eldest of four children. Nègre was sent to Paris about 1839 to study painting. In the studio of Paul Delaroche (1797–1856) he had among his fellow students Charles Daubigny and Adolphe Yvon (1817–1893) and also three young men who, like

Nègre, were destined to become photographers: Henri Dufresne (1828–1903), Gustave Le Gray (1820–1882), and Henri Le Secq (1818–1882). In 1843 Nègre completed his studies under Dominique Ingres and exhibited for the first time at the Salon. From 1848 to 1853 he was regularly accepted by the Salon. The critic Théophile Gautier took note of his painting *Universal Suffrage* (1849); in 1850 one of the eighteen paintings that Nègre exhibited won a third-class medal; and in 1851 (twelve paintings accepted) and 1852 he won gold medals. In 1852 the government purchased some of his entries. That year he was appointed professor of drawing at the Ecole Supérieure du Commerce. He seemed to be on his way to a successful career as a painter in the academic tradition.

But already (about 1844) Nègre had begun to experiment with photography, and although he at first approached the new invention from the viewpoint of painting, he was soon deeply interested in its technical aspects. Influenced by the treatises of Le Gray and the work of Louis Blanquart-Evrard (1802–1872), he began experimenting in the spring of 1850 with the paper-negative process. In January 1851 Nègre was a founding member of the first French photographic society, the Société Héliographique (renamed in 1855 the Société Française de Photographie), which published on 9 February 1851 the first issue of its journal, *La lumière* (after 1855 the *Bulletin de la Société Française de Photographie*). That spring he invented a combination of lenses that made it possible to take near-instantaneous photographs in the street. He was one of the first to photograph such subjects as chimney sweeps, rag-men, and organ grinders.

Nègre soon became concerned with the photographing of buildings and monuments. In the summer of 1852 he began on his own a three- to four-year project of photographing major Paris monuments. The previous summer (June 1851) the Historical Monuments Commission had expressed interest in such projects and had given commissions to three of Nègre's photographer friends (Le Gray, Le Secq, and Edmond Baldus [1813–1882]), as well as to two other photographers. But Nègre's two-month tour of the Midi, begun in August 1852, which led to the publication of his *Midi de la France*, a collection of some two hundred photographs on which much of his reputation rests, was created and financed by himself. Although he failed in 1858 to persuade Napoleon III to undertake a gigantic project of photographing the world's cultural treasures, Nègre did receive some government commissions: to photograph Chartres cathedral (1854–1855), as well as certain Louvre works (1858–1859), and, in May 1859, to prepare a photographic record of the newly opened Imperial Asylum, created by Empress Eugénie in the Bois de Vincennes for disabled artisans. He published in 1861 the results of this latter commission in an album of some sixty plates, *L'Asile Impérial de Vincennes*. By 1854 Nègre had become involved in the newly invented photogravure process to which he contributed (1856) and to which he eventually gave himself over almost entirely, although he never ceased to paint. For his patented process, he was awarded a first-class medal at the Paris exposition of 1855.

Despite years of effort, Nègre failed to win the prize established for the best photogravure process, although he was patronized by a number of artists and architects. Nor did he win the nomination to the Legion of Honor that he coveted. By 1860 his failing health required that he spend an increasing amount of time in the Midi (he had never married). In 1863 he retired to Nice, where he had been given an appointment as a drawing master at the Lycée Impérial. He maintained a studio at Nice, but this was a period of artistic decline, although he won a silver medal at the Paris international exposition of 1867. Nègre died at Grasse, 16 January 1880, and was at once forgotten except in his native town. Quite recently, however, he has been rediscovered and is today regarded as one of the greatest of the early photographers.

J. Borcoman, *Charles Nègre, 1820–1880* (Ottawa, 1976); Y. Christ, *L'age d'or de la photographie* (Paris, 1965); F. Heilbrun, "Charles Nègre et la photographie d'architecture," *MHF* no. 110 (1980); G. Mauner, "Charles Nègre, painter-photographer," *History of Photography* 1 (1977); R. A. Sobieszek, "Photography and the Theory of Realism in the Second Empire," in *One Hundred Years of Photographic History: Essays in Honor of Beaumont Newhall*, Van Deren Coke, ed. (Albuquerque, N.M., 1975).
Related entry: NADAR.

NERVAL, GERARD DE (pseudonym of GERARD LABRUNIE) (1808–1855), romantic poet and short story writer; born 22 May 1808, at Paris. Although Gérard de Nerval died in the early part of the Second Empire, it is to this period (1852–1855) that his finest works belong. His commitment to literature had been a long-standing one. With other of the major romantic writers, Nerval had participated in the battle of Victor Hugo's *Hernani* (1830). His translation of *Faust* (1828) had been highly praised by Goethe himself. He had collaborated with Alexandre Dumas père in the writing of romantic plays. And he had written literary and musical criticism that was impressive in its breadth and perceptiveness. His appreciations of Hector Berlioz (1803–1869), Richard Wagner (1813–1883), and Gaetano Donizetti (1797–1848) anticipated later essays by Charles Baudelaire and Théophile Gautier. Nerval's father was a military surgeon in Napoleon's armies; his mother died when Nerval was two. The boy was raised by an uncle and rejected his father when he reappeared after the wars. He studied at the Lycée Charlemagne where he formed a lifelong friendship with Gautier. In 1834 he inherited a small fortune from his grandmother and initiated a hopeless love for an English woman, Jenny Colon. At Paris he was one of the *noctambules*, a frequenter of the Bohemian Café Momus, in company with Félix Nadar, Gautier, Charles Asselineau (1820–1874), Alphonse Karr (1808–1890), and Jules Champfleury.

By 1852, the spells of mental illness (probably schizophrenia) that had plagued Nerval since at least 1841 were increasing in frequency and intensity. Twice (1853 and 1854) he attended the clinic of the famous psychiatrist, Dr. Emile Blanche (died 1893), at Passy in the Hôtel de Lamballe. Curiously, it was at this period in his life that Nerval's literary output increased and that his creative genius was at its peak. In 1852 he published collections of short stories (*Lorely*,

Les nuits d'octobre, *La Bohême galante*, *Sylvie*) and some of his finest poetry, in particular the poem for which he is best known, *El desdichado*, published by Alexandre Dumas in his periodical, *Le mousquetaire*. In 1853 appeared *Contes et facéties* and *Les petits châteaux de Bohême*, the latter a polymorphous work composed of poetry and anecdotal prose, partly autobiographical and evocative of Nerval's early bohemian days in Paris.

In the last year of his life (1854) Nerval produced his masterpieces: *Les filles du feu* and *Aurélia*. *Les filles du feu* is a collection of prose narratives, essays, and a one-act play, as well as a series of poems entitled *Les chimères*. In spite of its disparate nature, the work represents Nerval's spiritual autobiography, as it retraces themes that had recurred throughout his writings. *Aurélia*, Nerval's last work, subsumes the essence of his thought and stands as the *summum* of his art. As in the rest of his work, the theme of the quest dominates, a quest for self and for salvation. As Nerval's *persona* journeys from darkness to light, Aurélia, the incarnation of woman as all-powerful goddess, intercedes for the poet and leads him to salvation.

By 1855, Nerval had slipped once again into madness. At 5 A.M. of the morning of 25 January 1855, he was found hanging from a railing in the rue de la Vieille Lanterne (now the site of the Théâtre Sarah Bernhardt, place du Châtelet). It seems probable that he had hanged himself in despondency over the failure of his talent. He was buried at state expense. Among other major works by Nerval written during the Second Empire are *Les illuminés ou les précurseurs du socialisme* (1852) and *Le rêve et la vie* (1855).

R. E. Jones, *Gérard de Nerval* (New York, 1974); S. A. Rhodes, *Gérard de Nerval*: *Poet, Traveler, Dreamer* (New York, 1951); J. Richer, *Nerval, expérience et création* (Paris, 1963); N. Rinsler, *Gérard de Nerval* (London 1973); B. Sowerby, *The Disinherited*: *The Life of Gérard de Nerval* (London, 1973).

Dorothy E. Speirs

Related entries: BAUDELAIRE; CHAMPFLEURY; DORE; GAUTIER; NADAR.

NEWSPAPERS. See PRESS REGIME.

NICE AND SAVOY, territories lying between France and Sardinia, permanently acquired for France by Napoleon III as payment for French assistance in the unification of Italy. When France joined Sardinia in 1859 in a war to drive the Austrians from Italy, Napoleon III had an objective of his own, the annexation of Nice and Savoy to France. The acquisition of these territories would, he thought, "heal the wounds inflicted on France in 1815." Various factors, however, caused Napoleon III to make peace with Austria (the Preliminaries of Villafranca) before he had achieved all objectives of the Italian War. When leaving Italy, Napoleon III told the king of Sardinia that he would not take Nice and Savoy since Austria still occupied the province of Venetia.

The French nation was confused by the Italian War. It had been expensive in money and in French lives. Yet the emperor returned from his victories empty-handed. After a brief period of expectant silence, the French press began speculating about the compensation that had to be paid to France, and by the beginning of 1860 discussion began to center on the possibility that France might be given Nice and Savoy. Napoleon III, a ruler intensely concerned with public opinion, realized that the nation had to be given the compensation it wanted. The solution to his difficulty lay in the events taking place in Italy.

Despite the provisions of Villafranca that the princes of central Italy were to be restored to their thrones and the pope to the Romagna, the northern third of his states, Count Camillo Benso Cavour (1810–1861), the Sardinian prime minister, arranged with the provisional rulers of these territories that they organize independent governments and petition Sardinia for annexation. As a result, there was a stalemate in Italy. In January 1860 Cavour felt it was time to reach an accommodation with France. He informed Napoleon III that he was ready to give France Nice and Savoy in return for French protection while Sardinia annexed central Italy. It was not to be that simple, however. Distrust of Napoleon III was widespread, and the European great powers had already begun to react, asserting their right to be consulted under the Treaties of 1814–1815. Russia, Austria, and Prussia insisted that depriving the princes of central Italy of their states was an unacceptable attack on legitimate monarchy. Austria was further incensed by the despoliation of the pope. Britain, suspicious of French ambitions, was infuriated at the prospect of divesting Sardinia of the territories of Nice and Savoy. Switzerland, with the support of Britain, declared itself vitally concerned. The Treaty of Vienna of 1815 had placed the northern half of the Duchy of Savoy (Chablais and Faucigny) within the neutrality of Switzerland. Although the region concerned remained under the sovereignty of Sardinia, when war threatened Swiss troops were to enter Upper Savoy, physically protecting it. The British feared that with these arrangements swept away, France would control all of the western passes of the Alps.

France and Sardinia, however, were determined to complete their arrangement. Russia did not feel that the developments in Italy justified a war and turned its back on the entire development. Prussia, while unhappy, had its own plans for German national unification under Prussian control and no wish to antagonize France. Austria was on the verge of bankruptcy and feared civil disorder in Hungary. The Austrian government therefore informed Napoleon III that it would take no action in Italy. The British government was faced with a choice. It could continue to support Switzerland and possibly succeed in halting the French annexation of Savoy; however, this would have cost Sardinia the support of France for its annexation of central Italy. The British government therefore contented itself with protests. Under these circumstances Edouard Thouvenel, the new French foreign minister, rapidly pressed the demand for Nice and Savoy, beginning in February 1860 and culminating in the Treaty of Turin of 24 March 1860, which required plebiscites to be held in Nice and Savoy to determine the will of the populations involved. Every sampling of public opinion in the two territories indicated almost universal support for annexation to France. Nevertheless, at this critical moment, Napoleon III decided he could leave nothing to chance. He ordered the French troops in Lombardy, still there since the war of the previous year, to march home through Nice and Savoy. On 15–16 April while voting took place in Nice, and on 22–23 April, while voting occurred in Savoy, the two provinces were occupied by the French army. The vote for annexation was overwhelming in both territories, as it would most probably have been under any other circumstances. The locations of the French troops during the hours of balloting, the secret ballots used, and the counting of the ballots by officials who had previously been appointed by Sardinia suggest that the plebiscites were indeed honest. Nice and Savoy were formally transferred to France on 14 June 1860. The central Italian provinces joined Sardinia without significant international protest. And the question of the neutralized areas was resolved through normal diplomatic channels, France promising not to fortify Chablais or Faucigny. Interestingly, Paris justified the annexation of Nice and Savoy solely in balance-of-power terms, making no reference to the principle of nationalities.

G. Dethan, ''Réactions anglaises à l'annexion de la Savoie,'' *Revue de Savoie*, special number (1960); P. Guichonnet, *Histoire de l'annexion de la Savoie à la France* (Paris, 1983); L. Monnier, *L'annexion de la Savoie à la France et la politique Suisse, 1860* (Geneva, 1932); P. Scherer, ''British reaction to the French annexation of Nice and Savoy,'' *International Review of History and Political Science*, 2 no. 1 (1965); M. W. Sholofsky, ''The French Annexation of Savoy and Nice in 1860 and European Diplomacy'' (Ph.D. diss., University of Pennsylvania, 1974); G. Wright, ''Persigny and the Annexation of Nice and Savoy [letters],'' *JMH* 10 (1938).

Mark W. Sholofsky

Related entries: CHAMBERY; COBDEN-CHEVALIER TREATY; ITALIAN WAR; MONT CENIS; NATIONALITIES; PUBLIC OPINION; REVISION; THOUVENEL; VILLAFRANCA.

NIEL, ADOLPHE (1802–1869), marshal of France; chiefly responsible for the reform of French military institutions in 1868; born at Muret (Haute-Garonne), 4 October 1802. Niel studied at the Ecole Polytechnique and the Ecole d'Application (Metz), 1821–1823, and was promoted to captain of engineers 1831 and *chef de bataillon* December 1837, following the siege of Constantine (Algeria) in which he played a distinguished part. For his contribution to the fortification of Paris, he was promoted to colonel in 1846. During the siege of Rome by the French in the summer of 1849, Niel, as chief of staff for General Jean Baptiste Vaillant, directed the artillery fire in such a way as to spare the historic and artistic monuments of the city. Two months later (July 1849), he was named general of brigade and charged with carrying the keys of Rome to Pope Pius IX at Gaeta. Returned to France, he became director of engineers at the Ministry of War and in 1852 *conseiller d'état en service extraordinaire*.

The outbreak of the Crimean War opened a new field to Niel's talents. Named general of division (30 April 1853), he commanded the engineers corps in the Baltic under General Baraguay d'Hilliers (1795–1878) and directed the siege of Bomarsund. Following the fall of that fortress on 15 August 1854, Niel was appointed aide-de-camp to Napoleon III. As the siege of Sebastopol dragged on, the emperor sent him (January 1855) to survey the works and to report; however, the death of General Michel Brice Adrien Bizot (b. 1795) led on 11 April to Niel's taking command of the engineers. Having already designated the Malakov Tower as the key to the Russian defense, he directed the approach works and chose the moment for General Pélissier's successful attack. On 18 September 1855 Niel was named grand cross of the Legion of Honor. Queen Victoria awarded him the Order of the Bath.

In 1857 Niel gave an indication of another side of his talents when he spoke for the government in the legislative debate on a new military penal code, firmly rejecting reforms proposed by the Left. He was named to the Senate on 9 June 1857. Shortly afterward, the approaching war against Austria engaged his interest. It was Niel who officially requested of King Victor Emmanuel of Sardinia the hand of his daughter, Clotilde, in marriage to Prince Napoleon. He took the opportunity of the trip to study the terrain where the war was likely to be fought and put his knowledge to good use at the Battle of Magenta (where he shared credit with Marshal M.E.P. de MacMahon for the victory) and at Solférino where his IV Corps (commanded by Niel since 23 April 1859) formed the French right wing and forced an enemy two times its strength to withdraw. His reward was a marshal's baton (25 June 1859). Niel's subsequent criticism of Marshal François Canrobert for having failed to give him proper support at Solférino led to an acrimonious dispute between the two and might have resulted in a duel had the emperor not intervened.

A member and president of the Conseil Général of the Haute-Garonne and (from 1860) commander of the VI Territorial Corps at Toulouse, Niel was available when, following Prussia's unexpectedly decisive victory over Austria at Sadowa in July 1866, Napoleon III decided the French army must be reformed to meet the new challenge. In January 1867 Niel succeeded Marshal Randon as minister of war. He threw himself into the task with energy, adopting the chassepot rifle, expediting its production, and preparing a project of military reform, which, had it been adopted by the legislature, might well have averted the disaster of 1870. In the prolonged and bitter debate, Niel revealed not only patience and flexibility but also a first-rate oratorical talent. To Jules Favre's reproach, "Vous voulez donc faire de la France une caserne," the marshal retorted, "Prenez garde d'en faire un vaste cimetière." The reform law was voted and effectuated by a decree of 1 February 1868, but neither Napoleon III nor his minister of war, who had perhaps shown more optimism than was justified during the discussion, had been able to prevent its emasculation by modification and amendment. Although reproached by the emperor for his concessions, Niel was renamed minister following the cabinet changes of July 1869. He set about establishing the new Garde Mobile and reforming the general staff. His energy and determination might still have saved something. But Niel had long been ill from a bladder stone (the same illness from which Napoleon III suffered). He died at Paris 13 August 1869 during a series of operations. The emperor was himself too ill at the time to attend the funeral.

Related entries: ARMY REFORM; BAZAINE; CANROBERT; CHASSEPOT; MACMAHON; PELISSIER; RANDON; SAINT-ARNAUD; VAILLANT.

O

OATH, to the emperor; required under the Second Empire. The constitution of January 1852, as modified by the *sénatus-consulte* of 25 December 1852, required ministers, members of the Senate, Corps Législatif, and Conseil d'Etat, officers of the army and navy, magistrates, and all public functionaries to take, on assuming office, an oath: "Je jure obéissance à la Constitution et fidélité à l'empereur." Regulations were established by decree of 8 March 1852. Two of the three republican candidates elected in February 1852 refused the oath and were held to have resigned their seats. A third took it and was seated. In the elections of 1857 and the by-elections of 1858, republican candidates took the oath on election as decided in 1857 by a Paris committee against the opposition of the "men of 1848." The *sénatus-consulte* of 17 February 1858 required that a candidate henceforth subscribe to the oath, in writing, before posing his candidacy. Although maintained in this form until the end of the Second Empire, the oath did not prevent a steady increase in the number of successful opposition candidacies.
Related entries: LES CINQ; CORPS LEGISLATIF; ELECTIONS; REPUBLICANISM.

OFFENBACH, JACQUES (1819–1880), composer; creator of a new musical form, the operetta, which came to epitomize the Second Empire; born at Cologne, 20 June 1819. Offenbach was the seventh child, and the second son (a third, Michael, would die in 1840), of Isaac Eberst, a wandering minstrel, cantor, and bookbinder, who by about 1802 was known as the Offenbacher ("from Offenbach-on-Main") or, simply, Offenbach. In November 1833 Isaac took his two older sons, Julius, who played the violin, and Jakob, a cellist, to Paris where he secured entrance to the Conservatoire for the latter, who was both more precocious and ambitious than his brother. Soon the two boys were known as Jules and Jacques, and although Offenbach never lost his German accent, he became fluent in French and in every respect a Frenchman and a Parisian.

In December 1834 Offenbach left the Conservatoire. After playing in several orchestras, he joined that of the Opéra Comique. There he became a protégé of the famous composer Fromental Halévy (1799–1862), wrote music constantly (some of his waltzes were played in 1836 at the Jardin Turc by the popular dance band leader, Louis Jullien [1812–1860]), and became ever more bored. In 1838 he abandoned the orchestra pit for the salon circuit, playing jointly composed pieces with a new friend, Friedrich von Flotow (1812–1883). Offenbach flourished in the atmosphere of wealth and fashion that he loved and to which his wit, irreverence, and versatility were well suited. He acquired pupils, published songs, and gave a first successful public concert (with his brother Jules) in January 1839. Longing for a theater career, he had his first opportunity when asked by Anicet Bourgeois (1806–1871) to write incidental music for his play, *Pascal et Chambord*. Although the resulting vaudeville (2 March 1839) failed, Offenbach remained undiscouraged. His concerts in France and Germany with the fabled pianist Anton Rubinstein (1829–1894), Franz Liszt (1811–1886), and the popular Paris tenor Gustave Roger (1815–1879) won him a reputation as well as an acquaintanceship with Herminie de Alcain, stepdaughter of the London concert agent John Mitchell. On 14 August 1844 Offenbach married Herminie (then seventeen) after meeting the family's conditions of conversion to Roman Catholicism and the undertaking of an English concert tour, which culminated successfully with a performance at Windsor Castle.

The ten years between 1845 and 1855 were difficult for Offenbach. His efforts to have a work accepted by the Opéra Comique failed, and a commission from Adolphe Adam (1803–1856) for a comic opera to be performed at the Opéra National was frustrated by the 1848 Revolution. Offenbach fled for a year to Cologne with his family. In 1850 he was engaged by the director of the Comédie Française, Arsène Houssaye (1815–1896), at 6,000 francs per year as musical director and orchestra conductor at the Théâtre Français, but his first true success in the theater did not come until 28 October 1853, with *Pépito* (librettists Jules Moinaux [1825–1895] and Léon Battu [1829–1857]) at the Variétés. Although Florimond Hervé (1825–1892) accepted in 1855 an Offenbach operetta, *Oyayaie*, for his new (1854) Théâtre des Folies Nouvelles, the composer had decided on the daring step of securing a theater of his own.

Offenbach was motivated by a number of considerations. He was, first of all, convinced that it was almost impossible to have his works performed by others. He was intrigued by the opportunities offered by the approaching world's fair at Paris. But he had also become aware of a vacuum in Parisian musical life. No longer was there a clear distinction between opera and opéra comique (except for the technical point that the latter used spoken dialogue). Somewhere between opéra comique, as it had become in its desire to be "serious," and vaudeville, which was essentially a collection of musical numbers in a light comedy format, there was now room for a new musical form, already pioneered by Adam in *Si j'étais roi* (1852) and by Victor Massé (1822–1884; *Les noces de Jeanette*, 1853). Finally, Offenbach must have hoped that his political connections were sufficient to win him the license required for opening a theater. He had met Louis Napoleon at a presidential reception in 1849; he had been complimented by the now emperor's cousin, Prince Napoleon, for a schottische composed for the Théâtre Français; and he had dedicated a collection of songs to the prince's sister, Princess Mathilde. Above all, Offenbach was on good terms with Napoleon III's half-brother and close associate, Auguste de Morny, himself a theater buff. Undoubtedly Morny did intervene, for on 15 June 1855 Offenbach's bid was accepted over those of twenty others for a dilapidated wooden structure (the Théâtre Marigny) on the Champs Elysées, not far from the Palais de l'Industrie. One of Offenbach's partners in the venture was the newspaper publisher Hippolyte de Villemessant, whose *Le Figaro* had just been launched.

Acquisition of the Bouffes Parisiens (as he named it) was the turning point in Offenbach's career. His good fortune continued when Ludovic Halévy agreed to help write the libretto for a curtain raiser, *Entrez, messieurs et mesdames*. The opening bill of 5 July 1855 consisted of four short pieces, including *Les deux aveugles* (libretto by Moinaux). Success was immediate and complete. The tiny theater was crammed night after night, and Offenbach's reputation was made. Moreover, on 31 August 1855 another star was born: Hortense Schneider made her Paris debut at the Bouffes Parisiens. The Marigny theater had to be abandoned for the winter in favor of a more weather-resistant hall, the Théâtre des Jeunes Elèves (Théâtre Comte) in the Passage Choiseul, which Offenbach bought from Charles Comte (c. 1820–1884), son of the founder, and which he had enlarged and renovated by the architect Théodore Ballu (1817–1885). The new Bouffes Parisiens (*salle d'hiver*) opened 29 December 1855 with *Ba-ta-clan* (whose libretto was the first written entirely by Halévy for Offenbach). A parody of the grand opera style of Giacomo Meyerbeer, *Ba-ta-clan* was Offenbach's first great success. Meyerbeer himself attended, without ill feeling, and Morny was frequently in the audience. In the summer of 1856 the Bouffes moved back to the Théâtre Marigny for the season, but from the winter of 1856–1857 it would remain at the Passage Choiseul. Toward the end of 1856, Offenbach, who had presented on 12 June 1856 *Les dragées de baptême* in honor of the christening of the prince imperial, was commanded to perform *Les deux aveugles* at the Tuileries.

Offenbach intended the Bouffes Parisiens to serve as an outlet for new talent. And so, in addition to his own music, and such composers as Adam, Rossini, and Mozart, he presented works by Jules Duprato (1827–1892), Léon Gastinel (1823–1906), Emile Jonas (1827–1905), and Léo Delibes. In the summer of 1856, Offenbach staged a contest for young composers. The committee of judges, which included Fromental Halévy, Eugène Scribe, and Charles Gounod, shared the prize (at Halévy's insistence) between Georges Bizet (1838–1875), Halévy's favorite student, and Charles Lecocq (1832–1918), an event that greatly embittered Lecocq. Offenbach was now popular and successful, but he was not without problems. Since before 1850, his slight frame (he was just over 5 feet tall and never weighed 100 pounds) had been attacked by the rheumatism and gout whose complications would eventually end his life. Moreover, his lavishness and poor business sense had brought the Bouffes Parisiens close to bankruptcy, a situation not much alleviated by a successful British and French provincial tour in 1857. But once more a *deus ex machina* was at hand.

Orphée aux enfers was Offenbach's first *succès folle*, and it arrived at just the right time. The music was written at Ems—which the composer often visited—in the summer of 1858. Because regulations governing the theater had recently been relaxed, Offenbach was able for the first time to write a two-act operetta for a large cast. Halévy, now secretary for Algerian affairs, agreed very reluctantly to help Hector Crémieux (1828–1892) with the libretto. Lise Tautain and the comedian Bache were engaged to play the roles of Eurydice and John Styx (Hortense Schneider was not available). Offenbach's friend Gustave Doré assisted Charles Antoine Cambon (1802–1875) and Charles Bertall (1820–1881) with the sets and costumes. The debut on 21 October 1858 was not, however, quite the success that was required. Then, several weeks later, a scathing attack by Offenbach's adversary, the critic Jules Janin, which accused the composer of profanation of sacred antiquity, swung the balance, and only exhaustion of the cast after the two hundred twenty-eighth performance led to a temporary removal of the piece on 5 June 1859. By then its music was known all over France, and in April 1860 it was restaged as a gala at the Théâtre des Italiens, the emperor having consented to be present. Some months before, on 14 January 1860, Offenbach had become a naturalized Frenchman. Napoleon III, who had personally intervened to secure the naturalization decree, wrote to compliment the composer on the April performance of *Orphée aux enfers* and, on 15 August 1861, named him knight of the Legion of Honor.

In other ways, 1860 was a momentous year for Offenbach. In a musical sketch on 6 February 1860, *Le musicien de l'avenir*, he satirized Richard Wagner (1813–1883), who never forgave him. That fall Offenbach, Halévy, and Crémieux collaborated, at Morny's request, on an idea of Morny's for a vaudeville entitled *M. Choufleuri restera chez lui*. After a trial run at the Palais d'Orsay (where Morny, as president of the Corps Législatif, had apartments), the play was produced with considerable success as part of a double bill at the Bouffes Parisiens on 14 September 1861 with Bache in the lead role. It was in this same year that Halévy met an old school friend, Henry Meilhac, at the Théâtre des Variétés and entered into a collaboration that was to prove extraordinarily fruitful for both men and for Offenbach. At the end of 1860, Offenbach presented his only ballet, *Le papillon* (Opéra, 26 November). Marie Taglioni (1808–1884), the great ballerina of the romantic era, had become the patroness of a remarkable young French dancer, Emma Livry (1842–1863). Taglioni choreographed the production; J.H.V. de Saint-Georges (1799–1875) wrote the book. Livry, the illegitimate daughter of a talented sixteen-year-old dancer in the Opéra's corps de ballet, had made her debut 20 October 1858 in *La sylphide*. The forty-two performances of Offenbach's ballet represented her great success. Napoleon III, who attended *Le papillon*, requested a second performance a few days later. Tragically, in November 1862 Livry was terribly burned when her costume caught fire during rehearsals for a new ballet, *La muette de Portici*. She died eight months later after much suffering, but her memory would be preserved by future generations of ballet lovers.

Not all of Offenbach's productions succeeded, and not all of his luck was good. In January 1862, for reasons of health and financial management, he gave up direction of the Bouffes Parisiens (his eventual successor, 1869, would be Comte, who in 1865 married Offenbach's eldest daughter; in 1863 the theater was torn down and rebuilt). Also in 1862 the birth of Offenbach's son, Auguste Jacques, was balanced by a disastrous fire, which destroyed the seaside house at Etretat where the composer delighted in entertaining his friends: Morny (Auguste Jacques' godfather), the photographer Félix Nadar, Edmond About, Edouard Manet (who painted Offenbach's portrait), Bizet, Delibes, Doré, the painter Edouard Detaille (1848–1912), Crémieux, Villemessant, and the writers Guy de Maupassant (1850–1893) and Alphonse Karr (1808–1890). Built originally with the proceeds from *Orphée aux enfers*, the Villa Orphée was rebuilt, although for the next few years Offenbach experienced a series of failures and semi-successes, including an attempt at grand opera, *Les fées du Rhin* (libretto by Charles Nuitter [1828–1899] and Etienne Tréfeu, Vienna, 4 February 1864). However, *Les bavards* (libretto by Nuitter; Bouffes Parisiens, 20 February 1863) was a success, and that year Offenbach was among those invited to the *séries* at Compiègne.

La belle Hélène, one of Offenbach's greatest successes, was the first major collaboration of Halévy and Meilhac. Morny contributed a few lines and proved helpful with the censors. And Hortense Schneider was engaged to create the role of Hélène. The operetta (Variétés, 17 December 1864) was a smash hit from the first night. Offenbach, Meilhac, Halévy, and Schneider became the accredited entertainers of the Second Empire, and Offenbach reached the pinnacle of his career. Other triumphs followed: *Orphée* was again revived (the noted courtesan, Cora Pearl [Emma Crouch], sang Cupid in its five hundredth performance); *La vie parisienne* (libretto by Meilhac and Halévy; Palais Royal 31 October 1866) began its run of nearly two hundred performances before *Barbe Bleue* (Meilhac and Halévy; Variétés, 5 February 1866; with Hortense Schneider as Boulotte) had left the stage. And on 12 April 1867 *La Grande Duchesse de Gérolstein* opened at the Variétés, in the midst of the great Paris world's fair. It was the most sensational of Offenbach's successes, the peak of his collaboration with Meilhac and Halévy, and Hortense Schneider's apogee. Napoleon III attended soon after the premiere and again a few nights later. The operetta enjoyed nearly three hundred performances. It marked, however, the turning point of Offenbach's career. After 1867 there were to be more failures than successes, although Offenbach continued the frenetic pace, which was to use up some forty-three librettists in seventy-seven stage productions from 1852 to 1870. *La Périchole* (Meilhac-Halévy; Variétés, 6 October 1868, with Hortense Schneider) and *Les brigands* (Meilhac and Halévy; Variétés, 10 December 1869) counted among the successes. But *Robinson Crusoé* at the Opéra Comique 23 November 1867 with Célestine Galli-Marié (1840–1905), creator of Mignon (1866) and Carmen

(1875), was a disappointment. Offenbach's last Second Empire production, *La romance de la rose*, opened at the Bouffes Parisiens on 11 December 1869.

The Franco-Prussian War was an unmitigated disaster for the German-born composer. Attacked by both sides (Eugénie struck his name off the list for promotion in the Legion of Honor), he moved his family to Spain after Sedan, and during the Commune he toured Europe. Offenbach's career never regained its pre-1870 brilliance. Musical tastes had changed; satire lost favor to escapism; Lecocq's light, lyrical touch won the day; and Halévy and Meilhac followed that composer's rising star. Ruined financially, Offenbach continued to live in luxury (he had always been something of a dandy), but a tour of America in 1876 failed to restore his finances although he had always been popular there (a tune from *Geneviève de Brabant* [Tréfeu; Bouffes Parisiens, 19 November 1859; American premiere 1868] became the U.S. Marine Corps hymn). His last triumph came in 1879 with *La fille du tambour major*. The previous year he had begun at last to compose the opera he had always dreamed of writing. *Les contes d'Hoffmann* was performed 10 February 1881 at the Opéra Comique, four months after Offenbach's death at Paris on 5 October 1880. It would have 1,422 performances at the Opéra Comique before being moved (1974–1982) to the Opéra.

Offenbach's reputation was long a casualty of the final debacle of the Second Empire. He was attacked for reflecting and even for contributing to the supposed decadence of the era. His operettas were either condemned for their frivolity or interpreted as serious satire of the regime. In reality, Offenbach was not a political satirist. Politics held no interest for him, and it would have been absurd to have attacked a society to which he owed everything. Emile Zola, who modeled Nana on Hortense Schneider, viewed Offenbach and his work with contempt, as did the great romantic composer Hector Berlioz. But such critics missed the point. The Second Empire public applauded Offenbach not for his hedonism or for his decadence but for those same qualities we admire today: his wit, irrepressible energy, meticulous craftsmanship, and consummate theatricality. Offenbach was, above all, an entertainer, and it was largely because of his efforts and successes that operetta became an established genre, rooted in nineteenth-century opéra comique but reaching toward the Broadway musicals of our own day.

F. Bruyas, *Histoire de l'opérette en France, 1855–1965* (Lyons, 1974); J. Bruyr, *L'opérette* (Paris, 1962); A. Decaux, *Offenbach, roi du Second Empire*, 3d ed. (Paris, 1975); A. Faris, *Jacques Offenbach* (London, 1980); J. Harding, *Folies de Paris: The Rise and Fall of French Operetta* (London, 1979), and *Jacques Offenbach: A Biography* (London, 1980); M. S. Mackinlay, *The Origin and Development of Light Opera* (London, 1927); H. A. Parys, *Histoire anecdotique de l'opérette* (Brussels, 1945).

Related entries: CARVALHO; CONCERT LIFE; DELIBES; HALEVY; MEIL-HAC; MEYERBEER; SCHNEIDER; SCRIBE.

OIDIUM, PHYLLOXERA, diseases of the vine that struck France at the beginning and the end of the Second Empire. The years from about mid-century were a golden age for French wine makers. Not only did a "vine revolution" almost double the acreage devoted to viticulture in such regions as Languedoc, Beaujolais, and Corbières, but French per capita consumption of wine greatly increased (from 51 liters in 1848 to 77 in 1872), and wine making, the second-most-important French industry after textiles, became one of the major speculations of the period as trade liberalization and railroads opened the world market.

The results in Bordeaux were spectacular, especially after the Cobden-Chevalier commercial treaty of 1860. British imports of claret tripled at once, although the increase was from a very low base. An extraordinary number of Bordeaux chateaux changed hands during this period, the new owners reviving the custom of adding their names to those of the estates. Thus Château Mouton became Château Mouton-Rothschild when bought by Baron Nathaniel de Rothschild in 1853, and Château Lafite became Château Lafite-Rothschild with its purchase on 8 August 1868 by Baron James de Rothschild for over 4 million francs. There were other notable sales during the Second Empire: Boyd-Cantenac (1852), Palmer (1853, to the Pereires, for 425,000 francs; they replanted the vineyard, which had been wiped out by the oïdium, and built the present chateau), Cantenac-Brown (1860, to Armand Lalande); Pontet-Canet (1865, to Herman Cruse, for 700,000 francs), Lynch-Bages (1865, to Maurice Cayrou), Durfurt-Vivens (1866), Rausan-Ségla (1866), Ducru Beaucaillou (3 March 1866 to the wife of Nathaniel Johnston, for 1 million francs), and Lascombes (1867, to Gustave Louis A. V. Chaix d'Est-Ange [1800–1876]). The Second Empire stood at the center of the greatest era of expansion for the Bordeaux chateaux. During these years the Bordeaux wine trade (négociant, courtier, propriétaire, régisseur, maître de chai) assumed its present form. The owners spent freely to ensure the quality of their wine, a special "bordeaux" bottle was devised, and in 1855 Médoc and Sauternes wines were classified (according to the price they commanded), a classification that, although criticized, has not yet been replaced. Three great Bordeaux wine houses were founded: by Alphonse Delor in 1865, Octave Calvet in 1870, and Edouard Kressmann in 1871 (he had come to Bordeaux in 1858). Prices rose from an average 30 francs per hectoliter for wine in cask in 1852 to 145 francs in 1854 and a peak 221 francs in 1862. Bordeaux vintages of the Second Empire years are still celebrated, especially those of 1848, 1858 (perhaps the finest), 1864 (superb), 1868, 1869, and 1870.

But there was another side to the history of French viticulture during these years. One reason for the remarkable increase in the price of wine by 1854 was the fall in production resulting from the appearance of a powdery mildew, called the oïdium in Europe, a fungus that settles on vines, destroying their leaves, flowers, and finally the clusters. It covers everything it attacks with a whitish powder, and grapes burst open, dry up, or fall victim to a grey-colored rot. It apparently originated in the United States where native vines had developed varying levels of immunity. As it spread in Europe, it wreaked heavy destruction on the vitis vinifera. It made its first appearance there in 1846 but caused greatest damage after 1852. Yields fell to one-fifth their pre-1850 level, and the price of wine rose precipitously. This blight was finally overcome in the late 1850s by dusting the vines with sulphur powder, and 1863 Bordeaux production again exceeded 2 million hectoliters (in 1869 it was 4.5 million), but in the Oise and Lorraine the vine disappeared.

The phylloxera, another native of America, first appeared in France, in the Gard, in 1865. It is a yellow aphid or plant louse that lives by sinking its pointed snout into vine roots and sucking their sap, and which probably entered France on American vines. Unlike the powdery mildew, it kills the vine. It finally brought about the destruction of nearly every vineyard in Europe between the 1860s and the 1930s, seriously affecting France, where it was identified in 1868. This aphid was appropriately named *phylloxera* (Greek for dry leaves) *vastatrix* (Latin for devastator). Over two generations, all of the vineyards of Europe had to be replanted, a task of enormous proportions and unprecedented expense, estimated at 12 billion francs for France alone. Unlike the powdery mildew, this determined aphid resisted all chemical solutions, despite the efforts of such noted scientists as Louis Pasteur. In the 1870s and 1880s a palliative was discovered: carbon bisulphide, injected into the earth around vines, killed many aphids but not their eggs. The final solution that gained widespread acceptance by 1890 was to graft vinifera vines onto American root stocks that were resistant to phylloxera attacks. Since a chemical compound that will kill the lice and their eggs without killing the vine has never been discovered, grafting is still the only means in France of ensuring the survival of vinifera vines, except for such areas as the Camargue, and parts of the Aude and the Gard.

Between the early 1850s when powdery mildew struck and the 1880s when the phylloxera spread far beyond the Midi, the French wine industry enjoyed a golden age of adequate production and high prices. It participated in the great economic expansion of the 1860s resulting from railroads, free trade, and gold discoveries. The wealth it earned at this juncture helped it to survive the enormous losses heaped on it by the phylloxera.

A. Charles, "La viticulture en Gironde et le commerce des vins de Bordeaux sous le Second Empire," *Revue historique de Bordeaux et du département de la Gironde* 11 (1962); C. Higounet, ed., *La seigneurie et le vignoble de Château Latour*, 2 vols. (Paris, 1974); R. Laurent, *Les vignerons de la Côte d'Or au XIXe siècle* (Paris, 1957–1958); R. Lebeau, "Le Jura méridional sous le Second Empire," *Visages de l'Ain* 24 (1971); L. A. Loubère, *The Red and the White: A History of Wine in France and Italy in the Nineteenth Century* (State University of New York, 1978); G. Ordish, *The Great Wine Blight* (New York, 1972); I. Stevenson, "The Diffusion of Disaster: The Phylloxera Outbreak in the Department of the Hérault, 1862–1880," *Journal of the History of Geography* 6 (January 1980).

Leo A. Loubère

Related entries: COBDEN-CHEVALIER TREATY; PASTEUR.

OLLIVIER, EMILE (1825–1913), republican politician who rallied to the Second Empire and formed the first government of the Liberal Empire; born at Marseilles, 2 July 1825. Ollivier's father, Démosthène Ollivier, was a merchant, a democrat, and a republican who brought his family to Paris in 1839. Educated at the Collège Sainte Barbe, Emile became a practicing lawyer shortly before the Revolution of 1848. His brief political career under the Second Republic revealed a basic moderation (as commissioner at Marseilles he used troops against the radicals in June 1849) and provided the occasion for a lasting enmity with Georges Haussmann, future prefect of the Seine. Démosthène's futile attempt at Paris to organize resistance to the coup d'état in December 1851 resulted in his exile until 1860, a punishment that would have been more severe had it not been for the intervention of his friend, Prince Napoleon. For Emile the years until 1857 were politically inactive. He interested himself in music, becoming a champion of Richard Wagner (his future brother-in-law), practiced law for a small clientele, and on 22 October 1857 married Florence Blandine, daughter of Franz Liszt and the comtesse d'Agoult (Daniel Stern).

In 1857 Ollivier reentered the political arena. Supported vigorously by Léonor Havin, August Nefftzer, and *Le siècle*, he was elected 5 July to the Corps Législatif from Paris, defeating Louis Antoine Garnier-Pagès (1803–1878), an "homme de 1848." Taking the oath, he played from 1858 to 1863 a leading role as one of the handful of republicans in the chamber (*les Cinq*). He was an extraordinarily seductive orator, endowed with a musical voice and characterized by southern verve and spontaneity, which made him one of the greatest political orators of the nineteenth century, excelled only by Antoine Berryer and rivaled only by Jules Favre. Although Ollivier consistently urged a restoration of liberty, he had come, perhaps as early as 1859, to feel that the form of government was relatively unimportant. He was sympathetic to the reforms initiated by Napoleon III on 24 November 1860. Fearing revolution and reaction equally, Ollivier was prompted by an ultraconservative speech of the Alsatian deputy Emile Keller (1828–1909) on 13 January 1861 to suggest the following day his support of the reforms and the possibility of his rallying to a liberal Empire. Of the republicans, only Alfred Darimon was to follow Ollivier in this path, but Auguste de Morny, the astute president of the Corps Législatif, proved eager to facilitate Ollivier's conversion (the two men met privately for the first time in 1862). Despite the growing doubts of the republicans and Victor Fialin Persigny's opposition, Ollivier won reelection from Paris on 1 June 1863 (thanks largely to the efforts of his close friend, Emile de Girardin) but refused to call on the emperor. Morny succeeded, however, in having Ollivier named *rapporteur* of the coalitions law of 1864. The republican orator not only drafted the project but was perhaps chiefly responsible for its passage when Napoleon III wavered in the face of heavy opposition. This circumstance further widened the breach between Ollivier and his former friends, who remained unwilling to accept even desirable legislation from the hated Empire and regarded his actions as treason. From this moment dated the enmity toward Ollivier of Jules Simon (1814–1896) and the formal break with Favre. On 27 March 1865, the same month as Morny's death, Ollivier stated in the Corps Législatif his relative disinterest in the form of government and his willingness to vote the address. Several months later (6 May) he visited the Tuileries where he was received by Empress Eugénie, the emperor being on a visit to Algeria. Thereafter Darimon and Ollivier were no longer invited to republican meetings.

On 27 June 1865 Napoleon III and Ollivier met, and the latter urged further reforms, particularly freedom of the press and of elections. This was, as well, the theme of an amendment to the address that was moved by Ollivier at the beginning of 1866 and defeated 206 to 63. Although the legislative session of 1866–1867 marked Ollivier's final break with the republicans (he was now spoken of as a minister), among prominent bonapartists he had the support only of Alexandre Walewski, Victor Duruy, and Prince Napoleon, nor was he trusted or followed by a majority of the Tiers Parti. Neither Adolphe Thiers nor Louis Buffet was his friend. Contacts between Ollivier and the emperor were renewed in January 1867 (they had two conversations), but while there was sympathy and even affection between the two, neither was ready to take the final step. Ollivier set difficult conditions, including freedom of the press, a constitutional change permitting ministers to be deputies, and the abandonment of army reform. For his part Napoleon III greatly feared losing the power to preserve order and, to him the same thing, to ensure the continuation of the dynasty. He was unwilling to abandon Eugène Rouher, who now rightly saw Ollivier as a dangerous rival. The reforms of 19 January 1867 were partial therefore and did not involve a change of men, despite the efforts of Walewski and Persigny at the end of 1866. Walewski failed in his efforts to have Ollivier named *rapporteur* of the proposed law on the press and was himself soon forced by Rouher to resign as president of the Corps Législatif. When Ollivier on 12 July 1867 savagely attacked Rouher ("vice-empereur sans responsabilité") and demanded suppression of the Ministry of State, the emperor chose to express publicly his support for the beleaguered minister. The next year Ollivier opposed army reform and demanded examination by the Corps Législatif of the budget of the city of Paris. But he also defended the cause of free trade.

It was unfortunate for both Napoleon III and Ollivier that their negotiations of 1867 did not succeed. Although ambitious, excited by pomp, impressionable, and impulsive, Ollivier was also warm, generous, and candid, a sentimental optimist who inspired love in those about him. He would form a touching attachment to the emperor, many of whose ambitions he shared: free trade, the cause of nationalities (to an even greater extent than Napoleon III), social reform (although with less conviction), Saint-Simonianism, solution to the German question by peaceful means, and a liberal, anti-clerical Empire (Orleanist bonapartism?) as the middle way between anarchy and reaction. The fact remains, however, that Napoleon III, balancing between contradictory forces, did not abandon Rouher until forced to do so by the elections of 1869. In the interval the minister of state tried with some success not only to discredit Ollivier but to frustrate the reforms proposed by the emperor. The year 1869 was decisive for Ollivier. Rejected definitively by the republicans (he had refused to subscribe to a monument for the 1851 martyr, Jean Baptiste Baudin), he was defeated at Paris in the elections, despite publication on 3 March 1869 of his apologia for the negotiations of 1867 (*A Report to the Electors of the Third District of the Seine* or *19 January 1867*), but won in the Var, where Napoleon III refused to permit an official candidate to oppose him. That same year he remarried (Marie Thérèse Gravier). Ollivier largely orchestrated the legislative campaign that now pressed inexorably toward establishment of a liberal Empire. On 31 October 1869 he traveled in disguise from his property at Saint Tropez to Compiègne and on 27 December accepted the emperor's invitation to form a government.

But the cabinet of 2 January 1870, in which Ollivier took the justice portfolio for himself, was not a parliamentary government nor did it have a prime minister. In fact, Ollivier had become a bonapartist, accepting dual responsibility for ministers, to the Corps Législatif but also to the emperor, and taking strong measures against revolutionary unrest. Yet his election to the Académie Française 7 April 1870 and the result of the plebiscite in May, sanctioning the new liberal constitution, seemed to promise success, although it might be objected that Ollivier lacked the coolness of head and the natural weight of a true statesman. The plebiscite had itself created for the new government, which had stood so firm in January against the agitation of Henri Rochefort and the radical press during the Victor Noir affair, a grave political embarrassment by alienating the Center-Left faction of the Tiers Parti. Nevertheless, Ollivier was determined to press ahead toward decentralization (one of the first victims of the Liberal Empire was the autocratic prefect of the Seine, Haussmann), freedom of higher education, and even social innovation (he envisaged, in consultation with Frédéric Le Play and others, a *chambre du travail* composed equally of workers, employers, and economists). It was the crowning irony of Ollivier's life, however, that, despite his sincere pacifism, he was to be made, for psychological and political reasons, the scapegoat for the tragic events of the summer of 1870. Doubly ironic was the seal he himself put to this fate by the choice of words with which he announced to the Corps Législatif his acceptance (''avec un coeur légère'') of the war willed by Otto von Bismarck. Favoring the return of Napoleon III to Paris after the military disasters of August, and possibly a new coup d'état against the Left, Ollivier was forced to call an extraordinary session of the Corps Législatif on 9 August. In the vote of confidence that followed, only the ministers voted for themselves. It was the most humiliating overthrow of a government in French history. That same month Ollivier left France for Italy, from which he did not return until 1872. Throughout the remainder of his long life, he would attempt without success to alter by historical argument (*L'Empire libéral*) a condemnation that came from the deepest and least rational wells of the national psyche. He died at Saint-Gervais-le-Bains (Haute-Savoie), 20 August 1913.

S. Mastellone, ''Emile Ollivier et la guerre de 1859,'' *RHD* (July–September 1959); E. Ollivier, *Journal, 1846–1869*, 2 vols., ed. Theodore Zeldin and Anne Troisier de Diaz (Paris, 1961), *Démocratie et liberté* (Paris, 1867), *Le 19 janvier* (Paris, 1869), *Le ministère du 2 janvier: Mes discours* (Paris, 1875), *Lettres de l'exile, 1870–1874* (Paris, 1921), *Lamartine* (Paris, 1874), *L'église et l'état au concile du Vatican*, 2 vols. (Paris, 1879); *L'Empire libéral: Etudes récits, souveniers*, 18 vols. (Paris, 1895–1918); M.-T.

Ollivier, *J'ai vécu l'agonie du Second Empire* (Paris, 1970); P. Reynaud, "Le drame de l'homme de 1870: Emile Ollivier," *Historia* (March 1966); P. Saint-Marc, *Emile Ollivier, 1825–1913* (Paris, 1950); G. O. Troisier, *Autour d'Emile Ollivier: Souvenirs de sa fille* (Paris, 1965); T. Zeldin, *Emile Ollivier and the Liberal Empire of Napoleon III* (New York, 1963).

Related entries: BONAPARTISM; BUFFET; *LES CINQ*; COALITIONS LAW; CORPS LEGISLATIF; DARIMON; FAVRE; HOHENZOLLERN CANDIDACY; LIBERAL EMPIRE; MORNY; NATIONALITIES; PERSIGNY; PLEBISCITE; PRESS REGIME; PRINCE NAPOLEON; REFORM; REPUBLICANISM; ROUHER; THIERS; TIERS PARTI; WALEWSKI.

OPERA, the chief monument of the rebuilding of Paris under the Second Empire, designed by Charles Garnier, and built 1861–1874. From at least 1857 Napoleon III and Haussmann intended to replace the old opera of the rue Le Peletier (built by Charles Rohault de Fleury in 1821 of used materials) with a magnificent new structure that would provide a worthy home for the Paris company, then reputed to be the best in the world, and constitute as well the great monument of the proposed transformation of Paris. Haussmann early chose as the site the angle formed by two new streets, Auber and Halévy, just off the boulevard des Capucines. Mindful of the 1858 attempt on the emperor's life by Felice Orsini in the narrow street outside the old opera, the prefect further bounded the proposed site (rues Scribe, Gluck, and Meyerbeer). He had already begun construction from the south (in 1854) of an access way (avenue Napoléon III, now the avenue de l'Opéra) but continued to conceal his plans from the cost-conscious municipal council. However, the minister of state, Achille Fould, had in 1857 appointed the architect of the old opera to design the new one and in September 1860 a commission confirmed the site, which in the end proved a very cramped and difficult one. Alexandre Walewski, Fould's successor, found Fleury's plans too "mean" (the architect had already completed designing the uniform façades of the future Place de l'Opéra). On 29 November 1860 a design competition was announced. Within the stipulated month's deadline, 171 entries were received, including one from the Empress Eugénie. The jury of eminent architects finding no submission satisfactory (the empress' favorite, Eugène Viollet-le-Duc, did not place), five contestants were requested to submit more detailed designs. From these on 29 May 1861 the jury unanimously chose the plan of Garnier, who had placed fifth in the initial competition.

Discovery of a spring beneath the site delayed the project for a year while water was drained and a covered concrete reservoir constructed on which the building could be placed. The first excavation was on 27 August 1861; the first stone laid on 21 July 1862; plans displayed at the Salon, 1863; opening of the first part of the avenue Napoléon III, 1864; scaffolding and screens removed from the nearly completed facade, 15 August 1867; opening of the second part of the avenue Napoléon III, 1867; Jean Baptiste Carpeaux's sculptural group unveiled, 27 July 1869. The roof of the opera was put in place just before the Franco-Prussian War of

1870, but the building remained an empty shell, not to be inaugurated until 5 January 1875 (the approach avenue was completed in 1878).

At a cost of 35,400,000 francs, Garnier had created not only the largest theater in the world (172 meters long, 101 meters wide, and 69 meters high, higher than the Arc de Triomphe de l'Etoile) but one of the most magnificent. He wished, he had said, to create a "style Napoleon III." Certainly many aspects of the Second Empire were reflected in the structure; its taste for pomp, opulence, and display; its eclecticism (the building combined classical and Renaissance elements, among others), materialism, and modernity (for all its magnificence the great amphitheater of the opera was simply a plaster box suspended in a vast iron cage).

The "Palais Garnier," as it is called in our day, was constructed around movement through the building. Through the facade, decorated by the statuary groups of Eugène Guillaume ("La musique"), François Jouffroy ("La poésie lyrique"), Jean Joseph Perraud ("Le drame lyrique"), and Carpeaux ("La danse") streamed the ticket holders, while the subscribers, in all their magnificence, entered by the *porte-cochère* on the east. The two streams met in the Stair Hall, ascended the Grand Staircase, whose ceiling was painted by Isadore Pils, mingled in the Grand Foyer (decorated by Paul Baudry, who also painted the amphitheater ceiling), and dispersed in the amphitheater (2156 seats) where seeing and being seen took precedence over acoustics. The emperor, to avoid a repetition of the Orsini *attentat*, could enter by his own carriageway (on the west) and reach his box directly through the imperial pavilion, which today houses the library and museum of the opera. Few appreciated Garnier's design in his own day (an exception was Théophile Gautier), and all his life the architect had to defend himself against a charge of overdecorating. Some Frenchmen remain reticent, but in general the Opéra of Paris, restored and modernized in 1936–1937 and in 1952, has come to be accepted as an architectural masterwork of the nineteenth century, and its stage, 100 feet wide and 112 feet deep, remains the largest in the world.

E. About, *Peintures décoratives du grand foyer de l'Opéra: Notice biographique et description* (Paris, 1876); C. Garnier, *Le théâtre* (Paris, 1871), and *Le nouvel Opéra de Paris*, 2 vols. (Paris, 1878–1881); J. Mallet, "Un centenaire: l'Opéra de Paris," *AMN* 47 (October 1974); M. Steinhauser, *Die Architektur der Pariser Oper* (Munich, 1969).
Related entries: GARNIER; MEYERBEER; PARIS, REBUILDING OF.

OPERA IN FRANCE, 1852–1870. See MEYERBEER.

OPERETTA. See OFFENBACH.

OPINION. See PUBLIC OPINION.

L'OPINION NATIONALE, the newspaper of Adolphe Guéroult (1810–1872). With Emile de Girardin and Auguste Nefftzer, Guéroult was perhaps the most influential journalist of the Second Empire. Republican in sympathy, he was editor in chief of *La presse* from 1857 to 1859, and, although he had been one of those arrested at the coup d'état of December 1851, he defended in that paper the Italian policy of Napoleon III. In 1859 the emperor decided for various reasons to permit Guéroult, with whom he had had a private interview, to establish a new republican newspaper. Napoleon III hoped to have at Paris a daily republican journal that would champion his foreign policy, in particular the cause of nationalities, and would be sympathetic to the opening he was then offering to the left-wing opposition. Guéroult, a Saint-Simonian, was prepared to be sympathetic to any government that would show concern for the subjected nationalities of Europe and for the working class of France.

L'opinion nationale appeared 1 September 1859 at the extremely low subscription price of 40 francs per year (the usual price at the time was 54 francs). This was later increased, however, to a point above that of many other newspapers. The new journal announced its independence and its intention to be less an opposition newspaper than an avant-garde one, proposing solutions to problems and drawing the government along. In addition to his advocacy of the principle of nationalities and of a new European order, which would mark the eclipse of the absolutist powers (Russia and Austria), Guéroult, a friend of Prince Napoleon, championed left-wing bonapartism, arguing for a reconciliation of the Empire, anti-clerical Jacobinism, and social reform. Guéroult, an opposition deputy from 1863 to 1869 and influential in shaping the Paris opposition candidacies of 1863, would later support Emile Ollivier and the Liberal Empire. He showed a particular interest in economic topics. In October 1861 *L'opinion nationale* took up the cause of sending a delegation of French workers to the London world fair of 1862. From 15 September 1859 it campaigned actively for French annexation of Nice and Savoy, the only newspaper to do so for five months. And Guéroult's paper was, of course, a staunch advocate of French withdrawal from Rome and the ending of papal temporal power.

Although not well received by the other newspapers and not immune to government *avertissements, L'opinion nationale* soon had a solid clientele—the lower middle class—and a respectable circulation (17,300 in August 1861, 14,000 in 1866, and 9,500 in March 1869). With its high patronage, *L'opinion nationale* began life fully and impressively staffed. Among its political collaborators and contributors were the following: Clément Duvernois (1836–1879), Alexandre Bonneau (b. 1820), Félix Mornand (1815–1867), Paul Mathiez Laurent (Laurent de l'Ardèche, 1793–1877), Joseph Vilbort (b. 1829), Charles Louis Chassin (1831–1901), Gustave Naquet (1819–1889), and Jules Antoine Castagnary (1830–1888). Writers on literary topics included Jules Levallois (1829–1903; literary critic 1859–1872), Hector Malot (1830–1907), and Ferdinand de Lasteyrie (1810–1879). Francisque Sarcey (1828–1899) was drama critic from 1859 to 1867; he was succeeded by Jules Claretie (1840–1913), a determined opponent of the regime. Jacques Babinet (1794–1872), a physicist and astronomer, was science editor. Alexis Jacob Azevedo (1813–1875) edited the music *feuilleton* from 1859. Edmond About fulminated in the columns of *L'opinion nationale* against clericals and ultramontanes (advocates of papal sovereignty). The paper, which began its life by publishing Champfleury's daring *Mascarade de la vie parisienne*, also published novels by Paul Féval (1817–1887) and Pierre Alexis de Ponson du Terrail (1829–1871), and it was for *L'opinion nationale* that Charles Baudelaire wrote in 1863 his celebrated appreciation of Eugène Delacroix. *L'opinion nationale* was one of the most brilliant successes of the journalism of its day. The newspaper's identification with the Liberal Empire, however, and, for a long time, with the cause of Prussia, proved heavy burdens, and it survived the fall of the Empire by only six years.

Related entries: LABOR REFORM; MARINONI; NATIONALITIES; PALAIS ROYAL GROUP; PRESS REGIME; PRINCE NAPOLEON; PUBLIC OPINION; REPUBLICANISM; *SIECLE*.

ORGANISTS. See CAVAILLE-COLL.

ORLEANISM, the ideology associated with the liberal constitutionalism of the July Monarchy (1830–1848). Orleanism cannot be said to have come into being until the establishment of the July Monarchy and, in some ways until its overthrow, but the nationalistic, individualistic, and revolutionary ways of the junior branch of the Bourbons could be seen in the eighteenth century. The liberal thinking of Benjamin Constant (1767–1830) was important in its background, but the dominant figure of the last years of the July Monarchy, François Guizot (1787–1874), was perhaps its greatest shaper. Guizot was bourgeois and protestant. Orleanism, therefore, could never be traditionally aristocratic or Catholic. Orleanism was monarchical, but the sovereignty of the state was shared by various organs of government and based on popular approval. Unlike the philosophy of the legitimists, which saw society as the base of the nation, the Orleanists were individualistic. They wished to defend the rights of the individual before the law but were social conservatives, having little interest in the political and economic interests of the lower classes. They did not know the people or trust them. In an age of growing democracy, they were constitutional without being democratic, preferring a strict property franchise, which accounted for the overthrow of Louis Philippe in 1848.

During the Second Republic and the Second Empire, Orleanism further developed with the writings of Victor, duc de Broglie (1785–1870), and his son, Albert (1821–1901); Guillaume, baron de Barante (1782–1866); Joseph de Cléon, comte d'Haussonville (1809–1884); Charles de Rémusat (1797–1875), and Adolphe Thiers. The great Orleanist families constituted an elite openly contemptuous of Napoleon III and many of his ministers. The *Journal des débats* and, after 1858, the *Courrier du dimanche* (edited by Grégory Ganesco) were the Orleanist newspapers, and the *Revue des deux mondes* its journal. The princes of Orleans (the sons of Louis Philippe) represented various political tendencies, the duc d'Aumale (1822–1897) being the most popularly oriented, the duc de Nemours (1814–1896) the most legitimist. Louis Philippe's grandson, the comte de Paris (1838–1894), who had succeeded to his position as pretender with the death of his father in 1842, might be regarded as the most neutral. Less devoted, however, to the cause of monarchy than to that of parliamentarianism, much of Orleanism could, under the Empire, participate in a liberal coalition, reaching out to the republican Right as well as to liberal Catholicism (Charles de Montalembert). Nevertheless, having neither a popular nor a parliamentary base, the Orleanists constituted a very ineffective opposition, especially during the first years of the Second Empire. Many, in fact, rallied to Napoleon III in the name of order. Those who remained in opposition could do little more than harass the regime in their salons (those, for example, of Mme. Casimir-Perier, and of the duchesse de Galliera), their books (many were historians), and in the Institute, especially the Académie Française. The beginning of political reform in November 1860 made possible a somewhat more effective opposition, particularly after the elections to the Corps Législatif in 1863, for although Orleanist candidates were generally defeated, Adolphe Thiers was elected and became a powerful voice. However, while Orleanism played an important part in the transition (1860–1869) from the authoritarian to the parliamentary Empire, its role was less important than that of the Tiers Parti.

G. de Broglie, *L'Orléanisme: La ressource libérale de la France* (Paris, 1981); J.Lhomme, *La grande bourgeoisie au pouvoir, 1830–1880* (Paris, 1960); E. Beau de Loménie, *Les responsabilités des dynasties bourgeoises* (Paris, 1943); J. Plumyène, "La France orléaniste," *Contrepoint* 29 (1979).

Marvin L. Brown, Jr.

Related entries: ACADEMIE FRANCAISE; DECENTRALIZATION; ELECTIONS; *JOURNAL DES DEBATS*; LEGITIMISM; LIBERALISM; MONTALEMBERT; MORNY; ORLEANS DECREES; PREVOST-PARADOL; REFORM; *REVUE DES DEUX MONDES*; THIERS, TIERS PARTI; UNIVERSAL MANHOOD SUFFRAGE.

ORLEANS, BISHOP OF, perhaps the most influential—and controversial— prelate of the Second Empire. Mgr. Félix Dupanloup accepted on 16 April 1849 appointment as bishop of Orleans, partly because the proximity of that diocese to Paris would enable him to continue his many activities as educator, orator, polemicist, and politician.

Although authoritarian by nature and cool toward the Second Republic, Dupanloup was the only bishop present at Paris who refused to rally to the regime of Louis Napoleon following the coup d'état of December 1851. He would not share in the spoils distributed the following year to the dioceses from expropriated Orleanist property, and he warned his coreligionists of the price they would pay in future for the privileges then being granted them by the government. Dupanloup reproached Louis Veuillot, of whom he was a passionate and inveterate opponent, not only for his enthusiastic acceptance of the coup d'état but also for his intransigent brand of Catholicism, which the bishop of Orleans fought through brochures, episcopal directives, letters, and the journals *Ami de la religion* and the *Correspondant*. Dupanloup was unable to draw a majority of the bishops in this direction, but his vigorous defense of the "pagan classics," which Veuillot had attacked in *L'Univers* as unsuitable subjects of study for young Catholics, was a factor in his election to the Académie Française in May 1854.

The events of 1859–1860 in Italy brought Dupanloup once more into the political arena. He defended the temporal power of the pope in a stream of publications, the most important being two letters in reply to Vicomte Arthur La Guéronnière, a *Protestation* (30 September 1859, against Sardinian annexation of the Romagna), and *La souveraineté pontificale* (1860; Pius IX wrote to congratulate him). The conflict between the bishop and the government worsened. He was brought to trial in 1860 for a letter written to the *Constitutionnel*, but his lawyers, Antoine Berryer and Jules Dufaure (1798–1881), won the case. Dupanloup then further irritated the authorities with a funeral oration for the victims of Castelfidardo. Only in 1862 did relations improve, after Garibaldi's filibuster against Rome had been repulsed.

It was, however, Dupanloup's brochure *La Convention du 15 Septembre et l'encyclique du 8 décembre 1864* that spread his name throughout the world. This brochure did much to mitigate the consternation caused by the *Syllabus of Errors* of Pius IX. Dupanloup explained that the *Syllabus* was meant to censure only certain aspects of modern civilization, certain kinds of "progress" and abuses of reason, and that it should be regarded as an ideal that might never be fully realized in this world. The brochure was translated into several languages and went through many editions. Over 630 bishops indicated their approval. Although some intransigent Catholics were offended by this "Anti-Syllabus," Pius IX responded with a letter of congratulations. After all, Dupanloup had already demonstrated his opposition to all enemies of religion by successfully opposing Emile Littré's election to the Académie Française in 1863, publishing in 1866 a work entitled *L'athéisme et le péril social*, and making Voltaire a particular bête noir.

Dupanloup failed to duplicate at Vatican Council I, whose convocation he had advocated (*Lettre sur le future concile oecuménique*, July 1867), the successes he had achieved as a moderate leader in the episcopal assemblies at Rome of 1862 and June 1867. On the eve of the council, he damaged his cause by publishing (11 November 1869) a brochure that argued that a definition of papal infallibility would be inopportune. This appeal to public opinion, followed by his hectic activity at the council (on 26 April 1870 he wrote directly to the pope), aroused suspicions and ill will among a number of his coreligionists. Dupanloup accepted the doctrine of infallibility personally but feared its definition in terms envisaged by Pius IX would be prejudicial to episcopal dignity, conducive to schism among Catholics, offensive to other Christians, and at variance with contemporary attitudes. Thus he went so far as to request Napoléon Daru, indirectly, and Emile Ollivier, directly, to apply French pressure on the council's deliberations—all to little avail. Dupanloup left Rome before the final vote, and, on his return to France, was soon caught up in the events of the Franco-Prussian War.

R. Aubert, *"Mgr. Dupanloup et le Syllabus,"* *RHE* 51 (1956); F. Dupanloup, *Oeuvres choisies*, 6 vols. (Paris, 1862); M. B. Hassett, "Dupanloup on the Roman Question," Ph.D. diss., St. Louis University, 1967; J. Maurain, *La politique ecclésiastique du Second Empire* (Paris, 1930).

Raymond L. Cummings

Related entries: DUPANLOUP; GALLICANISM; GAUME; LA GUERON-NIERE; PIE; POSITIVISM; ROMAN QUESTION; *SYLLABUS OF ERRORS*; VATICAN COUNCIL; VEUILLOT.

ORLEANS DECREES, the dispossession of the Orleans family in France by Louis Napoleon during the period of dictatorship following the coup d'état of December 1851. Two decrees were signed by the prince president on 22 January 1852 and published in the official newspaper, *Le moniteur*, on 23 January. The first required the sale by the Orleans family of all its properties in France within a year; the second confiscated without compensation those properties that Louis Philippe had bequeathed to his sons on 7 August 1830, several days before becoming king. Probably on the advice of Victor Fialin Persigny, Louis Napoleon argued that Louis Philippe's bequest had been fraudulent and the state was merely reclaiming what it possessed by right. The legal argument was largely specious, although there were precedents for the government's action. Louis Napoleon's motives were certainly political. Overestimating the influence of Orleanism and resenting its role in shaping British opinion against him, the prince president wanted to deprive the family of its immense resources in France. He had been advised against the decree by his ministers, who on 9 January had demanded that jurists be consulted (Louis Napoleon had at first agreed, then changed his mind), and by Princess Mathilde. The strength of the adverse reaction perhaps surprised him, however. Four ministers resigned: August de Morny, Achille Fould, Eugène Rouher, and Pierre Magne (although without real acrimony, all soon returning to high posts). The *procureur général* of the Cour de Cassation also resigned. Charles de Montalembert broke with the regime. And a damaging pun made the rounds of Paris society ("c'est le premier vol de l'aigle"). But Louis Napoleon persisted. He constrained, with some difficulty, the Conseil d'Etat to reject appeals arising from the decrees (June), insisting that the conseillers were, in this matter, not magistrates but politicians. On 12 April the Orleans properties of Neuilly and Monceau were seized, the latter going half to the state, half to the Pereire brothers. The proceeds, which were well in excess of 30 million francs, were put to impeccable use, supporting workers' mutual aid societies, constructing housing for workers (by decree of 22 January 10 million francs were assigned to improve unsanitary housing), providing pensions for the infirm, and supplementing the endowments of the Legion of Honor and of the church. Later Rouher would arrange for certain Orleans heirs-through-marriage to have income from their portions of the confiscated estates.

E. Reverchon, *Les décrets du 22 janvier 1852* (Paris, 1871); V. Wright, "Le conseil d'état et l'affaire de la confiscation des biens d'Orléans en 1852," *Etudes et documents*, fascicule 2.

Related entries: AUTHORITARIAN EMPIRE; ORLEANISM; PRINCE PRESIDENT.

ORSINI, FELICE (1819–1858), the Italian patriot whose attempted assassination of Napoleon III in 1858 helped to precipitate French intervention in Italy the following year. On the evening of 14 January 1858, three bombs were thrown at the imperial *carrosse* as it drew up before the opera, rue Le Peletier, on the occasion of the retirement of the famed French baritone Jean Etienne August Massol (1802–1887). Neither the empress nor the emperor was hurt, although the carriage was overturned and 156 persons were wounded, of whom 8 died. The leader of the band of four Italian conspirators, all of whom were arrested within hours, was Felice Orsini, a former agent of Giuseppe Mazzini. Orsini had recently arrived in Paris from England where he had acquired the bomb used in the attack, as well as an English passport. He had hoped by his act to give the signal for a revolution in France that would spread to Italy and result in Italian liberation from Austrian control. Orsini blamed Napoleon III for the restoration of the pope in 1849 and for having betrayed the Italian cause. The consequences of the *attentat* were momentous. Relations with Britain were severely strained; a period of greatly increased repression followed in France; and, ultimately, France lent armed assistance to Sardinia to drive Austria from the peninsula.

For many, the horror and indignation of French opinion at the assassination attempt seemed to provide an opportunity to destroy the virus of revolution before it could burst into renewed life. Napoleon III for the moment agreed. France was divided (27 January) into five military districts, each under control of a marshal of France. A Conseil Privé was established (1 February), and on 7 February General Charles Espinasse (1815–1859), a firm advocate of repression, was named minister of the interior. A harsh law of 27 February (*loi de la sûreté générale* or *loi des suspects*) permitted imprisonment, deportation, or exile without trial of anyone previously condemned for political crimes related to the events of 1848, 1849, and 1851, and fining or imprisonment of others found guilty of conspiracy to act against the government. Some three hundred to five hundred were deported, mostly to Algeria, although none were associated with Orsini's act. Two newspapers were suppressed; *Le siècle* was saved only by a personal appeal to the emperor by Léonor Havin. But whatever the advice of such "men of December" as Jules Baroche, Napoleon III soon halted the move toward military dictatorship. Claude Delangle (1797–1869) replaced Espinasse (June 1858), the law of general security, which had been reluctantly approved by the Conseil d'Etat by a vote of 31 to 27, was allowed to lapse (although it was not repealed); and, perhaps most significant, the trial of Orsini was turned by the French emperor into an occasion for preparing public opinion (and his own entourage) for intervention in Italy.

Orsini was encouraged to write a letter through his lawyer, Jules Favre, calling on Napoleon III to "deliver Italy" and warning that until the peninsula was free, neither Europe nor the emperor could rest secure (11 February). This letter was read at the trial and published 25 February in the *Moniteur*, much to the surprise of the country. On 11 March Orsini wrote a second letter, meant for publication at Turin, condemning political murder, and recommending civic virtues to Italian youth as the only means of freeing Italy. Although Napoleon III and Eugénie would have spared him had it been feasible, Orsini was guillotined 13 March with his accomplice, Pieri. Four months later, the meeting of Napoleon III and of Cavour at Plombières initiated the events that would lead to the unification of Italy.

A. Dansette, *L'attentat d'Orsini* (Paris, 1964); A. Lefèvre, "Les retombées londoniennes de l'attentat d'Orsini (1858): Deux victimes inattendues: Lord Palmerston et le Comte de Persigny," *RHD* 86 (April–September 1972); M. St. John Packe, *Orsini: The Story of a Conspirator* (Boston, 1957); P. Pompili, "Le reprecussioni dell'attentato di Felice Orsini nell' opinione pubblica francese," *RSR* 61 (October–December 1974); R. L. Williams, *Manners and Murders in the World of Louis Napoleon* (Seattle: University of Washington, 1976); V. Wright, "La loi de sûreté générale de 1858," *RHMC* (July–September 1969).

Related entries: FAVRE; ITALIAN WAR; NAPOLEON III: ASSASSINATION ATTEMPTS; PIETRI; PLOMBIERES; REFORM.

P

PALAIS ROYAL GROUP, Parisian workers sympathetic to the regime of Napoleon III, active in the early 1860s; named after the residence of Prince Napoleon, who inspired and facilitated much of the group's activity. Also influential were former Saint-Simonians like Michel Chevalier and publicists like Adolphe Guéroult (1810–1872). The Palais Royal workers regarded the Empire as the best source for reform of workers' conditions. They included paid government agents and other bonapartist loyalists, as well as republicans who had been alienated by the conservative bourgeois leadership of the Second Republic. Their views converged with those of the erstwhile revolutionary republican, Armand Lévy (1827–1891), who had also rallied to the Empire in the name of reform favoring workers. Prominent in the group were printing workers, such as J. J. Blanc and A. Coutant, and the anti-clerical tinsmith Chabaud, its leading spokesman. Chabaud headed the Workers' Commission, which organized a delegation of workers to the London Exposition in 1862. This exercise in government-funded working-class representation was repeated in 1867 at the Paris Exposition, where Chabaud also had a role. Chabaud refused to run as a workers' candidate in the 1863 general elections to the Corps Législatif but announced his candidacy in the 1864 by-election to oppose that of Henri Tolain and, according to one interpretation, to discredit Tolain's candidacy among republicans. Thereafter he and Tolain, another leader of the workers' delegation of 1862, parted ways, Tolain to emphasize an autonomous labor movement and Chabaud to stress reform through petition to the government.

Palais Royal workers wrote pamphlets, *brochures ouvrières*, published with orange covers, as well as numerous articles and letters for *L'opinion nationale* and for the "Chroniques ouvrières" of the pro-government newspaper *Le pays*. In these they expressed their views on social questions. Their most famous pamphlet was their first, entitled *Le peuple, l'empereur et les anciens partis*, written in 1861 in response to the duc d'Aumale's (1822–1897) *Lettre sur l'histoire de France*, circulating in factories, which compared the bonapartist regime unfavorably with that of the July Monarchy. The Palais Royal authors—Chabaud, B. V. Viguier (a proofreader), Berthelemy (a printer), Coquard (a bookbinder) and Leroy (a printing worker)—argued that Napoleon III had demonstrated sincere concern for workers' conditions, as well as sensitivity for nationalist aspirations of peoples abroad, notably in Italy, whereas the July Monarchy had done nothing for oppressed peoples abroad and, like the bourgeois republicans, had no real interest in the people's welfare. The authors of this pamphlet blamed the current poverty of workers on the incumbents of high office sympathetic to former regimes and on the workers' failure to inform the government of their needs. Chabaud and other Palais Royal workers advocated appeal to the government rather than politics or independent labor organizing as the most effective way of securing freedom to strike, organizaton of *chambres syndicales*, vocational education, and free instruction on the primary level. The Palais Royal pamphlets (under such titles as *L'organisation des travailleurs par les corporations nouvelles*, and *Les cahiers populaires*) favored the formation of trade organizations supported, at least initially, by the state. Chabaud was an especially fervent partisan of secular education, having apparently remarked on one occasion that having no education was better than "being corrupted and brutalized by that given by priests and the religious orders." Palais Royal propagandists were skeptical of reform through political involvement, since they claimed that politics served the interests of the bourgeoisie without improving the workers' lot in any significant way.

Although clearly favored and at least partly financed by the government, the Palais Royal tendency seems to have been an honest response on the part of some workers to the social question. Support for the position of the Palais Royal group may have been widespread on occasion. However, the group had very little impact on the main direction of the Paris workers' movement of the 1860s and therefore has received scant attention from historians. Prince Napoleon's interest proved ephemeral; the Palais Royal group and its activities were soon forgotten.

G. Duveau, *La pensée ouvrière sur l'éducation pendant la Seconde République et le Second Empire* (Paris, 1948); D. I. Kulstein, "The Attitude of French Workers towards the Second Empire," *FHS* (Spring 1962), "Bonapartist Workers during the Second Empire," *International revue of social history*, no. 2 (1964), and *Napoleon III and the Working Class: A Study of Government Propaganda under the Second Empire* (Los Angeles, 1969); A. Thomas, *Le Second Empire, 1852–1870*, vol. 10 of J. Jaurès, ed., *Histoire socialiste, 1789–1900* (Paris, 1907).

George J. Sheridan, Jr.
Related entries: BONAPARTISM; CANDIDATURE OUVRIERE; COALITIONS LAW; FIRST INTERNATIONAL; LABOR REFORM; LA RICAMARIE; *LIVRET D'OUVRIER;OPINION NATIONALE*; PRINCE NAPOLEON; PROUDHON; REPUBLICANISM; SAINT-SIMONIANISM; TOLAIN; VARLIN.

PARIS, REBUILDING OF. The Paris of the Second Empire underwent significant development and reconstruction. The administrative reforms of 1859 extended the limits of the capital to embrace the inner suburbs and thereby increased the number of arrondissements from twelve to twenty and doubled the area of the city. The public works program and the alliance of government and private enterprise transformed the infrastructure of streets, drains, sewers and water supply. By the creation of new arteries, buildings, and parks, the physiognomy of Paris was permanently altered. Although the work of deeper forces should not be overlooked, although the achievements of previous and succeeding regimes should not be underestimated, and although the financial methods used and even the aesthetics of the architecture can be questioned, the accomplishment was real and lasting.

Historians have offered two kinds of explanation for the major public works program of the Second Empire. The most frequently invoked stresses the roles of Napoleon III and Georges Haussmann and attributes to them mixed motives: aesthetic, political, practical, and strategic. Emperor and prefect sought to embellish the capital, improve its communications, make it healthier and safer from insurrection. Undoubtedly, too, the desire to provide jobs was not entirely absent. Just as important, however, is the functionalist explanation that sees the rebuilding as the necessary self-stabilizing of an urban system faced with unprecedented problems. Everywhere in Europe, urbanization and industrialization forced municipalities to come to grips with problems that threatened order and life. In the first half of the nineteenth century, Paris's population doubled to reach just over a million by 1851. Population densities, moreover, were uneven. The four arrondissements of the Right Bank center contained over a third of the capital's inhabitants, and it was there that the cholera outbreaks of 1832 and 1849 had struck most severely. Under the Second Empire, and in the 1850s in particular, immigration to Paris increased. Between 1851 and 1856, the annual migration from the countryside to the towns reached 135,000, nearly a half (45 percent) of whom came to the capital. At the same time, the growth of industry made Paris by far the largest industrial center in France, responsible for roughly 40 percent of the value of French industrial production by the mid-century, a percentage that was to increase in the following decades. Parisian industry was dominated by small, artisanal concerns (only 11 percent of enterprises employed more than ten workers) and by textiles, and, especially, tailoring, cabinet-making, and other luxury trades. At the same time, however, the first half of the nineteenth century witnessed the growth of large-scale enterprise, and by 1848 Paris and its inner suburbs had no fewer than 424 large firms that employed more than 50 workers each, most of which (85 percent) were within the confines of the pre-1859 city. The economic geography of the city was also in rapid evolution. Industrial development was strongest in the north and east, especially around the La Villette basin and the Saint Martin canal, but the Right Bank center continued to be the principal area for light and luxury industries. Under the Second Empire, these tendencies were accentuated, as was the westward movement of business and bourgeois residential quarters.

The consequence of these demographic and economic changes was a series of interconnected urban problems. The concentration of industry and population in the Right Bank center led to serious overcrowding and sanitary problems—the death rate at Paris was higher than at London (29.3 per thousand as opposed to 26.1)—and seemed to pose a political threat since it was within Paris that many insurrections originated. Communications within the capital were strained; the east-west axis of streets was defective because the rue de Rivoli, begun by Napoleon I, stopped at the Tuileries, and the north-south axis was blocked by the densely populated Ile de la Cité. Water communications had been transformed by the completion of the Paris canals in the 1820s, but the Seine still awaited improvements. The new railway termini further congested the thoroughfares and disrupted patterns of settlement. Urban growth strained and often polluted water supplies. In 1850 only fifty-three hundred households had their own piped water; the rest relied on public fountains (which used only half as much water as the ornamental fountains) or the city's twenty thousand water carriers. Growth also swamped the inadequate drains and sewage disposal systems. There was, for example, only 1 kilometer of underground sewer for every 3 kilometers of street. The solution to these manifold problems necessitated the alliance of government, private enterprise, and technical expertise. This was effected by Napoleon III and Haussmann.

Whereas previous public works had been intended to palliate economic and political crises in the capital, they were now used massively to help sustain prosperity and to solve the problems that resulted from anarchic growth. The street network was improved, its length increased by 20 percent, asphalt employed for surfacing, and major streets built or widened to unheard of widths. Five new bridges were constructed over the Seine: the Pont Napoléon (now the Pont National), the Pont de la Gare (now the Pont de Bercy), the Pont du Point du Jour (now the Pont d'Auteuil), and the Ponts de l'Alma and de Solférino. Six others were rebuilt. The main effort was concentrated on the improvement of communications within the congested core and between the core and the outskirts. The result was that access to the railway termini was improved, the east-west and north-south axes were cleared (*la grande croisée*: rue de Rivoli, intersected north-south by the boulevards de Strasbourg, de Sébastopol, and Saint Michel), and work begun on the exterior boulevards (boulevards Malesherbes, Haussmann, de Magenta, du Prince Eugène [now Voltaire], Richard Lenoir [built over the Canal St. Martin], Mazas [now Diderot], Henri Quatre, de l'Hôpital, du Point Royal, du Montparnasse, des Invalides). The new boulevard Saint Germain opened an east-west path through the Left Bank. Perhaps the most ambitious of these schemes was the massive expropriation and demolition of property on the Ile de la Cité and the building of new public edifices that reduced the population there from fifteen thousand to five thousand and changed the heart of the city. Important steps were also taken to improve water supplies and drains. There were 700 kilometers of water pipes in 1852; by 1869, 852 kilometers had been added, and a new drainage system with 560 kilometers of drains had been installed, including nine great collectors, a system unparalleled in the world at that time (these were storm, not sanitary, sewers; human excrement was still carried away nightly in special carts). Haussmann freed Paris from its dependence on the Seine for drinking water, tapping neighboring springs for an ample supply.

The regime also endowed the capital with seven new markets, including Les Halles Centrales (a first priority) and the Abattoirs Généraux de La Villette. Napoleon III was especially anxious that Paris should have public parks like London's, and he personally supervised the remodeling of the "aristocratic" Bois de Boulogne to the west of the city (with its monumental avenues of approach, the avenue de l'Impératrice [now avenue Foch] and the avenue de l'Empereur [now avenues du Président Wilson, Georges Mandel, and Henri Martin]), and the "proletarian" Bois de Vincennes to the east. Also constructed were parks within the city: the Parc des Buttes Chaumont and the Parc de Monceau on the Right Bank and the Parc de Montsouris on the Left Bank (the Butte du Trocadéro was also leveled, and a public garden laid out there). In addition Haussmann created some twenty-one treed squares. A number of monumental buildings were erected, including four major theaters (most notably Charles Garnier's Opéra), fifteen churches, seventy schools, a half-dozen town halls (*mairies*), two major railroad stations (du Nord and d'Austerlitz), and six huge barracks (including the Préfecture de Police). The building of a new Hôtel Dieu hospital was begun, the Tribunal de Commerce erected, the new Louvre completed (another top priority), and the present reading room of the Bibliothèque Nationale constructed in glass and iron. Finally, in addition to numerous restorations and *dégagements*, Haussmann, with his passion for monumental perspectives, endowed the city with some of its most impressive *carrefours*: the places du Louvre, Château d'Eau (now place de la République), Voltaire (now Léon Blum), de l'Opéra, du Théâtre Français (now de l'Odéon), de l'Alma, Malesherbes, du Trocadéro, de l'Hôtel de Ville, du Châtelet, de l'Etoile, Saint Michel, and du Parvis Notre Dame, as well as the squares Saint Jacques, Louis XVI, des Innocents, and du Temple. The square Saint Jacques resulted from the fact that the hill on which the tower stood had to be lowered to permit the extension eastward of the rue de Rivoli (Haussmann, it should be noted, was the first to map Paris and its terrain accurately through triangulation).

Haussmann and Napoleon III did not succeed alone, of course, but relied on collaborators like Adolphe Alphand and Eugène Belgrand (1810–1878), both government engineers, and Isaac and Emile Pereire and Louis Frémy (1807–1891), who were financiers. Private enterprise, indeed, participated in public works and rebuilding. Housing construction accelerated from an annual average of 262 houses in the 1821–1850 period to an annual average of 4,752 under the Second Empire.

There were unquestionably flaws in the achievement. Working-class housing received pitifully few incentives from an administration preoccupied with building for the wealthy, and care was not taken to prevent the appearance of new slums. The shifting center of gravity of the capital from east to west was accentuated, and the Right Bank continued to attract more industry, commerce, and inhabitants than the Left (population on the Right Bank increased by nearly a third but by only a fifth on the Left). This, however, was a secular trend. More important, the attention lavished on public works in the city contrasted with the uncontrolled growth of the outer suburbs, new centers for the displaced working-class populations of the inner city. And even within the city, the problems of water supply and drainage had been only partly solved. Paris remained an unhealthy place in the last third of the century. The public works program had proved extremely costly—2,500 million francs according to Haussmann's estimates—and servicing the city's debt absorbed no less than 44 percent of its budget in 1870. Protests over costs and the prefect's financial methods, indeed, were the chief cause of his dismissal early in 1870. Haussmann's gamble, however, was based on the expectation that Paris would grow and prosper. He and Napoleon III played a part in ensuring that it did.

J. Bastié, *La croissance de la banlieu parisienne* (Paris, 1964); A. Castelot, "Haussmann, destructeur ou sauveur de Paris?" *Historia* 328 (March 1974); B. Chapman, "Baron Haussmann and the Planning of Paris," *Town Planning Review* 24 (1953); L. Chevalier, *La formation de la population parisienne au XIXe siècle* (Paris, 1952); Conservatoire National des Arts et Métiers, *Evolution de la géographie industrielle de Paris et sa proche banlieu au XIXe siècle*, 2 vols. (Paris, 1976); A. Dansette, "L'oeuvre du baron Haussmann," *RDM* (October 1974); G. Duby, ed., *Histoire de la France urbaine*, vol. 4: *La ville de l'age industriel* (Paris, 1983); I. A. Earls, "Napoleon III as Emperor-Architect," *PWSFH* 4 (1976); J. Gaillard, *Paris, la ville, 1852–1870* (Paris, 1977); Louis Girard, *La nouvelle histoire de Paris: la Deuxième République et le Second Empire* (Paris, 1981), and *La politique des travaux publics du Second Empire* (Paris, 1952); R. Héron de Villefosse, "Survol du Paris d'Haussmann," *RDM*, no. 5 (1970); C. Leonard, *Lyon transformed: Public Works of the Second Empire, 1853–1864* (Berkeley: University of California, 1961); H. Malet, "Paris avant Haussmann," *RDM*, 1 August 1953; *MHF*, no. 102 (1979); D. H. Pinkney, *Napoleon III and the Rebuilding of Paris* (Princeton, 1958); A. Sutcliffe, *The Autumn of Central Paris: The Defeat of Town Planning, 1850–1970* (London, 1977).

Barrie M. Ratcliffe

Related entries: ALPHAND; BOIS DE BOULOGNE: DAVIOUD; GARNIER; GRANDS MAGASINS; HALLES CENTRALES; HAUSSMANN; INTERNATIONAL EXPOSITIONS; LABROUSTE; OPERA; PEREIRE; RAILROADS; TUILERIES-LOUVRE; VIOLLET-LE-DUC.

PARIS, TREATY OF, 1856. See CONGRESS OF PARIS.

PARLIAMENT. See CORPS LEGISLATIF.

PARNASSIAN MOVEMENT. See LECONTE DE LISLE.

PASDELOUP, JULES (1819–1887), pianist, composer, and conductor; born at Paris, 15 September 1819. His father, François, was deputy conductor of the Opéra Comique orchestra. At the Conservatoire (1829–1833) Pasdeloup studied piano under Pierre Zimmermann (1785–1853) and composition under Michele Enrico Carafa de Colobrano (1787–1872), winning the first prize for piano. On graduation, his father having died, he gave lessons, played concerts and composed. From 1841 he was lecturer in solfège at the Conservatoire and from 1840 to 1850 lecturer in piano. In 1855 he was appointed professor of choral music (*ensemble*) at the Conservatoire, a position he would hold until 1868, when he gave up all teaching responsibilities. In 1860 Pasdeloup was named to share with François Bazin (1816–1878) direction of the Paris choral society, the Orphéon. In that capacity he succeeded Charles Gounod as director of music education in the communal schools of Paris.

Discouraged by the unsympathetic attitude of the Conservatoire's orchestra toward young composers, Pasdeloup founded in 1852 the Société des Jeunes Artistes to perform new music as well as recognized masterpieces. This orchestra of sixty-two was drawn from the best of the Conservatoire's students and had a choir of forty, conducted by Antoine Batiste (1820–1876), whose sister was the mother of Léo Delibes. The society's first concert was given in the Salle Herz on 20 February 1853. In 1856 Daniel Auber (1782–1871), director of the Conservatoire from 1842 until his death, became patron of the Jeunes Artistes, whose name was changed to the Société des Jeunes Artistes du Conservatoire Impérial de Musique. Pasdeloup's venture was an artistic success; the Jeunes Artistes gave first performances of symphonies by Gounod and Camille Saint-Saëns, introduced Schumann's first symphony to France (1857), and played the Wedding March from Wagner's *Lohengrin*. Although patronage meant free use of instruments and rehearsal rooms, by 1861 the deficit (which Pasdeloup had borne) rose to 77,000 francs. The conductor reacted to the crisis in a way that was to change the nature of French concert life.

In 1861 Pasdeloup rented the Cirque Napoléon (recently built by architect Jacques Hittorff [1792–1867] to seat almost five thousand) for a series of Sunday afternoon Concerts Populaires de Musique Classique. He enlarged the orchestra to over one hundred musicians (fifty-six strings and twenty-five wind, including forty-four Conservatoire *premier prix* winners), and priced admissions in the range of 3 francs to 75 centimes, thus making symphonic music available for the first time to the lower-middle and working classes. From the first concert, on 27 October 1861, the format was an unqualified success. After three concerts had made a profit, Pasdeloup engaged the hall for a further series, ending 13 April 1862. The program of the first concert was typical: Weber's overture to *Oberon*, Beethoven's "Pastoral" symphony, Mendelssohn's violin concerto (with Delphin Alard [1815–1888] as soloist; eventually all of the famous soloists of the day would perform in the Concerts Populaires), Haydn's "Austrian Hymn," and Méhul's overture to *Le jeune Henri*. Pasdeloup was not without musical daring. On 7 March 1866 he played the septuor from *Les Troyens* of Hector Berlioz (1803–1869) and in 1868 an excerpt from the same composer's *Roméo et Juliette*, and he frequently performed the works of German composers yet unfamiliar in France, in particular excerpts from Wagner (the march from Act

2 of *Tannhäuser* on 10 May 1862; the overture to *Der fliegende Holländer* on 25 December 1864). But the great achievement of the Concerts Populaires, imitated throughout the world, was to broaden greatly the concert-going audience and introduce it to symphonic music, with the result that younger composers were encouraged to break away from the near monopoly exercised until then by the musical theater.

In 1866–1867 Pasdeloup attempted unsuccessfully to add to the Concerts Populaires a series, at the new (1866) Salle de l'Athénée, of music for choir and orchestra. He presented Haydn's *Seasons*, Mendelssohn's *Athalie*, and Handel's *Ode to Saint Cecile*. But the experiment proved too costly and was abandoned after one season. In 1868 Pasdeloup founded the Société des Oratorios, which gave the first Paris performance of Bach's *Saint Matthew Passion* (first part). That same year (October) he followed Léon Carvalho as director of the Théâtre Lyrique but was unable to halt its decline. His attempt to familiarize French ears with Wagner (*Rienzi*, April 1869) may have contributed to the final failure of the Théâtre Lyrique in January 1870.

For Pasdeloup the years of the Second Empire were years of success and achievement. As *régisseur* (from 1848) of the Chateau de Saint Cloud, he was able to meet the leading figures of the day and to function as an impresario for the regime. For the supervisor of fine arts, Comte Emilien Nieuwerkerke (1811–1892), he organized concerts at the Louvre, for the prefect of the Seine, Baron Georges Haussmann, he arranged concerts at the Hôtel de Ville, and for the emperor's cousin, Princess Mathilde, he presented musical soirées. A knightship in the Legion of Honor inevitably followed, but the Franco-Prussian War, in which Pasdeloup fought as a member of the National Guard, proved to be an irreversible turning point. The Concerts Populaires, revived in 1871, now faced strong competitors, especially the Nouveau Concerts of Charles Lamoureux (1834–1899), who, as a boy of seventeen, had played violin in the orchestra of the Jeunes Artistes. In 1884 Pasdeloup gave up the struggle. He died at Fontainebleau, 13 August 1887.

E. Bernard, "Jules Pasdeloup et les Concerts Populaires," *RM* 57 (1971); A. Jullien, "Jules Pasdeloup et les Concerts Populaires," in *Musique: Mélanges d'histoire et de critique* (Paris, 1896).
Related entry: CONCERT LIFE.

PASSBOOK, WORKER'S. See LIVRET D'OUVRIER.

PASTEUR, LOUIS (1822–1895), chemist and microbiologist; among the most innovative and influential scientists of the Second Empire and one whose career was marked by brilliant solutions to both theoretical problems and practical problems in industry and medicine; born 27 December 1822 at Dôle. Pasteur came from a family of tanners. His father, Jean Joseph Pasteur, served in the renowned Third Regiment of Napoleon I before entering the tanning trade and finally leasing his own tannery in Arbois (1827). Louis was educated at the Collège d'Arbois (1831–1839), the Collège Royal de Besançon (1840–1842), and the Ecole Normale Supérieure, from which he received his doctorate (in physics and chemistry) in 1847. During the next decade, Pasteur established a scientific reputation based on fundamental research in crystallography, particularly with respect to the relation between molecular asymmetry and optical activity. He taught chemistry at the University of Strasbourg from 1849 to 1854 and was professor of chemistry and dean of the newly created Faculty of Sciences at Lille from 1854 to 1857. This faculty had been established specifically to focus teaching and research on local industrial interests and, consequently, whatever relationship between science and society Pasteur may have perceived previously, his profound dedication to the practical applications of science dates from the Lille period.

Politically conservative and authoritarian by nature, Pasteur welcomed the coup d'état of 1851 and subscribed to Louis Napoleon's conception of imperial glory. Pasteur remained a devoted supporter of the Empire and, after his former teacher, the chemist Jean Baptiste Dumas (whom Napoleon had made a senator), presented him to the emperor in 1863, he developed personal ties to both Napoleon III and the Empress Eugénie. Invited to spend a week as their guest at Compiègne in 1865, he delighted the royal couple with microscopic demonstrations and lectures on fermentation, molecular asymmetry, and microbes. They followed his career with great interest thereafter. Pasteur exerted considerable, at times controversial, influence on the French academic establishment through his tenure as administrator and director of scientific studies at the Ecole Normale (1857–1867), as professor of chemistry at the Sorbonne (1867–1874), and as director of the laboratory of physiological chemistry at the Ecole Normale (1867–1888). Although he complained of inadequate state support of science, particularly when compared to the situation in Germany, Pasteur was granted impressive laboratory facilities and generous research budgets by the imperial government after 1867. Elected to the Académie des Sciences in 1862 and made knight of the Legion of Honor in 1853, he was promoted to commander by the emperor in 1868, following his enforced resignation as associate director of the Ecole Normale in 1867 in the wake of a student demonstration in favor of Charles Augustin Sainte-Beuve. Pasteur's eminence derives from his manifold scientific accomplishments.

Fermentation. Stimulated in part by a request in 1856 by a Lille manufacturer to solve certain difficulties besetting his production of alcohol from beet sugar, Pasteur began an intensive investigation of fermentation. In contrast to the then predominant view that fermentation was a chemical reaction, Pasteur established that the conversion of sugar into alcohol, wine into vinegar, and milk sugar into lactic acid (among other cognate processes) were essentially physiological actions associated with the life functions of specific microscopic organisms (such as yeast). The experimental techniques he developed to cultivate and study these microorganisms and to demonstrate that substances in the fermenting mediums served as food for them were rapidly exploited to solve a wide variety of practical as well as theoretical problems. Pasteur's elucidation of the process by which vinegar is produced (for which he took out a patent in 1861) freed French manufacturers from the uncertainties of their traditional practices and rationalized the French vinegar industry. His studies on the diseases of wine were of even greater significance. Pasteur demonstrated (1864) that the various undesirable alterations of wine—rendering them bitter, sour, oily—were each due to a specific microorganism and, moreover, that these organisms could be destroyed by subjecting wine to controlled heating in closed vessels without damage to bouquet, taste, or appearance. This process of preserving wine, which was soon shown effective in protecting numerous other beverages and foods, became known internationally as pasteurization and gained for Pasteur the Grand Prix Medal of the international exposition of 1867 at Paris. In 1871, partly as a patriotic response to the Franco-Prussian War, he began a systematic study of beer in the hope of improving the French product and rendering it a serious competitor to its superior German rival. Although Pasteur's specific recommendations for new industrial procedures did not gain significant adoption, his general contributions toward the rationalization of the brewing industry, particularly his demonstration of the microbial origin of beer diseases and his methods for preventing them, were recognized, and they stimulated the Dane J. C. Jacobsen to create in the late 1870s a splendid laboratory in his Carlsberg brewery (which soon became a major international center of biochemical research).

Spontaneous Generation. The controversy over spontaneous generation had been rekindled in France in 1859 with the publication of a book by the respected Rouen naturalist Félix Pouchet (1800–1872) in which he claimed to have successfully produced microorganisms by adding artificially produced (and hence presumably germ-free) air or oxygen to boiled (and presumably sterile) hay infusions under mercury. Pouchet's findings caused sufficient stir to induce the Académie des Sciences to establish the Alhumbert Prize of 2,500 francs for the best experimental resolution of the spontaneous generation debate. The prize was won by Pasteur in 1862 on the basis of a series of technically brilliant experiments he had performed during 1860–1861. Pasteur demonstrated that microorganisms that appeared under experimental conditions owed their origin either to contaminated apparatus and materials or to airborne germs and argued that the laboratory mercury Pouchet used could have been the source of the observed microorganisms. Pasteur was widely considered in France to have refuted decisively the doctrine of spontaneous generation. There were, however, a number of unresolved issues, and he was forced to defend his position repeatedly against Pouchet and others throughout the 1860s and 1870s. Moreover the debate had considerable extrascientific implications and was followed with great public interest. Spontaneous generation—as also Darwinian evolution—was associated in the Second Empire with materialism, atheism, and radical political and social ideas, and Pasteur was seen as a defender of church and state. Although he claimed that his opposition to spontaneous generation derived from experimental considerations alone, it is clear that his conservative political and religious views buttressed and perhaps influenced his scientific opinion in this instance. Finally, in addition to strengthening his position among the French scientific elite, Pasteur's experiments were important contributions to microbiological theory and technique.

Silkworm Diseases. By 1865 the silkworm industry in France was near ruin, owing to a disease that had begun to attack the silkworm nurseries in the early 1850s. The situation was sufficiently serious for the Ministry of Agriculture to appoint a commission to study *pébrine*, as the disease was called because of the black spots that appeared on afflicted worms. At the insistence of Dumas, who was from Alais (now Alès), one of the most important centers of sericulture, Pasteur agreed to head the investigation. For the next five years Pasteur immersed himself in the problem, spending long periods each year away from Paris in a field laboratory (in effect, a research silkworm nursery) he established in the environs of Alais. Pasteur and his collaborators succeeded in demonstrating that the blight actually consisted of two separate diseases, *pébrine* and *flacherie*, which were dependent on the presence of specific microorganisms. Most important, he devised a technique of egg selection whereby eggs could be selected from healthy moths and those of diseased moths rejected on the basis of microscopic examination of moth tissue to detect the presence or absence of bacterial infection. Pasteur's technique aroused considerable mistrust and opposition, and a proposal by Marshal Jean Baptiste Vaillant, minister of the emperor's household, provided the scientist with an opportunity to demonstrate the effectiveness of his method. Pasteur was invited to supervise the seeding of the prince imperial's estate at Villa Vicentina, near Trieste, whose silkworm industry had been devastated by *pébrine* and *flacherie*. His success was striking and the egg selection method, as well as Pasteur's suggestions for maintaining appropriate environmental conditions in silkworm nurseries, came to be widely applied not only in France but in Austria and Italy as well. Napoleon III was sufficiently impressed with Pasteur's scientific and industrial achievements to issue a decree in July 1870, which, had it not been nullified by events, would have made Pasteur a senator.

Medicine. Although Pasteur's major contributions to medicine were made after the Second Empire, their importance requires mention. His work on fermentation and infectious silkworm diseases and his attacks on spontaneous generation prepared Pasteur for a sustained investigation of medical issues in general and of the germ theory of disease in particular. Joseph Lister, who introduced antiseptic surgery in the 1860s, cited Pasteur's studies on the microbial agents responsible for fermentation as the basis for his own achievement in preventing infection in the operating room. During the 1870s and 1880s, Pasteur, despite a debilitating stroke suffered in October 1868, produced a series of brilliant experimental demonstrations of the role played by microorganisms and viruses in the transmission and development of diseases such as anthrax, puerperal fever, fowl cholera, and rabies. His discovery of a vaccine against anthrax—prepared from an attenuated culture of the anthrax bacillus—and his famous demonstration of its effectiveness in an internationally reported field trial at Pouilly-le-Fort in

1881 signaled a major victory against a disease that had exacted a significant economic toll in France (and Europe). Pasteur's successful efforts in producing vaccines against other diseases, most notably rabies, laid the groundwork for the developing science of immunology.

Pasteur was an ardent advocate of increased state support for science. He was particularly critical of the scant government provision for laboratory research (most of the major laboratories were privately financed, often inadequately), and in *Le budget de la science* (1868) he attacked national indifference in this crucial area. His arguments gained the emperor's support for the construction of a major new laboratory of physiological chemistry at the Ecole Normale. Pasteur's own successes, however, underscored the more general paucity of government support for science, and he continued in his efforts to secure greater public expenditures in this domain, arguing that inadequate government support had cost the nation its preeminent scientific status of the early decades of the nineteenth century. Pasteur attributed France's defeat in the Franco-Prussian War in part to Prussia's superior endowment of scientific and technological training and, most significant, to Germany's brilliantly organized network of well-funded research laboratories. Although Pasteur's close association with the Second Empire and his lack of enthusiasm for republicanism rendered him politically unpopular after the fall of Napoleon III (he was defeated in his 1876 attempt to gain election to the senate as a conservative from Arbois), Pasteur's scientific and personal eminence continued unabated. The last decades of his life witnessed sustained scientific achievement, substantial government pensions, and numerous honors and awards, including election to the Académie Française in 1882, replacing, ironically, Emile Littré whose doctrine of positivism he opposed. The Institut Pasteur was established in 1888. Pasteur died 28 September 1895 at Villeneuve-l'Etang, near Paris.

F. Dagognet, *Méthodes et doctrines dans l'oeuvre de Pasteur* (Pasteur, 1967); A. Delaunay, "Pasteur au présent: Cent cinquième anniversaire de la naissance de Louis Pasteur," *Médecine et hygiène* 31 (1973); R. J. Dubos, *Louis Pasteur: Free Lance of Science* (Boston, 1950); J. Farley, "The Social, Political, and Religious Background of the Work of Louis Pasteur," *Annual Review of Microbiology* 32 (1978); J. Farley and G. L. Geison, "Science, Politics, and Spontaneous Generation in Nineteenth-Century France: The Pasteur-Pouchet Debate," *Bulletin of the History of Medicine* 48 (1974); J. Nicolle, *Pasteur: Sa vie, sa méthode, ses découvertes* (Paris,1969), and *Louis Pasteur* (New York, 1966).

Martin Fichman

Related entries: BERNARD; BERTHELOT; DARWINISM IN FRANCE; DUMAS; DURUY; OIDIUM, PHYLLOXERA; POSITIVISM.

LA PATRIE, a Paris daily newspaper, founded in 1841, one of a trio of semi-official journals during the Second Empire (the others were *Le pays* and *Le constitutionnel*). *La patrie* originally was considered part of the conservative Left. It assumed a careful opposition to the July Monarchy. During the Revolution of 1848, it had supported the Second Republic. After 1850, political expediency and the bonapartist ties of its owner (since 1844), Théodore Delamarre (1796–1870), moved the newspaper to partisanship for Louis Napoleon. Delamarre, who sat in the Corps Lég latif from 1852 to 1857, was a former banker, concerned with profits. Having bought *La patrie* at a very low price, he made it a "*journal économique*," close to business and even to speculative interests. Aspiring to attract as large a circulation as possible, Delamarre subordinated political principles to stories with a broad appeal. *La patrie* was the best-informed paper on the subject of crimes, catastrophes, accidents, and sensational news. Although Delamarre performed a number of services for the regime, receiving and printing official notices and news releases, directing and inspiring numerous articles, *La patrie* occasionally received *avertissements*—once for presuming to discuss the constitution of January 1852. Among the collaborators of the newspaper were Ernest Dréolle (1829–1887; an editor in chief), Edouard Fournier (1819–1880), Philippe Cucheval-Clarigny (1822–1895), Paulin Limayrac (1817–1868), and Robert Mitchell (1839–1916). Notable editors were Amédée de Césèna (1810–1889) and Limayrac. Gravely ill in 1866, Delamarre sold the newspaper to a group of political financiers. Throughout the Empire, *La patrie* was the least important of the semiofficial newspapers and played only a minor role in influencing public opinion. Its circulation was 24,500 in July 1858, 22,905 in August 1861, and 11,500 in March 1869.

Natalie Isser

Related entries: CONSTITUTIONNEL; MARINONI; *MONITEUR UNIVERSEL; PAYS*; PRESS REGIME.

LE PAYS, one of three semiofficial daily Paris newspapers during the Second Empire (the others were *La patrie* and *Le constitutionnel*). Founded in 1849 as the paper of Alphonse de Lamartine (1790–1869), *Le pays* was directed by Lamartine's protégé, Arthur de La Guéronnière, but moved nevertheless toward Louis Napoleon. After condemning the coup d'état of December 1851, the newspaper, owned (from 1850 until 1861) by the financier Jules Mirès, adopted openly a policy of loyal support for the new regime. On 1 December 1852 *Le pays* added to its masthead the title *Journal de l'Empire*. The government freely intervened in the selection of personnel and the formulation of policies. When a financial scandal forced Mirès into liquidation in 1861, Napoleon III's half-brother, Auguste de Morny, acquired a controlling interest in the company that owned both *Le pays* and *Le constitutionnel*. The columns of *Le pays* were open not only to government press releases and special announcements but also to articles inspired by the emperor and his ministers. Adolphe Granier de Cassagnac was director and editor in chief from 27 April 1859 until 1863 and again from 1866. During the interval, Pierre Grandguillot (1829–1891) directed both *Le pays* and *Le constitutionnel*, assisted by political director Auguste Chevalier (1809–1868), brother of the economist. Under the guidance of Granier de Cassagnac and his son Paul (1842–1904), from 1866, *Le pays* became a passionate and polemical defender of the Empire, an ultra voice that was sometimes embarrassing even to the regime. Among contributors and collaborators were Auguste Vitu (1823–1891), Ernest Dréolle (1829–1887), Jules Barbey d'Aurevilly (who wrote the literary chronicle), Joseph Méry (1798–1865; drama critic), Paulin Limayrac (1817–1868), Louis Enault (1824–1900), Paul Féval (1817–1887), and Robert Mitchell (1839–1916). *Le pays* never entered the front rank of influential newspapers during the Second Empire. Its circulation was 8,850 in July 1858, 7,000 in August 1861, 3,000 in 1866, and 2,800 in March 1869.

Natalie Isser

Related entries: CONSTITUTIONNEL; GRANIER DE CASSAGNAC; LA GUERONNIERE; MARINONI; MIRES; *MONITEUR UNIVERSEL; PATRIE*; PRESS REGIME.

PELISSIER, AIMABLE (DUC DE MALAKOV) (1794–1864), conqueror of Sebastopol (1855), marshal of France, ambassador; born at Maromme (Seine-Inférieure) to a peasant family of modest means. After studies at Saint Cyr, Pélissier began a military career that embraced almost every major war and expedition of the Restoration and of the July Monarchy: Napoleon's Hundred Days campaign (1815), the Spanish expedition (1823), the assistance given Greek insurgents against Turkey (1828–1829), the Algiers expedition of 1830, the siege of Antwerp during Belgium's struggle for independence (1832), and the conquest of Algeria (1839–1851). From 1819, when he was named to the general staff following a brilliant examination, until 1850, when he was promoted general of division, Pélissier's advance was irresistible. Not renowned for his tactical skills, he soon gained a reputation for energy, audacity, and even brutality (the asphyxiation of some six hundred Algerian insurgents by fire in 1845). Knight of the Legion of Honor from 1823, several times decorated, Pélissier replaced General Alphonse Henri d'Hautpoul (1789–1865) as interim governor of Algeria on 10 May 1851.

In his new position, Pélissier accepted the coup d'état of December 1851. On 7 December he put Algeria under martial law and offered himself as a guarantor of order. Replaced shortly after as governor by General Jacques Louis Randon, he organized and successfully executed the Kabylie expedition, took Laghouat, and forced the submission of the southern tribes (1852). His reputation made (he was named grand cross of the Legion of Honor 25 December 1854), Pélissier was the inevitable choice to succeed General François Certain Canrobert as commander of the French forces in the Crimea as the war against Russia (1854–1856) ran down in the interminable siege of Sebastopol. Taking command 16 May 1855, he pressed the siege with his accustomed vigor. Despite a bloody check on 18 June, the French carried the key defense of the Malakov Tower less than three months later (8 September 1855). It was the decisive event of the war, and it made Pélissier a marshal of France (12 September). Napoleon III's gratitude was soon further expressed. Returned to Paris following the war, Pélissier was given the title duc de Malakov (22 July 1856) and in March 1857 was voted a hereditary income of 100,000 francs per year by the Corps Législatif. His marriage the next year to a twenty-five-year-old wealthy Spanish woman (arranged by her distant relative, Empress Eugénie) produced a daughter. Vice-president of the Senate (14 December 1856), member of the first Conseil Privé (1 February 1858), Pélissier, who was popular in Britain (he had been named Knight of the Garter in June 1856), was sent as ambassador to that country on 22 March 1858 to restore good relations seriously disturbed in the aftermath of the attempt on Napoleon III's life by Felice Orsini. He replaced Victor Fialin Persigny. The outbreak of war with Austria in 1859 soon interrupted Pélissier's appointment. He was recalled 23 April 1859 to take command at Nancy of an army designated to watch the Rhine during the fighting in Italy. At the conclusion of the war, Pélissier was further honored by his nomination to the post of chancellor of the Legion of Honor (July 1859), succeeding the duc de Plaisance. His last service to the Empire was to accept nomination as governor general of Algeria (23 November 1860). A rude and somewhat uncouth man, whose brother, Philippe Xavier (1812–1887), was also a distinguished general, Pélissier had a lighter side, which reflected itself in witty poeticizing and even song writing. He died at Algiers, 22 May 1864.

General Derrécagaix, *Le Maréchal Pélissier, duc de Malakoff* (Paris, 1911); P. Guiral and R. Brunon, eds., *Aspects de la vie politique et militaire en France au milieu du XIXe siècle à travers la correspondence reçue par le Maréchal Pélissier (1828–1864)* (Paris, 1968); R. M. Johnston, *Memoirs of "Malakoff,"* 2 vols. (London, 1906).

Related entries: ALGERIA; ARMY REFORM; BAZAINE; CANROBERT; CRIMEAN WAR; MACMAHON; NIEL; RANDON; SAINT-ARNAUD; VAILLANT.

PEREIRE, EMILE, and **PEREIRE, ISAAC,** leading figures in Parisian finance who had variegated and remarkable careers as journalists, railway magnates, and company promoters. Emile was born 3 December 1800 at Bordeaux and died 6 January 1875 at Paris; Isaac was born 25 November 1806 at Bordeaux, and died 12 July 1880 at the chateau of Armainvilliers (Seine-et-Marne). The brothers founded the Crédit Mobilier and presided over its destinies until forced to resign in 1867, and they controlled a score of major companies in France and abroad that the Mobilier had established or supported. Both were deputies during the Second Empire.

In their own time, the Pereires were controversial figures, both lauded and condemned for their success and for their methods. Many of the easy epithets that were applied to them in their lifetimes have subsequently been applied by historians. Antisemitic critics seized on the fact that, like Jules Mirès, the Pereires were Sephardic Jews from Bordeaux (of Spanish descent, they were the grandsons of one of the inventors of a sign language for deaf mutes and sons of a maritime underwriter). For many, they, like Michel Chevalier and Prosper Enfantin (1796–1864), were Saint-Simonians who sought in their later careers to apply ideas and ideology they had imbibed in contact with the sect at Paris between 1826 and 1832. For others they were journalists and pamphleteers who profited from the opportunities offered by the return of prosperity in the 1850s. For still others the Pereires, with their ostentatious wealth (a mansion on the rue Saint Honoré, an impressive art collection, and a chateau at Armainvilliers) were parvenus, outsiders who arrived with the new political elite of the Second Empire and who failed when the Empire went into decline.

None of these labels is wholly accurate. As for their Jewishness, the brothers had long assimilated, ceased to be orthopraxis, and their children married outside the faith. As for their Saint-Simonianism, the commitment of the two had been unequal: Emile, the more original and astute, the one who usually planned while Isaac executed, had never adhered to the sect, and it was Isaac who followed its leader Enfantin until 1832. Besides, there was little that was original in Saint-Simonian ideas on banking or on the economy in general. The Pereires had certainly been financial journalists in the early years of the July Monarchy and the themes they developed in their writings then—ideas on credit, public finance, and tariff policy—they were to attempt to apply under the Second Empire. But with minor exceptions they had ceased their journalistic activities in the 1830s. They were not outsiders in 1852 when they set up their Crédit Mobilier. Under the July Monarchy, they had become leading railway magnates, building Paris's first suburban lines (Paris-Saint-German) and joining with James de Rothschild to organize the Compagnie du Chemin de Fer du Nord and the Paris-Lyons railway. In the 1840s Heinrich Heine (1797–1856) called Emile Pereire the ''Pontifex Maximus'' of French railways.

The Crédit Mobilier is the most controversial of the Pereires' creations under the Second Empire. Whatever judgment is made on that institution, the Pereires left behind them a mixture of successes and failures. They created and directed the successful Compagnie Générale Transatlantique. They helped to establish and to direct three major French railway companies—those of the West, East, and Midi (the last, established in 1852 and in July granted the Bordeaux-Cette [now Sète] concession, was inaugurated in 1857 as the only great line not departing from Paris)—but their efforts to control French railroads collapsed with the failure of the Compagnie du Grand Central de France and the subsequent reorganization of 1857. They also lost out in their struggle with other groups for through-routes to Italy and Switzerland (as in the case of the Paris-Méditer-ranée-Lyon route, where Pereire interests were overwhelmed between 1852 and 1857). They built successful railways in parts of Austria, Spain, and Switzerland but were outmaneuvered by the Rothschild group for concessions in other areas. And their Russian railway concession proved a disaster. They contributed to urban and port development in Paris and Marseilles. In the capital, through the Compagnie Immobilière de Paris (1854), they helped extend and develop the rue de Rivoli and to create the Monceau quarter. They built the Grand Hôtel and Grand Hôtel du Louvre, set up the Grands Magasins du Louvre, and amal-gamated the gas and omnibus companies (Compagnie Générale des Omnibus de

Paris, March 1855, and Société Parisienne d'Eclairage et de Chauffage par le Gaz, 1856). To mark their contribution to Paris, the municipal council named a boulevard and a square after them. These Parisian activities proved costly to the Crédit Mobilier because a heavy investment was made in commercial and luxury residential developments when construction costs were rising and the market was saturated. In the 1860s, the Compagnie Immobilière transferred its center of activity to Marseilles where by 1863 the Pereires had won their long struggle with Mirès but encountered strong opposition from Paulin Talabot, who succeeded in keeping the Pereires' Midi railway company from linking up with the city.

The Pereires also exerted some influence over economic policy. Introduced to Louis Napoleon in 1852 by Victor Fialin Persigny, who saw them as a means of challenging the Orleanist dominance of finance and who shared many of their ideas, such as recourse to loans rather than taxes as a means of raising government revenue (long-term borrowing against future income), they were among those who proposed the 1854 Bineau loan, the first flotation not to use the *haute banque* as an intermediary. An early proponent of modern tariffs, Emile Pereire played a role in persuading Napoleon III to sign the Anglo-French commercial treaty of 1860. The Pereires also advocated low interest rates, cheap money, abundant credit, limited liability, and reform of the Bank of France. These efforts failed, however, and an attempt to end the bank's monopoly of issue by acquiring the Banque de Savoie was frustrated in 1863–1864, although the Pereires did provoke the important banking inquiry of 1865. Napoleon III may well have sympathized with many of these ideas, but the Pereires' methods and penchant for speculation bolstered an impressive coalition against them (Rothschild, Pierre Magne, Jules Baroche, Jean Mocquard, Eugène Rouher, Achille Fould) that the emperor could not ignore, and by 1862 he inclined toward the Rothschilds, whose resources the Pereires could not match. Nevertheless, Napoleon III requested that the brothers, who had long sat on their departmental conseils généraux, contest the elections of 1863. Both were elected to the Corps Législatif and rewarded on 13 August 1864 by promotion to the rank of officer of the Legion of Honor. Lacking oratorical gifts, neither played an important role, and both withdrew in 1869. By then the Crédit Mobilier had failed (1867), and the Pereires had fallen from their eminence. They retained some of their holdings, however, and a significant part of their fortune.

J. Bouvier, "Les Pereire et l'affaire de la Banque de Savoie, 1860–1864," *Cahiers d'histoire* 4 (1962); L. Girard, "Le chemin de fer Sète-Marseille, 1861–1863," *RHMC* (April–June 1955); G. Pereire, ed., *Oeuvres d'I. et E. Pereire*, 3 vols. (Paris, 1913); B. M. Ratcliffe, "Les Pereire et le Saint-Simonisme," *EcS* (July 1971), "Some Jewish Problems in the Early Careers of Emile and Isaac Pereire," *Jewish Social Studies* 34 (1972), and "Railway Imperialism: The Example of the Pereires' Paris-Saint-Germain Company, 1835–1846," *Business History* 18 (1976); P. de Rivoire d'Heilly, "Une élection exemplaire sous le Second Empire," *RA* no. 174 (1976).

Barrie M. Ratcliffe

Related entries: BANKING; BEHIC; COBDEN-CHEVALIER TREATY; COMPAGNIE GENERALE TRANSATLANTIQUE; CREDIT MOBILIER; FOULD; GOVERNMENT FINANCE; MIRES; MORNY; PARIS, REBUILD-ING OF; PERSIGNY; RAILROADS; ROTHSCHILD; ROUHER; SAINT-SI-MONIANISM; SCHNEIDER, E.; TALABOT.

PERSIGNY, VICTOR FIALIN, DUC DE (1808–1872), friend and confidant of Napoleon III, politician, minister, diplomat, and senator; born Victor Fialin at Saint-Germain-Lespinasse (Loire), 11 January 1808 (the same year as Louis Napoleon). Raised by an uncle after his father, who had lost the remains of his estate through speculation, joined Napoleon I's Grande Armée, and was killed at the Battle of Salamanca (1812), Persigny (he adopted, about 1832, the long-disused family name and began to style himself first vicomte and, in 1848, comte) joined the army (1825), graduating in 1828 at the head of his class from the cavalry school at Saumur. He was soon converted from royalism to repub-licanism and as a consequence was discharged from the army at the beginning of the July Monarchy. In 1831 a chance encounter with Prince Louis Napoleon Bonaparte at Augsburg (their carriages passed in the street) led, according to Persigny's account, to an almost religious experience from which Persigny emerged a fervent bonapartist and an active propagandist for the cause. The two men met at Louis Napoleon's home near Arenenberg, Switzerland, in 1835. Thereafter their destinies were closely linked. No one else had a greater influence on Louis Napoleon's life between 1835 and 1852. Persigny made the final plans for the first attempt to overthrow Louis Philippe's regime (at Strasbourg in October 1836) and set the date. After the failure of that *attentat*, Persigny escaped, wandered briefly in Germany, and then made his way to England where he wrote *Relation de l'entreprise du Prince Napoléon Louis* (1837). Reunited with the prince that year, Persigny joined him in his English exile, wrote *Lettres de Londres: Visite au Prince Louis* (1840), and participated in the *attentat* of Bou-logne in August 1840. This time both men were sentenced to imprisonment, Louis Napoleon to life in the fortress of Ham and Persigny to twenty years at Doullens. When Persigny's eyesight was threatened by illness, he was transferred to a hospital at Versailles and thereafter had virtual freedom of movement. He used the time to write an elaborate memoir, *L'utilité des pyramides d'Egypte* (1844), proving that the purpose of the pyramids had been to protect the Nile Valley against invasion by the desert sand. Through his friend, Frédéric, comte de Falloux (1811–1886), Persigny could have had his freedom for the asking but refused to make the request. He was released from prison following the Revolution of 1848.

From 1848 until the establishment of the Second Empire, Persigny worked tirelessly on Louis Napoleon's behalf. He played a major role in the latter's election to the Constituent Assembly (4 June 1848) and as president of the Second Republic (10 December 1848). It was against his impetuous friend's advice that the prince wisely declined to accept his seat in June. Consequently he was absent from France during the street fighting of the June Days. Following 10 December, Persigny was rewarded for his services. He was assigned a high position in the general staff of the Paris National Guard, appointed aide-de-camp to the president, and named (1849) to the Legion of Honor. He was himself elected to the Legislative Assembly in May 1849 from the Nord and the Loire departments, opting for the latter. In the assembly he vigorously defended the cause of the prince president and helped to secure the appointment of Falloux as minister of education. Persigny was sent in the summer of 1849 on a special mission to Germany and early the following year was appointed minister to Prussia but returned to Paris before the end of 1850. He was one of the principal conspirators of the coup d'état of December 1851 (Persigny had advised Louis Napoleon not to swear loyalty to the constitution). His task on 2 December was, together with General Charles Espinasse (1815–1859), to take over the Palais Bourbon and to close the session of the Legislative Assembly.

Persigny's influence during the following year was a dominant one. He advised Louis Napoleon to confiscate much of the property of the Orleans family in France (Orleans decrees) and succeeded Auguste de Morny as minister of the interior when the latter resigned in protest on 22 January 1852. Persigny also served on the constitutional commission and on the commission that formulated the new electoral regime. With Eugène Rouher, he designed the system for administrative control of the press. It was Persigny who secured for the new regime a civil list of 25 million francs (equal to that of the Bourbons). He presided over the elections of February 1852 and persuaded Louis Napoleon to appoint Baron Georges Haussmann as prefect of the Seine. Always impetuous, Persigny argued for an early proclamation of the Second Empire. Undoubtedly his orchestration of the demonstrations that marked Louis Napoleon's tour of France in the autumn of 1852 contributed to bringing that proclamation about. The minister's role was also important in the establishment of the Crédit Mobilier in November 1852. Louis Napoleon amply rewarded his old friend. When Persigny married the granddaughter of Marshal Ney in May 1852, he received the title of comte and a wedding gift of 500,000 francs. On 11 December 1852 he was named commander of the Legion of Honor and on the last day of the month was appointed to the Senate.

Persigny's loyalty and his devotion to bonapartism were beyond question. For him, democratic Caesarism was an article of faith. There could be no question of a restoration of liberties until the regime had been accepted and the opposition had become in France, as it was in Britain, a loyal one. Despite his willingness to accept official candidates from all groups, Persigny remained adamantly opposed to parties, which he saw as little less than sedition against the regime. And yet his aim was to create, out of the combat of the elections, a popularly based, homogeneous bonapartist party. In economic matters he was Saint-Simonian by sympathy and adventurous by nature. He championed the Pereire brothers against their conservative opponents (it was he who introduced Isaac

and Emile Pereire to Napoleon III) and advanced the theory of productive expenditures (that improvements resulting from government spending would stimulate the economy, thus increasing tax revenues). Persigny had many excellent
qualities. He was loyal, energetic, idealistic, intelligent, bold, politically courageous, and personally honest and decent. But his defects were equally large.
He was tactless, impetuous, impatient, and hard to work with. His inability to
control his tongue combined with the lack of a sense of humor to give him more
than a touch of ridiculousness, of which he was completely unaware. Self-
righteous, he tended greatly to exaggerate his own importance. Above all, he
was a poor politician, unable or unwilling to accept that politics is the art of the
possible. As a result, Persigny was always *plus royaliste que le roi* and, after
the initial months, a growing embarrassment to his master.

In June 1854 Napoleon III asked his prickly minister of the interior to exchange
that post for a ministry without portfolio. Resentful, Persigny resigned, citing
reasons of health, and was succeeded by Adolphe Billault. But the eclipse was
brief. In May 1855 the Anglophile ex-minister was named ambassador to Britain,
replacing Alexandre Walewski, who had been appointed foreign minister. Persigny, who had helped to persuade Napoleon III to send the French fleet eastward
in the 1853 crisis that had led to the Crimean War, proved a strong supporter
of the British alliance and, despite the friction resulting from the attempt on the
emperor's life in January 1858 by Felice Orsini and the embarrassments caused
by the ambassador's frivolous young wife, proved an effective and popular
diplomat. His service was recognized by promotion to the rank of grand cross
of the Legion of Honor on 16 June 1857 (he had been named grand officer in
June 1854). Persigny's recall and the appointment in his place of Marshal Aimable Pélissier, duc de Malakov, on 23 March 1858, probably owed as much to
Walewski's irritation at Persigny's insistence on reporting directly to the emperor
as to any other factor. Persigny, having refused the offer of the vice-presidency
of the Senate, returned to London in April 1859 on Pélissier's recall for service
in the war against Austria that was about to begin. His relations with his friend,
Lord Palmerston, who was then prime minister, were excellent, and the ambassador contributed to the negotiation at the end of 1859 of the commercial
treaty between Britain and France (Cobden-Chevalier treaty), which initiated an
era of relative free trade in Europe (Persigny had been an advocate of trade
liberalization since 1852). He also presided over the very difficult period of
adjustment that followed French annexation of Nice and Savoy in June 1860.
But political developments in France necessitated the ambassador's recall at the
end of November 1860, a move that pleased the opposition conservatives, annoyed at Persigny's relationship with Palmerston.

Named once again to the Ministry of the Interior on 26 November 1860
following Napoleon III's reform decree of that month, Persigny introduced a
period of relative liberalization, particularly concerning administration of press
controls, and urged the prefects to cultivate men of the old parties. But his
feelings were undoubtedly mixed, and he had no desire to see a basic alteration

of the authoritarian regime. The minister's true propensities were revealed in his circular of September 1861 instructing the prefects to prepare lists of "dangerous men" and in his opposition (November 1861) to financial reform, favored even by such authoritarian figures as Rouher and Jules Baroche. Persigny now gave full vent to his intense anti-clericalism. He congratulated Prince Napoleon on his anti-papal Senate speech of 1 March 1861 and in October 1861 clamped down hard on the charitable Society of Saint Vincent de Paul. As one of the politicians most hated by the Catholic party, Persigny figured prominently in the cabinet crisis of October 1862. He was to have been dismissed along with Foreign Minister Edouard Thouvenel but remained as the result of a compromise that followed the protest of several ministers. He therefore conducted one final election, that of 1863, and won a decisive victory over his clerical opponents. But Napoleon III was discontent with the large increase in the opposition vote, and Persigny was blamed not only for the violence of his attacks but also for an inattention to detail, which may have cost the government half of the lost seats. Moreover, the minister had many enemies, in particular Empress Eugénie, Morny, Achille Fould (whom, with the help of Walewski, Haussmann, and Morny, he had toppled from a position of dominant influence at the end of 1860), Billault, Jules Baroche, Rouher, and Edouard Drouyn de Lhuys. Napoleon III's postelection decision to turn in a liberal direction added to the need for change. On 23 June 1863 Persigny resigned. On 13 September he received the title of duke.

Persigny's political career ended in June 1863. He remained a senator, a *conseiller général* of the Loire, and a member of the Conseil Privé, but the advice he continued to offer was usually ignored. In particular he urged a firmer hand with Prussia and a reinvigoration of the authoritarian Empire. His relations with Eugénie, whose marriage to Louis Napoleon he had opposed, grew worse, reaching a nadir at the end of 1867 when she accidentally read a letter from Persigny to the emperor warning against her influence and urging her exclusion from meetings of the Council of Ministers. Alarmed at the physical decline of his master and the growing influence of Rouher, Persigny called in a Senate speech of March 1866 for a change of policy and a continuation of reform. Together with Walewski he sought conditions that would make possible the creation of a broad *union dynastique* and tried to persuade Napoleon III to replace Rouher with Emile Ollivier. But Persigny was no convert to a parliamentary regime, which he attacked in a Senate speech of 12 March 1867. In 1868 he urged the Corps Législatif to reject the proposed liberal press law. It was only after the elections of 1869 that Persigny, in a mood of realism, adopted a truly reformist policy, which he expressed in a letter to Ollivier of 3 June 1869 that was published without his consent by the *Constitutionnel*, and even then his preference was for a "paternal government" of "toutes les vertus." It seems doubtful in fact that Persigny expected the Liberal Empire of his friend Ollivier to endure. Doubtless the old conspirator was still contemplating a coup d'état when the Franco-Prussian War at last ended the drama.

True to his almost mystical bonapartism, Persigny in the Conseil Privé vigorously opposed the idea of Napoleon III's return to Paris after the initial military defeats. After the fall of the Empire, fearing his life to be in danger, he took his family to London. In July 1871 he returned to France, but shortly afterward suffered a stroke, went to Nice to recover his health, and died there on 13 January 1872. Persigny's last years had been unhappy. He was greatly grieved at the breakdown of his marriage, although the fault was his wife's (they had five children), and at the seeming forgetfulness of his services by the former emperor. Napoleon III was himself desperately ill, and by a final irony a letter from him to his old friend, remembering services of the past, arrived at Nice shortly after Persigny's death. Thus the lives of master and servitor remained intertwined until the end. Not the least, in fact, of values to be gained from a study of Persigny's career is the insight it affords into the mind and character of Napoleon III, his political skill, tact, independence of mind, kindness, and loyalty to those who served him.

S. B. Barnwell, "The Duc de Persigny, 1808–1872" (Ph.D. diss., University of California, Berkeley, 1955); P. Chrétien, *Le Duc de Persigny* (Strasbourg, 1943); Comte M. H. de Laire d'Espagny [Persigny's secretary], ed., *Mémoires du Duc de Persigny*, 2d ed. (Paris, 1896); H. Farat, *Persigny: un ministre de Napoléon III* (Paris, 1957).

Related entries: AUTHORITARIAN EMPIRE; BAROCHE; BILLAULT; BONAPARTISM; COBDEN-CHEVALIER TREATY; COUP D'ETAT; ELECTIONS; FOULD; HAUSSMANN; LOUIS NAPOLEON; MAGNE; MAUPAS; MORNY; OLLIVIER; PEREIRE; PREFECTS; PRESS REGIME; PRINCE NAPOLEON; ROUHER; SAINT VINCENT DE PAUL, SOCIETY OF; SECOND EMPIRE; WALEWSKI.

LE PETIT JOURNAL, newspaper founded 1 February 1863 by Moïse (Polydor) Millaud, who thereby greatly contributed to the emergence of the modern French press. Millaud's initial fortune had been made through journalism, and it was to journalism that he returned after years of financial and commercial speculation. *Le petit journal* was innovative in a number of ways. Its price of 5 centimes, or 1 sou (a giant sou crowned the newspaper building on opening day), was lower than that of any other paper in the world, partly a reflection of the fact that as a nonpolitical journal, the newspaper escaped the stamp tax of 6 centimes per copy. It was sold not by subscription and through the post but on a daily basis, by its own small army of criers. A well-organized system of agents and distribution by small vehicles ensured its availability in the villages at the same price as at Paris and in the other large cities. Thus for the first time a newspaper reached the peasants on a major scale. *Le petit journal* marked the birth of the French information press. It was designed to appeal to those with little or no interest in politics and therefore sought not to mold opinion but to express what everyone was thinking and to keep the public informed, without political comment, of all the new developments, in regard to which reporters were to cultivate an air of knowing more than anyone else.

Millaud's formula for ensuring a large readership was simple and effective:

a lead article in the form of a chronicle and gossip column, a summary of cases heard in the courts, a potpourri of facts, reviews, and special features, and the installment of a novel. From 1863 to 1869, the chronicle was written by one of the principal founders of the paper, Léo Lespès (1815–1875), under the pseudonym Timothée Trimm (changed in early 1869, when Lespès gave up the column and its editorship became collective, to Thomas Grimm). One of the first and most popular novelists to contribute was Pierre Alexis Ponson du Terrail, whose *Rocambole* series was prolonged interminably. Other collaborators and contributors included Henri Escoffier (1837–1891; an editor from 1863 to 1873), Emile Zola, Edouard Drumont (1844–1917), Eugène Paz (1837–1901; wrote on health and gymnastics), Aurélien Scholl (1833–1902), Charles Monselet (1825–1888), Louis Blanc (1811–1882), Alfred Assollant (1827–1886), and Edmond About.

The growth of *Le petit journal* was phenomenal, despite the appearance of numerous competitors, including, in 1863, *Le moniteur universel du soir* or *Le petit moniteur*, which in 1869 stole Lespès for a salary of 100,000 francs. In the first year, circulation reached 150,000 copies. By 1865 it was 200,000 and by 1869 260,000. On occasion 300,000 or even 400,000 copies were sold. But profits did not offset the huge expenses involved. The newspaper was greatly in debt to Hippolyte Marinoni, who had developed and supplied the rotary presses that made so large a circulation possible. By 1869 Millaud was forced to sell his stock in *Le petit Journal*. In 1870 his affairs were liquidated, and in 1871 he died. Under successive owners (Emile de Girardin from 1872, Marinoni from 1874, and Cassignel from 1902) the newspaper continued to flourish, reaching in 1880 a circulation of 582,000, four times that of its nearest rival and one-quarter of the total for all Paris dailies. In 1893 the circulation was 900,000. Under Ernest Judet, *Le petit Journal* would become the journal of the nationalists during the Dreyfus affair.

M. Martin, "La réussite du *Petit journal* ou les débuts du quotidien populaire," *Bulletin du Centre de l'Histoire de France Contemporaine*, 3 (1982).

Related entries: GIRARDIN; MARINONI; MILLAUD; *MONITEUR UNIVERSEL*; NEFFTZER; PRESS REGIME; VILLEMESSANT.

PHOTOGRAPHY. See NADAR.

PHYLLOXERA. See OIDIUM, PHYLLOXERA.

PICARD, ERNEST (1821–1877), republican politician, one of the first to be elected during the Second Empire; born at Paris, 24 December 1821. A successful lawyer during the early years of the Second Empire, Picard moved from Orleanist bourgeois liberalism to republicanism. Associated with Léonor Havin and the democratic newspaper *Le siècle*, he was elected to the Corps Législatif as an independent in a by-election of May 1858, subsequently resigning from *Le siècle*. As a member of the small republican group, *les Cinq*, Picard specialized in matters of finance and administration, attacking the policies of Baron Georges

Haussmann (in 1865 he first revealed the *bons de délégation* device by which the prefect had obtained what were, in effect, unauthorized loans) and demanding freedom of the press with a wit and lightness of touch that endeared him to Parisians. Easily reelected in 1863, Picard did not follow Emile Ollivier, his boyhood friend, in moving toward reconciliation with the Empire. He took advantage of the new law on the press to assist in establishing (June 1868) a newspaper, *L'électeur libre*, whose first number was seized. Although reelected in two constituencies in 1869, Picard was suspected by the radical Left of excessive moderation and in fact emerged as leader in the Corps Législatif of those republicans who were not irreconcilably opposed to the Empire (*gauche ouverte*). He voted against the declaration of war in July 1870. Picard died at Paris 13 May 1877.

E. Picard, *Les Cinq, 1859–1860* (Paris, 1886), *Les Cinq, 1861–1863* (Paris, 1882), *L'Union Libérale, 1864–1869* (Paris, 1889), *Le ministère Ollivier, la république, 1870–1871* (Paris, 1890), and *Mon journal* (Paris, 1892); M. Reclus, *Ernest Picard, 1821–1877: Essai de contribution à l'histoire du parti républicaine* (Paris, 1912).

Related entries: CINQ; HAUSSMANN; REPUBLICANISM.

PIE, LOUIS (1815–1880), cardinal, bishop of Poitiers (1849–1880); with Mgr. Félix Dupanloup the best-known bishop of the French church during the Second Empire, and one of the finest orators of his era; born 26 September 1815 at Pontgouin, in the diocese of Chartres. Pie was the leading proponent of ultramontanism (supremacy of Rome) among the French bishops, many of whom harbored Gallican sentiments. In 1856 he adopted the Roman liturgy for his diocese, into which he also introduced many religious orders. Legitimist in his politics and intransigent in his religion, he distrusted the imperial regime and denounced liberal Catholicism and naturalism. His exceptionally sharp condemnation of Napoleon III's Italian policy attracted wide attention, in particular his pastoral letter of February 1861 with its words, "Wash your hands, O Pilate!" a reference, it was believed, to the emperor. The letter was referred to the Conseil d'Etat, and in the end Pie was constrained to urge his clergy to show moderation. Ultramontanes welcomed the publication in 1864 of his *Third Synodal Instructions*, which attacked a variety of modern ideas deemed contrary or injurious to Christianity. Pie praised and defended Pius IX's *Syllabus of Errors*, which appeared later in the same year. He expressed regret that Dupanloup's famous interpretation of the *Syllabus* had failed to state what the document was after having explained at length what it was not. As president of the commission on faith at Vatican Council I (1869–1870), he played an important role in shaping the dogmatic constitution *Dei filius*, which dealt with various fundamental articles of faith, rejected current errors, and defined the relation between faith and reason. He strongly supported the definition of the doctrine of papal infallibility. Cardinal Pie died at Angoulême, 18 May 1880.

L. Baunard, *Histoire du Cardinal Pie, évêque de Poitiers*, 2 vols. (Paris, 1886); J. M. Besse, *Le Cardinal Pie* (Paris, 1903); E. Catta, *Le doctrine politique et sociale du*

Cardinal Pie, 1815–1882 (Paris, 1959), and "Mgr. Edouard Pie, Pie IX, le *Syllabus* et le premier Concile du Vatican d'après les oeuvres de l'évêque de Poitiers," *Pie IX* 3 (July 1974); Pie, *Oeuvres complètes*, 10 vols. (Poitiers and Paris, 1894).

Raymond L. Cummings

Related entries: DUPANLOUP; FALLOUX LAW; GALLICANISM; INFAL-LIBILITY, DOCTRINE OF; MORTARA AFFAIR; PIUS IX; ROMAN QUES-TION; ROULAND; *SYLLABUS OF ERRORS*; VATICAN COUNCIL; VEUILLOT.

PIETRI, PIERRE MARIE (1809–1864) and **PIETRI, JOACHIM** (1820–1902), Corsican brothers who were Paris prefects of police a total of ten years during the Second Empire. Pierre Marie was born 23 May 1809 at Sartène, Corsica. He studied law at Aix and was admitted to the bar at Paris. Pietri, before the Revolution of 1848, was an advanced republican, a member of the Société des Droits de l'Homme, and an associate of Alexandre Ledru-Rollin (1807–1874). He was, in fact, named commissioner in Corsica by the provisional government and elected from there to the Constituent Assembly, third on a list of six that included three Bonapartes. Until mid-October 1848 he voted with the extreme Left. But when Louis Napoleon Bonaparte posed his candidacy for president of the Second Republic, Pietri rallied to him and to the party of order, voting subsequently for the suppression of the clubs and for the expedition to Rome. More and more closely attached to the prince president, he did not sit in the Legislative Assembly but was named successively prefect of the Ariège (1849), the Doubs, and the Haute-Garonne (1851).

Following the coup d'état of December 1851 and the appointment (22 January 1852) of C. E. de Maupas as minister of police, Pietri replaced the latter as Paris prefect of police. He not only kept his balance in the consequent internecine quarrels but helped to bring about the dismissal of Maupas and the suppression of the Ministry of Police (June 1853). Thereafter he retained Napoleon III's confidence until the attempt on the emperor's life by Felice Orsini in January 1858. Pietri was named knight of the Legion of Honor in 1851 and grand officer on 17 June 1856 and was appointed to the Senate on 9 June 1857. Supported by Jules Baroche, he successfully held off the attempts of the powerful prefect of the Seine, Baron Georges Haussmann, to enlarge his own powers at the expense of the police prefecture. But the Orsini *attentat* was fatal to the then prefect of police. "Votre police se fait joliment bien," the emperor greeted him after the bombs had exploded. The Italophile Pietri remained at the prefecture only long enough to assist Napoleon III in his propaganda use of the assassination attempt (it was he who encouraged Orsini to write the letter subsequently published in *Le moniteur*) before his replacement on 7 February 1858 by Symphorien Casimir Joseph Boittelle (1813–1897; prefect of police 1858–1866). In 1860 Pietri was sent as government commissioner to organize the annexation of Nice and Savoy to France. In 1862 he astounded everyone by calling, in the Senate, for individual liberty, freedom of the press and elections, and withdrawal of the

French expeditionary force from Rome in order to ''conjurer les tempêtes formées par la politique de temporisation et d'immobilité.'' He was appointed prefect of the Gironde in 1863 with special instructions to organize the elections of that year and was rewarded with the grand cross of the Legion of Honor. Pierre Marie Pietri died at Paris, 28 February 1864.

Two years later, Joachim Pietri, Pierre Marie's younger brother, succeeded to the police prefecture, whose powers had been somewhat diminished by the decree of 10 October 1859 enlarging the responsibilities of the prefect of the Seine. Joachim was born at Sartène, Corsica, 25 February 1820. He studied law at Paris before returning to practice at Sartène. With the help of his brother, he entered government administration in 1848, serving successively as subprefect at Argentan and at Brest and as prefect of the Ariège, the Cher, and the Hérault. Following the coup d'état, he was appointed prefect of the Nord. On 21 February 1866 he replaced Boittelle, who had resigned, as prefect of police. The final years of the Empire were tumultuous ones for the Paris police, punctuated by such events as the Baudin, Victor Noir, and Rochefort affairs and the disturbances accompanying the elections of 1869. Pietri acted in most cases firmly and with skill and must be credited at least in part with the fact that order was maintained (as, for example, in the case of the abortive demonstration of 26 October 1869 against the delay in convening the Corps Législatif). In April–May 1870 his police uncovered a final plot against the emperor. Pietri, commander of the Legion of Honor from 11 August 1864, was named grand officer on 13 August 1867 and appointed to the Senate on 27 July 1870 (Emile Ollivier's government had allowed him to retain his position as prefect of police after 2 January). Because of the Franco-Prussian War, the decree was never promulgated. Pietri vigorously but unsuccessfully argued for the return of Napoleon III to Paris after the defeats of August and helped to persuade the Empress Eugénie to flee Paris following the revolution of 4 September. He himself went into exile until the conclusion of peace. Pensioned in April 1873 for infirmities contracted during his government service, he was elected senator from Corsica in 1879 but was defeated in January 1885. A distant relative, Franceschini Pietri (died 1915) accompanied Napoleon III and Eugénie into exile as their confidential secretary and after years of loyal service was buried in the imperial mausoleum at Farnborough, on the stairs leading to the vault where Napoleon III, the prince imperial, and Eugénie are now buried.

Related entries: AMNESTY; BAUDIN; HAUSSMANN; MAUPAS; NAPOLEON III: ASSASSINATION ATTEMPTS; VICTOR NOIR AFFAIR; ORSINI; REPUBLICANISM; ROCHEFORT.

PILS, ISIDORE (1813–1875), painter and watercolorist, chiefly noted for his scenes of military life; born at Paris, 19 July 1813. Pils studied in the *atelier* of François Picot (1786–1868) and at the Ecole des Beaux-Arts, where he won the Prix de Rome in 1838. During the 1840s he was hospitalized several times for tuberculosis but at the end of the decade had achieved recognition by his paintings

Passage of the Beresina (1848) and *Rouget de Lisle Singing the "Marseillaise" for the First Time* (1849). Reproductions of the latter ensured his popularity. As an exhibitor at the Salons from 1846, Pils possessed characteristics calculated to win him the attention and patronage of the imperial government. His themes (the army, the church, the nobility of the poor) were appropriate and his style (a moderate realism) unthreatening. *The Death of a Sister of Charity* was bought by the state for 4,000 francs in May 1851. At the 1853 Salon, Empress Eugénie purchased Pils' *The Prayer at the Hospice*, and thereafter he was a court favorite. His moderate and sympathetic treatment of the theme of poverty recommended him to the regime, while his growing interest in military topics made him particularly useful as a sort of official realist.

Pils' earliest commissioned painting (in 1852) was especially appropriate: *Soldiers Distributing Bread to the Poor* (it was hung in the Ministry of the Interior). Although his poor health prevented his going in person to the Crimea during the war with Russia, Pils reconstructed scenes from that conflict in such paintings as *Trench before Sebastopol* (1855), *Disembarkment of the French Army in the Crimea* (1857), and *Battle of the Alma* (1861). The first won him a second-class medal; for *Disembarkment*, he was awarded a first-class medal and named to the Legion of Honor (16 August 1857); and the *Battle of Alma* (purchased by the Ministry of State) was rewarded with the *grande médaille d'honneur*. Although Pils was commissioned to help decorate the churches of Sainte Clotilde and Saint Eustache and to paint the ceiling over the grand staircase of the new Opéra (*The City of Paris Encouraging the Arts* and *Apollo Charming the Beasts with his Lyre*), it was military scenes that absorbed his interest during the 1860s. A frequent visitor to the camps at Vincennes and Châlons, the artist also represented other scenes in the lives of the sovereigns (*Fete Given to the Emperor and the Empress at Algiers 1860* [1867]).

Pils was greatly rewarded during the Second Empire. He was named professor at the reorganized Ecole des Beaux-Arts on 10 December 1863 and was a member of the Salon jury from 1864 through 1868. At the international exposition of 1867, he won a first-class medal. He was made an officer of the Legion of Honor 1 July 1867 and was elected to the Académie des Beaux-Arts in the place of his former teacher, Picot, on 7 November 1868. This contemporary fame was followed by a profound neglect; only recently has his work been reappraised in the context of a realism that he never abandoned and that won high honors for the first time in his person. Pils (whose brother Edouard Aisné Pils, 1823–1852, was also a talented painter) died at Douarnenez (Finistère), 3 September 1875.

L. Becq de Fouquières, *Isidore Alexandre Auguste Pils: Sa vie et ses oeuvres* (Paris, 1876); Gabriel P. Weisberg, "In Search of State Patronage: Three French Realists and the Second Empire—1851–1871," in *Essays in Honor of H. W. Janson* (New York, 1982), and *The Realist Tradition: French Painting and Drawing, 1830–1900* (Cleveland, 1980).

Related entries: GUYS; MEISSONIER.

PINARD, PIERRE ERNEST (1822–1909), functionary and politician, *procureur général, conseiller d'état*, minister, and deputy; born at Autun, 10 October 1822. After receiving his law degree at Paris and gaining admission to the bar there, Pinard entered government service, first in the provinces (Tonnerre, May 1849–December 1851; Troyes, December 1851–December 1852; Reims, December 1852–October 1853) and then, from 29 October 1853, at Paris where he became *substitut du procureur général* 15 April 1859. It was Pinard who argued the government's case against both Gustave Flaubert (for *Madame Bovary* in April 1857) and Charles Baudelaire (for *Les fleurs du mal* in August 1857). On 3 October 1861 he was assigned as *procureur général* to Douai.

At Paris Pinard had been extremely fortunate in the cases falling to his dossier, notably those of Doudet, Pescatore, and of the duc d'Aumale versus Mme. de Clercq. He had been named to the Legion of Honor in November 1858. Now at Douai, his good fortune continued, for it was there that the Jules Mirès case was heard on appeal in April 1862. The *procureur général's* eloquence, his high-minded attack on financial corruption, and his devotion to religion won him promotion to officer of the Legion of Honor (12 August 1862) and brought him to the attention of the emperor. Pinard, who had accepted the coup d'état of December 1851 because he feared social war, was sympathetic to the imperial regime. On 5 May 1866 he was recalled to Paris to take a place on the Conseil d'Etat. As a *conseiller* Pinard had ample opportunity to prove his loyalty and usefulness, playing an important role in the formulation of the law revising criminal penalties and procedures (May 1867) and the law on the press (May 1868). During 1866–1867 he was one of the few *conseillers* willing to support Napoleon III's plan to reform army recruitment by ending the system of replacement that permitted the well-to-do to avoid military service.

By the time the press law that Pinard had helped to draft came before the Corps Législatif, he had passed from the Conseil d'Etat to the ministry, having been named minister of the interior on 14 November 1867. Eugène Rouher, the powerful minister of state, had placed the *conseiller* tenth on the list he had prepared for Napoleon III's guidance, arguing that Pinard lacked the requisite weight and administrative experience. It was a shrewd judgment, but Rouher's opposition may have had another motive. The new minister of the interior, despite his innate conservatism, had shown a certain flexibility toward reform. He favored enlarging the government's majority by appealing to those who would accept the regime without its authoritarianism. Moreover, Pinard's friends had unwisely promoted him as a possible successor to Rouher. The minister of state had placed his own man, Gaston de Saint-Paul, in the Ministry of the Interior as director general and successfully shielded him there by the weight of his prestige and indispensability to the emperor. Pinard, through inexperience, made an already difficult situation worse. Although in his new capacity he defended before the legislature the laws on the press and public meetings, he was also determined to apply these new regulations strictly. His personal war against Henri Rochefort's scurrilous newspaper, *La lanterne*, contributed to giving that former vaudevillian a sudden ascendancy. But it was the Baudin affair that brought an end to Pinard's ministry. Having unwisely, if dutifully, prosecuted a number of Paris newspapers for their efforts to build a monument through public subscription to Victor Baudin, the deputy who had been killed while resisting the 1851 coup d'état, Pinard greatly overreacted on 3 December 1868 to a planned demonstration at Baudin's grave, flooding Paris with troops and arresting some sixty persons. He then compounded the error by sending a triumphal telegram to his prefects, which made it appear that public order had been seriously threatened. The diminutive minister became a Parisian laughingstock and was constrained to leave the ministry when it was remade on 17 December. Thus the career of one of the few new men to reach high rank in the imperial regime was checked.

Unwilling to be interred in the Senate, Pinard, who had been promoted to commander of the Legion of Honor 14 August 1868, contested the elections of May 1869 on a program calling for an intimate alliance of order and of liberty. Elected to the Corps Législatif from the Nord, he supported Emile Ollivier and the Liberal Empire but without ceasing to be in certain respects an authoritarian bonapartist (in February 1870 he stated his opinion that a meeting could not be considered private unless all of the people present knew each other; in June he supported the continued appointment of mayors by the government). Pinard voted for war with Prussia. At the fateful midnight meeting of the Corps Législatif on 3–4 September, his was the only voice raised in defense of the Empire against the Left's motion calling for its overthrow. Unsuccessful in reviving his political career following the overthrow of the Empire, Pinard returned to the practice of law. He died at Bourg in 1909.

J. Brelot, "P. E. Pinard, 1822–1909," *Visages de l'Ain*, 12 (1959); C. Pichois, "Un épisode oublié de la bataille Réaliste: Montalembert, le substitut Pinard, et Charles Baudelaire," *RHLF* 59 (1959); P. E. Pinard, *Mon journal*, 2 vols. (Paris, 1892); N. Salvaterra, "Magistrat austère ou poète licencieux?" *Visages de l'Ain* 12 (1959).

Related entries: BAUDIN; CONSEIL D'ETAT; PRESS REGIME; REFORM; ROCHEFORT; ROUHER.

PISSARRO, CAMILLE (1830–1903), Impressionist painter; born at Saint Thomas in the West Indies to a French *émigré* shopkeeper and his Creole wife. Pissarro was sent to boarding school in Passy for his early studies from 1842 to 1847. He then returned to Saint Thomas to work with his father in his general store. His interest in drawing was first developed when he went off with the Danish painter Fritz Melbye to Venezuela. Pissarro returned to France in 1855, in time to view the international exposition, where he admired the works of Jean Baptiste Camille Corot. He spent a short time at the Ecole des Beaux-Arts and attended the Académie Suisse, where he later met Claude Monet. His early works (mostly no longer extant) were of tropical landscapes painted from memory. He also began to paint landscapes in several areas near Paris, in Montmorency, La Roche-Guyon, and La Varenne-Saint-Hilaire, showing the influence of Corot. It was these paintings for which he would become best known. After being rejected by the jury of the Salons of 1861 and 1863 (a Montmorency landscape had been accepted in the Salon of 1859), Pissarro participated in the Salon des Refusés of 1863, showing three paintings. He was accepted once more in the Salon of 1864 as a pupil of Corot. Thereafter he would exhibit in every Salon of the Second Empire except for that of 1867, receiving his first critical attention in 1866.

In Pissarro's landscapes such as *The Hermitage at Pontoise* (1867, Wallraf-Richartz Museum, Cologne), the pervasive light is reminiscent of Corot's early landscapes, but there is also an emphasis on structure, stressing the rectangular composition of the buildings and the division of the canvas. There is, as well, a greater intensity of local color than would be found in Corot's paintings. This can be attributed to the influence of Gustave Courbet, whose realism and more materialist concerns were made manifest in the heaviness and tangibility of the objects depicted, especially from 1866, the year that marked Pissarro's break with Corot. There is also a correspondence to some of the positivist ideas of Hippolyte Taine published in *The Philosophy of Art* in 1867. Pissarro's dual interests in light and structure can be seen in the *Jallais Hill near Pontoise* (1867, Metropolitan Museum of Art, New York). Charles François Daubigny, Pissarro's friend and source of inspiration in such works as *The Ferry at La Varenne-Saint-Hilaire* (1864, Louvre, Paris), was able to persuade the jury to accept *Jallais Hill* at the Salon of 1868, where it was seen and admired by Emile Zola. During this period, Pissarro met at times with the group of artists and writers of which Edouard Manet was the leader at the Café Guerbois. At these gatherings, the discussions affirmed the convictions as to the nature of painting of the future Impressionists, Monet, Alfred Sisley (1839–1899), Pierre Auguste Renoir, Edgar Degas, and Pissarro, and strengthened their resolve to exhibit as a group. This led to the first Impressionist exhibition of 1874 in which all, except Manet but including Paul Cézanne (1839–1906), participated.

After living in Pointoise, Pissarro moved to Louveciennes where he found fresh motifs to paint. *The Road to Versailles at Louveciennes—Rain Effect* (1870, Sterling and Francine Clark Institute, Williamstown, Massachusetts) brings him even closer to the aims of Impressionism. The spontaneity of brushwork and the depiction of a particular weather condition that is of an ephemeral character but caught here momentarily in process are Impressionist values more fully realized in Pissarro's paintings of the 1870s and 1880s. The viewpoint and the quickly narrowing pathway are features that can also be seen in the works of Monet during this period.

Pissarro fled to London during the Franco-Prussian war, joining Monet there and meeting the dealer Paul Durand-Ruel (1831–1922), himself a refugee. Unfortunately, during the time of Pissarro's absence from Louveciennes, many of the paintings left there were destroyed by the Prussians who occupied the town. After his return to Louveciennes in 1871, Pissarro reacquainted himself with Cézanne, whom he had first met in 1861 at the Académie Suisse. Their association and mutual interests proved to be artistically stimulating and important for both. Pissarro died at Paris, 12 November 1903.

K. Adler, *Camille Pissarro, a Biography* (London, 1978); A. Berman, "Camille Pissarro: A Gentle Visionary of the Everyday," *Smithsonian*, 12, no. 3 (1981); K. S. Champa, *Studies in Early Impressionism* (New Haven, 1973); J. Rewald, *Pissarro* (New York, 1963), and *The History of Impressionism*, 4th ed. (New York, 1973).

Beverley Giblon

Related entries: COROT; COURBET; DAUBIGNY; DEGAS; MANET; MONET; POSITIVISM; RENOIR; SALON DES REFUSES.

PIUS IX, holder of the longest papal reign (1846–1878) in history; born Giovanni Maria Mastai-Ferretti, 13 May 1792, Senigallia, Italy. As bishop of Spoleta (1827–1832) during the uprisings of 1831 in the states of the church, he persuaded the rebels who had retreated into his diocese, one of whom was Louis Napoleon, to lay down their arms in exchange for help in returning home safely. His conciliatory yet firm episcopal policy at Spoleta and later at Imola (1832–1846), a more important diocese containing many radicals, won him praise and a reputation for at least moderately liberal inclinations. Elected pope on 17 June 1846 on the death of Gregory XVI, he inaugurated a series of reforms that aroused unprecedented enthusiasm and extravagant hopes not only in the Papal States but also among liberals throughout the peninsula. Outside Italy, too, Catholics were encouraged. Mgr. Félix Dupanloup, who visited Rome, found Pius full of praise for Charles de Montalembert and his struggle for liberty of education in France. The new pope's popularity was enhanced by his affability, wit, benign appearance, beautiful voice, and obvious goodwill. He hoped to be able to satisfy his subjects by consulting them and by improving the administration of the government of his provinces rather than by changing its structure. His sympathies, coupled with his predilection for moderate solutions, led him to appreciate the Italian desire for a diminution of Austrian influence in the peninsula, to seek a customs union, and to consider the feasibility of a defensive league of Italian states, but he did not accept the formula of a unitary or confederated kingdom. Such an arrangement could inhibit or destroy his temporal power and thereby jeopardize his religious mission. The dichotomy between popular expectations and papal intentions reached disastrous proportions in 1848, when liberals and radicals pushed Pius to a constitutionalism that he judged incompatible with his need for spiritual independence and toward a war with Austria, which, as the head of a universal church, he believed he could not declare. His flight to Gaeta in the Kingdom of Naples (24–25 November, 1848) was followed by the proclamation of a republic at Rome. It took a French expeditionary force to restore him to his possessions. Louis Napoleon, now president of the Second Republic, sought to persuade Pius to preserve constitutionalism and to grant further concessions, but the pope, chastened by recent experiences, could not be pressed, now or later, to go beyond administrative reform. Liberal government, he had concluded, was inherently pernicious, nationalism subversive. Thus he and Louis

Napoleon, inextricably bound by virtue of the prominent position of the church in France and the protective presence in Rome of a French garrison, which for political reasons could not be withdrawn, were fated to clash whenever Napoleon moved in a liberal or national direction. French liberal Catholics would also have to labor under the burden of papal disapproval. With rare exceptions, as in the controversy over the Falloux education law (1850), Pius henceforth saved his sympathy and support for ultramontane, intransigent Catholics (those who looked to Rome for leadership).

Pius applauded the coup d'état of December 1851, for it struck a blow at both republicanism and parliamentarianism. Although he was more circumspect in his reaction to the creation of the Second Empire in 1852, he could only delight in the favors showered on the church by the imperial government during its early years. The apogee of the alliance between pope and emperor coincided with the apogee of the authoritarian Empire in 1856, after the French victories in the Crimean War (1854–1856). Pius, represented by his cardinal-legate, acted as godfather of the prince imperial in the presence of almost the entire French episcopacy at his baptism on 14 June 1856. Nevertheless, some tension had existed from the beginning. Pius had not acceded to Napoleon III's wish to be consecrated by the pope at the time of his coronation in 1853, for Napoleon III had not acceded to the papal wish to see the Organic Articles, which asserted Gallican rights, abrogated. The pope had caused disappointment by excusing himself on the grounds of infirmity from marrying Napoleon III and Eugénie and from personally attending their son's baptism. More serious were the government's persistent Gallican tendencies, though muted, and the emperor's Italian sympathies. The latter, long a cause for papal suspicion of the imperial government, became more manifest with the Franco-Sardinian alliance of January 1855 and especially with the session of 8 April 1856 of the Congress of Paris. The Holy See was offended to see Napoleon III providing Sardinia with an international forum at the session for attacks on the pontifical government while virtually suppressing shortly thereafter a report drawn up by the French envoy to Rome defending the papal rule. Henceforth the Italian question would poison relations between Paris and Rome.

Although the assassination attempt against Napoleon III in January 1858 by Felice Orsini threw the church and state together against radicalism, the Mortara affair in the same year aggravated French anti-clericalism and irritated the emperor. Obstinately giving his religious convictions priority over his diplomatic interests, Pius defied public opinion throughout Western Europe by refusing to return Edgardo Mortara to the Jewish parents from whom he had been spirited. The following April, Pius was skeptical when, on the outbreak of war between France and Austria over Italy, the imperial government assured him that it would defend the temporal power. He was furious at the end of 1859 at Napoleon III's efforts to persuade him to relinquish the Romagna, which had revolted in June on the withdrawal of the Austrian forces stationed there. He not only refused to relinquish the Romagna, he excommunicated those connected in any way with the events leading to its union with Sardinia by virtue of plebiscites in March 1860. His conviction that Napoleon was collaborating with "the Revolution" deepened when French troops at Rome failed to prevent the Sardinian army from seizing the Marches and Umbria in September 1860. To the surprise of listeners, Pius, an emotional man, at times could not repress expressions of sympathy for the national cause, but he was inflexible in refusing to bend before actions that from his perspective were contrary to international law and carried out under the banner of a liberal, anti-clerical ideology disdainful of the temporal power and dedicated to restricting church influence in Italy or wherever else it could prevail. His quarrel with Napoleon III aroused for the first time since the coup d'état a serious parliamentary opposition in France.

When Montalembert argued in 1863 in behalf of the compatibility of Catholicism with liberal government, Pius privately reproached him. The following year he issued his encyclical *Quanta cura*, with its controversial accompanying *Syllabus of Errors*, which baldly challenged many beliefs that were widely held, especially by liberals, but were deemed by the papacy to be spiritually, morally, and socially corrosive. Negative stances such as these were, from the beginning of his pontificate, complemented by positive efforts to spread the faith through missionary activity (vigorous in French colonies) and to protect the church through concordats. The Holy See concluded concordats with Russia (1847), Spain (1851, 1859), Austria (1855), Portugal (1857), several German, and a number of Latin American states. Pius also recreated a hierarchy in England (1850) and the Netherlands (1853) and established over two hundred new dioceses and vicariates apostolic. Of capital importance was his centralization of ecclesiastical authority in the papal office at the expense of Gallicanism and all other expressions of church autonomy and regalian tradition. In France this effort benefited from his own immense prestige (increased by his tribulations), from the growth of religious orders, such as the Benedictines, who were dedicated to ultramontanism, from the eclipse of the legitimate Bourbon dynasty to which Gallican loyalties had been especially attached, and from the desire of the lower clergy to escape episcopal autocracy by looking for relief to the Holy See. The unsteady Gallican stance of the Second Empire was unable to counter Rome's steady push to extend papal jurisdiction more effectively over the entire church. Ultramontanism swept to its climax with the definition of the doctrine of infallibility at Vatican Council I (1869–1870).

The Franco-Prussian War (1870–1871) brought to an end both the Vatican Council and the French occupation of Rome. Despite quarrels with Napoleon III, Pius had continued to rely on his troops to protect Rome and its surrounding area, known as the Patrimony of St. Peter. Unofficial negotiations between Rome and Turin to solve the Roman Question had sputtered out in 1861, and the September Convention (1864) of Napoleon III with the Italian government, aimed at extricating his garrison from the territory, had floundered before the aggressive maneuvers of Garibaldi in 1867. When the last French troops left in August 1870, nothing remained to bar the Italians from taking Rome, which they entered on 20 September 1870. Pius proclaimed himself a prisoner of the Vatican, refusing to leave its confines for the rest of his life.

Pius IX had succeeded in fostering, especially in France, a unique attachment to the pope as the leader of the Catholic world. He had inspired devotion among the clergy and significant portions of the laity by his words and example. At the same time, his doctrinaire approach had encouraged anti-clericalism, supplied his enemies with ammunition, alienated intellectuals from the church, and provoked both political opposition and diplomatic isolation. Despite rumors of serious illness (he suffered from epileptic seizures), Pius survived the Second Empire and the emperor with whom so many events of his pontificate were linked. He died at Vatican City, 7 February 1878.

R. Aubert, *Le pontificat de Pie IX, 1846–1878* (Paris, 1952); F. J. Coppa, *Pope Pius IX* (Boston, 1979); E. E. Y. Hales, *Pio Nono: A Study in European Politics and Religion in the Nineteenth Century* (Garden City, N.Y., 1954); G. Martina, *Pio IX: chiesa e mondo moderno* (Rome, 1976); J. Maurain, *La politique ecclésiastique du Second Empire de 1852 à 1869* (Paris, 1930).

Raymond L. Cummings
Related entries: DUPANLOUP; GALLICANISM; INFALLIBILITY, DOCTRINE OF; MONTALEMBERT; MORTARA AFFAIR; PIE; ROMAN QUESTION; SOLESMES; *SYLLABUS OF ERRORS*; *UNIVERS*; VATICAN COUNCIL; VEUILLOT.

PLEBISCITE, together with universal manhood suffrage the key political concept of the Second Empire. Bonapartism posited authoritarian government sanctioned by popular approval, expressed regularly in elections, exceptionally in plebiscites. The plebiscite had, however, two distinctions. It was the primary sanction invoked at the beginning of a reign, and it could be initiated only by the ruler. At the coup d'état of 2 December 1851, Louis Napoleon promised that the French people would be consulted on the overthrow of the Legislative Assembly. It was understood that if the results of the vote were unfavorable, he would summon a new assembly and retire from the scene. Voting was to be open, on registers in each *mairie*, but the reaction to this proposal was so negative that Louis Napoleon decreed a secret ballot, its first use in France. Great administrative pressure was exerted to ensure a favorable result, and Auguste de Morny, minister of the interior, organized propaganda committees to operate throughout the country under the supervision of a central committee headed by a marshal of Napoleon I, Remi Joseph Isidore Exelmans (1775–1852). The opposition was not allowed to campaign. Moreover, since the voting extended over two days, efforts could be made to shepherd would-be abstainers to the polls. The legitimists were, in fact, instructed by their leaders to abstain, but this instruction was only partly obeyed. On 21 and 22 December 1851 almost 10 million registered voters were called on to approve or reject the proposition, "The people wish the maintenance of the authority of Louis Napoleon and delegate to him the powers necessary to establish a constitution on the bases proposed in his proclamation of 2 December.'' The results were decisive. Over 7 million voted yes, fewer than 650,000 no. Only one canton (that of Vernoux) cast a majority of no votes. Obviously many republicans, even the most radical, had voted for Louis Napoleon. And yet, the no balloting had been heavy in the cities (in Paris, 80,000 versus 132,000 yes). In at least eight departments, government support was below 60 percent, and in republican departments (Gard, Hérault, Aude, Pyrénées-Orientales, Gers, Lot-et-Garonne, Tarn) as in the largely republican east (Burgundy and the Jura), no votes were numerous. The army in Algeria, to which a number of dissident individuals and even units had been sent, cast 13,680 no ballots as well as 31,405 yes. Moreover, about 1.7 million registered voters abstained, especially in the cities (at Paris almost 80,000 of 291,000) and in departments where legitimists or republicans were numerous (Finistère, Morbihan, Ille-et-Vilaine, Seine-Inférieure, Bouches-du-Rhône, Gard, Hérault, and Vendée). In five departments fewer than 50 percent of registered voters cast yes ballots. All of the flaws of the plebiscite as a political device were revealed: its susceptibility to government manipulation, the moral pressure exerted on voters by the fact that they had no real choice, and the lack of a continuing control after the vote. Nevertheless, the results, which were officially communicated to Louis Napoleon on 31 December 1851 by Jules Baroche, acting president of the Commission Consultative, left no doubt that the overwhelming majority of Frenchmen approved the coup d'état.

It was to be the same with the establishment of the Second Empire in November 1852. The constitution of January 1852 affirmed that ''the president of the Republic is responsible before the French people, to whom he has always the right to appeal.'' On the initiative of Louis Napoleon, the Senate therefore proposed by article 8 of the *sénatus-consulte* of 7 November 1852 that the nation be asked to affirm the proposition that ''the people wish the reestablishment of the imperial dignity in the person of Louis Napoleon Bonaparte with heredity in his direct descendants, legitimate and adoptive, and give him the right to regulate the order of succession to the throne in the Bonaparte family.'' The voting took place on 21 and 22 November 1852. Almost 8 million voted yes; only some 250,000 no ballots were cast. But more than 2 million abstained, particularly in such legitimist and Orleanist departments as the Vendée, Maine-et-Loire, Morbihan, Bouches-du-Rhône, Rhône, and Gironde. Although even more government pressure had been exerted than in 1851, the results, determined by an extraordinary session of the Corps Législatif and conveyed to Louis Napoleon at Saint Cloud the night of 1–2 December 1852, confirmed that the nation wished the reestablishment of the Empire.

The final plebiscite of the Second Empire occurred under particularly interesting circumstances. On 21 March 1870, Napoleon III proposed that a *sénatus-consulte* incorporate new constitutional principles to reflect the reforms that had taken place since 1860. He does not appear to have intended that the *sénatus-consulte* should be submitted to a plebiscite, and he rejected the initial suggestion of Eugène Rouher to that effect. Rouher wished to confirm the plebiscitary basis of the new regime, but the emperor still thought of the plebiscite as a device by which reigns were to be inaugurated. However, when Napoleon Daru, a leader of the Tiers Parti, added his voice, Napoleon III in early April acceded. Daru, who favored a parliamentary government, apparently saw the plebiscite as a means of guaranteeing the reforms. Louis Buffet, another leader of the Center-Left faction of the Tiers Parti, soon disillusioned his colleague. Although both Buffet and Daru had agreed that the plebiscitary principle should be incorporated in the new constitution as it had been in that of 1852 (the plebiscite, and the continued responsibility of the ministers to the emperor were all that remained of the authoritarian Empire by 1870), the Center-Left regarded the plebiscitary power as being in contradiction with a parliamentary regime and considered it to be a continuing threat to the reforms. This point of view was effectively advanced by the republican Jules Grévy (1807–1891) during an interpellation in the Corps Législatif. When Napoleon III refused to agree not to call a plebiscite without the consent of the legislature, Buffet and Daru resigned (8–9 April 1870). On 20 April the Senate unanimously adopted the constitution (*sénatus-consulte*), whose final article stated that it would be submitted to the nation for approval. Preparations for the plebiscite went forward in the midst of great confusion. It was a war of committees. Many republicans urged abstention; the bishops generally advocated an affirmative vote; the legitimists and Orleanists (and Adolphe Thiers) called for a vote of no. Prince Napoleon, who initially had favored the plebiscite, now changed his mind because, he argued, the regime to be confirmed was not truly a parliamentary one. Among authoritarian bonapartists particularly active in support of the plebiscite were the former prefect Eugène Janvier de la Motte and his friend Louis Napoléon Suchet, duc d'Albufera (1813–1877). On 30 April, discovery of a plot to assassinate Napoleon III was announced. On 8 May 1870 (this time balloting was to take place on a single day), the voters were asked to respond to the proposition, "The people approve the liberal reforms made to the constitution since 1860 by the emperor with the assistance of the great state bodies, and ratify the *sénatus-consulte* of 20 April 1870." Although the army cast 41,000 no votes (to 254,000 yes) and Paris voted no (180,000 to 138,000, with 83,000 abstentions), and the yes majority was less than 60 percent in eighteen departments (less than 50 percent in seven), the overall results were little less satisfying to Napoleon III than had been those of 1851 and 1852. More than 7,350,000 voted yes, about 1.5 million no, and somewhat less than 1.9 million abstained. Formerly Catholic and legitimist areas voted for the Empire. Although the bourgeoisie were divided and the workers in the big cities voted no except at Strasbourg, Reims, Douai, Dunkerque, Valenciennes, Roubaix, Mulhouse, Amiens, and Versailles, the peasants, except for the richer ones, voted massively for the regime. "J'ai mon chiffre," remarked Napoleon III with satisfaction. Several days of rioting at Paris were easily contained, and many republicans yielded to a profound discouragement. It is also possible that Otto von

Bismarck, Prussian president of council, was prompted by this striking political success of Napoleon III to accelerate the diplomatic activity that was to lead in a few months to the Franco-Prussian War and to the fall of the Second Empire.

M. Boivin, *Elections et plébiscites, 1848–1914* (Rouen, 1971).

Related entries: AUTHORITARIAN EMPIRE; BONAPARTISM; CONSTITUTION; COUP D'ETAT; ELECTIONS; LIBERAL EMPIRE; SECOND EMPIRE; SENATE; UNIVERSAL MANHOOD SUFFRAGE.

PLOMBIERES, Vosges health resort (Plombières-les-Bains) at which Napoleon III and the Sardinian president of council, Count Camillo Benso di Cavour (1810–1861), met on 20 July 1858 to plot war against Austria. Galvanized by Felice Orsini's unsuccessful attempt on his life, 14 January 1858, Napoleon III arranged the secret meeting with Cavour. At Plombières, the two men conspired to make war on Austria for the liberation of Italy. According to the only contemporary account of the meeting (Cavour to King Victor Emmanuel II, 24 July 1858), it was agreed that France would aid Sardinia in driving Austria out of the peninsula if Austria could be made to appear the aggressor; that as a result of the war, Lombardy and Venetia would be added to Sardinia to form a kingdom of Northern Italy; that this kingdom would be united with perhaps three other Italian states in a confederation nominally headed by the pope; that France would receive Savoy and perhaps Nice; and that Napoleon's cousin, Prince Napoleon, would marry Clotilde, the young daughter of King Victor Emmanuel of Sardinia. This oral agreement, translated into the Treaty of Turin of January 1859, became the starting point for events that led on 3 May to the Franco-Sardinian-Austrian War, perhaps the major turning point of Second Empire history. Some historians have described the Plombières meeting, held without the knowledge of even the French foreign minister, Alexandre Walewski, as the first act of the *Realpolitik* that would dominate Europe after 1870.

F. Valsecchi, "Plombières," *Il Risorgimento*, (October 1958); M. Walker, ed., *Plombières* (New York, 1968).

Related entries: CONNEAU; ITALIAN CONFEDERATION; ITALIAN WAR; NATIONALITIES; NICE-SAVOY; ORSINI; ROMAN QUESTION; VENETIA; VILLAFRANCA; WALEWSKI.

POLAND. See POLISH QUESTION.

POLICE, MINISTRY OF. See MAUPAS.

POLISH QUESTION, arising from the continuing resistance of the Poles to rule by Prussia, Austria, and especially Russia. The Treaties of 1815 had created a Polish kingdom (Congress Poland), intending it to be a more or less autonomous state under the Russian crown (other Poles continued to live as Prussian subjects in Posen and as Austrians in Galicia). On 26 February 1832, however, following an unsuccessful revolt in Russian Poland (1830–1831), Nicholas I unilaterally revoked the clauses of 1815 concerning Congress Poland and proclaimed that the kingdom henceforth would be an integral part of the Russian Empire (in May 1847, it was declared a Russian province). A ruthless policy of Russification followed. As an aspirant to power in France, Louis Napoleon criticized French inactivity during the 1830–1831 revolt and championed Polish national rights. Moreover, although an advocate of revising the Treaties of 1815, he could not accept Nicholas' actions of 1832 or the combined decision of Prussia, Russia, and Austria in November 1846 to incorporate Cracow into the Austrian Empire, following a failed revolt there in February against Austrian rule. As Napoleon III (from December 1852), Louis Napoleon had other reasons for a pro-Polish policy: the sympathy of Catholics in France for their Polish coreligionists; the influence of Alexandre Walewski (ambassador to Britain, 1851–1855; minister of foreign affairs, 1855–1860; and the illegitimate son of Napoleon I and Madame Walewska); and the cool relations existing between France and Russia as a result of Nicholas' reluctance to recognize the title "Napoleon III" and his insistence in December 1852 on addressing the new emperor not as *mon frère* but simply as *mon ami*.

During the Crimean War (1854–1856), it seems likely that Napoleon III would have accepted, perhaps even welcomed, extension of the war with an aim to liberate Poland. To this the British would not agree. At the peace, France moved immediately to improve relations with Russia, and the Congress of Paris ignored the Polish question in response to Russian insinuations that Alexander II, the new czar, would introduce ameliorations there. Later, when Napoleon III sought help from Russia in his plans for evicting Austria from the Italian peninsula, it was in his interest to keep the Polish question quiet. However, the elements in France most sympathetic to the emperor's Italian policy were also the most sympathetic to Poland. Moreover, whatever the czar's intentions (he introduced in 1861, much to Napoleon III's relief, a seemingly sincere policy of conciliating his Polish subjects), discontent in Poland simmered and grew, while the large community of Polish *émigrés* at Paris, led by Prince Adam Czartoryski (1770–1861), kept the question alive, especially on the political Left. Ironically, too, the very success of nationalism in Italy after 1858 inspired the Poles to emulation. On 15 January 1863 the Russians began to conscript Polish youth. During the night of 22 January, a massive revolt began.

Napoleon III had no desire to intervene in Poland in 1863. Not only was he convinced that the revolt could not succeed, but he wished to preserve the entente established since 1856 with Russia. On this position, he was increasingly isolated within the court itself, opposed both by the Left (Prince Napoleon) and the Catholic Right (including Empress Eugénie). The foreign minister, Edouard Drouyn de Lhuys, proved, moreover, to be a not very helpful ally when, seeking a diversion by protesting Prussia's agreement of 8 February to cooperate along its Polish border with Russia (Alvensleben Convention), he succeeded instead in making an international question of the revolt. From that point, Napoleon

III's preferred policy of procrastination became increasingly untenable. On more than one occasion since 1849, he had regarded the Polish question as a proper matter for consideration by a European congress. Now he suggested to his old enemy, Austria, the possibility of an alliance whose aim would be an independent Poland and a consequent reorganization of Europe. Was it war, or a congress he had in mind? As it turned out, the result was neither. Convinced, rightly or wrongly, that French opinion now required some action on behalf of Poland, Napoleon III soon discovered that Austria and Britain would go no further than diplomatic protest. On 6 March, London proposed that a collective note be sent to St. Petersburg; on 26 March, Vienna declined an alliance with France; on 17 April, similar notes protesting Russian actions in Poland were delivered at St. Petersburg by the French, British, and Austrian governments. Russia rejected these but hinted to the French in May that it would not object to discussing the Polish question at a European congress if every other European question were also discussed there. On 17 June, in a second round of notes, Britain, France, and Austria proposed an armistice and a conference looking toward restoration of the 1815 treaties (and intentions) in Russian Poland. These proposals were brutally rejected by Russia as the process of repression continued. A final French protest of early August may be considered to mark the end of the Franco-Russian entente. Unwilling to go to war without British help and perhaps misled by Russian response to the first notes of protest, Napoleon III on 4 November 1863 proposed a general congress of Europe's rulers to discuss a variety of problems, including that of Poland. The British, their suspicions of Napoleonic France more heated than ever, bluntly declined on 25 November.

The crisis of 1863 had nefarious results for France and for Europe. Unaided, the Poles were defeated before the end of the year, and the revolt died away between January and April 1864. France found itself isolated, having quarreled with Russia while frightening Britain and failing to reach agreement with Austria. The basis had been laid for cooperation between Prussia and Russia (although a revival of the old Holy Alliance had not proved possible), and it was largely his pique over Britain's attitude and the fate of his congress proposal that prompted the French emperor to remain neutral in the first phase of Bismarck's war against Denmark (February 1864). Although the peace of the graveyard settled over Poland, the Polish question did not completely disappear. On 6 June 1867 a Pole named Berezowski fired on Czar Alexander II, visiting Paris for the world fair, as he rode at the side of Napoleon III. The attempt failed, but no bravado on the part of the emperor could conceal that for him and for the Second Empire, the Polish question, irresolvable and tragic, had been an important factor in the diplomatic failure that would culminate in the debacle of 1870.

S. Bóbr-Tylingo, "Les conversations du Baron de Hübner à Paris, 1863," *Antemurale* 16 (1972), "L'influence de l'entourage de Napoléon III sur sa politique polonaise en 1863," *RHMC* 9 (July–September 1962), "Un mémorandum française d'octobre 1863," *Antemurale* 20 (1976), "Napoléon III et le problème polonais, 1830–1859," *Revue internationale d'histoire politique et constitutionnelle* 5, n.s. nos. 19–20 (July–December

1953), "Napoléon III et la question polonaise, 1860–1862," *Revue internationale des doctrines et des institutions* (April–June 1959), *Napoléon III, l'Europe et la Pologne en 1863–1864* (Rome, 1963), "Le problème polonais au début de la Guerre de Crimée," *Antemurale* 25 (1975), *La Russie, l'Eglise, et la Pologne, 1860–1866: rapports des consuls français* (Rome, 1969), and, "Sept rapports des agents français sur la Pologne en 1863," *Antemurale*, 15 (1971); M. Fridieff, "L'opinion publique française et l'insurrection polonaise de 1863," *Le monde slave* 2 (1938), and 3 (1938); M. Handelsmann, *Les idées françaises et la mentalité politique de la Pologne au 19e siècle* (Paris, 1927); E. Ollivier, "Napoléon III et Bismarck en Pologne," *RDM* 4 (1901).

Related entries: ALLIANCE POLICY; CONGRESS OF PARIS; CONGRESS POLICY; DROUYN DE LHUYS; NATIONALITIES; PRINCE NAPOLEON; PUBLIC OPINION; REVISION; WALEWSKI.

PONSON DU TERRAIL, PIERRE ALEXIS, VICOMTE DE (1829–1871), prolific writer of popular novels; born 8 July 1829 at Montmaur (near Grenoble). Son of a family that traced its ancestry to the fifteenth century and to Bayard, France's most celebrated knight, Ponson du Terrail, although intended for the navy, came to Paris at the age of nineteen to begin a literary career. By 1850 he had chosen as his vehicle the serialized novel (the *roman feuilleton*) at a time when this literary form seemed on the verge of disappearing. Two great masters of the popular novel, Frédéric Soulié and Honoré de Balzac, had just died; another, Eugène Sue (1804–1857), had turned his attention to novels of socialistic propaganda and was soon to flee the country because of his opposition to the regime that came into power following the coup d'état of 2 December 1851. Only Alexandre Dumas père (1802–1870) continued his work as a *feuilletonniste*, but he never again enjoyed the success that had come with his *Monte Cristo* (1844). Further, the partisans of serious literature sensed this decline and rejoiced. Charles Augustin Sainte-Beuve, in particular, ferociously attacked what he termed the "industrial literature" of Sue and Soulié.

In spite of this opposition, Ponson du Terrail took up all the typical themes and characters of the popular novel, expressing the hardships and desires of the working classes, and popularizing the idea of social reform, albeit in a somewhat melodramatic style. He achieved an enormous success, almost singlehandedly rescuing the *roman feuilleton* from extinction. His first work, *Les coulisses du monde*, appeared in 1852, and for the next eighteen years Ponson du Terrail produced novels without respite. Never using assistants or ghostwriters, he composed over seventy novels, rising at 4 A.M., writing for five or six hours each morning, and often publishing several novels simultaneously in such newspapers as *La patrie, Le petit journal, L'opinion nationale*, and *La petite presse*. So numerous were his characters and so vast his canvas that Ponson du Terrail was obliged to have small wax figurines of each of his characters specially made. He kept them near his work table, destroying the figures as he killed off the corresponding characters in his novels. The facility with which he wrote was remarkable. Edmond de Goncourt noted in his *Journal* in 1861 that Ponson du

Terrail habitually said to the directors of newspapers in which his immense novels were appearing: "Let me know three installments in advance if my novel is boring your readers, and I'll finish it off in one installment." What was perhaps his most popular work, *Rocambole: Les drames de Paris*, began in *La patrie* in 1857. Almost overnight its popularity eclipsed even that of Sue's *Les mystères de Paris*. Enthusiasm for Rocambole was so great that his creator was virtually obliged to continue inventing adventures for him, becoming, in effect, a pioneer of the adventure story without end. When *La patrie* announced the forthcoming conclusion of one of the Rocambole stories, *L'héritage mystérieux*, the director of the newspaper received a letter threatening him with death if Ponson du Terrail did not produce a continuation of the novel featuring the same characters.

Ponson du Terrail's success continued unabated until 1870 when, faithful to the memory of his warrior ancestor, he declared himself unable to accept the defeat of France in its war with Germany. Raising a band of volunteers on his property near Orleans, the author joined Léon Gambetta in Bordeaux and organized a team of *francs-tireurs*. Some time after the squad was disbanded, Ponson du Terrail died, on 20 June 1871, under circumstances that have remained mysterious, although it is thought that smallpox was the cause of his death. Of the seventy novels produced by Ponson du Terrail during the Second Empire, some of the most popular were: *Les coulisses du monde* (1852), *Les cavaliers de la nuit* (1852), *La baronne trépassée* (1853), *La cape et l'épée* and *Bavolet* (1856), *Les drames de Paris* (the *Rocambole* series; 1857–1867); *La jeunesse du Roi Henri* (1860), *Les nuits de la Maison Dorée* (1862), *Les bohêmes de Paris* (1863), *Les bohémiennes de Londres* (1864), *Les écoliers de Paris* (1867), *La bohémienne du grand monde* (1867), and *Le forgeron de la Cour-Dieu* (1869).

A. Praviel, "Le Vicomte Ponson du Terrail," *Le correspondant* (1929).

Dorothy E. Speirs

Related entries: ERCKMANN-CHATRIAN; PETIT JOURNAL.

POSITIVISM, the doctrine founded by Auguste Comte (1798–1857). Positivism, as developed by Comte and his disciples before and during the Second Empire, exerted considerable influence on the formulation or reexamination of a number of disciplines, most notably sociology and philosophy. Comte's fundamental premise is that positive, or scientific, knowledge is legitimately confined to empirical verification of the laws of behavior governing natural (including social) phenomena. His six-volume *Cours de philosophie positive* (1830–1842) is an elaborate examination of the historical development of human knowledge predicated on the Law of the Three Stages. Comte held that all human conceptions pass successively through three stages or modes: the theological (or animistic) stage, the metaphysical (or abstract) stage, and the positive (or scientific) stage. In the theological stage, men regard natural processes as the product of the direct action or will of anthropomorphic gods. In the metaphysical stage, divine intervention is replaced by the causal efficacy of abstract powers or forces that govern phenomena. In the positive stage, man rejects the earlier claims of theology and metaphysics (of penetrating to the essence of things) and realizes that true scientific knowledge must be limited to verifiable statements describing phenomena and their observed relationship. Noting that the various branches of knowledge have developed historically at different rates, Comte was led to establish a hierarchy of sciences ranked in terms of their approach to the positive state: mathematics (the most fully positive), astronomy, physics, chemistry, biology, and sociology (the least positive). Each science, dealing with increasingly more complex phenomena, draws on the theories established by the science(s) preceding it in the hierarchy and adds laws unique to its own subject matter. In this sense, each science is dependent on, but not strictly reducible to, the sciences below it. Comtean positivism is not merely theoretical. It is also practical. For Comte, the ultimate aim of all science is prediction for the sake of action. The more closely a given subject approaches the positive stage, the more accurately will the laws governing its particular phenomena be known and, hence, the greater will be the ability of the scientist to predict (though not in a narrowly deterministic sense) the course of future events. Prediction was most reliable in astronomy, the science (apart from mathematics) that Comte considered to have been most fully purged of theological and metaphysical modes of thought. The other sciences were all enmeshed to varying degrees in prepositive concepts, and a primary task of the *Cours* was to indicate the methodological pathways by which all the sciences would be rendered positive. Sociology was at once the least positive and, potentially, the most valuable of the sciences, and it is in his analysis of social phenomena that some of Comte's most original and enduring contributions are to be found. Following the *philosophes* and the comte de Saint-Simon (1760–1825), he argued that the increasingly rapid advance of science, industrial development, and organization in Europe since the Middle Ages had gradually undermined the traditional political and religious authority that had governed human social behavior. Positive sociology was to be the crowning human science, free from the errors and prejudices that marred prior social theorizing. It would provide an outline (prediction) of the new social system appropriate to a scientific and industrial civilization while generating practical proposals for the reorganization of society to achieve the desired state. The superiority of Comtean sociology to pronounce on the most appropriate institutions, sentiments, and rituals for a new social order presumably lay in its grounding in the laws governing human biological (including psychological) behavior and those laws, verified by historical and comparative study, governing the nature and development of human societies. This positive blueprint, moreover, ideally ensured harmony of the interests of all classes. Political and economic control rightly lay in the hands of those (bankers, managers, manufacturers) whose expertise best equipped them to deal with industrial organization. The abuse of temporal power would be prevented by the ultimate authority of the spiritual power (the sociologists) whose function was to inculcate the conviction that the leaders of industrial society were merely agents performing their social function for the benefit of all. Positive education, by subordinating egoism to altruism, would, in Comte's view, train all members of industrial society to live and act in harmony and thereby prevent the conflicts inherent in a society preoccupied with material interests only. Comte considered the increasing concentration of temporal power among industrial capitalists as the best means of securing industrial efficiency and increased productivity. It was, thus, not the industrial or financial techniques of capitalism that he criticized but rather its failure to develop an effective agency of moral control to ensure that all members of society would benefit fully from industrialization. The priesthood of positivism, by its control of education and direction of public opinion, would provide the basis for enlightened social policy and thereby ensure that the spiritual power would constitute a wholly effective check on the abuse of temporal power and that progress and order would develop in tandem.

In 1848 Comte founded the Positivist Society as a forum for political discussion and positivist activities aimed at the reorganization of society. Although not initially opposed to the establishment of the Second Republic, Comte's authoritarian predilections and deep commitment to social order led him to support fully Louis Napoleon's coup d'état of December 1851. His conviction that the imperial regime provided a more appropriate political climate than either democracy or parliamentary government for preparing for the advent of positivist society provoked Emile Littré and others to break with Comte and form, from 1852, a rival group of dissident or so-called scientific positivists. In addition to their dismay at Comte's facile sacrifice of the political liberties of the Second Republic, the Littréists felt that Comte had betrayed the philosophical foundation of positivism. They considered his *Système de politique positive* (1851–1854), which elaborates the religion of humanity (with Comte as high priest) in minutely prescribed rituals for public and domestic behavior, as indicative of Comte's relapse into a subjective and theological mode of thinking and sought to propagate an objective positivism shorn of these later religious accretions. The orthodox positivists, led by Pierre Laffitte (1823–1893) after Comte's death in 1857, preached the full Comtean gospel and, with their English codisciples (under the leadership of Richard Congreve), defended the unity of Comte's work and were effective agents for the diffusion of positivism by means of public lectures, periodical literature, and positivist organizations and "churches." Laffitte was the most successful proselytizer of Comtean doctrine and by the 1880s attracted large audiences, most notably at his public lectures at the Collège de France.

Although the Second Empire has frequently been designated an age of positivism by historians, such a generalization ignores the ambiguities of the doctrine and the vigor of the opposition to it in the latter years of the Empire. The profound schism among Comte's immediate disciples renders any clear definition of positivism, and hence of its precise historical influence, problematic. Nevertheless, it remains clear that the positivist outlook informed the thought of persons of the stature of Ernest Renan, Hippolyte Taine, Emile Littré, and Claude Bernard. The journal *La philosophie positive*, founded by Littré and the *emigré*

Russian scientist Grégoire N. Wyrouboff (1843–1913) in 1867, brought the doctrine before a wider educated public and emphasized its sociological and political implications, particularly after the outbreak of the Franco-Prussian War. Positivism continued to exert an influence in philosophical and scientific circles, most notably in the founding of sociology as an academic discipline, during the late nineteenth century. Finally, despite Comte's own staunch imperial sympathies, most of his disciples were republican supporters. Littré was particularly active in republican circles during the 1860s and 1870s and was influential in introducing certain positivist educational, social, and philosophical precepts into the political strategy and doctrine of the formative years of the Third Republic, primarily through his influence on the views of Léon Gambetta and Jules Ferry (1832–1893).

D. G. Charlton, *Positivist Thought in France during the Second Empire* (New York, 1959); J. Eros, "The Positivist Generation of French Republicanism," *SR*, n.s. 3 (1955); L. Laudan, "Towards a Reassessment of Comte's 'Méthode Positive,' " *Philosophy of Science* 38 (1971); W. M. Simon, *European Positivism in the Nineteenth Century* (Ithaca, N.Y., 1963), and "The 'Two Cultures' in Nineteenth-Century France: Victor Cousin and Auguste Comte," *JHI* 26 (1965).

Martin Fichman

Related entries: BERNARD; BERTHELOT; DARWINISM IN FRANCE; DUMAS, J. P.; GAMBETTA; LE PLAY; LITTRE; PASTEUR; RENAN; REPUBLICANISM; SAINTE-BEUVE; SAINT-SIMONIANISM; TAINE; ZOLA.

PREAULT, ANTOINE AUGUSTIN (1809–1879), romantic sculptor; born at Paris, 6 October 1810. Préault studied for a short time with Pierre Jean David d'Angers (1788–1856), the classical sculptor of large bronze portraits, statues, and medallions, and was a friend of the realist Honoré Daumier, but his own spirit was that of a romantic. Some of his early works in plaster, shown beginning in 1833, have not survived since they were not executed in a more permanent material such as bronze. The relief *La tuerie* (Musée de Chartres), a rather strange and complicated work composed of fragmented figures, was accepted in the 1834 Salon but not cast until 1850. His work was thereafter refused until 1848. During this time, he received some commissions for works with religious subject matter. The movement away from classical themes and treatment is further revealed in his wooden *Christ* (Eglise Saint Gervais et Saint Protais), shown in 1848, 1849, and 1850. The expressive forms are full of energy and passion, recalling medieval crosses. The material links it with the simple life and ordinary people, giving it a more personal and contemporary feeling. Like most other sculptors of the time, Préault, although a republican, did not lack for government commissions. The public works projects of the Second Empire, and especially the rebuilding of Paris, guaranteed ample scope for monumental sculpture. Préault did saints for three Parisian churches (Saint Gervais, Sainte Clotilde, and Saint Paul et Saint Louis) and a number of decorative groups, including for the Pont d'Iéna (1859). It was his reliefs, however, that marked him as an exceptional artist and sparked an interest in him by the avant-garde of the Second Empire.

The theme of Ophelia, popular with many artists of a romantic bent, including Eugène Delacroix (*Death of Ophelia*, 1853, Louvre, Paris), was treated by Préault in an unusual interpretation. The life-size relief *Ophelia* was sculpted in clay in 1843, shown in the Salon of 1850, and finally cast in bronze in 1876 (Musée des Beaux-Arts, Marseilles). It was meant to lie on the ground and not to be suspended on a wall, thus making it seem more actual, as though the figure were lying supine in the water. Furthermore, it is a sunken relief, which creates darker shadows, making it seem as though Ophelia is submerged even deeper in the murky water. Her head is placed at an awkward and contorted angle, and the water appears to be swirling around her with repeated sinuous curves that anticipate later symbolism and art nouveau. Ophelia's death is not portrayed as a time of final and peaceful calm but rather as tragedy and struggle, as she clutches at the drapery being pulled from her by the rushing water.

During the Second Empire, Préault was occupied primarily with large marble figures commissioned by the state—for example, that for Versailles, *J. H. Mansart* (1852–1859), and *André Chénier* (1855) for the Cour Napoléon of the Louvre.

He created many large bronze medallions, including two (commissioned for the emperor in 1853) of *Dante* and *Virgil* (Louvre). Both are based on Renaissance models, but Préault's own sculptural powers are evident in the linear emphasis, the strongly modeled forms, and the manipulation of light and shadow. Other large medallions were commemorative of contemporary figures such as the romantic landscape painter Paul Huet (1804–1869), for whose tomb in the Cimetière Montparnasse Préault sculpted a sensitively modeled likeness, or Delacroix (*Eugène Delacroix*, 1864, Louvre). The expressive values Préault explored served as inspiration for Auguste Rodin (1840–1917), and the enigmatic features stimulated the ideas of Odilon Redon (1840–1916). Préault died at Paris, 11 January 1879.

L. Benoist, *La sculpture Romantique* (Paris, 1928); J. Locquin, "Un grand statuaire Romantique: Auguste Préault, 1809–1879," *La renaissance de l'art français*, no. 11 (November 1920); R. Mirolli, *Nineteenth-Century French Sculpture: Monuments for the Middle Class* (Louisville, 1971).

Beverley Giblon

Related entries: BARYE; CARPEAUX; RUDE.

PREFECTS, key administrative personnel of the Second Empire. Before December 1851 the prefects had been simply agents for executing the will of the minister of the interior. The decree of 25 March 1852, however, considerably enlarged their powers and role and would remain their basic charter until 1964.

Under the Second Empire, the prefect administered his department. He named a wide variety of officials, including (from 1854) primary school teachers, members of the *conseils académiques*, and (from 1855) mayors and assistant mayors (*adjoints*) of towns having populations smaller than three thousand. He drew up the budgets for those towns, had to approve their financial decisions, and could dismiss a mayor or dissolve a municipal council and appoint an administrative commission to function until a new council had been named. He could make decisions on more than a hundred local matters and was responsible for the maintenance of order. The prefect reported to Paris concerning all state agents. He enforced the laws and also exercised surveillance over newspapers and all associations and was empowered to close the cafés and cabarets if public order was threatened. From 1854 the prefects directed the municipal police in communes with populations smaller than forty thousand (at Paris there was a separate prefect of police).

The Second Empire prefect played a major social role. He was not only the center of his department's social life but was also responsible for the policy of social amelioration so important to Napoleon III. Finally, he was the chief political agent of the regime. The prefect both reported on public opinion (every three months; later, monthly) and was charged with shaping and guiding it. His dual political role was to win his department to bonapartism and to make the elections. The prefect was expected to choose reliable candidates, as well as to secure their election. Assisting him in these tasks, he had a council, a *chef de cabinet*, and (from 1865) a secretary-general. The material rewards were considerable. The eight first-class prefects received 40,000 francs per year; the eighteen second-class posts commanded 30,000 francs and the others 20,000.

Following the coup d'état of December 1851, eight prefects resigned and six were dismissed. The emperor made the final decision on all appointments. Most came from the bourgeoisie and were sons of functionaries. They were well educated (usually in law) and generally conscientious and hard working. Although only a minority were true bonapartists, they were loyal to Napaleon III and tended to hold their posts for long periods; two hundred twenty men would serve as prefects during the Second Empire in the eighty-seven departments. Twenty-four prefects kept their posts more than ten years and two for the entire Empire. Baron Georges Haussmann was prefect of the Seine from 1853 to 1870, Eugène Janvier de la Motte of the Eure from 1856 to 1868, and Claude Vaïsse (1799–1864) of the Rhone from 1853 to 1863. Nevertheless, fifty-two prefects were dismissed between 1854 and 1870 (twelve were fired and five reassigned by the Liberal Empire, 3 January 1870).

The prefects of the Second Empire represented a number of political nuances. Some were traditional conservatives, hostile to all social innovation; some wanted the authoritarian regime to draw its strength directly from the people; others would have imposed social reform from above; and still others sought a true rapprochement with the working class.

The final appraisal of the successes and failures of the prefects under the Second Empire has yet to be made. Certainly the typical Second Empire prefect was not a despot. He had too many powerful rivals for that, including the deputies, ministers, and *conseillers généraux*, and was, besides, at the disposition of the minister of the interior, who could easily overrule him. Nor was he necessarily the implacable enemy of the notables; after all, the prefect also belonged to that privileged group. Political reform and the advance of decentralization steadily reduced the prefectural power throughout the Second Empire, and increasingly the prefect's role became more that of an administrator and animator of economic life than that of a political agent. Yet in the latter area there were achievements as well, notably the conquest of the West for bonapartism.

Archives de France, *Les préfets du II ventôse an VIII au 4 Septembre 1870: Répertoire nominative et territorial* (Paris, 1982); B. Le Clère and V. Wright, *Les préfets du Second Empire* (Paris, 1973); B. Le Clère, "Rouher et les préfets du Second Empire," *AMN* 50 (July 1975).

Related entries: AUTHORITARIAN EMPIRE; BONAPARTISM; CHEVREAU; COUP D'ETAT; DECENTRALIZATION; ELECTIONS; HAUSSMANN; JANVIER DE LA MOTTE; LIBERAL EMPIRE; MAUPAS; PERSIGNY; PIETRI; PRESS REGIME; PUBLIC OPINION; ROUHER.

LA PRESSE, Emile de Girardin's first major daily newspaper and one of the earliest Parisian *journal d'affaires*. Although Girardin founded *La presse* in July 1836, he did not obtain full control of it until 1845. The newspaper pioneered mass commercial journalism in France. Relying on advertising rather than on subscriptions as the basis of revenue, Girardin reduced the subscription price to 40 francs, or half that of other newspapers, and was thus able to expand circulation rapidly. Appealing to businessmen and to a liberal clientele, *La presse* was one of the best-tailored Paris newspapers, a field of battle open to all opinions. Girardin was himself peripatetic in his political allegiance, shifting support from the Republic to Louis Napoleon and then, after the coup d'état of December 1851, enlisting *La presse* in the ranks of the opposition, somewhat to the right of the republican *Le siècle*. Plagued by *avertissements* and restrictions and annoyed at his inability to express his opinions freely, Girardin resigned from the editorial staff and in December 1856 sold his newspaper for 825,000 francs to Moïse Millaud, who in early 1859 sold in turn to the financier Félix Solar (1815–1871) for 750,000 francs.

As an evening paper, *La presse* continued under the direction of Auguste Nefftzer. *Gérant* from 1844, he had long been a political writer for the newspaper and would serve as editor in chief from 1856 to November 1857. Nefftzer was a Protestant, an Alsatian noted for his knowledge of German affairs. Attracted to the staff were writers well known for their opposition to the Empire: Alphonse Peyrat (1812–1891), Charles-Edmond (1822–1899), Théophile Gautier (drama and art critic until 1855), and Alfred Darimon, who wrote on economic affairs. Other collaborators and contributors included Nestor Roqueplan (1804–1870), Jules Vallès (1832–1885), Eugène Pelletan (1813–1884), Paulin Limayrac (1817–1868; wrote the literary chronicle briefly after Gautier's 1855 departure), Paul de Saint-Victor (1827–1881; dropped his title and served as drama critic from

1856 to January 1868), Jean Jouvin (1810–1886; succeeded Saint-Victor), Alfred Assollant (1827–1886), Emile Boutmy (1835–1906), Paul Féval (1817–1887), A. Erdan (Alexander André Jacob, 1826–1878), and Ernest Feydeau. Nefftzer was soon forced to resign by Prince Napoleon, one of the financial investors. Although the prince originally had sponsored Nefftzer's appointment, he had come to regard him as too Orleanist. Nefftzer was succeeded as editor in chief by Peyrat (Protestant, anti-clerical) who was also ousted after his support of republican candidates to the Corps Législatif in 1857 caused suspension of the newspaper for two months. (*La presse* and *Le siècle* had jointly published a list of candidates for Paris.) Adolphe Guéroult assumed leadership, only to leave in 1859 to found his own paper, *L'opinion nationale*. Under him, *La presse* was the only major newspaper, except for *Le siècle*, to support fully Napoleon III's 1858–1859 intervention in Italy. Nefftzer returned June 1858 as *secrétaire de rédaction* but left in 1861 to found *Le temps* (Solar was briefly chief editor from December 1860). The constant turnover of personnel damaged the journal's style and influence, and its circulation rapidly declined, until by April 1859 it had fewer than ten thousand subscriptions and mounting financial problems.

At this critical point in the history of *La presse*, Girardin returned unexpectedly as editor in chief (1 December 1862). He found himself surrounded by new younger writers such as Clément Duvernois (1836–1879), Jules Ferry (1832–1893), Darimon, and Auguste Jean Marie Vermorel (1841–1871), who were openly critical of the government. Articles by Duvernois earned the paper two *avertissements* in 1866. Important backers demanded prudence from the editors and writers, which led to the resignation of Girardin and many of his journalists. Philippe Cucheval-Clarigny (1822–1895) took over as chief editor, but *La presse* continued to decline. Its circulation, which had been 19,900 in April 1853 and about 40,000 in 1855–1857, fell steadily, to 23,000 in February 1858, 21,000 in July 1858, fewer than 10,000 in April 1859, and 9,000 in March 1869 (after a brief recovery to 18,000 in 1860–1861). In the final years of the Second Empire, the paper's political influence became negligible as, more concerned with its commercial success, it ignored political controversy.

A. Sirven, *Journaux et journalistes: "La presse," "La liberté"* (Paris, 1866).

Natalie Isser

Related entries: GIRARDIN; *LIBERTE*; MARINONI; MILLAUD; NEFFTZER; *OPINION NATIONALE*; PRESS REGIME; PRINCE NAPOLEON; *SIECLE*; *TEMPS*.

PRESS REGIME, under the Second Empire a determined and wide-ranging effort to control the media, which in mid-nineteenth-century France included press services (such as Havas), newspapers, brochures, cartoons, and the theater. Napoleon III, with his great interest both in knowing and shaping public opinion, wished not only to scrutinize but also to manipulate the media of his day. On no other point was he more determined. And of all channels of communication during the Second Empire, newspapers were by far the most significant. Anxious to create a bonapartist opinion and to restrict effective opposition to one that did not question the existence of the regime (a loyal opposition), the government actively subsidized newspapers while seeking, both at Paris and in the provinces, to preserve the illusion of diversity in the press. Opposition papers were not only permitted but even encouraged, provided that their opinions were neither too radical nor too polemical and that there was no criticism of the Empire itself. To ensure that these restraints were maintained was the major purpose of Second Empire press legislation, which, incidentally, applied only to periodical publications dealing with politics or political economy. Otherwise there was complete freedom of publication (except for licensing of printers and booksellers, and regulation of *colportage*, or book peddling, and of the theater, all of which predated the Empire). But the nonpolitical press could not deal, even tangentially, with forbidden topics.

Government and press relations were determined by the decree of 17 February 1852, issued during the period of dictatorship following the coup d'état and therefore having the effect of law. For the most part this decree merely codified existing regulations and practices. Newspapers required prior government authorization in order to exist, and this authorization had to be renewed with any change of publisher or chief editor, both of whom had to be approved by the government. A monthly deposit (bond) was necessary, varying from 15,000 to 50,000 francs or more. Every paper was subjected to high postal rates and to a special stamp tax (which after 1852 was 6 centimes per copy in Paris, 3 in the provinces). In addition to these restrictions, the government could withhold permission for a paper's sale on the public way (the newspaper kiosk was an invention of the Second Empire, from 1857, as were the newsstands established in railway stations by Louis Hachette). A paper that was permitted to publish had to be careful not to commit any of the *délits* established by the laws of 1819, 1835, and of the Empire itself (1852, 1866), including publication of false news or documents or unsigned articles or (until 1861) accounts of parliamentary debates or (from 1866) discussions of the constitution. In addition to codifying existing legislation, the decree of 1852 also innovated in two ways: first, by consigning the determination of *délits* to judges (the correctional tribunal) rather than to juries and, second, by establishing an ingenious administrative regime, joint invention of Victor Fialin Persigny and Eugène Rouher, which paralleled the judicial one. Article 32 of the 1852 decree provided that papers could be suspended either as the result of two convictions for *délits* within less than two years (a convicted chief editor would have to step down for three years) or as a result of the operation of a system of *avertissements*, or warnings. If an article was deemed "excessive, dangerous or disagreeable," the offending newspaper would receive an *avertissement*. If the editor did not reform his ways, another warning would be forthcoming, and the paper could be suspended for two months. A third *avertissement* might mean permanent suspension. Brochures also had to receive permission before publication and were required to pay a special tax.

The administration rewarded friendly newspapers. It contributed funds to establish or to ensure the existence of favorable journals or purchased large numbers of subscriptions in order to guarantee their income. Semiofficial and friendly papers were given exclusive press releases and officials often used these almost as bribes for cooperation. The paid publication of administrative announcements (*annonces*) was another form of subvention. A newspaper's financial stability often was determined, in fact, by a variety of government subsidies. Newspapers in the provinces were usually dependent on the goodwill of the prefects, who rigorously exercised their authority over them. To help create a favorable political climate, a system of syndication was also used. A particularly favorable article or editorial that had been printed in a Paris newspaper frequently appeared in various provincial papers signed by different editors. If political controversy engaged public discussion, officials sometimes gave friendly editors special documents and dossiers to help them elucidate the Empire's position.

During the Second Empire, the press was supervised by a special office, the Direction Générale de la Librairie, at first within the Ministry of Police and then under the minister of the interior. Headed until 1854 by Pierre Latour-Dumoulin (1823–1888) and then for several years by Arthur de la Guéronnière, the Direction proliferated *avertissements* during the first half of the Empire: ninety-one from January 1852 to June 1853, thirty-two from June 1853 to March 1854, and fifty-seven from March 1854 to February 1858. Of course, periodic amnesties could, and did, erase accumulated *avertissements*. Yet only three important papers were suppressed during the Second Empire, and suspensions were few since the government was reluctant to offend stockholders. Under the Empire, the publication of newspapers became big business, requiring a large amount of capitalization and necessitating massive circulation to ensure dividends for the investor. New technology (such as the railroads and the rotary presses of Hippolyte Marinoni) combined with new forms of journalism (the *petite presse*, symbolized by Hippolyte de Villemessant's *Le Figaro*; the *presse d'information*, represented by Moïse Millaud's *Le petit journal*) to make this possible, and the economic factor caused journalists to practice political caution in order to build huge circulations. These financial considerations effectively tempered independent political opinions and made the papers more circumspect and moderate in their tone. And they leant force to perhaps the most effective device of control, the *avis officieux*. Officials who had already obtained from all publishers and chief editors blank letters of resignation usually needed no more than an interview and a few words of advice to achieve their ends.

As time passed, authoritarian restrictions gradually lessened, partly because they were no longer needed to the same extent, mostly because of the growing demand for political reform. In his decree of 24 November 1860, Napoleon III promised a relaxation, which was effected by the *sénatus-consulte* of 2 February 1861 and by a law of 2 July 1861. Newspapers would no longer be suppressed on a third warning (or after two judicial convictions)—this to save *Le siècle* and *L'opinion nationale*. And henceforth they could print legislative debates, if they did so *in extenso* for each topic and did not offer comment. Although the emperor told Emile de Girardin in 1863 that he would never permit a free press and although at the end of 1867 ten newspapers were convicted for having discussed a parliamentary debate, 1860 marked a turning point and initiated a process that culminated in the promulgation on 11 May 1868 of a new press law removing most of the restrictions imposed sixteen years earlier. Preliminary authorization to found a newspaper was no longer necessary; it was merely required that the name of proprietor and publisher be posted and the required bond deposited. Licenses were no longer needed for printers and booksellers. And the administrative regime of *avertissements* and *avis officieux* was abolished (it had, in fact, ceased to function from 19 January 1867 when the emperor had promised the new press legislation). Libertarians protested the retention of a stamp tax, although it was reduced to 5 centimes (France was alone among major Western states to have such a tax), and the fact that *délits* were still determined by judges, who could suspend or suppress a paper, rather than by a jury, although fines were substituted for imprisonment. Moreover, newspapers could still be required to print government communiqués, and articles had to be signed. But the fact was that even the law of May 1868 would not have passed the Corps Législatif without the government's insistence and that Napoleon III shared with many of his conservative legislators a grave misgiving about the freedom that had been granted and that led almost immediately to a proliferation of newspapers such as Henri Rochefort's *La lanterne*, whose stances were far from reassuring. A truly free press in France would have to wait for another thirteen years and the law of 1881.

H. Avenel, *Histoire de la presse française depuis 1789 jusqu' à nos jours* (Paris, 1900); C. Bellanger et al., eds., *Histoire générale de la presse française* (Paris, 1969); R. Bellet, *Presse et journalisme sous le Second Empire* (Paris, 1967); I. Collins, *The Government and Newspaper Press in France, 1814–1881* (Paris, 1959); J. J. Darmon, *Le colportage de librairie en France sous le Second Empire* (Paris, 1972); A. Decaux, *La littérature au tribunal sous le Second Empire* (Monaco, 1963); L. Hatin, *Bibliographie historique et critique de la presse périodique en France, 1631–1865* (Paris, 1866); N. Isser, *The Second Empire and the Press* (The Hague, 1974); D. I. Kulstein, "Government Propaganda and the Press during the Second Empire," *Gazette*, no. 2 (1964); M. Martin, "Presse, publicité, et grandes affaires sous le Second Empire," *RH* (1976); M. Palmer, *Des petits journaux aux grandes agences: naissance du journalisme, 1863–1914* (Paris, 1983); R. L. Smith, "The Rise of the Mass Press in Nineteenth-Century France," *Journalism Quarterly* 53 (Spring 1976); G. Weill, *Le journal: Origines, évolution, et rôle de la presse périodique* (Paris, 1936); G. Wright, "La presse politique en province, 1860–1870," *R.1848* (September 1938).

Natalie Isser

Related entries: BAUDIN; *CONSTITUTIONNEL*; *CORRESPONDANT*; *FIGARO*; *FRANCE*; GIRARDIN; GRANIER DE CASSAGNAC; HACHETTE; HAVIN; *JOURNAL DES DEBATS*; LA GUERONNIERE; *LANTERNE*; *LIBERTE*; MARINONI; MILLAUD; *MONITEUR UNIVERSAL*; NEFFTZER; *OPINION NATIONALE*; *PATRIE*; *PAYS*; PERSIGNY; *PETIT JOURNAL*; PRE-

FECTS; *PRESSE*; PREVOST-PARADOL; PUBLIC OPINION; REFORM; *RE-VUE DES DEUX MONDES*; ROCHEFORT; ROUHER; *SIECLE*; *TEMPS*; *UNIVERS*; VEUILLOT; VILLEMESSANT.

PREVOST-PARADOL, LUCIEN ANATOLE (1829–1870), academic and journalist, one of the most brilliant publicists of the Second Empire; born at Paris, 8 July 1829, the son of a singer and actress of the Comédie Française. After particularly outstanding studies at the Ecole Normale Supérieure, where Ernest Taine was a friend and classmate, Prévost-Paradol rose to public prominence during the 1850s as a liberal critic of the authoritarian Empire. Obtaining the doctorate in 1855, Prévost-Paradol taught French literature with great success at the University of Aix but resigned in 1856 to replace Jean Lemoinne (1815–1892) in writing the political bulletin for the Orleanist newspaper the *Journal des débats*. Thus he followed the path of a number of promising academics during the Second Empire from university to journalism, men like Edmond About, Alfred Assollant (1827–1886), Paul Challemel-Lacour (1827–1896), Taine, and Jean Jacques Weiss (1827–1891). In 1860 Prévost-Paradol went briefly to *La presse*, but soon returned to the *Journal* before leaving for *Le courrier du Dimanche* (founded in 1858 by Grégory Ganesco [1833–1877]). Although adept at working within the censorship rules, Prévost-Paradol was jailed and fined in 1860 for a pamphlet, *Les anciens partis*, in which he stated that the oldest party was "the alliance of demagogy and despotism." The affair made his reputation. On 2 August 1866, however, *Le courrier du Dimanche* was suppressed as the consequence of an article written by the young journalist. The previous year Prévost-Paradol had been elected (7 April 1865) to the Académie Française over his journalist colleague Jules Janin, a result seen as a protest against the Empire, especially since it was thought that Napoleon III expected to be honored for his *Histoire de Jules César*. He was the youngest of the Immortals.

Never an irreconcilable enemy of the regime, Prévost-Paradol employed his newspaper columns to argue for a return to parliamentary liberties and to suggest that France should emulate English political institutions. Closely associated with Adolphe Thiers, he was an early proponent of the Union Libéral, working to bring moderates of all persuasions into a coalition designed to reestablish a liberal politics supposedly destroyed by the Revolution of 1848. Distrustful of democracy, which he believed threatened France's intellectual elite and natural leadership, Prévost-Paradol criticized the Empire as a demagogic manifestation of a dangerous egalitarian impulse emanating from a revolutionary tradition supported by a "deep layer of rural imbecility and provincial bestiality." He also argued that democratic considerations had led the regime to pursue a political economy meant to promote material wealth, thereby lowering the general state of public morality and diverting attention from the community's loss of liberty. One possible remedy, he insisted, would be a true and effective decentralization. He wanted parliamentary government, maximum individual liberties, and separation of church and state.

Pessimistic about the future, Prévost-Paradol concluded that France's recent history indicated a decline in national vigor. In *La France nouvelle* (1868), an essay that greatly influenced a later generation of liberals, he suggested that Europe in general was being eclipsed by the spread of Anglo-Saxon peoples over the globe while an aggressive Germany threatened to replace France as the preeminent continental power. To confront this situation, he recommended that France return to its traditional elites for leadership and implement a policy of imperialism in North Africa to provide not only a challenge supportive of national unity but the living space necessary for an enlarged and reinvigorated population. As a candidate for the Corps Législatif from Nantes in the elections of 1869, Prévost-Paradol was crushingly defeated as he had been at Paris in 1857. The experience filled him with dread of the newly revived revolutionary party. The continuing political reforms since 1860 and the advent of the Liberal Empire allowed him to rally to the regime. He served on the commissions to investigate decentralization and higher education. A supporter of the North during the U.S. Civil War, he solicited and received appointment as minister to the United States (12 June 1870). However, condemned by many for his change of politics, depressed at his reception in Washington, overwhelmed by the summer heat, and, above all, deeply shaken by the seeming inevitability of war between France and Prussia, Prévost-Paradol in the night of 11 July 1870 shot himself in the chest. He died almost instantly. Among his major works are *Essais de politique et littérature* (Paris, 1859 and 1863), and *Etudes sur les moralistes français* (Paris, 1865).

P. Dominique, ''Prévost-Paradol polémiste,'' *Ecrits de Paris*, no. 202 (1962); P. Guiral, *Prévost-Paradol (1829–1870): Pensée et action d'un libéral sous le Second Empire* (Paris, 1955), ''Un écrivain libéral du Second Empire, Prévost-Paradol,'' IH 16 (1954), and ''Prévost-Paradol et l'Italie [1863],'' *RST* 14 (July–December 1968); P. Senart, ''Prévost-Paradol,'' *RDM* no. 7 (1970).

Stuart L. Campbell

Related entries: DECENTRALIZATION; *JOURNAL DES DEBATS*; LIBERAL EMPIRE; LIBERALISM; ORLEANISM; PRESS REGIME; REFORM.

PRINCE IMPERIAL, NAPOLEON EUGENE LOUIS JOSEPH (1856–1879), only child of Napoleon III and Eugénie de Montijo; heir to the throne of the Second Empire; born at the Tuileries, 16 March 1856. The empress had been in labor for twenty-two hours before the birth at 3:15 A.M. For Napoleon III, who had ordered priority given to saving the life of the mother, the birth of his son during the Congress of Paris (ending the Crimean War) was an apogee. He proclaimed a general amnesty and, together with Eugénie, stood as sponsor for every legitimate child born in France that day. Poets, including Théophile Gautier, hymned the new prince. The city of Paris, which had presented to the imperial family an elaborate cradle designed by the city's architect, Victor Baltard (1805–1874), illuminated. The baptism, at Notre Dame on 14 June, was magnificent. The baby received a golden apple from his absent godfather, Pope Pius

IX (the queen of Sweden was godmother). On the following day, a Sunday, Paris was again illuminated, theaters were free to the public, and a carnival atmosphere prevailed. Before the great banquet that evening at the Hôtel de Ville, Napoleon III bestowed the grand cross of the Legion of Honor on his friend and arch-bonapartist Victor Fialin Persigny. The prince imperial became at once the center of bonapartist hopes and a major obstacle to those of his cousin Prince Napoleon, who only with great difficulty had been persuaded to sign the *acte de naissance* and to attend the baptism.

Until 1863 the prince was under the authority of his English nanny, Miss Shaw (whom Queen Victoria had recommended), his governess (*Gouvernante des Enfants de France*), Mme. Bruat (wife of Admiral Armand Joseph Bruat [1796–1855]), and two assistant governesses, Mmes. Bizot and de Brancion, each, like Mme. Bruat, widow of a high officer dead in the Crimea. The wet nurse was a Burgundian peasant, brought to Paris for the task. Dr. Barthez headed the medical staff but was little heeded.

On his seventh birthday, in 1863, the prince imperial received his first tutor (*précepteur*), François Monnier, professor at Paris' Collège Rollin. In the summer of 1867, the Maison du Prince Impérial was organized under the stern supervision of General Charles Auguste Frossard (1807–1875), assisted by four military aides-de-camp. As *Gouverneur du Prince Impériale* Frossard to some extent checked the tendency of the emperor to spoil "Loulou," as the prince was known in family circles. Monnier, bridling at the general's authority, resigned. He was replaced, on the advice of education minister Victor Duruy, by a young *normalien* and professor at the lycée of Grenoble, Augustin Filon (b. 1841), son of the historian Auguste Filon (1800–1875).

When Filon took over his tasks on 4 September 1867 at Saint-Cloud, the prince imperial was recovering from an injury to his hip resulting from a gymnasium mishap. An abscess had developed, giving rise to concern and necessitating an operation by the celebrated surgeon Auguste Nélaton (1807–1873). In fact, the prince's health was not particularly good, and this had combined with his disposition, the difficulties of his position, and the weaknesses of his first tutor to retard his educational development. It was decided that a Professor Edeline from the fashionable Lycée Bonaparte (now Condorcet) should teach the prince imperial as if he were in fact a member of his appropriate class at the lycée and even rank him (secretly) in comparison with his invisible classmates. Thus Filon became, in effect, a *répétiteur*. The experiment had a limited success. But Edeline, falling ill, was replaced in the fall of 1868 by Cuvelier, professor at the lycée of Vanves, and a disastrous effort was made to accelerate the pace of the prince's education, abandoning the lycée tie. Despite the participation of the young Ernest Lavisse, the prince imperial continued to resist intellectual exercises, although he did show a flair for drawing.

Another aspect of the prince's education proceeded more smoothly, however. Napoleon III well understood the need to associate his son closely with the army and to keep him at the center of attention. The prince imperial was placed in a saddle almost before he could walk and was inscribed when he was eight months old on the roll of the 1er Régiment de Grenadiers de la Garde Impériale. At three he attended a military review mounted on his own pony. And at four (August 1860) he was taken by his mother to the military camp at Châlons. In October 1869 the emperor designated General Frossard, who had formal charge of the prince's military education, as official guardian in the absence of the empress. The prince imperial appeared regularly at public functions from 1858. The experience was not always a happy one. During a distribution of academic prizes at the Sorbonne in August 1868, the son of General Louis Eugène Cavaignac (1802–1857) refused to accept his award from the prince and was applauded by the students. On the other hand, in Corsica with his mother in August 1869 for the centenary of the birth of Napoleon I, the prince imperial was received with great enthusiasm.

At the outbreak of the Franco-Prussian War, the fourteen-year-old prince accompanied his father to the front and with him observed the skirmish at Sarrebruck (Saarbrücken) on 2 August. Before joining MacMahon's ill-fated advance toward Metz, the emperor sent his son to the Belgian frontier and on 3 September ordered him to cross into Belgium. The prince's retainers obeyed the imperial orders despite Eugénie's instructions that her son not "run away." On 6 September, the prince imperial landed at Dover from Ostend. His mother joined him at Hastings two days later, and before the end of the month they had moved into Camden Place at Chislehurst. On 20 March 1871 at Dover, they greeted Napoleon III on his release from German captivity.

The tragedy of 1870–1871 seemed to work a transformation in the prince imperial, who became an ambitious, energetic, and hard-working young man, especially after entering Woolwich Military Academy in the fall of 1872 (an earlier attempt to study physics and math at King's College, London, on his father's advice, had failed). Eugénie was preparing to visit her son at Woolwich on the morning of 9 January 1873 when Napoleon III died suddenly in the midst of a series of operations to crush a bladder stone. On 15 April the bonapartists acclaimed the prince imperial as pretender, and on 16 March 1874 thousands gathered at Camden Place to cheer his majority on the occasion of his eighteenth birthday. The following February, the prince, who had been very popular at Woolwich, graduated seventh in a class of thirty-four, despite having had to study and take exams in English. He was first in riding and fencing.

The prince imperial was by 1875 a soldier first and foremost. What else he was remains unclear. A pious Catholic and opposed both to parliamentary government and absolute monarchy, he was variously considered clerical and Gallican, reactionary and liberal. He hoped one day to rule but understood that while developing his propaganda he must wait until the Third Republic discredited itself. Between the influences of Prince Napoleon and Eugène Rouher, he preferred the latter (Rouher divided his time between Paris and Camden Place), and in February 1876 he broke formally with Prince Napoleon on the occasion of the French elections of that year.

Patience was required, but in the meantime it was necessary to achieve a military reputation. At the beginning of 1879, the prince imperial persuaded a reluctant Eugénie, who, with her friend Queen Victoria, persuaded an even more reluctant British administration (Rouher had also disapproved), to allow him to participate in the war against the Zulus, which Britain had just undertaken in southern Africa. The prince's status was to be that of a distinguished visitor attached to the general staff of the Royal Artillery. He sailed for South Africa on 27 February 1879 and on 1 June departed with a reconnaissance party of six cavalrymen under Acting Captain Carey, who seems to have assumed that the prince imperial was in command and who unwisely allowed him to order an afternoon rest near high grass. When a war party of forty to fifty Zulus, some armed with rifles, suddenly emerged from cover within yards of the patrol, each man leaped into his saddle, but that of the prince broke. He fell, his horse bolted, and, having lost his sword, he was left alone to face the Zulus with his revolver and a spear he had recovered. He fell beneath some seventeen spear wounds, all in front. As a mark of respect for his courage, the Zulus did not mutilate his body.

With the death of the prince imperial, bonapartism ceased to be a significant force, although in his will the prince had designated Victor Bonaparte, eldest son of Prince Napoleon, as his successor. Eugénie, whose relationship with her son had been extremely close, buried him with full honors, in the presence of the British royal family, at St. Mary's Church, Chislehurst, on 12 July 1879. In the spring she visited the spot where he had been killed. Queen Victoria erected a monument to the memory of the prince imperial in St. George's Chapel at Windsor. Later (1881) Eugénie bought a larger property, Farnborough Hill, at Farnborough, forty miles from Chislehurst, and built a Premonstratensian (later Benedictine) monastery and a mausoleum, to which were transferred in January 1888 the remains of Napoleon III and of the prince imperial, and where they, and those of Eugénie herself, still rest.

A. Augustin-Thierry, *Le Prince Impérial* (Paris, 1935); "Centenaire de la mort du Prince Impérial," *SN* 42 (1979); H. Chaudet and S. Desternes, "Les Zoulous tuent le Prince Impériale," *Historia* 391 (June 1979), and *Louis, Prince Impérial, 1856–1879* (Paris, 1957); A. Decaux, *Le Prince Impérial* (Paris, 1964); A. Filon, *Memoirs of the Prince Imperial* (London, 1913); J. Philippon, *Le Prince Impérial, 1856–1879* (Paris, 1979); M. Rostand, *Napoléon IV* (Paris, 1928); *Souvenir napoléonien*, special issue, 35 (1972); E.E.P. Tisdall, *The Prince Imperial: A Study of His Life among the British* (London, 1959).

Related entries: BONAPARTISM; CHISLEHURST; EUGENIE; PRINCE NAPOLEON; ROUHER.

PRINCE NAPOLEON (1822–1891), usual designation during the Second Empire of Napoleon Joseph Charles Paul Bonaparte, known as Jérôme, second child of Napoleon I's brother Jérôme and of his second wife (1807), Princess Frédérique of Württemberg; born at Trieste, 9 September 1822, two years after the birth of his sister, Mathilde. His nickname Plom Plom or, later, Plon Plon, came perhaps from an infantile attempt to pronounce his name or perhaps from the fact that he was a plump baby. Prince Napoleon was raised at Rome by his grandmother, Laetitia Bonaparte (Madame Mère), until the involvement by his first cousins, Louis Napoleon and Napoleon Louis Bonaparte, in the Romagna insurrection of 1831 led to his expulsion from the Papal States. Thereafter he lived with his father at Florence and at Lausanne. From 1835 to 1837, Prince Napoleon studied at Geneva before spending three years (1837–1840) at the military school of Ludwigsburg in Württemberg.

In November 1835 and again during April and May 1836, Prince Napoleon and Mathilde visited their cousin Louis Napoleon at Arenenberg in Switzerland. The latter, then twenty-seven, took a liking to the thirteen-year-old Plon Plon, teaching him Latin and math. They did not meet again until the fall of 1846, although they continued to correspond. In the meantime Prince Napoleon, despite his aversion to discipline, graduated first in his class from military school but chose to resign from the general staff of the Württemberg army and to join his father at Florence, from where he traveled to Germany, Britain, and Spain, where in February 1843 he met Eugénie de Montijo, the future empress of France, at a Madrid ball. Unlike others in the family, Prince Napoleon approved of his cousin's attempts to overthrow the July Monarchy. He tried unsuccessfully to visit Louis Napoleon in prison at Ham and in the autumn of 1846 joined him for several months in England, where they became friends. In May 1847 Prince Napoleon's older brother, Jérôme, died at Florence. In September he accompanied his father, who had received permission to return temporarily to Paris.

Prince Napoleon welcomed the Revolution of 1848. Rallying to the Republic, he was elected from Corsica to the Constituent Assembly in April 1848. He sat with the moderate republicans and voted on most issues with the Right. When Louis Napoleon was elected president in December 1848, he appointed the prince's father, Jérôme (1784–1860), governor of the Invalides (23 December). At his own request, Prince Napoleon was named ambassador to Spain on 10 February 1849. En route to his post, he asserted at Bordeaux that his cousin was under the control of reactionaries and that he would run in twenty *arrondissements* in the next elections. Louis Napoleon publicly disavowed him (10 April 1849) and when a short time later the prince returned to Paris without permission, the French government, which had been requested by Queen Isabella to recall the ambassador as persona non grata, interpreted his action as a resignation. A two-year chill in relations between Prince Napoleon and Louis Napoleon followed. The prince was elected from Corsica to the Legislative Assembly in May 1849, sitting this time with the "advanced republicans." Victor Hugo would later claim that in November 1851 Prince Napoleon urged that his cousin be arrested. He was excluded from preparations for the coup d'état, which, as a republican, he disapproved, and following 2 December 1851 he retired from politics, having narrowly escaped exile. The plot against Louis Napoleon's life at Marseilles on 23 September 1852 provided, however, the occasion for a reconciliation of the two cousins.

The establishment of the Second Empire in December 1852 raised Prince Napoleon and his father (Prince Jérôme) to an eminence they did not refuse. The former was designated *prince français*, appointed by right to the Senate and Conseil d'Etat, and named grand cross of the Legion of Honor and general of division. The question of the succession raised difficulties, however, which in November 1852 led to Prince Jérôme's resignation as president of the Senate (he had been appointed 18 January 1852). On 18 December 1852, Napoleon III by decree fixed the succession (failing a direct or adoptive male issue of his own) in the male line of Prince Jérôme. Nevertheless, in the first great crisis of the regime, the Crimean War, Prince Napoleon proved something less than a pillar of support. Having shown real administrative ability in supervising preparations for the Paris international exposition of 1855, the prince coveted command of the French field army in the war. Named instead to command a division, he left Marseilles on 10 April 1854 and served bravely and well in the Crimea at the battles of the Alma and Inkerman. But Prince Napoleon had opposed the Crimean campaign as being favorable primarily to British interests and had argued for a war to liberate Poland. He was also critical of the French dispositions around Sebastopol. On sick leave for dysentery, he insisted, against Napoleon III's advice, on returning to Paris, where he arrived 10 February 1855, to give the emperor a ''true account'' of events. As a result, his enemies were able to accuse him of cowardice and to circulate a new nickname—''Craint Plomb.'' Prince Napoleon was also unjustly accused of publishing at Brussels a brochure critical of the Crimean campaign. The birth of the prince imperial on 16 March 1856 was another blow. The prince, who was a witness to the birth, seems to have taken the event very badly. He had been among those who had opposed Louis Napoleon's marriage to Eugénie. Now was added to her Catholicism and conservatism—both anathema to Prince Napoleon—the fact that she and her son were a bar to the throne. During 1856 and 1857, the prince sought escape in a long North Sea scientific cruise on board the *Reine Hortense* (an account by Charles-Edmond [1822–1899] was published in 1857), but he also served as emissary during the Neufchâtel crisis of 1857, traveling to Berlin to persuade King Frederick William IV to give up his claim to the duchy. In 1857 he was rewarded for his services in organizing the international exposition by appointment as a free member of the Académie des Beaux-Arts. And in the same year he paid a last visit to the most famous of his many mistresses, Rachel, the great tragedienne, then dying near Cannes. (Prince Napoleon flaunted his mistresses, including such notorious courtesans as Cora Pearl and Anna Deslions.) The year 1857 ended with yet another quarrel over the succession and with the refusal (1 February 1858) of the prince and his father, whom he dominated, to serve on the newly constituted Conseil Privé.

A new chapter opened in Prince Napoleon's life when Napoleon III decided to intervene in Italy. At Plombières in July 1858, the emperor proposed as a condition for his alliance with Sardinia against Austria the marriage of the prince to Clotilde, the teenage daughter of Sardinia's King Victor Emmanuel II. Prince Napoleon approved the marriage and also—as an enthusiastic champion of nationalities and a friend of Italy—the proposed war against Austria. In the fall of 1858, he was sent by Napoleon III to Warsaw to initiate the negotiations that culminated in a secret Franco-Russian alliance of 3 March 1859. On 24 June 1858, the prince, as agreed during the regency discussions of the previous year, had accepted the newly created post of minister for Algeria and the colonies, a vice-royalty plan for Algeria having failed, partly as the result of Prince Napoleon's insistence that he must spend three to four months of each year in Paris in order to treat directly with Napoleon III. Now the prince urged action in Italy on an increasingly reluctant emperor concerned with a hostile European opinion. On 13 January 1859 he left Paris for Turin; from 26 to 28 January he negotiated and signed an alliance with Sardinia; and on 30 January 1859 he married Clotilde at Turin. On 3 February Paris received the newlyweds coldly. A month later, on 8 March 1859, Prince Napoleon expressed his disapproval of Napoleon III's tactics of delay (a congress was about to be proposed and accepted) by resigning his ministry. The war came, however. The prince commanded an army corps for the defense of Tuscany and served as a diplomatic intermediary. Although disapproving the decision, he helped to secure the peace preliminaries of Villafranca 11–12 July 1859. Hurt because his troops had been left in Italy, he refused a direct command from the emperor to attend with Clotilde the victory parade in Paris on 14 August 1859.

It is possible that throughout 1860, Prince Napoleon dreamed of an Italian throne, for he was now the head of his house, Prince Jérôme having died on 24 June 1860 (from 25 January to 15 February 1861, the prince's half-brother, Jérôme, who had married an American, Elizabeth Patterson, would lose his suit in the French courts to regain his legitimacy). Instead a united Italy emerged. But it was an Italy without Rome. Prince Napoleon prided himself on his violent anti-clericalism and on his reputation as a freethinker. Thus he became through 1861 and 1862 a source of embarrassment to the regime in regard to the delicate Roman Question. On 1 March 1861, the prince in a three-hour Senate speech vigorously attacked papal temporal power and sketched a "Vatican City Plan" by which Rome could become the capital of Italy. Napoleon III, pleased that his cousin had, for the first time, defended the coup d'état, privately congratulated him, while making some reservations. But it became necessary for the minister of state, Adolphe Billault, to disassociate the government from Prince Napoleon's remarks. Another problem arose when the prince sought to be elected grand master of the Masonic Lodge, in which he took a great interest, against the incumbent, Prince Lucien Murat (1803–1878), a defender of the papal temporal power. To avoid a duel between the two men, Napoleon III twice adjourned the election scheduled for May 1861, and in January 1862 he named to the post Marshal Bernard Pierre Magnan (1791–1865), who was not even a Mason. More trouble resulted when the duc d'Aumale (1822–1897), replying to Prince Na-

poleon's Senate speech, launched a violent personal attack in a published brochure. The prince, who would have permitted the brochure to circulate (he was
overruled), rejected Napoleon III's suggestion that he go to Belgium and provoke
a duel. That summer and fall (2 June–10 October 1861), Prince Napoleon and
Clotilde spent traveling on the steam yacht *Jérôme Napoléon*. After visiting
Lisbon and the Azores, the prince arrived in the United States where the Civil
War had just begun, met President Abraham Lincoln at Washington, visited
behind the Confederate lines on a safe conduct, and traveled widely in the United
States and Canada (his sympathies were clearly with the North) before returning
to New York City on 18 September.

On 22 February 1862 Prince Napoleon spoke again in the Senate. This time
he stressed the revolutionary nature of bonapartism, called for freedom of the
press and of election, and even seemed to question the hereditary basis of the
imperial regime. He was shouted down by the normally staid senators (but later
published his speech in a widely circulated brochure), and Napoleon III immediately expressed his disapproval. The prince, in the Senate on 23 February,
''explained'' his remarks. That year, as president of the French section, he
visited the international exposition in London, having played a role in arranging
for a delegation of French workers to be sent there. The rising of the Poles
against their Russian masters in January 1863 created new tensions. On 20
February 1863 Prince Napoleon called on his cousin to intervene on behalf of
the Poles and thus to remake the map of Europe. When the prince repeated his
plea in the Senate on 18 March 1863, Billault refuted him (22 March) and was
congratulated by Napoleon III, who replied to his cousin's protest with a very
strong letter on 29 March. Perhaps at the government's request, Prince Napoleon
embarked with his wife on another long journey, this time to Italy, Egypt (where
in June he visited the Suez Canal works), and Syria (26 April–6 July 1863). He
was therefore absent from France during the elections of May 1863 and the
further reforms that followed in June.

On his return to France, Prince Napoleon once again made up the quarrel with
his eternally indulgent cousin. He was less flexible in his relations with Eugénie,
churlishly refusing to deliver the toast to her at a banquet on 15 November 1863.
Nevertheless a new task was found for him. As he had expressed disapproval
of the fact that the commission charged with publishing the correspondence of
Napoleon I (7 September 1854–December 1863) had included in the fifteen
volumes it had published certain unflattering material, the prince was named to
head a new commission, which sat from 3 February 1864 to 22 November 1869
and completed the undertaking in thirty-two volumes. During 1864 he defended
the Suez Canal Company and its project in a Senate speech. He agreed also to
Emile Ollivier's request that he be reconciled to August de Morny, but the latter
died in March 1865. Meanwhile another storm was brewing. While Prince Napoleon approved the reforms that Napoleon III had initiated in 1860, he was
always impatient for greater and more rapid progress toward a democratic Empire. At the beginning of May 1865, the emperor left for a visit to Algeria. On

15 May, Prince Napoleon, in Ajaccio, Corsica, where he had gone to dedicate a statue to Napoleon I, called for the establishment of a parliamentary regime of absolute liberty. He attacked the Bourbons and certain other royalists, renounced an Austrian alliance, praised the victory of the North in the U.S Civil War, and renewed his condemnation of papal temporal power, asserting that the time had come to "capture" Rome, the "last fortress of the Middle Ages." The prince immediately published his speech, which had not been seen by the government before its delivery. Responding to French public opinion, Napoleon III on 23 May wrote from Algiers a letter of reprimand, which he instructed Eugénie, as regent, to publish. The evening of the day that the letter appeared in the *Moniteur* (27 May), Prince Napoleon resigned all of his offices, including the vice-presidency of the Conseil Privé and the presidency of the commission, to prepare for the 1867 Paris international exposition. Although Napoleon III, in a letter written following his return to Paris, reaffirmed his personal friendship for the prince, the latter retired briefly to his Swiss property (the Chateau de Prangins on Lake Leman). He returned to Paris in December 1865 for the funeral of his republican friend, Jacques Alexandre Bixio (1808–1865), and was once again reconciled with the emperor.

This new reconciliation (June 1866) came on the eve of the war between Prussia and Austria, during which the prince was attached as an observer at the headquarters of his father-in-law, King Victor Emmanuel I of Italy (Italy was the ally of Prussia in the war). Prince Napoleon, who fully agreed with Napoleon III's policy in regard to Italy and Prussia, also agreed that Prussia's overwhelming victory at Sadowa in July 1866 required a reform of the French army. He was a member of the mixed commission that immediately, but with very limited success, attacked the problem. On 23 October 1867 the prince was accorded the honor of meeting Emperor Francis Joseph of Austria-Hungary on his arrival at Paris and received from him the Order of Saint Stephen. Touring Germany, Austria-Hungary, Rumania, and European Turkey during the first half of 1868, Prince Napoleon would take alarm at the ambitions of the North German chancellor, Otto von Bismarck, with whom he talked in Berlin. The prince was more pleased with the progress of politics in France. He had been delighted at the reform measures of January 1867 but criticized the retention of Eugène Rouher in the government. The return of French troops to Rome and the events of Mentana (November 1867) disturbed him, and he retired for several months to Prangins. The result of the elections of May 1869 (Prince Napoleon had opposed retention of official candidacy) at last opened the door to the final liberalization of the Empire, which he had long favored and which he again affirmed in a memo sent to Napoleon III immediately following the elections and in a Senate speech of August 1869 during the debate on the reform *sénatus-consulte*, which the prince did not believe went far enough. Although Rouher, the newly appointed president of the Senate, disputed Prince Napoleon's remarks, Napoleon III this time did not disavow his cousin. Prince Napoleon played an important role in the negotiations that led to the constitution of a liberal ministry by his friend

Ollivier on 2 January 1870. But, as always, the prince urged more sweeping change. On 4 March 1870 the emperor rejected a memo from his cousin proposing a true parliamentary regime. And Prince Napoleon rejected the plebiscite consequently proposed to sanction the new constitution since it would not install a fully "democratic" government. On 2 July 1870, the prince left with some friends for a cruise to the North Cape. Alarmed, however, at news of deteriorating relations between France and Prussia, he was back at Paris on 21 July, accompanied Napoleon III to Metz, and, after the initial defeats, to Châlons where, at the council of war of 17 August, he argued for a return of the emperor and the army to Paris. When this sensible expedient was rejected, Prince Napoleon reluctantly undertook (19 August) a mission to Florence to seek Italian help. But he had no illusions and on word of Sedan retired to Prangins.

An appraisal of Prince Napoleon must take into account his ambition, his ideas, and his character, while remembering that he was perhaps the most hated and calumniated man of the Second Empire. Bearing a marked resemblance to the great Napoleon, the prince coveted a historical role and lived, while awaiting his opportunity, the life of a grand prince. He was a man of considerable culture, a brilliant if sarcastic conversationalist, a ruthless critic who delighted in assembling writers, artists, and intellectuals, even those who opposed the regime. On 14 February 1860 he inaugurated a splendid town house on the avenue Montaigne, built for him from 1856 by the architect Alfred Nicolas Normand (1822–1909) in the style of a Pompeian villa (this Palais Pompéien or Villa Diomède, where the prince entertained lavishly but did not live, would be sold in March 1865 and demolished in 1891). From June 1860 he also had at his disposal the Palais Royal and, ten miles from Paris, the Chateau de Meudon, in whose gardens, originally laid out by Le Nôtre, he maintained a small zoo.

There seems no reason to doubt the sincerity of the ideas Prince Napoleon so vigorously and persistently advanced. He wanted an idealized version of Napoleon I's Consulate, a democratic, Jacobin, authoritarian, anti-clerical republic whose president (undoubtedly himself in due course) would be elected by the people and could recommend his successor to them. Saint-Simonian by propensity, an advocate of free trade, the prince desired an improvement in the workers' lot and for several years (from 1861) actively propagandized among them on his cousin's behalf through the Palais Royal Group. It was politics, however, and foreign policy that absorbed most of Prince Napoleon's energies. His Napoleonic republic would advance the cause of nationalities, liberating Poland, securing the unity of Italy, and bringing about the end of papal temporal power—thus the *bonapartisme de gauche*, which earned the prince his titles of "César déclassé," "Jérôme Egalité," or "the Red Prince." He cultivated, too, the image of a freethinker, although he was not at all an atheist, merely a violent anti-clerical, a "spiritualist," and a Gallican in the mode of Napoleon I's Concordat of 1801. More significant than the ideas, however, was the character of the man who held them. He had many admirable qualities—intelligence, culture, energy, administrative abilities, eloquence, strength of will, and both physical and political courage. He was incorruptible, devoid of sycophancy, and capable of loyalty, generosity, affection, and charm. Among his close friends were Ernest Renan, Ollivier, Maxime Du Camp (1822–1894), George Sand (who in addition to sharing his ideas liked and admired him), Edmond About, Charles Augustin Sainte-Beuve, Jacques Alexandre Bixio (1808–1865), Emile de Girardin, and Adolphe Guéroult (1810–1872), whose newspaper, *L'opinion nationale* (established September 1859), was often taken to be Prince Napoleon's voice at Paris. But the prince had far more enemies than friends, and his faults largely negated his strengths. He was essentially spoiled, a man who rejected discipline and who had never learned self-control. In Morny's words, he lacked good sense. Consequently he was impatient and impetuous, unpredictable, incapable of teamwork and perhaps even of sustained effort. His lack of tact, fits of anger, and intemperate language ensured his isolation and the futility of his efforts, and this, in turn, further embittered him, for he was always seeking a more important role, always convinced that he could save everything, suffering because he wanted to do some great thing and leave behind a name. And yet he was never disloyal to his cousin, never failed to rally to him in times of adversity, and Napoleon III throughout his reign displayed an almost unvarying indulgence toward him. It is impossible to say what kind of ruler Prince Napoleon would have been, although it is tempting to guess that the liberty he so cherished would have fared less well under him than under his cousin. But the question is certainly academic, for the prince was incapable of the political finesse that could have gained and retained power.

After Sedan Prince Napoleon proposed to join Napoleon III in captivity at Wilhelmshöhe, but the ex-emperor declined. He did go to Chislehurst in early October 1870 to offer his help to Eugénie, which was refused. Until Napoleon III's death, the prince continued to correspond with him and to plot his restoration. In January 1873 he attended his cousin's funeral. But the prince imperial chose Rouher for mentor and in his will (1879) named Prince Napoleon's eldest son, Victor, as his successor. When Victor at last accepted this charge (in May 1884), most bonapartists rallied to him, but Prince Napoleon resisted, and the movement was split. Although elected in May 1876 to the Chamber of Deputies from Ajaccio, Corsica (defeating Rouher), from 1885 the prince was a spent political force, and in 1886 he was expelled from France. By that same year, he had rallied to the Third Republic, asking only for a revision of its constitution, and no longer sought a restoration of the Empire. He died at Rome, 18 March 1891, refusing on his deathbed to see the eldest son whom he had disinherited and whose ideas were the exact opposite of his own. He left three children by Clotilde, and they are the source of the present Bonaparte pretenders: Napoleon Victor Jérôme Frédéric, born at the Palais Royal, 18 July 1862; Napoleon Louis Joseph Jérôme, born at the Château de Meudon, 16 July 1864; and Marie Laetitia Eugénie Catherine Adélaïde, born at the Palais Royal, 20 December 1866.

F. S. B. Bac, *Le Prince Napoléon* (Paris, 1932); M. C. Déjean de la Batie, "La Maison Pompéienne du Prince Napoléon, Avenue Montaigne," *GBA* 118 (1976); E.

d'Hauterive, "La mission du Prince Napoléon en Italie (1866)—lettres inédites," *RDM* 27 (May 1925), "Mission du Prince Napoléon à Varsovie (1858)," *RDM* 45 (June 1928), and ed., *Napoléon III et le Prince Napoléon: Correspondence inédite* (Paris, 1925); J. E. Jordan, "Matrimony and Machiavellianism: The Marriage of Prince Napoleon," *PAPS* (20 August 1971), and "Prince Napoleon Bonaparte and the Unification of Italy" (Ph.D. diss., University of California, Berkeley, 1965); Prince Napoleon, "Les préliminaires de la paix, 11 Juillet 1859: Journal de ma mission auprès de l'Empereur d'Autriche," *RDM* (August 1909); C. A. Zarur, "Prince Napoleon (Jerome) during the Second Empire" (Ph.D. diss., Georgetown University, 1965).

Related entries: ALGERIA; BAROCHE, BILLAULT; BONAPARTISM; CONSEIL PRIVE; CRIMEAN WAR; EUGENIE; FOULD; GALLICANISM; GIRARDIN; INTERNATIONAL EXPOSITIONS; ITALIAN WAR; LIBERAL EMPIRE; LOUIS NAPOLEON; MAGNE; MATHILDE; MORNY; NATIONALITIES; NEFFTZER; OLLIVIER; *OPINION NATIONALE*; PALAIS ROYAL GROUP; PERSIGNY; POLISH QUESTION; PRINCE IMPERIAL; RACHEL; REFORM; REPUBLICANISM; ROMAN QUESTION; ROUHER; SECOND EMPIRE; SENATE; VILLAFRANCA; WALEWSKI.

PRINCE PRESIDENT, the title by which Louis Napoleon Bonaparte was known as president of the Second Republic from December 1848 to December 1852. The title was used only occasionally and informally from 10 December 1848 until the coup d'état of 2 December 1851, but the constitution of January 1852 stated in its article 2, "Le gouvernement de la République Française est confié pour six ans au Prince Louis Napoléon Bonaparte, président actuel de la République."

Louis Napoleon was elected president of France 10 December 1848. Long a self-proclaimed republican, he had returned to Paris on 24 September 1848 from self-imposed exile in England to accept a seat in the Constituent Assembly to which he had been elected. Although the little man with a pronounced German accent seemed unimposing, he had a number of political advantages. These began with his name but included also his good fortune in having been outside France during the tragic June Days and the fact that prominent figures like Adolphe Thiers, having no chance themselves to gain election, found it politic to support a Bonaparte whom they hoped to control. Louis Napoleon appealed to these men as a proponent of order, to the church by his promises concerning the pope and French education, to the workers by his "socialism," to all Frenchmen by his demand for a vigorous French role in the world, and, perhaps above all, to the middle class by his nonreactionary conservatism. He received 5,534,520 votes to 1,442,302 for his only real rival, the republican General Louis Eugène Cavaignac (1802–1857). On 20 December Louis Napoleon swore an oath to defend the Republic against all who would attack it illegally.

Lacking a party of his own, the new president turned of necessity to the leaders of the dynastic opposition under the July Monarchy. From the first, however, he gave evidence of a disquieting independence, and his presidency can be divided into two periods. During the first, emphasis was given to the struggle for order, an emphasis that Louis Napoleon, in a letter to his leftward-leaning cousin, Prince Napoleon, firmly supported—"à chaque jour sa tache; la sécurité d'abord; ensuite les améliorations." Fearing an uprising by the Left, the president had General Nicolas Changarnier (1793–1877) blanket Paris with troops during the night of 28–29 January 1849. The threat passed, and shortly afterward the Constituent Assembly reluctantly voted its own dissolution. Only two "parties" contested the elections of May 1849 to the Legislative Assembly: the "party of order" and the Left ("party of republican solidarity"). The moderates who had made the Republic won barely seventy seats, the Left 180, while the party of order won some five hundred. On 13 June Louis Napoleon decisively crushed an attempted uprising by the Left at Paris. "Il est temps," he declared, "que les bons se rassurent et que les méchants tremblent." The Assembly voted a new and harsher press law, gave the government the right to suspend all political clubs for a year, and declared a state of siege. Fearing revolution, the middle class sought, through the Falloux education law, to cement an alliance with the church. And yet the threat continued and was reflected in the by-elections of 10 March and 28 April 1850 in which the Left garnered two-thirds of the vote and won twenty of thirty seats. Louis Napoleon named Jules Baroche as minister of the interior, and the new minister created a commission whose purpose was to revise the electoral law. Intending to deny the vote to those whom Thiers called "the vile multitude," the commission succeeded—probably inadvertently—in disenfranchising (31 May 1850) 3 million of 10 million adult Frenchmen. A new press law of 16 July 1850 reestablished for newspapers the need to post bond and buy tax stamps and required that henceforth all articles touching on politics, philosophy, or religion be signed.

Louis Napoleon signed these measures, although without enthusiasm for the Falloux and electoral laws, but there is evidence that the events of the spring of 1850 marked a turning point in his attitude. Convinced that the Assembly would join him in repression but not in reform, he began to cultivate a personal following, and the emphasis changed subtly from a struggle for order to a struggle for control. Already, on 31 October 1849, he had reacted to opposition within his cabinet to his Roman policy by dismissing it and naming another within which appeared names that would be major ones in the government of the Second Empire: M. F. Esquirou de Parieu (1815–1893), Achille Fould, and Eugène Rouher. Significantly, the president did not designate a successor to Odilon Barrot (1791–1873) as premier but himself played that role. From October 1849 the "party of the Elysée" began to form. Bonapartist names like that of Alexandre Walewski appeared in diplomatic circles. A Bonapartist organization, the Société du Dix Décembre, flourished, and Victor Fialin Persigny conducted active propaganda (there were several bonapartist newspapers). Relations between president and Assembly steadily worsened, especially in regard to the size of the civil list. Although the Orleanist notables regarded the president with contempt, he was, in fact, a dangerous opponent. Given to conspiracy, Louis Napoleon cultivated the army, while appealing directly to public opinion through a number of visits to the provinces. On 9–10 January 1851, he threw down the gauntlet by dismissing General Changarnier from his double command of the Paris National Guard and army. This act marked the final break between Louis Napoleon and Thiers, but while Changarnier had been the champion of the Assembly, the parliamentarians were unable to do anything in his behalf other than to censure the government for its actions.

It seems probable that Louis Napoleon did not intend to destroy the Republic if it could be altered legally to accord with majority opinion. On 10 April 1851 he named a new government (including Baroche, Rouher, Fould, General Jacques Louis Randon, and Pierre Magne) designed to conciliate the Assembly and to work toward a constitutional revision that would permit the president to seek reelection in 1852. Undoubtedly this accorded with the wishes of the country, for there was widespread fear of disorder attending the election within a space of several months of both a president and a new Legislative Assembly. On 19 July the proposal was approved 446 to 270, 97 votes short of the required three-quarters majority. Louis Napoleon yielded to pressure from his entourage and reluctantly gave the signal for a coup d'état.

The coup d'état of 2 December 1851 did not at once end the Republic, of which it formally designated Louis Napoleon prince president, nor is the evidence by any means conclusive that Louis Napoleon was determined from the outset to restore the Empire. Nevertheless, the major political event of 1852, aside from the decrees of 22 January confiscating Orléans property in France, was the steady progress toward the proclamation of the Second Empire. The decisive event was undoubtedly the president's tour of central and southern France in September and October. On 2 December 1852 Louis Napoleon exchanged the title of prince president for that of Emperor Napoleon III.

A. Dansette, *Louis Napoléon à la conquête du pouvoir* (Paris, 1961); J. M. Merriman, *The Agony of the Republic: The Repression of the Left in Revolutionary France, 1848–1851* (New Haven, 1978); F. A. Simpson, *The Rise of Louis Napoleon* (London, 1925); A. J. Tudesq, *L'élection présidentielle de Louis Napoléon Bonaparte, 10 décembre 1848* (Paris, 1965), and "La légende napoléonienne en France en 1848," *RH* 243 (1957). *Related entries:* COUP D'ETAT; FALLOUX LAW; LOUIS NAPOLEON; ORLEANS DECREES; REPUBLICANISM; ROMAN QUESTION; SECOND EMPIRE; THIERS.

PRINCIPALITIES. See RUMANIAN UNITY.

PRIVY COUNCIL. See CONSEIL PRIVE.

PROUDHON, PIERRE JOSEPH (1809–1865), radical social philosopher and critic of contemporary politics; creator of the theoretical foundations of anarchism; born at Besançon, 15 January 1809, of artisan and peasant parents. Proudhon worked as a printer until middle age and then lived from his writing. Although he had some formal education, he was largely self-taught and his learning was irregular, although vast. He gained considerable notoriety through his early books, especially *Qu'est-ce que la propriété?* (1840), which made strikingly radical attacks on nearly every sort of political and economic theory.

During much of the period of the Second Republic, Proudhon edited and was the principal writer of a series of daily newspapers: *Le représentant du peuple, Le peuple,* and *La voix du peuple.* His outspoken and highly effective criticism of the government, politicians, and current political ideas gained for the papers a very wide circulation—and the animosity of the government, which repeatedly prosecuted, then suppressed each one in turn. Proudhon's journalism and his pamphlets and books gained similar attention, both popular and repressive, for him individually. He was imprisoned from 1849 to 1852 for his newspaper attacks on Louis Napoleon, president of the Republic. While in prison he continued to publish frequent radical polemics, but his condemnation did cut short other, less successful efforts, such as his service (since June 1848) in the National Assembly and his experiment with mutual financial cooperation in a ''people's bank.'' Thereafter, as a matter of principle he avoided all political activity except that accomplished with his pen. In addition to his correspondence (fourteen volumes), Proudhon published twenty-six volumes during his lifetime; twelve more were published posthumously.

Proudhon's prison works included two of particular importance, *Les confessions d'un révolutionnaire* (1849) and *Idée générale de la révolution au XIXe siècle* (1851), in which he examined France's six decades of experience with revolution and the full range of political systems advocated and tried in the period. With impressive critical and rhetorical force, he assaulted all of them as fraudulent and delusory. His most severe attacks were directed at democracy in its several variants, including those of socialism. Both critical reason and experience convinced him that none of the systems sought by others could possibly yield the benefits claimed for them. All would necessarily prove self-destructive, and all would, whatever their intentions, deny humanity the rights vital to it. Very much the child of the revolution he condemned, Proudhon carried democratic and socialist thought to their logical extremes, leading to an egalitarianism in which none could have economic or political power over another. This was anarchy, a term he was the first to use with a positive meaning, rather than that of the chaos others expected a lack of government inevitably would produce.

Having repudiated the Second Republic as a vile fraud, Proudhon scarcely regretted its overthrow by Louis Napoleon Bonaparte. While Proudhon despised the latter and had frequently attacked him in print, he initially supposed that Louis Napoleon's ''revolutionary Caesarism'' might bring some immediate and desirable benefits to the people, a hope that he gave up within a few months. Thereafter he remained an outspoken opponent of the emperor, although most of his voluminous published work was directed at other targets. Early in the Second Empire, tactical considerations caused Proudhon to support organized opposition by democrats. Later his disgust with both the Empire and the opposition caused him to reject any conventional political action (in the 1863 elections he called for abstention). In his last years, he became convinced that cleavage between the bourgeois and plebeian classes was unbridgeable, requiring social revolution by the latter acting on their own.

Proudhon's greatest work, *De la justice dans la révolution et dans l'Eglise* (3 vols., 1858), brought immediate suppression and another prison sentence, which he avoided through exile in Belgium until an amnesty permitted his return in 1862. The radical critique of the authoritarian state and church, which led to this condemnation, went beyond attack on particular institutions and beliefs. Proudhon assailed most ideas about the human condition because they abstract from life's actuality so that generalizations simplify and make regular what really is complex and varied. He believed that from such ideas comes institutional domination of humanity, by both clearly authoritarian regimes and those supposedly free. The latter require conformity to laws and administrative decisions, which may, as general rules, seem just but inevitably fail to account for the infinite variety of the human condition and will. *De la justice* tried to provide principles that would be at once certain and completely adaptable to individual circumstance: "Justice...is respect, spontaneously felt and reciprocally guaranteed, for human dignity, in whatever person and whatever circumstance it finds itself jeoparidized, and at whatever risk its defense exposes us to....Right is for each one the faculty of requiring of others respect for the human dignity in his person;—duty, the obligation for each one to respect this dignity in another." Because it was necessary, in Proudhon's judgment, to choose between justice and the church, he became a pioneer of modern French anti-clericalism.

Although often gloomy about the present and near future, Proudhon had a profound faith in the capacity of humanity to overcome natural obstacles to material and spiritual well-being, if only the dominance of man by man could be ended. Individuals freely giving their efforts to collective endeavors, for the mutual and equitable benefit of all, could accomplish everything. To this end he developed in his last books, especially *Du principe fédératif* (1863) and *De la capacité politique des classes ouvrières* (1865), a vision of a confederation of communities cooperating without anybody having imperative power and of a workers' movement that would effect its own moral transformation and that of humanity through its collective effort to complete a social revolution. He remained opposed to strikes as a method of working-class action.

On 19 January 1865 Proudhon died, just as an international workers' movement was being formed. He appears to have been influential among French workers during the Second Empire, but from the closing years of the Empire and especially after the Paris Commune, he was eclipsed by others, many of whom followed Marx in angry repudiation of Proudhon as a mere petty bourgeois. Workers' movements, especially the revolutionary syndicalism of the early twentieth century, have sometimes seemed to share much of Proudhon's vision but without his influencing them directly. Intellectuals have been more often and directly attracted to him, especially when they have become disillusioned with conven-

PUBLIC OPINION

tional views like those he attacked so resolutely. In his own day, he influenced both Alfred Darimon and Léon Gambetta.

At his best, Proudhon's critical work has few rivals in penetration, originality, or eloquence; his profound and creative humanism makes his theory an important contribution to social and moral thought. On the other hand, he was often prolix and too preoccupied with elaborating his positions in great detail. His intelligence was closely circumscribed in some directions, so that he was blind or biased in key respects, notably in his bitter anti-feminism, his somewhat xenophobic viewpoint (he opposed both German and Italian unification), and his inadequate understanding of how industrialization changed society. Most prevailing intellectual and political perspectives, especially those of Marxism and conservatism, have been hostile to his views. With such hostility and his own faults, Proudhon has often been spoken of but infrequently known or esteemed.

G. Cogniot, *Proudhon et la démagogie bonapartiste* (Paris, 1958); P. B. Crapo, "Proudhon's Conspiratorial View of Society," *JES*, 11 (September 1981); D. Guérin, *Proudhon, oui et non* (Paris, 1978); P. Hauptmann, *La philosophie sociale de P. J. Proudhon* (Grenoble, 1980); and [P. Hauptmann] *Pierre Joseph Proudhon: Sa vie et sa pensée, 1809–1849* (Paris, 1982); R. L. Hoffman, *Revolutionary Justice: The Social and Political Theory of P. J. Proudhon* (Carbondale, Ill., 1972); E. S. Hyams, *Pierre Joseph Proudhon: His Revolutionary Life* (New York, 1979); P. J. Proudhon, *Oeuvres complètes de P. J. Proudhon* (Paris, 1923–1959); L. Spear, "Pierre Joseph Proudhon and the Myth of Universal Suffrage," *Canadian Journal of History* 10 (December 1975).

Robert L. Hoffmann

Related entries: BONAPARTISM; CANDIDATURE OUVRIERE; COURBET; FIRST INTERNATIONAL; GAMBETTA; LABOR REFORM; LA RICAMARIE; POSITIVISM; REPUBLICANISM; TOLAIN.

PUBLIC MEETINGS. See COALITIONS LAW.

PUBLIC OPINION, for Napoleon III a vital political consideration to be understood, respected, and guided. Elections to the Corps Législatif were managed, and until 1861 the debates could not be published, nor could public meetings be held. Press opinion, even in democratic countries, usually is not a good reflection of general public opinion, and during the Second Empire the press was controlled and directed to a great extent. Also, in order to survive, many papers had to submit to bribery by the French government and by such foreign governments as those of Prussia, Italy, and the North and South in the U.S. Civil War. On one occasion, Hippolyte de Villemessant, the editor of *Le Figaro*, proudly exhibited to a group of friends the latest edition of his paper, saying, "Here's the best number we've ever had. Every line is bought and paid for." Many journals were frankly government papers, but even those of the Orleanist or republican opposition had to tread cautiously to avoid closure. Therefore, although Napoleon III did read the newspapers, he had no illusions about their reflection of general public opinion. Wanting always to avoid strong public opposition, he turned to a system of secret periodic reports from the prefects and the *procureurs généraux*. The prefects headed the departments and sent in quarterly and, later, monthly reports on opinion to the minister of the interior. These reports were brief, limited mostly to local affairs, and after 1865 consisted of just four-page forms to be filled in. The most important source for full, unbiased information on opinion for the emperor's use were the secret periodic reports of the *procureurs généraux* in the twenty-eight judicial districts of France. These chief prosecutors were ordered to send in unbiased secret reports to the minister of justice every three months on public opinion on all important questions and on economic conditions, especially during the cotton famine of 1861–1865. At the time of France's participation in the Austro-Sardinian War, weekly pro- cureur and prefect reports were ordered (May–July 1859) because of their im- portance. Summaries of many of the procureur reports were made for the emperor's use. In one cabinet meeting in October 1862, where a debate took place on the question of public opinion on the Roman Question, Napoleon III silenced the ministers by saying, "I also, Gentlemen, feel the pulse of France twice a day; I know her sentiments, and I shall not abandon the pope." Hence for contem- porary policy formulation and for later historical use, these voluminous procureur reports on opinion were and are very valuable.

Once asserted vaguely or clearly, what effect did public opinion have on international and national affairs? As to foreign affairs, it hastened the end of the Crimean War in 1856, delayed the beginning of the Austro-Sardinian War in 1859, was a factor behind the Villafranca armistice (1859) that brought an end to that war, prevented the French government from abandoning the pope's temporal power (1862), forced the government to protest in favor of the insurgent Poles (1863) but refused to go to their defense, held the emperor back from intervening in the Austro-Prussian War after Prussia's victory at Sadowa (1866), pressed the French government to return French troops to Rome in 1867, forced the emasculation of the urgent army reform bill (1868) down to a ridiculous mobile guard, and then, to the contrary, expressed loud and widespread demands for war against Prussia in 1870. Often public opinion did not understand the complexities of foreign affairs. It wanted sympathy to be expressed for the Poles without helping them, and by weakening the needed army bill, it caused France to lose the Franco-Prussian War into which it had propelled the Empire initially. Then opinion heaped all the blame for defeat on Napoleon III, who had urged a strong army bill. In domestic affairs, the rumbling dissatisfaction over the commercial treaty with Britain and other foreign affairs in 1859 and 1860, highlighted by the election of five opposition republicans in 1857, led to the decree of 24 November 1860, which in turn began the long period of transition from the authoritarian regime to the Liberal Empire. Undoubtedly the emperor's reading of public opinion (not least important through the elections of 1863 and 1869) contributed strongly to this result, which was given final popular approval in the plebiscite of May 1870.

M. P. Abernethy, "The French Administrative Information System: An Evaluation

Based on the Reports of the *procureurs généraux* during the Second Empire'' (Ph.D. diss., University of Texas, 1979); A. Armengaud, *L'opinion publique en France et la crise nationale allemande en 1866* (Paris, 1962); L. M. Case, ''French Opinion and Napoleon III's Decision after Sadowa,'' *POQ* 13 (Fall 1949), and *French Opinion on War and Diplomacy during the Second Empire* (Philadelphia, 1954); G. Dethan, ''Napoléon III et l'opinion française devant la question romaine, 1860–1870,'' *RST* (1957); A. Lorant, *Le compromis Austro-Hongrois et l'opinion française en 1867* (Geneva, 1971); A. Masson, ''L'opinion française et les problèmes coloniaux à la fin du Second Empire,'' *RFHO*, nos. 3–4 (1962); M. P. Renouvin, ''La presse française devant les événements et les problèmes italiens (janvier 1858–février 1861),'' *BSHM* (October–December 1961).

Lynn M. Case

Related entries: ADDRESS; ARMY REFORM; BONAPARTISM; CORPS LEGISLATIF; ELECTIONS; HOHENZOLLERN CANDIDACY; LABOR REFORM; MEXICAN EXPEDITION; PLEBISCITE; POLISH QUESTION; PREFECTS; PRESS REGIME; REFORM; ROMAN QUESTION; UNIVERSAL MANHOOD SUFFRAGE.

PUVIS DE CHAVANNES, PIERRE (1824–1898), muralist and painter of mythological, allegorical, and religious subject matter; born at Lyons, 14 December 1824. Son of a mining engineer, Puvis de Chavannes was schooled in the classics with the intention of entering the Ecole Polytechnique. He became a painter instead, studying with Henri Scheffer (1798–1861) after an uneventful trip to Italy in 1846. In 1848 he went to Italy again, then spent two weeks in Eugène Delacroix's studio, and later three months with Thomas Couture. He was less impressed with either than he was with Théodore Chassériau's frescoes in the Cour des Comptes of the Palais d'Orsay done between 1844 and 1848. The first work of Puvis accepted at the Salon of 1850 was a *Pieta* (location unknown), but his works were rejected thereafter until 1859. In the 1850s, he painted portraits, religious themes, and Oriental scenes. A pendant pair of allegories, *Concordia (La paix)* and *Bellum (La guerre)*, were shown in the Salon of 1861. Puvis won the second-class medal for the category of history painting, and *Concordia* was bought by the state and subsequently donated to the city of Amiens. Puvis donated *Bellum* so the two could remain together in the new Musée de Picardie in Amiens, and then in 1863 two more works, *Work* and *Repose*, were added. These paintings clearly show Puvis' inspiration in the lucid presentation of the themes as allegories. The works are enormous in scale and are framed by a border of flowers and allegorical devices that give them the appearance of cartoons for tapestries. The colors are pale and restricted, the figures classically posed and fixed. Puvis is aiming at the generalized and the universal rather than the particular. The compositions convey a sense of harmonious balance and serenity. They also, especially the latter two, begin to show Puvis' awareness of the flatness of walls and the intention not to create a window into deep space. Instead the figures are disposed horizontally, with the planes compressed, recalling Greek friezes or the frescoes of Piero della Francesca. The medium used, oil mixed with wax, further emphasizes this flatness with its matte finish and large, unmodulated surfaces.

Subsequently Puvis was commissioned to paint eight more works for Amiens (in 1865) and thereafter was firmly established as a painter of large, decorative projects. He also produced reduced versions of his larger mural decorations, which were shown at the international exposition of 1867. Puvis continued to receive commissions for large murals, which he treated with even greater simplification and generalization, reducing still further the color range and intensity. This can be seen in his paintings in the Panthéon depicting the life of Saint Genevieve, executed in 1874–1878 when it was still the Church of Saint Genevieve. The majestic simplicity of the scheme indicates the path Puvis was to follow for the next two decades. These classicist characteristics of clarity, serenity of mood, simplification, and synthesis were much admired by Georges Seurat and Paul Gauguin. Puvis was named to the Legion of Honor in 1867. By the end of the Second Empire, he had already laid claim to the title of the most successful decorative painter of the late nineteenth century. He died at Paris, 24 October 1898.

L. d'Argencourt et al., *Puvis de Chavannes, 1824–1898* (Ottawa, 1977); R. J. Wattenmaker, *Puvis de Chavannes and the Modern Tradition* (Toronto, 1975).

Beverley Giblon

Q

QUATRE SEPTEMBRE, overthrow of the Second Empire, 4 September 1870. On the afternoon of 1 September, recognizing the impossibility either of defending the besieged city of Sedan or of escaping from it with his army, Napoleon III ordered the raising of a white flag. The next day he met with the Prussian king, William I, and his chief minister, Otto von Bismarck, and signed the instrument of surrender. The first word of this disaster reached Paris by telegraph about 6 P.M., 2 September, and was conveyed to the regent, Empress Eugénie. The Corps Législatif met at 3:30 P.M. the following day. The chief minister, Charles Guillaume, comte de Palikao (1796–1878), adopting an optimistic tone, admitted to a defeat at Sedan but concealed its full extent. Nevertheless, Jules Favre, speaking for the Left, hinted at a forthcoming motion that would proclaim the fall (*déchéance*) of the dynasty and call for transferring power to General Louis Jules Trochu (1815–1896), the military governor of Paris. At 4:30 P.M. the Corps Législatif adjourned. Shortly after, a telegram from Napoleon III was received, confirming the events at Sedan. Meeting for over two hours immediately after, the Council of Ministers was unable to agree on a course of action beyond informing Paris of the situation and calling the Corps Législatif to convene at noon on 4 September. Thus was lost by the essentially right-wing government whatever chance might still have existed of saving the Liberal Empire by an agreement with the moderate opposition.

By the time the Council of Ministers had adjourned, crowds were gathering in various parts of the city. Unwilling to wait until the following day, the Corps Législatif assembled under its president, Eugène Schneider, at midnight. Palikao confirmed that Napoleon III was a prisoner but insisted that the government must have more time to prepare its proposals. Before the Corps Législatif could adjourn, however, Favre presented, for consideration at the next sitting, the Left's proposal that in view of the *déchéance* of the dynasty, a commission be elected by the Corps Législatif to exercise power. Only Pierre Ernest Pinard spoke to defend the Empire.

At 1:30 A.M., 4 September, Parisians learned from government placards of the events at Sedan. Meeting at 8 A.M., the Council of Ministers decided to propose that the Corps Législatif elect a five-member *conseil de régence*, presided by Palikao as lieutenant-general, which subsequently would name the ministers. At 12:30 P.M., a delegation consisting of Louis Buffet, Comte Napoleon Daru, and Charles Louis Henri Kolb-Bernard (1798–1888) urged Eugénie to relinquish her powers of regency. She replied that she would abide by the decision of her ministers. The Corps Législatif convened at 1:15 P.M. to choose among three proposals: Favre's of the previous day, the government's (with *conseil de régence* changed to *conseil de gouvernement*), and a compromise motion presented by Adolphe Thiers, proposing election by the Corps Législatif of a five-member *commission de gouvernement et de défense nationale* but also the summoning, when possible, of a constituent assembly. The three motions were referred to a single commission, and the sitting of the Corps Législatif was suspended (1:30 P.M.). The commission opted for Thiers' proposal. In the meantime, a mob had invaded the Palais Bourbon, preventing the Corps Législatif from resuming its sitting. When a formal statement of *déchéance* of the dynasty by Léon Gambetta failed to resolve the chaos, he and Favre, in order to prevent the establishment of a socialist republic, led most of the mob and part of the Corps Législatif across Paris to the Hôtel de Ville where at about 4 P.M. a republic was proclaimed. The government was to consist of the Paris deputies in the Corps Législatif, plus Gambetta, Ernest Picard, Jules Simon and, at 5 P.M., Trochu. Eugénie never forgave Trochu, whom she had come to despise, for his role, believing that he had betrayed her and the Empire.

During these events, the Senate had been meeting under the presidency of Eugène Rouher, who, when Jules Baroche opposed his proposal to lift the sitting, simply left the chamber. The Senate, which had already voted its unanimous support for the dynasty, dispersed. From afternoon a huge crowd had surrounded the Tuileries. Recognizing that the palace could not be defended without bloodshed and unwilling to initiate civil war, Eugénie yielded to the entreaties of her friends, the Austrian ambassador, Prince Richard Metternich (1829–1895), and the Italian ambassador, Chevalier Costantino Nigra (1828–1907), and of her faithful servitor, Joachim Pietri, prefect of police, and slipped away to the home of the imperial family's American dentist, Dr. Thomas W. Evans (1823–1897), where she spent the night. That evening, some two hundred deputies met in the president's quarters of the Palais Bourbon but followed Thiers' advice and adjourned without resistance at the request of the new government. The next day, while Eugénie quietly left Paris in Evans' carriage and Napoleon III arrived at Wilhelmshöhe to begin his captivity, the Corps Législatif was dissolved and the Senate abolished. Almost nineteen years after the coup d'état of 2 December 1851, the Second Empire, its army and its emperor prisoners, had been overthrown by a bloodless Paris revolution.

J. Brunet-Moret, *Le Général Trochu, 1815–1896* (Paris, 1955); R. Gossez, "Le 4 Septembre: initiatives et spontanéité" in *Actes du 76e Congrès des Sociétés Savantes, 1951* (Paris, 1952); A. Guérin, "Il y a cent ans: La fin d'un régime," *RPP* (February 1970); E. A. Jeloubovskaia [or Zhelubovskaia], *La chute du Second Empire et la naissance de la Troisième République en France*, trans. J. Champenois (Moscow, 1959); I. Loiseau,

"Bazaine et le 4 Septembre," *RDM*, 1 January 1967; J. Mercier and D. Mercier, *4 Sepembre 1870: Napoléon III quitte la scène* (Paris, 1967); E. Peyron, "Le rôle de l'Impératrice Eugénie en Septembre–Octobre 1870," *R. 1848*, 18 (1920–1921); R. Recouly, *Le 4 Septembre* (Paris, 1930); Roger L. Williams, *The French Revolution of 1870– 1871* (New York, 1969).

Related entries: EUGENIE; FAVRE; FRANCO-PRUSSIAN WAR; GAMBETTA; LIBERAL EMPIRE; OLLIVIER; SEDAN.

R

RACHEL, stage name of ELISA RACHEL FELIX (1821–1858), the greatest tragedienne of the Second Empire; born toward the end of February 1821 in a wayside inn at Munf, Switzerland. Her parents were Jewish peddlers of French citizenship. Discovered singing in the streets of Lyons, Rachel was brought to Paris in 1831, where she studied religious music and then acting. Her first stage appearance in 1833 led to coaching by the actor Isidore Samson (1793–1871), who secured her admission to the Conservatoire at the end of October 1836. She made her debut at the Gymnase in *La Vendéenne* on 24 April 1837 and was engaged at the Comédie Française, against the resistance of most of the *sociétaires*, early in 1838. Her debut (12 June 1838) was as Camille in *Horace*. She seemed destined to be ignored when the critic Jules Janin, who had already noted her Gymnase performance, effusively hailed her in the *Journal des débats* of 10 September 1838. Her career from that moment soared.

Unprepossessing in appearance, Rachel had a true if essentially indescribable genius for classical tragedy, which almost single-handedly she restored to eminence in France. Her greatest roles were of Camille in *Horace*, Emilie in *Cinna*, Hermione in *Andromaque*, Eriphile in *Iphigénie*, Aménaïde in *Tancrède*, Monime in *Mithridate*, Roxane in *Bajazet*, and, above all, Phèdre (from 1843). In the many other roles she played (including Molière comedies), her success was not as great, although she undertook plays by such contemporary authors as Delphine Gay (Mme. de Girardin, 1804–1855), Ernest Legouvé (1807–1903), Eugène Scribe, Victor Hugo, Alexandre Dumas fils, Emile Augier, François Ponsard (1814–1867), Pierre Lebrun (1785–1873), Isidore Latour de Saint-Ybars (1810–1891), Auguste Maquet (1813–1888), Jules Lacroix (1809–1887), Armand Barthet (1820–1874), Hippolyte François Marie Romand (b. 1808), August Barbier (1805–1882), and Prosper Dinaux (1795–1859). Some thirteen roles were created for her, the last being Scribe's *La czarina* (1855).

Despite her qualities of intelligence, character, vivacity, and sense of humor, Rachel was increasingly blamed for a lack of improvement and an unseemly greed for money. The first undoubtedly followed from her extreme precocity; the second led to unfortunate consequences. Certainly the actress was linked with a number of eminent, often prosperous, men of her time: Alfred de Musset

(1810–1857), the prince de Joinville (1818–1900), Louis Véron (1798–1867; director of the Opéra), Alexandre Walewski (from 1843 to 1846; she had a son by him in 1844), Emile de Girardin (in 1846 while still Walewski's mistress), Louis Napoleon Bonaparte (in Britain the summer of 1846; as president of the Second Republic, he patronized her career), Arthur Bertrand (in 1847; son of Napoleon I's companion in exile; she had a son by him), Prince Napoleon (in the autumn of 1846 and again from 1848), and François Ponsard (in 1853).

Her fame established, Rachel proved adept under the management of her father, Jacob Félix, at extorting favorable terms from the Comédie Française. Not only was she earning by 1849 in excess of 60,000 francs per year but she had also the right to an annual four- to six-months leave. Organizing her own troupe (all four of her sisters, Sarah [1819–1877], Lia [1828–1907], Rebecca [1829–1854], and Dinah [1836–1909], were actresses), she toured the provinces and abroad. In 1849, she gave seventy-nine performances in ninety days; a year's leave in 1853–1854 was spent triumphantly touring Russia (despite the mounting tensions that would soon lead to the Crimean War), where she earned 400,000 francs for herself and 100,000 for her troupe, returning to France in a state of complete exhaustion. After numerous quarrels and two resignations, she finally left the Comédie Française at the end of 1854. In the course of these episodes, Rachel lost not only her health but the support of many of her former admirers, including Janin, who in 1855 hailed the rising Italian star, Adelaide Ristori (1822–1906).

After a last Paris performance on 23 July 1855 and a defiant attendance on the arm of Prince Napoleon at a performance by Adelaide Ristori, Rachel departed for a disastrous tour of America organized by her brother, Raphaël (1825–1872). The tour was designed to emulate the recent success of Jenny Lind (1821–1887) and would have involved two hundred performances in fifteen months, each for a fee of 6,000 francs. But the Americans, without an understandng of French or an interest in classical tragedy, could not appreciate Rachel's genius, and the rigors of the climate completed the undermining of her health. After a last performance at Charleston, South Carolina, on 17 December 1855, she broke her engagement and returned to France. Her doctors sent her to Nice, then to Egypt. She returned to Le Cannet (near Cannes) and there died of tuberculosis on 3 January 1858. The Théâtre Français was closed the following day and again on the occasion of the impressive funeral at Paris 11 January. A generation after her death, Rachel would be remembered with immediacy and praised with ef-fusion. Even the career of the incomparable Sarah Bernhardt (1844–1923), which began at the Théâtre Français in 1862, could not eclipse that of perhaps the greatest French tragedienne of the nineteenth century.

R. Bailly and C. Fournier, "Rachel 'la grande,' " *RDM* n.s., no. 5 (1971); F. de Bernardy, "Une tragédienne, mère d'un petit-fils de Napoléon,"*Historia*, no. 93 (1954); B. Falk, *Rachel the Immortal* (New York, 1935); P. Hagenauer, *Rachel, princesse de théâtre et coeur passionné* (Paris, 1957); M. Pollitzer, *Trois reines de théâtre: Mlle. Mars, Marie Dorval, Rachel* (Paris, 1958); "Rachel," in *Revue d'histoire du théâtre* 10

(1958); J. Richardson, *Rachel* (London, 1956); N. Toussaint du Wast, *Rachel: Amours et tragédie* (Paris, 1980).

Related entries: AUGIER; DUMAS FILS; PRINCE NAPOLEON; SARDOU; SCRIBE; THEATER.

RADICALISM. See REPUBLICANISM.

RAILROADS, a key economic development of the Second Empire and one of the chief shaping forces of the era. The crises of 1847 and 1848 had paralyzed the development of a railroad system so painfully begun under the July Monarchy. It was one of the major achievements of the Second Empire that by 1870 the plan proposed by the law of 11 June 1842 had been completed and a sizable network of secondary lines had joined the six main lines of the system. The rapidity and efficiency of the transformation were directly related to the perception of the regime that the railroads, as instruments of public policy and of commercial and industrial expansion, should be subject primarily to administrative rather than legislative bodies. It would be a point of honor in the Liberal Empire of 1869–1870 that railroad concession become the business of the legislature, but by that time the basic work of construction and transformation had been accomplished.

From the beginning, French railway planning was characterized by the notions of state cooperation and eventual state ownership, as well as state control over the plan of the system, and safeguards. These characteristics informed and to some extent explain the policies and the success of the Second Empire in railroad building. In 1850 there were some 3,000 kilometers in exploitation, divided among twenty-eight companies; by 1870 there would be 17,500 kilometers and only six companies. At the end of 1852 6,900 kilometers had already been conceded, 2,000 of these in 1852 itself. Among the first acts of the regime had been the refloating in January 1852 of the lines that would later constitute the Paris-Lyons-Mediterranean line (P.L.M.). In fact, during the period of dictatorship, concessions long in abeyance were made with an eye to the establishment of companies large enough to be efficient but not so large as to create monopolies. The Rothschild-controlled line to the north was the earliest, healthiest, and best designed of all the great lines and served as a model for the rationalization of the system. The Compagnie du Nord was permitted to absorb several lines, as was, in March 1852, the Compagnie d'Orléans. The Compagnie de l'Est was formed in 1853, merging in 1854 with the Compagnie Strasbourg-Bâle. The fusions that resulted in the Compagnie de l'Ouest were authorized in June 1855.

There was widespread speculation and bitter rivalry. Isaac and Emile Pereire, Auguste de Morny, Paulin Talabot, and James de Rothschild competed for control of a line from Paris to the Mediterranean. (Talabot, with Rothschild support, won, besting the Pereires between 1852 and 1857.) At the beginning of 1853, Morny floated the idea of a Grand Central Railroad, and it was from the collapse of this scheme several years later that emerged a general reorganization of the system by a convention of 11 April 1857 and a law of 19 June 1857. Thus six great companies came to enjoy regional monopolies: North (Nord), East (Est), West (Ouest), PLM, Orleans, and Southern (Midi). Moreover, in return for granting leases of ninety-nine years and offering aid in the meeting of the railroads' enlarged responsibilities, the government required the building of subsidiary feeder networks and imposed *cahiers du charges* favorable to the public and to governmental traffic. Eventual return of ownership to the state was built into all concessions. The economic crisis of 1857 led to demands for a revision of these agreements. The task fell to Alfred Charles Ernest Franquet de Franqueville (1809–1876), director general of railroads, who on 25 November 1858 concluded a new series of conventions. The organizing principle was a division of all railroad lines into one of two categories, old and new. The government offered guarantees of interest to the new (secondary) lines attached to the old. Profitable old lines, however, at a certain level of profit, would be required to turn excess profit to the account of the new line and by that degree lessen the participation of the state. The state would share in profits beyond 8 percent for the old lines and 6 percent on the new. Profit sharing, however, was not foreseen before 1872, and the guarantees were not to come into effect until 1865.

The conventions, while rational in principle, constituted an accountant's nightmare. The two strongest networks, the North and the PLM, did not have to avail themselves of the state guarantees. The lines of the East and South, however, were fertile sources of conflict between government and companies. The multiplication of new lines (after the *deuxième réseau* came a *troisième*) wrecked the 1858 conventions, which were amended, modified, and extended between 1863 and 1869. The most important change was the offering of guarantees to the old networks for the purpose of modernizing practice and equipment. By 1870 the French railway system had achieved its twentieth-century pattern, closely resembling the contemporary picture since post–World War II nationalization has reduced the network of secondary lines achieved between 1870 and 1890.

On the material level, the building of the French rail network during the Second Empire was a tremendous achievement. Steadily the average of kilometers built each year increased: 593 from 1852 to 1855, 781 from 1856 to 1860, 826 from 1861 to 1865, and 844 from 1866 to 1869. By the end of 1858 the *grand réseau* was complete: 8,700 kilometers had been built of 15,000 conceded. Another 1,000 to 2,000 kilometers were planned. Then came the secondary lines and, on 12 July 1865, a law for railroads of local interest (forty concessions by 1870 for 2,100 kilometers, of which 300 were built before the end of the Empire). By 1853 Paris was linked with the German frontier. During the Crimean War, the linkage with the Mediterranean occurred. By 1859 the network had reached Italy and by 1860 Spain. Thus some 15,000 kilometers were added to the French railroad network between 1852 and 1870 at a cost to the state of about 600 million francs and to private enterprise of more than 6 billion francs.

In addition to helping with the financing and construction of the railroads, the state continued the work begun under the July Monarchy of entering into international agreements governing security regulations, identity and interchangeability of equipment, arrivals, and departures. Such conventions had been signed with Switzerland in 1845 and Bavaria in 1848 and during the Second Empire were signed with Belgium and the Netherlands, 14 December 1852; Luxembourg, 10 June 1957; Bavaria, 3 July 1857; Sardinia, 30 August 1858 and 15 November 1858; Belgium, 20 September 1860, 1 July 1863, 15 January 1866, 22 March 1869, 9 July 1869, 25 November 1869, 18 March 1870, and 11 May 1870; Italy, 7 May 1862 and 3 February 1868 (the Alpine tunnel); Prussia (and the Zollverein), 2 August 1862; and with Prussia, 18 July 1867 and 26 April 1870. Schedules were tied to marine schedules and postal service.

The consequences for Second Empire France of this prodigious railroad development were many. Speculators and investors profited, of course. Company income, which was 100 million francs in 1852, reached 800 million francs by 1869. Moreover, France replaced Britain in promoting railroad development on the Continent (except for Germany and Scandinavia). These activities, at home and abroad, were perhaps the primary stimulant for the revolution in credit and banking that occurred in France during the Second Empire. Within France the impact of the railroads and of their construction on trade, commerce, and manufacture can hardly be expressed quantitatively, although it was great. By 1869 the French railroads had 4,870 locomotives, and production exceeded domestic demand; from 1853 to 1869, the number of *wagons* increased from 41,000 to 137,000; and French production of iron rails averaged 117,000 tons per year from 1854 to 1872. Steel and iron were also needed for bridges, where wood had been replaced as a structural medium about 1858. The building of the railroads and their exploitation provided many jobs: 137,000 *cheminots* by the end of the Second Empire, earning an average 1,000 francs per year for a twelve-hour day. Internal trade and commerce was stimulated (only certain river traffic actually diminished in competition with the railroads). In 1870, French railroads carried two times more passengers and merchandise than in 1858. Transit merchandise amounted to about 306 million francs in value annually between 1847 and 1856 and was of the order of 723 million in 1864. The external commerce of France between 1847 and 1856 approximated 3.136 billion francs annually; in 1864 it was of the order of 7.329 billion.

In this transformation, the railroad had some large if not exactly definable role. Other effects are even less quantifiable. First was the success of government policy in putting all parts of the nation in touch with each other, as well as making them more easily controllable from the Parisian center (letter writing became twice as popular as it had been). Mental horizons broadened and changed (for example, popular excursions to the sea began). Not only were peasants freed from their isolation and from the danger of local food shortages, but availability of fertilizer began the transformation of agriculture. Book peddling was dealt a severe blow, but Hachette's *bibliothèques de gares* made their appearance. Liberalization of the tariff system undoubtedly was influenced by the exigencies and possibilities of railroad development. And if local fairs suffered as a consequence of railroad development, that same development made possible the great international expositions of the mid-nineteenth century. It has also been argued that the impulsion to modernization of Paris came from the fact that the railroad facilitated internal emigration and concentration. Certainly the physiognomy of Paris was shaped by the great railway stations and their surrounding equipment yards, and neighboring *quartiers* very often possessed characteristics and populations derived from the regions they served. Finally, the transformation of the great ports during the Second Empire was related to the revolution in land transport.

Only in regard to the military potential of the railroad is the French record unimpressive, for the failures of 1870 largely cancel the use made of rail facilities during the Crimean and Italian wars. Although there are still disagreements about the matter, the Saint-Simonian vision of the railroad as an instrument of social change and regeneration seems to have been realized with singular success by the regime of Napoleon III, the Saint-Simonian on horseback.

M. Blanchard, "Les grandes étapes du réseau ferroviaire française," *RDM* (1941), and "La politique ferroviaire du Second Empire," *Annales d'histoire économique et sociale* 6 (1934); R. B. Carlisle, "Les chemins de fer, les Rothschild et les Saint-Simoniens," *EcS* (July 1971); F. Caron, *Histoire de l'exploitation d'un grand réseau: La Compagnie du Chemin de Fer du Nord, 1846–1937* (Paris, 1973); F. Crouzet, "Essor, déclin, et renaissance de l'industrie française des locomotives, 1838–1914," *RHES* 55 (1977); P. Dauzet, *Le siècle des chemins de fer en France* (Paris, 1948); L. Girard, "L'affaire du chemin de fer Sète-Marseille (1861–1863)," *RHMC* (April–June 1955); A. Lefèvre, *Sous le Second Empire: Chemins de fer et politique* (Paris, 1951); H. Vincenot, "L'époque héroïque du chemin de fer," *Historia* 357 (August 1976).

Robert B. Carlisle

Related entries: ARLES-DUFOUR; BANKING; BELGIAN RAILROADS AFFAIR; COBDEN-CHEVALIER TREATY; COMPAGNIE GENERALE TRANSATLANTIQUE; CREDIT MOBILIER; ECONOMIC CRISES; GOVERNMENT FINANCE; HACHETTE; INTERNATIONAL EXPOSITIONS; MESSAGERIES IMPERIALES; MONT CENIS; PEREIRE; ROTHSCHILD; SAINT-SIMONIANISM; *SOCIETES PAR ACTIONS*; SUEZ CANAL; TALABOT.

RANDON, JACQUES LOUIS (1795–1871), marshal of France, governor of Algeria (1851–1859), and minister of war (1851 and 1859–1867); born at Grenoble, 25 March 1795, son of a merchant. Randon served in Napoleon's army, fought at Borodino and Leipzig, and reached the rank of captain. Although forced into retirement in 1815 as a bonapartist, his conscience would not allow him to support Napoleon against Louis XVIII on the former's return from Elba. In July 1830 Randon reentered the army as a cavalryman. In April 1838 he became colonel of the Second African Chasseurs. It was in Algeria that he made his reputation as an efficient and reliable officer. In March 1848 he was director of Algerian affairs at the Ministry of War. Louis Napoleon, as president of the

Second Republic after 10 December 1848, attempted to advance him, but Randon declined to lead the French expeditionary force to Rome in the spring of 1849 on the ground that he was a Protestant, and he refused appointment to the Austrian embassy, claiming a lack of training in diplomacy. Louis Napoleon named him to command the Third Division at Metz and in August 1850, during a tour of the region, promoted him to grand officer of the Legion of Honor. Randon declined to accept the Ministry of War at the beginning of January 1851 since his first duty would have been to dismiss General Nicolas Changarnier (1793–1877) from his double command of the National Guard and the Paris army, but he accepted the post on Louis Napoleon's urging a short time later (24 January 1851), Changarnier having been dismissed.

Randon might well have played the role in the coup d'état of 2 December 1851 that was to fall to General Leroy de Saint-Arnaud, but although he placed achievement of a strong government above constitutional niceties, the war minister's conscience would not allow him to commit an act of flagrant illegality. He therefore declined the soundings that were made of him and was replaced as minister of war by Saint-Arnaud in the cabinet of 26 October 1851. Randon learned of the coup only at its execution, but he accepted it and was named governor of Algeria 11 December 1851, a post he had declined previously (General Aimable Pélissier was then interim governor). In this new position, Randon was active and popular. Laghouat and Tugghutt were occupied, roads opened, *sous préfectures* and *commissariats* created (as was an Arab college and schools of practical medicine). Viaducts were built, artesian wells drilled, mines dug, forests cleared, and, on 8 April 1857, a railroad network decreed. For these achievements, Randon, who had been a senator since 31 December 1852 and grand cross of the Legion of Honor from 24 December 1853, was named marshal of France on 18 March 1856 (at the same time as Generals François Canrobert and Pierre Bosquet [1810–1861]).

In dealing with those transported to Algeria for resistance to the coup d'état or in connection with the attempt on Napoleon III's life by Felice Orsini in January 1858, Randon exercised a relative moderation. Indignant, however, at the appointment of Prince Napoleon as minister for Algeria and the colonies, he resigned his governorship in June 1858.

Randon did not play an active role in the Italian War of 1859. Rather, when Marshal Jean Baptiste Vaillant took over Randon's command (since 23 April 1859) of the Army of the Alps, Randon replaced the marshal as minister of war (5 May 1859). He was to retain that post until 20 January 1867. It was a difficult ministry, coinciding with the war in Italy and with the Mexican, Chinese, Syrian, and Indochinese expeditions. In a time of growing economic and financial problems, Randon had to find the resources for an active military policy, which included a continuing occupation of Rome and the never-ending pacification of Algeria. The minister and Napoleon III worked harmoniously together (it was Randon who introduced Victor Duruy to the emperor), although Randon was, with Pierre Magne and Alexandre Walewski, one of Empress Eugénie's "clan," and an advocate of indefinite French occupation of Rome. But Prussia's victory over Austria at Sadowa in July 1866 altered circumstances. Already in 1859, following the Italian War, Napoleon III had attempted to reform the French army. Little had been accomplished. Now the task was urgent. In replacing Randon with Marshal Adolphe Niel, the emperor was motivated by a number of considerations: Randon's age, his lack of confidence in a reserve army (shared by Marshal Vaillant), and the public perception that the minister was to blame for the lack of military preparation that had led to French humiliation after Sadowa. (Ironically, Randon was one of those in the cabinet who, following Sadowa, had favored a French show of strength along the Rhine.) There was injustice in this, compounded by the inability of the government, for political reasons, to defend Randon's record, although Napoleon III expressed his sympathy and permitted the marshal's apologia to be printed in the *Moniteur*.

Resentful and in declining health, Randon retired from public life. At the outbreak of war with Prussia in 1870, the emperor appealed to him to resume the governorship of Algeria and to cover with his prestige the necessary withdrawal of troops. But ministerial resistance and Randon's ill health prevented his performing this final service to the Empire. Following 4 September, he retired to Geneva where he died on 13 January 1871, just two weeks before the capitulation of Paris.

H. de Larègle, "Napoléon III et le Maréchal Randon: Lettres et documents inédits," *Corr.* 240 (1910); Comte J. L. C. A.Randon, ed., *Mémoires du Maréchal Randon*, 2 vols. (Paris, 1875–1877); A. Rastoul, *Le Maréchal Randon, 1795–1871, d'après ses mémoires et ses documents inédits* (Paris, 1890).

Related entries: ALGERIA; ARMY REFORM; BAZAINE; CANROBERT; CHINA EXPEDITION; INDOCHINA; ITALIAN WAR; MACMAHON; MEXICAN EXPEDITION; NIEL; PELISSIER; ROMAN QUESTION; SADOWA; SAINT-ARNAUD; SYRIAN EXPEDITION; VAILLANT.

REALISM. See CHAMPFLEURY.

RECOGNITION QUESTION (U.S. Civil War), the diplomatic issue of European recognition of the Confederate States of America during the U.S. Civil War. The question took two forms: recognition of Southern belligerent status and recognition of the Confederate States as an independent sovereign state. The Confederate States actively sought these recognitions while the United States tried to prevent them. Because of similar commercial, maritime, and political interests, France and Great Britain followed a common policy toward the Civil War. Presidents of both belligerents transformed the domestic conflict into an international one when they appealed to the law of nations in issuing proclamations establishing privateers (Confederate States, April 17, 1861) and a blockade (United States, April 19, 1861). To protect their citizens and commerce and to clarify their rights as nonbelligerents, Great Britain (May 14, 1861) and France (June 10, 1861) issued identical proclamations of neutrality, which extended recognition to the Confederate States as a de facto government with full belligerent rights. The Confederate States, considering this to be a first step toward diplomatic recognition and possible intervention in the war, accepted the acts; for the same reasons, U.S. Secretary of State William H. Seward refused to acknowledge them. Nevertheless in London and Paris, U.S. diplomats consistently demanded neutral treatment. The French government's proclamation forbade its subjects from participating in the war, limited belligerent maritime use of French ports, and prohibited enhancement in France of the fighting ability of belligerent warships. It also obligated the French government to apply its internal laws to enforce the neutrality.

The question of full diplomatic recognition reached an overt diplomatic level in 1862–1863 at the time of the two efforts by France to secure mediation of the American conflict, and for the same reasons. The culmination was the Roebuck affair (May–July 1863). Napoleon III granted an interview to John H. Roebuck, who had introduced a recognition resolution in the British Parliament. During a subsequent debate in the House of Commons, Roebuck quoted the emperor as willing to join Great Britain in recognizing the Confederate States. The Northern victories at Vicksburg and Gettysburg (July 1863) and the French occupation of Mexico City (June 1863) intervened; Roebuck's resolution never came to a vote. French foreign minister Edouard Drouyn de Lhuys, who had moderated Napoleon III's original statement and, arguing the exigencies of the Mexican expedition, had refused to communicate it to Great Britain, now had to face the U.S. reaction. Seward, secure in the recent victories, informed his representative in Paris that should Napoleon III "violate the sovereignty you represent, your functions will be suspended." This was the most delicate diplomatic moment between Washington and Paris during the war. Fortunes of the battlefields, however, precluded any further French initiative to recognize the Confederate States. The gradual French economic recovery and the development of the Mexican expedition enabled Drouyn de Lhuys to assume the initiative in American affairs. He applied a strict neutrality, using the argument of French vulnerability in Mexico to impose his policy on the emperor and on the Council of Ministers. He and Seward arrived at an unofficial neutrality in both the Mexican and Civil War affairs. Drouyn de Lhuys upheld neutrality particularly in maritime activities. When Confederate warships began to use French ports (August 1863), he restricted them by strengthening French rules (January 1864). When he received proof that the Confederate Navy, at the emperor's initiative, was building warships in Nantes and Bordeaux, he again used the Mexican situation to persuade his master (who, while not sympathetic to slavery, hoped for a Southern victory that would be compatible with his *politique des nationalités*, free his hands in Mexico, and prevent the otherwise inevitable thrust of Yankee power into Latin America) to prevent delivery of the ships (December 1863–February 1864). His success earned Seward's gratitude and at war's end the United States entered no claims against France before the Geneva Arbitration Tribunal. Moreover, Drouyn de Lhuys' policy silenced Seward's threats prompted by the recognition question during the Roebuck affair and enabled him (3 June 1865) to elicit from the U.S. secretary of state a clear promise to continue United States neutrality toward Mexico.

D. B. Carroll, *Henri Mercier and the American Civil War* (Princeton, 1971); L. M. Case and W. F. Spencer, *The United States and France: Civil War Diplomacy* (Philadelphia, 1970); C. Fohlen, "Les historiens devant la politique Américaine du Second Empire," *RHMC* 21 (January–March 1974); B. Karsky, "Les libéraux français et l'émancipation des esclaves aux Etats-Unis, 1852–1870," *RHMC* 21 (October–December 1974); J.S. Larregola, *Le gouvernement français, face à la Guerre de Sécession* (Paris, 1970); T. A. Sancton, "The Myth of French Worker Support for the North in the American Civil War," *FHS* 11 (Spring 1979).

Warren F. Spencer

Related entries: COTTON FAMINE; DROUYN DE LHUYS; MEDIATION PROPOSALS (U.S. CIVIL WAR); MEXICAN EXPEDITION; THOUVENEL.

REFORM, the process of liberalization through which Napoleon III attempted, between 1860 and 1869, to crown the edifice of the 1852 constitution. By 1858 the political mood of the Second Empire had begun to change noticeably, for many reasons. The revolution of 1848–1849 and the social crisis of 1849–1852 were now almost ten years in the past. Prosperity and economic expansion had received a serious check in the recession of 1857. Victory in the Crimean War had been followed not by European reconstruction but by a pervasive sense of malaise. The elections of 1857 revealed both a resurgence of republicanism and of worker resistance to co-optation by the regime. And yet many of the most important policies of Napoleon III (nationalities, tariff reform, public works) found more support on the Left than on the Right. Moreover, forces and contradictions within the regime from the beginning had held out the possibility of change. A dictatorship based on popular sovereignty expressed through universal manhood suffrage but without freedom of press or of association, simultaneously dependent on the masses and an elite of whom only a minority were bonapartists, was unlikely to resist change indefinitely. From the beginning Napoleon III himself speculated on crowning the edifice (restoring personal freedom once favorable conditions existed). Undoubtedly he excluded ministerial responsibility, true parliamentary government, and complete freedom of the press. In fact, as the intense if indirect post-Crimean War debate on government objectives indicated, the emperor aligned neither with the view of the conservative Catholic Right as expressed in *L'Univers* nor with those of the Left as represented by *Le siècle* but rather with the moderate policies advocated by the *Journal des débats* and the *Revue des deux mondes*. The Orsini *attentat* of 14 January 1858 offered an opportunity for tightening the regime's control. After six months, however, this approach was rejected, and Napoleon III turned to Italy and, consequently, to a policy of conciliating the Left, which included a broad amnesty and acceptance of a new republican newspaper, *L'opinion nationale* of Adolphe Guéroult (1810–1872), which supported the government's desire to liberate the Italian peninsula from Austrian control.

The Italian War of May–July 1859 contributed to further change. Although opposition, whether Right or Left, remained too weak to be a major factor, growing friction between the regime and French clerics over the Roman Question and between the bourgeoisie and the government over tariff policy in general and the Cobden-Chevalier commercial treaty of 1860 with Britain in particular combined with the emperor's need to lessen his personal isolation and to secure more effective legislative assistance as, at the beginning of 1860, he turned the main focus of his attention from foreign affairs to the complexities of economic policy. Moreover, both August de Morny and Alexandre Walewski urged reforms that would extend personal liberties and enlarge the powers of control of the Corps Législatif, while Prince Napoleon, the emperor's cousin, continued to advocate a truly democratic form of bonapartism. On 24 November 1860, with only the support of Walewski and of Prosper de Chasseloup-Laubat in the new cabinet, Napoleon III issued his first reform decree. It reestablished the annual speech from the throne at the beginning of the legislative session, permitted an address to the throne by the chambers in reply, granted to them a limited right of interpellation during preparation of the address, appointed two ministers without portfolio to join with the minister presiding the Conseil d'Etat in responding to queries made at that time and in presenting projects of law to the chambers, and promised legislation permitting publication of the debates of the Senate and Corps Législatif. A further decree of February 1861 allowed preliminary discussion of projects of law in secret session by the Corps Législatif with government commissioners participating. In addition, the Corps Législatif henceforth could consider amendments (but not vote them) even if they had been rejected by a *commission* or by the Conseil d'Etat. The year ended with a *sénatus-consulte* (December 1861) giving the Corps Législatif greater control over budgets.

If these concessions were intended to end the reform question by giving to the legislative bodies an extended power of control (procedures) without major alterations in the constitution of 1852 (structures), they failed. Perhaps the greatest single result was a revival of political life. In the elections of May 1863, which may be regarded as a plebiscite on the issue of further reform, the opposition made significant gains. Despite earlier signs of a turn to the Right ("decapitation" of the Society of St. Vincent de Paul in October 1861; the cabinet changes of October 1862), and the fact that the government had still an immense majority in the Corps Législatif, Napoleon III reacted to the electoral setback by a pronounced liberal orientation, notwithstanding the staunch opposition of such champions of authoritarianism as Adolphe Billault, Achille Fould, Jules Baroche, Victor Fialin Persigny, Eugène Rouher, and Pierre Magne. Persigny was dismissed as minister of the interior and, in effect, from politics. Armand Béhic was appointed minister of public works and Victory Duruy minister of education. The minister of state (first Billault and then, on Billault's death a few months later, Rouher) was charged by decree of 23 June 1863 with sole responsibility (assisted by the minister presiding the Conseil d'Etat) for representing the government before the chambers.

These were the last political reforms to be enacted for three years, although the government's liberal economic policies were vigorously developed, and the coalitions law of May 1864 (part of Napoleon III's effort to woo the workers) constituted a first step toward establishing the right to strike. At meetings of 9 November 1865 and 7 and 11 March 1866, the Conseil Privé and the Council of Ministers rejected efforts to secure a reintroduction of interpellation and a more liberal press law. That same month, however, the Tiers Parti's proposal to amend the address in order to call for further reform received 63 votes in the Corps Législatif, while Persigny, in the Senate, also called for further change. The emperor, who had shown a more flexible attitude than his ministers, decided, following another combined meeting of the Conseil Privé and the Council of Ministers on 4 July, that there should be further procedural reform. A *sénatus-consulte* of 18 July 1866 allowed the Corps Législatif to sit as long as it wished and extended its right of amendment.

Although the *sénatus-consulte* of July 1866 declared discussion of the constitution (except by the Senate) to be at an end (in May 1865 the emperor had firmly repudiated the theory publicly advanced by Prince Napoleon of progress toward liberty through dictatorship), many factors continued to favor reform. As a legislative device and especially as a substitute for interpellation, the address had proved inadequate. Economic conditions worsened after 1862, the year in which former prefect of police Pierre Marie Pietri startled opinion by advocating in a Senate speech the restoration of individual liberties and of freedom of the press and the withdrawal of French troops from Rome. Foreign policy reverses continued: Mexico, Rome, Poland, and, above all, Sadowa. At the same time that these developments encouraged a movement to bring the emperor under control, the political system of the authoritarian Empire disintegrated. Adolphe Thiers, elected to the Corps Législatif in 1863, emerged as a political force or at least as a serious nuisance to the regime, while the Tiers Parti continued its demand for a "liberal Empire" of legislative control and full personal liberty. Fearing union between liberals and Orleanists, Georges Haussmann and Persigny now joined with Walewski in urging further reform. Napoleon III hesitated and failed to reach agreement with Emile Ollivier in the early winter of 1867. But he had seemed to countenance the Tiers Parti and, although still fearing loss of power to control events, published on 20 January 1867, against the advice of his ministers, the decree that was intended to crown the edifice definitively and thus end France's *apprentissage de la liberté* by restoring all liberties compatible with the 1852 constitution. The address was suppressed and interpellation reintroduced in the Corps Législatif and the Senate. In March, the Senate was also granted the right to request reconsideration of a bill by the Corps Législatif. Moreover, laws were promised restoring freedom of press and of public assembly.

This was indeed as far as the constitution could be changed without altering its fundamental nature. Arguably, the momentum was now so great that reform of the authoritarian Empire must have yielded to creation of a Liberal Empire. Specific events were to contribute to this result, however, and ensure the failure of reform to save the constitution of 1852: the dramatic decline in Napoleon III's health from the summer of 1865; continued economic and foreign policy reverses; the rebirth of a revolutionary movement; the dearth of new men; the policies of Rouher, increasingly dedicated to preserving all that could be saved of the authoritarian regime; the influence of Empress Eugénie; and, especially, the delay in enacting the promised laws on the press and public assembly (it required the best efforts of Walewski, Charles Jean, marquis de La Valette, and Eugène Schneider to persuade the emperor to persevere against his own doubts and the clamor of the authoritarian Right). Moreover, the relative freeing of the press and of public opinion that resulted from these laws contributed to the outcome of the elections of 1869 and to the political situation from which emerged, between May 1869 and May 1870, the Liberal Empire.

F. Choiseul, "La presse française face aux réformes de 1860," *RHMC* 27 (July-September 1980); J. Dülffer, "Vom autoritären zum liberalen Bonapartismus: Der politische Systemwechsel in Frankreich, 1858–1860," *HZ* 230 (June 1980); G. Dupuigrenet-Desroussilles, "La portée des mesures de libéralisation prises en 1860," *EcS* 4 (1970); Roger L. Williams, *The French Revolution of 1870–1871* (New York, 1969); T. Zeldin, *The Political System of Napoleon III* (New York, 1958), and *Emile Ollivier and the Liberal Empire of Napoleon III* (New York, 1963).

Related entries: ADDRESS; AUTHORITARIAN EMPIRE; BONAPARTISM; COALITIONS LAW; CONSTITUTION; CORPS LÉGISLATIF; CROWNING THE EDIFICE; DURUY; ELECTIONS; FOULD; LABOR REFORM; LIBERAL EMPIRE; LIBERALISM; MINISTER OF STATE; MORNY; PRINCE NAPOLEON; OLLIVIER; ORLEANISM; PERSIGNY; PLEBISCITE; PRESS REGIME; REPUBLICANISM; ROUHER; SENATE; THIERS; TIERS PARTI; WALEWSKI.

REGENCY. See CONSEIL PRIVE.

RENAN, ERNEST (1823–1892), historian, Hebrew scholar, philologist, critic, moralist, and hagiographer of science; born at Tréguier in Brittany on 28 February 1823, the last of three children in a grocer's family. After his father's death in 1828 by drowning (which may have been suicide) Renan was raised by his mother's relatives and became very close to his sister Henriette. In spite of the semipoverty of his family, he was educated for the priesthood, entering the Saint Sulpice seminary at Paris in 1845. At the age of twenty-two, Renan had fulfilled his mother's dream; at the age of twenty-six, he dashed that dream. In 1849, after much soul searching and with sympathetic support only from his sister, he renounced his vocation. This spiritual pilgrimage was amply recorded at the time in writings that were not published for half a century: an autobiography, *Cahiers de jeunesse* (published 1906–1907), an unfinished novel, *Ernest et Beatrix* (published in 1914), and *L'avenir de la science* (written in 1848, published in 1890).

Renan supported himself in the secular world by journalism, government employment, and writing. Securing academic certification in 1849 and the doctorate in 1852, he became a tutor at the Collège Stanislas and the Pension Crouzet at Paris in 1849, traveled to Italy for Louis Napoleon's government in 1850, and procured a minor post in the department of Oriental manuscripts at the Bibliothèque Nationale in 1851. In that same year he began his lifelong association with the *Revue des deux mondes* and, in 1853, with the *Journal des débats*. In 1856 he married Cornélie Scheffer, niece of the painter Ary Scheffer (1795–1858). That same year he was elected to the Académie des Inscriptions et Belles Lettres in place of the historian Augustin Thierry (1795–1856). Two years later, Renan was named to a national committee charged with writing a literary history of France. From this moment his many publications provided their author with a comfortable living.

Those writings had also made Renan the obvious candidate for the chair of Hebraic, Chaldean, and Syrian languages at the Collège de France, vacant since 1857. Not until 1859, however, could the government bring itself to make the appointment, fearing the outcry that would result from the Catholic party. But Renan had, in his fashion, rallied to Napoleon III. He accepted appointments and was a good friend of the emperor's cousin, Prince Napoleon. Moreover, the Italian War of 1859 brought the regime and the French clericals into conflict. That year, Renan was nominated to the vacant chair by Gustave Rouland, then minister of education. Pending confirmation, he was named to the Legion of Honor and sent on an archaeological mission to the East. His sister Henriette, who accompanied him, died during the trip.

On 23 February 1862 Renan gave his inaugural lecture at the Collège de France, on the theme of the Semitic peoples in the history of civilization. Amid considerable uproar (the majority of the students were favorable to him), the lecturer referred to Jesus as ''an incomparable man, so great that, although in our day everything should be judged from the point of view of positive science, I would not contradict those who, struck by the exceptional character of his work, would call him God.'' Four days later the course was suspended, and on 11 June 1864, following the publication (1863) of *Vie de Jésus*, in which he explicitly rejected the divinity of Christ, Renan was dismissed, an action that the new minister of education, Victor Duruy, was unable to prevent. In the name of academic freedom, Renan rejected a proffered consolation post as assistant director of the department of manuscripts in the Bibliothèque Impériale. Already marked by his widely publicized renunciation of the priesthood, Renan was now stamped as an apostate, beloved by liberals and despised by conservatives. His books were banned from public libraries as subversive, but the famous critic, Charles Augustin Sainte-Beuve, defended him in the Senate, and not only would Renan be reinstated at the Collège de France in 1871, but he would become its head in 1883.

Three main themes characterized Renan's oeuvre: science as religion, secularized history and philology of Semitic religions and Christianity, and magisterial literary commentary on contemporary French culture and politics. Renan's faith in science was central to his life, personality, and output. This faith in science lay at the core of his repudiation of the priesthood, of his skeptical yet enthusiastic temperament, and of his formal scholarship. For Renan science embraced all human intellectual inquiry—not just the natural science fields of mathematics, physics, chemistry, and biology but also, and even particularly, such areas as history, philosophy, philology, and literary criticism. Science for Renan was a moral force that compelled him to wage his lifelong crusade against the allegedly superstitious and repressive ecclesiastical establishment and that shaped his commitment to write secularized humanistic history and to educate the literate French public. From 1850 to 1870, the prime of Renan's creative life as opposed to the later period of his celebrity, he devoted himself to *Les origines du Christianisme*, of which *Vie de Jésus* was the first volume. The second, *Les Apôtres*, was published in 1866 and the third, *Saint Paul et sa mission*, in 1869. The eighth and final volume would appear in 1883. In 1869 Renan stood, without success, for election to the Corps Législatif. More liberal than his lifelong friend, Hippolyte Taine, or Sainte-Beuve, Renan was no democrat, and had he been elected he probably would have supported the Liberal Empire of Emile Ollivier.

Renan blamed France's defeat in the Franco-Prussian War of 1870 on the superiority of Prussian education, a theme he developed in *La réforme intellectuelle et morale* (1871). From 1871 to his death at Paris on 2 October 1892, Renan was cherished by all literary Frenchmen as a national treasure, an eloquent spokesman for progress and patriotism, even as he was still criticized by some for his humanistic elitism and cynicism. Among other works published by Renan during the Second Empire are *Histoire générale et système comparé des langues sémitiques* (1855), *Etudes d'histoire religieuse* (1857), and *Essais de morale et de critique* (1859).

R. M. Chadbourne, *Ernest Renan* (New York, 1968); P. Clarac, "Buloz, Renan, et la *Revue des deux mondes*," *RDM* (February 1979); A. Dansette, "Renan et le Second Empire," *Bulletin de la Société des Etudes Renaniennes*, no. 7 (1971); R. Debré, "Ernest Renan et Claude Bernard," *RDM*, no. 1 (January 1977); H. Girard and H. Moncel, *Bibliographie des oeuvres d 'Ernest Renan* (Paris, 1923); J. Onno, "Le renouveau de l'exégèse biblique en France de 1860 à 1914: Renan et les origines du modernisme," *IH* 40 (May 1978, September 1978); H. Psichari, ed., *Oeuvres complètes de Renan*, 10 vols. (Paris, 1947–1961); E. Renan, *Souvenirs d'enfance et de jeunesse*, ed. Jean Pommier (Paris, 1959); D. R. Stevenson, "Ernest Renan, Anachronism or Precursor?" *PWSFH* 1 (March 1974); H. W. Wardman, *Ernest Renan: A Critical Biography* (Paris, 1964).

David R. Stevenson

Related entries: BERNARD; BERTHELOT; DARWINISM IN FRANCE; DURUY; GALLICANISM; GOBINEAU; *JOURNAL DES DEBATS*; POSITIVISM; *REVUE DES DEUX MONDES*; TAINE.

RENOIR, PIERRE AUGUSTE (1841–1919), Impressionist painter; born at Limoges, 25 February 1841. Renoir's four-year apprenticeship from 1854 to 1858 as a porcelain painter was significant in establishing his craftsmanlike approach, his tonality based in part on the eighteenth-century colorism of François

Boucher, the importance of drawing, and the use of fine brushes to achieve delicate effects. His brief period at the Ecole des Beaux-Arts (1862) was augmented with some time in the studio of Charles Gleyre (1808–1874), where he met Frédéric Bazille (1841–1870), Claude Monet, and Alfred Sisley (1839–1899), and with copying in the Louvre, where he met Henri Fantin-Latour. His very early works, from about 1864, were portraits, and indeed it is as a figuralist that Renoir achieves renown.

As with other future Impressionists, the decade of the 1860s was a formative one in which assimilation of ideas and experimentation were the foremost goals. Renoir looked to Narcisse Diaz, Jean Baptiste Camille Corot, Gustave Courbet (whom he met in 1865), and Fantin but also to Dominique Ingres. In the summers, he painted with friends in the Forest of Fontainebleau. Some of these influences can be seen in the portrait of *Mlle Romaine Lacaux* (1864, Cleveland Museum of Art) where the delicacy of touch and color, the linear precision, simplification, and condensation of space are held in an acceptable balance. The silvery tones recall Corot, but a comparison could also be made with the *Girl in White* of James Whistler (1834–1903), which was exhibited in the Salon des Refusés. *Mother Anthony's Inn* (1866, National Museum, Stockholm), with its tangible, bulky plastic figures, makes Renoir's debt to Courbet evident, but his own refined touch tempers this with a softness that becomes more characteristic of his work in the next decades. Renoir was rejected for the Salons of 1866 and 1867 but exhibited in all others under the Empire from 1864. He also developed a taste for decorative painting (for example, for the hotel of Prince George Bibesco in 1868).

Renoir's association with Monet and Sisley encouraged him to work more out of doors and to set his figures in a landscape that retained the freshness of close observation and the direct effects of light. This new development can be seen in *Lise Holding a Parasol* (1867, Folkwang Museum, Essen, West Germany), a painting with strong affinities to Monet's *Women in the Garden*. It was admired by Emile Zola when he saw it in the Salon of 1868. *Alfred Sisley and His Wife* (1868, Wallraf-Richartz Museum, Cologne) also moves in the direction of figures integrated in a light-filled environment. The palette is brighter, and the pose and expression convey a mood of happiness, an indication of the *joie de vivre* so prevalent in Renoir's oeuvre. The close association of Monet and Renoir in 1869 was instrumental in the production of paintings by both artists of a similar scene in *La Grenouillère* (1869, National Museum, Stockholm). Again, the interest in painting out of doors, observing the motif directly and recording it with a sense of liveliness in the painterly treatment of the figures and their surroundings, is Renoir's major preoccupation. The full potential of his concerns for light, color, and large-scale figures in an outdoor setting would be realized with outstanding results in the later Impressionist works—for example, *Moulin de la Galette* (1876, Louvre, Paris), and *Luncheon of the Boating Party* (1881, Phillips Collection, Washington), the culmination of the explorations of the late 1860s. Renoir died at Cagnes Calpes-maritimes, 3 December 1919.

K. S. Champa, *Studies in Early Impressionism* (New Haven, 1973); F. Daulte, *Auguste Renoir, catalogue raisonné de l'oeuvre peint* (Lausanne, 1971); J. Maxon, *Paintings by Renoir* (Chicago, 1973); J. Rewald, *The History of Impressionism*, 4th ed. (New York, 1973).

Beverley Giblon

Related entries: DAUBIGNY; DEGAS; DIAZ DE LA PENA; MANET; MONET; PISSARRO.

REPUBLICANISM, the broad, anti-dynastic persuasion of Napoleon III's opponents on the Left. There was no definitive ideology that united the various republican factions. Republicans included socialists like Louis Blanc (1811–1882), Etienne Cabet (1788–1856), and Eugène Sue (1804–1857); revolutionaries like Auguste Blanqui (1805–1881) and Charles Delescluze (1809–1871); liberals and moderates like Jules Favre, Ernest Picard, Jules Grévy (1807–1891), and Jules Simon (1814–1896); working-class leaders like Henri Tolain; radicals like Alexandre Ledru-Rollin (1807–1874), François Raspail (1794–1878), Auguste Vacquerie (1819–1895), Gustave Tridon (1841–1871), Etienne Vacherot (1809–1897), Jules Vallès (1832–1885), Léon Gambetta, Paul Challemel-Lacour (1827–1896), and Auguste Vermorel (1841–1871); and artists, writers, and intellectuals like Emmanuel Arago (1812–1896), Pierre Leroux (1797–1871), Champfleury, Jules Claretie, Gustave Courbet, Honoré Daumier, Jules Michelet (1798–1874), Félix Nadar, Pierre Joseph Proudhon, Emile Littré, Edgar Quinet (1803–1875), Victor Schoelcher (1804–1893), Marcellin Berthelot, George Sand, Victor Hugo, and Emile Zola. What united the republicans was hostility toward imperial government and, in many instances, bitterness toward the man whose rise to power had eclipsed their political careers and ended the various political and social experiments they had attempted under the abortive Second Republic. This latter consideration was especially important for the "men of 1848" (*les vieux*) like Jules Bastide (1800–1879), Armand Barbès (1809–1870), Adolphe Crémieux (1796–1880), Ledru-Rollin, Raspail, Hippolyte Carnot (1801–1888), Louis Garnier-Pagès (1803–1878), and Michel Goudchaux (1797–1862).

A few republican deputies in the Legislative Assembly of the Second Republic attempted to resist Louis Napoleon's coup d'état of 2 December 1851, but with little success. The repressive measures that followed ended the possibility of open opposition. It was even illegal to use the word *republican*. Moreover, republicans made up the bulk of the six thousand to ten thousand who, following the coup, were imprisoned, exiled, transported, or *surveillés*. Other factors worked to limit the effectiveness of republican opposition during the first half of the Second Empire: prosperity, memories of the crisis of 1852, and the early strength and successes of Napoleon III. There were republican salons (such as that of Marie de Flavigny, comtesse d'Agoult [1805–1876], known as Daniel Stern), and republican newspapers, although at first only *Le siècle* (edited by Léonor Havin) was tolerated at Paris, and several others in the provinces. By 1857, however, *L'estafette, Le courrier de Paris, Le siècle*, and *La presse* (edited by

Auguste Nefftzer) spoke for republicanism in the capital, and in September 1859, Napoleon III permitted his friend Adolphe Guéroult (1810–1872) to found yet another republican organ, *L'opinion nationale*. But these moderate newspapers cautiously advocated philosophical republican and anti-clerical positions without directly criticizing the government.

The bar provided another base for dissenters in these early years. Republican lawyers like Jules Favre found occasional platforms for articulating political opinions while defending those subjected to government prosecution. Occasional plots, assassination attempts, or disturbances (as at Trélazé, 27 August 1855) were easily frustrated. And so republicans were largely reduced to such tactics as smuggling subversive literature into France (particularly through Lille) or turning Paris funerals into political statements, as in the case of Mme. Raspail, Félicité de Lamennais (1782–1854), Pierre Jean David d'Angers (1788–1856), Pierre Béranger (1780–1857), and General Louis Eugène Cavaignac (1802–1857). On the other hand, it was during these silent years that the new generation of republicans, the realists, worked out effective doctrinal and organizational positions.

The main thrust of republican opposition developed progressively as parliamentary life was restored. In the second half of the Empire, a number of factors contributed to a resurgence of republicanism. The return of exiled leaders under successive amnesties, economic difficulties and other reverses for the regime (notably in foreign policy), Napoleon III's physical decline, fading memories of 1852, the regime's failure to recruit widespread support from the young, the impatience of urban workers, growing French restiveness under dictatorship, and opportunities provided by the emperor's liberal policies and by his cultivation of the Left (as in the case of Guéroult) in search of support for his foreign policy encouraged the republican cause. Republican stalwarts of 1848 at first refused to stand for election to the Corps Législatif or, if elected, would not take the oath required of deputies. In 1852 Carnot and Jacques Hénon (1802–1872) refused the oath after election and were not seated. The one republican deputy, Pierre Legrand (1804–1859), rallied to the Empire. Abandoning this abstentionist position in 1857–1858, five republicans (Favre, Emile Ollivier, Alfred Darimon, Ernest Picard, and Hénon), supported by several influential left-wing Paris newspapers, thrust aside *les vieux*, were elected, and took their seats in the Corps Législatif as *les Cinq*. Although these republican deputies were to some extent quarantined, the fact remained that republicanism had won five of ten Paris seats and had garnered a strong poll at Toulouse, Marseilles, Lille, Saint-Etienne, and Angers. In 1863 the number of republican deputies increased to some seventeen (including nine of the ten Paris representatives) as the republicans swept to victory in almost all the large cities and emerged as the chief source of opposition to the Empire.

The political program of the republican deputies included liberty of the press and of association, a free electoral process, restored parliamentary authority centered in the lower house, free elementary education, and disestablishment of the Catholic church. The republicans also opposed Baron Georges Haussmann's Paris policies and called for election of the Paris and Lyons municipal councils and for revision of the colonial regime. Lip-service was given to the principle of free trade unions, but the middle-class perspective of the republican deputies was indifferent to, if not opposed to, social reform. This moderate program would find its most definitive statement in Jules Simon's *La politique radicale*, published in 1868, and in the notion of *la moindre action, la liberté totale*, which the book popularized. Although the parliamentary republicans were thus more comfortable with liberal monarchists, with whom they formed a coalition in the 1860s known as the Union Libérale, than with radicals and socialists, they remained unreconciled to the Empire (with the exception of Ollivier and Darimon) despite the policy of liberalization that Napoleon III pursued after 1863.

In more philosophical terms, republicanism during these early years was won over to anti-clericalism (the choice was often seen as between religion and justice) and to positivism (largely as a result of the efforts and influence of Emile Littré). Strong in the cities, republicans also established bases in such regions as Mediterranean Languedoc and Burgundy and in such departments as Basse-Alpes, Jura, Var, Lot-et-Garonne, Gers, Nièvre, Cher, Allier, Creuse, Gard, Hérault, Aude, Tarne, and Pyrénées-Orientales. The agents of proselytization included returning exiles, Free Masons, doctors and veterinarians, polytechnic engineers (as among the railroad workers), teachers, and workers on the Tour de France. Students were won over in large numbers. The elections of 1869 returned some thirty republicans to the Corps Législatif.

But two developments radically changed the political scene on the Left in the last years of the Second Empire: a rebirth of revolutionary violence (from 1864) and the emergence of younger republican radicals who challenged the authority as well as the romantic and spiritualist notions of their elders. The influence of Auguste Blanqui, brother of the liberal economist, Adolphe Blanqui (1798–1854), had grown steadily at the expense of Proudhon's more complex and gradualist program. Sentenced to ten years' imprisonment in May 1848, Blanqui escaped from Belle Ile prison, was rearrested, and in 1857 was transferred to Corte, Sardinia, and, in April 1859, to Mascara, Algeria (consequence of the general security law of 1858). He was freed 16 August 1859 by the general amnesty. But *le vieux*, as he was now known, was back in jail again in June 1861, sentenced to four years for organizing a secret society. He would spend almost half of his life behind prison walls. Blanqui escaped in 1865 but not before turning the prison of Sainte Pélagie into a veritable school for radicalism. Among its alumni were Vacherot, Auguste Scheurer-Kestner (1833–1899), Vermorel, Arthur Ranc (1831–1908), Tridon, and the young Georges Clemenceau (1841–1929), who, as a medical student, visited there. Intensely anti-clerical and uninterested in Marxism, Blanqui hoped through such disciples as Raoul Rigault (1846–1871) to manipulate the bourgeoisie, seize power at Paris, and exercise a dictatorship until France was ready for a fundamental revolution. From Brussels he would occasionally make his way back into France. For his some twenty-five hundred armed followers, organized into sections, he wrote in 1867–1868 a handbook on armed insurrection.

Militancy on the Left increased steadily and dramatically following the elections of 1863. In January 1864 Ernest Picard made in the Corps Législatif the first public criticism of the coup d'état; in March 1865 the *Rive gauche* published a polemic against the Empire ("Les propos de Labienus") in the guise of a review of Napoleon III's *Histoire de Jules César* by Louis Auguste Rogeard (born 1820). That same year Alphonse Peyrat (1812–1891) became director of *L'avenir national*; and at the end of 1865 republican students rioted at Paris against the expulsion of six students for their activities at a congress at Liège where the French delegation had been mostly Blanquist. In December student demonstrations forced the withdrawal from the Théâtre Français of a play by Jules and Edmond Goncourt (*Henriette Maréchale*) backed by the emperor's cousin, Princess Mathilde. In January 1866 several students and workers were jailed for singing the "Marseillaise" and shouting "Vive la République!" In November 1866 police broke up a Blanquist meeting at the Café de la Renaissance, boulevard Saint Michel, and obtained the names of six hundred thirty revolutionaries. In October 1867 there were demonstrations on the occasion of Austrian emperor Francis Joseph's visit to Paris and in November at the tomb of Cavaignac in the Montmartre Cemetery. After the institution of a more liberal press regime in 1868, extreme journals, among them *Le réveil* of Delescluze and the notorious *La lanterne* of Rochefort, openly excoriated the government, while Léon Gambetta gained political prominence by defending Delescluze against prosecution by the government for having organized a subscription to build a monument to a martyr of the coup d'état, the deputy Victor Baudin. And the 1869 elections, which sent Gambetta, Jules Ferry (1832–1893), Désiré Bancel (1822–1871), and Rochefort to the Corps Législatif, were accompanied by four days of rioting at Paris.

Not all republicans were socialists, revolutionaries, or even radicals. Not all shared such radical aims as a single-house legislature, replacement of the standing army with a citizen militia that would elect its own officers, election of judges, elimination of taxes, obligatory primary education, or Jacobin democracy (the idea, expressed in Gambetta's Belleville Manifesto, of a contract, or *mandat impératif*, binding the elected deputy to the will of his constituency). Moreover, radicals were not only divided from the socialists; they were also divided among themselves on such issues as decentralization. The elections of 1869 had not been a great triumph for them, and both Gambetta and Ferry were destined steadily to moderate their views when confronted by such absurdities as Rochefort's pledge to consult his Belleville constituents every day. In the end what the radicals had in common was—in the words of Littré—that they were working toward the complete and absolute reformation of the political order in a democratic sense (Vacherot was their principal ideologue during the Second Empire).

Toward the end of the 1860s, the International Working Men's Association (formed in 1864) extended its hand to the extreme Left. The workers would help to overthrow the Empire; the republicans in turn would help to overthrow capitalism. This bargain the parliamentary republicans rejected as they rejected the *mandat impératif*, and when Gambetta at the end of 1869 failed to favor an uprising to force an earlier convocation of the newly elected Corps Législatif than was proposed by the government, the rupture between republican deputies and socialists was complete. As 1870 began, both revolution and republicanism seemed to have been contained. The events surrounding the murder in January by Prince Pierre Bonaparte (1815–1881) of a republican journalist, Victor Noir, failed to produce the expected violence, while Emile Ollivier, motivated in part by fear of revolution, presided over the creation of a Liberal Empire. The republicans had not succeeded in taking their program effectively to provincial France or in building constituencies outside the cities. The false optimism created by their urban electoral successes in 1869 was shattered by the plebiscite of May 1870 when French voters overwhelmingly endorsed the liberalized Empire. Discouraged, the republican deputies split into two roughly equal groups. One, led by Gambetta and Grévy, with a newspaper, *La tribune*, edited by Alexandre Glais-Bizoin (1800–1877) and Eugène Pelletan (1813–1884), was the *gauche fermée*, closed to all but republicans. The other, led by Picard, whose newspaper was *L'électeur libre*, was open to all who wished to continue working for democratic reform (*gauche ouverte*). In the end, only the debacle of the Franco-Prussian War (which Gambetta had opposed and to which republican opposition to effective military reform greatly contributed) gave republicanism the opportunity that might otherwise have been indefinitely adjourned. An attempted uprising of Blanquists at La Villette failed on 14 August (Blanqui had himself returned to Paris two days earlier), but on 4 September, Gambetta and Favre, in order to prevent the establishment of a socialist republic, led in the creation of a provisional government, which in the mid-1870s would become the Third Republic. As in the case of so many other developments, the Second Empire had proved a fruitful seedbed for republicanism, which, from 1852 to 1870, became a doctrine (anti-clericalism, positivism, Gambetta's *souches nouvelles*, and Ferry's concept of public opinion), gained a following, grew in political experience, and produced the leaders (Gambetta, Favre, Ferry, Simon, Grévy, Clemenceau, and Jules Méline [1838–1925]) of the first phase of the Third Republic.

H. Allain-Targé, *La république sous l'Empire* (Paris, 1939); K. Auspitz, *The Radical Bourgeoisie: The Ligue de l'Enseignement and the Origins of the Third Republic, 1866–1885* (Cambridge, 1982); C. Becker, "[Zola] républicain sous l'Empire, *Zola et l'esprit républicain* [Colloque Limoges, 1979]," *CN* 26 (1980); A. Combes, "La Franc-maçonnerie parisienne de 1862 à 1870," *Humanisme*, no. 124 (1978); M. Dommanget, *Blanqui et l'opposition révolutionnaire à la fin du Second Empire* (Paris, 1960); A. Dupront, "Jules Ferry opposant à l'Empire: quelques traits de son idéologie républicaine," *RH* (March 1936); J. Eros, "The Positivist Generation of French Republicanism," *SR*, n.s. 3 (1955); J. Gaillard, "Gambetta et la radicalisme [1869]," *RH* 256 (1976); L. M. Greenberg, *Sisters of Liberty: Marseille, Lyon, Paris, and the Reaction to a Centralized*

State, 1868–1871 (Cambridge, Mass., 1971); P. H. Hutton, *The Cult of the Revolutionary Tradition: The Blanquistes in French Politics, 1864–1893* (Berkeley, 1981); H. C. Payne and H. Grosshans, "The Exiled Revolutionaries and the French Political Police in the 1850s," *AHR* (July 1963); M. Sorre, "Les pères du radicalisme, expression de la doctrine républicaine à la fin du Second Empire," *RFSP* (October–December 1951); I. Tchernoff, *Le parti républicain au coup d'état et sous le Second Empire* (Paris, 1906); G. Weill, *Histoire du parti républicain en France de 1814 à 1870* (Paris, 1900).

Joel S. Cleland

Related entries: AMNESTY; BAUDIN; BONAPARTISM; *CANDIDATURE OUVRIERE*; *LES CINQ*; COALITIONS LAW; CORPS LEGISLATIF; COUP D'ETAT; DARIMON; DECENTRALIZATION; ELECTIONS; FAVRE; FIRST INTERNATIONAL; GAMBETTA; *HISTOIRE DE JULES CESAR*; HUGO; LABOR REFORM; LA RICAMARIE; LIBERAL EMPIRE; NAPOLEON III: ASSASSINATION ATTEMPTS; VICTOR NOIR; OATH; OLLIVIER; *OPINION NATIONALE*; PICARD; PIETRI; PLEBISCITE; POSITIVISM; *PRESSE*; PRESS REGIME; PRINCE NAPOLEON; PROUDHON; QUATRE SEPTEMBRE; REFORM; ROCHEFORT; SAND; *SIECLE*; TOLAIN.

RESTAURANTS. See DUGLERE.

REVISION, the policy ascribed to Napoleon III of attempting to change provisions of the Treaties of 1815 that had redrawn the boundaries of Europe after the Napoleonic Wars. As pretender to the French throne, Louis Napoleon had condemned these treaties because he thought that Frenchmen saw them as a symbol of defeat, because they had been made without and against France, and because they had ignored or opposed the principle of nationalities, which Louis Napoleon believed to be an irresistible idea of the day. In March 1849, less than three months after his election as president of the Second Republic, he suggested to Britain a general European congress for the purpose of modifying and consolidating the treaties "in connexion with the necessities of the existing generation." His proposal received no response, and although on the eve of the proclamation of the Second Empire, the prince president pledged not to seek changes in the treaties by war (Bordeaux speech, October 1852), suspicion persisted that his real purpose was acquisition of territory, especially the annexation of the Rhineland to France.

Although Napoleon III undoubtedly hoped someday to regain the areas France had retained in 1814 but had lost by the Second Peace of Paris in 1815 (Nice and Savoy in the south and Saarbrucken and Saarlouis in the east), there is no convincing evidence that his ambition went further or that he intended to rely on force. Rather, it would appear that his consistent policy was to bring about through a system of alliances and through conference diplomacy a remapping of Europe that would be to France's advantage but from which its territorial gains would be modest. Before the Empire, he had remarked (in 1849) to his English friend, Lord Malmesbury (1807–1889), that "the danger to Europe lay in the absolute necessity of modifying the treaties of 1815...before a war broke out.'' When war did break out between France and Britain on one side and Russia on the other (Crimean War, 1854–1856), Napoleon III professed himself ready to accept a revolutionary conflict whose aim would be to remake the settlement of 1815, particularly concerning Poland. Revisionism of that sort was not to the liking of his British ally, and the Congress of Paris, which ended the Crimean War, could not be converted into a congress of revision.

The Treaty of Paris of 1856 did, however, make revision more practicable because it made a revisionist power of Russia. In return for support or even for hope of support in abolishing the Black Sea clauses of that treaty, Russia might be persuaded (as indeed it was in 1858–1859 in regard to Italy) to accept changes to the 1815 treaties in Western Europe. Certainly the freeing of the Italian peninsula from Austrian control and the establishment of an Italian confederation constituted for Napoleon III one of the most desirable revisions to be made to the settlement of 1815. He would have preferred such changes to be made through conference diplomacy, but he accepted war and conventional diplomacy. In 1860 France made its first territorial acquisitions (Nice and Savoy) as compensation for the creation (March 1861) of an Italian Kingdom, which excluded only Rome and Venetia.

The French emperor continued to speculate on redrawing the map of Europe, most notably, perhaps, through the famous *vol d'oiseau* on which Empress Eugénie took the Austrian ambassador, Prince Richard Metternich (1829–1895), in May 1861. In the spring of 1863, during the Polish insurrection against Russia, Napoleon III proposed to Vienna an alliance that would have restored an independent Poland and brought about other changes. At the end of that year (4 November), he invited his fellow sovereigns to a general congress for the revision of the Treaties of 1815, which had, he said, ''ceased to exist.'' Britain at once declined.

Between the failure of his general congress proposal and Prussia's victory over Austria in the war of 1866, the French emperor continued to nurture schemes for the remapping of Europe, including partition of Schleswig between Denmark and Germany along ethnic lines, the union of Venetia with the new Italian Kingdom (perhaps by arranging compensation for Austria in the form of a dynastic tie to an independent Rumania), the reorganization of Germany, and even the creation of a Scandinavian or an Iberian union. Had the congress that was proposed in May 1866 on the eve of the Austro-Prussian War met, Napoleon III quite probably would have proposed a sweeping redistribution of territory in Europe, for which Turkey would have paid the bill.

The unexpectedly decisive Prussian victory at Sadowa in July 1866 completely altered the tone and nature of French revisionism. Although Napoleon III could claim satisfaction that the Treaties of 1815 (which at Auxerre in May 1866 he had yet once again denounced) should have been destroyed in central Europe, the fact is that the disturbance of the balance of power was a far more potent fact. Henceforth revision would mean compensation. In July and August, France unsuccessfully claimed the entire Rhineland (the Saar, Landau, Mainz, the Bavarian Palatinate, the extreme western part of the Grand Duchy of Hesse, and Luxembourg). In September (La Valette Circular), the French emperor pronounced himself satisfied without territorial acquisitions. But negotiations had already begun, looking toward the purchase of Luxembourg by France from the king of Holland and the securing of French rights in regard to Belgium should appropriate circumstances arise (Benedetti Memorandum). There was question, as well, of a future Rhenish buffer state.

The sudden interposition of Germany between France and Holland in the matter of Luxembourg nearly led to war in April 1867. The crisis marks the point, perhaps, at which revision as a major aim of French foreign policy was replaced by another—preservation of the status quo. France's search for an alliance with Italy and with Austria-Hungary in 1868–1870 had, above all, the objective of placing the Treaty of Prague, which had ended the Austro-Prussian War, under a collective guarantee. The conference that met early in 1869 to deal with an insurrection on Crete against Turkish rule was embraced by Napoleon III as a precedent for invoking the European concert in order to preserve rather than to change the existing treaties and relationships. French policy had come full circle, and there is additional irony in the fact that the Franco-Prussian War, when it came in July 1870, resulted at least partly from the perception at Paris of a threat to the status quo.

P. Bernstein, "The Economic Aspect of Napoleon III's Rhine Policy," *FHS* 1 (Spring 1960), and "The Rhine Policy of Napoleon III: A New Interpretation," *Lock Haven Bulletin* 1 (1962); W. E. Echard, "Conference Diplomacy in the German Policy of Napoleon III, 1868–1869," *FHS* 4 (Spring 1966); H. Geuss, *Bismarck und Napoleon III: Ein Beitrag zur Geschichte der preussisch-französischen Beziehungen, 1851–1871* (Cologne, 1959); H. Holborn, "Onckens Werk über die Rheinpolitik Napoleons III," *HZ* 139 (1929); G. Ritter, "Bismarck und die Rheinpolitik Napoleons III," *Rheinische Vierteljahresblätter* 15–16 (1950–1951).

Related entries: ALLIANCE POLICY; BELGIAN RAILROADS AFFAIR; CONGRESS OF PARIS; CONGRESS POLICY; CRETAN REVOLT; CRIMEAN WAR; DANISH WAR; *DES IDEES NAPOLEONIENNES;* ITALIAN WAR; LUXEMBOURG CRISIS; NATIONALITIES; NICE-SAVOY; POLISH QUESTION; RUMANIAN UNITY; SADOWA; VENETIA.

REVOLUTION OF 1870. See QUATRE SEPTEMBRE.

REVUE DES DEUX MONDES, semimonthly literary-scientific-philosophical-political review founded in 1829 and acquired in 1831 by François Buloz (1803–1877) after a suspension of one year. Purely literary at first, the review expanded its scope in 1833 but always retained a strong literary flavor. The *Revue des deux mondes*, with its annual subscription price of 50 francs (relatively less than for similar publications but still high for all but the most comfortable), struggled to survive until 1848. Thereafter its policies and viewpoints ensured an adequate level of support. Never a party organ, the review was associated with Orleanism (Victor, duc de Broglie [1785–1870], was a stockholder) and often seemed to echo the *Journal des débats*. It was a staunch defender of the July Monarchy, liberalism, parliamentary government, orthodox finance, free trade, and British institutions. Although in vogue during the Second Empire, the *Revue des deux mondes* did not have a mass circulation. It sold 9,500 copies per issue in July 1858, 12,400 in August 1861, and 16,000 in March 1869. Among journalists who were its collaborators were literary critics Gustave Planche (1808–1857), Charles Augustin Sainte-Beuve, Emile Montégut (1825–1896), and Jules Janin; music critic Paul Scudo (1806–1864); Jean Lemoinne (1815–1892); Philippe Cucheval-Clarigny (1822–1895); Germain Antonin Lefevre-Pontalis (1830–1903); Lucien Anatole Prévost-Paradol; Henri Alphonse Esquiros (1812–1876; the review's correspondent in Britain from 1857); Victor de Mars (*secrétaire de rédaction* until 1866); Paulin Limayrac (1817–1868); Paul Challemel-Lacour (1827–1896; for a while *gérant*); and Jean Jacques Weiss (1827–1891).

Following the coup d'état of December 1851, the *Revue des deux mondes* undertook a policy of moderate but firm opposition to the authoritarian Empire, particularly in its fortnightly political chronicle, the *chronique de la quinzaine*. Throughout the Second Empire, this chronicle was written by Charles de Mazade (1821–1893), except for the period 31 May 1858 through 30 March 1868 when the task was undertaken by Eugène Forcade (1820–1869). The latter, a Marseillais, one-time protégé of François Guizot (1787–1874), cousin of J.L.V.A. de Forcade La Roquette, and editor in 1850 of *La patrie*, had a particular interest in financial questions (from 1856 to 1868 he was director of the Rothschilds' *La semaine financière*). He campaigned tenaciously for political liberalization. The review was saved from the censors by its moderation, the skill of its writers, and perhaps by the support it gave to such favored causes of the Empire as free trade and Italian nationalism. An important article by Prévost-Paradol on the press in Britain and France (1 January 1858) skillfully evaded attack, but another by Forcade, on 15 October 1861, treating finances and the economy, earned an *avertissement* for the journal, although the article had only stated what the government was itself to admit two weeks later. After July 1866 Forcade became a staunch advocate of military reform to counter the growing threat from Prussia. Tragically, he died insane on 8 November 1869—a victim of syphilis—and thus did not see the arrival of the Liberal Empire.

In its own day the *Revue des deux mondes*, suspected by the government, was rejected by many of the younger generation who regarded it as somewhat outmoded. Certainly the review was cautious (as revealed by the treatment accorded Charles Baudelaire from 1855 through 1857) and parsimonious toward its writers (both Planche and Scudo died in near poverty). But with its *chronique de la quinzaine* and companion yearbook (*Annuaire de la Revue des deux mondes*, 1850–1868), the *Revue des deux mondes* is today an invaluable source for a study of the Second Empire, especially since the appearance in 1875 of a general index for its annual volumes, each of which averages some one thousand pages.

Directed throughout the Second Empire by Buloz and by his sons Louis (1842–1869) and Charles (1843–1905), the *Revue des deux mondes* has continued to be published down to our own day.

G. de Broglie, *Histoire politique de la "Revue des deux mondes," de 1829 à 1979* (Paris, 1979); H. Castille, *Cent ans de vie française à la "Revue des deux mondes"* (Paris, 1929); P. Clarac "Buloz, Renan, et la *Revue des deux mondes*," *RDM* (February, 1979); S. Jeune, "Le cent cinquantenaire d'une grande dame," *Revue française d'histoire du livre* 49 (January 1980).

Related entries: BAUDELAIRE; *JOURNAL DES DEBATS*; LIBERALISM; ORLEANISM; PRESS REGIME; PREVOST-PARADOL; RENAN; SAINTE-BEUVE.

RHINE POLICY. See REVISION.

ROCHEFORT, HENRI (1830–1913), journalist, writer for vaudeville, and politician; born at Paris, 31 January 1830, of a legitimist aristocratic father and a republican mother. Rochefort's father, whose family had been ruined in the Revolution, was a well-known vaudeville author, Edmond Rochefort. The son seems to have adopted the maternal political views but was more impressed by his father's lineage. Although educated at the Collège Saint Louis, Rochefort was constrained by his family's modest finances to seek a career early in his life. At the age of twenty, he began working as a clerk in the Hôtel de Ville, where he pursued his interest in art and the restoration of paintings and devised ways to allow himself time for writing light comedies for the vaudeville stage (eighteen in all, between 1856 and 1866). He also wrote for Eugène de Mirecourt (1812–1880), a pulp journalist, and for the satirical journal, *Le charivari*. In 1858 Rochefort founded, together with Jules Vallès (1832–1885), a short-lived newspaper, *La chronique parisienne*. Promoted in 1861 to *sous-inspecteur des beaux-arts* for the city of Paris, he nevertheless resigned from the Hôtel de Ville in order to pursue a journalistic career and in 1863 followed Aurélien Scholl (1833–1902) to *Le nain jaune*. Although Rochefort also wrote for *Le soleil* and for Hippolyte Villemessant's *L'événement*, it was on that publisher's literary weekly, *Le Figaro*, that he first made his reputation in 1864. He continued to contribute to *Le Figaro* after it had become a political daily, but his attacks on the regime became so biting that Villemessant, concerned for the welfare of his newspaper, helped his younger colleague to found his own journal, *La lanterne*, a scathingly demagogic weekly sheet that was almost a pamphlet. The new paper's success was beyond all expectations, and the government, threatened by its clever barbs and irreverent style, moved against it, seizing the eleventh issue (August 1868). Rochefort, faced with accumulating fines and prison sentences, fled to Belgium, where he continued to publish *La lanterne* and attempted to smuggle it in to France.

Rochefort, in the course of his career, had provoked a number of notorious duels. The first was with a Spanish officer over an article critical of the Spanish queen. In duels with Prince Achille Murat and, later, Paul Granier de Cassagnac (1842–1904), who had objected to an attack on the legend of Joan of Arc, Rochefort was wounded. In September 1868 he seriously wounded Ernest Baroche, son of Napoleon III's minister. These incidents added to the notoriety of the fiery writer. In June 1869 Rochefort, although in exile, ran for election to the Corps Législatif and very nearly defeated the moderate republican, Jules Favre, at Paris. Fierce election riots followed his defeat. At the beginning of November, the exiled journalist boldly crossed into France to contest a by-election. Given safe conduct by the emperor, he was successful at Belleville, and a reluctant administration permitted his return to Paris to assume his political duties. Isolated on the extreme Left of the chamber, Rochefort attracted little notice as a political orator, but, committed to the Jacobin idea of a *mandat impératif* (a binding contract to carry out the will of his constituents), he organized popular meetings at Belleville and La Villette and turned to his now-famous forte, journalism. Elected editor in chief of *La Marseillaise*, which he had founded and whose sale was forbidden on the public way, he became involved in the Victor Noir affair and by the violence of his polemics provoked the government into indicting and, with the consent of the Corps Législatif, prosecuting him. Despite street demonstrations, Rochefort was tried in absentia by the new government of Emile Ollivier, convicted on 22 January 1870, arrested (7 February), and sent to the prison of Sainte-Pélagie for six months, during which time the final drama of the Second Empire was played out. He was still there on 4 September when the crowds that had toppled the Empire set him free. Rochefort championed the Communards in 1870–1871. He was arrested and sentenced to imprisonment in New Caledonia, from which he made a dramatic escape. Returning to Paris, he denounced the Third Republic, shrilly supported General Georges Boulanger (1839–1891), and excoriated Alfred Dreyfus with vicious, anti-Semitic rhetoric. His extreme positions gradually eroded his influence, and he died in relative obscurity at Aix-les-Bains in 1913. His talents had been those of a vaudevillian, but history had given him a brief moment of importance.

H. Rochefort, *Les aventures de ma vie*, 5 vols. (Paris, 1896–1898), and *Les signes du temps* (Paris, 1868); R. L. Williams, *Henri Rochefort, Prince of the Gutter Press* (New York, 1966); A. Zevaès, *Henri Rochefort, le pamphlétaire* (Paris, 1946).

Natalie Isser

Related entries: ELECTIONS; *LANTERNE*; OLLIVIER; PRESS REGIME; RE-PUBLICANISM; VICTOR NOIR AFFAIR.

ROMAN QUESTION, an ideological and diplomatic conflict that after 1815, and especially from 1849 to 1870, pitted traditional Catholic values against liberal ideas arising out of the French Revolution. Before 1852 abortive revolutions in Italy had caused both France and Austria to send military expeditions to the Papal States, bringing into conjunction for the first time great-power rivalry and conflicts arising from the collision of national and secular ideals with Roman theocracy. In response, the great powers in 1831 compiled the Reform Memorandum. By its terms, the states of the church were to be secularized, the principle of elections was to be established on papal territory, and an elective council was to be created for the management of papal finances. However, Pope Gregory XVI (1831–1846) refused to implement these reforms. Pius IX, who succeeded Gregory on 16 June 1846, seemed disposed not only to adopt the provisions of the Reform Memorandum but also to support constitutional movements and national aspirations in Italy. When, however, a revolution at Rome in November 1848 forced the pope into exile and resulted in the formation of a republican government, Pius IX turned toward a conservatism that would dominate the remaining decades of his long pontificate.

Louis Napoleon Bonaparte, elected president of the French Second Republic in December 1848, would have preferred to avoid intervening at Rome, but he could not tolerate restoration of the pope by Austria, the solution to which Pius IX inclined. When all alternatives failed and Austrian action seemed imminent, the French government decided (April 1849) to send an expeditionary force under General Nicolas Charles Victor Oudinot (1791–1863), whose premature and unsuccessful attack on Rome at the end of the month engaged the issue of French military prestige. Rome fell to French force on 1 July, but few were completely happy with the course of events. Pius IX, resenting French pressure on him to make reforms, did not return to Rome until April 1850, when he named Cardinal Giacomo Antonelli (1806–1876) as his minister of state. Louis Napoleon, whose letter of 18 August 1849 to Edgar Ney (1812–1882), calling on the pope to carry out reforms at Rome, was ignored, found himself a prisoner, unable either to withdraw or to exert a decisive influence on Piux IX. At home the French president had to balance between conservative forces, which applauded the suppression of the Roman Republic, and liberal parties, which looked askance at cooperation with theocracy.

Restored to his former absolutist authority over an extensive territory embracing the midsection of the Italian peninsula, Pius IX became an intransigent opponent of modern ideas. Liberals in France and elsewhere proposed a compromise: The pope would surrender his temporal power over his subjects and thus enhance his spiritual power. Pius IX refused, suspecting that abandonment of temporal power would bring about the loss of states of the church to the Italian nationalists. There were other proposals. Rome could become an international city, enjoying the guarantee and financial support of either the great powers or of the Catholic countries. Or the pope could become a constitutional monarch, thus retaining temporal power while sharing it with his subjects. The pope, however, rejected constitutionalism in any form. Moderate Italian liberals, such as Count Camillo Benso di Cavour and Baron Bettino Ricasoli, considered the conflict to be irresolvable. The pope refused to abandon or even to attenuate his temporal authority. The nationalists believed that the Italian state could be founded only through the unification of the several states, the abolition of the temporal power, and the acquisition of Rome as the national capital.

Napoleon III, ruler of a Catholic nation that prided itself on being the "eldest daughter of the church," but heir as well to Napoleonic Gallicanism, the secular principles of the Revolution, and the principle of nationalities, favored neo-guelphism, the so-called Giobertian solution, advanced by the abbé Gioberti in 1848. It was Gioberti's idea that Italy would become a confederate state, each historic entity in the peninsula preserving its autonomy. The capital of the con-federation would be at Rome where the pope could serve as a presidential figure without great political power but enjoying the influence his spiritual office gave him. The pope rejected this idea, as did the Sardinian government when Napoleon III proposed it again in 1856. Thereafter, Cavour opted for war against Austria as the means of separating Pius IX and the other conservative Italian princes from Austrian support. Napoleon III met Cavour secretly at Plombières in July 1858 where the two men plotted a war against Austria that would have as its objective a greatly enlarged Sardinia and an Italian confederation free of Austrian influence. Napoleon III probably would have accepted some progress toward these aims through a European conference (the Italian question had been dis-cussed at a concluding session of the Congress of Paris in April 1856), but Vienna precipitated war in May 1859 by an ultimatum to Sardinia. Although Napoleon III won several military victories, a number of factors persuaded him to end the war suddenly (armistice of Villafranca, 11 July 1859). Not least important was the fact that revolutions, encouraged by Sardinia, had broken out in the papal provinces of the Romagna and Umbria (at Perugia). By the terms of Villafranca, the population of the Romagna was to be persuaded, without force, to return to papal jurisdiction (the revolt at Perugia had been crushed). An Italian confederation was to be established under the honorary presidency of the pope. Neither Pius IX nor his rebellious subjects proved cooperative, how-ever, and at length Napoleon III, after failing once again in his effort to bring the Roman Question before a European congress (the proposed congress foun-dered in December 1859 on the publication at Paris of a government-inspired pamphlet, *Le Pape et le congrès*, calling on the pope to give up his temporal power), was constrained to accept the annexation of Romagna to Sardinia (March 1860). Pius IX's intransigent opposition to this despoliation had political reper-cussions in France where the clericals launched a pro-papal campaign through 1860 and 1861. Nevertheless Napoleon III and his new pro-Italian foreign min-ister, Edouard Thouvenel, refused to intervene on behalf of the pope, although Frenchmen like General Louis Lamoricière (1806–1865) helped to reorganize the papal army. In August 1860 the French emperor was persuaded (Chambéry interview) to allow Sardinian troops to enter the remaining papal provinces of Umbria and the Marches en route to intercept Giuseppi Garibaldi, who, having overthrown the Neapolitan government, seemed to be intent on seizing Rome. Lamoricière's army was defeated at Castelfidardo (18 September 1860), and Umbria and the Marches passed under Sardinian control.

With the pope's temporal power now restricted to Rome and its immediate hinterland, the French government tried from late 1860 to 1864 to achieve a *modus vivendi*, but the proclamation of a Kingdom of Italy (March 1861), the death of Cavour (June 1861), Pius IX's absolute inflexibility, and such incidents as Garibaldi's filibustering expedition against Rome in August 1862 (defeated by Italian forces at Aspromonte) frustrated agreement.

By the early 1860s the Roman Question had seriously divided French politics. Against the more numerous Italianissimes (Victor Fialin Persigny, Prince Napoleon, Vincent Benedetti, Thouvenel, Charles Jean de La Valette, Achille Fould, Auguste de Morny, and Jules Baroche) were aligned the defenders of the pope, notably Empress Eugénie, Alexandre Walewski, and Eugène Rouher (from 1867). The dismissal of Thouvenel as French foreign minister in October 1862 and his replacemnt by Edouard Drouyn de Lhuys represented a qualified triumph for the latter group. During these years, elements of concern for Catholic opinion also could be discovered in such events as French intervention in Syria, China, Japan, Mexico, and Indochina and in French sympathy for the Poles in their 1863 revolt against Russia. Napoleon III would have made the Roman Question a key agenda item for the general European congress, which he unsuccessfully proposed in November 1863. In September 1864 the Italian government, reluctantly and probably insincerely, accepted a convention with France (the September Convention) by which Italy agreed to renounce Rome as the capital of Italy in return for French withdrawal from Rome. As a mark of good faith, Italy officially adopted Florence as its capital. At Rome a force of French volunteers (the Legion of Antibes) was assembled with the unofficial blessing of Paris. But the respite was brief. Pius IX protested vehemently against the September Convention and in December 1864 issued an encyclical, *Quanta cura*, accompanied by a *Syllabus of Errors*, eighty propositions that condemned progress and modernity. Thereafter the popular reaction in Italy, directed as much against France as against the papacy, conspired to a new march on Rome. The last French troops left Italy in December 1866. In October 1867 thousands of Italian volunteers led by Garibaldi entered papal territory. When Florence failed to act, Napoleon III was forced to intervene. At Mentana on 3 November 1867, the Garibaldians were routed by papal forces supported decisively by a French expeditionary force. Thus a French garrison returned to Rome.

At the end of 1867, Napoleon III tried yet once again to submit the Roman Question to a European congress, hoping to secure a collective guarantee and financial support for a papacy shorn of its temporal power. But the Prussian chancellor, Otto von Bismarck, refused his help in resolving a problem that he recognized as a source of weakness for France. None of the great powers was eager to become involved, and a pledge made by the French minister of state, Rouher, during parliamentary debate, that Italy would never be permitted to take Rome, ended the congress negotiations (December 1867). In fact, domestic political considerations now required the French emperor to conciliate clerical opinion. Meanwhile Pius IX, expecting new assaults on Rome, built up a large military force. The Roman Question became in these final years of the Second Empire a threat to French security, helping to frustrate negotiations with Austria and Italy aimed at creating a Triple Alliance againt Prussian expansion. Ironically, at the same moment when the last vestiges of his temporal power were crumbling, Pius IX summoned a great church council to which lay representatives were not invited and contrived to have it recognize the pope's absolute spiritual authority by confirming papal infallibility *ex cathedra* in matters of faith and morals. The Vatican Council was interrupted by the outbreak of the Franco-Prussian War. Following its initial defeats, France withdrew its garrison from Rome. On 20 September 1870, Italian troops stormed the Roman walls. The pontifical forces, after a brief resistance, withdrew into the confines of the Vatican. The Roman Question entered a new phase that would last until 1929.

P. Arcari, *La Francia nell' opinione publica italiana dal 1859 al 1870* (Milan, 1940); R. E. Cameron, "Papal Finance and the Temporal Power, 1815–1871," *Church History* 26 (1957); G. Dethan, "Napoléon III et l'opinion française devant la question romaine, 1860–1870," *RST* (1957); W. E. Echard, "Louis Napoleon and the French Decision to Intervene at Rome in 1849: A New Appraisal," *CJH* 9 (December 1974); F. Engel-Janosi, "The Return of Pius IX in 1850," *Catholic Historical Review* 36 (July 1950); M. J. McDonald, "The Vicariat Proposals: A Crisis in Napoleon III's Italian Confederative Designs," in N. Barker and M. Brown, Jr., *Diplomacy in an Age of Nationalism* (The Hague, 1971); J. Maurain, *La politique ecclésiastique du Second Empire* (Paris, 1930); C. Pagani, "L'Imperatrice Eugenia e la questione di Roma," *NALSA* 205 (1921); G. Roloff, "Frankreich, Preussen und der Kirchenstaat im Jahre 1866: Eine Episode aus dem Kampfe zwischen Bismarck und Napoleon," *Forschungen zur brandenburgischen und preussischen Geschichte* 51 (1939); G. Rothan, "La France et l'Italie, 1866–1870," *RDM* 66 (November–December 1884); I. Scott, "The Diplomatic Origins of the Legion of Antibes: Instrument of Foreign Policy during the Second Empire," in N. Barker and M. Brown, Jr., eds., *Diplomacy in an Age of Nationalism* (The Hague, 1971), and *The Roman Question and the Powers, 1848–1865* (The Hague, 1970); R. Ugolino, *Cavour e Napoleone III nell' Italia centrale: Il sacificio di Perugia* (Rome, 1973); M. Vaussard, *La fin du pouvoir temporel des papes* (Paris, 1964).

Ivan Scott

Related entries: CHAMBERY; CONGRESS POLICY; DROUYN DE LHUYS; DUPANLOUP; GALLICANISM; INFALLIBILITY, DOCTRINE OF; ITALIAN CONFEDERATION; ITALIAN WAR; LA TOUR D'AUVERGNE; LA VALETTE; MENTANA; NATIONALITIES; ORLEANS, BISHOP OF; PIUS IX; PLOMBIERES; PRINCE NAPOLEON; PUBLIC OPINION; ROUHER; SAINT VINCENT DE PAUL, SOCIETY OF; SEPTEMBER CONVENTION; *SYLLABUS OF ERRORS*; THOUVENEL; TRIPLE ALLIANCE; *UNIVERS*; VATICAN COUNCIL; VENETIA; VILLAFRANCA; WALEWSKI.

ROTHSCHILD, JAMES, BARON DE (1792–1868), head of the French-based branch of the Rothschild banking family during most of the Second Empire; born at Frankfurt, 15 May 1792, youngest and last surviving son of Mayer Amshel Rothschild (1744–1812). At the beginning of the nineteenth century, these sons had dispersed to the great centers of Europe: Nathan (1777–1836) to London, James (who had been born Jakob) to Paris in 1811, Salomon (1774–

1855) to Vienna, Karl (1788–1855) to Naples, Amschel (1773–1855) alone remaining in Frankfurt. From 1811 James carved out a position of preeminence in French banking, based initially on his success in persuading the Napoleonic regime to facilitate the transfer of English gold to Wellington's Spanish army across France. In 1821 he was appointed Austrian consul at Paris and in 1822, with his brothers, granted the title baron of the Austrian Empire. Under the July Monarchy, James reigned supreme over the business of government loans and played, unlike his English counterpart, a crucial role in the financing of railways. In particular, James collaborated with Isaac and Emile Pereire in constructing the first French railway (Paris-St. Germain) and, later, the lines of the Compagnie du Chemin de Fer du Nord, which, under Rothschild control, added greatly to the family's wealth. He also had a hand in the Paris-Strasbourg and Normandy lines. During this time, Baron James held sway in Fouché's former mansion on the rue Laffitte and his wife, Betty (d. 1886), portrayed by the painter Dominique Ingres, received Honoré de Balzac, her friend and protégé Heinrich Heine (1797–1856), and Gioacchino Rossini (1792–1868) in her salon while Marie Antoine Carême fed them from her kitchens. James himself was small, brusque, gauche, ugly, spoke heavily accented French, was reputed to be extremely irritable, but nonetheless possessed an energy and charm that many of his visitors purported to find attractive. The Revolution of 1848 brought near disaster to the Paris house, which was saved by London. At the same time, James was put under police surveillance by the provisional government, which feared that his withdrawal from France would spell economic doom for the new regime.

The advent of the Second Empire marked a curious chapter in the annals of the family, of the Baron James, and of the banking practices that the Rothschilds most notably represented. James generally had been thought second only to Nathan in ability. By 1855, Nathan of London, Karl of Naples (that house was liquidated in 1863), Salomon of Vienna, and Amschel of Frankfurt having died (three of the brothers died during 1855), James found himself the last male survivor of his generation of the family and, in effect, head of the family enterprises. The Paris branch by then was the richest of the family banks, with a combined capital in 1863 of perhaps 538 million francs (888 million in 1874). James had to face the pretensions of his able and aggressive protégés, the Pereires, and the frank hostility of many in the new regime who were suspicious of Rothschild ties with the Orleanist monarchy and resentful of the well-known role they had played in the defeat of Napoleon I. In the struggle with the Pereires, James would be victorious and before his death would have consolidated his always-good relations with the emperor—a circumstance symbolized by the splendid reception at the Rothschilds' chateau at Ferrières on 16 December 1862—but these victories would be won at the expense of principle. The Rothschilds would have to embrace the kind of banking ushered in by the Pereires and recognize that private banks could not by themselves resist the pressures or meet the demands of an expanding economy best served by institutions modeled on the Crédit Mobilier, the Société Générale, or the Crédit Industriel et Commercial.

From 1848 to the coup d'état of 2 December 1851, large affairs were at a standstill. Fortunes had been lost; political uncertainty had been great. The Rothschilds supported General Louis Eugène Cavaignac (1802–1857) but acquiesced without difficulty in the change of regimes. The great business of the July Monarchy had been railroads, and their problems awaited resolution. Among the first acts of the new government in January 1852 were concessions to newly floated companies to undertake the completion of the great railroad lines. The Rothschilds' Compagnie du Nord had survived the Revolution of 1848, while the Paris-Lyons, Lyons-Avignon, and Avignon-Marseilles lines had had to suspend work. Their reorganization was the occasion of confrontation between Paulin Talabot and the Pereires, both in different ways and at different times patronized by Rothschild. The struggle over these lines may have been the source of the Pereire-Rothschild antagonism that would grow more intense as the Second Empire evolved. The Empire, on a low political level, suspected the Rothschilds and the *haute banque* of playing the Bourse against speculators in the imperial entourage. On a higher political level, the regime believed it ought to be able to generate and to control credit directly if economic stagnation was to be overcome. That view was encouraged by the Pereires, who, out of their Saint-Simonian convictions about the need for heavy industry and transport as keys to economic and social regeneration, had argued (since the 1820s) for the "democratization" of credit (making it cheaper) and the mobilizing of capital for great public projects on a scale of which only the state was capable. Their goals, they believed, would be achieved through the cooperation of capital rather than the competition of capitalists. The Pereires also viewed Europe as a kind of common market of capital, while the Rothschilds for obvious reasons favored indigenous capital appeals restricted to a very few persons (the Rothschild bank had, for example, not many more than a thousand clients). In practical terms, the Pereires' policies suggested state loans by popular subscription of small amounts and banks organized as *sociétés anonymes*, inviting the participation of small savers as well as great investors. James de Rothschild was opposed to such policies out of principle and interest. He opposed the *société anonyme*, for example, because it was, he thought, irresponsible in its anonymity. But it is also true that the firm he headed had been the regulator of credit in the July Monarchy. If James opposed a loan, it was not floated; if he resisted a railroad concession, it did not take place. State-encouraged public companies implied a restraint on the operations of a private banker and exposed him to the dangers of a publicity that throughout their history was shunned by the Rothschild firms.

These issues were joined with the founding in November 1852 of the Crédit Mobilier. Despite assurances from the emperor about the continuing importance of the Rothschilds to the regime, the banking career of James in his last sixteen years can be understood largely as a reaction to the Pereire influence and to the financial revolution they attempted to accomplish largely at Rothschild expense.

Until 1855 Rothschild would appear to acquiesce in the new state of affairs, solidifying the position and holdings of the Compagnie du Nord, concentrating on commercial matters, and leaving the field of industry to the newcomers. But in reality the strongly worded memo that Baron James sent to Napoleon III on 15 November 1852 warning him against the Crédit Mobilier scheme marked the break in relations with his former collaborators, the Pereires.

Between 1855 and 1857, the major confrontation took place. Rothschild, and his nephews abroad, successfully rivaled the Pereires' Crédit Mobilier, not only in France but in Italy, Spain, and the Austrian Empire. Cavour in 1855 was not unwilling to court influences that would lessen the position of the Rothschilds in the Sardinian kingdom; the great Austrian allies, Metternich and von Gentz, had disappeared from power; the Austrian ambassador at Paris, Count Alexandre Hübner (1811–1892), was an ally of the Pereires. Venal Spanish ministries were willing to play the groups against each other for control of mercury mines and railroad concessions. But the great shock to the Rothschild interest was the acquisition of the northern Austrian railways by the Crédit Mobilier and the proposal to create an Austrian version of that institution. By the end of 1855, however, the Pereire proposal had been rejected in favor of the creation of the Kreditanstalt engineered by the Rothschilds, who also won control of the south Austrian and northern Italian railways. Fearing the attack of the Crédit Mobilier at Rome (the papacy, while dependent on the Neapolitan branch, had resented Rothschild conditions for financial aid), foreseeing the closure of the Neapolitan branch, and suspicious of an incursion into the affairs of the Ottoman Empire, Rothschild from 1855 took decisive steps to counter the Pereire challenge. Encouraged by Paulin Talabot, he found an instrument for attack and defense in the Réunion Financière, a syndicate of traditional bankers of the Orleanist period one-quarter of whose capital was Rothschild supplied. The Réunion drafted proposals (1856) for a new bank, which met initial resistance from the government, impressed by the Pereires' contention that the end of the Crimean War would be a dangerous stimulus to economic activity that would have to be discouraged. But by 1859 the Réunion had created the Société Générale (ancestor of the present CIC). The combined forces of the syndicate controlled the iron industry, and Napoleon III further restricted the Pereires by definitively blocking their perennial request for a huge bond issue by the Crédit Mobilier. The Pereires could not hold head against the resources of the Rothschilds. By 1857 the issue had been decided. On the other hand, James de Rothschild had been forced to adopt some of the tactics of his rivals and even to emulate the Crédit Mobilier itself. Clearly the future belonged to the new banks and to the new methods, including the device, adopted by Napoleon III in 1854–1855, of placing government loans directly. Nor did the consistent Rothschild efforts to maintain peace in Europe always succeed. The Sardinian loan of 1859 went to the Pereires largely because the Rothschilds imposed harsh conditions designed to discourage war. And the efforts to arrange the peaceful purchase of Venetia in 1866 failed.

Rothschild, who married the daughter of his brother Salomon, had four sons:

Alphonse (1827–1905; a regent of the Bank of France from 1855), Gustave (1829–1911), Edmond (1845–1934), and Salomon (1835–1864). Of Austrian nationality, he nevertheless was advanced to the rank of grand cross in the Legion of Honor. Although he abandoned orthodoxy, he remained a Jew and became a great philanthropist. He guided his house through troubled years and left it incomparably rich (an estimate suggests the total family worth reached $6 billion at its height; and newspapers on the occasion of James de Rothschild's death, at Paris on 15 November 1868, put his personal fortune at 1.7 billion francs, including the great art collection assembled at Ferrières). But at the same time Baron James witnessed in the last years of his life the displacement of the traditional merchant bank by the public credit institution and of personal influence by public policy.

D. Borne, "Le premier des Rothschild," *Histoire*, 43 (1982); J. Bouvier, *Les Rothschilds* (Paris, 1960 and 1983); B. Gille, *Histoire de la Maison Rothschild, 1848–1870* (Geneva, 1967); F. Morton, *The Rothschilds: A Family Portrait* (New York, 1962); A. Muhlstein, *Baron James: The Rise of the French Rothschilds* (New York, 1983); H. Schnee, *Rothschild: Geschichter einer Finanzdynastie* (Göttingen, 1961).

Robert B. Carlisle

Related entries: BANKING; CREDIT MOBILIER; FOULD; GOVERNMENT FINANCE; MIRES; PEREIRE; PERSIGNY; RAILROADS; SCHNEIDER, E.; *SOCIETES PAR ACTIONS*; TALABOT; ECONOMIC CRISES.

LES ROUGON-MACQUART, a series of twenty novels by Emile Zola, the leading writer of the French naturalist school. Subtitled "A Natural and Social History of the Second Empire," the novels, which were planned during 1868–1869 and appeared at regular intervals between 1871 and 1893, embody the principles behind the naturalist movement. Very early in his literary career, Zola had decided to write a major work that would mirror the society of the Second Empire, as Balzac's *Comédie humaine* had done for the Restoration. With this opus already in mind, he set out to analyze the underlying laws of social evolution that would provide the framework for his series and that ultimately became the foundation of naturalist doctrine. Zola found the scientific support he sought in Hippolyte Taine's positivistic social theory, in Charles Darwin's and Ernst Haeckel's ideas of heredity, and in contemporary medical tracts. Convinced that the novel must be scientifically based—that is, that the author's duty was to present a sort of biological analysis of his society—Zola began his account of the Rougon-Macquart family, studying the effects of heredity and environment on the physical and moral evolution of his characters. Using these principles, Zola examined the family of Adélaïde Fouque, whose two husbands, a peasant, Rougon, and subsequently a drunkard, Macquart, sired the children around whom the novels are centered.

Les Rougon-Macquart is remarkable in its scope. The novels cover the period of the Second Empire from the coup d'état of December 1851 to the last days of the Commune (1871), dealing with the effect of the imperial regime across the entire social spectrum and portraying the democratic aspect of the age in the rise of some members of the family from peasant origin to the highest levels of government and finance. In the first volume, *La fortune des Rougon* (1871), Zola outlined the machinations of Adélaïde Fouque's son, Pierre Rougon, as he makes his fortune in the days immediately following the coup d'état. The novel is set in the fictitious town of Plassans (in reality, Aix-en-Province) during the last months of the Second Republic. The atmosphere is tense as republican, legitimist, and bourgeois factions (the last represented by the Rougon family) anxiously await developments in the capital and maneuver to protect their interest. Pierre suppresses a popular revolt in Plassans during the insurrections of December 1851 and thus gains his fortune, unmoved by the tragedies about him. In the second volume, *La curée* (1872), Zola turned his attention to the world of Parisian financial speculators who flourished during the early 1860s. His portrait of unscrupulous financiers, making and losing vast fortunes in the rebuilding of Paris by Baron Haussmann, is generally unsympathetic. *Le ventre de Paris* (1873) is an elaborate description of Les Halles, the great central food market of Paris constructed in the 1850s. In the novel, Zola narrates the odyssey of Florent, a political prisoner who had been unjustly condemned to exile in Guyana as a militant republican in 1851. Florent escapes from the prison colony, returns to Paris, and becomes an inspector in the fish market of Les Halles. After further involvement in idealistic and ineffectual political intrigues (1858–1859), he is finally denounced and recaptured, a metaphor perhaps of the triumph of Second Empire materialism over republican idealism. *Le ventre de Paris* was the first of the Rougon-Macquart novels to be published by Charpentier, Zola's original publisher, Lacroix, having failed.

Zola devoted the next two novels, *La conquête de Plassans* (1874) and *La faute de l'abbé Mouret* (1875), to an examination of religious themes, giving in the first a portrait of politics in a provincial town (1858–1863), in the second a sketch of religion in a poverty-stricken rural area during the late 1860s, and in both a view of the priest as at worst manipulative and at best "unnatural." With *Son Excellence Eugène Rougon* (1876), Zola returned to the world of politics, portraying imperial intrigues at the highest levels of government in the 1860s. In fact, his chief model for Eugène Rougon, minister, was probably Eugène Rouher, Napoleon III's "vice-emperor." *L'assommoir* (1877), the next novel in the series, remains one of Zola's most popular works and had an enormous impact in its day. Moving from the world of bourgeoisie, priests, and politicians, Zola focused on Gervaise Macquart, a laundry woman, and presented through her the Parisian working class of the Second Empire, plagued by alcoholism and poverty. The pessimism and stark realism of the novel (in which Zola was the first modern writer to transcribe the vocabulary actually used by the workers of the time) earned him the reputation of being a pornographic writer, a reputation that was to follow him for the rest of his life. After *Une page d'amour* (1878), notable chiefly for some very evocative descriptions of Paris in the 1860s, Zola had another huge *succès de scandale* with *Nana* (1880). Nana, the daughter of

L'assommoir's Gervaise Macquart, is presented as the courtesan par excellence, a symbol of the working class taking its revenge on the decadent rich. As Nana casts off one man after another, Zola uncovers different aspects of Second Empire society. After being kept by a rich banker, she becomes mistress to an actor and leads others to dishonor and suicide, before she herself dies while the Paris crowds march down the boulevards shouting, "To Berlin! To Berlin!" at the commencement of the disastrous 1870 war with Prussia.

In *Pot-Bouille* (1882), Zola returned to the world of the Paris haute bourgeoisie, uncovering the petty treacheries and infidelities of the inhabitants of an outwardly highly respectable apartment house whose name is the title of the novel. The protagonist of *Pot-Bouille*, Octave Mouret, reappears in the next novel of the series, *Au Bonheur des Dames* (1883), as the owner of one of the large department stores that were beginning to spring up in Paris during the Second Empire. Zola combines his plot—basically a love story—with an analysis of the ruinous effects of this sort of *grand capitalisme* on the small businessmen of Paris in the period 1864–1869. After *La joie de vivre* (1884), a partly autobiographical, psychologically oriented work set on the Normandy coast, Zola returned to his analysis of the working classes, this time to a study of the struggle between labor and management in a community of coal miners in northern France. *Germinal* (1885), one of Zola's most famous novels, traces the career of Gervaise's son, Etienne Lantier, as he organizes a union among the miners and leads them out on strike. Starving and finally dominated by government troops, the strikers are forced back to work. Nevertheless the novel ends on a note of optimism, in which Zola, through Etienne, expresses his belief in a vague utopian socialism for the society of the future.

In his early years, Zola had spent a great deal of time in the studios of the young painters of the Second Empire, and he used these memories in *L'oeuvre* (1886), the story of the career and eventual suicide of the failed young artist Claude Lantier, in whom appear certain traits of the novelist's boyhood friend, Paul Cézanne (1839–1906). *La terre* appeared in 1887 and provoked an enormous scandal. Zola's avowed purpose in the novel was to depict as realistically as possible the life of the peasant during the Second Empire, in this case centered in the Beauce, a relatively prosperous grain-growing area around Chartres. For a public used to the idealized vision of the farmer presented in the past by George Sand and Jean-Jacques Rousseau, however, Zola's portrayal of venal, bestial people, interested only in acquiring and holding land, shocked even his disciples, some of whom launched a formal revolt. After a rather insipid love story (*Le rêve*, 1888) and a melodrama (*La bête humaine*, 1890), whose setting is the railroad industry that had grown up during the Second Empire, Zola returned to the world of high finance with *L'argent* in 1891. Aristide Rougon is the central character of what Zola called his "novel about the Stock Exchange." Around Rougon, the incarnation of the Second Empire financial speculator, revolve the thinly disguised characters who dominated financial circles and the banking wars in the late 1860s. Several of the Second Empire's prominent Jewish banking families (Isaac and Emile Pereire and the Rothschilds, for example) are easily recognizable. Many aspects of the main character himself—his energy and his tactical sense—are based on the career of Jules Mirès, another prominent Paris financier who was tried for fraud in 1861. And in the background are the Marxists, the avowed enemies of the Bourse and of its manipulators. *La débâcle* (1892) describes the last days of the Second Empire and the events of the Franco-Prussian War, as Zola's hero, Jean Macquart, suffers through the battles of Bazeilles and Sedan and fights on the barricades of the Paris Commune. It is in this novel that Zola makes his strongest statement about the Second Empire, contrasting a corrupt, worn-out society, symbolized in the person of the sick and aging emperor, to the bright future that lies ahead for the France of the Third Republic. Zola terminated his series with *Le Docteur Pascal* (1893), a return to the provinces and a restatement in novelistic form of his theories on heredity and of his unbounded faith in the advancement that science would bring to humanity.

Consistent with the naturalist theory he expounded, Zola's presentation of the society of the Second Empire is faithful. Moving from the government leaders and financial speculators to the unemployed of the Paris slums, Zola focused on all levels of French society and described them with an accuracy that came from careful documentation. For this reason, *Les Rougon-Macquart* stands out as an important document among the portrayals of the society of Napoleon III, although it should be remembered that Zola was an opponent of the Empire, that he wrote his novels in the early years of the Third Republic when true objectivity was very difficult, that his facts were often gathered from the experiences of that time rather than from those of the period 1850–1870 (for example, the strike of coal miners in *Germinal* is based on that at Anzin in 1884), and that his research was of necessity superficial.

Among editions of the Rougon-Macquart novels the best are: H. Mitterrand, ed., Pléïade ed., 5 vols. (Paris, 1960–1967); and P. Cogny, ed., L'Intégrale ed., 6 vols. (Paris, 1969). For general appraisals see: M. Claverie, ''La fête impériale [vue par Zola],'' *CN*, no. 45 (1973); M. Descottes, *Le personnage de Napoléon III dans 'Les Rougon-Macquart'* (Paris, 1970); A. Dupuy, ''Napoléon III jugé par Emile Zola,'' *MH* (February 1953), and ''Le Second Empire vu et jugé par Zola,'' *IH* (March–April 1953); H. Guillemin, *Présentation des 'Rougon-Macquart'* (Paris, 1964); N. Kranowski, *Paris dans les romans d'Emile Zola* (Paris, 1968); S. L. Max, *Les métamorphoses de la grande ville dans 'Les Rougon-Macquart'* (Paris, 1967); J. Rostand, ''L'oeuvre de Zola et la pensée scientifique,'' *Europe* (April-May 1968).

Dorothy E. Speirs

Related entries: BERNARD; CHAMPFLEURY; DARWINISM IN FRANCE; POSITIVISM; TAINE; ZOLA.

ROUHER, EUGENE (1814–1884), minister, senator, key political figure of the final years of the Second Empire; born at Riom (Auvergne), son of a lawyer, 30 November 1814. After taking his law degree at Paris, Rouher became one of the most distinguished of Riom's *avoués*, earning a reputation as a liberal in several cases involving the press. He married the daughter of Conchon, mayor of Clermont-Ferrand. Recommended to François Guizot (1787–1874) by Auguste de Morny, he ran unsuccessfully for election to the Chamber of Deputies in 1846 under Guizot's patronage. Following the Revolution of 1848, Rouher proclaimed himself an advanced republican and was elected to the Constituent Assembly from Puy-de-Dôme, thirteenth on a list of fifteen. The course of the revolution, combined with his natural bent toward authoritarianism and with the counsels of his ambition, soon persuaded the new deputy to turn to the right and, in particular, to the cause of Louis Napoleon Bonaparte, elected president of the Republic on 10 December 1848. Sent with an increased vote to the Legislative Assembly in 1849, Rouher, who had voted on 10 December for General Louis Eugène Cavaignac (1802–1857), rallied to the president and was, before the coup d'état, minister of justice (1849–1851). In that capacity he branded the Revolution of 1848 a catastrophe and defended (1850) the new electoral law, which drastically reduced the suffrage.

Although Rouher was one of those involved in the decision in principle to carry out the coup d'état of 2 December 1851, he was not party to the actual date or directly involved in its execution. Moreover, there is evidence that he was prepared to dissociate himself from the conspirators in the event of failure. On 3 December, he was named once again to head the Justice Ministry, and he served subsequently on the commissions that elaborated the 1852 constitution (at Louis Napoleon's behest, Rouher drafted the document, perhaps in a single night) and the electoral regime. Rouher may also have inspired Victor Fialin Persigny with the idea of controlling the press through the use of *avertissements*, and he clamped down vigorously on critics of the authoritarian regime, dismissing untrustworthy magistrates and helping to muzzle the press. But Rouher was not yet ready completely to suspend his own judgment in his master's service. On 22 January 1852, he resigned, together with Morny, Achille Fould, and Pierre Magne, in protest against the decrees confiscating Orléans property in France. He was, however, at once named to head a section of the Conseil d'Etat, where he distinguished himself from 1852 to 1855 in matters relating to legislation, justice, and foreign affairs.

By 1855 Rouher's virtues had brought him to the attention of the emperor. He was a symbol of strength, not only in his own imposing physique but also in his bias toward authoritarianism (in 1856 he would join Jules Baroche and Adolphe Billault in opposing a general amnesty). He was a pragmatist, a hater of extremes, convinced of the value of a cool head in both business and politics. Endowed with a remarkable memory and great powers of assimilation, he also had an enormous capacity for work and was, besides, honest, resourceful, and a superlative advocate. On 3 February 1855, Napoleon III named him minister of agriculture, commerce, and public works and on 18 June 1856 senator. In economic affairs, Rouher married an Orleanist predilection for free enterprise to the Napoleonic desire for government initiative and assistance. He presided over one of the greatest periods of French railroad construction and amalgamation, served on the commission for the 1855 Paris international exposition, and gave full support to Georges Haussmann's massive Paris public works projects. A free trader from at least 1851, he negotiated (with Baroche and Michel Chevalier on the French side) the commercial treaty of January 1860 with Britain. The greatest secrecy was preserved until the last moment, Mme. Rouher herself copying the essential documents. In January 1861 Rouher was named to negotiate the commercial treaty with Belgium (signed 1 May 1861, together with a navigation and literary convention). That same year he took over, in the absence of Prince Napoleon, the French commission for the London international exposition of 1862. In 1863 he negotiated the treaty of commerce with Italy, submitted to the emperor a report on professional education, and played a major role (with Baroche) in securing deregulation of the bakeries. Throughout this period, Rouher aligned himself with the financial conservatives (Fould, Baroche, James de Rothschild) against the innovators (Victor Fialin Persigny, Morny, Armand Béhic, and Isaac and Emile Pereire). He approved, for example, the financial reforms of December 1861 proposed by Fould and accepted by the emperor.

By June 1863 Rouher had won a well-deserved reputation as a specialist, and it was this rather than any particular eminence within the imperial entourage that led to his appointment on 23 June as minister presiding the Conseil d'Etat, replacing his close friend Baroche. Rouher had just been named interim minister of the interior as well when his great opportunity unexpectedly arrived. Billault, newly appointed minister of state and, by virtue of that position, chief government spokesman before the legislature, died suddenly in October. Only Rouher and Baroche seemed possible successors. On 18 October Rouher was chosen, chiefly because of his more vigorous personality. No one really expected that he could replace Billault, and the challenge was indeed formidable, for the authoritarian Empire was faltering, and the elections of 1863 had returned a number of powerful opposition speakers to the Corps Législatif. As an orator, however, Rouher compensated for a lack of polish, eloquence, and elevation with a remarkable force and clarity of exposition. He was an incomparable debater, a superlative advocate, and soon made himself indispensable to the regime. He was well rewarded, earning as much as 260,000 francs per year from his various official positions and winning nomination as officer of the Legion of Honor in 1856 and as grand cross on 25 January 1860. But neither wealth nor honors were a high priority with him. Power for its own sake most probably was but also a true affection for and unswerving devotion to the emperor and a sincere predilection for authoritarian government. To Rouher, parliamentary government in France was synonymous with disorder and bloodshed; what he desired above ideology was good government, sound finance, order, and social peace. He therefore undertook a stubborn defense of personal rule and of the constitution of 1852. His closest associate in this endeavor was Baroche, but other friends included Fould, Jérôme David, J.L.V.A. de Forcade La Roquette, Adolphe Vuitry, and Gustave Louis A. V. Chaix d'Est-Ange (1800–1876). Rouher's enemies were either those who rivaled him for power and access to the emperor or who opposed or came to oppose his unflinching authoritarianism, notably Persigny, Morny, Haussmann, Prince Napoleon, Alexandre Walewski, C. E. de Maupas (whom Rouher helped to dislodge as minister of police in 1852), and, above all, Emile Ollivier.

From 1863 to 1867, Rouher formulated the legalistic justification of official candidacy (in 1866, after the municipal elections, he dismissed 126 mayors considered unreliable), defended Haussmann and his methods (while insisting on treating him as a mere agent of execution), and in general resisted all movement toward a parliamentary regime, which he insisted was incompatible with universal suffrage ("L'Empereur n'a pas relevé le trône pour ne pas gouverner et livrer le pouvoir aux manoeuvres du régime parlementaire"). Rouher's notable speeches on these subjects include those of 11 January 1864 (defining his role in the government), 14 January 1864 (defending official candidacy), 31 March 1865 (defending the press regime of 1852), and 6 April 1865 (against naming mayors from the municipal councils). At the same time the minister of state had to defend the free-trade position against constant harassment by the protectionists, especially Adolphe Thiers and Auguste Pouyer-Quertier (1820–1891)(speech of 9 March 1866 on an amendment relative to an agricultural inquiry and of 19 and 20 May 1868 opposing the demand for renunciation of the 1860 treaties).

Despite the bond of affection that united the two men, relations between Rouher and the emperor were sometimes difficult. Napoleon III, determined to be the master, was often embarrassed by his dependence on Rouher, who also occasionally chafed at the restraints on him and more than once (as in April 1864 over French policy concerning the Danish duchies) offered his resignation. But the minister always ended by yielding. Rouher's role remained that of an imperial instrument, and his loyalty proved unbreakable. From 1866 Persigny and Walewski worked to dislodge him in favor of Ollivier. The minister of state effectively resisted, however, even to the point of failing to appear at a meeting arranged between himself and Ollivier at the Tuileries. In January 1867 Napoleon III decided on further reforms but against a change of men. Rouher again offered his resignation but then reconsidered (even the empress, who resented his influence and pragmatism, urged him to remain). The emperor added to his minister of state's already great burden by naming him (until 12 November 1867) interim finance minister in place of Fould, and Rouher succeeded in having a friend of Walewski replaced in the new cabinet with one of his own protégés.

Rouher's role in the carrying out of the reforms promised by the emperor on 19 January 1867 remains a subject of controversy. He met with Ollivier, proclaimed his good faith, and even made a reformist speech in the Corps Législatif. And yet it is clear that throughout 1867 and into the spring of 1868 Rouher worked to limit the reforms, to cast them in as conservative a light as possible, and to maintain the authoritarian regime. He blocked Ollivier as *rapporteur* of the press law, launched a personal attack on Walewski, and succeeded in having him replaced (March 1867) as president of the Corps Législatif. And he clashed violently with Ollivier, who on 12 July 1867 called for suppression of the Ministry of State and branded Rouher "un vice-empereur sans responsabilité." Yet while opposed to liberalization of the press laws, Rouher yielded to an emotional appeal by the emperor ("ainsi donc, vous aussi, vous voulez m'abandonner") and in February 1868 persuaded a reluctant Corps Législatif (speech of 4 February) to approve the measure. Earlier (in April 1867) it had been as a result of Rouher's support that Victor Duruy's liberal education law had passed, although much adulterated. Still the tension continued. When Napoleon III, perhaps out of irritation, chose Pierre Ernest Pinard as minister of the interior although he had been tenth on Rouher's list (memo to the emperor of 15 October 1867), Rouher worked to undermine the new minister, maintained an ally, Gaston de Saint-Paul, as director general of the ministry, and when Pinard faltered in the Baudin monument affair (Rouher had advised against responding to efforts by the Left to make a martyr of the deputy killed on the barricades in December 1851), the minister of state had the satisfaction of seeing Forcade La Roquette named to head the Ministry of the Interior.

Domestic politics, however, constituted only one front. Increasingly Rouher had to combat in the arena of foreign policy as well, and there his liabilities were greater. He had traveled little and taken small interest in other countries. His predilections in foreign policy reflected his domestic concerns: to preserve the status quo, maintain peace, encourage trade by lowering tariffs, and limit military expenditures. He was well disposed toward Britain, opposed to intervention in Poland. Concerning Italy he favored unification but also papal independence and wanted to see French troops withdrawn from Rome. As for Germany, Rouher regarded a confederation of the north as desirable and, at any rate, inevitable. Mexico was a particular embarrassment for him. He had had no part in the decision to intervene but on several occasions had to defend the government against charges of dishonorable motives and (at the end) of cravenly yielding to menaces from the United States.

If Jules Favre was Rouher's greatest foe concerning Mexico, it was chiefly with Thiers he had to reckon in regard to the government's German policy ("Vous n'avez plus de fautes à commettre"). Rouher replied to the latter in a series of powerful speeches, notably those of 16 March 1867 (defending Napoleon III's German policy: "il n'y avait pas eu une seule faute commise") and of 24 March 1867 (proclaiming, just before the eruption of the Luxembourg crisis, that there were no complications on the horizon). On Rome, the great adversary was Antoine Berryer, ardent champion of the papal temporal power. Rouher was, in fact, favorable to the church, while distrusting the ultramontanists. Goaded by Berryer (and in order to seal a new political alliance between the Church and the authoritarian Empire), the minister, who sometimes allowed himself to be carried away by his own eloquence, pronounced on 5 December 1867 his famous assertion that Italy would never be allowed to seize Rome.

Rouher was a member of the commission that prepared the military reforms of 1867–1868. His eyes fixed on the coming elections, he worked, in effect, against the emperor's reform plans for the army (speech of 27 December 1867) and dissuaded Napoleon III from holding elections in the summer of 1867 on the issue. Throughout ·1868 and in the first months of 1869, the minister of state's attention focused on the imminent elections to the Corps Législatif. Despite his earlier justification of himself for having accepted reforms he had once opposed (speech of 7 May 1868), the minister fully affirmed Napoleon III's appeal of 18 January 1869 that the bases of the constitution of 1852 no longer be considered open to question. Through the new *Journal officiel*, which he had recently established (first issue 1 January 1869), and by every other means still at his disposal, including official candidacy, Rouher fought for a government electoral triumph. His abandonment of Haussmann to the tender mercies of the Corps Législatif opposition in February–March 1869 undoubtedly can be seen in this light. The triumph did not materialize, however, and the minister of state was at last required, on 12 July 1869, to resign. Abandoning his earlier thought of reviving the office of *chancelier* for his loyal servitor, Napoleon III on 20 July named him president of the Senate in place of Raymond Troplong, who had recently died.

In the Senate, Rouher spoke on 2 August 1869 supporting the proposed *sénatus-consulte* (approved 6 September) on the ground that France could not stand still while liberal doctrines were sweeping Europe. He resisted the idea of a new constitution, however, and when forced to yield helped to persuade the emperor to hold a plebiscite on the reforms—and on the Empire. The great success of the plebiscite undoubtedly confirmed Napoleon III in his tendency to continue seeking advice from his former minister. Rouher seems to have expected to be recalled to power when Ollivier had proved unable to maintain his balance between Right and Left. He regarded the government of 2 January 1870 and the experiment of the Liberal Empire as a temporary aberration. In the meantime, he had occasion to pronounce funeral eulogies for Marshal Adolphe Niel, Admiral Jean Baptiste, baron Grivel (1778–1869), and Charles Augustin Sainte-Beuve, regretting the last's "suprême témérité" in dying a freethinker. And he continued to defend free trade.

The Franco-Prussian War ended Rouher's hopes. He approved the declaration of war and on 16 July 1870 delivered a speech full of confidence in French preparedness. He supported the overthrow of Ollivier's government on 9 August. At first he resisted the idea of the emperor's returning to Paris and of the army's falling back on the capital but became converted to that strategy during a visit to Châlons on 21 August. He was not able, however, to persuade the government. On 4 September 1870, Rouher presided over the final meeting of the Senate (it unanimously confirmed its allegiance to the dynasty), leaving the chair when his sensible proposal to raise the session was resisted, even by his intimate friend Baroche. He fled Paris to Calais, joined the empress in England, and founded a bonapartist paper there. While he was in exile, his private papers were seized by Prussian troops from his Auvergne country home of Cerçay (demolished in 1921) and transported to Berlin, where they remained until after World War I.

In 1871 Rouher returned to France to become the effective, if not the nominal, leader of bonapartism following the death in 1873 of Napoleon III, with whom he had several times conferred at Chislehurst. A staunchly bonapartist deputy from 1872 to 1881 (representing Riom after his defeat in 1876 by Prince Napoleon at Ajaccio, Corsica) he retired from active politics in 1879, following the death of the prince imperial, who had chosen him as his political mentor. Rouher died at Paris, 3 February 1884.

Rouher's historical reputation suffered with the fate of the Second Empire. In his novel *Son Excellence Eugène Rougon*, Emile Zola depicted the former minister as a man obsessed with power, an adventurer to whom the criminal coup d'état of December 1851 opened the path of opportunity. Power was certainly important to Rouher, but so, too, were loyalty to the emperor and devotion to authoritarian government in a country still threatened with revolution and disorder. A more measured criticism holds that the minister, working behind the back of his master, frustrated the reforms of 1867–1868 and thus ensured the debacle that followed. But this is to ignore both the degree of flexibility shown by Rouher and the fact that Napoleon III also had reservations and doubts concerning the pace and scope of reform. Following Ollivier's "*vice-empereur sans responsabilité*" attack, the emperor honored his beleaguered minister by personally decorating him on 13 July 1867 with the insignia in diamonds of the grand cross of the Legion of Honor (a distinction bestowed only on Rouher, Morny, and Walewski). Moreover, in a letter published in September 1867 in the *Moniteur*, Napoleon III asserted that he and his minister were in complete accord.

Although much less noted, Rouher's influence on foreign policy may well have been the most nefarious aspect of his period of dominance. His political credentials were solid, rooted in his own constituency of the Auvergne where he remained a popular, "democratic" figure, but his claims to competency in foreign affairs were much weaker. On more than one occasion Rouher's interventions proved disastrous. The bid for Luxembourg as French compensation for Prussian gains was largely his work, and it culminated in the crisis of April 1867. His 5 December 1867 speech on Rome contributed greatly to the failure of Napoleon III's efforts to arrange a congress on that issue so vital to French security. Most fatefully, Rouher's failure to give full support to the emperor's efforts in 1866–1868 to reform the French army lend great weight to what is perhaps the most damaging criticism of his historical role, his failure to balance politics with statesmanship.

M. E. Martin, "Eugène Rouher," *SN* 16 (1953); R. Schnerb, *Rouher et le Second Empire* (Paris, 1950).

Related entries: AUTHORITARIAN EMPIRE; BAKERIES, DEREGULATION OF; BAROCHE; BILLAULT; COBDEN-CHEVALIER TREATY; CONSEIL D'ETAT; CONSTITUTION; CORPS LEGISLATIF; DAVID; ELECTIONS; FOULD; HAUSSMANN; MAGNE; MINISTER OF STATE; MORNY; OLLIVIER; PERSIGNY; PINARD; PLEBISCITE; PRINCE IMPERIAL; PRINCE NAPOLEON; REFORM; THIERS; WALEWSKI.

ROULAND, GUSTAVE (1806–1878), lawyer and politician; minister of education and religion (1856–1863); minister presiding the Conseil d'Etat (1863–1864); governor of the Bank of France (from 1864); born at Paris 1 February 1806, son of a judge. Rouland attended the Collège Royal de Rouen, served as a deputy (1846–1848) and later as a prosecutor and judge. A practicing Catholic, he was a Gallican and enemy of ultramontanists. He was appointed minister of education 13 August 1856, following the death of Hippolyte Fortoul. Inexperience led to caution in his ministry, a transition between the vigorous ones of Fortoul and Victor Duruy. Unlike his predecessor, Rouland believed in encouraging mass schooling, which he regarded as a source of progress so long as it included a strong moral component. He shared Napoleon III's liberal paternalism, relating social solidarity with the well-being of the masses. From these notions arose a concern for special or vocational education. More than other ministers, he valued practical training for students, commissioned two important reports (1862, 1864) on the subject, and anticipated Duruy's *enseignement spécial*. He never resolved the ambivalence that has permeated French debates about the place of special education: whether it would be equal to other tracks in high school, whether it needed separate buildings, how it could be combined with intellectual curiosity or *culture générale*.

In the first years of his ministry, Rouland concentrated on mollifying members of the University offended by Fortoul's arbitrary attempts at reform. He gradually undid *bifurcation*, which secondary school teachers complained had lowered standards. Attempting to restore the morale of primary school teachers, he raised salaries and conducted an essay contest for teachers concerning their problems. Their responses revealed discontent with their own poverty and with the extent of clerical influence, demonstrated the existence of many articulate *instituteurs*, and has become an oft-cited historical source. Discipline over teachers remained firm—they were expected to support official candidates in the elections of 1857 and 1863—and public criticism of the ministry from *universitaires* actually increased during his regime, although his ministry was less authoritarian than that of his predecessor.

The major goal of Rouland's ministry was to check the growth of Catholic schools. At first, he made sure that the Falloux law and the congregation laws were interpreted rigorously and let municipalities know that he disapproved of their assignment of public high schools to one of the religious orders (a transference that usually saved the coffers of the town councils a large sum). By 1860 the consequences of Napoleon's pro-Italian policy and increasing worries about Catholic schools' expansion permitted more openly anti-clerical measures. Rouland's refusal of a Jesuit proposal to open a school in Brest in 1860 was an omen, for no school of an unauthorized religious order was permitted in the 1860s although scores had opened in the 1850s. In 1861 he required the Christian Brothers, who competed with the state notably in special education, to charge tuition in their schools; he consistently opposed free education in public schools and reduced the number of scholarships in them, a policy consistent with Napoleon III's fear that the educated poor would become socialists. His anti-clerical measures were not decisive, probably because the great transfer of public schools to the clergy followed immediately on the Falloux law and had been completed before his ministry. Moreover, despite his policies, Catholic schooling grew more rapidly than did lay schooling during his ministry. Rouland, like Fortoul and Duruy, occupied the Ministry of Education during a period of rapid growth in enrollment in French schools; that growth, however, owed more to social demand than it did to the efforts of any of the ministers. Except in the area of vocational education, Rouland was the least adventuresome of the three major educational ministers of the Second Empire.

The suspension of Ernest Renan's course at the Collège de France in January 1862 for "attacks on Christian belief" was the most dramatic event at the end of Fortoul's ministry. Succeeded by Duruy in the liberalization of the government that followed the elections of 1863, Rouland, who had been appointed a senator 14 November 1857, was named vice-president of the Senate and (18 October 1863–27 September 1864) minister presiding the Conseil d'Etat. He was appointed governor of the Bank of France on 28 September 1864, a position he held into the Third Republic. He died at Paris on 12 December 1878.

G. Rouland, *Discours et réquisitoires de M. Rouland* (Paris, 1853); G. Dutacq, *Rouland, ministre de l'instruction publique* (Paris, 1910).

Patrick J. Harrigan

Related entries: DUPANLOUP; DURUY; FALLOUX LAW; FORTOUL; GALLICANISM; GAUME.

ROUSSEAU, THEODORE (1812–1867), Barbizon landscape painter; born at Paris, 15 April 1812, the son of a tailor from the Jura region. Rousseau began to draw and paint at an early age. Determined to work from nature, he was unsatisfied with the academic training he received in his youth. He was the first of a group of artists to settle in the village of Barbizon, bordering on the Fontainebleau Forest, beginning in 1836, and was regarded as the leader. Works submitted by him to the Salon from 1836 through 1848 were systematically rejected. When Rousseau once again showed his work in 1849, he won the first-class medal. He received recognition in 1855 at the Paris international exposition, after which his works got a warmer reception from the public and the new middle class of collectors, although in the early 1860s he suffered another period of neglect and poverty. His message seemed familiar, easy to understand, and reflected seventeenth-century Dutch painting, which also appealed to bourgeois tastes.

Rousseau had spent the 1840s traveling throughout France, seeking areas of untamed forest and varying conditions of light, which he recorded in many drawings and sketches. He won the admiration of Charles Baudelaire and Théophile Thoré (1807–1869) and the friendship of Honoré Daumier. Among his other artist friends were Narcisse Diaz de la Peña, Antoine Louis Barye, and Jean François Millet, his closest associate. *Edge of the Forest of Fontainebleau at Sunset* (1850, Louvre, Paris) is a typical example of Rousseau's work at this time. While it recalls the Italian landscapes of Claude Lorrain, the Dutch landscapes of Ruysdael, and the English of Constable, it nevertheless brings a new approach to the native landscape of France. The trees are extraordinarily well observed and rendered, their large forms majestically framing the cattle below. The fading light can still be seen penetrating the foliage, dappling the leaves with spots of shimmering highlights. Rousseau's facture here shows a certain freedom, his impasto a thickness, adding to the tactile qualities of the deeply felt and closely observed qualities of nature in the clouds, water, animals, and especially the trees. These elements would have been studied in situ with drawings and sketches, while the final work would have been finished in the studio. This new value that Rousseau brings to the history of landscape painting is the result of his close contact with nature, which he depicts with a fidelity that does not permit the idealized compositions, themes, and content of the past. Another version, *The Forest of Fontainebleau, Morning* (1850, Wallace Collection, London), exhibited as a pendant to *Edge of the Forest*, is seen from a slightly different point of view. Both indicate a new attitude toward light and its variations at specific times of day, an approach that influenced the succeeding generation of Impressionists. Composition is handled innovatively in *Oak Trees, Apremont* (1850–1852, Louvre), where a single group of trees, isolated in the middle of the canvas, becomes the central focus as opposed to the traditional method of composition where trees act as framing devices, leading the eye toward a more distant vista. A late work, *Path in the Forest of Fontainebleau, Effect of Storm* (1860–1865, Louvre), a motif Rousseau returned to frequently, is painted over a long period of time, with attention to topographical detail. Yet characteristic of the artist's later period, it is infused with a poetic spirit, enlivened with visible brushwork, and heightened by the dramatic contrast of light and dark in the sky and on the majestic old trees.

Rousseau received a considerable degree of recognition in the 1860s. He was invited to stay at the Château de Compiègne in 1865 by Napoleon III. The next year the enterprising art dealer Paul Durand-Ruel (1831–1922), who had developed the new technique of seeking a monopoly of the artists he patronized, bought seventy of Rousseau's paintings, thus giving him security at last (in 1872 Durand-Ruel would purchase all of Edouard Manet's paintings—some twenty-three—for 35,000 francs). Rousseau was appointed president of the jury of the painting section at the Paris international exposition of 1867 and was much honored there, as well as being named officer of the Legion of Honor. By the time of his death, Rousseau had won the enduring reputation, shared with Jean Baptiste Camille Corot, of the most admired and influential landscape painter of mid-nineteenth-century France. Rousseau's work served to elevate landscape painting to a position where it could be respected for its own values, not merely as a setting for a historical or mythological event. His work was also important as a bridge between romanticism and Impressionism. He died at Barbizon, 22 December 1867.

J. Bouret, *The Barbizon School* (Greenwich, Conn., 1973); P. Dorbec, *Théodore Rousseau* (Paris, 1910); P. Durand-Ruel, "Mémoires de Paul Durand-Ruel," in L. Venturi, ed., *Les archives de l'Impressionnisme* (Paris, 1939); M. Laclotte, H. Toussaint, and M. T. de Forges, *Théodore Rousseau* (Paris, 1967).

Beverley Giblon

Related entries: COROT; DAUBIGNY; DIAZ DE LA PENA; MILLET.

RUDE, FRANCOIS (1784–1855), romantic sculptor; born at Dijon, 4 January 1784. Rude was not an outstanding sculptor, nor was he prolific, yet as the prime exponent of romanticist sculpture, which continued to exert its influence during the Second Empire, his major contributions should be considered. After early training in his native city, Rude began to study at Paris, entering the Ecole des Beaux-Arts. Although he won the Prix de Rome in 1812, no funds were available to enable him to go to Rome, and the fall of the Empire compounded his difficulties since it resulted in his exile to Brussels, where he remained for twelve years. In Brussels, he received help from Louis David (1748–1825), who was also exiled in Belgium. After his return to Paris, Rude submitted *Neapolitan Fisherboy* (Louvre, Paris) to the Salon of 1833. Jean Baptiste Carpeaux studied with Rude in 1853, and it was Rude's work that influenced his *Fisherboy* of 1858. It is noteworthy that Rude did not go to Italy to study Michelangelo or Roman antiquity as Carpeaux was later to do.

The work for which Rude is best known is *The Departure of the Volunteers of 1792* (commonly known as *La Marseillaise*), sculpted for the Arc de Triomphe de l'Etoile. Completed in 1836, it was his response to the Revolution of 1830, expressing passionate support for a just cause. The stirring cry to do battle is convincingly rendered in this high relief. The figures, dressed as Roman soldiers, spanning several generations, charge into space with dramatic gestures, recalling Eugène Delacroix's *Liberty at the Barricades*. The open composition and broken silhouette animate the atmosphere. The shout coming from the wide-open mouth of the winged Victory, the personification of France, explodes into the immediate area and is powerful enough to reverberate far into the distance, calling the volunteers to arms. Characteristic of Rude's sculpture is the classical strength in the structuring of the figures, derived from his early training, which is combined with the intensity of feeling and expression whose impetus is the sculptor's own romantic spirit.

Rude's major public monument of the Second Empire is his statue of *Maréchal Ney* (1852–1853), which stands in the place de l'Observatoire, where Ney was shot by a firing squad in 1815. This tribute to Napoleon's aide, typical of Second Empire commissions to restore some of the glory of the First Empire, does not represent a classical, idealized, heroic figure; rather, it attempts to recreate the actual presence of the soldier with his most revealing and expressive gesture. Attention to detail in the military dress and facial features is evident, but what gives the work its most vital quality, its living presence, is the openness and dynamism of the sculpture as it expands into space by means of dynamic spirals and diagonals. Its liveliness was the innovative feature that Auguste Rodin (1840–1917) later came to admire and that he would also exploit in his own work. Rude died at Paris, 3 November 1855, two weeks before the closing of the Paris international exposition whose sculpture section he dominated.

L. Benoist, *La sculpture Romantique* (Paris, 1928); J. Calmette, *François Rude* (Paris, 1920); P. Fusco and H. W. Janson, *The Romantics to Rodin: French Nineteenth-Century Sculpture from North American Collections* (Los Angeles, 1980); R. Mirolli, *Nineteenth-century French Sculpture: Monuments for the Middle Class* (Louisville, 1971).

Beverley Giblon

Related entries: BARYE; CARPEAUX; PREAULT.

RUMANIAN UNITY, the creation under French auspices of the state of Rumania between 1856 and 1866. In the nineteenth century, Rumania was composed of the Danubian Principalities of Muntenia (Wallachia) and Moldova (Moldavia), which moved during the reign of Napoleon III from Ottoman suzerainty to virtual independence by 1866. For the emergence of modern Rumania, a state of some 5 million inhabitants, the policies and ideas of the French emperor were critical, but the legend that he was the arbiter of southeastern Europe never approximated reality.

In the aftermath of the abortive revolutions of 1848 in the Danubian Principalities and the exile or imprisonment of the largely French-educated and French-inspired revolutionaries, Rumanian national aspirations appeared unpromising. However, the exile movement in Paris, Brussels, and London generated widespread European awareness of the Rumanians' plight under Ottoman and Russian tutelage. Among those in the French capital sympathetic to the Rumanian cause were Alphonse de Lamartine (1790–1869), Jules Michelet (1798–1874), Jules Favre, Alexandre Ledru Rollin (1807–1874), Edgar Quinet (1803–1875), and Alfred Dumesnil (1821–1894). Also sympathetic were liberal and republican press circles (such as Emile de Girardin's *La presse*), other Parisian exile groups (such as Adam Mickiewicz [1798–1855]), and even Pierre Joseph Proudhon.

The demise of the French Second Republic in 1851 brought temporary eclipse to Rumanian efforts in France since these were associated with a republicanism hostile to Napoleon III. A turning point in Franco-Rumanian relations came with the Crimean War and the emergence of active French interest in the Balkans. At the same time that the French emperor was preparing to develop his policy of nationalities in the context of an ambitious imperial foreign policy, Rumanian nationalists such as Ion C. Brătianu (1821–1891), who was arrested and imprisoned in connection with the Hippodrome plot of June 1853 to assassinate Napoleon III, were eschewing radicalism in favor of seeking the emperor's sometimes quixotic backing for the Rumanian cause. Brătianu also seems to have maintained direct ties with Prince Napoleon, the cousin of Napoleon III, even while imprisoned, and through him was able to present to the emperor two crucially timed memos (1855, 1857) on the national questions of eastern Europe. Napoleon III talked of securing independence for the Danubian Principalities as early as July 1853, and during the Crimean War, at the second Vienna conference of March-June 1855, he proposed their union. His motives included a sympathy for nationalities, a desire to revise the Treaties of 1815, and a wish to reinforce his contemplated actions in Italy. Perhaps the throne of a Rumanian state could be offered to a Hapsburg prince in return for Modena or Lombardy, which would be annexed to Sardinia.

At the Congress of Paris (February–April 1856) following the Crimean War, no decision on union could be reached, but the Principalities were placed under the guarantee of Europe, and a commission was instructed to sit at Bucharest to consult the wishes of assemblies (*divans*) to be elected in Moldavia and Wallachia for the purpose of expressing Rumanian opinion on union. By 1857 the powers had taken clear stands. Turkey, Austria, and Britain firmly opposed union; France vigorously favored it and was supported, for various reasons, by Russia, Prussia, and Sardinia. When the Ottoman government openly rigged the election of the Moldavian divan in July 1857, the latter powers, led by France on 5 August, broke relations with the Porte. On a visit to Britain that same month, Napoleon III agreed to abandon political union in return for new elections, but he reserved the right to work for administrative union (Pact of Osborne). The elections of September 1857 pronounced decisively for union. An ambassadorial conference met at Paris on 22 May 1858, and, thanks to the obstinate efforts of the French emperor, agreed (19 August) that Wallachia and Moldavia should have the same laws, customs, monetary system, military organization, and, in time of war, a common pennant, although each would be administered by an elective official (*hospodar*) chosen by the elected divan.

The convention of 1858, which established the new internal political order of the Principalities and marked the decisive breaking point with the old regime of perpetual foreign interference, therefore was due largely to French backing of the Rumanian cause. An influential role in this process was played by the French consul at Jassy (Moldavia) from 1855 to 1863, Victor Place (1822–1875), and the French ambassador at Constantinople, Edouard Thouvenel. From this step to the election of the same man as *hospodar* by both Principalities (January–February 1859) to the union of 1861, the route was carved out by a series of Rumanian faits accomplis, which, although not instigated or openly encouraged by the French, were made possible by Napoleon III's refusal to concur in any measures by the powers that would overturn the actions of the Rumanian union-ists. Thus, while the French emperor did not "make" Rumania, he did make it possible for the Rumanians to achieve their own ends in a remarkably short time. The first prince of the United Danubian Principalities, the French-educated Alexandru Ioan Cuza (1820–1873), was elected in 1859 and quickly seized on Napoleon III's predilection for nationalist causes to gain official union of Moldavia and Wallachia, as well as complete autonomy by 1862. A conference convened at Paris 6 September 1859 acknowledged Cuza's election, and in December 1861 the Porte accepted union of the Principalities, under the name Rumania, during the prince's lifetime. Further playing on French support, Cuza

was able to achieve significant internal changes by means of a benevolent plebiscitary autocracy patterned after Napoleon III's own methods (coup d'état, 2
May 1864). At the same time, a French military mission arrived in Rumania to
help organize the new army.

Cuza's ouster on 22 February 1866 by a coalition representing a wide spectrum
of political opinion raised the question of a successor. Napoleon III's role in the
choice of the new Rumanian prince—the French-connected Karl of the Catholic
Hohenzollern-Sigmaringen family—is not conclusively established, but it appears that the recommendation was made from within French court circles (for
example, by Mme. Hortense Cornu [1812–1875]). The key figure mediating
between the French (both court and press opinion) and the Rumanian coalition
was once more Brătianu, who was successful both in portraying Cuza to the
French as a Russophile and in bringing Karl to Rumania on 22 May 1866 after
his endorsement by plebiscite 20 April. Once more Napoleon III, who had always
favored a foreign prince for Rumania (and who seems briefly to have flirted yet
again with an exchange plan, this time of Rumania for Venetia, before deciding
for Karl), prevented counteraction by the irate Turks and Austrians. A conference
that met at Paris on 10 March 1866 was unable to secure election of a native
prince, and on 23 October Constantinople accepted the new fait accompli. Once
more the Rumanians took advantage of the situation to initiate and carry out
nationalist desiderata. But as it was to turn out, the arrival of Karl (known as
Prince Carol thereafter) signaled the decline of French influence in Rumania,
despite the new king's links to the French court and his apparent Francophilism
(his private secretary was a Frenchman). The French military mission was soon
replaced by a Prussian one; German financial interests superseded Parisian ones.
The fading Napoleonic presence in Rumania was also a consequence of the
concomitant rise of Otto von Bismarck and the disintegration of the Crimean
system. Despite the fact that Rumanian public sentiment was solidly and de-
monstratively on the French side when the Franco-Prussian War broke out in
1870, the end of the Second Empire passed in Rumania with remarkably little
reaction. By 1883, Rumania was part of the German alliance system, although
culturally France continued to hold sway in what Rumanians liked to refer to as
the "Paris of the Balkans."

D. Berindei, *Epoca unirii* (Bucharest, 1979); G. J. Bobango, *The Emergence of the
Romanian National State* (New York, 1979); J. C. Campbell, *French Influence and the
Rise of Roumanian Nationalism* (New York, 1971); N. Corivan, *La politica orientale di
Napoleon III e l'unione dei Principati Romeni* (Iasi, 1937); M. Emerit, *Madame Cornu
et Napoléon III* (Paris, 1937), and *Victor Place et la politique française en Roumanie*
(Bucharest, 1931); C. Iancu, "Napoléon III et la politique française à l'égard de la
Roumanie," *RHD* 88 (January–June 1974); G. Lebel, *La France et les Principautés
Danubiennes* (Paris, 1955).

Paul E. Michelson

Related entries: BOLGRAD; CONGRESS OF PARIS; CONGRESS POLICY;
CRIMEAN WAR; NATIONALITIES; POLISH QUESTION; REVISION;
VENETIA.

S

SADOWA (or KONIGGRATZ), the decisive battle of the Austro-Prussian or Seven Weeks' War. The war, which began 18 June 1866, was essentially a German civil war, despite the alliance of Italy with Prussia. It had been precipitated by Prussia's president of council, Otto von Bismarck, in order to exclude Austria from Germany and to permit Prussian dominance within a unified German state. Most German governments sided with Vienna. The decisive clash came on the morning of 3 July 1866 in Bohemia, between the villages of Sadowa and Königgrätz. The Battle of Sadowa, which involved some 220,000 men on each side, was the largest armed encounter before the great battles of the twentieth century and resulted in a resounding Austrian defeat.

Although Prussia's victory was widely attributed to superior weaponry (the needle-gun, cannons with rifled barrels) and use of such new instruments as the railroads and the telegraph, in reality the Austrians were deficient in leadership, both political and military, in strategic planning, and in tactical flexibility. While Prussia's chief of staff, General Helmuth von Moltke, daringly divided his forces into three armies, the Austrians moved into Bohemia in a concentrated mass. Early encounters (Gitschin) resulted in demoralizing Austrian losses. Under pressure from Vienna, the Austrian commander, Marshal Ludwig von Benedek, launched an all-out attack on the center Prussian army near Sadowa. Although he had followed the Napoleonic maxim of seizing the inner lines (which may have been outdated by this time), Benedek had failed to take advantage in Napoleonic fashion of the separation of Prussian forces during early skirmishes. The unusually large number of troops under single command made the Austrian army virtually unmaneuverable and hence an easy target for encirclement by the Prussians, whose three-pronged advance was coordinated by Moltke in a daring and ultimately successful strategy. The battle, at first fiercely contested, was decided by the arrival on the field of the army of Prussian Crown Prince Frederick William about 12:30 P.M. Soon the Austrian retreat became a rout. The Prussian armies had lost about two thousand dead, seven thousand wounded; the Austrian six thousand dead, seventeen thousand wounded, and twenty thousand prisoners. The way to Vienna was open.

Sadowa changed the situation of France in Europe. Napoleon III had foreseen the possibility of a war and had made it more likely by urging Italy to negotiate an alliance with Prussia. Encouraged by Europe's military experts, he perhaps expected a stalemate and hoped to intervene as mediator to maintain Central European weakness. Certainly before the war he negotiated arrangements that guaranteed Italy's acquisition of Venetia, whether the victory went to Prussia or to Austria. Other scholars have suggested that Napoleon III favored German unification under Prussia with or without compensations to France. His speech at Auxerre on 6 May 1866 might be interpreted in this sense. The startling Prussian victory both lessened the influence France's emperor could bring to bear and shortened the time in which he could use it. Vienna appealed for French mediation. In the hours after the battle, Napoleon III considered and rejected armed mediation, favored by Empress Eugénie, Edouard Drouyn de Lhuys (the foreign minister), and the minister of war, Marshal Jacques Louis Randon. The emperor's own ill health, overcommitment of French troops abroad (Algeria, Rome, and, especially, Mexico), and the strong pacifism of French public opinion have been adduced, not entirely convincingly, as reasons for the decision against intervention. Extremely important was Bismarck's moderation in halting at the Main River and according generous terms to Austria. By 10 July French policy was set. Failing a show of force from France, Bismarck was able to expedite the signature of the peace preliminaries (Nikolsburg, 29 July 1866) and the peace treaty (Prague, 23 August 1866). Later he would ignore Napoleon III's belated and possibly halfhearted demands for compensation. Italy, although defeated at Custozza (24 June 1866), did receive Venetia from Austria via France.

Sadowa has been called the hinge of the nineteenth century. It facilitated eventual German unification under Prussia (beginning with the creation of a North German Confederation) and taught the French that Prussia had become a dangerous neighbor. From 1866 through 1869, France embarked on an ambitious but only partially realized program of military reform, while successive crises and growing tensions led inexorably to the decisive contest, the Franco-Prussian War.

A. Armengaud, *L'opinion publique en France et la crise nationale allemande en 1866* (Paris, 1962); L. M. Case, "French Opinion and Napoleon III's Decision after Sadowa," *POQ* 13 (Fall 1949); G. A. Craig, *The Battle of Königgrätz* (Philadelphia, 1964); E. R. Defrasne, "L'armée française au lendemain de Sadowa," *Revue historique de l'armée* 24 (1968); W. von Groote and U. von Gersdorff, eds., *Entscheidung 1866: Der Krieg zwischen Osterreich und Preussen* (Stuttgart, 1966); R. Lill, "Die Vorgeschichte der preussisch-italienischen Allianz (1866)," *Quellen und Forschungen aus italienischen Archiven und Bibliotheken* 42–43 (1963); B. D. Loynd, "Bismarck and Napoleon III: The Diplomacy of the German Crisis of 1866" (Ph.D. diss., University of California, 1976); E. A. Pottinger, *Napoleon III and the German Crisis, 1865–1866* (Cambridge, Mass., 1966); P. Rain, "Sadowa," *RDM*, no. 14 (15 July 1966).

Ann Pottinger Saab

Related entries: ARMY REFORM; BENEDETTI; BIARRITZ INTERVIEW; CONGRESS POLICY; DANISH WAR; DROUYN DE LHUYS; LUXEMBOURG CRISIS; MENTANA; NATIONALITIES; PUBLIC OPINION; VENETIA.

SAIGON. See INDOCHINA.

SAINT-ARNAUD, LEROY DE (1801–1854), marshal of France, military executor of the coup d'état of 2 December 1851, commander of French forces in the first phase of the Crimean War; born at Paris, 20 August 1801, the son of a lawyer who had been a prefect under the Consulate and who died when his son was five. In 1811 Saint-Arnaud's mother married Forcade La Roquette. Their son, Jean, born in 1820, was also destined to be a minister of the Second Empire. Although Saint-Arnaud studied at the Lycée Napoléon, he enlisted as a private soldier in the army of Louis XVIII. Ten years later, his undisciplined life had prevented promotion, and he left the army for a wandering life of adventure and miscellaneous jobs, in the course of which he became an able musician and a master of four foreign languages. Returning to the army in February 1831, he served in the Vendée against the legitimist rebels of the duchesse d'Orleans, winning the patronage of Marshal Bugeaud (1784–1849), to whose staff he was named. However, Saint-Arnaud's disordered life and accumulating debts and love affairs again constrained him to leave the army (1836). Enlisted in the Foreign Legion, he soon distinguished himself for reckless courage—and ruthlessness—in Algeria. In 1837 he was named to the Legion of Honor for his role in the assault on Constantine. Three years later, he entered the Zouaves Regiment of the French army as chef de bataillon. Now consumed by ambition, his advance was rapid: colonel, October 1844, commander of the Legion of Honor and general of brigade, November 1847. By 1850 he was commandant of the province of Constantine.

In April 1851 Louis Napoleon, since December 1848 president of the Second Republic, sent his aide-de-camp Comte Emile Félix Fleury (1815–1884) to Algeria to reconnoiter for military men who would be reliable in the event of a showdown with the president's political opponents. Fleury, who had served under Saint-Arnaud, soon confirmed his earlier advice to Louis Napoleon concerning the ambitious African officer. He accompanied Saint-Arnaud on his successful campaign against rebels in the Petite Kabylie (10 May–16 June). This campaign served as a convenient pretext for Saint-Arnaud's promotion to general of division (major general), a promotion announced to him by a personal letter from Louis Napoleon of 30 June 1851. A month later, he was named to command the Second Division of the Army of Paris, where he arrived on 15 August. Although an intimate friend of Louis Philippe's son, the duc d'Aumale (1822–1897), Saint-Arnaud seems to have committed himself to the coup d'état after two interviews with the prince president, perhaps as early as 20 August. His motives were compounded of ambition and of a hatred for the Left, gained during the February Revolution of 1848, when he had found himself on leave in Paris, and during his service in Algeria, when he had been responsible for the transported Paris insurgents of June 1849. Realizing his indispensability (General Victor Castellane [1788–1862] had declined military leadership of the coup, as had General Jacques Louis Randon, then minister of war, while General Bernard Pierre Magnan [1791–1865] was not considered adequate to the task), Saint-Arnaud was able to obtain postponement of the coup d'état until after the Legislative Assembly had reconvened following summer vacations, and to ensure himself promotion to minister of war (26 October 1851).

The coup d'état was executed with ruthless efficiency by Saint-Arnaud, Auguste de Morny (no friend of the minister of war, whom he had known in Algeria), Magnan, and the prefect of police, C. E. de Maupas. Saint-Arnaud soon reaped his reward; he was appointed senator 26 January 1852. His offer to resign as minister of war following the Orleans decrees (confiscating property of the family in France) was refused by the prince president, whom Saint-Arnaud accompanied on the tour of central and southern France that preceded the proclamation of the Second Empire on 2 December 1852. On that occasion, Saint-Arnaud, Castellane, and Magnan were awarded marshal's batons. On 31 December Saint-Arnaud became *grand écuyer*. Speaking for the army, he unsuccessfully opposed the marriage of Napoleon III to Eugénie de Montijo. As minister of war, he reorganized the general staff, the gendarmerie, the artillery, the sanitary corps, the Ecole Polytechnique, the Prytanée Militaire, and the cavalry school. Together with Victor Fialin Persigny, he successfully resisted the ambitions of de Maupas during the latter's brief tenure as minister of police. It was during this period that Saint-Arnaud killed a fellow officer, General Louis Antoine Ange Cornemuse, in a duel resulting from the disappearance of 200,000 francs in bank notes left by Louis Napoleon on a fireplace mantel.

The outbreak of the Crimean War in March 1854 capped the career of Saint-Arnaud, by now sincerely devoted to the emperor, who, among other kindnesses, had provided a dowry for the marshal's daughter. Named to command the Armée de l'Orient (he was succeeded as minister of war by Marshal Jean Baptiste Vaillant 11 March), he embarked at the end of April for the Danube. When that campaign failed to bring a decisive confrontation with the Russians, Saint-Arnaud became an advocate of the Crimean expedition, which disembarked at Eupatoria on 14 September. Saint-Arnaud skillfully conducted the Battle of the Alma six days later, remaining in the saddle for twelve hours. The victory established his historical reputation. Perhaps an immediate assault on Sebastopol would have secured it beyond reproach; but the casualties and fatigue of the battle, the lack of cavalry, the ravages of cholera, and the need to maintain pace with the less mobile British forces motivated against this. By the time the armies moved toward Sebastopol (23 September), Saint-Arnaud was a dying man. Long wracked by a serious illness, he was now afflicted by dysentery. On 26 September, he surrendered command to General François Canrobert. On 29 September he died en route to France aboard the *Berthollet*. His remains reached Paris on 16 October, the day before Canrobert commenced the bombardment of Sebastopol, and were interred after a public funeral in a crypt of the Invalides. Napoleon III, genuinely moved by the death of "un ami dévoué," persuaded the Conseil d'Etat to award Saint-Arnaud's widow a pension of 20,000 francs. The marshal's brother, Louis Adolphe (1807–1873), a lawyer, *conseiller d'état* (1852), and senator (26 December 1857), later published Saint-Arnaud's correspondence.

L. Bertrand, *Un grand Africain: Le Maréchal de Saint-Arnaud* (Paris, 1941); J. Dinfreville, *L'effervescent Maréchal de Saint-Arnaud* (Paris, 1969); Q. L'Epine, *Le Maréchal Saint-Arnaud*, 2 vols. (Paris, 1929); L. A. Saint-Arnaud, ed., *Lettres du Maréchal de Saint-Arnaud, 1832-1854*, 2 vols. (Paris, 1858).

Related entries: ALGERIA; CANROBERT; COUP D'ETAT; CRIMEAN WAR; RANDON; VAILLANT.

SAINTE-BEUVE, CHARLES AUGUSTIN (1804–1869), critic and poet; the most distinguished literary critic of the Second Empire and perhaps of modern France; born at Boulogne-sur-Mer, 23 December 1804. Sainte-Beuve's father died two months before his son's birth. Sainte-Beuve was educated at Paris (Lycée Charlemagne) and studied medicine there from 1823 to 1826 before turning to literary journalism. An early friend of Victor Hugo, until they quarreled (1831) over Sainte-Beuve's attachment to the poet's wife, he began his career as a romantic in literature, an aspiring poet and novelist, and a freethinker. By the beginning of the Second Empire, however, his atheism, tempered by a sincere if unsuccessful search for faith (in Saint-Simonianism, the thought of Félicité de Lamennais [1782–1854], and Jansenism), had become anti-clericalism; his republicanism, disillusioned by the experience of 1848, had turned to political skepticism; and he had chosen criticism as his literary field. Moreover, while remaining a romantic at heart, he was willing to accept and even to encourage the new literature of realism, in the name of a scientism that became ever more prominent in his critical writings.

Sainte-Beuve's participation in 1836 in a government commission studying the nation's heritage resulted in his major work, *Port-Royal*, which he researched and began writing while teaching at Lausanne, Switzerland (1837). A study of the history and development of Jansenism and of the monastery at Port-Royal-des-Champs, the work appeared in five volumes from 1840 to 1859. As well, the 1830s and 1840s saw the publication in *Revue des deux mondes* of his first portraits of literary contemporaries, collected and published as *Critiques et portraits littéraires* (1836–1839) and *Portraits contemporains* (1846). In 1844, this scholarship resulted in the critic's election to the Académie Française, despite the opposition of Victor Hugo.

The year 1848 proved a decisive turning point in the life and career of Saint-Beuve. Badly treated by the Second Republic, he fled to a teaching appointment at Liège, Belgium, where he composed his study, *Chateaubriand et son groupe littéraire sous l'Empire* (published 1861), but returned to Paris in 1849 and accepted appointment as literary critic for *Le constitutionnel*, owned by Louis Véron (1798–1867). That year he published the first article in his famous series, the *Causeries du Lundi*. Thereafter Sainte-Beuve submitted an article on a literary or historical subject every week for approximately twenty years either to *Le constitutionnel* (1849–1852, 1861–1867), *Le moniteur universel* (1852–1858, 1867–1868), or *Le temps* (1869). This collaboration was interrupted only once, for a period of three years during his lectureship at the Ecole Normale. A collected edition of fifteen volumes was published from 1851 to 1862 and a second series, *Nouveaux Lundis* (13 volumes), from 1863 to 1870.

The coup d'état of December 1851 and the establishment of the Second Empire a year later were welcomed by Sainte-Beuve who hailed Napoleon III as "Saint-Simon on Horseback" and hoped that the Empire would secure order while ensuring social progress. The critic accepted the cross of the Legion of Honor, which he had twice refused from Louis Philippe. On 6 December 1852 he became an editor of the official newspaper, *Le moniteur universel*. Two years later, the government appointed him to the chair of Latin poetry at the Collège de France (13 December 1854). But Sainte-Beuve's earlier gloating over the fate of the Orleanists under the authoritarian Empire had earned him a considerable unpopularity. His first two lectures (March 1855) were so interrupted by turbulent students that he refused to show up for a third and never lectured again at the Collège although he retained the chair until his death (he published his lectures on Virgil in 1857). The government compensated him with an appointment to the Ecole Normale Supérieure 3 November 1857. The *normaliens*, an intellectually sophisticated group of students, were at least attentive to Sainte-Beuve's lectures on literary tradition and its interpretation, and Louis Pasteur, then assistant director, never missed a chance to attend. Not entirely suited to the role of pedagogue, however (he was a poor speaker), Sainte-Beuve completed only three years of his seven-year contract, returning in 1861 to *Le constitutionnel*, by then a semiofficial newspaper. It was in the same year that the critic began regularly to attend the Wednesday evening salon of Napoleon III's cousin, Princess Mathilde, whom he had met in 1844 but had not seen frequently before 1860. Mathilde, who presided over the most influential literary and artistic salon of the Second Empire, considered Sainte-Beuve her literary adviser and over the years became his most intimate friend and staunch supporter. In 1863 she tried unsuccessfully to have him appointed minister of education (the post went to Victor Duruy) and in 1865 used her influence to secure his appointment as senator (28 April), a post he coveted not because of its prestige or the possibility of a political role but because of the annual stipend of 30,000 francs.

Throughout the Second Empire, Sainte-Beuve's reputation and literary influence grew. His life centered around his research of the Monday *Causerie*. His commitment to submit a weekly article necessitated a vigorous work schedule. A monument to Sainte-Beuve's scholarship and industry, the *Causeries* provided his readers with accounts of and comments on leading French writers and personalities and on many lesser-known figures as well. The critic did not confine himself to discussions of literary figures but devoted *causeries* to ecclesiastics, statesmen, diplomats, and military heroes as well. He included essays on personalities from antiquity, the Middle Ages, and the seventeenth and eighteenth centuries. Stimulated at an early age by the poets of the sixteenth century, he took the opportunity to draw attention to the beauties of Ronsard, Montaigne, and Rabelais. Thus the variety of the subject matter as well as a passion for minutiae and exactitude ensured the importance for future audiences of Sainte-

Beuve's observations. As a literary critic, he pioneered the biographical method, attempting to trace the growth of genius by a close study of the individual mind. In 1864 he accepted the views of Hippolyte Taine, especially his theory of the determining influences of climate and *race*. But always a skeptic, Sainte-Beuve had little faith in the existence of truth except in the sense of historical accuracy and exactness. Perhaps that is a reason why his influence continues, while Taine's (whom Sainte-Beuve considered to be, together with Ernest Renan, the most admirable of contemporary French writers) has all but vanished.

Those who admire Sainte-Beuve's work do not always think as highly of his character. A lifelong bachelor, he remained emotionally dissatisfied and restless. He seemed often to change his opinions and was accused of opportunism. Although a friend of Gustave Flaubert, he condemned *Madame Bovary* for "vulgarity," even when the book and the author were under attack by the government in the courts. Although Charles Baudelaire revered the critic and was influenced by his early poetry (as were François Coppée and even Paul Verlaine [1844–1896]), Sainte-Beuve remained silent during the 1857 trial of Baudelaire for publishing *Les fleurs du mal* and in 1862 seemed to make fun of the poet's attempt to gain election to the Académie Française. Sainte-Beuve was much condemned for his treatment of Baudelaire (was it a reflection of the critic's incomprehension of Baudelaire's poetic genius?), but he remained the center of a literary circle whose biweekly dinners at the Restaurant Magny, beginning in 1862, grouped at first Sainte-Beuve, Paul Gavarni (whose idea it was), the Goncourt brothers, and Charles Philippe, marquis de Chennevières (1820–1899), to whom were soon added Flaubert, Renan, Taine, Théophile Gautier, and the critic Paul de Saint-Victor (1827–1881), as well as George Sand, Auguste Nefftzer, Edmond Scherer (1815–1889), the biologist Charles Philippe Robin (1821–1885), the chemist Marcellin Berthelot, and Ivan Turgenev (1818–1883), among others, on occasion.

The final years of the Empire were unhappy ones for Sainte-Beuve. He suffered from a kidney stone and declining health. Moreover, he had always had reservations about the regime and had retained some independence, writing for *Revue des deux mondes* from 1863 to 1868, refusing on principle to review Napoleon III's *Histoire de Jules César* (1865), and pressing the emperor, unsuccessfully, to take the opposition of the intellectuals more seriously. Sainte-Beuve only once attended an imperial reception at the Chateau of Compiègne (Princess Mathilde arranged the invitation), finding it "frivolous." He was, like Prosper Mérimée, basically apolitical. Besides, the literary critic chafed at the restrictions placed on individual liberty. At first a silent senator, he became more vocal as the regime veered toward clericalism after 1865.

In the last years of his life, Sainte-Beuve's relations with the clerical party steadily worsened. On 29 March 1867, during discussion of the primary education law, he rose in the Senate to defend Renan, to the accompaniment of cries of "You aren't here to do that!" In June he spoke again in defense of intellectual freedom. Opposing a petition that would have banned from public libraries "subversive" books by such authors as Voltaire, Rousseau, Proudhon, Renan, Sand, and Balzac, the orator invoked Napoleon III as "the régime's highest and most liberal authority." A group of Ecole Normale students sent him a letter of congratulations. Their leader was expelled; his friends went on strike; the government backed down; and the director, Désiré Nisard (1806–1888), and assistant director Pasteur were transferred. Since 1857 Sainte-Beuve had moved in a liberal direction and had come to regard the popular bonapartism of Prince Napoleon, cousin of the emperor, with admiration. A dinner he gave for the prince on 10 April 1868 at the Restaurant Magny created an uproar because the date fell on Good Friday (it had been chosen to fit the guest's schedule). On 7 May, Sainte-Beuve used the pretext of the new law on the press to speak in favor of intellectual freedom, and on 19 May he opposed the petition of an editor, Giraud, calling for liberty of higher education but really intended as an attack on the Paris Faculty of Medicine, which was condemned by the Catholic party for the materialism of its instruction (the minister of education, Victor Duruy, steering a difficult course between academic and political considerations, had in fact been compelled to annul a doctoral thesis "proving" the nonexistence of free will). The Senate had the wisdom to avoid intervening too directly in such matters and took no action on the petition. Sainte-Beuve continued his defense of Duruy. When the church castigated the minister's plan for secondary schools for women, the critic sent to *Le moniteur* (he had declined to leave the paper when it lost its official character) an article condemning the reactionary bishop of Montpellier. His editor having balked at certain expressions, Sainte-Beuve on 4 January 1869 published the article in the opposition *Le temps*. Princess Mathilde viewed the act as a form of treason and broke violently with her former confidant, who continued to publish articles in *Le temps*.

For the first time Sainte-Beuve was popular. But he did not break with the Empire or join the opposition, and his articles in *Le temps* were nonpolitical except for a letter of 7 September 1869 criticizing the government for its indifference to the hostility of the intellectuals. A reconciliation was planned between the critic and Princess Mathilde, but on 13 October 1869 Sainte-Beuve died following an operation. Even in death he created one last scandal, for he had insisted upon a civil funeral. Sainte-Beuve's works have continued to be an important source of information on the history of French literature from the Renaissance to the mid-nineteenth century. Historically accurate and precisely documented, his intellectual portraits reflect a unique ability to employ a historical framework in the service of critical evaluation and are a major reason for the fact that he remains France's most admired literary critic.

A. Bellessort, *Sainte-Beuve et le XIXe siècle* (Paris, 1954); A. Billy, *Sainte Beuve: Sa vie, son temps* (Paris 1952); J. Bonnerot, *Bibliographie de l'oeuvre de Sainte-Beuve*, 3 vols. (Paris, 1937–1952); G. Corbière Gille, *Critique de Sainte-Beuve* (Paris, 1973); P. Moreau, *La critique selon Sainte-Beuve* (Paris, 1964); M. Regard, *Sainte-Beuve* (Paris, 1959); C. Sainte-Beuve, *Correspondance générale de Sainte Beuve*, ed. J. Bonnerot, 18 vols. (Paris, 1935–1977), *Causeries du Lundi*, 15 vols. (Paris, 1857), *Nouveaux Lundis*,

13 vols. (Paris, 1863–1872), and *Les grands écrivains français*, ed. M. Allem, 22 vols. (Paris, 1926–1933).

Dolorès A. Signori

Related entries: ACADEMIE FRANCAISE; JANIN; MATHILDE; *MONITEUR*; *REVUE DES DEUX MONDES*; SENATE; TAINE.

SAINT-SAENS, CAMILLE (1835–1921), composer, pianist, organist, writer, and scholar; born at Paris, 9 October 1835. Gabriel Fauré aptly called Saint-Saëns the "most complete musician" of his time. Effortlessly, skillfully, and in a variety of styles, he wrote music for every medium: sacred compositions, operas and other stage works, songs, choral, orchestral, chamber, piano, and organ works, even incidental music for a film (in 1908, the first film score by a renowned composer). His impeccable technique as a pianist ranked behind only that of Franz Liszt (1811–1886) and Anton Rubinstein (1829–1894), and his astonishing musical memory and brilliant yet sensitive sightreading (including the reduction of orchestral scores) were unsurpassed. Eventually he performed on five continents. His mastery of the organ and his magnificent improvisations inspired from Liszt the epithet "king of organists." His astute writings on music, many of which were gathered in loosely structured books, embrace criticism, philosophy, scholarship, and anecdotal history. (He also wrote poetry, plays, and reports on his archaeological research and maintained an active interest in the sciences, particularly astronomy.) Through his activities as a performer, writer, editor, and teacher, he promoted not only progressive contemporaries such as Hector Berlioz (1803–1869), Liszt, and Richard Wagner (1813–1883) (although he ultimately reversed his position on Wagner) but also past masters, among them Jean Philippe Rameau, Marc Antoine Charpentier, Christoph Gluck, and various *clavecinistes*.

Brought up by his mother and her aunt, Saint-Saëns quickly evinced a precocity comparable to that of Mozart and Mendelssohn. He played the piano before his third birthday, wrote a piano piece at three, and performed in public at four. At ten he supplemented a program of challenging solos and concertos by offering to perform any of Beethoven's thirty-two piano sonatas from memory. He had composed a creditable symphony by fifteen. During his childhood, he studied piano with his great aunt and Camille Stamaty (1811–1870), organ with François A. P. Boëly (1785–1858), and composition with Pierre Maleden. From these teachers and through his own exploration, he learned the music of Bach, Handel, Haydn, Mozart, and Beethoven. At thirteen, he entered the Paris Conservatoire, where his instructors included organist François Benoist (1794–1878) and, for composition, Fromental Halévy (1799–1862).

The start of Saint-Saën's professional career coincided with the beginning of the Second Empire. His compositions, performances, and perceptive mind rapidly won the respect of the best musicians, among them Berlioz, Liszt, Charles Gounod, Georges Bizet (1838–1875), and Pauline Viardot. He was organist briefly at Saint Séverin, then at Saint Merri (1853–1857) and the Madeleine

(1857–1876). From 1861 to 1865, he was professor of piano at the Ecole Niedermeyer, a school for church musicians, where his pupils included Gabriel Fauré (1845–1924), who remained a lifelong friend and admirer. He composed prolifically throughout the Second Empire, producing numerous sacred vocal works, including a Mass (1856), the *Oratorio de Noël*, and some cantatas, roughly thirty songs (many to texts of Victor Hugo, a favorite poet), several attractive chamber pieces, three of his five symphonies (the first in 1851), two violin concertos (the first in 1859), three (of five) piano concertos, and the popular *Introduction et rondo capriccioso* for violin and orchestra. Although some of this music (notably the last-named work and the finales of the piano concertos) offers levity and spectacle in a manner commonly associated with the era, most is more subtle and refined. Many of his works remained unpublished until after 1870, and the Empire public knew Saint-Saëns mainly as a virtuoso performer, although in 1867 he was awarded the grand prize for musical composition at the Paris international exposition. At his frequent concerts, he programmed old and new concertos, chamber works, and solo piano music. Many listeners considered his elegant, reserved interpretations too dry.

In 1871 Saint-Saëns cofounded the Société Nationale de Musique, which successfully promoted young French composers. Admired by fellow musicians and gaining public acclaim (even more so outside of France), he would be elected to the Institut in 1881. Saint-Saëns composed and performed until the end of his long life and received many more honors, among them the grand cross of the Legion of Honor and honorary degrees from Cambridge and Oxford. But despite his continuing international celebrity and his acknowledged influence on Fauré and Ravel, he came to be considered passé by many younger musicians. He in turn vehemently opposed most new musical trends, particularly condemning Claude Debussy's achievement and the advent of atonality, though from the mid-1890s Saint-Saëns himself would essay a leaner compositional technique and experiment with modal writing, thereby anticipating to some degree the neoclassical movement.

Saint-Saëns's style is particularly difficult to summarize because of his versatility and wide-ranging eclecticism. Ever mindful of the classical principles that he absorbed in his youth and the French tradition of elegance, proportion, and clarity, he also assimilated the ideas of Schumann, Liszt, Wagner, and other contemporaries, Baroque practices, and the exotic music that he heard during his extensive travels. His music is characterized by meticulous craftsmanship, lively rhythms, a variety of textures (including masterful imitative counterpoint), interesting colors, and an underlying diatonicism against which chromaticism provides temporary contrast. Some works display cyclical techniques and thematic transformation. Most of all, Saint-Saëns's compositions reflect his fervent belief that music is form rather than expression; although they are criticized for lacking depth, the best are fitting tributes to his musical credo. Saint-Saëns died at Algiers, 16 December 1921.

D. Fallon, "The Symphonies and Symphonic Poems of Camille Saint-Saëns" (Ph.D.

diss., Yale University, 1973); J. Harding, *Saint-Saëns and His Circle* (London, 1965); S. T. Ratner, ''The Piano Works of Camille Saint-Saëns'' (Ph.D. diss., University of Michigan, 1972); E. Remberg, ''The Chamber Music of Saint-Saëns'' (Ph.D. diss., New York University, 1976); C. Saint-Saëns, *Ecole buissonière: Notes et souvenirs*, trans. E. G. Rich (Boston, 1919; reprinted 1969).

Jeffrey Cooper

Related entries: CAVAILLE-COLL; CONCERT LIFE.

SAINT-SIMONIANISM, the supposed social-economic doctrine that some historians have argued was influential in shaping Second Empire developments. By the time the Second Empire was established, the Saint-Simonian movement, a small group of young intellectuals who had built on the ideas of the comte de Saint-Simon after his death in 1825, had been dissolved for nearly twenty years. Most contemporaries, indeed, remembered less the theories and aims of Saint-Simonianism than the infamous celibate retreat to Ménilmontant in 1831 and the trial of its leaders and consequent collapse of the sect the following year. Prosper Enfantin (1796–1864), the sect's one-time leader, was already in late middle age and had retained the devotion of but a half-dozen former followers. During its brief existence, the sect had been marked by the intensity of commitment of its adherents, an intensity born of existential crisis, and by a series of bitter schisms and disavowals. After its collapse in 1832, erstwhile members continued repudiations and, more rarely, to effect reconciliations. They dispersed to follow diverse careers as intellectuals, journalists, engineers, and businessmen and to espouse very different theories and creeds.

It was asserted during the Second Empire, however, and many historians have subsequently claimed, that Saint-Simonian ideas in general and individual Saint-Simonians in particular exercised a powerful influence on government policy and on the economy in the 1850s and 1860s. In part at least, this is a myth, propagated by both left- and right-wing critics of the regime who thereby sought to attack policies and practices. Thus the journalist J. B. Capefigue (1801–1872), condemning the speculation of the period, blamed it on Saint-Simonians and Jews. The deputy August Pouyer-Quertier (1820–1891), an opponent of the liberal tariff policy, denounced what he termed the nefarious influence of Saint-Simonianism. When the Crédit Mobilier was on the verge of collapse in 1867, enemies of the regime celebrated the discomfiture of ''Saint-Simonian finance,'' and Raoul Boudon, the pamphleteer, lambasted Emile and Isaac Pereire, founders of the Crédit Mobilier, as ''Saint-Simonian pirates.'' This contemporary myth has been reinforced by contemporary scholars who see Saint-Simonian influence in Second Empire government policy. Others view the Saint-Simonians as a radical minority who, as entrepreneurs and engineers, were partly responsible for the more dynamic orientation of French capitalism at this time.

The validity of these claims depends on two propositions: that Saint-Simonian economic theories, either singly or collectively, had some originality and/or that those who had been involved in the sect still constituted a group after mid-century. The originality of their ideas, however, can be doubted. Certainly Saint-Simonians had been early and enthusiastic believers in an industrial future and in the need for some kind of central direction of the economy. They had also emphasized the importance of improving communications, of building canals and railways; however, these ideas and insights were neither original nor fully developed in their writings. Thus although they put emphasis on the importance of credit, they made no major contribution to banking theory, and only one of the techniques they proposed has any claim to originality—their plan for the issue of interest-bearing bank notes. Similarly, although they proposed that France build a network of railways, they did not anticipate the role railways would play and offered no solutions to the practical problems posed by railway building. After the breakup of the sect, many of those who had been involved in the movement continued to use Saint-Simonian catchwords such as *promotion of the happiness of the most numerous and poorest class* or *the liberating power of economic growth and the mastery of nature*. It is even possible that in Saint-Simonianism they had imbibed an enthusiasm for achievement, a confidence in what they were doing, that bolstered their later careers. This ideology, however, was little different from the confidence in the established order and progress possessed by others in the political and business elite.

The reputed influence of Saint-Simonianism might still be feasible if ex-members of the sect retained some sense of identity, some cohesion as a group, some idea of themselves as an elite working through the government to direct an economic development that would, for example, improve the lot of the masses. After the dissolution of 1832, however, ex-members did not constitute a group with shared memories, ideas, and outlook. Leaders of the sect had quarreled before the final breakup, and they continued to disagree. Enfantin and Michel Chevalier, who had been second in the Saint-Simonian hierarchy, saw each other only rarely in subsequent years. There was, then, no dedicated group of reformers working through the system to achieve Saint-Simonian ends. Indeed, whenever former Saint-Simonians met together, they failed to agree on means or on ends. When, in the heady days of March 1848, some sixty of them met to decide what they could do together, they found they could not agree on any common action, and the meeting broke up in disarray. The only truly Saint-Simonian achievement of the Second Empire was the beginning in 1865 of the publication of the forty-seven volumes of the collected works of Saint-Simon and of Enfantin.

It is true that a number of high-profile figures during the Second Empire had been involved, in varying degrees, in the sect prior to 1832. These included Chevalier, a senator and economic policy adviser; Paulin Talabot, who created a vast industrial empire and built railways in France and abroad; the Pereires and their Crédit Mobilier; and François Barthélemy Arlès-Dufour, a leading figure in the Lyons business community. But these were a minority of ex-Saint-Simonians. Others remained hostile to the established order as a political and economic system. Pierre Leroux (1797–1871), Edouard Charton (1807–1890), and Jean Reynaud (1806–1863) turned toward socialism and Gustave Biard

(d. 1852) toward communism. It might even be claimed—and a number of Saint-Simonians did so at the time—that those who achieved prominence and success, who adopted what the young Chevalier had once castigated as "bourgeois dress and the horrible round hat," did so by abandoning the most original of Saint-Simonian ideas, such as sexual emancipation, women's liberation, the abolition of inheritance, the improvement of the workers' lot, or the achievement of a new religious synthesis.

Some less-publicized members of the sect continued to pursue these less fashionable ideas. Both Olinde Rodrigues (1794–1851), one of the founders of Saint-Simonianism (Saint-Simon's secretary and a cousin of the Pereires), and Emile Vinçard sought to foster the cause of the working class, while others, like Gustave d'Eichthal (1804–1886), went on searching for a religion that would unite rather than divide humanity. For the rest, figures as diverse as the painter Rosa Bonheur, the composer Félicien David (1810–1876), the industrialist Eugène Schneider, the engineer Eugène Flachat (1802–1873), and the chemist Jean Baptiste Dumas have been signaled as Saint-Simonians. As for Napoleon III himself, although he certainly wanted through economic development to improve the condition of the lower classes, there is no direct evidence that he was influenced by Saint-Simonian thought.

Some of the innovations of the period that many contemporaries and some scholars associated with Saint-Simonianism owed little to its theories. This is true, for instance, of the Crédit Mobilier, which was a synthesis of previous experiments in France and abroad and owed more to the banker Jacques Laffitte (1767–1844) than to Saint-Simon. The Anglo-French commercial treaty of 1860, which both Emile Pereire and Chevalier helped bring about, owed little to the sect, which had not even discussed tariffs, let alone free trade. And if the Suez Canal owed something to ex-Saint-Simonians, some of whom had spent four miserable years in Egypt (1833–1837), and to Enfantin, who had set up a study group to build a Suez canal in 1846, it did not owe much. No ex-Saint-Simonian played any role in the company of Ferdinand de Lesseps (1805–1894), and none was invited to the canal opening in 1869.

The complexity of thinking, the psychological and intellectual experience that Saint-Simonianism represented for those who went through it in the late 1820s and early 1830s cannot be reduced to the actions of a handful of prominent figures under the Second Empire. There were, in fact, as many one-time adherents in the ranks of opponents of the regime as among its supporters. Besides, it is quite possible that those Saint-Simonians who achieved fame and success would have had similar achievements even if they had not passed through the experience. As Metternich had said earlier, they were "young men too out of the ordinary not to have a future." And in their rise to success, they discarded radical aspects of Saint-Simonianism that may have been the sect's most important attribute.

R. B. Carlisle, "The Birth of Technocracy: Science, Society, and Saint-Simonians," JHI 35 (July–September 1974), and "Les chemins de fer, les Rothschild et les Saint-Simoniens," EcS 5 (1971); S. Charléty, Histoire du Saint-Simonisme, new ed. (Paris,

1931); J. C. Eclabar, "The Saint-Simonians in Industry and Economic Development," *American Journal of Economy and Sociology* 38 (January 1979); M. Lévy-Leboyer, "La banque Saint-Simonienne et la première industrialisation française," *ASMP*, 127th year (1974); F. E. Manuel, *The Prophets of Paris* (Cambridge, Mass., 1962); B. M. Ratcliffe, "The Economic Influence of the Saint-Simonians: Myth or Reality?" *PWSFH* 5 (1977), and "Saint-Simonism and Messianism: The Case of Gustave d'Eichthal," *FHS* 9 (Spring 1976); G. Taboulet, "Le rôle des Saint-Simoniens dans le percement de l'Isthme de Suez," *EcS* 5 (1971); J. Walch, "Les Saint-Simoniens et les grandes entreprises du XIXe siècle," *EcS* 4 (1970); G. Weill, "Les Saint-Simoniens sous Napoléon III," *REN* 4 (1913).

Barrie M. Ratcliffe

Related entries: ARLES-DUFOUR; BANKING; CHEVALIER; INTERNATIONAL EXPOSITIONS; PEREIRE; POSITIVISM; RAILROADS; TALABOT.

SAINT VINCENT DE PAUL, SOCIETY OF, a charitable and religious organization of Catholic laymen founded at Paris in 1833 by Frédéric Ozanam (1813–1853) in association with a number of friends and fellow law students. The purpose of the organization was to fortify the faith of its members through service to the poor, prayers, spiritual readings, fellowship, discussion, and participation in religious festivals. Charitable visitations to the poor in their homes received the highest priority, for Ozanam and his colleagues believed that such good works inspired an infectious faith and love. Contributions by the members, yearly fees from honorary members, and donations by subscribers who acted as benefactors provided the requisite funds. Ozanam did not organize the society in accord with a social or political ideology or with the intention of restructuring the social system of his day. Modestly he hoped to help some unfortunates immediately instead of waiting for a sweeping regeneration of society to eliminate inequities for all. Nevertheless, the society's work was not devoid of social implications for, as Ozanam expected, it forced those drawn into contact with working-class misery to contemplate causes and remedies, and was soon feeding recruits to the Catholic social movement.

At a general meeting on 8 December 1835, the feast of the Immaculate Conception, the society adopted its rules and title. The basic Vincentian unit was the conference, normally connected with a parish that gave it its name. A succession of councils composed of delegates representing units below ascended to a general council, which first appeared under that name in 1840. The general council established broad policy for the largely autonomous conferences, conferred official status on them (a process known as aggregation) after a probationary period, and stood at the head of an international association as conferences spread throughout Europe and even to the United States in the 1840s. The ranking officer of the general council held the post of president-general; a legitimist, Adolphe Baudon (1819–1888), held that position from 1847 into the 1880s. Like his predecessor, J. Gossin, also a legitimist, he adhered to the rule of the society prohibiting it from engaging in politics, but reaction to the June Days of 1848, the death of Ozanam in 1853, and the rapid expansion in membership, which shrunk its student component to a small minority, gave the society a markedly conservative political complexion during the Second Empire.

While all of the conferences emphasized visits to the poor, individual chapters sponsored a wide variety of activities, especially in the cities. Hospital and institutional visits, hostels and other types of workers' lodgings, improvement of workers' housing, patronage for apprentices, mutual aid societies, evening courses, and similar endeavors occupied the members, who also furnished personnel and leaders for other Catholic enterprises, such as the association to have Sunday observed as a day of rest. In the process of grouping together for charitable activities the most energetic, influential, well-off Catholics, the society had created an organization of significant national influence. Legitimists, unable to engage in public service because of their opposition to the Empire, found an outlet in the society. It is not surprising that a number of imperial officials resented the competition of the St. Vincent de Paul Society and other religious organizations in areas of public assistance and feared their independence and potential for political opposition. These organizations were vulnerable under laws prohibiting combinations, and in 1850, 1852, and 1854 the government requested that they seek legal authorization. Victor Fialin Persigny, minister of the interior from 1852 to 1854, recognized the social contributions of the Vincentians but increasingly regarded them as politically dangerous. Baudon advised the conferences to comply with the request that they seek authorization whenever the prefects so insisted and also counseled them to furnish full information about their rules, meetings, membership, and activities. The general council decided that since bonapartist views were not well enough represented among its members, it should recruit for the council several Catholics devoted to the regime. Civil servants and government supporters were present throughout the society, but legitimists remained prominent by virtue of their social preeminence, wealth, and numbers.

Imperial efforts aimed at getting the religious associations and orders to seek authorization were not pursued with vigor. Few bothered to apply. During the 1850s, the society enjoyed steady growth unimpeded by the government. By 1861 more than thirteen hundred conferences were functioning in France alone with a total membership of over thirty-two thousand but probably well below the one hundred thousand often given. The general council administered a budget of some 5 million francs. Although the society generally abided by its rule prohibiting politics, Persigny, back again as minister of the interior in 1860, believed that it was involved with more than charity; conspiracy lurked in the wings. After all, the society united militant Catholics of all parties, directed a national network of councils and chapters by means of a hierarchical structure centered in Paris, and included conferences dominated by legitimists, especially in the west. It was spreading at a time when Napoleon's Italian policy, with its disastrous effect on the temporal power of the pope, was severely straining church-state relations. Indiscreet statements by legitimists, imprudent acts, such as the refusal of a gift from the Empress Eugénie, as well as some efforts to arouse opposition to the government's foreign policy confirmed Persigny's belief that the society was a menace to the regime. His circular of October 1861 to the prefects required all non-authorized charitable organizations, including the Masons, to seek authorization. The Society of St. Vincent de Paul was the main target. In November the government suppressed its general council; the council would be allowed to reconstitute itself only if it accepted a president-general nominated by Napoleon III, something it refused to do. Most of the conferences sought authorization as Baudon advised, though between three hundred and four hundred refused and disbanded in protest. Eugénie organized the Society of the Prince Imperial to help fill the gap created by the crippling of the Vincentians. Bishop Félix Dupanloup wrote two pamphlets against the government's actions; Catholic militants agitated in the press and the legislature. They were officers without troops, however, for the masses did not stir. Individual conferences struggled on in a disorganized fashion deprived of direction (even the provincial councils were suppressed) and deserted by civil servants, government partisans, and those who had joined out of self-interest. More disturbing was the disinclination of young Catholics to enroll. When the government began to demonstrate more tolerance in 1868, the society revived somewhat but no longer displayed its old vigor. Despite the restoration of the general council, the society's growth in France after 1870 was slow. As a worldwide organization, it was far from dead, however. By 1960, it counted some twenty-one thousand conferences with approximately three hundred thousand members.

A. Foucault, *Histoire de la Société de Saint-Vincent-de-Paul* (Paris, 1933); J. Schall, *Adolphe Baudon, 1819–1888* (Paris, 1897); L. J. Wheeler, "The Conflict between the Government of Napoleon III and the Society of Saint Vincent de Paul, 1860–1862" (Ph.D. diss., University of Georgia, 1972).

Raymond L. Cummings

Related entries: LEGITIMISM; LE PLAY; PERSIGNY; ROMAN QUESTION; SOCIAL CATHOLICISM.

SALON DES REFUSES, the section of the exhibition of fine arts (Salon) of 1863 reserved for works rejected by the jury. By 1863 the Salon had become an event of critical importance for French artists. It represented the opportunity to be seen, to win awards, and to become established. The importance of the Salons ensured that the method of selection—by a jury representing the Académie des Beaux-Arts—would be resented by those whose works were rejected. From the beginning there had been private counterexhibitions (for example, that of Gustave Courbet in 1855) and consideration of how to incorporate these into the Salons, which were held annually from 1830 through 1856, biennially from 1857 to 1863. As new artistic styles emerged (realism, pre-Impressionism) criticism grew that the Salon juries systematically rejected submissions that did not satisfy their criteria of subject matter and finish.

In April 1861 artist-critic Théodore Véron proposed that all submitted works should be displayed in categories of merit determined by the jury, even down

to a class of *oeuvres mauvaises*. The controversy sharpened when it was announced that for the 1863 Salon, artists would be limited to three entries each
(as in 1852 and 1853) and that (as in 1851) artists who had won first-class or
second-class medals at previous Salons would share with those who had been
named to the Legion of Honor the privilege of exhibiting without having to
submit their entries to the jury. On 1 March Gustave Doré and Edouard Manet
presented a petition to Alexandre Walewski (minister of state) requesting more
liberal rules. Misgivings concerning the new regulations seemed justified when
it was known in April that of some five thousand entries, almost half had been
rejected.

It was in this atmosphere of controversy that Napoleon III in late April visited
the Palais de l'Industrie, where the Salons were held (then known as the Palais
des Champs Elysées), in order to view the rejected entries. On 24 April the
Moniteur announced that by a command of the emperor, a section of the Salon
would be set aside for the rejected works in order that the public might decide
for itself concerning their merit. Director of Museums Comte Emilien Nieuwerkerke (1811–1892), who in that same year was appointed to the newly created
post of superintendent of fine arts with control over all government art programs,
gave the rejected artists the opportunity to remove their entries. More than six
hundred did so, with the result that perhaps fewer than five hundred chose to
exhibit in the Salon des Refusés.

The Salon opened to the public on 1 May 1863, the Salon des Refusés on 15
May. No official catalog was printed for the latter, although an incomplete one
was assembled by a committee of the artists. Despite an admission charge of 1
franc (except for Sundays), the public responded with enthusiasm, estimates of
attendance at the Salon des Refusés ranging from four thousand to seven thousand
on busy days. Henri Fantin-Latour, whose *Féerie* hung in the Salon des Refusés,
also exhibited in the regular Salon. Camille Pissarro exhibited three paintings
(*Landscape*, *Study*, and *Village*), Johann Jongkind (1819–1891) three (*Effect of
Winter*, *Dutch Canal*, *Ruins of Rozemond*), and James Whistler (1834–1903)
one (*Woman in White* or *Dame blanche*). Edouard Manet, all three of whose
submissions had been rejected by the jury, exhibited *Young Man in Costume of
a Majo*, *Mlle Victorine in Costume of an Espada*, and, most notably, *Luncheon
on the Grass*. For those whose secret hope was to bury the obstreperous artists
under a weight of ridicule, there was some cause for congratulation. Manet's
Luncheon on the Grass was an especial focus of scandal and derision. But in
perspective it is clear that the avant-garde gained greatly from the Salon des
Refusés. For the first time, the public could discern artistic trends. And as these
seemed to have been systematically excluded from the official Salon, the Academy itself appeared to represent a particular style. It might even be argued that
modern art in France was launched by the Salon des Refusés of 1863.

The year 1863 also witnessed a government effort to reform and to liberalize
the Salons (which were henceforth to be held annually) and the Ecole des Beaux-
Arts. In August it was announced that for 1864, artists would be limited to two

entries each, thus permitting more of them to exhibit, and that three-quarters of the jury would be elected by artists who were members of the Academy, or of the Legion of Honor, or holders of medals from previous Salons. The remaining quarter would be named by the government. Moreover, this jury would also choose the award winners. Some one hundred artists, including Charles François Daubigny and Constant Troyon (1810–1865), wrote the emperor to thank him for these reforms. Although the Salon des Refusés was repeated in 1864, only 529 artists were judged too weak to participate in the regular Salon and only 286 of those elected to exhibit a total of 375 works in the special section established for them. It is possible that the leaders of the 1863 Salon des Refusés were deliberately admitted in 1864 to the regular Salon. At the official awards ceremony, Marshal Jean Baptiste Vaillant, the minister of fine arts, took care to praise originality. If such was indeed the strategy, it succeeded. The Salon des Refusés would not be repeated again during the Second Empire.

Discontent continued, however. Although a lenient jury accepted 3,559 works in 1865, the jury for the 1866 Salon accepted only 3,338 (1,998 paintings). There was a storm of protest. Emile Zola, writing in Hippolyte de Villemessant's newspaper L'événement under the pseudonym "Claude," joined his boyhood friend Paul Cézanne (1839–1906), whose submission (his first) had been rejected, in criticizing the jury and calling for another Salon des Refusés. The appeal was ignored. In 1867 the annual Salon was held in conjunction with the international exposition of that year at Paris. The jury had been slightly modified: one-third were appointed, two-thirds elected by artists holding medals from previous Salons or belonging to the Legion of Honor; an attempt to have a third of the jury chosen by the Academy had failed. Once again there were many rejections. Except for Edgar Degas and Berthe Morisot (1841–1895), all Impressionist submissions were refused. Of three thousand French works entered, two thousand were rejected. When Nieuwerkerke did not respond to a petition for a new Salon des Refusés, Manet exhibited in his own pavilion. For the 1868 Salon, the jury was elected by all artists who had previously exhibited (except for the Salon of 1848, when there had been no jury). The jury's decisions in 1869 (under the influence of Jean Léon Gérôme) prompted renewed protest, again without results. In the final Salon of the Second Empire, although the Impressionists were well represented, the exclusion of Claude Monet led Daubigny to resign from the jury and Théodore Véron once again to demand a Salon des Refusés. Thus despite the obviously good intentions of the emperor, the art wars of the Second Empire continued unabated until the end.

A. Boime, "The Salon des Refusés and the Evolution of Modern Art," Art Quarterly 32 (1969), "The Teaching Reforms of 1863 and the Origins of Modernism in France," Art Quarterly, n.s. 1 (Autumn 1977), and The Academy and French Painting in the Nineteenth Century (London, 1970); E. G. Holt, ed., The Art of All Nations: 1850–1873: The Emerging Role of Exhibitions and Critics (New York, 1981); J. C. Sloane, French Painting between the Past and the Present: Artists, Critics, and Traditions from 1848 to

1870 (Princeton, 1951); D. Wildenstein, ed., "Le Salon des Refusés de 1863: Catalogue, études, et documents," *GBA* 66 (September 1965); E. Zola, *L'oeuvre* (Paris, 1886).
Related entries: COURBET; INTERNATIONAL EXPOSITIONS; MANET; MATHILDE; VAILLANT; VIOLLET-LE-DUC.

SAND, GEORGE (pseudonym of AMANDINE AURORE LUCIE DUPIN, baronne DUDEVANT, 1804–1876), novelist and playwright; born 1 July 1804, at Paris. By the beginning of the Second Empire, George Sand had already produced over thirty novels and plays in which are reflected the major philosophical currents of the first half of the century: the romantic longings of the early years, the surge toward democracy of 1830, and the optimism of 1848. Throughout her numerous works, her faith in a socially conscious religion and her belief in fundamental human goodness remained strong and unshaken. Too, as she reached middle age, Sand was an extremely well-known figure, having scandalized Paris with her numerous affairs and enjoyed the friendship of a great many of the major literary figures of the day. She had corresponded with Louis Napoleon and visited him at Ham, where he was imprisoned (1840–1846), but while approving the socialist inspiration of his book, *L'extinction du paupérisme*, which he had sent her, Sand made clear her opposition to a revival of authoritarian rule. During the Revolution of 1848, she enthusiastically supported the advanced republicans but became increasingly disillusioned and by the time of the coup d'état (December 1851) was prepared to submit to the new regime without approving it, since she believed that Louis Napoleon's election as president in 1848, although she had opposed it, reflected the will of the French people. For a time, it was thought that Sand herself would be arrested in view of her long history of republican and socialist leanings. Instead, she sought an interview with Louis Napoleon to plead for her friends. She saw him twice between January and March 1852 and was impressed by his generosity (he granted all her requests for clemency) and by his professed goals. Sand was, besides, an intimate friend of Louis Napoleon's cousin, Prince Napoleon, who visited her often at Nohant, her country home. While continuing her prolific literary career, she spent much time interceding on behalf of various prisoners, assisting their families, sending aid to exiles, and drawing up petitions, constantly appealing to Prince Napoleon, Empress Eugénie, and Princess Mathilde, the emperor's cousin.

In 1854, Sand's *Histoire de ma vie* began to appear in the Paris papers and delighted readers with her account of a half-century of memories. After a trip to Italy in 1855, Sand published (1856) *La Daniella*, a vehemently anti-papist novel, which did little to endear its author to the imperial censors. In fact, the result was a warning delivered to *La presse*, in which the novel was being serialized. Three new plays, also written in 1856, were not particularly well received, much to Sand's chagrin, since the aid she continued to give to the families of political exiles was putting considerable strain on her financial resources. More novels and plays followed, and scandal—to which Sand was no stranger—came once again in 1858 with *Elle et lui*, an autobiographical novel based on her Venetian affair with Alfred de Musset (1810–1857). François Buloz (1803–1876), the director of *Revue des deux mondes*, hesitated for some time before agreeing to publish the work, in which Musset was portrayed in a rather unfavorable light. When *Elle et lui* finally appeared, the poet's brother, Paul de Musset (1804–1880), was infuriated and retaliated with his novel, *Lui et elle*, in which he reversed the roles, fiercely attacking George Sand.

By 1861, Sand was once again in financial distress. Her great friend, Charles Augustin Sainte-Beuve, suggested that the Académie Française award her the Gobert prize of 20,000 francs. Alfred de Vigny lent his influential name to her cause, but François Guizot (1787–1874) opposed her, on the basis that she had in the past made scandalous comments about marriage and property (Sand did, in fact, stand for equality of education for women, for civil rights, and for equality in marriage, including the right of divorce, but she was far from a true feminist, particularly in regard to politics, which she considered a male domain). In the end, the prize was given to Adolphe Thiers, and only six of the twenty-four votes were in Sand's favor. Jules Sandeau (1811–1883), her former lover, did not even put in an appearance at the voting. The imperial court, which continued to extend its protection to Sand, was displeased with this result, and the empress suggested that Sand be elected to the Académie Française itself. However, in a pamphlet entitled "Pourquoi les femmes à l'Académie?" Sand declined the offer, expressing her respect, but stating that she had no desire to be linked to a body of men whose attitudes were old-fashioned and out of touch with contemporary thought.

It was about this time that George Sand invited Alexandre Dumas fils for a stay at her chateau in Nohant, which she now preferred to Paris, thereby consolidating a ten-year friendship. Together they produced several plays: Dumas turned Sand's *François le Champi* (1847) into a play, *Le fils naturel*, while her *Claudie* (1851) became the basis for his *Les idées de Madame Aubray* and *Denise*. For her part, Sand took Dumas' play, *Le mariage de Victorine*, and turned it into a novel, *Le Marquis de Villemer*, from which he then helped her to construct a second play. As a play, *Le Marquis de Villemer* created yet another *succès de scandale* in 1864. Sand, angered by the religious intolerance of the imperial government and outraged by the threat to free speech, clearly expressed her anti-clerical sentiments. At the premiere, she received the enthusiastic support of bands of students and workmen, who feared an organized demonstration against the play. However, there was none, and the production grossed over 5,000 francs at the Odéon at a time when 1,500 francs was considered more than acceptable. Sand continued in her anti-clerical vein with *Mademoiselle La Quintinie*, serialized in the *Revue des deux mondes* from the late spring of 1863. The novel was devoured by the Paris youth of the universities, who hailed Sand as a champion of the opposition. She herself, as a mark of her break with Rome, had had her two daughters baptized as Protestants, and she had many anti-clerical, republican friends, including the photographer Félix Nadar, for whose son, Paul, she was godmother.

In spite of the protection she had received, Sand remained unreconciled to the Second Empire, putting little faith in Napoleon III's liberalism. She had previously praised his Italian policy in two pamphlets (one of them devoted to Garibaldi), but she blamed Napoleon for having made a hasty peace after the French triumphs at Magenta and Solferino in 1859. Thus, in *Monsieur Sylvestre* (1865) as in *Valvèdre* (1861), she remained critical, incarnating her social theories in the characters of her novels. Yet in spite of her antipathy to the regime, the more liberal policies that emerged toward the end of the Second Empire softened her attitude to some extent, and she professed herself satisfied with the arrival of the Liberal Empire in 1869–1870. Early in 1870, the *Revue des deux mondes* began to publish Sand's *Malgré tout*. A wicked character, Mlle. d'Ortosa, was rumored to have been inspired by the Empress Eugénie, whose intransigent Catholicism and its supposed effect on her husband's policies had long troubled the author. Distressed, Eugénie asked Gustave Flaubert to approach Sand on the subject. He did so and was assured that no allusion to the empress had been intended. Sand viewed the danger of war with Prussia arising out of the German question with mounting apprehension after 1866. When she became aware of the aggressive stand taken in July 1870 by the French foreign minister, she begged Prince Napoleon to reason with him, but her appeal was unsuccessful. It was at this time that Sand modified her attitude to Thiers. She had long regarded him as the main architect of the July Monarchy and as a self-satisfied bourgeois. However, as Thiers continued to plead for caution and moderation, Sand came to view him as a sane man amid imprudent radicals, the one true statesman of the opposition. She regarded the French declaration of war as a criminal folly. After the defeats, she did not share Léon Gambetta's view that the war might still be won, and she welcomed, in a letter published in *Le siècle*, the decision for peace. She opposed the Commune, fearing that radicalism would destroy the republic as clericalism had ruined Christianity. Sand died at Nohant, 8 June 1876, content in the knowledge that the Third Republic had emerged from the chaos of the *année terrible*.

The collected works of George Sand fill 105 volumes. Of novels written during the Second Empire may be cited the following: *L'histoire du véritable Gribouille* (1851), *Le château des désertes* (1851), *Metalla* (1852), *Les Mississipiens* (1852), *Procope le Grand* (1853), *La marquise* (1853), *Les maîtres sonneurs* (1853), *La filleule* (1853), *Jean Ziska* (1853), *Adriani* (1854), *Lucie* (1854), *Mont Revêche* (1855), *Le diable aux champs* (1856), *Les beaux messieurs de Bois-Doré* (1858), *Les dames vertes* (1859), *Laure* (1859 and 1864), *L'homme de neige* (1859), *Jean de La Roche* (1860), *Flavie* (1860), *Tamaris* (1861), *Antonia* (1861), *La famille de Germandre* (1861), *La ville noire* (1861), *Autour de la table* (1862), *Confessions d'une jeune fille* (1865), *Flavie* (1866), *Le dernier amour* (1867), *Cadio* (1868), *Mlle. Merquem* (1868), *Pierre qui roule* (1869), *Le beau Laurence* (1870), and *L'autre* (1870). Of plays produced during the Second Empire may be cited the following: *Claudie* (1851), *Le démon du foyer* (1852), *Les vacances de Pandolphe* (1852), *Mauprat* (1853), *Molière* (1853),

Le pressoir (1853), *Flaminio* (1854), *Le Maître Favilla* (1855), *Françoise* (1856), *Comme il vous plaira* (1856), *Evenor et Leucippe* (1856), *Lucie* (1856), *Les légendes rustiques* (1858), *Narcisse* (1859), *Marguerite de Saint-Gemme* (1859), *Constance Verrier* (1860), *Les beaux messieurs de Bois-Doré* (1862), *Le pavé (1862)*, *Les dames vertes* (1863), *Le drac* (1864), *Le lis du Japon* (1864), *Le théâtre de Nohant* (1864), and *Le Don Juan de village* (1866).

P. Arnold, "Le socialisme illuminé de George Sand," *Question de* (Paris), no. 12 (1976); J. Barry, *Infamous Woman: The Life of George Sand* (New York, 1977); C. Cate, *George Sand* (New York, 1975); P. Cousteix, "Le socialisme de George Sand," *Ours*, no. 89 (1978); E. Dolléans, *Féminisme et mouvement ouvrier: George Sand* (Paris, 1951); G. Lubin, "George Sand et les Bonaparte," *SN*, 43, no. 309 (1980); F. Mallet, "George Sand n'a pas changé d'opinions politiques entre 1848 et 1871," *Europe* 56 (1978); G. S. Manifold, "George Sand: A Stage History" (Ph.D. diss., University of California, 1983); A. Maurois, *Lelia: The Life of George Sand*, trans. from 1952 French ed. (London, 1953); E. Modum, "Les idées litéraires et politiques de George Sand et de Gustave Flaubert, d'après leur correspondance," *Bulletin de l'Association des Amis de George Sand*, no. 1 (1978); *RHLF* 76 (July–August 1976; special issue on George Sand); G. Sand, *Correspondance de George Sand*, ed. G. Lubin, 15 vols., to date (Paris, 1964–); R. Winegarten, *The Double Life of George Sand, Woman and Writer* (New York, 1978).

Dorothy E. Speirs

Related entries: DUMAS FILS; FLAUBERT; REPUBLICANISM; SAINT-BEUVE; THEATER.

SARDOU, VICTORIEN (1831–1908), dramatist, one of the most applauded playwrights of the Second Empire; born 7 September 1831 at Paris. Having no desire to pursue a career in medicine, Sardou abandoned his studies and turned to his chief interest, the theater. Supporting himself as a copyist, bookseller's clerk, and tutor, he wrote his first play, *La taverne des étudiants*, in 1854. Although it failed miserably, Sardou was not discouraged. With the assistance of the famous actress Pauline Virginie Déjazet (1798–1875), he presented *Les premières armes de Figaro* at the opening of the Théâtre Déjazet, 17 September 1859. This first successful venture led to a second the following year with the production of *Les pattes de mouche* at the Gymnase. Its popularity extended to Britain, where two different adapations were staged at Drury Lane in 1860 and at the St. James Theatre in 1861. The same month, May 1860, *Monsieur Garat* premiered, to run for three months at the Théâtre Déjazet. Its success did much to bolster Sardou's theatrical reputation.

In the early 1860s, Sardou continued to compose witty, well-constructed, and diverting comedies of manners and intrigue, much in the style of Eugène Scribe and Alexandre Dumas fils: *Nos intimes* (Vaudeville, 1861), *Les ganaches* (Gymnase, 1862), *Les pommes du voisin* (Palais Royal, 1864), and *Nos bons villageois* (Gymnase, 1866). *Piccolino*, staged at the Gymnase in 1861, drew full houses and was a brilliant success. *La papillone* (Théâtre Français, 1862), *Les prés Saint-Gervais* (Théâtre Déjazet, 1862), and *Les diables noirs* (Vaudeville, 1863) did not fare as well. Nor did *Bataille d'amour* (Opéra Comique, 1863), written in collaboration with Karl Daclin and set to music by Auguste Emmanuel Vaucorbeil (1821–1884), or *Le dégel* (Théâtre Déjazet, 1864), the last play written by Sardou for his friend Virginie Déjazet. A celebrated dramatist, nevertheless, Sardou was decorated with the rosette of the Legion of Honor shortly after the premiere of *Les diables noirs*. To this same period belong two further minor works: *Don Quichotte* (Gymnase, 1864) and *Le Capitaine Henriot* (Opéra Comique, 1864), which was written in collaboration with Gustave Vaëz (1812–1862) and set to music by François Auguste Gevaërt (1828–1908). Many of Sardou's plays were to become the inspiration for operas, both during the Second Empire and later (for example, Puccini's *Tosca*).

Sardou composed three comedies in the 1860s that were particularly successful with French audiences: *Les vieux garçons* (Gymnase, 1865), *La famille Benoîton* (Vaudeville, 1865), and *Maison neuve* (Vaudeville, 1864). All were pungent satires on some phase of society in Paris toward the end of the Second Empire. Not inclined toward the *pièce de thèse* as were Emile Augier and Dumas fils, Sardou gently ridiculed the money-making parvenus and the false morality of the times. Although a member of the circle of Félix Nadar, Sardou was also a habitué of the salon of Napoleon III's cousin, Princess Mathilde, and his reputation was acknowledged at court. On four separate occasions, his plays were performed at the chateau of Compiègne, one of the imperial residences. Of those performed, however (*Les prés Saint-Gervais, Les ganaches, Nos intimes,* and *La famille Benoîton*), only the first was favorably received by the select audience.

Patrie! the first of Sardou's dramas and one of his finest plays, was staged at the Porte Saint Martin in 1869. It marked the revival of the historical drama, interest in which had waned toward the end of the Second Empire. Later rewritten in collaboration with Louis Gallet (1835–1898) as a lyrical drama, it would be set to music by Emile Paladilhe (1844–1926) and staged at the Opéra (1886). *Le roi carotte*, originally written before the war and set to music by Jacques Offenbach, would not be produced until 1872 at the Théâtre de la Gaîté. The range of Sardou's craft extended from rhymed vaudeville, through farcical, dramatic, and satirical comedy to historical tragedy. After the fall of the Second Empire, he continued to compose comedies, dramas, and libretti, many of which were adapted for both the British and the American stage. Among other Sardou plays performed during the Second Empire were *Les gens nerveux* (Palais Royal, 1859), *Les femmes fortes* (Vaudeville, 1860), *L'écureuil* (Vaudeville, 1861), and *La perle noire* (Gymnase, 1862). Sardou died at Paris, 8 November 1908.

J. A. Hart, *Sardou and the Sardou Plays* (Philadelphia, 1913); G. Moulu, *La vie prodigieuse de Victorien Sardou* (Paris, 1931).

Dolorès A. Signori

Related entries: MATHILDE; RACHEL; THEATER.

SCHLESWIG-HOLSTEIN QUESTION. See DANISH WAR.

SCHNEIDER, EUGENE (1805–1875), industrialist, entrepreneur and politician; director of the metallurgical-machinery firm Le Creusot and vice-president and president of the Corps Législatif under Napoleon III; born 30 March 1805 at Bidestroff (formerly in the Meurthe, today Moselle). His father, Antoine, was a notary, landowner, and member of the conseil général of the Meurthe. Schneider was educated at the collège of Nancy and at the Conservatoire des Arts et Metiers in Paris, where he attended night classes from 1822. Initially a commercial agent for a wool-spinning firm of Reims, he joined his elder brother Adolphe (1802–1845) as an employee of the Seillière bank in Paris in the 1820s and in 1827 became director of the Montvilliers forge at Bazeilles, where he demonstrated exceptional managerial talent. In 1836, he and Adolphe became joint directors of the ailing mining-metallurgical firm of Le Creusot (Saône-et-Loire), which they, along with their employer Seillière, and the forge master Boigues (Adolphe's father-in-law), purchased from Manby and Wilson for 2.68 million francs.

Under the direction of the Schneiders, Le Creusot, whose exploitation had begun with Ignace de Wendel in 1782, became a leading producer of iron and machinery in France. In 1838 and 1839, respectively, it achieved national fame by producing the first French locomotive and steamboat, and in 1840 (when it employed 1,250 workers and 600 miners) one of the firm's engineers, François Bourdon (1797–1865), invented the steam-driven hammer. Eugène Schneider directed these achievements as the head of the firm's technical operations, while his brother Adolphe, the senior partner, managed commercial affairs. In 1840 and again in 1846, Eugène visited Britain, where he was impressed by the large size of workshops, permitting extensive economies in comparison with their French counterparts. After his brother's accidental death in 1845, leaving Eugène as the firm's sole director, he applied the lessons of his British visit to his own factories. Producing iron and sheet metal, rails, locomotives, machinery, armaments, bridge parts, and steamboats—the last two in factories at Chalon-sur-Saône—an output valued at some 35 million francs in 1867, the Schneider enterprise became one of the largest industrial undertakings in France by the time of the Second Empire and the leading French producer of locomotives, steel rails, machinery, and arms, accounting for 10 percent of French iron production in 1869 (Wendel accounted for 11 percent). Much, though by no means all, of the ore and coal used in the firm's shops was mined in nearby pits owned and operated by the Schneider Company, making it one of the more integrated firms as well. This growth was reflected in the assets of the firm, which increased from 6 million francs in 1847 to 27 million in 1873—most of which was owned by the Schneider family from 1855—and in the number of employees, which reached some ten thousand by 1870. This spectacular growth derived in part from the transport revolution, especially from the demand for rails and rolling stock, but it was also, not least, the result of Eugène Schneider's outstanding direction. Known for his flexibility and sense of the concrete, he excelled both as technician and as entrepreneur. In 1854 the Société des Ingénieurs Civils applauded his technical achievements by making him a member by acclamation while his fellows in the business community sought his participation in a variety of joint ventures. He was vice-president of the PLM railroad company, regent of the Bank of France from 1854, and in 1864 first president of the Comité des Forges. As a partner of the Seillière-Demachy-Schneider bank (successor to the old Seillière establishment), he helped to found the Société Générale in May 1864 and served as its president. Although an ally of Paulin Talabot and Baron James de Rothschild against the unorthodox Pereire brothers, Schneider was very much a modernizer in his business outlook. In 1867 he adopted the Bessemer converter in his factories, and after 1860 he adapted to the increased competition following negotiation of the treaty of commerce with Britain rather than simply fighting the free trade tendencies of the regime as he had at first done, notably through *Le moniteur industriel*. Later, in fact, he would admit that Napoleon III had been right in his tariff policy. In 1865 Schneider justly boasted from the tribune of the Corps Législatif of receiving an order for fifteen locomotives from a British railway company, demonstrating his firm's ability to compete even in the homeland of the industrial revolution.

The ascent of Le Creusot to a position of international prominence coincided with Eugène Schneider's elevation to high political office. In 1845 he was elected to the Chamber of Deputies to succeed his brother and remained a deputy until 1848. In 1851 President Louis Napoleon Bonaparte appointed him minister of agriculture and commerce, a position he held from 24 January to 10 April. After the coup d'état of 2 December 1851, he was made a member of the Consultative Commission and in 1852 was again elected deputy of the Saône-et-Loire for the district of Autun, this time to the Corps Législatif as an official candidate. In March 1852 Napoleon III appointed him vice-president of that body, where he served until his appointment as president in April 1867, replacing comte Alexandre Walewski. Although accused by more radical elements of representing the forces of reaction, Schneider gained the respect of a wide spectrum of the Corps Législatif for his judicious handling of controversy. Historians generally have regarded his politics as moderately liberal and pro-imperial, pointing out his role in persuading the emperor not to abandon the liberal press law in 1868 and in convincing him to dismiss Eugène Rouher in 1869. When Napoleon III named the conservative Jérôme David vice-president of the Corps Législatif (1869), Schneider offered his resignation, but it was refused. Schneider's election to the presidency of the Corps Législatif in December 1869, when the legislators were first allowed to choose their own officers, indicated the extent of respect for him among the deputies. His moderation and tact were tested most severely on the afternoon of 4 September 1870 when he presided over the last meeting of the legislature in the face of invading crowds (after Sedan he had shown a willingness to lead the Corps Législatif in substituting itself for the disintegrating regime). Forced to adjourn the meeting, Schneider was in no condition to preside the final meeting of the rump of the Corps Législatif that night. He withdrew from national politics but remained a close friend and consultant of Adolphe

Thiers, who sought his assistance in 1873 for manufacturing steel cannons to modernize the French army.

Besides his reputation as industrialist and politician, Schneider was known as a philanthropic employer with a progressive vision. His Saint-Simonian sympathies inclined him in this direction, and his beneficence extended to the town of Le Creusot (population 25,000), which historians have described as one with the factory, as well as to the workers of the Schneider enterprise. In addition to parks, walkways, and *cités ouvrières*, the Schneiders built several schools— including one for professional training of *cadres*—a church, and a hospital to provide free health care for workers and their families. The family's contributions to the town kept its inhabitants among the most literate, well housed, well fed, and generally healthy urban populations in nineteenth-century France, despite rapid growth. The town's prosperity and social peace also reflected Schneider's progressive management. He regarded his workers as assets to his enterprise, whose capacities should be developed through appropriate education and job training and whose devotion should be cultivated through a "totally moral administration." Le Creusot was renowned for its high wages, which were scaled in such a way as to stimulate productivity and to reward talent and skill. The firm's disciplinary methods—warning, suspension, and expulsion—were considered advanced in comparison with the system of fines practiced elsewhere.

Whatever its extent, this progressive management was essentially paternalistic and stopped short of allowing workers participation in the direction of their social services, even when these were funded out of their own pockets. The firm's celebrated *caisse de prévoyance*, used to pay for workers' funerals, to help support the church and the schools, and to give an income to workers with long illnesses, was controlled by the directors of the enterprise, even though it was funded by a 2.5 percent levy on workers' wages. In 1870 Schneider decided to test by plebiscite this unilateral control, expecting workers to confirm standing practice. Instead, the votes favored workers' control, while the majority of workers abstained from expressing their views and seemed, by doing so, to accept the outcome of the ballot. Schneider subsequently dismissed the vocal, articulate machinist Adolphe Alphonse Assi (1840–1886), who had led the campaign for workers' control, and provoked a partial strike (January). Refusing to negotiate, Schneider called for and received government troops to protect the "freedom to work," and the strike was quickly broken. A second strike, over demands that included shorter working days and higher pay, failed in April after twenty-three days. Since Schneider was president of the Corps Législatif at the time of these incidents, they provoked accusations of abuse of power, especially from the extreme Left. Once a leading example of the philanthropic employer, Schneider, whose personal income was estimated at 1.5 million francs in 1870, became for many a symbol of the alliance of capital, especially big capital, with the state against the interests of workers. Certainly he represented a dynasty, allied by marriage to the aristocracy, as well as to the Lebaudy family (sugar refineries), the Mame family (publishers), and even the Wendels, who under

Baron Alexis Charles de Wendel (1809–1870) represented the other major French metallurgical interest during the Second Empire. Schneider's nephew sat in the Corps Législatif, and his son and grandsons would follow him in parliament, while a son-in-law would serve as minister under the Third Republic.

Eugène Schneider died on 27 November 1875 at Paris, leaving behind him his widow, Constance Le Moine des Mares, a Protestant to whom he had been married since 1837, his son, Henri (born 1840), who succeeded him as director of the enterprise, and his daughter, Félicie, widow of Alfred Desseilligny, twice a member of de Broglie cabinets. A funeral cortege of thirty thousand persons and a statue erected in Schneider's honor at Le Creusot, through the contributions of fifteen thousand persons, testified to the extent of his popularity and renown.

P. Ponsot, *Les grèves de 1870 et la Commune de 1871 au Creusot* (Paris, 1958); J. A. Roy, *Histoire de la famille Schneider et du Creusot* (Paris, 1962).

George J. Sheridan, Jr.

Related entries: BANKING; COBDEN-CHEVALIER TREATY; COMITE DES FORGES; CORPS LEGISLATIF; DUPUY DE LOME; LA RICAMARIE; MARTIN; PEREIRE; RAILROADS; ROTHSCHILD; SAINT-SIMONIANISM; TALABOT.

SCHNEIDER, HORTENSE (1833–1920), actress, singer, and courtesan; born 30 April 1833 at Bordeaux. Schneider's father was a German master tailor who married a French woman and later died of drink. The child wanted desperately to be an actress, studied singing for several years, appeared first on a Bordeaux stage at age sixteen, joined a provincial troupe, and made her professional debut at Agen (Lot-et-Garonne) on 15 May 1853 as Inès in *La favorite*. In 1855 Schneider had been singing for two years at Angers, when she came to Paris and was introduced by her current lover, who was in the cast of Jacques Offenbach's *Les deux aveugles*, to the composer. Offenbach hired her at 200 francs a month to sing in his newly acquired theater, the Bouffes Parisiens. Her debut on 31 August 1855 in a curtain raiser, *Une pleine eau*, and in Offenbach's *Le violoneux*, was a triumph, despite a bad attack of stage fright. Although Schneider's beauty was slightly flawed and her voice small, she excelled in projection and enunciation, had real talent as an actress, and possessed a genuine star quality.

After *Le violoneux*, Schneider appeared at the Bouffes Parisiens in *Trombalcazar* (3 April 1856) and *La rose de Saint-Flour* (12 June 1856) before going to the Théâtre des Variétés in September 1856, on the expiration of her contract with Offenbach. After two seasons at the Variétés, she signed, in August 1858, a contract with the Théâtre du Palais Royal, where she would remain until 1864. A number of factors led to the exclusion of Schneider from Offenbach's wildly successful *Orphée aux enfers* (21 October 1858): her contractual obligations, her demand for 500 francs a month, and the fact that she had just had a baby by her lover, the duc de Gramont-Caderousse. Discouraged at the slow pace of her career and saddened by the lingering death of the duc de Gramont-Caderousse, then in his thirties, of tuberculosis, Schneider was preparing to leave the stage when Offenbach persuaded her, for a salary of 2,000 francs a month, to play Helen in *La belle Hélène* (17 December 1864, Variétés). This first major collaboration of Offenbach, Ludovic Halévy, and Henri Meilhac marked the beginning of Hortense Schneider's real fame. As actress and courtesan, she went thereafter from success to success: as Boulotte in *Barbe-Bleue* (5 February 1866, Variétés), for which she was paid 300 francs a night; as Métella in *La vie parisienne* (21 October 1866, Palais Royal); and, especially, as the duchess in *La Grande Duchesse de Gérolstein* (12 April 1867, Variétés), for which she was paid 4,500 francs a night. In that year of the great Paris world's fair, Schneider became the toast of Europe and the enchantress of kings, some of whom rushed directly from the railroad station to the theater.

A visit to London in 1868 was followed by *La Périchole* (6 October 1868, Variétés), and *La diva* (22 March 1869, Bouffes Parisiens), the last two Offenbach operettas in which Schneider was to sing. *La Périchole* was her final undoubted triumph. After 1870 she sang at the Palais Royal again (1871), at Saint Petersburg (1872), and once more at the Variétés (1873), before retiring to live the quiet life of a wealthy bourgeois (she had been given a legacy of 50,000 francs in October 1865 in the will of the duc de Gramont-Caderousse). Hortense Schneider died at Paris on 6 May 1920 in the same year that saw the disappearance of another long-lived symbol of the Second Empire, the Empress Eugénie.

M. Rouff and T. Casevitz, *Hortense Schneider: La vie de fête sous le Second Empire* (Paris, 1931).

Related entry: OFFENBACH.

SCRIBE, EUGENE (1791–1861), dramatist and librettist; born at Paris, 24 December 1791. By the beginning of the Second Empire, Scribe was already a much-celebrated playwright. In a single decade alone (from 1820 to 1830), he had written well over one hundred plays for the Paris stage, working often in collaboration with other playwrights or librettists: Germain Delavigne (1790–1868), Mélesville (1787–1865), and Ernest Legouvé (1807–1903). By attacking romanticism when it was most popular, Scribe earned several million francs and won great popularity. Both the comedies of manners and the historical and political comedies written later in his life reflected the solid bourgeois values of honesty, filial obedience, and morality. This, and his popularity, led to his appointment during the Second Empire to the municipal council of Paris. Still in the favor of audiences in the 1850s, Scribe was severely criticized by younger writers and their allies in the press. Victorien Sardou was an exception; the plays of Scribe were the subject of careful analysis by Sardou before he composed his first major success, *Les premières armes de Figaro*, in 1859.

During the last decade of his life, Scribe continued to dominate vaudeville and to appear on the more serious stages, both with his own plays and those written in collaboration with Ernest Legouvé: *Bataille de dames* (Théâtre Français, 1851), and *Les doigts de fée* (Théâtre Français, 1858). Scribe's stage sense and his flair for the well-made play recommended him to an astonishing variety of composers of opera. Adolphe Adam used him as librettist for seven operas; Daniel Auber (1782–1871) for thirty-eight, including *Marco Spada, ou la fille du bandit* and *Le cheval de bronze* (both produced in 1857); Vincenzo Bellini (1801–1835) for one (*La sonnambula*); Luigi Cherubini (1760–1842) for one; Gaetano Donizetti (1797–1848) for five, including *Elisir d'amore* and *La favorite*; Charles Gounod for one (*La nonne sanglante*, 1854); Fromental Halévy (1799–1862) for six, including *La Juive* and *Le Juif errant* (1852); Giacomo Meyerbeer for five, including *Les Huguenots*, *Le prophète* and *L'Africaine* (produced 1865); Gioacchino Rossini (1792–1868) for two; Franz von Suppé (1819–1895) for one; and Giuseppe Verdi (1813–1901) for two, *Les vêpres siciliennes* (1855) and *Un ballo in maschera* (1859).

Among other works composed by Scribe during the Second Empire may be listed the drama *La czarine* (Théâtre Français, 1855) and a number of comedies: *Mon étoile* (Théâtre Français, 1854), *Feu Lionel, ou qui vivra verra* (Théâtre Français, 1858), *Les trois Maupins, ou la veille de la régence* (Gymnase, 1858), *Rêves d'amour* (Théâtre Français, 1859), *La fille de trente ans* (Vaudeville, 1859), and *La frileuse* (Vaudeville, 1861). In addition, Scribe composed the libretti of a large number of operettas, including: *Les mystères d'Udolphe* (Opéra Comique, 1852), *Marco Spada* (Opéra Comique, 1852), *La lettre au Bon Dieu* (Opéra Comique, 1853), *Le nabab* (Opéra Comique, 1853), *L'étoile du nord* (Opéra Comique, 1854), *La fiancée du Diable* (Opéra Comique, 1854), *Jenny Bell* (Opéra Comique, 1855), *Manon Lescaut* (Opéra Comique, 1856), *La chatte métamorphosée en femme* (music by Jacques Offenbach, Bouffes Parisiens, 1858), *Broskovan* (Théâtre Lyrique, 1858), *Les trois Nicolas* (Opéra Comique, 1858), *Les petits violons du roi* (Théâtre Lyrique, 1859), *Yvonne* (Opéra Comique, 1859), *Le nouveau Pourceaugnac* (Bouffes Parisiens, 1860), *Barkouf* (music by Offenbach, Opéra Comique, 1860), *La Circassienne* (Opéra Comique, 1861), *Madame Grégoire* (Théâtre Lyrique, 1861), *La beauté du Diable* (Opéra Comique, 1861), *La fiancée du roi de Garbe* (Opéra Comique, 1864), and *L'ours et la pacha* (Opéra Comique, 1870). Scribe's complete works fill seventy-six volumes. He died at Paris on 20 February 1861.

N. Arvin, *Eugène Scribe and the French Theater, 1815–1860* (New York, 1924); H. Koon and R. Switzer, *Eugène Scribe* (Boston, 1980).

Dolorès A. Signori

Related entries: GOUNOD; MEYERBEER; OFFENBACH; THEATER.

SECOND EMPIRE, officially proclaimed 2 December 1852, one year after the coup d'état that had destroyed the Second Republic. Actions by Louis Napoleon immediately following the coup d'état appeared to indicate an intent to restore imperial government to France in the near future. On 1 January 1852, there was a *Te Deum* at Notre Dame, and decrees were issued restoring the imperial eagle to the French flag and ordaining that the prince president's effigy would appear on the coinage. On that day, too, Louis Napoleon moved his official residence from the Elysée to the Tuileries Palace. On 24 January, titles of nobility were restored by decree and a constitution formally promulgated that, with little change, could become the basis for an imperial regime. In signing the constitution, the president for the first time had signed himself "Louis Napoléon" rather than "Louis Napoléon Bonaparte." On 17 February, the birthday of Napoleon I was decreed the national holiday of France. On 5 May, the death of the first emperor (whose works Louis Napoleon had ordered to be published) was solemnly celebrated. And on 10 May, the imperial eagles were distributed to the army.

Still, Louis Napoleon hesitated to take the step that many had condemned as the fatal error of his uncle. Efforts by the imperialists, led by Victor Fialin Persigny, to organize public opinion through the conseils généraux were inconclusive. But a tour by Louis Napoleon of central and southern France (the regions least favorable to him) in September and October 1852, during which Persigny, without the prince president's knowledge, encouraged numerous demonstrations, was decisive. In a speech at Bordeaux on 9 October, where the prefect, Georges Haussmann, had masterfully orchestrated the reception, Louis Napoleon attempted to lay to rest the greatest fear associated with a restoration of the Empire when he proclaimed "L'Empire, c'est la paix." By 16 October the issue had been decided. Several days after his return to Paris, the Senate was convoked to deliberate on a restoration of the Empire. The prince president had already decided on the title "Napoleon III," reasoning that it did not imply legitimacy but simply recognized that there had been a reign, however brief, of Napoleon I's son, the King of Rome. On 7 November, reflecting Louis Napoleon's wishes, the Senate voted a *sénatus-consulte* that restored the Empire under Napoleon III and called for a plebiscite to confirm the decision. Only one senator, Louis Napoleon's friend and a former tutor of his brother, the republican Narcisse Vieillard (1791–1857), voted no. The plebiscite on 21–22 November was decisive: 7,824,189 voted for the Empire, 253,145 were opposed. But there were 63,326 spoiled ballots and 2,062,798 abstentions, the latter particularly numerous in the west where legitimism was strong. At Paris there were 54,000 *no* votes as well as 209,000 *yes*. Nevertheless, it is clear that while Persigny may have helped to crystallize a sentiment for restoring the Empire, he did not create it. The decision was genuinely popular in a country that just two years before had seemed poised on the brink of anarchy and civil war.

Louis Napoleon would have liked to have been crowned by the pope at Notre Dame as had been his uncle, but Pius IX, whose relationship with his protector was delicate, declined. Nor could the emperor, for various reasons, accept the pope's invitation to come to Rome. And so the negotiations dragged on until ended by the Crimean War (1854–1856). In regard to the reaction of the great powers, the outcome was happier. Favorable to the coup d'état, they were not pleased with the reestablishment of the Empire. It stirred memories of the first Napoleon's military conquests, especially in the mind of Czar Nicholas I of Russia. Austria's efforts, however, to organize a common front that would extract guarantees from France failed as a consequence of Britain's decision to accept the reassurances already given by Louis Napoleon. In the end, only Nicholas carried out even the anodine sanction of addressing the new emperor not as "brother" but as "friend." ("Tell the emperor," Napoleon III observed to the Russian ambassador, "that I am pleased; we must accept our families, but we choose our friends.") On 25 December 1852 a *sénatus-consulte* modified the constitution in order to adapt it to the imperial form, the succession having been fixed by previous decree in the line of Prince Jérôme Bonaparte (1784–1860), failing a direct or adoptive male heir.

S. Blot, "Le Second Empire, sa préparation," *La nouvelle revue*, vols. 105–108 (1930); A. Dansette, "Le rétablissement de l' Empire," *RDM*, nos. 18 and 19 (1965); H. Daniel Thomas, "The Reactions of the Great Powers to Louis Napoleon's Rise to Power in 1851," *CHJ* 13 (June 1970).

Related entries: AUTHORITARIAN EMPIRE; BONAPARTISM; CONSEIL D'ETAT; CONSTITUTION; COUP D'ETAT; FETE NATIONALE; *DES IDEES NAPOLEONIENNES*; LOUIS NAPOLEON; PERSIGNY; PLEBISCITE; PRINCE NAPOLEON; PRINCE PRESIDENT; SENATE; UNIVERSAL MANHOOD SUFFRAGE.

SEDAN, town in the Ardennes (on the Meuse River) where Napoleon III suffered his final defeat during the Franco-Prussian War and was taken prisoner together with the Army of Châlons. The Sedan campaign began on 23 August 1870 when Marshal Marie Edme Patrice de MacMahon, commander of the army that had formed at the great military camp of Châlons-sur-Marne following the defeats of August and the investment of Marshal Achille Bazaine's Army of the Rhine in Metz, determined to march eastward from Reims to the relief of Bazaine. MacMahon, who was under pressure from Paris to relieve Metz, had received a message from Bazaine that he intended to break out to the north, toward Montmédy. The Army of Châlons (about 100,000 men, 419 cannon) began its advance toward Metz already weary and demoralized. MacMahon, who made a most ineffective use of his cavalry for reconnaissance, did not at first realize that the German chief of staff, Helmuth von Moltke, had created from elements of Charles Frederik von Steinmetz's First Army and Frederick Charles' Second Army a new force, the Army of the Meuse, commanded by Albert, crown prince of Saxony. This Fourth Army, combined with the Third Army of Prussia's Crown Prince Frederick William, began to close on the French as they moved eastward. In the meantime, other German troops tightened their vise on Strasbourg, Metz, Verdun, and Phalsbourg and on 25 August took the Châlons base that MacMahon had recently left (about 100 miles east of Paris).

Although Napoleon III had abandoned command on 13 August, for reasons of health, he was prevented for political reasons from returning to Paris. He and his fourteen-year-old son, the prince imperial, therefore accompanied Mac-Mahon's army. This was an additional reason for confusion since the relationship between the emperor and his marshal was uncertain, at least in MacMahon's mind. The latter seems to have felt (although he never sought clarification) that Napoleon III retained final command authority. On 27 August MacMahon at last realized his danger, but the comte de Palikao, who had formed a government on 10 August (following the overthrow of Emile Ollivier), urged him and his weary men on. The previous day, the French emperor had sent the prince imperial to Mézières, only an hour from the Belgian frontier. On 28 August, as two German armies totaling some 220,000 men closed in on Paris, the French government opened the subscription to a war loan of 1 billion francs.

On 30 August, General Charles de Failly (1810–1892), commanding the vanguard of the Army of Châlons, was defeated at Beaumont while Napoleon III looked on. This action marked the cutting off of MacMahon's line of retreat, although the marshal, nourishing his illusions, appears to have reached the decision as well to give his men, exhausted by days of slogging through rain and mud, a brief rest at the small and obsolete fortress of Sedan. Provisions were short; three armies, totaling 250,000 men, with 500 cannon, were closing in on the French; and Sedan, located 7 miles south of the Belgian frontier and surrounded by hills, was not only far too cramped (it would have been crowded with 15,000 troops); it was also a potential trap.

Nevertheless, on 31 August the Army of Châlons began to take up its positions, which roughly resembled the letter J, around Sedan. VII Corps of General Félix Douay (1816–1879) was north of the city between the Calvaire of Illy (which, because it was the highest point in the area, would prove to be the strategic key to the coming battle) and the village of Floing. I Corps of General Auguste Ducrot (1817–1882), next in line, faced east, guarding the heights above the Givonne Valley. South of Ducrot was XII Corps of General Barthélemy Lebrun (1809–1889), which was to hold the French line as far south and west as the suburb of Bazeilles. V Corps, under General Emmanuel Félix Wimpffen (1811–1884), which had suffered badly at Beaumont on 30 August, was held in reserve. Hardly had the French taken up these positions when the Germans began to probe them in force. If MacMahon did not understand the situation, Moltke certainly did. He had ordered the newly created Meuse Army to advance along the right (or west) bank of the Meuse in order to turn the French flank, while the Third Army was to advance north in order to cut the French line of retreat to Mézières. In attendance with the two German armies were Moltke, Albrecht von Roon (the minister of war), Chancellor Otto von Bismarck, and King William I of Prussia. That night it was the Germans, not the French, who placed their cannon on the hills above Sedan.

The actual battle began about 4 A.M. on 1 September when the Bavarian Corps, under General von der Tann, attacked the French outpost at Bazeilles but were at first repulsed by French marines. Still, an important bridge there was not blown up even though MacMahon had ordered its destruction. This omission would contribute to the loss of Bazeilles to the Bavarians by the early afternoon after vicious fighting in which the civilian populace involved itself. (In retaliation the German troops burned the town and shot a number of civilians.)

One flank of the French army had thus been turned, and the possibility of further retreat was sharply reduced. With the fall of Bazeilles, the German attack began to develop northward, with the Third Army engaged against the troops of Douay's VII Corps along the hills above the Givonne. Here the overwhelming superiority of German artillery, with its greater range and superior percussion fuses, proved devastating. Before noon, a shell fragment wounded MacMahon in the leg as he was observing the last of the fighting at Bazeilles. This incident led to paralyzing confusion in the French ranks. MacMahon passed on his command to Ducrot, the ablest of the French generals of the Army of Châlons. Ducrot immediately ordered a general retreat in the direction of Illy as a preliminary to retirement to the stronger fortress of Mézières. As the operation began, however, General Wimpffen appeared with a letter from the comte de Palikao naming him to command the Army of Châlons in case MacMahon should be unable to carry on. Wimpffen promptly rescinded Ducrot's order, thus ensuring the defeat and destruction of the army, since the Germans in late afternoon would cut the Sedan-Mézières road, the last avenue of escape.

Wimpffen nevertheless proceeded with his now completely unrealistic plan to attempt a counterattack at Bazeilles in order to break out of the German ring to the south and then continue the march to the aid of Bazaine. Due to growing disorganization in the French ranks, however, nothing came of the attempt, and a massive and spontaneous French retreat into Sedan itself began at mid-afternoon. The fall of the Calvaire of Illy turned this movement into a rout. The last French attempt to avert complete disaster was the desperate one made by General Auguste Margueritte (1823–1870), whose cavalry division was ordered to attack and break through the German lines at Floing. Margueritte, who was fatally wounded before the attack began, was spared the sight of his heroic troopers' decimation. Yet in spite of repeated failure, the attack was pressed again and again.

By late afternoon of 1 September, the Army of Châlons had abandoned the field altogether and fallen back in complete disarray into the dubious shelter of Sedan. Napoleon III, who had arrived by train at Sedan on the evening of 30 August, had spent the morning of 1 September seeking death in the midst of his troops. Now, as shells rained on the town, he realized clearly (as did Eugénie at Paris) the political advantages that would follow from his death in the rubble of a fortress defended to the last. But he was unwilling to sacrifice the lives of almost ninety thousand men to that end. He therefore resumed authority and, despite Wimpffen's objections, sought an armistice. After an uncoordinated attack led personally by Wimpffen failed, he reluctantly accepted the emperor's decision. A white flag was raised, and Napoleon III wrote in his own hand to King William I of Prussia: "Mon frère, n'ayant pu mourir à la tête de mes troupes, je dépose mon épée au pied de votre majesté." On the morning of 2 September, after the French emperor had met with Bismarck, Moltke, and William I, the capitulation was signed. The German terms were harsh, even vindictive. The Army of Châlons (39 generals, 2,300 officers, 84,000 men; 25,000 had been captured in battle and some 10,000 had escaped into Belgium) was forced to lay down its arms without conditions. It was to be marched into captivity until the war should end. On the other hand, Napoleon III refused to negotiate with Bismarck, pronouncing himself a simple prisoner of war. At 11 A.M. the armistice terms went into effect. At 6 P.M. word of the disaster reached the French government. Two days later, on 4 September, a revolution at Paris overthrew the Second Empire. The next day Napoleon III arrived at Wilhelm-shöhe, his place of captivity.

The causes of the French defeat were numerous. First, the Army of Châlons, although it fought well, was outnumbered by more than two to one. Second, because of the indecision of Palikao and MacMahon and his staff, the French maneuvered themselves into a hopeless position, a position in which they had no choice but to fight under the most adverse conditions. By contrast, German maneuver and deployment were smoothly and masterfully executed with little if any indecision at the top level of command. Finally, the German artillery, which outranged French guns in addition to being armed with shells equipped with percussion fuses, completely overpowered the French artillery and then played havoc with troop concentrations. Perhaps the French could have overcome any one of these disadvantages, but in combination they proved fatal. Through the last years of his life, Napoleon III accepted full responsibility for the disaster.

General H. Castelnau, "Sédan et Wilhelmshöhe [Castelnau's journal, ed. by Louis Sonolet]," *La revue de Paris*, 36, 15 October, 1 November 1929; A. Dupuy, *Sedan et l'enseignement de la revanche* (Paris, 1975); General B. L. Joseph Lebrun, *Bazeilles-Sedan* (Paris, 1891); Baron A. Verly, *Souvenirs du Second Empire: Les étapes doulou-reuses: L'empereur de Metz à Sedan* (Paris, 1908); H. Welschinger, "En évoquant Sedan: Cent ans après la bataille," *IH* 32 (1970).

Eric A. Arnold, Jr.

Related entries: BAZAINE; CHISLEHURST; FRANCO-PRUSSIAN WAR; MACMAHON; QUATRE SEPTEMBRE.

SENATE, the appointive body that, under the constitution of 14 January 1852, exercised constituent power, judged the constitutionality of laws, supervised the constitution, and advised the emperor. The Senate first convened at the Palais du Luxembourg 30 March 1852; it met for the last time on 4 September 1870.

Cardinals, marshals, admirals, and, with imperial consent, French princes were senators by right for life. Others were appointed by the emperor (up to 150 by the *sénatus-consulte* of 25 December 1852). In the revised constitution of May 1870, the number of senators was to be no more than two-thirds that of the number of deputies. Appointment was for life. A senator was not removable and, by the *sénatus-consulte* of 25 December 1852, received an annual stipend of 30,000 francs. Seventy-two senators were named in January 1852 and a second group in March 1853. One-quarter were army officers. The Institute, business, the prefectoral corps, and the two chambers of the legislature of the July Mon-archy provided many of the others. And as many as possible of the few survivors of the aristocracy and leadership of the First Empire were appointed. The Senate always contained a higher proportion of authentic bonapartists than did the Corps Législatif.

The constitution stated, "The Senate is the guardian of the fundamental pact and of public liberties. No law may be promulgated without having been submitted to it." The Senate could annul any acts or projects, including administrative decisions, that compromised the defense of the territory or were held to violate or infringe on the constitution, morals and religion, freedom of cults, inviolability of property, or the principle of nonremovability of magistrates. The Senate could also interpret and complete the constitution, especially in regard to the colonies. But any fundamental change required popular approval by plebiscite. Modification of the constitution took the form of *sénatus-consultes*. The Senate was also empowered to receive petitions and to pose, in reports to the emperor, the bases of projects of law "of a national character." Senators established the civil list at the beginning of each reign by a special *sénatus-consulte*; it was with their consent ("*avis conforme*") that martial law was maintained or that the Corps Législatif was dissolved by the emperor; and during dissolution, the Senate, on proposition of the emperor, took measures necessary for the good functioning of the government. The Senate could put ministers in accusation.

The emperor convoked and prorogued the Senate, determined the length of its sessions, and could himself preside. He appointed for each year a president and vice-president from among the senators. The Senate was presided successively by: Jérôme Napoleon (brother of Napoleon I), to November 1852; Raymond Troplong, November 1852–2 March 1869; Adrien Marie Devienne (1802–1883), March–July 1869 (acting president); and Eugène Rouher, 20 July 1869–4 September 1870. A *sénateur grand référendaire* and a *secrétaire du sénat* dealt with administration. The Senate was divided into five *bureaux* at the beginning of each session. Sittings were secret. An act to be examined for constitutionality came usually from the government (via the minister of state) and was supported by *conseillers d'état* assigned to that task. It could be referred immediately to a general debate and a vote or sent to a *commission* (formed by the *bureaux*) and thus reported to the full Senate via a *rapporteur*. No amendments were possible, the proposition being simply "the Senate opposes" or "the Senate does not oppose promulgation." The vote was open. More than one-half of the senators being present, a simple majority decided. The president then sent the results to the minister of state. Acts could also be denounced by petition read in general session. Other petitions were considered by special *commissions* and might be referred to pertinent ministers.

Modification of the constitution through a *sénatus-consulte* could be proposed either by the emperor or by ten senators. In the first instance, the proposal would be introduced and supported by "government orators" (*conseillers d'état*), then discussed in the *bureaux*, a *commission*, and finally by the full Senate. If the initiative was the Senate's, the project required approval of three *bureaux*. It would then be sent, after general discussion, to the Conseil d'Etat (if the Senate so wished) and to a *commission* formed for the purpose. Amendments were sent to the *commission* to be included in its report. Amendments raised after the report had been presented needed support of five senators to be read and developed. *Sénatus-consultes* were sanctioned and promulgated by the emperor at his pleasure. In the case of initiative of a law held in writing by a senator to be "of great national interest," a *commission* was named (with the consent of at least three *bureaux*) and its report sent to the minister of state before being discussed and voted by the full Senate.

Although probably meant to be an independent body, the Senate was never free of government supervision. The government had the right to be represented in all deliberations by *conseillers d'état*; the minister of state was notified in advance of the orders of the day; and government orators had the right to be heard when they wished. Care was taken to prevent the Senate from claiming a real legislative role. For example, in 1852 when some senators demanded the right of reply to government speeches, in 1855 when others attacked the policies of the minister of public instruction, and in January 1856 when an attempt was made to change the regent's oath to include a promise to respect the concordat and the organic articles, the Senate was quickly called to order and reminded that it was to behave as an appeals court and not as a house of lords. Subsequently, however, the body proved more self-effacing than had been intended, making no attempts to initiate laws or reforms, despite government injunction to do so.

For the Senate, the evolution toward the Liberal Empire meant a gradual transformation into the upper house of a parliamentary regime, although the thrust toward those changes came from elsewhere. By decree of 24 November 1860, the Senate received, as did the Corps Législatif, the right of address and publicity of debate, rights that contributed in 1861 to the sharp debate on the Roman Question (speech of Prince Napoleon; proposed amendment to the address in favor of the temporal power of the pope, which was defeated 79 to 61). A *sénatus-consulte* of 18 July 1866 provided that the constitution could not be discussed except by the Senate and that petitions tending to interpret or to modify the constitution could be presented to the Senate only with approval of three of its *bureaux* and publicized only as part of the *compte rendu* of the sitting. Nevertheless, change continued. By decree of 19 January 1867, the Senate received the right of interpellation (with approval of at least two *bureaux*). The *sénatus-consulte* of 23 March 1867 provided that before pronouncing on the constitutionality of a law, the Senate could request a new deliberation by the Corps Législatif in the following session.

From 1867 some voices of warning or of opposition were heard in the Senate in addition to those of Prince Napoleon. Victor Fialin Persigny on occasion offered advice concerning the constitution. Charles Augustin Sainte-Beuve, the distinguished literary critic, spoke on 29 March 1867 in defense of Ernest Renan, to cries (led by Marshal François Canrobert) of "You are not here to do that!" and in June against a petition that would have banned books deemed subversive from the public libraries. On 7 May 1868 he again defended intellectual liberty (the pretext was the new law on the press) and on 19 May spoke against a petition by an editor, Giraud, which, while calling for liberty of higher education, was really an attack on the Paris Faculty of Medicine accused by the clerical party of materialism. On this occasion, the Senate wisely decided not to intervene in such matters, and the petition was not acted on. At the beginning of 1869, Senator Charlemagne Emile de Maupas, prefect of police during the coup d'état and disappointed rival of Rouher, called for parliamentary responsibility. In fact the Liberal Empire and the final transformation of the Senate was at hand.

The *sénatus-consulte* of 6 September 1869 provided that ministers would have free access to the Senate. Restraints were removed from the right of interpellation. Meetings were made public, and the Senate became master of its own organization and procedures, while receiving a suspensory veto. Future modifications of relations among the public powers henceforth would be by *sénatus-consultes*. The constitution of 21 May 1870, based on the *sénatus-consulte* of 20 April, approved by the plebiscite of 8 May, deprived the Senate of its constituent powers but made it a full partner in the legislative process, except for initiation of money bills. Ministers were responsible to the Senate as well as to the Corps Législatif and to the emperor. The Senate remained an appointive body; however, French princes no longer sat by right, and the emperor could name no more than twenty senators in any one year, nor could he any longer preside by right, although he continued to appoint the president and vice-president. Through all change, the Senate remained loyal to Napoleon III and to the basic tenets of bonapartism. On 4 September 1870, with the overthrow of the Empire, it quietly dispersed without awaiting, as Jules Baroche had proposed, the arrival of the mob. The Senate's last act had been a vote of support for the emperor.

Related entries: ADDRESS; BONAPARTISM; CONSEIL D'ETAT; CONSTI-TUTION; CORPS LEGISLATIF; LIBERAL EMPIRE; MINISTER OF STATE; MINISTRY; OATH; PLEBISCITE; PRINCE NAPOLEON; REFORM; RO-MAN QUESTION; ROUHER; SAINTE-BEUVE; TROPLONG.

SENATUS-CONSULTE. See SENATE.

SENEGAL, French colony and sphere of influence in West Africa with origins going back to the seventeenth century. It was the nucleus of what by 1906 would have evolved into French West Africa. During the Second Empire, *Sénégal-et-Dépendances* also included small French enclaves in what later became Mauritania, Mali, Guinea-Conakry, Ivory Coast, and Gabon.

As a territorial entity, French Senegal barely existed in 1852. Direct French rule was confined to miniscule French enclaves and islands. The two principal French settlements were Saint-Louis, the capital, located on N'Dar Island near the mouth of the Senegal River, and Gorée Island, off Cape Verde, about 200 kilometers south of Saint-Louis. By its position, Saint-Louis gave the French control over the Senegal River at least so far as European powers were concerned. The French held a few other posts along this river, particularly Bakel, the principal one in the upper river. It was cut off from Saint-Louis during the nine-month dry season when the Senegal River east of Podor is reduced to a trickle. The second major entrepôt, Gorée, served as the headquarters for French trade with the coast south of Cape Verde. Gorée also served as the principal base of the French West African Naval Squadron. After 1843, the new French posts of Assinie and Grand Bassam on the Ivory Coast and Gabon at the mouth of the Gabon estuary were also attached to the government of Senegal. From 1854 to 1858 the colonial administration of Senegal was split; Gorée and its dependencies were separated from the authority of the governor of Senegal. Then in 1858 Gorée and the French sphere as far south as Sierra Leone were returned to the jurisdiction of Saint-Louis, but the *comptoirs* of Assinie, Grand Bassam, and Libreville continued to be administered by the commandant of the French West African Naval Squadron whose principal base continued to be Gorée.

The European treaty system, confirmed as recently as the Treaty of Vienna of 1815, recognized that the West African coast from Arguin in northwestern Mauritania to the northern reaches of Sierra Leone was an exclusive French sphere except for British Gambia and Portuguese Guinea. What the European treaty system overlooked, however, was that these French forts and *comptoirs* had very little control over the African peoples and the state systems that they had elaborated in the hinterland. The heartland of Senegal proper (that is, the plain extending from the Senegal River on the north to the Gambia River on the south) was the homeland of the Woloff and the related Serrer peoples who, possibly as early as the fourteenth century, had constituted the Djoloff Empire. In the seventeenth century, pressures caused by the Atlantic slave trade had resulted in the break-up of this empire and the emergence of its principal provinces as independent states. These included the Woloff states of Walo (situated in the delta of the Senegal River east and northeast of Saint-Louis), Cayor (extending inland and along the Atlantic coast south of Walo and Saint-Louis to Cape Verde), and Baol (east of Cape Verde and South of Cayor). A rump Djoloff continued to exist in the arid sahel east of Cayor. Cape Verde itself had been settled by Woloff tributaries of Cayor. In 1790 they declared independence and formed what the French authorities would call the Lébou Republic. Directly east of Cape Verde were some acephalous settlements of Serrer-Nones, including the village of Thiès, the future railway junction. Then southeast to the Saloum estuary were the two Serrer kingdoms of Sine and Saloum. With the exception of the Lébou, these states all had monarchical forms of government.

The northern boundary of Senegal, the Senegal River, was one of the few true ethnolinguistic and even economic boundaries in precolonial Africa. It marked a separation between the Arabic and Berber nomads to the north and the black sedentary farmers to the south. There was much movement across this border. The social organization of the southern Mauritanian emirates had points in common with the social organization of the Woloff and Serrer societies. In recent years, there had been a tendency on the part of the Mauritanians to expand south of the river at the expense particularly of the Woloffs. The French would end this process, thus turning the lower and middle course of the Senegal River into a colonial boundary, which became an international frontier.

By virtue of their possessions along the Senegal River and south from its mouth along the Atlantic coast, the French had become participants (and by no means the dominant participant) in what was a very complex trading and socio-political system, which they barely understood. At various times after the successful settlement of Saint-Louis in 1659 and the seizure of Gorée from the Dutch in 1688, the French had considered schemes for conquering the hinterland peoples and turning Senegal into a true territorial colony, but these schemes had always come to naught. In recent years, between 1817 and 1830, an attempt to found indigo and cotton plantations in Walo had led to a spectacular and costly failure and demands by some French parliamentarians that France sell or even abandon its claim to Senegal. But later a special Interministerial Commission on French Colonies, which met on and off in the autumn and winter of 1850–1851, decided not only to retain all the French colonies then in existence but to make yet another attempt at tightening up French rule in Senegal.

The latest plan for putting the French presence on a stronger footing was partly the idea of a former governor, Louis Edouard Bouët-Willaumez (1808–1871), and partly that of a number of wholesale merchants (dealing in Senegalese gum arabic and unshelled groundnuts) led by the Bordeaux-based Maurel and Prom Company. Their plan involved: (1) suppression of the three Mauritanian-dominated gum trading stations (*escales*) situated along the lower Senegal River and their replacement by small but well-garrisoned French forts that would command free-trade zones where trade in gum and in all other commodities could take place at all times free of all African-imposed taxes and restrictions; (2) permission for the French wholesalers to open trading stations in these free-trade zones where they could deal directly with the African producers without any required use of middlemen; (3) reduction and eventual elimination of all taxes, duties, and navigation tolls payable by the French authorities or private parties to African rulers and other officials; (4) requiring that all the African rulers recognize that the French were the sovereign possessors of the Senegal River; and (5) preventing the Mauritanians from raiding the left bank sedentary societies, this to encourage the peasantry in the latter to grow groundnuts for the colonial market without molestation. A corollary of this last point, directed at the future groundnut-producing sedentary societies, called for French intervention to prevent the *tyed-dos* (crown soldiers in the Woloff and Serrer monarchies) from interfering with groundnut culture. This, then, was the basic blueprint that guided French actions in Senegal during the Second Empire, the realization of which was to a great extent the accomplishment of the engineer officer Louis Léon César Faidherbe, governor from 1854 to 1861 and from 1863 to 1865.

What must be borne in mind is that no one during the Second Empire, least of all Faidherbe, envisaged the total conquest of Senegal as if it were Algeria. The unarticulated policy of the French was to institute a kind of directed nonrule backed by force. Its aim was to end intertribal warfare and the domination of the Woloffs by the Mauritanians and to curb the exactions of groups within the sedentary societies so that the peasantry could produce unmolested for the French market. The French embarked on this plan in 1854 without realizing that the Senegalese societies in question were undergoing major structural changes, including the gradual replacement of traditional ruling elites with new ones sanctioned not so much by custom as by reforming, particularly Tijjani, Islam. In addition, the fact that the French inaugurated their new policy just as El-Hadj Omar Tall, a native Toucouleur from Fouta-Toro, was beginning a state-building *jihad* had repercussions that no one in 1854 could have suspected. (The Toucouleur, who inhabited much of the south bank of the Senegal River for about 600 kilometers east of Walo, were the first West Africans to be thoroughly Islamized and had already established the Fouta-Toro Confederation.) Two varieties of imperialism, French and Toucouleur-Islamic, thus came into violent conflict, particularly in Fouta-Toro and in the upper Senegal. The result was a limited French victory and a division of spheres, with Omar confining his state-building activities to the east of the upper Senegal while conceding the area west of Bafoulabé to the French. Meanwhile, revolutionary Islamic fervor gained other societies in the French sphere. From his base at Nioro-du-Rip, Maba Diakhou attempted to conquer the Serrer states, and Lat Dior became the strong man of Cayor. In many areas, the gains of these and other leaders were facilitated unwittingly by the French whose plan, even though very limited, contributed to weakening the traditional structures of authority and compromising the traditional rulers.

After 1858 and because of the increasing importance of groundnuts (first exported to France in 1843), the French authorities turned away from the Senegal River and began to look southward along the Atlantic coast and inland. Faidherbe attempted to ''pacify'' Cayor, while Pinet-Laprade, commandant of Gorée after 1858 and then governor of Senegal from 1865 to 1869, attempted to bring Baol, Sine, and Saloum into the French orbit and to halt the state-building activities of Maba-Diakhou in this zone. He also strengthened the French presence in the Casamance River and founded strategic entrepôts along the coast of Guinea at Boké in 1865 and at Benty and Boffa in 1866. Attempts at actual conquest were restricted for budgetary reasons; nonrule backed by force seemed to be the cheapest and the easiest way to fulfill French economic and political objectives. In 1864, in fact, Faidherbe expressed the view that French rule should consist of nothing more than two axes: the first, a series of fortified trading posts extending up the Senegal River from its mouth and then overland, from its source, to the Niger River at Bamako; and the second, the Atlantic Coast from Saint-Louis to Sierra Leone, including French forts at the mouths of the principal rivers and estuaries. He also proposed that the British be induced to exchange Gambia for Assinie, Grand Bassam, and possibly Libreville and that the Portuguese be bought out. Thus, the French would have unbroken claim to the coast and to the interior. Although the result would be a compact colony equipped with the pincers with which to crush African independence, Faidherbe, at least at the time he proposed this plan, seems not to have considered serious conquest.

One must not be fooled by the Algerian-style administrative terminology that Faidherbe introduced into the government of Senegal or by his remarks made in 1859 that "Senegal should be nothing more than a subdivision of Algeria." Although Faidherbe may have considered that this terminology would serve as a blueprint for the future, it was a facade with little substance in the 1850s and 1860s. The reference to Algeria must be understood as part of a plea that with the dissolution of the short-lived (1858–1860) Ministry of Algeria and the Colonies, Senegal should be transferred to the jurisdiction of the Ministry of War, which had traditional responsibility for Algeria, rather than being returned to the Ministry of the Navy, which had traditional responsibility for the French colonies.

That French rule in Senegal in the 1850s and 1860s was more a question of nonrule backed by force than a system of structured colonial domination (for which Napoleon III had, in general, little enthusiasm) is brought home by the difficulties of all sorts that beset the future admiral and minister of the navy Captain Jean Bernard Jauréguiberry (1815–1887) during the short period (from December 1861 to May 1863) that he served as governor of Senegal. His attempt to give substance to Faidherbe's terminology led to much resistance on the part of the native Africans and to full-scale war with Fouta-Toro. Jauréguiberry was recalled before he could elaborate his own variety of nonrule. Faidherbe's return to the governorship in August 1863 brought calm, which again deteriorated when he had left finally in May 1865.

The numerous administrative reforms, public works projects, and educational achievements accomplished by the governors of Senegal during the Second Empire seemed impressive primarily because so little had been accomplished before, even if most of these projects had been anticipated well before 1852. Moreover, they were almost completely centered on Saint-Louis and Gorée, hence giving an early impetus to what would be the very urban nature of French colonialism. Oddly enough, neither the settlement of Dakar after 1857 nor the construction of the first modern port facilities there was considered very necessary or important by Faidherbe or by the drafters of the plan of 1854. The initial justification for the formal annexation of Dakar and the establishment of the port was to force the newly formed Messageries Impériales shipping company to recoal on French territory the ships that it planned to operate between France and South America rather than at Saint Vincent in the Portuguese Cape Verde Islands. Only Pinet-Laprade, who as commandant of Gorée developed Dakar's first grid plan and supervised the construction of the port facilities (inaugurated 4 November 1866), and Jauréguiberry had the vision to perceive the future importance of Dakar. The French commercial interests centered on Gorée Island preferred to set up shop at Rufisque, 22 kilometers down the coast from Dakar, when they needed to move to the mainland. Indeed, the population of Dakar would not surpass that of Rufisque until 1922, and then primarily because Dakar had been made the administrative capital of French West Africa.

In short, the Second Empire period in Senegalese history represents military and politically a period characterized by much warfare, which nevertheless left most of the Senegalese societies independent if shaken. Yet the social weakening that resulted from this violence led to internal mutations within these societies, which in some cases led to revolutionary change. The real French conquest would not come until the 1880s, as was the case in other parts of tropical Africa. However, when the real conquest came, the younger generation of proconsuls could look to the Second Empire period, particularly to the governorship of Faidherbe, for lessons and precedents.

From an economic point of view, the Second Empire witnessed the introduction of the groundnut monoculture in Senegal. It witnessed an attempt at limited economic development and urban improvement in the original French settlements. By emphasizing communications with the upper Senegal and the mid-Niger region, the Second Empire gave a Sudanic thrust to French expansion, which would be continued by the imperialists of the Third Republic. Thus, the Second Empire represented for Senegal a transitional period between the era of mercantile trade and the era of full colonial rule.

L. C. Barrows, "Faidherbe and Senegal: A Critical Discussion," *African Studies Review* 19 (1976), "Faidherbe's Islamic Policy in Senegal, 1854–1865," *French Colonial Studies* (1977), "Jauréguiberry and Senegal (1861–1863)," in A. A. Heggoy, ed., *Proceedings of the French Colonial Historical Society* (Athens, Ga., 1976), "The Merchants and General Faidherbe: Aspects of French Expansion in Senegal in the 1850s," *RFHO* 61 (April 1974), and "Some Paradoxes of Pacification: Senegal and France in the 1850s and 1860s," in R. Dumett and B. K. Swartz, *West African Culture Dynamics: Archaeological and Historical Perspectives* (The Hague, 1980); F. Brigaud, *Histoire du Sénégal* (Dakar, 1964); E. A. Charles, *Precolonial Senegal: The Jolof Kingdom, 1800–1890* (Boston, 1977); L. G. Colvin, *Historical Dictionary of Senegal* (Metuchen, N.J., 1981); P. Curtin, *Economic Change in Precolonial Africa*, 2 vols. (Madison, Wisc. 1975); Y. J. Saint-Martin, "Le Second Empire et l'Islam au Sénégal," *AMN* 44 (January 1974).

Leland C. Barrows

Related entries: ALGERIA; CHASSELOUP-LAUBAT; FAIDHERBE; INDOCHINA; MESSAGERIES IMPERIALES.

SEPTEMBER CONVENTION, an agreement between the Italian and French governments signed on 15 September 1864 that appeared to resolve the Roman Question to the mutual satisfaction of both countries. France had maintained a protecting garrison at Rome since 1849 when the Roman Republic (a result of the Italian revolutions of 1848) had been suppressed by a French military expedition. In April 1850 the pope returned to Rome after an exile of approximately a year and one-half. The Austro-Sardinian War of 1859 resulted in the expulsion of Austria from all of Italy except Venetia. Within a year, the papacy had lost all of its territories except the city of Rome and its environs, the Campagna. In March 1861, with the proclamation of the newly formed Kingdom of Italy, the

Italian government asked Napoleon III to withdraw the French garrison from Rome. Thus began the negotiations that led to the September Convention. Napoleon III had no sympathy for the pope's pretensions to temporal power, but he did not dare to risk exposing him to danger by withdrawing the French garrison, nor could he lightly antagonize the clerical party in France or the pro-Roman opinion within his own entourage. Edouard Thouvenel, who had succeeded comte Alexandre Walewski as foreign minister in January 1860, recognized these problems but very much wished to secure a French withdrawal from Rome. Had Count Camillo Benso di Cavour (1810–1861), the Sardinian prime minister, lived, it is possible a way could have been found, but Cavour's death in June 1861 removed the guarantee that France required and brought negotiations to an end, although Paris did recognize the new Italian Kingdom on 16 June 1861. In the summer of 1862, Giuseppi Garibaldi (1807–1882), who two years earlier had overthrown the government of the Kingdom of the Two Sicilies, began to organize a filibuster against Rome with the motto ''Rome or Death!'' On 25 August he crossed from Sicily to the mainland, but four days later he was besieged on a height called Aspromonte at the toe of the Italian peninsula. Attempting to prevent a clash between his men and government troops, he was wounded in the foot and taken into custody, treated by a French specialist, and amnestied with his followers on 5 October. Unfortunately for Franco-Italian relations, this decisive action of the Italian government was followed on 10 September by a circular issued by General Giacomo Durando (1807–1894), Italian foreign minister, to the effect that while actions such as Garibaldi's would be resisted, Italy must and would have Rome for its capital. The Durando Circular led directly to the dismissal of Thouvenel in mid-October, his replacement by Edouard Drouyn de Lhuys, and a suspension for almost two years of negotiations between Paris and Turin on the Roman Question. And yet an agreement was imperative. In mid-1864, talks began once again, involving Napoleon III, Gioacchino Pepoli (1825–1881), Chevalier Costantino Nigra (1828–1907), and Drouyn de Lhuys. The key to agreement was to find a guarantee acceptable to French public opinion. It was found in the understanding that Italy would adopt Florence in place of Turin as its permanent capital. This arranged, the terms of the convention were little different from those agreed to almost four years earlier by Thouvenel and Cavour.

By the September Convention, Italy agreed not to attack Rome and to impede all attacks against the city. France agreed to evacuate its troops from Rome within two years of the convention's going into effect. In that time a pontifical army would be organized capable of defending Rome; Italy would offer no objection to this and would assume a proportional part of the debt of the Roman state. A secret annex to the convention required that Italy transfer its capital from Turin to some other city as evidence that it renounced Rome as the future capital of Italy, and a protocol stipulated that the convention would go into effect from the time that the Italian government should have decreed the transfer of its capital from Turin. King Victor Emmanuel complained that his ministers had deceived him but nonetheless agreed to the transfer of capital to Florence. The Italian chamber of deputies, after angry debates that were attended by riots at Turin, voted in favor of the convention. It was, however, at best a stopgap. The most that could be hoped for at Paris was a respite of a number of years, during which Italian attention would be directed toward Venetia rather than Rome. But even that hope was not to be realized.

L. M. Case, *Franco-Italian Relations, 1860–1865: The Roman Question and the Convention of September* (Philadelphia, 1932); C. M. Lovett, "Milano e la Convenzione di Settembre," *Nuova rivista storica* 59 (January–April 1975); N. Miko, "Zur Geschichte der Konvention vom 15 September 1864 zwischen Frankreich und Italien," *Römische historische Mitteilungen* 2 (1957–1958); R. Mori, "Il ritiro delle truppe francesi da Roma in attuazione della Convenzione di Settembre 1866," *Rivista storia della Chiesa in Italia* (1964); P. Paolini, "A proposito della convenzione italo-francese del Settembre 1864: Rassegna di studi," *Provincia di Lucca* 12 (1972), 13 (1973).

Ivan Scott

Related entries: CHAMBERY; DROUYN DE LHUYS; MENTANA; PIUS IX; ROMAN QUESTION; THOUVENEL; VENETIA; VILLAFRANCA.

LE SIECLE, moderate republican Paris daily newspaper, founded 1836. During the Second Empire *Le siècle* had the largest circulation and was probably the most influential political newspaper in France. Its director (1851–1868) was Léonor Havin. Its principal writers included Emile de la Bédollière (1812–1883), Taxtile Delord (1815–1877), Louis Jourdan (1810–1881), Edmond Texier (1816–1887), Léon Plée (1815–1879), Pierre Lanfrey (1828–1877), Philibert Audebrand (1816–1906), Eugène Pelletan (1813–1884), and Ferdinand de Lasteyrie (1810–1879). *Le siècle* was the only republican newspaper permitted to publish at Paris following the coup d'état of 2 December 1851. The influence of its stockholders, the persuasion of its friends at court, including Napoleon III's half-brother Auguste de Morny, who had a financial interest in the paper, and the hope that under Havin *Le siècle* would prove a moderate counterweight to the more extreme Left all contributed to this decision. Although several other republican newspapers were later authorized, *Le siècle* benefited from its temporary monopoly to increase its circulation greatly between 1853 and 1855. The newspaper avoided all direct attacks on the government. Instead it eulogized the principles of the Revolution of 1789, condemned aristocratic pretensions, spoke for some of the poor's grievances, and was especially vociferous in its anti-clericalism. Voltairean in tone, *Le siècle* clashed violently with the clerical newspaper *L'univers*, especially in November 1853, April 1855, and from 1858 concerning the miracles of Lourdes. In 1867 Havin raised money by public subscription to erect a statue to Voltaire, that most notorious of freethinkers.

Le siècle was a potent force in Parisian politics, helping to elect the five republican opponents of the Empire (*les Cinq*) in 1857 and to defeat the government's candidates at Paris in 1863. The newspaper received frequent *avertissements* but was never suppressed, although it required a face-to-face appeal by Havin to Napoleon III in 1858 to prevent suppression following Orsini's attempt on the emperor's life. A factor in its reprieve was undoubtedly the pro-Italian sympathies it had shown since 1856. Thereafter the newspaper vociferously proclaimed its pro-Italian sympathies and opposition to papal temporal power. Local officials complained about the tone of *Le siècle*'s articles, fearful of its popularity in the provinces. But in fact the newspaper gradually came to be regarded as an official opposition and a quasi-ally of the Empire. The stern republican leader, General Louis Eugène Cavaignac (1802–1857), had perhaps foreseen this in resigning earlier from *Le siècle*'s supervisory committee. *Le siècle*'s circulation was 21,325 in April 1853, 36,886 in July 1858, 52,300 in August 1861, 42,000 in 1866, and 35,514 in February 1870. In June 1870 it began the serialization of *La fortune des Rougon*, first of Emile Zola's Rougon-Macquart novels.

A. Sirven, *Journaux et journalistes: "Le siècle"* (Paris, 1866).

Natalie Isser

Related entries: HAVIN; MARINONI; *OPINION NATIONALE*; PRESS REGIME; REPUBLICANISM.

SOCIAL CATHOLICISM, the movement of Catholics in France to alleviate or solve in accord with Catholic concepts the problems of poverty, the exploitation of the working class, the advance of de-Christianization and immorality among the urban poor, unsanitary and demoralizing living conditions in cities affected by changing techniques of production, and other social ills. It had roots almost as old as socialism itself. The legitimist prefect and political economist, Alban de Villeneuve-Bargemont, initiated social Catholicism in French conservative circles in the 1820s and 1830s with his economic treatises and proposals for agricultural colonies to ease the misery of the proletariat. Concurrently, Philippe Buchez (1796–1865), a convert and ex-Saint-Simonian who sought to synthesize his new religious beliefs, old social principles, and the ideals of the French Revolution, stood at the head of a democratic current among social Catholics. He and his followers formed a disciplined school of Catholic socialists, while others on the Catholic Left were influenced by Charles Fourier (1772–1837) or by Félicité de Lamennais' *l'Avenir*. Although Lamennais' primary interest in 1830–1831 was not the social question, he brought to Catholic consciousness the idea of "modern slavery," and his colleagues, especially Charles de Coux (1787–1864), criticized a system that concerned itself with the production of goods but not with their equitable distribution and that concentrated on material values to the exclusion of the spiritual and the human.

Prior to 1848 the gulf between conservative social Catholics and those on the democratic Left was not impassable. Coux and various liberal Catholics, such as Frédéric Ozanam (1813–1853) and those connected with the *Correspondant*, made attempts to establish contacts between them. Articles by legitimists, liberals, and advanced democrats appeared side by side in the columns of the *Correspondant*. Ozanam's Society of St. Vincent de Paul, founded in 1833, brought men from all social levels into contact with the world of working-class misery. All social Catholics, before and during the Second Empire, were in agreement in their opposition to change by way of violence and in their rejection of class struggle, which they saw as an evil to be avoided. They stressed the moral law, spiritual conversion, strengthened family ties, associations to protect worker interests, state intervention, and a variety of other approaches. They unanimously recoiled from the concept of a state-directed economy. The Society of St. Francis Xavier, established in 1840 as a society for adult Catholic workers, opened its meetings to speakers of various political persuasions, democrats and future democrats, such as Ozanam, despite the fact that most of its militants were legitimists. For a small fee, the society provided substantial medical aid, Christian education, and, through its "Oeuvre du Travail," legal and job placement assistance. An undogmatic but faithful legitimist, Armand de Melun (1807–1877), formulated in 1839–1840 a system of patronage for young workers that would be embraced by Catholic social conservatives until the close of the nineteenth century. He first directed the "Oeuvre du Patronage des Apprentis" of the Society of St. Vincent de Paul and then organized his own patronage program alongside that of the society.

The promise of a rapprochement between the church and the workers, of a synthesis of social Catholicism and socialism, of a merger of the major currents of social Catholicism, appeared capable of realization during the heady days following the February Revolution of 1848. Workers respected priests; Catholic conservatives and Christian socialists hailed the Republic. Buchez was elected head of the Constituent Assembly on 5 May. But the revolutionary euphoria began to dissipate in the face of incidents of violence in April and May and collapsed as class struggle erupted in June. In an atmosphere of antagonism, the centrist position of men such as Charles de Coux crumbled. Ozanam attached himself to the democratic Left. Social democrats and social conservatives moved further apart as the conservatives took fright at adventuresome plans for social reform. Then Louis Napoleon's coup d'état of December 1851, by virtually destroying the democratic movement, left the social conservatives practically alone to shoulder the burden of involving Catholicism with the care of the poor and exploited.

Social Catholicism had always been a small minority movement within the French church. The modest but significant gains it was making prior to 1848 were made despite the indifference, sometimes the suspicion and hostility, of most Catholics, including liberal Catholics, who believed that the poor constituted a divinely ordained part of any social structure, that they should be helped simply by acts of charity, and that laissez-faire economists were correct in their dismal assessment of the necessary fate of the working classes. Few bishops thought beyond alms giving; they hesitated, for one thing, to intrude in affairs, such as social economics, beyond their competence, especially when liberals denounced the clergy for interfering in secular matters, even when they dared to ask that Sunday be made a legal day of rest. Nevertheless, the hierarchy did defend private property and did attack socialism. They ascribed working-class violence to false ideas rather than to faulty institutions. Catholic nobles, bourgeoisie, and peasants alike participated wholeheartedly in the reaction after June 1848 against the ''red'' spectre that threatened to redistribute property and wealth. The flight of nominal Catholics into the church, which they viewed as a bulwark of order, further retarded the development of its social ideas all during the Second Empire, and beyond. Social Catholicism under Napoleon III also suffered from Catholic preoccupation with other questions: threats to the temporal power of the pope, the progress of positivism, the internecine quarrel of the handful of liberal Catholics with intransigent Catholic leaders like Louis Veuillot. Thus social Catholicism, while by no means extinct during the Second Empire, showed far less vitality than before. The Society of St. Francis Xavier lost the sympathy of the workers and, with that, its dynamism. Both it and the Society of St. Vincent de Paul fell under the control of their conservative elements. The social conservatives retained their commitment to help the poor, but their efforts were timid, and they had even less confidence than before in the reliability of the working class. Much of the credit for the achievements that were made by the conservatives must go to Armand de Melun, who skillfully maneuvered during the Second Republic and the Second Empire to secure the passage of social legislation.

Napoleon III's personal concern with social problems affected social Catholicism, for he both sponsored projects it desired and sought to control and derive credit for whatever was done. He collaborated closely with Melun in drawing up and executing the decree-law of 26 March 1852 that laid down the provisions under which mutual aid societies (*sociétés de secours mutuels*) could be established in each commune. These societies, which had a marked effect on the working class of the Second Empire, especially before 1860, for a slight fee ensured their members help in case of sickness, injury, or infirmity and provided for funeral expenses. It was also expected that the contact between the workers and employers (admitted as honorary members) would make it easier for workers to find jobs. Although controlled in accord with Napoleon III's ideas, Melun's influence can be seen in their Christian aspects (curates were to cooperate closely with them), their being voluntary instead of obligatory, and their precise limits. He opposed their being tied in with cooperatives, but he did favor linking *patronages d'apprentis* to them and extending their benefits to women and children.

A main thrust of social Catholicism during the Empire was that of patronage, which gave members of the ''superior classes'' supervision, normally control, over the organizations into which workers were recruited. Conservative social Catholics expended much effort in establishing *patronages d'apprentis*, which constituted a religious and social apostolate seeking to preserve working-class children from immoral influences and to arrange for their vocational training. Sometimes the patrons also set up workshops and lodgings for them. Most of the apprentices came from artisan families, some from the petty bourgeoisie. The activity of Catholics in this direction failed to contain the anti-clericalism that had flared up after 1848 or the spread of de-Christianization among the workers, who were becoming increasingly resentful of upper-class patronage just at the time Catholics were relying heavily on it. German social Catholics advised their French colleagues on several occasions to support worker control of worker organizations, but few Frenchmen would take the risk. It was not until 1870 that Catholic leaders meeting at Versailles decided, on a motion by Melun, to start to phase out the word *patronage* from their projects.

Catholics had begun even before 1870 to listen more attentively to what the workers were saying. In the 1860s the Catholic *Société d'Economie Charitable* discussed purely charitable matters less and less. Melun sought to turn it more toward social prescriptions and in 1863 brought before it the question of the right of workers to form unions before the matter was posed in the Corps Législatif. The society decided that the law prohibiting unions should be abrogated but still favored mixed syndicates of masters and workers to arbitrate salary disputes. Melun himself modified his earlier opposition to unemployment compensation. There was, therefore, a slow ideological evolution among the minority of socially aware Catholics. In addition to work with the patronages and mutual aid societies, this small group had founded some saving institutions for workers; sponsored a few consumer cooperatives; opened day care centers (subsidized by the state starting in 1854), evening courses, and several professional schools; and, under the direction of a yeoman Catholic social worker, Augustin Cochin (1823–1872), organized an "exhibition of domestic economy" as part of the international exposition at Paris in 1867. These and some other scattered projects recruited sixty thousand to seventy thousand workers and touched still more. More disturbing than the unimpressive numbers was the fact that the workers involved showed little initiative and no leadership capacity within their class. Despite their unspectacular record, however, the Catholic social conservatives had shown admirable persistence during the Second Empire under adverse conditions. False starts, such as those connected with the unsuccessful agricultural colonies, and mistaken attachments such as the commitment to patronage, were not total losses. Without the experience provided by social Catholics prior to 1870, the vigorous Christian democracy of later years would have had far greater difficulty in developing.

J. B. Duroselle, *Les débuts du catholicisme social en France, 1822–1870* (Paris, 1951); H. Guitton, *Le catholicisme social* (Paris, 1945); E. Labrousse, *Le mouvement ouvrier et les idées sociales en France de 1815 à la fin du XIXe siècle* (Paris, 1948); M. Leroy, *Histoire des idées sociales en France: d'Auguste Comte à P. J. Proudhon* (Paris, 1954); F. Provinciali, "Il primo cattolicesimo sociale in Francia," *Civitas*, 32, no. 2 (1981); J. Touchart, *Aux origines du catholicisme social: Louis Rousseau, 1787–1856* (Paris, 1968); M. H. Vicaire, "Les ouvriers parisiens en face du catholicisme de 1830 à 1870," *Schweizerische zeitschrift für Geschichte* 1 (1951); G. Weill, *Histoire du mouvement social en France, 1852–1902* (Paris, 1924).

Raymond L. Cummings

Related entries: CORRESPONDANT; EXTINCTION DU PAUPERISME; GALLICANISM; LABOR REFORM; LEGITIMISM; LE PLAY; LIBERALISM; MONTALEMBERT; PALAIS ROYAL GROUP; PIUS IX; ROMAN QUESTION; SAINT VINCENT DE PAUL, SOCIETY OF; VEUILLOT.

SOCIALISM. See REPUBLICANISM.

SOCIAL LEGISLATION. See LABOR REFORM.

SOCIETES PAR ACTIONS, a form of business organization that flourished under the Second Empire, becoming ever more numerous, larger, and more powerful. Two types of joint stock companies were recognized by the commercial code of 1807, the *société anonyme* and the *société en commandite par actions*. The *société anonyme* was a corporation in the modern sense, a legal person whose shareholders enjoyed limited liability, managed by employees answerable to the shareholders or their representatives. The formation of a *société anonyme* (SA) required government authorization, which could be obtained only after a long procedure in which the Conseil d'Etat made the final decision. Since the conseil adopted a cautious attitude toward SAs, they were authorized only in limited numbers, most of them large enterprises promoted by recognized men of substance. For those promoters who failed to receive authorization for SAs or who renounced the attempt, there existed an alternative, the *société en commandite par actions* (CPA), a combination of the partnership and the corporate forms of business organization. The head (*gérant*) of the enterprise was subject to unlimited liability but also exercised absolute control over the enterprise. His only responsibility to the shareholders was to render a periodic accounting of the financial state of the enterprise. The shareholders, envisioned as passive partners, enjoyed limited liability but were enjoined from exercising the slightest control over the enterprise. CPAs had one great advantage: they did not require the consent of the government for their foundation and hence were exempt from the whole range of restrictions imposed by the Conseil d'Etat on SAs. Because authorization as an SA was so difficult to obtain, the CPA was pressed into service by promoters as a corporate substitute, and they appeared in large numbers beginning in the 1830s.

During the period 1852 to 1867, 217 SAs were formed, an average of 14 per year, figures that were much the same as under the July Monarchy. Most of the largest business enterprises in France were SAs, including railroads (the PLM railroad, formed in 1857 by the merger of a number of previously authorized lines and capitalized at 588 million francs, was the largest enterprise in France), insurance companies, mining and metallurgical enterprises, steamship lines, and real estate development companies connected with the rebuilding of Paris and other French cities. And during the Second Empire, the Conseil d'Etat permitted some large Parisian banks to be founded as SAs, albeit reluctantly and usually under pressure, including the Crédit Mobilier in 1852, the Crédit Foncier (1852), the Comptoir d'Escompte (1854), the Crédit Industriel et Commercial (1859), and the Société Générale (1864).

CPAs were generally smaller than SAs, but they were far more numerous; 3,147 were founded for the period 1852–1867, though many of these were stillborn, and many others enjoyed only an ephemeral existence. Almost one-half (1,539) were founded during the boom of 1853–1856, many solely to fleece unsuspecting shareholders. Because of the formation of so many CPAs with fraudulent intent, the government undertook to impose numerous restrictions on them by the law of 17 July 1856, which helped to curb their founding and effectively ended the CPA as a vehicle for large-scale enterprise, both fraudulent and legitimate. Enterprises utilizing the CPA form were quite varied. There were many banks, particularly in view of the hostile attitude of the Conseil d'Etat and the Bank of France to the authorization of banks as SAs. Among these was Jules Mirès' Caisse Générale des Chemins de Fer (1856), capitalized at 50 million francs, which had been refused authorization as an SA. The large metallurgical establishment of the Schneider brothers at Le Creusot (1836) was also a CPA, as was the giant metallurgical combine of Chatillon-Commentry (1845), until it succeeded in gaining authorization as an SA on its third attempt in 1862.

The law of 1856 restricting the CPA intensified demands for liberalizing French corporate law, to which the imperial regime responded as part of its general liberalization policies after 1860, and prodded by the liberalization of English company law. The first step was the law of 23 May 1863, which created yet a third type of joint stock company, the *société à responsabilité limitée* (SARL), which resembled the SA but did not require government authorization. The major drawback was that the capital of the SARL was limited to 20 million francs or less. The SARL was abolished in 1867, but before its disappearance in mid-1867, 338 SARLs were founded, including the Crédit Lyonnais (1863) and the important locomotive manufacturing enterprise of Fives-Lille (1865). The law of 24 July 1867, passed in response to growing pressure for liberalization, inaugurated a new era. A general incorporation law, it laid down the conditions under which SAs and CPAs, as well as cooperative societies, could be founded. The law abandoned government authorization, except for life insurance companies. This law remained the basic statute governing joint stock enterprise for the next one hundred years.

C. E. Freedeman, *Joint-Stock Enterprise in France, 1807–1867: From Privileged Company to Modern Corporation* (Chapel Hill, N.C., 1979); D. Nourredine, "Les origines de la libération des sociéte de capitaux à responsabilité limitée, 1856–1863," *RHMC*, 28 (April 1981).

Charles E. Freedeman

Related entries: BANKING; COMPAGNIE GENERALE TRANSATLANTIQUE; CONSEIL D'ETAT; CREDIT MOBILIER; MESSAGERIES IMPERIALES; MIRES; PEREIRE; RAILROADS; ROTHSCHILD; SCHNEIDER, E.; TALABOT.

SOLESMES, Benedictine abbey, also known as the Abbey of Saint-Pierre, located in the village of Solesmes in western France. Founded as a priory of the Benedictines in the early eleventh century, it was suppressed during the French Revolution, acquired by rich proprietors, and purchased in 1832 by a local priest, Prosper Guéranger (1805–1875). In 1833 Guéranger established there a Benedictine community, which was canonically confirmed by Gregory XVI in a papal brief of 1 September 1837 that also granted Solesmes the status of an abbey. The ancient Benedictine order, restored now to the nation, would have Solesmes as its mother abbey in France. Named the first abbot in October 1837, Dom Guéranger placed Solesmes in the forefront of a strong movement of liturgical renewal. At this time, a profusion of local neo-Gallican liturgies, many of which derived from eighteenth-century innovations, were creating confusion in the French church. As many as nine different Breviaries and Missals were in use in some dioceses. Guéranger launched a veritable campaign of articles and books (the most famous being his *Institutions liturgiques*), which attacked the validity of the Gallican liturgies while exalting the Roman liturgy as the true repository of the uninterrupted Catholic tradition. Alongside the *Institutions liturgiques*, published in three volumes between 1840 and 1851, Guéranger produced *L'année liturgique*, a widely consulted, encyclopedic commentary, with doctrinal explanations, on the seasons, feasts, and ceremonies of the church year. Its last volumes were completed after his death by his disciples, especially Dom Lucien Fromage. By 1864, with the support of Popes Gregory XVI and Pius IX, the crusade fought by the monks of Solesmes in favor of the Roman liturgy had triumphed in eighty out of ninety-one dioceses. After 1875, liturgical unity prevailed throughout the nation.

Perhaps the most renowned aspect of the liturgical revival led by Solesmes was its reform and restoration of the pure Gregorian chant. Once again Dom Guéranger provided the inspiration. Although a start had been made at Reims and Cambria in the mid-nineteenth century, the monks at Solesmes nurtured the real renaissance of Gregorian music. Complying with Guéranger's instructions to restore the sacred music on the basis of the best and most ancient manuscripts, Dom Jausions (1834–1870) and Dom Pothier (1835–1925) completed in 1864 a *Directorium chori* for use at Solesmes. The work thus begun led to publications, continuing into contemporary times, that have restored to the Catholic church a venerable liturgical art and spread the fame of Solesmes throughout the musical world.

Guéranger, the abbot of Solesmes during the entire Second Empire, lent his considerable prestige to the antiliberal, ultramontane (supremacy of Rome) Catholic position, which his championing of the Roman liturgy did much to strengthen. He was an ardent defender of papal infallibility, in behalf of which he wrote several works at the time of Vatican Council I.

P. Combes, *Histoire de la restauration du chant grégorien d'après des documents inédits* (Solesmes, 1969); *Dom Guéranger, abbé de Solesmes*, by a Benedictine monk of the Congregation of France, Dom Paul Delatte, 2 vols. (Paris, 1909–1910); A. Gough, ''The Roman Liturgy, Gregorian Plain-Chant, and the Gallican Church,'' *Journal of Religious History*, 11 (December 1981); A. Ledru, *Dom Guéranger, abbé de Solesmes, et Mgr. Bouvier, évêque du Mans* (Paris, 1911); Dom L. Soltner, *Solesmes et Dom Guéranger, 1805–1875* (Sablé, 1974).

Raymond L. Cummings

Related entries: GALLICANISM; LACORDAIRE; PIE; PIUS IX; ROMAN QUESTION; VATICAN COUNCIL.

SPANISH THRONE QUESTION. See HOHENZOLLERN CANDIDACY.

STEEL. See COMITE DES FORGES.

STRIKES. See LA RICAMARIE.

SUEZ CANAL, one of the greatest engineering achievements of the nineteenth century. Constructed over ten years from 1859, it provided the first direct maritime route between the Mediterranean and the Red Sea and was largely the result of the combined efforts of Ferdinand de Lesseps (1805–1894) and Napoleon III. France's long-standing interest in the canal project, notable during the reign of Louis XIV, was revived with Bonaparte's Egyptian campaigns. But British opposition to the scheme led Egyptian viceroys (Mehemet Ali, 1811–1849, and Abbas, 1849–1854) to rebuff proposals by the Saint-Simonians during the stay in Egypt (1833–1837) of Prosper Enfantin (1796–1864), by the Austrian government in 1844, and by the Saint-Simonian-inspired Société Internationale des Etudes du Canal de Suez founded in Paris in 1846. The British, who had developed an overland route from the Mediterranean to the Red Sea in the 1830s and who built an Alexandria-Cairo-Suez railroad 1856 to 1858, thought the project impractical but also feared an extension of French influence. De Lesseps, until 1849 a diplomat, had established during his years in consular service at Cairo (1832–1837) a friendship with one of Mehemet Ali's sons, Saïd. When Saïd became viceroy, de Lesseps returned to Egypt. Responding to a memorandum of 15 November from de Lesseps, Saïd granted his old friend a firman of concession (dated 30 November 1854 and formally signed 19 May 1855) permitting him to found the Compagnie Universelle du Canal Maritime de Suez. With the moral support of the viceroy and a land grant of 83,000 hectares, the company would construct a canal open to all shipping and administer it for ninety-nine years. At the end of that period, Egypt, which had been assured 15 percent of the company's annual profits after the payment of dividends, might purchase the canal.

The requirement that Turkey ratify the concession was the occasion for rival lobbying in Constantinople over the next decade by de Lesseps and the British government, especially when the latter was headed by Lord Palmerston. Not believing the canal to be economically feasible, the British concluded that French motives were political. These fears were not unreasonable, although they were misplaced. In reality, de Lesseps was an internationalist who wanted his water way to be neutral. Until 1859 Napoleon III's concern for the entente with Britain would lead him publicly to treat de Lesseps' activities as a private business dealing. However, the award of the grand cross of the Legion of Honor to Saïd (22 December 1854) and the numerous conversations de Lesseps had with Napoleon III and Eugénie were private expressions of support. The emperor believed that keeping France out of the affair was the best path to success. On 5 January 1856, Saïd signed an act of concession extending the firman of 1854 to include the construction of a freshwater canal between the maritime canal and the Nile.

The viceroy was to supply four-fifths of the workers for the project. Unsuccessful in a direct appeal to British public opinion in June 1857 and stalemated in his search for the sultan's sanction by successive British ambassadors at Constantinople (Lord Stratford de Redcliffe to 1858 and then Sir Henry Bulwer), de Lesseps incorporated the Compagnie Universelle in Paris in November 1858 with a proposed capitalization of 200 million francs, offered 400,000 shares at 500 francs each, and began the construction of the northern terminus of the canal the next year (25 April 1859) on a beach where Port Saïd now stands. While the 52 percent of shares reserved for Frenchmen was quickly subscribed (mostly by middle-class investors, sometimes for nationalistic reasons), French bankers and international investors remained aloof. The London *Times* ridiculed the project, and many thousands of shares remained unsold. These were purchased in 1860 by Saïd, who thus acquired 45 percent of the initial shares, a heavy burden on Egypt. Escalating costs, lack of capital, and British pressure on the sultan, who ordered a halt to construction in October 1859, endangered the project to the point that Napoleon III for the first time intervened officially. The French ambassador at Constantinople, Edouard Thouvenel, was instructed to help de Lesseps but without quarreling with Britain (3 November 1859). This permitted both sultan and viceroy to turn a blind eye to continued construction, and the waters of the Mediterranean, via Lakes Manzala and Balla, flowed into Lake Timsah in 1862.

The succession of Ismail as viceroy of Egypt in January 1863 offered a fresh opportunity for Britain to press its opposition to the canal, to the size of Saïd's land grant, and to the use of forced labor, on which de Lesseps relied from 1861 to 1864 since *fellahin* labor was tied up in cotton production as a consequence of the American Civil War. Bulwer now demanded an end to this practice, which the Porte commanded on 6 April 1863. The new British tactic was obviously to destroy de Lesseps' company by depriving it of labor. Perhaps a new group, including British financiers, would then have taken over. Certainly Napoleon III's half-brother, Auguste de Morny, was involved in such a scheme. But the French emperor again made his support of de Lesseps known, and the engineer stood firm against the Porte's orders and Ismail's demand for the immediate transfer of lands and the freshwater canal to Egypt. A rancorous public debate between the company and Egyptian foreign minister Nubar Pasha was terminated only by an agreement to submit to Napoleon III's arbitration. His decision, recommended 6 July 1864 by a commission chaired by former foreign minister Thouvenel, proposed an end to the *corvée*, the return of 60,000 hectares of land to Egypt, the transfer of the freshwater canal when the maritime canal was completed, and, all important, an indemnity to the company of 84 million francs. By 1866 the company and Egypt had finally resolved their differences in two conventions (30 January, 22 February), and on 14 March the Porte recognized Saïd's concession of 1856, the subsequent agreements, and the work in progress on the canal. To compensate for lost manpower, de Lesseps turned to French engineering (the only major engineering problem of a sea-level canal was the moving of vast quantities of sand and soil). Two Polytechniciens, Paul Borel (d. 1869) and Alexandre Lavalley (1821–1892), created steam-driven dredgers and elevators. These machines, designed and built in France, enabled the work to progress steadily from 1865. A final crisis, when the second offering of shares failed in 1867, was surmounted when Napoleon III authorized a lottery loan (June 1868), thus effectively saving the enterprise for the third time.

Nevertheless, the canal's financial difficulties resulted in two reductions (1859, 1866), in the projected depth and width of the 168-kilometer channel, which in the end cost more than two times as much and took five years longer to build than planned. But de Lesseps' energy and enthusiasm and his untiring public relations efforts (he had even founded his own journal, *Isthme de Suez*) proved equal to the task. The Suez Canal was inaugurated 16–18 November 1869 by Eugénie and de Lesseps on board *L'aigle*, leading a flotilla of sixty-seven ships carrying representatives of the European powers (including Emperor Francis Joseph of Austria-Hungary) on a voyage from Port Saïd to Suez. Its opening at once reduced the distance from Marseilles to India by 56 percent and to Australia by 21 percent.

C. M. Bellet, "A propos de Suez: L'arbitrage de Napoléon III (1864)," *RPP* (December 1951); A. Blumberg,"An early project for a Suez Canal: The Aborted Plan of 1847," *Mariner's Mirror* 68 (August, 1982); D. F. Bradshaw, "A Decade of British Opposition to the Suez Canal Project, 1854–1864," *JTH* 9 (1978), and "Stephenson, de Lesseps, and the Suez Canal Project, 1854–1864," *JTH* 4 (1977–1978); G. Edgar-Bonnet, *Ferdinand de Lesseps: Le diplomate, le créateur de Suez* (Paris, 1951), and "Le Canal de Suez," *RDM* (July and August 1982); D. A. Farnie, *East and West of Suez: The Suez Canal in History, 1854–1956* (New York, 1969); M. Gamichon, "La genèse du Canal de Suez: Napoléon III et Ferdinand de Lesseps," *AMN* 46 (July 1974, January 1975); J. Georges-Picot, "Napoléon III et le Canal de Suez," *SN* 41 (1978); D. S. Landes, *Bankers and Pashas: International Finance and Economic Imperialism in Egypt* (Cambridge, Mass., 1958); F. de Lesseps, *Recollections of Forty Years*, 2 vols. (London, 1887); J. Pudney, *Suez: De Lesseps' Canal* (New York, 1969); G. Spillman, *Napoléon III, prophète méconnu* (Paris, 1972); G. Taboulet, "Aux origines du Canal de Suez: Le conflit entre F. de Lesseps et les Saint-Simoniens," *RH* (July–December 1968), and "Le rôle des Saint-Simoniens dans le percement de l'Isthme de Suez," *EcS* 5 (1971); F. P. Voisin, *Le Canal de Suez*, 6 vols. (Paris, 1902–1906).

Christopher English

SYLLABUS OF ERRORS, a document issued by Pius IX in 1864 listing eighty propositions condemned as false by the papacy. Arranged in ten sections of unequal length, the propositions were appended to the encylical *Quanta cura*, which appeared on 8 December 1864. The idea of developing a document that would clearly identify the principal errors of the day and condemn them goes back to 1849, but a commission appointed in 1854 to carry out the task was proceeding slowly until Mgr. Olympe Gerbet (1798–1864), bishop of Perpignan, presented to his diocese a pastoral instruction in 1860 citing eighty-five modern concepts deemed pernicious. Impressed, Pius IX referred Gerbet's work to a new commission of theologians to serve as a guide for a similar declaration to be made by Rome. Among the issues troubling various French Catholics at this time was the pragmatic approach of the papacy to the problem of liberty in society, which, for instance, saw Rome attacking freedom of religion in Sardinia but tolerating it in Belgium. They desired the proclamation of a more coherent policy. Concurrently, bitterness was deepening at Rome against the liberal ideology, which was justifying Sardinia's seizure of papal territory and inspiring its appropriation of monastic properties, actions against the clergy, toleration of Protestant efforts to proselytize among Catholics, and other measures consistent with the principle of laicism. When Pius submitted his commission's work to the bishops assembled in Rome in 1862 for the canonization of a group of Japanese martyrs, Bishop Félix Dupanloup of Orleans led those who were opposed to any kind of sweeping condemnation of modern ideas. Cardinal Giacomo Antonelli, the papal secretary of state, also favored moderation, arguing that it would be a mistake to provide Napoleon III with a pretext to withdraw his troops from Rome. The French government, warned by associates of Bishop Henri Maret of the draft presented to the fathers at Rome, ordered its ambassador there to counsel against publication. This opposition, plus a furor of criticism in the anti-clerical press following the revelation of the proposed condemnations by a Turin weekly, caused the pope to hesitate. He established still another commission, instructing it to extract from his past encyclicals, allocutions, and letters statements rejecting the errors in question. Ultramontane bishops in France (those whose primary loyalty was to Rome), certain cardinals, and members of the Holy Office persisted in agitating for a declaration. Pius finally moved in 1864, after Charles de Montalembert's enthusiastic praise of liberalism at the Catholic congress in Malines, Belgium, in 1863, Pius' own illness in 1864 and the September Convention negotiated by Napoleon III in 1864 as prelude to the withdrawal of French troops from Rome. The last, concluded with Sardinia without papal knowledge, convinced Pius that little was to be gained from deferring to France.

Among the errors denounced by the *Syllabus*, some, such as pantheism, naturalism, and rationalism, were relatively uncontroversial. It was proclaimed erroneous to hold that philosophy need not submit to the magisterium of the church and that the methods and principles of scholastic theology were no longer relevant. Public opinion, however, focused primarily on the sections dealing with indifferentism and toleration, civil society, the rights of the church, and modern liberalism. Rejecting the thesis that one religion was as good as another, the *Syllabus* condemned the propositions that salvation could be found in any religion, that everyone should "profess the religion that his reason leads him to consider true," that it was no longer useful that Catholicism be considered the only state religion. It denounced separation of church and state, rebellion against legitimate princes, the principle that ecclesiastical rights and immunities derive from the state and that the state must prevail in disputes between the two authorities, the denial of the church's right to possess and employ temporal power, education divorced from church authority, the dissolubility of marriage, and, most dramatic, the belief that the "Roman Pontiff can and must make his peace with progress, liberalism and modern civilization and come to terms with them" (proposition 80). Attached to each condemned proposition was a reference to a previous condemnation of it by Pius IX.

In France, intransigent Catholics greeted the *Syllabus* with joy while liberal Catholics were dismayed. Anti-clerics delighted at being able to seize on a string of papal propositions that, divorced from their qualifying context in allocutions and other documents, served to confirm their charges of Catholic obscurantism, intolerance, and arrogance. Initially at least, few troubled to determine that proposition 80, for example, referred to the allocution *Jamdudum cernimus* (1861), which specifically proscribed the type of "progress, liberalism and modern civilization" embraced by the Sardinian government. Jules Baroche, the French minister for religious affairs, asserted that the propositions were "contrary to the principles on which the constitution of the Empire rests" and refused to permit bishops to transmit them to the clergy, although newspapers were allowed to print the encyclical and the *Syllabus* unofficially. Bishop Maret and Bishop Georges Darboy (1813–1871) of Paris tried, without success, to get Baroche to negotiate with Rome to obtain modifications or clarifications of the papal pronouncements. It was amid controversy, confusion, ultramontane exultation, and liberal Catholic disarray that there appeared in January 1865 the pamphlet *La Convention du 15 septembre et l'Encyclique du 8 décembre* of Bishop Dupanloup of Orleans. Dupanloup had just finished writing a protest against the September Convention when *Quanta cura* and the *Syllabus* appeared. Quickly, in collaboration with Augustin Cochin (1823–1872), he formulated a second part, placing the most controversial propositions of the *Syllabus* in context and interpreting the document in the light of a distinction between the thesis, which represented the ideal in a completely Catholic society, and the hypothesis, which involved the practical arrangements necessary once the religious consensus has broken down. Catholics, he explained, were expected to adjust to the constitutions and liberties of their particular states. This interpretation met with an enormous positive response from moderate and liberal Catholics throughout the world. Although denounced by Louis Veuillot and disparaged by anti-clericals, it won papal approval. Even so, the *Syllabus* continued to embarrass liberal Catholics and served to reinforce the anti-clerical currents that, swelling under the Second Empire, especially among republicans, burst forth during the first decades of the Third Republic.

R. Aubert, "Mgr. Dupanloup et le *Syllabus*," *RHE* 51 (1956), and "La réaction du *Correspondant* au *Syllabus*," in *Etudes de droit et d'histoire: Mélanges Mgr. H. Wagnon* (Louvain, 1976); E. Catta, "Mgr. Edouard Pie, Pie IX, le *Syllabus* et le premier Concile du Vatican d'après les oeuvres de l'évêque de Poitier," *Pio IX* 3 (July 1974, 1976, 1977);

E. Papa, Il Sillabo *di Pio IX e la stampa francese, inglese e italiana* (Rome, 1968); A. Quacquarelli, *La crisi della religiosità contemporanea del* Sillabo *al Concilio Vaticano* (Bari, 1946).

Raymond L. Cummings

Related entries: CORRESPONDANT; GALLICANISM; INFALLIBILITY, DOCTRINE OF; MARET; MONTALEMBERT; ORLEANS, BISHOP OF; PIE; PIUS IX; ROMAN QUESTION; SOCIAL CATHOLICISM; VATICAN COUNCIL; VEUILLOT.

SYRIAN EXPEDITION, the 1860 intervention by France, on behalf of Europe, to end an outbreak of sectarian violence in Syria. Since the Crusades, France had acted to protect Roman Catholic interests in this province of the Ottoman Empire. More recently (Napoleon Bonaparte's Egyptian expedition, 1798–1799; Adolphe Thiers' support of the Egyptian viceroy, Mehemet Ali, 1840), the powers had suspected France of imperial designs in the area. News of a recurrence in May 1860 of communal violence between the leading minorities, Roman Catholic Maronites, concentrated north of Palestine between the twin mountain ranges of the Lebanon, and Moslem Druses, reached Paris in June. Fears of a massacre of the Christians, either promoted by or acquiesced in by local Ottoman officials, led French foreign minister Edouard Thouvenel on 6 July to urge the Porte to restore order and the five powers signatory to the Treaty of Paris of 1856 to join with Turkey in establishing a commission that would inquire into the causes of the civil war and the actions of local officials, decide on reparations for the victims, and recommend a new administrative structure to succeed that of 1842, which had established separate districts for Maronites and Druses under a single Ottoman governor. Hoping to forestall international intervention, the Porte sent Fuad Pasha, minister of foreign affairs, to Beirut with unlimited powers to maintain order and to dispense justice. But news of the massacre of five hundred Christians in Damascus on 9 July, bringing Christian casualties to twelve thousand, determined Paris to act militarily. Ottoman and British reservations were overcome during a conference that met at Paris from 26 July. A protocol, signed by Thouvenel and the British, Austrian, Russian, Prussian, and Turkish ambassadors at Paris on 3 August and formalized as a convention on 5 September, sanctioned a French force of six thousand to occupy Syria for six months in support of Fuad Pasha. It would be increased if necessary by another six thousand troops from France or elsewhere. However, Fuad's skill in acting independently and in exploiting rivalries among the powers largely neutralized the French force, commanded by General Charles Marie Napoléon Beaufort d'Hautpoul (1804–1890). Between its arrival on 16 August 1860 and its withdrawal (after Thouvenel had won a four-month extension of its mandate) on 5 June 1861, the expeditionary force was confined largely to garrison duties around Beirut. Suspicions that France intended a permanent occupation were strong in London. Whether Napoleon III was working toward the creation of a client state, perhaps a *royaume* *arabe* under Algerian Emir Abd-El-Kader, awaits confirmation; however, Paris argued publicly (as in the emperor's open letter of 29 July 1860 to Victor Fialin Persigny, then his ambassador to Britain) that French motives were entirely disinterested and humanitarian. Moreover, every effort was made to stress the European dimension of the intervention.

While ambassadors of the five powers and Turkey continued to consult in Paris and in Constantinople, the International Commission at Beirut held twenty-nine sessions between 5 October 1860 and 4 May 1861. Its members (Léon Philippe Béclard represented France) seldom agreed on either procedures or recommendations. Conflict between the major protagonists, France and Britain, came to a head on the issue of the future administration of Lebanon. Béclard argued for a separate Maronite district presided over by a native Christian governor (*un seul chef unique et indigène*), in all likelihood a member of the Shehab dynasty deposed in 1842. The British representative, a consistent supporter of the Druses, proposed separate jurisdictions for Maronites, Druses, and Greek Orthodox, based on the precedent of 1842. The two plans were referred to the conference of ambassadors in Constantinople, which reached a compromise (*règlement* of 9 June 1861). Rejecting the precedent of 1842, it proposed a single Christian governor for the Lebanon but without requiring that he be a native. Denied an *indigène*, France accepted the nomination of Daoud Pasha, a respected Armenian Christian, and was reassured by the Porte's reiteration of its grant (*hatti hamayum*) in 1856 of full legal rights to Turkey's Christian subjects. With some minor adjustments proposed by France in 1864 (although once again Paris failed to win nomination of a native Christian governor), the 1861 *règlement* remained the basis for the Lebanon's administration until France assumed its League of Nations mandate in 1922.

F. Choisel, "L'expédition de Syrie (1860)," *Revue de la cavalerie blindée*, 107 (1979); D. Cohen, "Une souscription des Juifs de France en faveur des Chrétiens d'Orient en 1860," *RHMC* (July–September 1977); G. Dunn, "The French Intervention in Syria, 1860–1861" (Ph.D. diss., University of Texas, 1940); M. Emerit, "La crise syrienne et l'expansion économique française en 1860," *RH* 207 (April–June 1952); Commandant L. Grandin, *Les Français en Syrie, 1860–1861* (Paris, 1891).

Christopher English

Related entries: ALGERIA; CHINA EXPEDITIONS; CONGRESS POLICY; INDOCHINA; LA VALETTE; MEXICAN EXPEDITION; SUEZ CANAL; THOUVENEL.

T

TAINE, HIPPOLYTE (1828–1893), historian, philosopher, and critic; born at Vouziers in the Ardennes mountains on 21 April 1828. His father was a solicitor; his grandfather had been a subprefect. Taine was uprooted by the death of his father (1840) to be raised by his devoted mother and sisters in Paris. After losing his religious faith while in his teens, thus straining but not severing family ties, Taine began a promising but ultimately frustrating academic career. At the Ecole Normale Supérieure (1848), his record was brilliant and his abilities highly praised by his teacher, the philosopher Etienne Vacherot (1809–1897). But Taine could not accept the prevailing doctrines, and he failed his examinations for the *agrégation*. After an inferior assignment as substitute teacher at the Collège de Nevers (1851–1852), he was assigned to Poitiers (1852) and then to Besançon, where he was demoted to teaching the lower grades. Exasperated at last by this treatment and by the close supervision to which secondary school teachers were subjected, Taine obtained leave to complete his doctoral dissertation. When his psychology thesis ("Les sensations") was rejected, he turned to an inoffensive topic, receiving his doctorate for a thesis on *La Fontaine et ses fables* (1853; published 1860). Taine did not continue his academic career but, as with a number of other Second Empire academics, turned instead to literature and to journalism, publishing his first article in the *Revue de l'instruction publique* in 1855.

Taine's pessimism about human nature had prevented his being horrified by Louis Napoleon's coup d'état in December 1851. The subsequent plebiscite, he argued, while not justifying the coup did give to the new regime the right to be obeyed. Taine had signed the required oath, much to the disgust of his close liberal associates. Moreover, he frequented the salon of his long-time friend, Princess Mathilde, Napoleon III's cousin. But the regime distrusted his independence (he wrote for the liberal *Journal des débats* and *Revue des deux mondes*) and found his confrontation with traditional religion embarrassing. He was appointed examiner at the military academy of Saint-Cyr in 1863, then shortly afterward dismissed, by Minister of War Jacques Louis Randon, despite the emperor's mild protest. However, in 1864 Taine was named to replace Eugène Viollet-le-Duc as professor of the history of art at the reorganized Ecole des

Beaux-Arts, after the latter's unhappy experience there. Taine remained at the school for twenty years, leaving his impress as teacher and art critic. His political ideas remained unchanged. Not a democrat, he also rejected the authoritarian regime, favored decentralization, and admired British institutions, which, after a six-week visit, he treated brilliantly in his influential five-volume *Histoire de la littérature anglaise* (1863–1869).

The main thrust of Taine's *oeuvre* can be characterized as deterministic and positivistic. Taine presumed to search for the grand all-encompassing vision by developing a supposedly scientific method of discovery and analysis in which the individual personality, event, and reality are embedded in and shaped by the milieu. This search, this intellectual goal, stood against the metaphysical dualism (spirit versus matter, reason versus emotion) that prevailed in the Christian establishment, and it also opposed the analytical and fragmented perspective (specialized and narrow vantage point) that prevailed in the emerging scientific community. Taine's approach to the study of history and culture was moral but not religious, philosophical but not theological, humanistic but not social scientific; he was materialist, atheist, and pessimist but without abandoning individualist, humanist, and Christian values. In his arraignment of nineteenth-century French philosophers, *Les philosophes classiques au XIXe siècle en France* (1857), which catapulted him to prominence, Taine blasted Victor Cousin (1792–1867) and his followers for subordinating morality to science and concrete common sense to abstract language. In his magisterial history of English literature, which stamped him as one of the leading literary critics of the time, Taine elaborated his notion that the individual (Shakespeare, for example) both represented and was shaped by his society and culture ("race," Taine called it).

Already a pessimist in 1867 concerning France's future role in the world, Taine was in Dresden, gathering material for a work on Germany, when the Franco-Prussian War began. After the French defeat, he tried to assess the reasons for the disaster in his six-volume, unfinished, *Les origines de la France contemporaine* (1875–1893), and in the process developed a pessimistic view of the French Revolution, which pitted him against his former comrades in the struggle for science and progress. He declared that a quasi-metaphysical spirit of revolution had infected France and imperiled Western civilization. Taine died at Paris, 5 March 1893.

Since Taine's work was literary and not sociological, based on moral and not scientific assumptions, his histories and literary criticisms today seem obsolete. And yet Taine's monistic view and holistic approach, and especially his insistence on rooting the individual in the group and on the primacy of the moral question, continue to command the allegiance of the French intellectual world. Among others of his works published during the Second Empire are: *Voyage aux eaux des Pyrénées* (1855), *Essai sur Tite-Live* (1856), *Essais de critique et d'histoire* (1858–1865), *Philosophie de l'art dans les Pays-Bas* (1865), *Philosophie de l'art en Italie* (1866), *De l'idéal dans l'art en Grèce* (1869) (much of Taine's writing on art was later drawn together in his *Philosophie de l'art*, published in

1882), *Notes sur Paris* (1867), *Vie et opinions de Frédéric Thomas Graindorge* (1868), and *De l'intelligence* (1870).

A. Chevrillon, *Taine, la formation de sa pensée* (Paris, 1932); A. Cresson, *Hippolyte Taine: Sa vie, son oeuvre, avec un esquisse de sa philosophie* (Paris, 1951); J. Godechot, "Taine, historien de la Révolution française," *Romantisme*, 11, no. 32 (1981); S. J. Kahn, *Science and Aesthetic Judgement: A Study in Taine's Critical Method* (London, 1953); M. Leroy, *Taine* (Paris, 1933); A. A. Eustis, *Hippolyte Taine and the Classical Genius* (Berkeley, 1951); H. Taine, *Carnets de voyage: Note sur la province* (1863–1865) (Paris, 1897), and *Vie et correspondance*, 4 vols. (Paris, 1901–1907).

David R. Stevenson

Related entries: BERNARD; CHAMPFLEURY; GOBINEAU; MATHILDE; POSITIVISM; RENAN.

TALABOT, PAULIN (1799–1885), one of the most dynamic and successful of French industrialists; born at Limoges, 18 August 1799. Talabot enjoyed a business career that spanned over half a century. Like some other pioneers of the new metallurgical industry that emerged in France from the 1840s, like Eugène Schneider, manager of the Le Creusot ironworks, and Jean François Cail (1804–1871), the machine builder, he triumphed over relatively modest origins to create an industrial empire. The empire he built extended beyond coal and iron and even beyond France's borders. Indicative of the importance of his interests are the positions he held on the boards of directors of major metallurgical, mining, transport, and banking enterprises by 1881. In that year, he was on the boards of the South Austrian railway, the Société Générale bank, the Société des Transports Maritimes à Vapeur (a shipping company), and the Société Métallurgique du Saut-du-Tarn. He was honorary managing director of the Paris-Lyons-Mediterranean Railway Company (PLM) and chairman of the boards of the Denain-Anzin metallurgical complex, the Compagnie des Docks de Marseille, the Mokta el Hadid iron mining company in Algeria, and the Krivoli-Rog mining company in Russia.

It should not be thought, however, that Talabot was unique as an entrepreneurial type. There were other empire builders in the European industrialization process who exhibited similar verve and self-confidence, men like Camphausen in Germany and Cockerill in Belgium. Even in France, Talabot shared traits and a career pattern with other successful ironmasters like Paul Benoist d'Azy (1796–1880), the Jacksons, Pierre Emile Martin (1824–1915), and Charles de Wendel (1809–1870). These were the entrepreneurs who forged a modern French metallurgical industry and were thus the agents—and the products—of a technological and structural revolution. They introduced large-scale production based on the use of mineral fuel, steam engines, and the latest techniques. Through expansion and amalgamation, they built up the dozen or so large enterprises that, by the time of the Second Empire, came to dominate the French market. It was mainly due to their efforts that French metallurgy increased its production by a factor of twelve while reducing its prices by nearly half between 1814 and 1864.

This new type of ironmaster possessed two qualities: the technical know-how that enabled him successfully to adopt the high-cost technology and the business acumen that enabled him to grapple with the problem of raising capital and the marketing problems posed by the widening range of his products and the growing competition that resulted from the transport revolution. By force of circumstances, this type of innovating ironmaster was also an empire builder. He had an interest in securing optimal supplies of raw materials, in building the canals and railways that carried his goods and, in the case of the railway, constituted a vital market for his products. Individually and as a group, ironmasters early acquired political power, first in alliance with the landed interest, then through their own pressure groups like the Comité des Forges. Alphonse de Lamartine (1790–1869) complained in 1838 about ''the eighty ironmasters who get away with tyrannizing the country.'' They were thus disproportionately represented in the Chamber of Deputies. Of the thirty-eight deputies who were industrialists in 1848, no fewer than seventeen were ironmasters. Schneider, indeed, was minister of commerce during the presidency of Louis Napoleon, and both he and Talabot would have political careers during the Second Empire.

It should not be thought, either, that, whatever his organizational abilities or his vision, Talabot achieved success alone. He achieved it, first, with the help of his brothers. His father, François, a magistrate at Limoges, had five sons, of whom one, Auguste, followed his father in a legal career, and another, Edmond, who was the only Talabot to become a Saint-Simonian cultist, died of the cholera in 1832. The other three sons, Jules, Léon, and Paulin, followed business careers and worked closely together. Léon and Paulin possessed a second advantage; they were trained at the Ecole Polytechnique, the foremost engineering school in the world in the early nineteenth century. Paulin was also to benefit from the lifelong friendship and collaboration of another graduate of the Polytechnique, Charles Didion (1803–1882). Finally, to succeed in the rapidly changing metallurgical industry at this time, an ironmaster needed to secure alliances with politically and financially powerful groups. Talabot thus owed his start to the patronage of Marshal Soult (1769–1851), the Napoleonic soldier who after 1815 pursued a business (and later political) career. He owed his early success to the financial support of James de Rothschild, the most powerful merchant banker in the capital, and his successful empire building owed much to the alliance of Rhône valley interest and Parisian finance: Schneider (Le Creusot), J. François Bartholony (1796–1881; Paris-Orleans Railway), Martin (Fourchambault), Jules Hochet (industrial complex of Saint-Etienne).

After graduating from the Ecole des Ponts et Chaussées, which he attended after the Polytechnique, Talabot commenced his career modestly as a government engineer (he retired as *ingénieur en chef* in March 1862). It was only in 1830 that Soult, who with his associates owned the Midi metallurgical concerns of Alais (now Alès) and Saut-du-Tarn, invited Léon and Paulin to collaborate with him in his plans for expansion. This collaboration was to be the beginning of the Talabot business empire in the Rhône valley. The first two decades of the

Talabots' career, however, were not entirely successful, and many of Paulin's projects proved stillborn. His attempt to amalgamate Alais with the Grand-Combe coal mining company in the Gard failed, as did his proposal for the creation of a new metallurgical complex near Bône in Algeria. Construction of the Lyons-Avignon railway, whose concession a Talabot company secured in 1846, was not even started when the company collapsed in the following year. Talabot also joined with Prosper Enfantin (1796–1864) and others to set up a study group for a Suez canal (Société Internationale des Etudes du Canal de Suez), and Talabot carried out a study of the proposed waterway, but his 1847 project for a Suez-to-Alexandria route was too long and expensive and was, besides, overtaken by the mid-century economic crisis. Nonetheless, despite the failure of these plans, Talabot was cementing the relations and laying the bases that would enable him to build an empire during the reign of Napoleon III. He also had some successes. In 1837 he finally organized the company that by 1840 built the railway to link the ironworks at Alais with the Rhône river, the Alais-Beaucaire line. This was the first Talabot company to secure the financial backing of the Rothschild bank. Talabot and Didion also planned the route and organized the company for the Avignon-Marseilles railway. This company obtained the concession in 1843 and, although it suspended construction work in 1847, it was to be the springboard for Talabot's career as railway magnate and represented the first step toward achievement of the PLM.

It was after 1848 that Talabot's career was most successful. Under the Second Empire, he continued to collaborate with the Rothschild group and combatted the attempts of Emile and Isaac Pereire to control the railway to Marseilles, establish rival networks like the Grand Central, and take over Jules Mirès' enterprises in Marseilles where Talabot had important interests. He and his brothers were part of the Rothschild group (Réunion Financière) that set up the Société Générale pour Favoriser le Développement de l'Industrie et du Commerce, a major new joint stock bank, in 1864. The Société Générale controlled the Crédit Industriel et Commercial bank, which Talabot had also helped to establish in 1859 (he named three of the first administrators), despite the opposition of Eugène Rouher. In heavy industry the Talabots had a number of remarkable achievements. In 1849 they organized the merger of the Anzin mining company with the Denain ironworks. By 1869 Denain-Anzin was the tenth largest French metallurgical concern. In 1855 Paulin Talabot reorganized and expanded the Grand-Combe complex, which, with its six coal and six iron-ore mines, became France's second largest mining company. He also continued to seek new iron-ore supplies around the Mediterranean basin, as did a number of other leading French ironmasters at this time. He was responsible for the Mokta el Hadid mining company in Algeria, an enterprise that was to be financed in part by the Société Générale. His activities included the Marseilles dock company, which he helped establish in 1859, the Messageries Impériales (which had Marseilles as its principal port), the Forges de Firminy, the Constructions Mécaniques de La Ciotat, and the Société Algérienne. Abroad, his interests included Belgian coal mines and railways in Lombardy and Venetia (Compagnie de l'Haute Italie). Arguably his greatest achievement, however, was the fusion of companies to form the Paris-Lyon-Méditerranée railway, a fusion completed in 1857. From 1862 to 1882 Talabot would preside as director general over the destinies of the PLM, which, with a capital of 400 million francs in 1881, was not only France's biggest railway company but its largest joint stock enterprise. To achieve this project, envisaged since 1843, Talabot had had to triumph over the competition of the Pereires, whom he also prevented from extending their Midi railway to Marseilles.

In 1863 Talabot, long a member of the Conseil Général of the Gard, was elected as an official candidate to the Corps Législatif. In August 1864 he was named commander of the Legion of Honor. Although not a very vocal member of the legislature, he was reelected in 1869 (in the second round of voting). A protectionist and, in 1860, president of the Association pour la Défense du Travail National, he had later changed his mind on the issue of free trade. After 1870 he devoted himself entirely to business matters. Talabot died at Paris, 21 March 1885.

Paulin Talabot's career demonstrates that France produced entrepreneurs as creative and as energetic as those of other countries. His career is also a striking illustration of the remarkable modernization and concentration taking place in French metallurgy in the mid-nineteenth century. That he did not achieve his success alone but in a complex set of interlocking groupings with others showed the importance for success in big business in general and heavy industry in particular of alliances between enterprise, capital and politics.

A. A. Ernouf, *Paulin Talabot, sa vie, son oeuvre, 1799–1885* (Paris, 1886); R. E. Cameron, *France and the Economic Development of Europe, 1800–1914* (Princeton, 1961); B. Gille, *Recherches sur la formation de la grande entreprise capitaliste (1815–1848)* (Paris, 1959), and "Minerais algériens et sidérurgie métropolitaine; espoirs et réalités (1845–1880)," *RHS* 1 (1960).

Barrie M. Ratcliffe

Related entries: ARLES-DUFOUR; BANKING; BEHIC; COMITE DES FORGES; MESSAGERIES IMPERIALES; MIRES; PEREIRE; RAILROADS; ROTHSCHILD; SAINT-SIMONIANISM; SCHNEIDER, E.; *SOCIETES PAR ACTIONS.*

TANNHAUSER, opera by Richard Wagner (1813–1883); its Paris premiere in 1861 became a cause célèbre. Wagner had first come to Paris, with his wife, Minna, in September 1839, hoping to emulate the great success of Giacomo Meyerbeer. Although Meyerbeer provided him with letters of introduction, Wagner lived a life of poverty in what was then the musical center of Europe, supporting himself by songwriting and arranging and by writing articles. Before returning to Germany in April 1842, however, he composed his first successful opera, *Rienzi*, as well as his second, *Der fliegende Holländer. Tannhäuser* was produced at Dresden in 1845. The events of 1848–1849 led to Wagner's exile from Germany. He visited Paris briefly in 1849, again from February to July 1850 (it was in September of the latter year that he broke with Meyerbeer), in 1851 for several months, and from 7 to 21 October 1853. The occasion of the 1853 visit, as of others, was to see the celebrated pianist and composer Franz Liszt (1811–1886), Wagner's friend and patron, with whose daughter, Cosima, he would later begin a notorious love affair. Wagner was once more at Paris (for five days) in 1855, en route to London, and again for two weeks in January 1858, during which he failed to arrange production of *Tannhäuser* either at the Opéra or the Théâtre Lyrique.

By 1858 Wagner had become a subject of controversy at Paris. Some had termed him "the Courbet of music," a designation disputed by Jules Champfleury in an article ("On Realism—a Letter to Mme Sand") published in *L'artiste* in 1855. When Napoleon III met Emperor Francis Joseph of Austria at Stuttgart in September 1857, *Tannhäuser* was performed, and thereafter fragments of Wagner's music were played occasionally in France—for example, the overture to *Tannhäuser* at a Paris concert of 29 January 1858. A rather beleaguered group of French Wagnerians had begun to emerge. The group would come to include Champfleury, Charles Baudelaire, Henri Fantin-Latour, Théophile Gautier, Emile Zola, Charles Gounod, Camille Saint-Saëns, Léo Delibes, Gérard de Nerval, Edouard Manet, and Emile Ollivier. Ollivier in 1857 married Cosima's sister, Blandine, thus becoming, thirteen years later, Wagner's brother-in-law. It was he who protected the composer's literary rights in France. Champfleury and Baudelaire were perhaps the most devoted to Wagner's music, hailing it as both "romantic" and "modern."

In the fall of 1859, Wagner was once again at Paris. This time he arranged a series of concerts at the Théâtre des Italiens (25 January, 1 and 8 February 1860), featuring excerpts from his major operas—*Der fliegende Holländer*, *Lohengrin*, and *Tannhäuser*. The concerts ran a large deficit but attracted great attention. Hector Berlioz, unable to accept Wagner's music, nevertheless admitted his genius. On 27 January 1860 Champfleury published an article defending the composer, but Jacques Offenbach, in his irreverent way, poked fun at the Wagnerian pretensions in a musical sketch, *Le musicien de l'avenir* (Bouffes Parisiens, 6 February), an offense for which the egomaniacal German never forgave him. Wagner pressed his case, publishing (1860) a collection of his four principal librettos, introduced by a "Lettre sur la musique." He now had a powerful champion, Princess Pauline Metternich, whose husband, Prince Richard de Metternich (1829–1895), had been appointed Austrian ambassador to France in December 1859. The Metternichs, who would remain at their Paris post until 1872, had quickly become favorites of Napoleon III and Eugénie. Achille Fould, as minister of state, had resisted the princess's efforts to have *Tannhäuser* produced at the Opéra, but his successor (in November 1860), Alexandre Walewski, was more sympathetic. Urged by Princess Metternich, her allies at court, and such other Wagnerians as Ollivier, the emperor at last ordered the first premiere at Paris of a Wagner opera. Berlioz, who had vainly sought since 1858 to have *Les Troyens* produced, was understandably resentful.

The Opéra de Paris did not occupy in 1861 the splendid Palais Garnier, whose construction had not yet begun. Its quarters on the rue Le Peletier had been built in 1821 by Charles Rohault de Fleury of used materials and would continue to house the company until 1873. If Wagner were now to present *Tannhäuser und der Sängerkrieg auf Wartburg* (such was the opera's full name) at Paris, he must first subscribe to a number of conventions: that the work be translated into French, that it not be conducted by its composer, and that it contain a ballet at the beginning of the second act. The last convention was especially significant. At Paris, ballet was at least as popular as opera and had become by mid-century an elaborate spectacle that was placed late enough in the opera to permit gentlemen arriving fashionably late to admire the pretty ballet dancers. By the end of January 1861, Wagner had completed his revisions. He refused, however, to conform to convention in regard to the ballet, instead extending the Bacchanale and Venusberg scene at the beginning of act 1. A first-rate cast was engaged, including Marie Sass (1834–1907) as Elisabeth and Albert Niemann (1831–1917), the German tenor chosen by Wagner to sing the role of Tannhäuser. A large crowd attended the opening performance on 13 March 1861, including many friends of Princess Metternich. But when the latecomers arrived, their frustration at having missed the ballet undoubtedly fueled the disturbances, led by members of the Jockey Club, which disrupted the evening. On 18 March, despite certain cuts by the composer, the tumult continued even after the arrival of the emperor and empress. The third performance (on 24 March) having been no calmer, Wagner withdrew his work. The sets, which were to have been used in another opera commissioned for the purpose, were destroyed in a fire during the night of 19–20 July 1861. There were many reasons for the *Tannhäuser* fiasco: conservative French musical tastes, resentment of Princess Metternich's pushiness, Wagner's stubbornness concerning the ballet, his refusal to employ a claque, and his ill-advised attempt to bypass the rule against composers conducting their own work at the Opéra. The Opéra's conductor, Louis Dietsch (1808–1865), seems not to have distinguished himself in his conducting of *Tannhäuser*.

Although no other opera by Wagner would be produced at Paris during the remainder of the Second Empire until 1869, the failure of *Tannhäuser* did not mark an end to the Wagnerian controversy in France. Gounod saw the event as a short-term setback but a triumph in the long run ("God grant me a failure like that"). Baudelaire on 1 April 1861 published a spirited defense of Wagner ("Richard Wagner et *Tannhäuser* à Paris") in the *Revue européenne*, the bonapartist paper *Jeune France* also defended the composer, and Wagner himself (in *Bericht über die Aufführung des "Tannhäuser" in Paris*, 1861) distinguished between the fairness of the "true public" and the antics of the Jockey Club clique. Wagner returned to Paris in January 1862, and it was there that he completed the libretto of *Die Meistersinger von Nürnberg* (his final visit would be to southern France from December 1865 to January 1866). On 10 May 1862 Pasdeloup played the march from act 2 of *Tannhäuser* at one of his Concerts Populaires, and it was well received. Georges François Hainl (1807–1873), as conductor of the Société des Concerts du Conservatoire from 10 January 1864, included Wagner in that orchestra's repertoire. Wagnerians, like Fantin-Latour, persisted. Fantin-Latour's lithograph and painting, *"Tannhäuser*: Venusberg'' (1862) were his first important mature compositions inspired by imagination. On 25 December 1864, the painter, who had missed the *Tannhäuser* premiere (he had had tickets for the cancelled fourth performance), heard for the first time the overture to *Der fliegende Holländer* at a Pasdeloup concert. That conductor, as director of the Théâtre Lyrique, presented Wagner's opera *Rienzi* in April 1869. It failed, but, in the end, not even the tragedy of the Franco-Prussian War could extinguish the enthusiasm of some Frenchmen for *"le musicien de l'avenir.''*

L. Guichard, *La musique et les lettres au temps du Wagnérisme* (Paris, 1963); S. Huebner, *"Lohengrin* in Paris: Wagner and the *Revanchards,''* *History Today* 31 (November 1981); V. d'Indy, *Richard Wagner et son influence sur l'art musical français* (Paris, 1930); E. Schlumberger, *"Tannhäuser* à Paris (1861),'' *CA*, no. 330 (1979); G. D. Turbow, ''Wagnerism in France, 1839–1870: A Measure of a Social and Political Trend'' (Ph.D. diss., University of California, 1965).

Related entries: FANTIN-LATOUR; MEYERBEER; PASDELOUP.

TARIFFS. See COBDEN-CHEVALIER TREATY.

LE TEMPS, one of the great newspapers of modern France; established during the Second Empire. On 25 April 1861 Auguste Nefftzer revived the name, which had been carried by several previous Paris newspapers. Associated with him as *gérant*, director, and editor in chief was Adrien Hébrard (1834–1914), whose brother, Jacques (b. 1841), would also be *gérant* of the paper. Protestant and Alsatian influences were strong at *Le temps*, which was intended to be the French equivalent of the *Times* of London. In fact, it quickly rivaled the *Journal des débats* in its variety of erudite writers. Less scholarly in expression than that paper but far more elevated in subject and style than *La presse*, its major appeal was to opponents of the regime. Nevertheless, the political opinions of *Le temps*, as with other opposition newspapers, were very circumspect. As Hébrard stated in the introductory issue, the newspaper's program would be to support universal suffrage, advocate liberty, and plead for complete freedom of speech and conscience without subscribing to any party or faction. *Le temps* posted its correspondents widely and encouraged their objectivity. Louis Blanc (1811–1882) sent reports from England and the young Georges Clemenceau (1841–1929) from the United States. One of *Le temps*' more important editors, the Protestant Edmond Scherer (1815–1889), was a man capable of writing on a wide variety of subjects and of giving an electric air to the paper. Among the collaborators of the newspaper were the following: Charles Dollfus (1827–1913), Gustave Isambert, Edouard Hervé (1835–1899), Henri Brisson (1835–1912), Ferdinand

Lasteyrie (1810–1879), Charles-Edmond (1822–1899), Clément Duvernois (1836–1879), Hector Pessard (1836–1895), A. Erdan (Alexandre André Jacob, 1826–1878), Xavier Aubryet (1827–1880), and the geographer Louis Vivien de Saint-Martin (1802–1897). Louis Ulbach (1822–1889) and Francisque Sarcey (1828–1899) were drama critics, the latter from 1867. In 1864 *Le temps* enlisted Paul Armand Challemel-Lacour (1827–1896) to write on philosophy and Gustave Courcelle-Seneuil (1813–1892) for finance. Daniel Stern (comtesse d'Agoult, 1805–1876) also contributed, and in 1868 Charles Augustin Sainte-Beuve brought from *Le moniteur universel* his celebrated column, "Causeries du lundi," much to the disgust of his friend, Princess Mathilde.

In 1867–1868 Jules Ferry (1832–1893) published in *Le temps* his attack on the financial methods of Baron Georges Haussmann, "Les comptes fantastiques d'Haussmann." The newspaper also represented progressive business interests by its defense of free trade. It contributed to the fund to erect a memorial to Victor Baudin at the end of 1868 and counseled abstention in the plebiscite of May 1870. Understandably, *Le temps* did not escape censure (*avertissement*) by the government despite its relative moderation and the fact that it had been launched at a time when restrictions on the press were beginning to be relaxed. It received its first *avertissement* in February 1866. *Le temps* became increasingly significant as the Empire declined. Its circulation was 3,178 in August 1861, 10,000 in 1864, and 11,000 in March 1869. After 4 September it would become one of the great newspapers of the Third Republic.

Tables du journal "Le temps" (Paris, 1966–1967).

Natalie Isser

Related entries: MARINONI; NEFFTZER; PRESS REGIME.

THEATER. During the Second Empire, as during all previous regimes since the Revolution, plays required authorization before production (at Paris by the ministry exercising jurisdiction over the fine arts; in the provinces by the prefects) and could be prohibited if considered objectionable or even withdrawn after performances had begun if deemed a threat to public order. These provisions were confirmed by decree of 31 December 1852 and were continued beyond 1870. However, by decree of 6 January 1864, the requirement for preliminary authorization to establish a theater (law of 1806) was rescinded. During the first half of the Empire, the censors took their assignment seriously, rejecting many scripts that contained political or social criticism. *La dame aux camélias* (1852) by Alexandre Dumas fils was a case in point. At the same time, the eventual acceptance of the play demonstrated the rather arbitrary manner in which theater censorship functioned; Dumas fils needed only to await bureaucratic change within the ministry before his play was staged.

In the 1860s, the policy regarding censorship was more liberally interpreted, and playwrights who broached contemporary social issues—adultery, love, marriage, divorce, illegitimacy—could do so with less fear of outright rejection of their work. Treatments of such themes varied, but more often than not playwrights chose a comic form: the comedy of manners, the satirical comedy, the farce. To entertain, not to preach, seemed to be the order of the day, and authors like Alexandre Dumas fils, Victorien Sardou, Eugène Scribe, and Eugène Labiche were very successful in serving up gentle critique of contemporary *moeurs* in the palatable form of the social comedy. The comic opera and vaudeville (short comedies using popular songs) were equally as popular, and audiences responded enthusiastically to the productions of Ludovic Halévy and Henri Meilhac, many of which were set to the music of Jacques Offenbach. Even more aristocratic circles took an interest in contemporary theatrical fare. Octave Feuillet was invited to stage salon comedies for the empress. Napoleon III's half-brother, Auguste de Morny, and Jean Mocquard, *chef de cabinet* of the emperor, were both greatly interested in the theater. Other playwrights of the day—Emile Augier, Sardou, Labiche—were honored with membership in the Legion of Honor. Moreover, not all of the theater produced during the Second Empire has passed into oblivion. Plays of Scribe, Sardou (*Divorçones!*), Labiche (*Un chapeau de paille d'Italie*), and Dumas fils, sometimes in translation, are still part of theater repertoire.

G. Bapst, *Essai sur l'histoire du théâtre* (Paris, 1893); R. Boutet de Monvel, *Les Variétés, 1850–1870* (Paris, 1905); J. Claretie, *La vie moderne au théâtre* (Paris, 1869, 1875); P. Spencer, "Censorship of Literature under the Second Empire," *CHJ* 3 (1949); "Théâtre," *Larousse du XIXe siècle*, vol. 15.

Dolorès A. Signori

Related entries: AUGIER; BANVILLE; BAUDELAIRE; CLARETIE; COPPEE; DUMAS FILS; ERCKMAN-CHATRIAN; FEUILLET; FEYDEAU; FLAUBERT; GAUTIER; GONCOURT; HALEVY; JANIN; LABICHE; MEILHAC; MOCQUARD; MORNY; OFFENBACH; RACHEL; SAND; SARDOU; SCHNEIDER, H.

THEATRE LYRIQUE. See CARVALHO.

THIERS, ADOLPHE (1797–1877), historian, journalist, leading politician, and minister under the Orleans Monarchy, opponent of the Second Empire; born at Marseilles, 16 April 1797. Abandoned at birth by his father, Thiers was raised in frugal circumstances by his mother and grandmother, attending the Marseilles lycée on a partial scholarship. He studied law at Aix, moving to Paris in 1821 to begin his career as journalist, art critic, and historian. As first editor of *Le national*, Thiers helped bring about the Revolution of 1830. He then entered the legislature where his rise was rapid. He served as president of the cabinet in 1836 and again in 1840, when he perhaps helped pave the way for the Second Empire by having the ashes of Napoleon returned to France. But he was also responsible for the arrest of Louis Napoleon at Bologne that August. Thiers pushed for political reform under the Orleans monarchy, but in the legislature of the Second Republic he became a leader of the forces of order. Overestimating the power of the Left and underestimating, perhaps, that of Louis Napoleon

Bonaparte, Thiers backed the future emperor for president of the Republic and hosted his victory banquet on election night (10 December 1848). Thiers wielded considerable political influence during 1849, but by 1850 his influence was restricted to the legislative branch, and in 1851 he was among those exiled at the coup d'état of 2 December.

Thiers returned from an eight-month exile to spend the next eleven years on his multivolume *Histoire du Consulat et de l'Empire* (1845–1862). He gradually regained political influence, however, aided by his well-attended salon, his seat since 1833 in the Académie Française, and his ties with members of the press, especially Lucien Anatole Prévost-Paradol. Thiers favored Napoleon III's alliance with England in the Crimean War, and his favorable comments on the successful conclusion of this "just" war won him from the emperor the title of "our illustrious national historian." But he broke sharply with Napoleon III in 1858 when the emperor turned to support in Italy of what Thiers termed the *politique des nationalités*. Thiers tried in vain, through his strong influence on the foreign minister, Alexandre Walewski, to prevent the break with Austria. Even the reacquisition of Savoy and Nice was not enough to reconcile Thiers, who was above all an advocate of national glory, to the principle of nationalities. As early as 1859–1860, he began to warn of the danger to France if this principle were accepted in Germany. This lost him some of his friends on the Left, for whom Italian unity was a holy cause, but it also brought new allies from among Catholics outraged at the consequences for the pope of Napoleon III's Italian policy. The commercial treaty of 1860 with Britain also created potential allies for Thiers among outraged protectionists, for although a proponent of British political liberalism, in economic matters he was an unwavering supporter of tariff protection, as well as of a strong French merchant marine. The decree of 24 November 1860, a step toward political liberalization in France, was hailed by some as reflecting Thiers' influence, and throughout 1861–1862 he was increasingly consulted by legislators on methods of parliamentary opposition. In 1863, his historical study completed, Thiers allowed himself to be persuaded by Auguste Nefftzer of *Le temps* to seek election to the Corps Législatif as a republican. He was perhaps influenced as well by the attacks launched against him by the minister of the interior, Victor Fialin Persigny. Despite Persigny's efforts, Thiers was elected at Paris. He promised to oppose Napoleon III and the Empire but within the constitution.

From 1863 Thiers played a key role in the gradual revival of French parliamentary government. His ideal was for parliament, firmly in the hands of a prime minister, to rule, rather than the people, whom he feared and for whom he felt contempt. His hero was Napoleon I, whose centralization of France he fully approved. Carefully but insistently Thiers pushed for the liberties he termed, in his famous speech of 11 January 1864, necessary in the modern state. These included not only personal security and the free exchange of ideas but also free elections and a ministry responsible to the majority in the lower house of the legislature. Government spokesman Eugène Rouher, recognizing the strength that a man of Thiers' prestige and respectability lent to the still very small opposition minority, began to single him out for personal attack, thus initiating a duel that increasingly absorbed public attention. Thiers, who had seen the significance of the 1863 elections to be that he would now be at grips with the emperor, was perhaps not too much mistaken in regarding the restoration of the tribune in the Corps Législatif at the beginning of 1867 as meant for himself (he complained that it was too tall for his diminutive five foot two inches).

But if Thiers' goals remained political—"a progress in our institutions"—it was his series of speeches on foreign affairs that first won him the ear of the country. These began in January 1864, when, in concert with other opposition leaders, he tried to dissuade the government from sending Austrian archduke Maximilian to Mexico, pointing out that the costs would be much higher and the return of French forces much later than the government projected. But the main theme of Thiers' foreign policy speeches was the danger threatening France in Europe as a result of French support for nationalism. His most dramatic effort to change the course of imperial foreign policy came on 3 May 1866 when the Austro-Prussian conflict was imminent. Thiers warned in a Corps Législatif speech, that the abandonment of traditional policies based on balance of power concepts had destroyed the respect for international law painfully built up in preceding decades. Raising the specter of a new empire of Charles V, he asked how the government would explain to future generations France's fostering the growth of two great powers (Germany and Italy) on its doorstep and stressed his belief that no territorial gain for France could compensate for that growth. France, he argued, should use its influence to restrain Italy, leaving Austria free to deal with Prussia. Thiers felt this would also promote the best interests of the middle German states, which did not wish to be absorbed by Prussia. Thiers' oratory was so effective that a desire to counter it was perhaps one of the motives for a speech that Napoleon III gave at Auxerre three days later. The emperor found that public opinion was not with him, but this did not lead to an adoption of Thiers' views. After Prussia's decisive victory over Austria at Sadowa, Thiers strongly urged that France use its role as mediator to intercede for the smaller German states and limit Prussian gains as much as possible rather than seek anything for itself, but again his views were not adopted. After the failure of French efforts to gain territorial compensation, however, Thiers found his prestige greatly enhanced. In a final indictment of the Mexican affair in July 1867, he was able to link demands for more powers for the legislature to the need for more control over foreign policy. In a speech of 4 December 1867, demanding that Italy be made to respect its treaty obligations on Rome, he pushed Rouher to declare the following day that France would never abandon the pope. Thiers' republican allies could not swallow his defense of the pope, and Thiers himself was rather dismayed by such actions of Pope Pius IX as publication of the *Syllabus of Errors* in December 1864. But he insisted that foreign policy must take states as they were and that in the long run the chances for liberal governments would be improved in a peaceful Europe where treaties were respected and borders secure.

For the next three years, Thiers, who only sporadically attended meetings of the Corps Législatif, spoke little on foreign policy issues, feeling France's only course was to "arm quietly and threaten no one." He took almost no part in the debate over the military reform bill. He saw the need for improved armaments, was greatly interested in military matters, and broke regularly with the Left on the issue of military spending in each annual budget debate, but he also had great faith in France's traditional military setup and in its generals, and he did not see the value of Marshal Adolphe Niel's plans for greatly increasing the number of trained men available. Throughout his career Thiers would prefer a relatively small, long-term-enlistment professional army. He spoke strongly, however, for liberalization of the press laws and continued to promote and inspire the growth of the Tiers Parti. Thiers could have led this growing faction, for he had resisted the blandishments of Auguste de Morny, but he was unwilling to accept anything less than supreme power. Moreover, his arrogance and his extreme demands (the abandonment of the principle of nationalities and the complete acceptance of parliamentary government) were further barriers. In the elections of 1869, Thiers was opposed at Paris not only by the official candidate, for whose benefit the government gerrymandered the district, but also by a socialist to his left. But he managed to win in the runoff election, and he had the satisfaction of seeing his old foe Rouher forced to resign when the new legislature convened.

Thiers was not a member of the Emile Ollivier ministry finally appointed the following January, but he was generally considered a strong influence on it, and especially on Louis Buffet and Napoléon Daru, ministers of finance and foreign affairs, respectively. Empress Eugénie could never shake the erroneous belief that Thiers and his friends still plotted to restore the house of Orleans, but in fact in the early months of 1870, Thiers, who had stood clear of the Orleanist-legitimist quarrel and attempts at fusion, had high hopes of gaining his political goals without a change of dynasty. These hopes were somewhat dashed by the plebiscite that May, which led to the resignation of Buffet and Daru, but Thiers still retained some influence on Ollivier and others of the cabinet.

The news of the Hohenzollern candidacy for the Spanish throne was as much a shock to Thiers as to anyone else at Paris; his reaction was to do everything possible to resolve the crisis without war. He made a final lonely effort the night of 15 July 1870 when he opposed the granting of war credits and insisted that the legislature be shown the diplomatic dispatches before being asked to make an irrevocable decision. For the last time he appealed to the legislators to "know how to wait," to bide their time against Prussia, and to fight only in defense of south Germany when France would have Europe on its side. Without such aid, Thiers privately doubted military victory for France, although it is open to debate whether he realized the extent of French unpreparedness. It was one of the finest hours of a man not usually gifted with prophetic vision. He was frightened of the railroads, a defender of papal temporal power (although himself a free-thinker), fearful of democracy, contemptuous of Baron Georges Haussmann's modernization of Paris (which he attacked in a speech of 23 February 1869), and almost completely blind to the emerging social question.

Thiers left the Palais Bourbon the night of 15 July amid insults and cries of treason. But he was a man of vast abilities, inexhaustible energy, and monumental self-confidence, and his strengths far outweighed his faults of pessimism, egoism, and a lack of physical courage. When the course of the war turned against France, this politician, who was said to be able to understand anything and who was certainly one of the most persuasive speakers of his time, found his opinions and support solicited from every side. From 22 August 1870, he served on the Committee for Defense, and he was arguing for the withdrawal of Marshal Marie Edme Patrice de MacMahon's army toward Paris when the news of Sedan arrived. The Corps Législatif at its meeting of 4 September 1870 would have adopted Thiers' motion for creation of a Committee of National Defense to replace the imperial government had its session not been interrupted by the invasion of a mob. Jules Favre and Léon Gambetta led the demonstrators off to the Hôtel de Ville to proclaim a republic, while the rest of the legislators chose Thiers to preside. He persuaded them to ''retire with dignity.'' His subsequent role belongs to the history of the Third Republic: the negotiation of an armistice, the war on the Commune, the ''liberation of the territory.'' But he would never have been chosen for this role without his seven-year debate with the Empire. He died at Saint-Germain-en-Laye, 3 September 1877.

J. M. S. Allison, *Monsieur Thiers* (New York, 1932); M. A. Calman, ed., *Discours parlementaires de M. Thiers*, 16 vols. (Paris, 1879–1889); R. Christophe, *Le siècle de Monsieur Thiers* (Paris, 1966); J. M. Knapp, "Adolphe Thiers and the Revolutions of 1830, 1848, and 1870" (Ph.D. diss., University of Pennsylvania, 1973); J. Lucas-Dubreton, *Aspects de Monsieur Thiers* (Paris, 1948); H. Malo, *Monsieur Thiers* (Paris, 1932); C. H. Pomaret, *Monsieur Thiers et son siècle* (Paris, 1948); G. Roux, *Thiers* (Paris, 1948); R. Schnerb, "La politique fiscale de Thiers," *RH* 201 (1949), 202 (1950); W. A. Shepard, "Adolphe Thiers and French Foreign Policy under the Second Empire" (Ph.D. diss., University of Pennsylvania, 1974).

Winyss A. Shepard

Related entries: BUFFET; CORPS LEGISLATIF; DARU; ELECTIONS; LIBERAL EMPIRE; LIBERALISM; NATIONALITIES; OLLIVIER; ORLEANISM; PERSIGNY; PRESS REGIME; REFORM; ROUHER; TIERS PARTI.

THOMAS, AMBROISE (1811–1896), opera composer, second only to Charles Gounod in French public esteem during the Second Empire; born at Metz, 5 August 1811. Thomas' parents were both music teachers, and he enjoyed a brilliant career at the Paris Conservatoire (1828–1832), where he studied piano with Pierre Zimmermann (1785–1853), harmony and accompaniment with Victor Charles Paul Dourlen (1780–1864), and composition with Jean François Le Sueur (1760–1837) before winning the Prix de Rome in 1832. At Rome he became a friend of Dominique Ingres, director of the Villa Medici and, like Thomas, an admirer of Mozart and of Beethoven. On his return to Paris (1835), the young composer turned, as was customary in the middle of the nineteenth century, to the musical stage. His first opéra comique, *La double échelle*, was performed in 1837. By 1851 Thomas had won a degree of popularity with a dozen light operas. That year he was elected to the Académie des Beaux-Arts in place of Gasparo Spontini (1774–1851), defeating Hector Berlioz (1803–1869), Félicien David (1810–1876), Louis Clapisson (1808–1866), and Louis Niedermeyer (1802–1861).

During the 1850s Thomas' reputation grew with a series of moderately successful opéras comiques: *La Tonelli* (Opéra Comique, 30 March 1853; libretto by Elie Sauvage [1814–1871]); *La cour de Célimène* (Opéra Comique, 11 April 1855; libretto by Joseph Bernard Rosier [1804–1880]); *Psyché* (Opéra Comique, 26 January 1857; libretto by Jules Barbier [1822–1882] and Michel Carré [1819–1872]; influenced by Gounod's *Sapho*); *Le carnaval de Venise* (Opéra Comique, 9 December 1857; libretto by Sauvage; influenced by Victor Massé [1822–1884]); and *Le roman d'Elvire* (Opéra Comique, 4 February 1860; libretto by Alexandre Dumas père [1802–1870] and Adolphe de Leuven [1800–1884]; failure). Leuven, an ardent bonapartist and a lifelong friend of Alexandre Dumas fils, would be director of the Opéra Comique from December 1862 to 1874. In 1856 Thomas replaced Adolphe Adam (1803–1856) as professor of composition at the Conservatoire, and in 1858 he was named officer of the Legion of Honor.

Thomas had shown great versatility and eclecticism during the decade. From 1860 to 1866, he underwent the influence in particular of Gounod's extremely successful opera, *Faust* (1859). A long pause in Thomas' operatic creativity ended on 17 November 1866 when the Opéra Comique presented *Mignon* (libretto by Barbier and Carré). The cast was an extremely strong one: Célestine Galli-Marié (1840–1905) created Mignon (and would later create Carmen), and Marie Cabel (1827–1885) sang Philine. The opera, a worldwide success, was destined for perennial popularity in France where more than a thousand performances would have been given at the Opéra Comique by 1894. Sixteen months later, *Hamlet* clearly reflected the influence of Gounod's *Roméo et Juliette*. Produced at the Opéra 9 March 1868, *Hamlet* was the occasion of the debut on that stage of the great Swedish soprano Christine Nilsson (1843–1921), who created the role of Ophélie and was later incomparable in that of Mignon. Others in the splendid cast were Jean Baptiste Faure (1830–1914), Louis Guéymard (1822–1880; the Opéra's leading tenor until 1868), and Armand Castelmary (1834–1897). *Mignon* and *Hamlet* put the seal on Thomas' already considerable reputation. In August 1868 he was named commander of the Legion of Honor (in 1894 he would be the first composer to reach the rank of grand cross), and in 1871, on the death of Daniel Auber (1782–1871), he would be named director of the Conservatoire.

During the Second Empire, Thomas was ranked with Gounod, Wagner, and Verdi. Indeed, Verdi respected his music, as did also Berlioz, Gounod, Georges

Bizet (1838–1875), and Jules Massenet (1842–1912). Thomas' acceptance of the conventions that governed French opera was praised rather than criticized in an era when even Gonoud was thought by some to be too Wagnerian. Working within those conventions, Thomas raised opéra comique to a higher level of sentiment and lyricism than had been achieved by Auber, and his *Hamlet* was hailed as the worthy heir at the Opéra of the works of Giacomo Meyerbeer and of Fromental Halévy (1799–1862). But Thomas' later works proved slight, and today only *Mignon* keeps his musical reputation alive outside France. He died at Paris, 12 February 1896.

M. Cooper, *Charles Louis Ambroise Thomas* (London, 1957); M. Curtiss, *Bizet and His World* (London, 1959).
Related entries: CARVALHO; DELIBES; GOUNOD; MEYERBEER; OFFENBACH; *TANNHAUSER*; VIARDOT.

TOUR D'AUVERGNE, LA. See LA TOUR D'AUVERGNE.

THOUVENEL, EDOUARD ANTOINE (1818–1866), the youngest and probably the ablest foreign minister of the Second Empire; born at Verdun, 11 November 1818. Thouvenel came from a well-known and honorable bourgeois family of Lorraine. His grandfather, Nicholas Thouvenel, was a lawyer in the provincial parlement, and his father, Louis Thouvenel, was a *maréchal de camp* under Napoleon I and later, under Louis Philippe, was *commandant adjoint* of the École Polytechnique.

Having received his *bachelier-ès-lettres* at Paris in 1835, Thouvenel went on to the Ecole de Droit, where he received the bachelor of law in 1838 and the masters degree (*license*) in law in 1839. Still only twenty years old, he was already determined to go into the diplomatic service and as a unique preparation took a trip to the Near East via the Danube River, through Austria, Hungary, and Wallachia, to Constantinople and back through Greece and Italy. Finally in 1841 Thouvenel obtained his first modest diplomatic appointment as an unpaid supernumerary in the *direction politique* of the French Ministry of Foreign Affairs. From this bottom rung he eventually was to climb to the top position in the ministry. In the meantime, he had exciting assignments along the way. After serving as French attaché in Belgium (1844–1845), he became secretary of legation in Greece in 1845, and in 1849 President Louis Napoleon Bonaparte promoted him to minister at the head of the Athens legation. On this assignment, he had to deal with the famous affair of Don Pacifico, a British subject whose home had been sacked by an Athenian mob in 1847. Because Greece stalled on paying damages to Pacifico and debt installments to England, the British fleet took custody of Greek ships and blockaded Greek ports. When France sent Baron Jean Baptiste Gros (1793–1870) to Athens as mediator, Thouvenel facilitated his efforts, to no avail. Greece had to accept the harsh British terms in 1850. Because Britain had become so hostile to Thouvenel, he had to ask for reassignment and become minister to Bavaria later in 1850. There his duties lasted only about a year; after the coup d'état of 2 December 1851, Louis Napoleon had him appointed as chief of the *direction politique* of the Foreign Ministry, where he had begun initially in 1841 at the lowest level. Here his duties were to keep the foreign minister informed, to compose all outgoing instructions, and, though not required, to write personal letters to the French diplomats abroad. It was during Thouvenel's directorate that the Crimean War broke out in March 1854. In the preceding year, before the declaration, it was Thouvenel's circular of 15 July 1853 that presented to the world the allied case against Russia. In April 1855, after a disagreement with Edouard Drouyn de Lhuys, then foreign minister, Thouvenel resigned his post and took the assignment (May 1855) of ambassador to Turkey, an allied country in the Crimean War.

In Constantinople, Thouvenel was to encounter the bitter rivalry of Viscount Stratford de Redcliffe, the British ambassador, who had already engineered the recall of two previous French ambassadors. Both the French and British governments were critical of Stratford, but he was retained in that post because of his knowledge of and influence in that critical area. For his part, Thouvenel played an important role in the composition of the sultan's *firman* (decree) on domestic reforms and in the formulation of a new constitution for the Danubian Provinces (Rumania), giving a shadowy union to the two provinces. When Moldavia rejected the union plan in fraudulent elections and Turkey, supported by Stratford, refused to hold new elections, Thouvenel broke off French relations with the Ottomans and boarded ship to go home (5–6 August 1857). This caused Turkey to relent and hold new elections. Thouvenel then returned to the embassy, and Stratford soon resigned, leaving the French ambassador victor. In 1859 Thouvenel was made a senator, a lifetime position, and in early 1860 he was called home to become France's foreign minister at the early age of forty-one, succeeding comte Alexandre Walewski.

While Thouvenel was foreign minister (1860–1862), his most important and persistent problem was that of the Italian states. He and Napoleon III tended to be sympathetic toward Italian nationalism and opposed to papal resistance to it. Curiously, the Italian question brought Thouvenel's initial ministerial appointment and eventually his dismissal from that office. Early in 1860, by correspondence with Count Benso di Cavour, Sardinia's prime minister, Thouvenel gave French assent to new plebiscites in Parma, Modena, the Romagna, and Tuscany, which approved their annexation to the Kingdom of Sardinia. In return, by the Treaty of Turin (March 1860) with Sardinia, he obtained the annexation of Savoy and Nice to France by similar plebiscites. For these new French acquisitions, the emperor awarded Thouvenel the grand cross of the Legion of Honor. Soon after these Sardinian acquisitions came the Garibaldi expedition through Sicily and southern Italy, the fall of Naples, and the flight of King Francis II. Converging on this was a similar invasion southward by Sardinia through the papal provinces of Umbria and the Marches and the reception of the southern provinces by King Victor Emmanuel of Sardinia from the hands of Garibaldi. Again plebiscites confirmed the annexation by Sardinia of these territories, excluding Rome and the Patrimony of Saint Peter. Thouvenel had been opposed to the Sardinian move southward and ordered a gentle semibreak in relations by recalling the French minister from Turin but leaving a chargé d'affaires in the legation. When the united Kingdom of Italy was proclaimed in March 1861, Thouvenel did not at first recognize it, but he began a secret negotiation with Cavour for an agreement that France would withdraw its protective troops from Rome in return for Italy's promise not to attack papal Rome or permit any other attack. Before the conclusion of this arrangement, Cavour died (June 1861), and Thouvenel, to prevent the Italian radicals from taking over the new kingdom's government and attacking Rome and Venetia, persuaded the emperor to recognize the Kingdom of Italy, while leaving the French garrison at Rome. This gained for Thouvenel the permanent hostility of Empress Eugénie. Finally, Garibaldi organized another drive to take Rome from the pope. Even though the Italian government stopped him at Aspromonte (in August 1862), it spoiled its own advantage by demanding its annexation of Rome rather than just the French military evacuation of the Holy City. This led Napoleon III to take a harder line toward Italy to gain clerical support in the coming elections of 1863. Thouvenel was dismissed from the cabinet in October 1862 as the sacrificial lamb to the clericals.

Over this same period of Thouvenel's ministry, he had had to deal with the U.S. Civil War. His most famous act was his protest in December 1861 against the North's seizure of Mason and Slidell from the British ship *Trent*. It was this note, rather than the British protest, that solved the crisis peacefully by the release of the two men. Thouvenel remained slightly pro-North during his ministry and in August 1862 was suggesting to the French minister at Washington, Baron Henri Mercier de L'Ostende (b. 1816), a plan of a union of two separate confederations with a joint senate and diplomatic services, similar to that of the United Provinces of Moldavia and Wallachia. As to the Mexican expedition, Thouvenel was not enthusiastic about it. He learned that the emperor was mistaken about a strong Mexican monarchist sentiment and advised against the selection of Maximilian as the future ruler. This may also have contributed to his own dismissal in October 1862.

After leaving office, Thouvenel still retained his Senate seat and was active in the debates of that body, becoming, in 1865, the Senate's *grand référendaire* (chief administrator). He also served as president of the administrative council of the Chemin de Fer de l'Est. One of his last duties, in 1864, was to serve as the president of the arbitration commission that acted for Napoleon III in settling a dispute between the Suez Canal Company and the viceroy of Egypt. Exhausted by his earlier diplomatic duties and alarmed by the growing power of Prussia in Germany and by the Prussian victory over Austria at Sadowa (July 1866), Thouvenel rapidly declined in health. He died at the age of forty-eight on 18 October 1866 from a combination of asthma and a weakened heart.

L. M. Case, *Edouard Thouvenel et la diplomatie du Second Empire* (Paris, 1976); L. M. Case, ''Thouvenel et la rupture des relations diplomatiques franco-sardes en 1860,''

RHMC 7 (1960), "A Duel of Giants in Old Stambul: Stratford versus Thouvenel," *JMH* 35 (1963), and "Deux journées dans la vie d'un ministre français des affaires étrangères," *RHD*, nos. 2–4 (April–December 1981); L. M. Case and W. F. Spencer, *The United States and France: Civil War Diplomacy* (Philadelphia, 1970); L. Thouvenel, *Episodes d'histoire contemporaine, 1844–1845, 1851–1852* (Paris, 1892), *Nicolas 1er et Napoléon III, les préliminaires de la Guerre de Crimée, 1852–1854* (Paris, 1891), *Trois années de la question d'Orient, 1856–1859* (Paris, 1897), *Pages de l'histoire du Second Empire (1854–1866)* (Paris, 1903), and *Le secret de l'empereur, correspondance confidentielle et inédite échangée entre M. Thouvenel, le duc de Gramont et le général comte de Flahaut, 1860–1863*, 2 vols. (Paris, 1889).

Lynn M. Case

Related entries: DROUYN DE DHUYS; ITALIAN CONFEDERATION; MEDIATION PROPOSAL (U.S. CIVIL WAR); MEXICAN EXPEDITION; MINISTRY; NICE AND SAVOY; RECOGNITION QUESTION (U.S. CIVIL WAR); ROMAN QUESTION; SUEZ CANAL; SYRIAN EXPEDITION; WALEWSKI.

TIERS PARTI, from 1864 the dynastic opposition under the Second Empire, accepting the dynasty but not the authoritarian regime. The elections of 1863 crushed the Orleanist-dominated Union Libérale (which had attempted to bring together moderate opponents of the regime) but returned some forty deputies who were to become the nucleus of the Tiers Parti. These included liberal official candidates like Jules Brame (1808–1878), J.P.E.N. Chevandier de Valdrôme (1810–1878), Charles Louvet (1806–1882), and Alexis Emile Segris (1811–1880); Catholics and protectionists like Charles Louis Henri Kolb-Bernard (1798–1888) and Ignace Plichon (1814–1888); and independents who had served in the previous Corps Législatif like Emile Ollivier and Louis Buffet. Most, but not all, were bonapartists.

The term Tiers Parti was used from 1864 and had become current by 1865, when Ollivier gave a dinner at which he began to draw together a liberal Empire party. The Tiers Parti deputies maintained liaison on the right with Adolphe Thiers and his followers, who would grudgingly accept the dynasty only if the regime became truly a parliamentary one, and on the left with the more moderate republicans. Thiers could have led the Tiers Parti but declined (in fact he only sporadically attended sessions of the Corps Législatif), although he exercised an influence through Buffet, whom he advised, and through such speeches as that of January 1864 in which he demanded the five necessary freedoms (freedom of the press, free elections, the right of interpellation, ministerial responsibility, and individual liberty). Buffet was probably the most influential man in the Tiers Parti but was too committed to a parliamentary regime to be acceptable to the emperor, while Ollivier was disliked by both Buffet and Thiers and widely distrusted.

The Tiers Parti first won wide attention in the early spring of 1866. In mid-March an amendment to the address was drafted by Ollivier, Buffet, Chevandier de Valdrôme, and J.D.A. de P., comte de Chambrun (1821–1899), protesting loyalty to the dynasty as France's guarantee of order and urging Napoleon III to continue the reforms begun in 1860 (there had been no further movement since the coalitions law of May 1864 and no political reforms since June 1863). Only men loyal to the dynasty were asked to sign, and forty-two did so. Thiers did not, but he helped to secure signatures. Moved by Ollivier on 17 March, the amendment was defeated two days later by a vote of 206 to 63 (of which thirteen were republicans). During the debate, however, Eugène Rouher had stated the government's intention to introduce more reforms when the time was right, and the emperor himself had seemed to countenance the liberal agitation. The Tiers Parti was truly launched. In 1869 would come both its triumph and the revelation of its divisions.

A. Darimon, *Histoire de douze ans, 1857–1869* (Paris, 1883), *Histoire d'un parti: Le Tiers Parti sous l'Empire, 1863–1866* (Paris, 1887), and *Les 116 et le ministère du 2 janvier* (Paris, 1889).

Related entries: ADDRESS; AUTHORITARIAN EMPIRE; BONAPARTISM; BUFFET; CORPS LEGISLATIF; CROWNING THE EDIFICE; DARIMON; DARU; ELECTIONS; LIBERAL EMPIRE; LIBERALISM; OLLIVIER; ORLEANISM; PLEBISCITE; REFORM; THIERS.

TOLAIN, HENRI (1828–1897), engraver on bronze, founding member of the First International, and leader of the Proudhonian group of French workers in the 1860s; born 18 June 1828 to a dance master in Paris. Tolain was educated at a mutual school until, at age eleven, he was apprenticed to a bronze engraver. He remained employed in this trade until 1860, when he began doing his own custom work. In 1867 and 1868 he kept accounts for a master tinsmith. Tolain emerged in this decade as a highly articulate and principled spokesman for an independent workers' movement. In a letter published in the 17 October 1861 issue of *L'opinion nationale*, he proposed election of worker delegates to the 1862 international exposition at London. His suggestion was taken up by the imperial government, and Tolain was made secretary of the delegation. While in London he contacted British trade unionists and was impressed by the achievement of their independent unions. After returning to Paris, he became involved in the workers' candidacies for election to the Corps Législatif. In the general election of 1863, he stood briefly as a candidate himself but withdrew before the polling date to support two other workers running for office. After the election, he wrote *Quelques vérités sur les élections de Paris,* which emphasized the need for an autonomous workers' organization and outlined a program for the workers' movement. In a Paris by-election of March 1864, he stood alone as a worker candidate against a bonapartist and a republican, receiving only 424 votes, and in February he had a major role—the most influential, according to Edouard Dolléans—in the drafting of the Manifesto of the Sixty, which justified workers' candidacies. Most historians interpret his participation in these candidacies as a sign of his separation from the Palais Royal workers, although some contemporaries claimed the reverse.

Tolain's developing autonomist ideology emerged most clearly on the international scene. During a visit to London in the summer of 1863 to join workers of that city in support of the Polish revolution, he proposed the organization of an international association of workers. The idea took shape on 28 September 1864 at Saint Martin's Hall, where English and French workers together established the First International along lines of a project formulated by Tolain. As leading secretary of the Paris Bureau, assisted by Ernest Fribourg and Charles Limousin (1840–1909) in a group collectively called the "Gravilliers" (from the street location of their office), Tolain articulated an essentially laborist conception of a workers' organization influenced by Proudhonian mutualism. In 1865 he led the Gravilliers in protesting the London General Council's selection of Henri Lefort, republican journalist and supporter of workers' candidacies, as the International's official representative to the French press. Tolain and his group opposed this appointment ostensibly on the grounds that it violated the autonomy of each national delegation, but some historians have seen this opposition as motivated equally by laborist concerns. In the same year, the Gravilliers favored limiting membership in the International to manual workers, thus excluding "workers of the mind." Tolain proposed an amendment at the 1866 Geneva congress allowing only manual workers to participate as voting delegates in the association. Both efforts failed. Tolain and his group did succeed, however, in resisting collectivist tendencies in the International in its initial years. In fact, the Proudhonian mutualist ideology, of which he was the leading spokesman, prevailed in the first two congresses of the International, preventing the association from making a resolution in favor of collectivized property until 1869.

In 1867–1868, however, after Tolain and other members of the Paris Bureau of the International were charged with and convicted of participating in a nonauthorized association of more than twenty persons, their place was taken by a second Bureau more sympathetic to collectivism. Eugène Varlin (1839–1871), leading voice of this group, called its position "nonauthoritarian communism," to emphasize continued resistance to centralized state control. Varlin's growing influence was reflected in the International's adoption of a resolution favoring communal appropriation of landed property at the Basel congress in 1869, over the opposing votes of Tolain and only three other delegates. Tolain's "reformist" views were clearly out of touch with the militant working-class majority by this date, both abroad and at home. Indeed, the more revolutionary Varlin dominated working-class politics and social actions by the end of the Empire. Tolain's association with the International, moreover, was becoming tenuous. Although he took an active part in the events surrounding the fall of the Empire and the establishment of the Republic (he was arrested in August 1870 for his activity in the International, served as assistant mayor of the eleventh arrondissement of Paris after 4 September and was elected to the National Assembly in February 1871), he rallied to the Versailles government after the election of a Paris Commune in March and subsequently was expelled from the International. Tolain ended his career as a member of the Senate of the Third Republic, to which he had been elected in 1876. There he supported Léon Gambetta and was *rapporteur* for the 1884 law on trade unions.

Tolain was an active supporter of cooperative societies, an advocate of freedom of meeting and association, and a partisan of federalist organization of government and of workers' societies. A Proudhonian "before having read Proudhon" (which he did seriously only in 1865–1866—according to Georges Duveau—to prepare for the Geneva congress of the International), Tolain opposed the imposition of all authority from above or from outside the working class. A notable theme of his writings and speeches was the danger of concentration and organization of capital "in powerful financial and industrial associations," reigning "despotically" as a new aristocracy, as a result of commercial freedom. This danger could be avoided only by the organization of *chambres syndicales* composed exclusively of workers. Although Tolain also favored freedom to strike, he did not look favorably on strikes until 1867. In that year he joined the other secretaries of the Paris Bureau in supporting the demands of striking miners of Fuveau and of striking spinners and weavers of Roubaix, taking issue, however, with destruction of machines by the latter. He and the other Gravilliers were especially supportive of the striking bronze workers of Paris, for whom Tolain traveled to London in 1867 to procure solidarity funds. By 1868 Tolain came to regard strikes "to defend one's rights" as a "holy war."

Tolain defended the nuclear family, with the wife freed of paid work and remaining at home to take care of children and household. His views on education reflected this attachment to a familial ideal. An intelligent, largely self-taught worker, he was an enthusiastic proponent of education for workers, especially vocational instruction. Although he seems to have supported free, compulsory instruction on the primary level at the time of signing the Manifesto of the Sixty, he expressed strong reservations about state-financed education at the Geneva congress of the International in 1866. Fearing uniformity of thought in a state-controlled system of education, he and the other Proudhonian delegates preferred leaving the instruction of children to the mother and father of the family. At the Lausanne congress the following year, he was willing to admit a limited degree of state intervention but only to assist the father unable to provide for his children's educational needs on his own. Tolain's educational views apparently also separated him from Varlin and other "nonauthoritarian communists," who continued to support free, compulsory education for all, financed by the state. As a Freemason and enemy of all a priori thinking, Tolain opposed religious teaching in the schools. In the 1880s he would support the Ferry laws.

Tolain was also a peace activist, again largely in the context of the International. He and his fellows of the Paris Bureau stated their resistance to permanent standing armies as a threat to peace in 1866 and advised workers to remain neutral in conflicts between governments in order to focus their energies on their "social and political emancipation." In 1867 the Gravilliers responded to threats of war over Luxembourg and to an appeal of German workers by proclaiming the international solidarity of workers. In the same year, Tolain signed a manifesto of the International Disarmament League calling for general disarmament and for the organization of national militias instead of permanent armies. Tolain did show some reluctance to support affiliation of the International with the League of Peace and Liberty, however, presumably to protect the independence of the workers' organization from the influence of this largely middle-class group.

Tolain's views on culture have been given some attention, especially by Duveau. These had a rather traditional, moralist, and austere tone. He despised ''bourgeois and banal'' eloquence and resisted proposals to simplify spelling, defending the integrity of the traditional French language. An enemy of pornography and sensationalist journalism and literature, he preferred novels that were didactic and morally elevating to those that were sentimental. Tolain expressed these views and views on other issues in numerous articles in *Le courrier français*, *La tribune ouvrière*, *La presse ouvrière* and *La fourmi*, as well as in his speeches to the International. To contemporaries and historians alike, he was clearly one of the most articulate working-class leaders of the 1860s. Tolain died at Paris, May 1897.

George J. Sheridan, Jr.

Related entries: CANDIDATURE OUVRIERE; COALITIONS LAW; FIRST INTERNATIONAL; LABOR REFORM; LA RICAMARIE; PALAIS ROYAL GROUP; PROUDHON; VARLIN.

TRADE. See COBDEN-CHEVALIER TREATY.

TREATIES OF 1815. See REVISION.

TRIPLE ALLIANCE, a proposed military alliance of France, Austria, and Italy against Prussia that was the objective of unsuccessful negotiations between 1867 and 1870. At the beginning of his reign, Napoleon III had regarded Austria as an irreconcilable enemy of Napoleonic policies. That analysis was certainly accurate while French policies included revision of the Treaties of 1815, advancement of the cause of nationalities, and creation of a concert of Europe devoted to change rather than to conservation. By 1867, however, much had changed. Austria had been evicted from Italy by France and from Germany by Prussia. Prussia, by the magnitude of its victory at Sadowa in July 1866, had emerged as a threat to the European balance of power. Napoleon III was in physical decline, while foreign policy reverses (in Mexico, for example) had seriously diminished his prestige. The authoritarian Empire was in the process of being transformed into a parliamentary regime. And experience had shown, at Rome and in the Luxembourg crisis, that no arrangement between France and Prussia was possible. Moreover, Napoleon III understood that if Bismarck should attempt to incorporate the south German states into the North German Confederation established after Sadowa, French opinion would demand war. Under these circumstances, serious negotiations between Paris and Vienna became possible.

In April 1867, during the Luxembourg crisis and again in August 1867 at

Salzburg, where he met with Austrian emperor Francis Joseph, Napoleon III unveiled the prospect of a Franco-Austrian alliance. In July 1868 he presented Vienna with an alternative to what he called an active alliance. If Austria did not want an understanding designed to lead to war with Prussia, perhaps it would prefer a passive alliance, one designed to bring about a European congress that would place the Treaty of Prague, which had ended the Austro-Prussian War of 1866, under the sanction of Europe. This alternative was preferred at Vienna, where Count Ferdinand von Beust (1809–1886) was foreign minister. Beust obtained French consent to postponing the congress proposal until autumn, and he suggested that the purpose of the meeting should be to discuss not the German question but disarmament. This latter proposal was not particularly welcome at Paris, but the French government was more amenable to Beust's insistence that if war were to come between Prussia on the one hand and France and Austria on the other, it should come over the Eastern question and not over Germany. Moreover, Vienna clearly desired that Italy be included in any understanding so that in the event of war, Austria would not face invasion from the south.

Toward the end of December 1868, on a hint from Beust, preparation of a draft treaty began. On 31 December 1868, in an interview with King Victor Emmanuel I of Italy's aide-de-camp, General Etienne Türr (b. 1824), Napoleon III proposed a triple alliance of France, Austria, and Italy, with a European congress as its immediate objective. In fact, Türr had already visited Vienna where an alliance had been discussed. On 1 March 1869, following the successful conclusion of a European conference on Crete (9–20 January 1869), which had restored the status quo on the island where a revolt against Turkish rule had been in progress for years and invoked the principle of mediation of dangerous quarrels, the French government produced a first draft treaty of alliance. If Austria were to be at war with Russia, France would place an observation corps on the Rhine and would enter the war on Austria's side if Russia were joined by Prussia. If France were to be at war with Prussia, Austria would place an observation corps in Bohemia and would enter the war on France's side if Russia joined Prussia. Italy in either latter case would join its allies in the war and would be rewarded with the South Tyrol and a solution to the Roman Question. This was too strong a commitment for Austria, which declined in April 1869. On 10 May 1869 Eugène Rouher, French minister of state, prepared a second draft treaty, which merely committed the parties to agree in advance that in the event of a European war, they would conclude an offensive and defensive alliance whose exact conditions would be determined at that time. Finally, after some five or six drafts had been exchanged and examined, agreement was reached. The three states would mutually guarantee each other's territory, they would envision concluding an alliance in the event of a general war, and they would not engage in negotiations with other states without first informing each other in advance. But now Italy posed two conditions for its acquiescence: France must withdraw from Rome, and the results of the 1866 war, including the North German Confederation, must be guaranteed. These conditions, in particular the first, were unacceptable at Paris. And so, in the end, all that remained of the negotiations was an exchange of letters. In a letter to Francis Joseph on 24 September 1869, Napoleon III promised not to start negotiations with any other power before agreeing with Austria and to help Austria if it were attacked. Victor Emmanuel, in his letter of about 25 September to Napoleon III, stated his acceptance of the principle of an alliance but repeated that Italy could not enter into any engagement until the problem of Rome had been resolved. Francis Joseph's letter has been lost, but it seems almost certainly to have eluded commitment.

It seems possible that Napoleon III had reason to hope for some Austrian assistance in the event of war with Prussia. His interview with Archduke Albrecht at Paris in March 1870 and the interview of General Barthélemy Louis Joseph Lebrun (1809–1889) with Francis Joseph at Vienna on 14 June gave some encouragement to this hope. But there were three qualifications: France must not be seen as the aggressor, must win initial victories, and must be willing to fight the war in southern Germany. Even then, it is not at all certain that the Hungarians (since 1867 Austria had been officially "Austria-Hungary") would have agreed to war. These qualifications seem to have escaped the attention of Antoine, duc de Gramont, the French ambassador at Vienna, who on 15 May 1870 was appointed foreign minister and informed, some time after, of the Triple Alliance negotiations, which since 1867 had been conducted in strictest secrecy. Perhaps the greatest illusion was, however, that an effective alliance between Austria and France had ever been possible. France wanted an alliance against Prussia; Austria wanted one against Russia. The claims were incompatible. In the end the illusion of a Triple Alliance, wittingly or unwittingly encouraged by Gramont, became part of the chain of events that for France led in July 1870 to the disaster of the Franco-Prussian War.

W. E. Echard, "Conference Diplomacy in the German Policy of Napoleon III, 1868–1869," *FHS* 4 (Spring 1966); D. W. Houston, "The Negotiations for a Triple Alliance between France, Austria, and Italy, 1869–1870" (Ph.D. diss., University of Pennsylvania, 1959); R. Mori, "La prima fase delle trattative per la triplice alleanza (1868–1869)," *SP* (April–June and July–September 1966); V. L. Tapié, *Autour d'une tentative d'alliance entre la France et l'Autriche, 1867–1870* (Vienna, 1971).

Related entries: ALLIANCE POLICY; ARMY REFORM; BELGIAN RAILROADS AFFAIR; CONGRESS POLICY; CRETAN REVOLT; DARU; FRANCO-PRUSSIAN WAR; GRAMONT; LA TOUR D'AUVERGNE; LA VALETTE; LUXEMBOURG CRISIS; POLISH QUESTION; REVISION.

TROPLONG, RAYMOND (1795–1869), jurisconsult, president of the Cour de Cassation, president of the Senate, and the most significant bonapartist ideologue during the Second Empire. La Gorce portrayed him as a man of the pen who legitimized a work of force (the coup d'état of December 1851) and who made the constitution of 1852 viable by his explanations of it. Troplong possessed the gifts of profound vagueness and intelligent generalization that allowed him to interpret an imprecise constitution, drawing on his thorough understanding of jurisprudence, without revealing the document's obscurities and contradictions. Troplong was born at Saint-Gaudens (Haute-Garonne), 8 October 1795. His father was a professor of the humanities. The younger Troplong pursued a career in law, completing his education in the early years of the Restoration. He never forsook his father's professorial interests, however, and throughout his life his attention was divided between his functions as a magistrate and historical study and commentary on the law.

Beginning his career in the public prosecutor's office at Sartène, Troplong moved to similar posts at Corte, Alençon, and Bastia and subsequently spent brief periods as solicitor-general at Bastia and Nancy. In 1832 he was named president of the court at Nancy. Then in 1843 he was appointed first president of the appeals court at Paris. Throughout this period, he read and studied the commentators on both Roman and French law. He wrote extensively on civil law, and his treatises, gathered in twenty-seven volumes under the title, *Droit civil française suivant l'ordre des articles du Code, depuis et y compris le titre de la vente*, had considerable success and are noted for their stylistic eloquence and clarity, their historical method and perspective, and their philosophical expansiveness. His work, both as magistrate and as historian, was widely respected, bringing him election to the Académie des Sciences Morales (1840) and appointment to the Chamber of Peers of the July Monarchy (1846).

Louis Napoleon Bonaparte, as president of the Second Republic, appointed Troplong to the court of Paris and after the coup named him to the Commission Consultatif and the commission to prepare a constitution. In January 1852 he was appointed an original senator. When Jérôme Bonaparte resigned as president of the Senate in November 1852, Troplong succeeded him. He would hold that post until his death, combining it with the presidency of the Cour de Cassation and thus laying claim to combined stipends of 195,000 francs per year. In 1858, although he had been among those who opposed the marriage of Napoleon III to Eugénie de Montijo, Troplong was named by the emperor to the Conseil Privé and awarded the grand cross of the Legion of Honor. Frequently identified as a partisan of a strong executive, Troplong produced a small work in 1853 entitled *Du principe d'autorité depuis 1789*. The argument of this piece was fairly simple. For sixty years France had struggled with revolution and disorder, and only with the reestablishment of the Empire had it found internal peace. Maintenance of order and peace was possible only through the principle of authority: "power is the commencement of liberty; without power, one can count on anarchy." The mere attainment of power was insufficient, however, for power must be based on popular confidence. And the Empire had the confidence of the people for they found in it a monarchy, the most natural form of government for the French in that it ensured a respect for order, hierarchy, and stability but a monarchy that did not threaten a return to the Old Regime. Rather, the Empire incorporated the Republic. The Empire, and the Empire alone, could reconcile the old and new France. Through the principle of authority, the Empire would be the regulator of the Revolution and the organizer of democracy. Not surprisingly, Troplong in church matters was a Gallican, suspicious of Rome and of the ultramontane party. Twice in 1852, Troplong drew on these general ideas as reporter (*rapporteur*) to the Senate for commissions working on constitutional revisions: first in explaining the *sénatus-consulte* reestablishing the Empire with the approval of the people expressed in a plebiscite and then defending the imperial proposal to limit the powers of the Corps Législatif in matters of commerce, tariffs, and public works. And throughout his tenure, he frequently articulated his point of view in explaining to the Senate how a proposal from the throne or a law voted in the Corps Législatif should be considered. He was one of the grand old men of the Second Empire, and his was a consistently clear voice of conservative bonapartism. As a result of this devotion, Troplong was twice defeated for election to the Orleanist-dominated Académie Française—by Victor, duc de Broglie (1785–1870), in 1855 and by Alfred Cuvillier-Fleury (1802–1887) in 1866. Troplong's death at Paris on 1 March 1869 was a significant loss to a regime then in full decline.

William E. Duvall

Related entries: AUTHORITARIAN EMPIRE; BONAPARTISM; CONSTITUTION; SECOND EMPIRE; SENATE.

TUILERIES-LOUVRE, center of government and of the imperial court during the Second Empire. These two royal palaces were given their modern aspect between 1852 and 1865. Less than a month after seizing power in 1851, Louis Napoleon established his official Paris residence in the Tuileries, the great palace built by Catherine de Medicis. Already, as president, he had sponsored the restoration (authorized in 1848) by Jacques Duban (1797–1870) of the Salon Carré and of the Salle des Sept Cheminées in the adjacent and even more ancient palace of the Louvre and had pushed forward the long-delayed clearance of the slum that had grown up between the two royal residences. Following his successful coup d'état, the prince president opened a credit for completing this work of *dégagement* (13 December). In March 1852 he secured a further credit of 25 million francs and decreed that the "Nouveau Louvre" should be completed within five years. It was a project second on his list of priorities only to the new central market (the Halles) and completion of the rue de Rivoli.

For centuries, from its conception in 1565, the idea had persisted of linking the Tuileries and the Louvre. Henri IV completed the task on the south, next to the river (Galerie du Bord de l'Eau or Grand Gallery). Charles Percier and P.F.L. Fontaine, the architects of Napoleon I, built the Pavillon de Marsan on the north to match the Pavillon de Flore and began construction of the northern link along the rue de Rivoli (Galerie du Nord), but in 1815 a gap of 800 feet remained. Napoleon III completed the task, first through the architect Louis Visconti (1791–1853) and then, on Visconti's death, through Hector Lefuel (1810–1881). Visconti had solved the problem posed by the fact that the linking galleries on the north and the south would not be parallel by designing six internal pavilions paired north and south (Turgot, Richelieu, Colbert, Mollien, Daru, and Denon, the latter still retaining today on its front the only sculptural representation [by Simart] of Napoleon III still existing in Paris). Excavations began in May 1852; the first cornerstone was posed by the emperor 25 July 1852. By 1853 some three thousand workmen were employed, Napoleon III often visiting the site to make suggestions. An elaborate inauguration took place 14 August 1857. From 1863 to 1865, Lefuel tore down and rebuilt the Pavillon de Flore, employing Jean Baptiste Carpeaux as sculptor, as well as the western part of the Galerie du Bord de l'Eau. He also redesigned the facade of the Pavillon de Marsan in a style that has been criticized for its extravagance but that certainly reflected Second Empire tastes. Two gates (one by Duban, the other—Porte de l'Empereur—by Lefuel) and the huge Guichets du Carrousel (also by Lefuel) pierced the reconstructed Galerie du Bord de l'Eau, the Guichets crowned with a high relief by Antoine Louis Barye of Napoleon III on horseback (removed in 1870). Lefuel also added to the north side of the Galerie (on the west) another internal pavilion (the Pavillon des Etats). In 1861 electric lamps were installed, to illuminate the Cour de Carrousel, renamed the Place Napoléon III.

The "Nouveau Louvre," incorporating the Tuileries, was the center of the court of the Second Empire and of much of its political, social, and cultural activity. Although the palace (Tuileries) was generally dark and gloomy, not even furnished with running water during most of the Empire, the private apartments on the garden side of the south wing were lavishly rebuilt and decorated by Lefuel between 1858 and 1860, especially those of the empress on the second floor. From his office below, Napoleon III governed France (the Tricolor flying from the Pavillon de l'Horloge announced when he was in residence). Also in the Tuileries was the Throne Room. Receptions were held in the state apartments on the Cour du Carrousel side of the south wing, entered through the Pavillon de l'Horloge. In the Salle des Maréchaux, which occupied the second floor of the Pavillon d l'Horloge, above the entrance vestibule, the Corps Législatif and the Senate first met in combined session on 29 March 1852 (thereafter, at the beginning of each year, they assembled in the Grande Salle du Louvre). Also in the Salle des Maréchaux took place the civil marriage of Napoleon III and Eugénie, and here were held the four great annual balls of the social season between January and Lent, culminating in that of 1867 for the emperors of Austria and Russia and the kings of Prussia, Sweden, and Italy, during the international exposition of that year at Paris. For the exposition an external stairway was built, allowing guests direct access from the Salle des Maréchaux to the Tuileries Gardens. Military reviews were held in the place Napoléon III. The ministries of State, Algeria (briefly), and the Imperial Household (Maison de l'Empereur) were housed in the new pavilions, as was the Administration of the Telegraph. The additions also accommodated a printing office and stables and made possible an expansion of the art museum, for which the Second Empire acquired in 1861 the bulk of the collection of objets d'art of the Renaissance and of antiquity belonging to the marquis de Campana (during the Empire, the Louvre's collections were quadrupled). The magnificent Tuileries Gardens were traditionally open to the public. During the Second Empire the income from their concessions was donated to the retirement funds of the Sèvres and Gobelins factories.

Center of the Second Empire during its glory, the Tuileries also witnessed the tragedy of its closing hours. From the palace, the empress made her escape to England on Sunday, 4 September 1870. Nor did the Tuileries itself long survive the Empire. Gutted by fire in the last days of the Commune of 1871, it was never rebuilt, although Lefuel reconstructed the two corner pavilions from 1871 to 1876.

C. Aulanier, *Histoire du Palais et du Musée du Louvre: Le Pavillon de Flore* (Paris, 1971), and *Le nouveau Louvre de Napoléon III* (vol. 4 of *Histoire du Palais et du Musée du Louvre* (Paris, 1953); H. Clouzot, *Des Tuileries à Saint-Cloud: L'art décoratif du Second Empire* (Paris, 1925); J. Hillairet, *Le palais royal et impérial des Tuileries et son jardin* (Paris, 1965).

Related entry: PARIS, REBUILDING OF.

U

ULTRAMONTANISM. See GALLICANISM.

UNIONS. See COALITIONS LAW.

L'UNIVERS, conservative Catholic daily newspaper. In 1833 Abbé Jacques Paul Migne (1800–1875) founded a small Catholic sheet in Paris. Very shortly, under lay leadership, it became the key Catholic journal in France and remained so until 1914. Throughout its existence, its actual subscription list was small, but its editorials became the inspiration for reactionary expressions of all kinds, including sermons. Louis Veuillot was not associated with the paper until the late 1830s and then only as an occasional contributor. In 1843, however, he became the principal figure in its operation, though a priest, Melchior Du Lac, was a greater force than generally has been recognized. Charles de Coux (1787–1864) was designated editor along with Veuillot during the years before 1848 in order to promote Catholic unity and to serve as a check on Veuillot, who as early as 1844 was imprisoned for a month because of journalistic excesses. The proprietor, Taconet, for decades ensured its existence. After 1848 Veuillot was completely unchecked and for quite a few years accommodated his journal to what appeared to be a president and emperor favorable to Catholic reaction and ultramontanism (papal sovereignty). Veuillot complicated matters among Catholics by his quarrels with various bishops, notably Mgr. Marie Sibour (1792–1857), archbishop of Paris, with whom he disputed the role of the classics in education.

Having supported the emperor during the Crimean War, Veuillot attacked Napoleon III's increasing support of the cause of Italian unification at the expense of Pope Pius IX. For publishing on 28 January 1860 the pope's encyclical condemning the enemies of temporal power, *L'Univers* was suspended. It did not appear again until 1867, although to some degree another journal of Taconet, *Le monde*, took its place. The revival of Veuillot's paper on 19 February 1867 was the result of a personal decision by the emperor. *L'Univers* continued its ultramontane and reactionary role until 1870. The high-water mark was its coverage of the Vatican Council in 1870 and its triumphant announcement of the doctrine of papal infallibility, though the Franco-Prussian War promptly dimmed this triumph. Despite the controversial nature of the polemics in which the journal was constantly engaged, its literary nature was long of high quality. If it ever took a cue from any other journal, it was from *Civiltà cattolica*. *L'Univers* had a circulation of 3,500 in 1855, 5,000 in June 1858, 4,150 in December 1867, and 4,290 in March 1869.

J. Gadille, "Autour de Louis Veuillot et de *L'Univers*," *Cahiers d'histoire* (1969); B. W. Ghezzi, "*L'Univers* and the Definition of Papal Infallibility" (Ph.D. diss., University of Notre Dame, 1969).

Marvin L. Brown, Jr.

Related entries: DUPANLOUP; GALLICANISM; GAUME; INFALLIBILITY, DOCTRINE OF; LOURDES; MONTALEMBERT; MORTARA AFFAIR; PIE; PIUS IX; PRESS REGIME; ROMAN QUESTION; *SYLLABUS OF ERRORS*; VATICAN COUNCIL; VEUILLOT.

UNIVERSAL MANHOOD SUFFRAGE, the political basis of the Second Empire. The great problem for France since the Revolution had been to reconcile popular sovereignty with effective and orderly government. Louis Napoleon believed that he had found the solution, at least for a transitional period, in the fusion of bonapartist leadership with universal manhood suffrage. The people, when properly apprised of their interest, would endorse a strong ruler whose responsibility would then be to effect the Napoleonic ideas. This popular endorsement would come regularly in legislative elections, irregularly in plebiscites on precise issues. During the intervals, an authoritarian government would act, more or less freely, in the name of the people—thus "democratic Caesarism."

As one of the nineteenth century's most skillful politicians, Louis Napoleon well understood the pragmatic potential of these ideas. He was perhaps the first European leader to recognize that in an agricultural society, the application of universal manhood suffrage would have a conservative rather than a radical effect. He knew as well the emotional impact of the suffrage issue. As president of the Second Republic, he had reluctantly accepted a new electoral law (31 May 1850), prepared by the conservatives, which by excluding some 3 million voters, ended universal manhood suffrage as established in 1848. On the eve of the coup d'état, however, Louis Napoleon called, unsuccessfully, for the abrogation of this law. The defeat of his proposal by the Legislative Assembly on 4 November 1851 became yet another weapon in the prince president's arsenal. The proclamation of 2 December 1851, which announced the coup d'état, also declared the restoration of universal manhood suffrage, a restoration formalized by article 36 of the constitution of January 1852.

The operation of universal manhood suffrage during the Second Empire was regulated by a decree-law of 2 February 1852. With the exception of those convicted of certain specified offenses, every Frenchman twenty-one years of age or older who had lived at least six months in his commune could vote (some 10 million). It is true that the right to vote could be withheld not only from

those with criminal convictions, but also from those convicted of political misdemeanors (ranging from rebellion to membership in a club), attacks against
property, or *outrages à la religion.* There is no evidence, however, that any
systematic attempt was made to alter the principle of universal manhood suffrage
by applying these exclusions. On the other hand, great efforts were made to
keep abreast of and to influence public opinion, to control the press, and to
manage elections. Nevertheless, it seems probable that Napoleon III was sincere
in his support of universal manhood suffrage. Often throughout his reign he
acted even against his own judgment to comply with what he assumed to be the
popular will. Moreover, the unprecedented political evolution of the Second
Empire from an authoritarian to a liberal regime attests to the emperor's willingness to give to French public opinion what it desired, despite his insistence
that the ruler, once endorsed, had an obligation to carry forward only right
ideas—that is, to execute the Rousseauist general will.

No demand was made during the Second Empire for extension of the vote to
women.

P. Braud, *Le suffrage universel contre la démocratie* (Paris, 1980); M. Flory, "L'appel
au peuple napoléonien," *Revue internationale d'histoire politique et constitutionnelle*
(July–September 1952).

Related entries: AUTHORITARIAN EMPIRE; BONAPARTISM; COALI-
TIONS LAW; CONSTITUTION; CORPS LEGISLATIF; COUP D'ETAT; DE-
CENTRALIZATION; ELECTIONS; *DES IDEES NAPOLEONIENNES*;
LIBERAL EMPIRE; LIBERALISM; ORLEANISM; PLEBISCITE; PRE-
FECTS; PRESS REGIME; PUBLIC OPINION; REFORM; REPUBLICANISM.

U.S. CIVIL WAR. See RECOGNITION QUESTION.

V

VAILLANT, JEAN BAPTISTE, COMTE (1790–1872), marshal of France, minister of war (1854–1859), and minister of the imperial household (1860–1870); born at Dijon, 6 October 1790. A graduate of the Ecole Polytechnique and of the Ecole d'Application du Génie, Vaillant campaigned under Napoleon I from 1812 to 1815 and was named to the Legion of Honor in 1813 for his great courage on the battlefield. He later served as an engineer during the Algiers expedition (1830) and the siege of Antwerp (1833). Colonel from 1833, he directed construction of fortifications in Algeria (1834–1838). Subsequently, as general of brigade, he commanded the Ecole Polytechnique from 1838 to 1840. He helped to fortify Paris during the 1840s (directing the work from 1845) and was promoted to lieutenant general. In 1849, as second in command of the French expeditionary force to Rome, he directed the successful siege of the city, winning promotion to grand cross of the Legion of Honor, 12 July 1849.

Vaillant was not interested in politics. He was prepared to serve the existing regime and therefore rallied readily to Louis Napoleon following the coup d'état of December 1851. He was named senator on 26 January 1852 in the initial appointments list, marshal of France on 11 December 1852 (following proclamation of the Empire), and grand marshal of the palace on 1 January 1853. Shortly after, he was awarded the title of comte. On 11 March 1854, Vaillant succeeded Marshal Leroy de Saint-Arnaud as minister of war on the latter's appointment to command French forces in the war against Russia. He held the post for five years, reorganizing the military schools and, in fact, much of the army's structure, and creating several specialized corps. In July 1856 he served briefly as interim minister of public instruction. In 1853 he had been elected to the Académie des Sciences as a *membre libre*. It was to Vaillant (later a member of the Conseil Privé) that Napoleon III intended to confide the presidency of the Council of Ministers if he had persevered in his intention of going in person to the Crimea early in 1855.

At the beginning of the war against Austria (1859), Vaillant organized for the first time the transport of French troops by rail and then surrendered his ministry to Marshal Jacques Louis Randon, partly as a consequence of his failure to prepare the army for the war, partly in order to serve under the emperor's command as major general of the Army of the Alps (4 May 1859). Having participated in the Solférino campaign, it was he who on 8 July signed the cease-fire accord with General Hesse. Two days later, Vaillant received command of the five corps of the French occupation army. He did not return to France until 5 June 1860. On 24 November he reentered the cabinet as minister of the imperial household (*maison de l'empereur*), a post to which was added in June 1863 responsibility for fine arts.

As minister of fine arts, Vaillant presided over a tumultuous period in the history of the French art establishment. Wishing to liberalize instruction at the Ecole des Beaux-Arts while at the same time giving it a greater sense of unity and direction, the government had appointed an investigatory commission in March 1862. On 13 November 1863, an imperial decree introduced important changes. New courses were proposed, adding variety to the classical regimen; the Prix de Rome was altered to exclude competitors over twenty-five, to shorten their stay abroad from five years to two, and to allow them to choose countries other than Italy as their place of study; control of the Ecole des Beaux-Arts was removed from the Académie des Beaux-Arts and confided directly to the minister of fine arts; and one man, a professor of aesthetics and art history, was designated to supervise instruction within a standardized curriculum. Finally, foreigners became admissible to the Ecole although ineligible for the Prix de Rome. This attempt at liberalization through centralization failed, partly because the first professor of aesthetics was the architect Eugène Viollet-le-Duc, and it was per-ceived that he and comte Emilien Nieuwerkerke (1811–1892), the superintendent of fine arts, had inspired the decree. Both were enemies of the art establishment. Viollet-le-Duc was prevented by student interruptions (29 January 1864) from delivering his inaugural lecture and never took up his post. That same month Vaillant signed the decree ending the requirement for government authorization to establish a theater (6 January 1864). The year 1864 was also when a reformed jury first presided over the annual Salon (members of the Academy had been removed from direct power in selecting the paintings to be shown and in awarding prizes). The 1865 jury accepted Edouard Manet's controversial painting, *Olym-pia*. Also in the summer of 1864 the government extended official authorization to the Union Centrale des Beaux-Arts Appliqués à l'Industrie. Napoleon III wished to promote a closer relation between industry and the fine arts, and he was eager to encourage the sort of individual initiative represented by the Union. Vaillant obtained in 1869 a decree authorizing the government to transfer art objects from Paris museums to those in the provinces. Other lasting reforms concerning the fine arts were introduced during his administration. The minister was well rewarded. His various administrative, military, and legislative stipends totaled 250,000 francs per year.

Vaillant was a member of Emile Ollivier's government of 2 January 1870 but without responsibility for fine arts and without invitation to attend meetings of the Council of Ministers. Although he had shown little sympathy with Napoleon III's plans to reform the army in 1868–1869, lacking confidence in reserve troops, the marshal was one of those who encouraged the emperor to go to war against Prussia in 1870. For a short time after the fall of the Empire, he remained a member of the committee for the defense of Paris, but on 22 October he was ordered into exile. He returned to Dijon, dying on 4 June 1872. Vaillant left his modest estate to organizations he had served: the Bureau des Longitudes (1862), the Société d'Horticulture, the Société d'Acclimatation, and the Société Protectrice des Animaux.

A. Boime, "The Teaching Reforms of 1863 and the Origins of Modernism in France," *Art Quarterly*, n.s. 1 (Autumn 1977); Colonel Gondinet, "Le Maréchal Vaillant, 1790–1872," *Vauban* 14 (1977).

Related entries: ITALIAN WAR; SALON DES REFUSES; VIOLLET-LE-DUC.

VARLIN, EUGENE (1839–1871), bookbinder, Parisian labor activist, organizer of cooperatives, and member of the Paris Commune; born 5 October 1839 in the hamlet of Voisins in the Seine-et-Marne department, son of an agricultural laborer. Varlin was apprenticed as a bookbinder and practiced that trade in Paris during the 1860s. He quickly emerged as the bookbinders' leading spokesman, representing them at the London Exposition of 1862 and the Paris Exposition of 1867, as well as leading them in two strikes in 1864 and 1865, the first successful, the second a failure. In addition, he was wholeheartedly committed to the cooperative movement, sponsoring an independent savings cooperative for the bookbinders in 1865 and later creating two cooperatives open to all workers: La Ménagère, a consumers' cooperative, and La Marmite, a cooperative restaurant. When trade unions emerged at the end of the 1860s, he wrote articles in support of their strikes and solicited contributions to their funds, but he envisioned unions as transcending these immediate labor concerns in the future and transforming themselves into producers' cooperatives. This metamorphosis, in effect a social revolution, could not, he felt, take place until a political revolution brought about a republican form of government in France.

To prepare further the terrain for a social revolution, Varlin helped found the Paris branch of the International Working Men's Association in 1865 (the First International). He attended most of the International's congresses, where he exhibited a refreshing independence of thought. Although he shared the International's commitment to cooperatives, he unsuccessfully sought to have it endorse state-supported education and equal employment opportunity for women. When in 1869 the International accepted collectivization of agricultural property, Varlin was among those voting for it. He believed that collectivism and the cooperative ideal were compatible, though many people subsequently considered them to be mutually exclusive. Varlin, who was an exceptionally talented organizer, reorganized the International at Paris in December 1869. Twice on trial for his activities with the International, Varlin fled France in April 1870 to avoid a one-year prison term.

With the proclamation of a republic in September 1870, Varlin returned to Paris and immediately dedicated himself to defending the city against the Prussians. He served first as commandant of the 193rd National Guard Battalion and subsequently as a food supply organizer in the seventeenth *arrondissement*. Although the hoped-for political revolution had now taken place, Varlin urged members of the International to delay the social revolution until the invaders were repulsed. He served the Commune on its finance, subsistance, and intendance committees and vigorously sought to keep this revolution from falling back on socialist formulas inherited from the French Revolution. During the final week of the Commune, Varlin energetically directed the fighting at various barricades and when taken prisoner on the last day of the combat (28 May) was summarily executed as he shouted, "Long Live the Republic! Long Live the Commune!"

J. Bruhat, *Eugène Varlin: Militant ouvrier, révolutionnaire et Communard* (Paris, 1975); M. Foulon, *Eugène Varlin, relieur et membre de la Commune* (Clermont-Ferrand, 1934); E. Varlin, *Pratique militante* (Paris, 1977).

Julian Archer

Related entries: COALITIONS LAW; FIRST INTERNATIONAL; LABOR REFORM; LA RICAMARIE; *LIVRET D'OUVRIER*; PALAIS ROYAL GROUP; PROUDHON; REPUBLICANISM; TOLAIN.

VATICAN COUNCIL I, the twentieth general council, the first to meet since the Council of Trent three centuries before. It solemnly opened in St. Peter's Basilica on 8 December 1869 and adjourned after voting the doctrine of papal infallibility on 18 July 1870. Pius IX intended that the council should reassemble to continue its labors but deemed this inexpedient after the Italian occupation of Rome on 20 September 1870 following French defeat in the Franco-Prussian War that had begun on 19 July. Approximately 770 cardinals, patriarchs, bishops, abbots, and heads of religious orders participated, some 70 of them French. Contrary to ancient custom, princes were not invited to send *oratores* to represent them, though they were free to despatch envoys to the council. A further innovation was the appointment, starting in 1865, of preparatory commissions to compose draft constitutions (*schemata*) dealing with a wide range of church concerns for the council's eventual consideration. Although the question of papal infallibility was not part of the original formal agenda, the expectation that it would be brought before the council had stirred controversy before it met and divided the assembled prelates into groups that, though by no means homogeneous, were sufficiently distinct by virtue of their position on infallibility to be recognized as constituting the majority and the minority. The minority or opposition numbered approximately 140, or about 18 percent of those in attendance. Among the French the proportion of those in opposition was considerably higher, somewhere around 40 percent. German bishops took the lead in opposing infallibility, but the French were also prominent, especially Archbishop Georges Darboy (1813–1871) of Paris, Félix Dupanloup of Orleans, Jacques Ginoulhiac (1806–1875) of Grenoble, and Cardinal Jacques Mathieu (1796–1875) of Besançon. Archbishops Deschamps of Malines (Belgium) and Henry Manning of

Westminster were leaders of the majority, with Bishop Louis Pie of Poitiers, Claude Plantier (1813–1875) of Nîmes, and Cardinal Ferdinand Donnet (1795–1882) of Bordeaux important among the French members of this group. A third party of French bishops, hoping to find a compromise definition of infallibility, gathered about Cardinal Henri Bonnechose (1800–1883) of Rouen and included, among others, Joseph Guibert (1802–1886) of Tours, Théodore Forcade (1816–1885) of Nevers, and Archbishop Charles Lavigerie (1825–1892) of Algiers.

The minority were poorly represented on the four elected commissions (or deputations) that council procedure, established by Pius IX, stipulated should recast the *schemata* after examining amendments to them proposed in debate. Electoral committees had formed about Dupanloup for the minority and Manning for the majority. Manning exploited the strength at his disposal to produce a bloc vote for twenty-four names, which excluded the minority from the key deputation on faith (*de Fide*), a tactic disapproved of by Pie, who placed second among the twenty-four elected to the deputation, and by Pius IX himself, who had had the good sense to name three of the opposition and Cardinal Bonnechose to the appointed commission, *de Postulatis*, established to consider written agenda proposals from the prelates. Offended by what they considered to be unfair treatment, the anti-infallibilists were inclined to be more critical of proposals than they would otherwise have been. The French members of the group were especially energetic in protesting anything that appeared to inhibit free and full discussion. After debate began on the first *schema* presented, *de Fide*, the minority felt somewhat reassured, for six sessions (general congregations) of discussion carrying the deliberations into January demonstrated that there would be an opportunity for serious criticism. After *de Fide* was remitted to its deputation on 10 January for substantial redrafting, the council turned to matters of church discipline, which many had believed would be the principal concern of the council when the idea of convoking one was first broached. Once again the criticism of the prepared *schemata* was sharp and prolonged: on the Episcopal Office (14–25 January), on the Clerical Life (25 January–8 February), on the Little Catechism (10–22 February). Frequently the positions taken had nothing to do with the speakers' stand on infallibility, though the division over this issue did manifest itself. The ultramontane preference for a centralized church under papal sovereignty often clashed with the desire of others for diversity, as can be seen in Dupanloup's opposition to a single catechism for the entire church. The protracted discussions taxed the assembly's patience and prompted Pius IX to decree a new procedure on 22 February, which provoked minority protests against two of its provisions, that permitting closure by majority vote and that basing council decisions on majority vote rather than on "moral unanimity." Backed by an international committee codirected by Darboy, Dupanloup drew up one of the protests, which thirty French and twenty other bishops signed.

On the other side, French ultramontanes were prominent among those petitioning, first, that the question of infallibility be added to the agenda, and second, after this was done on 6 March, that it be considered early, out of its proper order. Pius IX hesitated to accede but finally agreed on 29 April. Pie of Poitiers opened the debate on 13 May. Irritated by the tactics of the opposition, the pope had already, regrettably and unnecessarily, made his own sentiments clear when he wrote a letter to Dom Prosper Guéranger (1805–1875) congratulating him on his publication *De la monarchie pontificale*, written to counter Mgr. Henri Maret's earlier work questioning the existence of a separate papal infallibility. Thereafter Pius IX sporadically lent his prestige to the majority prelates.

From early January, the French bishops opposed to the definition had acted to persuade their government to intervene in the affairs of the council. Comte Napoléon Daru, foreign minister in the cabinet of Emile Ollivier, had had close contact with liberal Catholics associated with the journal *Le correspondant*, particularly with Charles de Montalembert. Although Daru favored strong measures to support the anti-infallibilists, Ollivier and the majority of the ministers did not, for they considered the questions at issue theological rather than political. Nevertheless, the cabinet was sufficiently concerned that the church might seek to justify church supremacy in mixed politico-religious affairs to send a cautionary note to the Holy See in February and a memorandum of protest, supported by the principal European powers, on 4 April. The memorandum threatened no sanctions and was further weakened by Daru's resignation on a domestic issue 9 April. Like Daru, Napoleon III, to whom Darboy wrote two letters from Rome, would have preferred more forceful intervention; he transferred Bishop Ginoulhiac from Grenoble to Lyons during the council to manifest his support for the minority. The French infallibilists and the Tiers Parti also made representations to the government; both Lavigerie and Forcade made excursions to Paris during the discussions.

The lengthy debates in a time period cut short by political events and the intense activity of the minority regarding infallibility resulted in the council's promulgating only two constitutions, both of them more moderately worded than would have been the case had the opposition been less energetic. In dealing with faith, reason, and modern errors, the constitution *Dei filius*, voted on 24 April, not only recognized the importance of reason but also the need for each science to follow its own principles and methods. The constitution *Pastor aeternus*, voted on 18 July 1870, unequivocally proclaimed the primacy of papal jurisdiction within the church but narrowly defined papal infallibility. A test vote on *Pastor aeternus* on 13 July produced 451 for (*placet*), 88 against (*non placet*), and 62 conditional approvals (*placet juxta modum*). The final vote, which had to be either for or against, saw 533 in favor and only 2 against. Approximately 60 bishops had departed prior to the vote rather than publicly oppose, 25 of them French. The other 45 French prelates had voted *placet*. Unlike their German colleagues, most of the French minority had opposed the definition not on grounds of historical or doctrinal criticism but on pastoral grounds, because they held it to be inopportune. An aggrandizement of papal authority, they believed, might excite public opinion, alarm governments, and repel Protestants and Eastern Christians. Some, however, such as Ginoulhiac, Félix, Les Cases (1819–1880) of Constantine, and Maret doubted that scripture or church tradition supported a separate papal infallibility. All of the hierarchy eventually submitted to the council's decisions, the French episcopate being especially quick to adhere.

R. Aubert, *Vatican I* (Paris, 1964); T. Caffrey, "Consensus and Infallibility: The Mind of Vatican I," *Downside Review* 88 (April 1970); J. Gadille, "L'épiscopat français au premier Concile du Vatican," *RHEF* 56 (July–December 1970), and *Albert du Boys: Ses souvenirs du Concile du Vatican, 1869–1870: L'intervention du gouvernement impérial à Vatican I* (Louvain, 1968); A. B. Hasler, *Pius IX (1846–1878): Päpstliche Unfehlbarkeit und 1. Vatikanisches Konzil* (Stuttgart, 1977); J. Hoffman, "Histoire et dogme: La définition de l'infallibilité pontificale à Vatican I à propos de l'ouvrage de A. B. Hasler," *Revue des sciences philosophiques et théologiques*, 62 (October 1978), 63 (January 1979); R. Palanque, *Catholiques libéraux et gallicanes face au Concile du Vatican, 1867–1870* (Aix-en-Provence, 1962); A. Riccardi, *Neo-galicanesimo e cattolicismo borghese: Henri Maret e il Concilio Vaticano I* (Bologna, 1976); I. Sivrić, *Bishop J. G. Strossmayer: New Light on Vatican I* (Chicago, 1975).

Raymond L. Cummings

Related entries: CORRESPONDANT; DARU; GALLICANISM; PERE HYACINTHE; INFALLIBILITY, DOCTRINE OF; MARET; MONTALEMBERT; OLLIVIER; ORLEANS, BISHOP OF; PIE; PIUS IX; ROMAN QUESTION; *SYLLABUS OF ERRORS*; *UNIVERS*; VEUILLOT.

VENETIA, a territory in northeastern Italy that Napoleon III failed to wrest from Austria in the Italian War of 1859. In 1815, as part of the territorial settlement imposed by the great powers, the city of Venice and its mainland provinces were joined to the Duchy of Milan (Lombardy) to become the Kingdom of Lombardy-Venetia, which was placed under the sovereignty of the Austrian emperor. Thereafter a vice-regent at Milan ruled the kingdom with delegated powers. In May 1859, on going to war in alliance with Sardinia against Austria, Napoleon III vowed to "free Italy from the Alps to the Adriatic." But while as a result of the war Austria ceded Lombardy to Sardinia, it retained Venetia, which, after the Franco-Sardinian victories at Magenta and Solferino, remained sheltered behind the imposing fortifications of the Quadrilateral. By the terms of the Villafranca peace preliminaries, Venetia was to become part of an Italian confederation. Apprehension that Austria could use this arrangement as a means to reassert influence in Italy undoubtedly lent force to the annexationist movements in central Italy, which, together with Giuseppi Garibaldi's conquest of the south, delivered to Sardinia before the end of 1860 all of the peninsula except Rome and Venetia.

From 1861 Venetia became an important diplomatic question. The Italian government, with French support, attempted unsuccessfully to purchase the province or to acquire it in some other peaceful way, such as through an exchange of territories involving the Danubian Principalities (Rumania). Napoleon III brooded over his failure to keep his promise of 1859. In his interview with the Prussian foreign minister, Otto von Bismarck, at Biarritz in October 1865, the French emperor quite probably revealed his enthusiasm for the redemption of

Venetia and certainly encouraged Italy to negotiate an offensive and defensive alliance with Prussia, signed on 8 April 1866. Perhaps he hoped to force Austria to relinquish Venetia under threat of a war, but Napoleon III also took steps to ensure that if war were to come, Italy would be certain of gaining the province whether it won or lost. It was also in France's interest that King Victor Emmanuel I of Italy not take more than Venetia (Italy had designs on the Tyrol and Istria as well). And so when Florence declined an Austrian offer of Venetia in exchange for Italian neutrality and when Vienna in effect vetoed a proposed congress to avert war between Germany and Prussia, Napoleon III entered into a secret agreement with Austria (12 August 1866). In exchange for French neutrality, Austria would cede Venetia to France, even if it won the war. In this way, the French emperor hoped to contain Italy's ambitions (which, if unchecked, might have repercussions at Rome where France was obligated by the September Convention to withdraw its protecting garrison by the end of 1866), while ensuring that the undertaking of 1859 would be completed. Prussia's overwhelming victory at Sadowa served to emphasize, however, the embarrassment of its Italian ally at having to accept Venetia through France as intermediary. Italy had in fact made little military progress against Austria (on 20 July 1866 it was defeated at the naval battle of Lissa). Although General Enrico Cialdini entered Venetia on 8 July, six days earlier Vienna, in seeking French mediation, had committed itself to ceding the province to France. An armistice was signed between Austria and Italy on 12 August and a peace treaty on 3 October. Following ratification on 12 October, Austria at once began the transfer of Venetia to France, under the terms of a convention signed at Vienna on 24 August. Following a plebiscite on 21–22 October, France, in the person of a single general, handed the province over to Italy. Once again, however, Napoleon III received no gratitude for his services, which many Italians regarded as humiliating for their country. Moreover, the acquisition of Venetia by Italy had the unwelcome result for France of focusing Italian attention once again on Rome.

Atti del XLIII [October 1966] Congresso di Storia del Risorgimento italiano (Rome, 1968); N. Barker, "Austria, France, and the Venetian Question, 1861–1866," *JMH* 36 (June 1964); N. Blakiston and R. Blass, *Il problema Veneto e l'Europa, 1859-1866* (Venice, 1966); J. W. Bush, Jr., "Napoleon III, Venetia, and the war of 1866," in L. Vincitorio, ed., *Crisis in the "Great Republic"* (New York, 1969), and *Venetia Redeemed: Franco-Italian Relations, 1864–1866* (Ithaca, N.Y., 1967); D. Caccamo, "L'Italia, la questione del Veneto e i Principati Danubiani (1861–1866)," *SP* 19 (September 1980); E. Nicolardi, "Napoleone III garanti all' Italia la sicurezza da tutti gli attachi," *Messagero veneto* (January 1973).

Ivan Scott

Related entries: BIARRITZ INTERVIEW; CHAMBERY; CONGRESS POLICY; ITALIAN CONFEDERATION; ITALIAN WAR; NATIONALITIES; NICE-SAVOY; ROMAN QUESTION; RUMANIAN UNITY; VILLAFRANCA.

VERNE, JULES (1828–1905), novelist and playwright, inventor of science fiction; born 8 February 1828 at Nantes. As the eldest son of a lawyer, Verne was sent to Paris to study law so that he might follow in his father's footsteps. However, he developed a passion for writing and began to frequent the salon of Mme. Barrère, through whom he made a number of literary contacts, among them Alexandre Dumas père, Théophile Gautier, and Emile de Girardin. His play, *Les pailles rompues*, was produced at the Gymnase in 1850 under Dumas père's auspices. For the next ten years, while earning his living as a stockbroker (he had refused to return to Nantes and to his father's law office), Verne persisted in his literary vocation, although he enjoyed very little success, producing in collaboration with various authors (such as Michel Carré, 1819–1872) some eight or nine comedies, a drama, and six libretti for such composers as Aristide Hignard (1822–1898). From 1852 to 1855, Verne experienced a certain measure of financial stability through his having been given the post of secretary to Emile Perrin (1814–1885), administrator of the Paris Théâtre Lyrique, quite possibly through the good offices of Dumas père once again. During this period, he turned his hand to prose fiction, publishing novellas (*Les premiers navires de la marine mexicaine*, 1851; *Martin Paz*, 1852) in the periodical *Le musée des familles*. Even in these early works, the style and themes that were later to make Verne world famous are apparent: the use of exotic settings and exciting events narrated with skill and immediacy and with a scrupulous attention to factual details, gleaned from the many trips he was to take during his lifetime (to Holland, Denmark, Scandinavia, Morocco, Algeria, Spain, Italy, England, Scotland, and to the United States on board the *Great Eastern* in 1867).

In 1861, Dumas père introduced Verne, who had just completed the manuscript of *Cinq semaines en ballon*, to the publisher Jules Hetzel (1814–1886) whose list included such republican authors as George Sand and Victor Hugo. From this meeting came a lifelong friendship and a contract, by which Verne promised Hetzel three volumes per year at almost 2,000 francs per book, originally destined to be published in Hetzel's children's periodical, *Le magasin d'éducation et de recréation*. With certain modifications (such as two novels per year instead of three after 1871), this agreement lasted until Hetzel's death and produced sixty-three volumes in the series *Voyages extraordinaires*. *Cinq semaines en ballon*, published in 1863, was Verne's first major success, and it heralded a new kind of fiction—the science novel—in which strict factual accuracy was respected within a plot handled with consummate narrative skill and in which problems were posed and solutions predicted that were shortly to come to pass, as in the announced discovery of the source of the Nile within months of its fictional discovery by Verne's balloonists. *Cinq semaines* was probably inspired by the author's friendship with Félix Nadar, photographer and aeronaut. In July 1863 Verne was secretary of Nadar's Society for the Encouragement of Aerial Locomotion by Means of Heavier-Than-Air Machines, and in October of that year Nadar's great balloon, *Le Géant*, made its maiden flight.

Verne's novels continued to appear at the rate of approximately two per year and were received with enthusiasm by the public who waited avidly for the serialized novels to appear in the *Magasin* (*Le désert de glace: Les aventures du Capitaine Hatteras*, 1864–1866; *Vingt mille lieues sous les mers*, 1869–1870) and in the *Journal des débats* (*De le terre à la lune: Trajet direct en quatre-vingt-dix-sept heures*). Fortune followed, if not recognition from the scholarly world or peace of mind in an unhappy marriage contracted in 1857. Hetzel continually improved the terms of Verne's contract as success followed success and intervened on his behalf, with the result that the author, who was also recommended by Ferdinand de Lesseps (1805–1894), was named to the Legion of Honor on 13 August 1870, in the last decree signed by the Empress Eugénie, then regent. Verne, an avowed republican since 1848, only reluctantly accepted the honor from a regime he detested. On the outbreak of war with Prussia in 1870, he joined the home guard (*Garde Mobile*) in his town of Le Crotoy and patrolled the estuary of the Somme with a small cannon on his sailing boat. He voiced his disapproval, however, of the Commune, which he viewed as a divisive "communist"-inspired movement. Nevertheless, it is interesting to note that Verne later rewrote novels written by Paschal Grousset (1845–1909), and bought by Hetzel, to assist that impoverished radical in exile in England. During this period, he kept up his literary production, with perhaps his greatest success coming in 1873, when *Le tour du monde en quatre-vingt jours* appeared in *Le temps*, tripling that newspaper's circulation during the serialization. He collaborated in making a play from the novel, and *Le tour du monde* alternated every two years at the Théâtre du Châtelet with another of Verne's great triumphs, *Michel Strogoff* (novel 1876, play 1880) uninterrupted until 1926.

Beginning in the mid-1870s, Verne was translated into many languages and, by 1953, was the fourth most translated author in the world, after Stalin, Lenin, and Simenon. Critics have increasingly found in his work (only half of which was completed by 1886) greater complexity than had at first been suspected. They point to Verne's misogyny, his social satire (as of financial speculation during the Second Empire), and his underlying pessimism about the interaction of men and machines. Plagued by failing health after 1890 and by persistent family problems, Verne died at Amiens, 24 March 1905.

Among other major theatrical works written by Verne during the Second Empire are the following: *Colin maillard* (1853), *Les compagnons de Marjolaine* (1855), and *L'auberge des Ardennes* (1860). Among his novels are: *Le voyage au centre de la terre* (1864); *The Blockade Runner* (1865); *Les enfants du Capitaine Grant* (1867–1868); *Autour de la lune* (1869–1870); *Les Anglais au Pôle Nord* (1870); *Les naufragés de l'air* (1870); *L'Ile mystérieuse* (first part, 1870); and *Une ville flottante* (1871; based on his voyage on the *Great Eastern*). Verne also wrote, in collaboration with Théophile Lavallée (1804–1866), a *Géographie illustrée de la France* (1867–1868).

M. Allote de La Faye, *Jules Verne*, trans. from the French (New York, 1956); J. Chesneaux, *The Political and Social Ideas of Jules Verne*, trans. from the French (London,

1972); *Europe* (April–May 1955); J. Jules-Verne, *Jules Verne*, trans. from the French (New York, 1976); M. Soriano, *Jules Verne* (Paris, 1978); S. Vierne, *Jules Verne et le roman initiatique* (Paris, 1973).

                                                                                        Dorothy E. Speirs

VEUILLOT, LOUIS (1813–1883), author and editor of the clerical journal, *L'Univers*; born in Boynes (Loiret), 11 October 1813. The first literate member of a peasant family, Veuillot became a highly successful literary man and the personification of ultramontane (papal supremacy) clericalism. In 1838, jaded with the artificialities of Paris, he went on a vacation to Rome and ever after was a fiery champion of Roman Catholicism. In 1843 he assumed control of *L'Univers* and until his death was thoroughly identified with this arm of militant Catholicism. Having gone to prison for a month during the July Monarchy, Veuillot's role in 1848 and during the rise of Louis Napoleon Bonaparte was significant. "Catholic-before-all" and increasingly reactionary, he leaned toward the legitimist cause during the 1840s. Louis Napoleon, however, by restoring the pope to Rome in 1849, more and more seemed to Veuillot to be filling the role of a latter-day Charlemagne. Veuillot's accommodation to and support for Napoleon III increased during the early 1850s, reaching its height during the Crimean War, which *L'Univers* represented as a crusade. By the end of the war, however, as Napoleon III began to favor the cause of Italian unification, Veuillot foresaw the abandonment of the papacy and reacted accordingly. Despite his devotion to the Empress Eugénie, he turned against Napoleon during the 1859 war with Austria, and in January 1860 *L'Univers* was suppressed.

Veuillot had suffered personal tragedy in the mid-1850s with the death of his wife and four of his six daughters. The suppression of his journal was another blow, but from 1860 to 1867 he was able more fully to follow the role of *écrivain*, the term by which he consistently described himself. His *Vie de Notre Seigneur Jésus-Christ* (1864) was a notable answer to Ernest Renan and was regarded by Veuillot as his principal work, but his *Les odeurs de Paris* (1866) and many other political-religious-social writings, as well as his poetry and fiction, were favorites of the French public. Finally, as liberalism became the key to Napoleon's survival, *L'Univers* was able to appear again (1867), and another three years of criticism of the Empire's pro-Italian policy followed.

It is hard to name persons who inspired the independent-minded Veuillot, but the Spaniard Donoso Cortés left an early and profound mark on him. Pope Pius IX was the key to all his stands, and the very length of Pius' pontificate had much to do with Veuillot's career. Veuillot traveled many times to Rome, but the most notable of these voyages was during 1869–1870, when he played an important part in coordinating the victory of the *infaillibilists*. Even as the Prussians were beginning to threaten Paris in 1870, Veuillot seemed at least equally distressed about the erection of a monument in Paris to Voltaire, who symbolized much of what he hated. Education had preoccupied Veuillot during much of the Second Empire, and the Falloux compromise of 1850 long distressed him. The height of his distress was the battle precipitated by the Abbé Joseph Gaume in which he became engaged in 1852–1853 with his own archbishop, M.D.A. Sibour (1792–1857), about the study of the classics rather than the church fathers. Keeping *L'Univers* going during 1870–1871 at more than one city, Veuillot's identity with the cause of the comte de Chambord became complete. His lack of charity toward opponents caused the pope to censure him in due course, a heavy blow for Veuillot, who died the same year as Chambord, at Paris, 7 April 1883.

M. L. Brown, Jr., *Louis Veuillot: French Ultramontane Catholic Journalist and Layman, 1813–1883* (Durham, N.C., 1977); C. Foucard, *L'aspect méconnu d'un grand lutteur: Louis Veuillot devant les arts et les lettres*, 2 vols. (Paris, 1979); R. J. Hesbert, *Ca et là dans les oeuvres de Louis Veuillot* (Paris, 1982); N. Isser, "The Mortara Affair and Louis Veuillot," *PWSFH* (1980).

Marvin L. Brown, Jr.

Related entries: CHAMBORD; DUPANLOUP; GALLICANISM; GAUME; INFALLIBILITY, DOCTRINE OF; LEGITIMISM; MORTARA AFFAIR; PIUS IX; ROMAN QUESTION; *L UNIVERS*; VATICAN COUNCIL.

VIARDOT, PAULINE (1821–1910), mezzo-soprano, composer, and teacher; born Michelle Ferdinande Pauline Garcia, at Paris, 18 July 1821. Her father was the celebrated tenor and voice teacher, Manuel Garcia (1775–1832). The Garcias were an extraordinary opera dynasty. Viardot's elder sister was the legendary soprano, Madame Maria Malibran (1808–1836), tragically dead at twenty-eight of injuries suffered when she fell from her horse; her brother, Manuel (1805–1906), himself a baritone, became perhaps the greatest singing teacher of the nineteenth century. Viardot traveled widely with her family and learned her music initially from them (both she and Malibran studied voice with their father). But Viardot was also an accomplished pianist and composer, having studied harmony and composition with Anton Reicha (1770–1836) and piano with Franz Liszt (1811–1886). She made her concert debut at Brussels, where the family then lived, in 1837 and her stage debut at London on 9 May 1839 as Desdemona in *Otello* of Gioacchino Rossini (1792–1868). She sang Cinderella in Rossini's *La cenerentola* at London and later that year sang both roles, as well as Tancrède and Rosina in the same composer's *Tancrède* and the *Barber of Seville*, at Paris' Théâtre des Italiens. In 1840 she married Louis Viardot (1800–1883), journalist and impresario, who had been director of the Italiens since 1838.

Viardot's husband having in an uncommon act of probity resigned his directorship, the couple lived an itinerant life. During the 1840s, Viardot sang at Vienna, Dresden, Berlin, and, principally, St. Petersburg, which she first visited in 1843. By then she had met the two composers with whom her career would be most intertwined, Charles Gounod (at Rome) and Giacomo Meyerbeer (at Berlin). The latter was even more impressed by Viardot than he had been by Malibran, and he promised the singer a major role in his next Paris production. True to his word, Meyerbeer wrote *Le prophète* (Opéra, 16 April 1849) with

Viardot in mind, and her creation of Fidès, a role she was to sing more than two hundred times, established her reputation not only at Paris but also at London's Covent Garden (1848–1851, 1854–1855), at Berlin, and at St. Petersburg.

The next decade marked the culmination of Viardot's singing career. Meyerbeer, Fromental Halévy (1799–1862), and Gluck were her composers, and she excelled in such dramatic roles as Valentine in *Les Huguenots* (Meyerbeer), Rachel in *La Juive* (Halévy), and Alice in *Robert le Diable* (Meyerbeer). The pinnacle was perhaps the famous version by Hector Berlioz (1803–1869) of Gluck's *Orfeo ed Euridice* (Théâtre Lyrique, 19 November 1859). Between 1859 and 1862, Viardot sang the role of Orpheus 150 times to great acclaim. It was a fitting end to a stage career during which she had sung with and rivaled the greatest voices of her generation: Luigi Lablache (1794–1858), Giovanni Battista Rubini (1795–1854), Antonio Tamburini (1800–1876), Giulia Grisi (1811–1869), Giovanni Matteo Mario (1810–1883), Fanny Persiani (1812–1867), and Marietta Alboni (1826–1894).

Viardot was distinguished from her operatic contemporaries not by her voice, which was less than perfect, but by her intelligence, personality, skills as an actress, and accomplishments in a variety of fields. As a pianist she could, in 1851, have been appointed head of department at the Cologne Conservatory. She was an excellent painter and an impressive linguist, speaking French, Italian, Spanish, German, and English well. She composed three operettas and sixty songs, in addition to pieces for piano and violin. Perhaps above all, she moved as an equal among the intellectual and cultural elite of her day, who admired her artistry even more than did the general public, and who praised her extravagantly, as in the case of Théophile Gautier. Gounod, Berlioz, Alfred de Musset (1810–1857), Ary Scheffer (1795–1858), and Ivan Turgenev (1818–1883) fell in love with her. Robert Schumann (1810–1856) and George Sand were her close friends. Viardot's Paris salon, at no. 50, rue de Douai (Hôtel Viardot), gathered Paul Delaroche (1797–1856), Gustave Doré, Léon Bonnat (1833–1922), Carolus-Duran (1837–1917), Ernest Renan, Gustave Flaubert, Charles Dickens (1812–1870), Henri Martin (1810–1883), Jules Simon (1814–1896), Ambroise Thomas, César Franck (1822–1890), Edouard Lalo (1823–1892), Camille Saint-Saëns, Prince Adam Czartoryski (1770–1861), Prince Troubetzkoï, Daniel Manin (1804–1857), and the comtesse d'Agoult (Daniel Stern, 1805–1876). Turgenev, who had loved Pauline Viardot since 1843, lived upstairs for thirty years, although she would never agree to leave her husband for him, an experience that became the basis of Turgenev's most famous play, *A Day in the Country*.

But Viardot's true world was music, and there her contributions were enduring. She established the prototype of the modern mezzo-soprano and was one of the main conduits through which Russian music reached the West. Always interested in struggling composers, she helped to launch Gounod's operatic career (*Sapho*, 1859), as well as that of Jules Massenet (1842–1912). In 1859 at Baden-Baden, she sang Cassandra in the only public performance of excerpts from the first act of Berlioz's *Les Troyens*, and the next year, at the request of Richard Wagner (1813–1883), she sang Isolde in a private hearing at Paris of *Tristan und Isolde* (act 2), with Wagner singing Tristan. She was the first (in 1860) to sing Leonore in Beethoven's *Fidelio* in French. It was for Viardot that Brahms wrote his "Alto Rhapsody," which she sang for the first time at Jena on 3 March 1870.

As with her physical appearance, so with her voice, Viardot's distinction came less from physical endowments than from the play of will and intelligence on them. Her natural range was perhaps two octaves, but by application she extended it to more than three, and her repertoire was very wide. The result was inevitable. When she sang the title role in the 1861 revival at the Opéra of Gluck's *Alceste*, the limitations of her voice were already apparent, although she was a sensation. In 1863 Viardot retired but continued to give occasional concerts at Stuttgart or at Baden-Baden where she settled until 1870 and where she met Brahms. In March 1870 she sang *Orfeo ed Eurydice* at Weimar. Her career was now that of a teacher. During the Franco-Prussian War, Viardot was at London, but in 1871 she returned to Paris where she continued to compose and to teach until her death on 18 May 1910. Her daughter, Louise (1841–1918), was a contralto and her son, Paul (b. 1857), a violinist.

A. Fitzlyon, *The Price of Genius: A Biography of Pauline Viardot* (London, 1964); J. M. Levien, *The Garcia Family* (London, 1932; revised 1948 as *Six Sovereigns of Song*); T. Marix-Spire, "Gounod and His First Interpreter, Pauline Viardot," *Musical Quarterly* 21 (1945).

Related entries: CARVALHO; GOUNOD; MEYERBEER.

VICTOR NOIR AFFAIR, the murder by Prince Pierre Bonaparte, Napoleon III's cousin, of the journalist Yvan Salmon on 10 January 1870. Prince Pierre Napoléon Bonaparte (1815–1881), third son of Lucien Bonaparte, had had a turbulent and violent career in Italy and South America, Albania, and on the island of Corfu, before settling in Paris in 1848. A republican of the extreme Left in the Legislative Assembly (1849–1851), he was disconcerted by the coup d'état of December 1851 and retired to private life, dividing his time thereafter between Corsica and his country home at Auteuil. Although awarded the title of prince at the establishment of the Second Empire, he was held at arm's length by the emperor, who ignored his offers of service, did not summon him to court, and remained aloof from his marriage in Belgium in 1868 to a working-class French woman with whom he had lived since 1853 and by whom he had had two illegitimate children. This *mésalliance* cost the prince his civil list stipend of 100,000 francs per year. Pierre Bonaparte's violent and unpredictable nature made him a constant threat of embarrassment to the regime.

Thinking himself insulted by an article published in a Corsican newspaper, *La revanche*, Pierre Bonaparte published on 30 December 1869 in a rival paper, *L'avenir de la Corse*, a letter attacking the editors of *La revanche*. Henri Rochefort's newspaper, *La Marseillaise*, entered the fray, with the result that the prince, on 9 January 1870, challenged Rochefort to a duel. In the meantime

Paschal Grousset (1845–1909), an editor of *La Marseillaise* and the Paris representative of *La revanche*, had decided, independently of Rochefort, to send
his own challenge for allusions made in Pierre Bonaparte's letter of 30 December.
Grousset chose as his seconds Ulric de Fonvielle (1833–1911) and a young man
attached to *La Marseillaise*, Yvan Salmon. Born in 1848, Salmon was the brother
of Louis Noir, a writer, and in fact called himself Victor Noir. As a reporter
for several left-wing newspapers, he had proved useful on occasion for his brawn.
Early in the afternoon of 10 January, the two men, both armed, presented
themselves at Pierre Bonaparte's home, where the prince was ill with flu. Shortly
after, Victor Noir, followed by Fonvielle, staggered from the house, shot near
the heart, and died a few minutes later in a pharmacy to which he had been
carried. Grousset, who had been waiting on the street, had been joined in the
meantime by a second group of men, also armed, en route to call on the prince
on Rochefort's behalf.

On his return from a hunt later that afternoon, Napoleon III received word of
the incident. Greatly disturbed, he agreed at once to his cousin's arrest, but
Pierre Bonaparte had already surrendered himself voluntarily to the police at
Auteuil. A trial was immediately decided on, the date was set nine days later
for 21 March. Pending the trial, both Pierre Bonaparte and Grousset were detained, the former in comfortable lodgings at the Conciergerie, the latter secretly.
In the meantime, the Left, as was to be expected, seized on the murder. Announcing it in his newspaper on 11 January, Rochefort had virtually issued a
call to arms (for which he would later be sentenced to six months imprisonment).
There were disturbances in Paris that evening. Victor Noir's funeral, at Neuilly
on the following day, was turned into a huge political demonstration despite the
wishes of the family. Apprehensions of revolution proved groundless, however.
The republican deputies in the Corps Législatif did not attend. Only a tiny
minority of the demonstrators contemplated violence, and the ministry of Emile
Ollivier having massed troops on the Champs Elysées, the postfuneral procession
dispersed without further incident. On 17 January the Corps Législatif, by a vote
of 222 to 34, authorized the prosecution of Rochefort, then a deputy. Despite
riots in Paris on 17–18 January, the journalist was convicted in absentia on 22
January and arrested at Paris on 7 February. Riots again followed and a few
barricades rose in the city on 8 and 9 January, but order was quickly restored.

The trial was held at Tours, 21–27 March, before the High Court of Justice,
which, under the *sénatus-consulte* of 4 June 1858, was alone competent to try
members of the imperial family. The thirty-six jurors, chosen by lot from eighty-
nine names similarly chosen one from each departmental conseil général, had
to decide between conflicting testimonies. Both sides agreed that the interview
had been brief, that Pierre Bonaparte, who had expected to be called on by
Rochefort's seconds, was surprised to hear the name of Paschal Grousset, and
that he had brusquely refused the latter's challenge, rejecting a letter offered
him on Grousset's behalf by Fonvielle and Noir. The prince, however, insisted
that Victor Noir had replied by striking him and that he had fired his revolver

in self-defense. Grousset testified that Pierre Bonaparte had slapped Victor Noir and then fired without provocation. Prince Pierre Bonaparte's uncontrollable temper and violent nature counted against him, but the gathering of armed men at his house, the complete perversion of the dueling code by Rochefort and Grousset, and, above all, the violence of the witnesses against the prince at his trial proved decisive. The fact that it was indeed Noir who had struck Pierre Bonaparte was established, and while the prosecuter, M.E.A. Grandperret (1818–1890), conducted himself with fairness, he and the jurors showed much deference to the prince, who was found innocent of both murder and attempted murder, although he was required to pay 25,000 francs to the Salmon family. The verdict of acquittal was cheered outside the courtroom, and Pierre Bonaparte, rejecting the emperor's private request that he leave France, retired to his rented property in the Ardennes. As the 25,000 francs were refused by Victor Noir's family, the prince entrusted it with the mayor of Tours, to be used for charity. Grousset continued a campaign in *La Marseillaise*, which earned him several convictions. The affair and its outcome (both the emperor and Ollivier had hoped for a sentence of one to two years) contributed significantly to the unpopularity of the imperial family and to the growth of a revolutionary party.

P. Bastid, "L'affaire Victor Noir," *RPP* 72 (1970); A. Decaux, "Pierre Bonaparte assassine Victor Noir," *Historia* 391 (June 1979); A. Le Milinaire, "Vallès et l'enterrement de Victor Noir," *Annales de Bretagne* 77 (1970); P. Mermet, "L'assassinat de Victor Noir," *MH*, no. 91 (1957); A. Zévaès, *L'affaire Pierre Bonaparte: Le meurtre de Victor Noir* (Paris, c. 1929).

Related entries: BAUDIN; OLLIVIER; REPUBLICANISM; ROCHEFORT.

VIE DE CESAR. See HISTOIRE DE JULES CESAR.

VIGNY, ALFRED, COMTE DE (1797–1863), romantic poet and playwright; born 27 March 1797 at Loches. Although Vigny's greatest triumphs as a playwright and poet were behind him by the beginning of the Second Empire (he had been a member of the Académie Française since 1845), he remained nonetheless a figurehead of the romantic movement, admired by a new generation of poets and novelists, among them Charles Baudelaire, Charles Leconte de Lisle, and Gustave Flaubert.

Vigny had stood for election as deputy from the Charente in 1848 and 1849 but had been badly beaten on both occasions. Disappointed at not being able to take an active part in government, he left Paris to live on his Charente country estate in semiseclusion. The creation of the Second Empire gave new life to his political ambitions, for Vigny was delighted to see France return to a more authoritarian regime. Whereas republican writers like Victor Hugo and George Sand saw in Louis Napoleon a potential dictator and longed for a return to republican government, Vigny saw in the future emperor, whom he had known for a number of years, a leader who would fight against the forces of "materialism and communism'' and who would free France from the influence of an uncensored, hence unbridled, press.

In October 1852, during the triumphal tour that preceded the reestablishment of the Empire, Louis Napoleon invited the poet to Angoulême. Vigny returned to Paris with visions of an important appointment. Having completely disavowed any socialistic ideas that he might previously have expressed, he went so far as to send notes to the government, giving names of officials whom he suspected of harboring anti-imperialist sentiments. In spite of his efforts, Vigny received no appointment.

Once and for all, he gave up his dream of a political role and returned to his literary pursuits. He published poems in *Revue des deux mondes* and devoted much of his time to the Académie, attending meetings and lobbying for the elections of writers whom he felt had well served the arts. With Hugo and Alphonse de Lamartine temporarily absent and with Alfred de Musset's death in 1857, Vigny was the leading light among the Immortals. Although far from being widely celebrated in the years before his death, Vigny's influence on younger poets was underlined in an article published by Charles Augustin Sainte-Beuve. Many solicited his advice, among them Leconte de Lisle, who asked not only Vigny's counsel but also his aid in obtaining a state pension. Vigny's major work during the Second Empire was the composition of the eleven poems that were published posthumously, in 1864, under the title *Les destinées: Poèmes philosophiques*. These poems, six of which appeared in the poet's lifetime in the *Revue des deux mondes*, represent the evolution of his personal philosophy as it moved from an attitude of doubt and despair to an acceptance of the human condition and finally to a proclamation of faith in the future of the human spirit. Vigny died at Paris, 17 September 1863. His daily jottings, thoughts, and drafts of unfinished works were published in 1867 as *Journal d'un poète*.

P. G. Castex, *Vigny* (Paris, 1969); P. Flottes, *Vigny et sa fortune littéraire* (Bordeaux, 1970); *Revue de Pau et du Béarn*, no. 6 (1978); M. Toesca, *Vigny, ou la passion de l'honneur* (Paris, 1972).

Dorothy E. Speirs

VILLAFRANCA, Venetian town where peace preliminaries were signed 11 July 1859 ending the Italian War of France and Sardinia against Austria. The Franco-Sardinian victory at Solferino on 24 June 1859 secured Lombardy, whose capital had already been occupied by the allied forces. However, a number of factors encouraged Napoleon III to end the war short of complete victory. He was concerned at the state of the French army, the strength of Austrian forces in the Quatrilateral fortresses of Peschiera, Mantua, Verona, and Legnago, and, especially, the mobilization of Prussian forces on the Rhine. The French emperor was also unhappy at Sardinian encouragement of revolution throughout Italy, including the Papal States. Besides, opinion in France was now eager for peace. Already, on the eve of Solferino, Napoleon III had warned that it might be necessary to end the war. Shortly after the battle, whose horror seems greatly to have affected him, he began efforts to secure European support for peace terms and to arrange an armistice (achieved 8 July). On 10 July General E. F. Fleury (1815–1884) carried a letter of the emperor to Francis Joseph's headquarters at Verona. The next day, 11 July, the two rulers met at Villafranca.

Already predisposed to terms by defeat and suspicion of Prussia, the Austrian emperor was further influenced by Napoleon III's suggestion that Europe was about to intervene. That evening Francis Joseph received from Prince Napoleon and accepted Napoleon III's draft of peace terms. Lombardy, without the Quadrilateral, would be ceded by Austria to France; Venetia would remain Austrian; both sides would grant amnesty to all who had engaged in war against them; dispossessed Italian rulers could return to their thrones but not by force; an Italian confederation, including Venetia, would be established under the honorary presidency of the pope. The prohibition of force was understood but not stated, as was the intention that the agreement should ultimately be ratified by a European congress. Warned but not consulted, the Sardinian king, Victor Emmanuel, realistically accepted the Villafranca agreement insofar as it concerned him. Count Camillo Benso di Cavour, however, angrily resigned as prime minister, retiring temporarily from the political scene. The Treaty of Zurich (signed 10 November, following a conference that had begun on 8 August) formally ended the war on the basis of the Villafranca agreement. Contemporaries would argue, with much justification, that Villafranca ensured the unification of Italy, which Napoleon III had opposed, since a confederation containing Venetia would be dominated by Austria, and Italian patriots therefore had no choice but to seek annexation to Sardinia. French annexation of Nice and Savoy and the creation of the Kingdom of Italy (March 1861) may therefore be regarded as long-range consequences of Villafranca, several of whose provisions were destined not to be fulfilled.

G. Hadju-Villa, "La critique des 'préliminaires de paix' de Villafranca par Louis Kossuth," *RHMC* 23 (January–March 1976); Prince Napoleon, "Les préliminaires de la paix, 11 juillet 1859: Journal de ma mission auprès de l'Empereur d'Autriche," *RDM*, 1 August 1909; A. J. P. Taylor, "European Mediation and the Agreement of Villafranca, 1859," *EHR* 201 (1936); R. Ugolini, *Cavour e Napoleone III nell'Italia centrale: Il sacrificio di Perugia* (Rome, 1973); F. Valsecchi, "Villafranca, ovvero la fine della diplomazia," *NALSA* (September 1959), and "La paix de Zurich (1859)," *RHMC* 7 (1960).

Related entries: CHAMBERY CONGRESS POLICY; ITALIAN CONFEDERATION; ITALIAN WAR; NATIONALITIES; NICE-SAVOY; ROMAN QUESTION; VENETIA; WALEWSKI.

VILLEMESSANT, HIPPOLYTE DE (1812–1879), journalist and businessman, founder of *Le Figaro*; born at Rouen, 22 April 1812. Like Emile de Girardin, Villemessant was a bastard. Baptized at fourteen, he took his mother's name, and at the age of eighteen he married. After a succession of business failures at Blois, Tours, and Nantes, Villemessant came to Paris (1839) and turned his hand to journalism. His first newspaper, *La sylphide* (1840), failed. From 1840 to 1848 he wrote the fashion column of *La presse*. After the Revolution of 1848, Villemessant established, in succession, three short-lived legitimist and reactionary newspapers. Then on 2 April 1854, he launched, with his sons-in-law, Gustave Bourdin and Jean Jouvin (1810–1886), *Le Figaro*, a weekly literary review. The immediate and continuing success of this paper provided Villemessant with a base from which he would originate or finance a large number of journals, including *La gazette de Paris*, *Le grand journal* (later renamed *Paris-magazine*; rival of Moïse Millaud's *Le petit journal*), *L'événement* (a nonpolitical daily at 10 centimes founded November 1865 and suspended 15 November 1866 for printing a political article), *Le petit Figaro* (founded in October 1867 after *Le Figaro*, which became a daily in November 1866, had changed from a literary to a political journal), and *Le diable à quatre* (launched to capitalize on the success of the first *La lanterne* of Henri Rochefort, which Villemessant had helped to finance).

Not himself a journalist so much as an administrator and businessman (he was an investor in Offenbach's first theater, the Bouffes Parisiens), Villemessant was notorious for his flamboyance, his propensity for lawsuits and duels (three in ten years), his political opportunism (although generally supposed to be a legitimist, on occasion he claimed Orleanist sympathies and, as a friend of Napoleon III's half-brother, August de Morny, often seemed to favor the Empire), and his hard way with writers. Villemessant was able to recognize and to attract to his journal an endless succession of talented men, but their tenure at his paper was usually brief. Although hated by many, especially on the Left, and frequently treated with contempt, *Le Figaro* appears increasingly in retrospect to have been a significant development in French journalism. Villemessant held control of it (except for several months following a notorious duel involving *Le Figaro* journalist Henri de Pène [1830–1888]) from 1854 until 1875. He died at Monte Carlo, 11 April 1879.

J. Castelnan, "Un grand journaliste du siècle dernier: Hippolyte de Villemessant," *Les oeuvres libres*, 15 May 1949; J. Goldorp, "Hippolyte de Villemessant, créateur du *Figaro*," *Ecrits Paris*, no. 266 (1968); J. Morienval, *Les créateurs de la grande presse en France: Emile de Girardin, H. de Villemessant, Moïse Millaud* (Paris, 1934); H. de Villemessant, *Mémoires d'un journaliste*, 6 vols. (Paris, 1872–1878).
Related entries: FIGARO; GIRARDIN; MILLAUD; *PETIT JOURNAL*.

VIOLLET-LE-DUC, EUGENE (1814–1879), architect and archaeologist, chiefly noted for his restorations of medieval buildings; born at Paris, 27 January 1814. His father was a government functionary who counted a number of architects among his relatives. After studying from 1830 to 1832 in the offices of the architect Achille Leclère (1785–1853), Viollet-le-Duc, who had become interested in medieval (Gothic) civil, religious, and military architecture, refused to enter the Ecole des Beaux-Arts (then under domination of the classicists), one of the very few architects of the day to do so. Instead, he studied Greek and

Roman art in Italy and Sicily (1836–1837) and then, at the suggestion of his father, traveled in southern France making an inventory of historical monuments. In 1839 he was employed by the newly formed Commission des Monuments Historiques (1837) to restore the abbey church at Vézelay (Burgundy). At the same time he was attached to the Service des Edifices Diocésains. From 1840 to the establishment of the Second Empire, Viollet-le-Duc immersed himself in medieval restorations: the Sainte Chapelle at Paris, first in collaboration with Jean Baptiste Lassus (1807–1857) under the supervision of Jacques Duban (1797–1870) and later alone; the abbey church at Vézelay and the Eglise Saint Pierre-sous-Vézelay; the churches of Saint Pierre and of Montréale (Yonne); the city halls of Saint-Antonin (Tarn-et-Garonne) and of Narbonne; and the churches of Poissy (Seine-et-Oise), Semur (Côte-d'Or), and Saint Michel at Carcassonne. Following a competition (1845), Viollet-le-Duc and Lassus were charged with the restoration of the Cathedral of Notre Dame at Paris and the construction of a new sacristy. When Lassus died in 1857, Viollet-le-Duc continued the work alone, designing the central spire and the great altar, as well as the treasury adjoining the cathedral. In 1846 he was chosen to restore the abbey church of Saint Denis. Earlier (April 1844) he had been appointed to reconstruct the walled city of Carcassonne. In 1849 he began work on the cathedral of Amiens and the *salle synodale* of Sens. During these years, Viollet-le-Duc became an expert on Gothic architecture and developed the theories that made him the leader of the French romantic rationalist school, which sought to merge the structural rationalism of Henri Labrouste with a sense of evolving historical style. Viollet-le-Duc thought that there had been a steady progress in structural efficiency from the Greeks through the Romans to the Gothic. For him, the Renaissance represented a backward step. It should therefore be leaped and an effort made to marry nineteenth-century materials and techniques to the Gothic. These theories Viollet-le-Duc expressed throughout his life in an impressive series of writings, notably his *Dictionnaire raisonné de l'architecture française du XIe au XVIe siècle* (10 vols., 1853–1869), *Essai sur l'architecture militaire au Moyen Age* (1854), and *Dictionnaire du mobilier français de l'époque carlovingienne à la Renaissance* (6 vols., 1858–1878).

On the proclamation of the Second Empire, Viollet-le-Duc quickly entered imperial circles. A friend of Princess Mathilde, and introduced to the court by Prosper Mérimée, he constituted a counterweight to the influence of the classical architect Hector Lefuel (1810–1881) and the eclectic Charles Garnier. He became a favorite of both Napoleon III and Eugènie, a frequent guest at the Château de Compiègne, and a close crony of the emperor in his military and archaeological pursuits, as well as a trusted adviser of the empress. It was in this capacity as a courtier that Viollet-le-Duc carried out such duties as the decoration of Notre Dame for the wedding of Napoleon III and Eugénie, the design of decorations for the imperial train, and the staging at Compiègne of the plays of which the empress was so fond.

From 1850 the tempo of work at Carcassonne accelerated as funds were made available. Restoration of the cathedral was completed in 1860, but work on the fortifications, begun in 1852, continued beyond Viollet-le-Duc's lifetime. In 1853 the architect was named one of three inspector generals of the Service des Edifices Diocésains. In this capacity, he continued his work on the basilica and funerary monuments of Saint Denis (which remained in his charge until his death) and conducted or supervised the restoration of Notre Dame de Châlons-sur-Marne and the cathedral of Laon. He was also architect of the diocesan buildings of Reims and of Amiens (1849–1874). In 1857, Viollet-le-Duc, at the request of the emperor and empress, undertook to restore the donjon of the ruined Château de Pierrefonds (near Compiègne) as a lodge. This accomplished (1858–1861), he began total reconstruction of the chateau as an imperial residence. The basic work was completed by 1866, but matters of detail would occupy him until his death, and some were never to be completed. In 1862 he restored the church of Saint Sernin (Toulouse) and in 1863 the Château Coucy. Throughout this period (1855–1874), he was involved as well in completion of the cathedral of Clermont-Ferrand.

The life of a courtier is not always a happy one, however. In 1861 Viollet-le-Duc entered the competition for architect of the new Paris Opéra. Although supported by Eugénie, he did not place; the prize went to Charles Garnier, who at one time had worked in the older architect's offices to earn needed money. Two years later Viollet-le-Duc was influential, together with Emilien Nieuwerkeke (1811–1892), then superintendent of fine arts, in obtaining a decree reorganizing the Académie des Beaux-Arts. The major purpose of the reform was to free the Ecole des Beaux-Arts from Academy control and to transform it into a true professional art school, offering for the first time basic instruction. To this end, three *ateliers* were assimilated into the Ecole (those of Alexandre Cabanel, Jean Léon Gérôme, and the realist Isidore Pils), and on 18 November 1863 Viollet-le-Duc was named professor of art history and aesthetics with commission to supervise and to reorganize the curriculum, giving it a sense of direction, making it more intellectually rigorous, and thus bringing it nearer to the predilections of romantic rationalism. The students, perceiving a heavy-handed government interference, reacted with a boisterous demonstration that so disrupted Viollet-le-Duc's inaugural lecture (29 January 1864) that he was hardly able to say a word. The lecture was never given; the architect was soon replaced by Hippolyte Taine; and the material that he had gathered for his courses became part of his *Entretiens sur l'architecture* (2 vols., Paris, 1863).

Despite these setbacks, Viollet-le-Duc lived a life of prodigious activity through the latter half of the Second Empire, continuing his restorations (to the list must be added the ramparts at Avignon, the Porte Saint André at Autun, the *capitole* at Toulouse, the Château d'Eu, and the cathedrals of Lausanne and of Reims), and his career as a watercolorist (he had won a first-class medal in 1855). In addition he collaborated with the journal *Le XIXe siècle*, as he had done since its founding (his uncle was the painter and art critic Etienne Jean Delécluze [1781–1863]), and taught courses at the Ecole Nationale de Dessin. Honors followed. His *Dictionnaire raisonné de l'architecture française* was awarded the Institute's prize in 1860 and 1861. Named to the Legion of Honor in 1849, he was promoted to officer on 30 July 1858 and to commander on 14 August 1869. He received in 1863 a gold medal from the Royal Institute of British Architects. But Viollet-de-Duc's fame rested on his reputation as an archaeologist and a theorist. He built little that was new: the Notre Dame sacristy, an apartment building on the rue de Liège (1846–1848), his own house on the rue Condorcet (1862), parish churches at Carcassonne (Saint Gimer, 1852) and Aillant-sur-Tholon (1865–1867), and the tomb of Auguste de Morny in Père Lachaise Cemetery (1865–1866). It may also have been Viollet-le-Duc who inspired Napoleon III to demand that the pavilions of the new central market (les Halles Centrales) be umbrellas of iron and glass. Certainly his influence was great and is reflected in such facts as the increase in the number of stained glass factories in France from 4 in 1836 to 150 in 1863.

The fall of the Second Empire constituted a decisive break in Viollet-le-Duc's career. During the siege of Paris, he commanded engineers and subsequently became an "advanced" republican, although his political career remained municipal in scope. Because of his reputation as a freethinker, he was constrained to resign from most of his diocesan responsibilities. Viollet-le-Duc died suddenly at his country house at Lausanne, Switzerland, 17 September 1879, and was buried without religious ceremony.

M. Bataille, "Viollet-le-Duc, jardinier des pierres," *Archeologia*, no. 6 (1965); P. Boudon, H. Damisch, and P. Deshayes, eds., *Analyse du 'Dictionnaire raisonné de l'architecture française du XIe au XVIe siècle' par E. Viollet-le-Duc* (Paris, 1978); P. Deshayes, "Viollet-le-Duc au Grand Palais," *Esprit*, 4 (1980); F.T. Harlow, "Viollet-le-Duc and the Preservation of National Patrimony," *Nineteenth Century* 6 (1980); B. Keating, "Viollet-le-Duc, the Maligned Restorer," *Horizon* 22 (1979); *MHF*, N.S., 2 (1965); N. Pevsner, *Ruskin and Viollet-le-Duc: Englishness and Frenchness in the Appreciation of Gothic Architecture* (London, 1970); D. D. Reiff, "Viollet-le-Duc and Historic Restoration: The West Portals of Notre Dame," *Journal of the Society of Architectural Historians* 30 (1971); I. Tagliaventi, *Viollet-le-Duc e la cultura archittonica del rivivals* (Bologna, 1976).

Related entries: COMPIEGNE; GARNIER; MERIMEE; PARIS, REBUILDING OF; VAILLANT.

VITICULTURE. See OIDIUM, PHYLLOXERA.

VUITRY, ADOLPHE (1813–1885), *conseiller d'état*, governor of the Bank of France, minister presiding the Conseil d'Etat (1864–1869), and senator; born at Sens, 31 March 1813, to a rich and cultivated bourgeois family. His father, Paul Julien Marin Vuitry (1786–1879), was a deputy and supporter of François Guizot (1787–1874) during the July Monarchy. Vuitry graduated from the Ecole Polytechnique as an engineer but then took a law degree and was briefly an *avocat* attached to the court of appeals at Paris. Soon afterward he entered Guizot's government as a subcabinet official in the Ministry of Justice and Cults before being named *maître des requêtes* in the Conseil d'Etat (1842). His report on communal administration (1850) won him attention, but in 1851 he briefly left the Conseil d'Etat to be under-secretary in the Ministry of Finance under his friend Achille Fould. Conservative in politics (although liberal in economics), an Orleanist at heart, and unsympathetic toward certain aspects of bonapartism, which he found too tainted with democracy and socialism, Vuitry nevertheless rallied to Louis Napoleon Bonaparte as a man of order and following the coup d'état of December 1851 accepted appointment on 25 January 1852 as one of the original *conseillers d'état* under the constitution of 1852.

Vuitry soon gave evidence of his independence when in June 1852 he joined seven other *conseillers* to oppose the decrees by which Louis Napoleon in January had confiscated property of the Orleans family in France. Although General Leroy de Saint-Arnaud would have removed all eight, including—reluctantly—Vuitry, Louis Napoleon refused, and the *conseiller's* disgrace was mild and short. In 1857 Vuitry was appointed to preside over the financial section of the Conseil d'Etat. The following year he joined with M. F. Esquirou de Parieu (1815–1893) and Gustave Louis A. V. Chaix d'Est-Ange (1800–1876) in supporting Michel Chevalier's opposition within the Conseil d'Etat to the proposed law of general security, which was to be submitted to the Corps Législatif following Felice Orsini's attempt on Napoleon III's life (the Conseil d'Etat sanctioned the law but by a vote of only 31 to 27, a majority of the *conseillers en service ordinaire* voting against). Despite this and Vuitry's election on 15 March 1862, with Orleanist support, to the Académie des Sciences Morales et Politiques, his loyalty to the emperor was never in doubt. In March 1863 he was named governor of the Bank of France. Shortly after, to permit his continued association with the Conseil d'Etat, he was appointed (15 May 1863) *conseiller d'état en service ordinaire hors section*. And on the promotion of his friend Eugène Rouher to minister of state, Vuitry became, on 18 October 1863, an honorary vice-president of the conseil. Together with the two other vice-presidents named on the occasion (Chaix d'Est-Ange and J.L.V.A. de Forcade La Roquette), Vuitry assisted Rouher in shepherding proposed legislation through the Corps Législatif and the Senate. Chiefly responsible for financial and commercial matters, he performed the task with skill but much preferred the role of functionary to that of politician. On 28 September 1864 he was named to replace Gustave Rouland as minister presiding the Conseil d'Etat (Rouland became governor of the Bank of France). That same year, Vuitry was appointed grand officer of the Legion of Honor (officer, 1858; commander, 1860).

Unlike Jules Baroche, who had dominated the Second Empire's Conseil d'Etat from its creation until June 1863, Vuitry considered himself to be above all a *conseiller d'état*, and although he accepted that the conseil should serve the emperor, he sought his ends not by bending the will of his fellow *conseillers* but by seeking conciliation through tact and freedom of discussion. He was, in fact, one of the very few men of top quality to have been recruited to the regime after the coup d'état. In November 1866 Napoleon III chose him to be part of the commission named to study army reform following Prussia's victory over Austria at Sadowa, and he expressed during the commission's deliberations grave misgivings concerning the emerging Niel law. Conservative in politics, Gallican in religion (he was himself an agnostic), Vuitry could nevertheless accept the movement of the regime toward parliamentarianism. The dismissal of Rouher following the elections of 1869 seemed, however, to present a good opportunity for retirement, and on 16 July 1869 he resigned from the Conseil d'Etat, of which he had been a member for twenty-seven years. Four days later, he was named to the Senate. The political career from which he had derived great honors, culminating in his appointment as grand cross of the Legion of Honor on 4 August 1867, was over, except for his membership of the Conseil Général of the Yonne. In 1869 one of his three daughters married Henri Germain (1824–1905), newly elected deputy and founder of the Crédit Lyonnais (Vuitry's wife was the daughter of Charles Wangel Bret, a Second Empire prefect and senator).

Vuitry was one of the most respected men of the Second Empire, notable for his ability, character, and integrity even among those whom recent research has shown not to have deserved the opprobrium to which they were long subjected under the Third Republic. Following the overthrow of the Empire, he devoted himself to writing on pre-Revolutionary French financial history and to his duties (from 1871) as president of the Paris-Lyons-Mediterranean Railroad. Vuitry died at Saint-Donain (Yonne), 23 June 1885.

L. Aucoc, *Discours prononcé aux funérailles de M. Vuitry* (Paris, 1885); A. Cucheval-Clarigny, *Notice sur la vie et les travaux de M. Aldolphe Vuitry* (Paris, 1887); A. de Foville, "Notice sur la vie et les travaux de M. Adolphe Vuitry," in *Ecole Polytechnique: Livre du centenaire* (Paris, 1897); A. Vuitry, *Rapports et discours* (Paris, 1887).

Related entries: BANKING; BAROCHE; BILLAULT; CONSEIL D'ETAT; FOULD; GOVERNMENT FINANCE; MAGNE; ROUHER.

W

WAGNER IN FRANCE. See *TANNHAUSER*.

WALEWSKI, COMTE ALEXANDRE (1810–1868), diplomat and politician; born at Walewice Castle (Poland), 4 May 1810, the illegitimate son of Napoleon I and Countess Marie Walewska. On the death of her husband, who had assumed paternity, Marie Walewska married Marshal Philippe d'Ornano, but, following her own death a short time later, Walewski was raised in Poland by his mother's brother. The boy studied at Geneva and Warsaw. Affected by romantic nationalism, he escaped from Poland to France, returning to participate in the uprising of 1830–1831 against Russian rule, during which he was sent to London by the revolutionary government in an attempt to gain diplomatic support for the Polish cause. Stranded and destitute following the collapse of the insurrection, Walewski emigrated to France where he lived with his stepfather, became a naturalized citizen (17 July 1833), and served in the French army in Algeria. In 1837, however, he went on the inactive list (he resigned from the army in 1841), returning to Paris to make his fortune, for by this time he had spent his inheritance.

In the late 1830s, Walewski failed to establish himself in politics, journalism, and the theater (he may have collaborated with Alexandre Dumas fils in writing *Mademoiselle de Belle-Isle* in 1839, and his five-act comedy, *L'école du monde ou la coquette sans savoir*, played with no great success at the Théâtre Français in January 1840). He came, however, under the patronage of Adolphe Thiers and in 1840 began a diplomatic career. His three-year liaison with the celebrated tragedienne Rachel (a son was born in November 1844) had just ended in March 1846 when Walewski was sent as French minister to Florence. There he met and married (in May 1846) Marianne (Marie Anne) Ricci, the daughter of a Polish *émigré* family of aristocratic (Poniatowski) background. This second marriage (Walewski's first wife, Caroline Montague, a daughter of the earl of Sandwich, had died in 1834), while it brought no great dowry, was to prove a very good one. On 28 February 1847 the young diplomat was sent to the tip of South America where the Argentine Confederation was just beginning to take shape. In September 1847 he returned to Paris, in time to experience the Revolution of 1848. That revolution revealed two significant characteristics of Walewski's attitude that differed from his earlier years: he favored conservatism over liberalism and established governments over revolutionary ones, especially if the latter were nationalist; and he had become of distinctly clerical inclination, with a disposition toward ultramontanism (the sovereignty of the pope).

This new orientation was amply demonstrated by Walewski's enthusiastic attachment to Louis Napoleon Bonaparte, the cousin whom he had met in London in May 1831 but whom he barely knew at the time of the latter's election as president of the Second Republic in December 1848. The sudden emergence of Louis Napoleon did much to make the fortune of a man who until then had remained a relatively obscure diplomat. Walewski was promoted in rapid succession through a series of diplomatic posts (minister to Tuscany, 26 January 1849; minister to Naples, 17 April 1850; ambassador to Spain, 20 February 1851). In June 1851, en route to Madrid, he exchanged posts with General Jacques Aupick (1789–1857), who had been the prince president's second choice (his first was Joseph, comte de Flahaut [1785–1870]) as ambassador to Britain. The Walewskis were successful at London, where Lord Palmerston was to be a lifelong friend of the young diplomat. When Louis Napoleon carried out his coup d'état on 2 December 1851, it was Walewski who persuaded the British government to accept the fait accompli. Already an ardent Anglophile, he played a significant role in negotiating the Crimean alliance between France and Britain, although he disapproved of Napoleon III's policy concerning the Holy Places and worked hard to avert the Crimean War.

Relations between Walewski and the foreign minister, Edouard Drouyn de Lhuys, had long been difficult. The ambassador had coveted the appointment that went to Drouyn de Lhuys in 1852, and by the beginning of 1854 a personal animosity had developed. On 8 May 1855 Walewski succeeded Drouyn de Lhuys at the Quai d'Orsay. His ministry was destined to be one of confusion and vacillation between the stronger and better managed ones that preceded and followed. Fundamentally, Walewski was at odds with Napoleon III, who desired to revise the Treaties of 1815 in France's favor at the particular expense of Russia and Austria. Although the foreign minister remained an Anglophile and devoted to Poland, his first duty was now to France, and he feared the consequences for his adopted country of a revolutionary policy, which he sought to counter with a conservative, pacific, and clerical one of his own. In essence, Walewski hoped to supplement the British alliance with a conservative one on the Continent, to prevent a French adventure in Italy, and to give unflagging support to the pope. He began his ministry by attempting unsuccessfully to break the British alliance (or at least to limit its restrictions on France) while the Crimean War was still in progress and by attempting (too quickly) to formulate an entente with Russia. Rebuffed in this effort (although he did succeed in bringing an end to the war after the fall of Sebastopol despite British objections and in reducing the influence of the British ambassador at Paris, Lord Cowley [1804–1884]), Walewski made a disastrous president of the Congress of Paris, where in a spectacular display of mismanagement he infuriated in turn the very powers (Prussia, Austria, and

Russia) he most sought to cultivate. Not only did he fail to alter Napoleon III's policy, but he was lampooned mercilessly, even by his own subordinates, for his ineptitude. Although named grand cross of the Legion of Honor on 3 March 1856, the foreign minister found himself thwarted in every instance by Napoleon III's anti-Austrian designs. Walewski was outflanked, reversed, or undermined by the emperor concerning the treaty guaranteeing the peace settlement of 1856 against Russia, the unification of the Danubian Principalities (Rumania), the *Cagliari* affair (Naples, June 1857 to August 1858), and, above all, the events leading up to the war with Austria in 1859, including the Plombières meeting of the French emperor and Sardinia's Count Benso di Cavour (held without Walewski's knowledge). These events combined with the Bolgrad question (1856–1857), the aftermath of Felice Orsini's January 1858 attempt on Napoleon III's life, and the emperor's assistance in 1859 to Ferdinand de Lesseps' Suez Canal Company to weaken seriously the Anglo-French alliance. Reflecting his uncertainty and impotence, Walewski issued vague, noncommittal, or contradictory instructions to his agents. Foreign diplomats at Paris complained about unsatisfactory interviews with him and began to bypass him in order to speak directly with Napoleon III. Torn between resigning on principle and persisting in office for its prestige, Walewski tendered his resignation on seven different occasions before it was at last accepted following publication at Paris in December 1859 of a semiofficial brochure, *Le pape et le congrès*, which called on the pope to give up his temporal power. On 4 January 1860 Walewski was succeeded by Edouard Thouvenel.

The Walewskis were never out of official favor, however. Marianne Walewski, who became Napoleon III's mistress in July 1857 following the tenure of Virginia di Castiglione (1837–1899), managed the situation with superb tact and even retained Eugénie's friendship. Walewski, too, was tactful, ignoring not only the liaison but continuing to pass over in silence the uncomfortable fact that he, not the emperor, was a son of Napoleon I. (Walewski discouraged all observations concerning his physical resemblance to the first Napoleon.) Nevertheless, while sincerely attached to each other, Napoleon III and Walewski were never really close, and the former foreign minister's advice was rarely heeded: to break relations with Russia and to aid the Poles in 1863; to adopt at once in 1866 a war or peace policy toward Prussia; to ally with Austria (Walewski was a close friend of Austria's ambassador at Paris, Prince Richard Metternich [1829–1895]); and, above all, to keep French troops indefinitely at Rome. On this last issue Walewski was one of ''Eugénie's clique,'' together with Pierre Magne, and Marshal Jacques Louis Randon, and he helped to bring about the dismissal of Thouvenel in October 1862.

Ironically Walewski's greatest influence was to come after his term at the Quai d'Orsay and in the area of domestic politics. Following his resignation, the former foreign minister was named to the Conseil Privé and on 24 November 1860 was appointed minister of state and of fine arts. In this capacity, he presided over the planning of the new Opéra, drafted the copyright law, and arranged the premiere in France of Richard Wagner's *Tannhäuser*. The change in the nature of the Ministry of State in June 1863 required Walewski's replacement by Adolphe Billault on 23 June. He returned to the Senate, to which he had been named on 26 April 1855, but the death of Auguste de Morny left vacant the presidency of the Corps Législatif. Relinquishing his Senate seat, Walewski was elected to the lower house from the Landes on 29 August 1865 and named president of that body on 1 September, even before the verification of powers had been completed. The new president by now had the reputation of a liberal. He had perhaps never ceased to be an Orleanist at heart and had certainly continued his friendship and contacts with Thiers. Together with Prosper de Chasseloup-Laubat, Walewski had, alone of all the ministers, supported Napoleon III's reform decree of November 1860. In April 1864 he advised the emperor to continue on the same path. In 1866 he tried without success to persuade Napoleon III to replace Eugène Rouher with Emile Ollivier, arguing that only Ollivier was capable of liberalizing the system and warning that if Rouher continued in office, the reforms announced in January 1867 would prove ineffective. Although the effort failed, Walewski did present his friend Ollivier to the emperor. Unfortunately, Walewski lacked the qualities necessary for a president of the Corps Législatif. He was easily outmaneuvered by Rouher, shouted down by the majority when he attempted to show impartiality toward the opposition, and forced to resign on 29 March 1867. Walewski had failed to obtain Ollivier's appointment as *rapporteur* of the promised new press law, but he did help to persuade Napoleon III the following year not to abandon that legislation. In the late summer of 1868, the Walewskis toured Germany. At a Strasbourg hotel on 27 September 1868, Walewski died of a massive heart attack.

It seems probable that Walewski's historical reputation has suffered from the attacks of his many enemies (including Victor Fialin Persigny, Rouher, Morny, and Achille Fould, whose financial reforms Walewski opposed in 1861), the vitriol of the gossips, and his own defects. He was ponderous, often pompous, ambitious, and opportunistic. But in the dearth of leadership that afflicted the Empire, Walewski had qualities to be valued: loyalty, honesty, moderation, common sense, and sound judgment. His advice would be missed in the years that remained to the Second Empire.

F. de Bernardy, *Alexandre Walewski, 1810–1868: Le fils polonais de Napoléon* (Paris, 1976), and ''Alexandre Walewski et la question italienne,'' *RHD* 90 (July–December 1976); J. R. Bloomfield, ''Count Walewski's Foreign Ministry, 1855–1860'' (Ph.D. diss., University of Pennsylvania, 1972); Comte d'Ornano, *La vie passionante du Comte Walewski, fils de Napoléon* (Paris, 1953); P. Poirson, *Walewski, fils de Napoléon* (Paris, 1943).

James R. Bloomfield

Related entries: ALLIANCE POLICY; BILLAULT; CHAMBERY; CONGRESS OF PARIS; CORPS LEGISLATIF; CRIMEAN WAR; DROUYN DE LHUYS; FOULD; GALLICANISM; ITALIAN CONFEDERATION; ITALIAN WAR; MINISTER OF STATE; MORNY; PRINCE NAPOLEON; NATION-

ALITIES; OLLIVIER; PERSIGNY; PLOMBIERES; POLISH QUESTION; RACHEL; REFORM; ROMAN QUESTION; ROUHER; RUMANIAN UNITY; THIERS; THOUVENEL; VAILLANT; VILLAFRANCA.

WINE. See OIDIUM, PHYLLOXERA.

WINTERHALTER, FRANCOIS XAVIER (1805–1873), portrait painter; born at Menzenschwand, Baden, 20 April 1805. Little is known of Winterhalter's early life except that he studied in Munich and Italy. The year of his birth and the spelling of his birthplace are in doubt. He arrived at Paris in 1834, showed in the Salon of 1835, and was commissioned to paint portraits of the royal family and the court of Louis Philippe, after making his reputation in 1837 with the painting *The Decameron*. He left for England in 1848 and returned to France in 1853 where he was once more welcomed with many commissions for portraits of the court ladies and the imperial family. His manner of painting and handling of the paint resulted in a considerable number of uninspired likenesses that seemed to concentrate primarily on imitating the luxurious fabrics of the sitter's costume. His portraits of the Empress Eugénie are more praiseworthy for their function as documents of the taste and fashions of the period than as major works of art. *The Empress Eugénie in Eighteenth-Century Costume* (1854, Estate of Germain Seligmann, New York) illustrates the empress' interest in reviving aspects of eighteenth-century court life. The empress is depicted in profile, set against an imaginary landscape, treated with the charm and delicacy of coloring of eighteenth-century French portraits, recalling the English portrait tradition as well. In fact, Théophile Gautier compared Winterhalter to Sir Thomas Lawrence. Equally concerned with representing the opulence of costume, the wealth of the sitters, and their status in a large-scale painting is Winterhalter's rendering of *The Empress Eugénie Surrounded by Her Ladies-in-Waiting* (1855, Musée National du Château, Compiègne), exhibited in the Salon of 1855, and owned by the empress. Although there is an attempt to present the figures as individuals with attention to particular facial features, the ladies all seem to share an expression of cloying sweetness. Winterhalter was named a member of the awards jury for the Salon of 1855. His long association with the imperial family and the court (he painted the Empress Eugénie at least nine times) brought him considerable recognition, although contemporary critics were unimpressed. He returned to Germany in 1870 and died at Frankfurt, 9 July 1873.

A. Dayot, "Winterhalter—painter to the Second Empire," *International Studio* 91 (October 1928); F. Wild, *Nekrologe und Verzeichnisse der Gemälde von Franz und Hermann Winterhalter* (Zurich, 1894).

Beverley Giblon

Related entry: COMPIEGNE.

WORKERS' CANDIDACY. See CANDIDATURE OUVRIERE.

WORKER'S PASSBOOK. See LIVRET D'OUVRIER.

WORKINGMEN'S INTERNATIONAL. See FIRST INTERNATIONAL.

WORLD'S FAIRS. See INTERNATIONAL EXPOSITIONS.

WORTH, CHARLES FREDERICK (1825–1895), dressmaker to Eugénie and to the high society of the Second Empire; founder of modern Parisian *haute-couture*; born in 1825 at Bourne, Lincolnshire. Because Worth's father, a solicitor, had lost his property through speculation, Worth had to leave school at eleven and seek work. At thirteen he was apprenticed for seven years to Swan and Edgar, retailers in Piccadilly. Fascinated by the Paris fashions he had studied in magazines, Worth went to the French capital in 1846 with no knowledge of the language and only 117 francs in his pocket. He was successful in finding a job at Gagelin and Opigez, a fashionable fabric retailer on the rue de Richelieu (at that time the center of Paris dressmaking). Although it was assumed that women would make dresses for women, Worth soon was creating costumes for his wife, a former Gagelin *demoiselle de magasin*, to model and was allowed to establish a dressmaking department. In 1851 his design for a dress train won first prize at the Crystal Palace Exposition at London. Ambitious and discontent with his position at Gagelin, Worth in 1858 accepted the offer of a wealthy Swedish friend, Otto Dobergh, to set him up in business at no. 7, rue de la Paix. Dobergh would manage the business affairs of the House of Worth until the end of the Second Empire.

Worth's shop on the rue de la Paix, which at first had some twenty employees, served a moderately well-off middle-class clientele, but the English dressmaker aspired to greater things. His opportunity came in 1860 when he persuaded Princess Pauline Metternich, wife of the newly appointed Austrian ambassador, to buy one of his gowns. Princess Pauline, a vivacious woman who once called herself "the best dressed monkey in Paris," was a friend of Empress Eugénie, who shortly after bought her first Worth creation, and from that moment the couturier's fortune was made. Soon he was director of Paris fashion, in demand by the *haute-monde* of France and Europe. After 1864 he made all of Eugénie's evening dresses (she was neither as extravagant nor as daring in matters of dress as legend would have it). By 1867 the Maison Worth employed some twelve hundred and was dressing nobility and royalty in France, Russia, Austria, Spain, and Italy (even Queen Victoria bought several gowns), as well as the wives of American millionaires. The material rewards were considerable. Worth acquired a house off the Champs Elysées and a villa at Suresne. As a young man, he had spent his leisure hours in museums and art galleries; now he was able to assemble an important art collection.

Worth's success had a more significant side. It was he who pioneered the use of fashion models (*mannequins*) and who created the modern fashion salon, elegant, decorated, and lit to simulate the conditions in which the dress would be worn. This innovation in marketing was his great achievement, although he boasted of having dethroned the crinoline, and it was he who created almost singlehandedly the fashionable aura that still clings to the rue de la Paix. Moreover, Worth's concern for materials (lace, lyons silk) undoubtedly had a major impact on several French industries. His sumptuous, extravagant designs (the simplest could cost 1,600 francs) reflected the taste of the era. Worth, who once designed and made a dinner gown for Mme. Octave Feuillet in one day, was considered by many to be a creative artist, a pretension insisted on by the couturier (who imposed his taste on his clients) and satirized by Emile Zola in the character M. Worms in *La curée*. Worth died at Paris, 12 March 1895. His two sons, Jean Philippe and Gaston, both naturalized Frenchmen, continued the business, whose premises Worth had converted into a military hospital during the siege of Paris, 1870–1871.

J. Jacquinot, "Au Musée Jaquemart-André: Constantin Guys, Nadar et Worth, animateurs de la vie parisienne," *JAA* 13 (1959); E. Saunders, *The Age of Worth, Couturier to the Empress Eugénie* (Bloomington, Ind., 1954); A. Trèves, "La vie parisienne au temps de Guys, Nadar, et Worth," *Peintre*, no. 194 (1959); J. P. Worth, *A Century of Fashion* (Boston, 1928).

Related entries: CRINOLINE; EUGENIE.

Z

ZOLA, EMILE (1840–1902), journalist, art critic, and naturalist novelist; born at Paris, 2 April 1840, of a French mother and a Venetian-born soldier and civil engineer, Francesco Zola. Shortly after his birth, the family moved to Aix-en-Provence where Francesco planned to build a municipal dam and a canal to distribute the water. On 28 March 1847, before the project was completed, Zola's father died suddenly, leaving Emile to be raised by his mother and grandmother. The family began a gradual but steady descent into poverty. Neither this nor frail health seems, however, to have prevented Zola from having a happy childhood at Aix. In February 1858 he joined his mother at Paris where she had gone to seek help from friends of her husband. Although Zola received a scholarship at the Lycée Saint Louis, he felt out of place and in the summer of 1859 twice failed his baccalaureate examination. This academic failure meant early and severe difficulties for the young provincial at Paris, since he had neither training nor connections for a good job. In order to support himself and his mother, Zola took a series of low-paying jobs and for a short time was a customs clerk. Quitting the latter job to be a writer, he lived in a Paris slum during 1861–1862. Then in early 1862, after eighteen months of unemployment, Zola's fortunes took a turn for the better when he became a clerk (in the shipping department) and subsequently director of advertising (*chef de publicité*) at the publishing house of Louis Hachette. That same year (31 October) he became a naturalized Frenchman.

The Hachette position was a turning point in Zola's life. There he came to know prominent writers and critics, including Edmond Duranty, Edmond About, and Hippolyte Taine. Taine's writings would soon have a profound influence on the development of Zola's thinking and on his literary values, shaping his naturalist philosophy and style, with its scientific empiricism and its search for the causes of events. From Zola's Hachette contacts also dates his career as a journalist. In 1864 and 1865 he contributed to *Le petit journal*, the *Revue française*, *La vie parisienne*, and Hippolyte de Villemessant's *Le Figaro*. In December 1864 Jules Hetzel (1814–1886) published Zola's first book, *Contes à Ninon*, a collection of romantic short stories. A first novel, *La confession de Claude*, appeared at the end of November 1865 and created so much notoriety for the author that he was given to understand by the new Hachette management (Louis Hachette had died in 1864) that he would be advised to devote himself full time to his novels. On 31 January 1866, Zola took up a new position as writer of a sort of literary gossip column for Villemessant's *L'événement* (founded in November 1865).

In the early 1860s Zola's friends were almost entirely young painters and sculptors in rebellion against the Académie des Beaux-Arts and its rules (his first contact with Edmond and Jules de Goncourt came in February 1865 and with Charles Augustin Sainte-Beuve in June 1865, while his close friendship with Gustave Flaubert could not have had its beginnings earlier than 1869). Paul Cézanne (1839–1906) was a childhood friend from Aix who, after a first visit in 1861, came to Paris in November 1862. Through Cézanne, Zola met Antoine Guillemet (1843–1918, a minor landscape painter), Camille Pissaro, Frédéric Bazille (1841–1870), and Claude Monet. At the Salon des Refusés in 1863, the writer was infuriated by the sneers of the crowd at such works as Edouard Manet's *Déjeuner sur l'herbe*. His sympathy grew when he was introduced in February 1866 to the group of artists who met at the Café Guerbois on Friday evenings. This Batignolles group, whose regulars in 1866 were Guillemet, Bazille, and Henri Fantin-Latour, would come to embrace most of the painters later to be called Impressionists. Zola found an affinity with their views (he had already, in the summer of 1865, published his famous definition: "A work of art is a corner of the universe viewed through a temperament") and grew concerned at rumors of the exclusion of the rebel painters from the Salon of 1866. Having obtained from Villemessant a commission to write about the Salon under the pseudonym Claude, Zola on 27 April 1866 published in *L'événement* a first article, attacking the judges by name even before the exhibition opened and demanding a new Salon des Refusés. In a fourth article (7 May), the critic defended Manet. It was too much, and Villemessant insisted that the series be completed in two more articles. But Zola had gained additional notoriety and a new lifelong friend, Manet, to whom Duranty and Guillemet now introduced him (Manet painted Zola's portrait in the winter of 1867, and they were close friends from 1868).

Zola was an anti-establishment rebel, and it was this rather than any socialist ideas that led him to republicanism and to a bitter hostility toward the Second Empire. His first book had been published by a republican, Hetzel, and he would write in the later 1860s for a variety of leftist opposition newspapers, including *Le rappel*, *Le globe*, *La tribune*, and *La cloche*. When *L'événement* was suppressed in November 1866 for printing a political article, Villemessant did not hire Zola to write for *Le Figaro*, now a daily newspaper. Another period of hardship began for the writer, which contributions to *Le Gaulois*, the *Revue contemporaine*, and *L'illustration* barely alleviated. In 1866 Zola published *Mes haines* (a collection of his criticism), *Mon salon*, and *Le voeu d'une morte*. The next year, in addition to a pamphlet on Manet and a potboiler written for the money (*Les mystères de Marseille*), he published (at Lacroix's, in November

1867) his first great novel, *Thérèse Raquin*. Although denounced as pornographic, the book soon went into a second edition, for which Zola in April 1868 wrote a preface justifying the work and explaining his naturalist viewpoint. At the end of 1864 or the beginning of 1865, the writer had begun a relationship with Gabrielle Alexandrine Meley, whom he married on 31 May 1870.

In the autumn of 1868, Zola had the idea of writing a series of novels that would take the form of the history of a family (the Rougon-Macquart) and would portray the social history of the Second Empire while developing the chief theory of naturalism—that human actions are determined by such material factors as physiology and milieu. Albert Lacroix (1834–1903) agreed to put Zola on a retainer in return for two volumes each year for five years. The first novel, *La fortune des Rougon*, was begun in May 1869. Its serialization commenced in *Le siècle* on 28 June 1870, but the outbreak of war with Prussia led to a temporary suspension on 10 August. In the meantime (May–July 1870) Zola wrote a second volume, *La curée*. The novelist had been one of the few to oppose the war hysteria that had gripped France in July 1870. Excused from military service because of myopia and his status as sole son of a widow, Zola, along with his mother and new wife, left Paris on 7 September and spent most of the war in Marseilles and Bordeaux. His attempt to obtain a position in the provisional government failed, and, after the armistice with the victorious Germans, he returned to Paris where he witnessed the Commune, reestablished his soaring literary career, played a memorable role in the Dreyfus affair, and died of asphyxiation from a faulty fireplace on 29 September 1902.

Zola's greatest fame as a writer was established during the Third Republic, but it was in the years of the Second Empire that his character was formed (hypersensitive, melancholic, hypochondriac, superstitious, misanthropic, ambitious, isolated), that his genius awakened, and that he conceived the great project that was to occupy him until the early 1890s, the twenty volumes of the Rougon-Macquart series.

C. Baker, "[Zola] républicain sous l'Empire," *CN* 26 (1980); C. B. Jennings, "Le troisième règne: Zola et la révolution Copernicienne en litérature," *RHLF* 80 (May 1980); I. N. Ebin, "Manet and Zola," *GBA* (June 1945); *Europe* (April–May 1968); I. M. Frandon, *La pensée politique de Zola* (Paris 1959); H. Guillemin, *Zola: Légende ou vérité?* new ed. (Paris, 1979); F. W. J. Hemmings, *The Life and Times of Emile Zola* (London, 1977), and *Zola* (New York, 1953); B. de Jouvenel, *Vie de Zola* (Paris, 1979); A. Lanoux and S. Lorenzi, *Zola ou la conscience humaine* (Paris, 1980); H. Mitterand, *Bibliographie chronologique et analytique (1859–1881)* (Paris, 1968), and "Un jeune homme de province à Paris: Emile Zola de 1858 à 1861," *CN*, no. 11 (1958); H. Mitterand and H. Suwala, *Emile Zola journaliste* (Paris, 1962); J. Rewald, *Cézanne et Zola* (Paris, 1936); J. Richardson, *Zola* (London, 1978); P. Walker, *Emile Zola* (London, 1968); E. Zola, *Oeuvres complètes*, ed. Maurice Le Blond, 50 vols. (Paris, 1927–1929), and *Correspondance d'Emile Zola* (1858–1872), 2 vols. (Montreal, 1978, 1980).

Eric A. Arnold, Jr.

Related entries: BERNARD; CHAMPFLEURY; MANET; POSITIVISM; PRESS REGIME; REPUBLICANISM; *LES ROUGON-MACQUART*; SALON DES REFUSES; TAINE.

Chronology of the French Second Empire

1852

POLITICAL/DIPLOMATIC/MILITARY

Installation of Louis Napoleon as president following coup d'état of 2 December 1851 (1/1)
New constitution signed, published in *Moniteur* (14-15/1)
Confiscation of Orleans property in France (22-23/1)
Electoral regime decreed (2/2)
Elections to Corps Législatif (29/2-1/3)
Oath of allegiance to Louis Napoleon prescribed (8/3)
Billault named president of Corps Législatif (22/3)
Powers of prefects increased (24/3)
End of martial law and of the period of dictatorship (27/3)
Legislative session begins (29/3)
Michelet and other professors dismissed for refusing oath (Mar.; others resign, 10/5)
Charlemagne affair in French dispute with Turkey over the Holy Places (Apr.)
First deportations to a new penal colony at Cayenne (Apr.)
Protocol of London, settling the succession in the Elbe Duchies (8/5)
Plot to assassinate Louis Napoleon (Reine Blanche) revealed (1/6)
Legislative session ends (28/6)
Law regulating election and organization of *conseils généraux* (7/7)
Amnesty of Thiers and of others exiled following coup d'état (8/8; proclaimed during first celebration of *fête de l'Empereur* in 39 years, 15/8)
Louis Napoleon tours central and southern France (14/9-16/10); speech at Bordeaux (9/10)
London conference on the Greek throne (20/10-20/11)
Senate submits proposal for restoration of the Empire to a plebiscite (7/11)
Plebiscite approves restoration of the Empire (21-22/11); extraordinary legislative session (25/11-3/12)
Troplong succeeds King Jérôme (resigned) as president of the Senate (Nov.)
Second Empire proclaimed; Louis Napoleon becomes Napoleon III (1-2/12)
Sénatus-consulte modifying the constitution in an imperial sense (25/12)

SOCIAL/ECONOMIC

Railroad concessions granted: Paris-Lyons (5/1), Dijon-Besançon (9/2), Paris-
  Cherbourg, Cette (Sète)-Bordeaux
Credits for a telegraph system authorized (6/1)
Railroad fusions authorized: with Compagnie du Nord (19/2); in center and west
  (27/3); of five companies (8/7)
Foundation laid for Crédit Foncier (28/2 and 28/3)
Decree regulating *monts de piété* (pawn shops) (24/3)
Establishment of an unemployment office at Paris (25/3)
Louis Napoleon inaugurates the Paris-Strasbourg railroad (July)
Concession of the Courrières mines (5/9)
Crédit Mobilier established (17-20/11)
Banque Foncière de Paris becomes Crédit Foncier (10/12)
Speculation by Pereire brothers on their Crédit Mobilier stock (Dec.)
Paris-Creil railroad inaugurated

PARIS

''New Louvre'' ordered completed within five years (26/3; work begins, May;
  cornerstone laid, 25/7)
Construction of Palais de l'Industrie authorized (30/3; work begun by Viel)
Cession of Bois de Boulogne to city of Paris (8/7; work begins)
Decision made to build Rues de Rennes and des Ecoles (July)
Levelling of Tour St. Jacques area authorized (July)
Chemin de Fer de Ceinture decreed (10/12)
Napoleon III inaugurates the Cirque Napoléon (11/12)
Completion of Rue de Rivoli across the Place de l'Oratoire decreed (Dec.)
Enlargement of Baltard's Halles Centrales project ordered; *mairie* of Montrouge built
Completed: Gare de Lyon, Gare Montparnasse, Rue Bonaparte

PUBLICATIONS

BLANC: *Histoire de la Révolution française*
COMTE: *Catéchisme positiviste*
DURY: *Histoire de la Grèce antique*; *Histoire de la France*
GAUTIER: *Emaux et camées*
HUGO: *Napoléon le Petit*
LAMARTINE: *Histoire de la Restauration*; *Graziella*
LITTRE: *Conservation, révolution et Positivisme*
MARX: *Le 18 Brumaire de Louis Napoléon*
MERIMEE: *Nouvelles*
NERVAL: *Lorely*; *Les illuminées*
PROUDHON: *La révolution sociale démontrée par le coup d'état du 2 décembre*
TURGENEV: *Récits d'un chasseur*
Librairies Plon and Larousse founded

JOURNALISM

Press regime decreed (17/2)
Government issues first *avertissement* (9/4)
Amnesty decree: *avertissements* cancelled (9/12)
Founding of *La revue contemporaine*

THEATER

AUGIER: *Diane* (Théâtre Français, 19/2)
BANVILLE: *Le feuilleton d'Aristophane* (Odéon, 26/12)
DUMAS FILS: *La dame aux camélias* (2/2); *Le régent Mustel*
LABICHE: *Le misanthrope et l'Auvergnat* (Palais Royal, 19/8)
MURGER: *Le bonhomme jadis* (Théâtre Français, 21/4)
PONSARD: *Ulysse* (Théâtre Français, 18/6; incidental music by Gounod)

PAINTING/SCULPTURE/PHOTOGRAPHY

BARYE: "Jaguar et lièvre"
GAVARNI: *Masques et visages* (lithographs; completed 1858)
RUDE: "Tombeau de Godefroy Cavaignac"

MUSIC

ADAM: *Si j'étais roi* (Théâtre Lyrique, 4/9); *Orfa* (Opéra, 29/12; ballet); *La poupée de Nuremberg* (Théâtre Lyrique, 21/2)
AUBER: *Marco Spada* (Opéra Comique, 21/12; debut of Caroline Duprez)
GOUNOD: Incidental music for Ponsard's *Ulysse* (18/6)
L. HALEVY: *Le Juif errant* (Opéra, 23/4)
Invention of piano accordion by Bouton

ACADEMIC

Montalembert and Alfred de Musset received at the Académie Française
Berryer elected to the Académie Française
Lycée reform, establishing *bifurcation* (10/5)
At Bibliothèque Impériale Léopold Delisle begins study of modern paleography

SCIENTIFIC/TECHNOLOGICAL

Foucault's pendulum experiment demonstrates motion of the earth; he invents the gyroscope
Photolitho book illustration specimens by N.B. Lerebour and Alfred Lemercier in *Lithophotographie*
Société Aérostatique de France founded
Charles Gerhardt pioneers atomic notation with his *New theory of organic compounds*

1853

POLITICAL/DIPLOMATIC/MILITARY

Russia, Austria and Prussia recognize the Empire (11/1)
Civil and religious marriage of Napoleon III and Eugénie (29-30/1)
Moniteur announces amnesty of 4312 political prisoners (1/2)
Opening of legislative session: Napoleon III announces reduction of 20,000 in army
    strength (14/2)
Menshikov arrives at Constantinople (28/2)
Napoleon III orders French fleet to Greece (19-20/3)
Report of government's commission on *colportage* (Apr.)
Menshikov delivers Russian ultimatum to Turkey (5/5); rejected (10/5)
Napoleon III offers Britain an alliance against Russia (24/5)
Closing of legislative session (28/5)
Napoleon III orders French fleet to sail toward Dardanelles (31/5)
British and French fleets ordered to Bessica Bay (2/6)
Ministry of police abolished (21/6)
Russian troops occupy Danubian Principalities (2-5/7)
Vienna Conference formulates Vienna Note (24-25/7)
Subjugation of Kabylia (Algeria) completed (July)
Russia accepts Vienna Note (3/8)
First celebration under the Empire of the *fête napoléonienne* (15/8)
Turkey modifies Vienna Note (19/8)
Nesselrode's "violent interpretation": Russia rejects Turkey's modifications of the
    Vienna Note (7/9)
British and French ships enter Dardanelles (14-15/9)
French fleet ordered to the Bosphorus (25/9)
France rejects "Buol Project" (28/9)
French occupy New Caledonia (Sept.)
Turkey declares war on Russia (5/10)
British and French fleets enter the Bosphorus (Oct.)
Russia declares war on Turkey (1/11)
Russians destroy Turkish fleet at Sinope (30/11)
British and French fleets at Constantinople (Nov.)
Vienna Conference adopts Vienna Protocol (5/12)
Palmerston resigns as British home secretary (14/12); resumes post (23/12)

SOCIAL/ECONOMIC

Concession of mines at Lens, Béthune and Noeux (15/1)
With aid of Crédit Mobilier Morny establishes Compagnie du Grand Central de France
    (Apr.)
Concession of Lyons-Geneva Railroad (May)
Government launches large-scale scheme for model housing for workers (May)
Law tripling capital of Comptoir d'Escompte and converting it into a private bank
    (10/6)
Mirès forms Caisse Générale des Chemins de Fer (1/7)

Concession of Paris-Mulhouse-Nancy Railroad (17/8)
Poor harvest, severe food shortage (Sept.)
Cholera at Paris (Oct.)
Free medical home care established for Paris poor (6/11)
Duties reduced on coal, iron and rails (22/11)
Caisse du Boulangerie established for Paris and region (27/12)
First nature reserve established, Forest of Fontainebleau
First electrical manufacturing company: Société Générale d'Electricité (Paris)
Silkworm disease reduces value of silk crop to about one-third
Continued decline in French oyster production

PARIS

Panthéon reconsecrated as Eglise Sainte Geneviève (2/1)
Haussmann named prefect of the Seine (23/6)
Napoleon III inaugurates Boulevard de Strasbourg (16/12)
Reconstruction of the Petit Point and of Pont Notre Dame
Construction of military prison, Rue de Cherche Midi
Beginning of restoration of Tour Saint Jacques
Place Saint Pierre de Montmartre laid out
Beginning of Construction of Rue des Ecoles
Completion of Rue Soufflot
Cirque National renamed Cirque de l'Impératrice

PUBLICATIONS

COUSIN: *Du vrai, du beau* (July)
GOBINEAU: *Essai sur l'inégalité des races humaines* (completed 1855)
HUGO: *Les châtiments*
LECONTE DE LISLE: *Poèmes antiques* (Mar.)
MIGNET: *Notices historiques* (Apr.)
MUSSET: *Comédies et proverbes; Histoire d'un merle blanc*
NERVAL: *Petits châteaux de Bohême*
SAND: *Les maîtres sonneurs* (Aug.)
TAINE: *Essai sur les fables de La Fontaine*
THIERRY: *La formation et les progrès du tiers-état* (Apr.)

JOURNALISM

Le mercure de France discontinues publication

THEATER

AUGIER: *Philiberte* (Gymnase, 19/3)
DUMAS FILS: *Diane de Lys* (Gymnase, 15/11)
PONSARD: *L'honneur et l'argent* (Odéon, 11/3)
SAND: *Mauprat* (Odéon, 28/11); *Molière; Le pressoir*

PAINTING/SCULPTURE/PHOTOGRAPHY

CHASSERIAU: "Le tepidarium"
GEROME: "Idylle"
HEBERT: "Le baiser de Judas"
MEISSONIER: "Le lecteur"
MILLET: "Moissoneurs"
NADAR opens his studio
RUDE: "Marshal Ney" (statue; unveiled 7/12)

MUSIC

ADAM: *Le sourd ou l'auberge pleine* (Opéra Comique, 2/2)
F. HALEVY: *Le nabab* (1/9)
OFFENBACH: *Pepito* (Variétés, 28/10)
THOMAS: *La tonelli* (Opéra Comique, 30/3)
VERDI: *Luisa Miller* (Opéra, 2/2)
First concert of Société des Jeunes Artistes du Conservatoire (20/2)

ACADEMIC

Reorganization of Conservatoire des Arts et Métiers (10/11)

SCIENTIFIC/TECHNOLOGICAL

Gerhardt synthesizes acetylsalicylic acid (but not in pure form)
Telegraph completed between Dover and Ostende

1854

POLITICAL/DIPLOMATIC/MILITARY

British and French fleets enter Black Sea (3-4/1); confine Russian ships to port (6/1)
Napoleon III writes Czar Nicholas, proposing peaceful solution (29/1); czar replies
    intransigently (9/2)
Vienna Protocol accepted by France, Britain, Prussia, Austria (9/4)
Allies demand immediate Russian withdrawal from Danubian Principalities (27/2)
Legislative session opens (2/3); authorizes 250 million franc war loan (3-11/3)
France and Britain declare war on Russia (27-28/3)
French and British occupy Athens and the Pireus (25/5)
Allied forces disembark at Varna (29/5)
Garde Impériale reestablished (May)
End of legislative session (1/6)
Austria demands Russia evacuate Principalities (3/6)
Billault replaces Persigny as minister of the interior (24/6)
Russia withdraws from Principalities (June-July)
Allied war council decides on Crimean campaign (18/7)

Britain accepts (29/7) the war aims (Four Points) negotiated in June by France and
    Austria; formalized (8/8)
British and French fleets take and destroy Bomarsund on Åland Islands (15/8)
Austrians occupy Principalities; Allies embark at Varna for Crimea (Aug.); disembark
    near Eupatoria (13-18/9)
Allied victory at the Alma (20/9)
Death of French field commander Marshal Saint-Arnaud (29/9)
Siege of Sebastopol begins (25-30/9)
Allied victory at Balaclava (25/10) and Inkermann (5/11)
Morny succeeds Billault as president of Corps Législatif (14/11)
Russia accepts Four Points as basis of negotiations (14/11)
Franco-Austrian-British treaty of alliance signed (2/12)
Faidherbe appointed governor of Senegal (16/12)
Franco-Austrian convention guarantees status quo in Italy during the war (22/12)
Corps Législatif begins its 1855 session (26/12)

SOCIAL/ECONOMIC

Franco-Belgian commercial treaty (21/2)
Compagnie de l'Est and Compagnie Paris-Lyons permitted to fuse with other railroad
    lines (20/4)
Abolition of *mort civile* (31/5)
First French agricultural competition (June)
Law renewing obligation of workers to carry *livrets* (22/6)
Law permitting private telegraph (22/6)
Government undertakes to give example of Sunday as a day of rest (July)
Government takes over Crédit Foncier (July)
As result of oïdium, duties on imported wines almost eliminated (30-31/8)
End of food shortages (Oct.)
500 million franc war loan voted (28/12)—first state loan to be issued direct to the
    public
Regular maritime service to Algeria inaugurated
Cholera epidemic

PARIS

Haussmann empowered to prepare plans for Paris sewage system; charges Belgrand
    with exploring sources of Paris water supply (Apr.); reports to Paris council (4/8)
Beginning of construction of Halles Centrales (May) and of decoration of Hôtel de
    Ville by Delacroix and Ingres
Decree authorizing clearance of area around Hôtel de Ville (29/7)
Lefuel named to direct construction of New Louvre (29/7)
Completion of Rue de Rivoli and construction of Boulevard du Centre (later
    Sebastopol) authorized (Sept.)
Municipal police reorganized (Sept.)
Macadam first used at Paris (Rue Bergère)
Alphand put in charge of transforming Bois de Boulogne (5/12)

Steeple of Sainte Chapelle restored
Reconstruction of Pont d'Austerlitz and restoration of Point Neuf
Reconstruction of Pont des Invalides begun (completed 1855)
Completion of Boulevard Mazas, Rues des Halles Centrales, des Arts, Asselin, Baran,
    Barque, Bachelet, Biron-Montmartre.
Founding of Société Zoologique d'Acclimatation
Completion of Eglises Saint Eugène, Sainte Cécile and Caserne du Prince Eugène
Enlargement of Rue de l'Oratorio

PUBLICATIONS

ABOUT: *La Grèce contemporaine*
ARAGO: Collected works (Apr.)
BERNARD: *Recherches expérimentelles sur le grand sympathique*
CHAMPFLEURY: *Les bourgeois de Molinchart*; *Contes d'automne* (May)
COMTE: *Système de politique positive* (completed)
GAUTIER: *Constantinople*
GOBINEAU: *Essai sur l'inégalité des races humaines* (completed)
GONCOURT: *Histoire de la société française pendant la Révolution*
MIGNET: *Charles-Quint* (June)
MUSSET: *Contes*
NERVAL: *Les chimères*; *Les filles du feu*; *Aurélia*
SAND: *Histoire de ma vie*; *Lucie*
JULES SIMON: *Le devoir*
VIOLLET-LE-DUC: *Essai sur l'architecture militaire du Moyen Age*
Félibrige founded by Mistral and others (21/5)
Decree opening credit for publication of correspondence of Napoleon I

JOURNALISM

First issue of weekly *Le Figaro* (2/4)
Girardin speaks in defense of freedom of the press (June)
Revue de Paris founded

THEATER

AUGIER: *Le gendre de M. Poirier*
DUMAS FILS: *La conscience* (Odéon, 4/11)
FEUILLET: *Péril en la demeure* (Gymnase, 8/3; and Théâtre Français, 19/4/55)
SAND: *Flaminio* (Gymnase, 13/10)
SARDOU: *La taverne des étudiants* (Odéon, 1/4)

PAINTING/SCULPTURE/PHOTOGRAPHY

CARPEAUX: "Hector imploring the gods" (statue)
COURBET: "La rencontre: Bonjour, M. Courbet"
DORE: Illustrations for Rabelais' collected works

MILLET: "Le glaneur"
Disderi patents small format photography (*cartes de visite*)

MUSIC

BERLIOZ: *L'enfance du Christ* (10/12)
GOUNOD: *La nonne sanglante* (Opéra, 18/10)
MEYERBEER: *L'étoile du Nord* (Opéra Comique, 16/2)
SAINT-SAENS: "Symphony no. 1 in E-flat major"
VERDI: *Il Trovatore* (Théâtre Italien, 23/12)
Académie Impériale de Musique placed under state subsidy and control (July)

ACADEMIC

Education law establishes *bifurcation* (14/6)
Claude Bernard elected to Académie des Sciences (26/6)
Dupanloup received at the Académie Française (Nov.)
Halévy elected perpetual secretary of Académie des Beaux-Arts
Silvestre de Sacy elected to Académie Française

SCIENTIFIC/TECHNOLOGICAL

Khedive of Egypt grants concession for Suez Canal (30/11); formally signed (19/5/55)
Telegraph opened between Paris and Bastia, Corsica (Nov.)
First industrial production of aluminum (by Sainte-Claire-Deville)
Berthelot synthesizes glycerine, lays basis of thermochemistry
Bernard discovers glycogenic function of liver and role of vasodilator nerves; chair
    created for him at Paris Faculty of Sciences

1855

POLITICAL/DIPLOMATIC/MILITARY

Sardinia enters war against Russia, signs military convention (26/1)
Rouher minister of public works, Magne finance minister (3/2)
Palmerston forms his government (6/2)
Napoleon III decides to go to the Crimea (Feb.)
Death of Czar Nicholas I (2/3)
Second Vienna Conference (15/3-4/6)
Law reorganizing military recruitment (*loi de la dotation*) (26/4)
End of legislative session (14/4)
Napoleon III and Eugénie on state visit to Britain (15-21/4)
Napoleon III abandons plan to go to the Crimea (26/4)
Attempt on Napoleon III's life by Pianori (28/4)
Napoleon III rejects counterpoise as solution to Black Sea Question, and Drouyn de
    Lhuys resigns as foreign minister (4/5); succeeded by Walewski (8/5)
Law on organization of local government gives more power to the executive (5/5)

Pélissier takes command of French forces in the Crimea (16/5)
Persigny named ambassador to Britain (May)
Failure of Allied assault on Sebastopol defenses (18/6)
Extraordinary legislative session begins (2/7); authorizes 750 million franc loan (9/7);
    adjourns (13/7)
Allied victory at the Tchernaya (16/8)
Queen Victoria and Prince Albert on state visit to France (18-27/8)
Disturbance at Trélazé (near Angers) (27/8)
Attempt on life of Napoleon III by Delmarre (8/9)
French take Malakov Fort, key to Sebastopol (8/9)
Russians destroy their fleet, evacuate Sebastopol (9/9)
Danes abrogate separate constitution for Schleswig-Holstein (2/10)
Buol-Bourqueney Memorandum (concerning peace terms) (14/11)
Napoleon III writes Queen Victoria, proposing a broadened war (22/11)
Kars falls to Russians after a long siege (26/11)
Contacts begin between Morny and Gorchakov (Nov.)
Victor Emmanuel of Sardinia and Cavour on state visit to France (Nov.); Napoleon III
    asks Cavour what he can do for Italy (Dec.)
Publication of brochure *D'une nécessité d'un congrès* (27/11)
Austrian ultimatum delivered at St. Petersburg (28/11)

SOCIAL/ECONOMIC

Compagnie Générale Maritime established (25/2)
Paris Compagnie Générale des Omnibus established (Mar.)
Concession of Paris-Lyons railroad line (7/4)
Trademark law (2/5)
Devastating floods from Bordeaux to Toulouse (June)
Railroad mergers authorized to create Compagnie de l'Ouest (June)
Grand Magasins du Louvre opens (9/7)
Poor harvest, rising prices; credit of 10 million francs opened for public works and
    relief (Sept.)
Crédit Mobilier prohibited from issuing stocks (Sept.)
Commission named to inquire into railroad accidents (Nov.)
Concession of Bruay and Marles mines (29/11)
Compagnie des Petites Voitures granted monopoly of *voitures de place* (Dec.)
Founding of Asiles de Vincennes and du Vesinet for workers convalescing after
    hospital
Cholera epidemic

PARIS

City commission authorizes Haussmann to prepare detailed plan for water supply
    (12/1)
Law on Paris public works (2/5)
International exposition at Paris (15/5-15/11)
City of Paris issues 60 million franc loan (14/6)—oversubscribed

Hôtel du Louvre completed (July)
Completion of Pont de l'Alma
Restoration of Eglise Saint Sulpice
Opening of Rue de Crimée
Sauvageot Collection purchased for the Louvre

PUBLICATIONS

ABOUT: *Tolla*
BARBEY D'AUREVILLY: *L'ensorcelée*
GRATRY: *Connaissance de Dieu*
JANET: *La famille*
LE PLAY: *Les ouvriers européens*
MERIMEE: *Mélanges historiques et littéraires*
NERVAL: *La bohême galante; La rêve et la vie* (helps launch Symbolism)
SAND: *Mont Revèche*
TAINE: *Voyage aux eaux des Pyrénées*

JOURNALISM

Clash between *Le siècle* and *L'Univers* (Apr.)
Montalembert and friends take over direction of *Le correspondant* (Oct.)
Foundation of *Journal du dimanche*, *Journal pour tous* (Hachette), and *Revue
  française*.

THEATER

AUGIER: *Ceinture dorée* (Gymnase, 3/2); *Le mariage d'Olympe* (Vaudeville, 17/7)
DUMAS FILS: *Le demimonde* (Gymnase, 29/3)
SCRIBE: *La czarina* (Théâtre Français, 15/1; last role created by Rachel)
Rachel's last Paris performance (23/7)
Adélaïde Ristori takes Paris by storm in S. Pellicos' *Francesca da Rimini*

PAINTING/SCULPTURE/PHOTOGRAPHY

BONHEUR: "La fenaison en Auvergne"
COURBET: "L'atelier"; Courbet opens a "Pavillon du Réalisme" for Paris world's
  fair

MUSIC

ADAM: *Le houzard de Berchini* (Opéra Comique, 17/10)
AUBER: *Jenny Bell* (Opéra Comique, 2/6)
BERLIOZ: *Te Deum* (Saint Eustache, 30/4)
GOUNOD: *Messe solenelle de Sainte Cecile* (Saint Eustache, 22/11)
L. HALEVY: *Jaguarita l'Indienne* (Théâtre Lyrique, 14/5)

OFFENBACH: *Le violoneux* (Bouffes Parisiens, 31/8; Paris debut of Hortense
   Schneider)
VERDI: *Les vêpres siciliennes* (Opera, 13/6)
Opening of Offenbach's Bouffes Parisiens theater (5/7)
Champfleury defends Wagner in article in *L'artiste*
Manuel Garcia invents laryngoscope

ACADEMIC

Berryer received at Académie Française (Feb.) and Sacy (28/6)
Duc de Broglie and Legouvé elected to Académie Française (1/13) and Ponsard (24/3)
Decree reorganizing the Institute ("Academic coup d'état") (14/4)
Taine publishes his first article in *Revue de l'instruction publique*

SCIENTIFIC/TECHNOLOGICAL

Napoleon III discreetly approves Lesseps' Suez project (Jan.)
Telegraph completed from London to the Crimea (Apr.)
International Statistical Congress meets at Paris, forms a commission to work for
   uniform system of weights and measures (Sept.)
Three French armored floating batteries engage in naval action (Kinburn, Crimea,
   16/10)
Berthelot synthesizes alcohol
Foucault experiments on induced currents
Hirn develops superheat (steam engine)
Leverrier begins publications in *Annales de l'Observatoire de Paris*

1856

POLITICAL/DIPLOMATIC/MILITARY

Napoleon III suggests a conference on Russian counterproposal to Austrian ultimatum
   (13/1)
Czar decides to accept the peace preliminaries proposed by Austria (15/1)
Britain accepts the peace preliminaries (29/1); they are signed (1/2)
Sultan issues reform decree concerning his Christian subjects (18/2)
Congress of Paris (25/2-16/4)
Judicial execution in China of a French missionary (29/2)
Beginning of legislative session (3/3)
Walewski proposes unification of Danubian Principalities (8/3)
Birth of Prince Imperial; all political *condamnés* amnestied on condition of accepting
   the regime (16/3)
Treaty of Paris signed (30/3)
Italy discussed at Congress of Paris (8/4); Clarendon's mediation proposal adopted
   (14/4); Declaration of Paris accepted (16/4)
Britain, France, Austria sign secret treaty guaranteeing treaty of Paris (15/4)
Napoleon III proposes an Anglo-French-Russian alliance (23/5)
Baptism of Prince Imperial (14/6)

End of legislative session (2/7)
Sénatus consulte establishes machinery for a regency (8/7)
Allies evacuate Crimea (12/7)
Morny named ambassador to Russia (July)
Trade treaty with Siam (15/8)
Failure of royalist coup at Neufchâtel; Napoleon III suggests a conference (Sept.)
5-power conference on Greece at London (Sept.)
Britain and France break relations with Naples (28/10)
Franco-Spanish boundary treaty (2/12)
Chinese burn European factories (14/12)
Conference on Bolgrad begins at Paris (31/12)
Austria decides to evacuate Danubian Principalities (Dec.)

SOCIAL/ECONOMIC

Creation of Réunion Finançière by the Rothschilds to oppose Crédit Mobilier (Jan.)
All *émissions finançières* suspended until end of year (9/3)
Corps Lègislatif adopts municipal tax on vehicles, systematizes earlier tariff reductions (May)
Floods in south and near Lyons (May); Napoleon III visits the area (June)
Government proposes ending all prohibitions in foreign trade but meets fierce resistance (June) and withdraws (Oct.)
Reform of legislation concerning commercial societies (26/7)
Poor harvest (Sept.)
Financial crisis (began in Germany Sept.) at height (6/10)
Crédit Mobilier creates railroad companies in northern Italy and Russia (Sept.); gains concession of Kaiser Franz Josef Orient Bahn (Oct.)
Napoleon III donates 100,000 francs to set up soup kitchens (7/11)
Inauguration of Maison Eugénie Napoléon (28/12)

PARIS

Napoleon III inaugurates Pont de l'Alma (2/4)
Creation of Pré-Catelan (29/6) and of Cascade de Longchamp, Bois de Boulogne
Construction of Eglise Saint Marcel
Demolition of the pompes Notre Dame
Construction of Prince Napoleon's Roman house, avenue Montaigne
Population of Paris 1,174,347
Opening of Grand Café Parisien; closing of Café de Paris

PUBLICATIONS

BANVILLE: *Les odelettes*
BAUDELAIRE: Vol. 1 of his translation of Poe, *Histoires extraordinaires*
FLAUBERT: *Mme Bovary* (Oct.)
GAUTIER: *Emaux et camées* (expanded edition)
HUGO: *Les contemplations* (Apr.; completed 1857)

JANIN: *Les petits bonheurs*
LABOULAYE: *Histoire politique des Etats Unis*
LAMARTINE: *Cours de littérature* (Mar.)
LAPRADE: *Symphonies*
LAROUSSE: *Nouveau dictionnaire de la langue française*
MICHELET: *L'oiseau* (Mar.)
JULES SIMON: *La religion naturelle*
TOCQUEVILLE: *L'Ancien Régime et la Révolution* (June)
TURGENEV: *Rudin*

JOURNALISM

First issue of Duranty's *Le Réalisme* (15/11); ends publication May 1857
Girardin sells *La presse* to Millaud for 825,000 francs (Dec.)
Revue critique d'histoire et de littérature founded

THEATER

BANVILLE: *Le beau Léandre* (Vaudeville, 27/9)
DUMAS FILS: *L'Orestie* (Porte Saint Martin, 5/1)
PONSARD: *La Bourse* (Odéon, 6/5)

PAINTING/SCULPTURE/PHOTOGRAPHY

INGRES: "La source"

MUSIC

DELIBES: *Deux sous de charbon* (Folies Nouvelles, 9/2; his first operetta); *Six demoiselles à marier* (Bouffes Parisiens, 12/11)
MASSE: *La Reine Topaze* (Théâtre Lyrique, 27/12)
OFFENBACH: *Les dragées de baptême* (Bouffes Parisiens, 12/6)
Léon Carvalho's first Théâtre Lyrique production (1/3)
First public performance of Debain's harmonichorde (18/3)
First concert of the Société des Jeunes Artistes (conductor, Pasdeloup, 7/12)

ACADEMIC

Received at the Académie Française: Legouvé (29/3), Duc de Broglie (3/4), Ponsard (4/12)
Elected to the Académie Française: Falloux and Biot (Apr.)
Berlioz elected to the Académie des Beaux-Arts (21/6)
Rouland named minister of public instruction (13/8)

SCIENTIFIC/TECHNOLOGICAL

Definitive firman of viceroy of Egypt conceding Suez enterprise to de Lesseps (5/1)

Patent law modifies regulations concerning *brevets d'invention* (31/5)
Pasteur develops germ theory of disease; becomes professor at University of Paris
Bessemer process patented
English chemistry student William Perkins accidentally invents world's first synthetic
　　dye (mauve) from coal tar
Neanderthal Man fossils found in Rhineland Germany; Broca upholds their uniqueness
　　vs. Virchow

1857

POLITICAL/DIPLOMATIC/MILITARY

Archbishop of Paris Sibour assassinated by a priest (3/1)
End of conference on Bolgrad (6/1)
Cour de Cassation rules that administrative authorization is required for distribution of
　　ballots (Jan.)
Flaubert prosecuted for *Madame Bovary* but acquitted (Jan.)
Legislative session begins (16/2)
Conference on Neufchâtel opens at Paris (5/3; ends 25/5)
Austria evacuates Danubian Principalities (Mar.)
Britain, France, U.S. agree to send plenipotentiaries to China (Mar.)
Beginning of Sepoy Mutiny against British in India (10/5)
Sénatus-consulte adds six new deputies to Corps Législatif (29/5)
End of legislative session and dissolution of Corps Législatif (29/5)
Corps Législatif elections (21-22/6)
Beginning of decisive Kabylia campaign in Algeria (May; ends in triumph July)
Beginning of *Cagliari* affair (25/6)
Government announces arrest of Tibaldi *et al.* (13/6) for plot to kill the emperor (28/6)
Morny returns as president of Corps Législatif after his embassy to Russia (July)
France, Sardinia, Russia, Prussia break relations with Turkey over Moldavian elections
　　(5-6/8)
Napoleon III and Eugénie on state visit to Britain (6-10/8; "Pact of Osborne")
Moldavian elections annulled (27/8)
British and French fleets blockade Canton (Aug.)
Napoleon III meets Alexander II at Stuttgart and, later, the German princes (26-28/9)
Divans of Danubian Principalities pronounce for union under a foreign prince (Oct.)
William becomes regent of Prussia for Frederick William IV (Oct.)
By-elections (22/11)
Corps Législatif meets to examine credentials of newly elected deputies (28/11;
　　adjourns 3/12)
Portuguese seize French ship *Charles-et-Georges* as a slaver (29/11; dispute resolved
　　25/10/58)
France calls on Sardinia to curb radical press (4/11; rebuffed)
Anglo-French forces take Canton (28-29/12)
Napoleon III offers passage through France to British troops en route to India (Dec.)
Faidherbe founds Dakar

SOCIAL/ECONOMIC

Subsidies granted to the three major transatlantic services (1/1)
Decree reorganizing the merchant marine (26/1)
Decree establishing a railroad network for Algeria (8/4)
Convention rationalizing railroad system (11/4)
Inauguration of Chemin de Fer du Midi (at Toulouse), linking Atlantic and
    Mediterranean (Bordeaux-Sète); and of railroads from Paris to Chaumont and
    Rennes (Apr.)
Law governing establishment of foreign companies in France (30/5)
Law extending privileges of Bank of France for 30 years (9/6)
Decree authorizing Chemin de Fer des Ardennes (10/6)
Franco-Russian trade treaty (14/6)
Laws on the Gascogne Landes; ratifying partition of Grand Central Railroad; fusing
    Paris-Lyons and Lyons-Marseilles lines; and projecting a secondary rail network
    (19/6)
Law establishing protection of trademarks and industrial patents (23/6)
Concessions granted to Compagnies du Chemin de Fer du Nord and de l'Ouest (26/6),
    and to Chemins de Fer Pyrénéens and Compagnie du Midi (1/8)
U.S. economic crisis reaches Europe (Aug.)
Convention with Denmark concerning Sound Dues (28/8)
Bank of France discount reaches 10% (Nov.)

PARIS

Longchamp race track inaugurated (26/4)
Inauguration of Vincennes Asile des Ouvriers Convalescents (31/7)
Napoleon III inaugurates New Louvre (14/8) and the Halles Centrales
Inauguration of Eglise Sainte Clotilde (30/11)
Châlons military camp established
Reconstruction of Pont Saint Michel
Disengagement of Palais des Thermes
Opening of Rues des Annelets, Ardennes, l'Arcade-Montmartre, and Cadran

PUBLICATIONS

ABOUT: *Germaine*; *Le roi des montagnes*
BANVILLE: *Odes funambulesques*
BAUDELAIRE: *Les fleurs du mal* (June); Baudelaire convicted of obscenity, 20/8; fine
    reduced on petition to the empress (Nov.)
BERANGER: *Dernières chansons*
CHAMPFLEURY: *La succession de Camus*; *Le Réalisme*
FLAUBERT: *La tentation de Sainte Antoine*
MICHELET: *L'insecte* (Oct.)
RENAN: *Etudes d'histoire religieuse*
THIERRY: *L'histoire des Gaulois*
VALLES: *L'argent*

JOURNALISM

La presse warned for publishing an article by George Sand offensive to the pope (Mar.)
Sainte-Beuve writes a defense of ''modern poetry'' (Oct.)
Monde illustré established
Semaine politique founded (5/7)

THEATER

BANVILLE: *Le cousin du roi* (Odéon, 11/4)
DUMAS FILS: *La question d'argent* (Gymnase, 31/1)
LABICHE: *L'affaire de la Rue de Lourcine* (Palais Royal, 26/5)

PAINTING/SCULPTURE/PHOTOGRAPHY

COURBET: ''Les demoiselles des bords de la Seine''
DAUBIGNY: ''Journée de printemps''
GEROME: ''Le duel de pierrot'' (begun; completed 1859)
MEISSONIER: ''L'amateur de tableaux''
MILLET: ''Les glaneuses''
TH. ROUSSEAU: ''Bords de la Loire''
VERNET: ''Daniel dans la fosse aux lions''
Delacroix begins decoration of Saint Sulpice (completed 1861)
Ferrier makes his first small photographic portraits (*cartes de visite*) at Nice

MUSIC

DELIBES: *Maître Griffard* (Théâtre Lyrique, 3/10; his first opera)
SAINT-SAENS becomes organist at La Madeleine (7/12)
THOMAS: *Psyché* (Opéra Comique); *Le Carnaval de Venise* (Opéra Comique, 9/12)

ACADEMIC

Received at the Académie Française: Biot (Feb.), Falloux (Mar.)

SCIENTIFIC/TECHNOLOGICAL

King Victor Emmanuel (Sardinia) inaugurates work on Mont Cenis tunnel (31/8)
Suez Canal project discussed at Constantinople (Dec.)
Marc Antoine Gaudin makes artificial sapphires
Invention of *papier à pâte de bois*
Foucault invents reflecting telescope with silvered mirror
Sainte Claire Deville prepares magnesium industrially
Pasteur proves lactic fermentation of milk is caused by living organisms
First French street (Rue Impériale, Lyons) lit permanently by electricity
Bernard begins ''modern'' investigation of glycogen production by the human liver

1858

POLITICAL/DIPLOMATIC/MILITARY

Anglo-French force enters Canton (5/1)
Attempt on Napoleon III's life by four Italians led by Orsini (14/1)
Opening of legislative session (18/1)
France demands curbs on press and refugees in Sardinia (20/1; refused)
Decree establishing martial law (27/1)
Decree establishing a Conseil Privé and provisions for a regency (1/2)
General security law presented to Corps Législatif (1/2); passed (19/2); promulgated
    (27/2)
General Espinasse named minister of interior, Boitelle minister of police (7/2)
Orsini writes Napoleon III (11/2); *Moniteur* publishes Orsini's letter (25/2)
Bernadette sees first vision at Lourdes (11/2); spring begins to flow (25/2); last
    appearance of the vision (16/7)
Candidates for election required to take the oath (17/2)
Orsini convicted (26/2), executed (13/3)
Republican demonstration suppressed at Châlons (9/3)
Pélissier replaces Persigny as French ambassador to Britain (Mar.)
Faidherbe launches expedition in the Cayor (Senegal) (Mar.)
Paris by-elections to Corps Législatif—Favre elected (25-26/4)
Picard elected, second round of by-elections (9-10/5)
End of legislative session (8/5)
Allies take Pei Ho forts and arrive at Tientsin (20/5)
Conference on Danubian Principalities meets at Paris (22/5; ends 16/8)
Moniteur announces suspension of general security law (25/5)
Delangle replaces Espinasse as minister of interior—end of state of emergency (14/6)
Ministry of Algeria created—Prince Napoleon minister (24/6)
Beginning of Mortara affair (24/6)
Franco-Chinese treaty of Tientsin (27/6)
Napoleon III and Cavour meet at Plombières (20/7)
Visit of Queen Victoria to Cherbourg (4-5/8)
Franco-Spanish expedition in Cochinchina (Sept.)
Prince Napoleon and Alexander meet at Warsaw (Sept.)
Moniteur chides those alarmed at the situation in Italy (Dec.) (*La presse* hints at war
    with Austria, 22/11)

SOCIAL/ECONOMIC

End of Crimean War tax (*décime de guerre*) (1/1)
Decree deregulating Paris butcheries (24/2)
Decree requiring charitable institutions to sell their property (May)
Crédit Mobilier fails to pay a dividend (May)
Government agrees for fifty years to guarantee return on investment in secondary
    railroad lines (June; law passed 11/6/59)
Inauguration of Grand Napoléon Docks and inner basin at Cherbourg and of Paris-
    Cherbourg Railroad (Aug.)

Expiration of suspension of tariffs on grain—*échelle mobile* not restored (30/9)

Completion of Pont de Culoz across the Rhone, linking France and Savoy (Sept.)

Franco-Japanese commercial treaty (9/10)

Foreign ships permitted for one year to transport food to Algeria (Oct.)

Contract labor system for blacks suspended by decree pending an inquiry (Oct.)

Commission of inquiry into silkworm disease appointed

Business paralyzed by rumors of war (end of year)

PARIS

Contract between government and City of Paris for construction of second *réseau* of streets (18/3; voted as a law, May)

Fontaine des Palmiers (Châtelet) moved (21/4)

Decree instituting Caisse des Travaux de Paris (14-19/11)

Decree permitting expropriated proprietors to keep the part of their property not incorporated in the public way (27/11)

Demolition of Pont au Change

Restoration of Eglise Saint Germain des Près

Construction begun: Ave. du Trocadéro (Mar.); Eglise Saint Bernard de la Chapelle (10/8); Pont Solférino; flèche of Notre Dame

Construction completed: Bd. de Sébastopol (inaugurated 5/4); Hôtel des Ventes (begun 1851); Eglise Saint Michel; Rues des Arts, Burcq, and Cretet

PUBLICATIONS

ABOUT: *Trente et quarante*

CHAMPFLEURY: *Les amoureux de Sainte Périne*

DAUDET: *Les amoureuses*

FEYDEAU: *Fanny*

FEUILLET: *Le roman d'un jeune homme pauvre*

GAUTIER: *Le roman de la momie*; *Poésies complètes*

GONCOURT: *Histoire de Marie Antoinette*; *Portraits intimes du 18e siècle*

GUIZOT: *Mémoires pour servir à l'histoire de mon temps* (first vol.; completed 1867)

JANET: *Histoire de la philosophie morale et politique*

LECONTE DE LISLE: *Poésies complètes*

MICHELET: *L'amour*

PREVOST-PARADOL: *De la liberté des cultes en France*

PROUDHON: *De la justice dans la Révolution et dans l'Eglise*

QUINET: *Histoire de mes idées*; *Oeuvres complètes*

SAND: *Elle et lui*

SEGUR (Comtesse): *Les petites filles modèles*

TAINE: *Essais de critique et d'histoire* (Mar.)

VAPEREAU: *Dictionnaire des contemporains* (first edition)

Government begins publication of correspondence of Napoleon I (Mar.)

JOURNALISM

Article of Prévost-Paradol in *Revue des deux mondes* on press in France and Britain (1/1)

Le reveil founded by Granier de Cassagnac (1/1)
Revue germanique et française founded (31/1)
Semaine politique becomes *Courrier du Dimanche* (9/5)
Eugène de Forcade editor of *Revue des deux mondes*' "Chronique" (May)
Patrie argues for freedom of press (June)
Montalembert tried (25/11) for article in *Le correspondant*; convicted, he is pardoned
    by Napoleon III (Dec.)
Baudelaire on "Le haschich," *Revue contemporaine*

THEATER

AUGIER: *Les lionnes pauvres* (Vaudeville, 22/5)
DUMAS FILS: *Le fils naturel* (Gymnase, 16/1)
LABICHE: *Un grain de café* (Palais Royal, 3/11)
SARDOU: *Séraphine* (Gymnase, 29/11)
Death of Rachel at 38 (3/1; funeral at Paris, 11/1)

PAINTING/SCULPTURE/PHOTOGRAPHY

GAVARNI: *Masques et visages* (lithographs; completed)
MANET: "Le buveur d'absinthe"
Boudin persuades Monet to paint from nature

MUSIC

BERLIOZ: *Les Troyens* (completed, Apr.)
FRANCK: *Messe solennelle*
GOUNOD: *Le médecin malgré lui* (Théâtre Lyrique, 15/11)
OFFENBACH: *Orphée aux enfers* (Bouffes Parisiens, 21/10)
Debut of Emma Livry in *La sylphide* (20/10)

ACADEMIC

Emile Augier elected to Académie Française (Jan.)
Claude Bernard gives his first lecture at Collège de France in his course on
    experimental method (16/10)

SCIENTIFIC/TECHNOLOGICAL

Compressed-air drill invented by Augustin Sommeiller (Jan.)
London-Constantinople telegraph completed (May)
De Lesseps forms Suez Canal Company (subscription opened 5-30/11)
Beginning of dispute between Pasteur and Pouchet regarding spontaneous generation
Invention of fuchsine dye by Verguin
Invention of *injecteur de vapeur* by Giffard
Bernard discovers function of vaso-constrictor nerves, publishes *Leçons sur la
    physiologie et la pathologie du système nerveux*

Ferdinand P.A. Carré invents mechanical absorption refrigerator, using liquid ammonia (patent 1859)

1859

POLITICAL/DIPLOMATIC/MILITARY

At New Year's reception Napoleon III regrets Franco-Austrian relations have deteriorated (1/1)
Franco-Sardinian alliance secretly signed at Turin (26-28/1; dated 16/12/58)
Prince Couza elected hospodar of Moldavia (17/1); of Wallachia (5/2)
Marriage of Prince Napoleon and Princess Clotilde at Turin (30/1); return to Paris (3/2)
Opening of legislative session (7/2)
French occupy Saigon (16-18/2)
Secret Franco-Russian treaty of alliance (3/3)
Russia proposes congress on Italy (16/3)
Chasseloup-Laubat replaces Prince Napoleon (resigned 8/3) as minister for Algeria (24/3)
Cavour accepts principle of general disarmament (18/4)
Austrian ultimatum to Sardinia (23/4)
Austrian troops cross the Ticino; Grand Duke of Tuscany overthrown (27/4)
Revolt in Parma (1/5)
France declares war on Austria (3/5)
Napoleon III leaves for Italy—Eugénie regent (10/5)
War loan of 500 million francs (May)
End of legislative session (27/5)
Battle of Magenta (4/6)
Napoleon III and Victor Emmanuel enter Milan (8/6)
Revolution in the Romagna (11/6)
Duke of Modena overthrown (15/6)
Revolt suppressed at Perugia (Umbria) (20/6)
Chinese violate treaty of Tientsin (21-25/6)
Battle of Solferino (24/6)
Prussia partially mobilizes (June)
Franco-Austrian armistice (6/7) and peace preliminaries (Villafranca, 11-12/7)
Cavour resigns (13/7)
Peace congress, Zurich (8/8-Sept.)
Victory parade, Paris, and amnesty (15/8)
Conference on Danubian Principalities meets at Paris (6/9)
Napoleon III agrees at Saint-Sauveur that Sardinia can have Parma (9/9)
Biarritz Memorandum (9/9)
Dupanloup's *Protestation* attacks Sardinia's annexation of the Romagna (30/9)
Napoleon III discusses military reform with his marshals (Oct.)
Britain and France prepare an expedition to China (Oct.)
Billault minister of interior (1/11)
Treaty of Zurich signed (10/11)
Britain agrees to Sardinian annexation of central Italy (25/11)

Publication of *Pape et le congrès* (22/12)
Napoleon III advises pope to cede the Romagna (31/12)
Proposed congress on Italy "postponed" (Dec.)

SOCIAL/ECONOMIC

Founding of Société Générale de Crédit Industriel et Commercial (May)
Napoleon III receives Cobden and Chevalier (27/10)
First adhesive postage-due stamp

PARIS

Decree establishing a floating debt for the city (6/1)
Law annexing banlieu to the city signed (6/6)
City commission approves plan for water supply and sewers (Mar.)
Labruste begins construction of new Bibliothèque Impériale (1/6)
Inauguration of Pont Solférino and Square Louvois (8/8)
Decree increasing powers of prefect of the Seine (10/10)
Completion of the great collector sewer
Completion of Rue Arago, Gare de Vincennes, and Asile du Pecq (for convalescents)
Reconstruction of Pont au Change begins
Rue de Magenta laid out
Opening of popular restaurant Le Petit Ramponneau

PUBLICATIONS

ABOUT: *La question romaine*
ERCKMANN-CHATRIAN: *Illustre Docteur Mathéus*
TH. GAUTIER: *Histoire de l'art dramatique en France*
GOBINEAU: *Trois ans en Asie*
GONCOURT: *L'art au XVIIIe siècle*
HUGO: *La légende des siècles* (first part)
LECONTE DE LISLE: *Le chemin de la croix*
LEVASSEUR: *Histoire des classes ouvrières en France*
MICHELET: *La femme*
MISTRAL: *Mireio* (2/2; translated as *Mireille*, 1861)
RENAN: *Essais de morale et de critique*
SAND: *L'homme de neige*
VACHEROT: *La démocratie*
Translation of Shakespeare by François Victor Hugo begun (18th and last vol., 1866)

JOURNALISM

Publication of *L'Empereur Napoléon III et l'Italie* (4/2)
Granier de Cassagnac abandons *Le reveil* (18/2)
Guéroult founds *L'opinion nationale* (1/9)
Publication of Montalembert's *Pie IX et la France en 1849 et 1859* (Oct.)

First issue of Vapereau's *L'année littéraire* (published through 1869)
Founding of *Paris journal*; *La femme*; *La revue européene*; *Gazette des beaux-arts*
Solar buys controlling interest in *La presse* for 750,000 francs
Baudelaire's "Salon de 1859" in *Revue française*

THEATER

ABOUT-SARCEY: *Risette* (Gymnase, 8/8)
AUGIER; *Un beau mariage* (Gymnase, 3/3)
DUMAS FILS: *Le père prodigue* (Gymnase, 30/11)
LABICHE: *Les petites mains* (Vaudeville, 28/11)
SARDOU: *Les gens nerveux* (Palais Royal, 4/11)
At Cirque Napoléon Jules Léotard performs first flying trapeze act (12/11)
Mlle Déjazet takes direction of Théâtre des Folies Nouvelles, which becomes Théâtre Déjazet
French tightrope walker Charles Blondin crosses Niagara Falls on a tightrope (30/6)

PAINTING/SCULPTURE/PHOTOGRAPHY

BOUDIN: "Pardon de Sainte Anne"
BRETON: "The recall of the gleaners"
COROT: "Macbeth"
GEROME: "Les gladiateurs"; "Mort de César"
INGRES: "Le bain turc" (begun; completed 1863)
MANET: "L'enfant aux cerises"
MEISSONIER: "Les bravi"
MILLET: "L'angélus"
PUVIS DE CHAVANNES: "Retour de chasse"
WHISTLER: "At the piano"

MUSIC

GLUCK-BERLIOZ: *Orféo ed Euridice* (Théâtre Lyrique, 19/11)
GOUNOD: *Faust* (Théâtre Lyrique, 19/3); "Ave Maria"
MEYERBEER: *Le pardon de Ploërmel* (Opéra Comique, 4/4)
Orphée aux enfers (OFFENBACH) removed after 228 performances (5/6)

ACADEMIC

Taine reads controversial paper on semitic races and monotheism to the Académie des Inscriptions (11/3)
Laprade received at the Académie Française (17/3)

SCIENTIFIC/TECHNOLOGICAL

Work begins on Suez Canal; founding of Port Saïd (25/4)
Napoleon III instructs his foreign minister to aid de Lesseps (3/11)

R. L. Gaston Planté constructs first practical storage-cell battery (of lead)

Anthropological Society founded at Paris

First high seas ironclad (wooden-hulled) warship, *La gloire*, launched (at Toulon, 24/12)

Steamroller, invented by Louis Lemoine (27/5), used in construction of Bois de Boulogne

Pasteur disproves theory of spontaneous generation, shows some microorganisms are anaerobic

1860

POLITICAL/DIPLOMATIC/MILITARY

Moniteur publishes Napoleon III's 31 Dec. letter to Pius IX and Pius IX's 1 Jan. allocution (11/1)

Walewski resigns (4/1); Thouvenel succeeds him as foreign minister (5/1; takes up duties, 24/1)

Cavour again Sardinian prime minister (16/1)

Britain proposes interim Italian solution (''Four Points'') (17/1)

Article in *Patrie* calls for annexation of Nice and Savoy (25/1)

L'Univers suppressed (29-39/1)

Reestablishment of *gouvernement général* of Algeria (10/2)

France claims Nice and Savoy (24/2; Sardinia agrees, on condition of a plebiscite, 3/3)

Opening of legislative session (1/3)

Plebiscites in Tuscany, the Romagna opt for annexation to Sardinia (11/3)

Switzerland appeals to signatories of 1815 concerning Chablais-Faucigny (19/3)

Treaty of cession of Nice-Savoy signed (24/3)

Gros and Elgin sail for China (26/4)

Anglo-French expedition reaches China (May; first battle, 12/8)

Garibaldi lands in Sicily (11/5; takes Palermo, 6/6; Messina, 26/7)

In Syria beginning of massacres of Maronites by the Druses (29/5)

Nice-Savoy transferred to France (14/6; following plebiscites, 12/6)

At Baden Napoleon III meets German princes (15-17/6)

Death of Jérôme Bonaparte (24/6)

Massacre of Christians at Damascus (9-11/7)

France proposes Anglo-French force prevent Garibaldi crossing the Straits (14/7; Britain declines)

France proposes a European force be sent to Syria (17/7)

End of legislative session (20/7)

Conference on Syria meets at Paris (26/7-3/8)

French troops land in Syria (Lebanon) (16/8; pacification complete, Nov.)

Garibaldi crosses Straits of Messina (18/8; enters Naples, 7/9)

Chambéry interview (28/8)

Sardinian troops invade Papal States (10-11/9; Castelfidaro, 18/9)

France recalls minister from Turin (12/9)

Napoleon III and Eugénie leave Paris for Algeria (15/9; back in Paris, 22/9)

Anglo-French take Taku forts (21/8; defeat Tartar army [China], 18 and 21/9)

Allies take Peking (12-15/10)

Warsaw meeting of Francis Joseph, Alexander II, William (20-27/10)

Second treaty of Tientsin (24-25/10)

Failure of Napoleon III to secure reform of French army (Oct.)

French fleet prevents Sardinian blockade of King Francis II (Naples) at Gaëta (Oct.); siege begins (3/11)

Plebiscites in Marches, Umbria (4-5/11; annexation proclaimed, Dec.)

Garibaldi and Victor Emmanuel enter Naples (7/11; Garibaldi to Caprera, 9/11)

Napoleon III reveals his reform plans to his ministers (22/11); publishes reform decree (24/11); ministerial changes (26/11)

Walewski replaces Fould as minister of state; Magne and Billault ministers without portfolio (23/11)

Pélissier named governor of Algeria (Nov.)

Decree adding wide cultural responsibility to Ministry of State (5/12)

Marseilles municipal elections (5/12; liberals protest irregularities)

SOCIAL/ECONOMIC

Napoleon III announces his economic policy in a letter to Fould (5/1; published in *Moniteur*, 15/1)

Cobden-Chevalier treaty signed (22/1; published, 23/1; effective, 1/10)

Government promises 40 million francs to industry to help in adjustment to new tariffs (Mar.; law adopted, 1/8)

Crédit Foncier authorized to loan to departments, communes, and *syndicats* (7/7)

Money tight throughout Europe (Oct.)

British subjects not required to have passports in France after 1/1/61 (16/12)

Concession of Cavin and Ostricourt mines (19/12)

First postal order

Bazar de l'Hôtel de Ville founded

Comptoir d'Escompte annexes Crédit Agricole

Creation of Conférences Populaires (Entrétiens) de la Rue de la Paix

France opens branch of Comptoir d'Escompte in Shanghai

PARIS

Extension of city limits effective (1/1); population 1,525,942

Scaffolding removed from Notre Dame's new flèche (Jan.)

Haussmann proposes tapping springs of Dhuis and Surmelin for Paris water supply (Apr.; accepted, 18/5)

Work begins on: Théâtre Impériale (Pl. du Châte.et), Bd. du Prince Eugène, Eglise Saint Augustin

Construction completed: Pont au Change and Fontaine Sainte Michel (inaugurated, 15/8), Eglise Saint Eugène (inaugurated, 20/12), Prince Napoleon's Maison Pompéienne (begun, 1856) on Ave. Montaigne, annex to Ecole des Beaux-Arts, Hôtel de la Paix (later, Grand Hôtel), and Rues Chardonnière, du Château des Rentiers, du Chemin des Dames, and des Cloys

Cour de Cassation rules on expropriations (12/6)

Cession of Bois de Vincennes to City of Paris (24/7)

New Opéra authorized (29/9; design competition opened, 29/11)
Jardin Zoologique d'Acclimatation (Bois de Boulogne) opened to public (9/10)
Haussmann given right to sit in Conseil d'État and (for consideration of Paris affairs)
   the Council of Ministers (22/12)
Enlargement of Théâtre Français
Restoration of Théâtre de la Porte Saint Martin
Bronze fountain placed at entrance to Grotte de la Fontaine Médicis, Palais du
   Luxembourg
Decree forbids organ grinders to play on Paris streets

PUBLICATIONS

BARBEY D'AUREVILLY: *Les prophètes du passé* (enl. ed.)
BAUDELAIRE: *Les paradis artificiels*
DURANTY: *Le malheur d'Henriette Gérard*
ERCKMANN-CHATRIAN: *Contes fantastiques*
GONCOURT: *Les hommes de lettres*; *Les maîtresses de Louis XV*
JANET: *Etudes sur la dialectique dans Platon et Hégel*
MENDES (CATULLE): *Le roman d'une nuit*
MONTALEMBERT: *Les moines d'Occident* (first vol.; completed 1877)
RENAN: *Mission de Phénicie*
SAINTE-BEUVE: *Port-Royal*
SAND: *Jean de la Roche*; *Flavie*; *Théâtre*
SEGUR: *Mémoires d'un âne*
TAINE: *La Fontaine et ses fables*
TURGENEV: *On the eve*
Circular of minister of education inviting formation of societies to establish public
   libraries (31/5)

JOURNALISM

Temporary relaxation in press restrictions by Persigny (11-20/12)
Duveyrier's brochure *L'Empereur François Joseph et l'Europe* (Dec.)
Champfleury's "La mascarade de la vie parisienne" (*Opinion nationale*; begun 1859)
   suspended on government orders
Laprade's "Pro aris et focis" (*Correspondant*)
Founding of *Le monde*; *Le tour du monde*; *La mode illustrée*; *La revue nationale*
Girardin's brochure *Le décret du 24 novembre* (Dec.)

THEATER

AUGIER: *L'aventurière* (Théâtre Français, 10/4)
DUMAS FILS: *L'envers d'une conspiration* (Vaudeville, 4/6); *La dame de Monsoreau*
   (Ambigu, 19/11)
FEUILLET: *Le cheveublanc* (Gymnase, 16/3); *La tentation* (Vaudeville, 19/3); *Ce qui
   plaît aux femmes* (Vaudeville, 30/7)

LABICHE: *La sensitive* (Palais Royal, 10/3); *Les deux timides* (Gymnase, 16/3); *Le voyage de M. Perrichon* (Gymnase, 10/9)
Léotard successful at Cirque de l'Impératrice

PAINTING/SCULPTURE/PHOTOGRAPHY

DEGAS: "Spartan boys and girls exercizing"
MANET: "Le guitariste"; "Portrait de M. et Mme Manet"

MUSIC

DONIZETTI: *Rita ou le mari battu* (Opéra Comique, 7/5)
GOUNOD: *Philémon et Baucis* (Théâtre Lyrique, 18/2)
OFFENBACH: *Le papillon* (Opéra, 26/11; with Emma Livry); gala performance of *Orphée aux enfers* at Théâtre des Italiens, Napoleon III attending (Apr.)
SAINT-SAENS: *Oratorio de Noël*
THOMAS: *Le roman d'Elvire* (Opéra Comique, 2/2)
WAGNER: Conducts concerts of his works at Théâtre des Italiens (25/1, 1/2, 8/2)

ACADEMIC

Lacordaire elected to Académie Française (2/2)

SCIENTIFIC/TECHNOLOGICAL

Weather bulletins from Britain sent via Paris to the Continent (1/9)
Napoleon III sponsors a biennial science prize of 20,000 francs (22/12)
Berthelot publishes *Chimie organique fondée sur la synthèse*
Lenoir develops an internal combustion engine using illuminating gas, but without compression (patented 24/1)
Lancereaux identifies diabetes as a pancreas disorder
Pasteur sterilizes milk at 125°C.
Great aquarium of the Jardin d'Acclimatation built
Founding of *La revue archéologique*

1861

POLITICAL/DIPLOMATIC/MILITARY

French defeat Annamites near Saigon (1/1)
William I becomes King of Prussia (2/1)
French fleet leaves Gaëta (19/1; city falls to Sardinians, 13-14/2)
Senate meets in extraordinary session (22/1)
Sénatus-consulte adopted establishing publicity of legislative debate (2/2)
France purchases a third of Monaco for 4 million francs (announced, 5/2)
Beginning of legislative session (4/2)
First volume of *Livres jaunes* (6/2)

Conference on Syria reconvened at Paris (19/2)

Mgr. Pie, Bishop of Poitier, in a pastoral letter compares Napoleon III to Pilate (27/2)

Organic decrees altering organization of Corps Législatif (3/2 and 28/2)

Debate on Rome begins in Senate (28/2) and in Corps Législatif (11/3; ends, 22/3)

Saigon province conquered (Feb.)

Prince Napoleon in Senate speech attacks papal temporal power (1/3)

Franco-Italian boundary treaty (6/3)

Senate defeats pro-papal amendment to Address, but 61 vote for it (7/3)

Emile Keller's pro-papal speech (13/3)

Ollivier announces his willingness to rally to a liberal Empire (14/3)

Kingdom of Italy established (14/3)

Paris conference extends French mandate in Syria to 5 June (15/3)

Body of Napoleon I placed in completed Invalides crypt (2/4)

Circular forbids priests to meddle in politics (11/4)

U.S. Civil War begins (12/4; North declares blockade, 19/4)

Decree on administrative decentralization (13/4)

Last French troops leave Syria (5/6)

Death of Cavour (6/6)

Constantinople conference signs convention establishing a new government for the
    Lebanon (9/6)

France declares neutrality in U.S. Civil War (10/6)

France recognizes Kingdom of Italy (24/6)

End of legislative session (27/6)

William I at Compiègne (6/10)

All charitable societies required to be authorized (18/10)

Anglo-Franco-Spanish convention on intervention in Mexico (31/10)

Trent incident (8/11)

General council of Society of Saint Vincent de Paul dissolved (Nov.)

Senate meets in special session to prepare financial reform (2/12)

France protests U.S. actions in *Trent* incident (3/12; reaches U.S., 25/12)

Death of Prince Albert (14/12)

French take citadel of Bien Hoa in Cochinchina (18/12)

U.S. decides to release Mason and Slidell, ending *Trent* affair (26/12)

Jauréguiberry replaces Faidherbe in Senegal (Dec.)

SOCIAL/ECONOMIC

Mirès arrested for speculation (17/2; sentenced, 11/7; conviction quashed on appeal,
    28/12)

Strasbourg-to-the-Rhine (Kehl) railroad inaugurated (6/4)

Compagnie Générale Maritime reorganized as Compagnie Générale Transatlantique
    (21/4)

Franco-Turkish commercial treaty (29/4)

Franco-Belgian commercial treaty (1/5)

Sliding scale (*échelle mobile*) of tariffs on grain imports abolished (15/6)

Bank of France monopoly of bank note issue extended for thirty years (19/6)

Network of secondary rail lines for France and a rail system for Algeria projected
    (June)

Napoleon III ends recruitment of "voluntary" black labor in Africa (1/7)

Fould writes Napoleon III a letter critical of government finances (29/9)

Poor harvest in France (Sept.); economic crisis threatens (Oct.)

Cobden-Chevalier treaty in full effect (1/10)

Publication of Tolain's letter calling for a workers' delegation to London world's fair in 1862 (17/10)

Napoleon III promises financial reforms, appoints Fould finance minister (announced, 15/11)

Decree requiring requests for extraordinary credits to go through finance minister (1/12); *sénatus-consulte* requiring legislative approval of extraordinary credits (31/12)

Completion of Canal du Midi (Languedoc), connecting Atlantic and Mediterranean

PARIS

Report by Haussmann on Paris water supply (4/5)

Napoleon III purchases Campana collection for the Louvre (11/5)

Garnier wins Opéra design competition (29/5; unanimously adopted, 2/6)

Bd. Malesherbes inaugurated by Napoleon III and Haussmann (13/8)

Excavations begin for Opéra (27/8)

Demolition of Pavillon de Flore

Establishment of a bd. on a vault covering the Canal St. Martin (Richard Lenoir)

Electric lights installed Place du Carrousel

Construction begun: Eglise de la Trinité

Construction completed: Parc Monceau (Jan.-Sept.), Eglise Russe, Eglise Saint Etienne du Mont (restored), Pont Saint Louis (replacing an existing bridge of same name), Passage Mirès, tomb of Napoleon I (Invalides)

PUBLICATIONS

BAUDELAIRE: Second edition of *Les fleurs du mal*

COUSIN: *Histoire générale de la philosophie*

DAUDET: *La double conversion*

DUCAMP: *L'homme au bracelet d'or*

ERCKMANN-CHATRIAN: *Maître Daniel Rock*

FEYDEAU: *Sylvie*

GONCOURT: *Soeur Philomène*

HOFFMANN: *Contes fantastiques*

MACE: *Histoire d'une bouchée de pain*

MICHELET: *Le mer*

QUINET: *Merlin l'enchanteur*

SAND: *Tamaris*; *Antonia*; *Le Marquis de Villemer*

SIMON: *L'ouvrière*

TURGENEV: *Une nichée de gentilshomme*

VEUILLOT: *Les libres penseurs*

JOURNALISM

Guéroult publishes brochure arguing for freedom of press

Baudelaire's "Richard Wagner et *Tannhäuser* à Paris," *Revue européen* (1/4)
Seizure in all bookstores of Duc d'Aumale's *Lettre sur l'histoire de France* (13/4)
Forcade criticizes government finances in *Revue des deux mondes* (Apr.; the journal is warned, Oct.)
Favre in Corps Législatif calls for freedom of the press (June)
Law modifying the press regime (2/7)
Napoleon III tells Girardin he'll never agree to freedom of the press (Dec.)
Founding of: *Revue fantaisiste* (15/2; Parnassian movement), *Le temps* (25/4; by Nefftzer), *Le travail* (22/12); *Le boulevard* (Carjat)

THEATER

ABOUT: *Un mariage à Paris* (Vaudeville, 5/7)
AUGIER: *Les effrontés* (Théâtre Français, 1/10)
LABICHE: *La poudre aux yeux* (Gymnase, 19/10)
MEILHAC: *La vertu de Célimène* (Gymnase, 1/5)
MUSSET: *On ne badine pas avec l'amour* (Théâtre Français, 18/11)
ST. REMY (MORNY): *M. Choufleuri restera chez lui* (Bouffes Parisiens, 14/9)
SARDOU: *Nos intimes* (Vaudeville, 16/11)

PAINTING/SCULPTURE/PHOTOGRAPHY

BAUDRY: "L'assassinat de Marat"
BOUGUEREAU: "La paix"
CARRIER-BELLEUSE: "Mme Marie Lauren"
COROT: "Orphée, le repos"
COURBET: "Combat de cerfs"
DAUBIGNY: "Le village"
DORE: Illustrations for Dante's *Inferno*
GEROME: "Portrait de Rachel"
MEISSONIER: "Solférino"; "Le peintre"
MILLET: "L'attente"
PUVIS DE CHAVANNES: "Bellum et concordia"

MUSIC

AUBER: *La Circassienne* (Opéra Comique, 2/2)
MEYERBEER: *Le prophète* (Opéra, 16/4)
OFFENBACH: *La chanson de Fortunio* (Bouffes Parisiens, 5/1)
First PASDELOUP concert (27/10)
WAGNER: *Tannhäuser* (Opéra, 13/3; withdrawn, 25/3)

ACADEMIC

Lacordaire received at the Académie Française (24/1)
Institute awards its 20,000-franc biannual prize to Thiers for his *Histoire du Consulat et de l'Empire* (29/5)

At Lyons Mlle J.V. Daubré becomes first woman *bachelière-ès-lettres* (18/8)
Laprade dismissed from Lyons University for poem published by *Le correspondant*
  25/4 attacking the government (14/12)

SCIENTIFIC/TECHNOLOGICAL

Ironclad warships *Solférino* and *Magenta* launched (June)
Pasteur continues work on anaerobic microbes, publishes *Mémoire sur les corpuscles
  organisés qui existent dans l'atmosphère*
Explanation of aphasia by Broca (*Remarques sur le siège de la faculté du langue
  articulé*)

1862

POLITICAL/DIPLOMATIC/MILITARY

French expeditionary force lands in Mexico at Vera Cruz (7/1)
Opening of legislative session (27/1)
Convention of Soledad (Mexico; 19/2)
In Senate Prince Napoleon and Pietri call for freedom of press and election (22/2;
  Napoleon III expresses his disapproval)
Corps Législatif rejects proposal of income for Palikao for his China services (28/2)
Franco-Prussian treaty of commerce, navigation, and copyright (29/3)
Spain and Britain opt out of Mexican intervention (Orizaba meeting, 9/4)
Japanese embassy received at Paris (13/4)
Franco-Spanish boundary treaty (14/4)
France declares war on government of Juarèz in Mexico (16/4)
Opening of London world's fair (1/5)
French defeated at Puebla, Mexico (5/5)
Three eastern provinces of Cochinchina ceded by Annam to France (3-5/6)
End of legislative session (27/6)
Napoleon III confers title of duke on Morny (July)
Liberal conferences of Rue de la Paix (Deschanel) suppressed (July)
Garibaldi, advancing on Rome, defeated by Italian army at Aspromonte (29/8)
General Forey and 2500 French troops land in Mexico (28/8)
Conference at Constantinople concerning Serbia (Aug.)
Italian foreign minister Durando claims Rome as capital of Italy (Durando Circular)
  (10/9)
Bismarck becomes president of Prussian Council of Ministers (23/9)
"Cabinet crisis": Thouvenel replaced by Drouyn de Lhuys as foreign minister
  (13-16/10)
France invites Britain and Russia to join her in mediating U.S. Civil War (30/10;
  Britain declines, 13/11)
LaValette replaced at Rome by La Tour d'Auvergne and Benedetti at Turin by Sartiges
  (Oct.)
Prince of Nagato (Japan) fires on English and French vessels (15-19/11)
Conference at London on succession to Greek throne and cession of Ionian Islands
  (4/12)

Drouyn de Lhuys rejects Bismarck's bid for an entente (25/12)
Opening of a national subscription for Lamartine
Henri Dunant's *Souvenirs de Solférino* lays foundations for International Red Cross

SOCIAL/ECONOMIC

Law enabling refunding of debt from 4-1/2% to 3% (8/2; conversion in Mar.)
Fould announces his financial program (24/2)
Workers' committee organized to choose delegation to London world's fair (Feb.;
    delegation leaves Paris, 19/7)
Strike of Paris typesetters (25/3; new strike in July; Napoleon III pardons strike
    leaders, 23/11)
Inauguration of Saint-Nazaire to Central America maritime service (14/4)
Mirès acquitted after new trial and released (21/4)
Decree setting rules of public accountability and permitting proposal of a *budget
    rectificatif* (31/5)
Franco-Prussian-Zollverein commercial treaty (2/8)
Three million francs made available for building secondary railroads (Aug.)
Concession of Liéven mines (15/9)
Cotton mills of Seine Inférieure begin to lay off workers (Sept.; "cotton famine" at its
    height, Oct.; public subscription for unemployed workers, Dec.)
Decree requiring authorization of mine mergers (23/10)
Napoleon III feted at Rothschild estate, Ferrières (16/12; event hailed as sign of return
    to financial orthodoxy)
Commission named to prepare a copyright law (28/12)
Fould requests supplementary credits, mostly for Mexican intervention (Dec.)
First section of Algerian railroad opened

PARIS

Chemin de Fer de Ceinture opened (14/7)
Cornerstone of Opéra laid (21/7)
Inauguration of Théâtre Impérial (Théâtre du Châtelet, 19/8); Théâtre de la Gaieté
    (3/9); Théâtre Lyrique (Théâtre de la Ville, 30/10); Théâtre des Folies Dramatiques
    (30/12)
Work begins on reservoir for waters from Dhuis and Surmelin (1/9)
Napoleon III inaugurates Bd. du Prince Eugène (7/12)
Notre Dame reconsecrated, following restoration (24/12)
Completion of new facade of Théâtre Français
Fontaine Médicis displaced and Luxembourg Orangerie destroyed to allow extension of
    Rue Soufflot
Rue Lafayette prolonged (for second time)
"La Grande Croisée" completed

PUBLICATIONS

ABOUT: *Homme à l'oreille cassé*; *Nez d'un notaire*; *Théâtre impossible*

DURANTY: *La canne de Mme Désireux*
ERCKMANN-CHATRIAN: *Le fou Yogof*
FLAUBERT: *Salammbô*
GONCOURT: *La femme au XVIIIe siècle*
HUGO: *Les misérables* (3/4; first instalment)
JANET: *La philosophie du bonheur*
LABOULAYE: *Les Etats Unis et la France*
LECONTE DE LISLE: *Poèmes barbares*
MICHELET: *La sorcière*
PREVOST-PARADOL: *Nouveaux essais de politique et de littérature*; *Quelques pages d'histoire contemporaine*
PROUDHON: *Théorie de l'impôt*
RENAN: *De la métaphysique et de son avenir*
ROCHEFORT: *Les petits mystères de l'Hôtel des Ventes*
THIERS: *Histoire du Consulat et de l'Empire* (20th and last volume)
TURGENEV: *Fathers and sons*
VILLIERS DE L'ISLE-ADAM: *Isis*

JOURNALISM

Le travail suppressed (2/3; replaced by *Le matin*)
First issue of Guéronnière's *La France* (8/8)
Girardin returns as chief editor of *La presse* (1/12)
Le temps brings unemployment in Rouen cotton mills to public attention (Dec.)
Marcellin founds *La vie parisienne*
Le Figaro publishes "Lettres de Junius" of Duchesne and Delvau

THEATER

ABOUT: *Gaetana* (Odéon, 2/1; republican demonstrations force withdrawal after four performances)
AUGIER: *Le fils de giboyer* (Théâtre Français, 1/12; anticlerical, it creates a furor but is popular)
DAUDET: *La dernière idole* (Odéon, 4/2)
LABICHE: *Les petits oiseaux* (Vaudeville, 1/4)
MEILHAC-HALEVY: *Les brébis de Panurge* (Vaudeville, 24/11)
SARDOU: *Le papillonne* (Théâtre Français, 11/4); *La perle noire* (Gymnase, 12/4); *Les ganaches* (Gymnase, 29/10)
Debut of Sarah Bernhardt at Théâtre Français (11/8)

PAINTING/SCULPTURE/PHOTOGRAPHY

CARPEAUX: "Ugolin et ses fils"
DORE: Illustration of Perrault's *Contes*
MANET: "Lola de Valence"; "La musique aux Tuileries"
MILLET: "The potato planters"
Campana collection (Musée Napoleon III) displayed at Palais de l'Industrie (1/5)

MUSIC

BERLIOZ: At Baden Baden conducts first performance of *Béatrice et Bénédict* (9/8)
F. DAVID: *Lalla-Roukh* (Opéra Comique, 12/5)
GOUNOD: *Le reine de Saba* (Opéra, 28/2)
OFFENBACH: *M. et Mme Denis* (Bouffes Parisiens, 11/1; gives up management of
   the Bouffes, Jan.)
Funeral of F. Halévy (24/3)
Inauguration of Concerts des Champs Elysées (May)
Debut of Galli-Marié at Opéra Comique (12/8) and of Adelina Patti at Théâtre Italien
   (17/11)
Emma Livry fatally burned during rehearsal at Opéra (19/11)

ACADEMIC

Renan appointed to chair of Hebrew, Collège de France (Jan.; suspended for calling
   Jesus "an incomparable man," 26/2)
Elected to Académie Française: Albert de Broglie (20/2), Dufaure (3/3)
Duruy, *inspecteur général* of education, introduces contemporary history into school
   curricula (Oct.)
Beginning of Paris public libraries
Thiers establishes at Académie Française a triennial prize of 3000 francs

SCIENTIFIC/TECHNOLOGICAL

Etienne Lenoir builds first motor car with an internal combustion engine (powered by
   illuminating gas, May)
Electric safety lamp exhibited by Dumas and Benoît (8/9)
Imperial Observatory issues first daily international meteorological bulletin (Nov.)
Berthelot synthesizes acetylene
Foucault measures speed of light
Bernard discovers role of vaso-motor nerves
Beau de Rochas invents four-cycle engine
French translation of Darwin: *De l'origine des espèces*
Reynaud's disease described by P. Edouard Reynaud
La Compagnie Parisienne Ancienne Maison Michaux et Cie, Paris, begins regular
   series production of bicycles

1863

POLITICAL/DIPLOMATIC/MILITARY

New electoral boundaries set (4/1)
France offers to mediate U.S. Civil War; proposes talks without an armistice (9/1;
   declined by the North, 6/2)
Beginning of legislative session (12/1)
Polish insurrection begins (22/1)

In *Moniteur* Napoleon III denounces land tenure practices in Algeria (22/1); announces his "Arab Kingdom" policy (6/2)

Alvensleben Convention announced (8/2); France asks Britain and Austria to join in protest (21/2; declined by Britain, 1/3)

Eugénie takes Austrian ambassador on a *vol d'oiseau* of map of Europe (21/2)

Convention regulating Franco-Spanish frontier (27/2)

Britain proposes collective note to Russia on Poland (6/3; delivered, 17/4, reply, 26/4)

Siege of Puebla, Mexico, begins (10/3; falls to the French, 18/5)

Prince William of Schleswig-Holstein named King George of Greece (30/3; confirmed by protocol of London, 5/6—Britain to cede Ionian Islands to Greece)

Sénatus-consulte establishing property in Algeria as collective right of the tribes promulgated (22/4)

Battle of Camerone, Mexico (30/4)

France suggests conference on Poland (4/5)

Corps Législatif dissolved (7/5); election campaign begins (10/5)

First round of elections (31/5-1/6)

Britain, France, Austria propose conference on Poland (17/6; second round of notes, 20/6; Russia rejects conference, 1/7)

Decree designating minister of state as sole spokesman for the government (23/6; cabinet remade—Billault minister of state)

Lee defeated at Gettysburg (1-3/7; Vicksburg surrenders to Grant, 4/7)

Anglo-French squadron bombards points in Japan (15-20/7)

Bazaine named to command of French forces in Mexico (16/7)

Cambodia becomes a French protectorate (11/8)

Roman Catholic congress, Malines, Belgium (19/8)

Final French note on Poland (Aug.)

Persigny made a duke (9/9)

Maximilian, pressed by Napoleon III (19/9), agrees to accept Mexican throne (3/10)

France takes possession of Loyalty Islands (24/9)

Unexpected death of Billault (13/10; state funeral, 17/10; Rouher minister of state, 18/10)

Geneva conference founds Red Cross (26/10)

Napoleon III proposes European congress (4/11; Britain declines, 25/11)

Legislative session opens (5/11)

Treaty of London cedes Ionian Islands to Greece (14/11)

Denmark adopts single constitution for entire realm (Nov.)

Thiers speaks for first time in Corps Législatif, which approves 300 million franc loan (24/12)

SOCIAL/ECONOMIC

Franco-Italian commercial treaty (17/1)

Boucicaut acquires full ownership of Bon Marché (31/1)

Government asks for five million francs to aid those suffering from "cotton famine" (Jan.)

Franco-Japanese convention (20/5)

Law on *sociétés anonymes* makes limited liability possible (23/5)

Decree freeing Paris bakery trade from government control (22/6)

Crédit Lyonnais founded (6/7)
Decree approving fusions with P.L.M. railroad (16/7)
Treaty abolishing Scheldt dues (16/7)
Corps Législatif approves 300 million franc loan (24/12)
Perrier Water introduced commercially by Source Perrier

PARIS

Te Deum celebrating reconsecration of Notre Dame (15/8)
New statue of Napoleon I (in costume of a Roman emperor) is placed on Vendôme
  Column (3/11)
First Grand Prix de Paris, at Longchamp
Construction begun: Gare du Nord, Marché du Temple (completed 1865), Asile Sainte
  Anne
Pont de Bercy replaced with a stone bridge
Creation of Parc des Buttes Chaumont
Completion of Rues Ferrus, Cabanis, Broussais

PUBLICATIONS

ABOUT: *Madelon*
CLARETIE: *Une drôlesse*
DUMAS PERE: *Madame de Chamblay*
ERCKMANN-CHATRIAN: *Madame Thérèse*
FEUILLET: *Histoire de Sybille*
FROMENTIN: *Dominique*
GAUTIER: *Le Capitaine Fracasse*
HOUSSAYE: *Les femmes du temps passé*
LITTRE: *Dictionnaire de la langue française* (first *livraison*); *Auguste Comte et la
  philosophie positive*
MICHELET: *Les femmes de la Révolution*
PROUDHON: *Du principe fédératif*
RENAN: *Vie de Jésus* (on sale 27/6)
SAND: *Mademoiselle de la Quintinie*
TAINE: *Histoire de la littérature française* (begun; completed 1869)
VERNE: *Cinq semaines en ballon*
Death of Vigny (Sept.)

JOURNALISM

First issue of Millaud's *Petit journal* (1/2) and of Aurélien Scholl's *Nain jaune* (16/5)
Founding of Villemessant's *Grand journal* (16/11), Nadar's *L'aéronaute*, and the
  Courrier français
First instalment in *Le Figaro* of Baudelaire's "Peintre de la vie moderne" (26/11)
In *Revue des deux mondes* Mazade calls for France to leave Mexico as soon as
  possible

THEATER

BANVILLE: *Diane au bois* (Odéon, 16/10)
FEUILLET: *Montjoye* (Gymnase, 24/10)
LABICHE: *Célimare le bien-aimé* (Palais Royal, 27/2); *Le commode de Victorine*
    (Palais Royal, 23/12)
SARDOU: *Les diables noirs* (Vaudeville, 28/11)

PAINTING/SCULPTURE/PHOTOGRAPHY

BOUGUEREAU: "Sainte Famille"
CARPEAUX: Bust of Princess Mathilde
COURBET: "Chasse au renard"
DORE: Illustrations for *Don Quixote*
MANET: "Mlle Victorine en costume d'Espada"; "Le déjeuner sur l'herbe";
    "Olympia"
MILLET: "Man with a hoe"
WHISTLER: "Symphony in white"
Opening of Salon des Refusés (15/5)
Death of Delacroix (13/8)

MUSIC

BERLIOZ: *Les Troyens* (part 2) (Théâtre Lyrique, 4/11)
BIZET: *Pêcheurs de perles* (Théâtre Lyrique, 30/9)
OFFENBACH: *Les bavards* (Bouffes Parisiens, 20/2)
VERDI: *Rigoletto* (Opéra, 24/12)
Thérésa hired at Café Moka as *chanteuse de chansonnettes*

ACADEMIC

Received at Académie Française: Albert de Broglie (26/2), Octave Feuillet (26/3)
Elected to Académie Française: Dufaure and Carné (23/4)
Duruy minister of public instruction (23/6); reestablishes study of philosophy in the
    lycées (June), introduces contemporary history (Aug.)
Decree reorganizing Ecole des Beaux-Arts (13/11)

SCIENTIFIC/TECHNOLOGICAL

Sommeiller's compressed air drill used in digging Mont Cenis tunnel (Jan.)
Turkey demands end of forced labor at Suez (6/4)
International conference (Paris) discusses U.S.-Europe telegraph cable (5/5)
Nadar founds Society for Encouragement of Heavier-than-Air Machines (July)
Lenoir drives his motor car through Paris at 4 mph (Sept.)
Nadar's balloon *Le géant* ascends with fourteen passengers (4/10)
Reorganization of French telegraph system (14/12)
First electric lighthouse, Cap de la Hève

First international postal congress (Paris)
Sphygmograph invented by M.E.J. Marey to study the pulse
First steamroller manufactured in series (by Gellerat et Cie, Paris)
First self-propelled submarine, *Le plongeur* (420-ton, compressed air) launched at Rochefort, but proves impracticable

1864

POLITICAL/DIPLOMATIC/MILITARY

Arrest of Greco and others for plotting to kill Napoleon III (3/1)
Thiers in Corps Législatif calls for "the four necessary liberties" (11/1)
Britain suggests Anglo-French intervention in German-Danish dispute and a conference (24/1)
Austro-Prussian-Danish War begins (1/2)
Tolain's "Manifeste des soixante" published in *L'opinion nationale* 17/2; launches idea of workers' candidacies
Archduke Maximilian at Paris (5/3)
France accepts a conference on Schleswig-Holstein (11/3; meets, 25/4; ends in failure, 22/6)
Carnot and Garnier-Pagès, republicans, elected at Paris in by-elections (20/3)
Rouher threatens to resign over France's Danish policy (1/4)
At Miramar Maximilian formally accepts Mexican throne (10/4; arrives Vera Cruz, 29/5)
Death of Pélissier (22/5)
End of legislative session (28/5)
Alabama sunk by *Kearsage* in duel off Cherbourg (19/6)
Les misérables, *Madame Bovary*, and other French novels on Index (20/6)
Danish War recommences (26/6, after armistice of 9/5; new armistice, 18/7)
Decree reorganizing government of Algeria (7/7)
Fall of Peking—virtual end of Taiping rebellion after fourteen years (18/7)
Trial of the *Treize* (July; convicted, Aug. and on appeal, 7/12)
Geneva conference on protection of war wounded (8/8; concludes 22/8 with formal establishment of Red Cross)
King of Spain visits France (16/8)
Death of Enfantin (31/8)
Liberal Catholic congress at Malines, Belgium (Aug.)
Sherman occupies Atlanta (1/9)
Western fleets attack Japanese forts, Strait of Shimonoseiki (4-6/9)
MacMahon governor of Algeria (8/9)
September Convention signed (15/9)
Vuitry president of Conseil d'Etat (27/9)
Benedetti ambassador to Prussia (4/10)
Treaty of Vienna signed, ending Danish War (30/10)
Lincoln reelected president of U.S. (8/11)
Italian chamber authorizes transfer of capital to Florence (19/11; riots at Turin)
Publication of papal encyclical *Quanta cura*, with *Syllabus of errors* attached (8/12)
Death of Mocquard (12/12)

Sherman enters Savannah (21/12)
Père Hyacinthe at the Madeleine

SOCIAL/ECONOMIC

Establishment of Comité des Forges (Feb.)
Corps Législatif votes law on *caisse des retraites* (Apr.)
Decree authorizing Société Générale (4/5)
Coalitions law voted (25/5)
Reforestation law (8/6)
Inauguration of Le Havre–N.Y. steamship service (15/6)
Franco-Japanese convention (20/6)
Franco-Swiss commercial and copyright treaty (30/6)
Strike of Paris book binders (June; successfully concluded, Sept.)
First Deauville "season" begins (15/8)   `
London meeting lays foundation of International Workingmen's Association (First
   International) (28/9; established in France by end of year)
Société Marseillaise de Crédit Industriel et Commercial founded (Sept.)
Financial crisis in Europe (Oct.); crops fail
Bank of France absorbs Banque de Savoie, despite Pereires' efforts (19/11)
Publication of Isaac Pereire's *La Banque de France et l'organisation du crédit en
   France* (Dec.)
Moniteur announces moratorium on loans (Dec.)
Lentil industry moves to Lorraine to escape pests
Bank of France issues 50-franc note

PARIS

Public foyer and staircase of honor inaugurated at Théâtre Français (16/3)
Solemn consecration of restored Notre Dame by Archbishop Darboy (20/5)
Napoleon III orders construction of New Hôtel Dieu begun (31/7)
Completion of: Tribunal de Commerce, Eglise Saint Augustin
Inauguration of Avenue de Saint-Cloud

PUBLICATIONS

ABOUT: *Le progrès*
BAUDELAIRE: "Petits poèmes en prose" (*L'artiste*); "Le spleen de Paris" (*Revue
   de Paris*)
COUSIN: *Histoire de philosophie*
DUMAS PERE: *Le San Félice*
ERCKMANN-CHATRIAN: *L'ami Fritz, Histoire d'un conscrit de 1813*
FUSTEL DE COULANGES: *La cité antique*
GONCOURT: *Renée Mauperin; Germinie Lacerteux*
JANIN: *Le matérialisme contemporain en Allemagne*
JOANNE: *Dictionnaire des communes de la France*
LABOULAYE: *Paris in America*

LE PLAY: *La réforme sociale*
MICHELET: *La Bible de l'humanité*
SAND: *Laure*
SEGUR (Comtesse de): *Les malheurs de Sophie*
TAINE: *Le Positivisme anglais: Etude sur Stuart Mill*
VERNE: *Voyage au centre de la terre*
VIGNY: *Les destinées* (posthumous; philosophical poem)
ZOLA: *Contes à Ninon* (Nov.; his first book)
Dialogue aux enfers entre Montesquieu et Machiavel (one of the sources of the later
    myth of the ''Protocols of Zion'')

JOURNALISM

First issue of *Journal illustré* (15/2)
Founding of: *Moniteur de la semaine*, *Journal politique*, *Moniteur du soir*, *Journal
    littéraire*, *Le globe* (Lockroy and Hippolyte Castille), *Rive gauche*, *Le
    contemporain*, *La vie parisienne* (Marcelin), *Le club* (Aurélien Scholl), *Lucifer*
Baron Brisse launches his ''chronique de la table,'' *Salle à manager*
Direction de la presse section of ministry of the interior suppressed (Nov.)

THEATER

AUGIER: *Maître Guérin* (Théâtre Français, 29/10)
BANVILLE: *Les fourberies de Nérine* (Vaudeville, 15/6)
BARBIER: *La fille maudite* (Ambigu, 25/6)
DUMAS FILS: *L'ami des femmes* (Gymnase, 5/3); *Les Mohicans de Paris* (Gaîté)
LABICHE: *La cagnotte* (Palais Royal, 22/2); *Moi* (Théâtre Français, 21/3)
SAND: *Le Marquis de Villemer* (Odéon, 29/2)
SARDOU: *Don Quichotte* (Gymnase, 25/7); *Les pommes du voisin* (Palais Royal,
    15/10); *Maison neuve* (Vaudeville, 3/12)
Decree permitting establishment of a theater without preliminary authorization (4/1)
Blondin at the Hippodrome

PAINTING/SCULPTURE/PHOTOGRAPHY

COROT: ''Souvenir de Mortefontaine''
DEGAS: ''Portrait de Manet''
FANTIN-LATOUR: ''L'hommage à Delacroix''
MANET: ''Episode d'un combat de taureaux''; ''Anges au tombeau du Christ''
MEISSONIER: ''L'Empereur Napoléon III à Solférino''; ''1814''
MILLET: ''La bergère et son troupeau''
MOREAU: ''Oedipe et le Sphinx''
NEUVILLE: ''Episode du combat de Magenta''
PUVIS DE CHAVANNES: ''Automne''
RODIN: ''L'homme au nez cassé''
ROUSSEAU: ''Chaumières sous les arbres''
Union Centrale des Beaux-Arts Appliqués à l'Industrie established (July)
Salon des Refusés repeated

MUSIC

GOUNOD: *Mireille* (Opéra, 19/3)
OFFENBACH: *La belle Hélène* (Variétés, 17/12)
Death of Meyerbeer at Paris (2/5)
Inauguration of the Athénée Musical (17/1; fails, 25/5)
Thérésa at the Alcazar

ACADEMIC

Students prevent Viollet-le-Duc from delivering his inaugural lecture at the Ecole des
    Beaux-Arts (29/1)
Received at the Académie Française: Carné (Feb.), Dufaure (7/4)
Duruy argues in a circular for free primary education (Feb.)
Opening at Sorbonne of free public evening courses (7/3)
Renan dismissed from Chair of Hebrew, Collège de France (11/6)
Taine named professor of art and esthetics at Ecole des Beaux-Arts (26/10)
Publication of Barbey d'Aurevilly's *Les quarante médaillons de l'Académie*

SCIENTIFIC/TECHNOLOGICAL

Commission chaired by Thouvenel named by Napoleon III to arbitrate dispute between
    Suez Canal Co. and Egypt (19/3; award announced, 6/7)
Convention signed for a telegraph cable Europe-South America (16/5)
Société d'Anthropologie de Paris accorded official recognition (21/6)
Martin open-hearth process for making steel developed
Pasteur invents "Pasteurization" (for wine; patented 11/4/65)
Lenoir receives world's first order for a motor car—from Czar Alexander II of Russia

1865

POLITICAL/DIPLOMATIC/MILITARY

Government forbids parts of *Quanta cura* to be read from pulpits (1/1; disobeyed by
    some bishops, 5/1)
Death of Proudhon (19/1)
Dupanloup publishes brochure explaining *Syllabus of errors* (Jan.)
Prince Napoleon named vice-president of Conseil Privé (Jan.)
Legislative session begins (15/2)
Publication of first instalment of Rogeard's "Les propos de Labiénus" (4/3;
    concluded, 18/3; Rogeard sentenced to jail and a fine, 25/3)
Death of Morny (10/3; state funeral, Père Lachaise, 13/3)
Ollivier in Corps Législatif speech moves toward the Empire (27/3)
La Valette minister of the interior (28/3)
General Lee surrenders at Appomatox Court House (9/4; news reaches Paris, 23/4)
Maximilian (Mexico) promulgates constitution (10/4)
Corps Législatif amendment to the Address (favoring temporal power) obtains 84 votes
    (13/4)

Sainte-Beuve named senator (30/4)
Napoleon III leaves France for Algeria; Eugénie regent (3/5; he returns, 10/6)
Prince Napoleon's Ajaccio speech (15/5; Napoleon III's reprimand published, 27/5;
    Prince Napoleon resigns his offices)
Ollivier talks with Napoleon III at the Tuileries (27/6)
End of legislative session (8/7)
Sénatus-consulte opens French citizenship to Algerian natives (14/7); Napoleon III
    talks of an ''Arab Kingdom'' (20/7)
Gastein Convention signed (14/8; France protests, 29/8)
Review of British fleet at Cherbourg and Brest (15-21/8; French fleet at Portsmouth,
    29/8-1/9)
Napoleon III urges a firmer policy on Maximilian (17/8), who orders guerillas shot,
    3/10; first executions, 16/10
Napoleon III ill at Châlons; stone diagnosed for first time (Aug.)
U.S. protests French intervention in Mexico (Aug.; demands withdrawal, Oct.)
Municipal council elections (Aug.)
''Nancy Program'' for decentralization (Aug.)
Walewski president of Corps Législatif (1/9)
Bismarck talks with Rouher and Drouyn de Lhuys at Paris (2/9), with Napoleon III at
    Biarritz (4-11/10; and again at Saint-Cloud, 3/11)
Death of Palmerston (18/10)
French evacuation of Rome begins—first stage (7/11)
Council of Ministers and Conseil d'État unanimously oppose granting right of
    interpellation (9/11)
Napoleon III publishes (Nov.) a letter to MacMahon of 20/6 calling for an ''Arab
    Kingdom''
Death of King Leopold, Belgium (10/12)
Riot by Paris Faculty of Medicine students (18/12) against expulsion of six students
    for their antireligious activities at student congress at Liège (Oct.)
France agrees to provide pope with a ''foreign legion'' for his defense (19/12; result
    will be ''Légion d'Antibes'')

SOCIAL/ECONOMIC

Paris bureau of First International established (Jan.)
World's fair at Paris decreed for 1867 (1/2)
Commercial treaties with: Sweden-Norway (14/2), Hanseatic cities (4/3), Mecklenburg
    (9/6), Spain (18/6), Netherlands (7/7)
Strike of Paris blacksmiths (May)
Legal recognition of bank check (14/6)
Strike of drivers of the Paris Compagnie des Petites Voitures (15/6)
Law concerning local railroads (*chemins de fer vicinaux*) (12/7)
Cholera at Marseilles (July) and Paris (22/9; at peak at Paris, Oct.; ends, Nov.)
Strike of Lyons construction workers (July)
Société Lyonnaise established (Sept.)
Congress of First International, London (Sept.)
Strike of 2000 Saint-Etienne velvet-makers (Oct.)
Decree requiring reduction of government expenditures (Nov.)

France proposes sanitary conference (Nov.)
Latin Monetary Union established (23/12)
Fould announces some of 1867's budget surplus will be used to amortize the debt
Le Printemps Department Store established
Investigation of Bank of France
Failure of Decazeville metallurgical firm
Phylloxera observed in southern France

PARIS

In three articles in *Journal des débats* Léon Say reveals Haussmann's financial
   methods (Jan.-Feb.)
In Corps Législatif Picard attacks Haussmann's *bons de délégations* (7/4; continues
   into June)
Grand Prix de Paris (Longchamp) won by French horse, "Gladiateur," earlier the
   victor at Epsom (11/6)
Law authorizing Paris to borrow 250 million francs for public works (12/7)
First water from the Dhuis reaches Paris (Oct.; reservoir constructed at Ménilmontant
   to hold it, 1863-1865)
Napoleon III authorizes reduction of Luxembourg Garden to permit construction of
   new streets (25/11; beginning of a public outcry)
First stamp auction, Hôtel Drouot (29/12)
Pont du Point du Jour begun (completed 1866)
Completion of *mairie* of 8th arrondissement
After driver's strike, Compagnie des Petites Voitures loses its monopoly
Publication begun of *Histoire générale de Paris*, a collection of original documents
Third of the "baths of Lutèce" discovered

PUBLICATIONS

ABOUT: *La vieille roche*
BARBEY D'AUREVILLY: *Un prêtre marié*
BAUDELAIRE: *Histoires grotesques et sérieuses* (trans. of Poe)
CHAMPFLEURY: *Histoire de la caricature antique*
ERCKMANN-CHATRIAN: *Waterloo*; *Histoire d'un homme du peuple*
GOBINEAU: *Les religions et les philosophes dans l'Asie Centrale*
LAROUSSE: *Grand dictionnaire universel du dix-neuvième siècle* (publication begun)
NAPOLEON III: *Histoire de Jules César* (preface published in *Moniteur*, 25/2; first
   volume on sale, 9/3)
PREVOST-PARADOL: *Etudes sur les moralistes français*
PROUDHON: *De la capacité politique des classes ouvrières*; *Du principe de l'art*
QUINET: *Histoire de la campagne*
SULLY-PRUDHOMME: *Stances et poèmes*
TAINE: *Philosophie de l'art* (completed 1869); *Nouveaux essais de critique et
   d'histoire*
TENOT: *La province en décembre 1851*
VERNE: *De la terre à la lune*
ZOLA: *La confession de Claude* (Nov.)

JOURNALISM

First issue of *L'avenir national* (2/1)
La rive gauche publishes "Les propos de Labiénus" (Mar.)
Founding of: *Candide* (May; Blanquiste); *Tribune ouvrière* (June; becomes *Presse ouvrière*, Aug., and *La fourmi*, Sept.); *L'événement* (Nov.; Villemessant); *L'art*; *Le soleil* (Millaud); *L'époque* (9/3; Feydeau); *La morale indépendante*
As regent Eugénie cancels all *avertissements* (June)
First issue of *Liberté* (15/7)
Avertissement to legitimist *Gazette de France* (Oct.)
La revue germanique becomes *La revue moderne*
First daily newspaper on economic affairs, *Le messager de Paris*

THEATER

BANVILLE: *La pomme* (Théâtre Français, 30/6; great success)
DUMAS FILS - E. de GIRARDIN: *Le supplice d'une femme* (Théâtre Français, 29/4)
FEUILLET: *La belle au bois dormant* (Vaudeville, 17/2)
FEVAL: *Jean qui rit* (Vaudeville, 25/3)
FEYDEAU: *Monsieur de Saint Bertrand* (Vaudeville, 25/4)
GIRARDIN: *Les deux soeurs* (Vaudeville, 12/8)
GONCOURT: *Henriette Maréchal* (Théâtre Français, 5/12; backed by Princess Mathilde; student demonstrations force its withdrawal, Dec.)
MUSSET: *Carmosine* (Odéon, 7/11)
SARDOU: *Les vieux garçons* (Gymnase, 2/1); *La famille Benoiton* (Vaudeville, 4/11)
Demolition of Théâtre des Folies Dramatiques

PAINTING/SCULPTURE/PHOTOGRAPHY

CABANEL: "Portrait de Napoléon III"
COURBET: "Proudhon et sa famille"
DORE: Illustrations for the Bible (Tours edition)
MEISSONIER: "Les cuirassiers de la Garde à Friedland"
MOREAU: "Le jeune homme et la mort"; "Jason"
PUVIS DE CHAVANNES: "Ave Picardia nutrix"
Eugénie signs decree naming Rosa Bonheur to Legion of Honor (8/6)
Laboulaye launches proposal which will later result in gift to U.S. of the Statue of Liberty
Exposition of works of Hippolyte Flandrin

MUSIC

MEYERBEER: *L'Africaine* (Opéra, 28/4)
OFFENBACH: *Jeanne qui pleure et Jean qui rit* (Bouffes Parisiens, 3/11)
VERDI: *Macbeth* (Théâtre Lyrique, 21/4; Paris version)
Opening of café-concert Ba-ta-clan

ACADEMIC

In throne speech Napoleon III announces intention to generalize primary education
  (15/2; *Moniteur* publishes Duruy's plan, 6/3; rejected by Conseil d'État, 8/3)
Prévost-Paradol elected to Académie Française (7/4)
Founding of Ecole Centrale d'Architecture

SCIENTIFIC/TECHNOLOGICAL

Inauguration of Paris-Lyons line for facsimile transmission by telegraph (*télégraphe
  autographique*) (16/2)
Britain-to-Bombay telegraph inaugurated (1/3)
First international telegraph conference (Mar.; at Paris, sixteen states, but not Britain;
  accord signed, May)
Berthelot invents the calorimètre
Claude Bernard, *Introduction à la médecine expérimentale*
Berthelot, *Leçons sur la thermochimie*
Marey analyzes cardiac and respiratory rhythms
Pasteur cures silkworm disease, saves French silk industry
Flammarion (astronomer), *Les mondes imaginaires et les mondes réels*

1866

POLITICAL/DIPLOMATIC/MILITARY

Opening of legislative session; Napoleon III announces decision to leave Mexico
  (22/1)
Cuza overthrown in Danubian Principalities (22-23/2); France proposes a conference at
  Paris (27/2; meets, 10/3; ends, 25/6)
Council of Ministers and Conseil Privé again reject further reform (7 and 11/3)
Britain (9/3) and Austria (16/3) reject French plan to exchange Danubian Principalities
  for Venetia
Amendment des quarante-cinq, calling for further reform, moved by Ollivier (17/3;
  defeated, 19/3)
Napoleon III encourages Italy to ally with Prussia (21/3; signed, 8/4)
Napoleon III abandons idea of an "Arab Kingdom" of Algeria (Mar.)
France announces 3-stage withdrawal from Mexico: Nov. 1866, Mar. and Nov. 1867
  (5/4; changed to one-stage [Mar. 1867], Dec.)
Divans elect Charles of Hohenzollern-Sigmaringen hospodar of Danubian Principalities
  (20/4; appears at Bucharest, 22/5; recognized by sultan, 24/10)
Thiers calls for resisting German unity (3/5; Rouher declares French neutrality,
  reaffirmed by letter of Napoleon III, 11/6)
Italy declines to pledge neutrality in return for Venetia (5-6/5)
At Auxerre Napoleon III attacks treaties of 1815 (6/5)
France proposes congress on German question (8/5; invitations, 24/5; rejected by
  Austria, 3/6)
Franco-Austrian treaty exchanging French neutrality for Venetia (to Italy) (12/6)
Prussia and Italy declare war on Austria (18/6)

End of legislative session (30/6)

Austrians decisively defeated at Sadowa (3/7)

Benedetti at Prussian headquarters (12/7); Bismarck declines French proposals (17/7;
    armistice, 22/7; peace preliminaries [Nicolsburg], 26/7; treaty of Prague, 23/8)

Sénatus-consulte extending Corps Législatif's power of amendment and forbidding
    further discussion of the constitution except by the Senate (18/7)

Law increasing powers of *conseils généraux* (18/7)

Napoleon III ill at Vichy (28/7)

Drouyn de Lhuys formulates French compensation demands (29/7; presented to Prussia
    and rejected, 3/8; repudiated by Napoleon III, 11/8; resignation of Drouyn de Lhuys
    accepted, 20/8)

Moustier named foreign minister (1/9)

Charlotte of Mexico at Paris (Aug.)

Napoleon III formally claims Luxembourg and initiates process for reforming French
    army (20/8)

Napoleon III advises Maximilian to abdicate (29/8; rejected, 19/9)

Chassepot rifle adopted (30/8)

Bismarck's secret military alliances with south German states (Aug.)

War begins between Crete and Turkey (11/9)

La Valette Circular (16/9)

Antibes Legion arrives at Rome (24/9)

Venetia ceded to France (12/10; transferred to France and by her to Italy, 19/10)

Military commission named (26/10)

Mass arrest of Blanquists, Café de la Renaissance (7/11)

France proposes to Prussia an alliance regarding Rome (25/11; rejected by Bismarck,
    Dec.)

French garrison leaves Rome (2-13/12)

Moniteur publishes proposals for army reform (12/12; general opposition)

Troplong named president of the Senate (27/12)

Failure of attempt to secure replacement of Rouher by Ollivier (Nov.-Dec.)

SOCIAL/ECONOMIC

Napoleon III announces an agricultural inquiry (22/1)

Prefects ordered to permit meetings of workers on occupational matters (Feb.)

Treaty on Danish navigation signed after conference at Paris (9/4)

Fall of Overend Bank, London, signals beginning of 1866-1867 economic crisis (11/5)

Treaties of commerce with Portugal (11/7), Austria (11/12)

Suppression of *courtiers en marchandises* (19/7)

Napoleon III proposes workers' accident insurance fund (26/7; study ordered, 1/8)

Congress of First International, Geneva (3-8/9)

Floods in the south (Sept.)

Opening of port of Dakar (4/11)

Commission named to encourage worker education (29/11)

Ending of tonnage dues in French ports except by reciprocity (29/12; effective, 1/1/67)

Cholera at Paris

Opening of Magasins Réunis

Official recognition of French Red Cross

PARIS

Saint Maur Market inaugurated (4/2)
Napoleon III modifies his decree regarding Luxembourg Garden, but protests continue
  (Feb.)
End of "taxi cab" monopoly of Compagnie des Petites Voitures (15/6)
Store for selling horse meat opens at Paris (9/7)
Le Figaro proposes a Paris museum (19/7; decision made to establish one at the Hôtel
  Carnavalet)
Construction completed: Pont du Point du Jour; Bd. Saint Germain; Halle aux Cuirs
Bd. Magenta begun
Restoration of facade of Hôtel de Ville
Square des Buttes Chaumont landscaped
Rue Turbigo prolonged
Paris population (census 1866) 2,150,916

PUBLICATIONS

BAUDELAIRE: *Les épaves*
CLARETIE: *Un assassin*
COPPEE: *Le reliquaire*
DAUDET: "Lettres de mon moulin" (in *L'événement*)
DUPANLOUP: *L'athéisme et le péril social*
ERCKMANN-CHATRIAN: *La guerre*; *La maison forestière*
GONCOURT: *Idées et sensations*
HUGO: *Les travailleurs de la mer* (on sale, 15/3); *Les chansons des rues et des bois*
LITTRE: *Auguste Comte et Stuart Mill*
MICHELET: *Histoire de France: Louis XV* (vol. 16)
NAPOLEON III: *Histoire de Jules César* (vol. 2; Dec.)
RENAN: *Les Apôtres*
ROCHEFORT: *Les Français de la décadence*
SAND: *Flavie*
SCHOLL: *Les cris de paon*
SIMON: *Le travail*
TAINE: *Voyage en Italie*; *Philosophie de l'art en Italie*
VALLES: *Les réfractaires*; *La rue*
VERLAINE: *Poèmes saturniens*
ZOLA: *Mes haines*
Copyright law voted (27/6)
First *Le Parnasse contemporain* (3/3)

JOURNALISM

First issue of Vermorel's *Courrier français* (20/5)
Girardin acquires *La liberté*, drops price to 10 centimes (June)
Courrier du Dimanche suppressed for publishing Prévost-Paradol article (2/8)
Founding of *La petite presse* (7/9) and *Revue de poche*
L'événement suppressed for publishing a "political" article (15/11)

THEATER

AUGIER: *La contagion* (Odéon, 17/3)
BANVILLE: *Gringoire* (Théâtre Français, 21/6)
DUMAS FILS: *Héloïse Paranquet* (Gymnase, 20/1); *L'affaire Clemenceau*
LABICHE: *Un pied dans le crime* (Palais Royal, 19/5)
MUSSET: *Fantasio* (Théâtre Français, 18/8)
PONSARD: *Le lion amoureux* (Théâtre Français, 18/1; great success)
ROCHEFORT: *La confession d'un enfant du siècle* (Vaudeville, Sept.)
SARDOU: *Nos bons villageois* (Gymnase, 3/10)
Opening of Théâtre des Délassements Comiques (15/2), Théâtre des Nouveautés (31/3; destroyed by fire, 3/11), Théâtre des Menus Plaisirs (15/12), Théâtre des Fantaisies Parisiennes, and Théâtre du Prince Impérial

PAINTING/SCULPTURE/PHOTOGRAPHY

CARRIER-BELLEUSE: "Angélina"
COROT: "L'église de Marissel"
COURBET: "La femme au perroquet"; "Remise de chevreuil"
DEGAS: First ballet scenes
FROMENTIN: "Tribu nomade en marche"
GEROME: "Cléopatre"
MANET: "Le fifre"; "L'acteur tragique"
MONET: "Camille"
MOREAU: "Jeune fille portant la tête d'Orphée"
In article on the Salon in *L'événement* Zola defends Manet (7/5)

MUSIC

DELIBES: *La source* (Opéra, 12/11)
OFFENBACH: *Barbe Bleue* (Variétés, 5/2); *La vie parisienne* (Palais Royal, 31/10; great success)
THOMAS: *Mignon* (Opéra Comique, 17/11; great success)
Decree making the Opéra a private enterprise, independent of the civil list
Opening of L'Athénée (concert hall)
Liszt at Paris
Gounod elected to Académie des Beaux-Arts

ACADEMIC

Prévost-Paradol received at the Académie Française (7/3)
Cuvillier-Fleury elected to Académie Française (12/4)
Suppression of the new section of the Académie des Sciences Morales et Politiques established Apr. 1855 (9/5)
In *L'opinion nationale* Jean Macé proposes a "Ligue de l'Enseignement" (founded, 15/11)

SCIENTIFIC/TECHNOLOGICAL

Sultan grants concession to the Suez Canal Company (19/3)
Nadar ascends in his balloon *Le Géant* (23/6)
International conference at Paris formulates sanitary regulations against cholera (23/6)
Great Eastern completes laying first successful Atlantic cable, Ireland to U.S. (27/7;
   "lost" cable of 1865 recovered and completed, 8/9)
Joret builds world's first steel bridge at Paris for 1867 world's fair

1867

POLITICAL/DIPLOMATIC/MILITARY

Interviews of Napoleon III with Ollivier (10 and 13/1)
Napoleon III reveals his reform plans to his cabinet (17/1); publishes them (19/1;
   cabinet remade, 20/1—Rouher finance minister)
Le siècle launches subscription to erect a monument to Voltaire (25/1)
Decree altering organization and procedures of Corps Législatif; tribune and
   interpellation restored (5/2)
Beginning of legislative session (14/2; Napoleon III calls for army reform)
France formally asks Dutch King to sell Luxembourg (28/2; he agrees, 19/3)
First interpellation in Corps Législatif (Feb.)
Project of army reform submitted to Corps Législatif (7/3; published, 8/3)
Sénatus-consulte grants Senate a one-year suspensive veto (12/3)
Bismarck reveals Prussian military alliances with south German states (19/3)
Walewski forced to resign as president of Corps Législatif (29/3; Schneider named to
   succeed him, 2/4)
Dutch king writes William I concerning Luxembourg (26/3)
French complete withdrawal from Mexico (Mar.)
Proposed laws on press and public meetings submitted to Corps Législatif (Mar.)
Bismarck interpellated in Reichstag concerning Luxembourg (1/4; beginning of
   Luxembourg crisis)
Napoleon III decides against war over Luxembourg (5/4)
Turks surrender fortress at Belgrade to the Serbs (18/4)
Russia proposes conference on Luxembourg (21/4; France accepts, 27/4; invitations,
   1/5; meets at London, 7-11/5; Prussia evacuates fortress, 8/9)
Corps Législatif votes "*récompense nationale*" of 500,000 francs for Lamartine (8/5)
Czar of Russia at Paris (1/6-11/6)
Pius IX gives first public hint of Vatican Council and Papal Infallibility (1/6)
King of Prussia at Paris (5/6-14/6)
Attempt on life of czar at Paris by Berezowski (6/6)
Maximilian executed by Juarès at Queretaro (19/6)
Three western provinces of Cochinchina annexed to France (25/6; treaty, 15/7)
Turkish sultan at Paris (30/6)
North German Confederation comes into being (1/7)
Ollivier in Corps Législatif calls Rouher "vice-emperor without responsibility" (12/7;
   Napoleon III awards Rouher the Grand Cross in diamonds, 13/7)
Law extending powers of municipal councils in local affairs (24/7)

End of legislative session (24/7)
Napoleon III meets at Salzburg with Francis Joseph and other German rulers (18-21/8)
At Lille Napoleon III alludes in a speech to "*des points noirs*" on the horizon (27/8)
Death of Fould (12/10)
Francis Joseph at Paris (23/10-4/11)
French defeat Garibaldi at Mentana (3/11)
Lord Lyons received as Britain's ambassador to France (9/11)
France proposes congress on Rome (9/11; pope accepts, 19/11; Italy agrees to prepare a program, 3/12)
Pinard minister of interior (13/11)
1868 legislative session begins (18/11; Napoleon III withdraws Niel project for army reform, submits proposal to change 1832 law)
In Corps Législatif Rouher, replying to a speech of Thiers' of 4/12, states Italy will never be allowed to take Rome (5/12; Italy rejects congress on Rome, 10/12)
Discussion on army reform in Corps Législatif (19/12)

SOCIAL/ECONOMIC

Bronze workers strike against efforts of employers to dissolve their mutual society (Feb.)
Strike of garment workers begins (31/3)
Abolition of imprisonment for debt (*contrainte par corps*) voted (15/4)
Opening of Asile Sainte Anne (1/5)
International monetary conference at Paris (17/6-9/7; gold standard agreement adopted)
Law dispensing *sociétés anonymes* from need for authorization (24/7)
French treaty of commerce with the pope (29/7)
Assemblées de la Passage Raoul begin (July; until Aug. 1869)
Second Congress of the International, Lausanne (2-7/9); Congress of Peace and Liberty, Geneva (9-12/9)
Pereires are forced to withdraw from management of Crédit Mobilier (Oct.)
French section of the International prosecuted (30/12)

PARIS

La Villette *abattoir* inaugurated (1/1)
International Exposition at Paris (1/4-3/11)
Picard, Berryer, Forcade attack Haussmann's finances (Apr.)
Inauguration of Parc des Buttes Chaumont (1/5)
Scaffolding removed from facade of the Opéra (15/8)
Haussmann signs contract with Crédit Foncier (8/11; approved by municipal commission, 2/12)
Work begins on project to bring water to Paris from the Vannes (Nov.)
In *Le temps* Ferry attacks Haussmann's finances (20/12)
Restoration of tombs of Saint Denis Basilica; restoration of Château de Saint Germain (museum installed)
Beginning of construction of Bd. Arago

PUBLICATIONS

ABOUT: *L'infâme et le Salon de 1866*
BANVILLE: *Odes funambulesques*
CHAMPFLEURY: *La comédie académique*; *La belle Paule*
CLARETIE: *Les derniers Montagnards*
DUMAS PERE: *Les blancs et les bleus*
ERCKMANN-CHATRIAN: *Blocus*; *Episode de la fin de l'Empire*
FEUILLET: *M. de Camors*
FEYDEAU: *La Comtesse de Châlis*
GAUTIER: *Voyage en Russie*
GONCOURT: *Manette Salomon*
GUIZOT: *Memoires* (May; final vol.)
HOUSSAYE: *Les femmes du diable*
LANFREY: *Histoire de Napoleon I* (Apr.; first vol.; first critical study)
LAPRADE: *L'éducation homicide*; *Plaidoyer pour l'enfance*
MISTRAL: *Calendau*; *Puemo nouveau*; *The golden shoes*
MUSSET: *Oeuvres posthumes*
NERVAL: *Oeuvres complètes*
OLLIVIER: *Démocratie et liberté*
QUINET: *Critique de la Révolution*; *France et Allemagne*
SIMON: *La liberté civile*; *L'ouvrier de 8 ans*
TAINE: *Notes sur Paris*
TURGENEV: *Fumées*
VIGNY: *Le journal d'un poète*
ZOLA: *Thérèse Raquin* (Nov.); *Edouard Manet* (June); *Les mystères de Marseille*
    (June and Oct.); begins preparatory work for Rougon-Macquart novels (end of year)
Death of Baudelaire (31/8)

JOURNALISM

Reappearance of *L'Univers* (19/2)
Copies of *Liberté* (Girardin) prohibited to be sold on the public way (Apr.)
Le Figaro becomes a political newpaper (May)
Founding of *La rue* (Vallès) and *L'éclair*

THEATER

DAUDET: *Le frère aîné* (Vaudeville, 19/12)
DUMAS FILS: *Les idées de Mme Aubray* (Gymnase, 16/5)
HUGO: *Hernani* (Théâtre Français, 20/6; revival; great success)
LABICHE: *La grammaire* (Palais Royal, 28/7)
PONSARD: *Galilée* (Théâtre Français, 7/3)
Théâtre de Belleville burns (10/12)

PAINTING/SCULPTURE/PHOTOGRAPHY

BAZILLE: ''Réunion de famille''

BONHEUR: "Mourons au bord de la mer"
BOUGUEREAU: "Soeur aînée"
BRETON (JULES): "La moisson"
CARPEAUX: "Pêcheur napolitain"
CEZANNE: "L'enlèvement"
FALGUIERE: "Vainqueur du combat de coqs"
FANTIN-LATOUR: "Portrait de Manet"
GEROME: "Marché d'esclaves"
HEBERT: "Feuilles d'automne"
ISABEY: "Episode de la Saint Barthélemy"
JONGKIND: "Vue de l'escaut à Anvers"
MANET: "L'exécution de l'Empereur Maximilien" (first version); "L'exposition de 1867"
MEISSONIER: "L'ordonnance"
MONET: "Femmes au jardin"
MORISOT: "Vue du Trocadéro"
RENOIR: "Diane chasseresse"
Death of Ingres (14/1); exposition of his paintings
Zola defends Manet in *Revue du XIXe siècle* (Jan.)
Opening of Manet's independent exhibition (24/5)
Death of Théodore Rousseau (22/12)
Paris world's fair introduces Japanese art to the West
Viollet-le-Duc's *Dictionnaire raisonné de l'architecture française* (vol. 1)

MUSIC

BIZET: *La jolie fille de Perthe* (Théâtre Lyrique, 26/12; failure)
GOUNOD: *Roméo et Juliette* (Théâtre Lyrique, 27/4)
OFFENBACH: *La Grande Duchesse de Gérolstein* (Variétés, 12/4; great success); *Robinson Crusoe* (Opéra Comique, 23/11)
VERDI: *Don Carlos* (Opéra, 11/3)

ACADEMIC

Funeral of Victor Cousin (24/1)
In senate speech Sainte-Beuve defends Renan (12/3)
Primary education law voted (10/4)
Cuvillier-Fleury received at the Académie Française (Apr.)
Elected to Académie Française: Favre (2/5), Gratry (May)
"Affair of the Ecole Normale" (July)
Duruy announces creation of a secondary education for girls (Oct.; courses opened in some twenty towns, Dec.)

SCIENTIFIC/TECHNOLOGICAL

Joseph Monier patents reinforced concrete (16/7)
Pasteur studies fermentation of wine

Charles Tellier begins experiments at Auteuil on "dry freezing" meat
Marinoni develops his rotary press
Edoux constructs two elevators for the Paris world's fair; calls them *ascenseurs*
George Leclanché invents first practical dry-cell battery
Hippolyte Mège-Mouries develops margarine at urging of Napoleon III (until 1869)
Bernard's *De la physiologie générale*

1868

POLITICAL/DIPLOMATIC/MILITARY

Osaka and Niogo opened to European commerce (1/1)
Corps Législatif votes army reform (14/1; Senate approves, 30/1; published, 4/2)
Discussion of press law begins in Corps Législatif (29/1; Cassagnac speaks against,
    31/1; Napoleon III decides for a free vote, 31/1, then changes his mind, 2/2; Rouher
    makes decisive speech for the bill, 4/2)
Students and police clash at Paris over banning of Hugo's *Ruy Blas* (18/2)
Disraeli British prime minister (29/2)
Right-wing bonapartist faction, the "Arcadiens," is formed (Feb.)
War on Crete resumes (Feb.)
Press law passed, 9/3; promulgated, 11/5
Discussion of law on public meetings begins in Corps Législatif (12/3; passed, 25/3;
    Senate approves, May; promulgated, 6/6)
Catholic opposition to Duruy grows (Mar.)
Disturbances (Toulouse, Bordeaux, etc.) over cost of living, Garde Mobile (Mar.)
Niel reports reformed French army ready for any eventuality (May)
First public meeting under new law (17/6, Salle du Wauxhall)
Pius IX issues invitations to Vatican Council (29/6; formally announced, 8/9)
Legislative session ends after record nine months (28/7)
Four-million franc indemnity approved for holders of Mexican bonds (July)
Napoleon III broaches alliance to Austria (July)
Son of General Cavaignac refuses to take his school prize from hands of Prince
    Imperial (10/8)
Grévy elected (16/8; Corps Législatif by-election)
Under French mediation Italy and Rome agree on sharing papal debt (Aug.)
Revolution in Spain (18/9; Queen Isabella deposed, 29/9; France recognizes new
    government, 25/10; Isabella at Paris, 6/11)
Death of Walewski (27/9)
Government wins 3 of 4 by-elections (Sept.)
Napoleon III and Eugénie leave Biarritz for last time (17/10)
Demonstration at Baudin's newly rediscovered tomb, Montmartre Cemetery, on All
    Soul's Day; subscription opened for a monument to Baudin (1/11)
Gambetta unsuccessfully defends newspaper editors tried for Baudin subscription
    (13-14/11 and 28/11) but makes his reputation
Death of Berryer (29/11)
Turkey breaks diplomatic relations with Greece over Crete (1/12); sends ultimatum
    (11/12; rejected, 15/12)
Bloody riots on Réunion (1/12)

Pinard, interior minister, overreacts to threat of leftist demonstration (3/12; replaced by
La Roquette, 17/12)
Gladstone British prime minister, Clarendon foreign secretary (9/12)
Moustier suffers heart attack; La Valette acting foreign minister (17/12)
Bismarck proposes conference concerning Crete (18/12; accepted by France, 21/12)
Napoleon III writes King of Italy proposing alliance of France, Italy, and Austria-
Hungary (31/12)

SOCIAL/ECONOMIC

Bank of France reserves reach a billion francs—the "*grève du milliard*" (Jan.)
Loan of 429 million francs requested by Magne (27/1); oversubscribed (Aug.)
French section of the International condemned on appeal and ordered dissolved (20/3;
new, more radical bureau also prosecuted, 22/5, convicted and ordered dissolved,
18-19/6)
Napoleon III approves report of Forcade La Roquette giving official character to
administrative tolerance of labor unions (31/3)
Strike of miners in Charleroi basin (Mar.)
Failure of attack on free trade in Corps Législatif (May)
Pereires return to administration of Compagnie Générale Transatlantique (June)
Corps Législatif votes law on construction of *chemins vicinaux* (June)
Two voluntary insurance funds established for workers—life, and accident, the latter
partly subsidized by the state (July)
Baron James de Rothschild buys Château Lafite for over 4 million francs (8/8; dies,
15/11)
Establishment of equality of witness for worker and employer in court (18/8)
Third congress of the International at Brussels (6-13/9; endorses nationalization of
industry)
Peace congress at Berne (24/9)
Bakunin founds Alliance Internationale de la Démocratie Sociale (Sept.)
Compagnie des Chemins de Fer de l'Est buys 2 Belgian railroads (8/12)
First meeting of Société des Agriculteurs de France (16/12)
Government inquiry concerning *livrets d'ouvriers*

PARIS

Government submits contract between city of Paris and Crédit Foncier to Corps
Législatif (Apr.)
Eglise Saint Augustin inaugurated (28/5)
Ferry's *Les comptes fantastiques d'Haussmann* (May)
Haussmann publishes a financial report in the *Moniteur* (18/6; reports to Corps
Législatif, June)
Siphon tube placed under the Seine, connecting the great sewer collectors (18/8;
siphon system completed, 2/11)
Establishment of the Théâtre de la Gaîté-Montparnasse

PUBLICATIONS

ABOUT: *Les mariages de Province*

ALTON-SHEE: *Mémoires*
COPPEE: *Intimités*
DAUDET: *Le petit chose*; *Marthe Varadès*
DUPANLOUP: *La femme chrétienne et française; Dernière réponse à M. Duruy*
ERCKMANN-CHATRIAN: *Histoire de la Révolution Française racontée par un paysan* (first of 4 vols.; completed 1870)
LABOULAYE: *Le Prince Caniche*
MICHELET: *La Montagne*
PONSON DU TERRAIL: *L'auberge de la Rue des Enfants Rouges*
PREVOST-PARADOL: *La France nouvelle*
QUINET: *Mémoires d'exil*
RENAN: *Questions contemporaines*
SAND: *Cadio*
TENOT: *Paris en Décembre 1851*; 5th printing of *La Province en Décembre 1851*
VACHEROT: *La religion*
ZOLA: Preface to 2nd ed. of *Thérèse Raquin* (15/4); *Madeleine Férat* (19/12); *Les mystères de Marseille* (3rd vol.; 11/7)

JOURNALISM

First issue of *L'éclipse* (26/1)
Ten Paris newspapers fined for discussing legislative debates (Jan.)
Napoleon III establishes his own newspaper, *L'époque*, with Duvernois as editor (Apr.)
Press law promulgated (11/5; see POLITICAL)
First issue of Rochefort's *La lanterne* (30/5)
Founding of : *La tribune* (14/6), *Le reveil* (Delescluze, 3/7), *Le Gaulois* (Pène and Tarbé, 5/7), *Le public* (a government paper; 15/11)
Eleventh issue of *La lanterne* seized (8/8; Rochefort convicted, 14/8 and 28/8; flees to Belgium)
Condemnation of Claretie for an article (11/8)
First issue of *Diable à quatre* (best of the imitations of *La lanterne*, 17/9)
Death of Havin (12/11)
Decree lays basis for a *Journal officiel* to assume functions of *Le moniteur universel* (16/11)

THEATER

ABOUT: *Histoire ancienne* (Théâtre Français, 31/10)
AUGIER: *Paul Forestier* (Théâtre Français, 25/1; great success)
MEILHAC-HALEVY: *Fanny Lear* (Gymnase, 23/8)
Debut of Coquelin Cadet, Théâtre Français (10/6)

PAINTING/SCULPTURE/PHOTOGRAPHY

BOUDIN: "La jetée du Havre"
COROT: "La femme à la perle"; "Un matin à Ville-d'Avray"; "Le soir"

COURBET: "L'aumône d'un mendiant"
DEGAS: "L'orchestre de l'Opéra de Paris" (comp. 1869)
DETAILLE: "La halte"
FALGUIERE: "Tarcinus, martyr chrétien"
FROMENTIN: "Arabes attaquant une lionne"
GEROME: "L'exécution du Maréchal Ney"
JONGKIND: "Vue de la Rivière d'Overschie près Rotterdam"
MANET: "Portrait de M. Emile Zola"; "Une jeune femme"
MONET: "Navires sortant des jettées du Havre"
PISSARRO: "La côte de Jallais"
RENOIR: "The skaters"; "Lise"
SISLEY: "Avenue de Châtaigniers près La-Celle-Saint-Cloud"
Barye elected to Académie des Beaux-Arts

MUSIC

LE COQ: *Fleur de thé* (Athénée, 11/4; great success); *Le carnaval d'un merle blanc*
   (Palais Royal, 30/12; success)
OFFENBACH: *Le château à Toto* (Palais Royal, 6/5); *La Périchole* (Théâtre des
   Variétés, 6/10)
SAINT-SAENS: "Concerto no. 2 in G Minor for piano and orchestra" (performed
   13/5)
THOMAS: *Hamlet* (Opéra, 9/3; debut of Christine Nilsson)
VERDI: *Giovanna d'Arco* (Théâtre Italien, 28/3; Paris premiere; failure)
Excerpts from Wagner's *Meistersinger* included in Pasdeloup's concert (12/10)
Death of Rossini (13/11)

ACADEMIC

Pope Pius IX joins Dupanloup in opposing secondary education for girls (Feb.)
Discussion in Senate of "materialism" in Paris Faculty of Medicine (Mar.-May)
Received at Académie Française: Gratry (Mar.), Favre (23/4)
Sainte-Beuve speaks in Senate on intellectual freedom (7/5 and 19/5)
Ecole Pratique des Hautes Etudes founded (31/7)

SCIENTIFIC/TECHNOLOGICAL

Death of Foucault
Bicycle (*vélocipède*) races at Saint-Cloud (31/5; earliest recorded)
Inauguration of railroad over Mont Cenis (15/6)
Napoleon III again saves Suez Canal Co.—authorizes a lottery (June)
Government grants 20-year concession to French Atlantic Telegraph Co. to lay cable
   to America (8/7)
Pasteur suffers a cerebral hemorrhage (Oct.)
Ducos Duhauron patents color photography process (Nov.)
Skeleton of Cro-Magnon Man found near Périgueux by Lartet
Flammarion's *Le pluralité des mondes habités*
Letourneau's *Physiologie des passions*

1869

POLITICAL/DIPLOMATIC/MILITARY

Invitations sent for a conference concerning Crete (2/1; meets, 9/1; concludes, 20/1)

Legislative session begins (18/1)

Belgian parliament nullifies cession of Belgian railroad lines to a French company
(13/2); "Belgian railroads affair" begins (Feb.)

France presents at Vienna a first draft of a Triple Alliance (1/3; declined, Apr.)

Deaths of Lamartine and Troplong (2/3)

Ollivier publishes *Le 19 janvier* (3/3)

Schneider again named president of the Corps Législatif (16/3)

Question of Belgian railroads submitted to a mixed commission (Mar.; Napoleon III
decides to make concessions, 27/4; dispute is resolved, May)

Corps Législatif dissolved (26/4)

In Senate the marshals offer reassurance concerning French military preparedness
(Apr.)

Electoral campaign begins (3/5; first round of elections, 23-24/5; second round, 6-7/6)

Rouher's second draft of a Triple Alliance (10/5)

Meeting of French prelates at Orleans demands canonization of Joan of Arc (15/5)

Persigny, Ollivier, Prince Napoleon advise the emperor to turn to new men (May)

Disturbances at Paris (8-10/6; end, 11/6; emperor and empress ride along boulevards)

Corps Législatif meets to verify credentials; Rouher promises reform proposals for
regular session (28/6)

116 deputies sign demand for interpellation on responsible government (6/7)

Rouher announces his resignation to the Corps Législatif and further reforms,
including responsible government (12/7)

Corps Législatif prorogued without date (13/7)

New government named (17/7: Ministry of State suppressed, Chasseloup-Laubat
president of Conseil d'État)

Rouher named president of Senate (20/7)

Gambetta rejects proposed reforms (July)

Senate meets to consider revision to the constitution (2/8; *sénatus-consulte* approved,
6/9; promulgated, 10/9)

Death of Marshal Niel (13/8; succeeded by Le Boeuf)

Unconditional amnesty granted political offenders (15/8)

Eugénie and Prince Imperial in Corsica—Napoleon III ill (Aug.)

French prelates attack Papal Infallibility: Maret, 19/9; Père Hyacinthe, 20/9 (leaves his
order in protest); Dupanloup, 11/11

Napoleon III promises to aid Austria if she is attacked (24/9)

Italy makes alliance dependent on French evacuation of Rome (25/9)

Corps Législatif convoked for 29/11 (3/10; threatened uprising at Paris fails to
materialize, 26/10)

Napoleon III and Ollivier meet secretly at Compiègne (31/10)

Following October "meeting of the people," Bd. de Clichy, leftist deputies break with
the extreme Left (15/11)

Four Paris by-elections (21-22/11; Rochefort elected)

Tiers Parti opened to all (26/11; with Napoleon III's approval, 163 join, 28/11)

Extraordinary session of Corps Législatif opened by the emperor (29/11; begins regular
    session, then is at once adjourned, 27/12)
Schneider elected president of Corps Législatif (1/12)
Vatican Council convenes at Rome (8/12)
Exchange of letters between Napoleon III and Francis Joseph (Dec.)
Napoleon III asks Ollivier to form a ministry (27/12; first attempt fails, 31/12)
Tiers Parti splits into two factions (Dec.)
Autonomists win Bavarian elections (Dec.)

SOCIAL/ECONOMIC

Following ''Assemblies of the Passage Raoul,'' workers list their demands for the
    government (Jan.)
On Napoleon III's initiative Corps Législatif accepts in principle suppression of *livret
    d'ouvriers* (23/3; proposal of law submitted, 31/3)
Corps Législatif passes law providing pensions for survivors of Napoleon I's armies
    (Apr.)
Loire coalminers' strike begins (12/6; miners and troops clash at La Ricamarie,
    15-16/6; strike ends, 24/6)
Miners' strike begins at Carmaux (Aveyron) (26/6)
Convention organizes a Franco-Belgian railway service (9/7)
Strike of Loire silk workers (July)
Napoleon III pardons 62 leaders of Loire miners' strike following their convictions
    (Aug.)
Meeting at Lausanne under presidency of Hugo of Ligue Internationale pour la Paix et
    la Liberté (14-18/9)
Strike of Elbeuf textile workers (Sept.)
Strike of employees of Paris *magasins de nouveautés* (6/10)
Miners' strike at Aubin (7/10; clash of troops and miners, 8/10)
Creation of Fédération Parisienne des Associations Ouvrières (Nov.)
Inquiry ordered into free trade (Nov.)
Varlin reorganizes Paris bureau of the International (Dec.)
La Samaritaine department store founded

PARIS

Debate begins in Corps Législatif on Paris finances (22/2; Thiers attacks Haussmann,
    23/2; Rouher admits irregularities, 26/2)
Corps Législatif approves, but on its own terms, Haussmann's contract with the Crédit
    Foncier (6/3; law published, 19/4)
Caisse des Travaux de Paris dissolved (19/4)
In Senate Haussmann defends his policies (Apr.)
City of Paris floats loan for 250 million francs (May)
Cornerstone laid for new Bon Marché store (9/9)
Demolition of Prince Napoleon's Palais Pompéien
Beginning of construction of Passy *mairie* (completed, 1879)
Construction of Louvre's Grand Staircase

PUBLICATIONS

BANVILLE: *Nouvelles odes funambulesques*
CATULLE MENDES: *Hesperus*; *Le soleil de minuit*
CHAMPFLEURY: *Les chats*; *Histoire de l'imagerie populaire*
COPPEE: *Poèmes modernes*; *La grève des forgerons*
DAUDET: *Lettres de mon moulin*
DELORD: *Histoire du Second Empire* (first vol.; completed, 1876)
DUMAS PERE: *Causeries sur l'Italie*
DUPANLOUP: *La femme studieuse*; *Second panégyrique de Jeanne d'Arc*
FEYDEAU: *Les aventures du Baron Féreste*
FLAUBERT: *L'éducation sentimentale*
GOBINEAU: *Histoire des Perses*
GONCOURT: *Madame Gervaisais*
HOUSSAYE: *Les parisiennes*
HUGO: *L'homme qui rit* (Apr.)
LECONTE DE LISLE: *Kain*
PONSON DU TERRAIL: *Rocambole en prison*
RENAN: *Saint Paul et sa mission*
SAND: *Pierre qui roule*
SIMON: *La peine de mort*; *La liberté de penser*
SULLY-PRUDHOMME: *Les solitudes*
TAINE: *Philosophie de l'art en Grece*
TENOT: *Les suspects en 1858*; 13th printing of *Paris en décembre 1851*
TURGENEV: *Les nouvelles Moscovites*
VERLAINE: *Fêtes galantes*
VERNE: *Vingt milles lieues sous les mers*
Death of Saint-Beuve (13/10)
Second issue of *Le Parnasse contemporain*

JOURNALISM

Journal officiel replaces *Moniteur* as the official newspaper (1/1)
Sainte-Beuve publishes in *Le temps* (4/1)
Founding of: *Le peuple* (Vallès, 4/2; 15 numbers); *Le rappel* (4/5); *Le lorgnon* (Scholl,
   1/10); *Le Père Duchêne* (3/12); *La Marseillaise* (Rochefort, 19/12); *Le réfractaire*
   (Vallès; 3 numbers); *Vélocipède illustré*
Revue contemporaine fined for discussing constitution (7/4)
General crackdown on the press

THEATER

AUGIER: *Le post-scriptum* (Théâtre Français, 1/5); *Lions et renards* (Théâtre
   Français, 6/12; failure)
COPPEE: *Le passant* (Odéon, 14/1; first great success for both Mlle Agar and Sarah
   Bernhardt; performed at Princess Mathilde's with Napoleon III present, 29/4)
DAUDET: *Le sacrifice* (Vaudeville, 11/2)

DEROULEDE (PAUL): *Juan Strenner* (Théâtre Français, 9/6)
DUMAS FILS: *Le filleul de Pompignac* (Gymnase, 7/5)
ERCKMANN-CHATRIAN: *Le Juif polonais* (Théâtre Cluny, 15/6; success)
FEUILLET: *Julie* (Théâtre Français, 4/5)
MEILHAC-HALEVY: *Froufrou* (Gymnase, 30/10; success)
SARDOU: *Patrie!* (Porte Saint Martin, 18/3; success)
New Théâtre Vaudeville inaugurated (23/4)
Debut of Blanche d'Antigny, Palais Royal (21/8)
Hippodrome burns (29/9)
Opening of Folies Bergère
First series of Claretie's *La vie moderne au théâtre*

PAINTING/SCULPTURE/PHOTOGRAPHY

BAZILLE: "Vue de village"
CARRIER-BELLEUSE: "Hébé"
CEZANNE: "Portrait d'Achille Emperaire"
COURBET: "L'hallali du cerf"
DEGAS: "Au Café de Châteaudun"; "Portrait de Mme Gaujelin"
FALGUIERE: "Ophélie"
GEROME: "Promenade du harem"
MANET: "Le balcon"; "Le départ du bateau de Folkestone à Boulogne"
MONET: "La grenouillère"
MOREAU: "Prométhée"
Unveiling of Carpeaux's Opéra sculpture "La danse" (27/7; ink thrown over it, 27/8)

MUSIC

FRANCK: "Les béatitudes" (begun; completed, 1879)
GOUNOD: *Faust* (Opéra version, 3/3)
OFFENBACH: *Vert-vert* (Opéra comique, 10/3); *Les brigands* (Variétés, 10/12; success)
Death of Berlioz (8/3)
Music publishing house of Durand founded

ACADEMIC

Creation at Ecole Pratique des Hautes Etudes of a fifth section, *sciences économiques* (30/1)
Physical education introduced into curricula of lycées and collèges (8/2)
Triple election to Académie Française: Champagny, Haussonville, Barbier (Apr.)
Reception of Claude Bernard at Académie Française—professes Positivisim (27/5)
Resignation of Duruy as minister of education (13/7)
Ecole Monge established

SCIENTIFIC/TECHNOLOGICAL

European end of French trans-Atlantic cable brought ashore at Brest (17/6; at Duxbury, Mass., 23/7; third Atlantic cable)

Eugénie leaves for Suez (30/9; Suez Canal opened, 16-18/11, in her presence)
First bicycle race on French roads (7/11; won by an Englishman)
Margarine first produced commercially
First utilization of hydroelectric power, by Bergès (28/9)
Wurtz's *Dictionnaire de chimie pure et appliquée* (completed, 1869)

1870

POLITICAL/DIPLOMATIC/MILITARY

Ollivier forms first cabinet of the Liberal Empire (2/1)
At Vatican Council 38 French prelates petition against Infallibility (5/1; rejected, 26/1)
Corps Législatif reconvenes (10/1; Gambetta remains intransigent)
Pierre Bonaparte kills Victor Noir (10/1; Rochefort in *La Marseillaise* calls for
    insurrection, 11/1; at Noir's funeral 100,000 gather, but disperse peacefully, 12/1)
Corps Législatif votes to allow Rochefort to be prosecuted (17/1; demonstrations at
    Paris, 17-18/1; Rochefort convicted and sentenced *in absentia*, 22/1; arrested, 7/2;
    barricades and rioting, 7-9/2)
Death of Victor, duc de Broglie (Jan.)
Official candidacy abandoned (26/2)
France cautions Pope on Infallibility (Feb.)
Commissions established on administrative reorganization of Paris, decentralization,
    and freedom of higher education (Feb.)
Ollivier seeks abrogation of the general security law (Feb.)
Napoleon III rejects Prince Napoleon's idea of a true parliamentary regime; denies him
    an interview (4/3)
Infallibility *schema* presented to Vatican Council (6/3)
Death of Montalembert (13/3)
Pierre Bonaparte's trial at Tours (begins, 21/3; acquitted, 27/3)
Napoleon III proposes constitutional changes (21/3; submitted to Senate, 28/3)
France and other powers protest against doctrine of Infallibility (4/4)
Buffet resigns from cabinet in protest against proposed (Apr.) plebiscite (8/4; Daru
    follows suit, 9/4)
Senate adopts *sénatus-consulte* establishing a new constitution and calling for a
    plebiscite on the reforms since 1860 (20/4)
Beaury and others arrested at Blois for conspiracy against Napoleon III's life (29/4;
    announced, 30/4)
Plebiscite on the Liberal Empire: 7,527,379 *oui*, 1,530,909 *non* (8/5; riots at Paris,
    8-11/5)
Gramont named foreign minister (15/5)
New constitution promulgated (21/5)
In Corps Législatif Picard organizes a *gauche ouvert* (May)
Debate on Infallibility arbitrarily closed at Vatican Council (3/6; doctrine adopted
    547-2, 18/7, with 25 French prelates abstaining; Vatican Council ends, 28/7)
Prévost-Paradol, having rallied to the Liberal Empire, named minister to U.S. (12/6)
Leopold of Sigmaringen agrees to accept Spanish throne (19/6)
Corps Législatif approves reduction by 10,000 of reserve component of annual military
    contingent; Ollivier assures legislators peace has never been as assured (30/6)

Prim promises Spain a king in three months (June)
Projected law on selection of mayors submitted to Corps Législatif (June)
Napoleon III examined by five doctors (1/7)
Girardin, Pasteur, Joachim Pietri named to Senate (July)
Corps Législatif votes 173-31 against allowing return of Orleans princes (2/7)
First word of Hohenzollern candidacy reaches Paris (3-4/7; widely known by 6th)

SOCIAL/ECONOMIC

Buffet obtains a number of protectionist decrees from the new cabinet (9/1)
Beginning of strike at Le Creusot (19/1; ends, 22/1; miners' strike, 21/3-12/4)
Execution of Tropman (19/1)
International once again dissolved in France and its leaders arrested (2/6; trial begins, 22/6; defendants convicted, 5/7)
Project of law deposed controlling working hours in mines and factories and creating an Inspectorat du Travail (26/6)
Crisis in agriculture as result of a 3-month drought (June)
Project of law deposed establishing a voluntary pension fund for workers (July)
Uprising fails at Marseilles—Crémieux arrested (8/8)
Gold standard suspended (*cours forcé des billets de banque*) (13/8)
Blanquist uprising fails at LaVillette (14/8)

PARIS

Haussmann dismissed as prefect of the Seine (5/1; succeeded by Henri Chevreau, 6/1; Haussmann stages his own ceremonial retirement, 10/1)
Napoleon III visits site of just-discovered Arènes de Lutèce; decides to let Rue Monge be built over it (15/4)

PUBLICATIONS

CLARETIE: *Armand Barbès: Etude historique et biographique*
COPPEE: *Poésies*
DELORD: *Histoire du Second Empire* (vol. 2)
SAND: *Le beau Laurence*
TAINE: *De l'intelligence*
VAPEREAU: *Dictionnaire des contemporains* (4th ed.)
VERLAINE: *La bonne chanson*
ZOLA: *La fortune des Rougon* (first instalment published in *Le siècle*, 28/6; publication suspended on order of the government, 10/8); *La curée* (written in course of the year)
Death of Jules de Goncourt (20/6)

JOURNALISM

Restrictions on foreign newspapers lifted (Jan.)

Appearance at Lyons of the journal *La décentralisation* and at Paris of the weekly
  Revue de la décentralisation (Feb.)
Napoleon III constrained to withdraw support from Duvernois' *L'époque* (Feb.)
Girardin sells *La liberté* to his nephew for one million francs (June)
Duc de Broglie publishes his father's manuscript, *Vues sur le gouvernement de
  France*, seized in 1860 (June)
Reduction by one centime of the stamp tax on newspapers proposed (June)
Suspended: *La Marseillaise* (25/7), *Le reveil* (10/8), *Le rappel* (11/8)

THEATER

COPPEE: *Les deux douleurs* (Théâtre Français, 20/4; in March the play was presented
  at Princess Mathilde's in the presence of Napoleon III and Eugénie)
HUGO: *Lucrèce Borgia* (Saint Martin, Feb.)
LABICHE: *Le plus heureux des trois* (Palais Royal, 11/1; great success); *Les trentes
  millions de "Gladiator"* (Variétés, 22/1)
SARDOU: *Fernande* (Gymnase, 8/3)
SCRIBE: *Le verre d'eau* (Théâtre Français, 7/1)

PAINTING/SCULPTURE/PHOTOGRAPHY

BAZILLE: "La toilette"; "L'atelier de l'artiste"
CEZANNE: "Nature morte à la pendule"
COURBET: "Stormy sea"
DEGAS: "Portrait de Mme Camus"
FANTIN-LATOUR: "Hommage à Manet: Un atelier à Batignolles"; "La lecture"
MANET: "Le repos"; "Portrait d'Eva Gonzalès"; "La leçon de musique"
MONET: "Sur la plage"; "La capeline rouge"
PISSARRO: "Le printemps aux toits rouges"
RENOIR: "Baigneuse"; "Femme d'Alger"
SISLEY: "Péniches sur le Canal Saint Martin"
Suppression of ministry of fine arts (24/8)

MUSIC

DELIBES: *Coppélia* (25/5)
SAINT-SAENS: "Concerto No. 3 in E-flat Major for piano and orchestra" (premiere,
  17/3, Salle Pleyel)
Death of Auber (11/5)

ACADEMIC

Received at Académie Française: Champagny (10/3), Haussonville (31/3)
Ollivier elected to Académie Française in place of Lamartine (8/4); Janin elected in
  place of Sainte-Beuve (14/4)
Death of Villemain, perpetual secretary of the Académie Française since 1834 (May)

774 CHRONOLOGY

Laboulaye forced by his students to give up his course at the Collège de France because he supported the plebiscite (May)

SCIENTIFIC/TECHNOLOGICAL

"Rediscovery" of ball-bearings by Suriray
Pasteur's *Etudes sur la maladie des vers-à-soie*

LAST MONTHS OF THE EMPIRE: JULY-SEPTEMBER 1870
July

6. Foreign minister Gramont delivers to Corps Législatif a strong statement, directed to Prussia, concerning the Hohenzollern candidacy.
11. Ambassador Benedetti has interview at Ems with Prussian king, William I.
12. Word that Leopold of Sigmaringen has renounced his candidacy to the Spanish throne is made known at Paris by the Spanish ambassador; but in the afternoon Napoleon III, Gramont, and Eugénie decide to present an additional demand that Prussia offer guarantees for the future.
13. Gramont announces to Corps Législatif the withdrawal of Leopold; French government decides not to press its additional demand; but in the meantime a reluctant Benedetti confronts William I at Ems; the king sends an account (Ems dispatch) by telegraph to Bismarck, who alters it to make it seem that the king and the ambassador had exchanged insults; in the evening Bismarck publishes the edited account in German newspapers.
14. French government decides to propose a congress, but publication of the Ems dispatch at Paris persuades it to opt for war.
15. In afternoon the government proposes war to Corps Législatif; Thiers urges restraint and delay; Ollivier makes his *coeur léger* speech; Minister of War Le Boeuf assures Corps Législatif the army is *"cinq fois prêt."*
16. Corps Législatif unanimously (with ten abstentions) votes to open war credits, mobilize the Garde Mobile, and prohibit press criticism of the military administration; La Tour d'Auvergne named ambassador to Austria (arrives at Vienna the 19th).
18. Austria announces her neutrality in the coming war.
19. France declares war on Prussia.
20. The South German states declare war on France.
21. Corps Législatif adjourns after authorizing a war loan of 500 million francs.
23. Eugénie named regent (assumes duties the 26th); Napoleon III issues his war proclamation (William I's on the 25th).
26. Government decides to recall French troops from Rome (last leave, 19/8; Italian army enters the city, 20/9).
28. Napoleon III leaves Paris with Prince Imperial by train from Saint-Cloud (assumes command of the army at Metz the 29th).

August

2. Frossard's corps takes heights overlooking Saarbrücken as Napoleon III and Prince Imperial watch; Steinmetz's First (Prussian) Army withdraws in good order and with few casualties.

4. In the south, Crown Prince Frederick William's Third Army surprises General Abel Douay's division of MacMahon's corps and defeats it near Wissembourg (Douay is killed); in the north, Frossard is forced to abandon Saarbrücken as Prussian invasion of Alsace and Lorraine begins.

5. Steinmetz defeats Frossard at Spichern; French retreat before combined force of Steinmetz's First Army and Frederick Charles' Second Army.

6. While Paris celebrates false rumor of a great victory over the Crown Prince, his Third Army defeats MacMahon's heavily outnumbered corps at Wörth-Fröschwiller and thus drives a wedge between the northern and southern French forces; MacMahon withdraws toward Nancy-Châlons, while Frossard's outnumbered forces are defeated at Forbach and Bazaine's corps withdraws toward Metz.

7. State of siege declared at Paris; Corps Législatif convoked for the 11th.

8. Date of convocation of the Corps Législatif advanced, under political pressure, to the 9th; Napoleon III suspends as too risky his order to the army to fall back on Châlons; Palikao recalled to Paris from Lyons.

9. Council of Ministers rejects idea (championed by Ollivier and Pietri) that the emperor should return to Paris; Napoleon III confides northern operations, centered on Metz, to Bazaine; Corps Législatif overthrows Ollivier's government; Prussia signs treaty with Britain guaranteeing Belgium's neutrality (similar treaty signed by France, the 11th).

10. Germans invest Strasbourg; Palikao forms a conservative government; Magne asks for war credits of one billion francs (750 million franc loan successfully floated, 24th); all French males age 25 to 35 called up.

12. Nancy occupied by Germans without resistance; Bavarian forces pass the Vosges; Napoleon III gives up command to Bazaine, but remains with the army.

14. Prussian First and Second Armies begin process of shutting Bazaine's forces in Metz: French defeated at Courcelles, Pange-Longueville, Colombey-Nouilly-Borny; Napoleon III leaves Metz; bombardment of Strasbourg begins; Toul invested; first *francs tireurs* appear.

15. French navy blockades the Baltic; state of siege declared in Algeria.

16. At Vionville (Mars-la-Tour) Prussian Second Army fights a drawn battle, prevents Bazaine from retreating toward Verdun; Napoleon III, Prince Imperial, and Prince Napoleon reach Châlons.

17. In the morning, MacMahon reaches Châlons with his troops (by the 20th, some 100,000); council of war at Châlons decides Napoleon III to return to Paris with Trochu, who is named military governor of the city; but after a telegram from Eugénie, the emperor "adjourns" his own return to the capital, where Trochu arrives at midnight to become president of the Comité de Défence.

18. Trochu fails to persuade the government to recall Napoleon III and the Châlons forces to Paris; Germans, with King William I observing, defeat Bazaine at Gravelotte (Rezonville) in early afternoon and at Saint-Privat in evening, and drive his army into Metz.

19. MacMahon ordered to march from Châlons to relief of Metz (telegraph line to Metz cut at 1 P.M.); Prince Napoleon leaves for Florence on Napoleon III's orders.

21. At Châlons, Rouher becomes convinced MacMahon should fall back on Paris and Napoleon III returns to the capital.

22. Rouher fails to persuade the government to recall Napoleon III and the army;

MacMahon is again ordered to relieve Metz, but, on receipt of a message from Bazaine, he has already decided to do so.

23. MacMahon begins his advance toward Metz with the Army of Châlons, pursued by the Germans; Napoleon III and Prince Imperial accompany him (Germans occupy Châlons the 25th).

26. French sortie repulsed at Metz; Napoleon III sends Prince Imperial to Mézières, near Belgian frontier.

29. Trochu orders expulsion of all Germans from Paris; subscriptions opened for war loan of one billion francs.

30. Failly, commanding MacMahon's vanguard, defeated at Beaumont as Napoleon III watches; cut off from retreat, MacMahon withdraws toward Sedan; Napoleon III arrives in the town that night by train.

31. Bazaine defeated at Metz and MacMahon at Carignan and in the Plain of Douzy; French retreat into Sedan; during the night the Germans mount cannon on the heights.

September

1. French defeated in decisive battles around Sedan, beginning at 4 A.M.; in afternoon Napoleon III resumes command, and, in order to avoid a slaughter, runs up the white flag and writes to William I.

2. Armistice signed—Napoleon III, his generals, and the Army of Châlons enter German captivity; first word of the defeat reaches Paris in early evening.

3. Corps Législatif meets in afternoon and again (briefly) at midnight; in second meeting Favre moves, just before adjournment, the *déchéance* of the regime.

4. Paris informed in early morning of the disaster at Sedan; Corps Législatif meets in early afternoon; as it deliberates, a mob invades the Palais Bourbon; Gambetta and Favre lead the demonstrators to the Hôtel de Ville where a moderate republic is proclaimed and a provisional government formed, including Trochu; Senate votes support for Napoleon III and then disperses; as 200,000 surround the Tuileries, Eugénie seeks refuge in house of Dr. Evans, the imperial dentist.

5. William I establishes his headquarters at Reims; in early morning Eugénie and Dr. Evans leave Paris in disguise; in evening Napoleon III arrives at Wilhelmshöhe, where he will spend his captivity.

6. Eugénie and Dr. Evans reach Deauville by railroad; Prince Imperial arrives at Dover; Victor Hugo, Louis Blanc return to Paris; Favre issues a defiant circular as foreign minister of the provisional government.

8. Eugénie reaches England.

19. Siege of Paris begins.

24. Eugénie and Prince Imperial move into Camden Place.

Index

Mornand, Félix (1815–1867), journalist, 452

Morny, Charles Auguste, duc de (1811–1865), politician, 8–9, 16, 25, 29, 45, 59, 62, 71, 98, 120, 125–26, 133–36, 138, 146–47, 158, 162, 174, 191, 211, 219, 231, 243, 245, 264, 281, 283, 288, 382, 401, 404, *418–21*, 441–43, 447, 456, 471, 477, 479, 492, 518, 521, 536, 544, 563, 572–74, 577, 588, 628, 637, 653, 656, 694, 697, 703

Morocco and Tunisia, 14, 180, 388, 684

Mortara affair, 408, *421–22*, 490

Mort civile, 34, 133

Mouchy, Antoine Juste Léon Marie de Noailles, duc de (b. 1841), politician, 354

Le mousquetaire, 434

Moustier, Lionel François René, marquis de (1817–1869), diplomat, 155, 345–46, 404

Mulhouse, 327, 494

Mun, Albert de (1841–1914), publicist, 350

Municipal commission (Paris). *See* Paris municipal commission

Municipal government, 66, 95, 121, 133, 136–37, 139, 142, 164, 175–76, 354, 356–57, 487, 503–4, 552, 574. *See also* Decentralization; Mayors; Paris municipal commission

Murat, Joachim (1843–1901), courtier, 94, 290, 354

Murat, Prince Lucien (1803–1878), 517

Murger, Henri (1822–1861), writer, 31, 36, 82, 233, 411, 424

Musée Carnavalet, 287

Music. *See* Concert life

Musset, Alfred de (1810–1857), writer, 7, 36, 424, 534–35, 604, 688, 692

Musset, Paul de (1804–1880), writer, 604

Mutual aid societies (*sociétés de secours mutuels*), 99, 327–28, 339–41, 363, 456, 599, 631–32. *See also* Cooperatives; Mutualism

Mutualism, 69, 235, 328, 526, 664. *See also* Cooperatives; Mutual aid societies

My-thô, battle of. *See* Saigon

Nadar, Félix (1820–1910), photographer, 31, 36, 38, 82, 184–85, 192, 261–62, 279, 295, 312, 396, *423–26*, 433, 443, 550, 604, 607, 684. *See also* Heavier-than-air flight

Le nain jaune 32, 127, 348, 559

Nancy, 65, 71, 247, 266, 296, 332, 346, 371, 473, 608, 669

Nancy movement, 176

Nantes, 56, 91, 213, 511, 542, 684, 693

Naples, Kingdom of. *See* Two Sicilies, Kingdom of

Napoleon, Louis. *See* Louis Napoleon

Napoleon, Prince. *See* Prince Napoleon

Napoleon I, 18, 35, 40, 81, 85, 97, 108, 117, 146, 163, 175, 188, 203, 230, 253, 262, 265, 282–83, 293, 299, 313, 331, 347–49, 364–65, 380, 385, 415, 429–30, 433, 462, 466, 472, 476, 485, 492, 496, 519–20, 539, 565, 581, 585, 614, 653–54, 659, 670, 676, 700, 702. *See also Des idées napoléoniennes*; Fête nationale; First Empire and Consulate; Napoleon I, centenary; Napoleon I, publication of his correspondence; Napoleonic Legend

Napoleon I, centenary, 140, 231, 355, 513

Napoleon I, publication of his correspondence, 400, 518, 614

Napoleonic Code. *See* Code Napoléon

Napoleonic Ideas. See Des idées napoléoniennes

Napoleonic Legend, 60, 114, 120, 298–99. *See also* Napoleon I

Napoleonic veterans, 140, 231. *See also* First Empire and Consulate

"Napoléon le Petit," 294–95

Napoleon III, assassination attempts, 210, 308, 314, *426–28*, 457–58, 484, 494, 515–16, 582. *See also* Beaury *complot*; Berejowski *attentat*; Greppo affair; Hippodrome plot; "Infernal machine" plot, Marseilles; Opéra Comique plot; Orsini, Felice; Pianori *attentat*; Reine Blanche affair; Théâtre Italien *attentat*; Tibaldi conspiracy

Napoleon III, health, 94, 115–16, 154, 247, 249, 251, 288, 354–55, 366, *428–30*, 479–80, 513, 546, 551, 586, 615, 666

Napoleon III, writings and speeches, 142, 288–90, 408. *See also Histoire de Jules César*; Speech from the throne

Naquet, Gustave (1819–1889), journalist, 452

Le nation, 278

Le national, 31, 231

National Guard, 32, 91, 122, 230, 232, 248, 250, 257, 382, 466, 477, 524, 540, 679

Nationalities, principle of. *See Politique des nationalités*

Naturalism, 50, 266–69, 568–71, 644, 707, 709. *See also* Rougon-Macquart novels

Naudin, Emilio (1823–1890), singer, 395

Navy and naval construction, 86, 104, 107, 132, 164, 196–98, 250, 252, 300–302, 311, 313, 379, 389–90, 542, 622, 625. *See also*

25, 136–37, 139, 141–42, 164, 244, 355, 357, 403, 439, 493–94, 508, 544–45, 614, 619–20, 670, 690. *See also* Constituent power, question of; *Sénatus-consulte* of 25 December 1852; *Sénatus-consulte* of 6 September 1869

Senegal, 86, 221–24, 388–89, *621–26*. *See also* Dakar; Faidherbe, Louis Léon César

Separation of church and state, 255–56, 332, 350, 352, 360, 413, 510, 551–52, 639. *See also* Clericalism and anticlericalism; "Free church in a free state"; Gallicanism

Sepoy mutiny (1857), 143

September Convention (1864), 187, 386, 491, 563, *626–28*, 639–40, 683

Serbia, 114

Sericulture. *See* Silk and silk industry

Séries de Compiègne. *See* Compiègne

Serpents Island, 59

Sète. *See* Bordeaux-Cette railroad concession

Seven Weeks War. *See* Austro-Prussian War

Seveste, Jules (d. 1854), impresario, 75

Sèvres, Museum and porcelainry, 672

Seward, William H., 384, 542–43

Shakespeare, 180, 185, 336, 644

Shipping, 45, 106–8, 196–97, 272–73, 388–90, 654. *See also* Compagnie des Messageries Impériales; Compagnie Générale Transatlantique; La Ciotat shipyards; Navy and naval construction; Ports

Siam and the Siamese embassy, 17, 262

Sibour, Marie D. A. (1792–1857), ecclesiastic, 673, 687

Sicily. *See* Two Sicilies, Kingdom of

Le siècle, 40, 69, 210–12, 216, 264, 287–88, 447, 457, 481, 505–6, 508, 543, 550, 605, *628–29*, 709

Siemens-Martin process, 104, 313, 379. *See also* Bessemer process

Silk and silk industry, 19, 102–3, 159, 340, 383, 469, 706. *See also Pébrine* epidemic

Silver and gold. *See* Monetary standards and agreements

Simart, Pierre Charles (1806–1857), sculptor, 671

Simonis-Empis, A. D. F. J. (1795–1868), writer and administrator, 7

Simon, Jules (1814–1896), politician, 23, 176, 194, 212–15, 235, 240, 447, 532, 550, 552, 554, 688

Sinope, 156

Sireuil, Forges de, 379

Sisley, Alfred (1839–1899), painter, 169, 376, 409, 488, 549

La situation, 32

1688 et 1830, 366

Sixth correctional chamber, 41

Slavery and slave trade, 221, 542

Sliding scale. *See Echelle mobile*

Social Catholicism, 81, 196, 255, 309, 327, 350, 352, 377, 598, *629–32*

Social insurance, 56, 238, 329, 340, 610, 632. *See also* Mutual aid societies; Pensions

Socialists and socialism, 19, 34, 40, 61, 69, 89, 218–19, 225, 228, 237, 254, 256, 294, 337, 347, 350, 412–14, 422, 434, 498, 522–27, 532, 550, 552–54, 570, 579, 596, 603, 630–31, 656, 664, 678–79, 692, 698, 708. *See also* First International; Marx and Marxism; Republicans and republicanism; Saint-Simonianism

Social legislation. *See* Labor reform

Sociedad General de Credito Mobiliario Español, 153

Società di Credito Mobiliare, 153

Société Alard Franchomme. *See* Société de Musique de Chambre

Société Bourgault-Ducoudray, 112

Société Chorale d'Amateurs de Guillot de Sainbris, 112

Société d'Acclimatation, 58, 188, 678

Société d'Anthropologie de Paris, 167

Société de Biologie, 49–50, 85

Société d'Economie Charitable, 632

Société de Musique de Chambre, 111

Société de Musique de Chambre Armingaud. *See* Quatuor Armingaud-Jacquard

Société des Aéronautes. *See* Heavier-than-air flight

Société des Agriculteurs de France, 188

Société des Aquafortistes, 227

Société des Concerts de Chant Classique, 112

Société des Concerts du Conservatoire, 110–11, 651

Société des Derniers Quatuors de Beethoven, 111

Société des Forges et Chantiers de la Méditerranée, 45, 198

Société des Jeunes Artistes, 110, 270, 465–66

Société des Journaux Associés, 125–26

Société des Oratorios, 112, 466

Société des Quatuors de Mendelssohn. *See* Quatuor Armingaud-Jacquard

Société des Quatuors Français, 111

About the Editor

WILLIAM E. ECHARD is Associate Professor of History at Glendon College of York University in Toronto. His earlier works include *Napoleon III and the Concert of Europe* and articles published in *French Historical Studies* and the *Canadian Journal of History*.